001.56
St   Sternberg, Martin L
        American sign language:
        a comprehensive...

DATE DUE			

AMERICAN SIGN LANGUAGE

AMERICAN SIGN LANGUAGE

A Comprehensive Dictionary

Martin L. A. Sternberg, Ed.D.

ILLUSTRATED BY HERBERT ROGOFF

HARPER & ROW, PUBLISHERS, New York

Cambridge, Hagerstown, Philadelphia, San Francisco
London, Mexico City, São Paulo, Sydney

1817

To
Edna S. Levine
cherished friend,
with love and admiration

The investigation for this volume was supported in part by a grant, RD-1298-S, during its initial stages, 1963 and 1964, from the Vocational Rehabilitation Administration, Department of Special Education and Rehabilitative Services, United States Department of Education.

Designed by Lydia Link

Library of Congress Cataloging in Publication Data

Sternberg, Martin L   A
    American sign language.
    Bibliography: p.
    Includes indexes.
    1. Sign language—Dictionaries. I. Title.
HV2475.S77 1981   001.56   75-25066
ISBN 0–06–014097–6   85 10 9 8 7 6

Contents

Acknowledgments

American Sign Language: A Comprehensive Dictionary is the culmination of a period of endeavor which goes back to 1962. Dr. Elizabeth Peet, late Dean of Women and Professor of Romance Languages at Gallaudet College, Washington, D.C., first inspired me to compile this work, and she offered the initial guidance and encouragement.

Dr. Edna S. Levine, Professor Emeritus at New York University, provided continuing help and support after Dr. Peet's death. She assisted in the design of the dictionary format, and was instrumental in obtaining a two-year grant from the Rehabilitation Services Administration to demonstrate the feasibility of the project. This book is dedicated to her.

Herbert Rogoff, an illustrator of uncommon ability, labored with me for many years on the eight thousand illustrations in this book, which were drawn from many thousands of Polaroid photographs depicting the signs. His style and approach to illustration in this demanding area have influenced the work of many other people in the field.

William Stokoe, my much-admired colleague and friend from my Gallaudet days, has been kind enough to permit his seminal monograph, "The Study and Use of Sign Language" to be used here, with slight revisions, as an Introduction to the dictionary. His work through the years has generated so much scholarly activity in American sign language that it would be difficult to do justice to the subject in the short space allotted here. He and James Bourg, a Gallaudet College colleague, have made available to me an early computer printout of titles in the general area of sign language, and this has in turn formed the basis for the Bibliography in the book.

The Foreign Language Indexes, developed to make the book accessible to deaf people and hearing workers of other lands, was a joint contribution of many talented and dedicated people. They are listed in the General Editorial Committee, but I would be remiss not to single out Elena Radutzky, Lynn Clark, Judith Clifford, and Lawrence Healy for special thanks.

Norma Schwartz and Jean Calder both kept the thousands of drawings and entry cards in their homes for several years while they worked on mounting and checking. Judith Clifford also provided shelter for the bulk of the manuscript during the Foreign Index phase. All these people made unique sacrifices, and it is difficult to express my thanks in adequate terms.

My publishers, Harper & Row, deserve a medal of honor for the patience and encouragement that have marked their long relationship with me while the book was taking shape. Harold Grove, my long-suffering editor, heads the list of people to whom I am indebted. William Monroe, Lydia Link, Dolores Simon, Millie Matacia, and Barbara Hufham also deserve special mention.

Theodora S. Zavin provided valuable legal assistance from the very beginning of this project. Leo Rosen and Kenneth S. Kauffman shared their expertise in copyright and related matters, and helped keep this very considerable undertaking on a businesslike basis.

My friends Dr. Salvatore diMichael and Dr. Boyce R. Williams both merit a very special thank-you. It was they who provided the very earliest guidance in the shaping of this project, and, through the years, have maintained a lively interest in its development.

An undertaking of this scope, and covering such a long period of time in its development, cannot escape certain built-in hazards. Among these are new signs and new applications for old ones. It has not always been possible to include them. Older signs, too, tend sometimes to fall into disuse. Their inclusion in the dictionary may be useful, however, as historical benchmarks in sign development. Like a history book, this work will never really be finished. I accept full responsibility for what is included and for what is not, and urge my colleagues everywhere to draw my attention to material which I may include in a later edition.

Martin L. A. Sternberg, Ed.D.

Foreword

This dictionary of the language of signs is a significant addition to the published works on manual communication and brings further dignity to the communication medium of deaf people.

Presentation of the components of the language of signs in true dictionary form complete to entry titles, pronunciation, parts of speech, rationale description, and cross references with other entries, imparts to the volume important values. Its usefulness to rehabilitation as a language training tool is readily apparent. The deaf reader with language problems will be greatly benefited in his search for word knowledge by the finely executed word-sign illustrations. The hearing reader who is learning the language of signs so that he may better serve deaf people will find helpful the alphabetical word-sign order.

It is interesting to know that the development of the dictionary was generative. A supposed 2,000 American sign vocabulary expanded in research to over 5,000 entries.

The Vocational Rehabilitation Administration is very pleased to have had a part in making available to deaf people and to hearing people who serve them this advanced reference document on the language of signs. My special thanks go to Martin L. A. Sternberg and Dr. Edna S. Levine of New York University and the many other persons who labored to make this dictionary possible.

Mary E. Switzer
Commissioner of Vocational Rehabilitation

General Editorial Committee

Editorial Staff

Edna S. Levine, Ph.D., Litt.D., *Project Director*; Professor Emeritus, New York University, New York, N.Y.

Martin L. A. Sternberg, Ed.D., *Principal Research Scientist and Editor-in-Chief;* Former Adjunct Assistant Professor, New York University; Adjunct Associate Professor of Deaf Education and Consulting Program Director, University College, Adelphi University, Garden City, N.Y.

Herbert Rogoff, *Illustrator*; Former Associate Research Scientist, New York University, New York, N.Y.; Member, Society of Illustrators; Former Director of Public Relations, M. Grumbacher, Inc., New York, N.Y.

William F. Marquardt, Ph.D., *Linguist*; Late Professor of English Education, New York University, New York, N.Y.

Joseph V. Firsching III, *Project Secretary*

Consulting Committee

Elizabeth E. Benson, Litt.D., *Chief Consultant*; Late Dean of Women and Professor of Speech, Gallaudet College, Washington, D.C.

Leon Auerbach, *Senior Consultant*; Professor of Mathematics, Gallaudet College, Washington, D.C.

Special Consultants

Charles L. Brooks, *Vocational Signs*
Nancy Frishberg, Ph.D., *Editorial*
Emil Ladner, *Catholic Signs*
Max Lubin, *Jewish Signs*
The Rev. Steve L. Mathis III, *Protestant Signs*
Jerome D. Schein, Ph.D., *Editorial*
Edward L. Scouten, *General Signs*
William C. Stokoe, Ph.D., *Editorial*
Joseph P. Youngs, Jr., LL.D., *General Signs*

Illustration Assistants

Ann Silver, *Senior Illustration Assistant*
Jack Fennell
Jean Worth

Illustration Processing

Norma Schwartz, *Senior Illustration Processor* (Mounting)
Jean Calder, *Illustration Processor* (Mounting)

Bibliography

James W. Bourg, *Coordinator, Bibliographic Database*
William C. Stokoe, Ph.D., *Consultant*
Claudia Gomez, *Typist*

Foreign Language Indexes

Elena Radutzky, *Editor*
Lynn Clark, *Senior Consultant*
Judith M. Clifford, *Senior Consultant*
Lawrence A. Healy, *Senior Consultant*

Lucia Carbajal, *Foreign Language Consultant*
Nancy de Conciliis, *Foreign Language Consultant*
Eva Glatz, *Foreign Language Consultant*
Mitsuko Hasegawa, *Foreign Language Consultant*
Karen Herschell, *Foreign Language Consultant*
Michiko Kosaka, *Foreign Language Consultant*
Deborah Sontag, *Foreign Language Consultant*
Charles Stern, *Foreign Language Consultant*
Mary Ellen Tracy, *Foreign Language Consultant*

Joseph V. Firsching III, *Data Processing Coordinator*
Frank Burkhardt, *Programming Consultant*
Ardele Frank, *Data Processing*
Rosemary Nikolaus, *Data Processing*
Bernice Schwartz, *Data Processing*
Rosalee Truesdale, *Data Processing*

Editorial Assistants

Lilly Berke, Edna Bock, Jean Calder (*Senior*), Nancy Chough,
Judith M. Clifford, Arlene Graham, Pat Rost, Norma Schwartz,
Patrice Smith, Mary Ellen Tracy

Secretarial/Clerical/Typing

Edna Bock, Carole Goldman, Carole Wilkins

The Study and Use of Sign Language

by William C. Stokoe, Jr.

Introductory

American education of the deaf began with sign language, but for more than a hundred years "signing" has been strictly prohibited in a few schools, discouraged and neglected in the rest. It has been treated as unsuitable behavior, something to be ashamed of or repressed, instead of as an object of study and a language to use. Educated deaf persons have been decrying this treatment of sign language since it began, and for a decade or so they have been joined by linguists and sociologists; but textbooks and materials now in use and the direction of most research in special education indicate that prejudice against the use of sign language and ignorance of its relation to English have not materially lessened. However, there are signs of change: growing discontent with the low level of achievement reached by the deaf child in school, new interest in sign language from linguistics and related sciences, and greater need to conserve human resources as we confront the problems of our time. There is no need for most of the thousands of deaf children about to enter school to leave at sixteen or eighteen with virtually no reading ability. In the following pages we will take a positive, not a negative, view of sign language. It will be the center of attention, not as an object of interest to the specialist in language, but as the central feature in the complex sociolinguistic and psycholinguistic system that makes the deaf person part of general American culture and at the same time part of a special group. To see sign language in this way it will be necessary first to examine the ways language may be presented to the eye instead of to the ear, next to point out the contrasts and parallels between speech and sign language. Then the relation of sign language to the education of deaf persons will be considered in the light of bilingualism. This use of two or more languages with, it may be, different degrees of profi-

First prepared in 1970 for the ERIC Clearinghouse for Linguistics. Revised in 1971 for the National Association of the Deaf. Copyright © 1971 by William C. Stokoe, Jr., and used, with slight revisions, by permission.

ciency in different situations, has been the object of important research in recent years and has an obvious relevance to sign language,
to English, and to the sociolinguistic functioning of deaf people. Finally we will look at steps that concerned teachers can take to apply
research most appropriate to their classrooms and to carry out research of their own of the most practical kind. What does *this* deaf
child know and understand? What does he most need to have explained to widen his grasp? How do I reach him? These are the
questions that teachers must ask and answer for themselves. And
these are the questions that this study addresses. The teacher knows
English, but the deaf child starting school (unlike the hearing child)
may not. The deaf child under the right conditions may know sign
language the way a hearing child knows standard English, or Spanish,
or the nonstandard dialect of the ghetto; but the teacher too often
knows no sign language and may even have been taught to hate and
fear it. Sign language cannot be learned as a living, working language
from these pages, but it is hoped that teachers, sign language interpreters, deaf persons, and others reading them may find a new understanding of what this language is like, of how it relates to English, and
of its importance in the intellectual and psychosocial development of
deaf persons. Even more important it is a language that can be learned
by the parents of a deaf child and so become the way to more normal
parent-child communication and mental and linguistic development;
for the deaf child will "pick it up" from his peers, and an adult's
example and guidance become much needed balancing factors.

Sight, Language, and Speech

Education for the deaf confronts a central fact: sight instead of hearing is the sense that conveys language symbols to the person who
cannot hear. In the history of systematic education of the deaf this fact
has not always been squarely faced. The French pioneers l'Épée and
Sicard, in harmony with the empirical and scientific spirit of the
Enlightenment, founded their teaching on this fact. Visibly distinct
signals were built into their rigorous intellectual program of instruction. But even in l'Épée's lifetime Samuel Heinicke challenged the
French approach, insisting that words, that is, ideas, could never be
presented inside the mind without sounds. Their exchange of letters
began in 1780.[1] Paris, Leipzig, Vienna, and Zurich—the whole intellectual world of Europe—were involved. The decision of the Rector
and the Fellows of the Academy of Zurich in l'Épée's favor in 1783
did not end the controversy, though the fact remains that eyes, not
ears, are the deaf person's prime symbol receivers.

Modern heirs of Heinicke follow a train of reasoning that with-
draws from that fact. He began by teaching deaf-mutes to make
sounds, thence "to read and speak clearly and with understanding."
Like all readers they had to use their eyes, but he contended that the

written symbols had meaning for them only through association with the sounds that they had been taught to produce. He and teachers of the deaf before and since his time also have their pupils try to associate the sounds that they make (and that they must suppose others also make) with visible facial movements—to lipread.

Language taught by these procedures is speech, but speech with a difference: seeing the oral action of persons speaking, and making the sounds one has been taught to make. Various ways of using these procedures dominate American education of the deaf. Users of "the pure oral method" postpone reading and writing instruction until lipreading and voice production have been practiced for several years. Proponents of "the natural method" do not teach language analytically nor synthetically but "naturally" as situations arise for its use in the classroom of deaf pupils with a hearing teacher. "The oral method" differs from the other two chiefly in that reading and writing instruction accompany lipreading and speaking. In theory there is nothing for the deaf child to see when any of these procedures is in use except for the lip movements of the teacher and other pupils. In fact there is a wealth of information presented to the eyes. Besides the inevitable gesturing of the teacher there are her other actions, the room itself and all the objects in it, not to mention the activity of a handful or a double handful of bright-eyed children. American education of deaf people gambles that all this and more information can be integrated and understood by means of spoken English as it is learned from visual inspection of a speaker's face. In normal circumstances speech and language do perform this function. Many readers will have had some contact with a three- or four-year-old's "Why? What's that for? Why're you doing that? What's that thing? Where's he going?" But the oral method usually begins only after the six- or seven-year-old child is in school, and then with the expectation that in one full year of instruction the average deaf child will have a lipreading and speaking vocabulary of fifty words.

The question arises whether, used in this way, the deaf child's eyes and mind are being put to anything like efficient use. This question and other considerations have turned attention to the sign language of deaf people. American Sign Language is directly derived from the language of signs that inspired l'Épée and Sicard and that was used by the generations of deaf people they instructed in eighteenth and nineteenth century France. It is the language of deaf adults in North America and has been their language for one hundred and fifty years. It has been put to special uses recently by hearing persons where speech will not work: in noisy locations, under water, and in airless space. It is also one part of the whole field of *semiotics,* sign and symbolic communication of all kinds, in which many sciences now have an interest. Used simultaneously with spoken English, it is the language in which deaf persons achieve a higher education.

The Nature of Sign Language

Sign language uses sight, as lipread speech does, but uses it in a radically different way. Sounds—vowels and consonants along with differences in intonation—are the elements of language received by the normal ear. What is "read" by a deaf person who has learned to do so is the positions of the lips, teeth, and tongue producing these sounds. But the elements of sign language are things seen exactly as they are done. They do not divide into vowels and consonants but into three kinds of elements. These are places, or *tabs,* different from each other but all recognizable as where the sign starts or acts or ends; designators *(dez),* the appearance of the hand or hands that make the sign; and *sigs,* the action itself.[2]

Just as vowels and consonants in some sequences but not in others make syllables of English and one or more syllables make words, so the elements of sign language combine in some ways and not in others to make *signs.* Signs are considered to "have meaning" just as words are, but here some of the common misunderstandings of sign language have their beginning. The usual notion, fostered by all the older English-Sign handbooks, is that a sign represents a word of English and conversely that each English word listed "has a sign." The truth is different. Linguistics, the scientific study of languages as systems complete in themselves, has made it perfectly clear that no word-for-word translation of one language into another is possible. And this is true both because the semantic areas covered by words that translate each other are not congruent and because the syntactic combinations open to a word in one language are not the same ones open to a similar word in another. A sign may have some of the meanings and uses of an English word but not of others. Likewise a word may translate a sign occurring in some contexts but not in others. This being so, there may be even more divergence between constructions, the phrases and sentences of the two languages, than between words and signs.

The possibilities of difference in structure between something said in standard English and the same idea expressed in sign language have been exaggerated and misrepresented. It is possible for an expression in signs to be exactly parallel to an expression in English—of that more later. It is also possible for the constructions expressing "the same thing" to be quite different in the two languages. This has led some users of sign language as well as its detractors to claim that it is "ungrammatical," or "has no grammar." Unfortunately this notion, uncorrected by any real knowledge about language, is repeated in many textbooks used in training teachers of deaf children and is widely believed. Again the truth is otherwise.

The signs of sign language can occur in the same order as the words in an English sentence, or they can occur in quite different order. The sign sentence may seem to omit signs for words that are essential in the English sentence. Again the sign sentence may have signs where the English sentence has no equivalent word. Sign language grammar or syntax has its rules as well as its lexicon or vocabulary of signs, and both rules and lexicon differ from the rules and lexicon of English.

Seen as a whole system, however, sign language is quite like English or any other language. Its elements contrast with each other (visibly instead of audibly). They combine in certain ways, not in others. These combinations, signs, "have meaning" as words or morphemes do. Constructions combining signs, like constructions combining words, express meanings more completely and complexly than single signs or words can. These constructions or syntactic structures are systematic, rule-governed structures. But there is a unique set of rules for making sign language constructions just as there is for making standard English constructions, nonstandard English constructions, or the constructions of any language.

Before looking at the extreme differences between sign language constructions and English, we should go more fully into the possibility of similarity. One thing that makes parallel constructions in the two languages possible is the general agreement that many signs and words do in fact form approximately equivalent pairs. The most important reason, however, that sign language constructions can be made to duplicate the order of English constructions is really incidental to sign language. There is a third way for language to be presented to sight—different both from the appearance of a speaker's face and from the combinations of the elements of signs. This third way is usually known as fingerspelling, though it has also been called manual English, dactylology, the manual alphabet, and chirologia. It is usually very closely associated with sign language in use; though in the "Rochester Method," an experimental, recently revived method, fingerspelling exclusive of signs is used to teach and communicate with deaf children.[3]

Fingerspelling works of course by virtue of the existence of alphabetic writing, and there is some evidence that its use—perhaps more for secret communication than for serving deaf persons—is as old as the practice of scratching, carving, and writing letters. When it is combined with sign language the differences between sign language and English grammar and vocabulary can be eliminated. Words that have no counterpart in sign language, like *the, a, an, of,* and all the forms of *be,* are simply fingerspelled.

It also serves as an important link between the two languages for the bilingual American deaf person. New signs are coined, and many old ones have been formed by using the manual alphabet "hand" as dez and moving it in a certain way in a certain place. Thus the first letter of the English word becomes the dez element of the new sign. The signs for five of the days of the week, color names, personal names, and many other signs are made in this way.

Without this link, to the linguist interested in the grammars of the two, sign language and English seem to differ enormously. But

with it, to a deaf American, shifting from one language to the other
is so easy that it is usually done without conscious notice. But here
a sociolinguistic distinction must be made. The deaf person who
sometimes uses a sign and sometimes uses a fingerspelled word that
translates the sign is one who has achieved a higher educational level
than the signer who uses the same sign (and knows its meaning, of
course) but does not know that English has an equivalent word.

The conditions, then, under which a sign language sentence will
preserve the order of an English sentence are (1) the free use of
fingerspelling with signs, (2) the sign language user's competence to
produce the English structure, and (3) occasions that call for English-
like sign language instead of the colloquial or casual variety. Such
occasion may be the signed interpretation for a deaf audience of a
formal lecture or the natural tact of a deaf signer when conversing
with a hearing viewer who is unfamiliar with colloquial signs. However, on other occasions, when the named conditions are not present,
sign language sentences may show a wide departure from the patterns
of standard English—but it should be borne in mind that colloquial
English, not to mention nonstandard dialectal varieties, may also
depart from the models of grammatical sentences shown in school-
books. Two examples of such divergence will be examined in detail.

The first example is furnished by one way of signing a simple,
basic sentence in English: *He saw me.* This sentence is called simple
and basic because its syntax has been described by a small number of
explicit rules for expanding "S" into terminal symbols. Leaving aside
all explanation of the meaning and the sounds that result, we may use
these three rules to generate *he saw me:*

S	→	NP + VP	S, structure or sentence
			NP, noun phrase
(1)	NP →	Pro	VP, verb phrase
			Pro, pronoun
VP →	VT + NP		VT, transitive verb

Figure 1 shows the structure these rules generate and, below the
terminal symbols, the words in order:

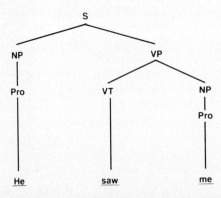

Figure 1

There should be no difficulty in relating the series of rules and the diagram to terminology used traditionally in parsing sentences. The first rule describes the structure Subject + Predicate, the third rule describes the predicate as Transitive Verb + Object.

The difficulty arises when the sign sentence is put beside the English. All that an observer sees is what the manuals of sign language would call one sign, but the sign is one this writer has not found in any of them. The "sign" for "see" is described in the manuals somewhat as follows: "The V-hand held up so that the fingertips are opposite the signer's eyes, back of the hand outward, is moved away from the face a short distance." Instead of this, the signer whose sentence is *he saw me* holds the V-hand pointing obliquely out at about head level, looking at it, and with a flick of the wrist bends the fingertips toward himself.

Using the same rules for the signed sentence as for the English sentence, we are forced to observe that two of the three symbols are not expanded, those called "Pro" in Figure 2:

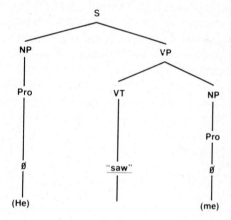

Figure 2

This will not do, although it seems to have a counterpart in English:

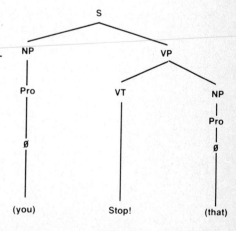

Figure 3

The speaker and hearer of English understand perfectly that *Stop!* may be expanded into *You stop!* or *Stop that!* or *You stop that!*, which in fact may occur instead of *Stop!* Thus all four of these English S's have the same underlying structure and presumably the same meaning.

In the case of *He saw me,* however, the parties to the exchange understand exactly what this sentence says to the English reader: "A person, not the transmitting or receiving one, which person (masculine) both writer and reader could fully identify if necessary, saw the transmitting person." Some would add that since *He saw me* is a declarative sentence it also includes this meaning: "I'm telling you that . . ." In the English form of course there are at least two other bits of meaning that can be separated out and shown to relate to the surface form: *saw* has a form that indicates the seeing took place in time past, and *me* redundantly indicates what its position also tells, that it is the object. Another form, *he,* announces that it is the subject, but exactly what person, man or boy, it stands for is outside this kind of grammatical analysis. When we use an example like *He saw me* in a discussion of language we must suppose that the sentence is spoken where the speaker and hearer can both indicate and understand the meaning of *he* through glances of their eyes. (Just how much sign language, or more properly *kinesics,* is necessary for efficient speech among hearing persons is beyond the subject of this discussion.) Or if the center of attention is written English, we must suppose that *He saw me* is taken out of a series of sentences which more exactly identifies who *he* is.

In the sign language the same kind of supposition is necessary. Since the sign sentence is translated "He saw me," the meaning "past" in the sentence must have come from a signed sentence occurring earlier in a real sign language conversation or story.

Though we can now account for the element "past" of the sign sentence in the same way used to account for the reference of *he* in the English sentence, the problem remains to explain how a signer makes his sentence mean "he saw me." He does so (a) by changing the way of making the sign "see" (which also means "I see"), (b) by starting the changed sign "see" with the hand held where it would be to sign "him" or "her," and (c) by moving the sign's prominent feature, the fingertips, toward himself, "me."

To sum up the comparison, or contrast rather, of the sign language and English sentences more rules are needed. First for the English, tense and object marking are specified by rules too:

$$S \rightarrow NP + VP$$

(2) $NP \rightarrow Pro$ (+ Obj, in context VP)

$$VP \rightarrow VT + NP$$

$$VT \rightarrow V + Past$$

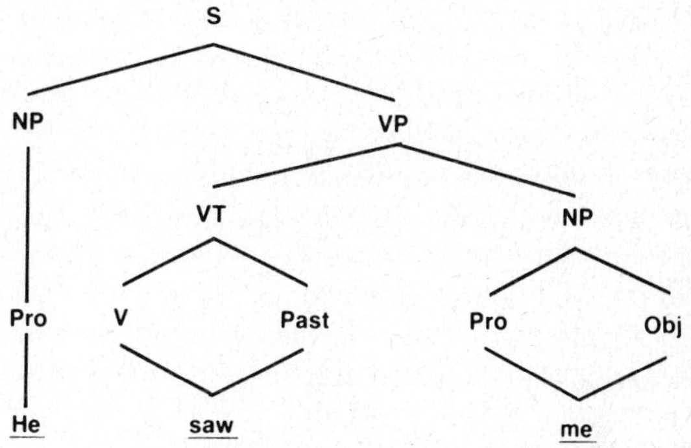

```
                          S
            ┌─────────────┴─────────────┐
           NP                           VP
            │              ┌─────────────┴─────────────┐
            │             VT                           NP
            │          ┌───┴───┐                    ┌───┴───┐
           Pro         V      Past                 Pro     Obj
            │          └───┬───┘                    └───┬───┘
           He             saw                          me
```

Figure 4

This is still a very simple structure, but the sentence in sign language is not. To describe it requires more and different categories, as Figure 5 shows:

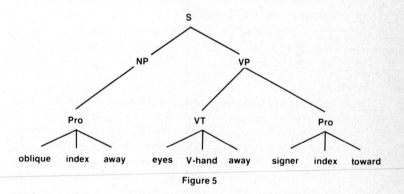

Figure 5

If these elements are put together in a sign language way, we get a three-sign sentence with the same order as in English. But the sign sentence we have been considering may be described as a transformation, or at least as a complex morphological change, by the action of which the Verb branch is changed almost out of recognition because

of its occurrence with the two Pronoun branches. All of the material
on the left of the double arrow below symbolizing transformation is
consolidated into the three sign elements to the right:

<u>oblique</u> + index + away (= "he")
+
(3) eyes + <u>V-hand</u> + away (= "saw") $\rightleftarrows$ oblique + V-hand + toward
+
signer + index + <u>toward</u> (= "me") ("he") "saw" ("me")

A number of other grammars of this one sign sentence could be
written, but two points should be quite clear from this tentatively
suggested description: sign language has just as much grammatical
structure as English, perhaps more; and to the person who knows sign
language it conveys exactly as much meaning as does the English
sentence to one who knows English. And one point further. Just as
He saw me! He saw me. He saw me? and other intonations than these
suggested ones have definite and different meanings for many English
speakers, so the sign sentence can be varied with head and eye movements and modifications in the way the hand moves to indicate question, surprise, emphasis, and other meanings.

The second pair of sentences to be compared seems to show more
complication on the English side. Grammarians who speak of generation and transformation would say that there is a base structure
behind or underlying the sentence, *There's a man in there,* and point
out that a transformation has made it what it is on the surface. They
might write rules like these to generate that base:

S	$\rightarrow$	NP	+ VP	
NP	$\rightarrow$	Det	+ N	Det, determiner
(4) VP	$\rightarrow$	Copula	+ Adv	Adv, adverb
Adv	$\rightarrow$	Adv	+ Adv	

Following the rules generates this structure, which describes the base:

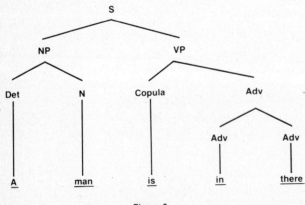

Figure 6

Various transformational rules to derive a *there*-sentence from a base have been proposed. (Part of the educational value of this kind of grammar is the practice it gives the proposer.) One proposal is to consider that two bases are transformed by embedding one in the other. This requires the generation of another base: **There's something.* (The asterisk indicates that the sentence is suppositious.) Then *something* is replaced by the first base (rule: something =S). The diagram shows the first stage of the embedding:

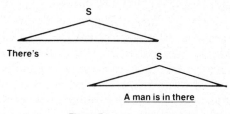

Figure 7

A deletion rule requires us to remove *is,* and the result is: *There's a man in there.* The sign language sentence that "says" the same thing seems to be much simpler in structure. It uses only two signs, "man" and "there." It has no article-determiner and no copula. (Sign language like most of the world's languages does not translate *be* overtly, but in English-like signing all the eight forms of *be* are fingerspelled.) In this sentence the sign that glosses the English adverb *there,* means "in there," because the signer would be pointing to a door or wall— *the man* is not in sight. In the English sentence . . . *a man there* means "where you can see him too." Thus the actual situation in which it is used determines whether this sign means "there" or "in there"— a not unusual way for a language form and its situational meaning to relate.

    In spite of the absence of articles and copula or linking verbs, in spite of its having just two signs, the signed equivalent of "There's a man in there" is an extremely difficult structure to describe. What makes it so is that both signs composing it appear at exactly the same time. The rule S → "man" + "there" does not work; since X + Y means "X followed by Y." But the rule S → "there" + "man" is just as powerless to explain what happens. Neither of the structures below can be the basic structure because they too imply left-to-right order:

$$S \rightarrow X + Y, \text{ or}$$
$$S \rightarrow Y + X, \text{ or}$$

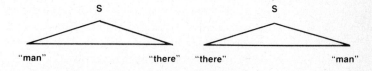

Figure 8

Order is meaningful in sign language of course just as it is in all languages. The difference between "you forgot" and "forgot you," signed, is just like the difference between these two English sequences. Sign language like English has XY and YX as possible orders in its syntax, but nothing in our normal conventions of writing can show the third order sign language also has. The displays $\overset{X}{Y}$ and $\overset{Y}{X}$ show a superiority that implies priority of one symbol over the other; but no such priority can be found in sign language itself. What looks like a typist's error could show how the sign language sentence is made: $\mathbf{X}$. But microscopic examination of a typist's strikeover will tell us which key was hit first. Two signs performed at the same time contain no clues to help a detective. A speaker might cry, "In there! In there!" —to which a listener replies, "What?" and gets the answer, "A man!" With this to go on, grammarians will argue that beneath all this excitement lies the English-language competence of speaker and listener, that their competence has quietly generated this base, *a man (is) in there,* and that two different deletion rules have operated to let the first speaker make his outcry and his answer. But deletion, substitution, combination, and permutation transforms do not describe the sign language sentence we have here.

The point is not that generative-transformational grammars are inadequate. "All grammars leak"; no theorist of language has yet adequately described the way languages work inside their own systems, let alone the way they work socially, in human groupings. The point instead is that sign language, far from having no grammar, has such interesting and unusual structure and system that it challenges all theories of grammar. The difference seen in just two pairs of sentences should warn us that everything we know about English, right or wrong, must be questioned all over again before we apply it to sign language.

Equally important is the fact that languages are much easier to learn and use than to describe or explain. Every natural language used (now or in the past) has been learned and learned thoroughly by every child, bright, normal, or dull, who is born among its users—provided that he can hear.

The elements of a sign language are perfectly clear and understandable to anyone who can see. The combinations of these elements are signs that have meaning for all who use the language. Having meaning, the signs then can be used to translate English words, but translate them no better nor worse than the words of any language can translate the words of another. The combinations of the signs make sentences, but make them in two ways. With fingerspelling freely used, the sign sentence may be a close or exact replica of an English sentence. But in casual and informal styles the sign sentences may be slightly, mildly, or wildly different in structure.

Social Implications of Sign Language

In the preceding section we saw that sign language order is sometimes like, sometimes unlike, the order of an English sentence. Education of deaf persons is also both like and unlike American education in general. William Labov says, ". . . the fundamental role of the school is to teach reading and writing of standard English."[4] But the schools he takes in the aggregate play their role on the solid stage of language competence. An American child comes to school after four or five years of intensive language learning and use. As some would say, he has mastered the rules, that is, he has the competence to generate and to understand countless sentences. Labov might add: ". . . in some standard or nonstandard dialect of English." Others would say that the child has completely learned the sound subsystem, is nearly done learning the inventory of grammatical forms and their combinations, but is only well started on learning the semantic system of the language spoken where he grew to school age.

A deaf child probably has not learned any of this. The school for him undertakes teaching him literacy of course, but it assumes first an additional role—to teach him English as his native language. What surprises linguists like Labov when they learn of it, and shocks compassionate teachers like Herbert Kohl,[5] is that *no school for deaf children uses sign language to perform either role.* It would take too much time away from the study of sign language to go into the language methods and rationalizations that *are* in use, and much of the educational literature is vague or worse about language anyway. Time is better spent in looking at the sociolinguistic facts of life in silence.

One of the most important uses of language is the formation and preservation of social groups. The term *group* can be given its widest meaning, for language has critical functions in the intimate group of two (though perhaps the smallest group is one person thinking) as well as in the largest national or supernational groups: "Western Civilization," "The Free World," "Socialist Peoples' Republics." If the extremes are too remote to be convincing, one has only to think of the inclusive and divisive effect of the one word *black* in American society of the late sixties.

The grossest social effect of sign language is to make deaf persons using it immediately visible and visibly "different." Conversely, its nonuse hides the deaf person or group from detection as different by a casual observer. An unreasonably high valuation put on this hiding effect has worked along with outmoded language theories to keep sign language out of schools. Nevertheless these facts remain: those who cannot hear must use eyes instead of ears to receive information, and in this respect alone they are different from hearing persons; communication with others by lipreading and acquired speech is no more "normal" than communication by signing; deaf persons whether educated orally or left alone sign to each other.

Thus deaf persons constitute a social group both by the difference of not hearing and by the social working of language. But this is grouping by separation from hearing society, and deaf people form groups just as people generally do, in part by the joining operation of language. Possession of a common language joins people most strongly, just as different languages divide. A minority group, the oral deaf, using no signs or fingerspelling, find more affinity with those few hearing persons who actively promote the language of lipread and acquired speech. These deaf persons have little contact with the larger group of deaf persons whose language is sign language. That this group is small is attested by such studies as Pierre Gorman's 1961 Cambridge University thesis[6] and indirectly by the results of broad surveys both in Britain[7] and Finland[8]: among deaf pupils leaving school, speech intelligibility and understanding of what is said to them is no more than ten percent.

However, using sign language in itself is far from making a single homogeneous group. Just as among users of any language, there are all kinds of levels or groupings both determined by language and best discerned by examining the evidence provided by language. Because of the fact that language changes, the most important of these distinctions is age. Children, teenagers, and adults who use sign language are in far more complete communication within these age levels than across them. The case of infants is somewhat different, as in any language community. The fortunate ones—from a language standpoint—have deaf parents and possibly deaf brothers and sisters. Thus their early sign language puts them into perfectly natural communication within their families. Once the sign language user joins a group of age mates—and those whose sign language acquisition is not a family affair often learn it then—his language is theirs and stays so for a lifetime.

Another kind of language grouping, observed among speakers of all languages, is found, too, among signers. Persons of the same age group sign alike except that those of the same sex sign more alike. Obviously physiological causes can be found for the difference in men's and women's voices; but when the focus is language and not speech, the sexual differences in vocabulary, grammatical rules, and every part of the system can be observed. Here the observer who comes new to signing is at an advantage. One of his first impressions will be of the difference between the signing of men and of women, a difference he may describe as angular, sharp versus round, smooth, or graceful. The reader may doubt that there is a similar difference in male and female language among speakers of English unless he has heard and noted this difference in other English dialects than his own.

A third kind of grouping, a more precisely interpersonal relationship that language accomplishes, it does through style levels. Martin Joos calls these "The Five Clocks" in his book of the same name.[9] As five clocks can be set to tell different times, style levels of language can be set—are set—to tell different things of importance about the relation of speaker and addressee. These levels he calls "intimate, casual, consultative, formal, and frozen," arranged as a central norm and opposite tendencies. Consultative style joins two people through language despite their differences, because "two heads are better than one." Its vocabulary, sentence structure, manner of production, and information content can be taken as standard for the language. In casual style, the language itself implies "we're friends," and therefore much information may be left out that belongs in consultative. Also in casual style, slang is not only permitted but required. In the other direction, formal style treats the addressee almost as if he wasn't there —he isn't able to reply because now he is one of an audience or other formal group. All the connections must be clear in this variety of language along with every bit of information, and since interruptions are not expected or allowed, *careful* is the obvious characterization of formal style.

Intimate style comes very close to being a contradiction to some widely used definitions of language because it is not universal but is an exclusive social vehicle, a possession shared only by those who know the rules which generate it. For intimate style is private language. Husbands and wives, to take one kind of group, have a special vocabulary (pet names) as many have observed; but a clearing of the throat with a certain intonation or a grunt or a word that would have minimal meaning in other circumstances—these have more force in an intimate group than whole paragraphs of formal language can have.

Frozen style is the imaginative label Joos gives to the style as (good) prose and poetry. He does not call it "literary" probably because in casual or consultative exchanges we take that word to mean artificial, artsy-craftsy, or hoked up. "Frozen" seems a chilly label until we think of how our standard of eating has improved since benefactors of mankind have spent the time and care needed to give us frozen foods. From his discussion of this style Joos launches into a description of literature, its nature, uses, and production, by creating some. This is still pertinent to the study of sign language and of the utmost importance to every person who has contact with deaf people. Sign language is not written, but it has a literature. Careful language characterizes formal style, but artistic language (frozen style) has more than just care behind it. Many peoples whose culture does not include writing have songs, poems, stories, charms, histories, and liturgies. Sign language users too have artistic forms of expression, and objects to express in them. Two of the most intensively developed at the present time are fortunately widely accessible to nonsigning audiences. One is a union of sign language and interpretative dancing in which signs naturally (really with consummate artistry) merge into the total movement of the dancers. The other is the National Theater of the Deaf—visible on television and on national and international tours. This too is a natural development from pantomime and from the pioneering of Washington's Gallaudet College Dramatic Club in the fifties and sixties.

All five of these styles are found in use among signers, and recognizing them has tremendous implications for the study of sign language. First of course is the conviction that recognition of them brings: if sign language works intimately, casually, and so forth, even as it divides and unites its users by age, and as its structures come from its self-contained system, then surely it is a language of the depth and complexity that only languages have, a language well worth study. Second, when its "frozen style" embodies artistic achievements that make critics of drama and dance jump to their feet and wildly applaud, the parents and teachers of deaf children must come to realize that using signs does not "cut off" the heights but opens new ranges to be conquered. And third, for the study of sign language itself the five styles, the five clocks, are indispensable instruments.

A very creditable first attempt has been made by Elizabeth McCall to explain the syntax of sign language in "A Generative Grammar of Sign."[10] She writes phrase structure rules and transformational rules to generate some sentences of sign language she observed in use. One shortcoming is that the signs and sign activity, the elements of sign, are not described. Instead the sentences she collected are recorded as sequences of English words used to translate the signs observed. But the use of "the five clocks" could have prevented a more serious flaw than that. In the signing she observed at picnics and other social occasions the persons were friends, fellow workers, immediate relatives, and intimates of each other, as is learned from Miss McCall's introduction and from the internal evidence of the sentences themselves. It is a safe bet, then, if not a certainty, that the sign language she observed was all on the casual and intimate levels, never even rising to the consultative, since persons not on casual terms do not go to such gatherings, or if they do, as Joos points out, they stay on strangers' footing a few seconds at most, the time for a formal introduction, and response. Then, since the characteristics of casual style are ellipsis and slang and those of intimate are extraction (of information the intimate already knows) and jargon, any attempt to write the grammar of sign language and its (partial) lexicon from this data is bound to describe something quite different from the standard (consultative or formal) sign language, the sign language that might be used to advantage in schools. Indeed the first two rules (p. 22) of Miss McCall's grammar show more things left out (parentheses) than left in the base structures:

1. $S \rightarrow \begin{Bmatrix} G \\ (Adv_e) \end{Bmatrix} + (NP) + Pred + (T)$ G, "global gesture"
                                                                          T,   time sign

2. $G \rightarrow \begin{Bmatrix} (Adv_e) \\ G_2 \end{Bmatrix} + G_1$

The same procedure would result in a much elided rule for English sentences. Suppose we overhear a conversation between husband and wife that goes like this:

"Dear."
"Engh."
"Checks."
"N't goin' that way."

Then a panel of experts on English might translate it into as follows, with parenthetical parts to show the information left out because the addressee already knows it:

"Dear, (I would like to remind you of an errand.)."
"Engh (=Yes, I hear you; what is it? I'm listening.)."
"(I am almost out of blank) *checks,* (and I must do the accounts tonight. Would you stop at the bank on your way to work and get some.)."
"(Sorry, I have to drive Charley to the airport and I will) *not* (be) *going that way."*

Finally if we were to write rules for English sentences that would convey this information, with parentheses to indicate what was left out of them when they were spoken, we would probably get a generative grammar of English much like the first generative grammar of signs.

Two other ranges that Joos relates to the five styles are those of scope and responsibility. By scope he means that a user of a language may be understood only *locally,* in some wider *provincial* region, or anywhere that the language is used. From *standard,* the scope again narrows to *conservative* or all the way to *puristic.* Education and a variety of experiences are usually the means of changing local and provincial ways of using language to standard, but personal preference accounts for the later narrowing if it occurs. There is frequent reference among sign users to other signers' "home sign" and some condescension in discussion of these local and provincial manners of signing. Ironically, though, the makers of handbooks and teachers of sign language (to adults or college students, since school children are not supposed to use it) are conservative or even purist in attitude; and their descriptions of "the right way" to make signs can depart as far from standard as regional practices do in another direction. Standard of course is not a matter of legislation, but of currency. Frederick Schreiber, widely known late Executive Secretary of the National Association of the Deaf, was born and raised in Brooklyn and taught school in Texas. He knew the sign dialects of New York and of the Southwest, but living in the national capital area and visiting every state in the course of his work, he used a variety of sign language that is understood everywhere, that is, standard. When he discussed, and other national leaders of the deaf community discuss standardization of sign language as part of the work of their agencies, they are not trying to stop the tides of language change but only to recognize that there are local, provincial, standard, conservative, and puristic kinds of sign language and that one who studies standard is on the surest ground.

The other range is responsibility. Just as in a person's way of speaking we detect character, so is it done in sign language. The smooth operator, the promoter, the perpetual victim, the hail-fellow-well-met, and all the other types that we associate with a way of using language are to be found in the sign language community too. One does not have to be a native signer or expert in sign language to recognize the general indications. This kind of language difference Joos calls responsibility; and we judge it of course by the way a person talks, looks, and acts, so that it is a language difference tied to many other indications.

Bilingualism: Sign Language and English

Bilingualism, "the constant (oral) use of two languages," may be looked at from either end of the sociolinguistic telescope. It is a complicated social and political problem with a linguistic center and an explosive potential, when people of two different language stocks live under one government. It is also a valuable individual skill. The study of sign language requires looking in both directions. The deaf population of the United States suffers the same irritation, frustration, even loss of basic rights as other minority language groups. The deaf individual, however, faces a unique problem: one of the two languages he needs to use is not oral.

The broad social aspect of bilingualism has many facets when looked at closely. Canadian bilingualism involves two languages of high prestige and the rivalry of French, British, and North American cultural values. In other bilingual situations only one of the languages may have the prestige of worldwide use, while the other remains little known and perhaps unwritten. In the past, obviously, the world language would be that of the dominant group and the local language remain that of the governed. In the present world it is possible, however, to find the language of the emerging nationality made official, and English, French, Dutch, or Arabic reduced to secondary status.

These are but a few of the possibilities of combination, but for deaf people the pattern is still most like that of the past. Sign language is not written, though now it may be. It is little known either to the general public or to those whose study is language. It is frequently excluded from school and religious instruction—outlawed in some of the United States—though it should be said that several religious groups have been and are its staunchest supporters. For deaf people in other countries the bilingual situation can be even less advantageous. Colonialism, imperialism, and racism—words occurring oftener now in hot debate than in cool study—do summon up a social attitude that can be discerned in much official policy regarding sign language. Here for instance are the words of a royal commission to examine "the place if any of 'manual communication' in the education of deaf children" in Britain (emphasis added):

> Clearly *the major risks* associated with the use of a combined method which includes signing would be eliminated if the signs were themselves chosen from a systematic language *with normal grammatical structure.*[11]

The chairman of the commission has amplified this in a recent address:

> Everybody knows what is commonly said about signing, that it may impede, may retard, the development of language. I think there is some misunderstanding about this, if I may give my personal opinion. The notion is that signing is more natural, that signing is easier than the mother tongue. Up to a point this is true, but if signing is to be a means of educating the children, the question is whether it is in the hands of teachers who understand what they are doing and have the skill to put it into practice; and how far the signing is itself linguistic.[12]

The commonly held notion that "the mother tongue" (anyone's mother tongue) is the sole repository of "normal grammatical structure" and the only language that can be "linguistic" is a concept well known to anthropologists, who call it ethnocentrism. When it is used to deny that some other language is "systematic" and to impute to the out-group using the language a deficiency of mental functioning, this notion comes perilously close to racism. The study of the grammatical system of sign language as well as its semantic and symbolic systems is the best way to replace such supersitition and prejudice with useful knowledge. One way to begin is to read the essays "The Linguistic Community" and "Sign Language Dialects" by Professor Carl Croneberg. Himself a member of the community he writes of, he has freed himself of ethnocentric bias by studies in anthropology and linguistics. Moreover he was born in Sweden and has native fluency in Scandinavian as well as in American sign language, besides combining a scholar's grasp of Swedish and English with a clear style. His essays appear as Appendix C (pp. 297–311) and Appendix D (pp. 313–319) in *A Dictionary of American Sign Language on Linguistic Principles.*

Social bilingualism is important to an understanding of American education of deaf people, but the bilingual development of the individual deaf person is crucial. Indeed he faces more than the classic bilingual dilemma. The member of a minority language group (which may in this case be a nonstandard dialect-using group) has the choice of staying monolingual and remaining a second- or third-class citizen socially and economically. If he tries to shift to the other tongue, he may either succeed and shut himself off from his background and incur social and psychic costs, or fail and be rejected by the dominant group with equally serious consequences. Ideally, of course, he should grow up where he can use both languages with about equal frequency with native speakers of each, a situation hard to realize.

The person who cannot hear does not even have these choices. The chances are against his growing up in a family using sign language, and therefore he must reach school age *without knowing any real use of language.* Even with sign language learned from the cradle or from his first association with older deaf children he may not receive any formal education, because the schools and teachers may reject signing. Instead he may be taught to pronounce sounds and perhaps lipread them, to recognize and to write letters, and possibly to fingerspell. All of this activity of course is English-language based and designed to make him a monolingual user of English. Early resistance or failure on his part to function like a native speaker of English—dropping out—more than likely consigns him, not to a depressed economic status, but to a life in an institution.

As is often the case, the good sense and adjustment to reality of the linguistic minority exceeds that of well meaning officialdom. None or very few of those whose native language is sign language suppose that a monolingual life in a deaf community is an open option—although there was a short-lived movement in the last century to set aside some of the southwest territory for a deaf state with the language of signs its official language. While the authorities try to enforce monolingual functioning in a vocal-symbol language, wiser heads in the deaf community strive for maximally effective bilingualism. The higher the level of competence in reading and writing English the sign language user can attain the better his life in the bilingual situation. Acquired speech and lipreading skills are also valued assets that no deaf person despises. The objection of the deaf is to a formal educational program which concentrates on these two "oralist" skills alone when all evidence shows that reasonable proficiency in them is attainable by very few individuals, and that for most even a dozen years of full-time effort brings frustration and failure. Meanwhile the language competence in English, read and written and understood, that could be fostered through use of the deaf child's sign language competence is lost.

From the point of view of one who cannot hear, bilingualism can be more a challenge than a dilemma. Direct personal communication with one's friends will naturally (in every sense of the word) be in sign language. One does not have this kind of relationship with foreigners, and all speakers of all oral languages will always be in a sense foreign to one who must listen with the eyes. But consultative and formal participation with others is almost exclusively in English, the language of the general culture, which affords the only way into that culture and all its benefits. Therefore the person who cannot hear will learn just as much English as well as circumstances allow.

The main question for all those who have a hand in shaping these circumstances is this: will the deaf individual reach his maximum competence in English better if he is forced into apparent monolingual use of the language or if his need for bilingual development is acknowledged and satisfied? This question is a somewhat different way of stating an issue that has been in controversy since the eighteenth century. The earliest debate in the *oralist-manualist* controversy was philosophical, as much concerned with the nature of speech and language and perception as with practical matters of instruction. In modern times the debate has degenerated to advocacy of specific educational methods and to advancement of the interests of segments of the learned professions. At one time or another otologists, speech therapists, clinical psychologists, audiologists, phoneticians, psychometrists, pediatricians, psychiatrists, reading specialists, and every other kind of educational specialists have joined the clamor. The philosophical depth of the earlier debate is covered with fragments of psychological theories of all kinds, and even these are obscured by statistical procedures good in themselves but being applied to irrelevant information.

Linguistics and sociolinguistics at least provide a different way of looking at the issue. In the first place linguistics as an anthropological science starts from the position that language is part of the cultural activity of communication. Therefore difference in the way people communicate, in the things that they do, is seen as data to be studied and not as a deviation, error, deprivation, primitivism, or degeneracy. Second, sociolinguistic studies have shown over and over again that bilingualism, diglossia, and other intimate combinations of languages in the individual and in society are facts of life. From a sociolinguistic viewpoint the bilingual language competence of deaf persons may be compound or complex; in contrast, the psychological model behind much current educational policy calls the language of deaf persons a pathological condition.

Fortunately some teachers' practice is better than their theory, but bad theory can still adversely affect practice. A teacher may understand a complicated statement, explanation, or request presented entirely in sign language and respond appropriately; but this teacher is all too likely to tell an observer that the pupil thus communicating "has no language." What we are to understand from this statement requires explanation: 1. By "language" the teacher means the competence in English needed (a) to understand grammatical sentences presented in the teacher's voice or in print or writing and (b) to generate grammatical sentences and produce them in the pupil's own voice or writing. 2. By "no language" the teacher means that (a) the pupil's responses to written or spoken sentences are inappropriate or lacking, (b) that the pupil's production is in some way or ways not grammatical, or (c) both of these. 3. By "has no language" the teacher implies that the pupil is as much out of place in an ordinary elementary classroom as a two-year-old would be in second grade. 4. By using "language" as the token for "(correct) English language" and not allowing it to stand for "sign language" or for anything other than "correct English," the teacher is guilty through ignorance (no excuse) of falsely condemning the pupil to a subhuman or at least socially inferior category. 5. This teacher is also confessing and excusing failure—who can be blamed for not teaching anything to a child who "has no language?"

But this teacher is on the side of the angels. This teacher at least has studied or learned enough sign language to understand the pupil perfectly when he signs. What this teacher says and thinks about "language" are the residue of teacher education and textbooks, and this teacher's not using sign language to address the pupil and to help him learn English are doubtless the enforced policy of the school. The study of sign language could free such a teacher from the fear and ignorance that equate all knowledge and thought with a single language.

But such a teacher is unfortunately not typical, not in even a substantial minority. The response to the first appearance of a deaf pupil's sign language is often such utter rejection that it is ever afterwards hidden from teachers. This does not keep teachers from saying however that the pupil "has no language." Sociolinguistics could at least tell these teachers that even in a one-hundred-percent American community there are other languages than English and other varieties of English than theirs in constant use. Teachers and those in special education programs who will become teachers of the deaf can find other benefits too in the study of sign language and the findings of linguistics. We will have more to say about this later.

The greatest obstacle to second language learning is lack of opportunity. There must be a great many persons, among them teachers, who would like to know another language if only they could find someone to teach them. The good fortune of finding a person one spends minutes or hours with every day to learn from as a native informant seems remote. Nevertheless, every teacher of deaf persons is faced with such riches to the point of embarrassment. An older deaf pupil knows far more sign language (vocabulary *and* structure) than any teacher imagines. Indeed, the pupil has probably become extremely skillful in hiding this knowledge because of the attitude of the school and teachers.

So, if such a teacher has a genuine desire to learn sign language, the problem is not to find one who knows it but to persuade those who know it that using sign language is permissible, even desired, behavior. A pupil who is halting, at a loss, almost inarticulate in English may be fluent, imaginative, even eloquent in sign language. Of course one who resolves to learn the pupils' language must first accept the fact that it is a language, must be undisturbed by its differences from English, and must make the pupil-informant comfortable in the communicative situation. In some cases it may be easier to find an informant not in the pupil-teacher relationship. Many teachers will find colleagues (in the vocational department), dormitory supervisors, or deaf parents of their pupils easier to approach and to learn from. For it is a difficult reversal of roles. There are many references in the writing of deaf persons to the kind of behavior (often unconscious) from hearing persons which effectively and finally checks their attempts to speak: it is the looks on the faces of those standing near when they venture to produce speech sounds. Just as clearly the deaf person perceives the kind of effect his production of signs has always elicited in the oral school environment. The classroom teacher who is at least open to being convinced that there is a case for the study of sign language has only to be attentive, sympathetic, encouraging. But this kind of attitude may be dead against the policy of the school and so will have to be carefully considered.

Classroom Research and Applications

Once contact is made and a teacher is in a situation where the study of sign language can begin, progress may be rapid. Besides being in more direct communication with pupils the teacher who knows sign language is able to engage in fruitful research of a directly applicable kind. Contrastive study of sign language and English has barely begun as a formal activity so that any teacher with deaf children is in a position to anticipate the professional researcher. The first kind of contrast noted by everyone who encounters a new language is vocabulary matching. "What is the sign for ——?" is a question asked hundreds of times by those learning sign language. But the kind of information gathering and information storage this question represents has only limited usefulness. If there really was a definite answer each time it is asked, if there should be exactly one sign for every English word the asker knows, there would be no sign language but only a simple one-for-one code to represent standard English.

A more effective way to study contrasts may be put like this: given sign A and word B that translate each other, what are the differences in the way they are used? The question is open ended. A complete answer requires a full description of each language. Yet some useful information can be discovered by asking it. For example, the third word in "from Chicago to New York" is equivalent to the third sign in this four-sign translation: "from Chicago to New-York." The sign written as "to" is made by touching or approaching one index fingertip with the other. But in translating "he forgot to pay," no sign is used for the third word. Three signs render the sentence in sign language. Then the sign language sentence may be retranslated in various ways: (1) "Him forget pay" will occur when the translator has an open or hidden animosity toward sign language and its "native speakers." It is quite unreliable translation. (2) "He forgot pay," or "He forgot paid" are more likely to occur when the translator is more at home in sign language than in his second language—remember that the English speaker in a billion or so patterns like this one has never failed to hear a /t/ between the two verbs and never failed to produce the /t/, but the deaf translator has never heard it. Then there is (3) "He overlooked paying" which may occur if the translator wants to keep the number of words equal to the number of signs and also wants to keep the translation grammatical and idiomatic in English since it is so in sign language.

The large matter of contrast between mutually translating items can be broken into more detailed questions. And the teacher studying sign language can apply the answers immediately. One thing to look for is a one-to-two contrast. Some words in English take two signs to translate, for example, *discuss:* "discuss about." Some signs of sign language require two-word English translations: C@ (the cupped hand circles in front of the face): "search for." No one has yet made a full study of these contrasting sets of singles and doubles, and the teacher of deaf children with a real interest in sign language is in a better position to study them than are most graduate students in linguistics.

The teacher too stands to be the most important consumer of this kind of research result, and the teacher's pupils are in line to receive the most benefit. Contrasts of the kind just considered are clear to a native speaker of English who studies sign language and who notes them. They are part, too, of the bilingual deaf signer whose English proficiency would be classed as "native." But to deaf pupils in a classroom or doing homework there is no such clear-cut contrast between the patterns of one language and the patterns of the other. They will blithely write, "I searched the word in the dictionary." Or, "We discussed about Viet Nam." Any experienced teacher of deaf pupils can list a great many more examples of each of these two mix-ups. The teacher who makes a study of sign language will know how to take steps toward reducing their production and increasing the proportion of grammatical combinations the pupils can produce. The algorithm here is a bilingual one: "See, here's the way we sign it; but when we write it or say it in English, we take out this sign and put in these words." How much and how fast the English production of pupils so taught will improve may be viewed optimistically or pessimistically, but there is good evidence that just having a teacher who knows and makes known to the class that they are dealing with two language systems, not one, will pay educational and social dividends. Another approach is to look for pairs of English words that occur together in the same order but when translated take the opposite order in signs (e.g., *plane reservation:* "reservation plane"), or for pairs that admit no separation in one language but must be separated in the other.

Besides these syntactic contrasts which are relatively easy to discover and deal with, there are other language system differences that need study. English has a unique tense system. Every finite verb in English has to be marked for past tense or be unmarked. Sign language, however, does not use verbs as time indicators at all; but signers like everyone else must deal with time. Again the classroom teacher is in position to be a front-line psycholinguistic researcher.

How do children who use sign language deal with time, as their sense of time, their concepts for dealing with it, and their language symbols for time concepts are developing? The work of the Swiss psychologist Jean Piaget on children's growth in handling space, time, equivalence, proportion, and the like is pertinent here, as is the application of it Hans Furth has made in his studies with deaf school children. Furth's book is somewhat misleadingly entitled. In *Thinking Without Language*[13] he is concerned to show how deaf children's ability to perform mental operations can be far in advance of their proficiency in oral and written English. That their competence in sign language has much to do with this ability he never doubts.

Or one may move from these syntactic-semantic contrasts to semantic differences. So common a matter as degree is treated in a totally different way in the two languages. The English speaker has at his command all the resources of paralanguage ("tone of voice," etc.) and kinesics ("body language") he shares with other users of his dialect. Thus he can say "good!" with intonations and voice features and facial expression and gestures that will modify the effect of the word he utters in several ways. But in addition to these paralinguistic and kinesic modifications, he also has most of the time a wide range of words to choose from. Instead of *good* with whatever his voice and body added to it, he could have said, *OK, fine, right, excellent, wonderful* or *first rate.* A different choice of word presumably would also modify the effect of what the speaker says.

All the users of English whom the speaker is in frequent contact with are also in complete control (though it may be outside their awareness) of both these scales of modification, the paralinguistic and the word choice. Like the speaker they know how to read the result of both ranges at once—does *wonderful* with lower than normal pitch, falling intonation, and a sigh of resignation indicate a more or a less negative reaction than *good* spoken with false heartiness, speeded up tempo, clipped resonance, and a grimace? In contrast with all of this is the sign language user's communication of similar ranges of meanings. The first and most striking difference is vocabulary size. Sign language has in many semantic areas only a single sign to express what English has a whole series of words for. Despite this difference, everyone who makes a study of the communication of persons using sign language notes with surprise the subtlety and precision of their interchange. Sign language seems to have no need for large numbers of closely related separate items of vocabulary because one sign can so easily be modified to express many degrees of meaning. Sincerity, intensity, interest, and other nuances are part of the signer's performance of the sign. The size, speed, tension, precision, and duration of the actions involved in signing are all variable at will, and all are used and understood as message-bearing fractions of total communicative activity—but again outside the awareness of the users.

This contrast between English and sign language vocabulary size and function has a rough analogy in two mechanics' toolboxes. One has a complete set of wrenches of fixed size to fit each different size of nut or bolt head he expects to come across. The other has just one adjustable wrench which will open wide enough for the largest nut and can be made to fit anything smaller.

This contrast of English and sign language needs much more study. In fact it would be better to treat it as a hypothesis. The testing of its truth by observing sign language and English in operation is research any teacher working with deaf pupils may undertake. Here too the opportunity to apply what one finds out is waiting. Those pupils who are found to be adept at conveying to each other finely shaded meanings have real semantic skill and should be apt learners when shown how to put the same messages across in standard English —once the teacher has worked out the full details of the contrasted patterns.

In this contrastive study there is material of the most valuable kind. What the pupils are saying to each other is by all odds the most interesting matter. What the lesson is about—what Dick said to Jane —what the teacher says—these things are just not even in the same universe of discourse. One real objective of sign language study is the ultimate ability of the teacher to participate in the real, intimate, vital communication of deaf pupils, imparting all the knowledge and understanding that a teacher's experience and training can add, and ultimately to show them how all that they have to impart may be put into English appropriate to the message.

Interesting as sign language is as a system, tantalizingly like other languages and fascinatingly different, the real value to be found in the study of sign language is a human not an abstract scientific value. All language is unique. Inexhaustible and wonderful as the universe is, only man in it possesses language, which is both a measure of man's potential and an indication of the open-endedness of that potential. So powerful indeed is the combination of human mind and language that even when deprived of one of the five senses, hearing, the human mind with sign language reaches heights of achievement we are only beginning to study.

NOTES

1. An account of the early controversy is given in Christopher B. Garnett, Jr.'s *Exchange of Letters Between Samuel Heinicke and Abbé Charles Michel de l'Épée,* New York: Vantage, 1968. See also Jules Paul Seigel, "The Enlightenment and the Evolution of a Language of Signs in France and England," *Journal of the History of Ideas,* 30 (1969), 96–118.

2. For detailed description of sign language elements, combination, and lexicon, see the author's "Sign Language Structure: An outline of the visual communication systems of the American deaf," *Studies in Linguistics: Occasional Papers 8* (1960); and Stokoe, Casterline, and Croneberg, *A Dictionary of American Sign Language on Linguistic Principles,* Washington, D.C.: Gallaudet College Press, 1965.

3. For a full discussion of five modes of manual communication see the summary of O'Rourke's presentation in Stokoe, "CAL Conferences on Sign Languages," *The Linguistic Reporter,* April 1970. Reprints available from National Association of the Deaf, Silver Spring, Md. 20910.

4. William Labov, *The Study of Non-standard Dialects,* Washington, D.C.: CAL/ERIC, 1969.

5. Herbert R. Kohl, *Language and Education of the Deaf,* New York: Center for Urban Education, 1966.

6. Pierre Gorman, "Certain Social and Psychological Difficulties Facing the Deaf Person in the English Community" (unpubl. Ph.D. diss.) Cambridge University, 1961.

7. M. M. Lewis, *The Education of Deaf Children,* London: Her Majesty's Stationery Office, 1968.

8. Jaakko Pesonen, *Phoneme Communication of the Deaf,* Helsinki: Annales Academiae Scientiarum Fennicae, 1968.

9. New York: Harcourt Brace Jovanovich, 1967.

10. (M.A. thesis, unpublished), University of Iowa, 1965.

11. Lewis, *op. cit.*

12. From a speech by Lewis at the Royal National Institute for the Deaf Conference at Edinburgh, quoted in *Hearing* 24, no. 4 (April 1969), 102.

13. New York: Vantage, 1966.

Pronunciation Guide

Symbol	Example	Symbol	Example
a	cat	o͞o	groove
ā	name	ou	plow, clout
â	hair, rare	t͟h	think, wrath
ä	balm, palm, father	t͟h	those, neither
e	berry, pet	u	cup, hut
ē	eat, tee	û(r)	turn
ēr	hear	z͟h	visionary
i	kitten, sit	ə	Indicates sound in un-
ī	kite, like		accented syllables, as:
n͡g	ring, fling		a <u>in</u> about
o	pop, rotten		e <u>in</u> the
ō	coat, open		i <u>in</u> readily
ô	pall, claw		o <u>in</u> calorie
oi	boil		u <u>in</u> circus
o͝o	took, hook		

Condensed and adapted from *The Random House College Dictionary*. Revised Edition.
New York: Random House, 1968, 1975. Used by permission.

Abbreviations

adj.	Adjective
adv.	Adverb, adverbial
adv. phrase	Adverbial phrase
arch.	Archaic
cf.	Confer. L., compare (with other entries)
colloq.	Colloquial, colloquialism. Informal or familiar term or expression in sign
eccles.	Ecclesiastical. Of or pertaining to religious signs. These signs are among the earliest and best developed, inasmuch as the first teachers of deaf people were frequently religious workers, and instruction was often of a religious nature.
e.g.	*Exempli gratia.* L., for example
i.e.	*Id est.* L., that is
interj.	Interjection
L.	Latin
loc.	Localism. A sign peculiar to a local or limited area. This may frequently be the case in a given school for deaf children, a college or postsecondary program catering to their needs, or a geographical area around such school or facility where deaf persons may live or work.
obs.	Obscure, obsolete
pl.	Plural
poss.	Possessive
prep.	Preposition
prep. phrase	Prepositional phrase
pron.	Pronoun
q.v.	*Quod vide.* L., which see
sl.	Slang
v.	Verb
v.i.	Verb intransitive

viz.	*Videlicet.* L., namely
voc.	Vocational. These signs usually pertain to specialized vocabularies used in workshops, trade and vocational classes and schools.
v.t.	Verb transitive
vulg.	Vulgarism. A vulgar term or expression, usually used only in a colloquial sense.

Explanatory Notes

I. Entries

Arrangement of entries

All entries have been arranged in alphabetical order. These include proper nouns, abbreviations, combining forms, and compounds of two or more words. All material appearing in bold-face type is to be regarded as an entry. Each entry has a code number, appearing in brackets.

Where more than one sign may exist for an entry, the entry-word is repeated and becomes a separate and distinct entry in the dictionary, with appropriate explanatory and illustrative matter, as well as cross-references to similar entry-words.

In the case of multiple entries of the same word, each entry is numbered consecutively, with the number appearing immediately after the entry-word. In general, an attempt is made to give the earliest and most original sign first, so that successive signs for the same word may be better understood and remembered as derivatives of the first one.

Pronunciation

There is no final authority on pronunciation. The particular pronunciation key used in this dictionary is derived and condensed from *The Random House College Dictionary,* revised edition. New York: Random House, 1968, 1975. Syllabification and pronunciation appear in parentheses. The main accent is indicated by a heavy accent mark, ′, while the secondary accent is indicated by a lighter accent, mark, ′.

Parts of speech

The parts of speech are indicated abbreviated in italics. In the case of a verb, the principal parts of the verb are also given, in small capital letters.

Sign rationale

This term, admittedly imprecise semantically, refers to the explanatory material in parentheses which follows the part of speech. This material is an attempt to link the entry-word iconographically with the sign as described verbally. It is a device to aid the user of the dictionary to remember how a sign is formed.

Verbal description

The sign and its formation are described verbally. Such terms as "S" hand, "D" position, "both 'B' hands," refer to the positions of the hand or hands as they are depicted in the American Manual Alphabet on page xlv.

Terms such as "counterclockwise," "clockwise," refer to movement from the signer's orientation. Care should be taken not to become confused by illustrations which appear at first glance to contradict a verbal description. In all cases the verbal description should be the one of choice, with the illustration reinforcing it. The reader should place himself mentally in the position of the signer, i.e., the illustration, in order to assume the correct orientation for signing a word.

Cross-referencing

Cross-references are found at the end of the verbal description, following the italicized *Cf.* These are given in small capital letters.

It is important to be aware at all times that cross-references, like the entry-words from which they spring, are to be regarded as sign-related material and not as mere English words.

II. Illustrations

A. Illustrations appearing in sequence should not be regarded as separate depictions of parts of a sign. They are fluid and continuous, and should be used in conjunction with the verbal description of a sign, for they illustrate the main features of the sign as one movement flows into the next.

B. Arrows, broken or solid, indicate direction of movement. Again, they are designed to reinforce the verbal description and, where confusion may arise, the reader is cautioned to review the verbal description, always keeping himself mentally in the position of the illustration (the signer).

C. As a general rule, a hand drawn with dotted or broken lines indicates the sign's initial movement or position of the hand. This is especially true if a similar drawing appears next to it using solid lines. This indicates terminal position in the continuum.

D. Groups of illustrations have been arranged as far as possible in visually logical order. They are read from left to right, or from top to bottom. Where confusion is possible, they have been captioned with letters A, B, C, etc.

E. Small lines outlining parts of the hand, especially when they are repeated, indicate small, repeated, or wavy or jerky motion, as described in the verbal section of an entry. ANTICIPATE is an example.

F. Arrows drawn side by side but pointing in opposite directions indicate repeated movement, as described in the verbal section of an entry. APPLAUD is an example.

G. Illustrations giving side or three-quarter views have been so placed to afford maximum visibility and to avoid foreshortening problems. The user of the dictionary should not assume a similar orientation when making the sign. As a general rule, the signer faces the person he is signing to.

H. Inclusion of the head in the figures permits proper orientation in the formation of certain signs. The head is omitted where there is no question of ambiguity.

III.   Bibliography

The bibliography is arranged in alphabetical sequence by author, each entry numbered consecutively. A subject index (page 872), listing sources under Learning and Teaching of Sign Language, and Language Description and Analysis, gives the bibliography entry number only.

IV.   Appendixes: Foreign-language indexes

There are seven foreign-language indexes in the Appendix: French-English; German-English; Italian-English; Japanese-English; Portuguese-English; Russian-English; and Spanish-English. Each index is alphabetized in the particular language, with the English word-equivalent appearing beside it, followed by the code number of the entry as found in the main part of the dictionary. Where there are variations of a sign, e.g., MOTHER 1 and MOTHER 2, only the first entry is listed. Aside from frequently untranslatable semantic nuances, it must be re-emphasized that the entries as they appear in the dictionary are sign-related material, not mere English words.. The principal mission of the indexes is to aid non-English-speaking readers, deaf and hearing, to see, through the illustrations, how foreign words are signed in American Sign Language.

American
Manual
Alphabet

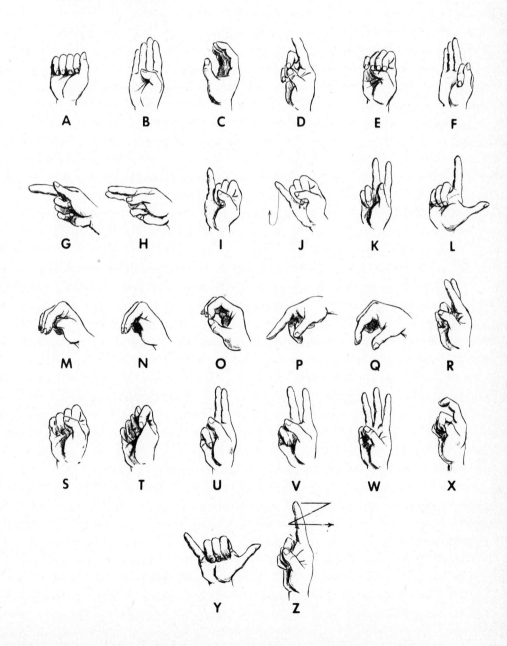

AMERICAN SIGN LANGUAGE

A

A (ā; unstressed ə), *adj. or indef. article.* The right "A" hand, held at chest level, moves a short distance to the right.

ABANDON 1 (ə băn′ dən), *v.,* -DONED, -DONING. (To throw something aside.) Both "S" hands are held with palms facing at chest level and then thrown down and to the left, opening into the "5" position. *Cf.* CAST OFF, DEPOSIT 2, DISCARD 1, FORSAKE 3, LEAVE 2, LET ALONE, NEGLECT.

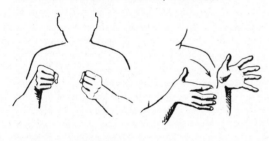

ABANDON 2, *v.* (To toss up and out.) Both "S" hands, held at chest level with palms facing, are swung down slightly and then up into the air toward the left, opening into the "5" position. *Cf.* CAST OUT, DISCARD 2, EVICT.

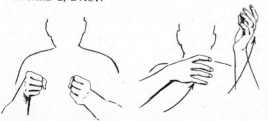

ABBREVIATE 1 (ə brē′ vĭ āt′), *v.,* -ATED, -ATING. (To squeeze or condense into a small space.) The "C" hands face each other, with the right hand nearer to the body than the left. Both hands draw together and close deliberately, squeezing an imaginary object. *Cf.* BRIEF 2, CONDENSE, MAKE BRIEF, SUMMARIZE 1, SUMMARY 1.

ABBREVIATE 2, *v.* (To make short; to measure off a short space.) The index and middle fingers of the right "H" hand are placed across the top of the index and middle fingers of the left "H" hand, and move a short distance back and forth, along the length of the left index finger. *Cf.* BRIEF 1, SHORT 1, SHORTEN.

ABBREVIATION (-shən), *n.* See ABBREVIATE 1 or 2.

ABDICATE (ăb′ də kāt′), *v.,* -CATED, -CATING. (Throwing up the hands in a gesture of surrender.) Both "A" hands are held palms down before the chest and then thrown up in unison, ending in the "5" position. *Cf.* CEDE, DISCOURAGE 1, FORFEIT, GIVE UP, LOSE HOPE, RELINQUISH, RENOUNCE, RENUNCIATION, SURRENDER 1, YIELD.

[A–8]

ABDUCT (ăb dŭkt′), *v.*, -DUCTED, -DUCTING. (The hand, partly concealed, takes something surreptitiously.) The index and middle fingers of the right hand, somewhat curved, are placed under the left elbow. As they move slowly along the left forearm toward the left wrist, they close a bit. *Cf.* EMBEZZLE, EMBEZZLEMENT, KIDNAP, ROB 1, ROBBERY 1, STEAL 1, SWIPE, THEFT 1, THIEF 1, THIEVERY.

[A–9]

ABHOR (ăb hôr′), *v.*, -HORRED, -HORRING. (To push away and recoil from; avoid.) The two open hands, palms facing left, are pushed deliberately to the left, as if pushing something away. An expression of disdain or disgust is worn. *Cf.* AVOID 2, DESPISE 1, DETEST 1, HATE 1, LOATHE.

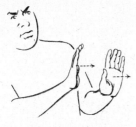

[A–10]

ABILITY (ə bĭl′ ə tĭ), *n.* (An affirmative movement of the hands, likened to a nodding of the head, to indicate ability or power to accomplish something.) Both "A" hands, held palms down, move down in unison a short distance before the chest. *Cf.* ABLE, CAN 1, CAPABLE, COMPETENT, COULD, FACULTY, MAY 2, POSSIBLE.

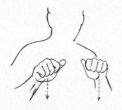

[A–11]

ABLE (ā′ bəl), *adj.* See ABILITY.

[A–12]

ABOLISH 1 (ə bŏl′ ĭsh), *v.*, -ISHED, -ISHING. (Wiping off.) The left "5" hand, palm up, is held slightly above the right "5" hand, held palm down. The right hand swings up, just brushing over the left palm. Both hands close into the "S" position, and the right is brought back with force to its initial position, striking a glancing blow against the left knuckles as it returns. *Cf.* ANNIHILATE, CORRUPT, DEFACE, DEMOLISH, DESTROY, HAVOC, PERISH 2, REMOVE 3, RUIN.

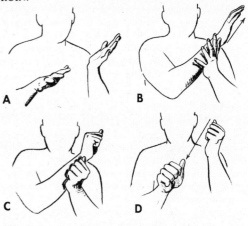

[A–13]

ABOLISH 2, *v.* (Removing.) The right "A" hand, resting in the palm of the left "5" hand, moves slightly up and away, describing a small arc. It is then cast downward, opening into the "5" position, palm down, as if removing something from the left hand and casting it down. *Cf.* ABSENCE 2, ABSENT 2, ABSTAIN, CHEAT 2, DEDUCT, DEFICIENCY, DELETE 1, LESS 2, MINUS 3, OUT 2, REMOVE 1, SUBTRACT, SUBTRACTION, TAKE AWAY FROM, WITHDRAW 2.

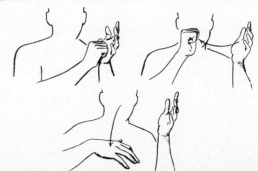

[A–14]

ABOUT 1 (ə bout'), *prep.* (Revolving about.) The left hand is held at chest height, all fingers extended and touching the thumb, and all pointing to the right. The right index finger circles about the left fingers several times. *Cf.* CONCERNING, ELECTRIC MOTOR, OF.

[A–15]

ABOUT 2, *adv.* The left hand is held at chest level in the right angle position, with fingers pointing up and the back of the hand facing right. The right fingers are swept up along the back of the left hand. *Cf.* ALMOST, NEARLY.

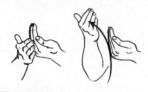

[A–16]

ABOVE (ə bŭv'), *adv.* (One hand moves above the other.) Both hands, palms flat and facing down, are held before the chest. The right hand circles horizontally above the left in a counterclockwise direction. *Cf.* OVER 1.

[A–17]

ABRAHAM (ā' brə hăm', -həm), *(eccles.),* *n.* (The hand is stayed in the execution of Isaac.) The upraised right hand, grasping an imaginary knife, is stopped at the wrist by the left hand as it begins to descend.

[A–18]

ABSENCE 1 (ăb' səns), *n.* (A disappearance.) The right open hand, palm facing the body, is held by the left hand and is drawn down and out, ending in a position with fingers drawn together. The left hand, meanwhile, may close into a position with fingers also drawn together. *Cf.* ABSENT 1, DEPLETE, DISAPPEAR, EMPTY 1, EXTINCT, FADE AWAY, GONE 1, MISSING 1, OMISSION 1, OUT 3, OUT OF, VANISH.

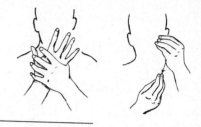

[A–19]

ABSENCE 2, *n.* (Removing.) The right "A" hand, resting in the palm of the left "5" hand, moves slightly up and away, describing a small arc. It is then cast downward, opening into the "5" position, palm down, as if removing something from the left hand and casting it down. *Cf.* ABOLISH 2, ABSENT 2, ABSTAIN, CHEAT 2, DEDUCT, DEFICIENCY, DELETE 1, LESS 2, MINUS 3, OUT 2, REMOVE 1, SUBTRACT, SUBTRACTION, TAKE AWAY FROM, WITHDRAW 2.

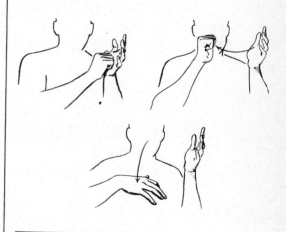

[A–20]

ABSENT 1 (-sənt), *adj.* See ABSENCE 1.

[A–21]

ABSENT 2, *adj.* See ABSENCE 2.

[A-22]

ABSENT-MINDED (mĭn' dĭd), *adj.* (The mind is gone.) The index finger of the right hand, palm back, touches the forehead (the modified sign for **THINK**, *q. v.*). The right open hand, palm facing the body, is held by the left hand and is drawn down and out, ending in a position with fingers drawn together. The left hand, meanwhile, has closed into a position with fingers also drawn together. *Cf.* ABSENCE 1.

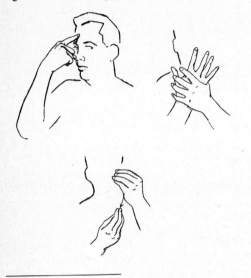

[A-23]

ABSOLUTE (ăb' sə lōōt'), *adj.* (Coming forth directly from the lips; true.) The index finger of the right "D" hand, palm facing left, is placed against the lips. It moves up an inch or two and then describes a small arc forward and away from the lips. *Cf.* ABSOLUTELY, ACTUAL, ACTUALLY, AUTHENTIC, CERTAIN, CERTAINLY, FAITHFUL 3, FIDELITY, FRANKLY, GENUINE, INDEED, POSITIVE 1, POSITIVELY, REAL, REALLY, SINCERE 2, SURE, SURELY, TRUE, TRULY, TRUTH, VALID, VERILY.

[A-24]

ABSOLUTELY (ăb' sə lōōt' lĭ), *adv.* See ABSOLUTE.

[A-25]

ABSOLUTION 1 (ăb' sə lōō' shən), *(eccles.)*, *n.* (Blessed; forgiveness.) The "A" hands are held near the lips, thumbs up and almost touching. Both hands move down and out simultaneously, ending in the "5" position, palms down. The right hand, palm flat, facing down, is then brushed over the left hand, held palm flat and facing up. This latter action may be repeated twice. *Cf.* BLESS 1, FORGIVE 1.

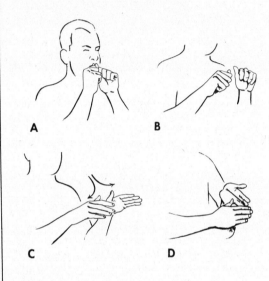

A   B

C   D

[A-26]

ABSOLUTION 2, *(eccles.)*, *n.* (The sign of the cross.) The right hand, palm flat and facing left, describes a cross in front of the face.

[A-27]

ABSTAIN (ăb stān'), *v.*, -STAINED, -STAINING. (Removing.) The right "A" hand, resting in the palm of the left "5" hand, moves slightly up and away, describing a small arc. It is then cast downward, opening into the "5" position, palm down, as if removing something from the left hand and casting it down. *Cf.* ABOLISH 2, ABSENCE 2, ABSENT 2,

CHEAT 2, DEDUCT, DEFICIENCY, DELETE 1, LESS 2, MINUS 3, OUT 2, REMOVE 1, SUBTRACT, SUBTRACTION, TAKE AWAY FROM, WITHDRAW 2.

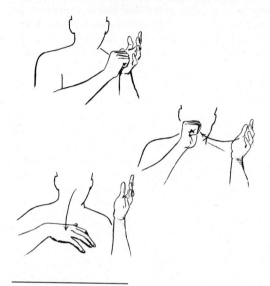

[A–28]

ABSTINENCE (ăb′ stə nəns), *(eccles.), n.* (Wiping from the mouth, in the sense of fasting.) The thumb of the right "A" hand, held upright, is wiped across the lips, from left to right.

[A–29]

ABSURD (ăb sûrd′, -zûrd′), *adj.* (Thoughts flickering back and forth.) The right "Y" hand, thumb almost touching the forehead, is shaken back and forth across the forehead several times. *Cf.* DAFT, FOLLY, FOOLISH, NONSENSE, RIDICULOUS, SILLY, TRIFLING.

[A–30]

ABUNDANCE (ə bŭn′ dəns), *n.* (A full cup.) The left hand, in the "S" position, is held palm facing right. The right "5" hand, palm down, is brushed outward several times over the top of the left, indicating a wiping off of the top of a cup. *Cf.* ABUNDANT, ADEQUATE, AMPLE, ENOUGH, PLENTY, SUBSTANTIAL, SUFFICIENT.

[A–31]

ABUNDANT (ə bŭn′ dənt), *adj.* See ABUNDANCE.

[A–32]

ACCEPT (ăk sĕpt′), *v.,* -CEPTED, -CEPTING. (A taking of something unto oneself.) Both open hands, palms down, are held in front of the chest. They move in unison toward the chest, where they come to rest, all fingers closed. *Cf.* WILLING 1.

[A–33]

ACCIDENT (ăk′ sə dənt), *n.* (A befalling.) Both "D" hands, index fingers pointing away from the body, are simultaneously pivoted over so that the palms face down. *Cf.* BEFALL, CHANCE, COINCIDE 1, COINCIDENCE, EVENT, HAPPEN 1, INCIDENT, OCCUR, OPPORTUNITY 4.

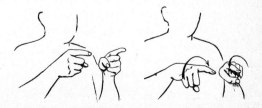

[A-34]

ACCLAIM 1 (ə klām'), *v.*, -CLAIMED, -CLAIMING. (An issuance from the mouth.) Both index fingers are placed at the lips, with palms facing the body. They are rotated once and swung out in arcs, until the left index finger points somewhat to the left and the right index somewhat to the right. Sometimes the rotation of the fingers is omitted in favor of a simple swinging out from the lips. *Cf.* ACCLAMATION, ANNOUNCE, ANNOUNCEMENT, DECLARE, MAKE KNOWN, PROCLAIM, PROCLAMATION.

[A-37]

ACCOMPANY (ə kŭm' pə ni), *v.*, -NIED, -NYING. (To go along with.) Both "A" hands, knuckles together and thumbs up, are moved forward in unison, away from the chest. *Cf.* TOGETHER, WANDER AROUND WITH, WITH.

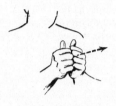

[A-38]

ACCOMPLISH 1 (ə kŏm' plish), *v.*, -PLISHED, -PLISHING. (Penetrating the heights.) The "D" hands, palms back, are held at each side of the head, near the temples. With a pivoting motion of the wrists, the hands swing up and around, simultaneously, to a position above the head, with palms facing out. *Cf.* ACHIEVE 1, ATTAIN, PROSPER, SUCCEED, SUCCESS, SUCCESSFUL, TRIUMPH 2.

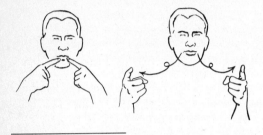

[A-35]

ACCLAIM 2, *v., n.* (Good words coming from the mouth; clapping hands.) The fingertips of the right hand, palm flat and facing the body, are brought up to the lips, so that they touch (part of the sign for GOOD, *q.v.*). The hands are then clapped together several times. *Cf.* APPLAUD, APPLAUSE, APPROBATION, APPROVAL, APPROVE, CLAP, COMMEND, CONGRATULATE 1, CONGRATULATIONS 1, PRAISE.

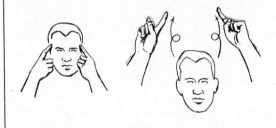

[A-39]

ACCOMPLISH 2, *v.* (Bring to an end.) The left hand, fingers together and pointing forward, is held palm facing right. The right, palm down, fingers also together, moves along the top of the left, goes over the tip of the left index finger, and drops straight down, indicating a cutting off or a finishing. This sign is also used to indicate the past tense of a verb, in the sense of accomplishing an action or state of being. *Cf.* ACHIEVE 2, COMPLETE 1, CONCLUDE, DONE 1, END 4, EXPIRE 1, FINISH 1, HAVE 2, TERMINATE.

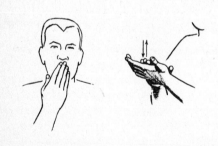

[A-36]

ACCLAMATION (ăk' lə mā' shən), *n.* See ACCLAIM 1.

[A–40]

ACCORD (ə kôrd'), *n.* (Agreement; of the same mind; thinking the same way.) The index finger of the right "D" hand, palm back, touches the forehead (the modified sign for THINK, *q.v.*), and then the two index fingers, both in the "D" position, palm down, are brought together so they are side by side, pointing away from the body (the sign for SAME). *Cf.* ACQUIESCE, ACQUIESCENCE, AGREE, AGREEMENT, COINCIDE 2, COMPLY, CONCUR, CONSENT.

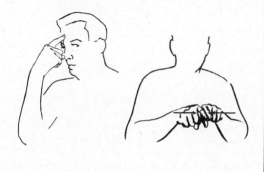

[A–41]

ACCORDING (TO) (ə kôr' dǐng), *adv.* (A likeness; a sameness.) Both index fingers, held together at one side of the body near waist level, point forward. As they travel to the other side of the body they separate an inch or two and come together again. *Cf.* ALSO 1, AS, DUPLICATE 2, SAME AS, TOO.

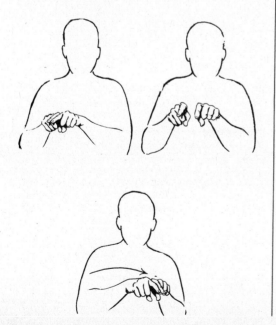

[A–42]

ACCOUNT (ə kount'), *n.* (A bank or charge account —act of signing the name on paper.) The index finger and thumb of the right hand go through the natural motion of scribbling across the left palm. Then the fingers of the right "H" hand, palm facing down, are thrust against the left palm, as if placing the name on a piece of paper. As an alternate, the closed fingers of the right hand may be thrust into the left palm. *Cf.* CHARGE 2.

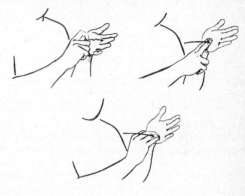

[A–43]

ACCUMULATE 1 (ə kū' myə lāt'), *v.*, -LATED, -LAT-ING. (Gathering in.) The right "5" hand, its little finger edge touching the upturned left palm, is drawn in an arc toward the body, closing into the "S" position as it sweeps over the base of the left hand. *Cf.* COLLECT, EARN, SALARY, WAGES.

[A–44]

ACCUMULATE 2, *v.* (A gathering together.) The right "5" hand, fingers curved and palm facing left, sweeps across and over the upturned left palm, several times, in a circular movement. *Cf.* GATHER 1, GATHERING TOGETHER.

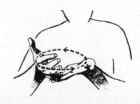

[A–45]

ACCUMULATE 3, *v.* (Assemble all together.) Both "5" hands, palms facing, are held with fingers pointing out from the body. With a sweeping motion they are brought in toward the chest, and all fingertips come together. This is repeated. *Cf.* ASSEMBLE, ASSEMBLY, CONFERENCE, CONVENE, CONVENTION, GATHER 2, GATHERING, MEETING 1.

[A–46]

ACCURATE 1 (ăk′ yə rĭt), *adj.* (The fingers come together precisely.) The thumb and index finger of each hand, palms facing, the right above the left, form circles. They are brought together with a deliberate movement, so that the fingers and thumbs now touch. Sometimes the right hand, before coming together with the left, executes a slow clockwise circle above the left. *Cf.* EXACT 1, EXACTLY, EXPLICIT 1, PRECISE, SPECIFIC.

[A–47]

ACCURATE 2, *adj.* The right index finger, held above the left index finger, comes down rather forcefully so that the bottom of the right hand comes to rest on top of the left thumb joint. *Cf.* CORRECT 1, DECENT, EXACT 2, JUST 2, PROPER, RIGHT 3, SUITABLE.

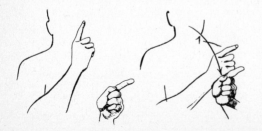

[A–48]

ACCUSE 1 (ə kuz′), *v.,* -CUSED, -CUSING. (The blame is firmly placed.) The right "A" hand, thumb pointing up, is brought down firmly against the back of the left hand, held palm down; the right thumb is then directed toward the person or object to blame. When personal blame is acknowledged, the thumb is brought in to the chest. *Cf.* BLAME, FAULT 1, GUILTY 1.

[A–49]

ACCUSE 2, *v.* (A fingering of someone.) The "D" hand, index finger pointing at an imaginary culprit, moves away from the body in short, stabbing steps.

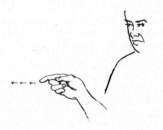

[A–50]

ACCUSTOM (ə kŭs′ təm), *v.,* -TOMED, -TOMING. (Bound down to custom or habit.) Both "S" hands, palms down, are crossed and brought down in unison before the chest. *Cf.* BOUND, CUSTOM, HABIT, LOCKED, PRACTICE 3.

[A-51]

ACHE (āk), *n., v.,* ACHED, ACHING. (A stabbing pain.) The "D" hands, index fingers pointing to each other, are rotated in elliptical fashion before the chest—simultaneously but in opposite directions. *Cf.* HARM 1, HURT 1, INJURE 1, INJURY, MAR 1, OFFEND, OFFENSE, PAIN, SIN, WOUND,

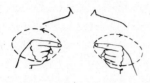

[A-52]

ACHIEVE 1 (ə chēv'), *v.,* -CHIEVED, -CHIEVING. (Penetrating the heights.) The "D" hands, palms back, are held at each side of the head, near the temples. With a pivoting motion of the wrists, the hands swing up and around, simultaneously, to a position above the head, with palms facing out. *Cf.* ACCOMPLISH 1, ATTAIN, PROSPER, SUCCEED, SUCCESS, SUCCESSFUL, TRIUMPH 2.

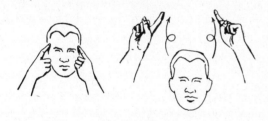

[A-53]

ACHIEVE 2, *v.* (Bring to an end.) The left hand, fingers together and pointing forward, is held palm facing right. The right, palm down, fingers also together, moves along the top of the left, goes over the tip of the left index finger, and drops straight down, indicating a cutting off or a finishing. This sign is also used to indicate the past tense of a verb, in the sense of achieving an action or state of being. *Cf.* ACCOMPLISH 2, COMPLETE 1, CONCLUDE, DONE 1, END 4, EXPIRE 1, FINISH 1, HAVE 2, TERMINATE.

[A-54]

ACID (ăs' ĭd), *n., adj.* (Something sour or bitter.) The right index finger is brought sharply up against the lips, while the mouth is puckered up as if tasting something sour. *Cf.* BITTER, DISAPPOINTED 1, LEMON 1, PICKLE, SOUR.

[A-55]

ACORN (ā' kôrn, ā' kərn), *n.* (The thumbtip, representing a nut or acorn, is bitten.) The right thumbtip is placed between the teeth. It is sometimes moved out from the mouth after being placed in it, but this is optional. *Cf.* NUT.

[A-56]

ACQUIESCE (ăk' wĭ ĕs'), *v.,* -ESCED, -ESCING. (Agreement; of the same mind; thinking the same way.) The index finger of the right "D" hand, palm back, touches the forehead (the modified sign for THINK, *q.v.*), and then the two index fingers, both in the "D" position, palm down, are brought together so they are side by side, pointing away from the body (the sign for SAME). *Cf.* ACCORD, ACQUIESCENCE, AGREE, AGREEMENT, COINCIDE 2, COMPLY, CONCUR, CONSENT.

[A–57]

ACQUIESCENCE (ăk′ wĭ ĕs′ əns), *n.* See ACQUI-
ESCE.

[A–58]

ACQUIRE (ə kwīr′), *v.*, -QUIRED, -QUIRING. (A
grasping and bringing forward to oneself.) Both
hands, in the "5" position, fingers curved, are
crossed at the wrists, with the left palm facing right
and the right palm facing left. They are brought in
toward the chest, while closing into a grasping "S"
position. *Cf.* GET, OBTAIN, PROCURE, RECEIVE.

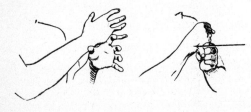

[A–59]

ACROSS (ə krôs′, ə krŏs′), *prep., adv.* (A crossing
over.) The left hand is held before the chest, palm
down and fingers together. The right hand, fingers
together, glides over the left, with the right little
finger touching the top of the left hand. *Cf.* CROSS
3, OVER 2.

[A–60]

ACT 1 (ăkt), *v.*, ACTED, ACTING, *n.* (Motion or
movement, modified by the letter "A" for "act.")
Both "A" hands, palms out, are held at shoulder
height and rotate alternately toward the head. *Cf.*
ACTOR, ACTRESS, DRAMA, PERFORM 2, PERFORM-
ANCE 2, PLAY 2, SHOW 2.

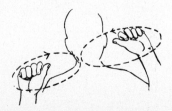

[A–61]

ACT 2, *v.* (An activity.) Both open hands, palms
down, are swung right and left before the chest. *Cf.*
ACTION, ACTIVE, ACTIVITY, BUSY 2, CONDUCT 1,
DEED, DO, PERFORM 1, PERFORMANCE 1, RENDER
2.

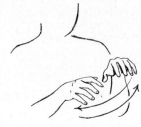

[A–62]

ACTION (ăk′ shən), *n.* (An activity.) See ACT 2.

[A–63]

ACTIVE (ăk′ tĭv), *adj.* (Activity.) See ACT 2.

[A–64]

ACTIVITY (ăk tĭv′ ə ti), *n.* See ACT 2.

[A–65]

ACTOR (ăk′ tər), *n.* (Male acting individual.) The
right hand moves to the forehead and grasps an
imaginary cap brim (MALE root sign). The sign for
ACT 1 is then given. This is followed by the sign for
INDIVIDUAL: Both hands, fingers together, are
placed at either side of the chest and are moved
down to waist level. *Note:* The MALE root sign is
optional.

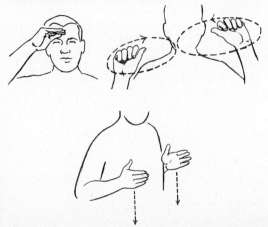

[A–66]

ACTRESS (ăk′ trĭs), *n.* (Female acting individual.) The thumb of the right "A" hand moves down along the line of the right jaw from ear to chin (FEMALE root sign). The sign for ACT 1 is then given. This is followed by the sign for INDIVIDUAL: Both hands, fingers together, are placed at either side of the chest and are moved down to waist level. *Note:* The FEMALE root sign is optional.

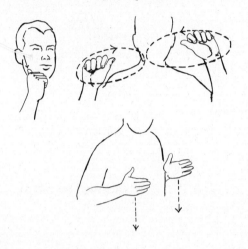

[A–67]

ACTUAL (ăk′ chŏŏ əl), *adj.* (Coming forth directly from the lips; true.) The index finger of the right "D" hand, palm facing left, is placed against the lips. It moves up an inch or two and then describes a small arc forward and away from the lips. *Cf.* ABSOLUTE, ABSOLUTELY, ACTUALLY, AUTHENTIC, CERTAIN, CERTAINLY, FAITHFUL 3, FIDELITY, FRANKLY, GENUINE, INDEED, POSITIVE 1, POSITIVELY, REAL, REALLY, SINCERE 2, SURE, SURELY, TRUE, TRULY, TRUTH, VALID, VERILY.

[A–68]

ACTUALLY (ăk′ chŏŏ ə lĭ), *adv.* (Truly.) See AC-TUAL.

[A–69]

ADAM (ăd′ əm), *(arch.), n.* ("A," father.) The right "A" hand is swung up until the thumb touches the forehead, near the right temple, in a modified version of FATHER, *q.v.*

[A–70]

ADD 1 (ăd), *v.,* ADDED, ADDING. (To bring up all together.) The two open hands, palms and fingers facing each other, with the left hand above the right, are brought together, with all fingers closing simultaneously. This sign is used mainly in the sense of adding up figures or items. *Cf.* ADDITION, AMOUNT 1, SUM, SUMMARIZE 2, SUMMARY 2, SUM UP, TOTAL.

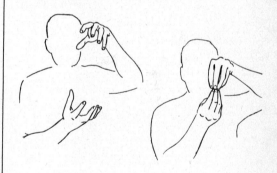

[A–71]

ADD 2, *v.* (A mathematical symbol.) The two index fingers are crossed in the sign for PLUS. *Cf.* ADDI-TION, PLUS, POSITIVE 2.

[A–72]

ADD 3, *v.* (Adding on.) The index and middle fingers of the right "H" hand, palm up, are swung up and over until they come to rest on the index and middle fingers of the left "H" hand, held palm down. *Cf.* ADDITION, EXTEND 1, EXTRA, GAIN 1, IN-CREASE, ON TO, RAISE 2.

[A–73]

ADD 4, *v.* (One hand is added to the other; an addition.) Both hands, palms facing, are held fingers together, the left a bit above the right. The right hand is brought up to the left until their fingertips touch. *Cf.* BESIDES, FURTHER 2, MORE, MOREOVER 2.

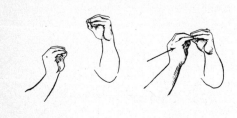

[A–74]

ADDITION (ə dish′ ən), *n.* See ADD 1, 2, or 3.

[A–75]

ADDRESS 1 (ə dres′), *n., v.,* -DRESSED, -DRESSING. (A gesture of an orator.) The right open hand, palm facing left, is held above and to the right of the head. It pivots on the wrist, forward and backward, several times. *Cf.* LECTURE, ORATE, SPEECH 2, TALK 2, TESTIMONY.

[A–76]

ADDRESS 2 (ăd′ rĕs), *n.* (A place where one eats and sleeps.) The closed fingers of the right hand are placed against the lips (the sign for EAT), and then, opening into a flat palm, against the right cheek (resting the head on a pillow, as in SLEEP). The head leans slightly to the right, as if going to sleep in the right palm, during this latter movement. *Cf.* HOME, RESIDENCE 1.

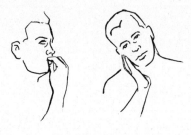

[A–77]

ADDRESS 3, *n., v.* (Same rationale as for LIFE 1, with the initials "L.") The upturned thumbs of the "A" hands move in unison up the chest. *Cf.* ALIVE, DWELL, EXIST, LIFE 1, LIVE 1, LIVING, MORTAL, RESIDE.

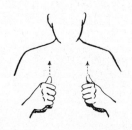

[A–78]

ADEPT (ə dĕpt′), *adj.* (A sharp-edged hand.) The right hand grasps the little finger edge of the left firmly. As it leaves this position, moving down and out, it assumes the "A" position, palm facing left. *Cf.* EXPERIENCE 1, EXPERT, SHARP 4, SHREWD, SKILL, SKILLFUL.

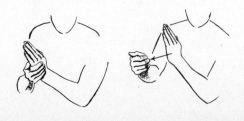

[A–79]

ADEQUATE (ăd′ a kwĭt), *adj.* (A full cup.) The left hand, in the "S" position, is held palm facing right. The right "5" hand, palm down, is brushed outward several times over the top of the left, indicating a wiping off of the top of a cup. *Cf.* ABUNDANCE, ABUNDANT, AMPLE, ENOUGH, PLENTY, SUBSTANTIAL, SUFFICIENT.

[A–80]

ADJACENT (ə jā′ sənt), *adj.* (One hand is near the other.) The left hand, cupped, fingers together, is held before the chest, palm facing the body. The right hand, also cupped, fingers together, moves a very short distance back and forth, as it is held in front of the left. *Cf.* BESIDE, BY 1, CLOSE (TO) 2, NEAR 1, NEIGHBOR, NEIGHBORHOOD, VICINITY.

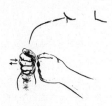

[A–81]

ADJUST (ə jŭst′), *v.,* -JUSTED, -JUSTING. (To change positions.) Both "A" hands, thumbs up, are held before the chest, several inches apart. The left hand is pivoted over so that its thumb points to the right. Simultaneously, the right hand is moved up and over the left, describing a small arc, with its thumb pointing to the left. *Cf.* ALTER, ALTERATION, CHANGE 1, CONVERT, MODIFY, REVERSE 2, TRANSFER 1.

[A–82]

ADMIRE 1 (ăd mīr′), *v.,* -MIRED, -MIRING. (Drawing out the feelings.) The thumb and index finger of the right open hand, held an inch or two apart, are placed at mid-chest. As the hand moves straight out from the chest the two fingers come together. *Cf.* LIKE 1, REVERE 1.

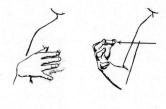

[A–83]

ADMIRE 2, *(eccles.), (rare), v.* The right open hand faces the chest, with thumb and index finger touching the mid-chest. The hand is drawn straight out and away, while the thumb and index finger come together and touch. The "H" position is next assumed and, with a sweeping motion, the index and middle fingers describe an arc directed inward to the forehead. *Cf.* HONOR 2.

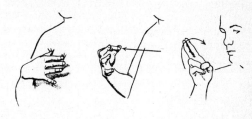

[A–84]

ADMISSION 1 (ăd mĭsh′ ən), *n.* (Getting something off the chest.) Both hands are held with fingers touching the chest and pointing down. They are then swung up and out, ending with both palms facing up before the body. *Cf.* ADMIT 1, CONCEDE, CONFESS, CONFESSION 1.

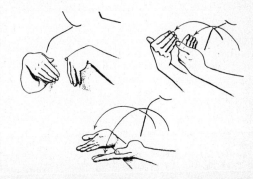

[A–85]

ADMISSION 2, *n.* (A nicking of or making a notch in the pocketbook, in the colloquial sense. This sign is used in the sense of ADMISSION to a theatre or public event.) The knuckle of the right "X" finger is nicked against the palm of the left hand, held in the "5" position, palm facing right. *Cf.* CHARGE 1, COST, DUTY 2, EXCISE, EXPENSE, FEE, FINE 2, IMPOST, PENALTY 3, PRICE 2, TAX 1, TAXATION 1, TOLL.

[A–86]

ADMIT 1 (ăd mĭt´), *v.,* -MITTED, -MITTING. See ADMISSION 1.

[A–87]

ADMIT 2, *v.* (Opening or leading the way toward something.) The open right hand, held up before the body, sweeps down in an arc and over toward the left side of the chest, ending in the palm-up position. Reversing the movement gives the passive form of the verb, except that the hand does not arc upward but rather simply moves outward in a small arc from the body. *Cf.* INVITATION, INVITE, INVITED, USHER, WELCOME.

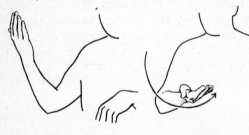

[A–88]

ADMONISH 1 (ăd mŏn´ ĭsh), *v.,* -ISHED, -ISHING. (Tapping one to draw attention to danger.) The right hand taps the back of the left several times. *Cf.* CAUTION, FOREWARN, WARN.

[A–89]

ADMONISH 2, *v.* (A scolding with the finger.) The right index finger shakes back and forth in a natural scolding movement. *Cf.* REPRIMAND, REPROVE, SCOLD 1.

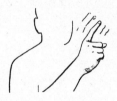

[A–90]

ADOLESCENCE (ăd´ ə lĕs´ əns), *n.* (The spirits bubbling up.) The fingertips of both open hands, placed on either side of the chest just below the shoulders, move up and off the chest, in unison, to a point just above the shoulders. This is repeated several times. *Cf.* ADOLESCENT, YOUNG, YOUTH, YOUTHFUL.

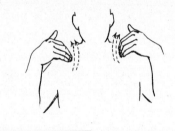

[A–91]

ADOLESCENT (ăd´ ə lĕs´ ənt), *adj.* See ADOLESCENCE.

[A–92]

ADOPT (ə dŏpt´), *v.,* -DOPTED, -DOPTING. (Taking unto oneself.) The right hand, palm out, is extended before the chest, index finger and thumb in an open position, the other fingers separated and pointing up. The hand is drawn in toward the chest, and the index and thumb close at the same time, indicating something taken to oneself. *Cf.* APPOINT, CHOOSE 1, SELECT 2, TAKE.

[A-93]

ADORE (ə dōr'), v., -DORED, -DORING. (Worshiping.) The hands are clasped together, with the left cupped over the right. Both are brought in toward the body, while the eyes are shut and the head is bowed slightly. This sign is most often used to describe religious adoration. *Cf.* AMEN, DEVOUT, PIOUS, WORSHIP.

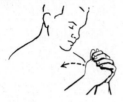

[A-94]

ADORN (ə dôrn'), v., -DORNED, -DORNING. (The hands describe the flounces of draperies.) Both "C" hands, palms out, are held somewhat above the head. They move out and down in a series of successive arcs. *Cf.* DECORATE 1, ORNAMENT 1, TRIM 1.

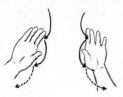

[A-95]

ADVANCE (ăd văns', -väns'), n., v., -VANCED, -VANCING. (Moving forward, step by step.) Both hands, in the right angle position, palms facing, are held before the chest, a few inches apart, with the right hand slightly behind the left. The right hand is brought up, over and forward, so that it is now ahead of the left. The left hand then follows suit, so that it is now ahead of the right. *Cf.* PROGRESS 1.

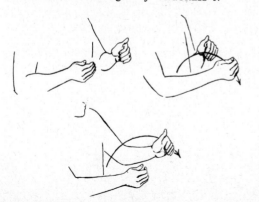

[A-96]

ADVANCED (ăd vănst'), adj. (Something high up.) Both hands, in the right angle position, are held before the face, about a foot apart, palms facing. They are raised abruptly about a foot, in a slight outward curving movement. *Cf.* HIGH 1, PROMOTE, PROMOTION.

[A-97]

ADVICE (ăd vīs'), n. (Take something, *advice*, and disseminate it.) The left hand, held limp in front of the body, has its fingers pointing down. The fingers of the right hand, held all together, are placed on the top of the left hand, and then move forward, off the left hand, assuming a "5" position, palm down. *Cf.* ADVISE, COUNSEL, COUNSELOR, INFLUENCE 4.

[A-98]

ADVISE (ăd vīz'), v., -VISED, -VISING. See ADVICE.

[A-99]

ADVOCATE (ad' və kāt'), v., -CATED, -CATING. (One hand upholds the other.) Both hands, in the "S" position, are held palms facing the body, the right under the left. The right hand pushes up the left in a gesture of support. *Cf.* ENDORSE 2, INDORSE 2, SUPPORT 2.

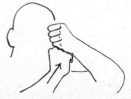

[A–100]

AFFILIATE 1 (ə fil′ i āt′), *v.*, -ATED, -ATING. (Joining together.) Both hands, held in the modified "5" position, palms out, move toward each other. The thumbs and index fingers of both hands then connect. *Cf.* ANNEX, ASSOCIATE 2, ATTACH, BELONG, COMMUNION OF SAINTS, CONCERN 2, CONNECT, ENLIST, ENROLL, JOIN 1, PARTICIPATE, RELATIVE 2, UNION, UNITE.

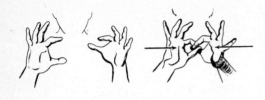

[A–101]

AFFILIATE 2, *n.* The sign for AFFILIATE 1 is made, followed by the sign for INDIVIDUAL: The open hands, placed at the sides of the chest, move down in unison, to waist level.

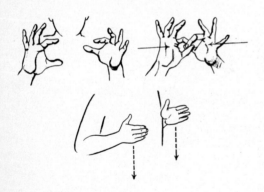

[A–102]

AFRAID (ə frād′), *adj.* (The heart is suddenly covered with fear.) Both hands, fingers together, are placed side by side, palms facing the chest. They quickly open and come together over the heart, one on top of the other. *Cf.* COWARD, FEAR 1, FRIGHT, FRIGHTEN, SCARE(D), TERROR 1.

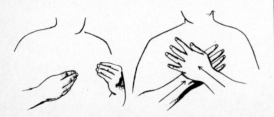

[A–103]

AFRICA (ăf′ rə kə), *n.* (A flattened nose.) The middle finger, after touching the tip of the nose, revolves in a counterclockwise direction around the face and comes to rest on the tip of the nose again. (This sign is considered somewhat improper and offensive.) *Cf.* NEGRO 2.

[A–104]

AFTER 1 (ăf′ tər, äf′-), *prep.* (Something occurring *after* a fixed place in time, represented by the hand nearest the body.) The right hand, held flat, palm facing the body, fingertips pointing left, represents the fixed place in time. The left hand is placed against the back of the right, and moves straight out from the body. The relative positions of the two hands may be reversed, with the left remaining stationary near the body and the right moving out.

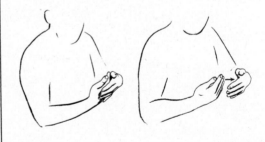

[A–105]

AFTER 2, *prep.* (One hand is after or behind the other.) Both hands, in the "A" position, are held knuckles to knuckles. The right hand moves back, describing a small arc, and comes to rest against the left wrist. *Cf.* BACK 1, BACKSLIDE, BEHIND.

[A-106]

AFTER A WHILE (hwīl), *adv. phrase.* (A moving on of the minute hand of the clock.) The right "L" hand, its thumb thrust into the palm of the left and acting as a pivot, moves forward a short distance. *Cf.* AFTERWARD, LATER 1, SUBSEQUENT, SUBSEQUENTLY.

[A-107]

AFTERNOON (ăf´ tər nōōn´, äf´ -), *n., adj.* (The sun is midway between zenith and sunset.) The right arm, fingers together and pointing forward, rests on the back of the left hand, its fingers also together and pointing somewhat to the right. The right arm remains in a position about 45° from the vertical.

[A-108]

AFTERWARD (ăf´ tər wərd, äf´ -), *adv.* See AFTER A WHILE.

[A-109]

AGAIN (ə gĕn´), *adv.* The left hand, open in the "5" position, palm up, is held before the chest. The right hand, in the right-angle position, fingers pointing up, arches over and into the left palm. *Cf.* ENCORE, REPEAT.

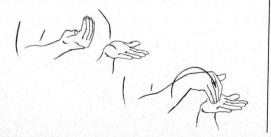

[A-110]

AGAINST (ə gĕnst´, -gänst´), *prep.* (Opposed to; restraint.) The tips of the right fingers, held together, are thrust purposefully into the open left palm, whose fingers are also together and pointing forward. *Cf.* OPPOSE.

[A-111]

AGE 1 (āj), *n.* (Age, in the sense of chronological age; the beard of an old man.) The right hand grasps an imaginary beard at the chin and pulls it downward. *Cf.* ANTIQUE, OLD.

[A-112]

AGE 2, *n.* (Time in the abstract, indicated by the rotating of the "T" hand on the face of a clock.) The right "T" hand is placed palm to palm in the open left hand. It describes a clockwise circle and comes to rest again in the left palm. *Cf.* EPOCH, ERA, PERIOD 2, SEASON, TIME 2.

[A-113]

AGO (ə gō´), *adj., adv.* (Something past, behind.) The upraised right hand, in the "5" position with palm facing the body, is held just above the right shoulder and is thrown back over it. *Cf.* FORMERLY, ONCE UPON A TIME, PAST, PREVIOUS, PREVIOUSLY, WAS, WERE.

[A–114]

AGONY (ăg′ ə nĭ), *n.* (A clenching of the fists; the rise and fall of pain.) Both "S" hands, tightly clenched, revolve about each other, slowly and deliberately, while a pained expression is worn. *Cf.* BEAR 3, DIFFICULT 3, ENDURE 1, PASSION 2, SUFFER 1, TOLERATE 2.

[A–115]

AGREE (ə grē′), *v.,* -GREED, -GREEING. (Of the same mind; thinking the same way.) The index finger of the right "D" hand, palm back, touches the forehead (the modified sign for THINK, *q.v.*), and then the two index fingers, both in the "D" position, palms down, are brought together so they are side by side, pointing away from the body (the sign for SAME). *Cf.* ACCORD, ACQUIESCE, ACQUIESCENCE, AGREEMENT, COINCIDE 2, COMPLY, CONCUR, CONSENT.

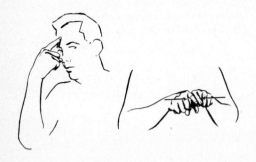

[A–116]

AGREEMENT (-mənt), *n.* See AGREE.

[A–117]

AHEAD (ə hĕd′), *adv.* (One hand moves *ahead* of the other.) The two "A" hands are placed side by side in front of the chest with thumbs and knuckles touching, and the thumbs pointing outward from the body. The right "A" hand moves ahead until its heel rests on the left knuckles.

[A–118]

AID (ād), *n., v.,* AIDED, AIDING. (Helping up; supporting.) The left "S" hand, thumb side up, rests in the open right palm. In this position the left hand is pushed up a short distance by the right. *Cf.* ASSIST, ASSISTANCE, BENEFIT 1, BOOST, GIVE ASSISTANCE, HELP.

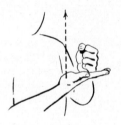

[A–119]

AIM (ām), *v.,* AIMED, AIMING, *n.* (A thought directed upward, toward a goal.) The left "D" hand, palm facing the body, is held above the head, to represent the goal. The index finger of the right "D" hand, after touching the forehead (modified sign for THINK, *q.v.*), moves slowly and deliberately up to the tip of the left index finger. *Cf.* AMBITION, ASPIRE, GOAL, OBJECTIVE, PERSEVERE 4, PURPOSE 2.

[A-120]

AIR (âr), *n*. (Creating a breeze with the hands.) Both hands, in the "5" position, palms facing, are held at face height. Pivoting at the wrists, they wave back and forth, fanning the face.

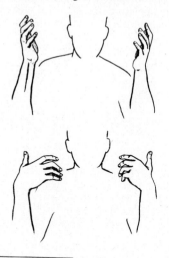

[A-121]

AIRPLANE 1 (âr′ plān′), *n*. (The wings of the airplane.) The "Y" hand, palm down and drawn up near the shoulder, moves forward, up and away from the body. Either hand may be used. *Cf.* FLY 1, PLANE 1.

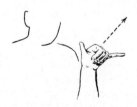

[A-122]

AIRPLANE 2, *n*. (The wings and fuselage of the airplane.) The hand assumes the same position as in AIRPLANE 1, but the index finger is also extended, to represent the fuselage of the airplane. Either hand may be used, and the movement is the same as in AIRPLANE 1. *Cf.* FLY 2, PLANE 2.

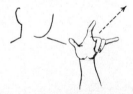

[A-123]

ALAS (ə lăs′, ə läs′), *interj*. (The hands are thrown out and wrung together.) Both hands, palms facing out and fingers wide open, are thrown out from the face. They are then brought together, one over the other, and wrung. This is accompanied by a troubled expression.

[A-124]

ALGEBRA (ăl′ jə brə), *n*. (A multiplying, modified by the letter "A.") Both "A" hands, palms facing outward, move toward each other and cross. The motion is repeated several times.

[A-125]

ALIKE (ə līk′), *adv*. (Matching fingers are brought together.) The outstretched index fingers are brought together, either once or several times. *Cf.* IDENTICAL, LIKE 2, SAME 1, SIMILAR, SUCH.

[A-126]

ALIVE (ə līv′), *adj*. (The fountain [of LIFE] wells up from within the body.) The upturned thumbs of the "A" hands move in unison up the chest. *Cf.* ADDRESS 3, DWELL, EXIST, LIFE 1, LIVE 1, LIVING, MORTAL, RESIDE.

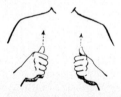

[A-127]

ALL 1 (ôl), *adj., n., pron.* (Encompassing; a gathering together.) Both hands are held in the right angle position, palms facing the body, and the right hand in front of the left. The right hand makes a sweeping outward movement around the left, and comes to rest with the back of the right hand resting in the left palm. *Cf.* ENTIRE, UNIVERSAL, WHOLE.

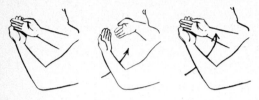

[A-128]

ALL 2, *adj., n., pron.* (An inclusion, in the sense of a total number.) The left hand is held in the "C" position, fingers pointing right. The right hand, in the "5" position, fingers facing out from the body, palm down, is held above the left. With a horizontal swing to the right, the right hand describes an arc, as the fingers close and are thrust into the left "C" hand, which closes over it. *Cf.* ALTOGETHER, INCLUDE, INCLUSIVE, WHOLE (THE).

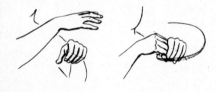

[A-129]

ALL AFTERNOON (ăf′ tər nōōn′, ăf′ -), *adv. phrase.* (The sun, at its zenith, travels across the sky to sunset position, at the horizon.) The left arm is held before the chest, with the hand extended, fingers together, and palm facing down. The right elbow rests on the left hand, with the right hand extended, palm facing out. The right arm, using its elbow as a pivot, moves slowly down until it reaches the horizontal. *Cf.* AFTERNOON.

[A-130]

ALL ALONG (ə lông′, əlŏng′), *adv. phrase.* (From a point up and over.) In the "D" position, palms down, both index fingers touch the right shoulder and then are brought up and over, ending in a palm-up position, pointing straight ahead of the body. *Cf.* ALL THE TIME, EVER SINCE, SINCE, SO FAR, THUS FAR.

[A-131]

ALL DAY (dā), *phrase.* (From sunrise to sunset.) The left arm is held before the chest, palm down, fingers together. The right elbow rests on the back of the left hand. The right hand, palm up, pivoted by its elbow, describes an arc, from as far to the right as it can be held to a point where it comes to rest on the left arm, indicating the course of the sun from sunrise to sunset.

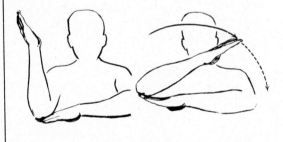

[A-132]

ALL MORNING (môr′ nĭng), *adv. phrase.* (The sun, at sunrise position, rises until it reaches its zenith.) The right arm is held horizontally before the body, palm up and fingers together. The left hand, palm facing the body, is placed in the crook of the right elbow, and the right arm rises slowly until it reaches the vertical.

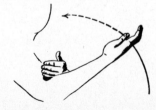

[A-133]

ALL NIGHT (nīt), *adv. phrase.* (The sun, having set over the horizon, continues around the other side of the earth, until it reaches the opposite horizon.) The left arm is held before the chest, hand extended, fingers together, palm down. The right arm rests on the back of the left hand, with palm down, fingers extended and together. The right hand, pivoted at its wrist, describes a sweeping downward arc until it comes to a stop near the left elbow. *Cf.* LATE AT NIGHT.

[A-134]

ALLOW (ə lou'), *v.,* -LOWED, -LOWING. (A permissive upswinging of the hands, as if giving in.) Both hands, palms facing and fingers pointing away from the body, are held at chest level, almost a foot apart. With an upward movement, using their wrists as pivots, the hands sweep up until the fingers point almost straight up. *Cf.* GRANT 1, LET, LET'S, LET US, MAY 3, PERMISSION 1, PERMIT 1, TOLERATE 1.

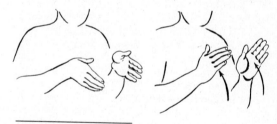

[A-135]

ALL RIGHT (rīt), *phrase.* (A straightening out.) The right hand, fingers together and palm facing left, is placed in the upturned left palm, whose fingers point away from the body. The right hand slides straight out along the left palm, over the left fingers, and stops with its heel resting on the left fingertips. *Cf.* O.K. 1, PRIVILEGE, RIGHT 1, RIGHTEOUS 1, YOU'RE WELCOME 2.

[A-136]

ALL THE TIME (tīm), *adv. phrase.* See ALL ALONG.

[A-137]

ALL YEAR; ALL YEAR 'ROUND (yĭr; round), *(colloq.), adv., v. phrase.* (Encircling the planet.) The left hand, in the "S" position, knuckles facing right, is encircled by the right index finger, which travels in a clockwise direction. It makes one revolution and comes to rest atop the left hand. *Cf.* AROUND THE WORLD, ORBIT 1.

[A-138]

ALMIGHTY (ôl mī' tĭ), *adj.* (All, strong.) The sign for ALL 1 is made. This is followed by the sign for STRONG: The palms of the hands are placed flat against the chest, and then, with a forceful movement, both hands are drawn out and a bit down, each closing into the "S" position.

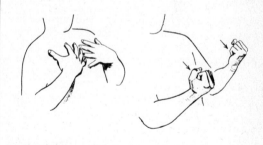

[A-139]

ALMOST (ôl' mōst, ôl mōst'), *adv.* The left hand is held at chest level in the right angle position, with fingers pointing up and the back of the hand facing right. The right fingers are swept up along the back of the left hand. *Cf.* ABOUT 2, NEARLY.

[A–140]

ALONE (ə lōn′), *adj.* (One, wandering around in a circle.) The index finger, pointing straight up, palm facing the body (the number *one*), is rotated before the face in a counterclockwise direction. *Cf.* LONE, ONE 2, ONLY, SOLE, UNITY.

[A–141]

ALONG (ə lông′, ə lŏng′), *prep.* (Describing motion or direction.) The index finger of the "D" hand, palm facing left, is pointed straight out from the body. It moves away from the body in a curving, somewhat zigzag manner.

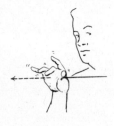

[A–142]

ALPHABET (ăl′ fə bĕt′), *n.* (The movement of the fingers in fingerspelling.) The right hand, palm out, is moved from left to right, with the fingers wriggling up and down. *Cf.* DACTYLOLOGY, FINGERSPELL-ING, MANUAL ALPHABET, SPELL, SPELLING.

[A–143]

ALSO 1 (ôl′ sō), *adv.* (A likeness; a sameness.) Both index fingers, held together at one side of the body near waist level, point forward. As they travel to the other side of the body they separate an inch or two and come together again. *Cf.* ACCORDING (TO), AS, DUPLICATE 2, SAME AS, TOO.

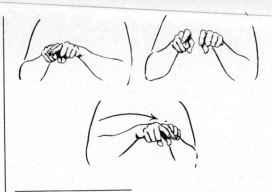

[A–144]

ALSO 2, *adv.* The right "5" hand, palm facing the body, fingers facing left, moves from left to right, meanwhile closing until all its fingers touch around its thumb. *Cf.* AND, MOREOVER 1.

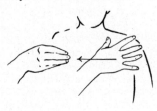

[A–145]

ALTAR 1 (ôl′ tər), *(eccles.)*, *n.* (A table for kneeling.) The sign for TABLE is made: Both hands, held flat, palms down, touch at the thumbs. They are drawn apart about a foot (to represent the table top). The two index fingers, pointing down, move down simultaneously an inch or two, retract their course, move in toward the body, and again move down an inch or two (the table's four legs). The right index and middle fingers, bent at the knuckles, are then thrust into the upright palm of the left hand (to represent the act of kneeling).

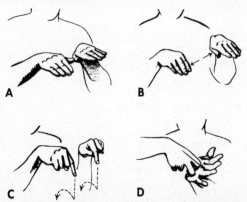

A   B

C   D

[A–146]

ALTAR 2, *(eccles.)*, *n.* (A table for Mass.) The sign for ALTAR 1 is made; and then the two "F" hands, palms out, are drawn up and together, so that the thumbs and index fingers of both hands touch before the face (bringing the Host to the lips in Roman Catholic practice). *Cf.* MASS.

[A–147]

ALTER (ôl' tər), *v.*, -TERED, -TERING. (To change positions.) Both "A" hands, thumbs up, are held before the chest, several inches apart. The left hand is pivoted over so that its thumb points to the right. Simultaneously, the right hand is moved up and over the left, describing a small arc, with its thumb pointing to the left. *Cf.* ADJUST, ALTERATION, CHANGE 1, CONVERT, MODIFY, REVERSE 2, TRANSFER 1.

[A–148]

ALTERATION (-ā' shən), *n.* See ALTER.

[A–149]

ALTHOUGH (ôl thō'), *conj.* (A divergence or a difference; the opposite of SAME.) The index fingers of both "D" hands, palms facing down, are crossed near their tips. The hands are drawn apart. *Cf.* BUT, HOWEVER 1, ON THE CONTRARY.

[A–150]

ALTOGETHER (ôl' tə gĕth' ər), *adv.* (All; the whole.) The left hand is held in the "C" position, fingers pointing right. The right hand, in the "5" position, fingers facing out from the body, palm down, is held above the left. With a horizontal swing to the right, the right hand describes an arc, as the fingers close and are thrust into the left "C" hand, which closes over it. *Cf.* ALL 2, INCLUDE, INCLUSIVE, WHOLE (THE).

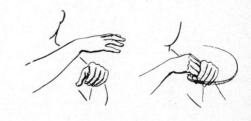

[A–151]

ALWAYS (ôl' wāz, -wĭz), *adv.* (Around the clock.) The index finger of the right "D" hand points outward, away from the body, with palm facing left. The arm is rotated clockwise.

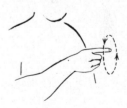

[A–152]

AM 1 (ăm; *unstressed* əm), *v.* (Part of the verb to BE.) The tip of the right index finger, held in the "D" position, palm facing left, is held at the lips, and the hand moves straight out and away from the lips. *Cf.* ARE 1, BE 1, IS 1.

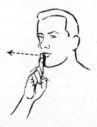

[A-153]

AM 2, *v.* (The "A" hand.) The tip of the right thumb, in the "A" position, palm facing left, is held at the lips. Then the hand moves straight out and away from the lips.

[A-154]

AMAZE (ə māz'), *v.*, -MAZED, -MAZING. (The eyes pop open in amazement.) Both hands are held in modified "O" positions with thumb and index fingers of each hand near the eyes. These fingers suddenly flick open, and the eyes simultaneously pop open wide. *Cf.* AMAZEMENT, ASTONISH, ASTONISHED, ASTONISHMENT, ASTOUND, SURPRISE 1.

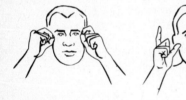

[A-155]

AMAZEMENT (-mənt), *n.* See AMAZE.

[A-156]

AMBITION (ăm bĭsh' ən), *n.* (A thought directed upward, toward a goal.) The left "D" hand, palm facing the body, is held above the head, to represent the goal. The index finger of the right "D" hand, after touching the forehead (modified sign for THINK, *q.v.*), moves slowly and deliberately up to the tip of the left index finger. *Cf.* AIM, ASPIRE, GOAL, OBJECTIVE, PERSEVERE 4, PURPOSE 2.

[A-157]

AMBITIOUS 1 (ăm bĭsh' əs), *adj.* (Rubbing the hands together in zeal or ambition.) The open hands are rubbed vigorously back and forth against each other. *Cf.* ANXIOUS 1, ARDENT, DILIGENCE 1, DILIGENT, EAGER, EAGERNESS, EARNEST, ENTHUSIASM, ENTHUSIASTIC, INDUSTRIOUS, METHODIST, ZEAL, ZEALOUS.

[A-158]

AMBITIOUS 2, *adj.* (The self is carried uppermost.) The right "A" hand, thumb up, is brought up against the chest, from waist to breast. *Cf.* EGOTISM 1, SELF 2.

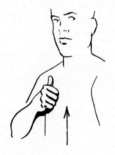

[A-159]

AMEN (ā' mĕn', ä' -), *(eccles.)*, *interj.* (Worshiping.) The hands are clasped together, with the left cupped over the right. Both are brought in toward the body, while the eyes are shut and the head is bowed slightly. *Cf.* ADORE, DEVOUT, PIOUS, WORSHIP.

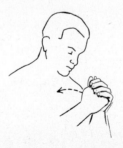

[A-160]

AMERICA (ə mĕr′ ə kə), *n.* (The fences built by the early settlers as protection against the Indians.) The extended fingers of both hands are interlocked, and are swept in an arc from left to right as if encompassing an imaginary house or stockade. *Cf.* UNION, THE.

[A-161]

AMIABLE (ā′ mĭ ə bəl), *adj.* (A crinkling-up of the face.) Both hands, in the "5" position, palms facing back, are placed on either side of the face. The fingers wiggle back and forth, while a pleasant, happy expression is worn. *Cf.* CHEERFUL, CORDIAL, FRIENDLY, JOLLY, PLEASANT.

[A-162]

AMID (ə′ mĭd′), *prep.* (Wandering in and out.) The right index finger weaves its way in and out between the outstretched fingers of the left hand. *Cf.* AMIDST, AMONG, MIDST.

[A-163]

AMIDST (ə′ mĭdst′), *prep.* See AMID.

[A-164]

AMONG (ə mŭng′), *prep.* See AMID.

[A-165]

AMOUNT 1 (ə mount′), *n.* (To bring up all together.) The two open hands, palms and fingers facing each other, with the left hand above the right, are brought together, with all fingers closing simultaneously. This sign is used mainly in the sense of adding up figures or items. *Cf.* ADD 1, ADDITION, SUM, SUMMARIZE 2, SUMMARY 2, SUM UP, TOTAL.

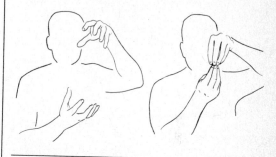

[A-166]

AMOUNT 2, *n.* (Throwing up a number of things before the eyes; a display of fingers to indicate a question of how many or how much.) The right hand, palm up, is held before the chest, all fingers touching the thumb. The hand is tossed straight up, while the fingers open to the "5" position. *Cf.* HOW MANY?, HOW MUCH?, NUMBER 2.

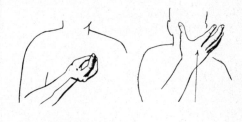

[A-167]

AMPLE (ăm′ pəl), *adj.* (A full cup.) The left hand, in the "S" position, is held palm facing right. The right "5" hand, palm down, is brushed outward several times over the top of the left, indicating a wiping off of the top of a cup. *Cf.* ABUNDANCE, ABUNDANT, ADEQUATE, ENOUGH, PLENTY, SUBSTANTIAL, SUFFICIENT.

[A-168]

AMUSING (ə mū´ zǐng), *adj.* (A smiling face.) The extended index fingers are placed at the corners of the mouth and then drawn away to either side of the face, while the signer smiles appropriately.

[A-169]

ANCESTORS 1 (ăn´ sĕs tĕrz), *n. pl.* (A series of parents, in the past.) The upright open hands are held facing each other before the right shoulder, right palm facing left, left palm facing right. In this position the hands move back over the shoulder, alternately executing a series of up-down, circular motions.

[A-170]

ANCESTORS 2, *n. pl.* The upright, right open hand, palm facing left, moves back over the right shoulder in a series of up-down, circular motions. (This is similar to the sign for ANCESTORS 1, except that only the right hand is used.)

[A-171]

AND (ănd; *unstressed* ənd; ən), *conj.* The right "5" hand, palm facing the body, fingers facing left, moves from left to right, meanwhile closing until all its fingers touch around its thumb. *Cf.* ALSO 2, MOREOVER 1.

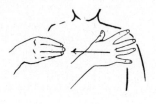

[A-172]

ANGEL (ān´ jəl), *n.* (A winged creature.) The fingertips of both hands rest on the shoulders, and then the hands go through the motions of flapping wings, pivoting up and down from the wrists, and held at shoulder level. The eyes are sometimes rolled upward, indicating something celestial.

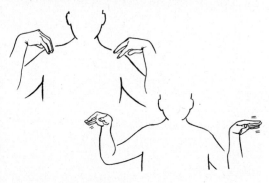

[A-173]

ANGER (ăn´ gər), *n.* (A violent welling-up of the emotions.) The curved fingers of the right hand are placed in the center of the chest, and fly up suddenly and violently. An expression of anger is worn. *Cf.* ANGRY 2, ENRAGE, FURY, INDIGNANT, INDIGNATION, IRE, MAD 1, RAGE.

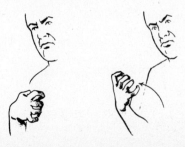

[A–174]

ANGLE (ăn′ gəl), *n., v.,* -GLED, -GLING. (The natural sign.) Both hands, palms flat and fingers straight, are held in front of the body at right angles to each other with fingertips touching, the left fingertips pointing to the right and the right fingertips pointing forward. *Cf.* CORNER 1.

[A–175]

ANGRY 1 (ăn′ grĭ), *adj.* (Wrinkling the brow.) The "5" hand is held palm toward the face. The fingers open and close partly, several times, while an angry expression is worn on the face. *Cf.* CROSS 1, CROSSNESS, FIERCE, ILL TEMPER, IRRITABLE.

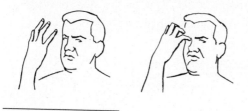

[A–176]

ANGRY 2, *adj.* See ANGER.

[A–177]

ANIMAL 1 (ăn′ ə məl), *n.* (Something with four legs that breathes.) With palms facing the body, both hands are placed on the chest, with one on top of the other, right fingers facing left and left fingers right. In this position both are moved alternately on and off the chest (signifying the rise and fall of the chest in breathing). The index and middle fingers of both hands are next brought into play, pointing downward, one in front of the other, and describing a walking motion outward from the body.

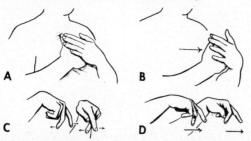

[A–178]

ANIMAL 2, *n.* (A modification of the breathing movement described in ANIMAL 1.) With the curved fingertips of both hands resting on either side of the chest, acting as anchors, the arms are moved alternately toward and away from each other.

[A–179]

ANNEX (ə nĕks′), *v.,* -NEXED, -NEXING. (Joining together.) Both hands, held in the modified "5" position, palms out, move toward each other. The thumbs and index fingers of both hands then connect. *Cf.* AFFILIATE 1, ASSOCIATE 2, ATTACH, BELONG, COMMUNION OF SAINTS, CONCERN 2, CONNECT, ENLIST, ENROLL, JOIN 1, PARTICIPATE, RELATIVE 2, UNION, UNITE.

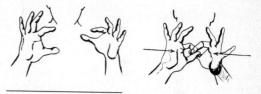

[A–180]

ANNIHILATE (ə nĭ′ ə lat′), *v.,* -LATED, -LATING. (Wiping off.) The left "5" hand, palm up, is held slightly above the right "5" hand, held palm down. The right hand swings up, just brushing over the left palm. Both hands close into the "S" position, and the right is brought back with force to its initial position, striking a glancing blow against the left knuckles as it returns. *Cf.* ABOLISH 1, CORRUPT, DEFACE, DEMOLISH, DESTROY, HAVOC, PERISH 2, REMOVE 3, RUIN.

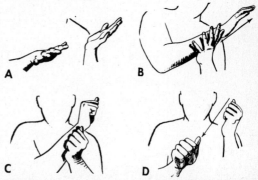

[A-181]

ANNOUNCE (ə nouns'), *v.*, -NOUNCED, -NOUNCING. (An issuance from the mouth.) Both index fingers are placed at the lips, with palms facing the body. They are rotated once and swung out in arcs, until the left index finger points somewhat to the left and the right index somewhat to the right. Sometimes the rotation of the fingers is omitted in favor of a simple swinging out from the lips. *Cf.* ACCLAIM 1, ACCLAMATION, ANNOUNCEMENT, DECLARE, MAKE KNOWN, PROCLAIM, PROCLAMATION.

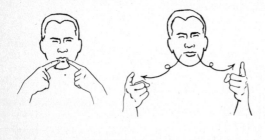

[A-182]

ANNOUNCEMENT (-mənt), *n.* See ANNOUNCE.

[A-183]

ANNOY 1 (ə noi'), *v.*, -NOYED, -NOYING. (Obstruct, block.) The left hand, fingers together and palm flat, is held before the body, facing somewhat down. The little finger side of the right hand, held with palm flat, makes one or several up-down chopping motions against the left hand, between its thumb and index finger. *Cf.* ANNOYANCE 1, BLOCK, BOTHER 1, CHECK 2, COME BETWEEN, DISRUPT, DISTURB, HINDER, HINDRANCE, IMPEDE, INTERCEPT, INTERFERE, INTERFERENCE, INTERFERE WITH, INTERRUPT, MEDDLE 1, OBSTACLE, OBSTRUCT, PREVENT, PREVENTION.

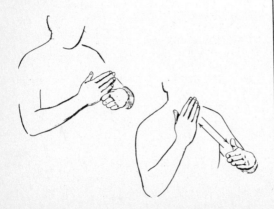

[A-184]

ANNOY 2, *(rare), v.* (A clouding over; a troubling.) Both "B" hands, palms facing each other, are rotated alternately before the forehead. *Cf.* ANNOYANCE 2, ANXIOUS 2, BOTHER 2, CONCERN 1, FRET, PROBLEM 1, TROUBLE, WORRIED, WORRY 1.

[A-185]

ANNOYANCE 1 (ə noi' əns), *n.* See ANNOY 1.

[A-186]

ANNOYANCE 2, *(rare), n.* See ANNOY 2.

[A-187]

ANNUAL (ăn' yo͞o əl), *adj.* (Several years brought forward.) This sign is actually a modification of the sign for YEAR, *q.v.* The ball of the right "S" hand, moving straight out from the body, palm facing left, glances over the thumb side of the "S" hand, which is held palm facing right. As this contact is made, the right index finger is flung straight out, and the right hand, in this new position, continues forward. This is repeated several times, to indicate several years. *Cf.* EVERY YEAR, YEARLY.

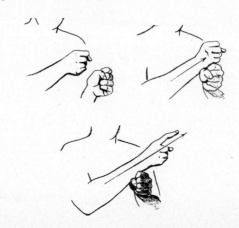

[A-188]

ANNUL (ə nŭl'), *v.*, -NULLED, -NULLING. (A cancel-ing out.) The right index finger makes a cross on the open left palm. *Cf.* CANCEL, CHECK 1, CORRECT 2, CRITICISM, CRITICIZE, FIND FAULT 1, REVOKE.

[A-189]

ANOINT 1 (ə noint'), *(eccles.)*, *v.*, -NOINTED, -NOINTING. (A pouring of water over the head.) An imaginary cup of water is tilted and poured over the head.

[A-190]

ANOINT 2, *(eccles.)*, *v.* (A crossing of the forehead.) In the "A" position, the right thumbnail is kissed, and then is used to describe a small cross on the forehead.

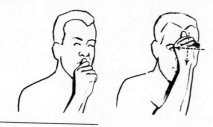

[A-191]

ANOTHER (ə nŭth' ər), *adj.* (Moving over to *an-other* position.) The right "A" hand, thumb up, is pivoted from the wrist and swung over to the right, so that the thumb now points to the right. *Cf.* OTHER.

[A-192]

ANSWER 1 (ăn' sər; än' -), *n., v.*, -SWERED, -SWER-ING. (Directing a reply from the mouth to someone.) The tip of the right index finger, held in the "D" position, palm facing the body, is placed on the lips, while the left "D" hand, palm also facing the body, is held about a foot in front of the right hand. The right index finger, swinging around, moves toward and stops in a pointing position a few inches from the left index fingertip. *Cf.* MAKE RESPONSE, REPLY 1, RESPOND, RESPONSE 1.

[A-193]

ANSWER 2, *n.* (The letter "R"; coming out of the mouth.) Both "R" hands are held before the face, with the right "R" hand at the lips and behind the left "R" hand. Both hands move forward simultane-ously, describing a small upward arc. *Cf.* REACTION, REPLY 2, REPORT, RESPONSE 2.

[A-194]

ANTICIPATE (ăn tĭs' ə pāt'), *v.*, -PATED, -PATING. (A thought awaited.) The tip of the right index finger, held in the "D" position, palm facing the body, is placed on the forehead (modified THINK, *q. v.*). Both hands then assume right angle positions, fingers facing, with the left hand held above left shoulder level and the right before the right breast. Both hands, held thus, wave to each other several times. *Cf.* ANTICIPATION, EXPECT, HOPE.

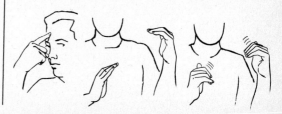

[A-195]

ANTICIPATION (-pā′ shən), *n.* See ANTICIPATE.

___

[A-196]

ANTIQUE (ăn tēk′), *adj.* (Old; the beard of an old man.) The right hand grasps an imaginary beard at the chin and pulls it downward. (This sign is used only in the sense of an adjective; as a noun it would be spelled out with the fingers. *Cf.* AGE 1, OLD.

___

[A-197]

ANTLERS (ănt′ lərs), *n. pl.* (The branching of the antlers from the head.) Both hands, in the "5" position, palms up, are placed at the head, thumbs resting on the head above the temples. *Cf.* DEER, ELK, MOOSE.

___

[A-198]

ANXIETY (ăng zī′ ə ti), *n.* (The heart pounds.) The open left hand is held in front of the heart, palm toward the body. The right "S" hand moves forcefully back and forth between the heart and the left palm, representing the heart pounding beneath one's clothing.

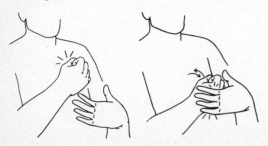

[A-199]

ANXIOUS 1 (ăngk′ shəs, ăng′ shəs), *adj.* (Rubbing the hands together in zeal or ambition.) The open hands are rubbed vigorously back and forth against each other. *Cf.* AMBITIOUS 1, ARDENT, DILIGENCE 1, DILIGENT, EAGER, EAGERNESS, EARNEST, ENTHUSIASM, ENTHUSIASTIC, INDUSTRIOUS, METHODIST, ZEAL, ZEALOUS.

___

[A-200]

ANXIOUS 2 *adj.* (A clouding over; a troubling.) Both "B" hands, palms facing each other, are rotated alternately before the forehead. *Cf.* ANNOY 2, ANNOYANCE 2, BOTHER 2, CONCERN 1, FRET, PROBLEM 1, TROUBLE, WORRIED, WORRY 1.

___

[A-201]

ANY 1 (ĕn′ ĭ), *adj., pron.* The "A" hand, palm out, moves down in an S-shaped curve to a point a bit above waist level.

[A–202]

ANY 2, *adj., pron.* The "A" hand, palm down and thumb pointing left, pivots around on the wrist, so the thumb now points down.

[A–203]

ANYHOW (ĕn′ ĭ hou′), *adv.* Both hands, in the "5" position, are held before the chest, fingertips facing each other. With an alternate back-forth movement, the fingertips are made to strike each other. *Cf.* ANY-WAY, DESPITE, DOESN'T MATTER, HOWEVER 2, IN-DIFFERENCE, INDIFFERENT, IN SPITE OF, MAKE NO DIFFERENCE, NEVERTHELESS, NO MATTER, WHER-EVER.

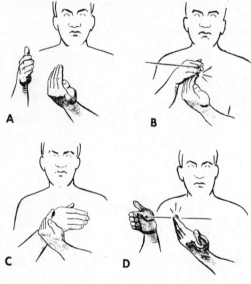

A   B

C   D

[A–204]

ANYONE (ĕn′ ĭ wŭn′), *pron.* (*Any* and *one.*) After forming either of the two signs for ANY, the "A" hand, moving up a bit, assumes the "1" position ("D"), palm out.

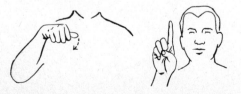

[A–205]

ANYTHING (ĕn′ ĭ thĭng′), *pron.* (Something shown in the hand.) The sign for either ANY 1 or ANY 2 is made. The outstretched right hand, palm up and held before the chest, is dropped slightly and brought over a bit to the right. *Cf.* APPARATUS, INSTRUMENT, MATTER, OBJECT 1, SUBSTANCE 1, THING.

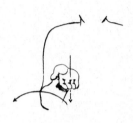

[A–206]

ANYWAY (ĕn′ ĭ wā′), *adv.* See ANYHOW.

[A–207]

APART (ə pärt′), *adv.* (The hands are moved *apart.*) Both hands, in the "A" position, thumbs up, are held together, with knuckles touching. With a delib-erate movement they come apart. *Cf.* DIVORCE 1, PART 3, SEPARATE 1.

[A–208]

APE (āp), *n.* (The scratching of apes.) Both hands go through the natural motion of scratching the sides of the chest. *Cf.* MONKEY.

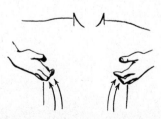

[A–209]

APOLOGIZE 1 (ə pŏl′ ə jīz′), *v.*, -GIZED, -GIZING. (The heart is circled, to indicate feeling, modified by the letter "S," for SORRY.) The right "S" hand, palm facing the body, is rotated several times over the area of the heart. *Cf.* APOLOGY 1, CONTRITION, PENITENT, REGRET, REGRETFUL, REPENT, REPENTANT, RUE, SORROW, SORROWFUL 2, SORRY.

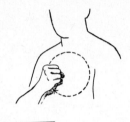

[A–210]

APOLOGIZE 2, *v.* (A wiped-off and cleaned slate.) The right hand wipes off the left palm several times. *·Cf.* APOLOGY 2, EXCUSE, FORGIVE 2, PARDON, PAROLE.

[A–211]

APOLOGY 1 (ə pŏl′ ə jĭ), *n.* See APOLOGIZE 1.

[A–212]

APOLOGY 2, *n.* See APOLOGIZE 2.

[A–213]

APPARATUS (ăp′ ə rā′ təs; -răt′ əs), *n.* (Something shown in the hand.) The outstretched right hand, palm up and held before the chest, is dropped slightly and brought over a bit to the right. *Cf.* ANYTHING, INSTRUMENT, MATTER, OBJECT 1, SUBSTANCE 1, THING.

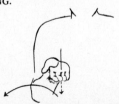

[A–214]

APPARENT (ə păr′ ənt, ə pâr′ -), *adj.* (Something presented before the eyes.) The open right hand, palm flat and facing out, with fingers together and pointing up, is positioned at shoulder level. Pivoting from the wrist, the hand is swung around so that the palm now faces the eyes. Sometimes the eyes glance at the newly presented palm. *Cf.* APPARENTLY, APPEAR 1, LOOK 2, SEEM.

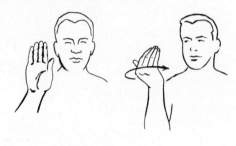

[A–215]

APPARENTLY (ə păr′ ənt lē, ə pâr′ -), *adv.* See APPARENT.

[A–216]

APPEAR 1 (ə pir′), *v.*, -PEARED, -PEARING. See APPARENT.

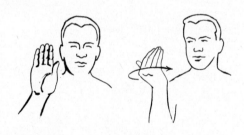

[A–217]

APPEAR 2, *v.* (Popping up before the eyes.) The right index finger, pointing up, pops up between the index and middle fingers of the left hand, whose palm faces down. *Cf.* POP UP, RISE 2.

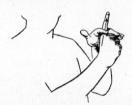

[A–218]

APPEAR 3, *v.* (Face to face.) The left hand, fingers together, palm flat and facing the eyes, is held a bit above eye level. The right hand, fingers also together, is held in front of the mouth, with palm facing the left hand. With a sweeping upward movement the right hand moves toward the left, which moves straight up an inch or two at the same time. *Cf.* APPEARANCE, BEFORE 3, CONFRONT, FACE 2, FACE TO FACE, PRESENCE.

[A–219]

APPEARANCE (ə pĭr′ əns), *n.* See APPEAR 3.

[A–220]

APPETITE (ăp′ ə tīt′), *n.* (The upper alimentary tract is outlined.) The right "C" hand, palm facing the body, is placed with fingertips touching mid-chest. In this position it moves down a bit. *Cf.* CRAVE, DESIRE 2, FAMINE, HUNGARIAN, HUNGARY, HUNGER, HUNGRY, STARVATION, STARVE, STARVED, WISH 2.

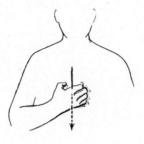

[A–221]

APPLAUD (ə plôd′), *v.,* -PLAUDED, -PLAUDING. (Good words coming from the mouth; clapping hands.) The fingertips of the right hand, palm flat and facing the body, are brought up to the lips, so

that they touch (part of the sign for GOOD, *q.v.*). The hands are then clapped together several times. *Cf.* ACCLAIM 2, APPLAUSE, APPROBATION, APPROVAL, APPROVE, CLAP, COMMEND, CONGRATULATE 1, CONGRATULATIONS 1, PRAISE.

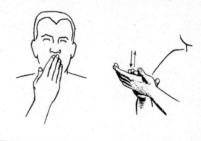

[A–222]

APPLAUSE (ə plôz′), *n.* See APPLAUD.

[A–223]

APPLE (ăp′ əl), *n.* (A chewing of the letter "A," for *apple.*) The right "A" hand is held at the right cheek, with the thumb tip touching the cheek and palm facing out. In this position the hand is swung over and back from the wrist several times, using the thumb as a pivot.

[A–224]

APPLY 1 (ə plī′), *v.,* -PLIED, -PLYING. (Bringing oneself forward.) The right index finger and thumb grasp the clothing near the right shoulder (often the lapel of a suit or the collar of a dress) and tug it up and down gently several times. Sometimes one tug only is used. *Cf.* CANDIDATE, OFFER 2, RUN FOR OFFICE, VOLUNTEER.

[A–225]

APPLY 2, *v*. (Directing one's attention forward; applying oneself; concentrating.) Both hands, fingers pointing up and together, are held at the sides of the face. They move straight out from the face. *Cf*. AT-TEND (TO), ATTENTION, CONCENTRATE, CONCENTRATION, FOCUS, GIVE ATTENTION (TO), MIND 2, PAY ATTENTION (TO).

[A–226]

APPOINT (ə point′), *v*., -POINTED, -POINTING. (Taking unto oneself.) The right hand, palm out, is extended before the chest, index finger and thumb in an open position, the other fingers separated and pointing up. The hand is drawn in toward the chest, and the index and thumb close at the same time, indicating something taken to oneself. *Cf*. ADOPT, CHOOSE 1, SELECT 2, TAKE.

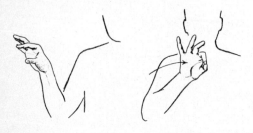

[A–227]

APPOINTMENT (ə point′ mənt), *n*. (A binding of the hands together; a commitment.) The right "S" hand, palm down, is positioned above the left "S" hand, also palm down. The right hand circles above the left in a clockwise manner and is brought down on the back of the left hand. At the same instant both hands move down in unison a short distance. *Cf*. ENGAGEMENT.

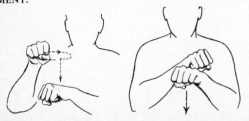

[A–228]

APPORTION (ə pōr′ shən), *v*., -TIONED, -TIONING. (A splitting apart or dividing.) The two hands are crossed, with the right little finger resting on the left index finger. Both hands are dropped down and separated simultaneously, so that the palms face down. *Cf*. DIVIDE 1, SHARE 2.

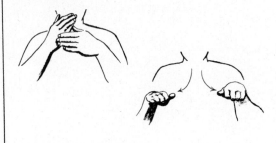

[A–229]

APPRECIATE (ə prē′ shĭ āt′), *v*., -ATED, -ATING. (A pleasurable feeling on the heart.) The open right hand is circled on the chest, over the heart. *Cf*. ENJOY, ENJOYMENT, GRATIFY 1, LIKE 3, PLEASE, PLEASURE, WILLING 2.

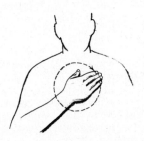

[A–230]

APPROACH (ə prōch′), *v*., -PROACHED, -PROACHING. (Coming close to.) Both hands are held in the right angle position, fingers facing each other, with the right hand held between the left hand and the chest. The right hand slowly moves toward the left. *Cf*. NEAR 2, TOWARD 2.

[A-231]

APPROBATION (ăp′ rə bā′ shən), *n.* (Good words coming from the mouth; clapping hands.) The fingertips of the right hand, palm flat and facing the body, are brought up to the lips, so that they touch (part of the sign for GOOD, *q.v.*). The hands are then clapped together several times. *Cf.* ACCLAIM 2, APPLAUD, APPLAUSE, APPROVAL, APPROVE, CLAP, COMMEND, CONGRATULATE 1, CONGRATULATIONS 1, PRAISE.

[A-232]

APPROVAL (ə prōō′ vəl), *n.* See APPROBATION.

[A-233]

APPROVE (ə prōōv′), *v.*, -PROVED, -PROVING. See APPROBATION.

[A-234]

APRON (ā′ prən), *n.* (Something worn at midriff.) The "L" hands, index fingers pointing down, palms facing the body, are placed in the center of the chest and are drawn apart, outlining the apron.

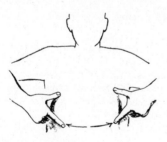

[A-235]

ARBOR PRESS (är′ bər prĕs), *(voc.).* (The handle of the arbor press is moved down. The arbor press is a special type of punch-press used in the vocational departments of some schools for the deaf.) The right

"S" hand, palm facing left, is held a foot above the upturned left palm, which is representing the press platform. The right hand, as if grasping an imaginary handle, swings in a bit toward the body and down in an arc, over the left hand, until it stops a few inches above it.

[A-236]

ARCH (ärch), *n.* (The curve of the arch.) Both outstretched hands, fingers together, are placed before the face. As they are brought up in unison, they describe a natural arch before the face, ending with the fingertips of both hands touching.

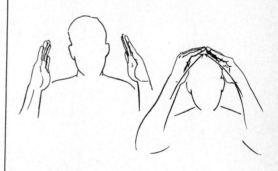

[A-237]

ARCHBISHOP (ärch′ bĭsh′ əp), *(eccles.),* *n.* (A high bishop.) Both hands, in the right angle position, fingers facing, move straight up from a point near eye level (the sign for HIGH). The ring finger of the right hand, held in the "S" position; is then kissed (the sign for BISHOP, Catholic).

[A–238]

ARCHERY (är′ chə ri), *n.* Go through the natural motion of drawing back an arrow on a bow. The arrow may be released.

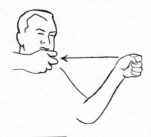

[A–239]

ARDENT (är′ dənt), *adj.* (Rubbing the hands together in zeal or ambition.) The open hands are rubbed vigorously back and forth against each other. *Cf.* AMBITIOUS 1, ANXIOUS 1, DILIGENCE 1, DILIGENT, EAGER, EAGERNESS, EARNEST, ENTHUSIASM, ENTHUSIASTIC, INDUSTRIOUS, METHODIST, ZEAL, ZEALOUS.

[A–240]

ARE 1 (är), *v.* (Part of the verb to BE.) The tip of the right index finger, held in the "D" position, palm facing left, is held at the lips, and the hand moves straight out and away from the lips. *Cf.* AM 1, BE 1, IS 1.

[A–241]

ARE 2, *v.* This is the same sign as for ARE 1, except that the "R" hand is used.

[A–242]

AREA (âr′ i ə), *n.* (The letter "A"; the limitations or borders of the area.) The "A" hands, palms facing down, are positioned with thumbtips touching. They separate, move in toward the body, and then come together again at the thumbtips. The movement describes a square or a circle.

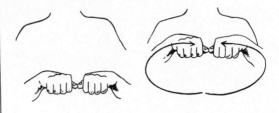

[A–243]

ARGUE (är′ gū), *v.,* -GUED, -GUING. (An expounding back and forth.) The index fingers here represent the two sides of the argument. First the left index finger is slapped into the open right palm, and then the right makes the same movement into the left palm. This is repeated back and forth several times. *Cf.* ARGUMENT, CONTROVERSY, DEBATE, DISPUTE.

[A–244]

ARGUMENT (-mənt), *n.* See ARGUE.

[A–245]

ARID (ăr′ id), *adj.* (A dryness, indicated by a wiping of the lips.) The "X" finger is drawn across the lips, from left to right, as if wiping them. *Cf.* BORE 1, DROUGHT, DRY, DULL 2.

[A-246]

ARISE 1 (ə rīz´), v., -ROSE, -RISEN, -RISING. (Rising up.) Both upturned hands, held at chest level, rise in unison, to about shoulder height. Cf. RISE 3, STAND 3.

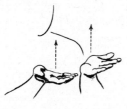

[A-247]

ARISE 2, v. (Getting onto one's feet.) The upturned index and middle fingers of the right hand, representing the legs, are swung up and over in an arc, coming to rest in the upturned left palm. Cf. ELEVATE, GET UP, RAISE 1, RISE 1, STAND 2, STAND UP.

[A-248]

ARITHMETIC (ə rĭth´ mə tĭk), n. (A multiplying.) The "V" hands, palms facing the body, alternately cross and separate, several times. Cf. CALCULATE, ESTIMATE, FIGURE 1, MULTIPLY 1.

[A-249]

ARM (ärm), n. (Describing the physical length of the arm.) The back of the right hand travels along the length of the outstretched left arm, from shoulder to wrist.

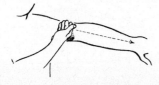

[A-250]

ARMS (ärmz), n. pl. (Bearing arms.) Both "A" hands, palms facing the body, are placed at the left breast, with the right hand above the left, as if holding a rifle against the body. Cf. SOLDIER.

[A-251]

ARMY (är´ mǐ), n. (A group of arms-bearers or soldiers.) The sign for ARMS is made. The "C" hands, palms facing each other, then pivot around on their wrists so that the palms now face the body (a class or category, all together as one unit). Cf. MILITARY.

[A-252]

AROUND (ə round´), adv. (Circling around.) The left hand, all fingers pointed up and touching, is encircled by the right index finger, pointing down and moving clockwise.

[A-253]

AROUND THE WORLD (wûrld), adv. phrase. (Encircling the planet.) The left hand, in the "S" position, knuckles facing right, is encircled by the right index finger, which travels in a clockwise direction. It makes one revolution and comes to rest atop the left hand. Cf. ALL YEAR, ALL YEAR 'ROUND, ORBIT 1.

[A–254]

AROUSE (ə rouz′), *v.*, -ROUSED, -ROUSING. (Opening the eyes.) Both hands are closed, with thumb and index finger of each hand held together, extended, and placed at the corners of the closed eyes. Slowly they separate, and the eyes open. *Cf.* AWAKE, AWAKEN, WAKE UP.

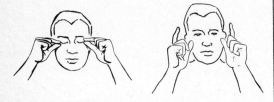

[A–255]

ARRANGE (ə rānj′), *v.*, -RANGED, -RANGING. (Placing things in order.) The hands, palms facing, fingers together and pointing away from the body, are positioned at the left side and held about a foot apart. With a slight up-down motion, as if describing waves, the hands travel in unison from left to right. *Cf.* ARRANGEMENT, CLASSED 2, DEVISE 1, ORDER 3, PLAN 1, POLICY 1, PREPARE 1, PROGRAM 1, PROVIDE 1, PUT IN ORDER, READY 1, SCHEME, SYSTEM.

[A–256]

ARRANGEMENT (ə rānj′ mənt), *n.* See ARRANGE.

[A–257]

ARREARS (ə rirz′), *n. pl.* (Pointing to the palm, where the money should be placed.) The index finger of one hand is thrust into the upturned palm of the other several times. *Cf.* DEBIT, DEBT, DUE, OBLIGATION 3, OWE.

[A–258]

ARREST 1 (ə rĕst′), *v.*, -RESTED, -RESTING. (Seizing someone by the clothing.) The right hand quickly grasps the clothing at the left shoulder.

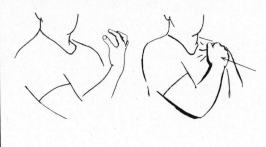

[A–259]

ARREST 2, *v.* (A stopping or cutting short.) The little finger edge of the right hand is thrust abruptly into the upturned left palm, indicating a cutting short. *Cf.* CEASE, HALT, STOP.

[A–260]

ARRIVAL (ə rī′ vəl), *n.* (Arrival at a designated place.) The right hand, palm facing the body and fingers pointing up, is brought forward from a position near the right shoulder and placed in the upturned palm of the left hand (the designated place). *Cf.* ARRIVE, REACH.

[A–261]

ARRIVE (ə rīv′), *v.*, -RIVED, -RIVING. See ARRIVAL.

[A-262]

ART (ärt), *n*. (Drawing on the hand.) The little finger of the right hand, representing a pencil, traces a curved line in the upturned left palm. *Cf*. DRAW 1, MAP.

[A-263]

ARTIST (är′ tĭst), *n*. (An individual who draws.) The sign for ART is made, followed by the sign for INDIVIDUAL: Both hands, fingers together, are placed at either side of the chest and are moved down to waist level.

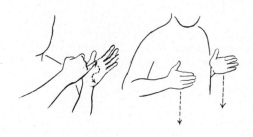

[A-264]

AS (ăz; *unstressed* əz), *adv*. (A likeness; a sameness.) Both index fingers, held together at one side of the body near waist level, point forward. As they travel to the other side of the body they separate an inch or two and come together again. *Cf*. ACCORDING (TO), ALSO 1, DUPLICATE 2, SAME AS, TOO.

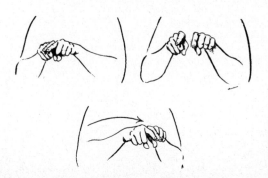

[A-265]

ASCEND (ə sĕnd′), *(arch.)*, *v*., -CENDED, -CENDING. (Rising.) The right open hand, palm up, moves slowly up. *Cf*. CLIMB 2, LADDER.

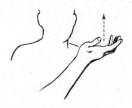

[A-266]

ASCENSION (ə sĕn′ shən), *(eccles.)*, *n*. (A rising.) The right index and middle fingers, representing the legs, are positioned in the upturned left palm. The right hand moves slowly up and off the left. *Note:* This sign is considered vulgar by some; it is at best used in a colloquial sense. *Cf*. EASTER 2, RESURRECTION.

[A-267]

ASHAMED 1 (ə shāmd′), *adj*. (The color rises in the cheek; an attempt is made to hide the head.) The backs of the fingers of the right hand, held in the right angle position, are placed against the right cheek. The hand moves up along the cheek, pivoting at the wrist, so that the fingers finally point to the rear. *Cf*. BASHFUL 1, IMMODEST, IMMORAL, SHAME 1, SHAMEFUL, SHAME ON YOU, SHY 1.

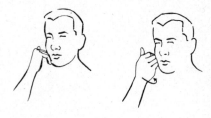

[A-268]

ASHAMED 2, *adj*. Similar to ASHAMED 1, but both hands are used, at either cheek. *Cf*. BASHFUL 2, SHAME 2, SHY 2.

[A–269]

ASH WEDNESDAY (ăsh wĕnz´ di), *(eccles.).* (The placing of the ashes on the forehead.) The right thumb and index fingers, describing a small cross, place imaginary ashes upon the forehead.

[A–270]

ASIA (ā´ zhə, ā´ shə), *n.* (Slanting eyes.) The index fingers draw back the corners of the eyes, causing them to slant. *Cf.* CHINA 1, CHINESE, ORIENTAL.

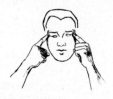

[A–271]

ASK 1 (ăsk, äsk), *v.,* ASKED, ASKING. (Pray tell.) Both hands, held upright about a foot in front of the chest, with palms facing and fingers pointing straight up, are positioned about a foot apart. Moving toward the chest, they come together until they touch, as if in prayer. *Cf.* CONSULT, INQUIRE 1, REQUEST 1.

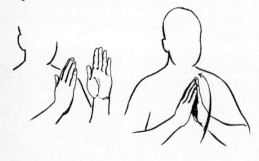

[A–272]

ASK 2, *(colloq.), v.,* (Fire a question.) The right hand, held in a modified "S" position with palm facing out, assumes a position with the thumb rest-

ing on the fingernail of the index finger. The index finger is flicked out and forward, usually directed at the person being asked a question. Reversing the direction so that the index finger flicks out toward the speaker indicates the passive voice of the verb, *i.e.,* to be ASKED. *Cf.* EXAMINATION 2, INQUIRE 2, INTERROGATE 2, INTERROGATION 2, QUERY 2, QUESTION 2, QUIZ 2.

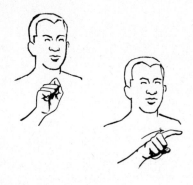

[A–273]

ASK 3, *v.* (Firing questions.) The index fingers of both "D" hands repeatedly curve and straighten out as the hands are alternately flung forward and back, as if firing questions. *Cf.* EXAMINATION 3, INQUIRE 3, INTERROGATE 1, INTERROGATION 1, QUERY 1, QUESTION 3, QUIZ 3.

[A–274]

ASK ALMS (ämz), *(arch.), v. phrase.* (Holding out the hand and begging.) The right open hand, palm up and fingers slightly cupped, is moved up and down by the left hand, positioned under it. *Cf.* BEG 1, BEGGAR, PANHANDLER.

[A–275]

ASLEEP (ə slēp'), *adv.* (The eyes are closed.) The fingers of the right open hand, facing the forehead, are placed on the forehead. The hand moves down and away from the head, with the fingers closing so that they all touch. The eyes meanwhile close, and the head bows slightly, as in sleep. *Cf.* DOZE, NAP, SLEEP 1.

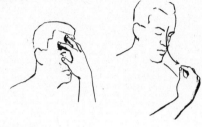

[A–276]

ASPIRE (ə spīr'), *v.*, -PIRED, -PIRING. (A thought directed upward, toward a goal.) The left "D" hand, palm facing the body, is held above the head, to represent the goal. The index finger of the right "D" hand, after touching the forehead (modified sign for THINK, *q.v.*), moves slowly and deliberately up to the tip of the left index finger. *Cf.* AIM, AMBITION, GOAL, OBJECTIVE, PERSEVERE 4, PURPOSE 2.

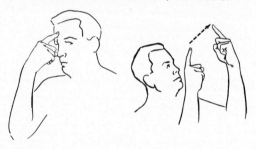

[A–277]

ASSEMBLE (ə sĕm' bəl), *v.*, -BLED, -BLING. (Assemble all together.) Both "5" hands, palms facing, are held with fingers pointing out from the body. With a sweeping motion they are brought in toward the chest, and all fingertips come together. This is repeated. *Cf.* ACCUMULATE 3, ASSEMBLY, CONFERENCE, CONVENE, CONVENTION, GATHER 2, GATHERING, MEETING 1.

[A–278]

ASSEMBLIES OF GOD, *(eccles.)*. (God the Father.) The thumb of the right "A" hand touches the forehead (a contraction of the MALE sign, *q.v.*), and then the hand opens up, the palm flattens and the fingers point straight up. In this position the right hand is raised above the head and then brought down somewhat, in an arc toward the forehead. The head may bow slightly as the hand is lowered, to signify reverence.

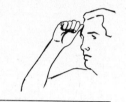

[A–279]

ASSEMBLY (ə sĕm' blĭ), *n.* See ASSEMBLE.

[A–280]

ASSIST (ə sĭst'), *n.*, *v.*, -SISTED, -SISTING. (Helping up; supporting.) The left "S" hand, thumb side up, rests in the open right palm. In this position the left hand is pushed up a short distance by the right. *Cf.* AID, ASSISTANCE, BENEFIT 1, BOOST, GIVE ASSISTANCE, HELP.

[A–281]

ASSISTANCE (ə sĭs' təns), *n.* See ASSIST.

[A–282]

ASSOCIATE 1 (ə sō' shĭ āt'), *v.*, -ATED, -ATING. (Mingling with.) Both hands are held in modified "A" positions, thumbs out. The left hand is positioned with its thumb pointing straight up, and the right hand, with its thumb pointing down, revolves above the left thumb in a counterclockwise direction. *Cf.* EACH OTHER, FELLOWSHIP, MINGLE 2, MUTUAL 1, ONE ANOTHER.

[A-283]

ASSOCIATE 2, *v.* (Joining together.) Both hands, held in the modified "5" position, palms out, move toward each other. The thumbs and index fingers of both hands then connect. *Cf.* AFFILIATE 1, ANNEX, ATTACH, BELONG, COMMUNION OF SAINTS, CONCERN 2, CONNECT, ENLIST, ENROLL, JOIN 1, PARTICIPATE, RELATIVE 2, UNION, UNITE.

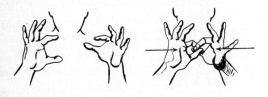

[A-284]

ASSOCIATION (ə sō′ si ā′ shən), *n.* (A grouping together.) Both "C" hands, palms facing, are held a few inches apart at chest height. They are swung around in unison, so that the palms now face the body. *Cf.* AUDIENCE 1, CASTE, CIRCLE 2, CLASS, CLASSED 1, CLUB, COMPANY, FAMILY 2, GANG, GROUP 1, JOIN 2, ORGANIZATION 1.

[A-285]

ASSORT (ə sôrt′), *v.*, -SORTED, -SORTING. (Separating to classify.) Both hands, in the right angle position, are placed palms down before the body, knuckles to knuckles. They pull apart or separate, once or a number of times. *Cf.* PART 2, SEPARATE 2.

[A-286]

ASSORTED (ə sôr′ tid), *adj.* (Separated many times; different.) The "D" hands, palms down, are crossed at the index fingers or are held side by side. They separate and return to their initial position a number of times. *Cf.* DIFFERENCE, DIFFERENT, DIVERSE 1, DIVERSITY 1, UNLIKE, VARIED.

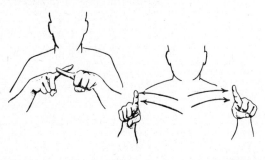

[A-287]

ASSUME (ə soom′), *v.*, -SUMED, -SUMING. (To take up.) Both hands, held palms down in the "5" position, are at chest level. With a grasping upward movement, both close into "S" positions before the face. *Cf.* PICK UP 1, TAKE UP.

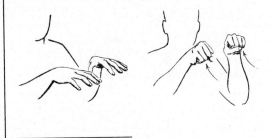

[A-288]

ASTONISH (ə stŏn′ ish), *v.*, -ISHED, -ISHING. (The eyes pop open in amazement.) Both hands are held in modified "O" positions with thumb and index fingers of each hand near the eyes. These fingers suddenly flick open, and the eyes simultaneously pop open wide. *Cf.* AMAZE, AMAZEMENT, ASTONISHED, ASTONISHMENT, ASTOUND, SURPRISE 1.

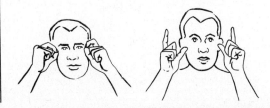

[A-289]

ASTONISHED, *adj.* See ASTONISH.

[A-290]

ASTONISHMENT (-mənt), *n.* See ASTONISH.

[A-291]

ASTOUND (ə stound'), *v.,* -TOUNDED, -TOUNDING. See ASTONISH.

[A-292]

AT (ăt; *unstressed* ət; ĭt), *prep.* The left hand is held at eye level, palm facing out and fingers together. The right hand, palm down, fingers also together, moves over to the left, so that the right fingertips come to touch the back of the left hand. This sign is seldom used; most signers prefer to spell out "AT" on the fingers.

[A-293]

AT A LOSS (lôs, lŏs), *phrase.* (The mind is frozen; the thought is frozen.) The index finger of the right "D" hand, palm facing the body, touches the forehead (modified THINK sign, *q.v.*). Both hands, in the "5" position, palms down, are then suddenly and deliberately dropped down in front of the body. A look of surprise is assumed at this point, and the head jerks back slightly. *Cf.* DUMFOUNDED 1, JOLT, SHOCKED 1, STUMPED.

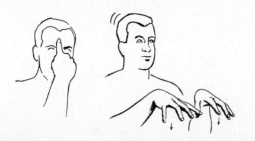

[A-294]

ATTACH (ə tăch'), *v.,* -TACHED, -TACHING. (Joining together.) Both hands, held in the modified "5" position, palms out, move toward each other. The thumbs and index fingers of both hands then connect. *Cf.* AFFILIATE 1, ANNEX, ASSOCIATE 2, BELONG, COMMUNION OF SAINTS, CONCERN 2, CONNECT, ENLIST, ENROLL, JOIN 1, PARTICIPATE, RELATIVE 2, UNION, UNITE.

[A-295]

ATTACK (ə tăk'), *n., v.,* -TACKED, -TACKING. (Striking against.) The clenched right hand strikes against the open left palm.

[A-296]

ATTAIN (ə tān'), *v.,* -TAINED, -TAINING. (Penetrating the heights.) The "D" hands, palms back, are held at each side of the head, near the temples. With a pivoting motion of the wrists, the hands swing up and around, simultaneously, to a position above the head, with palms facing out. *Cf.* ACCOMPLISH 1, ACHIEVE 1, PROSPER, SUCCEED, SUCCESS, SUCCESSFUL, TRIUMPH 2.

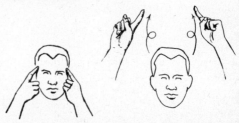

[A-297]

ATTEMPT 1 (ə tĕmpt′), *n., v.,* -TEMPTED, -TEMPT-ING. (Trying to push through.) The "A" hands, palms facing before the body, are swung around and a bit down, so that the palms now face out. The movement indicates an attempt to push through a barrier. *Cf.* EFFORT 1, ENDEAVOR, PERSEVERE 1, PERSIST 1, TRY 1.

[A-298]

ATTEMPT 2, *n., v.* (Trying to push through, using the "T" hands, for "try.") This is the same sign as ATTEMPT 1, except that the "T" hands are employed. *Cf.* EFFORT 2, PERSEVERE 2, TRY 2.

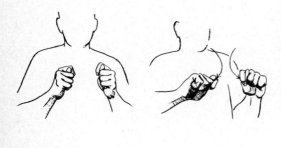

[A-299]

ATTEND (TO) (ə tĕnd′), *v.,* -TENDED, -TENDING. (Directing one's attention forward; applying oneself; concentrating.) Both hands, fingers pointing up and together, are held at the sides of the face. They move straight out from the face. *Cf.* APPLY 2, ATTENTION, CONCENTRATE, CONCENTRATION, FOCUS, GIVE AT-TENTION (TO), MIND 2, PAY ATTENTION (TO).

[A-300]

ATTENTION (ə tĕn′ shən), *n.* See ATTEND (TO).

[A-301]

ATTITUDE (ăt′ ə tūd′, -tŏŏd′), *n.* (The letter "A"; the inclination of the heart.) The right "A" hand describes a counterclockwise circle around the heart, and comes to rest against the heart.

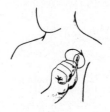

[A-302]

ATTORNEY (ə tûr′ ni), *n.* (A law individual.) The upright right "L" hand (for LAW), resting palm against palm on the upright left "5" hand, moves down in an arc, a short distance, coming to rest on the base of the left palm. The sign for INDIVID-UAL is then added: Both hands, fingers together, are placed at either side of the chest and are moved down to waist level.

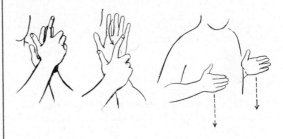

[A-303]

ATTRACT (ə trăkt′), *v.,* -TRACTED, -TRACTING. (Bringing everything together, to one point.) The open "5" hands, palms down and held at chest level, draw together until all the fingertips touch. *Cf.* AT-TRACTION, ATTRACTIVE 1.

[A-304]

ATTRACTION (ə trăk′ shən), *n.* See ATTRACT.

[A-305]

ATTRACTIVE 1 (ə trăk′ tĭv), *adj.* See ATTRACT.

[A-306]

ATTRACTIVE 2, *adj.* (Literally, a good face.) The right hand, fingers closed over the thumb, is placed at or just below the lips (indicating a tasting of something GOOD, *q.v.*). It then describes a counterclockwise circle around the face, opening into the "5" position, to indicate the whole face. At the completion of the circling movement the hand comes to rest in its initial position, at or just below the lips. *Cf.* BEAUTIFUL, BEAUTY, EXQUISITE, PRETTY, SPLENDID 3.

[A-307]

ATTRIBUTE 1 (ə trĭb′ ūt), *v.,* -UTED, -UTING. (Something which weighs down or burdens one with responsibility.) The fingertips of both hands, placed on the right shoulder, bear down. *Cf.* BEAR 4, BURDEN, OBLIGATION 1, RELY 1, RESPONSIBILITY 1, RESPONSIBLE 1.

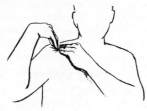

[A-308]

ATTRIBUTE 2, *v.* (Something which weighs down or burdens, modified by the letter "R," for "responsibility.") The "R" hands bear down on the right

shoulder, in the same manner as ATTRIBUTE 1. *Cf.* RESPONSIBILITY 2, RESPONSIBLE 2.

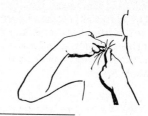

[A-309]

AUDIENCE 1 (ô′ dĭ əns), *n.* (A grouping together.) Both "C" hands, palms facing, are held a few inches apart at chest height. They are swung around in unison, so that the palms now face the body. *Cf.* ASSOCIATION, CASTE, CIRCLE 2, CLASS, CLASSED 1, CLUB, COMPANY, FAMILY 2, GANG, GROUP 1, JOIN 2, ORGANIZATION 1.

[A-310]

AUDIENCE 2, *n.* (People, indicated by the rotating "P" hands.) The "P" hands, side by side, are moved alternately in continuous counterclockwise circles. *Cf.* HUMANITY, PEOPLE, PUBLIC.

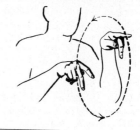

[A-311]

AUNT (ănt, änt), *n.* (A female, defined by the letter "A.") The "A" hand, thumb near the right jawline (see sign for FEMALE), quivers back and forth several times.

[A–312]

AUSTRALIA (ô strāl' yə), *n.* (The turned back brim of an Australian hat.) The fingertips of the right "B" hand are placed against the forehead with palm toward the face. The hand is then drawn away from the face and turned so that the palm faces outward. The open hand then strikes back against the right side of the head.

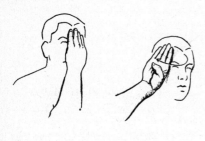

[A–313]

AUTHENTIC (ô thĕn' tĭk), *adj.* (Coming forth directly from the lips; true.) The index finger of the right "D" hand, palm facing left, is placed against the lips. It moves up an inch or two and then describes a small arc forward and away from the lips. *Cf.* ABSOLUTE, ABSOLUTELY, ACTUAL, ACTUALLY, CERTAIN, CERTAINLY, FAITHFUL 3, FIDELITY, FRANKLY, GENUINE, INDEED, POSITIVE 1, POSITIVELY, REAL, REALLY, SINCERE 2, SURE, SURELY, TRUE, TRULY, TRUTH, VALID, VERILY.

[A–314]

AUTHORITY (ə thôr' ə tĭ, -thŏr' -), *n.* (Holding the reins over all.) The "A" hands, palms facing, move alternately back and forth, as if grasping and manipulating reins. The left "A" hand, still in position, swings over so that its palm now faces down. The right hand opens to the "5" position, palm down, and swings over the left which moves slightly

to the right. *Cf.* CONTROL 1, DIRECT 1, GOVERN, MANAGE, MANAGEMENT, MANAGER, OPERATE, REGULATE, REIGN, RULE 1.

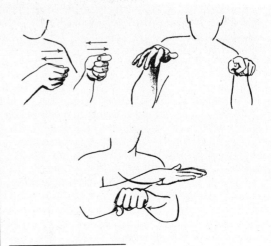

[A–315]

AUTOMOBILE (ô' tə mə bēl', ô' tə mō' bēl, -mə bēl'), *n.* (The steering wheel.) The hands grasp an imaginary steering wheel and manipulate it. *Cf.* CAR, DRIVE.

[A–316]

AUTUMN 1 (ô' təm), *n.* (The falling of leaves.) The left arm, held upright with palm facing back, represents a tree trunk. The right hand, fingers together and palm down, moves down along the left arm, from the back of the wrist to the elbow, either once or several times. This represents the falling of leaves from the tree branches, indicated by the left fingers. *Cf.* FALL 1.

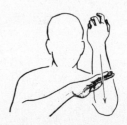

[A–317]

AUTUMN 2, *n.* (A chopping down during harvest time.) The left arm is held in the same manner as in AUTUMN 1. The right hand, fingers together and palm facing down, makes several chopping motions against the left elbow, to indicate the felling of growing things in autumn.

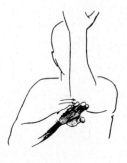

[A–318]

AVARICIOUS (ăv´ ə rĭsh´ əs), *adj.* (Scratching the palm in greed.) The right fingers scratch the upturned left palm several times. A frowning expression is often used. *Cf.* GREEDY 2, SELFISH 2, STINGY 2, TIGHTWAD 2.

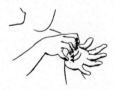

[A–319]

AVERAGE (ăv´ ər ĭj, ăv´ rĭj), *n., adj., v.,* -AGED, -AGING. (Halfway between top and bottom.) The right open hand, held upright, palm facing left, rests its little finger edge across the index finger edge of the downturned, open left hand. In this position the right hand moves back and forth several times, rubbing the base of the little finger along the edge of the left hand. *Cf.* MEAN 3.

[A–320]

AVIATOR (ā´ vi ā´ tər, ăv´ ĭ-), *n.* (An individual who flies a plane.) The sign for either AIRPLANE 1 or AIRPLANE 2 is made, and this is followed by the sign for INDIVIDUAL 1: Both hands, fingers together, are placed at either side of the chest and are moved down to waist level. *Cf.* FLIER, PILOT.

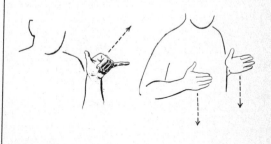

[A–321]

AVOID 1 (ə void´), *v.,* -VOIDED, -VOIDING. (Ducking back and forth, away from something.) Both "A" hands, thumbs pointing straight up, are held some distance before the chest, with the left hand in front of the right. The right hand, swinging back and forth, moves away from the left and toward the chest. *Cf.* EVADE, EVASION, SHIRK, SHUN.

[A–322]

AVOID 2, *v.* (To push away and recoil from; avoid.) The two open hands, palms facing left, are pushed deliberately to the left, as if pushing something away. An expression of disdain or disgust is worn. *Cf.* ABHOR, DESPISE 1, DETEST 1, HATE 1, LOATHE.

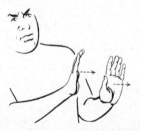

[A–323]

AWAKE (ə wāk′), *v., adj.*, -WOKE or -WAKED, -WAKING. (Opening the eyes.) Both hands are closed, with thumb and index finger of each hand held together, extended, and placed at the corners of the closed eyes. Slowly they separate, and the eyes open. *Cf.* AROUSE, AWAKEN, WAKE UP.

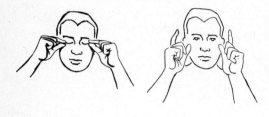

[A–324]

AWAKEN (ə wā′ kən), *v.*, -ENED, -ENING. See AWAKE.

[A–325]

AWARD (ə wôrd′), *n., v.*, -WARDED, -WARDING. (A giving of something.) Both "A" hands, with index fingers somewhat draped over the tips of the thumbs, are held palms facing in front of the chest. They are pivoted forward and down, in unison, from the wrists. *Cf.* BEQUEATH, BESTOW, CONFER, CONSIGN, CONTRIBUTE, GIFT, PRESENT 2.

[A–326]

AWARE OF, *adj. phrase.* (Something important inside the head.) The signer pats his forehead significantly, as he might pat his pocket if it held money.

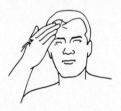

[A–327]

AWAY (ə wā′), *adj., adv.* (Motion away from or off.) The fingers of the downturned, open right hand rest on the back of the fingers of the downturned, open left hand. Then the right hand moves up and forward, turning so that its palm faces the body. *Cf.* OFF 1.

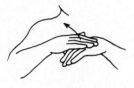

[A–328]

AWFUL (ô′ fəl), *adj.* (Throwing out the hands.) Both hands, their fingertips touching their respective thumbs, are held, palms facing each other, near the temples. They are thrown out before the face, assuming "5" positions, palms still facing. *Cf.* CALAMITOUS, CATASTROPHIC, DANGER 1, DANGEROUS 1, DREADFUL, FEARFUL, TERRIBLE, TRAGEDY, TRAGIC.

[A–329]

AWKWARD (ôk′ wərd), *adj.* (Clumsy in gait; all thumbs.) The "3" hands, palms down, move alternately up and down before the body. *Cf.* AWKWARDNESS, CLUMSINESS, CLUMSY 1, GREEN 2, GREENHORN 2, NAIVE.

[A–330]

AWKWARDNESS, *n.* See AWKWARD.

B

BABY (bā' bǐ), *n., adj., v.,* -BIED, -BYING. (The rocking of the baby.) The arms are held with one resting on the other, as if cradling a baby. They rock from side to side. *Cf.* DOLL 2, INFANT.

[B-2]

BACHELOR (băch´ ə lər, băch´ lər), *n.* (The letter "B.") The right "B" hand, held with palm facing left and fingers pointing up, touches the left side of the mouth and then moves back across the lips to touch the right side of the mouth.

[B-3]

BACK 1 (băk), *adv.* (One hand is after or behind the other.) Both hands, in the "A" position, are held knuckles to knuckles. The right hand moves back, describing a small arc, and comes to rest against the left wrist. *Cf.* AFTER 2, BACKSLIDE, BEHIND.

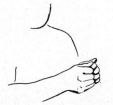

[B-4]

BACK 2, *n.* (The natural sign.) The right hand moves over the right shoulder to tap the back. *Cf.* REAR 1.

[B-5]

BACK AND FORTH, *adv. phrase.* (The natural sign.) The right "A" hand, palm facing left and thumb held straight up, moves back and forth repeatedly from left to right. *Cf.* TRANSPORTATION.

[B-6]

BACKBITE (băk´ bīt´), *v.,* -BIT, -BITTEN, -BITING. (Striking down against.) Both "A" or "X" hands are held before the chest, the right above the left. The right hand strikes down and out, hitting the left thumb and knuckles with force. *Cf.* BASE 3, CRUEL 1, HARM 2, HURT 2, MAR 2, MEAN 1, SPOIL.

[B-7]

BACKGROUND (băk′ ground′), *n.* (The area below.) Both hands, in the "5" position, palms down, are held before the chest, the right under the left. The right hand moves under the left in a counterclockwise fashion. *Cf.* BASIS 2, BELOW 1, BOTTOM, FOUNDATION.

[B-8]

BACKSLIDE (băk′ slīd′), *v.*, -SLID, -SLIDING. See BACK 1.

[B-9]

BAD 1 (băd), *adj.* (Tasting something, finding it unacceptable, and turning it down.) The tips of the right "B" hand are placed at the lips, and then the hand is thrown down. *Cf.* GRAVE 2, NAUGHTY, WICKED.

[B-10]

BAD 2 (colloq.), *adj.* The right "I" hand is held, palm facing forward, in front of the right shoulder. From this position, the right hand moves slightly to the right.

[B-11]

BAGGAGE (băg′ ĭj), *n.* (The natural sign.) The downturned right "S" hand grasps an imaginary piece of luggage and shakes it up and down slightly, as if testing its weight. *Cf.* LUGGAGE, SUITCASE, VALISE.

[B-12]

BAKE (bāk), *v.*, BAKED, BAKING, *n.* (Placing the bread in the oven.) The downturned right "B" hand, representing the bread, is thrust slowly forward under the downturned left hand, representing the oven. *Cf.* OVEN.

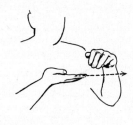

[B-13]

BAKER (bā′ kər), *n.* (Kneading dough.) Both hands grasp the edge of an imaginary piece of rolled dough and lift it, in a forward-and-up motion. This is followed by the sign for INDIVIDUAL: Both open hands, palms facing each other, move down the sides of the body, tracing its outline to the hips.

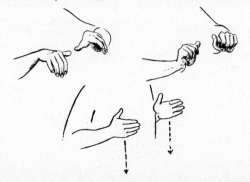

[B-14]

BALANCE 1 (băl´ əns), *n., v.,* -ANCED, -ANCING. (The natural sign.) The extended right index and middle fingers are placed across the extended index and middle fingers of the left hand, which is held with thumb edge up and fingers pointing forward. In this position the right hand rocks back and forth, as if balancing.

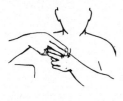

[B-15]

BALANCE 2, *n., v.* (The scales.) Both open hands, held palms down in front of the body, move alternately up and down, imitating a pair of scales. *Cf.* SCALE 3.

[B-16]

BALD (bôld), *adj.* (A bald patch.) The middle finger of the open right hand makes several circles on the back of the left "S" hand, which is held with palm facing down. *Cf.* BARE 1.

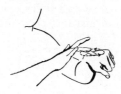

[B-17]

BALL 1 (bôl), *n.* (The rhythmic swaying of the feet.) The downturned index and middle fingers of the right "V" hand swing rhythmically back and forth over the upturned left palm. *Cf.* DANCE, PARTY 2.

[B-18]

BALL 2, *n.* (The shape.) The curved open hands are held with fingertips touching, as if holding a ball. *Cf.* ORB, ROUND 1, SPHERE.

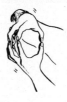

[B-19]

BALONEY (bə lō´ ni), *(sl.), n.* The right "S" hand is held with its thumb edge over the tip of the nose, palm facing left; in this position the right hand is then twisted forcefully to the left, until the palm faces down.

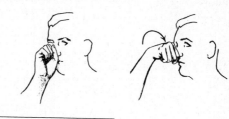

[B-20]

BAN (băn), *v.,* BANNED, BANNING, *n.* (A modification of LAW, *q.v.;* "against the law.") The downturned right "D" or "L" hand is thrust forcefully into the left palm. *Cf.* FORBID 1, FORBIDDEN 1, PROHIBIT.

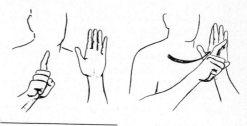

[B-21]

BANANA 1 (bə nan´ ə), *n.* (The natural sign.) Go through the motions of peeling a banana, the left index representing the banana and the right fingertips pulling off the skin.

[B–22]

BANANA 2, *n.* (Peeling a banana.) The left "AND" hand is held with fingers pointing up, representing a banana, while the left hand moves as if peeling the skin downward.

[B–23]

BANDAGE (băn′ dǐj), *n., v.,* -AGED, -AGING. (Applying a Band-Aid.) The index and middle fingers of the right hand are drawn across the back of the downturned, left "S" hand, as if smoothing a Band-Aid. *Cf.* BAND-AID.

[B–24]

BAND-AID (bănd′ ād), *n.* See BANDAGE.

[B–25]

BANDIT (băn′ dǐt), *n.* (A mustachioed thief.) The fingertips of both "H" hands, palms facing the body, are placed above the lips and are drawn slowly apart, describing a mustache. Sometimes one hand only is used. This is followed by the sign for INDIVID-UAL: Both open hands, palms facing each other, move down the sides of the body, tracing its outline to the hips. *Cf.* BURGLAR, BURGLARY, CROOK, ROB 3, ROBBER 1, STEAL 3, THEFT 3, THIEF 2.

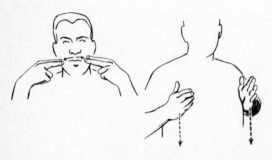

[B–26]

BANISH (băn′ ǐsh), *v.,* -ISHED, -ISHING. (A slap in the face.) The right hand slaps the back of the left a glancing blow, and its momentum continues it beyond the left hand. *Cf.* INSULT 2.

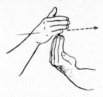

[B–27]

BANKRUPT (băngk′ rŭpt, -rəpt), *n., adj.* (The head is chopped off.) The tips of the right fingers are thrust forcefully into the right side of the neck. *Cf.* BROKE.

[B–28]

BANNER (băn′ ər), *n.* (The waving.) The right "B" hand is held up, palm facing left and right elbow resting on the back of the downturned left hand. The right "B" hand waves back and forth, imitating the waving of a flag. *Cf.* FLAG.

[B–29]

BANQUET (băng′ kwǐt), *n., v.,* -QUETED, -QUET-ING. (Placing food in the mouth.) Both closed hands alternately come to the mouth, as if placing food in it. *Cf.* DINNER, FEAST.

[B–30]

BAPTISM (băp′ tǐz əm), *(eccles.), n.* (The sprinkling of water on the head.) The right hand sprinkles imaginary water on the head. *Cf.* SHOWER.

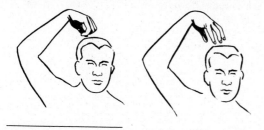

[B–31]

BAPTIST (băp′ tǐst), *(eccles.), n.* (The immersion.) Both "A" hands, palms facing and thumbs pointing up, swing over simultaneously to the left, with the thumbs describing a downward arc. *Cf.* BAPTIZE.

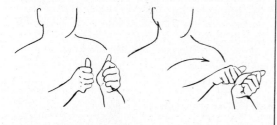

[B–32]

BAPTIZE (băp tīz′, băp′ tīz), *v.,* -TIZED, -TIZING. See BAPTIST.

[B–33]

BARE 1 (băr), *adj.* (A bald patch.) The middle finger of the open right hand makes several circles on the back of the left "S" hand, which is held with palm facing down. *Cf.* BALD.

[B–34]

BARE 2, *adj.* (Devoid of everything on the surface.) The middle finger of the downturned right "5" hand sweeps over the back of the downturned left "A" or

"S" hand, from wrist to knuckles, and continues beyond a bit. *Cf.* EMPTY 2, NAKED, NUDE, OMISSION 2, VACANCY, VACANT, VOID.

[B–35]

BARK (bärk), *v.,* BARKED, BARKING, (The opening and closing of the dog's mouth.) The hands are positioned palm against palm before the body, with the fingertips pointing forward. With the bases of the hands always touching and serving as a hinge, the hands open and close repeatedly, with the stress on the opening movement, which is sudden and abrupt. *Cf.* SCOLD 3.

[B–36]

BAR MITZVAH (bär mǐts′ və), *(eccles.).* (The phylactery straps are wound around the left arm at age 13 to remind the Jew to keep the law.) The right hand winds an imaginary phylactery (tefilin) strap around the left arm. The sign for OLD is then made, followed by the sign for 13.

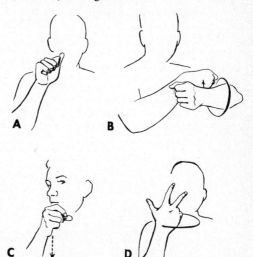

[B–37]

BARN (bärn), *n.* (The shape of the building.) The open hands are held with fingertips touching, so that they form a pyramid a bit above eye level. From this position, the hands separate and move diagonally downward for a short distance; then they continue straight down a few inches. This movement traces the outline of a roof and walls. *Cf.* DOMICILE, HOUSE, RESIDENCE 2.

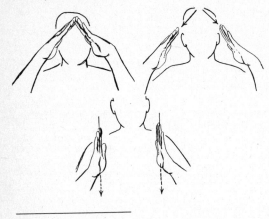

[B–38]

BARREL (băr′ əl), *n.* (Opening a barrel.) The right fist acts as a hammer, striking its little finger edge down against the upturned edge of the left fist, which moves in a counterclockwise circle as if around a barrel hoop.

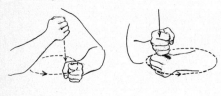

[B–39]

BASE 1 (bās), *n., adj.* (Motion downward.) The "A" hand is held in front of the body, thumb pointing upward. The hand then moves straight downward several inches. Both hands may be used. *Cf.* LOW 1.

[B–40]

BASE 2, *n., adj.* (Motion downward.) The right-angle hands are held up before the head, fingertips pointing toward each other. From this position, the hands move down in an arc. *Cf.* DEMOTE, LOW 2, LOWER.

[B–41]

BASE 3, *adj.* (Striking down against.) Both "A" or "X" hands are held before the chest, the right above the left. The right hand strikes down and out, hitting the left thumb and knuckles with force. *Cf.* BACK-BITE, CRUEL 1, HARM 2, HURT 2, MAR 2, MEAN 1, SPOIL.

[B–42]

BASEBALL (bās′ bôl′), *n.* (Swinging a bat.) Both "S" hands, the right behind the left, grip an imaginary bat and move back and forth over the right shoulder, as if preparing to hit a baseball. *Cf.* BAT, BATTER.

[B–43]

BASHFUL 1 (băsh′ fəl), *adj.* (The color rises in the cheek; an attempt is made to hide the head.) The backs of the fingers of the right hand, held in the right angle position, are placed against the right cheek. The hand moves up along the cheek, pivoting at the wrist, so that the fingers finally point to the rear. *Cf.* ASHAMED 1, IMMODEST, IMMORAL, SHAME 1, SHAMEFUL, SHAME ON YOU, SHY 1.

[B–44]

BASHFUL 2, *adj.* Similar to BASHFUL 1, but both hands are used, at either cheek. *Cf.* ASHAMED 2, SHAME 2, SHY 2.

[B–45]

BASIS 1 (bā′ sĭs), *n.* (Rays of influence emanating from a given source.) All the right fingertips, including the thumb, are positioned on the tip of the up-turned thumb of the left "A" hand. The right hand, opening into the downturned "5" position, moves forward from its initial position. Instead of its initial position on the left thumb, the right hand is frequently placed on the back of the downturned left "S" hand, moving forward as described above. *Cf.* CAUSE, EFFECT 1, INFLUENCE 2, INTENT 2, LOGIC, PRODUCE 4, REASON 2.

[B–46]

BASIS 2, *n.* (The area below.) Both hands, in the "5" position, palms down, are held before the chest, the right under the left. The right hand moves under the left in a counterclockwise fashion. *Cf.* BACK-GROUND, BELOW 1, BOTTOM, FOUNDATION.

[B–47]

BASKET (băs′ kĭt, bäs′ -), *n.* (The shape.) The left arm is held horizontally, the right index finger de-scribes an arc under it, from wrist to elbow, repre-senting the shape of a basket as it hangs on the left arm. *Cf.* EPISCOPAL, EPISCOPALIAN, STORE 3.

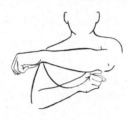

[B–48]

BASKETBALL (băs′ kĭt bôl′), *n.* (Shooting a basket.) Both open hands are held with fingers pointing down and somewhat curved, as if grasping a basketball. From this position the hands move around and up-ward, as if to shoot a basket.

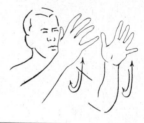

[B–49]

BASTARD (băs′ tərd), *n., adj.* (The letter "B.") The right "B" hand, held with palm facing left, fingers pointing up, strikes the middle of the forehead.

[B–50]

BASTE (bāst), *v.*, BASTED, BASTING. (The large stitches.) The right hand grasps an imaginary needle and sews large stitches on the upturned left palm.

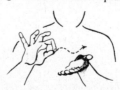

[B–51]

BAT (băt), *n., v.,* BATTED, BATTING. (Swinging a bat.) Both "S" hands, the right behind the left, grip an imaginary bat and move back and forth over the right shoulder, as if preparing to hit a baseball. *Cf.* BASEBALL, BATTER.

[B–52]

BATH (băth, bäth), *n.* (The natural sign.) The closed hands move up and down against the chest as if scrubbing it. *Cf.* BATHE, WASH 3.

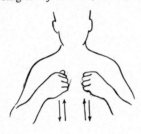

[B–53]

BATHE (bāth), *v.,* BATHED, BATHING. See BATH.

[B–54]

BATHROOM (băth' room', -room', bäth' -), *n.* (The natural signs.) The sign for BATH is made, and then the sign for ROOM: The open hands, palms facing and fingers pointing out, are dropped an inch or two simultaneously. They then shift their relative positions so that both palms face the body, with one hand in front of the other. In this new position they again drop an inch or two simultaneously.

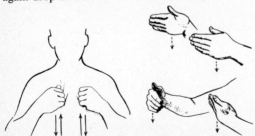

[B–55]

BATTER (băt' ər), *n.* (Swinging a bat.) Both "S" hands, the right behind the left, grip an imaginary bat and move back and forth over the right shoulder, as if preparing to hit a baseball. This is followed by the sign for INDIVIDUAL: Both open hands, palms facing each other, move down the sides of the body, tracing its outline to the hips. *Cf.* BASEBALL, BAT.

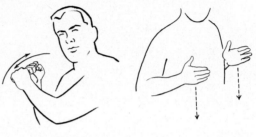

[B–56]

BATTLE (băt' əl), *n., v.,* -TLED, -TLING. (Two groups of individuals pulling back and forth.) Both open hands are held in front of the body, with palms toward the chest, fingers pointing toward each other, and thumbs extended upward. In this position the hands move from left to right several times.

[B–57]

BAWL 1 (bôl). *v.,* BAWLED, BAWLING. (Tears streaming down the cheeks.) Both index fingers, in the "D" position, move down the cheeks, either once or several times. Sometimes one finger only is used. *Cf.* CRY 1, TEAR 2, TEARDROP, WEEP 1.

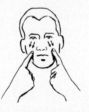

[B–58]

BAWL 2, *v.* (Tears gushing from the eyes.) Both "B" hands are held before the face, palms facing forward, with the backs of the index fingertips touching the face just below the eyes. From this position both hands move forward and over in an arc, to indicate a flow of tears. *Cf.* CRY 2, WEEP 2.

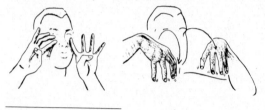

[B–59]

BAWL OUT, *v. phrase.* (Words coming out forcefully.) The "S" hands are held one atop the other, the right palm facing left and the left palm facing right. Both hands suddenly shoot straight out, opening to the "5" position. The sign is repeated once or twice.

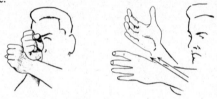

[B–60]

BE 1 (bē; *unstressed* bǐ), *v.,* BEEN, BEING. (Part of the verb to BE.) The tip of the right index finger, held in the "D" position, palm facing left, is held at the lips, and the hand moves straight out and away from the lips. *Cf.* AM 1, ARE 1, IS 1.

[B–61]

BE 2, *v.* (The "B" hand.) This is the same sign as for BE 1 except that the "B" hand is used.

[B–62]

BE 3, *(arch.), v.* The crooked index finger of the right "G" hand moves from right to left in front of the body.

[B–63]

BEAK (bēk), *n.* (The shape and movement of a beak.) The right thumb and index fingers are placed against the mouth, pointing straight out. They open and close. *Cf.* BIRD.

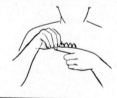

[B–64]

BEAN(S) (bēn), *n.* (The beans in a pod.) The tips of the four right fingers move up and down simultaneously as they move along the left index finger from knuckle to tip. This sign is used generally for different grains. *Cf.* GRAIN, OATMEAL, RICE.

[B–65]

BEANPOLE (bēn′ pōl′), *(sl.), n.* (A thin, tapering object is described with the little fingers, the thinnest of all.) The tips of the little fingers, touching, one above the other, are drawn apart. The cheeks may also be drawn in for emphasis. *Cf.* SKINNY, THIN 2.

[B–66]

BEAR 1 (bâr). *n*. (Scratching; the bear hug.) Cross the arms, placing the right hand on the left upper-arm and the left hand on the right upperarm; pull the hands across the arms toward the center, with a clawing movement.

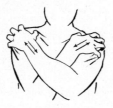

_____

[B–67]

BEAR 2, *v.*, BORE, BORNE, BEARING. (Coming from the uterus.) The open hands are held with both palms toward the body, the back of one hand resting against the palm of the other. From a position near the abdomen, the hands turn slightly upward or downward and push out away from the body.

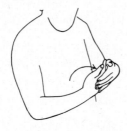

_____

[B–68]

BEAR 3, *v.*, BORE, BORN(E), BEARING. (A clenching of the fists; the rise and fall of pain.) Both "S" hands, tightly clenched, revolve about each other, slowly and deliberately, while a pained expression is worn. *Cf.* AGONY, DIFFICULT 3, ENDURE 1, PASSION 2, SUFFER 1, TOLERATE 2.

[B–69]

BEAR 4, *v.* (Something which weighs down or bur-dens one with responsibility.) The fingertips of both hands, placed on the right shoulder, bear down. *Cf.* ATTRIBUTE 1, BURDEN, OBLIGATION 1, RELY 1, RE-SPONSIBILITY 1, RESPONSIBLE 1.

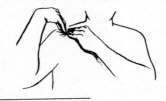

_____

[B–70]

BEARD 1 (bĭrd), *n*. (The natural sign.) The thumb and fingers of the right hand move down either side of the lower face, tracing the outline of a beard and coming together just below the chin.

_____

[B–71]

BEARD 2, *n*. (In need of a shave.) The fingers of both open hands move up and down along either cheek.

_____

[B–72]

BEAT 1 (bēt), *v.*, BEAT, BEATEN, BEATING. (The natural sign.) The left hand is held in a fist before the face, as if grasping something or someone. The right hand, at the same time, is held as if grasping a stick or whip; it strikes repeatedly at the imaginary object or person dangling from the left hand. *Cf.* PUNISH 2, WHIP.

[B-73]

BEAT 2, *v.,* (Forcing the head into a bowed position.) The right "S" hand, placed across the left "S" hand, moves over and down a bit. *Cf.* CONQUER, DEFEAT, OVERCOME, SUBDUE.

[B-74]

BEAT 3, *n.* (A blow is struck.) The right fist strikes the left palm. *Cf.* BLOW 2.

[B-75]

BEATEN (bē' tən), *adj.* (The head is forced into a bowed position.) The right "S" hand, palm up, is placed under and across the left "S" hand, whose palm faces down. The right "S" hand moves up and over, toward the body. This sign is used as the passive voice of the verb BEAT. *Cf.* CONQUERED.

[B-76]

BEAU (bō), *(colloq.), n.* (Heads nodding toward each other.) The "A" hands are placed together before the body with thumbs up. The thumbs wiggle up and down. *Cf.* COURTING, COURTSHIP, LOVER, MAKE LOVE 1, SWEETHEART 1.

[B-77]

BEAUTIFUL (bū' tə fəl), *adj.* (Literally, a good face.) The right hand, fingers closed over the thumb, is placed at or just below the lips (indicating a tasting of something GOOD, *q.v.*). It then describes a counterclockwise circle around the face, opening into the "5" position, to indicate the whole face. At the completion of the circling movement the hand comes to rest in its initial position, at or just below the lips. *Cf.* ATTRACTIVE 2, BEAUTY, EXQUISITE, PRETTY, SPLENDID 3.

[B-78]

BEAUTY (bū' tǐ), *n.* See BEAUTIFUL.

[B-79]

BEAUTY PARLOR (pär' lər). (Working on the hair.) The "S" hands, palms out, are positioned above the head. They move alternately toward and away from the head, as if pulling locks of hair. *Cf.* HAIRDRESSER.

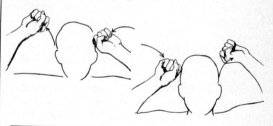

[B-80]

BE CAREFUL (kâr' fəl), *v. phrase.* (The "K" for *keep* in the sense of *keeping carefully.*) Both "K" hands are crossed, the right atop the left. The right hand moves up and down a very short distance, several times, each time coming to rest on top of the left. *Cf.* CAREFUL 3, TAKE CARE OF 1.

[B-81]

BECAUSE (bĭ kôz', -kŏz'), *conj.* (A thought or knowledge uppermost in the mind.) The fingers of the right hand or the index finger, are placed on the center of the forehead, and then the hand is brought strongly up above the head, assuming the "A" position, with thumb pointing up. *Cf.* FOR 2.

[B-82]

BECKON (bĕk' ən), *v.,* BECKONED, BECKONING. The right index finger makes a natural beckoning movement. *Cf.* COME 2.

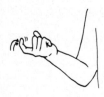

[B-83]

BECOME (bĭ kŭm'), *v.,* -CAME, -COME, -COMING. (To change from one position to another.) The palms of both hands, fingers closed and slightly curved, face each other a few inches apart, with the right above the left. They are pivoted around simultaneously, in a clockwise manner, so that their relative positions are reversed.

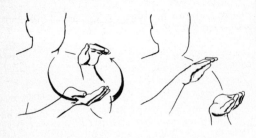

[B-84]

BECOMING (bĭ kŭm' ĭng), *adj.* (Something that agrees with.) Both hands, in the "D" position, index fingers pointing straight out, are held before the body, palms facing and several inches apart. They are swung down in unison until the palms face down —bringing the two index fingers almost together and side by side, in "agreement" with each other.

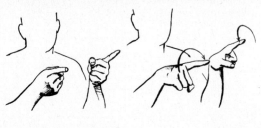

[B-85]

BED (bĕd), *n.* (A sleeping place with four legs.) The head is tilted to one side, with the cheek resting in the palm, to represent the head on a pillow. Both index fingers, pointing down, move straight down a short distance, in unison (the two front legs of the bed), and then are brought up slightly, and move down again a bit closer to the body (the rear legs).

[B-86]

BEDROOM (-rōͦm; -rŏͦm), *n.* The sign for BED is made, followed by the sign for ROOM. The open palms facing and fingers pointing out are dropped an inch or two simultaneously. They then shift their relative positions so that both palms face the body, with one hand in front of the other. In this new position they again drop an inch or two simultaneously. This indicates the four sides of a room. The "R" hands are often substituted for the open palms.

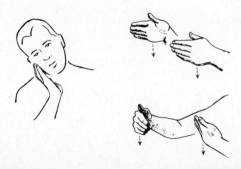

[B-87]

BEE (bē), *n.* (The bee's stinger is brushed away.) The index finger is placed on the cheek, and then the same hand makes a quick brushing motion off the cheek.

[B-88]

BEEF (bēf), *n.* (The fleshy part of the hand.) The right index finger and thumb squeeze the fleshy part of the open left hand, between thumb and index finger. *Cf.* FLESH, MEAT.

[B-89]

BEER (bĭr), *n.* (Raising a beer stein to the lips.) The right "Y" hand is raised to the lips, as the head tilts back a bit.

[B-90]

BEFALL (bĭ fôl'), *v.,* -FELL, -FALLEN, -FALLING. (A befalling.) Both "D" hands, index fingers pointing away from the body, are simultaneously pivoted over so that the palms face down. *Cf.* ACCIDENT, CHANCE, COINCIDE 1, COINCIDENCE, EVENT, HAPPEN 1, INCIDENT, OCCUR, OPPORTUNITY 4.

[B-91]

BEFORE 1 (bĭ fōr'), *adv.* (One hand precedes the other.) The left hand is held before the body, fingers together and pointing to the right. The right hand, fingers also together, and pointing to the left, is placed so that its back rests in the left palm. The right hand moves rather quickly toward the body. The sign is used as an indication of time or of precedence: *He arrived before me.*

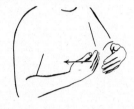

[B-92]

BEFORE 2, *(alt.), adv.* (One hand precedes the other.) The left hand, palm out and fingers together, is held before the body. The right, fingers also together, is placed back to back against the left, and moves rather quickly toward the body. The sign is used alternatively, but less commonly, than BEFORE 1.

[B-93]

BEFORE 3, *adv.* (Face to face.) The left hand, fingers together, palm flat and facing the eyes, is held a bit above eye level. The right hand, fingers also together, is held in front of the mouth, with palm facing the left hand. With a sweeping upward movement the right hand moves toward the left, which moves straight up an inch or two at the same time. *Cf.* APPEAR 3, APPEARANCE, CONFRONT, FACE 2, FACE TO FACE, PRESENCE.

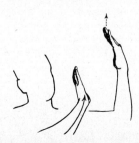

[B-94]

BEG 1 (bĕg), *v.*, BEGGED, BEGGING. (Holding out the hand and begging.) The right open hand, palm up and fingers slightly cupped, is moved up and down by the left hand, positioned under it. *Cf.* ASK ALMS, BEGGAR, PANHANDLER.

[B-95]

BEG 2, *v.* (An act of supplication.) With the right hand clasped over the left, both hands are shaken gently before the body. The eyes often are directed upward. *Cf.* BESEECH, ENTREAT, IMPLORE, PLEA, PLEAD, SUPPLICATION.

[B-96]

BEGGAR (bĕg' ər), *n.* (An individual who begs.) The sign for BEG 1 is made, followed by the sign for INDIVIDUAL: Both hands, fingers together, are placed at either side of the chest and are moved down to waist level. *Cf.* ASK ALMS, BEG 1, PANHANDLER.

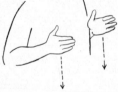

[B-97]

BEGIN (bĭ gĭn'), *v.*, -GAN, -GUN, -GINNING. (Turning a key to open up a new venture.) The right index finger, resting between the left index and middle fingers, executes a half turn, once or twice. *Cf.* COMMENCE, INITIATE, INSTITUTE 2, ORIGIN 1, ORIGINATE 1, START.

[B-98]

BEHIND (bĭ hīnd'), *prep.* (One hand is after or behind the other.) Both hands, in the "A" position, are held knuckles to knuckles. The right hand moves back, describing a small arc, and comes to rest against the left wrist. *Cf.* AFTER 2, BACK, BACKSLIDE.

[B-99]

BEHIND TIME, *phrase.* (Hanging back.) The "5" hand and forearm, hanging loosely and straight down from the elbow, move back and forth under the armpit. *Cf.* LATE, NOT DONE, NOT YET, TARDY.

[B-100]

BELCH (bĕlch), *n., v.*, BELCHED, BELCHING. (The natural sign.) The downturned "S" hand is positioned against the lower chest. It moves up suddenly for a short distance as the upper part of the body contracts slightly, as it does in emitting a belch.

[B-101]

BELIEF (bĭ lēf'), *n.* (A thought clasped onto.) The index finger touches the middle of the forehead (where the thought lies), and then both hands are clasped together. *Cf.* BELIEVE, CONVICTION 2, DOCTRINE 2.

[B-102]

BELIEVE (bǐ lēv'), *v.,* -LIEVED, -LIEVING. See BE-LIEF.

[B-103]

BELL 1 (běl), *n.* (The bell's reverberations.) The right fist strikes the front of the left hand, and then opens and moves away from the left in an undulating manner, to indicate the sound waves. *Cf.* RING 2.

[B-104]

BELL 2, *n.* (Ringing a small bell to summon someone.) An imaginary small bell is held in the hand and daintily shaken back and forth.

[B-105]

BELL 3, *n.* (Pressing the button of the bell.) The right thumb is thrust into the open left palm several times, indicating the pressing of a bell button.

[B-106]

BELONG (bǐ lông', -lŏng'), *v.,* -LONGED, -LONGING. (Joining together.) Both hands, held in the modified "5" position, palms out, move toward each other. The thumbs and index fingers of both hands then connect. *Cf.* AFFILIATE 1, ANNEX, ASSOCIATE 2, ATTACH, COMMUNION OF SAINTS, CONCERN 2, CONNECT, ENLIST, ENROLL, JOIN 1, PARTICIPATE, RELATIVE 2, UNION, UNITE.

[B-107]

BELONG TO, *v. phrase.* (Joining together with someone.) The sign for BELONG is made, followed by the sign for YOUR: The right "5" hand, palm facing out, moves straight out toward the person spoken to.

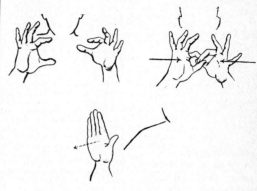

[B-108]

BELOVED (bǐ lŭv' ĭd), *adj.* (Clasping the heart.) The "5" hands are held one atop the other over the heart. Sometimes the "S" hands are used, in which case they are crossed at the wrists. *Cf.* CHARITY, DEVOTION, LOVE, REVERE 2.

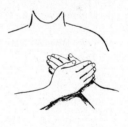

[B-109]

BELOW 1 (bǐ lō'), *adv.* (The area below.) Both hands, in the "5" position, palms down, are held before the chest, the right under the left. The right hand moves under the left in a counterclockwise fashion. *Cf.* BACKGROUND, BASIS 2, BOTTOM, FOUNDATION.

[B-110]

BELOW 2, *adv.* (Underneath something.) The right hand, in the "A" position, thumb pointing straight up, moves down under the left hand, held outstretched, fingers together, palm down. *Cf.* BENEATH 1, UNDER 1, UNDERNEATH.

[B-111]

BELOW 3, *adv.* (The area below.) The right "A" hand, thumb pointing up, moves in a counterclockwise fashion under the downturned left hand. *Cf.* BENEATH 2, UNDER 2.

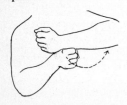

[B-112]

BENCH (bĕnch), *(arch.), n.* (The expanse of bench with its supports.) With both hands in the "S" position, the left hand is held before the chest, palm facing the body. The right hand is placed under the left wrist, and then, describing an arc, moves over to the left elbow, indicating supports. Both hands are then placed together, palm to palm, fingers pointing away from the body. They separate, to describe the expanse of bench.

[B-113]

BEND (bĕnd), *v.,* BENT, BENDING. (A bending back and forth.) Both hands, fingertips together, grasp and bend an imaginary object back and forth several times.

[B-114]

BENEATH 1 (bĭ nēth′, -nĕth′), *adv.* (Underneath something.) The right hand, in the "A" position, thumb pointing straight up, moves down under the left hand, held outstretched, fingers together, palm down. *Cf.* BELOW 2, UNDER 1, UNDERNEATH.

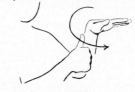

[B-115]

BENEATH 2, *adv.* (The area below.) The right "A" hand, thumb pointing up, moves in a counterclockwise fashion under the downturned left hand. *Cf.* BELOW 3, UNDER 2.

[B-116]

BENEDICTION 1 (bĕn ′ə dĭk′ shən), *(eccles.), n.* (The monstrance of the Roman Catholic Church.) Holding an imaginary monstrance, the sign of the cross is made. This is a Catholic sign.

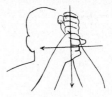

[B-117]

BENEDICTION 2, *n.* (Pronouncing a blessing over a kneeling figure.) The index finger of the right "D" hand is placed at the lips, to indicate the source of the blessing. Both hands then assume the "A" position, thumbs up and knuckles touching. They sweep down and out, opening to the "5" position, palms down, as if placing the hands on bowed heads. *Cf.* BLESS 2.

[B-118]

BENEFIT 1 (běn'ə fĭt), *v.*, -FITED, -FITING. (Helping up; supporting.) The left "S" hand, thumb side up, rests in the open right palm. In this position the left hand is pushed up a short distance by the right. *Cf.* AID, ASSIST, ASSISTANCE, BOOST, GIVE ASSISTANCE, HELP.

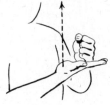

[B-119]

BENEFIT 2, *v.* (To get a profit; a coin popped into the vest pocket.) The sign for GET is made: Both outstretched hands, held in a grasping "5" position, close into "S" positions, with the right on top of the left. At the same time both hands are drawn in to the body. The thumb and index finger of the right hand, holding an imaginary coin, are then popped into an imaginary vest or breast pocket. Note: the sign for GET is sometimes omitted. *Cf.* GAIN 2, PROFIT.

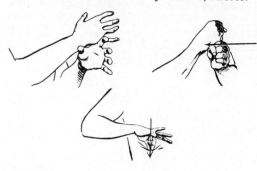

[B-120]

BENEVOLENT (bə něv' ə lənt), *adj.* (The heart rolls out.) Both right-angle hands roll over each other as they move down and away from their initial position at the heart. *Cf.* GENEROUS 1, GENTLE 1, GENTLE-NESS, GRACIOUS, HUMANE, KIND 1, KINDNESS, MERCY 1, TENDER 3.

[B-121]

BEQUEATH (bǐ kwēth´), *v.*, -QUEATHED, -QUEATH-ING. (A giving of something.) Both "A" hands, with index fingers somewhat draped over the tips of the thumbs, are held palms facing in front of the chest. They are pivoted forward and down, in unison, from the wrists. *Cf.* AWARD, BESTOW, CONFER, CONSIGN, CONTRIBUTE, GIFT, PRESENT 2.

[B-122]

BE QUIET 1 (kwi´ ət), *v. phrase.* (The natural sign.) The index finger is brought up against the pursed lips. *Cf.* CALM 2, HUSH, NOISELESS, QUIET 1, SI-LENCE 1, SILENT, STILL 2.

[B-123]

BE QUIET 2. (Quiet and peace.) The open hands are crossed before the mouth, the right palm facing left, left facing right. Then both hands, held palms down, move down from the mouth, curving outward to either side of the body. *Cf.* BE STILL, CALM 1, QUIET 2, SILENCE 2.

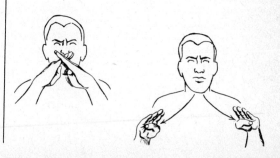

[B-124]

BE SEATED, *v. phrase*. (The act of sitting.) The extended right index and middle fingers are draped across the back of the same two fingers of the downturned left hand. The hands then move straight downward a short distance. *Cf.* CHAIR 1, SEAT, SIT 1.

[B-125]

BESEECH (bǐ sēch′), *v.*, -SOUGHT, -SEECHING. (An act of supplication.) With the right hand clasped over the left, both hands are shaken gently before the body. The eyes often are directed upward. *Cf.* BEG 2, ENTREAT, IMPLORE, PLEA, PLEAD, SUPPLICATION.

[B-126]

BESIDE (bǐ sīd′), *prep.* (One hand is near the other.) The left hand, cupped, fingers together, is held before the chest, palm facing the body. The right hand, also cupped, fingers together, moves a very short distance back and forth, as it is held in front of the left. *Cf.* ADJACENT, BY 1, CLOSE (TO) 2, NEAR 1, NEIGHBOR, NEIGHBORHOOD, VICINITY.

[B-127]

BESIDES (bǐ sīdz′), *adv.* (One hand is added to the other; an addition.) Both hands, palms facing, are held fingers together, the left a bit above the right. The right hand is brought up to the left until their fingertips touch. *Cf.* ADD 4, FURTHER 2, MORE, MOREOVER 2.

[B-128]

BEST (bĕst), *adj.* (The most good.) The fingertips of one hand are placed at the lips, as if tasting something (*see* GOOD), and then the hand is brought high up above the head into the "A" position, thumb up, indicating the superlative degree.

[B-129]

BE STILL, *v. phrase.* See BE QUIET 2.

[B-130]

BESTOW (bǐ stō′), *v.*, -STOWED, -STOWING. (A giving of something.) Both "A" hands, with index fingers somewhat draped over the tips of the thumbs, are held palms facing in front of the chest. They are pivoted forward and down, in unison, from the wrists. *Cf.* AWARD, BEQUEATH, CONFER, CONSIGN, CONTRIBUTE, GIFT, PRESENT 2.

[B-131]

BET (bĕt) *n., v.*, BET, BETTED, BETTING. (The placing or slamming down of bets by two parties.) Both open hands, palms up, are suddenly swung over in unison, to the palms-down position. Sometimes they are swung over one at a time. *Cf.* WAGER.

[B-132]

BETTER (bĕt´ ər), *adj.* (More good.) The fingertips of one hand are placed at the lips, as if tasting something (*see* GOOD). Then the hand is moved up to a position just above the head, where it assumes the "A" position, thumb up. This latter position, less high up than the one indicated in BEST, denotes the comparative degree. *Cf.* PREFER.

[B-133]

BETWEEN (bĭ twēn´), *prep.* (Between the fingers.) The left hand, in the "C" position, is placed before the chest, all fingers facing up. The right hand, in the "B" position, is placed between the left fingers and moves back and forth several times. This sign may also be made by pointing the left fingers to the right, with the left thumb pointing up, and the right hand making the same back and forth motion as before, with the right little finger resting on the left index finger.

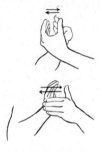

[B-134]

BEYOND (bĭ yŏnd´), *prep.* (One hand moves on to a place *beyond* the other.) Both hands, fingers together, and slightly cupped, are held before the chest, with the left hand in front of the right. The right hand moves up and over the left, and then straight out.

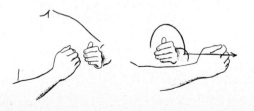

[B-135]

BIBLE 1 (bī´ bəl), *n.* (Literally, Jesus book.) The sign for JESUS is made: The left middle finger touches the right palm, and then the right middle finger touches the left palm (the crucifixion marks). The sign for BOOK is then made: The open hands are held together, fingers pointing away from the body. They open with little fingers remaining in contact, as in the opening of a book. This BIBLE sign signifies the Christian Bible. *Cf.* TESTAMENT 1.

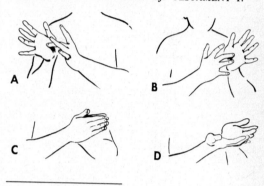

[B-136]

BIBLE 2, *n.* (Literally, holy book.) The right "H" hand makes a clockwise circular movement, and is then opened and wiped across the open left palm (something nice or clean with an "H," *i.e.,* HOLY). The sign for BOOK, as in BIBLE 1, is then made. This sign may be used by all religious faiths. *Cf.* TESTAMENT 2.

[B-137]

BIBLE 3, *n.* (Literally, Jewish book; the Old Testament.) The sign for JEW is formed: The fingers and thumb of each hand are placed at the chin, and stroke an imaginary beard, as worn by the old Jewish patriarchs or Orthodox rabbis. The sign for BOOK, as in BIBLE 1, is then made. *Cf.* HEBREW BIBLE, HOLY SCRIPTURE, JEWISH BIBLE, TESTAMENT 3.

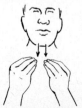

[B-138]

BICYCLE, (bī' sə kəl), *n., v.,* -CLED, -CLING. (The motion of the feet on the pedals.) Both hands, in the "S" position, rotate alternately before the chest. *Cf.* PEDAL, TRICYCLE.

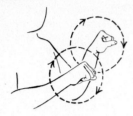

[B-139]

BID 1 (bĭd), *v.,* BADE, BAD or BID; BIDDEN or BID; BIDDING. (An issuance from the mouth.) The tip of the index finger of the "D" hand, palm facing the body, is placed at the closed lips. It moves around and out, rather forcefully. *Cf.* COMMAND, DIRECT 2, ORDER 1.

[B-140]

BID 2, *v., n.* (An offering; a presenting.) Both hands, slightly cupped, palms up, are held close to the chest. They move up and out in unison, describing a very slight arc. *Cf.* MOTION 1, OFFER 1, OFFERING 1, PRESENT 1, PROPOSE, SUGGEST, TENDER 2.

[B-141]

BID 3, *v.* (Words tumbling from the mouth.) The right index finger, pointing left, describes a continuous small circle in front of the mouth. *Cf.* DISCOURSE, HEARING, MAINTAIN 2, MENTION, REMARK, SAID, SAY, SPEAK, SPEECH 1, STATE, STATEMENT, TALK 1, TELL, VERBAL 1.

[B-142]

BIG 1 (bĭg), *adj.* (A delineation of something big, modified by the letter "L," which stands for LARGE.) Both "L" hands, palms facing out, are placed before the face, and separate rather widely. *Cf.* ENORMOUS, GREAT 1, HUGE, IMMENSE, LARGE.

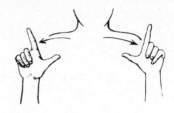

[B-143]

BIG 2, *adj.* (The height is indicated.) The right right-angle hand, palm facing the left, is held at the height the signer wishes to indicate. *Cf.* HEIGHT 2, HIGH 3, TALL 2.

[B-144]

BIG-HEADED (hĕd' ĭd), *(colloq.), adj.* (The natural sign.) Both downturned "L" hands are positioned with index fingers at the temples. They move away from the head rather slowly, indicating the size or growth of the head. The head is often moved slightly back and forth as the hands move away. An expression of superiority is assumed. *Cf.* BIG SHOT, CONCEITED, SWELL-HEADED.

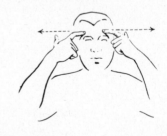

[B-145]

BIG SHOT (shŏt), *(sl.).* See BIG-HEADED.

[B–146]

BIG WORDS (wûrdz), *(sl.)*. (Large expanses of written material as they appear on the page.) The right "Y" hand, palm down, is placed on the left "G" hand, above the wrist. The right hand, in this position, arcs up and over, coming to rest on the left index finger. In this sign the two fingers of the right hand represent the widest possible space that can be indicated, and the left "G" hand represents a single line on the page.

[B–147]

BILLION (bĭl′ yən), *adj., n.* (A thousand thousand thousands.) The sign for THOUSAND is made three times: The tips of the right "M" hand are thrust into the upturned left palm three times, each time a little closer to the left fingertips.

[B–148]

BILL(S) 1 (bĭl), *n.* (The natural sign; drawing a bill from a billfold.) The right thumb and index finger trace the outlines of a bill on the upturned left palm. Or, the right thumb and fingers may grasp the base of the open left hand, which is held palm facing right and fingers pointing forward; the right hand, in this position, then slides forward along and off the left hand, as if drawing bills from a billfold. *Cf.* COIN(S) 1, DOLLAR(S) 1.

[B–149]

BILL(S) 2, *n.* (The shape of a coin.) The right index finger traces a small circle on the upturned left palm. *Cf.* COIN(S) 2, DOLLAR(S) 2.

[B–150]

BIND (bīnd), *v.*, BOUND, BINDING. (The act of tying.) Both hands, in the "A" position, go through the natural hand-over-hand motions of tying and drawing out a knot. *Cf.* FASTEN, KNOT, TIE 1.

[B–151]

BINOCULARS (bə nŏk′ yə lərz, bī-), *n. pl.* (The natural sign.) The "C" hands are held in front of the eyes. *Cf.* GOGGLES, OPERA GLASSES.

[B–152]

BIRD (bûrd), *n.* (The shape and movement of a beak.) The right thumb and index finger are placed against the mouth, pointing straight out. They open and close. *Cf.* BEAK.

[B-153]

BIRTH 1 (bûrth), *n*. (Presenting the baby from womb to hand; a coming out from the womb to the waiting hand.) The upturned right hand is brought forward from the stomach to the upturned left palm. *Cf.* BORN 1, NEE.

[B-154]

BIRTH 2, *n*. (The baby is presented.) Both open hands are held against the breast, one on top of the other, as if holding something to oneself. From this position the hands move out from the body and to either side, ending palms up. *Cf.* BORN 2.

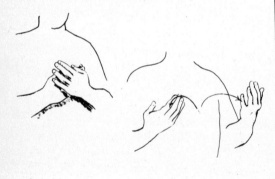

[B-155]

BIRTH 3, *n*. (The baby is brought forth from the womb.) Both cupped hands, palms facing the body, are placed at the stomach or lower chest, one on top of the other. Both hands are moved out and away from the body in unison, describing a small arc. *Cf.* BORN 3.

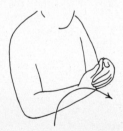

[B-156]

BIRTHDAY (bûrth′ dā′), *n*. The sign for BIRTH 1 or BIRTH 2 is made, followed by the sign for DAY: The left arm, held horizontally, palm down, represents the horizon. The right elbow rests on the back of the left hand, with the right arm in a perpendicular position. The right "D" hand, palm facing left, moves in an arc to the left until it is just above the left elbow.

[B-157]

BISCUIT (bĭs′ kĭt), *n*. (Act of cutting biscuits with a cookie mold.) The right hand, in the "C" position, palm down, is placed into the open left palm. It then rises a bit, swings or twists around a little, and in this new position is placed again in the open left palm. *Cf.* COOKIE, MUFFIN.

[B-158]

BISHOP 1 (bĭsh′ əp), *(eccles.)*, *n*. (Kissing the ring.) The extended index and middle fingers make the sign of the cross before the face. Then the ring finger of the right "S" hand is kissed. This is the sign for a Catholic bishop.

[B–159]

BISHOP 2, *n.* (The shape.) The downturned open hands, fingers together, move up from either side of the head, and the fingertips come together, forming an arch over the head, to describe the bishop's mitre. *Cf.* MITRE.

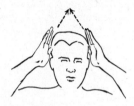

[B–160]

BITCH (bĭch), *(sl.)*, *n.* (The letter "B"; the "female" portion of the head.) The right "B" hand is brought up to the chin.

[B–161]

BITE (bīt), *n.*, *v.*, BIT, BITTEN, BITING. (The natural sign.) The index finger of the downturned hand is bitten.

[B–162]

BITTER (bĭt' ər), *adj.* (Something sour or bitter.) The right index finger is brought sharply up against the lips, while the mouth is puckered up as if tasting something sour. *Cf.* ACID, DISAPPOINTED 1, LEMON 1, PICKLE, SOUR.

[B–163]

BITTERNESS (bĭt' ər nĭs), *n.* The sign for BITTER is made. This is followed by the sign for -NESS: The downturned right "N" hand moves down along the left palm, which is facing away from the body.

[B–164]

BLACK (blăk), *adj.* (The darkest part of the face, *i.e.,* the brow, is indicated.) The tip of the index finger moves along the eyebrow.

[B–165]

BLACKBOARD (blăk' bōrd´), *n.* (Black, hard, write.) The sign for BLACK is made. This is followed by the sign for HARD: The bent right index and middle fingers strike the back of the left fist. Then the sign for WRITE is made: The right index finger and thumb, grasping an imaginary piece of chalk, write across the open left palm. *Cf.* SLATE.

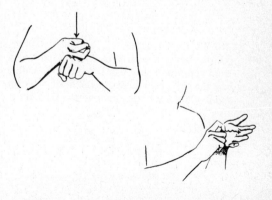

[B-166]

BLACKSMITH (blăk' smĭth´), *n.* (Striking an anvil with a hammer.) The left index finger, pointing forward from the body, represents the anvil. The right hand, grasping an imaginary hammer, swings down against the left index finger and glances off. This may be repeated. This is followed by the sign for INDIVIDUAL: Both open hands, palms facing each other, move down the sides of the body, tracing its outline to the hips. *Cf.* IRON 1, STEEL.

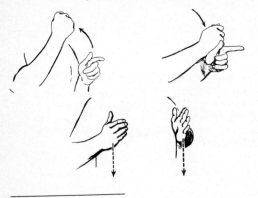

[B-167]

BLAME (blām), *v.,* BLAME, BLAMING, *n.* (The blame is firmly placed.) The right "A" hand, thumb pointing up, is brought down firmly against the back of the left hand, held palm down; the right thumb is then directed toward the person or object to blame. When personal blame is acknowledged, the thumb is brought in to the chest. *Cf.* ACCUSE 1, FAULT 1, GUILTY 1.

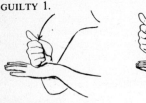

[B-168]

BLASPHEME 1 (blăs fēm´), *v.,* -PHEMED, -PHEMING. (Harsh words and a threatening hand.) The right hand appears to claw words out of the mouth. It ends in the "S" position, above the head, shaking back and forth in a threatening manner. *Cf.* CURSE 1, SWEAR 2.

[B-169]

BLASPHEME 2, *v.* (Harsh words thrown out.) The right hand, as in BLASPHEME 1, appears to claw words out of the mouth. This time, however, it turns and throws them out, ending in the "5" position. *Cf.* CALL OUT, CRY 3, CRY OUT, CURSE 2, SCREAM, SHOUT, SUMMON 1, SWEAR 3.

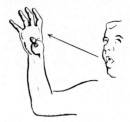

[B-170]

BLASPHEME 3, *(sl.), v.* (Curlicues, as one finds in cartoon-type swear words.) The right "Y" hand, palm down, pivots at the wrist along the "G" hand, from the wrist to the tip of the finger. *Cf.* CURSE 3, SWEAR 4.

[B-171]

BLEED (blēd), *v.,* BLED, BLEEDING, *adj.* (Blood trickles down from the hand.) The left "5" hand is held palm facing the body and fingertips pointing right. The right "5" hand touches the back of the left and moves down, with the right fingers wiggling. *Cf.* BLOOD.

[B-172]

BLESS 1 (blĕs), *v.*, BLESSED or BLEST, BLESSING. (Blessed; forgiveness.) The "A" hands are held near the lips, thumbs up and almost touching. Both hands move down and out simultaneously, ending in the "5" position, palms down. The right hand, palm flat, facing down, is then brushed over the left hand, held palm flat and facing up. This latter action may be repeated twice. *Cf.* ABSOLUTION 1, FORGIVE 1.

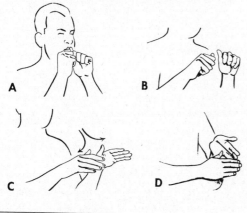

[B-173]

BLESS 2, *v.* (Pronouncing a blessing over a kneeling figure.) The index finger of the right "D" hand is placed at the lips, to indicate the source of the blessing. Both hands then assume the "A" position, thumbs up and knuckles touching. They sweep down and out, opening to the "5" position, palms down, as if placing the hands on bowed heads. *Cf.* BENEDICTION 2.

[B-174]

BLIND (blīnd), *adj.* (The eyes are blocked.) The tips of the "V" fingers are thrust toward the closed eyes. *Cf.* BLINDNESS.

[B-175]

BLINDNESS, *n.* See BLIND. This is followed by the sign for -NESS: The downturned right "N" hand moves down along the left palm, which is facing away from the body.

[B-176]

BLOCK (blŏk), *n.* (Obstruct, block.) The left hand, fingers together and palm flat, is held before the body, facing somewhat down. The little finger side of the right hand, held with palm flat, makes one or several up-down chopping motions against the left hand, between its thumb and index finger. *Cf.* ANNOY 1, ANNOYANCE 1, BOTHER 1, CHECK 2, COME BETWEEN, DISRUPT, DISTURB, HINDER, HINDRANCE, IMPEDE, INTERCEPT, INTERFERE, INTERFERENCE, INTERFERE WITH, INTERRUPT, MEDDLE 1, OBSTACLE, OBSTRUCT, PREVENT, PREVENTION.

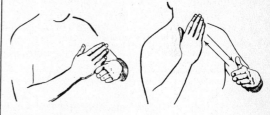

[B-177]

BLOCKING, *(sports)*, *n.* (Knocking one over.) The index and middle fingers of the right "H" hand are brought forcefully against the corresponding fingers of the left "H" hand, as a football player would throw himself against his opponent's legs.

[B-178]

BLOOD (blŭd), *n.* See BLEED.

[B-179]

BLOOM (blōōm), *n.* (Flowers or plants emerge from the ground.) The right fingers, pointing up, emerge from the closed left hand, and they spread open as they do. *Cf.* DEVELOP 1, GROW, GROWN, MATURE, PLANT 1, RAISE 3, REAR 2, SPRING 1.

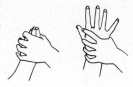

[B-180]

BLOSSOM (blŏs' əm), *n.* (The natural motion of smelling a flower.) The right hand, grasping an imaginary flower, holds it first against the right nostril and then against the left. *Cf.* FLOWER.

[B-181]

BLOW 1 (blō), *v.,* BLEW, BLOWN, BLOWING, *n.* (The blowing back and forth of the wind.) The "5" hands, palms facing and held up before the body, sway gracefully back and forth, in unison. The cheeks meanwhile are puffed up and the breath is being expelled. The nature of the swaying movement —graceful and slow, fast and violent, etc.—determines the type of wind. The strength of exhalation is also a qualifying device. *Cf.* BREEZE, GALE, STORM, WIND.

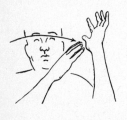 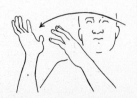

[B-182]

BLOW 2, *n.* (A blow is struck.) The right fist strikes the left palm. *Cf.* BEAT 3.

[B-183]

BLOW AWAY, *(colloq.), v. phrase.* (Blowing something away so that it no longer remains.) The signer blows into the upturned palm. *Cf.* NOTHING 3.

[B-184]

BLUE (blōō), *n., adj.* (The letter "B.") The right "B" hand shakes slightly, pivoted at the wrist.

[B-185]

BLUFF (blŭf), *n.* (A double face, *i.e.,* a mask covers the face.) The right hand is placed over the back of the left hand and pushes it down and a bit in toward the body. *Cf.* FAKE, HUMBUG, HYPOCRITE 1, IMPOSTOR.

[B–186]

BLURRY (blûr´ ĭ), *adj.* (One hand obscures the other.) The "5" hands are held up palm against palm in front of the body. The right hand moves in a slow, continuous clockwise circle over the left palm, as the signer tries to see between the fingers. *Cf.* UNCLEAR, VAGUE.

[B–187]

BLUSH (blŭsh), *v.*, BLUSHED, BLUSHING. (The red rises in the cheeks.) The sign for RED is made: The tip of the right index finger of the "D" hand moves down over the lips, which are red. Both hands are then placed palms facing the cheeks, and move up along the face, to indicate the rise of color. *Cf.* EMBARRASS, EMBARRASSED, FLUSH, MORTIFICATION.

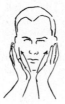

[B–188]

BOARD (bōrd), *n.* (The letter "B"; the Roman toga, a symbol of authority, draped across the shoulders.) The right "B" hand, palm facing left, moves from the right shoulder to the left shoulder. (This sign is used for "board of directors.")

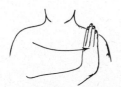

[B–189]

BOAST (bōst), *v.*, BOASTED, BOASTING. (Indicating the self, repeatedly.) The thumbs of both "A" hands are alternately thrust into the chest a number of times. *Cf.* BRAG, SHOW OFF 1.

[B–190]

BOAT (bōt), *n.* (The shape; the bobbing on the waves.) Both hands are cupped together to form the hull of a boat. They move forward in a bobbing motion.

[B–191]

BODY (bŏd´ ĭ), *n.* (The body is indicated.) One or both hands are placed against the chest and then are removed and replaced at a point a bit below the first. *Cf.* PHYSICAL.

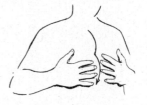

[B–192]

BONE (bōn), *n.* (The finger touches a brittle substance.) The index finger is brought up to touch the exposed front teeth. *Cf.* CHINA 2, DISH, GLASS 1, PLATE, PORCELAIN.

[B-193]

BOOK (boŏk), *n.* (Opening a book.) The open hands are held together, fingers pointing away from the body. They open with little fingers remaining in contact, as in the opening of a book. *Cf.* TEXTBOOK, VOLUME.

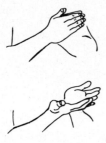

[B-194]

BOOKLET (boŏk′ lĭt), *n.* (A book with a narrow spine.) The left hand, fingers together, is held upright, palm facing right. The right hand wraps around the lower edge of the left and travels up to the little finger. This denotes a narrow object. The sign for BOOK is then made. Sometimes this latter sign is omitted. *Cf.* CATALOG, MAGAZINE, MANUAL, PAMPHLET.

[B-195]

BOOST (boōst), *v.,* BOOSTED, BOOSTING. (Helping up; supporting.) The left "S" hand, thumb side up, rests in the open right palm. In this position the left hand is pushed up a short distance by the right. *Cf.* AID, ASSIST, ASSISTANCE, BENEFIT 1, GIVE ASSISTANCE, HELP.

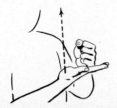

[B-196]

BORE 1 (bōr), *v.,* BORED, BORING, *n.* (A dryness, indicated by a wiping of the lips.) The "X" finger is drawn across the lips, from left to right, as if wiping them. *Cf.* ARID, DROUGHT, DRY, DULL 2.

[B-197]

BORE 2, *v.* (Act of boring a hole with a brace.) The left "S" hand, palm down, grasps an imaginary brace top. The right hand, also in the "S" position, palm facing left, rotates the brace, as if drilling something. *Cf.* DRILL 1.

[B-198]

BORING (bōr′ ĭng), *adj.* (The nose is pressed, as if to a grindstone wheel.) The right index finger touches the tip of the nose, as a bored expression is assumed. The right hand is sometimes pivoted back and forth slightly, as the fingertip remains against the nose. *Cf.* MONOTONOUS 1, TEDIOUS.

[B-199]

BORN 1 (bôrn), *adj.* (Presenting the baby from womb to hand; a coming out from the womb to the waiting hand.) The upturned right hand is brought forward from the stomach to the upturned left palm. *Cf.* BIRTH 1, NEE.

[B–200]

BORN 2, *adj.* (The baby is presented.) Both open hands are held against the breast, one on top of the other, as if holding something to oneself. From this position the hands move out from the body and to either side, ending palms up. *Cf.* BIRTH 2.

[B–201]

BORN 3, *adj.* (The baby is brought forth from the womb.) Both cupped hands, palms facing the body, are placed at the stomach or lower chest, one on top of the other. Both hands are moved out and away from the body in unison, describing a small arc. *Cf.* BIRTH 3.

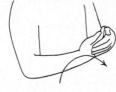

[B–202]

BORROW (bŏr′ ō, bôr′ ō), *v.,* -ROWED, -ROWING, (Bring to oneself.) The "K" hands are crossed and moved in toward the body.

[B–203]

BOTH (bōth), *adj., pron.* (Two fingers are drawn together.) The right "2" hand, palm facing the body, is drawn down through the left "C" hand. As it does, the right index and middle fingers come together. *Cf.* MUTUAL 2, PAIR.

[B–204]

BOTHER 1 (bŏ*th*′ ər), *v.,* -ERED, -ERING. (Obstruct, block.) The left hand, fingers together and palm flat, is held before the body, facing somewhat down. The little finger side of the right hand, held with palm flat, makes one or several up-down chopping motions against the left hand, between its thumb and index finger. *Cf.* ANNOY 1, ANNOYANCE 1, BLOCK, CHECK 2, COME BETWEEN, DISRUPT, DISTURB, HINDER, HINDRANCE, IMPEDE, INTERCEPT, INTERFERE, INTERFERENCE, INTERFERE WITH, INTERRUPT, MEDDLE 1, OBSTACLE, OBSTRUCT, PREVENT, PREVENTION.

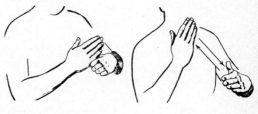

[B–205]

BOTHER 2, *v.* (A clouding over; a troubling.) Both "B" hands, palms facing each other, are rotated alternately before the forehead. *Cf.* ANNOY 2, ANNOYANCE 2, ANXIOUS 2, CONCERN 1, FRET, PROBLEM 1, TROUBLE, WORRIED, WORRY 1.

[B–206]

BOTTOM (bŏt′ əm), *n.* (The area below.) Both hands, in the "5" position, palms down, are held before the chest, the right under the left. The right hand moves under the left in a counterclockwise fashion. *Cf.* BACKGROUND, BASIS 2, BELOW 1, FOUNDATION.

[B-207]

BOUND (bound), *adj.* (Bound down to custom or habit.) Both "S" hands, palms down, are crossed and brought down in unison before the chest. *Cf.* ACCUSTOM, CUSTOM, HABIT, LOCKED, PRACTICE 3.

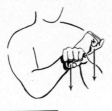

[B-208]

BOW 1 (bō), *n.* (The natural act of tying a bow tie.) The "U" hands go through the motions of tying and drawing out a bow tie. *Cf.* BOW TIE.

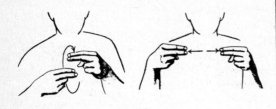

[B-209]

BOW 2 (bou), *v.,* BOWED, BOWING. (Act of bowing the head.) The right "S" hand, palm out, represents the head, and bows over and down.

[B-210]

BOWL 1 (bōl), *n.* (The natural shape.) The cupped hands form a bowl and move up a bit to indicate the height. *Cf.* POT.

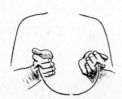

[B-211]

BOWL 2, *v.,* BOWLED, BOWLING. (The natural sign.) The right hand grasps an imaginary bowling ball and hurls it down the alley.

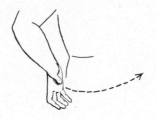

[B-212]

BOW TIE (bō´ tī). (The natural act of tying a bow tie.) The "U" hands go through the motions of tying and drawing out a bow tie. *Cf.* BOW 1.

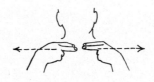

[B-213]

BOX 1 (bŏks), *n.* (The dimensions are indicated.) The open hands, palms facing and fingers pointing out, are dropped an inch or two simultaneously. They then shift their relative positions so that both palms face the body, with one hand in front of the other. In this new position they again drop an inch or two simultaneously. *Cf.* PACKAGE, ROOM 1, SQUARE 1, TRUNK.

[B-214]

BOX 2, *v.*, BOXED, BOXING. (The natural sign.) Both clenched fists go through the motions of boxing. *Cf.* FIGHT 2.

[B-215]

BOY 1 (boi), *n.* (A small male.) The MALE root sign is made: The thumb and extended fingers of the right hand are brought up to grasp an imaginary cap brim, representing the tipping of caps by men in olden days. The downturned right hand then indicates the short height of a small boy.

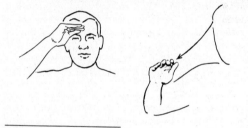

[B-216]

BOY 2, *n.* (A modification of the MALE root sign; the familiar sign for BOY 1.) The right hand, palm down, is held at the forehead. The fingers open and close once or twice. *Cf.* LAD.

[B-217]

BOY SCOUT (skout), *n.* (The salute.) The Boy Scout salute is given.

[B-218]

BRACE (brās), *n.*, *v.*, BRACED, BRACING. (The natural sign.) The thumb tips are thrust up against the edges of the upper teeth. *Cf.* BRIDGE 2.

[B-219]

BRAG (brăg), *v.*, BRAGGED, BRAGGING. (Indicating the self, repeatedly.) The thumbs of both "A" hands are alternately thrust into the chest a number of times. *Cf.* BOAST, SHOW OFF 1.

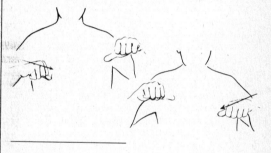

[B-220]

BRAID (brād), *n.*, *v.*, BRAIDED, BRAIDING. (Act of braiding the hair.) The "R" hands, placed palms out at the left temple, are alternately moved down, as if braiding the hair. *Cf.* CURL.

[B-221]

BRAIN (brān), *n.* (The natural sign.) The fingertips tap the side of the head several times.

[B-222]

BRANCH (brănch, bränch), *n.* (The shape.) The elbow of the upright right arm rests on the palm of the upturned left hand. This is the trunk. The right "5" fingers wiggle to imitate the movement of the branches and leaves. *Cf.* TREE.

[B-223]

BRAVE (brāv), *adj., n., v.,* BRAVED, BRAVING. (Strength emanating from the body.) Both "5" hands are placed palms against the chest. They move out and away, forcefully, closing and assuming the "S" position. *Cf.* BRAVERY, COURAGE, COURAGEOUS, FORTITUDE, HALE, HEALTH, HEALTHY, MIGHTY 2, STRENGTH, STRONG 2, WELL 2.

[B-224]

BRAVERY (brā' və rĭ), *n.* See BRAVE.

[B-225]

BRAYER (brā' ər), *(voc.), n.* (Manipulating the brayer.) An imaginary brayer, a small roller used for inking type, is grasped in the right "S" hand, and is rolled back and forth over the upturned left palm, representing the type.

[B-226]

BREAD (brĕd), *n.* (Act of cutting a loaf of bread.) The left arm is held against the chest, representing a loaf of bread. The little finger edge of the right hand is drawn down over the back of the left hand several times, to indicate the cutting of slices. *Cf.* COMMUNION·(HOLY) 2, HOLY COMMUNION 2, WINE 2.

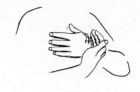

[B-227]

BREAK (brāk), *n., v.,* BROKE, BROKEN, BREAKING. (The natural sign.) The hands grasp an imaginary object and break it in two. *Cf.* FRACTURE.

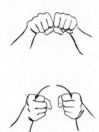

[B-228]

BREAKDOWN (-doun), *n.* (A collapsing.) Both "5" hands, fingertips joined before the chest, swing down so that the fingertips face down. *Cf.* CAVE IN, COLLAPSE.

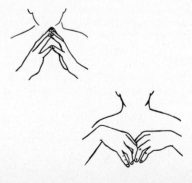

[B-229]

BREAKFAST (brĕk' fəst), *n.* (Morning food.) The sign for FOOD is given: The closed right hand goes through the natural motion of placing food in the mouth. This movement is repeated, followed by the sign for MORNING: The little finger edge of the left hand rests in the crook of the right elbow. The left arm, held horizontally, represents the horizon. The open right hand, fingers together and pointing up, with palm facing the body, rises slowly to an almost upright angle. The signs may also be reversed, as MORNING, FOOD.

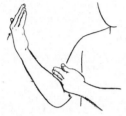

[B-230]

BREATH (brĕth), *n.* (The rise and fall of the chest in respiration.) The hands, folded over the chest, move forward and back to the chest, to indicate the breathing. *Cf.* BREATHE, RESPIRATION.

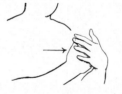

[B-231]

BREATHE (brĕth), *v.,* BREATHED, BREATHING. See BREATH.

[B-232]

BREEZE (brēz), *n.* (The blowing back and forth of the wind.) The "5" hands, palms facing and held up before the body, sway gracefully back and forth, in unison. The cheeks meanwhile are puffed up and the breath is being expelled. The nature of the swaying movement—graceful and slow, fast and violent, etc. —determines the type of wind. The strength of exhalation is also a qualifying device. *Cf.* BLOW 1, GALE, STORM, WIND.

[B-233]

BRIBE (brīb), *n., v.,* BRIBED, BRIBING. (Underhanded payment of money.) The right hand, grasping an imaginary dollar bill, moves under the downturned left hand.

[B-234]

BRIDGE 1 (brĭj), *n., v.,* BRIDGED, BRIDGING. (The shape and supports.) The left arm, held horizontally palm down, represents the shape of the bridge. The right upturned "V" fingers are thrust up against the downturned left wrist, and describing an arc, they move back and up against the midpoint of the forearm, close to the elbow.

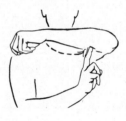

[B-235]

BRIDGE 2, *n.* (The natural sign.) The thumb tips are thrust up against the edges of the upper teeth. *Cf.* BRACE.

[B-236]

BRIEF 1 (brēf), *adj.* (To make short; to measure off a short space.) The index and middle fingers of the right "H" hand are placed across the top of the index and middle fingers of the left "H" hand, and move a short distance back and forth, along the length of the left index finger. *Cf.* ABBREVIATE 2, SHORT 1, SHORTEN.

[B-237]

BRIEF 2, *adj.* (To squeeze or condense into a small space.) Both "C" hands face each other, with the right hand nearer to the body than the left. Both hands draw together and close deliberately, squeezing an imaginary object. *Cf.* ABBREVIATE 1, CONDENSE, MAKE BRIEF, SUMMARIZE 1, SUMMARY 1.

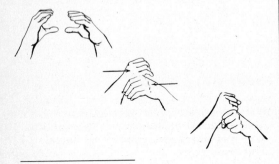

[B-238]

BRIGHT 1 (brīt), *adj.* (Rays of light clearing the way.) Both hands are held at chest height, palms out, all fingertips together. They open into the "5" position in unison, the right hand moving toward the right and the left toward the left. The palms of both hands remain facing out. *Cf.* BRILLIANCE 1, BRILLIANT 2, CLEAR, EXPLICIT 2, OBVIOUS, PLAIN 1.

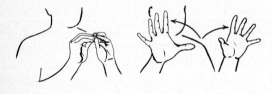

[B-239]

BRIGHT 2 *adj.* (Reflected glistening of light rays.) The left hand, held supinely before the chest, palm down, represents the object from which the rays glisten. The right hand, in the "5" position, touches the back of the left lightly and moves up toward the right, pivoting slightly at the wrist, with fingers wiggling. *Cf.* GLISTEN, SHINE, SHINING.

[B-240]

BRIGHT 3, *adj.* (The mind is bright.) The middle finger is placed at the forehead, and then the hand, with an outward flick, turns around so that the palm faces outward. This indicates a brightness flowing from the mind. *Cf.* BRILLIANT 1, CLEVER 1, INTELLIGENT, SMART.

[B-241]

BRIGHT 4, *adj.* (Light rays glistening upward.) Both "5" hands, palms facing out, are held before the chest. They move up and out, all fingers wiggling to convey the glistening of light rays upward. This sign is an alternate for BRIGHT 2 and GLISTEN. *Cf.* BRILLIANCE 2.

[B-242]

BRILLIANCE 1 (bril′ yəns), *n.* See BRIGHT 1.

[B-243]

BRILLIANCE 2, *n.* See BRIGHT 4.

[B-244]

BRILLIANT 1 (bril′ yənt), *adj.* See BRIGHT 3.

[B-245]

BRILLIANT 2, *adj.* See BRIGHT 1.

[B-246]

BRING (bring), *v.*, BROUGHT, BRINGING. (Carrying something over.) Both open hands, palms up, move in an arc from left to right, as if carrying something from one point to another. *Cf.* CARRY 2, DELIVER 2, FETCH, PRODUCE 1. TRANSPORT.

[B-247]

BRITAIN (brĭt´ ən), *n.* (The English are supposed to be handshakers.) The right hand grasps and shakes the left. *Cf.* BRITISH, ENGLAND, ENGLISH, GREAT BRITAIN.

[B-248]

BRITISH (brĭt´ ĭsh), *adj.* See BRITAIN.

[B-249]

BROAD (brôd), *adj.* (The width is indicated.) The open hands, fingers pointing out and palms facing each other, separate from their initial position an inch or two apart. *Cf.* WIDE, WIDTH.

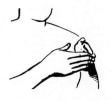

[B-250]

BROAD-MINDED (brôd´ mīn´ dĭd), *adj.* (The mind is open, or wide.) The index finger touches the forehead to indicate the MIND. Then the sign for BROAD is made: The open hands, fingers pointing out and palms facing each other, separate from their initial position an inch or two apart.

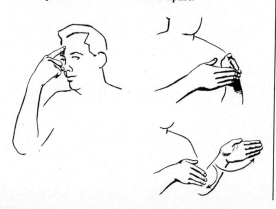

[B-251]

BROAD-SHOULDERED (shōl´ dərd), *adj.* (The width is indicated.) The index fingers of the "L" hands are placed on the shoulders, and then both hands move apart from the shoulders.

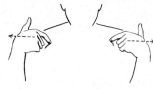

[B-252]

BROIL (broil), *v.*, BROILED, BROILING. (The dancing of the flames over the item being broiled.) The fingers of the right hand wiggle as the right hand passes back and forth over the upturned left, from base to fingertips.

[B-253]

BROKE (brōk), *(sl.), adj.* (The head is chopped off.) The tips of the right fingers are thrust forcefully into the right side of the neck. *Cf.* BANKRUPT.

[B-254]

BROOCH (brōch, brŏŏch), *n.* (The shape and location of the item.) The thumb and index finger of one hand form a circle, and are placed against the chest. The hand then moves down an inch. *Cf.* PIN 2.

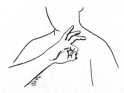

[B-255]

BROOM (brōōm, brŏŏm), *n.* (The natural sign.) The hands grasp and manipulate an imaginary broom. *Cf.* SWEEP.

[B-256]

BROTHER 1 (brŭth′ ər), *n.* (A male who is the same, *i.e.,* from the same family.) The root sign for MALE is made: The thumb and extended fingers of the right hand are brought up to grasp an imaginary cap brim, representing the tipping of caps by men in olden days. Then the sign for SAME 1 is made: The outstretched index fingers are brought together, either once or several times.

[B-257]

BROTHER 2, *(eccles.), n.* (The white collar-piece worn by religious brothers.) The thumb and index finger of one hand are placed just below the throat, and move down, describing the white hanging collar-piece. *Cf.* CHRISTIAN BROTHERS.

[B-258]

BROTHER-IN-LAW (brŭth′ ər in lô′), *n.* (The sign for BROTHER 1 is made, followed by the sign for IN: The fingers of the right hand are thrust into the left. The sign for LAW is then made: The upright right "L" hand, resting palm against palm on the upright left "5" hand, moves down in an arc, a short distance, coming to rest on the base of the left palm.

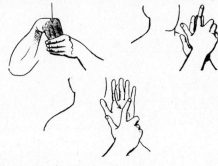

[B-259]

BROWN (broun), *adj.* The "B" hand is placed against the face, with the index finger touching the upper cheek. The hand is then drawn straight down the cheek.

[B-260]

BRUSH 1 (brŭsh), *n., v.,* BRUSHED, BRUSHING. (The natural sign.) Either hand, grasping an imaginary brush, brushes the clothes. *Cf.* CLOTHESBRUSH.

[B-261]

BRUSH 2, *n., v.* (The natural sign.) Either hand, grasping an imaginary brush, brushes the hair. *Cf.* HAIRBRUSH.

[B–262]

BRUSH 3, *n., v.* (The natural sign.) Either hand, grasping an imaginary brush, brushes the shoes. *Cf.* SHOEBRUSH.

[B–263]

BRUSH 4, *n., v.* (The natural sign.) The index finger is thrust back and forth in front of the exposed teeth. *Cf.* TOOTHBRUSH.

[B–264]

BUFFALO (bŭf′ ə lō′), *n.* (The horns.) The "Y" hand, pivoted at the wrist, is shaken slightly beside the head. This sign is used for both the animal and the city of Buffalo, in New York State.

[B–265]

BUG (bŭg), *(sl.), n.* (The quivering antennae.) The thumb of the "3" hand rests against the nose, and the index and middle fingers bend slightly and straighten again a number of times. *Cf.* INSECT 2.

[B–266]

BUILD (bĭld), *v.,* BUILT, BUILDING. (Piling bricks one on top of another.) The downturned hands are placed repeatedly atop each other. Each time this is done the arms rise a bit, to indicate the raising of a building. *Cf.* CONSTRUCT 1, CONSTRUCTION, ERECT.

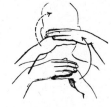

[B–267]

BUILDING (bĭl′ dĭng), *n.* The sign for BUILD is made, followed by the sign for HOUSE: The hands, forming a pyramid a bit above eye level, move down as they separate, and then they continue straight down a few inches.

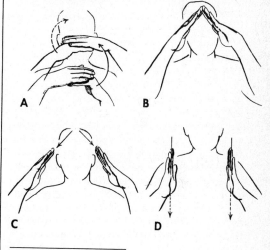

[B–268]

BULL (bool), *n.* (The flattened brow of the bull.) The "A" hand, palm facing the body, is placed at the forehead and rotated counterclockwise. This sign is sometimes used to indicate any male animal.

[B-269]

BUMP (bŭmp), *n.* (The shape.) The right index finger indicates a bump on the back of the left hand.

[B-270]

BURDEN (bûr′ dən), *n.* (Something which weighs down or burdens one with responsibility.) The fingertips of both hands, placed on the right shoulder, bear down. *Cf.* ATTRIBUTE 1, BEAR 4, OBLIGATION 1, RELY 1, RESPONSIBILITY 1, RESPONSIBLE 1.

[B-271]

BURGLAR (bûr′ glər), *n.* (A mustachioed thief.) The fingertips of both "H" hands, palms facing the body, are placed above the lips and are drawn slowly apart, describing a mustache. Sometimes one hand only is used. This is followed by the sign for INDIVIDUAL: Both open hands, palms facing each other, move down the sides of the body, tracing its outline to the hips. *Cf.* BANDIT, BURGLARY, CROOK, ROB 3, ROBBER 1, STEAL 3, THEFT 3, THIEF 2.

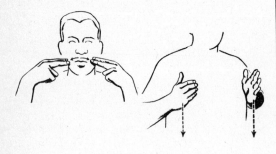

[B-272]

BURGLARY (bûr′ glə rĭ), *n.* See BURGLAR.

[B-273]

BURN (bûrn), *n., v.,* BURNED or BURNT, BURNING. (The leaping of flames.) The "5" hands are held with palms facing the body. They move up and down alternately, while the fingers wiggle. *Cf.* FIRE 1, FLAME, HELL 2.

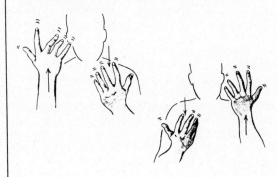

[B-274]

BURY (bĕr′ ĭ), *v.,* BURIED, BURYING. (The mound of a grave.) The downturned open hands, slightly cupped, are held side by side. They describe on arc as they are drawn in toward the body. *Cf.* CEMETERY, GRAVE 1.

[B-275]

BUSH (bŏosh), *n.* (The movement of bushes.) The "5" hands, held palm to palm, move back and forth against each other. The gaze is often directed through the fingers as they move back and forth. Sometimes the two hands are swung around after each back-and-forth movement.

[B-276]

BUSINESS (bĭz´ nĭs), *n.* (An activity of the hands, modified by the letter "B.") The upright right "B" hand glances back and forth against the left "S" hand, whose palm faces down. This sign is frequently made with both hands in the "S" position, employing the same movement as above.

[B-277]

BUSY 1 (bĭz´ ĭ), *adj.* (An activity of the hands.) The right "S" hand, palm out, glances back and forth against the left "S" hand, whose palm faces down. *Cf.* the alternate sign for BUSINESS.

[B-278]

BUSY 2, *adj.* (An activity.) Both open hands, palms down, are swung right and left before the chest. *Cf.* ACT 2, ACTION, ACTIVE, ACTIVITY, CONDUCT 1, DEED, DO, PERFORM 1, PERFORMANCE 1, RENDER 2.

[B-279]

BUT (bŭt; *unstressed* bət), *conj.* (A divergence or a difference; the opposite of SAME.) The index fingers of both "D" hands, palms facing down, are crossed near their tips. The hands are drawn apart. *Cf.* ALTHOUGH, HOWEVER 1, ON THE CONTRARY.

[B-280]

BUTTER (bŭt´ ər), *n., v.,* -TERED, -TERING. (The spreading of butter.) The tips of the fingers of the downturned right "U" hand are brushed repeatedly over the upturned left palm.

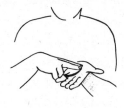

[B-281]

BUTTERFLY (bŭt´ ər flī´), *n.* (The natural sign.) The "5" hands, palms facing the body, are crossed and intertwined at the thumbs. The hands, hooked in this manner, move to and fro in vague figure-eights, while the individual hands flap back and forth.

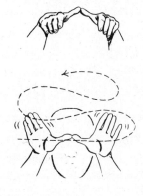

[B-282]

BUTT IN, *(sl.), v. phrase,* BUTTED, BUTTING. (The nose is poked into something.) The sign for NOSE is formed by touching the tip of the nose with the index finger. The sign for IN, INTO follows: The right hand, fingertips touching the thumb, thrust into the left "C" hand, which closes a bit over the right fingers as they enter. *Cf.* MEDDLE 2.

[B-283]

BUTTON 1 (bŭt´ ən), *n.* (The natural sign.) The index finger and thumb form a small circle and are placed against the mid-chest. In this position the hand may move down in a series of arcs, indicating individual buttons.

[B-284]

BUTTON 2, *(arch.), n.* (The round button sticks out from the clothing.) The thumb of the right "A" hand, pointing up, is rotated back and forth several times between the index and middle fingers of the left hand, whose palm faces down.

[B-285]

BUY (bī), *n., v.,* BOUGHT, BUYING. (Giving out money.) The sign for MONEY is made: The up-turned right hand, grasping some imaginary bills, is brought down into the upturned left palm, and then the right hand moves forward and up in a small arc, opening up as it does. *Cf.* PURCHASE.

[B-286]

BY 1 (bī), *prep.* (One hand is near the other.) The left hand, cupped, fingers together, is held before the chest, palm facing the body. The right hand, also cupped, fingers together, moves a very short distance back and forth, as it is held in front of the left. *Cf.* ADJACENT, BESIDE, CLOSE (TO) 2, NEAR 1, NEIGHBOR, NEIGHBORHOOD, VICINITY.

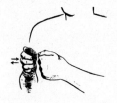

[B-287]

BY 2, *(rare), adv.* (Indicating agency or means by which something is accomplished or done.) Both "A" hands, palms facing and thumbs facing left, are moved over a bit to the left, in a small arc.

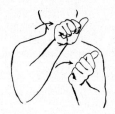

[B-288]

BY AND BY (bī´ ən bī), *n.* (Something ahead or in the future.) The upright, open right hand, palm facing left, moves straight out and slightly up from a position beside the right temple. *Cf.* FUTURE, IN THE FUTURE, LATER 2, LATER ON, SHALL, WILL 1, WOULD.

C

CABBAGE (kăb′ ĭj), *n*. (Head of cabbage.) Both "S" hands (or "A" hands) are knocked against the sides of the head simultaneously. As an alternate sign, the "C" hands may be employed.

[C–2]

CABINETMAKER (kăb′ ə nĭt mā′ kər), *n*. (Manipulating a carpenter's plane.) The hands grasp and manipulate an imaginary carpenter's plane. This is followed by the sign for INDIVIDUAL: Both open hands, palms facing each other, move down to the sides of the body, tracing its outline to the hips. *Cf.* CARPENTER.

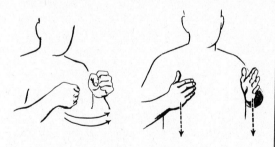

[C–3]

CAKE 1 (kāk), *n*. (The rising of the cake.) The fingertips of the right "5" hand are placed in the upturned left palm. The right rises slowly an inch or two above the left.

[C–4]

CAKE 2, *(loc.)*, *n*. (The letter "K," the last initial of an instructor of baking at a school for the deaf.) The middle finger of the right "K" hand touches the right cheek twice. *Cf.* PIE 2.

[C–5]

CAKE 3, *n*. The same position is assumed as in CAKE 1 except that the right hand moves up and down several times.

[C–6]

CALAMITOUS (kə lăm′ ə təs), *adj*. (Throwing out the hands.) Both hands, their fingertips touching their respective thumbs, are held, palms facing each other, near the temples. They are thrown out before the face, assuming "5" positions, palms still facing. *Cf.* AWFUL, CATASTROPHIC, DANGER 1, DANGEROUS 1, DREADFUL, FEARFUL, TERRIBLE, TRAGEDY, TRAGIC.

[C-7]

CALCULATE (kăl′ kyə lāt′), *v.*, -LATED, -LATING.
(A multiplying.) The "V" hands, palms facing the
body, alternately cross and separate, several times.
Cf. ARITHMETIC, ESTIMATE, FIGURE 1, MULTIPLY
1.

  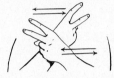

[C-8]

CALCULUS (kăl′ kyə ləs), *n.* (The "C" hands; multiplying or calculating.) The "C" hands, palms facing each other, are crossed at the wrists repeatedly.

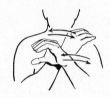

[C-9]

CALF (kăf, käf), *n.* (Small horns.) The index fingers
are wiggled slightly at the temples.

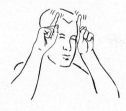

[C-10]

CALIFORNIA (kăl′ ə fôr′ nyə, -fôr′ ni ə), *n.* (Yellow
earrings, *i.e.,* gold, which was discovered in California.) The earlobe is pinched, and then the sign for
YELLOW is made: The "Y" hand, pivoted at the
wrist, is shaken back and forth repeatedly. *Cf.*
GOLD.

[C-11]

CALIPER (kăl′ ə pər), *(voc.), n.* (The natural sign.)
The curved index finger and thumb of the right "5"
hand close carefully and deliberately against the
edges of the left index finger, as if measuring its
thickness. *Cf.* GAGE, MICROMETER.

[C-12]

CALL 1 (kôl), *v.*, CALLED, CALLING. (To tap someone for attention.) The right hand is placed upon the
back of the left, held palm down. The right hand
then moves up and in toward the body, assuming the
"A" position. As an optional addition, the right
hand may then assume a beckoning movement. *Cf.*
SUMMON 2.

[C-13]

CALL 2 *n., v.* (The natural sign.) The cupped right
hand is held against the right cheek. The mouth is
slightly open.

[C-14]

CALLED, *adj.* (NAME, indicating who is named.)
The sign for NAME is made: The right "H" hand,
palm facing left, is brought down on the left "H"
hand, palm facing right. The hands, in this position,
move forward a few inches. *Cf.* NAMED.

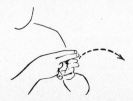

[C–15]

CALL OUT (kôl out), *v. phrase.* (Harsh words thrown out.) The right hand, as in BLASPHEME 1, appears to claw words out of the mouth. This time, however, it turns and throws them out, ending in the "5" position. *Cf.* BLASPHEME 2, CRY 3, CRY OUT, CURSE 2, SCREAM, SHOUT, SUMMON 1, SWEAR 3.

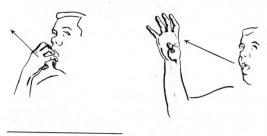

[C–16]

CALM 1 (käm), *adj., v.,* CALMED, CALMING. (Quiet and peace.) The open hands are crossed before the mouth, the right palm facing left, left facing right. Then both hands, held palms down, move down from the mouth, curving outward to either side of the body. *Cf.* BE QUIET 2, BE STILL, QUIET 2, SILENCE 2.

[C–17]

CALM 2, *adj.* (The natural sign.) The index finger is brought up against the pursed lips. *Cf.* BE QUIET 1, HUSH, NOISELESS, QUIET 1, SILENCE 1, SILENT, STILL 2.

[C–18]

CALVARY 1 (kăl′ vəri), *(eccles.), n.* (The cross on the mountain.) The back of the right "S" hand is

struck several times against the back of the left "S" hand to denote something hard, like a ROCK or a MOUNTAIN. The sign for CROSS 2 is then made: The right "C" hand, palm facing out, makes the sign of the cross. *Cf.* CROSS 2, CRUCIFIX.

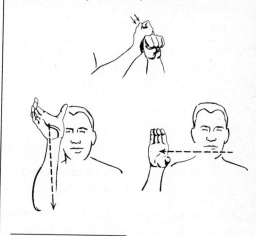

[C–19]

CALVARY 2, *(eccles.), n.* (An upward moving cross.) The left hand is held up before the body, fingers open and palm facing out. The right hand, in the same relative position, moves up the back of the left in an undulating manner until, situated slightly above the level of the left fingertips, it describes a cross.

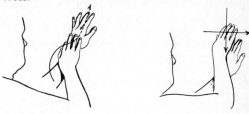

[C–20]

CAMEL (kăm′ əl), *n.* (The shape of the neck.) The two "C" hands are placed at the neck. The right hand, palm facing up, moves up and forward in a long undulating curve, as if tracing the camel's long neck.

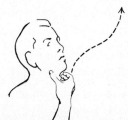

[C–21]

CAMERA 1 (kăm´ər ə, kăm´ rə), *n.* (The natural sign.) The eye peers through the viewfinder of an imaginary camera, and the index finger clicks the shutter. This sign is used for a camera of the 35 mm. type.

[C–22]

CAMERA 2, *n.* (The natural sign.) The signer peers down into the viewfinder of an imaginary camera held at the waist, and the thumb clicks the shutter. This sign is used for a camera of the box type.

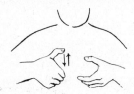

[C–23]

CAMP (kămp), *n.* (A collection of tents.) The sign for TENT is made several times: The tips of the index and middle fingers of both "V" hands are placed in contact. The hands move down, separating as they do. This describes the slanting top of a tent. Each time the sign is made, the hands are positioned an inch or two further to the right.

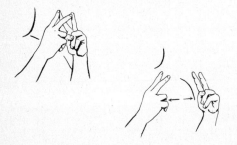

[C–24]

CAN 1 (kăn, kən), *v.* (An affirmative movement of the hands, likened to a nodding of the head, to indicate ability or power to accomplish something.) Both "A" hands, held palms down, move down in unison a short distance before the chest. *Cf.* ABIL-

ITY, ABLE, CAPABLE, COMPETENT, COULD, FACULTY, MAY 2, POSSIBLE.

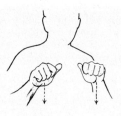

[C–25]

CAN(NING) 2, *n.* (Turning the cover of a jar.) The right hand is laid palm down over the upturned thumb edge of the left "S" hand. In this position the right hand twists in a clockwise circle, as if turning the cover of a jar. *Cf.* CONTAINER.

[C–26]

CANADA (kăn´ə də), *n.* (Shaking the snow from the lapel of an overcoat.) The hand grasps and shakes the right lapel. *Cf.* CANADIAN.

[C–27]

CANADIAN (kə nā´ di ən), *adj., n.* The sign for CANADA is made, followed by the sign for INDIVIDUAL: Both open hands, palms facing each other, move down the sides of the body, tracing its outline to the hips.

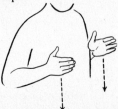

[C–28]

CANCEL (kăn´ səl), *n., v.,* -CELED, -CELING. (A canceling out.) The right index finger makes a cross on the open left palm. *Cf.* ANNUL, CHECK 1, CORRECT 2, CRITICISM, CRITICIZE, FIND FAULT 1, REVOKE.

[C–29]

CANDIDATE (kăn´ də dāt´, -dĭt), *n.* (Bringing oneself forward.) The right index finger and thumb grasp the clothing near the right shoulder (often the lapel of a suit or the collar of a dress) and tug it up and down gently several times. Sometimes one tug only is used. *Cf.* APPLY 1, OFFER 2, RUN FOR OFFICE, VOLUNTEER.

[C–30]

CANDLE (kăn´ dəl), *n., v.,* -DLED, -DLING. (Blowing the flame of the candle; the flickering flames.) The tip of the index finger of the right hand is placed at the lips and then it is placed at the base of the outstretched left hand, whose palm is facing out and whose fingers are wiggling to denote the flickering of flames.

[C–31]

CANDY 1 (kăn´ dĭ), *n.* (Titillating to the taste.) The fingertips of the right "U" hand, palm facing the

body, brush against the chin a number of times beginning at the lips. *Cf.* CUTE 1, SUGAR, SWEET.

[C–32]

CANDY 2, *n.* (Wiping the lips; licking the finger.) The right index finger, pointing left, is drawn across the lips from left to right.

[C–33]

CANNON 1 (kăn´ ən), *n.* (The recoil.) The right index finger points out and slightly upward. The right arm is jerked quickly forward and back, like the recoil of a cannon.

[C–34]

CANNON 2, *n.* (Describing the physical length.) The back of the right hand travels along the length of the outstretched left arm, from shoulder to wrist.

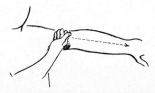

[C–35]

CANNOT 1 (kăn´ ŏt), *v.* (One finger encounters an unyielding quality in striking another.) The right index finger strikes the left and continues moving down. The left index finger remains in place. *Cf.* CAN'T, IMPOSSIBLE 1, UNABLE.

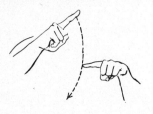

[C–36]

CANNOT 2, *v.* (Not able.) The sign for CAN is formed, followed by the sign for NOT: Both hands, fingers together and palms facing down, are held before the body with the right slightly above the left. They separate with a deliberate movement, the right hand moving to the right and the left moving to the left.

[C–37]

CANOEING (kə nōō´ ing), *n.* (The natural sign.) The hands, grasping an imaginary paddle, go through the motions of paddling a canoe. *Cf.* PADDLE.

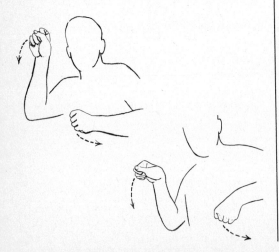

[C–38]

CAN'T (kănt, känt), *v.* See CANNOT 1, 2.

[C–39]

CAP (kăp), *n., v.,* CAPPED, CAPPING. (The natural sign.) The hand grasps the brim of an imaginary cap and pulls it down slightly.

[C–40]

CAPABLE (kā´ pə bəl), *adj.* (An affirmative movement of the hands, likened to a nodding of the head, to indicate ability or power to accomplish something.) Both "A" hands, held palm down, move down in unison a short distance before the chest. *Cf.* ABILITY, ABLE, CAN 1, COMPETENT, COULD, FACULTY, MAY 2, POSSIBLE.

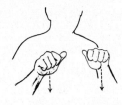

[C–41]

CAPACITY (kə păs´ ə tĭ), *n.* (The upper and lower limits are defined.) The right-angle hands, palms facing, are held before the body, the right above the left. They swing out 45 degrees simultaneously, pivoted from their wrists. *Cf.* LIMIT, QUANTITY 1, RESTRICT.

[C–42]

CAPITAL 1 (kăp´ ə təl), *n.* (The head indicates the head or seat of government.) The right index finger, pointing toward the right temple, describes a small clockwise circle and comes to rest on the right temple. *Cf.* GOVERNMENT, ST. PAUL (MINN.).

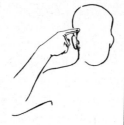

[C–43]

CAPITAL 2, *n.* (Slapping of paper money in the palm.) The upturned right hand, grasping some imaginary bills, is brought down into the upturned left palm a number of times. *Cf.* CURRENCY, FINANCES, FUNDS, MONEY 1.

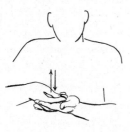

[C–44]

CAPSIZE (kăp sīz´), *v.,* -SIZED, -SIZING. (A turning over.) Both "5" hands are held before the body, facing each other, with the right a few inches above the left. They are both swung around and over so that their relative positions are now reversed.

[C–45]

CAPTAIN (kăp´ tən, -tĭn), *n.* (The epaulets.) The

fingertips of the downturned right "5" hand strike the right shoulder twice. *Cf.* OFFICER.

[C–46]

CAPTION (kăp´ shən), *n.* (The quotation marks are indicated.) The curved index and middle fingers of both hands, held palms out, move slightly to either side of the body, as if drawing quotation marks in the air. *Cf.* CITE, QUOTATION, QUOTE, SO-CALLED, SUBJECT, THEME, TITLE, TOPIC.

[C–47]

CAPTURE (kăp´ chər), *n., v.,* -TURED, -TURING. (Grasping something and holding it down.) Both hands, palms down, quickly close into the "S" position, the right on top of the left. *Cf.* CATCH 2, GRAB, GRASP, SEIZE.

[C–48]

CAR (kär), *n.* (The steering wheel.) The hands grasp an imaginary steering wheel and manipulate it. *Cf.* AUTOMOBILE, DRIVE.

[C–49]

CARD (kärd), *n.* (The natural sign.) The sides of the card are outlined with the thumb and index finger of each hand. *Cf.* TICKET 1.

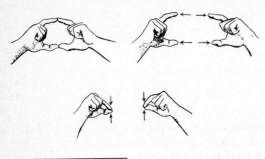

_____

[C–50]

CARDINAL (kär´ də nəl), *(eccles.)*, *n.* (A red bishop.) The sign for RED is made: The tip of the right index finger moves down across the lips. The "R" hand may also be used. This is followed by the sign for BISHOP 1: The ring finger of the right "S" hand is kissed. This is the sign for a Catholic bishop. The red refers to the cardinal's red hat or biretta.

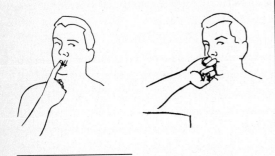

_____

[C–51]

CARD PLAYING (plā´ ǐng). (The action of dealing out cards.) The signer goes through the motions of dealing out imaginary playing cards. *Cf.* CARDS, DISTRIBUTE 2, PLAYING CARDS.

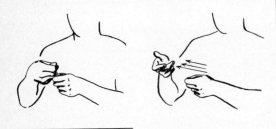

_____

[C–52]

CARDS (kärdz), *n. pl.* See CARD PLAYING.

[C–53]

CARE 1 (kâr), *n., v.,* CARED, CARING. (Slow, careful movement.) The "K" hands are crossed, the right above the left, little finger edges down. In this position they describe a small counterclockwise circle in front of the chest. *Cf.* CARE FOR, CAREFUL 1, TAKE CARE OF 3.

_____

[C–54]

CARE 2, *n., v.* With the hands in the same position as in CARE 1, they are moved up and down a short distance. *Cf.* CAREFUL 2, KEEP, MAINTAIN 1, MIND 3, PRESERVE, RESERVE 2, TAKE CARE OF 2.

_____

[C–55]

CARE FOR (fôr), *v. phrase.* See CARE 1.

_____

[C–56]

CAREFUL 1 (kâr´ fəl), *adj.* See CARE 1.

_____

[C–57]

CAREFUL 2, *adj.* See CARE 2.

_____

[C–58]

CAREFUL 3, *adj.* (The "K" for *keep* in the sense of *keeping carefully.*) Both "K" hands are crossed, the right atop the left. The right hand moves up and down a very short distance, several times, each time coming to rest on top of the left. *Cf.* BE CAREFUL, TAKE CARE OF 1.

[C-59]

CARELESS (kâr´ lĭs), *adj.* (The vision is side-tracked, causing one to lose sight of the object in view.) The right "V" hand, representing the vision, is held in front of the face, palm facing left. The hand, pivoted at the wrist, moves back and forth a number of times. *Cf.* HEEDLESS, RECKLESS, THOUGHTLESS.

[C-60]

CARIES (kâr´ ēz, -ĭēz´), *n.* (The hole in a tooth.) The right index finger "drills" into a tooth. The mouth is of course held wide open. *Cf.* CAVITY.

[C-61]

CARPENTER (kär´ pən tər), *n.* (Manipulating a carpenter's plane.) The hands grasp and manipulate an imaginary carpenter's plane. This is followed by the sign for INDIVIDUAL: Both open hands, palms facing each other, move down the sides of the body, tracing its outline to the hips. *Cf.* CABINETMAKER.

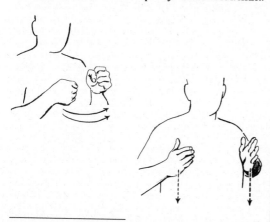

[C-62]

CARRIAGE 1 (kăr´ ij), *n.* (Holding the carriage.) The downturned hands grasp the handle bar of an imaginary carriage and move it forward and back once or twice.

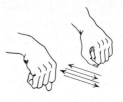

[C-63]

CARRIAGE 2, *n.* (The rolling wheels and the ears of the horse, defined by FINE or ELEGANT.) The index fingers of the "D" hands, pointing to each other, describe small circles in the air. They are then moved forward in unison and describe another series of circles, to define the wheels of the carriage. The "H" hands, palms facing out, are then placed at the sides of the head and the index and middle fingers of both hands move back and forth to describe the movement of a horse's ears. The thumb of the right "5" hand is then thrust into the chest—an act which indicates the "fineness" of the ruffled bosoms of ladies and shirt fronts of gentlemen of old. *Cf.* CART, CHARIOT.

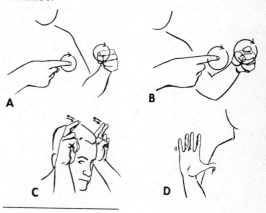

[C-64]

CARRY 1 (kăr´ ĭ), *v.,* -RIED, -RYING. (Act of conveying an object from one point to another.) The open hands are held palms up before the chest on the right side of the body. Describing an arc, they move up and forward in unison. *Cf.* CONVEY.

[C-65]

CARRY 2, *v.* (Carrying something over.) Both open hands, palms up, move in an arc from left to right, as if carrying something from one point to another. *Cf.* BRING, DELIVER 2, FETCH, PRODUCE 1, TRANSPORT.

[C-66]

CARS (kärz), *(arch.)*, *n. pl.* (Running along the tracks.) The "V" hands are held palms down. The right "V" moves back and forth over the left "V." *Cf.* RAILROAD 1, TRAIN 1.

[C-67]

CART (kärt), *n.* See CARRIAGE 2.

[C-68]

CARVE (kärv), *v.,* CARVED, CARVING. (Chipping or cutting out.) The right thumb tip repeatedly gouges out imaginary pieces of material from the palm of the left hand, held facing right. *Cf.* ENGRAVE, ETCH.

[C-69]

CASTE (kăst, käst), *n.* (A grouping together.) Both "C" hands, palms facing, are held a few inches apart at chest height. They are swung around in unison, so that the palms now face the body. *Cf.* ASSOCIATION, AUDIENCE 1, CIRCLE 2, CLASS, CLASSED 1, CLUB,

COMPANY, FAMILY 2, GANG, GROUP 1, JOIN 2, ORGANIZATION 1.

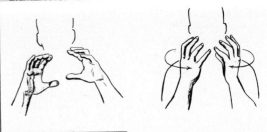

[C-70]

CAST OFF (kăst ôf´), *v. phrase,* CAST, CASTING. (To throw something aside.) Both "S" hands are held with palms facing at chest level and then thrown down and to the left, opening into the "5" position. *Cf.* ABANDON 1, DEPOSIT 2, DISCARD 1, FORSAKE 3, LEAVE 2, LET ALONE, NEGLECT.

[C-71]

CAST OUT (out), *(colloq.)*, *v. phrase.* (To toss up and out.) Both "S" hands, held at chest level with palms facing, are swung down slightly and then up into the air toward the left, opening into the "5" position. *Cf.* ABANDON 2, DISCARD 2, EVICT.

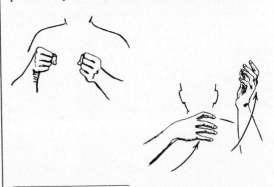

[C-72]

CAT (kăt), *n.* (The whiskers.) The thumbs and index fingers of both hands stroke an imaginary pair of whiskers at either side of the face. The right hand then strokes the back of the left, as if stroking the fur. This latter sign is seldom used today, however.

Also one hand may be used in place of two for the stroking of the whiskers.

act of catching.) Both hands quickly come together, as if catching a ball.

[C–73]

CATALOG (căt´ ə lôg´), *n.* (A book with a narrow spine.) The left hand, fingers together, is held upright, palm facing right. The right hand wraps around the lower edge of the left and travels up to the little finger. This denotes a narrow object. The sign for BOOK is then made: The hands are placed together, palm to palm, and then opened, as if opening a book. Sometimes this latter sign is omitted. *Cf.* BOOKLET, MAGAZINE, MANUAL, PAMPHLET.

[C–74]

CATASTROPHIC (kăt´ ə strŏf´ ĭk), *adj.* (Throwing out the hands.) Both hands, their fingertips touching their respective thumbs, are held, palms facing each other, near the temples. They are thrown out before the face, assuming "5" positions, palms still facing. *Cf.* AWFUL, CALAMITOUS, DANGER 1, DANGEROUS 1, DREADFUL, FEARFUL, TERRIBLE, TRAGEDY, TRAGIC.

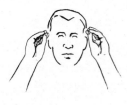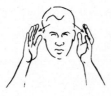

[C–75]

CATCH 1 (kăch), *n., v.,* CAUGHT, CATCHING. (The

[C–76]

CATCH 2, *v.* (Grasping something and holding it down.) Both hands, palms down, quickly close into the "S" position, the right on top of the left. *Cf.* CAPTURE, GRAB, GRASP, SEIZE.

[C–77]

CATCH 3, *v.* (Catching a ball.) Both hands go through the motions of catching a ball.

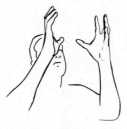

[C–78]

CATCHER (kăch´ ər), *n.* (One who catches a ball.) The sign for CATCH 3 is made, followed by the sign for INDIVIDUAL: Both open hands, palms facing each other, move down the sides of the body, tracing its outline to the hips.

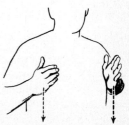

[C–79]

CATHOLIC (kăth´ ə lĭk, kăth´ lĭk), *adj.* (The cross.) The extended index and middle fingers make the sign of the cross before the face, moving down from the forehead and then across the face from left to right.

[C–80]

CAUGHT IN THE ACT 1 (kôt ĭn t͟hi ăkt), *v. phrase.* (A pinning down.) The left "D" finger represents the one who is caught. The curved index and middle fingers of the right hand, palm facing down, are thrust against the left "D" finger, impaling it. *Cf.* CONTACT 2, CORNER 2.

[C–81]

CAUGHT IN THE ACT 2, *v. phrase.* (Impaled on a stick, as a snake's head.) The "V" fingers are thrust into the throat. *Cf.* CHOKE 2, STRANDED, STUCK 2, TRAP.

[C–82]

CAUSE (kôz), *n., v.,* CAUSED, CAUSING. (Rays of influence emanating from a given source.) All the right fingertips, including the thumb, are positioned on the tip of the upturned thumb of the left "A" hand. The right hand, opening into the downturned "5" position, moves forward from its initial position.

Instead of its initial position on the left thumb, the right hand is frequently placed on the back of the downturned left "S" hand, moving forward as described above. *Cf.* BASIS 1, EFFECT 1, INFLUENCE 2, INTENT 2, LOGIC, PRODUCE 4, REASON 2.

[C–83]

CAUTION (kô´ shən), *n.* (Tapping one to draw attention to danger.) The right hand taps the back of the left several times. *Cf.* ADMONISH 1, FOREWARN, WARN.

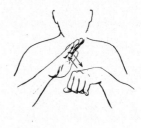

[C–84]

CAVE IN (kāv ĭn´), *v. phrase,* CAVED, CAVING. (A collapsing.) Both "5" hands, fingertips joined before the chest, swing down so that the fingertips face down. *Cf.* BREAKDOWN, COLLAPSE.

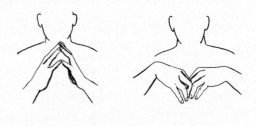

[C–85]

CAVITY (kăv´ ə tĭ), *n.* (The hole in a tooth.) The right index finger "drills" into a tooth. The mouth is of course held wide open. *Cf.* CARIES.

[C–86]

CEASE (sēs), *n., v.,* CEASED, CEASING. (A stopping or cutting short.) The little finger edge of the right hand is thrust abruptly into the upturned left palm, indicating a cutting short. *Cf.* ARREST 2, HALT, STOP.

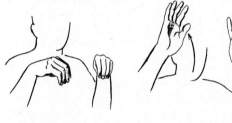

[C–87]

CEDE (sēd), *v.,* CEDED, CEDING. (Throwing up the hands in a gesture of surrender.) Both "A" hands are held palms down before the chest and then thrown up in unison, ending in the "5" position. *Cf.* ABDICATE, DISCOURAGE 1, FORFEIT, GIVE UP, LOSE HOPE, RELINQUISH, RENOUNCE, RENUNCIATION, SURRENDER 1, YIELD.

[C–88]

CELEBRATE (sĕl´ ə brāt´), *v.,* -BRATED, -BRATING. (Waving of flags.) Both upright hands, grasping imaginary flags, wave them in small circles. *Cf.* CELEBRATION, CHEER, REJOICE, VICTORY 1, WIN 1.

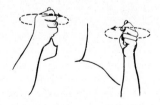

[C–89]

CELEBRATED (sĕl´ ə brā´ tĭd), *adj.* (One's fame radiates far and wide.) The extended index fingers rest on the lips (or on the temples). Moving in small, continuous spirals, they move up and to either side of the head. *Cf.* FAME, FAMOUS, PROMINENT 1, RENOWNED.

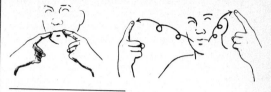

[C–90]

CELEBRATION (sĕl´ ə brā´ shən), *n.* See CELEBRATE.

[C–91]

CEMETERY (sĕm´ ə tĕr´ ĭ), *n.* (The mound of a grave.) The downturned open hands, slightly cupped, are held side by side. They describe an arc as they are drawn in toward the body. *Cf.* BURY, GRAVE 1.

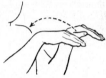

[C–92]

CENT (sĕnt), *n.* (The Lincoln head.) The right index finger touches the right temple and moves up and away quickly. This is "one cent." For two cents, the "2" hand is used, etc. *Cf.* CENTS, PENNY.

[C–93]

CENTER (sĕnt´ ər), *n., v.,* -TERED, -TERING. (The natural sign.) The downturned right fingers describe a small clockwise circle and come to rest in the center of the upturn left palm. *Cf.* CENTRAL, MIDDLE.

[C-94]

CENTRAL (sĕn´ trəl), *adj.* See CENTER.

[C-95]

CENTS, *n. pl.* See CENT.

[C-96]

CENTURY (sĕn´ chə ri), *n.* (One hundred years.) The sign for ONE HUNDRED is made: ONE and "C". This is followed by the sign for YEAR: The right "S" hand, palm facing left, represents the earth. It is positioned atop the left "S" hand, whose palm faces right, and represents the sun. The right "S" hand describes a complete circle around the left, and comes to rest in its original position. *Cf.* ONE HUNDRED YEARS.

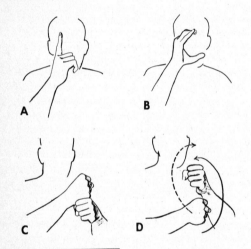

A   B

C   D

[C-97]

CERAMICS (sə răm´ iks), *n. pl.* (The wetness and softness of ceramic material before firing.) The fingers of both hands open and close against the thumbs a number of times. *Cf.* CLAY, DAMP, MOIST, WET.

[C-98]

CERTAIN (sûr´ tən), *adj.* (Coming forth directly from the lips; true.) The index finger of the right "D"

hand, palm facing left, is placed against the lips. It moves up an inch or two and then describes a small arc forward and away from the lips. *Cf.* ABSOLUTE, ABSOLUTELY, ACTUAL, ACTUALLY, AUTHENTIC, CERTAINLY, FAITHFUL 3, FIDELITY, FRANKLY, GENUINE, INDEED, POSITIVE 1, POSITIVELY, REAL, REALLY, SINCERE 2, SURE, SURELY, TRUE, TRULY, TRUTH, VALID, VERILY.

[C-99]

CERTAINLY (sûr´ tən li), *adv.* See CERTAIN.

[C-100]

CHAIN (chān), *n.* (The links.) The thumbs and index fingers of both hands interlock, separate, reverse their relative positions, and interlock again.

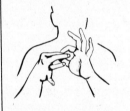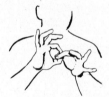

[C-101]

CHAIR 1 (châr), *n.* (The act of sitting.) The extended right index and middle fingers are draped across the back of the same two fingers of the downturned left hand. The hands then move straight downward a short distance. *Cf.* BE SEATED, SEAT, SIT 1.

[C-102]

CHAIR 2, *n.* (Act of sitting down; the legs of the chair.) Both hands, palms down, are held before the chest, and they move down a short distance in unison. The downturned index fingers are then thrust downward a few inches, moved in toward the body, and thrust downward once again, to represent the four legs of the chair. *Cf.* SIT 2.

pointing straight up, palms facing the body. They come together forcefully, moving down a bit as they do, and the knuckles of one hand strike those of the other. *Cf.* GAME 1, OPPORTUNITY 2, VERSUS.

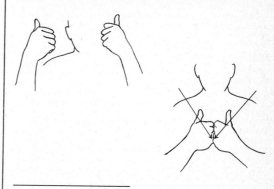

[C–103]

CHAIR 3, *n.* (A rocking chair.) The "L" hands, palms facing each other and about two feet apart, are held before the chest. They arc up and down toward the shoulders a number of times. The body is sometimes rocked back and forth in time with the movement of the hands. *Cf.* ROCKING CHAIR 1.

[C–104]

CHALK (chôk), *n.* (A white crayon.) The sign for WHITE is made: The open palm is placed on the chest, and it is drawn away, all fingertips coming together on the thumb. The length of chalk, represented by the left index finger, is next defined by the thumb and index finger of the right hand.

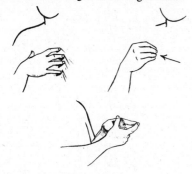

[C–105]

CHALLENGE (chăl´ ĭnj), *n., v.,* -LENGED, -LENGING. (Two individuals pitted against each other.) The hands are held in the "A" position, thumbs

[C–106]

CHAMPION (chăm´ pĭ ən), *(sports), n.* (The head is crowned.) The upturned left index finger represents the victorious individual. The downturned "5" hand, fingers curved, is brought down on the left index finger as if draping it with a crown. *Cf.* CROWNED.

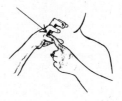

[C–107]

CHANCE (chăns, chäns), *n., v.,* CHANCED, CHANCING, *adj.* (A befalling.) Both "D" hands, index fingers pointing away from the body, are simultaneously pivoted over so that the palms face down. *Cf.* ACCIDENT, BEFALL, COINCIDE 1, COINCIDENCE, EVENT, HAPPEN 1, INCIDENT, OCCUR, OPPORTUNITY 4.

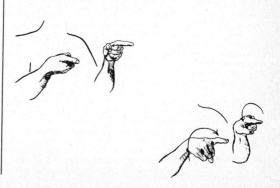

[C-108]

CHANGE 1 (chānj), *v.,* CHANGED, CHANGING, *n.* (The position of the hands is altered.) Both "A" hands, thumbs up, are held before the chest, several inches apart. The left hand is pivoted over so that its thumb points to the right. Simultaneously, the right hand is moved up and over the left, describing a small arc, with its thumb pointing to the left. *Cf.* ADJUST, ALTER, ALTERATION, CONVERT, MODIFY, REVERSE 2, TRANSFER 1.

[C-109]

CHANGE 2, *n., v.* The "A" hands are held before the chest, right behind the left. The right hand swings under the left.

[C-110]

CHANGEABLE (chăn' jə bəl), *adj.* (Changing again and again.) The "5" hands, fingers curved and palms facing, swing in unison, in alternate clockwise and counterclockwise directions, with the left and right hands alternating in front of each other. *Cf.* WISHY-WASHY.

[C-111]

CHANT (chănt, chänt), *n.* (A rhythmic, wavy movement of the hand, to indicate a melody; the movement of a conductor's hand in directing a musical performance.) The right "5" hand, palm facing left, is waved back and forth over the downturned left

hand, in a series of elongated figure-eights. *Cf.* HYMN 1, MELODY, MUSIC, SING, SONG.

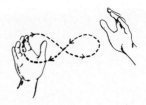

[C-112]

CHANUKAH (hä' nōō kä´), *(eccles.), n.* (The eight candles.) The upturned right index finger is placed at the pursed lips (a candle). The "4" hands, side by side, palms out before the face, separate slowly, making a total of eight candles, the symbol of this Jewish festival. *Cf.* MENORAH.

[C-113]

CHAPEL (chăp' əl), *n.* (The letter "C," set up on a firm foundation, as a building.) The base of the thumb of the right "C" hand is brought down to rest on the back of the downturned open left hand. The action may be repeated twice. *Cf.* CHURCH 1.

[C-114]

CHAPTER (chăp' tər), *n.* (A section of a page.) The palm of the left "C" hand faces right, representing a page. The fingertips of the right "C" hand, representing a section of the page, move straight down against the left palm.

[C-115]

CHARACTER 1 (kăr´ĭk tər), *n*. (The heart is defined by the letter "C.") The right "C" hand, palm facing left, describes a circle against the heart.

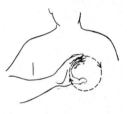

[C-116]

CHARACTER 2, *n*. The "C" is again placed on the heart, and then the index fingers outline the heart itself.

[C-117]

CHARGE 1 (chärj), *v.,* CHARGED, CHARGING, *n*. (Nicking into one.) The knuckle of the right "X" finger is nicked against the palm of the left hand, held in the "5" position, palm facing right. *Cf.* AD-MISSION 2, COST, DUTY 2, EXCISE, EXPENSE, FEE, FINE 2, IMPOST, PENALTY 3, PRICE 2, TAX 1, TAXA-TION 1, TOLL.

[C-118]

CHARGE 2, *v., n*. (A bank or charge account—act of signing the name on paper.) The index finger and thumb of the right hand go through the natural motion of scribbling across the left palm. Then the fingers of the right "H" hand, palm facing down, are thrust against the left palm, as if placing the name on a piece of paper. As an alternate, the closed

fingers of the right hand may be thrust into the left palm. *Cf.* ACCOUNT.

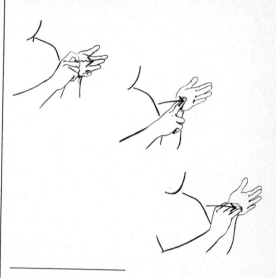

[C-119]

CHARIOT (char´ĭ ət), *n*. (The rolling wheels and the ears of the horse, defined by FINE or ELEGANT.) The index fingers of the "D" hands, pointing to each other, describe small circles in the air. They are then moved forward in unison and describe another series of circles, to define the wheels of the carriage. The "H" hands, palms facing out, are then placed at the sides of the head and the index and middle fingers of both hands move back and forth to describe the movement of a horse's ears. The thumb of the right "5" hand is then thrust into the chest—an act which indicates the "fineness" of the ruffled bosoms of la-dies and shirt fronts of gentlemen of old. *Cf.* CAR-RIAGE, CART.

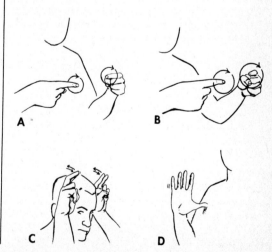

A   B

C   D

[C–120]

CHARITY (chăr′ ə tǐ), *n.* (Clasping the heart.) The "5" hands are held one atop the other over the heart. Sometimes the "S" hands are used, in which case they are crossed at the wrists. *Cf.* BELOVED, DEVOTION, LOVE, REVERE 2.

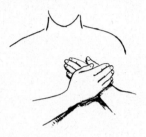

[C–121]

CHASE 1 (chās), *v.*, CHASED, CHASING. (The natural sign.) The "A" hands are held in front of the body, with the thumbs facing forward, the right palm facing left and the left palm facing right. The left hand is held slightly ahead of the right; it then moves forward in a straight line while the right hand follows after, executing a circular motion or swerving back and forth, as if in pursuit. *Cf.* PURSUE.

[C–122]

CHASE 2, *(voc.)*, *n.* (The printer's chase outlined.) The downturned index finger and thumb of each hand outline the square shape of a frame. *Cf.* FRAME.

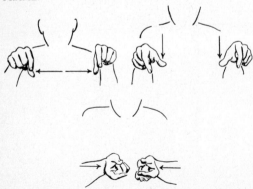

[C–123]

CHASTITY (chăs′ tə tǐ), *n.* (The letter "P," for PURE, passed over the palm to denote clean.) The right "P" hand moves forward along the palm of the upturned left hand, which is held flat, with fingers pointing forward. *Cf.* PURE 2.

[C–124]

CHAT (chăt), *n., v.,* CHATTED, CHATTING. (Words tossed back and forth.) The open hands are held side by side with palms up, fingers pointing forward and slightly curved. In this position the hands swing back and forth from side to side before the chest. *Cf.* CONVERSATION 2.

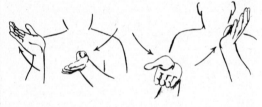

[C–125]

CHEAP 1 (chēp), *adj.* (A small amount of money.) The sign for MONEY is made: The upturned right hand, grasping some imaginary bills, is brought down into the upturned left palm a number of times. The downturned cupped right hand is then positioned over the upturned cupped left hand. The right hand descends a short distance but does not touch the left. *Cf.* INEXPENSIVE.

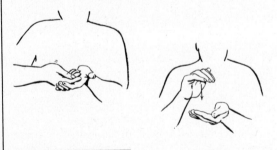

[C–126]

CHEAP 2, *(colloq.)*, *adj.* (Something easily moved,

therefore of no consequence.) The right fingertips slap the little finger edge of the upturned left hand.

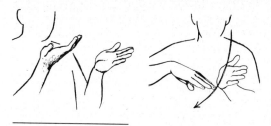

[C–127]

CHEAT 1 (chēt), *v.*, CHEATED, CHEATING. (Underhandedness.) The right hand, palm down, is held with index and little fingers pointing out. The left hand, in a similar position, is held above the right. The right hand moves forward repeatedly, each time emerging briefly from under the left hand. The positions may be reversed, with the left hand doing the movement, or both hands can move simultaneously. *Cf.* DECEIT, DECEIVE, DECEPTION, DEFRAUD, FRAUD, FRAUDULENT 1.

[C–128]

CHEAT 2, *v.*, CHEATED, CHEATING. (Removing.) The right "A" hand, resting in the palm of the left "5" hand, moves slightly up and away, describing a small arc. It is then cast downward, opening into the "5" position, palm down, as if removing something from the left hand and casting it down. *Cf.* ABOLISH 2, ABSENCE 2, ABSENT 2, ABSTAIN, DEDUCT, DEFICIENCY, DELETE 1, LESS 2, MINUS 3, OUT 2, REMOVE 1, SUBTRACT, SUBTRACTION, TAKE AWAY FROM, WITHDRAW 2.

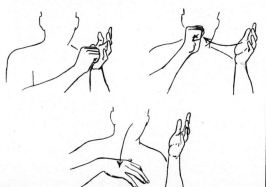

[C–129]

CHECK 1 (chĕk), *v.*, CHECKED, CHECKING. (A canceling out.) The right index finger makes a cross on the open left palm. *Cf.* ANNUL, CANCEL, CORRECT 2, CRITICISM, CRITICIZE, FIND FAULT 1, REVOKE.

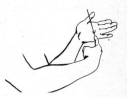

[C–130]

CHECK 2, *v.* (Obstruct, block.) The left hand, fingers together and palm flat, is held before the body, facing somewhat down. The little finger side of the right hand, held with palm flat, makes one or several up-down chopping motions against the left hand, between its thumb and index finger. *Cf.* ANNOY 1, ANNOYANCE 1, BLOCK, BOTHER 1, COME BETWEEN, DISRUPT, DISTURB, HINDER, HINDRANCE, IMPEDE, INTERCEPT, INTERFERE, INTERFERENCE, INTERFERE WITH, INTERRUPT, MEDDLE 1, OBSTACLE, OBSTRUCT, PREVENT, PREVENTION.

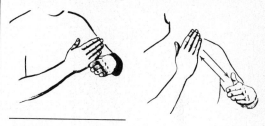

[C–131]

CHECK 3, *n.* (A bank check.) The sign for CARD is made: The sides of the card are outlined with the thumb and index finger of each hand. This is followed by the sign for MONEY: The back of the right hand, palm up and fingers touching the thumb, is placed in the upturned left hand.

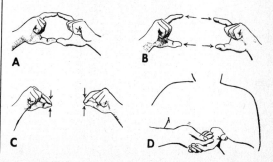

A   B

C   D

[C–132]

CHECK 4, *n.* (A baggage check or ticket.) The sign for CARD is made: The sides of the card are outlined with the thumb and index finger of each hand. This is followed by the sign for TICKET: The middle knuckles of the second and third fingers of the right hand squeeze the outer edge of the left palm, as a conductor's ticket punch. *Cf.* TICKET 2.

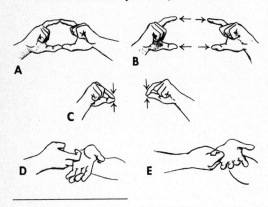

A **B**

C

D **E**

[C–133]

CHEEK (chĕk), *(colloq.), n.* (The cheek is indicated.) The knuckles of the right index and middle fingers are thrust or twisted against the right cheek. *Cf.* NERVE, NERVY.

[C–134]

CHEER (chîr), *n.* (Waving of flags.) Both upright hands, grasping imaginary flags, wave them in small circles. *Cf.* CELEBRATE, CELEBRATION, REJOICE, VICTORY 1, WIN 1.

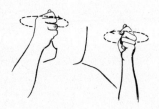

[C–135]

CHEERFUL (chîr´ fəl), *adj.* (A crinkling-up of the face.) Both hands, in the "5" position, palms facing back, are placed on either side of the face. The fingers wiggle back and forth, while a pleasant, happy expression is worn. *Cf.* AMIABLE, CORDIAL, FRIENDLY, JOLLY, PLEASANT.

[C–136]

CHEESE (chēz), *n.* (The pressing of cheese.) The base of the downturned right hand is pressed against the base of the upturned left hand, and the two rotate back and forth against each other.

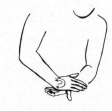

[C–137]

CHEF (shĕf), *n.* (Turning over a pancake.) The open right hand rests on the upturned left palm. The right hand flips over and comes to rest with its back on the left palm. This is the action of turning over a pancake. The sign for INDIVIDUAL then follows: Both open hands, palms facing each other, move down the sides of the body, tracing its outline to the hips. *Cf.* COOK, KITCHEN 1, PANCAKE.

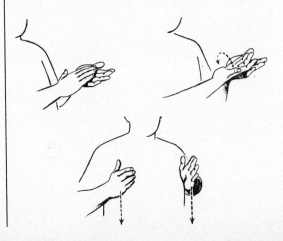

[C-138]

CHEMIST (kĕm´ ĭst), *n.* See CHEMISTRY. This is followed by the sign for INDIVIDUAL 1: Both open hands, palms facing each other, move down the sides of the body, tracing its outline to the hips.

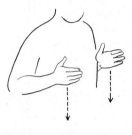

[C-139]

CHEMISTRY (kĕm´ ĭs trĭ), *n.* (Pouring alternately from test tubes.) The upright thumbs of both "A" hands swing over alternately, as if pouring out the contents of a pair of test tubes. *Cf.* SCIENCE 2.

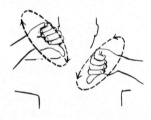

[C-140]

CHEST 1 (chĕst), *n.* (The chest is indicated.) One or both open hands are placed on the chest, either once or twice.

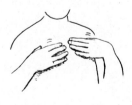

[C-141]

CHEST 2, *n.* (A wooden structure with drawers.) The sign for WOOD is made: The little finger edge of the open right hand moves back and forth in a sawing motion over the back of the downturned left hand. This is followed by an outlining of the top and sides of the chest. Finally the upturned "A" hands pull out an imaginary drawer. For a steel chest or a

chest of other material the sign for WOOD is either omitted or replaced by another qualifying sign.

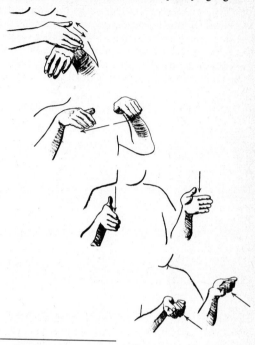

[C-142]

CHEW (cho͞o), *v.*, CHEWED, CHEWING. (The grinding of teeth.) The knuckles of the downturned right "A" hand are placed against those of the upturned left "A" hand. The two hands "grind" against each other, in opposite directions. *Cf.* MASTICATE.

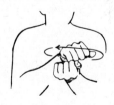

[C-143]

CHICAGO (shĭ kô´ gō, -kä´-), *n.* (The letter "C.") The right "C" hand, palm facing out, describes an inverted "S" curve, moving down as it does.

[C–144]

CHICKEN (chĭk´ ən, -ĭn), *n.* (The bill and the scratching.) The right index finger and thumb open and close as they are held pointing out from the mouth. (This is the root sign for any kind of bird.) The right "X" finger then scratches against the upturned left palm, as if scratching for food. The scratching is sometimes omitted. *Cf.* FOWL, HEN.

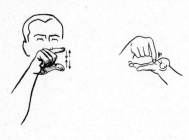

[C–145]

CHICKEN POX (pŏks). (The pocked face.) The right index and thumb describe pock marks on the right cheek.

[C–146]

CHIEF (chēf), *n., adj.* (The largest or greatest amount.) The sign for MUCH is made: The "5" hands, palms facing, fingers curved and thumbs pointing up, draw apart. The sign for the superlative suffix, "-EST," *q.v.,* is then made: The right "A" hand, thumb pointing up, quickly moves straight upward, until it is above the head. *Cf.* MAINLY, MOST, MOST OF ALL, PRINCIPAL 2.

[C–147]

CHILD (chīld), *n.* (The child's height.) The down-

turned right palm is extended before the body, as if resting on a child's head.

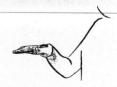

[C–148]

CHILDREN (chĭl´ drən), *n.* (Indicating different heights of children; patting the children on their heads.) The downturned right palm, held before the body, executes a series of movements from left to right, as if patting a number of children on their heads.

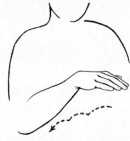

[C–149]

CHILLY (chĭl´ ĭ), *adj.* (The trembling from cold.) Both "S" hands, palms facing, are placed at the sides of the body. In this position the arms and hands shiver. *Cf.* COLD 1, FRIGID, SHIVER 1, WINTER 1.

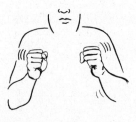

[C–150]

CHIN (chĭn), *n.* The chin is touched with the extended index finger.

[C–151]

CHINA 1 (chī′ nə), *n.* (Slanting eyes.) The index fingers draw back the corners of the eyes, causing them to slant. *Cf.* ASIA, CHINESE, ORIENTAL.

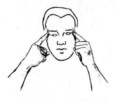

[C–152]

CHINA 2, *n.* (The finger touches a brittle substance.) The index finger is brought up to touch the exposed front teeth. *Cf.* BONE, DISH, GLASS 1, PLATE, PORCELAIN.

[C–153]

CHINESE (chī nēz′, -nēs′), *n., adj.* See CHINA 1.

[C–154]

CHIP IN (chĭp), *(colloq.), v. phrase,* CHIPPED, CHIPPING. (Paying in.) The "AND" hands are held about a foot apart in front of the body, with fingertips facing each other and palms toward the chest. From this position the hands move downward and toward each other in an arc. At the same time, both thumbs slide forward along the index fingers. *Cf.* POOL.

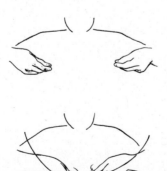

[C–155]

CHISEL (chĭz′ əl), *n., v.,* -ELED, -ELING. (Gouging out the wood.) The right "U" hand, palm down, is held before the chest. The index and middle fingers are swept down against the upturned left palm, and move forward against the palm.

[C–156]

CHOCOLATE (chôk′ ə lĭt, chŏk′-, chôk′ lĭt, chŏk′-), *n., adj.* The thumb of the right "C" hand, resting against the back of the downturned left "S" hand, makes a series of small counterclockwise circles.

[C–157]

CHOICE (chois), *n.* (Making a choice.) The left "V" hand faces the body. The right thumb and index finger close first over the left index fingertip and then over the left middle fingertip. *Cf.* EITHER 2.

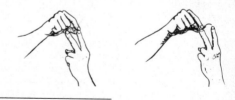

[C–158]

CHOKE 1 (chōk), *v.* CHOKED, CHOKING. (Catching one by the throat.) The right hand makes a natural movement of grabbing the throat. *Cf.* STUCK 1.

[C-159]

CHOKE 2, *v., n.* (Impaled on a stick, as a snake's head.) The "V" fingers are thrust into the throat. *Cf.* CAUGHT IN THE ACT 2, STRANDED, STUCK 2, TRAP.

[C-160]

CHOOSE 1 (chōōz), *v.,* CHOSE, CHOSEN, CHOOSING. (Taking unto oneself.) The right hand, palm out, is extended before the chest, index finger and thumb in an open position, the other fingers separated and pointing up. The hand is drawn in toward the chest, and the index and thumb close at the same time, indicating something taken to oneself. *Cf.* ADOPT, APPOINT, SELECT 2, TAKE.

[C-161]

CHOOSE 2, *v.* (The natural motion of selecting something from the hand.) The thumb and index fingers of the outstretched right hand grasp an imaginary object on the upturned left palm. The right hand then moves straight up. *Cf.* DISCOVER, FIND, PICK 1, SELECT 1.

[C-162]

CHRIST (krīst), *(eccles.), n.* The right "C" hand is placed against the left shoulder and slides down across the chest to the right hip. The movement from shoulder to hip outlines the band worn across the chest by royalty.

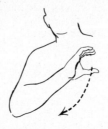

[C-163]

CHRISTIAN (krĭs´ chən), *n., adj.* (An individual who follows Jesus.) The sign for JESUS is made: Both "5" hands are used. The left middle finger touches the right palm, and then the right middle finger touches the left palm. This is followed by the sign for INDIVIDUAL: Both open hands, palms facing each other, move down the sides of the body, tracing its outline to the hips. Other ways to make this sign involve the signs for JESUS, and BELIEVER, FOLLOWER, or FRIEND. Another way is to make the signs for CHRIST and INDIVIDUAL.

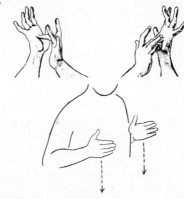

[C-164]

CHRISTIAN BROTHERS, *(eccles.), n.* (The white collar-piece worn by religious brothers.) The thumb and index finger of one hand are placed just below the throat, and move down, describing the white hanging collar-piece. *Cf.* BROTHER 2.

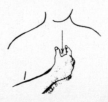

[C–165]

CHRISTIANITY (kris′ chĭ ăn′ ə tĭ), *n*. (Jesus, group.) The sign for JESUS is made: Both "5" hands are used. The left middle finger touches the right palm, and then the right middle finger touches the left palm. This is followed by the sign for GROUP 1: Both "C" hands, palms facing, are held a few inches apart at chest height. They are swung around in unison so that the palms now face the body.

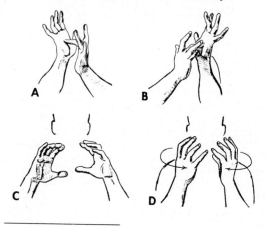

[C–166]

CHRISTMAS 1 (kris′ məs), *n*. (The shape of the wreath.) The right "C" hand, palm facing out, describes an arc from left to right. *Cf.* WREATH.

[C–167]

CHRISTMAS 2, *n*. (Jesus's birthday.) The sign for JESUS is made. This is followed by the sign for BIRTHDAY: The sign for BIRTH, 1, 2, or 3 is made, followed by the sign for DAY: The right "D" hand, pointing straight up, elbow resting on the downturned left hand, moves down to a horizontal position, describing the path of the sun across the sky, and comes to a rest atop the left arm.

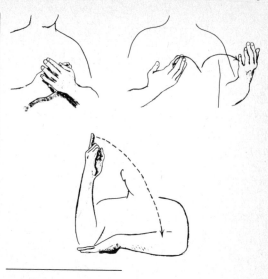

[C–168]

CHURCH 1 (chûrch), *n*. (The letter "C," set up on a firm foundation, as a building.) The base of the thumb of the right "C" hand is brought down to rest on the back of the downturned open left hand. The action may be repeated twice. *Cf.* CHAPEL.

[C–169]

CHURCH 2, *n*. ("Sunday house.") The fingertips of both hands are placed together to indicate the sloping roof of a house. The sign for SUNDAY is then made: The "5" hands, held side by side, palms out, before the body, move straight down a short distance. They may also move slightly out as they move down.

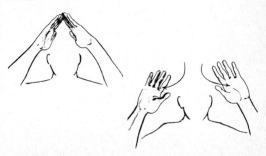

[C–170]

CIGAR 1 (sĭ gär´), *n.* (The shape.) The right hand, in the "1" position, is placed with the base of the thumb against the lips. The extended index finger indicates the cigar.

[C–171]

CIGAR 2, *n.* (The shape.) The right hand, in a grasping position and palm facing left, moves forward from the slightly open mouth, closing into the "S" position.

[C–172]

CIGARETTE (sĭg´ ə rĕt´, sĭg´ ə rĕt´), *n.* (The dimensions of the cigarette.) The index and little fingers of the right hand, palm facing down, are placed upon the left index finger, so that the right index finger rests on the knuckle of the left index finger and the right little finger rests on the tip of the left index finger.

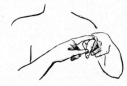

[C–173]

CINEMA (sĭn´ ə mə), *n.* (The frames of the film speeding through the projector.) The left "5" hand, palm facing right and thumb pointing up, is the projector. The right "5" hand is placed against the left, and moves back and forth quickly. *Cf.* FILM, MOTION PICTURE, MOVIE(S), MOVING PICTURE.

[C–174]

CIRCLE 1 (sûr´ kəl), *n., v.,* -CLED, -CLING. (The circle is described.) The index finger, pointing down or out, describes a circle. *Cf.* ROUND 2.

[C–175]

CIRCLE 2, *n., v.* (A grouping together.) Both "C" hands, palms facing, are held a few inches apart at chest height. They are swung around in unison, so that the palms now face the body. *Cf.* ASSOCIATION, AUDIENCE 1, CASTE, CLASS, CLASSED 1, CLUB, COMPANY, FAMILY 2, GANG, GROUP 1, JOIN 2, ORGANIZATION 1.

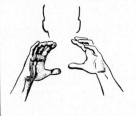

[C–176]

CITE (sīt), *v.,* CITED, CITING, (The quotation marks are indicated.) The curved index and middle fingers of both hands, held palms out, move slightly to either side of the body, as if drawing quotation marks in the air. *Cf.* CAPTION, QUOTATION, QUOTE, SO-CALLED, SUBJECT, THEME, TITLE, TOPIC.

[C–177]

CITIZEN (sĭt´ ə zən, -sən), *n.* The sign for INDIVIDUAL 1 is made: Both open hands, palms facing each other, move down the sides of the body, tracing its outline to the hips.

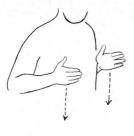

[C-178]

CITY (sĭt´ ĭ), *n.* (A collection of rooftops.) The fingertips of both hands are joined, the hands and arms forming a pyramid. The fingertips separate and rejoin a number of times. Both arms may move a bit from left to right each time the fingertips separate and rejoin. *Cf.* COMMUNITY 2, TOWN.

[C-179]

CLAP (klăp), *v.,* CLAPPED, CLAPPING, *n.* (Good words coming from the mouth; clapping hands.) The fingertips of the right hand, palm flat and facing the body, are brought up to the lips, so that they touch (part of the sign for GOOD, *q.v.*). The hands are then clapped together several times. *Cf.* ACCLAIM 2, APPLAUD, APPLAUSE, APPROBATION, APPROVAL, APPROVE, COMMEND, CONGRATULATE 1, CONGRATULATIONS 1, PRAISE.

[C-180]

CLASS (klăs, kläs), *n.* (A grouping together.) Both "C" hands, palms facing, are held a few inches apart

at chest height. They are swung around in unison, so that the palms now face the body. *Cf.* ASSOCIATION, AUDIENCE 1, CASTE, CIRCLE 2, CLASSED 1, CLUB, COMPANY, FAMILY 2, GANG, GROUP 1, JOIN 2, ORGANIZATION 1.

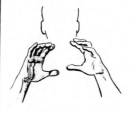

[C-181]

CLASSED 1, *v.* See CLASS.

[C-182]

CLASSED 2, *v.* (Placing things in order.) The hands, palms facing, fingers together and pointing away from the body, are positioned at the left side and held about a foot apart. With a slight up-down motion, as if describing waves, the hands travel in unison from left to right. *Cf.* ARRANGE, ARRANGEMENT, DEVISE 1, ORDER 3, PLAN 1, POLICY 1, PREPARE 1, PROGRAM 1, PROVIDE 1, PUT IN ORDER, READY 1, SCHEME, SYSTEM.

[C-183]

CLAW HAMMER, *(voc.), n. phrase.* (The natural sign.) The right "S" hand is held above the right shoulder, as if preparing to strike the left "S" hand, which is held below the right shoulder, thumb edge facing up. From this position the right hand moves forcefully in an arc toward the left hand.

[C-184]

CLAY (klā), *n.* (The softness.) The fingers of both hands open and close against the thumbs a number of times. *Cf.* CERAMICS, DAMP, MOIST, WET.

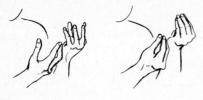

[C-185]

CLEAN 1 (klēn), *adj.* (Everything is wiped off the hand, to emphasize an uncluttered or clean condition.) The right hand slowly wipes the upturned left palm, from wrist to fingertips. *Cf.* IMMACULATE, NEAT, NICE, PLAIN 2, PURE 1, PURITY, SIMPLE 2.

[C-186]

CLEAN 2, *v.,* CLEANED, CLEANING. (Rubbing the clothes.) The knuckles of the "A" hands rub against one another, in circles. *Cf.* WASH 1.

[C-187]

CLEAR (klir), *adj.* (Rays of light clearing the way.) Both hands are held at chest height, palms out, all fingertips together. They open into the "5" position in unison, the right hand moving toward the right and the left toward the left. The palms of both hands remain facing out. *Cf.* BRIGHT 1, BRILLIANCE 1, BRILLIANT 2, EXPLICIT 2, OBVIOUS, PLAIN 1.

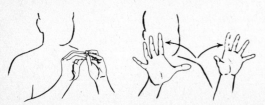

[C-188]

CLEVER 1 (klĕv´ ər), *adj.* (The mind is bright.) The middle finger is placed at the forehead, and then the hand, with an outward flick, turns around so that the palm faces outward. This indicates a brightness flowing from the mind. *Cf.* BRIGHT 3, BRILLIANT 1, INTELLIGENT, SMART.

[C-189]

CLEVER 2, *adj.* (Modification of CLEVER 1.) The right "5" hand, palm facing the signer, is placed with the tip of the middle finger touching the forehead. The hand swings quickly out and around, moving up an inch or two as it does so. *Cf.* SHARP 3.

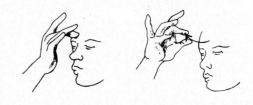

[C-190]

CLIENT 1 (klī´ ənt), *n.* (One who is advised.) The sign for ADVICE is reversed: The closed fingertips of the right hand rest on top of the downturned left hand. The right hand is brought in toward the chest, opening into the downturned "5" position. This is followed by the sign for INDIVIDUAL: Both open hands, palms facing each other, move down the sides of the body, tracing its outline to the hips.

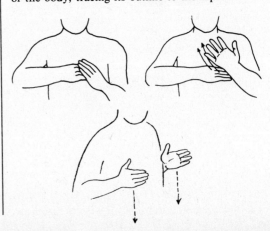

[C-191]

CLIENT 2, *n.* (The letter "C.") The "C" hands move down the sides of the body, as in INDIVIDUAL 1, *q.v.*

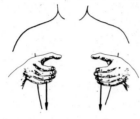

[C-192]

CLIMB 1 (klīm), *v.*, CLIMBED, CLIMBING, *n.* (One hand over the other.) One hand is lifted above the other, as if climbing a pole or tree.

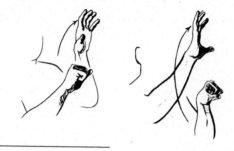

[C-193]

CLIMB 2, *v., n.* (Rising.) The right open hand, palm up, moves slowly up. *Cf.* ASCEND, LADDER.

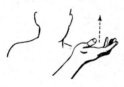

[C-194]

CLIMB 3, *v.* (Climbing up a ladder.) The left "V" hand, palm facing out, serves as the ladder. The right index and middle fingers "walk" up along the back of the left hand, starting at the wrist.

[C-195]

CLOAK (klōk), *n.* (The lapels are outlined.) The tips of the "A" thumbs outline the lapels of the cloak. *Cf.* COAT, OVERCOAT.

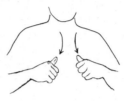

[C-196]

CLOCK (klŏk), *n.* (Time by the clock, indicated by the ticking of the clock or watch.) The curved right index finger taps the back of the left wrist several times. *Cf.* TIME 1, WATCH 3.

[C-197]

CLOSE 1 (*adj., adv.* klōs; *v.* klōz), CLOSED, CLOS-ING. (The act of closing.) Both "B" hands, held palms out before the body, come together with some force. *Cf.* SHUT.

[C-198]

CLOSE (TO) 2, *adj.* (One hand is near the other.) The left hand, cupped, fingers together, is held before the chest, palm facing the body. The right hand, also cupped, fingers together, moves a very short distance back and forth, as it is held in front of the left. *Cf.* ADJACENT, BESIDE, BY 1, NEAR 1, NEIGH-BOR, NEIGHBORHOOD, VICINITY.

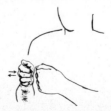

[C–199]

CLOSET (klŏz´ ĭt), *n., v.,* -ETED, -ETING. The extended index and middle fingers of the right hand strike across the back and then the front of the same two fingers of the left hand, which is held with palm facing the chest.

[C–200]

CLOTHES (klōz, klōthz), *n. pl.* (Draping the clothes on the body.) With fingertips resting on the chest, both hands move down simultaneously. The action is repeated. *Cf.* CLOTHING, DRESS, FROCK, GARMENT, GOWN, SHIRT, SUIT, WEAR 1.

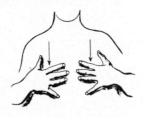

[C–201]

CLOTHESBRUSH (klōz´ brŭsh´, klōthz-´), *n.* (The natural sign.) Either hand, grasping an imaginary brush, brushes the clothes. *Cf.* BRUSH 1.

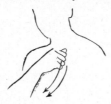

[C–202]

CLOTHESPIN (klōz´ pĭn´, klōthz´-), *n.* The index and thumb of the right hand squeeze the left index finger, first at the knuckle and then at the tip, indicating the position of the clothespin on a line.

[C–203]

CLOTHING (klō´ thǐng), *n.* See CLOTHES.

[C–204]

CLOUD(S) (kloud), *n.* (Black objects gathering over the head.) The sign for BLACK is made: The right index finger is drawn over the right eyebrow, from left to right. Both open hands are then rotated alternately before the forehead, outlining the shape of the clouds.

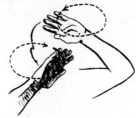

[C–205]

CLUB (klŭb), *n.* (A grouping together.) Both "C" hands, palms facing, are held a few inches apart at chest height. They are swung around in unison, so that the palms now face the body. *Cf.* ASSOCIATION, AUDIENCE 1, CASTE, CIRCLE 2, CLASS, CLASSED 1, COMPANY, FAMILY 2, GANG, GROUP 1, JOIN 2, ORGANIZATION 1.

[C–206]

CLUMSINESS (klŭm´ zǐ nǐs), *n.* (Clumsy in gait; all thumbs.) The "3" hands, palms down, move alternately up and down before the body. *Cf.* AWKWARD, AWKWARDNESS, CLUMSY 1, GREEN 2, GREENHORN 2, NAIVE.

[C–207]

CLUMSY 1 (klŭm´ zĭ), *adj.* See CLUMSINESS.

[C–208]

CLUMSY 2, *(colloq.), adj.* (The thickness of the skull is indicated, to stress intellectual density.) With the thumb of the right "C" hand grasped by the closed left hand, the right hand is swung in toward the body, describing a small arc as it moves. The space between the curved right fingers and the closed left hand indicates the thickness of the skull. *Cf.* DUMB 2, MORON, STUPID 2, THICK-SKULLED, UNSKILLED.

[C–209]

CLUTTER (klŭt´ ər), *v.,* -TERED, -TERING. (Scrambling or mixing up.) The downturned right hand is positioned above the upturned left. The fingers of both are curved. Both hands move in opposite horizontal circles. *Cf.* COMPLICATE, CONFUSE, CONFUSED, CONFUSION, DISORDER, MINGLE 1, MIX, MIXED, MIX UP, SCRAMBLE.

[C–210]

COAL (kōl), *n.* (A black mass.) The sign for BLACK is made: The right index finger moves over

the right eyebrow, from left to right. The hands then are brought together as if holding an imaginary ball.

[C–211]

COAST (kōst), *v.,* COASTED, COASTING. (The runners of a sled.) The curved index and middle fingers of the upturned right hand coast down along the back of the outstretched left hand.

[C–212]

COAT (kōt), *n.* (The lapels are outlined.) The tips of the "A" thumbs outline the lapels of the coat. *Cf.* CLOAK, OVERCOAT.

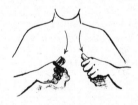

[C–213]

COAX (kōks), *v.,* COAXED, COAXING. (Shaking someone, to implant one's will into another.) Both "A" hands, palms facing, are held before the chest, the left slightly in front of the right. In this position the hands move back and forth a short distance. *Cf.* CONVINCE, INDUCE, PERSUADE, PERSUASION, PROD, URGE 2.

[C-214]

COBBLER (kŏb′ lər), *n.* (The stitching action of the sewing machine.) Both "D" hands, palms facing each other, are alternately crossed and pulled apart a number of times. Each time they come apart, the index fingers close tightly into the "X" position. The sign for INDIVIDUAL is then made: Both open hands, palms facing each other, move down the sides of the body, tracing its outline to the hips. *Cf.* COBBLING, SHOEMAKER, SHOEMAKING, SHOE REPAIR.

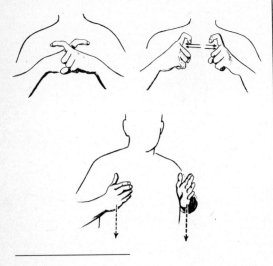

[C-215]

COBBLING, *n.* See COBBLER. The sign for INDIVIDUAL, however, is omitted.

[C-216]

COCA-COLA (kō′ kə kō′ lə), *(colloq.)* (A shot in the arm.) The right index finger is thrust into the left upper arm and the thumb wiggles back and forth a number of times, as if implanting a shot in the arm. *Cf.* COKE, DOPE, INOCULATE, MORPHINE, NARCOTICS.

[C-217]

COCK (kŏk), *n.* (The pecking beak and the comb of the cock.) The "Q" hand's back is placed against the lips, and the thumb and index fingers open and close, representing a beak. The thumb of the right "3" hand is then thrust against the forehead a couple of times, representing the comb. *Cf.* ROOSTER.

[C-218]

COERCE 1 (kō ûrs′), *v.,* -ERCED, -ERCING. (Forcing the head to bow.) The right "C" hand pushes down on an imaginary neck. *Cf.* COERCION 1, COMPEL 1, FORCE 1, IMPEL 1.

[C-219]

COERCE 2, *v.* (Pushing something forward.) The open right hand is held palm down at chin level, fingers pointing left. From this position the hand turns to point forward, and moves forcefully forward and away from the body, as if pushing something ahead of it. *Cf.* COERCION 2, COMPEL 2, FORCE 2, IMPEL 2.

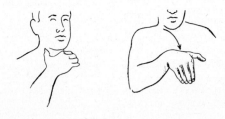

[C-220]

COERCION 1 (kō ûr′ shən), *n.* See COERCE 1.

[C-221]

COERCION 2, *n.* See COERCE 2.

[C-222]

COFFEE (kôf′ ĭ, kŏf′ ĭ), *n.* (Grinding the coffee

beans.) The right "S" hand, palm facing left, rotates in a counterclockwise manner, atop the left "S" hand, palm facing right.

[C–223]

COIN(S) 1 (koin), *(arch.)*, *n.*, (The natural sign; drawing a bill from a billfold.) The right thumb and index finger trace the outlines of a bill on the upturned left palm. Or, the right thumb and fingers may grasp the base of the open left hand, which is held palm facing right and fingers pointing forward; the right hand, in this position, then slides forward along and off the left hand, as if drawing bills from a billfold. *Cf.* BILL(S) 1, DOLLAR(S) 1.

[C–224]

COIN(S) 2, *n.* (The shape of a coin.) The right index finger traces a small circle on the upturned left palm. *Cf.* BILL(S) 2, DOLLAR(S) 2.

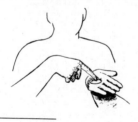

[C–225]

COINCIDE 1 (kō′ in sid′), *v.,* -CIDED, -CIDING. (A befalling.) Both "D" hands, index fingers pointing away from the body, are simultaneously pivoted over so that the palms face down. *Cf.* ACCIDENT, BEFALL, CHANCE, COINCIDENCE, EVENT, HAPPEN 1, INCIDENT, OCCUR, OPPORTUNITY 4.

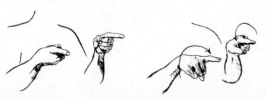

[C–226]

COINCIDE 2, *v.* (Agreement; of the same mind; thinking the same way.) The index finger of the right "D" hand, palm back, touches the forehead (the modified sign for THINK), and then the two index fingers, both in the "D" position, palm down, are brought together so they are side by side, pointing away from the body (the sign for SAME). *Cf.* ACCORD, ACQUIESCE, ACQUIESCENCE, AGREE, AGREEMENT, COMPLY, CONCUR, CONSENT.

[C–227]

COINCIDENCE (kō ĭn′ sə dəns), *n.* See COINCIDE 1.

[C–228]

COKE (kōk), *(colloq.)*, *n.* See COCA-COLA.

[C–229]

COLD 1 (kōld), *adj.* (The trembling from cold.) Both "S" hands, palms facing, are placed at the sides of the body. In this position the arms and hands shiver. *Cf.* CHILLY, FRIGID, SHIVER 1, WINTER 1.

[C–230]

COLD 2, *n.* (Wiping the nose.) The signer makes the motions of wiping the nose several times with an imaginary handkerchief. This is the common cold. *Cf.* HANDKERCHIEF.

[C–231]

COLLAPSE (kə lăps´), *v.,* -LAPSED, -LAPSING, *n.* (A collapsing.) Both "5" hands, fingertips joined before the chest, swing down so that the fingertips face down. *Cf.* BREAKDOWN, CAVE IN.

[C–232]

COLLAR (kŏl´ ər), *n.* (Outlining the collar.) The fingertips of both "Q" hands are placed at either side of the neck. They encircle the neck, coming together under the chin.

[C–233]

COLLECT (kə lĕkt´), *v.,* -LECTED, -LECTING. (Gathering in.) The right "5" hand, its little finger edge touching the upturned left palm, is drawn in an arc toward the body, closing into the "S" position as it sweeps over the base of the left hand. *Cf.* ACCUMULATE 1, EARN, SALARY, WAGES.

[C–234]

COLLEGE (kŏl´ ij), *n.* (Above ordinary school.) The sign for SCHOOL, *q.v.,* is made, but without the clapping of hands. The upper hand swings up in an arc above the lower. The upper hand may form a "C," instead of assuming a clapping position.

[C–235]

COLLIDE 1 (kə līd´), *v.,* -LIDED, -LIDING. The fists come together with force. *Cf.* COLLISION 1, CRASH, RUN UP AGAINST, WRECK.

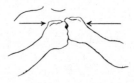

[C–236]

COLLIDE 2, *v.* (A coming together.) Both "5" hands, palms facing, are held about a foot apart in front of the chest. They both sweep upward in unison until their palms come together with force. *Cf.* COLLISION 2.

[C–237]

COLLISION 1 (kə lizh´ en), *n.* See COLLIDE 1.

[C–238]

COLLISION 2, *n.* See COLLIDE 2.

[C–239]

COLOGNE (kə lōn´), *n.* (Act of smelling and pouring.) The right "A" hand, holding the neck of an imaginary bottle, is placed at the nose. The hand is then tipped over slightly against the chest. *Cf.* PERFUME.

COLON (kō´ lən), *n.* (The marks of the colon.) The thumb and index fingers, holding an imaginary pencil, make colon marks in the air.

[C-241]

COLOR 1 (kŭl´ ər), *(rare), n.* (Mixing the colors on the palette.) The fingertips of the downturned right "B" hand rub against the upturned left palm in a clockwise-counterclockwise fashion.

[C-242]

COLOR 2, *(loc.), n.* The fingertips of the right "5" hand, palm facing the body, are placed against the chin and wiggle back and forth.

[C-243]

COLOR 3, *(rare), n.* (Bringing an object into view to observe its color.) The fingertips of the right "V" hand are thrust into the upturned left palm. They are then brought up quickly before the eyes.

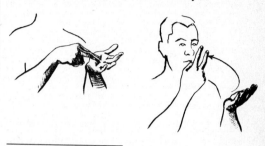

[C-244]

COMB (kōm) *n., v.,* COMBED, COMBING. (Act of combing the hair.) The downturned curved fingertips of the right hand, representing the teeth of the comb, are drawn through the hair.

[C-245]

COMBAT (*n.* kŏm´ băt, kŭm´ -; *v. also* kəm băt´), -BATED, -BATING. (The fists in combat.) The "S" hands, palms facing, swing down simultaneously toward each other. They do not touch, however. *Cf.* FIGHT 1.

[C-246]

COME 1 (kŭm), *v.,* CAME, COME, COMING. (Movement toward the body.) The index fingers, pointing to each other, are rolled in toward the body.

[C-247]

COME 2, *v.* (A beckoning.) The right index finger makes a natural beckoning movement. *Cf.* BECKON.

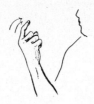

[C-248]

COME 3, *v.* (The natural sign.) The upright hand beckons.

[C-249]

COME BETWEEN, *v. phrase.* (Obstruct, block.) The left hand, fingers together and palm flat, is held before the body, facing somewhat down. The little finger side of the right hand, held with palm flat, makes one or several up-down chopping motions against the left hand, between its thumb and index finger. *Cf.* ANNOY 1, ANNOYANCE 1, BLOCK, BOTHER 1, CHECK 2, DISRUPT, DISTURB, HINDER, HINDRANCE, IMPEDE, INTERCEPT, INTERFERE, INTERFERENCE, INTERFERE WITH, INTERRUPT, MEDDLE 1, OBSTACLE, OBSTRUCT, PREVENT, PREVENTION.

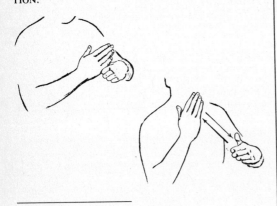

[C-250]

COME ON, *v. phrase.* (The natural beckoning motion.) One right-angle hand, held at shoulder level, palm facing the body, is moved toward the body in

a beckoning motion, while the signer assumes an appropriately encouraging or anxious expression.

[C-251]

COMFORT (kŭm´ fərt), *n., v.,* -FORTED, -FORTING. (A stroking motion.) Each downturned open hand alternately strokes the back of the other, moving forward from wrist to fingers. *Cf.* COMFORTABLE, CONSOLE, COZY.

[C-252]

COMFORTABLE (kŭmf´ tə bəl, kŭm´ fər tə bəl), *adj.* See COMFORT.

[C-253]

COMIC (kŏm´ ĭk), *n.* (The nose wrinkles in laughter.) The tips of the right index and middle fingers brush repeatedly off the tip of the nose. *Cf.* COMICAL, FUNNY, HUMOR, HUMOROUS.

[C-254]

COMICAL (kŏm´ ə kəl), *adj.* See COMIC.

[C-255]

COMMA (kŏm´ ə), *n.* (The natural sign.) The right thumb and index finger are held together. In this position they draw a comma in the air before the face.

[C–256]

COMMAND (kə mănd´), *n., v.,* -MANDED, -MAND-ING. (An issuance from the mouth.) The tip of the index finger of the "D" hand, palm facing the body, is placed at the closed lips. It moves around and out, rather forcefully. *Cf.* BID 1, DIRECT 2, ORDER 1.

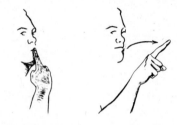

[C–257]

COMMANDMENTS (kə mănd´ mənts), *n. pl.* Hold up the left open hand, palm facing right; place the side of the right "C" hand against the left palm twice, the second time slightly lower than the first.

[C–258]

COMMENCE (kə mĕns´), *v.,* -MENCED, -MENCING. (Turning a key to open up a new venture.) The right index finger, resting between the left index and middle fingers, executes a half turn, once or twice. *Cf.* BEGIN, INITIATE, INSTITUTE 2, ORIGIN 1, ORIGINATE 1, START.

[C–259]

COMMEND (kə mĕnd´), *v.,* -MENDED, -MENDING. (Good words coming from the mouth; clapping hands.) The fingertips of the right hand, palm flat and facing the body, are brought up to the lips, so that they touch (part of the sign for GOOD, *q.v.*). The hands are then clapped together several times. *Cf.* ACCLAIM 2, APPLAUD, APPLAUSE, APPROBATION, APPROVAL, APPROVE, CLAP, CONGRATULATE 1, CONGRATULATIONS 1, PRAISE.

[C–260]

COMMUNICATE WITH, *v. phrase.* (Movement forward from, and back to, the mouth.) The tips of both index fingers, held pointing up, move alternately forward from, and back to, the lips. *Cf.* CONVERSATION 1, CONVERSE, TALK 3.

[C–261]

COMMUNICATION (kə mū´ nə kā´ shən), *n.* (The give-and-take.) The "O" hands, palms facing each other, move in alternating ellipses to and from the mouth. The "C" hands are also used.

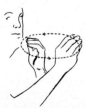

[C-262]

COMMUNION (HOLY) 1 (kə mūn´ yən), *(eccles.), n.* (The Blessed Sacrament.) The right thumb and index finger move as if placing the Sacred Host on the tip of the tongue; or they may trace a cross over the lips. *Cf.* EUCHARIST, HOLY COMMUNION 1.

[C-263]

COMMUNION (HOLY) 2, *(eccles.), n.* (Act of cutting a loaf of bread.) The left arm is held against the chest, representing a loaf of bread. The little finger edge of the right hand is drawn down over the back of the left hand several times, to indicate the cutting of slices. *Cf.* BREAD, HOLY COMMUNION 2, WINE 2.

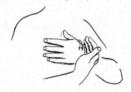

[C-264]

COMMUNION OF SAINTS (kə mūn´ yən əv sānts´), *(eccles.), n. phrase.* (Joining together.) Both hands, held in the modified "5" position, palms out, move toward each other. The thumbs and index fingers of both hands then connect. *Cf.* AFFILIATE 1, ANNEX, ASSOCIATE 2, ATTACH, BELONG, CONCERN 2, CONNECT, ENLIST, ENROLL, JOIN 1, PARTICIPATE, RELATIVE 2, UNION, UNITE.

[C-265]

COMMUNITY 1 (kə mū´ nə tĭ). *n.* (A collection of roofs; nearness to one another.) The sign for CITY or TOWN is made: The fingertips of the "B" hands

come together once or twice, to describe the slanting roofs. With the left open hand facing the body and fingers pointing right, the right hand, fingers pointing left, is then placed over the back of the left. This movement is then repeated, with the hands in reversed position, and the left hand placed over the back of the right.

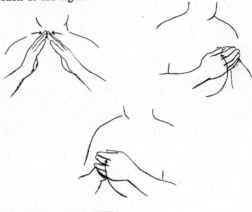

[C-266]

COMMUNITY 2, *n.* (A collection of rooftops.) The fingertips of both hands are joined, the hands and arms forming a pyramid. The fingertips separate and rejoin a number of times. Both arms may move a bit from left to right each time the fingertips separate and rejoin. *Cf.* CITY, TOWN.

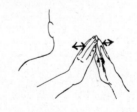

[C-267]

COMPANY (kŭm´ pə nĭ), *n.* (A grouping together.) Both "C" hands, palms facing, are held a few inches apart at chest height. They are swung around in unison, so that the palms now face the body. *Cf.* ASSOCIATION, AUDIENCE 1, CASTE, CIRCLE 2, CLASS, CLASSED 1, CLUB, FAMILY 2, GANG, GROUP 1, JOIN 2, ORGANIZATION 1.

[C–268]

COMPARE (kəm pâr′), *v.*, -PARED, -PARING. (Comparing both palms.) Both open hands are held before the body, with palms facing each other and fingers pointing upward. The hands then turn toward the face while the signer looks from one to the other, as if comparing them. *Cf.* CONTRAST 1.

[C–269]

COMPASSION (kəm păsh′ ən), *n.* (Feelings from the heart, conferred on others.) The middle finger of the open right hand moves up the chest over the heart. The same open hand then moves in a small, clockwise circle in front of the right shoulder, with palm facing forward and fingers pointing up. The signer assumes a kindly expression.

[C–270]

COMPEL 1 (kəm pĕl′), *v.*, -PELLED, -PELLING. (Forcing the head to bow.) The right "C" hand pushes down on an imaginary neck. *Cf.* COERCE 1, COERCION 1, FORCE 1, IMPEL 1.

[C–271]

COMPEL 2, *v.* (Pushing something forward.) The open right hand is held palm down at chin level, fingers pointing left. From this position the hand turns to point forward, and moves forcefully forward and away from the body, as if pushing some-

thing ahead of it. *Cf.* COERCE 2, COERCION 2, FORCE 2, IMPEL 2.

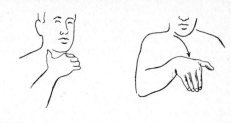

[C–272]

COMPETE 1 (kəm pēt′), *v.*, -PETED, -PETING. (Two opponents come together.) Both hands are closed, with thumbs pointing straight up and palms facing the body. From their initial position about a foot apart, the hands are brought together sharply, so that the knuckles strike. The hands, as they are drawn together, also move down a bit, so that they describe a "V." *Cf.* COMPETITION 1, CONTEND 1, CONTEST 1, RACE 1, RIVAL 2, RIVALRY 1, VIE 1.

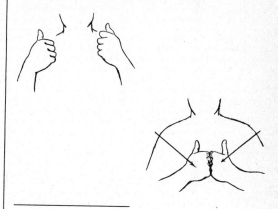

[C–273]

COMPETE 2, *v.* (Opposing objects.) The "A" hands are held side by side before the chest, palms facing each other and thumbs pointing forward. In this position the hands move alternately back and forth, toward and away from the body. *Cf.* COMPETITION 2, CONTEND 2, CONTEST 2, RACE 2, RIVAL 3, RIVALRY 2, VIE 2.

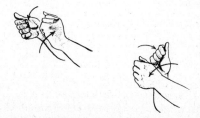

[C–274]

COMPETE 3, *v.* (The changing fortunes of competitors.) The "A" hands are held facing each other, thumbs pointing up in front of the body. Both hands are moved alternately backward and forward past each other several times. *Cf.* COMPETITION 3, CONTEND 3, CONTEST 3, RACE 3, RIVAL 4, RIVALRY 3, VIE 3.

[C–275]

COMPETENT (kŏm´ pə tənt), *adj.* (An affirmative movement of the hands, likened to a nodding of the head, to indicate ability or power to accomplish something.) Both "A" hands, held palms down, move down in unison a short distance before the chest. *Cf.* ABILITY, ABLE, CAN 1, CAPABLE, COULD, FACULTY, MAY 2, POSSIBLE.

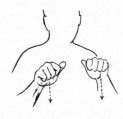

[C–276]

COMPETITION 1 (kŏm´ pə tĭsh´ ən), *n.* See COMPETE 1.

[C–277]

COMPETITION 2, *n.* See COMPETE 2.

[C–278]

COMPETITION 3, *n.* See COMPETE 3.

[C–279]

COMPLAIN 1 (kəm plān´), *v.,* -PLAINED, -PLAINING. (The hand is thrust into the chest to force a complaint out.) The curved fingers of the right hand are

thrust forcefully into the chest. *Cf.* COMPLAINT, OBJECT 2, OBJECTION, PROTEST.

[C–280]

COMPLAIN 2, *(sl.), v.* (Kicking.) Both "S" hands are held before the chest. Then the hands move sharply to the side, opening into a modified "V" position, palms down, as if "kicking." *Cf.* KICK 2, OBJECT 3.

[C–281]

COMPLAINT (kəm plānt´), *n.* See COMPLAIN 1.

[C–282]

COMPLETE 1 (kəm plēt´), *adj., v.,* -PLETED, -PLETING. (Bring to an end.) The left hand, fingers together and pointing forward, is held palm facing right. The right, palm down, fingers also together, moves along the top of the left, goes over the tip of the left index finger, and drops straight down, indicating a cutting off or a finishing. This sign is also used to indicate the past tense of a verb, in the sense of completing an action or state of being. *Cf.* ACCOMPLISH 2, ACHIEVE 2, CONCLUDE, DONE 1, END 4, EXPIRE 1, FINISH 1, HAVE 2, TERMINATE.

[C–283]

COMPLETE 2, *v.* (Wiping off the top of a container, to indicate its condition of fullness.) The downturned open right hand wipes across the index finger edge of the left "S" hand, whose palm faces right. The movement of the right hand is toward the body. *Cf.* FILL, FULL 1.

[C–284]

COMPLICATE (kŏm´ plə kāt´), *v.,* -CATED, -CATING. (Scrambling or mixing up.) The downturned right hand is positioned above the upturned left. The fingers of both are curved. Both hands move in opposite horizontal circles. *Cf.* CLUTTER, CONFUSE, CONFUSED, CONFUSION, DISORDER, MINGLE 1, MIX, MIXED, MIX UP, SCRAMBLE.

[C–285]

COMPLY (kəm plī´), *v.,* -PLIED, -PLYING. (Agreement; of the same mind; thinking the same way.) The index finger of the right "D" hand, palm back, touches the forehead (the modified sign for THINK, *q. v.*), and then the two index fingers, both in the "D" position, palms down, are brought together so they are side by side, pointing away from the body (the sign for SAME). *Cf.* ACCORD, ACQUIESCE, ACQUIESCENCE, AGREE, AGREEMENT, COINCIDE 2, CONCUR, CONSENT.

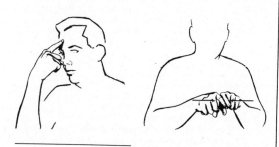

[C–286]

COMPOSE (kəm pōz´), *v.,* -POSED, -POSING. (Fashioning something with the hands.) The right "S"

hand, palm facing left, is placed on top of its left counterpart, whose palm faces right. The hands are twisted back and forth, striking each other slightly after each twist. *Cf.* CONSTITUTE, CONSTRUCT 2, CREATE, DEVISE 2, FABRICATE, FASHION, FIX, MAKE, MANUFACTURE, MEND 1, PRODUCE 3, RENDER 1, REPAIR.

[C–287]

COMPREHEND (kŏm´ pri hĕnd´), *v.,* -HENDED, -HENDING. (See rationale for UNDERSTAND 1.) The curved index finger of the right hand, palm facing the body, is placed with the fingernail resting on the middle of the forehead. It suddenly flicks up into the "D" position. *Cf.* UNDERSTAND 2, UNDERSTANDING, UNDERSTOOD.

[C–288]

CONCEDE (kən sēd´), *v.,* -CEDED, -CEDING. (Getting something off the chest.) Both hands are held with fingers touching the chest and pointing down. They are then swung up and out, ending with both palms facing up before the body. *Cf.* ADMISSION 1, ADMIT 1, CONFESS, CONFESSION 1.

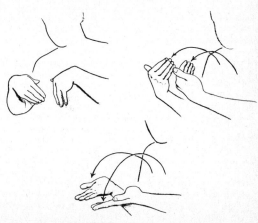

[C–289]

CONCEITED (kən sē´ tĭd), *(colloq.), adj.* (The natural sign.) Both downturned "L" hands are positioned with index fingers at the temples. They move away from the head rather slowly, indicating the size or growth of the head. The head is often moved slightly back and forth as the hands move away. An expression of superiority is assumed. *Cf.* BIG-HEADED, BIG SHOT, SWELL-HEADED.

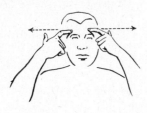

[C–290]

CONCEIVE 1 (kən sēv´), *v.,* -CEIVED, -CEIVING. (Thought reflected in a mirror.) The extended right index finger touches the forehead briefly. The right palm is then turned back and forth like a mirror before the face, as if reflecting a thought.

[C–291]

CONCEIVE 2, *v.,* -CEIVED, -CEIVING. (A thought coming forward from the mind, modified by the letter "I" for "idea.") With the "I" position on the right hand, palm facing the body, touch the little finger to the forehead, and then move the hand up and away in a circular, clockwise motion. The hand may also be moved up and away without this circular motion. *Cf.* CONCEPT 1, CONCEPTION, FANCY 2, IDEA, IMAGINATION, IMAGINE 1, JUST THINK OF IT!, NOTION, POLICY 2, THEORY, THOUGHT 2.

[C–292]

CONCEIVE 3, *(eccles.), v.* The right "AND" hand is held above the head, fingers pointing down; while the left "AND" hand is held before the body, fingers pointing up toward the right hand. The two hands then move toward each other, opening as they come together.

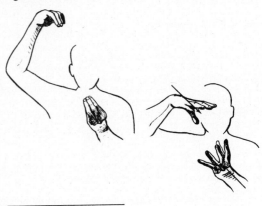

[C–293]

CONCENTRATE (kŏn´ sən trāt´), *v.,* -TRATED, -TRATING, *n.* (Directing one's attention forward; applying oneself; concentrating.) Both hands, fingers pointing up and together, are held at the sides of the face. They move straight out from the face. *Cf.* APPLY 2, ATTEND (TO), ATTENTION, CONCENTRATION, FOCUS, GIVE ATTENTION (TO), MIND 2, PAY ATTENTION (TO).

[C–294]

CONCENTRATION (kŏn´ sən tra´ shən), *n.* See CONCENTRATE.

[C–295]

CONCEPT 1 (kŏn´ sĕpt), *n.* (A thought coming forward from the mind, modified by the letter "I" for "idea.") With the "I" position on the right hand, palm facing the body, touch the little finger to the forehead, and then move the hand up and away in a circular, clockwise motion. The hand may also be moved up and away without this circular motion. *Cf.* CONCEIVE 2, CONCEPTION, FANCY 2, IDEA,

IMAGINATION, IMAGINE 1, JUST THINK OF IT!, NOTION, POLICY 2, THEORY, THOUGHT 2.

SAINTS, CONNECT, ENLIST, ENROLL, JOIN 1, PARTICIPATE, RELATIVE 2, UNION, UNITE.

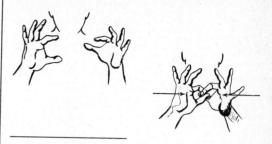

[C–296]

CONCEPT 2, *n.* (The letter "C;" an idea popping out of the head.) The right "C" hand is held near the right side of the forehead. It moves up and out a bit.

[C–297]

CONCEPTION (kən sĕp´ shən), *n.* See CONCEPT 1.

[C–298]

CONCERN 1 (kən sûrn´), *n., v.,* -CERNED, -CERNING. (A clouding over; a troubling.) Both "B" hands, palms facing each other, are rotated alternately before the forehead. *Cf.* ANNOY 2, ANNOYANCE 2, ANXIOUS 2, BOTHER 2, FRET, PROBLEM 1, TROUBLE, WORRIED, WORRY 1.

[C–299]

CONCERN 2, *n., v.* (Joining together.) Both hands, held in the modified "5" position, palms out, move toward each other. The thumbs and index fingers of both hands then connect. *Cf.* AFFILIATE 1, ANNEX, ASSOCIATE 2, ATTACH, BELONG, COMMUNION OF

[C–300]

CONCERNING (kən sûr´ nĭng), *prep.* (Revolving about.) The left hand is held at chest height, all fingers extended and touching the thumb and all pointing to the right. The right index finger circles about the left fingers several times. *Cf.* ABOUT 1, ELECTRIC MOTOR, OF.

[C–301]

CONCLUDE (kən klōōd´), *v.,* -CLUDED, -CLUDING. (Bring to an end.) The left hand, fingers together and pointing forward, is held palm facing right. The right, palm down, fingers also together, moves along the top of the left, goes over the tip of the left index finger, and drops straight down, indicating a cutting off or a finishing. This sign is also used to indicate the past tense of a verb, in the sense of concluding an action or state of being. *Cf.* ACCOMPLISH 2, ACHIEVE 2, COMPLETE 1, DONE 1, END 4, EXPIRE 1, FINISH 1, HAVE 2, TERMINATE.

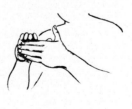

[C–302]

CONCUR (kən kûr´), *v.,* -CURRED, -CURRING. (Agreement; of the same mind; thinking the same way.) The index finger of the right "D" hand, palm back, touches the forehead (the modified sign for THINK, *q.v.*), and then the two index fingers, both in the "D" position, palm down, are brought together so they are side by side, pointing away from the body (the sign for SAME). *Cf.* ACCORD, ACQUI-ESCE, ACQUIESCENCE, AGREE, AGREEMENT, COIN-CIDE 2, COMPLY, CONSENT.

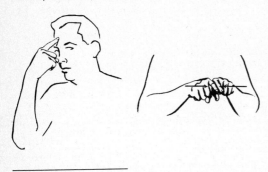

[C–303]

CONDENSE (kən děns´), *v.,* -DENSED, -DENSING. (To squeeze or condense into a small space.) The "C" hands face each other, with the right hand nearer to the body than the left. Both hands draw together and close deliberately, squeezing an imaginary object. *Cf.* ABBREVIATE 1, BRIEF 2, MAKE BRIEF, SUMMARIZE 1, SUMMARY 1.

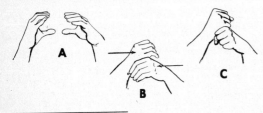

[C–304]

CONDUCT 1 (*n.* kŏn´ dŭkt; *v.* kən dŭkt´), -DUCTED, -DUCTING. (An activity.) Both open hands, palms down, are swung right and left before the chest. *Cf.* ACT 2, ACTION, ACTIVE, ACTIVITY, BUSY 2, DEED, DO, PERFORM 1, PERFORMANCE 1, RENDER 2.

[C–305]

CONDUCT 2, *n.* (One hand leads the other.) The right hand grasps the tips of the left fingers and pulls the left hand forward. *Cf.* GUIDE, LEAD 1.

[C–306]

CONFER (kən fûr´), *v.,* -FERRED, -FERRING. (A giving of something.) Both "A" hands, with index fingers somewhat draped over the tips of the thumbs, are held palms facing in front of the chest. They are pivoted forward and down, in unison, from the wrists. *Cf.* AWARD, BEQUEATH, BESTOW, CONSIGN, CONTRIBUTE, GIFT, PRESENT 2.

[C–307]

CONFERENCE (kŏn´ fər əns,), *n.* (Assemble all together.) Both "5" hands, palms facing, are held with fingers pointing out from the body. With a sweeping motion they are brought in toward the chest, and all fingertips come together. This is repeated. *Cf.* AC-CUMULATE 3, ASSEMBLE, ASSEMBLY, CONVENE, CONVENTION, GATHER 2, GATHERING, MEETING 1.

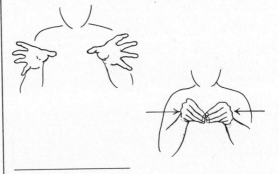

[C–308]

CONFESS (kən fĕs´), *v.,* -FESSED, -FESSING. (Getting something off the chest.) Both hands are held with fingers touching the chest and pointing down. They are then swung up and out, ending with both palms facing up before the body. *Cf.* ADMISSION 1, ADMIT 1, CONCEDE, CONFESSION 1.

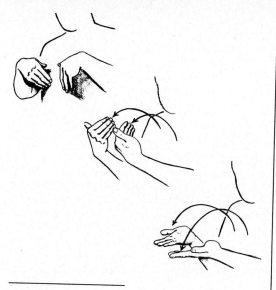

CONFESSION 1 (kən fĕsh´ ən), *n.* See CONFESS.

[C–310]

CONFESSION 2, *(eccles.), n.* (The grating through which confession is heard.) The fingers of the right open hand are spread slightly and placed with their backs resting diagonally across the front of the spread fingers of the left open hand, so as to form a grid held just to the side of the face, palms toward the face. *Cf.* CONFESSIONAL, PENANCE 2.

[C–311]

CONFESSIONAL (kən fĕsh´ ən əl), *adj., n.* See CONFESSION 2.

[C–312]

CONFIDENCE (kŏn´ fə dəns), *n.* (Planting a flag-pole, *i.e.,* planting one's trust.) The "S" hands grasp and plant an imaginary flagpole in the ground. This

sign may be preceded by BELIEVE, *q.v. Cf.* FAITH, TRUST.

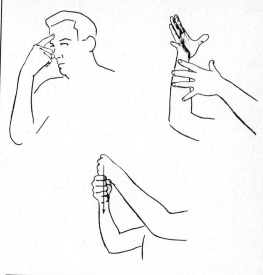

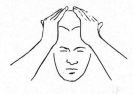

[C–313]

CONFIRMATION 1 (kŏn´ fər mā´ shən), *n.* The right-angle hands are placed against either temple, fingers pointing back over the head.

[C–314]

CONFIRMATION 2, *(eccles.), n.* (Part of the rubrics of conferring confirmation.) The thumb of the open right hand traces a cross on the forehead. Then the palm of the same open hand deals a blow to the right cheek.

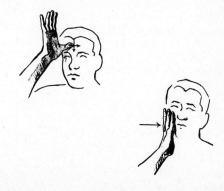

[C–315]

CONFRONT (kən frŭnt´), *v.*, -FRONTED, -FRONT-ING. (Face to face.) The left hand, fingers together, palm flat and facing the eyes, is held a bit above eye level. The right hand, fingers also together, is held in front of the mouth, with palm facing the left hand. With a sweeping upward movement the right hand moves toward the left, which moves straight up an inch or two at the same time. *Cf.* APPEAR 3, AP-PEARANCE, BEFORE 3, FACE 2, FACE TO FACE, PRES-ENCE.

[C–316]

CONFUSE (kən fūz´), *v.*, -FUSED, -FUSING. (Scrambling or mixing up.) The downturned right hand is positioned above the upturned left. The fingers of both are curved. Both hands move in opposite horizontal circles. *Cf.* CLUTTER, COMPLICATE, CON-FUSED, CONFUSION, DISORDER, MINGLE 1, MIX, MIXED, MIX UP, SCRAMBLE.

[C–317]

CONFUSED (kən fūzd´), *adj.* See CONFUSE.

[C–318]

CONFUSION (kən fū´ zhən), *n.* See CONFUSE.

[C–319]

CONGRATULATE 1 (kən grăch´ ə lāt´), *v.*, -LATED, -LATING. (Good words coming from the mouth; clapping hands.) The fingertips of the right hand, palm flat and facing the body, are brought up to the lips, so that they touch (part of the sign for GOOD, *q.v.*). The hands are then clapped together several times. *Cf.* ACCLAIM 2, APPLAUD, APPLAUSE, AP-

PROBATION, APPROVAL, APPROVE, CLAP, COM-MEND, CONGRATULATIONS 1, PRAISE.

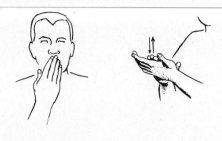

[C–320]

CONGRATULATE 2, *v.* (Shaking the clasped hands in triumph.) The hands are clasped together in front of the face and are shaken vigorously back and forth. The signer smiles. *Cf.* CONGRATULATIONS 2.

[C–321]

CONGRATULATIONS 1 (kən grăch´ ə lā´ shənz), *n. pl.* See CONGRATULATE 1.

[C–322]

CONGRATULATIONS 2, *n. pl.* See CONGRATULATE 2.

[C–323]

CONNECT (kə nĕkt´), *v.*, -NECTED, -NECTING. (Joining together.) Both hands, held in the modified "5" position, palms out, move toward each other. The thumbs and index fingers of both hands then connect. *Cf.* AFFILIATE 1, ANNEX, ASSOCIATE 2, ATTACH, BELONG, COMMUNION OF SAINTS, CON-CERN 2, ENLIST, ENROLL, JOIN 1, PARTICIPATE, RELATIVE 2, UNION, UNITE.

[C–324]

CONNECTION (kə nĕk´ shən), *n.* (The fingers are connected.) The index fingers and thumbs of both hands interlock, and the hands move back and forth from right to left. *Cf.* RELATIONSHIP 1.

[C–325]

CONNOTE (kə nōt´), *v.,* -NOTED, -NOTING. (Relative standing of one's thoughts.) A modified sign for THINK is made: The right index finger touches the middle of the forehead. The tips of the right "V" hand, palm down, are then thrust into the upturned left palm (as in STAND, *q.v.*). The right "V" hand is then re-thrust into the upturned left palm, with right palm now facing the body. *Cf.* IMPLY, INTEND, INTENT 1, INTENTION, MEAN 2, MEANING, MOTIVE 3, PURPOSE 1, SIGNIFICANCE 2, SIGNIFY 2, SUBSTANCE 2.

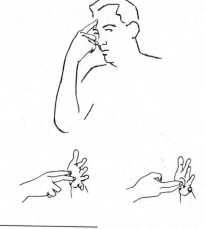

[C–326]

CONQUER (kŏng´ kər), *v.,* -QUERED, -QUERING. (Forcing the head into a bowed position.) The right "S" hand, placed across the left "S" hand, moves over and down a bit. *Cf.* BEAT 2, DEFEAT, OVERCOME, SUBDUE.

[C–327]

CONQUERED, *adj.* (The head is forced into a bowed position.) The right "S" hand, palm up, is placed under and across the left "S" hand, whose palm faces down. The right "S" hand moves up and over, toward the body. This sign is used as the passive voice of the verb CONQUER. *Cf.* BEATEN.

[C–328]

CONSCIENCE 1 (kŏn´ shəns), *n.* The index finger is shaken scoldingly at the heart. *Cf.* CONVICTION 1.

[C–329]

CONSCIENCE 2, *n.* (Shaking a warning finger at yourself.) The right "G" hand is held just above the right side of the head, with the index fingertip pointing toward the right temple. Then the hand drops toward the head but does not touch it. This movement is repeated several times.

[C–330]

CONSCIENCE 3, *n.* (A guilty heart.) The side of the right "G" hand strikes against the heart several times.

[C–331]

CONSCIOUS (kŏn´ shəs), *adj.* (Indicating the mind.) The fingertips of the open right hand are placed against the forehead. *Cf.* CONSCIOUSNESS, KNOWING.

[C–332]

CONSCIOUSNESS (kŏn´ shəs nĭs), *n.* The sign for CONSCIOUS is made. This is followed by the sign for -NESS: The downturned right "N" hand moves down along the left palm, which is facing away from the body.

[C–333]

CONSECRATION (kŏn´ sə krā´ shən), *(eccles.), n.* (In Mass.) The head is bowed while the right "A" hand, held palm inward, strikes the breast.

[C–334]

CONSECUTIVE (kən sek´ yə tĭv), *adj.* (One hand follows the other.) The "A" hands are used, thumbs pointing up. The right is positioned a few inches behind the left. The left hand moves straight forward, while the right follows behind in a series of

wavy movements. *Cf.* FOLLOW, FOLLOWING, SEQUEL.

[C–335]

CONSENT (kən sĕnt´), *n., v.,* -SENTED, -SENTING. (Agreement; of the same mind; thinking the same way.) The index finger of the right "D" hand, palm back, touches the forehead (the modified sign for THINK), and then the two index fingers, both in the "D" position, palm down, are brought together so they are side by side, pointing away from the body (the sign for SAME). *Cf.* ACCORD, ACQUIESCE, ACQUIESCENCE, AGREE, AGREEMENT, COINCIDE 2, COMPLY, CONCUR.

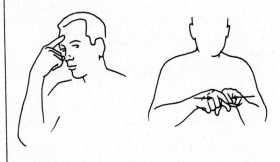

[C–336]

CONSIDER 1 (kən sĭd´ ər), *v.,* -ERED, -ERING. (A thought is turned over in the mind.) The index finger makes a small circle on the forehead. *Cf.* MOTIVE 1, RECKON, SPECULATE 1, SPECULATION 1, THINK, THOUGHT 1, THOUGHTFUL.

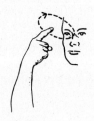

[C–337]

CONSIDER 2, *v.* (Turning thoughts over in the mind.) Both index fingers, pointing to the forehead, describe continuous alternating circles. *Cf.* CON-

TEMPLATE, PONDER, SPECULATE 2, SPECULATION 2, WEIGH 2, WONDER 1.

[C–338]

CONSIDER 3, *v.* (The scales move up and down.) The two "F" hands, palms facing each other, move alternately up and down. *Cf.* COURT, EVALUATE 1, IF, JUDGE 1, JUDGMENT, JUSTICE 1.

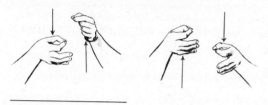

[C–339]

CONSIGN (kən sīn´), v., -SIGNED, -SIGNING. (A giving of something.) Both "A" hands, with index fingers somewhat draped over the tips of the thumbs, are held palms facing in front of the chest. They are pivoted forward and down, in unison, from the wrists. *Cf.* AWARD, BEQUEATH, BESTOW, CONFER, CONTRIBUTE, GIFT, PRESENT 2.

[C–340]

CONSISTENT (kən sis´ tənt), *adj.* (Coming together with regular frequency.) Both "D" hands are held with index fingers pointing forward, the right hand above the left. The right "D" hand is brought down on the left several times in rhythmic succession. *Cf.* FAITHFUL 1, REGULAR.

[C–341]

CONSOLE (kən sōl´), *v.,* -SOLED, -SOLING. (A stroking motion.) Each downturned open hand alternately strokes the back of the other, moving forward from wrist to fingers. *Cf.* COMFORT, COMFORTABLE, COZY.

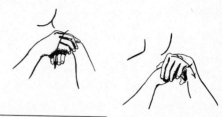

[C–342]

CONSTITUTE (kŏn´ stə tūt´, -tōōt´), *v.,* -TUTED, -TUTING. (Fashioning something with the hands.) The right "S" hand, palm facing left, is placed on top of its left counterpart, whose palm faces right. The hands are twisted back and forth, striking each other slightly after each twist. *Cf.* COMPOSE, CONSTRUCT 2, CREATE, DEVISE 2, FABRICATE, FASHION, FIX, MAKE, MANUFACTURE, MEND 1, PRODUCE 3, RENDER 1, REPAIR.

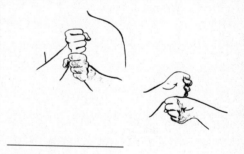

[C–343]

CONSTITUTION (kŏn´ stə tū´ shən, -tōō´-), *n.* (The letter "C.") The right "C" hand moves downward along the left palm, in two stages, from fingertips to wrist.

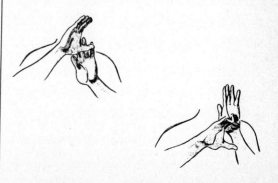

[C–344]

CONSTRUCT 1 (kən strŭkt′), *v.,* -STRUCTED, -STRUCTING. (Piling bricks one on top of another.) The downturned hands are placed repeatedly atop each other. Each time this is done the arms rise a bit, to indicate the raising of a building. *Cf.* BUILD, CONSTRUCTION, ERECT.

[C–345]

CONSTRUCT 2, *v.* (Fashioning something with the hands.) The right "S" hand, palm facing left, is placed on top of its left counterpart, whose palm faces right. The hands are twisted back and forth, striking each other slightly after each twist. *Cf.* COMPOSE, CONSTITUTE, CREATE, DEVISE 2, FABRICATE, FASHION, FIX, MAKE, MANUFACTURE, MEND 1, PRODUCE 3, RENDER 1, REPAIR.

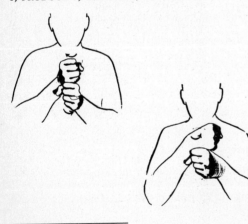

[C–346]

CONSTRUCTION (kən strŭk′ shən), *n.* See CONSTRUCT 1.

[C–347]

CONSULT (kən sŭlt′) -SULTED, -SULTING. (Pray tell.) Both hands, held upright about a foot in front of the chest, with palms facing and fingers pointing straight up, are positioned about a foot apart. Moving toward the chest, they come together until they touch, as if in prayer. *Cf.* ASK 1, INQUIRE 1, REQUEST 1.

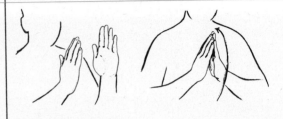

[C–348]

CONSUME 1 (kən sōōm′), *v.,* -SUMED, -SUMING. (The natural sign.) The closed right hand goes through the natural motion of placing food in the mouth. This movement is repeated. *Cf.* CONSUMPTION, DEVOUR, DINE, EAT, FEED 1, FOOD 1, MEAL.

[C–349]

CONSUME 2, *v.* (To use; the letter "U.") The right "U" hand describes a small clockwise circle. *Cf.* USE, USED, USEFUL, UTILIZE, WEAR 2.

[C–350]

CONSUMPTION (kən sŭmp′ shən), *n.* See CONSUME 1.

[C–351]

CONTACT 1 (kŏn′ tăkt), *n., v.,* -TACTED, -TACTING. (The natural movement of touching.) The tip of the middle finger of the downturned right "5" hand touches the back of the left hand a number of times. *Cf.* FEEL 1, TOUCH, TOUCHDOWN.

[C-352]

CONTACT 2, *v.* (A pinning down.) The left "D" finger represents the one who is caught. The curved index and middle fingers of the right hand, palm facing down, are thrust against the left "D" finger, impaling it. *Cf.* CAUGHT IN THE ACT 1, CORNER 2.

[C-353]

CONTAGIOUS (kən tā´ jəs), *adj.* (Catching a "bug.") The right hand closes into the "AND" position as it swoops abruptly down to touch its fingertips on the back of the prone left hand, as if catching an insect.

[C-354]

CONTAINER (kən tā´ nər), *n.* (Turning the cover of a jar.) The right hand is laid palm down over the upturned thumb edge of the left "S" hand. In this position the right hand twists in a clockwise circle, as if turning the cover of a jar. *Cf.* CAN(NING) 2.

[C-355]

CONTEMPLATE (kŏn´ təm plāt´, kən těm´ plāt), *v.,* -PLATED, -PLATING. (Turning thoughts over in the mind.) Both index fingers, pointing to the forehead, describe continuous alternating circles. *Cf.* CONSIDER 2, PONDER, SPECULATE 2, SPECULATION 2, WEIGH 2, WONDER 1.

[C-356]

CONTEMPT 1 (kən těmpt´), *n.* (The gaze is cast downward.) Both "V" hands, side by side and palms facing out, are swept downward so that the fingertips now point down. A haughty expression, or one of mild contempt, is sometimes assumed. *Cf.* LOOK DOWN, SCORN 1.

[C-357]

CONTEMPT 2, *(rare), n.* (The finger is flicked to indicate something petty, small; *i.e.,* to be scorned as inconsequential.) The right index finger and thumb are used to press the lips down into an expression of contempt. The right thumb is then flicked out from the closed hand. *Cf.* DESPISE 2, DETEST 2, DISLIKE, HATE 2, SCORN 2.

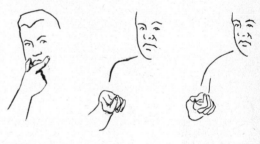

[C-358]

CONTEND 1 (kən těnd´), *v.,* -TENDED, -TENDING. (Two opponents come together.) Both hands are closed, with thumbs pointing straight up and palms facing the body. From their initial position about a foot apart, the hands are brought together sharply, so that the knuckles strike. The hands, as they are drawn together, also move down a bit, so that they describe a "V." *Cf.* COMPETE 1, COMPETITION 1, CONTEST 1, RACE 1, RIVAL 2, RIVALRY 1, VIE 1.

[C–359]

CONTEND 2, *v.* (Opposing objects.) The "A" hands are held side by side before the chest, palms facing each other and thumbs pointing forward. In this position the hands move alternately back and forth, toward and away from the body. *Cf.* COMPETE 2, COMPETITION 2, CONTEST 2, RACE 2, RIVAL 3, RIVALRY 2, VIE 2.

[C–360]

CONTEND 3, *v.* (The changing fortunes of competitors.) The "A" hands are held facing each other, thumbs pointing up in front of the body. Both hands are moved alternately backward and forward past each other several times. *Cf.* COMPETE 3, COMPETITION 3, CONTEST 3, RACE 3, RIVAL 4, RIVALRY 3, VIE 3.

[C–361]

CONTENT (kən těnt´), *adj.* (The inner feelings settle down.) Both "B" hands (or "5" hands, fingers together) are placed palms down against the chest, the right above the left. Both move down simultaneously a few inches. *Cf.* CONTENTED, GRATIFY 2, SATISFACTION, SATISFIED, SATISFY 1.

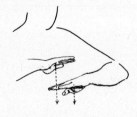

[C–362]

CONTENTED (kən těn´ tĭd), *adj.* See CONTENT.

[C–363]

CONTEST 1 (*n.* kŏn´ těst; *v.* kən těst´), *n., v.,* -TESTED, -TESTING. See CONTEND 1.

[C–364]

CONTEST 2, *n.* See CONTEND 2.

[C–365]

CONTEST 3, *n.* See CONTEND 3.

[C–366]

CONTINUE 1 (kən tǐn´ ū), *v.,* -TINUED, -TINUING. (Steady, uninterrupted movement.) The "A" hands are held with palms out, thumbs extended and touching, the right behind the left. In this position the hands move forward in a straight, steady line. *Cf.* ENDURE 2, EVER 1, LAST 3, LASTING, PERMANENT, PERPETUAL, PERSEVERE 3, PERSIST 2, REMAIN, STAY 1, STAY STILL.

[C–367]

CONTINUE 2, *v.* (Duration of movement from past to present.) The right "Y" hand is held palm down in front of the right shoulder and is then moved slowly down and forward in a smooth curve. *Cf.* STAY 2, STILL 1, YET 1.

[C–368]

CONTRADICT (kŏn´ trə dĭkt´), *v.,* -DICTED, -DICTING. (To think in opposite terms.) The sign for THINK is made: The right index finger touches the forehead. The sign for OPPOSITE is then made: The "D" hands, palms facing the body and index fingers touching, draw apart sharply. *Cf.* CONTRARY TO, DIFFER, DISAGREE.

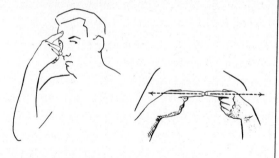

[C-369]

CONTRARY TO (kŏn′ trĕr ĭ tōō), *prep.* See CONTRADICT.

[C-370]

CONTRAST 1 (*n.* kŏn′ trăst; *v.* kən trăst′), -TRASTED, -TRASTING. (Comparing both palms.) Both open hands are held before the body, with palms facing each other and fingers pointing upward. The hands then turn toward the face while the signer looks from one to the other, as if comparing them. *Cf.* COMPARE.

[C-371]

CONTRAST 2, *n., v.* (Separateness.) The tips of the extended index fingers touch before the chest, the right finger pointing left and the left finger pointing right. The fingers then draw apart sharply to either side. *Cf.* OPPOSITE, REVERSE 1.

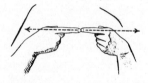

[C-372]

CONTRIBUTE (kən trĭb′ ūt), v., -UTED, -UTING. (A giving of something.) Both "A" hands, with index

fingers somewhat draped over the tips of the thumbs, are held palms facing in front of the chest. They are pivoted forward and down, in unison, from the wrists. *Cf.* AWARD, BEQUEATH, BESTOW, CONFER, CONSIGN, GIFT, PRESENT 2.

[C-373]

CONTRITION (kən trĭsh′ ən), *n.* (The heart is circled, to indicate feeling, modified by the letter "S," for SORRY.) The right "S" hand, palm facing the body, is rotated several times over the area of the heart. *Cf.* APOLOGIZE 1, APOLOGY 1, PENITENT, REGRET, REGRETFUL, REPENT, REPENTANT, RUE, SORROW, SORROWFUL 2, SORRY.

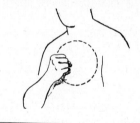

[C-374]

CONTROL 1 (kən trōl′), v., -TROLLED, -TROLLING. (Holding the reins over all.) The "A" hands, palms facing, move alternately back and forth, as if grasping and manipulating reins. The left "A" hand, still in position, swings over so that its palm now faces down. The right hand opens to the "5" position, palm down, and swings over the left which moves slightly to the right. *Cf.* AUTHORITY, DIRECT 1, GOVERN, MANAGE, MANAGEMENT, MANAGER, OPERATE, REGULATE, REIGN, RULE 1.

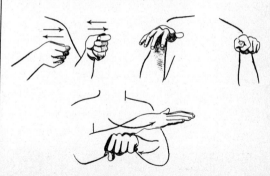

[C–375]

CONTROL 2, *n., v.* (Keeping the feelings down.) The curved fingertips of both hands are placed against the chest. The hands slowly move down as the fingers close into the "S" position. One hand only may also be used. *Cf.* SUPPRESS FEELINGS.

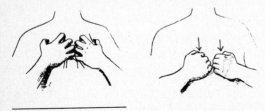

[C–376]

CONTROVERSY (kŏn´ trə vûr´ sǐ), *n.* (An expounding back and forth.) The index fingers here represent the two sides of the argument. First the left index finger is slapped into the open right palm, and then the right makes the same movement into the left palm. This is repeated back and forth several times. *Cf.* ARGUE, ARGUMENT, DEBATE, DISPUTE.

[C–377]

CONVENE (kən vēn´), *v.,* -VENED, -VENING. (Assemble all together.) Both "5" hands, palms facing, are held with fingers pointing out from the body. With a sweeping motion they are brought in toward the chest, and all fingertips come together. This is repeated. *Cf.* ACCUMULATE 3, ASSEMBLE, ASSEMBLY, CONFERENCE, CONVENTION, GATHER 2, GATHERING, MEETING 1.

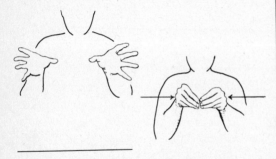

[C–378]

CONVENTION (kən vĕn´ shən), *n.* See CONVENE.

[C–379]

CONVERSATION 1 (kŏn´ vər sā´ shən), *n.* (Movement forward from, and back to, the mouth.) The tips of both index fingers, held pointing up, move alternately forward from, and back to, the lips. *Cf.* COMMUNICATE WITH, CONVERSE, TALK 3.

[C–380]

CONVERSATION 2, *n.* (Words tossed back and forth.) The open hands are held side by side with palms up, fingers pointing forward and slightly curved. In this position the hands swing back and forth from side to side before the chest. *Cf.* CHAT.

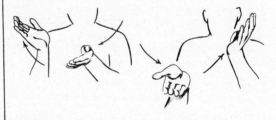

[C–381]

CONVERSE (kən vûrs´), *v.,* -VERSED, -VERSING. See CONVERSATION 1.

[C–382]

CONVERT (kən vûrt´), *v.,* -VERTED, -VERTING. (To change positions.) Both "A" hands, thumbs up, are held before the chest, several inches apart. The left hand is pivoted over so that its thumb points to the right. Simultaneously, the right hand is moved up and over the left, describing a small arc, with its thumb pointing to the left. *Cf.* ADJUST, ALTER, ALTERATION, CHANGE 1, MODIFY, REVERSE 2, TRANSFER 1.

[C–383]

CONVEY (kən vā´), *v.,* -VEYED, -VEYING. (Act of conveying an object from one point to another.) The open hands are held palms up before the chest on the right side of the body. Describing an arc, they move up and forward in unison. *Cf.* CARRY 1.

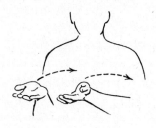

[C–384]

CONVICTION 1 (kən vĭk´ shən), *n.* The index finger is shaken scoldingly at the heart. *Cf.* CONSCIENCE 1.

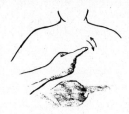

[C–385]

CONVICTION 2, *n.* (A thought clasped onto.) The index finger touches the middle of the forehead (where the thought lies), and then both hands are clasped together. *Cf.* BELIEF, BELIEVE, DOCTRINE 2.

[C–386]

CONVICTION 3, *n.* (Feel strongly.) The sign for FEEL 2 is made: The right middle finger, touching the heart, moves up an inch or two a number of times. This is followed by the sign for STRONG: Both "5" hands are placed palms against the chest.

They move out and away, forcefully, closing and assuming the "S" position.

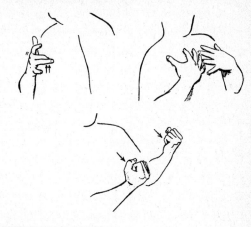

[C–387]

CONVINCE (kən vĭns´), *v.,* -VINCED, -VINCING. (Shaking someone, to implant one's will into another.) Both "A" hands, palms facing, are held before the chest, the left slightly in front of the right. In this position the hands move back and forth a short distance. *Cf.* COAX, INDUCE, PERSUADE, PERSUASION, PROD, URGE 2.

[C–388]

COOK (ko͝ok), *n.,v.,* COOKED, COOKING. (Turning over a pancake.) The open right hand rests on the upturned left palm. The right hand flips over and comes to rest with its back on the left palm. This is the action of turning over a pancake. The sign for INDIVIDUAL, for a noun, then follows: Both open hands, palms facing each other, move down the sides of the body, tracing its outline to the hips. *Cf.* CHEF, KITCHEN 1, PANCAKE.

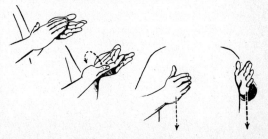

[C–389]

COOKIE (kŏok´ ĭ), *n.* (Act of cutting cookies with a cookie mold.) The right hand, in the "C" position, palm down, is placed into the open left palm. It then rises a bit, swings or twists around a little, and in this new position is placed again in the open left palm. *Cf.* BISCUIT, MUFFIN.

[C–390]

COOL (kōol), *adj., v.,* COOLED, COOLING. (Fanning the face.) Both open hands are held with palms down and fingers spread and pointing toward the face. The hands move up and down as if fanning the face.

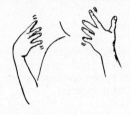

[C–391]

COOPERATE (kō ŏp´ ə rāt´), *v.,* -ATED, -ATING. (Joining in movement.) Both "D" hands, thumbs and index fingers interlocked, rotate in a counterclockwise circle in front of the body.

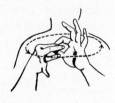

[C–392]

COP (kŏp), *(colloq.), n.* (The letter "C" for "cop"; the shape and position of the badge.) The right "C" hand, palm facing left, is placed against the heart. *Cf.* POLICE, POLICEMAN, SHERIFF.

[C–393]

COPULATE (kŏp´ yə lāt´), *v.,* -LATED, -LATING. (The motions of the legs during the sexual act.) The upturned left "V" hand remains motionless, while the downturned right "V" hand comes down repeatedly on the left. *Cf.* FORNICATE, SEXUAL INTERCOURSE.

[C–394]

COPY 1 (kŏp´ ĭ), *n., v.,* COPIED, COPYING. (The natural sign.) The right fingers and thumb close together and move onto the upturned, open left hand, as if taking something from one place to another. *Cf.* DUPLICATE 1, IMITATE, MIMIC, MODEL.

[C–395]

COPY 2, *v.* (The motion of removing something and transferring it.) The fingertips and thumb of the right hand are placed against the back of the left hand, which is held palm toward the face, fingers pointing up. The fingers of the right hand then close into the "AND" position, and move forward, away from the left hand, as they do.

[C–396]

COPY FROM, *v. phrase.* (The motion of removing something and transferring it.) The thumb tip and fingertips of the open right hand are spread and placed against the palm of the open left hand, which is held facing right with fingers spread and pointing up. The thumb and fingers of the right hand then

close into the "AND" position, and move to the right, away from the left hand, as they do.

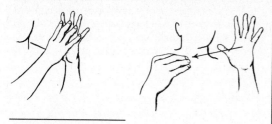

[C–397]

CORD (kôrd), *n.* (The natural sign.) The "I" hands are held palms facing the body, little fingertips pointing toward each other. Both little fingers revolve in small circles and draw apart slowly as they do.

[C–398]

CORDIAL (kôr´ jəl), *adj.* (A crinkling-up of the face.) Both hands, in the "5" position, palms facing back, are placed on either side of the face. The fingers wiggle back and forth, while a pleasant, happy expression is worn. *Cf.* AMIABLE, CHEERFUL, FRIENDLY, JOLLY, PLEASANT.

[C–399]

CORK (kôrk), *n.* (Removing a cork from a bottle.) The knuckle of the right index finger is withdrawn forcefully from the circle formed by the left "O" hand, as if removing a cork.

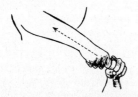

[C–400]

CORKSCREW (kôrk´ skro͞o′), *n.* (The natural sign.) The right "R" hand, fingers pointing forward, rotates in a corkscrew motion.

[C–401]

CORN (kôrn), *n.* (Scraping kernels from the corncob.) The extended left index finger points forward, representing the corncob, while the right thumb and index finger rub back and forth along the finger, as if scraping off kernels.

[C–402]

CORNER 1 (kôr´ nər), *n.* (The natural sign.) Both hands, palms flat and fingers straight, are held in front of the body at right angles to each other with fingertips touching, the left fingertips pointing to the right and the right fingertips pointing forward. *Cf.* ANGLE.

[C–403]

CORNER 2, *v.*, -NERED, -NERING. (A pinning down.) The left "D" finger represents the one who is caught. The curved index and middle fingers of the right hand, palm facing down, are thrust against the left "D" finger, impaling it. *Cf.* CAUGHT IN THE ACT 1, CONTACT 2.

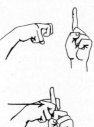

[C-404]

CORNER ROUNDER, *(voc.), n. phrase.* (Moving around a corner.) The right hand is held flat, palm facing the body and fingers pointing left. It moves slowly to the left, in front of, and around, the fingertips of the left hand, which is held with fingers pointing down and palm facing the body.

[C-405]

CORN-ON-THE-COB (kôrn, kŏb), *n.* (Act of eating an ear of corn.) The index fingers, touching each other, are brought up against the teeth. Both hands are pivoted around and back several times. One index finger may also be used, instead of two.

[C-406]

CORONET (kôr´ ə nĭt, -nĕt´, kŏr´ -), *n.* (The natural sign.) Both "C" hands, held in a modified position, with middle, ring, and little fingers extended and little finger edges down, are held over the head and slowly lowered, as if placing a crown on the head. *Cf.* CROWN 1.

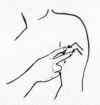

[C-407]

CORPORAL (kôr´ pə rəl), *n.* (Two stripes worn on the sleeve.) The index and middle fingers of the right "H" hand trace two parallel, inverted-V stripes on the left sleeve below the shoulder.

[C-408]

CORRECT 1, *adj.* The right index finger, held above the left index finger, comes down rather forcefully so that the bottom of the right hand comes to rest on top of the left thumb joint. *Cf.* ACCURATE 2, DECENT, EXACT 2, JUST 2, PROPER, RIGHT 3, SUITABLE.

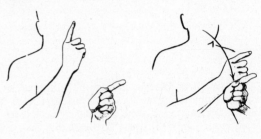

[C-409]

CORRECT 2 (kə rĕkt´), *v.,* -RECTED, -RECTING. (A canceling out.) The right index finger makes a cross on the open left palm. *Cf.* ANNUL, CANCEL, CHECK 1, CRITICISM, CRITICIZE, FIND FAULT 1, REVOKE.

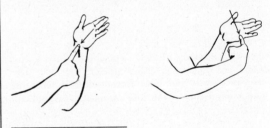

[C-410]

CORRESPOND (kôr´ ə spŏnd´), *v.,* -PONDED, -PONDING. The "AND" hands face each other, one slightly higher than the other. The two hands then move toward and past each other, opening as they do.

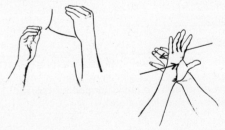

[C-411]

CORRIDOR (kôr´ ə dər, kŏr´ -), *n.* (The movement.) Both hands, palms facing and fingers together and extended straight out, move in unison away from the body, in a straight or winding manner. *Cf.* HALL,

HALLWAY, MANNER 2, METHOD, OPPORTUNITY 3, PATH, ROAD, STREET, TRAIL, WAY 1.

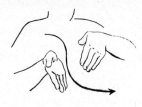

[C–412]

CORRUPT (kə rŭpt´), *adj.* The left "5" hand, palm up, is held slightly above the right "5" hand, held palm down. The right hand swings up, just brushing over the left palm. Both hands close into the "S" position, and the right is brought back with force to its initial position, striking a glancing blow against the left knuckles as it returns. *Cf.* ABOLISH 1, ANNIHILATE, DEFACE, DEMOLISH, HAVOC, PERISH 2, REMOVE 3, RUIN.

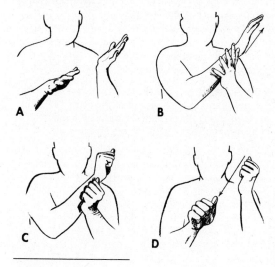

A　　　　　　　B

C　　　　　　　D

[C–413]

COSMETICS (kŏz mĕt´ĭks), *n. pl.* (Applying something to the face.) The thumbtip and fingertips of each hand are held together and rotated in small counterclockwise circles on both cheeks simultaneously. *Cf.* MAKE-UP.

[C–414]

COST (kôst, kŏst), *n., v.,* COST, COSTING. (Nicking into one.) The knuckle of the right "X" finger is nicked against the palm of the left hand, held in the "5" position, palm facing right. *Cf.* ADMISSION 2, CHARGE 1, DUTY 2, EXCISE, EXPENSE, FEE, FINE 2, IMPOST, PENALTY 3, PRICE 2, TAX 1, TAXATION 1, TOLL.

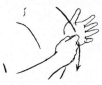

[C–415]

COSTLY (kôst´ lĭ), *adj.* (Throwing away money.) The right "AND" hand lies in the palm of the up-turned, open left hand (as if holding money). The right hand then moves up and away from the left, opening abruptly as it does (as if dropping the money it holds). *Cf.* DEAR 2, EXPENSIVE.

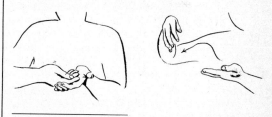

[C–416]

COTTON (kŏt´ ən), *n.* (White, pick.) The sign for WHITE is formed: The fingertips of the "5" hand are placed against the chest. The hand moves straight out from the chest, while the fingers and thumb all come together. Then the fingertips and thumbtip of the downturned, open right hand come together, and the hand moves up a short distance, as if picking something.

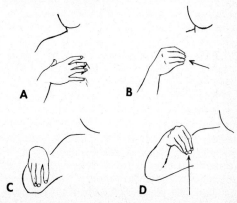

A　　　　　　　B

C　　　　　　　D

[C-417]

COUGH 1 (kôf), *n., v.,* COUGHED, COUGHING. (An irritation in the throat.) The fingertips of the right "V" hand are jabbed into the right side of the neck. The signer imitates coughing.

[C-418]

COUGH 2 (kôf, kŏf), *n., v.* (Indicating distress in the chest area.) The right hand, held cupped, palm down, is moved alternately forward and back in a small arc in front of the chest. The signer opens his mouth as if coughing and assumes a distressed expression.

[C-419]

COULD (kŏŏd), *v.* (An affirmative movement of the hands, likened to a nodding of the head, to indicate ability or power to accomplish something.) Both "A" hands, held palms down, move down in unison a short distance before the chest. *Cf.* ABILITY, ABLE, CAN 1, CAPABLE, COMPETENT, FACULTY, MAY 2, POSSIBLE.

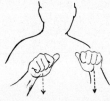

[C-420]

COUNSEL (koun´ səl), *n., v.,* -SELED, -SELING. (Take something, *counsel,* and disseminate it.) The left hand, held limp in front of the body, has its fingers pointing down. The fingers of the right hand, held all together, are placed on top of the left hand,

and then move forward, off the left hand, assuming a "5" position, palm down. This may be repeated. *Cf.* ADVICE, ADVISE, COUNSELOR, INFLUENCE 4.

[C-421]

COUNSELOR (koun´ sə lər), *n.* The sign for COUNSEL is made. This is followed by the sign for INDIVIDUAL: Both open hands, palms facing each other, move down the sides of the body, tracing its outline to the hips.

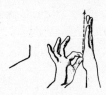

[C-422]

COUNT (kount), *v.,* COUNTED, COUNTING. The thumbtip and index fingertip of the right "F" hand move up along the palm of the open left hand, which is held facing right with fingers pointing up.

[C-423]

COUNTRY 1 (kun´ tri), *n.* (The elbow reinforcement on the jacket of a "country squire" type; also, a place where one commonly "roughs it," *i.e.,* gets rough elbows.) The open right hand describes a continuous counterclockwise circle on the left elbow. *Cf.* FARM 3.

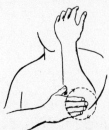

[C–424]

COUNTRY 2, *n.* (An established area.) The right "N" hand, palm down, executes a clockwise circle above the downturned prone left hand. The tips of the "N" fingers then move straight down and come to rest on the back of the left hand. *Cf.* LAND 2, NATION.

[C–425]

COURAGE (kûr´ ĭj, kŭr´ -), *n.* (Strength emanating from the body.) Both "5" hands are placed palms against the chest. They move out and away, forcefully, closing and assuming the "S" position. *Cf.* BRAVE, BRAVERY, COURAGEOUS, FORTITUDE, HALE, HEALTH, HEALTHY, MIGHTY 2, STRENGTH, STRONG 2, WELL 2.

[C–426]

COURAGEOUS (kə rā´ jəs), *adj.* See COURAGE.

[C–427]

COURT (kôrt), *n.* (The scales move up and down.) The two "F" hands, palms facing each other, move alternately up and down. *Cf.* CONSIDER 3, EVALUATE 1, IF, JUDGE 1, JUDGMENT, JUSTICE 1.

[C–428]

COURTEOUS (kûr´ tĭ əs), *adj.* (The ruffled shirt front of a gentleman of old.) The thumb of the right "5" hand is thrust into the chest. The hand then pivots down, with thumb remaining in place. This latter part of the sign, however, is optional. *Cf.* COURTESY, FINE 4, POLITE.

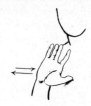

[C–429]

COURTESY (kûr´ tə sĭ), n. See COURTEOUS.

[C–430]

COURTING (kôrt´ ing), *(colloq.), n.* (Heads nodding toward each other.) The "A" hands are placed together before the body with thumbs up. The thumbs wiggle up and down. *Cf.* BEAU, COURTSHIP, LOVER, MAKE LOVE 1, SWEETHEART 1.

[C–431]

COURTSHIP (kôrt´ shĭp), *(colloq.), n.* See COURTING.

[C–432]

COUSIN (kŭz´ ən), *(f.), n.* (The letter "C" in female position.) The right "C" hand is shaken back and forth next to the right cheek.

[C–433]

COUSIN, *(m.), n.* (The letter "C" in male position.) The right "C" hand is shaken back and forth next to the right temple.

[C-434]

COVER 1 (kŭv´ ər), *n., v.,* -ERED, -ERING. (The natural sign.) The right hand, held curved and palm down, slides from fingertips to wrist over the back of the left hand, which is also held curved and palm down.

[C-435]

COVER 2, *n.* (The natural sign.) The open right hand lies over the upturned thumb edge of the left "S" hand. In this position the right hand turns in a clockwise direction several times, as if screwing on a cover. *Cf.* LID.

[C-436]

COVER 3, *n.* (The natural sign.) The open right hand, held palm down before the chest, moves downward, coming to rest atop the upturned thumb edge of the left "S" hand, as if to cover it.

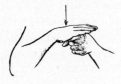

[C-437]

COVER 4, *v.* (One hand is hidden under the other.) The thumb of the right "A" hand, whose palm faces left, is placed against the lips. The hand then swings down and under the downturned left hand. The initial contact with the lips is sometimes omitted. *Cf.* HIDE.

[C-438]

COVET 1 (kŭv´ it), *v.,* -ETED, -ETING. (Grasping something and pulling it in.) The upturned "5" hands, held side by side before the chest, close slightly into a grasping position as they move in toward the body. *Cf.* DESIRE 1, LONG 2, NEED 2, WHAT, WILL 2, WISH 1.

[C-439]

COVET 2, *v.* (Biting the finger to suppress the feelings.) The tip of the index finger is bitten. The tip of the little finger is sometimes used. *Cf.* ENVIOUS, ENVY, JEALOUS, JEALOUSY.

[C-440]

COW (kou), *n.* (The cow's horns.) The "Y" hands, palms facing away from the body, are placed at the temples, with thumbs touching the head. Both hands are brought out and away simultaneously, in a gentle curve.

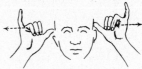

[C-441]

COWARD (kou´ ərd), *n.* (The heart is suddenly covered with fear.) Both hands, fingers together, are placed side by side, palms facing the chest. They quickly open and come together over the heart, one on top of the other. *Cf.* AFRAID, FEAR 1, FRIGHT, FRIGHTEN, SCARE(D), TERROR 1.

[C-442]

COZY (kō´ zǐ), *adj.* (A stroking motion.) Each downturned open hand alternately strokes the back of the other, moving forward from wrist to fingers. *Cf.* COMFORT, COMFORTABLE, CONSOLE.

[C-443]

CRACK (krăk), *v.*, CRACKED, CRACKING. (The natural movement.) The little finger edge of the right hand describes a zigzag on the upturned left palm.

[C-444]

CRACKED IN THE HEAD, *adj. phrase.* (The mind is cracked.) The forehead is touched with the index finger. The little finger edge of the right hand then traces a zigzag path on the upturned left palm. *Cf.* MENTALLY UNBALANCED 3.

[C-445]

CRACKER 1 (krăk´ ər), *n.* The thumb edge of the right fist strikes several times against the left elbow, while the left arm is bent so that the left fist is held against the right shoulder. *Cf.* MATZOTH, PASSOVER.

[C-446]

CRACKER 2, *n.* (Modification of CRACKER 1.) The elbow is brought down into the upturned palm, as if to break a cracker in it.

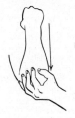

[C-447]

CRASH (krăsh), *n., v.,* CRASHED, CRASHING. The fists come together with force. *Cf.* COLLIDE 1, COLLISION 1, RUN UP AGAINST, WRECK.

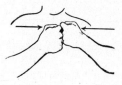

[C-448]

CRAVE (krāv), *v.,* CRAVED, CRAVING. (The upper alimentary tract is outlined.) The right "C" hand, palm facing the body, is placed with fingertips touching midchest. In this position it moves down a bit. *Cf.* APPETITE, DESIRE 2, FAMINE, HUNGARIAN, HUNGARY, HUNGER, HUNGRY, STARVATION, STARVE, STARVED, WISH 2.

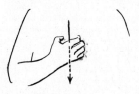

[C-449]

CRAZY 1 (krā´ zǐ), *adj.* (Turning of wheels in the head.) The open right hand is held palm down before the face, fingers spread, bent, and pointing toward the forehead. The fingers move in circles before the forehead. *Cf.* INSANE, INSANITY, MAD 2, NUTS 1.

[C–450]

CRAZY 2, *adj.* (Wheels in the head.) The sign for THINK is made. Then both index fingers, positioned one on top of the other and pointing to each other, spin around. *Cf.* NUTS 2.

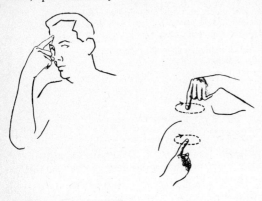

[C–451]

CRAZY 3, *adj.* (Turning of wheels in the head.) The right index finger revolves in a clockwise circle at the right temple. *Cf.* NUTS 3.

[C–452]

CREAM (krēm), *n.* (The motion of "skimming" cream.) The right hand is held slightly cupped and is moved repeatedly across the upturned, open left palm, as if skimming cream from the top of a container of milk.

[C–453]

CREATE (krē āt´), *v.,* CREATED, CREATING. (Fashioning something with the hands.) The right "S" hand, palm facing left, is placed on top of its left counterpart, whose palm faces right. The hands are twisted back and forth, striking each other slightly after each twist. *Cf.* COMPOSE, CONSTITUTE, CONSTRUCT 2, DEVISE 2, FABRICATE, FASHION, FIX, MAKE, MANUFACTURE, MEND 1, PRODUCE 3, RENDER 1, REPAIR.

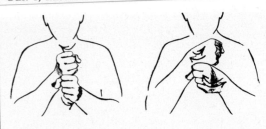

[C–454]

CREATOR (krē ā´ tər), *n.* The sign for CREATE, is made. This is followed by the sign for INDIVIDUAL: Both open hands, palms facing each other, move down the sides of the body, tracing its outline to the hips.

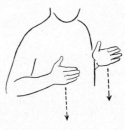

[C–455]

CREDIBLE (krĕd´ ə bəl), *adj.* (Fall for something, *i.e.,* swallowing the bait.) The right-angle hand is brought up toward the open mouth. *Cf.* GULLIBLE.

[C–456]

CRIME (krīm), *n.* (BAD; SIN.) The sign for BAD is made: The right fingertips are placed on the lips, and then the right hand is thrown down. This is followed by the sign for SIN: The "D" hands, palms facing the body, are positioned with index fingers pointing toward each other. The hands move in continuous ellipses, away from and toward each other. *Cf.* EVIL.

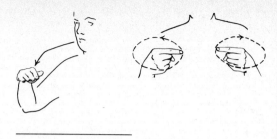

[C–457]

CRIPPLE (krĭp´ əl), *n.,v.,* -PLED, -PLING. (The uneven movement of the legs.) The downturned index fingers move alternately up and down. The body sways to and fro a little, keeping time with the movement of the fingers. *Cf.* LAME.

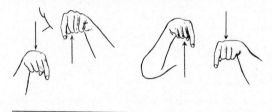

[C–458]

CRITICISM (krĭt´ ə sĭz´ əm), *n.* (A canceling out.) The right index finger makes a cross on the open left palm. *Cf.* ANNUL, CANCEL, CHECK 1, CORRECT 2, CRITICIZE, FIND FAULT 1, REVOKE.

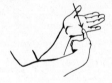

[C–459]

CRITICIZE (krĭt´ ə sĭz´), *v.,* -CIZED, -CIZING. See CRITICISM.

[C–460]

CROCHET (krō shā´), *v.,* -CHETED, -CHETING. (The act of crocheting.) The curved index fingers alternate in crossing each other several times.

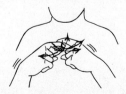

[C–461]

CROOK (krŏŏk), *n.* (A mustachioed thief.) The fingertips of both "H" hands, palms facing the body, are placed above the lips and are drawn slowly apart, describing a mustache. Sometimes one hand only is used. This is followed by the sign for INDIVIDUAL: Both open hands, palms facing each other, move down the sides of the body, tracing its outline to the hips. *Cf.* BANDIT, BURGLAR, BURGLARY, ROB 3, ROBBER 1, STEAL 3, THEFT 3, THIEF 2.

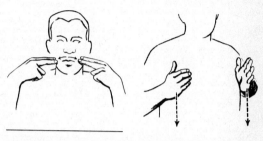

[C–462]

CROSS 1 (krôs), *adj.* (Wrinkling the brow.) The "5" hand is held palm toward the face. The fingers open and close partly, several times, while an angry expression is worn on the face. *Cf.* ANGRY 1, CROSSNESS, FIERCE, ILL TEMPER, IRRITABLE.

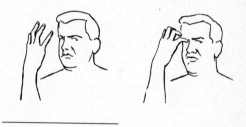

[C–463]

CROSS 2, *(eccles.), n.* (The cross on the mountain.) The back of the right "S" hand is struck several times against the back of the left "S" hand to denote something hard, like a ROCK or a MOUNTAIN, *q.v.* The sign for CROSS 2 is then made: The right "C" hand, palm facing out, makes the sign of the cross. *Cf.* CALVARY 1, CRUCIFIX.

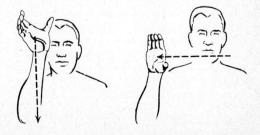

[C–464]

CROSS 3, *v.*, CROSSED, CROSSING. (A crossing over.) The left hand is held before the chest, palm down and fingers together. The right hand, fingers together, glides over the left, with the right little finger touching the top of the left hand. *Cf.* ACROSS, OVER 2.

[C–465]

CROSS 4, *v.* (Intersecting lines.) The extended index fingers move toward each other at right angles and cross. *Cf.* CROSSING, INTERSECT, INTERSECTION.

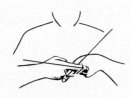

[C–466]

CROSSING (krôs´ ing), *n.* See CROSS 4.

[C–467]

CROSSNESS, *n.* See CROSS 1.

[C–468]

CROWD (kroud), *n., v.*, CROWDED, CROWDING. (The movement of many people.) Both open hands are held side by side, palms down. The hands are then moved forward while the fingers wiggle.

[C–469]

CROWDED, *adj.* (Squeezed in.) The "5" hands are held about a foot apart in front of the body, fingers pointing forward. The hands are slowly pushed toward each other without touching, as if compressing something into a smaller space. The signer assumes a strained expression.

[C–470]

CROWN 1 (kroun), *n.* (The natural sign.) Both "C" hands, held in a modified position, with middle, ring, and little fingers extended and little finger edges down, are held over the head and slowly lowered, as if placing a crown on the head. *Cf.* CORONET.

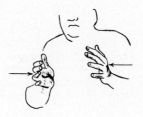

[C–471]

CROWN 2, *n., v.* (Placing a crown on the head.) The right hand, its thumb and fingers spread and curved, is placed with thumbtip and fingertips touching the top of the head, to represent a crown.

[C–472]

CROWNED (kround), *(sports), adj.* (The head is crowned.) The upturned left index finger represents the victorious individual. The downturned "5" hand, fingers curved, is brought down on the left index finger as if draping it with a crown. *Cf.* CHAMPION.

[C–473]

CRUCIFIX (krōō sə fĭks´), *n.* See CROSS 2.

[C–474]

CRUCIFY (krōō´ sə fī′), *v.,* -FIED, -FYING. (Nailing the hands to the cross.) The right index fingertip is pushed into the palm of the open left hand, which is held facing right; immediately following this, the little finger edge of the right fist is struck forcefully against the same open left palm, as if driving a nail. Then the above motions are repeated, using the left index finger and fist against the open right palm, which is held facing left. Finally, both open "5" hands are raised above the head and held there, palms facing forward, fingers spread and pointing up.

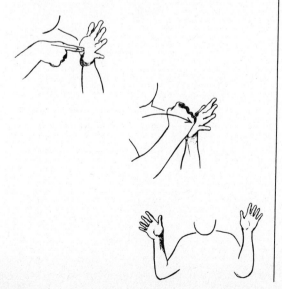

[C–475]

CRUEL 1 (krōō´ əl), *adj.* (Striking down against.) Both "A" or "X" hands are held before the chest, the right above the left. The right hand strikes down and out, hitting the left thumb and knuckles with force. *Cf.* BACKBITE, BASE 3, HARM 2, HURT 2, MAR 2, MEAN 1, SPOIL.

[C–476]

CRUEL 2, *adj.* (A heart that is rough.) The sign for HEART 1 is made: The index fingers outline either half of a small heart on the left side of the chest. Then the sign for ROUGH is made: The right thumbtip and fingertips are placed at the base of the upturned, open left palm. From this position they move forward forcefully, off and away from the left hand.

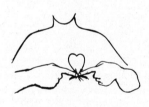

[C–477]

CRUEL 3, *adj*. The movements in TEASE 1, *q.v.*, are duplicated, except that the "G" hands are used. *Cf.* TEASE 3.

[C–478]

CRUSHING (krŭsh´ ing), *adj*. (The hands drop under a weight.) The upturned "5" hands, held before the chest, suddenly drop a short distance. *Cf.* HEAVY, WEIGHTY.

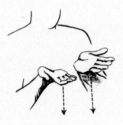

[C–479]

CRY 1 (krī), *v.*, CRIED, CRYING. (Tears streaming down the cheeks.) Both index fingers, in the "D" position, move down the cheeks, either once or several times. Sometimes one finger only is used. *Cf.* BAWL 1, TEAR 2, TEARDROP, WEEP 1.

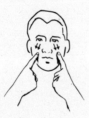

[C–480]

CRY 2, *v.* (Tears gushing from the eyes.) Both "B" hands are held before the face, palms facing forward, with the backs of the index fingertips touching the face just below the eyes. From this position both hands move forward and over in an arc, to indicate a flow of tears. *Cf.* BAWL 2, WEEP 2.

[C–481]

CRY 3, *v.* (Harsh words thrown out.) The right hand, as in BLASPHEME 1, appears to claw words out of the mouth. This time, however, it turns and throws them out, ending in the "5" position. *Cf.* BLASPHEME 2, CALL OUT, CRY OUT, CURSE 2, SCREAM, SHOUT, SUMMON 1, SWEAR 3.

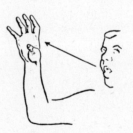

[C–482]

CRY OUT (krī out), *v. phrase*. See CRY 3.

[C–483]

CUNNING (kŭn´ ĭng), *n., adj.* (Acting undercover.) The right index finger passes slowly beneath the downturned, cupped left hand. The signer assumes a sly expression.

[C–484]

CUP (kŭp), *n.* (The natural sign.) The little finger edge of the right "C" hand rests on the palm of the upturned, open left hand. *Cf.* CUP AND SAUCER.

[C–485]

CUP AND SAUCER (kŭp, sô´ sər), *n. phrase.* See CUP.

[C–486]

CURIOSITY (kyŏŏr´ ĭ ŏs´ ə tĭ), *n.* See CURIOUS 3.

[C–487]

CURIOUS 1 (kyŏŏr´ ĭ əs), *adj.* (Directing the vision from place to place.) The right "C" hand, palm facing left, moves from right to left across the line of vision, in a series of counterclockwise circles. The signer's gaze remains concentrated and his head turns slowly from right to left. *Cf.* EXAMINE, INVESTIGATE 1, LOOK FOR, PROBE 1, QUEST, SEARCH, SEEK.

[C–488]

CURIOUS 2, *adj.* (Something which distorts the vision.) The "C" hand describes a small arc in front of the face. *Cf.* GROTESQUE, ODD, PECULIAR, QUEER 1, STRANGE 1, WEIRD.

[C–489]

CURIOUS 3, *(colloq.), adj.* (The Adam's apple.) The right thumb and index finger pinch the skin over the Adam's apple, while the hand wiggles up and down. *Cf.* CURIOSITY.

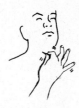

[C–490]

CURL (kŭrl), *n., v.,* CURLED, CURLING. (Act of curling or braiding the hair.) The "R" hands, placed palms out at the left temple, are alternately moved down, as if braiding the hair. *Cf.* BRAID.

[C–491]

CURRANT (kûr´ ənt), *n.* (Indicating the color and small size of the fruit.) The sign for RED is made: The index finger of the right "D" hand is drawn down across the lips several times. The thumb and index finger of the right "D" hand then grasp the tip of the little finger of the left "I" hand.

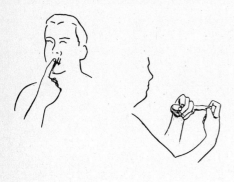

[C–492]

CURRENCY (kûr´ ən sĭ), *n.* (Slapping of paper money in the palm.) The upturned right hand, grasping some imaginary bills, is brought down into the upturned left palm a number of times. *Cf.* CAPITAL 2, FINANCES, FUNDS, MONEY 1.

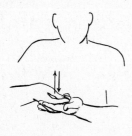

[C–493]

CURRENT (kûr´ ənt), *adj.* (Something right in front of you.) The upturned right-angle hands drop down rather sharply. The "Y" hands may also be used. *Cf.* IMMEDIATE, NOW, PRESENT 3.

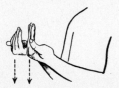

[C–494]

CURSE 1 (kûrs), *n., v.,* CURSED, CURSING. (Harsh words and a threatening hand.) The right hand appears to claw words out of the mouth. It ends in the "S" position, above the head, shaking back and forth in a threatening manner. *Cf.* BLASPHEME 1, SWEAR 2.

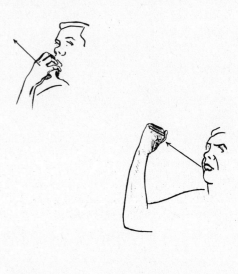

[C–495]

CURSE 2, *n., v.* (Harsh words thrown out.) The right hand, as in CURSE 1, appears to claw words out of the mouth. This time, however, it turns and throws them out, ending in the "5" position. *Cf.* BLASPHEME 2, CALL OUT, CRY 3, CRY OUT, SCREAM, SHOUT, SUMMON 1, SWEAR 3.

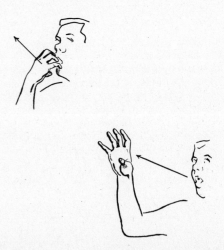

[C–496]

CURSE 3, *(sl.), n., v.* (Curlicues, as one finds in cartoon-type swear words.) The right "Y" hand, palm down, pivots at the wrist along the left "G" hand, from the wrist to the tip of the finger. *Cf.* BLASPHEME 3, SWEAR 4.

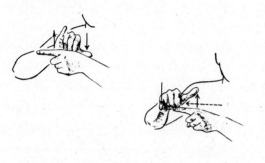

[C–497]

CURTAIN (kûr´ tən), *n.* (The drape of the curtain.) The "5" hands, palms out, trace the curtains on the window.

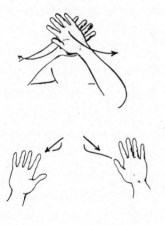

[C–498]

CUSTOM (kŭs´ təm), *n.* (Bound down to custom or habit.) Both "S" hands, palms down, are crossed and brought down in unison before the chest. *Cf.* ACCUS-TOM, BOUND, HABIT, LOCKED, PRACTICE 3.

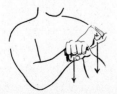

[C–499]

CUT (kŭt), *v.*, CUT, CUTTING. (Cutting the finger with a knife.) The extended right index finger makes a cutting motion across the extended left index finger. Both hands are held palms down.

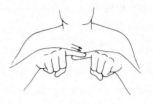

[C–500]

CUTE 1 (kūt), *adj.* (Titillating to the taste.) The fingertips of the right "U" hand, palm facing the body, brush against the chin a number of times, beginning at the lips. *Cf.* CANDY 1, SUGAR, SWEET.

[C–501]

CUTE 2, *adj.* (Tickling.) The open right hand is held with fingers spread and pointing up, palm facing the chest. In this position the fingertips wiggle up and down, tickling the chin several times.

[C–502]

CUT OFF, *v. phrase.* (The natural sign.) The right index and middle fingers grasp the extended left fingertips, as if to cut them off.

[C–503]

CYNIC (sĭn´ ĭk), *n.* (The nose is wrinkled in disbelief.) The right "V" hand faces the nose. The index and middle fingers bend as a cynical expression is assumed. This is followed by the sign for INDIVIDUAL: Both open hands, palms facing each other, move down the sides of the body, tracing its outline

to the hips. *Cf.* CYNICAL, DISBELIEF 1, DON'T BELIEVE, DOUBT 1, INCREDULITY, SKEPTIC 1, SKEPTICAL 1.

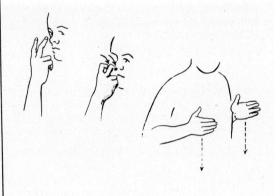

[C–504]

CYNICAL (sĭn´ ə kəl), *adj.* See CYNIC. The sign for INDIVIDUAL is omitted.

D

DACTYLOLOGY (dăk´ tə lŏl´ ə jĭ), *n.* (The movement of the fingers in fingerspelling.) The right hand, palm out, is moved from left to right, with the fingers wriggling up and down. *Cf.* ALPHABET, FINGER-SPELLING, MANUAL ALPHABET, SPELL, SPELLING.

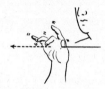

[D-2]

DAD (dăd), *(informal), n.* (Derived from the formal sign for FATHER 1, *q.v.*) The thumbtip of the right "5" hand touches the right temple a number of times. The other fingers may also wiggle. *Cf.* DADDY, FATHER 2, PAPA, POP 2.

[D-3]

DADDY (dăd´ ĭ), *n.* See DAD.

[D-4]

DAFT (dăft, däft), *adj.* (Thoughts flickering back and forth.) The right "Y" hand, thumb almost touching the forehead, is shaken back and forth across the forehead several times. *Cf.* ABSURD, FOLLY, FOOLISH, NONSENSE, RIDICULOUS, SILLY, TRIFLING.

[D-5]

DAILY (dā´ lĭ), *adj.* (Tomorrow after tomorrow.) The sign for TOMORROW, *q.v.,* is made several times: The right "A" hand moves forward several times from its initial resting place on the right cheek. *Cf.* EVERYDAY.

[D-6]

DAMN (dăm), *(ejac.), n., v.,* DAMNED, DAMNING. (The letter "D"; an emphatic movement.) The right "D" hand moves quickly to the right.

[D-7]

DAMP (dămp), *adj.* (The wetness.) The right fingertips touch the lips, and then the fingers of both hands open and close against the thumbs a number of times. *Cf.* CERAMICS, CLAY, MOIST, WET.

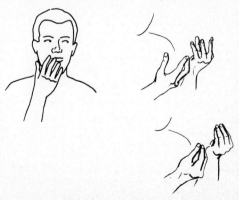

[D-8]

DANCE (dăns, däns), *n., v.,* DANCED, DANCING. (The rhythmic swaying of the feet.) The downturned index and middle fingers of the right "V" hand swing rhythmically back and forth over the upturned left palm. *Cf.* BALL 1, PARTY 2.

[D-9]

DANE (dān), *n.* (The letter "D"; the top or northern part of the body.) The right "D" hand, palm facing left, makes a small counterclockwise circle on the forehead. *Cf.* DENMARK.

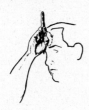

[D-10]

DANGER 1 (dān' jər), *n.* (Throwing out the hands.) Both hands, their fingertips touching their respective thumbs, are held, palms facing each other, near the temples. They are thrown out before the face, assuming "5" positions, palms still facing. *Cf.* AWFUL, CALAMITOUS, CATASTROPHIC, DANGEROUS 1, DREADFUL, FEARFUL, TERRIBLE, TRAGEDY, TRAGIC.

[D-11]

DANGER 2, *n.* (An encroachment; parrying a knife thrust.) The left "A" hand is held palm toward the body, knuckles facing right. The extended thumb of

the right "A" hand is brought sharply over the back of the left. *Cf.* DANGEROUS 2, INJURE 2, PERIL, TRESPASS, VIOLATE.

[D-12]

DANGEROUS 1 (dān' jər əs), *adj.* See DANGER 1.

[D-13]

DANGEROUS 2, *adj.* See DANGER 2.

[D-14]

DARK(NESS) (därk), *adj., n.* (Shutting out the light.) Both open hands are held in front of the face, the right palm over the right eye and the left palm over the left eye. The hands then move toward each other and slightly downward in a short arc, coming to rest one behind the other so that they hide the face. *Cf.* TWILIGHT.

[D-15]

DARN (därn), *v.,* DARNED, DARNING. (The threads are interwoven.) Both "5" hands, palms down, are brought slowly together, with the right sliding over the left. As they move together, the fingers wiggle. *Cf.* INFILTRATE, WEAVE.

[D-16]

DAUGHTER (dô' tər), *n*. (Female baby.) The FE-MALE prefix sign is made: The thumb of the right "A" hand traces a line on the right jaw from just below the ear to the chin. The sign for BABY is then made: The right arm is folded on the left arm. Both palms face up.

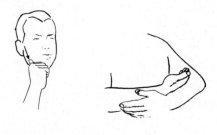

[D-17]

DAY (dā), *n., adj*. (The letter "D"; the course of the sun across the sky.) The left arm, held horizontally, palm down, represents the horizon. The right elbow rests on the back of the left hand, with the right arm in a perpendicular position. The right "D" hand, palm facing left, moves in an arc to the left until it is just above the left elbow.

[D-18]

DAY AFTER TOMORROW (tə môr' ō), *phrase*. (One tomorrow ahead.) The sign for TOMORROW, *q.v.*, is made, but as the "A" hand moves forward the index finger is presented.

[D-19]

DAY BEFORE YESTERDAY (yĕs' tər di, -dā´), *phrase*. (One yesterday in the past.) The sign for YESTERDAY, *q.v.*, is made, but as the "A" hand moves back the index finger is presented.

[D-20]

DAYDREAM (dā' drēm´), *n., v.*, -DREAMED, -DREAMING. (A thought wanders off into space.) The right curved index finger opens and closes quickly as it leaves its initial position on the forehead and moves up into the air. *Cf.* DISTRACTION, DREAM.

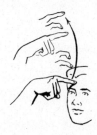

[D-21]

DAY OF ATONEMENT (ə tōn' mənt), *(eccles.)*. (Day of Sorrow.) The sign for DAY is made: The right "D" hand, palm facing left, is held high, with the right elbow resting in the palm or on the back of the left hand. The right arm describes a 45-degree arc as it moves from right to left. The sign for SORRY or SORROW is then made: The right "S" hand, palm facing the body, is rotated several times over the area of the heart. *Cf.* YOM KIPPUR.

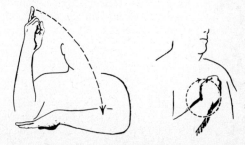

[D–22]

DAZZLE (dăz′ əl), v., -ZLED, -ZLING. (A glittering which leaves one wide-eyed.) The "5" hands, palms out, are held before the face. The fingers wiggle and the eyes are opened wide. The head is held slightly back.

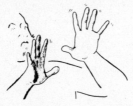

[D–23]

DEACON 1 (dē′ kən), (eccles.), n. (The letter "D.") The tip of the index finger of the right "D" hand traces a line from the left shoulder to the right hip.

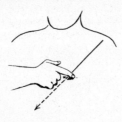

[D–24]

DEACON 2, (eccles.), n. The right "D" hand, palm facing the body, swings from the right shoulder to the left shoulder.

[D–25]

DEAD 1 (dĕd), adj. (Turning over on one's side.) The open hands, fingers pointing ahead, are held side by side, with the right palm down and the left palm up. The two hands reverse their relative positions as they move from the left to the right. Cf. DEATH, DIE 1, DYING, EXPIRE 2, PERISH 1.

[D–26]

DEAD 2, (sl.), adj. (An animal's legs sticking up in the air, in death.) Both hands are held with palms facing each other, and curved index and middle fingers presented. The hands pivot up a bit, simultaneously, assuming the "V" position as they do. Cf. DIE 2, PASS OUT.

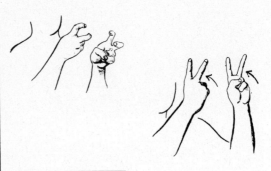

[D–27]

DEAF 1 (dĕf), adj. (Deaf and mute.) The tip of the extended right index finger touches first the right ear and then the closed lips.

[D–28]

DEAF 2 (dĕf), adj. (The ear is shut.) The right index finger touches the right ear. Both "B" hands, palms out, then draw together until their index finger edges touch.

[D–29]

DEAFNESS (dĕf′ nĕs), n. See DEAF 1. This is followed by the sign for -NESS: The downturned right

"N" hand moves down along the left palm, which is facing away from the body.

left hand, which is held with palm down and other fingers pointing right. *Cf.* LACK, MISSING 2.

[D–30]

DEAR 1 (dĭr), *adj.* (Stroking a person or the head of a pet.) The right hand strokes the back of the left several times. *Cf.* FOND 1, PET, STROKE 2, TAME.

[D–31]

DEAR 2, *adj.* (Throwing away money.) The right "AND" hand lies in the palm of the upturned, open left hand (as if holding money). The right hand then moves up and away from the left, opening abruptly as it does (as if dropping the money it holds). *Cf.* COSTLY, EXPENSIVE.

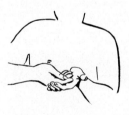

[D–32]

DEARTH (dûrth), *n.* The extended right index finger strikes against the downturned middle finger of the

[D–33]

DEATH (dĕth), *n.* See DEAD 1.

[D–34]

DEBATE (dĭ bāt'), *n., v.,* -BATED, -BATING. (An expounding back and forth.) The index fingers here represent the two sides of the argument. First the left index finger is slapped into the open right palm, and then the right makes the same movement into the left palm. This is repeated back and forth several times. *Cf.* ARGUE, ARGUMENT, CONTROVERSY, DISPUTE.

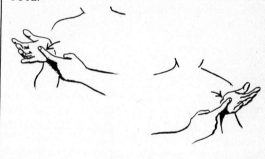

[D–35]

DEBIT (dĕb' ĭt), *n.* (Pointing to the palm, where the money should be placed.) The index finger of one hand is thrust into the upturned palm of the other several times. *Cf.* ARREARS, DEBT, DUE, OBLIGATION 3, OWE.

[D–36]

DEBT (dĕt), *n.* See DEBIT.

[D-37]

DECAY (dǐ kā'), *v.*, -CAYED, -CAYING. (Fingering the small pieces resulting from the breaking up of something.) The thumbs rub slowly across the fingertips of the upturned hands, from the little fingers to the index fingers, and then continue to the "A" position, palms up. *Cf.* DIE OUT, DISSOLVE, FADE, MELT, ROT.

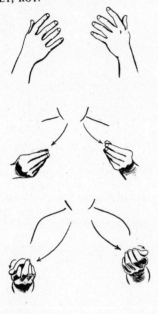

[D-38]

DECEIT (dǐ sēt'), *n.* (Underhandedness.) The right hand, palm down, is held with index and little fingers pointing out. The left hand, in a similar position, is held above the right. The right hand moves forward repeatedly, each time emerging briefly from under the left hand. The positions may be reversed, with the left hand doing the movement, or both hands can move simultaneously. *Cf.* CHEAT 1, DECEIVE, DECEPTION, DEFRAUD, FRAUD, FRAUDULENT 1.

[D-39]

DECEIVE (dǐ sēv'), *v.*, -CEIVED, -CEIVING. See DECEIT.

[D-40]

DECENT (dē' sənt), *adj.* The right index finger, held above the left index finger, comes down rather forcefully so that the bottom of the right hand comes to rest on top of the left thumb joint. *Cf.* ACCURATE 2, CORRECT 1, EXACT 2, JUST 2, PROPER, RIGHT 3, SUITABLE.

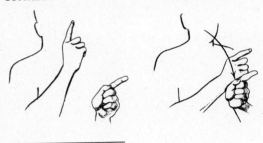

[D-41]

DECEPTION (dǐ sĕp' shən), *n.* See DECEIT.

[D-42]

DECIDE (dǐ sīd'), *v.*, -CIDED, -CIDING. (The mind stops wavering, and the pros and cons are resolved.) The right index finger touches the forehead, the sign for THINK, *q.v.* Both "F" hands, palms facing each other and fingers pointing straight out, then drop down simultaneously. The sign for JUDGE, *q.v.*, explains the rationale behind the movement of the two hands here. *Cf.* DECISION, DECREE 1, DETERMINE, MAKE UP ONE'S MIND, MIND 5, RENDER JUDGMENT, RESOLVE, VERDICT.

[D-43]

DECISION (dǐ sizh' ən), *n.* See DECIDE.

[D-44]

DECLARE (dǐ klâr'), *v.*, -CLARED, -CLARING. (An issuance from the mouth.) Both index fingers are placed at the lips, with palms facing the body. They are rotated once and swung out in arcs, until the left index finger points somewhat to the left and the right index somewhat to the right. Sometimes the rotation of the fingers is omitted in favor of a simple swinging out from the lips. *Cf.* ACCLAIM 1, ACCLAMATION, ANNOUNCE, ANNOUNCEMENT, MAKE KNOWN, PROCLAIM, PROCLAMATION.

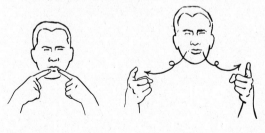

[D–45]

DECLINE 1 (dĭ klīn'), *n., v.,* -CLINED, -CLINING. (A downward movement.) The right "A" hand, held with thumb pointing up, moves straight downward in front of the body. Both "A" hands may also be used. *Cf.* DEGENERATION.

[D–46]

DECLINE 2, *v.* (Going down step by step.) The little finger edge of the open right hand is placed on the upper side of the extended left arm, which is held with the open left hand palm down. The right hand moves down along the left arm in a series of short movements. This is the opposite of IMPROVE, *q.v. Cf.* DETERIORATE, DETERIORATION, NOT IMPROVE.

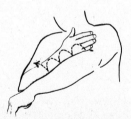

[D–47]

DECLINE 3, *v.* (The hands are shaken, indicating a wish to rid them of something.) The "5" hands, palms facing the body, suddenly swing around to the palms-down position. *Cf.* DON'T WANT.

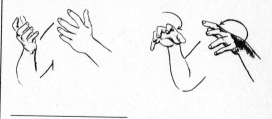

[D–48]

DECORATE 1 (dĕk' ə rāt'), *v.,* -RATED, -RATING. (The hands describe the flounces of draperies.) Both "C" hands, palms out, are held somewhat above the head. They move out and down in a series of successive arcs. *Cf.* ADORN, ORNAMENT 1, TRIM 1.

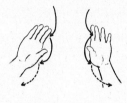

[D–49]

DECORATE 2, *v.* (Embellishing; adding to.) Both "O" hands, palms facing each other, move alternately back and forth in a curving up and down direction. The fingertips come in contact each time the hands pass each other. *Cf.* ORNAMENT 2, TRIM 2.

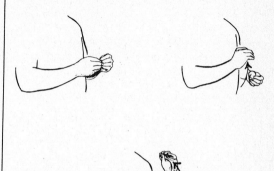

[D-50]

DECREASE (*n.* dē′ krēs; *v.* dĭ krēs′), -CREASED, -CREASING. (The diminishing size or amount.) With palms facing, the right hand is held above the left. The right hand moves slowly down toward the left, but does not touch it. *Cf.* LESS 1, REDUCE.

[D-51]

DECREE 1 (dĭk rē′), *n., v.,* -CREED, -CREEING. (The mind stops wavering, and the pros and cons are resolved.) The right index finger touches the forehead, the sign for THINK, *q.v.* Both "F" hands, palms facing each other and fingers pointing straight out, then drop down simultaneously. The sign for JUDGE, *q.v.,* explains the rationale behind the movement of the two hands here. *Cf.* DECIDE, DECISION, DETERMINE, MAKE UP ONE'S MIND, MIND 5, RENDER JUDGMENT, RESOLVE, VERDICT.

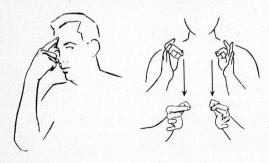

[D-52]

DECREE 2, *n.* (A series of LAWS as they appear on the printed page.) The upright right "L" hand, resting palm against palm on the upright left "5" hand, moves down in an arc, a short distance, coming to rest on the base of the left palm. *Cf.* LAW, LAWYER, LEGAL, PRECEPT.

[D-53]

DECREPIT (dĭ krĕp′ ĭt), *adj.* (Weakness.) The right "A" hand is held palm down before the body, as if grasping a cane. The hand wiggles back and forth as if weak and unsteady, while the head bobs up and down in a similarly shaky manner.

[D-54]

DEDUCT (dĭ dŭkt′), *v.,* -DUCTED, -DUCTING. (Removing.) The right "A" hand, resting in the palm of the left "5" hand, moves slightly up and away, describing a small arc. It is then cast downward, opening into the "5" position, palm down, as if removing something from the left hand and casting it down. *Cf.* ABOLISH 2, ABSENCE 2, ABSENT 2, ABSTAIN, CHEAT 2, DEFICIENCY, DELETE 1, LESS 2, MINUS 3, OUT 2, REMOVE 1, SUBTRACT, SUBTRACTION, TAKE AWAY FROM, WITHDRAW 2.

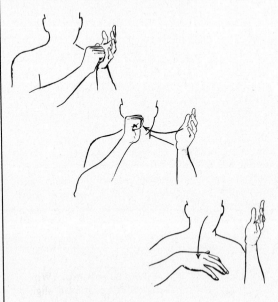

[D-55]

DEED (dēd), *n.* (An activity.) Both open hands, palms down, are swung right and left before the chest. *Cf.* ACT 2, ACTION, ACTIVE, ACTIVITY, BUSY 2, CONDUCT 1, DO, PERFORM 1, PERFORMANCE 1, RENDER 2.

[D–56]

DEEP (dēp), *adj.* (The "D" hand, movement downward.) The right "D" hand is held with index finger pointing down. In this position it moves down along the left palm, which is held facing right with fingertips pointing forward. *Cf.* DEPTH.

[D–57]

DEER (dĭr), *n.* (The branching of the antlers from the head.) Both hands, in the "5" position, palms up, are placed at the head, thumbs resting on the head above the temples. *Cf.* ANTLERS, ELK, MOOSE.

[D–58]

DEFACE (dĭ fās'), *v.*, -FACED, -FACING. (Wiping off.) The left "5" hand, palm up, is held slightly above the right "5" hand, held palm down. The right hand swings up, just brushing over the left palm. Both hands close into the "S" position, and the right is brought back with force to its initial position, striking a glancing blow against the left knuckles as

it returns. *Cf.* ABOLISH 1, ANNIHILATE, CORRUPT, DEMOLISH, DESTROY, HAVOC, PERISH 2, REMOVE 3, RUIN.

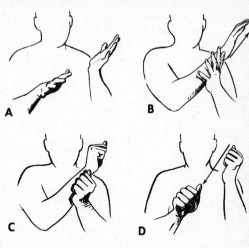

[D–59]

DEFEAT (dĭ fēt'), *v.*, -FEATED, -FEATING. (Forcing the head into a bowed position.) The right "S" hand, placed across the left "S" hand, moves over and down a bit. *Cf.* BEAT 2, CONQUER, OVERCOME, SUBDUE.

[D–60]

DEFEATED, *adj.* (Overpowered by great strength.) The right "S" hand (a fist) is held with palm facing the right shoulder. In this position it moves back toward the shoulder, pivoting from the elbow. The left "S" hand, at the same time, is held palm down with knuckles facing right, and is positioned below the right hand and over the right biceps.

[D-61]

DEFECATE (dĕf′ ə kāt′), *(sl., vulg.), v.,* -CATED, -CATING. (The passing of fecal material.) The left hand grasps the upturned right thumb. The right hand drops down and the right thumb is exposed. *Cf.* FECES.

[D-62]

DEFEND (dĭ fĕnd′), *v.,* -FENDED, -FENDING. (Hold down firmly; cover and strengthen.) The "S" hands, downturned, are held side by side in front of the body, the arms almost horizontal, and the left hand in front of the right. Both arms move a short distance forward and slightly downward. *Cf.* DEFENSE, FORTIFY, GUARD, PROTECT, PROTECTION, SHIELD 1.

[D-63]

DEFENSE (dĭ fĕns′), *n.* See DEFEND.

[D-64]

DEFER (dĭ fûr′), *v.,* -FERRED, -FERRING. (Putting off; moving things forward repeatedly.) The "F" hands, palms facing and fingers pointing out from the body, are moved forward simultaneously in a series of short movements. *Cf.* DELAY, POSTPONE, PROCRASTINATE, PUT OFF.

[D-65]

DEFICIENCY (dĭ fĭsh′ ən sĭ), *n.* (Removing.) The right "A" hand, resting in the palm of the left "5" hand, moves slightly up and away, describing a small arc. It is then cast downward, opening into the "5" position, palm down, as if removing something from the left hand and casting it down. *Cf.* ABOLISH 2, ABSENCE 2, ABSENT 2, ABSTAIN, CHEAT 2, DEDUCT, DELETE 1, LESS 2, MINUS 3, OUT 2, REMOVE 1, SUBTRACT, SUBTRACTION, TAKE AWAY FROM, WITHDRAW 2.

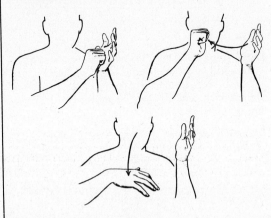

[D-66]

DEFINE 1 (dĭ fīn′), *v.,* -FINED, -FINING. (Unraveling something to get at its parts.) The "F" hands, palms facing and fingers pointing straight out, are held about an inch apart. They move alternately back and forth a few inches. *Cf.* DESCRIBE 1, DESCRIPTION, EXPLAIN 1.

[D-67]

DEFINE 2, *v.* This is the same sign as for DEFINE 1, except that the "D" hands are used.

[D–68]

DEFLATE (dĭ flāt′), *v.,* -FLATED, -FLATING. (A flattening.) The thumb of the right "C" hand rests on the back of the downturned left "B" hand. The fingers suddenly come down on the right thumb. *Cf.* DEFLATION.

[D–69]

DEFLATION (dĭ flā′ shən), *n.* See DEFLATE.

[D–70]

DEFLECT (dĭ flĕkt′), *v.,* -FLECTED, -FLECTING. (The natural motion.) The "G" hands are held side by side and touching, palms down, index fingers pointing forward. Then the right hand moves forward, curving toward the right side as it does. *Cf.* DEVIATE 2, GO OFF THE TRACK, STRAY, WANDER 1.

[D–71]

DEFRAUD (dĭ frôd′), *v.,* -FRAUDED, -FRAUDING. (Underhandedness.) The right hand, palm down, is held with index and little fingers pointing out. The left hand, in a similar position, is held above the right. The right hand moves forward repeatedly, each time emerging briefly from under the left hand. The positions may be reversed, with the left hand doing the movement, or both hands can move simultaneously. *Cf.* CHEAT 1, DECEIT, DECEIVE, DECEPTION, FRAUD, FRAUDULENT 1.

[D–72]

DEGENERATION (dĭ jĕn′ ə rā′ shən), *n.* (A downward movement.) The right "A" hand, held with thumb pointing up, moves straight downward in front of the body. Both "A" hands may also be used. *Cf.* DECLINE 1.

[D–73]

DEJECTED (dĭ jĕk′ tĭd), *adj.* (The facial features drop.) Both "5" hands, palms facing the eyes and fingers slightly curved, drop simultaneously to a level with the mouth. The head drops slightly as the hands move down, and an expression of sadness is assumed. *Cf.* DEPRESSED, GLOOM, GLOOMY, GRAVE 3, GRIEF 1, MELANCHOLY, MOURNFUL, SAD, SORROWFUL 1.

[D–74]

DELAY (dĭ lā′), *n., v.,* -LAYED, -LAYING. (Putting off; moving things forward repeatedly.) The "F" hands, palms facing and fingers pointing out from the body, are moved forward simultaneously in a series of short movements. *Cf.* DEFER, POSTPONE, PROCRASTINATE, PUT OFF.

[D–75]

DELETE 1 (dĭ lēt'), *v.*, -LETED, -LETING. (Removing.) The right "A" hand, resting in the palm of the left "5" hand, moves slightly up and away, describing a small arc. It is then cast downward, opening into the "5" position, palm down, as if removing something from the left hand and casting it down. *Cf.* ABOLISH 2, ABSENCE 2, ABSENT 2, ABSTAIN, CHEAT 2, DEDUCT, DEFICIENCY, LESS 2, MINUS 3, OUT 2, REMOVE 1, SUBTRACT, SUBTRACTION, TAKE AWAY FROM, WITHDRAW 2.

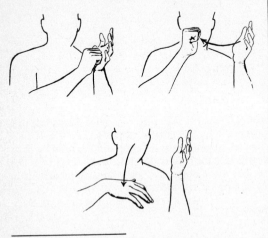

[D–76]

DELETE 2, *v.* (Scratching something out and throwing it away.) The fingertips of the open right hand scratch downward across the palm of the upright left hand. In one continuous motion, the right hand then closes as if holding something, and finally opens again forcefully and motions as if throwing something away. *Cf.* DISCARD 3, ELIMINATE.

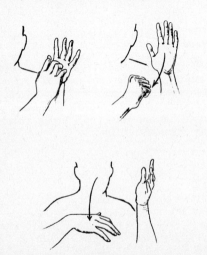

[D–77]

DELETE 3, *v.* (The printer flicks a piece of type out of the composing stick.) The thumb, positioned initially inside the closed hand, flicks out. The hand moves up a bit as the thumb makes its appearance. *Cf.* EXPUNGE.

[D–78]

DELICIOUS 1 (dĭ lĭsh' əs), *adj.* (Smooth to the taste.) The right middle finger is placed on the lips, and then the hand moves down and out a bit. As it does, the thumb rubs over the middle finger. Both hands may be used.

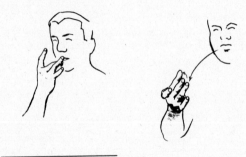

[D–79]

DELICIOUS 2, *adj.* (Licking the fingers.) The signer draws the fingertips of one open hand downward across the tip of the tongue, as if licking the fingers one at a time.

[D–80]

DELIGHT (dĭ līt'), *n.* (The heart is stirred; the spirits bubble up.) The open right hand, palm facing the body, strikes the heart repeatedly, moving up and off the heart after each strike. *Cf.* GAIETY 1, GAY, GLAD, HAPPINESS, HAPPY, JOY, MERRY.

DELIVER 1 (dǐ lǐv′ ər), *v.*, -ERED, -ERING. (Breaking the bonds.) The "S" hands, crossed in front of the body, swing apart and face out. *Cf.* EMANCIPATE, FREE 1, INDEPENDENCE, INDEPENDENT, LIBERATION, REDEEM 1, RELIEF, RESCUE, SAFE, SALVATION, SAVE 1.

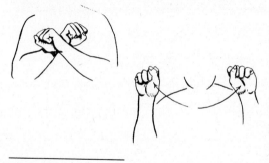

DELIVER 2, *v.* (Carrying something over.) Both open hands, palms up, move in an arc from left to right, as if carrying something from one point to another. *Cf.* BRING, CARRY 2, FETCH, PRODUCE 1, TRANSPORT.

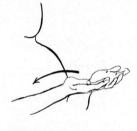

DEMAND (dǐ mănd′, -mänd′), *v.*, -MANDED, -MANDING. (Something specific is moved in toward oneself.) The palm of the left "5" hand faces right. The right index finger is thrust into the left palm,

and both hands are drawn sharply in toward the chest. *Cf.* INSIST, REQUEST 2, REQUIRE.

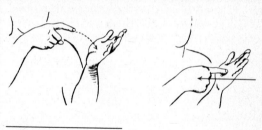

DEMOCRAT (dĕm′ ə krăt), *n.* (The "D" hand.) The right "D" hand is shaken back and forth several times before the right shoulder.

DEMOLISH (dǐ mŏl′ ĭsh), *v.*, -ISHED, -ISHING. (Wiping off.) The left "5" hand, palm up, is held slightly above the right "5" hand, held palm down. The right hand swings up, just brushing over the left palm. Both hands close into the "S" position, and the right is brought back with force to its initial position, striking a glancing blow against the left knuckles as it returns. *Cf.* ABOLISH 1, ANNIHILATE, CORRUPT, DEFACE, DESTROY, HAVOC, PERISH 2, REMOVE 3, RUIN.

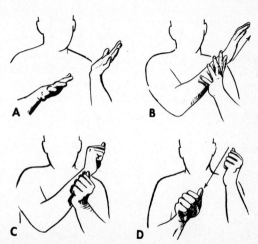

[D–86]

DEMON (dē′ mən), *n.* (The horns.) With the thumbs resting on the temples, the index and middle fingers of both hands open and close repeatedly. *Cf.* DEVIL, DEVILMENT, HELL 1, SATAN.

[D–87]

DEMONSTRATE (dĕm′ ən strāt′), *v.,* -STRATED, -STRATING. (Directing the attention to something, and bringing it forward.) The right index finger points into the left palm, held facing out before the body. The left palm moves straight out. For the passive form of this verb, *i.e.,* **BE SHOWN** or **DEMONSTRATED,** the movement is reversed: The left hand, palm facing in, is moved in toward the body, while the right index finger remains pointing into the left palm. *Cf.* DISPLAY, EVIDENCE, EXAMPLE, EXHIBIT, EXHIBITION, ILLUSTRATE, INDICATE, INFLUENCE 3, PRODUCE 2, REPRESENT, SHOW 1, SIGNIFY 1.

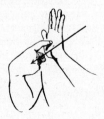

[D–88]

DEMOTE (di′ mōt), *v.,* -MOTED, -MOTING. (Motion downward.) The right-angle hands are held up before the head, fingertips pointing toward each other. From this position, the hands move down in an arc. *Cf.* BASE 2, LOW 2, LOWER.

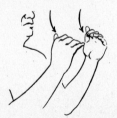

[D–89]

DENMARK (dĕn′ märk), *n.* (The letter "D"; the top or northern part of the body.) The right "D" hand, palm facing left, makes a small counterclockwise circle on the forehead. *Cf.* DANE.

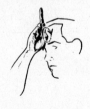

[D–90]

DENTIST (dĕn′ tist), *n.* (The teeth.) The index finger touches the lower teeth, and then the sign for INDIVIDUAL 1, *q.v.,* is made. Instead of the latter sign, the sign for DOCTOR, *q.v.,* may be made. Also, instead of the index finger alone, the middle finger and the index may both be used to touch the lower teeth.

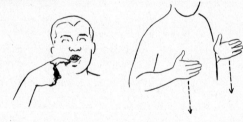

[D–91]

DENY 1 (di nī′), *v.,* -NIED, -NYING. (An emphatic NOT 2, *q.v.*) The thumbs of both "A" hands, positioned under the chin, move out simultaneously, each toward their respective sides of the body. The head may be shaken slightly as the hands move out.

[D-92]

DENY 2, *v.* (Turning down.) The right "A" hand swings down sharply, its thumb pointing down. Both hands are sometimes used here.

[D-93]

DEPART (dĭ p̈art'), *v.*, -PARTED, -PARTING. (Pulling away.) The downturned open hands are held in a line, with fingers pointing to the left, the right hand behind the left. Both hands move in unison toward the right. As they do so, they assume the "A" position. *Cf.* EVACUATE, FORSAKE 1, GRADUATE 2, LEAVE 1, RETIRE 1, WITHDRAW 1.

[D-94]

DEPEND 1 (dĭ pĕnd'), *v.*, -PENDED, -PENDING. (Hanging onto.) With the right index finger resting across its left counterpart, both hands drop down a bit. *Cf.* DEPENDABLE, DEPENDENT, HINGE 2, RELY 2.

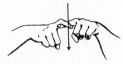

[D-95]

DEPEND 2, *v.* (One hand depending on the other.) The extended index and middle fingers of the downturned right hand rest across the back of their left counterparts. In this position the right fingers push down slightly on the left fingers.

[D-96]

DEPEND 3, *v.* (The letter "D"; DEPEND 1.) The base of the right "D" hand rests on the back of the downturned left "S" hand. Both hands move down simultaneously.

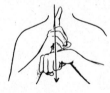

[D-97]

DEPENDABLE (dĭ pĕn' də bəl), *adj.* See DEPEND 1.

[D-98]

DEPENDENT (dĭ pen' dənt), *adj.* See DEPEND 1.

[D-99]

DEPLETE (dĭ plēt'), *v.*, -PLETED, -PLETING. (A disappearance.) The right open hand, palm facing the body, is held by the left hand and is drawn down and out, ending in a position with fingers drawn together. The left hand, meanwhile, may close into a position with fingers also drawn together. *Cf.* ABSENCE 1, ABSENT 1, DISAPPEAR, EMPTY 1, EXTINCT, FADE AWAY, GONE 1, MISSING 1, OMISSION 1, OUT 3, OUT OF, VANISH.

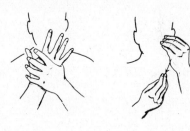

[D-100]

DEPOSIT 1 (dĭ pŏz' ĭt), *v.* (The natural motion.) The downturned "O" hands are brought down and to the left simultaneously from an initial side-by-side position near the right shoulder. *Cf.* PUT DOWN.

[D-101]

DEPOSIT 2, *v.* (To throw something aside.) Both "S" hands are held with palms facing at chest level and then thrown down and to the left, opening into the "5" position. *Cf.* ABANDON 1, CAST OFF, DISCARD 1, FORSAKE 3, LEAVE 2, LET ALONE, NEGLECT.

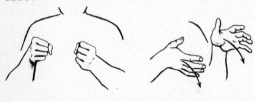

[D-102]

DEPRESSED (dĭ prĕst′), *adj.* (The facial features drop.) Both "5" hands, palms facing the eyes and fingers slightly curved, drop simultaneously to a level with the mouth. The head drops slightly as the hands move down, and an expression of sadness is assumed. *Cf.* DEJECTED, GLOOM, GLOOMY, GRAVE 3, GRIEF 1, MELANCHOLY, MOURNFUL, SAD, SORROWFUL 1.

[D-103]

DEPTH (dĕpth), *n.* (The "D" hand, movement downward.) The right "D" hand is held with index finger pointing down. In this position it moves down along the left palm, which is held facing right with fingertips pointing forward. *Cf.* DEEP.

[D-104]

DESCEND 1 (dĭ sĕnd′), *v.,* -SCENDED, -SCENDING. (Moving down in stages.) With the open hands fac-

ing each other and held aloft, index and middle fingers curved, the hands move down alternately before the body. This is the opposite of the sign for CLIMB 1, *q.v.*

[D-105]

DESCEND 2, *v.* (The natural sign.) With index finger pointing down, the right hand moves down.

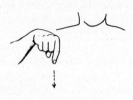

[D-106]

DESCENDANT (dĭ sĕn′ dənt), *n.* (Succeeding generations.) The downturned open left hand is held near the right shoulder, on which rest the fingertips of the right hand. The right hand swings over the back of the left, which then swings in turn over the back of the right. This movement may continue a number of times. *Cf.* OFFSPRING.

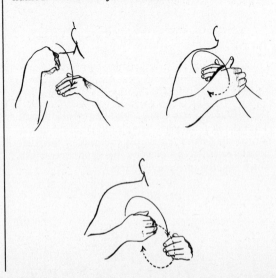

[D–107]

DESCEND LADDER, *v. phrase.* (Legs and arms bent in the natural motion.) The vertical "V" hands are held facing each other a bit above eye level, with fingertips bent. The hands then move down in alternating steps, as if descending a ladder.

[D–108]

DESCEND STAIRS, *v. phrase.* The open hands, held palms down, move alternately downward, step by step.

[D–109]

DESCRIBE 1 (dĭ skrīb'), *v.,* -SCRIBED, -SCRIBING. (Unraveling something to get at its parts.) The "F" hands, palms facing and fingers pointing straight out, are held about an inch apart. They move alternately back and forth a few inches. *Cf.* DEFINE 1, DESCRIPTION, EXPLAIN 1.

[D–110]

DESCRIBE 2, *v.* (The unraveling or stretching out of words or sentences.) Both open hands are held close to each other, with fingers open and palms facing and almost touching. As the hands are drawn apart, the thumb and index finger of each hand come together to form circles. This is repeated several times. *Cf.* EXPLAIN 2, FABLE, FICTION, GOSPEL 1, NARRATE, NARRATIVE, STORY 1, TALE, TELL ABOUT.

[D–111]

DESCRIBE 3, *v.* (The letter "D"; unraveling something.) The "D" hands, palms facing and index fingers pointing straight forward, are held an inch or two apart. They move alternately forward and back.

[D–112]

DESCRIPTION (dĭ skrĭp' shən), *n.* See DESCRIBE 1.

[D–113]

DESERVE (dĭ zûrv'), *v.,* -SERVED, -SERVING. Both "F" hands, palms facing each other, move apart, up, and together in a smooth elliptical fashion, coming together at the tips of the thumbs and index fingers of both hands. *Cf.* ESSENTIAL, IMPORTANT 1, MAIN, MERIT, PRECIOUS, PROMINENT 2, SIGNIFICANCE 1, SIGNIFICANT, VALUABLE, VALUE, VITAL 1, WORTH, WORTHWHILE, WORTHY.

[D–114]

DESIRE 1 (dĭ zīr'), *v.,* -SIRED, -SIRING, *n.* (Grasping something and pulling it in.) The upturned "5" hands, held side by side before the chest, close slightly into a grasping position as they move in toward the body. *Cf.* COVET 1, LONG 2, NEED 2, WANT, WILL 2, WISH 1.

[D–115]

DESIRE 2, *v., n.* (The upper alimentary tract is outlined.) The right "C" hand, palm facing the body, is placed with fingertips touching mid-chest. In this position it moves down a bit. *Cf.* APPETITE, CRAVE, FAMINE, HUNGARIAN, HUNGARY, HUNGER, HUNGRY, STARVATION, STARVE, STARVED, WISH 2.

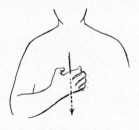

[D–116]

DESPISE 1 (dĭ spīz′), *v.,* -SPISED, -SPISING. (To push away and recoil from; avoid.) The two open hands, palms facing left, are pushed deliberately to the left, as if pushing something away. An expression of disdain or disgust is worn. *Cf.* ABHOR, AVOID 2, DETEST 1, HATE 1, LOATHE.

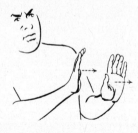

[D–117]

DESPISE 2, *v.* (The finger is flicked to indicate something petty, small; *i.e.,* to be scorned as inconsequential.) The right index finger and thumb are used to press the lips down into an expression of contempt. The right thumb is then flicked out from the closed hand. *Cf.* CONTEMPT 2, DETEST 2, DISLIKE, HATE 2, SCORN 2.

[D–118]

DESPITE (dĭ spīt′), *prep., n.* Both hands, in the "5" position, are held before the chest, fingertips facing each other. With an alternate back-forth movement, the fingertips are made to strike each other. *Cf.* ANYHOW, ANYWAY, DOESN'T MATTER, HOWEVER 2, INDIFFERENCE, INDIFFERENT, IN SPITE OF, MAKE NO DIFFERENCE, NEVERTHELESS, NO MATTER, WHEREVER.

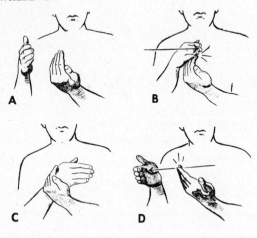

[D–119]

DESTROY (dĭ stroi′), *v.,* -STROYED, -STROYING. (Wiping off.) The left "5" hand, palm up, is held slightly above the right "5" hand, held palm down. The right hand swings up, just brushing over the left palm. Both hands close into the "S" position, and the right is brought back with force to its initial position, striking a glancing blow against the left knuckles as it returns. *Cf.* ABOLISH 1, ANNIHILATE, CORRUPT, DEFACE, DEMOLISH, HAVOC, PERISH 2, REMOVE 3, RUIN.

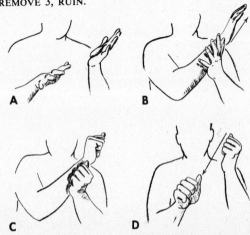

[D–120]

DESTRUCTION (dĭ strŭk' shən), *n.* See DESTROY.

[D–121]

DETACH (dĭ tăch'), *v.*, -TACHED, -TACHING. (An unlocking.) With thumbs and index fingers interlocked initially (the links of a chain), the hands draw apart, showing the break in the chain. *Cf.* DISCONNECT, PART FROM.

[D–122]

DETECT (dĭ tĕkt'), *v.*, -TECTED, -TECTING. (The eye is directed to something specific.) The right index finger touches the base of the right eye, and is then thrust into the upturned left palm. *Cf.* NOTE, NOTICE, OBSERVE 2.

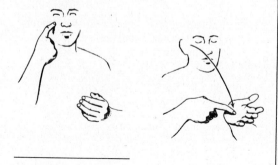

[D–123]

DETECTIVE 1 (dĭ tĕk' tĭv), *n.* (The badge.) The right "D" hand circles over the heart.

[D–124]

DETECTIVE 2, *n.* (The badge hung over the heart.) The right "T" hand moves down slightly from its

position on the heart. This movement is repeated a number of times.

[D–125]

DETERIORATE (dĭ tĭr' ĭ ə rāt'), *v.*, -RATED, -RATING. (Going down step by step.) The little finger edge of the open right hand is placed on the upper side of the extended left arm, which is held with the open left hand palm down. The right hand moves down along the left arm in a series of short movements. This is the opposite of IMPROVE, *q.v. Cf.* DECLINE 2, DETERIORATION, NOT IMPROVE.

[D–126]

DETERIORATION (dĭ tĭr´ ĭ ə rā' shən), *n.* See DETERIORATE.

[D–127]

DETERMINE (dĭ tûr' mĭn), *v.*, -MINED, -MINING. (The mind stops wavering, and the pros and cons are resolved.) The right index finger touches the forehead, the sign for THINK, *q.v.* Both "F" hands, palms facing each other and fingers pointing straight out, then drop down simultaneously. The sign for JUDGE, *q.v.*, explains the rationale behind the movement of the two hands here. *Cf.* DECIDE, DECISION, DECREE 1, MAKE UP ONE'S MIND, MIND 5, RENDER JUDGMENT, RESOLVE, VERDICT.

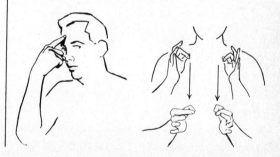

[D–128]

DETEST 1 (dĭ tĕst'), *v.,* -TESTED, -TESTING. (To push away and recoil from; avoid.) The two open hands, palms facing left, are pushed deliberately to the left, as if pushing something away. An expression of disdain or disgust is worn. *Cf.* ABHOR, AVOID 2, DESPISE 1, HATE 1, LOATHE.

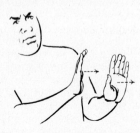

[D–129]

DETEST 2, *v.* (The finger is flicked to indicate something petty, small; *i.e.,* to be scorned as inconsequential.) The right index finger and thumb are used to press the lips down into an expression of contempt. The right thumb is then flicked out from the closed hand. *Cf.* CONTEMPT 2, DESPISE 2, DISLIKE, HATE 2, SCORN 2.

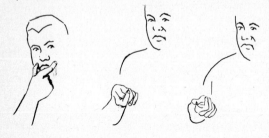

[D–130]

DETROIT (dĭ troit'), *n.* (The letter "D.") The right "D" hand moves down, describing a wavy "S."

[D–131]

DEVELOP 1 (dĭ vĕl' əp), *v.,* -OPED, -OPING. (Flowers or plants emerge from the ground.) The right

fingers, pointing up, emerge from the closed left hand, and they spread open as they do. *Cf.* BLOOM, GROW, GROWN, MATURE, PLANT 1, RAISE 3, REAR 2, SPRING 1.

[D–132]

DEVELOP 2, *v.* (The letter "D"; moving upward, as if in growth.) The right "D" hand is placed against the left palm, which is facing right with fingers pointing up. The "D" hand moves straight up to the left fingertips.

[D–133]

DEVELOP FILM (fĭlm), *v. phrase.* (The natural sign.) With the hands grasping the ends of an imaginary strip of film, the arms swing alternately up and down as if rinsing the film in a film bath.

[D–134]

DEVELOPMENT (dĭ vĕl' əp mənt), *n.* The sign for DEVELOP 2 is made. The -MENT suffix sign is then made: The downturned right "M" hand moves down along the left palm, which is facing away from the body.

[D–135]

DEVIATE 1 (dē′ vĭ āt′), *v.*, -ATED, -ATING. (Going astray.) The open right hand, palm facing left, is placed with its little finger edge resting on the upturned left palm. The right hand curves rather sharply to the left as it moves across the palm. *Cf.* WRONG 2.

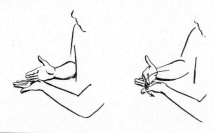

[D–136]

DEVIATE 2, *v.* (The natural motion.) The "G" hands are held side by side and touching, palms down, index fingers pointing forward. Then the right hand moves forward, curving toward the right side as it does. *Cf.* DEFLECT, GO OFF THE TRACK, STRAY, WANDER 1.

[D–137]

DEVIATION (dē′ vĭ ā′ shən), *n.* See DEVIATE 1.

[D–138]

DEVIL (dĕv′ əl), *n.* (The horns.) With the thumbs resting on the temples, the index and middle fingers of both hands open and close repeatedly. *Cf.* DEMON, DEVILMENT, HELL 1, SATAN.

[D–139]

DEVILMENT (dĕv′ əl mənt), *n.* See DEVIL.

[D–140]

DEVISE 1 (dĭ vīz′), *v.*, -VISED, -VISING, *n.* (Placing things in order.) The hands, palms facing, fingers together and pointing away from the body, are positioned at the left side and held about a foot apart. With a slight up-down motion, as if describing waves, the hands travel in unison from left to right. *Cf.* ARRANGE, ARRANGEMENT, CLASSED 2, ORDER 3, PLAN 1, POLICY 1, PREPARE 1, PROGRAM 1, PROVIDE 1, PUT IN ORDER, READY 1, SCHEME, SYSTEM.

[D–141]

DEVISE 2, *v.* (Fashioning something with the hands.) The right "S" hand, palm facing left, is placed on top of its left counterpart, whose palm faces right. The hands are twisted back and forth, striking each other slightly after each twist. *Cf.* COMPOSE, CONSTITUTE, CONSTRUCT 2, CREATE, FABRICATE, FASHION, FIX, MAKE, MANUFACTURE, MEND 1, PRODUCE 3, RENDER 1, REPAIR.

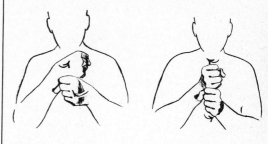

[D–142]

DEVOTION (dĭ vō′ shən), *n.* (Clasping the heart.) The "5" hands are held one atop the other over the heart. Sometimes the "S" hands are used, in which case they are crossed at the wrists. *Cf.* BELOVED, CHARITY, LOVE, REVERE 2.

[D–143]

DEVOUR (dĭ vour′), *v.*, -VOURED, -VOURING. (The natural sign.) The closed right hand goes through the natural motion of placing food in the mouth. This movement is repeated. *Cf.* CONSUME 1, CONSUMPTION, DINE, EAT, FEED 1, FOOD 1, MEAL.

[D–144]

DEVOUT (dĭ vout′), *adj.* (Worshiping.) The hands are clasped together, with the left cupped over the right. Both are brought in toward the body, while the eyes are shut and the head is bowed slightly. *Cf.* ADORE, AMEN, PIOUS, WORSHIP.

[D–145]

DIAMOND 1 (dī′ mənd, dī′ ə-), *n.* (The letter "D"; sparkling with scintillating rays of light.) The right "D" hand is shaken slightly as it is held slightly above the ring finger of the downturned left hand.

[D–146]

DIAMOND 2, *n.* (Fingering the gem.) The right thumb and index finger hold an imaginary diamond. The right hand moves around slightly, as if causing

the gem to catch the light and flash. An expression of pleasure is assumed, and the eyes follow the flashing of the stone.

[D–147]

DIAMOND 3, *n.* (A sparkling ring.) The downturned right "S" hand is shaken slightly over the ring finger of the downturned open left hand.

[D–148]

DIARRHEA (dī′ ə rē′ ə), *n.* (Repeated emptying of the bowels.) The upturned hands are poised side by side with their backs facing out and their fingertips resting on or just above the stomach. They swing down and out simultaneously. This is repeated several times.

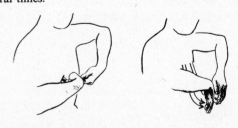

[D–149]

DICE (dīs), *n.* (The shaking and throwing of the dice.) The upturned right "A" hand shakes a pair of imaginary dice and throws them out. *Cf.* GAMBLE.

[D–150]

DICTIONARY 1 (dĭk′ shə nĕr′ ĭ), *n.* (The letter "D.") The right "D" hand is shaken slightly back and forth. This may be preceded by the sign for BOOK, *q.v.:* The open hands are held together, fingers pointing away from the body. They open with little fingers remaining in contact, as in the opening of a book.

[D–151]

DICTIONARY 2, *n.* (Thumbing the pages.) The right "D" hand moves across the left palm quickly, from the fingers to the base, several times, as if thumbing through the pages.

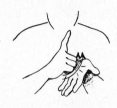

[D–152]

DIE 1 (dī), *v.,* DIED, DYING. (Turning over on one's side.) The open hands, fingers pointing ahead, are held side by side, with the right palm down and the left palm up. The two hands reverse their relative positions as they move from the left to the right. *Cf.* DEAD 1, DEATH, DYING, EXPIRE 2, PERISH 1.

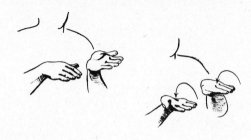

[D–153]

DIE 2 *(sl.), v.* (An animal's legs sticking up in the air, in death.) Both hands are held with palms facing each other, and curved index and middle fingers

presented. The hands pivot up a bit, simultaneously, assuming the "V" position as they do. *Cf.* DEAD 2, PASS OUT.

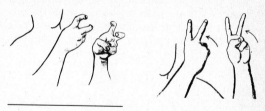

[D–154]

DIE OUT, *v. phrase.* (Fingering the small pieces resulting from the breaking up of something.) The thumbs rub slowly across the fingertips of the upturned hands, from the little fingers to the index fingers, and then continue to the "A" position, palms up. *Cf.* DECAY, DISSOLVE, FADE, MELT, ROT.

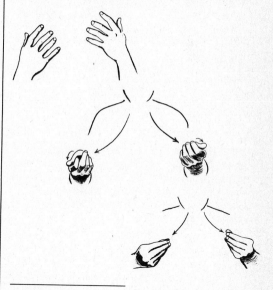

[D–155]

DIFFER (dĭf′ ər), *v.,* -FERED, -FERING. (To think in opposite terms.) The sign for THINK is made: The right index finger touches the forehead. The sign for OPPOSITE is then made: The "D" hands, palms facing the body and index fingers touching, draw apart sharply. *Cf.* CONTRADICT, CONTRARY TO, DISAGREE.

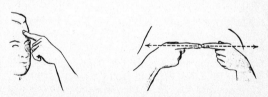

[D–156]

DIFFERENCE (dĭf′ ər əns, dĭf′ rəns,), *n.* (Separated many times; different.) The "D" hands, palms down, are crossed at the index fingers or are held side by side. They separate and return to their initial position a number of times. *Cf.* ASSORTED, DIFFERENT, DIVERSE 1, DIVERSITY 1, UNLIKE, VARIED.

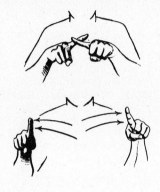

[D–157]

DIFFERENT (dĭf′ ər ənt, dĭf′ rənt), *adj.* See DIFFERENCE.

[D–158]

DIFFERENT OBJECTS (ŏb jĭkts). (The fingertips indicate many things.) Both hands, in the "D" position, palms out and index fingertips touching, are drawn apart. As they move apart, the index fingers wiggle up and down. *Cf.* DIVERSE 2, DIVERSITY 2, VARIOUS, VARY.

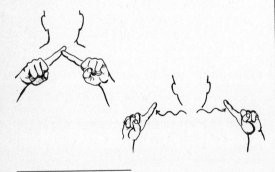

[D–159]

DIFFICULT 1 (dĭf′ ə kŭlt′), *adj.* (The knuckles are rubbed, to indicate a condition of being worn down.) The knuckles of the curved index and middle fingers of both hands are rubbed up and down against each other. Instead of the up-down rubbing, they may rub against each other in an alternate clockwise-counter-

clockwise manner. *Cf.* DIFFICULTY, HARD 1, HARDSHIP, POVERTY 2, PROBLEM 2.

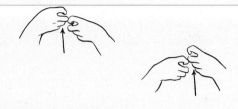

[D–160]

DIFFICULT 2, *adj.* (Striking a hard object.) The curved index and middle fingers of the right hand, whose palm faces the body or the left, are brought down sharply against the back of the downturned left "S" hand. *Cf.* HARD 2, SOLID.

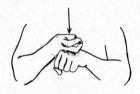

[D–161]

DIFFICULT 3, *adj.* (A clenching of the fists; the rise and fall of pain.) Both "S" hands, tightly clenched, revolve about each other, slowly and deliberately, while a pained expression is worn. *Cf.* AGONY, BEAR 3, ENDURE 1, PASSION 2, SUFFER 1, TOLERATE 2.

[D–162]

DIFFICULTY (dĭf′ ə kŭl′ tĭ, -kəl tĭ), *n.* See DIFFICULT 1.

[D–163]

DIG 1 (dĭg), *v.*, DUG *or* DIGGED, DIGGING. (The natural sign.) The slightly cupped right hand, palm up, goes through the motions of digging into a mound of earth and turning it over.

[D–164]

DIG 2, *v.* (The natural motion.) Both hands, in the "A" position, right hand facing up and left hand facing down, grasp an imaginary shovel. They go through the natural movements of shoveling earth—first digging in and then tossing the earth aside. *Cf.* SHOVEL, SPADE.

[D–165]

DILIGENCE 1 (dĭl' ə jəns), *n.* (Rubbing the hands together in zeal or ambition.) The open hands are rubbed vigorously back and forth against each other. *Cf.* AMBITIOUS 1, ANXIOUS 1, ARDENT, DILIGENT, EAGER, EAGERNESS, EARNEST, ENTHUSIASM, EN-THUSIASTIC, INDUSTRIOUS, METHODIST, ZEAL, ZEALOUS.

[D–166]

DILIGENCE 2, *(colloq.), n.* (Rationale obscure; possibly an emphasis on sharpness.) The upturned open right hand is poised with thumb resting on the chin and the middle finger bent back under the thumb. The middle finger suddenly flicks out sharply. An intense expression is assumed, with brows furrowed.

[D–167]

DILIGENT (dĭl' ə jənt), *adj.* See DILIGENCE 1.

[D–168]

DIN (dĭn), *n.* (A shaking which disturbs the ear.) After placing the index finger on the ear, both hands assume the "S" position, palms down. They move alternately back and forth, forcefully. *Cf.* NOISE, NOISY, RACKET, SOUND, THUNDER, VIBRATION.

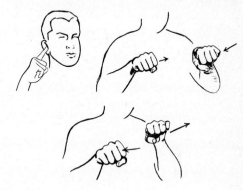

[D–169]

DINE (dīn), *v.*, DINED, DINING. (The natural sign.) The closed right hand goes through the natural motion of placing food in the mouth. This movement is repeated. *Cf.* CONSUME 1, CONSUMPTION, DEVOUR, EAT, FEED 1, FOOD 1, MEAL.

[D–170]

DINNER (dĭn' ər), *n.* (Placing food in the mouth.) Both closed hands alternately come to the mouth, as if placing food in it. *Cf.* BANQUET, FEAST.

[D–171]

DIOCESE (dī′ ə sēs′, sĭs), *(eccles.)*, *n.* (The letter "D"; encompassing.) The "D" hands are held side by side, palms facing out. The hands swing out and forward simultaneously, describing a circle, and come together with palms now facing the signer and little finger edges touching.

[D–172]

DIRECT 1 (dĭ rĕkt′, dī-), *v.*, -RECTED, -RECTING. (Holding the reins over all.) The "A" hands, palms facing, move alternately back and forth, as if grasping and manipulating reins. The left "A" hand, still in position, swings over so that its palm now faces down. The right hand opens to the "5" position, palm down, and swings over the left which moves slightly to the right. *Cf.* AUTHORITY, CONTROL 1, GOVERN, MANAGE, MANAGEMENT, MANAGER, OPERATE, REGULATE, REIGN, RULE 1.

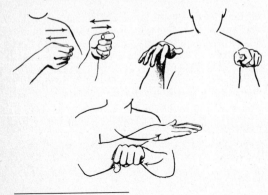

[D–173]

DIRECT 2, *v.* (An issuance from the mouth.) The tip of the index finger of the "D" hand, palm facing the body, is placed at the closed lips. It moves around and out, rather forcefully. *Cf.* BID 1, COMMAND, ORDER 1.

[D–174]

DIRECTION 1 (dĭ rĕk′ shən), *n.* (Alternate directions are indicated.) The right "D" hand, with palm out and index finger straight or slightly curved, moves a short distance back and forth, from left to right. *Cf.* WHERE 1.

[D–175]

DIRECTION 2, *n.* The open "5" hands, palms up and fingers slightly curved, move back and forth in front of the body, the right hand to the right and the left hand to the left. *Cf.* HERE, WHERE 2.

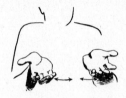

[D–176]

DIRT (dûrt), *n.* (Fingering the soil.) Both hands, held upright before the body, finger imaginary pinches of soil. *Cf.* EARTH 2, GROUND, SOIL 1.

[D–177]

DIRTY (dûr′ tĭ), *adj.* (A modification of the pig's snout groveling in a trough.) The downturned right hand is placed under the chin. Its fingers, pointing left, wiggle repeatedly. *Cf.* FILTHY, FOUL, IMPURE, NASTY, SOIL 2, STAIN.

[D–178]

DIRTY-MINDED (-mĭn′ dĭd), *(colloq.), adj.* (A thick layer of dirt on the mind.) The base of the right "C" hand rests on the back of the downturned open left hand. The right hand moves over the back of the left from its wrist to its knuckles.

[D–179]

DISAGREE (dĭs′ ə grē′), *v.,* -GREED, -GREEING. (To think in opposite terms.) The sign for THINK is made: The right index finger touches the forehead. The sign for OPPOSITE is then made: The "D" hands, palms facing the body and index fingers touching, draw apart sharply. *Cf.* CONTRADICT, CONTRARY TO, DIFFER.

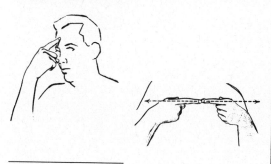

[D–180]

DISAPPEAR (dĭs′ ə pir′). *v.,* -PEARED, -PEARING. (A disappearance.) The right open hand, palm facing the body, is held by the left hand and is drawn down and out, ending in a position with fingers drawn together. The left hand, meanwhile, may close into a position with fingers also drawn together. *Cf.* ABSENCE 1, ABSENT 1, DEPLETE, EMPTY 1, EXTINCT, FADE AWAY, GONE 1, MISSING 1, OMISSION 1, OUT 3, OUT OF, VANISH.

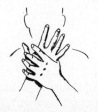

[D–181]

DISAPPOINT (dĭs′ ə point′), *v.,* -POINTED, -POINTING. (The feelings sink.) The middle fingers of both "5" hands, one above the other, rest on the heart. They both move down a few inches.

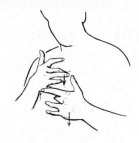

[D–182]

DISAPPOINTED 1, *adj.* (Something sour or bitter.) The right index finger is brought sharply up against the lips, while the mouth is puckered up as if tasting something sour. *Cf.* ACID, BITTER, LEMON 1, PICKLE, SOUR.

[D–183]

DISAPPOINTED 2, *adj.* (Coming up against a wall; a door is slammed in the face.) The open right hand is brought up sharply, and its back strikes the mouth and nose. The head moves back a bit at the same time. *Cf.* FRUSTRATED.

[D–184]

DISAPPOINTMENT (dĭs′ ə point′ mənt), *n.* Use any sign for DISAPPOINT, DISAPPOINTED 1, or DISAPPOINTED 2.

[D–185]

DISBELIEF 1 (dĭs bĭ lēf'), *n.* (The nose is wrinkled in disbelief.) The right "V" hand faces the nose. The index and middle fingers bend as a cynical expression is assumed. *Cf.* CYNIC, CYNICAL, DON'T BE-LIEVE, DOUBT 1, INCREDULITY, SKEPTIC 1, SKEPTI-CAL 1.

[D–186]

DISBELIEF 2, *n.* (The wavering.) The downturned "S" hands swing alternately up and down. *Cf.* DOUBT 2, DOUBTFUL, WAVER 2.

[D–187]

DISCARD 1 (*v.* dĭs kärd' ; *n.* dĭs' kärd), -CARDED, -CARDING. (To throw something aside.) Both "S" hands are held with palms facing at chest level and then thrown down and to the left, opening into the "5" position. *Cf.* ABANDON 1, CAST OFF, DEPOSIT 2, FORSAKE 3, LEAVE 2, LET ALONE, NEGLECT.

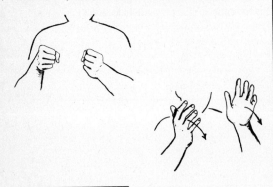

[D–188]

DISCARD 2, *v.* (To toss up and out.) Both "S" hands, held at chest level with palms facing, are swung down slightly and then up into the air toward

the left, opening into the "5" position. *Cf.* ABANDON 2, CAST OUT, EVICT.

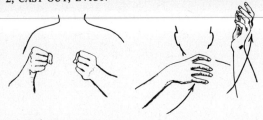

[D–189]

DISCARD 3, *v.* (Scratching something out and throwing it away.) The fingertips of the open right hand scratch downward across the palm of the up-right left hand. In one continuous motion, the right hand then closes as if holding something, and finally opens again forcefully and motions as if throwing something away. *Cf.* DELETE 2, ELIMINATE.

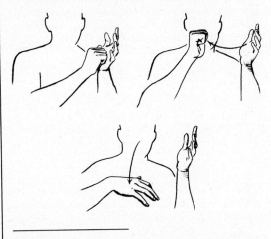

[D–190]

DISCHARGE 1 (dĭs chärj'), *v.,* -CHARGED, -CHARG-ING. ("Getting the axe"; the head is chopped off.) The upturned open right hand is swung sharply over the index finger edge of the left "S" hand, whose palm faces right. *Cf.* EXPEL 1, FIRE 2.

[D–191]

DISCHARGE 2, *v.* (To cut one down.) The right index finger strikes the tip of the upturned left index finger, in a right to left direction, causing the left index finger to bend slightly. *Cf.* EXPEL 2.

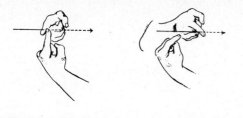

[D–192]

DISCIPLE (dǐ sī′ pəl), *n.* (JESUS, FOLLOW, INDIVIDUAL.) The sign for JESUS is made: Both "5" hands are used. The left middle finger touches the right palm, and then the right middle finger touches the left palm. This is followed by the sign for FOLLOW: The "A" hands are used, thumbs pointing up. The right is positioned a few inches behind the left. The left hand moves straight forward, while the right follows behind in a series of wavy, back-and-forth movements. Then the sign for INDIVIDUAL is made: Both open hands, palms facing each other, move down the sides of the body, tracing its outline to the hips.

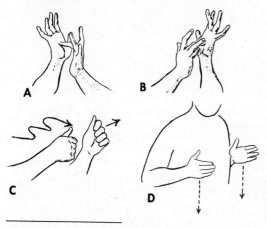

A   B

C

D

[D–193]

DISCIPLINE 1 (dĭs′ ə plĭn), *n., v.,* -PLINED, -PLINING. (Polishing or sharpening up.) The knuckles of the downturned right "A" hand are rubbed briskly back and forth over the side of the hand and index finger of the left "D" hand. *Cf.* DRILL 3, PRACTICE 1, TRAIN 2, TRAINING 1.

[D–194]

DISCIPLINE 2, *v.* (A modification of the striking movement.) The right index finger strikes the left elbow with a glancing blow. *Cf.* PENALTY 2, PENANCE 1, PUNISH 3.

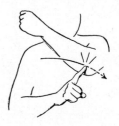

[D–195]

DISCIPLINE 3, *v.,* (A striking movement.) The right index finger makes a striking movement below the left "S" hand, which is held up, as if grasping a culprit. *Cf.* PENALTY 1, PUNISH 1.

[D–196]

DISCONNECT (dĭs′ kə někt′), *v.,* -NECTED, -NECTING. (An unlocking.) With thumbs and index fingers interlocked initially (the links of a chain), the hands draw apart, showing the break in the chain. *Cf.* DETACH, PART FROM.

[D-197]

DISCONTENTED (dĭs´ kən tĕn´ tĭd), *adj.* (NOT, SATISFIED.) The sign for NOT 1 is made: The crossed downturned open hands draw apart. The sign for SATISFIED then follows: The downturned "B" hands, the right above the left, are positioned on the chest. They move straight down simultaneously. *Cf.* DISSATISFACTION, DISSATISFIED.

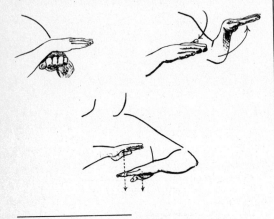

[D-198]

DISCOURAGE 1 (dĭs kûr´ ĭjd), *adj., v.,* -AGED, -AGING. (Throwing up the hands in a gesture of surrender.) Both "A" hands are held palms down before the chest and then thrown up in unison, ending in the "5" position. *Cf.* ABDICATE, CEDE, FORFEIT, GIVE UP, LOSE HOPE, RELINQUISH, RENOUNCE, RENUNCIATION, SURRENDER 1, YIELD.

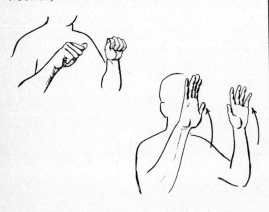

[D-199]

DISCOURAGE 2, *adj., v.* (The hands collapse in exhaustion.) Both "C" hands are placed either on the lower chest or at the waist. The palms face the body. They fall away into a palms-up position. At the same time, the shoulders suddenly sag in a very pro-

nounced fashion. An expression of weariness may be used for emphasis. *Cf.* EXHAUST, FATIGUE, TIRE, TIRED, WEARY.

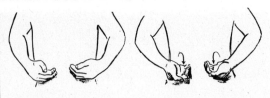

[D-200]

DISCOURSE (*n.* dĭs´ kôrs, dĭs kôrs´; *v.* dĭs kôrs´), -COURSED, -COURSING. (Words tumbling from the mouth.) The right index finger, pointing left, describes a continuous small circle in front of the mouth. *Cf.* BID 3, HEARING, MAINTAIN 2, MENTION, REMARK, SAID, SAY, SPEAK, SPEECH 1, STATE, STATEMENT, TALK 1, TELL, VERBAL 1.

[D-201]

DISCOVER (dĭs kŭv´ ər), *v.,* -ERED, -ERING. (The natural motion of selecting something from the hand.) The thumb and index fingers of the outstretched right hand grasp an imaginary object on the upturned left palm. The right hand then moves straight up. *Cf.* CHOOSE 2, FIND, PICK 1, SELECT 1.

[D-202]

DISCOVERY (dĭs kŭv´ ə rĭ), *n.* See DISCOVER.

[D-203]

DISCUSS (dĭs kŭs´), *v.,* -CUSSED, -CUSSING. (Expounding one's points.) The right "D" hand is held with the palm facing the body. It moves down repeatedly so that the side of the index finger strikes the upturned left palm. *Cf.* DISCUSSION 1.

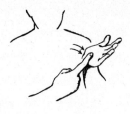

[D–204]

DISCUSSION 1 (dĭs kŭsh′ ən), *n.* See DISCUSS.

[D–205]

DISCUSSION 2, *n.* (Back and forth talk.) The "5" hands, palms facing and somewhat cupped, swing alternately toward and away from the face. Each time they move away they also swing down a bit. The movement is graceful and continuous.

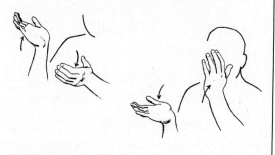

[D–206]

DISEASE 1 (dĭ zēz′), *n., v.,* -EASED, -EASING. (The sick parts of the anatomy are indicated.) The right middle finger rests on the forehead, and its left counterpart is placed against the stomach. The signer assumes an expression of sadness or physical distress. *Cf.* ILL, ILLNESS, SICK, SICKNESS.

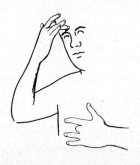

[D–207]

DISEASE 2, *n.* (Something inside is emphasized.) The "5" hands, palms facing the body, are positioned with middle fingers resting on the chest. The hands move alternately up and down.

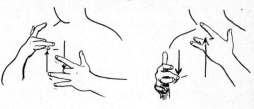

[D–208]

DISGUST (dĭs gŭst′), *n., v.,* -GUSTED, -GUSTING. (Turning the stomach.) The fingertips of the curved right hand describe a continuous circle on the stomach. The signer assumes an exaggerated expression of disgust. *Cf.* DISGUSTED, DISGUSTING, DISPLEASED, MAKE ME DISGUSTED, MAKE ME SICK, NAUSEA, NAUSEATE, NAUSEOUS, OBNOXIOUS, REVOLTING.

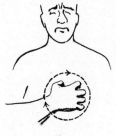

[D–209]

DISGUSTED (dĭs gŭs′ tĭd), *adj.* See DISGUST.

[D–210]

DISGUSTING (dĭs gŭs′ tĭng), *adj.* See DISGUST.

[D–211]

DISH (dĭsh), *n.* (The finger touches a brittle substance.) The index finger is brought up to touch the exposed front teeth. *Cf.* BONE, CHINA 2, GLASS 1, PLATE, PORCELAIN.

[D-212]

DISHONEST (dĭs ŏn′ ĭst), *adj.* (NOT, HONEST.) The sign for NOT 1 is made: The crossed downturned open hands draw apart. The sign for HONEST is then made: The index and middle fingers of the right "H" hand, whose palm faces left, move straight forward along the upturned left palm.

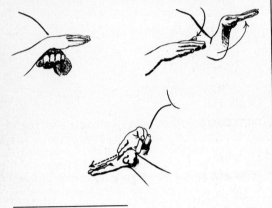

[D-213]

DISHWASHING (dĭsh′ wŏsh ĭng -wôsh-), *n.* (The natural sign.) The downturned right "5" hand describes a clockwise circle as it moves over the upturned left "5" hand. *Cf.* WASH DISHES.

[D-214]

DISJOIN (dĭs join′), *v.* (The natural motion of disconnecting.) The interlocked thumbs and index fingers of both hands snap open and apart as the hands are separated.

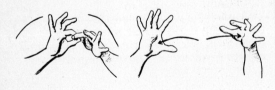

[D-215]

DISLIKE (dĭs līk′), *v.*, -LIKED, -LIKING, *(rare), n.* (The finger is flicked to indicate something petty, small; *i.e.,* to be scorned as inconsequential.) The right index finger and thumb are used to press the

lips down into an expression of contempt. The right thumb is then flicked out from the closed hand. *Cf.* CONTEMPT 2, DESPISE 2, DETEST 2, HATE 2, SCORN 2.

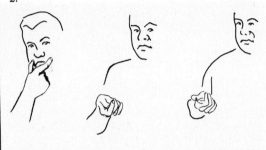

[D-216]

DISOBEDIENCE (dĭs′ ə bē′ dĭ əns), *n.* See DISOBEY.

[D-217]

DISOBEY (dĭs′ ə bā′), *v.*, -BEYED, -BEYING. (Turning the head.) The right "S" hand, held up with its palm facing the body, swings sharply around to the palm-out position. The head meanwhile moves slightly toward the left. *Cf.* DISOBEDIENCE, REBEL.

[D-218]

DISORDER (dĭs ôr′ dər), *n.* (Scrambling or mixing up.) The downturned right hand is positioned above the upturned left. The fingers of both are curved. Both hands move in opposite horizontal circles. *Cf.* CLUTTER, COMPLICATE, CONFUSE, CONFUSED, CONFUSION, MINGLE 1, MIX, MIXED, MIX UP, SCRAMBLE.

[D-219]

DISPATCH (dĭs păch′), *v.*, -PATCHED, -PATCHING. (Moving away from.) The fingertips of the right hand move off the top of the left hand. *Cf.* SEND AWAY 1.

DISPLAY (dĭs plā′), *v.,* -PLAYED, -PLAYING. (Directing the attention to something, and bringing it forward.) The right index finger points into the left palm, held facing out before the body. The left palm moves straight out. For the passive form of this verb, *i.e.,* BE SHOWN or DISPLAYED, the movement is reversed: The left hand, palm facing in, is moved in toward the body, while the right index finger remains pointing into the left palm. *Cf.* DEMONSTRATE, EVIDENCE, EXAMPLE, EXHIBIT, EXHIBITION, ILLUSTRATE, INDICATE, INFLUENCE 3, PRODUCE 2, REPRESENT, SHOW 1, SIGNIFY 1.

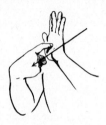

DISPLEASED (dĭs plēz′d), *adj., v.,* -PLEASED, -PLEASING. (Turning the stomach.) The fingertips of the curved right hand describe a continuous circle on the stomach. The signer assumes an exaggerated expression of disgust. *Cf.* DISGUST, DISGUSTED, DISGUSTING, MAKE ME DISGUSTED, MAKE ME SICK, NAUSEA, NAUSEATE, NAUSEOUS, OBNOXIOUS, REVOLTING.

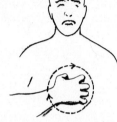

DISPOSE (dĭs pōz′), *v.,* -POSED, -POSING, *n.* (The feelings of the heart move toward a specific object.)

The tip of the right middle finger touches the heart. The open right hand, palm facing the body, then moves away from the heart toward the palm of the open left hand. *Cf.* DISPOSED TO, DISPOSITION, INCLINATION, INCLINE, INCLINED, TEND, TENDENCY.

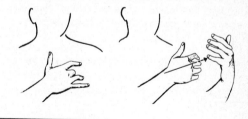

DISPOSED TO (dĭs pōzd′), *adj. phrase.* See DISPOSE.

DISPOSITION (dĭs′ pə zĭsh′ ən), *n.* See DISPOSE.

DISPUTE (dĭs pūt′), *n., v.,* -PUTED, -PUTING, (An expounding back and forth.) The index fingers here represent the two sides of the argument. First the left index finger is slapped into the open right palm, and then the right makes the same movement into the left palm. This is repeated back and forth several times. *Cf.* ARGUE, ARGUMENT, CONTROVERSY, DEBATE.

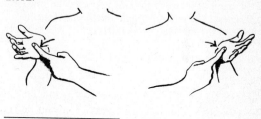

DISREGARD (dĭs′ rĭ gärd′), *v.,* -GARDED, -GARDING. (Thumbing the nose.) The index finger of the right "B" hand is placed under the tip of the nose. From this position the right hand moves straight forward, away from the face. *Cf.* IGNORE.

[D-227]

DISRUPT (dĭs rŭpt′), v., -RUPTED, -RUPTING. (Obstruct, bother.) The left hand, fingers together and palm flat, is held before the body, facing somewhat down. The little finger side of the right hand, held with palm flat, makes one or several up-down chopping motions against the left hand, between its thumb and index finger. Cf. ANNOY 1, ANNOYANCE 1, BLOCK, BOTHER 1, CHECK 2, COME BETWEEN, DISTURB, HINDER, HINDRANCE, IMPEDE, INTERCEPT, INTERFERE, INTERFERENCE, INTERFERE WITH, INTERRUPT, MEDDLE 1, OBSTACLE, OBSTRUCT, PREVENT, PREVENTION.

[D-228]

DISSATISFACTION (dĭs′ săt ĭs făk′ shən), n. (NOT, SATISFIED.) The sign for NOT 1 is made: The crossed downturned open hands draw apart. The sign for SATISFIED then follows: The downturned "B" hands, the right above the left, are positioned on the chest. They move straight down simultaneously. Cf. DISCONTENTED, DISSATISFIED.

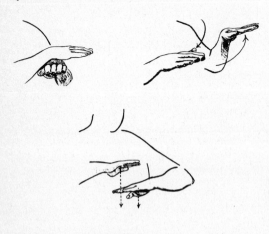

[D-229]

DISSATISFIED (dĭs săt′ ĭs fīd′), adj. See DISSATISFACTION.

[D-230]

DISSOLVE (dĭ zŏlv′), v., -SOLVED, -SOLVING. (Fingering the small pieces resulting from the breaking up of something.) The thumbs rub slowly across the fingertips of the upturned hands, from the little fingers to the index fingers, and then continue to the "A" position, palms up. Cf. DECAY, DIE OUT, FADE, MELT, ROT.

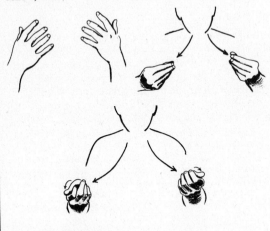

[D-231]

DISTANCE (dĭs′ təns), n. (Moving beyond, i.e., the concept of distance or "farness.") The "A" hands are held together, thumbs pointing away from the body. The right hand moves straight ahead in a slight arc. The left hand does not move. Cf. DISTANT, FAR, OFF 2, REMOTE.

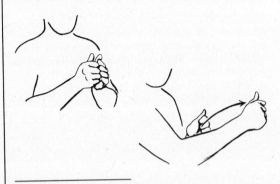

[D-232]

DISTANT (dĭs′ tənt), adj. See DISTANCE.

[D-233]

DISTRACTION (dĭs trăk′ shən), n. (A thought wanders off into space.) The right curved index finger opens and closes quickly as it leaves its initial position on the forehead and moves up into the air. *Cf.* DAYDREAM, DREAM.

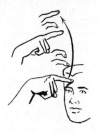

DISTRIBUTE 1 (dĭs trĭb' ūt), *v.,* -UTED, -UTING. (Giving out widely.) The "AND" hands are held with palms up and fingertips touching each other, the right fingertips pointing left and the left fingertips pointing right. From this position, the hands sweep forward and curve to either side, opening, palms up, as they do.

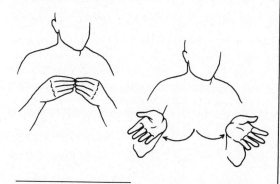

[D-235]

DISTRIBUTE 2, *v.* (The action of dealing out cards.) The signer goes through the motions of dealing out imaginary playing cards. *Cf.* CARD PLAYING, CARDS, PLAYING CARDS.

[D-236]

DISTRUST (dĭs trŭst'), *v.,* -TRUSTED, -TRUSTING. (Fending someone off.) The downturned left "S" hand, positioned near the left hip, moves several

times to the left a bit. Each time it moves the head moves slightly to the right.

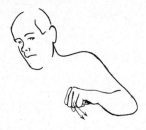

[D-237]

DISTURB (dĭs tûrb'), *v.,* -TURBED, -TURBING. (Obstruct, bother.) The left hand, fingers together and palm flat, is held before the body, facing somewhat down. The little finger side of the right hand, held with palm flat, makes one or several up-down chopping motions against the left hand, between its thumb and index finger. *Cf.* ANNOY 1, ANNOYANCE 1, BLOCK, BOTHER 1, CHECK 2, COME BETWEEN, DISRUPT, HINDER, HINDRANCE, IMPEDE, INTERCEPT, INTERFERE, INTERFERENCE, INTERFERE WITH, INTERRUPT, MEDDLE 1, OBSTACLE, OBSTRUCT, PREVENT, PREVENTION.

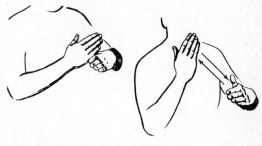

[D-238]

DIVE 1 (dīv), *v.,* DIVED or DOVE, DIVED, DIVING. (The natural motion.) The extended right index and middle fingertips are placed on the back of the same two fingers of the left hand, which is held palm down in front of the body. From this position the right hand moves upward and back in an arc, as if diving off the left hand.

[D-239]

DIVE 2, *n., v.* (The natural sign.) The hands are held together, in praying fashion. Always in contact, they swing down in an arc, as if diving into the water.

[D-240]

DIVERSE 1 (dĭ vûrs', dī-, dī' vûrs), *adj.* (Separated many times; different.) The "D" hands, palms down, are crossed at the index fingers or are held side by side. They separate and return to their initial position a number of times. *Cf.* ASSORTED, DIFFERENCE, DIFFERENT, DIVERSITY 1, UNLIKE, VARIED.

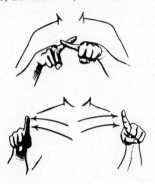

[D-241]

DIVERSE 2, *adj.* (The fingertips indicate many things.) Both hands, in the "D" position, palms out and index fingertips touching, are drawn apart. As they move apart, the index fingers wiggle up and down. *Cf.* DIFFERENT OBJECTS, DIVERSITY 2, VARIOUS, VARY.

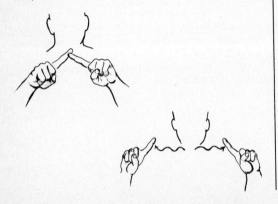

[D-242]

DIVERSITY 1 (dĭ vûr' sə tĭ, dī-), *n.* See DIVERSE 1.

[D-243]

DIVERSITY 2, *n.* See DIVERSE 2.

[D-244]

DIVIDE 1 (dĭ vīd'), *v.,* -VIDED, -VIDING. (A splitting apart or dividing.) The two hands are crossed, with the right little finger resting on the left index finger. Both hands are dropped down and separated simultaneously, so that the palms face down. *Cf.* APPORTION, SHARE 2.

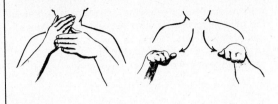

[D-245]

DIVIDE 2, *v.* (Separating or splitting apart.) The "D" hands, palms facing and index fingers pointing straight out, swing down sharply, moving toward their respective sides of the body. *Cf.* DIVISION.

[D-246]

DIVIDEND (dĭv' ə dĕnd'), *n.* (A regular taking in.) The outstretched open left hand, held palm facing right, moves in toward the body, assuming the "A" position, palm still facing right. This is repeated several times. *Cf.* INCOME, INTEREST 4, SUBSCRIBE, SUBSCRIPTION.

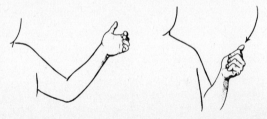

[D–247]

DIVINE (dĭ vīn'), *adj.* (The initial "D," cleanliness or purity.) The right "D" hand is held with index finger pointing up before the right shoulder. Then the downturned open right hand is passed across the upturned right hand from wrist to fingertips.

[D–248]

DIVISION (dĭ vĭzh' ən), *n.* See DIVIDE 2.

[D–249]

DIVORCE 1 (dĭ vōrs'), *n., v.*, -VORCED, -VORCING. (The hands are moved apart.) Both hands, in the "A" position, thumbs up, are held together, with knuckles touching. With a deliberate movement they come apart. *Cf.* APART, PART 3, SEPARATE 1.

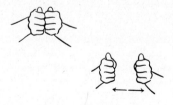

[D–250]

DIVORCE 2, *n., v.* (The hands, locked in marriage, come apart.) The clasped hands draw apart, into the "A" position, palms facing each other.

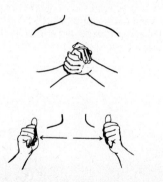

[D–251]

DIVORCE 3, *n., v.* (The letter "D"; a separating.) The "D" hands, palms facing and fingertips touching, draw apart.

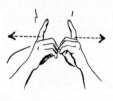

[D–252]

DIZZINESS (dĭz' ĭ nĭs), *n.* The sign for DIZZY is formed. This is followed by the sign for -NESS: The downturned right "N" hand moves down along the left palm, which is facing away from the body.

[D–253]

DIZZY (dĭz' ĭ), *adj.* (Images swinging around before the eyes.) The right "5" hand, palm facing the body and fingers somewhat curved, swings around in a continuous counterclockwise circle before the eyes.

[D–254]

DO (do͞o), *v.*, DOES, DID, DONE, DOING. (An activity.) Both open hands, palms down, are swung right and left before the chest. *Cf.* ACT 2, ACTION, ACTIVE, ACTIVITY, BUSY 2, CONDUCT 1, DEED, PERFORM 1, PERFORMANCE 1, RENDER 2.

[D-255]

DOCTOR (dŏk′ tər), *n.* (The letter "M," from "M.D."; feeling the pulse.) The fingertips of the right "M" hand lightly tap the left pulse a number of times. The right "D" hand may also be used, in which case the thumb and fingertips tap the left pulse. *Cf.* SURGEON.

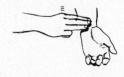

[D-256]

DOCTRINE 1 (dŏk′ trĭn), *n.* (A collection or listing is indicated by the open palm, representing a page.) The right "P" hand, for PRINCIPLE, is placed against the upper part of the open left hand, which faces right, fingers pointing upward. The right hand swings down to the lower part of the left palm. The "D" hand may be used instead of the "P." *Cf.* PRINCIPLE.

[D-257]

DOCTRINE 2, *n.* (A thought clasped onto.) The index finger touches the middle of the forehead (where the thought lies), and then both hands are clasped together. *Cf.* BELIEF, BELIEVE, CONVICTION 2.

[D-258]

DOESN'T MATTER, *v. phrase.* Both hands, in the "5" position, are held before the chest, fingertips

facing each other. With an alternate back-forth movement, the fingertips are made to strike each other. *Cf.* ANYHOW, ANYWAY, DESPITE, HOWEVER 2, INDIFFERENCE, INDIFFERENT, IN SPITE OF, MAKE NO DIFFERENCE, NEVERTHELESS, NO MATTER, WHEREVER.

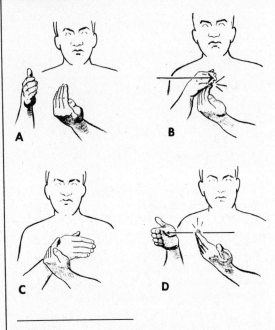

A   B

C   D

[D-259]

DOG 1 (dôg), *n.* (Patting the knee and snapping the fingers to beckon the dog.) The right hand pats the right knee, and then the fingers are snapped.

[D-260]

DOG 2, *(colloq.)*, *n.* (The dog's habit of scratching behind the ear.) The right "B" hand, imitating a paw, brushes the right ear repeatedly.

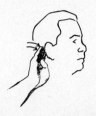

[D–261]

DOLL 1 (dŏl), *n.* (Pulling the nose.) The right "X" finger, resting on the nose, pulls the head with it as it moves down slightly. It does not leave its position on the nose. *Cf.* FOOL 2, HOAX, JOKE.

[D–262]

DOLL 2, *n.* (The rocking of the baby.) The arms are held with one resting on the other, as if cradling a baby. They rock from side to side. *Cf.* BABY, INFANT.

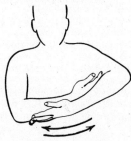

[D–263]

DOLLAR(S) 1 (dŏl' ər), *n.* (The natural sign; drawing a bill from a billfold.) The right thumb and index finger trace the outlines of a bill on the upturned left palm. Or, the right thumb and fingers may grasp the base of the open left hand, which is held palm facing right and fingers pointing forward; the right hand, in this position, then slides forward along and off the left hand, as if drawing bills from a billfold. *Cf.* BILL(S) 1, COIN(S) 1.

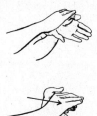

[D–264]

DOLLAR(S) 2, *n.* (The shape of a coin.) The right index finger traces a small circle on the upturned left palm. *Cf.* BILL(S) 2, COIN(S) 2.

[D–265]

DOMICILE (dŏm' ə səl, -sīl´), *n.* (The shape of the building.) The open hands are held with fingertips touching, so that they form a pyramid a bit above eye level. From this position, the hands separate and move diagonally downward for a short distance; then they continue straight down a few inches. This movement traces the outline of a roof and walls. *Cf.* BARN, HOUSE, RESIDENCE 2.

[D–266]

DONE 1 (dŭn), *v.* (Bring to an end.) The left hand, fingers together and pointing forward, is held palm facing right. The right, palm down, fingers also together, moves along the top of the left, goes over the tip of the left index finger, and drops straight down, indicating a cutting off or a finishing. This sign is also used to indicate the past tense of a verb, in the sense of accomplishing an action or state of being. *Cf.* ACCOMPLISH 2, ACHIEVE 2, COMPLETE 1, CONCLUDE, END 4, EXPIRE 1, FINISH 1, HAVE 2, TERMINATE.

[D–267]

DONE 2, *v.* (Shaking the hands to rid them of something.) The upright "5" hands, palms facing each other, are suddenly and quickly swung around to a palm-out position. *Cf.* END 3, FINISH 2.

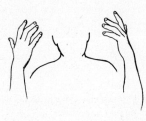

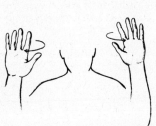

[D–268]

DONKEY (dŏng' kĭ), *n.* (The donkey's broad ear; the animal is traditionally a stubborn one.) The open hand, or the "B" hand, is placed at the side of the head, with palm out and fingers pointing straight up. The hand moves forward and back, pivoting at the wrist, as in the case of a donkey's ears flapping. Both hands may also be used, at either side of the head. *Cf.* MULE, MULISH, OBSTINATE, STUBBORN.

[D–269]

DO NOT 1, *v. phrase.* (The natural sign.) The crossed "5" hands, palms facing out (or down), separate and recross quickly and repeatedly. The head is usually shaken simultaneously. This sign is from NOT 1, *q.v. Cf.* DON'T 1.

[D–270]

DO NOT 2, *v. phrase.* The thumb of the right "A" hand is placed under the chin. From this position it is flicked outward in an arc. *Cf.* DON'T 2.

[D–271]

DON'T 1 (dōnt) *v.* See DO NOT 1.

[D–272]

DON'T 2, *v.* See DO NOT 2.

[D–273]

DON'T BELIEVE, *v. phrase.* (The nose is wrinkled in disbelief.) The right "V" hand faces the nose. The index and middle fingers bend as a cynical expression is assumed. *Cf.* CYNIC, CYNICAL, DISBELIEF 1, DOUBT 1, INCREDULITY, SKEPTIC 1, SKEPTICAL 1.

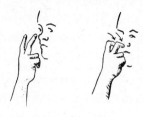

[D-274]

DON'T CARE 1, *(colloq.), v. phrase,* (Wiping the nose, *i.e.,* "Keeping the nose clean" or not becoming involved.) The downturned right "D" hand, index finger touching the nose, is suddenly flung down and to the right.

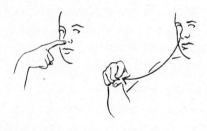

[D-275]

DON'T CARE 2, *(colloq.), v. phrase.* (The thoughts, *i.e.,* the concern for, is thrown away.) The fingertips of the closed right hand rest on the forehead. The right hand is suddenly flung down and to the right, opening into the downturned "5" position.

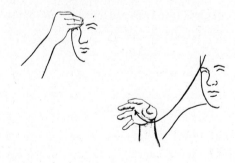

[D-276]

DON'T CARE 3, *(colloq.), v. phrase.* (A variation of DON'T CARE 2.) The thumb of the right "Y" hand touches the right ear. The right "Y" hand is then

flung down and to the right. *Cf.* DON'T CARE FOR 2, DON'T LIKE 1.

[D-277]

DON'T CARE FOR 1, *v. phrase.* (An indication of disdain.) The right "5" hand is placed over the heart, and the head moves back slightly to the right. An expression of disdain is assumed. *Cf.* DON'T LIKE 2.

[D-278]

DON'T CARE FOR 2, *(colloq.), v. phrase.* See DON'T CARE 3.

[D-279]

DON'T KNOW, *v. phrase.* (Knowledge is lacking.) The sign for KNOW is made: The right fingertips tap the forehead several times. The right hand is then flung over to the right, ending in the "5" position, palm out.

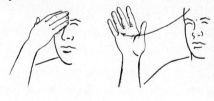

[D-280]

DON'T LIKE 1, *(colloq.), v. phrase.* See DON'T CARE 3.

[D-281]

DON'T LIKE 2, *v. phrase.* See DON'T CARE FOR 1.

[D–282]

DON'T TELL, *v. phrase.* (The sealing of the lips; keeping the words back.) The back of the thumb of the right "A" hand is placed firmly against the closed lips. The thumb, in this position, may move off the lips slightly and return again to the lips. *Cf.* PRIVACY, PRIVATE 1, SECRET.

[D–283]

DON'T WANT, *v. phrase.* (The hands are shaken, indicating a wish to rid them of something.) The "5" hands, palms facing the body, suddenly swing around to the palms-down position. *Cf.* DECLINE 3.

[D–284]

DOOR (dōr), *n.* (The opening and closing of the door.) The "B" hands, palms out and edges touching, are drawn apart and then come together again. *Cf.* DOORWAY, OPEN THE DOOR.

[D–285]

DOORBELL (dōr' bĕl'), *n.* (Pressing the button.) The ball of the extended right thumb is pressed forcefully into the open left palm, which faces right with fingers pointing forward.

[D–286]

DOORWAY (dōr' wā'), *n.* See DOOR.

[D–287]

DOPE (dōp), *(colloq.), n.* (A shot in the arm.) The right index finger is thrust into the left upper arm and the thumb wiggles back and forth a number of times, as if implanting a shot in the arm. *Cf.* COCA-COLA, COKE, INOCULATE, MORPHINE, NARCOTICS.

[D–288]

DOUBLE (dŭb' əl), *adj.* (Two fingers are brought up.) The right "V" fingers rest in the open left palm, and are then swung in an arc to an upright position. *Cf.* TWICE.

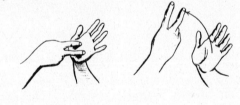

[D–289]

DOUBT 1 (dout), *n., v.,* DOUBTED, DOUBTING. (The nose is wrinkled in disbelief.) The right "V" hand faces the nose. The index and middle fingers bend as a cynical expression is assumed. *Cf.* CYNIC, CYNICAL, DISBELIEF 1, DON'T BELIEVE, INCREDULITY, SKEPTIC 1, SKEPTICAL 1.

[D-290]

DOUBT 2, *n., v.* (The wavering.) The downturned "S" hands swing alternately up and down. *Cf.* DISBELIEF 2, DOUBTFUL, WAVER 2.

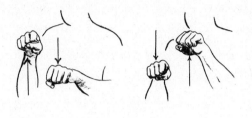

[D-291]

DOUBT 3, *n., v.* (On the fence.) One extended index finger makes a seesaw motion across the other.

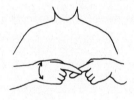

[D-292]

DOUBTFUL (dout′ fəl), *adj.* See DOUBT 2.

[D-293]

DOUGHNUT (dō′ nət), *n.* (The twisted pastry is eaten.) The right "R" hand is placed in the mouth.

[D-294]

DOWN (doun), *prep.* (The natural sign.) The right hand, pointing down, moves down an inch or two.

[D-295]

DOZE (dōz), *v.,* DOZED, DOZING, *n.* (The eyes are closed.) The fingers of the right open hand, facing the forehead, are placed on the forehead. The hand moves down and away from the head, with the fingers closing so that they all touch. The eyes meanwhile close, and the head bows slightly, as in sleep. *Cf.* ASLEEP, NAP, SLEEP 1.

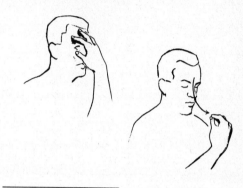

[D-296]

DRAG (drăg), *v.* DRAGGED, DRAGGING. (The natural action.) Both open hands, the right palm up and the left palm down, grasp an imaginary pole and pull it toward the body. *Cf.* DRAW 2, PULL 1.

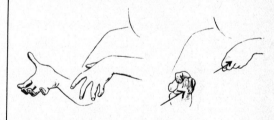

[D-297]

DRAMA (dra′ mə, drăm′ ə), *n.* (Motion or movement, modified by the letter "A" for "act.") Both "A" hands, palms out, are held at shoulder height and rotate alternately toward the head. *Cf.* ACT 1, ACTOR, ACTRESS, PERFORM 2, PERFORMANCE 2, PLAY 2, SHOW 2.

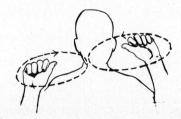

[D–298]

DRAW 1 (drô), *v.*, DREW, DRAWN, DRAWING. (Drawing on the hand.) The little finger of the right hand, representing a pencil, traces a curved line in the upturned left palm. *Cf.* ART, MAP.

[D–299]

DRAW 2, *v.* See DRAG.

[D–300]

DRAWER (drôr), *n.* (The natural sign.) The upturned hands grasp imaginary drawer pulls and pull the drawer toward the body.

[D–301]

DREAD (drĕd), *v.*, DREADED, DREADING. (The hands attempt to ward off something which causes fear.) The "5" hands, right behind left, move downward before the body, in a wavy motion. *Cf.* FEAR 2, TERROR 2, TIMID.

[D–302]

DREADFUL (drĕd′ fəl), *adj.* (Throwing out the hands.) Both hands, their fingertips touching their

respective thumbs, are held, palms facing each other, near the temples. They are thrown out before the face, assuming "5" positions, palms still facing. *Cf.* AWFUL, CALAMITOUS, CATASTROPHIC, DANGER 1, DANGEROUS 1, FEARFUL, TERRIBLE, TRAGEDY, TRAGIC.

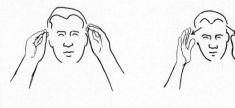

[D–303]

DREAM (drēm), *n.*, *v.*, DREAMED, DREAMT, DREAMING. (A thought wanders off into space.) The right curved index finger opens and closes quickly as it leaves its initial position on the forehead and moves up into the air. *Cf.* DAYDREAM, DISTRACTION.

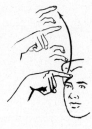

[D–304]

DRESS (drĕs), *n.*, *v.*, DRESSED, DRESSING. (Draping the clothes on the body.) With fingertips resting on the chest, both hands move down simultaneously. The action is repeated. *Cf.* CLOTHES, CLOTHING, FROCK, GARMENT, GOWN, SHIRT, SUIT, WEAR 1.

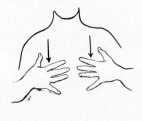

[D–305]

DRESSMAKER (drĕs′ mā′ kər), *n.* (A sewer of dresses.) The sign for DRESS is made, followed by the sign for SEW, *q.v.:* The right hand, grasping an imaginary needle, sews stitches on the upturned left

palm. This is followed by the sign for INDIVID-
UAL: Both open hands, palms facing each other,
move down the sides of the body, tracing its outline
to the hips.

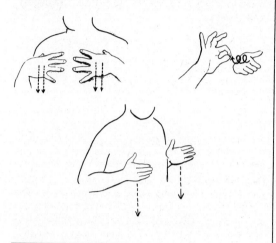

DRILL 1 (drĭl), *n.* (Act of boring a hole with a
brace.) The left "S" hand, palm down, grasps an
imaginary brace top. The right hand, also in the "S"
position, palm facing left, rotates the brace, as if
drilling something. *Cf.* BORE 2.

DRILL 2, *(voc.)*, *n., v.* (The natural sign.) The right
index finger is held pointing down. In this position
the hand spirals downward, imitating the motion of
a drill.

DRILL 3, *v.*, DRILLED, DRILLING. (Polishing or
sharpening up.) The knuckles of the downturned
right "A" hand are rubbed briskly back and forth
over the side of the hand and index finger of the left
"D" hand. *Cf.* DISCIPLINE 1, PRACTICE 1, TRAIN 2,
TRAINING 1.

DRINK 1 (drĭngk), *n., v.*, DRANK, DRUNK, DRINK-
ING. (The natural sign.) An imaginary glass is tipped
at the open lips.

DRINK 2, *n., v.*, (The act of drinking.) The thumbtip
of the right "Y" hand is tilted toward the mouth, as
if it were a drinking glass or bottle. The signer tilts
his head back slightly, as if drinking. *Cf.* DRUNK,
DRUNKARD, DRUNKENNESS, INTOXICATE, INTOXI-
CATION, LIQUOR 2.

DRIP (drĭp), *v.*, DRIPPED, DRIPPING. (The natural
sign.) The right "4" hand, palm facing the body and
fingers pointing left, moves down repeatedly from its
position below the right "S" hand, whose palm faces
the body with thumb edge up. *Cf.* LEAK.

[D–312]

DRIVE (drīv), *v.,* DROVE, DRIVEN, DRIVING, *n.* (The steering wheel.) The hands grasp an imaginary steering wheel and manipulate it. *Cf.* AUTOMOBILE, CAR.

[D–313]

DROP (drŏp), *v.,* DROPPED, DROPPING. (The natural sign.) The downturned right "S" hand, held at shoulder height, drops down, opening into the downturned "5" position.

[D–314]

DROUGHT (drout), *n.* (A dryness, indicated by a wiping of the lips.) The "X" finger is drawn across the lips, from left to right, as if wiping them. *Cf.* ARID, BORE 1, DRY, DULL 2.

[D–315]

DROWN 1 (droun), *v.* (The legs go under.) The index and middle fingers of the right "V" hand, palm facing the body, are drawn down between the index and middle fingers of the downturned left "4" hand.

The right index finger alone may be substituted for the "V" fingers.

[D–316]

DROWN 2, *v.* (The downward movement.) The downturned right hand, fingers touching thumb, is thrust down into the cup formed by the open left hand. The right hand continues straight down through this cup.

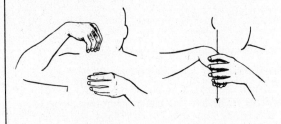

[D–317]

DRUG (drŭg), *n., v.,* DRUGGED, DRUGGING. (Mixing of medicine; rolling a pill.) The ball of the middle fingertip of the right "5" hand describes a small counterclockwise circle in the upturned left palm. *Cf.* MEDICINE, POISON 1, PRESCRIPTION.

[D–318]

DRUM (drŭm), *n., v.,* DRUMMED, DRUMMING. (The natural sign.) The hands play an imaginary drum.

[D–319]

DRUNK (drŭngk), *adj.* (The act of drinking.) The thumbtip of the right "Y" hand is tilted toward the mouth, as if it were a drinking glass or bottle. The signer tilts his head back slightly, as if drinking. *Cf.* DRINK 2, DRUNKARD, DRUNKENNESS, INTOXICATE, INTOXICATION, LIQUOR 2.

[D–320]

DRUNKARD (drŭngk' ərd), *n.* See DRUNK.

[D–321]

DRUNKENNESS (drŭngk' ən nĭs), *n.* See DRUNK.

[D–322]

DRY (drī), *adj., v.,* DRIED, DRYING. (A dryness, indicated by a wiping of the lips.) The "X" finger is drawn across the lips, from left to right, as if wiping them. *Cf.* ARID, BORE 1, DROUGHT, DULL 2.

[D–323]

DUCK (dŭk), *n.* (The broad bill.) The right hand is held with its back resting against the mouth. The thumb, index and middle fingers come together repeatedly, indicating the opening and closing of a broad bill. *Cf.* GOOSE.

[D–324]

DUE (dū, do͞o), *adj.* (Pointing to the palm, where the money should be placed.) The index finger of one hand is thrust into the upturned palm of the other several times. *Cf.* ARREARS, DEBIT, DEBT, OBLIGATION 3, OWE.

[D–325]

DULL 1 (dŭl), *adj.* (Knocking the head to indicate its empty state.) The "S" hand, palm facing the body, knocks against the forehead. *Cf.* DUMB 1, DUNCE, STUPID 1.

[D–326]

DULL 2, *adj.* See DRY.

[D–327]

DUMB 1 (dŭm), *adj.* See DULL 1.

[D–328]

DUMB 2, *(colloq.), adj.* (The thickness of the skull is indicated, to stress intellectual density.) With the thumb of the right "C" hand grasped by the closed left hand, the right hand is swung in toward the body, describing a small arc as it moves. The space between the curved right fingers and the closed left hand indicates the thickness of the skull. *Cf.* CLUMSY 2, MORON, STUPID 2, THICK-SKULLED, UNSKILLED.

[D-329]

DUMFOUNDED 1 (dŭm found′), *adj.* (The mind is frozen; the thought is frozen.) The index finger of the right "D" hand, palm facing the body, touches the forehead (modified **THINK** sign, *q.v.*). Both hands, in the "5" position, palms down, are then suddenly and deliberately dropped down in front of the body. A look of surprise is assumed at this point, and the head jerks back slightly. *Cf.* AT A LOSS, JOLT, SHOCKED 1, STUMPED.

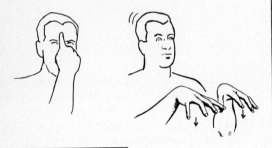

[D-330]

DUMFOUNDED 2, *(colloq.), adj.* (The mouth drops open.) The fingertips of both "V" hands are held curved and touching before the body, one hand above the other. Then the hands are suddenly drawn apart, and at the same instant the mouth drops open and the eyes open wide. *Cf.* FLABBERGASTED. OPEN-MOUTHED, SPEECHLESS, SURPRISE 2.

[D-331]

DUNCE (dŭns), *n.* See DULL 1.

[D-332]

DUPLICATE 1 (*adj., n.,* dū′ plə kĭt, dōō′-; *v.,* dū′ plə kāt′, dōō′-), -CATED, -CATING. (The natural sign.) The right fingers and thumb close together and move onto the upturned, open left hand, as if taking something from one place to another. *Cf.* COPY 1, IMITATE, MIMIC, MODEL.

[D-333]

DUPLICATE 2, *n.* (A likeness; a sameness.) Both index fingers, held together at one side of the body near waist level, point forward. As they travel to the other side of the body they separate an inch or two and come together again. *Cf.* ACCORDING (TO), ALSO 1, AS, SAME AS, TOO.

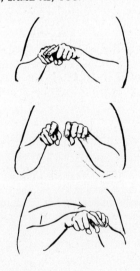

[D-334]

DURING (dyŏŏr′ ĭng, dŏŏr′-), *prep.* (Parallel time.) Both "D" hands, palms down, move forward in unison, away from the body. They may move straight forward or may follow a slight upward arc. *Cf.* IN THE MEANTIME, IN THE PROCESS OF, MEANTIME, WHILE.

[D–335]

DUTCH 1 (dŭch), *adj.* (The long pipe smoked by Netherlanders.) The right "Y" hand is held before the face, with thumbtip at the lips. It swings down and forward, outlining the shape of a long curved pipe. *Cf.* HOLLAND 1, NETHERLANDS 1.

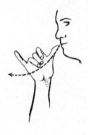

[D–336]

DUTCH 2, *adj.* (The hat worn by Netherlands women.) The hands, held open at either temple, grasp the points of the native female headgear. They swing upward a bit, as the fingers close over the thumbs. *Cf.* HOLLAND 2, NETHERLANDS 2.

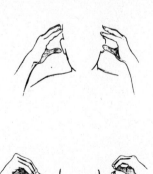

[D–337]

DUTY 1 (dū′ tĭ, dōō′-), *n.* (The letter "D"; bound down.) The base of the right "D" hand repeatedly strikes the back of the downturned left "S" hand. *Cf.* OBLIGATION 2.

[D–338]

DUTY 2, *n.* (Nicking into one.) The knuckle of the right "X" finger is nicked against the palm of the left hand, held in the "5" position, palm facing right. *Cf.* ADMISSION 2, CHARGE 1, COST, EXCISE, EXPENSE, FEE, FINE 2, IMPOST, PENALTY 3, PRICE 2, TAX 1, TAXATION 1, TOLL.

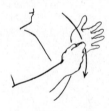

[D–339]

DWELL (dwĕl), *v.,* DWELLED, DWELLING. (A place where one lives.) The "A" hands, thumbs up, are placed on the sides, at waist level. They slide up the body in unison, to chest level. This is the sign for LIFE or LIVE, indicating an upsurging of life. *Cf.* ADDRESS 3, ALIVE, EXIST, LIFE 1, LIVE 1, LIVING, MORTAL, RESIDE.

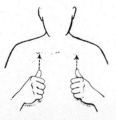

[D–340]

DYE (dī), *n., v.,* DYED, DYEING. (The garment or other object is lifted in and out of the dye.) The downturned hands, grasping an imaginary garment or other object, move up and down simultaneously.

[D–341]

DYING (dī′ ing), *adj.* (Turning over on one's side.) The open hands, fingers pointing ahead, are held side by side, with the right palm down and the left palm up. The two hands reverse their relative positions as they move from the left to the right. *Cf.* DEAD 1, DEATH, DIE 1, EXPIRE 2, PERISH 1.

E

[E–1]

EACH (ēch), *adj.* (Peeling off, one by one.) The left "A" hand is held palm facing the right. The knuckles of the right "A" hand are drawn repeatedly down the left thumb, from its tip to its base. *Cf.* EVERY.

[E–2]

EACH ONE, *pron. phrase.* (EVERY; ONE.) The sign for EVERY is made, followed by the sign for ONE. *Cf.* EVERYBODY, EVERYONE.

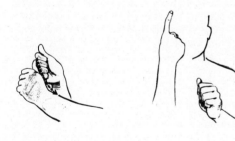

[E–3]

EACH OTHER, *pron. phrase.* (Mingling with.) Both hands are held in modified "A" positions, thumbs out. The left hand is positioned with its thumb pointing straight up, and the right hand, with its thumb pointing down, revolves above the left thumb in a counterclockwise direction. *Cf.* ASSOCIATE 1, FELLOWSHIP, MINGLE 2, MUTUAL 1, ONE ANOTHER.

[E–4]

EAGER (ē′ gər), *adj.* (Rubbing the hands together in zeal or ambition.) The open hands are rubbed vigorously back and forth against each other. *Cf.* AMBITIOUS 1, ANXIOUS 1, ARDENT, DILIGENCE 1, DILIGENT, EAGERNESS, EARNEST, ENTHUSIASM, ENTHUSIASTIC, INDUSTRIOUS, METHODIST, ZEAL, ZEALOUS.

[E–5]

EAGERNESS, *n.* See EAGER.

[E–6]

EAGLE (ē′ gəl), *n.* (The hooked beak and the wings.) The index finger of the right "X" hand is placed on the nose, either facing out or across it. The hands and arms then flap slowly, in imitation of the bird's majestic flight.

[E–7]

EAR (ĭr), *n.* (The natural sign.) The right index finger touches the right ear.

211

[E-8]

EARACHE (ĭr′ āk´), *n.* (A stabbing pain in the ear.) The sign for EAR is made, followed by the sign for ACHE: The "D" hands, index fingers pointing to each other and palms facing the body, are rotated in elliptical fashion before the chest—simultaneously but in opposite directions.

[E-9]

EARLY (ûr′ lĭ), *adj.* (The sun is coming up.) The little finger edge of the open right hand rests in the crook of the left elbow. (The right arm here represents the horizon and should therefore be held in a horizontal position.) The left "5" hand is held palm up and the left arm is held at a 45-degree angle from the horizontal. This represents the sun coming up over the horizon, and is a modified sign for MORNING, *q.v.,* but with no motion.

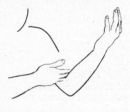

[E-10]

EARN (ûrn), *v.,* EARNED, EARNING. (Gathering in.) The right "5" hand, its little finger edge touching the upturned left palm, is drawn in an arc toward the body, closing into the "S" position as it sweeps over the base of the left hand. *Cf.* ACCUMULATE 1, COLLECT, SALARY, WAGES.

[E-11]

EARNEST (ûr′ nĭst), *adj.* (Rubbing the hands together in zeal or ambition.) The open hands are rubbed vigorously back and forth against each other. *Cf.* AMBITIOUS 1, ANXIOUS 1, ARDENT, DILIGENCE 1, DILIGENT, EAGER, EAGERNESS, ENTHUSIASM, ENTHUSIASTIC, INDUSTRIOUS, METHODIST, ZEAL, ZEALOUS.

[E-12]

EARRING (ĭr′ rĭng´), *n.* (The natural sign.) The right thumb and index finger press the right ear lobe.

[E-13]

EARTH 1 (ûrth), *n.* (The earth and its axes are indicated.) The downturned left "S" hand indicates the earth. The thumb and index finger of the downturned right "5" hand are placed at each edge of the left. In this position the right hand swings back and forth, while maintaining contact with the left. *Cf.* GEOGRAPHY, GLOBE 1, PLANET.

[E-14]

EARTH 2, *n.* (Fingering the soil.) Both hands, held upright before the body, finger imaginary pinches of soil. *Cf.* DIRT, GROUND, SOIL 1.

[E-15]

EARTHQUAKE (ûrth′ kwāk´), *n.* (Earth, noise.) The sign for EARTH 1 is made. This is followed by the sign for NOISE. After placing the index finger on the ear, both hands assume the "S" position, palms down. They move alternately back and forth forcefully.

[E–16]

EAST (ēst), *n., adj., adv.* (The letter "E"; the direction.) The right "E" hand moves toward the right.

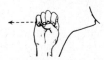

[E–17]

EASTER 1 (ēs′ tər), *n.* (The letter "E.") The right "E" hand, pivoted at the wrist, is shaken slightly.

[E–18]

EASTER 2, *n.* (A rising.) The right index and middle fingers, representing the legs, are positioned in the upturned left palm. The right hand moves slowly up and off the left. *Note:* This sign is considered vulgar by some; it is at best used in a colloquial sense. *Cf.* ASCENSION, RESURRECTION.

[E–19]

EASTER 3, *n.* (A modification of EASTER 1.) The right "E" hand swings in an arc from left to right.

[E–20]

EASY 1 (ē′ zĭ), *adj.* (The fingertips are easily moved.) The right fingertips brush repeatedly over their upturned left counterparts, causing them to move. *Cf.* FACILITATE, SIMPLE 1.

[E–21]

EASY 2, *(loc., colloq.), adj.* (Rationale obscure.) The thumb and index finger of the right "F" hand are placed on the chin.

[E–22]

EAT (ēt), *v.,* ATE, EATEN, EATING. (The natural sign.) The closed right hand goes through the natural motion of placing food in the mouth. This movement is repeated. *Cf.* CONSUME 1, CONSUMPTION, DEVOUR, DINE, FEED 1, FOOD 1, MEAL.

[E–23]

ECCENTRIC (ĭk sĕn′ trĭk), *adj.* -TRICALLY, *adv.* (Something which distorts the vision.) The "C" hand describes a small arc in front of the face.

[E–24]

EDUCATE (ĕj′ ŏo kāt′), *v.*, -CATED, -CATING. (Giving forth from the mind.) The fingertips of each hand are placed on the temples. They then swing out and open into the "5" position. *Cf.* INDOCTRINATE, INDOCTRINATION, INSTRUCT, INSTRUCTION, TEACH.

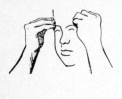 

[E–25]

EDUCATION (ĕj′ ŏo kā′ shən), *n.* (Taking knowledge from a book and placing it in the head.) The downturned fingers of the right hand are placed on the upturned left palm. They close, and then the hand rises and the right fingertips are placed on the forehead. *Cf.* LEARN.

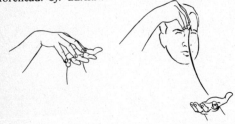

[E–26]

EDUCATOR (ĕj′ ŏo kā′ tər), *n.* The sign for EDUCATE is made. This is followed by the sign for INDIVIDUAL: Both open hands, palms facing each other, move down the sides of the body, tracing its outline to the hips. *Cf.* INSTRUCTOR, TEACHER.

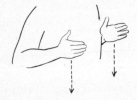

[E–27]

EFFECT 1 (ĭ fĕkt′), *n.* (Rays of influence emanating from a given source.) All the right fingertips, including the thumb, are positioned on the tip of the upturned thumb of the left "A" hand. The right hand, opening into the downturned "5" position, moves

forward from its initial position. Instead of its initial position on the left thumb, the right hand is frequently placed on the back of the downturned left "S" hand, moving forward as described above. *Cf.* BASIS 1, CAUSE, INFLUENCE 2, INTENT 2, LOGIC, PRODUCE 4, REASON 2.

[E–28]

EFFECT 2, *n.* (Swaying one to one's side.) The "A" hands, palms facing each other and the right positioned above the left, swing over simultaneously to the left side of the body. *Cf.* INFLUENCE 1.

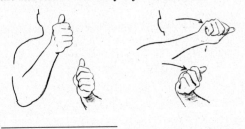

[E–29]

EFFORT 1 (ĕf′ ərt), *n.* (Trying to push through.) The "A" hands, palms facing before the body, are swung around and a bit down, so that the palms now face out. The movement indicates an attempt to push through a barrier. *Cf.* ATTEMPT 1, ENDEAVOR, PERSEVERE 1, PERSIST 1, TRY 1.

[E–30]

EFFORT 2, *n.* (Trying to push through, using the "T" hands, for "try.") This is the same sign as EFFORT 1, except that the "T" hands are employed. *Cf.* ATTEMPT 2, PERSEVERE 2, TRY 2.

[E-31]

EFFORT 3, *n.* (The letter "E"; attempting to break through.) Both "E" hands move forward simultaneously, describing a small, downturned arc.

[E-32]

EGG (ĕg), *n.* (Act of breaking an egg into a bowl.) The right "H" hand is brought down on the left "H" hand, and then both hands are pivoted down and slightly apart.

[E-33]

EGOTISM 1 (ē' gə tĭz´ əm, ĕg' ə-), *n.* (The self is carried uppermost.) The right "A" hand, thumb up, is brought up against the chest, from waist to breast. *Cf.* AMBITIOUS 2, SELF 2.

[E-34]

EGOTISM 2 *n.* (Repeated "I"s.) The "I" hands are alternately swung in toward and away from the chest. The movement is repeated a number of times.

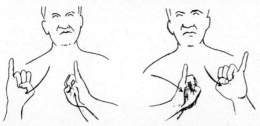

[E-35]

EGOTISM 3, *(colloq.)*, *n.* (A big "I.") The right "I" hand, palm facing left, rests on the chest. The left hand, wrapped loosely around the right little finger, is drawn straight up, as if to extend the right little finger.

[E-36]

EGYPT (ē' jĭpt), *n.* (The dark face.) The right fingertips rest initially on the nose. The right hand sweeps around the face, describing a counterclockwise circle and returning to its original position. *Cf.* EGYPTIAN.

[E-37]

EGYPTIAN (ĭ jĭp' shən), *n.* See EGYPT.

[E-38]

EIGHT (āt), *n., adj.* The thumbtip and middle fingertip touch, while the other fingers point straight up. The palm faces out from the body.

[E-39]

EIGHTH (āth), *adj.* (One over eight.) The "1" hand drops down a few inches, assuming the "8" position as it does.

[E–40]

EIGHT OF US, *phrase.* (Eight; encompassed.) The right "8" hand swings in an arc from the right shoulder to the left shoulder.

[E–41]

EITHER 1 (ē′ thər *or, esp. Brit.,* ī′ thər), *conj.* (Selection between two or among multiple choices.) The left "L" hand is held palm facing the body and thumb pointing straight up. The right index finger touches the left thumbtip and then the left index fingertip. *Cf.* OR 1.

[E–42]

EITHER 2, *adj.* (Making a choice.) The left "V" hand faces the body. The right thumb and index finger close first over the left index fingertip and then over the left middle fingertip. *Cf.* CHOICE.

[E–43]

EITHER 3, *conj.* (Considering one thing against another.) The "A" hands, palms facing and thumbs pointing straight up, move alternately up and down before the chest. *Cf.* OR 2, WHETHER, WHICH 1.

[E–44]

EJACULATE (ĭ jăk′ yə lāt′), *v.,* -LATED, -LATING. (The motion of ejecting.) The right hand is closed, with the thumb resting on the fingertips. The hand opens suddenly and quickly. This is repeated once or twice.

[E–45]

ELAPSE (ĭ lăps′), *v.,* -LAPSED, -LAPSING. (One hand passes the other.) Both "A" hands, palms facing each other, are held before the body, the right behind the left. The right hand moves forward, its knuckles brushing those of the left, and continues forward a bit beyond the left. *Cf.* GO BY, PASS 1.

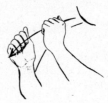

[E–46]

ELASTIC (ĭ lăs′ tĭk), *adj.* -TICALLY, *adv.* (Pulling apart.) Both "S" hands are pulled apart slowly, as if stretching something they are holding. *Cf.* STRETCH.

[E–47]

ELDER (ĕl′ dər), *adj., comparative degree.* The sign for OLD is made, followed by the comparative degree sign: The upturned right thumb moves up to a position in line with the right temple. *Cf.* OLDER.

[E–48]

ELDEST (ĕl′ dĭst), *adj., superlative degree.* The sign for OLD is made, followed by the superlative degree sign: The upturned right thumb moves up to a position above the level of the head. *Cf.* OLDEST.

[E–49]

ELECT (ĭ lĕkt′), *n., v.,* -LECTED, -LECTING (Placing a ballot in a box.) The right hand, holding an imaginary ballot between the thumb and index finger, places it into an imaginary box formed by the left "O" hand, palm facing right. *Cf.* ELECTION, VOTE.

[E–50]

ELECTION (ĭ lĕk′ shən), *n.* See ELECT.

[E–51]

ELECTRIC (ĭ lĕk′ trĭk), *adj.* (The points of the electrodes.) The "X" hands are held palms facing the body, thumb edges up. The knuckles of the index fingers touch each other repeatedly. *Cf.* ELECTRICITY, PHYSICS.

[E–52]

ELECTRICITY (ĭ lĕk′ trĭs′ ə tĭ), *n.* See ELECTRIC.

[E–53]

ELECTRIC MOTOR (mō′ tər), (Winding the coil around the armature.) The left hand, facing right, is held with fingers touching thumb. The right index finger moves in a continuous clockwise circle around the left fingers. The sign for ELECTRIC is often made first. *Cf.* ABOUT 1, CONCERNING, OF.

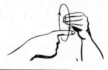

[E–54]

ELECTRIC OUTLET (out′ lət). (Plugging in.) Both "V" hands, palms facing each other, are held before the body. The right "V" hand, representing the prongs of a plug, is brought into an interlocking position with the left. *Cf.* ELECTRIC PLUG, SOCKET.

[E–55]

ELECTRIC PLUG (plŭg). See ELECTRIC OUTLET.

[E–56]

ELECTROCUTE (ĭ lĕk′ trə kūt′), *v.* -CUTED, -CUTING. (Applying the electrodes to the head.) Both index fingers, somewhat curved, are thrust into contact with the temples. *Cf.* ELECTROCUTION.

[E–57]

ELECTROCUTION, *n.* See ELECTROCUTE.

[E–58]

ELEGANT (el′ ə gənt), *adj.* (The feelings are titillated.) With the thumb resting on the upper part of the chest, the fingers are wiggled back and forth. *Cf.* FINE 1, GRAND 2, GREAT 4, SPLENDID 2, SWELL 2, WONDERFUL 2.

[E-59]

ELEPHANT (ĕl′ ə fənt), *n.* (The movement of the trunk.) The cupped downturned right hand is placed with its back resting on the nose. The hand moves down, out, and around, imitating the motion of the trunk in bringing food up to the mouth. The hand may also be moved in random undulations.

[E-60]

ELEVATE (ĕl′ ə vāt′), *v.*, -VATED, -VATING. (Getting onto one's feet.) The upturned index and middle fingers of the right hand, representing the legs, are swung up and over in an arc, coming to rest in the upturned left palm. *Cf.* ARISE 2, GET UP, RAISE 1, RISE 1, STAND 2, STAND UP.

[E-61]

ELEVATOR 1 (ĕl′ ə vā′ tər), *n.* (A rising platform.) With the downturned right "V" fingers standing on the upturned left palm, the left hand rises straight up.

[E-62]

ELEVATOR 2, *n.* (The letter "E"; the rising.) The right "E" hand, palm facing left and thumb edge up, rises straight up.

[E-63]

ELIMINATE (i lim ə nāt′), *v.*, -NATED, -NATING. (Scratching something out and throwing it away.)

The fingertips of the open right hand scratch downward across the palm of the upright left hand. In one continuous motion, the right hand then closes as if holding something, and finally opens again forcefully and motions as if throwing something away. *Cf.* DELETE 2, DISCARD 3.

[E-64]

ELK (ĕlk), *n.* (The branching of the antlers from the head.) Both hands, in the "5" position, palms up, are placed at the head, thumbs resting on the head above the temples. *Cf.* ANTLERS, DEER, MOOSE.

[E-65]

EMANCIPATE (i măn′ sə pāt′), *v.*, -PATED, -PATING. (Breaking the bonds.) The "S" hands, crossed in front of the body, swing apart and face out. *Cf.* DELIVER 1, FREE 1, INDEPENDENCE, INDEPENDENT, LIBERATION, REDEEM 1, RELIEF, RESCUE, SAFE, SALVATION, SAVE 1.

[E-66]

EMBARRASS (ĕm băr′ əs), *v.*, -RASSED, -RASSING. (The red rises in the cheeks.) The sign for RED is made: The tip of the right index finger of the "D" hand moves down over the lips, which are red. Both hands are then placed palms facing the cheeks, and move up along the face, to indicate the rise of color. *Cf.* BLUSH, EMBARRASSED, FLUSH, MORTIFICATION.

[E–67]

EMBARRASSED *adj.,* See EMBARRASS.

[E–68]

EMBEZZLE (ĕm bĕz′ əl), *v.,* -ZLED, -ZLING. (The hand, partly concealed, takes something surreptitiously.) The index and middle fingers of the right hand, somewhat curved, are placed under the left elbow. As they move slowly along the left forearm toward the left wrist, they close a bit. *Cf.* ABDUCT, EMBEZZLEMENT, KIDNAP, ROB 1, ROBBERY 1, STEAL 1, SWIPE, THEFT 1, THIEF 1, THIEVERY.

[E–69]

EMBEZZLEMENT (ĕm bĕz′ əl mənt), *n.* See EMBEZZLE. This is followed by the sign for -MENT: The downturned right "M" hand moves down along the left palm, which is facing away from the body.

[E–70]

EMBRACE (ĕm brās′), *v.,* -BRACED, -BRACING, *n.* (The natural sign.) The arms clasp the body in a natural hugging position. *Cf.* HUG.

[E–71]

EMOTION 1 (ĭ mō′ shən), *n.* (The welling up of feelings or emotions in the heart.) The right middle finger, touching the heart, moves up an inch or two a number of times. *Cf.* FEEL 2, FEELING, MOTIVE 2, SENSATION, SENSE 2.

[E–72]

EMOTION 2, *n.* (The letter "E"; that which moves about in the chest, *i.e.* the heart.) The "E" hands, palms facing in, are positioned close to the chest. Both hands describe alternate circles, the left hand clockwise and the right hand counterclockwise. The right hand alone may be used.

[E–73]

EMPEROR (ĕm′ pər ər), *n.* (The letter "E"; the sash worn by royalty.) The right "E" hand, palm facing left, moves down in an arc from the left shoulder to the right hip.

[E–74]

EMPHASIS (ĕm′ fə sĭs), *n.* (Pressing down to emphasize.) The right thumb is pressed down deliberately against the upturned left palm. Both hands move forward a bit. *Cf.* EMPHASIZE, EMPHATIC, STRESS.

[E–75]

EMPHASIZE (ĕm′ fə sīz′), *v.,* -SIZED, -SIZING. See EMPHASIS.

[E–76]

EMPHATIC (ĕm făt′ ĭk), *adj.* See EMPHASIS.

[E–77]

EMPLOY (ĕm ploi′), *v.,* EMPLOYED, EMPLOYING. (The letter "E"; striking the anvil.) The base of the right "E" hand strikes the back of the downturned left "S" hand.

[E–78]

EMPLOYMENT (ĕm ploi′ mənt), *n.* The sign for EMPLOY is followed by the -MENT suffix sign: The downturned right "M" hand moves down along the left palm, which is facing away from the body.

[E–79]

EMPTY 1 (ĕmp′ tĭ), *adj.* (A disappearance.) The right open hand, palm facing the body, is held by the left hand and is drawn down and out, ending in a position with fingers drawn together. The left hand, meanwhile, may close into a position with fingers also drawn together. *Cf.* ABSENCE 1, ABSENT 1, DE-PLETE, DISAPPEAR, EXTINCT, FADE AWAY, GONE 1, MISSING 1, OMISSION 1, OUT 3, OUT OF, VANISH.

[E–80]

EMPTY 2, *adj.* (Devoid of everything on the surface.) The middle finger of the downturned right "5" hand sweeps over the back of the downturned left "A" or "S" hand, from wrist to knuckles, and continues beyond a bit. *Cf.* BARE 2, NAKED, NUDE, OMISSION 2, VACANCY, VACANT, VOID.

[E–81]

ENCORE (äng′ kōr, än′-), *interj., n., v.,* -CORED, -CORING. The left hand, open in the "5" position, palm up, is held before the chest. The right hand, in the right angle position, fingers pointing up, arches over and into the left palm. *Cf.* AGAIN, REPEAT.

[E–82]

ENCOUNTER (ĕn koun′ tər), *v.,* -TERED, -TERING. (A coming together of two persons.) Both "D" hands, palms facing each other, are brought together. *Cf.* MEET.

[E–83]

ENCOURAGE (ĕn kûr′ ĭj), *v.,* -AGED, -AGING. (Pushing forward.) Both "5" hands are held, palms out, the right fingers facing right and the left fingers left. The hands move straight forward in a series of short movements. *Cf.* MOTIVATE, MOTIVATION, URGE 1.

[E–84]

END 1 (ĕnd), *n., v.,* ENDED, ENDING. (The little, *i.e.,* LAST, fingers are indicated.) With the hands in the "I" position, the tip of the right little finger strikes the tip of its left counterpart. The right index finger may be used instead of the right little finger. *Cf.* EVENTUALLY, FINAL 1, FINALLY 1, LAST 1, ULTI-MATE, ULTIMATELY.

[E–85]

END 2, *n., v.,* (A single little, *i.e.,* LAST, finger is indicated.) The tip of the index finger of the right "D" hand strikes the tip of the little finger of the left "I" hand. *Cf.* FINAL 2, FINALLY 2, LAST 2.

[E–86]

END 3, *n., v.* (Shaking the hands to rid them of something.) The upright "5" hands, palms facing each other, are suddenly and quickly swung around to a palm-out position. *Cf.* DONE 2, FINISH 2.

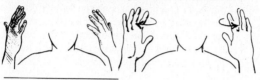

[E–87]

END 4, *n., v.* (Bring to an end.) The left hand, fingers together and pointing forward, is held palm facing right. The right, palm down, fingers also together, moves along the top of the left, goes over the tip of the left index finger, and drops straight down, indicating a cutting off or a finishing. This sign is also used to indicate the past tense of a verb, in the sense of ending an action or state of being. *Cf.* ACCOMPLISH 2, ACHIEVE 2, COMPLETE 1, CONCLUDE, DONE 1, EXPIRE 1, FINISH 1, HAVE 2, TERMINATE.

[E–88]

ENDEAVOR (ĕn dĕv′ ər), *n.* (Trying to push through.) The "A" hands, palms facing before the body, are swung around and a bit down, so that the palms now face out. The movement indicates an attempt to push through a barrier. *Cf.* ATTEMPT 1, EFFORT 1, PERSEVERE 1, PERSIST 1, TRY 1.

[E–89]

END OF THE LINE, *(colloq.), phrase.* (The end fingers.) The "I" hands face each other, with the left somewhat in front of the right. The right hand moves forward, and the right little finger touches the tip of its left counterpart as it passes by and continues beyond a bit.

[E–90]

ENDORSE 1 (ĕn dôrs′), *v.,* -DORSED, -DORSING. (Holding up.) The right "S" hand pushes up the left "S" hand. *Cf.* FAVOR, INDORSE 1, MAINTENANCE, SUPPORT 1, SUSTAIN, SUSTENANCE, UPHOLD, UPLIFT.

[E–91]

ENDORSE 2, *v.* (One hand upholds the other.) Both hands, in the "S" position, are held palms facing the body, the right under the left. The right hand pushes up the left in a gesture of support. *Cf.* ADVOCATE, INDORSE 2, SUPPORT 2.

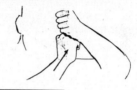

[E–92]

ENDORSE 3, *v.* ("Second"—two fingers.) The right "L" hand, held somewhat above the head, index finger pointing straight up, pivots forward a bit, so that the index finger now points forward. Used in parliamentary procedure. *Cf.* INDORSE 3, SECOND 2, SUPPORT 3.

[E–93]

ENDURE 1 (ĕn dyŏŏr′, -dŏŏr′), *v.,* -DURED, -DURING. (A clenching of the fists; the rise and fall of pain.) Both "S" hands, tightly clenched, revolve about each other, slowly and deliberately, while a pained expression is worn. *Cf.* AGONY, BEAR 3, DIFFICULT 3, PASSION 2, SUFFER 1, TOLERATE 2.

[E-94]

ENDURE 2, *v.* (Steady, uninterrupted movement.) The "A" hands are held with palms out, thumbs extended and touching, the right behind the left. In this position the hands move forward in a straight, steady line. *Cf.* CONTINUE 1, EVER 1, LAST 3, LAST-ING, PERMANENT, PERPETUAL, PERSEVERE 3, PERSIST 2, REMAIN, STAY 1, STAY STILL.

[E-95]

ENEMY (ĕn′ ə mĭ), *n.* (At sword's point.) The two index fingers, after pointing to each other, are drawn sharply apart. This is followed by the sign for INDIVIDUAL: Both open hands, palms facing each other, move down the sides of the body, tracing its outline to the hips. *Cf.* FOE, OPPONENT, RIVAL 1.

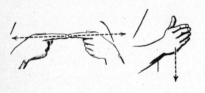

[E-96]

ENGAGED 1 (ĕn gājd′), *adj.* (The letter "E"; the ring finger.) The right "E" hand moves in a clockwise circle over the downturned left hand, and then comes to rest on the left ring finger.

[E-97]

ENGAGED 2, *adj.* (The natural sign.) The right hand goes through the natural motion of placing a ring on the left ring finger.

[E-98]

ENGAGEMENT (ĕn gāj′ mənt), *n.* (A binding of the hands together; a commitment.) The right "S" hand, palm down, is positioned above the left "S" hand, also palm down. The right hand circles above the left in a clockwise manner and is brought down on the back of the left hand. At the same instant both hands move down in unison a short distance. *Cf.* APPOINTMENT.

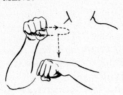 

[E-99]

ENGINE (ĕn′ jən), *n.* (The meshing gears.) With the knuckles of both hands interlocked, the hands pivot up and down, imitating the meshing of gear teeth. *Cf.* FACTORY, MACHINE, MACHINERY, MECHANIC 1, MECHANISM, MOTOR.

[E-100]

ENGLAND (ĭng′ glənd), *n.* (The English are supposed to be handshakers.) The right hand grasps and shakes the left. *Cf.* BRITAIN, BRITISH, ENGLISH, GREAT BRITAIN.

[E-101]

ENGLISH (ĭng′ glĭsh), *adj.* See ENGLAND.

[E-102]

ENGLISHMAN (ĭng′ glĭsh mən), *n.* (England, man.) The sign for ENGLAND is made. This is followed by the sign for MAN: The thumb and extended fingers of the right hand are brought up to grasp an imaginary cap brim, representing the tipping of a cap.

[E-103]

ENGRAVE (ĕn grāv'), *v.*, -GRAVED, -GRAVING. (Chipping or cutting out.) The right thumb tip repeatedly gouges out imaginary pieces of material from the palm of the left hand, held facing right. *Cf.* CARVE, ETCH.

[E-104]

ENGRAVER (ĕn grāv' ər), *n.* The sign for ENGRAVE is made. This is followed by the sign for INDIVIDUAL 1: Both open hands, palms facing each other, move down the sides of the body, tracing its outline to the hips.

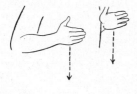

[E-105]

ENGROSS (ĕn grōs'), *v.*, -GROSSED, -GROSSING. (Drawing out.) The index and middle fingers of one hand are placed on the chest, while the same two fingers of the other hand are positioned in front of the mouth. Both hands move forward simultaneously, the index and middle fingers of each hand coming together as they do. *Cf.* FASCINATE 2, INTEREST 2.

[E-106]

ENJOY (ĕn joi'), *v.*, -JOYED, -JOYING. (A pleasurable feeling on the heart.) The open right hand is circled on the chest, over the heart. *Cf.* APPRECIATE, ENJOYMENT, GRATIFY 1, LIKE 3, PLEASE, PLEASURE, WILLING 2.

[E-107]

ENJOYMENT (ĕn joi' mənt), *n.* See ENJOY.

[E-108]

ENLIST (ĕn lĭst'), *v.*, -LISTED, -LISTING. (Joining together.) Both hands, held in the modified "5" position, palms out, move toward each other. The thumbs and index fingers of both hands then connect. *Cf.* AFFILIATE 1, ANNEX, ASSOCIATE 2, ATTACH, BELONG, COMMUNION OF SAINTS, CONCERN 2, CONNECT, ENROLL, JOIN 1, PARTICIPATE, RELATIVE 2, UNION, UNITE.

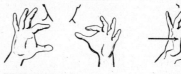

[E-109]

ENORMOUS (ĭ nôr' məs), *adj.* (A delineation of something big, modified by the letter "L," which stands for LARGE.) Both "L" hands, palms facing out, are placed before the face, and separate rather widely. *Cf.* BIG 1, GREAT 1, HUGE, IMMENSE, LARGE.

[E-110]

ENOUGH (ĭ nŭf'), *adj.* (A full cup.) The left hand, in the "S" position, is held palm facing right. The right "5" hand, palm down, is brushed outward several times over the top of the left, indicating a wiping off of the top of a cup. *Cf.* ABUNDANCE, ABUNDANT, ADEQUATE, AMPLE, PLENTY, SUBSTANTIAL, SUFFICIENT.

[E–111]

ENRAGE (ĕn rāj′), *v.*, -RAGED, -RAGING. (A violent welling-up of the emotions.) The curved fingers of the right hand are placed in the center of the chest, and fly up suddenly and violently. An expression of anger is worn. *Cf.* ANGER, ANGRY 2, FURY, INDIGNANT, INDIGNATION, IRE, MAD 1, RAGE.

[E–112]

ENROLL (ĕn rōl′), *v.*, -ROLLED, -ROLLING. See ENLIST.

[E–113]

ENTER (ĕn′ tər), *v.*, -TERED, -TERING. (Going in.) The downturned open right hand sweeps under its downturned left counterpart. *Cf.* ENTRANCE 1.

[E–114]

ENTHUSIASM (ĕn thōō′ zi ăz′ əm), *n.* (Rubbing the hands together in zeal or ambition.) The open hands are rubbed vigorously back and forth against each other. *Cf.* AMBITIOUS 1, ANXIOUS 1, ARDENT, DILIGENCE 1, DILIGENT, EAGER, EAGERNESS, EARNEST, ENTHUSIASTIC, INDUSTRIOUS, METHODIST, ZEAL, ZEALOUS.

[E–115]

ENTHUSIASTIC (ĕn thōō′ zi ăs′ tĭk), *adj.* See ENTHUSIASM.

[E–116]

ENTICE (ĕn tīs′), *v.*, -TICED, -TICING. (Tapping one surreptitiously at a concealed place.) With the left arm held palm down before the chest, the curved right index finger taps the left elbow a number of times. *Cf.* TEMPT, TEMPTATION.

[E–117]

ENTIRE (ĕn tīr′), *adj.* (Encompassing; a gathering together.) Both hands are held in the right angle position, palms facing the body, and the right hand in front of the left. The right hand makes a sweeping outward movement around the left, and comes to rest with the back of the right hand resting in the left palm. *Cf.* ALL, UNIVERSAL, WHOLE.

[E–118]

ENTRANCE 1 (ĕn trəns′), *n.* See ENTER.

[E–119]

ENTRANCE 2, *(sl.)*, *v.*, -TRANCED, -TRANCING. (The tongue drops out of the mouth; gawking.) The right thumb and curved index finger are placed in front of the open mouth. The right hand moves straight forward as the tongue comes out of the mouth a bit.

[E–120]

ENTREAT (ĕn trēt′), *v.*, -TREATED, -TREATING. (An act of supplication.) With the right hand clasped over the left, both hands are shaken gently before the body. The eyes often are directed upward. *Cf.* BEG 2, BESEECH, IMPLORE, PLEA, PLEAD, SUPPLICATION.

[E-121]

ENVIOUS (ĕn′ vĭ əs), *adj.* (Biting the finger to suppress the feelings.) The tip of the index finger is bitten. The tip of the little finger is sometimes used. *Cf.* COVET 2, ENVY, JEALOUS, JEALOUSY.

[E-122]

ENVIRONMENT 1 (ĕn vī′ rən mənt), *n.* (The surrounding area.) The downturned right hand circles around the upturned left, in a counterclockwise direction.

[E-123]

ENVIRONMENT 2, *n.* (The letter "E"; encircling the individual, represented by the index finger.) The right "E" hand travels around the upright left index finger.

[E-124]

ENVY (en′ vĭ), *n.* See ENVIOUS.

[E-125]

EPHPHETA (ə fe′ tə), *(eccles.)*, *n.* (Gr., "Be Thou Opened.") (The St. Andrew's Cross.) The right "E" hand, palm out, makes the sign of the cross. This is a form of blessing for the deaf, that the ears may be opened.

[E-126]

EPIPHANY (ĭ pĭf′ ə nĭ), *(eccles.)*, *n.* (The candle flame and the rays of light.) The index finger of the "D" hand is placed on the pursed lips, as if blowing

out a candle. The right hand is then raised above the head, with the fingertips and thumbtip touching, and palm facing out. The hand then moves down and a bit forward, opening into the "5" position, palm down. (The "candle" part of this sign is frequently omitted.) *Cf.* LIGHT 1, RAY.

[E-127]

EPISCOPAL (ĭ pĭs′ kə pəl), *adj.* (The surplice sleeve.) The left arm is held horizontally, the right index finger describes an arc under it, from wrist to elbow. *Cf.* BASKET, EPISCOPALIAN, STORE 3.

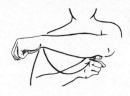

[E-128]

EPISCOPALIAN (ĭ pĭs′ kə pāl′ yən), *adj.* See EPISCOPAL. This is followed by the sign for INDIVIDUAL: Both open hands, palms facing each other, move down the sides of the body, tracing its outline to the hips.

[E-129]

EPISTLE (ĭ pĭs′ əl), *n.* (The stamp is affixed.) The right thumb is placed on the tongue, and is then pressed into the open left palm. *Cf.* LETTER, MAIL 1.

[E-130]

EPOCH (ĕp′ ək), *n.* (Time in the abstract, indicated by the rotating of the "T" hand on the face of a clock.) The right "T" hand is placed palm-to-palm in the open left hand. It describes a clockwise circle and comes to rest again in the left palm. *Cf.* AGE 2, ERA, PERIOD 2, SEASON, TIME 2.

[E-131]

EQUAL (ē′ kwəl), *adj., n., v.,* -QUALED, -QUALING. (Sameness is stressed.) The downturned "B" hands, held at chest height, are brought together repeatedly, so that the index finger edges or fingertips come into contact. *Cf.* EQUIVALENT, EVEN, FAIR 1, IMPARTIAL, JUST 1, LEVEL.

[E-132]

EQUIVALENT (ĭ kwĭv′ ə lənt), *adj.* See EQUAL.

[E-133]

-ER 1. (To form comparative degree.) The "A" hand, thumb extended upward, is raised slightly.

[E-134]

-ER 2. (Of occupation; hands are moved down the sides of the torso to denote the individual.) The heels of edgewise palms, fingers pointing outward, slide down the sides of the body. (The action is signed and then the "er" is added, to indicate the individual, as "write" and "er" for the writer.)

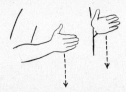

[E-135]

ERA (ĭr′ ə), *n.* See EPOCH.

[E-136]

ERASE (ĭ rās′), *v.,* -RASED, -RASING. (The natural sign.) The right hand, grasping an imaginary eraser, rubs it back and forth over the left palm.

[E-137]

ERECT (ĭ rĕkt′), *v.,* -RECTED, -RECTING. (Piling bricks one on top of another.) The downturned hands are placed repeatedly atop each other. Each time this is done the arms rise a bit, to indicate the raising of a building. *Cf.* BUILD, CONSTRUCT 1, CONSTRUCTION.

[E-138]

ERROR (ĕr′ ər), *n.* (Rationale obscure; the thumb and little finger are said to represent, respectively, right and wrong, with the head poised between the two.) The right "Y" hand, palm facing the body, is brought up to the chin. *Cf.* FAULT 2, MISTAKE, SACRILEGIOUS, WRONG 1.

[E-139]

ERUPT (ĭ rŭpt′), *v.,* -RUPTED, -RUPTING. (The upward explosion.) The left hand forms a cup, palm facing right. The right hand, fingertips together, shoots upward suddenly from its position within the left hand. As it emerges, the fingers open quickly. The sign is repeated. *Cf.* VOLCANO.

[E-140]

ESCAPE (ĕs kāp′), *v.*, -CAPED, -CAPING. (Emerging from a hiding place.) The downturned right "D" hand is positioned under the downturned open left hand. The right "D" hand suddenly emerges and moves off quickly to the right. *Cf.* FLEE.

[E-141]

ESPECIAL (ĕs pĕsh′ əl), *adj.* (Selecting a particular item from among several.) The index finger and thumb of the right hand grasp and pull up the left index finger. *Cf.* EXCEPT, EXCEPTION, SPECIAL.

[E-142]

ESSENTIAL (ə sĕn′ shəl), *adj.* Both "F" hands, palms facing each other, move apart, up, and together in a smooth elliptical fashion, coming together at the tips of the thumbs and index fingers of both hands. *Cf.* DESERVE, IMPORTANT 1, MAIN, MERIT, PRECIOUS, PROMINENT 2, SIGNIFICANCE 1, SIGNIFICANT, VALUABLE, VALUE, VITAL 1, WORTH, WORTHWHILE, WORTHY.

[E-143]

-EST, (Superlative suffix.) (Indicating height, or the top.) The right "A" hand, thumb pointing up, quickly moves straight upward, until it is above the head.

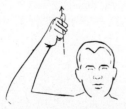

[E-144]

ESTABLISH (ĕs tăb′ lĭsh), *v.*, -LISHED, -LISHING. (To set up.) The right "A" hand, thumb up and palm facing left, comes down to rest on the back of the downturned left "S" hand. Before doing so, the right "A" hand may describe a clockwise circle above the left hand, but this is optional. *Cf.* FOUND, FOUNDED.

[E-145]

ESTIMATE (*v.* ĕs′ tə māt′; *n.* ĕs′ tə mĭt, -măt′), -MATED, -MATING. (A multiplying.) The "V" hands, palms facing the body, alternately cross and separate, several times. *Cf.* ARITHMETIC, CALCULATE, FIGURE 1, MULTIPLY 1.

[E-146]

ET CETERA (ETC.), *phrase.* (A continuing line.) The index fingers of both "L" hands touch each other before the body, with palms facing inward and thumbs pointing up. From this position the fingers move away from each other and draw wavy lines in the air as they do—the right hand moving to the right and the left hand to the left. *Cf.* SO FORTH.

[E-147]

ETCH (ĕch), *v.*, ETCHED, ETCHING. (Chipping or cutting out.) The right thumb tip repeatedly gouges out imaginary pieces of material from the palm of the left hand, held facing right. *Cf.* CARVE, ENGRAVE.

[E-148]

ETERNITY 1 (ĭ tûr′ nə tĭ), *n.* (Around the clock and ahead into the future.) The right index finger, pointing forward, traces a clockwise circle in the air. The downturned right "Y" hand then moves forward, either in a straight line or in a slight downward curve. *Cf.* EVER 2, EVERLASTING, FOREVER.

[E-149]

ETERNITY 2, *(rare)*, *n.* (The letter "E"; continuous motion.) The right "E" hand, palm out, moves in a continuous clockwise circle. *Cf.* EUROPE.

[E-150]

EUCHARIST (ū′ kə rĭst), *n.* (The Blessed Sacrament.) The right thumb and index finger move as if placing the Sacred Host on the tip of the tongue; or they may trace a cross over the lips. *Cf.* COMMUNION (HOLY) 1, HOLY COMMUNION 1.

[E-151]

EUROPE (yŏŏr′ əp), *n.* See ETERNITY 2.

[E-152]

EVACUATE (ĭ văk′ yŏŏ āt′), *v.*, -ATED, -ATING. (Pulling away.) The downturned open hands are held in a line, with fingers pointing to the left, the right hand behind the left. Both hands move in unison toward the right. As they do so, they assume the "A" position. *Cf.* DEPART, FORSAKE 1, GRADUATE 2, LEAVE 1, RETIRE 1, WITHDRAW 1.

[E-153]

EVADE (ĭ vād′), *v.*, -VADED, -VADING. (Ducking back and forth, away from something.) Both "A" hands, thumbs pointing straight up, are held some distance before the chest, with the left hand in front of the right. The right hand, swinging back and forth, moves away from the left and toward the chest. *Cf.* AVOID 1, EVASION, SHIRK, SHUN.

[E-154]

EVALUATE 1 (ĭ văl′ yŏŏ āt′), *v.*, -ATED, -ATING. (The scales move up and down.) The two "F" hands, palms facing each other, move alternately up and down. *Cf.* CONSIDER 3, COURT, IF, JUDGE 1, JUDGMENT, JUSTICE 1.

[E-155]

EVALUATE 2, *v.* (The letter "E"; weighing up and down.) The "E" hands, palms facing out from the body, move alternately up and down.

[E-156]

EVASION (ĭ vā′ zhən), *n.* See EVADE.

[E-157]

EVE (ēv), *(arch.)*, *n.* (A movement indicating the past, an exaggerated YESTERDAY, *q.v.*) The right "A" hand moves up in an arc toward the right side of the face. The right thumb comes in contact with the right cheek and continues beyond a bit.

[E-158]

EVEN (ē' vən), *adj.* (Sameness is stressed.) The downturned "B" hands, held at chest height, are brought together repeatedly, so that the index finger edges or fingertips come into contact. *Cf.* EQUAL, EQUIVALENT, FAIR 1, IMPARTIAL, JUST 1, LEVEL.

[E-159]

EVENING (ēv' nĭng), *n.* (The sun drops beneath the horizon.) The left hand, palm down, is positioned at chest height. The downturned right hand, held an inch or so above the left, moves over the left hand in an arc, as the sun setting beneath the horizon. *Cf.* NIGHT.

[E-160]

EVENLY MATCHED (măchd), *phrase.* (In balance.) The two right-angle hands, palms facing, move up and down alternately, for short distances.

[E-161]

EVENT (ĭ vĕnt'), *n.* (A befalling.) Both "D" hands, index fingers pointing away from the body, are simultaneously pivoted over so that the palms face down. *Cf.* ACCIDENT, BEFALL, CHANCE, COINCIDE 1, COINCIDENCE, HAPPEN 1, INCIDENT, OCCUR, OPPORTUNITY 4.

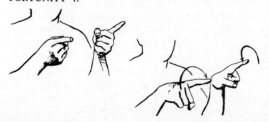

[E-162]

EVENTUALLY (ĭ vĕn' chŏo ə lĭ), *adv.* (The little, *i.e.,* LAST, fingers are indicated.) With the hands in the "I" position, the tip of the right little finger strikes the tip of its left counterpart. The right index finger may be used instead of the right little finger. *Cf.* END 1, FINAL 1, FINALLY 1, LAST 1, ULTIMATE, ULTIMATELY.

[E-163]

EVER 1 (ĕv' ər), *adv.* (Steady, uninterrupted movement.) The "A" hands are held with palms out, thumbs extended and touching, the right behind the left. In this position the hands move forward in a straight, steady line. *Cf.* CONTINUE 1, ENDURE 2, LAST 3, LASTING, PERMANENT, PERPETUAL, PERSEVERE 3, PERSIST 2, REMAIN, STAY 1, STAY STILL.

[E-164]

EVER 2, *adv.* (Around the clock and ahead into the future.) The right index finger, pointing forward, traces a clockwise circle in the air. The downturned right "Y" hand then moves forward, either in a straight line or in a slight downward curve. ETERNITY 1, EVERLASTING, FOREVER.

[E-165]

EVER 3, *adv.* (Around the clock again and again.) The index finger of the right "D" hand points outward, away from the body, with palm facing left. The arm is rotated clockwise.

[E-166]

EVERLASTING (ĕv' ər lăs' tĭng, -läs'-), *adj.* See EVER 2.

[E–167]

EVER SINCE (ĕv′ ər sĭns), *phrase.* (From a point up and over.) In the "D" position, palms down, both index fingers touch the right shoulder and then are brought up and over, ending in a palm-up position, pointing straight ahead of the body. *Cf.* ALL ALONG, ALL THE TIME, SINCE, SO FAR, THUS FAR.

[E–168]

EVERY (ĕv′ rĭ), *adj.* (Peeling off, one by one.) The left "A" hand is held palm facing the right. The knuckles of the right "A" hand are drawn repeatedly down the left thumb, from its tip to its base. *Cf.* EACH.

[E–169]

EVERYBODY (ĕv′ rĭ bŏd´ ĭ), *pron.* (EVERY, ONE.) The sign for EVERY is made, followed by the sign for ONE, *q.v. Cf.* EACH ONE, EVERYONE.

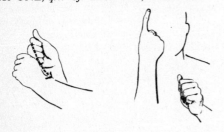

[E–170]

EVERYDAY (ĕv′ rĭ dā′), *adj.* (Tomorrow after tomorrow.) The sign for TOMORROW, *q.v.,* is made several times: The right "A" hand moves forward several times from its initial resting place on the right cheek. *Cf.* DAILY.

[E–171]

EVERYONE (ĕv′ rĭ wŭn´), *pron.* See EVERYBODY.

[E–172]

EVERY YEAR (yĭr), *phrase.* (Several years brought forward.) This sign is actually a modification of the sign for YEAR, *q.v.* The ball of the right "S" hand, moving straight out from the body, palm facing left, glances over the thumb side of the left "S" hand, which is held palm facing right. As this contact is made, the right index finger is flung straight out, and the right hand, in this new position, continues forward. This is repeated several times, to indicate several years. *Cf.* ANNUAL, YEARLY.

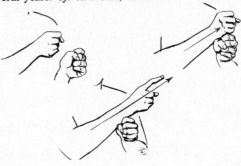

[E–173]

EVICT (ĭ vĭkt′), *v.,* -VICTED, -VICTING. (To toss up and out.) Both "S" hands, held at chest level with palms facing, are swung down slightly and then up into the air toward the left, opening into the "5" position. *Cf.* ABANDON 2, CAST OUT, DISCARD 2.

[E–174]

EVIDENCE (ĕv′ ə dəns), *n., v.,* -DENCED, -DENCING. (Directing the attention to something, and bringing it forward.) The right index finger points into the left palm, held facing out before the body. The left palm moves straight out. For the passive form of this verb, *i.e.,* BE SHOWN, the movement is reversed: The left hand, palm facing in, is moved in toward the body, while the right index finger remains pointing

into the left palm. *Cf.* DEMONSTRATE, DISPLAY, EX-
AMPLE, EXHIBIT, EXHIBITION, ILLUSTRATE, INDI-
CATE, INFLUENCE 3, PRODUCE 2, REPRESENT,
SHOW 1, SIGNIFY 1.

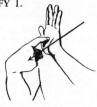

[E–175]

EVIL (ē' vəl), *n., adj.* (BAD; SIN.) The sign for
BAD is made: The right fingertips are placed on the
lips, and then the right hand is thrown down. This
is followed by the sign for SIN: The "D" hands,
palms facing the body, are positioned with index
fingers pointing toward each other. The hands move
in continuous ellipses, away from and toward each
other. *Cf.* CRIME.

[E–176]

EXACT 1 (ĭg zăkt'), *adj.* (The fingers come together
precisely.) The thumb and index finger of each hand,
palms facing, the right above the left, form circles.
They are brought together with a deliberate movement, so that the fingers and thumbs now touch.
Sometimes the right hand, before coming together
with the left, executes a slow clockwise circle above
the left. *Cf.* ACCURATE 1, EXACTLY, EXPLICIT 1,
PRECISE, SPECIFIC.

[E–177]

EXACT 2, *adj.* The right index finger, held above the
left index finger, comes down rather forcefully so

that the bottom of the right hand comes to rest on
top of the left thumb joint. *Cf.* ACCURATE 2, COR-
RECT 1, DECENT, JUST 2, PROPER, RIGHT 3, SUIT-
ABLE.

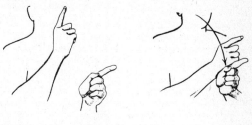

[E–178]

EXACTLY (ĭg zăkt' lĭ), *adv.* See EXACT 1.

[E–179]

EXAGGERATE 1 (ĭg zăj' ə rāt'), *v.,* -ATED, -ATING.
(Thoughts pop up and are added on to something.)
The right index finger moves straight up on the forehead. The sign for MORE is then made: The left
hand, fingers touching the thumb, and palm down,
moves down in an arc to come in contact with the
right hand, held in the same position but with palm
up. The sign is repeated with both hands reversing
their roles.

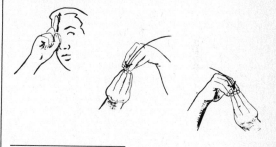

[E–180]

EXAGGERATE 2, *(sl.), v.,* -ATED, -ATING. (Stretching out one's words.) The left "S" hand, palm facing
right, is held before the mouth. Its right counterpart,
palm facing left, is moved forward in a series of short
up-and-down arcs.

[E-181]

EXAMINATION 1 (ĭg zăm´ ə nā´ shən), *n*. (A series of questions spread out on a page.) Both "D" hands, palms down, simultaneously execute a single circle, the right hand moving in a clockwise direction and the left in a counterclockwise direction. Upon completion of the circle, both hands open into the "5" position and move straight down a short distance. (The hands actually draw question marks in the air.) *Cf.* QUIZ 1, TEST.

[E-182]

EXAMINATION 2, *(colloq.), n.* (Fire a question.) The right hand, held in a modified "S" position with palm facing out, assumes a position with the thumb resting on the fingernail of the index finger. The index finger is flicked out and forward, usually directed at the person being asked a question. *Cf.* ASK 2, INQUIRE 2, INTERROGATE 2, INTERROGATION 2, QUERY 2, QUESTION 2, QUIZ 2.

[E-183]

EXAMINATION 3, *n*. (Firing questions.) The index fingers of both "D" hands repeatedly curve and straighten out as the hands are alternately flung forward and back, as if firing questions. *Cf.* ASK 3, INQUIRE 3, INTERROGATE 1, INTERROGATION 1, QUERY 1, QUESTION 3, QUIZ 3.

[E-184]

EXAMINATION OF CONSCIENCE (kŏn´ shəns), *(eccles.), phrase.* (The letter "E"; looking at oneself.) The right "E" hand, palm facing the body, is held before the eyes. It moves in a clockwise circle.

[E-185]

EXAMINE (ĭg zăm´ ĭn), *v.,* -INED, -INING. (Directing the vision from place to place.) The right "C" hand, palm facing left, moves from right to left across the line of vision, in a series of counterclockwise circles. The signer's gaze remains concentrated and his head turns slowly from right to left. *Cf.* CURIOUS 1, INVESTIGATE 1, LOOK FOR, PROBE 1, QUEST, SEARCH, SEEK.

[E-186]

EXAMPLE (ĭg zăm´ pəl, -zäm´ -), *n., v.,* -PLED, -PLING. (Directing the attention to something, and bringing it forward.) The right index finger points into the left palm, held facing out before the body. The left palm moves straight out. For the passive form of this verb, *i.e.,* BE SHOWN, the movement is reversed: The left hand, palm facing in, is moved in toward the body, while the right index finger remains pointing into the left palm. *Cf.* DEMONSTRATE, DISPLAY, EVIDENCE, EXHIBIT, EXHIBITION, ILLUSTRATE, INDICATE, INFLUENCE 3, PRODUCE 2, REPRESENT, SHOW 1, SIGNIFY 1.

[E-187]

EXCEED (ĭk sēd´), *v.,* -CEEDED, -CEEDING. (Rising above something.) Both hands, in the right-angle position, palms down, are held before the chest, with the right atop the left. The right hand arcs upward to a position about eight inches above the left. *Cf.* EXCESSIVE, PASSETH, SURPASS.

[E-188]

EXCELLENT (ĕk´ sə lənt), *adj.* (The hands gesture toward the heavens.) The "5" hands, palms out and arms raised rather high, are positioned somewhat above the line of vision. The arms move abruptly forward and up once or twice. An expression of pleasure or surprise is usually assumed. *Cf.* GRAND 1, GREAT 3, MARVEL, MARVELOUS, MIRACLE, O!, SPLENDID 1, SWELL 1, WONDER 2, WONDERFUL 1.

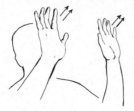

[E-189]

EXCEPT (ĭk sĕpt'), *prep., conj.* (Selecting a particular item from among several.) The index finger and thumb of the right hand grasp and pull up the left index finger. *Cf.* ESPECIAL, EXCEPTION, SPECIAL.

[E-190]

EXCEPTION (ĭk sĕp' shən), *n.* See EXCEPT.

[E-191]

EXCESSIVE (ĭk sĕs' ĭv), *adj.* See EXCEED.

[E-192]

EXCHANGE (ĭks chānj'), *v.,* -CHANGED, -CHANG-ING. (Exchanging places.) The right "A" hand, positioned above the left "A" hand, swings down and under the left, coming up a bit in front of it. *Cf.* INSTEAD OF 1, REPLACE, SUBSTITUTE, TRADE.

[E-193]

EXCISE (ĭk sīz'), *n., v.,* -CISED, -CISING. (Nicking into one.) The knuckle of the right "X" finger is nicked against the palm of the left hand, held in the "5" position, palm facing right. *Cf.* ADMISSION 2, CHARGE 1, COST, DUTY 2, EXPENSE, FEE, FINE 2, IMPOST, PENALTY 3, PRICE 2, TAX 1, TAXATION 1, TOLL.

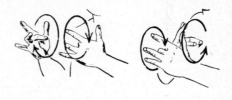

[E-194]

EXCITE (ĭk sīt'), *v.,* -CITED, -CITING. (The heart beats violently.) Both middle fingers move up alternately to strike the heart sharply. *Cf.* EXCITEMENT, EXCITING, THRILL 1.

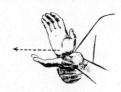

[E-195]

EXCITEMENT (ĭk sīt' mənt), *n.* See EXCITE.

[E-196]

EXCITING (ĭk sī' tĭng), *adj.* See EXCITE.

[E-197]

EXCLUDE (ĭk sklo͞od'), *v.,* -CLUDED, -CLUDING. (Push out.) The base of the cupped right hand, palm facing out, moves forward over the upturned left palm, from its base to its fingertips. *Cf.* EXCLUSION.

[E-198]

EXCLUSION (ĭk sklo͞o' zhən), *n.* See EXCLUDE.

[E-199]

EXCUSE (*n.* ĭk skūs'; *v.* ĭk skūz'), -CUSED, -CUSING. (A wiped-off and cleaned slate.) The right hand wipes off the left palm several times. *Cf.* APOLOGIZE 2, APOLOGY 2, FORGIVE 2, PARDON, PAROLE.

[E-200]

EXERCISE 1 (ĕk' sər sīz'), *v.,* -CISED, -CISING. (Typical calisthenic exercises.) The downturned "S" hands move back and forth simultaneously, and then up and down simultaneously. *Cf.* GYM.

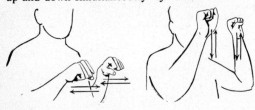

[E-201]

EXERCISE 2, *n.* (A section of a page.) The upturned open left hand represents the page. The little finger edge of the right right-angle hand is placed on the left palm near the fingertips. It moves up and over, in an arc, to the base of the left palm. *Cf.* LESSON.

[E-202]

EXHAUST (ĭg zôst'), *v.,* -HAUSTED, -HAUSTING. (The hands collapse in exhaustion.) Both "C" hands are placed either on the lower chest or at the waist. The palms face the body. They fall away into a palms-up position. At the same time, the shoulders suddenly sag in a very pronounced fashion. An expression of weariness may be used for emphasis. *Cf.* DISCOURAGE 2, FATIGUE, TIRE, TIRED, WEARY.

[E-203]

EXHAUSTED (-ĭd), *adj.* (A wiping-off motion, to indicate a condition of no longer being present.) The little finger edge of the right "5" hand, held palm facing the body, rests on the back of the downturned left hand. The right hand moves straight forward suddenly, closing into the "S" position, palm still facing the body. *Cf.* GONE 2.

[E-204]

EXHIBIT (ĭg zĭb' ĭt), *v.,* -ITED, -ITING. (Directing the attention to something, and bringing it forward.) The right index finger points into the left palm, held facing out before the body. The left palm moves straight out. For the passive form of this verb, *i.e.,* BE SHOWN, the movement is reversed: The left hand, palm facing in, is moved in toward the body, while the right index finger remains pointing into the left palm. *Cf.* DEMONSTRATE, DISPLAY, EVIDENCE, EXAMPLE, EXHIBITION, ILLUSTRATE, INDICATE, INFLUENCE 3, PRODUCE 2, REPRESENT, SHOW 1, SIGNIFY 1.

[E-205]

EXHIBITION (ĕk' sə bĭsh' ən), *n.* See EXHIBIT.

[E-206]

EXIST (ĭg zĭst'), *v.,* -ISTED, -ISTING. (The fountain [of LIFE] wells up from within the body.) The upturned thumbs of the "A" hands move in unison up the chest. *Cf.* ALIVE, DWELL, LIFE 1, LIVE 1, LIVING, MORTAL, RESIDE.

[E–207]

EXIT (ĕg′ zĭt, ĕk sĭt), *n.* (The natural motion of withdrawing, *i.e.,* taking *out,* of the hand.) The downturned open right hand, grasped loosely by the left, is drawn up and out of the left hand's grasp. As it does so, the fingers come together with the thumb. The left hand, meanwhile, closes into the "0" position, palm facing right. *Cf.* OUT 1.

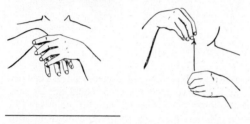

[E–208]

EXPAND (ĭk spănd′), v., -PANDED, -PANDING. (A large amount.) The "5" hands face each other, fingers curved and touching. They move apart rather quickly. *Cf.* GREAT 2, INFINITE, LOT, MUCH.

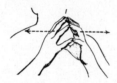

[E–209]

EXPECT (ĭk spĕkt′), v., -PECTED, -PECTING. (A thought awaited.) The tip of the right index finger, held in the "D" position, palm facing the body, is placed on the forehead (modified THINK, *q.v.*). Both hands then assume right angle positions, fingers facing, with the left hand held above left shoulder level and the right before the right breast. Both hands, held thus, wave to each other several times. *Cf.* ANTICIPATE, ANTICIPATION, HOPE.

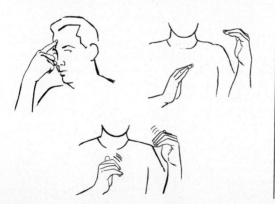

[E–210]

EXPECTORATE (ĭk spĕk′ tə rāt′), v., -RATED, -RAT-ING. (The flinging out of saliva.) The thumb and index finger, forming a circle, are placed at the lips. The index finger suddenly flicks open and away from the mouth. *Cf.* SPIT.

[E–211]

EXPEL 1 (ĭk spĕl′), v., -PELLED, -PELLING. ("Get-ting the axe"; the head is chopped off.) The upturned open right hand is swung sharply over the index finger edge of the left "S" hand, whose palm faces right. *Cf.* DISCHARGE 1, FIRE 2.

[E–212]

EXPEL 2, v. (To cut one down.) The right index finger strikes the tip of the upturned left index finger, in a right to left direction, causing the left index finger to bend slightly. *Cf.* DISCHARGE 2.

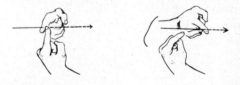

[E–213]

EXPENSE (ĭk spĕns′), *n.* (Nicking into one.) The knuckle of the right "X" finger is nicked against the palm of the left hand, held in the "5" position, palm facing right. *Cf.* ADMISSION 2, CHARGE 1, COST, DUTY 2, EXCISE, FEE, FINE 2, IMPOST, PENALTY 3, PRICE 2, TAX 1, TAXATION 1, TOLL.

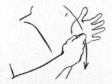

[E–214]

EXPENSIVE (ĭk spĕn′ sĭv), *adj.* (Throwing away money.) The right "AND" hand lies in the palm of the upturned, open left hand (as if holding money). The right hand then moves up and away from the left, opening abruptly as it does (as if dropping the money it holds). Cf. COSTLY, DEAR 2.

[E–215]

EXPERIENCE 1 (ĭk spir′ ĭ əns), *n.* (A sharp-edged hand.) The right hand grasps the little finger edge of the left firmly. As it leaves this position, moving down and out, it assumes the "A" position, palm facing left. Cf. ADEPT, EXPERT, SHARP 4, SHREWD, SKILL, SKILLFUL.

[E–216]

EXPERIENCE 2, *n.* (White hair.) The right fingertips gently pull the hair of the right temple. The movement is repeated.

[E–217]

EXPERT (*n.* ĕks′ pûrt; *adj.* ĭk spûrt′). See EXPERIENCE 1.

[E–218]

EXPIRE 1 (ĭk spīr′), *v.*, -PIRED, -PIRING. (Bring to an end.) The left hand, fingers together and pointing forward, is held palm facing right. The right, palm down, fingers also together, moves along the top of the left, goes over the tip of the left index finger, and

drops straight down, indicating a cutting off or a finishing. Cf. ACCOMPLISH 2, ACHIEVE 2, COMPLETE 1, CONCLUDE, DONE 1, END 4, FINISH 1, HAVE 2, TERMINATE.

[E–219]

EXPIRE 2, *v.* (Turning over on one's side.) The open hands, fingers pointing ahead, are held side by side, with the right palm down and the left palm up. The two hands reverse their relative positions as they move from the left to the right. Cf. DEAD 1, DEATH, DIE 1, DYING, PERISH 1.

[E–220]

EXPLAIN 1 (ĭk splān′), *v.*, -PLAINED, -PLAINING. (Unraveling something to get at its parts.) The "F" hands, palms facing and fingers pointing straight out, are held about an inch apart. They move alternately back and forth a few inches. Cf. DEFINE 1, DESCRIBE 1, DESCRIPTION.

[E–221]

EXPLAIN 2, *v.* (The unraveling or stretching out of words or sentences.) Both open hands are held close to each other, with fingers open and palms facing and almost touching. As the hands are drawn apart, the thumb and index finger of each hand come together to form circles. This is repeated several times. Cf. DESCRIBE 2, FABLE, FICTION, GOSPEL 1, NARRATE, NARRATIVE, STORY 1, TALE, TELL ABOUT.

[E–222]

EXPLICIT 1 (ĭk splĭs′ ĭt), *adj.* (The fingers come together precisely.) The thumb and index finger of each hand, palms facing, the right above the left, form circles. They are brought together with a deliberate movement, so that the fingers and thumbs now touch. Sometimes the right hand, before coming together with the left, executes a slow clockwise circle above the left. *Cf.* ACCURATE 1, EXACT 1, EXACTLY, PRECISE, SPECIFIC.

[E–223]

EXPLICIT 2, *adj.* (Rays of light clearing the way.) Both hands are held at chest height, palms out, all fingertips together. They open into the "5" position in unison, the right hand moving toward the right and the left toward the left. The palms of both hands remain facing out. *Cf.* BRIGHT 1, BRILLIANCE 1, BRILLIANT 2, CLEAR, OBVIOUS, PLAIN 1.

[E–224]

EXPLODE (ĭk splōd′), *v.,* -PLODED, -PLODING. (Burst apart.) The crossed "S" hands burst apart violently. *Cf.* EXPLOSION.

[E–225]

EXPLOSION (ĭk splō′ zhən), *n.* See EXPLODE.

[E–226]

EXPRESSION (ĭk sprĕsh′ ən), *n.* (The up-and-down movement of the facial features.) The "X" hands, palms facing, move alternately up and down on either side of the face.

[E–227]

EXPUNGE (ĭk spŭnj′), *v.,* -PUNGED, -PUNGING. (The printer flicks a piece of type out of the composing stick.) The thumb, positioned initially inside the closed hand, flicks out. The hand moves up a bit as the thumb makes its appearance. *Cf.* DELETE 3.

[E–228]

EXQUISITE (ĕks′ kwĭ zĭt, ĭk skwĭz′ ĭt), *adj.* (Literally, a good face.) The right hand, fingers closed over the thumb, is placed at or just below the lips (indicating a tasting of something GOOD, *q.v.*). It then describes a counterclockwise circle around the face, opening into the "5" position, to indicate the whole face. At the completion of the circling movement the hand comes to rest in its initial position, at or just below the lips. *Cf.* ATTRACTIVE 2, BEAUTIFUL, BEAUTY, PRETTY, SPLENDID 3.

[E–229]

EXTEND 1 (ĭk stĕnd′), *v.,* -TENDED, -TENDING. (Adding on.) The index and middle fingers of the right "H" hand, palm up, are swung up and over until they come to rest on the index and middle fingers of the left "H" hand, held palm down. *Cf.* ADD 3, ADDITION, EXTRA, GAIN 1, INCREASE, ON TO, RAISE 2.

[E–230]

EXTEND 2, *v.* (The hands move forward and open.) Both hands are held palms down, about a foot apart, thumbs resting on fingertips. The hands are extended forward in a slight arc, opening to the "5" position as they do. *Cf.* GIVE 1.

[E–231]

EXTINCT (ĭk stĭngkt'), *adj.* (A disappearance.) The right open hand, palm facing the body, is held by the left hand and is drawn down and out, ending in a position with fingers drawn together. The left hand, meanwhile, may close into a position with fingers also drawn together. *Cf.* ABSENCE 1, ABSENT 1, DEPLETE, DISAPPEAR, EMPTY 1, FADE AWAY, GONE 1, MISSING 1, OMISSION 1, OUT 3, OUT OF, VANISH.

 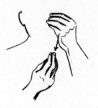

[E–232]

EXTRA (ĕks' trə), *adj.* See EXTEND.

[E–233]

EXTRAVAGANT (ĭk străv' ə gənt), *adj.* (Repeated giving forth.) The back of the upturned right hand, thumb touching fingertips, is placed in the upturned left palm. The right hand moves off and away from the left once or several times, each time opening into the "5" position, palm up. *Cf.* SPEND, SQUANDER, WASTE 1.

[E–234]

EXTREME UNCTION (ĭks trēm' ŭngk' shən), *(eccles.).* (The sign of the cross over the closed eyes.) The thumb of the right "A" hand traces a cross in front of the closed eyes.

[E–235]

EXULTATION (ĕg' zŭl tā' shən), *n.* (Waving a flag.) The right "A" hand goes through the natural movement of waving a flag in circular fashion. Preceding this, the right hand may go through the motion of grabbing the flagstaff out of the left hand. *Cf.* TRIUMPH 1, VICTORY 2, WIN 2.

[E–236]

EYE (ī), *n., v.,* EYED, EYING or EYEING. (The natural sign.) The right index finger touches the lower lid of the right eye.

[E–237]

EYEGLASSES (ī' glăs' əs), *n. pl.* (The shape.) The thumb and index finger of the right hand, placed flat against the right temple, move back toward the right ear, tracing the line formed by the eyeglass frame. *Cf.* GALLAUDET, THOMAS HOPKINS; GLASSES; SPECTACLES.

F

[F–1]

FABLE (fā' bəl), *n., adj.* (The unraveling or stretching out of words or sentences.) Both open hands are held close to each other, with fingers open and palms facing and almost touching. As the hands are drawn apart, the thumb and index finger of each hand come together to form circles. This is repeated several times. *Cf.* DESCRIBE 2, EXPLAIN 2, FICTION, GOSPEL 1, NARRATE, NARRATIVE, STORY 1, TALE, TELL ABOUT.

[F–2]

FABRICATE (făb' rə kāt´), *v.,* -CATED, -CATING. (Fashioning something with the hands.) The right "S" hand, palm facing left, is placed on top of its left counterpart, whose palm faces right. The hands are twisted back and forth, striking each other slightly after each twist. *Cf.* COMPOSE, CONSTITUTE, CONSTRUCT 2, CREATE, DEVISE 2, FASHION, FIX, MAKE, MANUFACTURE, MEND 1, PRODUCE 3, RENDER 1, REPAIR.

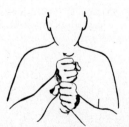

[F–3]

FACE 1 (fās), *n.* (The natural sign.) The index finger outlines the face, without touching it.

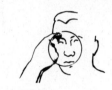

[F–4]

FACE 2, *v.,* FACED, FACING. (Face to face.) The left hand, fingers together, palm flat and facing the eyes, is held a bit above eye level. The right hand, fingers also together, is held in front of the mouth, with palm facing the left hand. With a sweeping upward movement the right hand moves toward the left, which moves straight up an inch or two at the same time. *Cf.* APPEAR 3, APPEARANCE, BEFORE 3, CONFRONT, FACE TO FACE, PRESENCE.

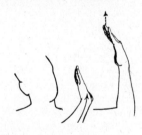

[F–5]

FACE TO FACE, *phrase.* See FACE 2.

[F–6]

FACILITATE (fə sĭl' ə tāt´), *v.,* -TATED, -TATING. (The fingertips are easily moved.) The right fingertips brush repeatedly over their upturned left counterparts, causing them to move. *Cf.* EASY 1, SIMPLE 1.

239

[F-7]

FACTORY (făk' tə ri), *n.* (The meshing gears.) With the knuckles of both hands interlocked, the hands pivot up and down, imitating the meshing of gear teeth. *Cf.* ENGINE, MACHINE, MACHINERY, MECHANIC 1, MECHANISM, MOTOR.

[F-8]

FACULTY (făk' əl tĭ), *n.* (An affirmative movement of the hands, likened to a nodding of the head, to indicate ability or power to accomplish something.) Both "A" hands, held palms down, move down in unison a short distance before the chest. *Cf.* ABILITY, ABLE, CAN 1, CAPABLE, COMPETENT, COULD, MAY 2, POSSIBLE.

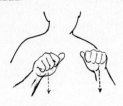

[F-9]

FADE (fād), *v.*, FADED, FADING. (Fingering the small pieces resulting from the breaking up of something.) The thumbs rub slowly across the fingertips of the upturned hands, from the little fingers to the index fingers, and then continue to the "A" position, palms up. *Cf.* DECAY, DIE OUT, DISSOLVE, MELT, ROT.

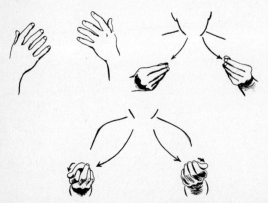

[F-10]

FADE AWAY (ə wā'), *v. phrase.* (A disappearance.) The right open hand, palm facing the body, is held by the left hand and is drawn down and out, ending in a position with fingers drawn together. The left hand, meanwhile, may close into a position with fingers also drawn together. *Cf.* ABSENCE 1, ABSENT 1, DEPLETE, DISAPPEAR, EMPTY 1, EXTINCT, GONE 1, MISSING 1, OMISSION 1, OUT 3, OUT OF, VANISH.

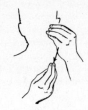

[F-11]

FAIL 1 (fāl), *v.*, FAILED, FAILING. (Tumbling down.) The open hands, palms facing the body, rotate around each other as they move downward and a bit outward from the body. *Cf.* FAILURE.

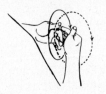

[F-12]

FAIL 2, *v.* (A sliding.) The right "V" hand, palm up, slides along the upturned left palm, from its base to its fingertips. *Cf.* FAILURE.

[F-13]

FAIL 3, *v.* The right "F" hand strikes forcefully against the open left palm, which faces right with fingers pointing forward. *Cf.* FLUNK.

[F–14]

FAILURE (fāl′ yər), *n.* See FAIL 1 or 2.

[F–15]

FAINT 1 (fānt), *adj.* (The knees buckle.) The right "V" hand is placed with fingertips resting in the upturned left palm. The knuckles of the "V" fingers buckle a bit. This motion may be repeated. *Cf.* FEEBLE, FRAIL, WEAK, WEAKNESS.

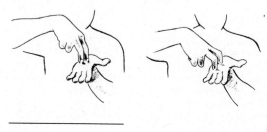

[F–16]

FAINT 2, *v.,* FAINTED, FAINTING. (Attempting to grasp something as one falls.) The downturned open hands, fingers somewhat curved, suddenly separate and close into the "S" position. The head, meanwhile, falls back a bit, and the eyes close.

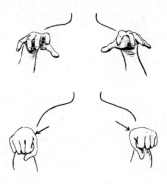

[F–17]

FAIR 1 (fâr), *adj.* (Sameness is stressed.) The downturned "B" hands, held at chest height, are brought together repeatedly, so that the index finger edges or fingertips come into contact. *Cf.* EQUAL, EQUIVALENT, EVEN, IMPARTIAL, JUST 1, LEVEL.

[F–18]

FAIR 2, *adj.* (The letter "F" at the midpoint of the mouth, *i.e.,* neither good nor bad.) The tip of the middle finger of the right "F" hand, whose palm faces left, touches the middle of the lips repeatedly.

[F–19]

FAIRY (fǎr′ ǐ), *(sl.), n.* (An effeminate gesture.) The extended right little finger touches the tip of the tongue and then wipes outward along the right eyebrow. This may be followed by slapping the right fingertips against the back of the limply held left wrist.

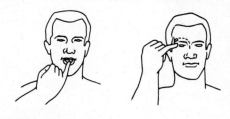

[F–20]

FAITH (fāth), *n.* (Planting a flagpole, *i.e.,* planting one's trust.) The "S" hands grasp and plant an imaginary flagpole in the ground. This sign may be preceded by BELIEVE, *q.v. Cf.* CONFIDENCE, TRUST.

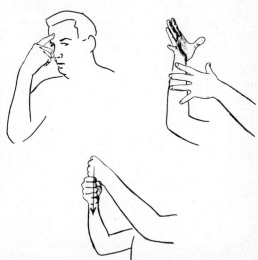

[F-21]

FAITHFUL 1 (fāth' fəl), *adj.* (Coming together with regular frequency.) Both "D" hands are held with index fingers pointing forward, the right hand above the left. The right "D" hand is brought down on the left several times in rhythmic succession. *Cf.* CONSISTENT, REGULAR.

[F-22]

FAITHFUL 2, *adj.* (A modification of FAITHFUL 1, above, with the "F" hands.) The "F" hands execute the same movements as in FAITHFUL 1.

[F-23]

FAITHFUL 3, *adj.* (Coming forth directly from the lips; true.) The index finger of the right "D" hand, palm facing left, is placed against the lips. It moves up an inch or two and then describes a small arc forward and away from the lips. *Cf.* ABSOLUTE, ABSOLUTELY, ACTUAL, ACTUALLY, AUTHENTIC, CERTAIN, CERTAINLY, FIDELITY, FRANKLY, GENUINE, INDEED, POSITIVE 1, POSITIVELY, REAL, REALLY, SINCERE 2, SURE, SURELY, TRUE, TRULY, TRUTH, VALID, VERILY.

[F-24]

FAKE (fāk), *v.,* FAKED, FAKING. (A double face, *i.e.,* a mask covers the face.) The right hand is placed

over the back of the left hand and pushes it down and a bit in toward the body. *Cf.* BLUFF, HUMBUG, HYPOCRITE 1, IMPOSTOR.

[F-25]

FALL 1 (fôl), *n.* (The falling of leaves.) The left arm, held upright with palm facing back, represents a tree trunk. The right hand, fingers together and palm down, moves down along the left arm, from the back of the wrist to the elbow, either once or several times. This represents the falling of leaves from the tree branches, indicated by the left fingers. *Cf.* AUTUMN 1.

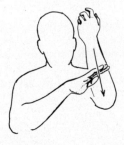

[F-26]

FALL 2, *n.* (A chopping down during harvest time.) The left arm is held in the same manner as in FALL 1. The right hand, fingers together and palm facing down, makes several chopping motions against the left elbow, to indicate the felling of growing things in autumn.

[F-27]

FALL 3, *n., v.,* FELL, FALLEN, FALLING. (Falling on one's side.) The downturned index and middle fingers of the right "V" hand are placed in a standing position on the upturned left palm. The right "V" hand flips over, coming to rest palm up on the upturned left palm.

[F–28]

FALL 4, *v.* (Falling on one's side.) The "V" hand, held palm down, flips over toward the right, to the palm-up position.

[F–29]

FALL BEHIND (bĭ hīnd'), *v. phrase,* FELL, FALLEN, FALLING. (One hand falls behind the other.) The "A" hands, thumbs up, are positioned knuckle to knuckle in front of the chest. The right "A" hand moves slowly and deliberately toward the chest, as close as possible to the left arm. *Cf.* LAG, RETARD.

[F–30]

FALL FOR, *(colloq.), v. phrase.* (Falling flat on one's face.) The right "D" hand, palm out, falls down into the upturned left palm. This sign is used in the sense of "falling for" someone, *i.e.,* becoming enamored of someone.

[F–31]

FALL IN LOVE WITH, *v. phrase.* (The heart is smitten and the affected person "slides into love.") The right middle finger is quickly placed against the

heart, as the body suddenly straightens up. The right "V" hand, palm up and fingers pointing away from the body, then slides over the upturned left palm, from its base to its fingertips.

[F–32]

FALSE 1 (fôls), *adj.* (Words diverted instead of coming straight, or truthfully, out.) The index finger of the right "D" hand, pointing to the left, moves along the lips from right to left. *Cf.* FALSEHOOD, FRAUDULENT 2, LIAR, LIE 1, PREVARICATE, UNTRUTH.

[F–33]

FALSE 2, *adj.* (The words are deflected from their normal straight path from the lips.) The right "D" hand, palm facing left, moves quickly in front of the lips, from right to left. *Cf.* FIB.

[F–34]

FALSE-FACED (fāst), *adj.* (Covering the real face.) Both hands are held open, with palms down. The right hand, from a position above the left, swings out and under the left, and then moves straight out. *Cf.* HYPOCRITE 2, TWO-FACED, UNDERHAND.

[F–35]

FALSEHOOD (fôls' hŏod), *n.* See FALSE 1.

[F–36]

FAME (fām), *n.* (One's fame radiates far and wide.) The extended index fingers rest on the lips (or on the temples). Moving in small, continuous spirals, they move up and to either side of the head. *Cf.* CELEBRATED, FAMOUS, PROMINENT 1, RENOWNED.

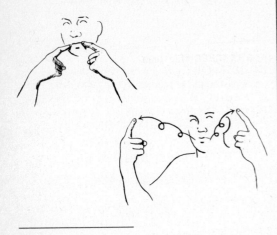

[F–37]

FAMILY 1 (făm' ə lĭ), *n.* (The letter "F;" a circle or group.) The thumb and index fingers of both "F" hands are in contact, palms facing. The hands swing open and around, coming together again at their little finger edges, palms now facing the body.

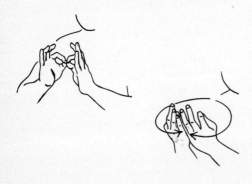

[F–38]

FAMILY 2, *n.* (A grouping together.) Both "C" hands, palms facing, are held a few inches apart at chest height. They are swung around in unison, so that the palms now face the body. *Cf.* ASSOCIATION, AUDIENCE 1, CASTE, CIRCLE 2, CLASS, CLASSED 1,

CLUB, COMPANY, GANG, GROUP 1, JOIN 2, ORGANIZATION 1.

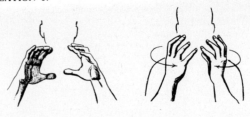

[F–39]

FAMINE (făm' ĭn), *n.* (The upper alimentary tract is outlined.) The right "C" hand, palm facing the body, is placed with fingertips touching mid-chest. In this position it moves down a bit. *Cf.* APPETITE, CRAVE, DESIRE 2, HUNGARIAN, HUNGARY, HUNGER, HUNGRY, STARVATION, STARVE, STARVED, WISH 2.

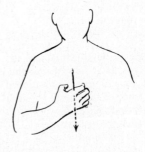

[F–40]

FAMOUS (fā' məs), *adj.* See FAME.

[F–41]

FANCY 1 (făn' sĭ), *adj.* Both hands are held with palms out and thumbs and fingers bent to form "claws." In this position the hands draw alternate circles in the air before the face.

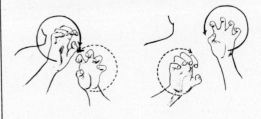

[F–42]

FANCY 2, *n.* (A thought coming forward from the mind, modified by the letter "I" for "idea.") With the "I" position on the right hand, palm facing the body, touch the little finger to the forehead, and then move the hand up and away in a circular, clockwise motion. The hand may also be moved up and away without this circular motion. *Cf.* CONCEIVE 2, CONCEPT 1, CONCEPTION, IDEA, IMAGINATION, IMAGINE 1, JUST THINK OF IT!, NOTION, POLICY 2, THEORY, THOUGHT 2.

[F–43]

FAR (fär), *adj.* (Moving beyond, *i.e.,* the concept of distance or "farness.") The "A" hands are held together, thumbs pointing away from the body. The right hand moves straight ahead in a slight arc. The left hand does not move. *Cf.* DISTANCE, DISTANT, OFF 2, REMOTE.

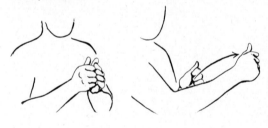

[F–44]

FAREWELL 1 (fâr′ wĕl′), *interj.* (Words extended politely from the mouth.) The fingertips of the right "5" hand are placed at the mouth. The hand moves away from the mouth to a palm-up position before the body. The signer meanwhile usually nods smilingly. *Cf.* GOODBYE 1, HELLO 1, THANKS, THANK YOU, YOU'RE WELCOME 1.

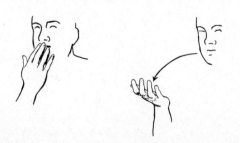

[F–45]

FAREWELL 2, *interj.* (A wave of the hand.) The right open hand waves back and forth several times. *Cf.* GOODBYE 2, HELLO 2, SO LONG.

[F–46]

FAR-FETCHED (fär′ fĕcht′), *adj.* (The mind wanders off into space or fantasy.) The index finger of the right "5" hand is placed at the right temple. The hand then moves toward the right in a series of clockwise spirals up and away from the head.

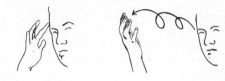

[F–47]

FARM 1 (färm), *n.* (The action of the plow's blade in making a furrow.) The open right hand is placed upright in a perpendicular position on the upturned left palm, with the little finger edge resting in the palm. The right hand moves forward along the left palm. As it does so, it swings over to a palm-down position, and moves off a bit to the right. *Cf.* PLOW.

[F–48]

FARM 2, *(sl.)*, *n.* (The stubbled beard commonly associated with an uncouth backwoods type.) The open right "5" hand is placed with thumb resting on the left side of the chin. The hand moves over to the right side of the chin, with the thumb always in contact with it.

[F–49]

FARM 3, *(colloq.)*, *n.* (The elbow reinforcement on the jacket of a "country squire" type; also, a place where one commonly "roughs it," *i.e.,* gets rough elbows.) The open right hand describes a continuous counterclockwise circle on the left elbow. *Cf.* COUNTRY 1.

[F–50]

FARMER 1 (fär′ mər), *n.* (Farm, individual.) The sign for FARM 1 is made. This is followed by the sign for INDIVIDUAL: Both open hands, palms facing each other, move down the sides of the body, tracing its outline to the hips.

[F–51]

FARMER 2, *(sl.)*, *n.* The sign for FARM 2 is made. This is followed by the sign for INDIVIDUAL, as in FARMER 1.

[F–52]

FARMER 3, *n.* The sign for FARM 3 is made. This is followed by the sign for INDIVIDUAL, as in FARMER 1.

[F–53]

FARMLAND (färm′ lănd), *n.* (An elbow patch; fingering the soil.) The sign for FARM 3 is made. This is followed by the sign for SOIL 1: Both hands,

held upright before the body, finger imaginary pinches of soil.

[F–54]

FARTHER (fär′ ŧhər), *comparative adj. and adv.* The sign for FAR is made: The "A" hands are held together, thumbs pointing up. The right hand moves straight ahead in a slight arc. The left hand does not move. This is followed by the sign for the comparative suffix -ER: The "A" hand, thumb extended upward, is raised slightly. *Cf.* FURTHER 1.

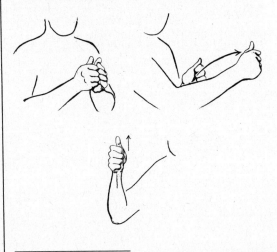

[F–55]

FARTHEST (fär′ ŧhist), *superlative adj. and adv.* The sign for FAR, as in FARTHER, is made. This is followed by the sign for the superlative suffix -EST: The right "A" hand, thumb pointing up, quickly moves straight upward, until it is above the head. *Cf.* FURTHEST.

[F-56]

FASCINATE 1 (făs′ ə nāt′), *v.*, -NATED, -NATING. (Drawing one out.) The index and middle fingers of both hands, one above the other, are placed on the middle part of the chest. Both hands move forward simultaneously. As they do, the index and middle fingers of each hand come together. *Cf.* INTEREST 1, INTERESTED 1, INTERESTING 1.

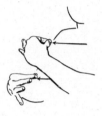

[F-57]

FASCINATE 2, *v.* (A modification of FASCINATE 1.) The same movements are employed, except that one of the hands is positioned in front of the mouth. *Cf.* ENGROSS, INTEREST 2.

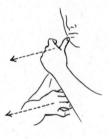

[F-58]

FASHION (făsh′ ən), *n.* (Fashioning something with the hands.) The right "S" hand, palm facing left, is placed on top of its left counterpart, whose palm faces right. The hands are twisted back and forth, striking each other slightly after each twist. *Cf.* COMPOSE, CONSTITUTE, CONSTRUCT 2, CREATE, DEVISE 2, FABRICATE, FIX, MAKE, MANUFACTURE, MEND 1, PRODUCE 3, RENDER 1, REPAIR.

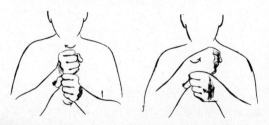

[F-59]

FASHIONABLE (făsh′ ən ə bəl), *(rare), adj.* (Embellishment.) Both hands, initially in the "O" position, palms out, are held with the fingertips in contact. Alternately, each hand opens into the "5" position, describes a small circle (the right clockwise and the left counterclockwise), and returns to its original position. *Cf.* STYLISH.

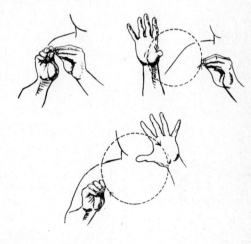

[F-60]

FAST 1 (făst), *adj.* (A quick movement.) The thumbtip of the upright right hand is flicked quickly off the tip of the curved right index finger, as if shooting marbles. *Cf.* IMMEDIATELY, QUICK, QUICKNESS, RAPID, RATE 1, SPEED, SPEEDY, SWIFT.

[F-61]

FAST 2, *v.*, FASTED, FASTING. (The "F" hand, zipping closed.) The thumb of the right "F" hand is drawn along the lips from left to right.

[F-62]

FASTEN (făs′ ən), *v.*, -ENED, -ENING. (The act of tying.) Both hands, in the "A" position, go through the natural hand-over-hand motions of tying and drawing out a knot. *Cf.* BIND, KNOT, TIE 1.

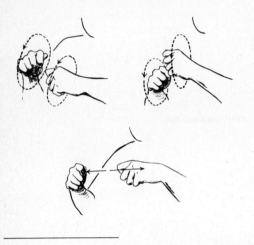

[F-63]

FAT 1 (făt), *adj.* (The swollen cheeks.) The cheeks are puffed out and the open "C" hands, positioned at either cheek, move away to their respective sides. *Cf.* STOUT.

[F-64]

FAT 2, *(colloq.), adj.* (The legs are spread wide to accommodate a wide torso.) The downturned right "Y" hand is placed in the upturned left palm, so that the right little finger supports the right hand. The right hand pivots forward on the little finger until the right thumb comes to rest on the left palm. The right hand then pivots forward again until the little finger comes to rest again on the left palm. The action is similar to the manipulation of a pair of dividers. *Cf.* OBESE.

[F-65]

FAT 3, *n.* (The drippings from a fleshy, *i.e.,* animal, substance. Used, however, to indicate both organic and inorganic types of oil.) The right thumb and middle finger grasp the fleshy part of the open left hand. The right hand moves straight down. This is repeated once or twice. *Cf.* FATTY, GRAVY, GREASE, GREASY, OIL 2, OILY.

[F-66]

FATHER 1 (fä′ thər), *n.* (Male who holds the baby.) The sign for MALE, *q.v.,* is made: The thumb and extended fingers of the right hand are brought up to grasp an imaginary cap brim, representing the tipping of caps by men in olden days. Both hands are then held open with palms facing up, as if holding a baby. This is the formal sign.

[F-67]

FATHER 2, *(informal), n.* (Derived from the formal sign for FATHER 1, *q.v.*) The thumbtip of the right "5" hand touches the right temple a number of times. The other fingers may also wiggle. *Cf.* DAD, DADDY, PAPA, POP 2.

[F-68]

FATHER 3, *n.* (The ecclesiastical collar.) The thumbs and index fingers of both hands indicate the shape of the collar as they move around the neck, coming together in front of the throat. Sometimes only one hand is used. *Cf.* PRIEST 1.

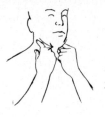

[F–69]

FATHER-IN-LAW, *n.* The sign for FATHER 1 or 2 is made. This is followed by the sign for LAW: The upright right "L" hand, resting palm against palm on the upright left "5" hand, moves down in an arc a short distance, coming to rest on the base of the left palm.

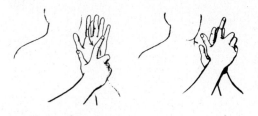

[F–70]

FATIGUE (fə tēg'), *n.* (The hands collapse in exhaustion.) Both "C" hands are placed either on the lower chest or at the waist. The palms face the body. They fall away into a palms-up position. At the same time, the shoulders suddenly sag in a very pronounced fashion. An expression of weariness may be used for emphasis. *Cf.* DISCOURAGE 2, EXHAUST, TIRE, TIRED, WEARY.

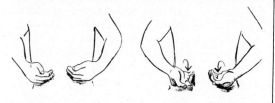

[F–71]

FATTY (făt' ĭ), *adj.* (The drippings from a fleshy, *i.e.,* animal, substance. Used, however, to indicate both organic and inorganic types of oil.) The right thumb and middle finger grasp the fleshy part of the open left hand. The right hand moves straight down.

This is repeated once or twice. *Cf.* FAT 3, GRAVY, GREASE, GREASY, OIL 2, OILY.

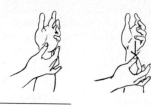

[F–72]

FAULT 1 (fôlt), *n.* (The blame is firmly placed.) The right "A" hand, thumb pointing up, is brought down firmly against the back of the left hand, held palm down; the right thumb is then directed toward the person or object to blame. When personal blame is acknowledged, the thumb is brought in to the chest. *Cf.* ACCUSE 1, BLAME, GUILTY 1.

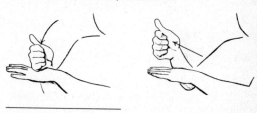

[F–73]

FAULT 2, *n.* (Rationale obscure; the thumb and little finger are said to represent, respectively, right and wrong, with the head poised between the two.) The right "Y" hand, palm facing the body, is brought up to the chin. *Cf.* ERROR, MISTAKE, SACRILEGIOUS, WRONG 1.

[F–74]

FAVOR (fā' vər), *n.* (Holding up.) The right "S" hand pushes up the left "S" hand. *Cf.* ENDORSE 1, INDORSE 1, MAINTENANCE, SUPPORT 1, SUSTAIN, SUSTENANCE, UPHOLD, UPLIFT.

[F-75]

FAVORITE 1 (fā′ vər ĭt), *adj.* (The thoughts are directed to a single thing.) The right index finger, placed initially at the forehead, palm facing the body, swings away, the palm coming around to face out, and the index finger coming to rest on the tip of the left upturned index finger.

[F-76]

FAVORITE 2, *(colloq.), adj.* (Something or someone which turns the head.) The open right "5" hand is placed with its index finger resting near the right temple, palm facing the left. The hand suddenly pivots sharply around and out toward the right, moving away from the head and ending in a position with the palm facing the head and held about a foot from it.

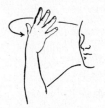

[F-77]

FAVORITE 3, *(colloq.), adj.* (Strongly attached or hooked on to.) With index fingers interlocked, both hands move forward a short distance. *Cf.* FOND 2.

[F-78]

FEAR 1 (fĭr), *n., v.,* FEARED, FEARING. (The heart is suddenly covered with fear.) Both hands, fingers

together, are placed side by side, palms facing the chest. They quickly open and come together over the heart, one on top of the other. *Cf.* AFRAID, COWARD, FRIGHT, FRIGHTEN, SCARE(D), TERROR 1.

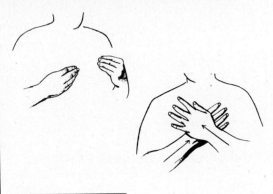

[F-79]

FEAR 2, *n., v.* (The hands attempt to ward off something which causes fear.) The "5" hands, right behind left, move downward before the body, in a wavy motion. *Cf.* DREAD, TERROR 2, TIMID.

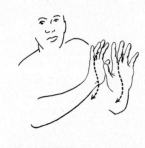

[F-80]

FEARFUL (fĭr′ fəl), *adj.* (Throwing out the hands.) Both hands, their fingertips touching their respective thumbs, are held, palms facing each other, near the temples. They are thrown out before the face, assuming "5" positions, palms still facing. *Cf.* AWFUL, CALAMITOUS, CATASTROPHIC, DANGER 1, DANGEROUS 1, DREADFUL, TERRIBLE, TRAGEDY, TRAGIC.

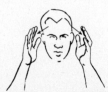

[F–81]

FEAST (fēst), *n.* (Placing food in the mouth.) Both closed hands alternately come to the mouth, as if placing food in it. *Cf.* BANQUET, DINNER.

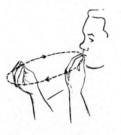

[F–82]

FEASTDAY (fēst′ dā), *n.* (**CARE, DAY.**) The sign for CARE 1 is made: The "K" hands are crossed, the right above the left, little finger edges down. In this position they describe a small counterclockwise circle in front of the chest. This is followed by the sign for DAY: The left arm, held horizontally, palm down, represents the horizon. The right elbow rests on the back of the left hand, with the right arm in a perpendicular position. The right "D" hand, palm facing left, moves in an arc to the left until it is just above the left elbow.

[F–83]

FECES (fē′ sēz), *(sl., vulg.), n.* (The passing of fecal material.) The left hand grasps the upturned right thumb. The right hand drops down and the right thumb is exposed. *Cf.* DEFECATE.

[F–84]

FED UP (fĕd ŭp), *adj. phrase.* (Full—up to the chin.) The downturned open right hand moves up until its back comes into contact with the underside of the chin. The signer assumes an expression of annoyance. *Cf.* FULL 2.

[F–85]

FEE (fē), *n.* (Nicking into one.) The knuckle of the right "X" finger is nicked against the palm of the left hand, held in the "5" position, palm facing right. *Cf.* ADMISSION 2, CHARGE 1, COST, DUTY 2, EXCISE, EXPENSE, FINE 2, IMPOST, PENALTY 3, PRICE 2, TAX 1, TAXATION 1, TOLL.

[F–86]

FEEBLE (fē′ bəl), *adj.* (The knees buckle.) The right "V" hand is placed with fingertips resting in the upturned left palm. The knuckles of the "V" fingers buckle a bit. This motion may be repeated. *Cf.* FAINT 1, FRAIL, WEAK, WEAKNESS.

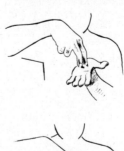

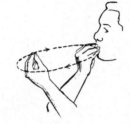

[F–87]

FEEBLE-MINDED (fē′ bəl mĭn′ dĭd), *adj. phrase.* (Weakness at the mind.) The fingers of the right "V" hand, placed at the right temple, collapse. The movement may be repeated. *Cf.* WEAK-MINDED.

[F–88]

FEED 1 (fēd), *v.,* FED, FEEDING. (The natural sign.) The closed right hand goes through the natural motion of placing food in the mouth. This movement is repeated. *Cf.* CONSUME 1, CONSUMPTION, DEVOUR, DINE, EAT, FOOD 1, MEAL.

[F–89]

FEED 2, *v.* (Placing food before someone; the action of placing food in someone's mouth.) The upturned hands, holding imaginary pieces of food, the right behind the left, move forward simultaneously, in a gesture of placing food in someone's mouth.

[F–90]

FEEL 1 (fēl), *v.,* FELT, FEELING. (The natural movement of touching.) The tip of the middle finger of the downturned right "5" hand touches the back of the left hand a number of times. *Cf.* CONTACT 1, TOUCH, TOUCHDOWN.

[F–91]

FEEL 2, *v.* (The welling up of feelings or emotions in the heart.) The right middle finger, touching the heart, moves up an inch or two a number of times. *Cf.* EMOTION 1, FEELING, MOTIVE 2, SENSATION, SENSE 2.

[F–92]

FEEL HURT (hŭrt), *v. phrase.* (The feelings are those which give pain, and cause the hand to be removed quickly from the source of this pain.) The sign for FEEL 2 is made, and then the right hand is thrown down and out, opening into the downturned "5" position. *Cf.* HURT 4.

[F–93]

FEELING (fē′ lĭng), *n.* See FEEL 2.

[F–94]

FEEL TOUCHED (tŭcht), *v. phrase.* (A piercing of the heart.) The tip of the middle finger of the right "5" hand is thrust against the heart. The head, at the same time, moves abruptly back a very slight distance. *Cf.* TOUCHED, TOUCHING.

[F-95]

FEET (fēt), *n. pl.* (The natural pointing sign.) The downturned index finger points, in turn, to the left and then the right foot.

[F-96]

FELLOWSHIP (fĕl' ō shǐp'), *n.* (Mingling with.) Both hands are held in modified "A" positions, thumbs out. The left hand is positioned with its thumb pointing straight up, and the right hand, with its thumb pointing down, revolves above the left thumb in a counterclockwise direction. *Cf.* ASSOCIATE 1, EACH OTHER, MINGLE 2, MUTUAL 1, ONE ANOTHER.

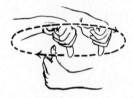

[F-97]

FEMALE (fē' māl), *n., adj.* (The bonnet string used by women of old.) The right "A" hand's thumb moves down along the line of the right jaw, from ear almost to chin. This outlines the string used to tie ladies' bonnets in olden days. This is a root sign to modify many others. *Viz:* FEMALE plus BABY; DAUGHTER, FEMALE plus SAME; SISTER, etc.

[F-98]

FENCE 1 (fĕns), *n.* (The interlocking nature of the fence's design; its shape.) The hands are held with interlocked fingers and palms facing the body. As they slowly separate, each moves to the side of the body, tracing the fence's course around an imaginary house or building.

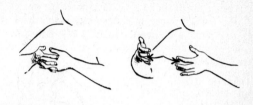

[F-99]

FENCE 2, *n.* (The upright posts.) The "5" hands, palms facing out, are held side by side in front of the body. They move apart in a series of up-down motions.

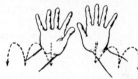

[F-100]

FENCE 3, *v.,* FENCED, FENCING. (The natural motion.) The right hand, holding an imaginary fencing implement, goes through the natural motion of fencing. The left hand may be held aloft, to add reality and naturalness to the sign.

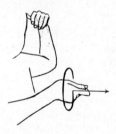

[F-101]

FETCH (fĕch), *v.,* FETCHED, FETCHING. (Carrying something over.) Both open hands, palms up, move in an arc from left to right, as if carrying something from one point to another. *Cf.* BRING, CARRY 2, DELIVER 2, PRODUCE 1, TRANSPORT.

[F-102]

FETTER (fĕt′ ər), *n., v.,* -TERED, -TERING. (The course of the chain or shackle around the ankles.) The right "X" finger describes a half-circle around the left wrist, and then the hands are switched and the movement repeated with the left "X" finger and the right wrist.

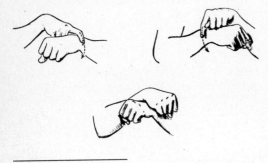

[F-103]

FEVER (fē′ vər), *n.* (The rise and fall of the mercury in the thermometer.) The index finger of the right "D" hand, pointing left, moves slowly up and down the index finger of the left "D" hand, which is held pointing up. *Cf.* TEMPERATURE, THERMOMETER.

[F-104]

FEW (fū), *adj.* (The fingers are presented in order, to convey the concept of "several.") The right "A" hand is held palm facing up. One by one the fingers open, beginning with the index finger and ending with the little finger. Some use only the index and middle fingers. *Cf.* RARE, SCARCE, SEVERAL, SUNDRY.

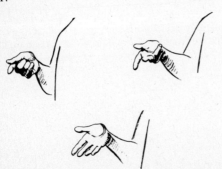

[F-105]

FEW DAYS AGO, A, *adv. phrase.* (Several yesterdays.) The right "A" hand is placed at the right cheek, thumb touching the cheek. Using the thumb as a pivot, the hand is swung back, gradually opening up the remaining fingers of the right hand, one by one, with the index finger first.

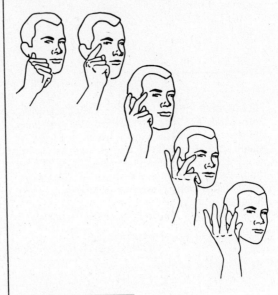

[F-106]

FEW SECONDS AGO, A, *adv. phrase.* (Time moved backward a bit.) The right "D" hand, palm facing the body, is placed in the palm of the left hand, which is facing right. The right hand swings back a bit toward the body, with the index finger describing an arc. *Cf.* JUST A MOMENT AGO, WHILE AGO 3.

[F-107]

FIB (fĭb), *n.* (The words are deflected from their normal straight path from the lips.) The right "D" hand, palm facing left, moves quickly in front of the lips, from right to left. *Cf.* FALSE 2.

[F-108]

FICTION (fĭk′ shən), *n.* (The unraveling or stretching out of words or sentences.) Both open hands are held close to each other, with fingers open and palms facing and almost touching. As the hands are drawn apart, the thumb and index finger of each hand come together to form circles. This is repeated several times. *Cf.* DESCRIBE 2, EXPLAIN 2, FABLE, GOSPEL 1, NARRATE, NARRATIVE, STORY 1, TALE, TELL ABOUT.

[F-109]

FIDDLE (fĭd′ əl), n., v., -DLED, -DLING. (The natural movement.) The hands and arms go through the natural motions of playing a violin. *Cf.* VIOLIN.

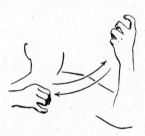

[F-110]

FIDELITY (fī dĕl′ ə tĭ, fə-), *n.* (Coming forth directly from the lips; true.) The index finger of the right "D" hand, palm facing left, is placed against the lips. It moves up an inch or two and then describes a small arc forward and away from the lips. *Cf.* ABSOLUTE, ABSOLUTELY, ACTUAL, ACTUALLY, AUTHENTIC, CERTAIN, CERTAINLY, FAITHFUL 3, FRANKLY, GENUINE, INDEED, POSITIVE 1, POSITIVELY, REAL, REALLY, SINCERE 2, SURE, SURELY, TRUE, TRULY, TRUTH, VALID, VERILY.

[F-111]

FIELD 1 (fēld), *n.* (An expanse of ground.) The sign for SOIL 1 is made: Both hands, held upright before the body, finger imaginary pinches of soil. The downturned open right "5" hand then sweeps in an arc from right to left. *Cf.* LAND 1.

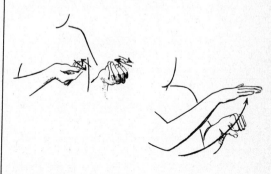

[F-112]

FIELD 2, *n.* (A fenced-in enclosure.) The "5" hands are held with palms facing the body and fingers interlocked but not curved. The hands separate, swinging first to either side of the body, and then moving in toward the body, tracing a circle and coming together palms out and bases touching. *Cf.* GARDEN, YARD 2.

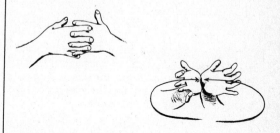

[F-113]

FIELD 3, *n.* (A straight, *i.e.*, special, path.) The hands are held in the "B" position, one above the other, with left palm facing right and right palm facing left. The little finger edge of the right hand moves straight forward along the index finger edge of the left. *Cf.* IN THE FIELD OF, SPECIALIZE, SPECIALTY.

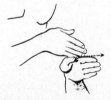

[F-114]

FIELD 4, *n.* (The letter "F"; straight line denotes a specific "line" or area of pursuit.) The thumb edge of the right "F" hand moves forward along the outstretched left index finger. *Cf.* PROFESSION 1.

[F-115]

FIERCE (fĭrs), *adj.* (Wrinkling the brow.) The "5" hand is held palm toward the face. The fingers open and close partly, several times, while an angry expression is worn on the face. *Cf.* ANGRY 1, CROSS 1, CROSSNESS, ILL TEMPER, IRRITABLE.

[F-116]

FIFE (fīf), *n.* (Playing a fife.) The thumbs and fingers of both hands grasp an imaginary fife and hold it to the mouth. The fingers move up and down, as if playing the instrument, and the signer purses his lips as if blowing. *Cf.* PICNIC 2.

[F-117]

FIGHT 1 (fĭt), *n., v.,* FOUGHT, FIGHTING. (The fists in combat.) The "S" hands, palms facing, swing down simultaneously toward each other. They do not touch, however. *Cf.* COMBAT.

[F-118]

FIGHT 2, *n., v.* (The natural sign.) Both clenched fists go through the motions of boxing. *Cf.* BOX 2.

[F-119]

FIGURE 1 (fĭg' yər), *n., v.,* -URED, -URING. (A multiplying.) The "V" hands, palms facing the body, alternately cross and separate, several times. *Cf.* ARITHMETIC, CALCULATE, ESTIMATE, MULTIPLY 1.

[F-120]

FIGURE 2, *n., v.* (Contours are indicated or outlined.) Both "A" hands, held about a foot apart before the face, with palms facing each other, move down simultaneously in a wavy, undulating motion. *Cf.* FORM, IMAGE, SCULPT, SCULPTURE, SHAPE 1, STATUE.

[F-121]

FILE 1 (fīl), *(voc.), n., v.* (The natural sign.) The index and middle fingers of the right "H" hand rub back and forth over the edge of the index finger of the left "H" hand, whose palm faces right.

[F–122]

FILE 2, *v.* (Impaling a piece of paper on a spike.) The right "V" hand is brought down over the up-turned left index finger.

[F–123]

FILL (fĭl), *v.* FILLED, FILLING. (Wiping off the top of a container, to indicate its condition of fullness.) The downturned open right hand wipes across the index finger edge of the left "S" hand, whose palm faces right. The movement of the right hand is toward the body. *Cf.* COMPLETE 2, FULL 1.

[F–124]

FILM (fĭlm), *n.* (The frames of the film speeding through the projector.) The left "5" hand, palm facing right and thumb pointing up, is the projector. The right "5" hand is placed against the left, and moves back and forth quickly. *Cf.* CINEMA, MOTION PICTURE, MOVIE(S), MOVING PICTURE.

[F–125]

FILTHY (fĭl′ thĭ), *adj.* (A modification of the pig's snout groveling in a trough.) The downturned right hand is placed under the chin. Its fingers, pointing

left, wiggle repeatedly. *Cf.* DIRTY, FOUL, IMPURE, NASTY, SOIL 2, STAIN.

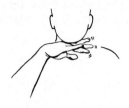

[F–126]

FINAL 1 (fī′ nəl), *adj.* (The little, *i.e.,* LAST, fingers are indicated.) With the hands in the "I" position, the tip of the right little finger strikes the tip of its left counterpart. The right index finger may be used instead of the right little finger. *Cf.* END 1, EVENTUALLY, FINALLY 1, LAST 1, ULTIMATE, ULTIMATELY.

[F–127]

FINAL 2, *adj.* (A single little, *i.e.,* LAST, finger is indicated.) The tip of the index finger of the right "D" hand strikes the tip of the little finger of the left "I" hand. *Cf.* END 2, FINALLY 2, LAST 2.

[F–128]

FINALLY 1 (fī′ nə lĭ), *adv.* See FINAL 1.

[F–129]

FINALLY 2, *adv.* See FINAL 2.

[F–130]

FINANCES (fĭ năn′ səs, fī′ năn səs), *n. pl.* (Slapping of paper money in the palm.) The upturned right hand, grasping some imaginary bills, is brought down into the upturned left palm a number of times. *Cf.* CAPITAL 2, CURRENCY, FUNDS, MONEY 1.

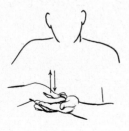

[F–131]

FIND (fīnd), *n., v.,* FOUND, FINDING. (The natural motion of selecting something from the hand.) The thumb and index fingers of the outstretched right hand grasp an imaginary object on the upturned left palm. The right hand then moves straight up. *Cf.* CHOOSE 2, DISCOVER, PICK 1, SELECT 1.

[F–132]

FIND FAULT 1 (fôlt), *v. phrase.* (A canceling out.) The right index finger makes a cross on the open left palm. *Cf.* ANNUL, CANCEL, CHECK 1, CORRECT 2, CRITICISM, CRITICIZE, REVOKE.

[F–133]

FIND FAULT 2, *(arch.), v. phrase.* (Selecting something by pulling it out of a receptacle or container.) The cupped left "C" hand is the container. The right

index finger and thumb are placed in this imaginary container and pull something out.

[F–134]

FINE 1 (fīn), *adj., interj.* (The feelings are titillated.) With the thumb resting on the upper part of the chest, the fingers are wiggled back and forth. *Cf.* ELEGANT, GRAND 2, GREAT 4, SPLENDID 2, SWELL 2, WONDERFUL 2.

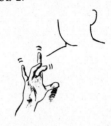

[F–135]

FINE 2, *n., v.,* FINED, FINING. (Nicking into one.) The knuckle of the right "X" finger is nicked against the palm of the left hand, held in the "5" position, palm facing right. *Cf.* ADMISSION 2, CHARGE 1, COST, DUTY 2, EXCISE, EXPENSE, FEE, IMPOST, PENALTY 3, PRICE 2, TAX 1, TAXATION 1, TOLL.

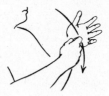

[F–136]

FINE 3, *adj.* (The fineness of sand or dust.) The index finger and thumb of the right "F" hand rub each other, as if fingering sand or dust.

[F–137]

FINE 4, *adj.* (The ruffled shirt front of a gentleman of old.) The thumb of the right "5" hand is thrust into the chest. The hand then pivots down, with thumb remaining in place. This latter part of the sign, however, is optional. *Cf.* COURTEOUS, COURTESY, POLITE.

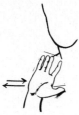

[F–138]

FINGER (fĭng' gər), *n.* (The natural sign.) The right index finger touches its left mate.

[F–139]

FINGERNAILS (fĭng' gər nāls´), *n. pl.* (The natural sign.) The left "5" hand is held palm facing the body. The right index finger runs over the left fingernails, beginning at the left index finger.

[F–140]

FINGERPRINT (fĭng' gər prĭnt´), *n., v.,* -PRINTED, -PRINTING. (The natural sign.) The right middle fingertip is pressed into the upturned left palm, and the right hand is pivoted back and forth, causing the middle fingertip to roll from side to side, to record the whole fingerprint.

[F–141]

FINGERSPELLING (fĭng' ger, spĕl ĭng), *n.* (The movement of the fingers in fingerspelling.) The right hand, palm out, is moved from left to right, with the fingers wriggling up and down. *Cf.* ALPHABET, DACTYLOLOGY, MANUAL ALPHABET, SPELL, SPELLING.

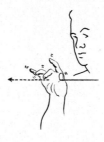

[F–142]

FINISH 1 (fĭn' ĭsh), *v.,* -ISHED, -ISHING. (Bring to an end.) The left hand, fingers together and pointing forward, is held palm facing right. The right, palm down, fingers also together, moves along the top of the left, goes over the tip of the left index finger, and drops straight down, indicating a cutting off or a finishing. This sign is also used to indicate the past tense of a verb, in the sense of finishing an action or state of being. *Cf.* ACCOMPLISH 2, ACHIEVE 2, COMPLETE 1, CONCLUDE, DONE 1, END 4, EXPIRE 1, HAVE 2, TERMINATE.

[F–143]

FINISH 2, *(colloq.), n., v.* (Shaking the hands to rid them of something.) The upright "5" hands, palms facing each other, are suddenly and quickly swung around to a palm-out position. *Cf.* DONE 2, END 3.

[F-144]

FINLAND (fĭn′ lənd), *n.* (The letter "F"; the uppermost part of the body, to indicate the northern or Scandinavian sector of Europe.) The right "F" hand moves in a small counterclockwise circle on the forehead. *Cf.* FINN.

[F-145]

FINN (fĭn), *n.* See FINLAND. The sign for INDIVIDUAL 1, *q.v.*, may also be added.

[F-146]

FIRE 1 (fīr), *n., v.,* FIRED, FIRING. (The leaping of flames.) The "5" hands are held with palms facing the body. They move up and down alternately, while the fingers wiggle. *Cf.* BURN, FLAME, HELL 2.

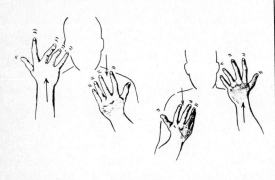

[F-147]

FIRE 2, *v.* ("Getting the axe"; the head is chopped off.) The upturned open right hand is swung sharply over the index finger edge of the left "S" hand, whose palm faces right. *Cf.* DISCHARGE 1, EXPEL 1.

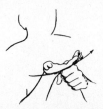

[F-148]

FIREMAN (fīr′ mən), *(loc.), n.* (The shape of the hat.) The open right hand, palm facing out, fingers together, is placed at the forehead.

[F-149]

FIRST 1 (fûrst), *adj.* (The first finger is indicated.) The right index finger touches the upturned left thumb. *Cf.* INITIAL, ORIGIN 2, PRIMARY.

[F-150]

FIRST 2, *adj.* (The natural sign.) The right "1" hand, palm facing left, is swung around so that the palm now faces the signer.

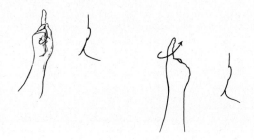

[F-151]

FISH 1 (fĭsh), *n.* (The natural motion.) The open right hand, palm facing left and fingers pointing forward, represents the fish. The open left hand, palm facing right and fingers also pointing forward, is positioned behind the right hand so that its fingertips rest against the base of the right hand. The right hand flaps back and forth, from right to left, moving very slightly forward meanwhile. The left hand remains in contact with the right, but its only movement is forward. The left hand may also be dispensed with.

FISH 2, *v.*, FISHED, FISHING. (The natural motion of fishing.) The hands grasp and shake an imaginary fishing rod. The right hand may also go through the motions of operating the fishing reel.

[F–153]

FIVE (fīv), *adj.* (The natural sign.) The five fingers of either hand are held up. The palm usually faces the person spoken to.

[F–154]

FIVE OF US, *n. phrase.* ("Five," all in a circle.) The right "5" hand swings in an arc from right shoulder to left shoulder.

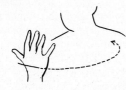

[F–155]

FIX (fĭks), *v.*, FIXED, FIXING, *n.* (Fashioning something with the hands.) The right "S" hand, palm

facing left, is placed on top of its left counterpart, whose palm faces right. The hands are twisted back and forth, striking each other slightly after each twist. *Cf.* COMPOSE, CONSTITUTE, CONSTRUCT 2, CREATE, DEVISE 2, FABRICATE, FASHION, MAKE, MANUFACTURE, MEND 1, PRODUCE 3, RENDER 1, REPAIR.

[F–156]

FLABBERGASTED (flăb' ər găst´ əd), *(colloq.), adj.* (The mouth drops open.) The fingertips of both "V" hands are held curved and touching before the body, one hand above the other. Then the hands are suddenly drawn apart, and at the same instant the mouth drops open and the eyes open wide. *Cf.* DUMFOUNDED 2, OPEN-MOUTHED, SPEECHLESS, SURPRISE 2.

[F–157]

FLAG (flăg), *n., v.*, FLAGGED, FLAGGING. (The waving.) The right "B" hand is held up, palm facing left and right elbow resting on the back of the downturned left hand. The right "B" hand waves back and forth, imitating the waving of a flag. *Cf.* BANNER.

[F–158]

FLAME (flām), *n., v.*, FLAMED, FLAMING. (The leaping of flames.) The "5" hands are held with palms facing the body. They move up and down alternately, while the fingers wiggle. *Cf.* BURN, FIRE 1, HELL 2.

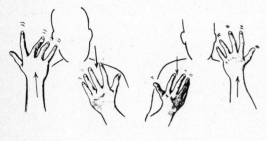

[F–159]

FLASHLIGHT (flăsh' līt'), *n.* (The natural sign.) The right hand holds an imaginary flashlight, and the thumb goes through the motion of flicking the switch. The downturned left hand is draped over the back of the downturned right hand, whose fingers are in contact with the right thumb and pointing straight out from the body. The right hand opens up into the downturned "5" position and moves straight out from under the left, in imitation of the rays of light from the flashlight.

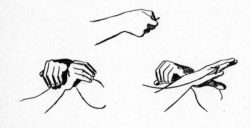

[F–160]

FLAT (flăt), *adj.* (The concept of flatness is emphasized.) The downturned hands, fingers together and pointing straight out from the body, are held side by side, about a foot apart. They drop down simultaneously an inch or two, and then move to the respective sides of the body—the right to the right side and the left to the left side. The initial dropping down of the hands is often omitted.

[F–161]

FLATBED PRESS, (flăt bĕd prĕs), *(voc.).* (The natural motion of feeding sheets of paper into the flatbed press.) The downturned open hands, held side by side, move over to the right, grasp an imaginary sheet of paper, and, moving to the left, feed it into the press. The movement is usually repeated.

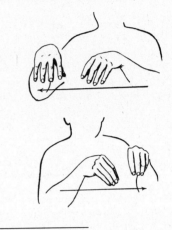

[F–162]

FLATIRON (flăt' ī' ərn), *n.* (The act of pressing with an iron.) The right hand goes through the motion of swinging an iron back and forth over the upturned left palm. *Cf.* IRON 2, PRESS 1.

[F–163]

FLATTER 1 (flăt' ər), *v.*, -TERED, -TERING. (Blinding one with sparkling words.) The downturned open hands are joined at the thumbtips. The fingers wiggle at random. Sometimes the hands sway up and down alternately, but in any case the thumbtips remain in contact at all times. *Cf.* FLATTERY 1.

[F–164]

FLATTER 2, *v.* (All eyes are directed to the signer, the one being flattered.) The "V" hands, palms facing the body, wave back and forth before the face. *Cf.* FLATTERY 2.

[F–165]

FLATTERY 1 (flăt′ ə ri), *n.* See FLATTER 1.

[F–166]

FLATTERY 2, *n.* See FLATTER 2.

[F–167]

FLEA 1 (flē), *n.* (The flea is killed by pressing it between the thumb nails.) The thumb nails are pressed together a number of times.

[F–168]

FLEA 2, *n.* (The flea is killed by pinching it.) The right thumb and index finger are pinched together deliberately once or twice.

[F–169]

FLEA 3, *n.* (Wetting the fingertip to make the insect stick to it and slapping the flea.) The right index finger is touched to the tongue, and then the right hand slaps the left arm at the elbow.

[F–170]

FLEE (flē), *v.*, FLED, FLEEING. (Emerging from a hiding place.) The downturned right "D" hand is positioned under the downturned open left hand. The right "D" hand suddenly emerges and moves off quickly to the right. *Cf.* ESCAPE.

[F–171]

FLESH (flĕsh), *n.* (The fleshy part of the hand.) The right index finger and thumb squeeze the fleshy part of the open left hand, between thumb and index finger. *Cf.* BEEF, MEAT.

[F–172]

FLIER (flī′ ər), *n.* (An individual who flies a plane.) The sign for either AIRPLANE 1 or AIRPLANE 2 is made, and this is followed by the sign for INDIVIDUAL: Both open hands, palms facing each other, move down the sides of the body, tracing its outline to the hips. *Cf.* AVIATOR, PILOT.

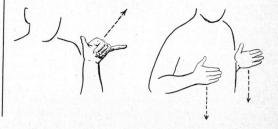

[F–173]

FLIP THE LID (flip ᵗhə lid), *(sl.)*, *v. phrase*, FLIPPED, FLIPPING. (The lid or cover of a pot pops off into the air.) This sign is used to indicate a loss of temper. The left "O" hand, thumb side up and palm facing right, is the pot. The downturned right hand, resting on the left, suddenly pops up and, pivoted at the wrist, moves up in a wavy manner. *Cf.* FLY OFF THE HANDLE.

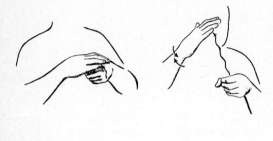

[F–174]

FLIRT (flûrt), *v.*, FLIRTED, FLIRTING. (Dazzling one with scintillating looks.) The "5" hands, thumbs touching, swing alternately up and down. The fingers sometimes wiggle, as in FLATTER 1, *q.v.*

[F–175]

FLOAT (flōt), *n.*, *v.*, FLOATED, FLOATING. (Resting on an object which bobs up and down on the water.) Both hands are held in the palms-down position. The right index and middle fingers rest on their left counterparts. The left hand moves forward in a series of bobbing movements, carrying the right hand along with it.

[F–176]

FLOOD (flŭd), *n.*, *v.*, FLOODED, FLOODING. (Rippling water rising.) The downturned "5" hands rise slowly as the fingers wiggle. The sign for WATER 2, *q.v.*, is sometimes given first.

[F–177]

FLOOR (flōr), *n.* (Boards arranged side by side.) The downturned open hands, fingers together, are held side by side at the left side of the body. They separate and come together repeatedly as they move toward the right.

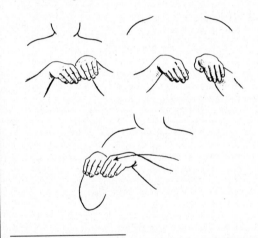

[F–178]

FLOUR 1 (flour), *n.* (The sign for WHITE; the grinding process.) The sign for WHITE is made: The right "5" hand is placed at mid-chest, palm facing the body. It moves off the chest, closing into the "O" position, palm still facing the body. The fingertips of the right hand, held palm down, move in a continuous counterclockwise circle on the upturned left palm.

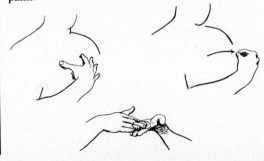

[F–179]

FLOUR 2, *n.* (The sign for WHITE; feeling the flour.) The sign for WHITE is made, as in FLOUR 1. The right hand then fingers an imaginary pinch of flour.

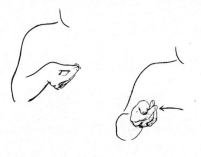

[F–180]

FLOWER (flou′ ər), *n.* (The natural motion of smelling a flower.) The right hand, grasping an imaginary flower, holds it first against the right nostril and then against the left. *Cf.* BLOSSOM.

[F–181]

FLUNK (flŭngk), *v.,* FLUNKED, FLUNKING. The right "F" hand strikes forcefully against the open left palm, which faces right with fingers pointing forward. *Cf.* FAIL 3.

[F–182]

FLUSH (flŭsh), *v.,* FLUSHED, FLUSHING. (The red rises in the cheeks.) The sign for RED is made: The tip of the right index finger of the "D" hand moves down over the lips, which are red. Both hands are then placed palms facing the cheeks, and move up along the face, to indicate the rise of color. *Cf.*

BLUSH, EMBARRASS, EMBARRASSED, MORTIFICATION.

[F–183]

FLY 1 (flī), *v.,* FLEW, FLOWN, FLYING. (The wings of the airplane.) The "Y" hand, palm down and drawn up near the shoulder, moves forward, up and away from the body. Either hand may be used. *Cf.* AIRPLANE 1, PLANE 1.

[F–184]

FLY 2, *v., n.* (The wings and fuselage of the airplane.) The hand assumes the same position as in FLY 1, but the index finger is also extended, to represent the fuselage of the airplane. Either hand may be used, and the movement is the same as in FLY 1. *Cf.* AIRPLANE 2, PLANE 2.

[F–185]

FLY 3, *n.* (Act of catching a fly.) The open right hand, poised over the raised left arm, quickly swoops down and grasps an imaginary fly resting on the left arm.

[F-186]

FLY OFF THE HANDLE, *(sl.), v. phrase.* See FLIP
THE LID.

[F-187]

FOCUS (fō' kəs), *n., v.,* -CUSED, -CUSING. (Directing one's attention forward; applying oneself; concentrating.) Both hands, fingers pointing up and together, are held at the sides of the face. They move
straight out from the face. *Cf.* APPLY 2, ATTEND
(TO), ATTENTION, CONCENTRATE, CONCENTRA-
TION, GIVE ATTENTION (TO), MIND 2, PAY ATTEN-
TION (TO).

[F-188]

FOE (fō), *n.* (At sword's point.) The two index
fingers, after pointing to each other, are drawn
sharply apart. This is followed by the sign for INDI-
VIDUAL: Both open hands, palms facing each
other, move down the sides of the body, tracing its
outline to the hips. *Cf.* ENEMY, OPPONENT, RIVAL
1.

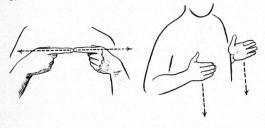

[F-189]

FOLD (fōld), *v.,* FOLDED, FOLDING. (The natural
sign.) The open hands, held palms up and at right
angles to each other, with the little finger edges
touching, close, with the right hand over the left, as
if folding something over.

[F-190]

FOLLOW (fŏl' ō), *v.,* -LOWED, -LOWING. (One hand
follows the other.) The "A" hands are used, thumbs
pointing up. The right is positioned a few inches
behind the left. The left hand moves straight forward, while the right follows behind in a series of
wavy movements. *Cf.* CONSECUTIVE, FOLLOWING,
SEQUEL.

[F-191]

FOLLOWING (fŏl' ō ĭng), *adj.* See FOLLOW.

[F-192]

FOLLY (fŏl' ĭ), *n.* (Thoughts flickering back and
forth.) The right "Y" hand, thumb almost touching
the forehead, is shaken back and forth across the
forehead several times. *Cf.* ABSURD, DAFT, FOOLISH,
NONSENSE, RIDICULOUS, SILLY, TRIFLING.

[F-193]

FOND 1 (fŏnd), *adj.* (Stroking a person or the head
of a pet.) The right hand strokes the back of the left
several times. *Cf.* DEAR 1, PET, STROKE 2, TAME.

[F-194]

FOND 2, *(colloq.), adj., adv.* (Strongly attached or hooked on to.) With index fingers interlocked, both hands move forward a short distance. *Cf.* FAVORITE 3.

[F-195]

FOOD 1 (fo͞od), *n.* (The natural sign.) The closed right hand goes through the natural motion of placing food in the mouth. This movement is repeated. *Cf.* CONSUME 1, CONSUMPTION, DEVOUR, DINE, EAT, FEED 1, MEAL.

[F-196]

FOOD 2, *n.* (Various things to eat.) The sign for FOOD 1 is made, followed by the sign for VARIOUS: The index fingers, pointing at each other, are drawn apart. As they do so, they wiggle slightly.

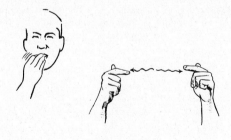

[F-197]

FOOL 1 (fo͞ol), *v.,* FOOLED, FOOLING. (Underhandedness.) The right index finger touches the nose. Then the downturned right hand, index and little

fingers extended, moves under the downturned left hand.

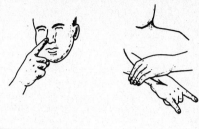

[F-198]

FOOL 2, *v.* (Pulling the nose.) The right "X" finger, resting on the nose, pulls the head with it as it moves down slightly. It does not leave its position on the nose. *Cf.* DOLL 1, HOAX, JOKE.

[F-199]

FOOLISH (fo͞o′ lĭsh), *adj.* (Thoughts flickering back and forth.) The right "Y" hand, thumb almost touching the forehead, is shaken back and forth across the forehead several times. *Cf.* ABSURD, DAFT, FOLLY, NONSENSE, RIDICULOUS, SILLY, TRIFLING.

[F-200]

FOOT 1 (fo͝ot), *n.* (The natural sign.) The signer points to his foot.

[F–201]

FOOT 2, *n.* (The length is indicated.) The "A" hands, palms down and thumbtips touching, are held before the chest. They separate until they are about a foot apart.

[F–202]

FOOTBALL 1 (foŏt′ bôl′), *n.* (The teams lock in combat.) The "5" hands, facing each other, are interlocked suddenly. They are drawn apart and the action is repeated.

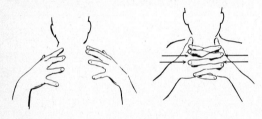

[F–203]

FOOTBALL 2, *n.* (The shape of the ball.) The "5" hands face each other, the right fingers in contact with their left counterparts. The hands are drawn apart into the "O" position, palms facing each other.

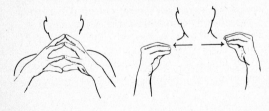

[F–204]

FOR 1 (fôr), *prep.* (The thoughts are directed outward, toward a specific goal or purpose.) The right index finger, resting on the right temple, leaves its position and moves straight out in front of the face. *Cf.* TO 2, TOWARD 3.

[F–205]

FOR 2, *prep.* (A thought or knowledge uppermost in the mind.) The fingers of the right hand or the index finger are placed on the center of the forehead, and then the hand is brought strongly up above the head, assuming the "A" position, with thumb pointing up. *Cf.* BECAUSE.

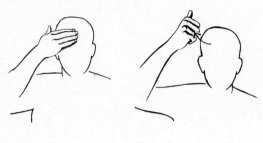

[F–206]

FORBID 1 (fər bǐd′), *v.,* -BADE *or* -BAD, -BIDDEN *or* -BID, -BIDDING. (A modification of LAW, *q.v.;* "against the law.") The downturned right "D" or "L" hand is thrust forcefully into the left palm. *Cf.* BAN, FORBIDDEN 1, PROHIBIT.

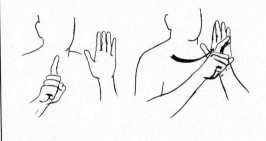

[F–207]

FORBID 2, *v.* (The letter "F"; the same sign as above.) The right "F" hand makes the same sign as in FORBID 1. *Cf.* FORBIDDEN 2.

[F–208]

FORBIDDEN 1 (fər bǐd′ ən), *v.* See FORBID 1.

[F–209]

FORBIDDEN 2, *adj.* See FORBID 2.

[F–210]

FORCE 1 (fōrs), *v.,* FORCED, FORCING. (Forcing the head to bow.) The right "C" hand pushes down on an imaginary neck. *Cf.* COERCE 1, COERCION 1, COMPEL 1, IMPEL 1.

[F–211]

FORCE 2, *v.* (Pushing something forward.) The open right hand is held palm down at chin level, fingers pointing left. From this position the hand turns to point forward, and moves forcefully forward and away from the body, as if pushing something ahead of it. *Cf.* COERCE 2, COERCION 2, COMPEL 2, IMPEL 2.

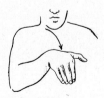

[F–212]

FORECAST (fōr' kăst', -käst'), *v.,* -CAST or -CASTED, -CASTING. (The vision is directed forward, into the distance.) The right "V" fingertips are placed under the eyes, with palm facing the body. The hand is then swung around and forward, moving under the downturned prone left hand and continuing forward and upward. *Cf.* FORESEE, FORE-

TELL, PERCEIVE 2, PREDICT, PROPHECY, PROPHESY, PROPHET, VISION 2.

[F–213]

FOREMAN (fōr' mən), *n.* (The eyes sweep back and forth.) The "V" hands, held crossed, describe a counterclockwise circle before the chest. This is followed by the sign for INDIVIDUAL: Both open hands, palms facing each other, move down the sides of the body, tracing its outline to the hips. *Cf.* Supervisor.

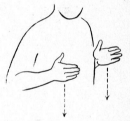

[F–214]

FORENOON (*n.* fōr' nōōn'; *adj.* fōr' nōōn´). (The sun comes over the horizon.) The little finger edge of the left hand rests in the crook of the right elbow. The left arm, held horizontally, represents the horizon. The open right hand, fingers together and pointing up, with palm facing the body, rises slowly to an almost upright angle. *Cf.* MORNING.

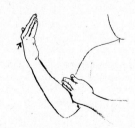

[F–215]

FORESEE (fōr sē'), *v.,* -SAW, -SEEN, -SEEING. See FORECAST.

[F-216]

FOREST (fôr' ĭst), *n.* (A series of trees.) The open right "5" hand is raised, with elbow resting on the back of the left hand, as in TREE, *q.v.* As the right hand swings around and back a number of times, pivoting at the wrist, the left arm carries the right arm from left to right. *Cf.* WOODS.

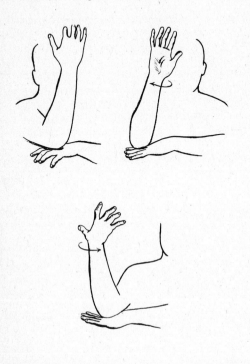

[F-217]

FORETELL (fōr tĕl'), *v.*, -TOLD, -TELLING. See FORECAST.

[F-218]

FOREVER (fôr ĕv' ər), *adv.* (Around the clock and ahead into the future.) The right index finger, pointing forward, traces a clockwise circle in the air. The downturned right "Y" hand then moves forward, either in a straight line or in a slight downward curve. *Cf.* ETERNITY 1, EVER 2, EVERLASTING.

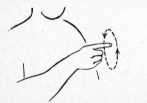

[F-219]

FOREWARN (fōr wôrn'), *v.*, -WARNED, -WARNING. (Tapping one to draw attention to danger.) The right hand taps the back of the left several times. *Cf.* ADMONISH 1, CAUTION, WARN.

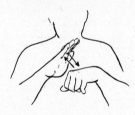

[F-220]

FORFEIT (fôr' fĭt), *n.* (Throwing up the hands in a gesture of surrender.) Both "A" hands are held palms down before the chest and then thrown up in unison, ending in the "5" position. *Cf.* ABDICATE, CEDE, DISCOURAGE 1, GIVE UP, LOSE HOPE, RELINQUISH, RENOUNCE, RENUNCIATION, SURRENDER 1, YIELD.

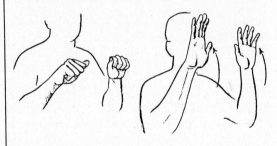

[F-221]

FORGET 1 (fər gĕt'), *v.*, -GOT, -GOTTEN, -GETTING. (Wiping knowledge from the mind.) The right hand, fingers pointing left, rests on the forehead. It moves off to the right, assuming the "A" position, thumb up and palm facing the signer's rear. *Cf.* FORSAKE 2.

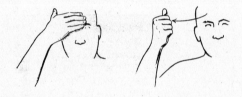

[F-222]

FORGET 2, *v.* (The thought is gone.) The sign for THINK is made: The index finger makes a small circle on the forehead. This is followed by the sign for GONE 1: The right open hand, palm facing the body, is held by the left hand and is drawn down and out, ending in a position with fingers drawn together. The left hand, meanwhile, has closed into a position with fingers also drawn together.

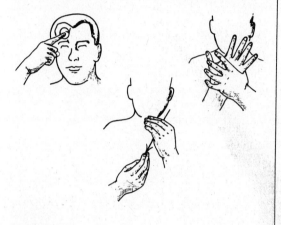

[F–223]

FORGIVE 1 (fər gĭv′), *(eccles.)*, *v.*, -GAVE, -GIVEN, -GIVING. (Blessed; forgiveness.) The "A" hands are held near the lips, thumbs up and almost touching. Both hands move down and out simultaneously, ending in the "5" position, palms down. The right hand, palm flat, facing down, is then brushed over the left hand, held palm flat and facing up. This latter action may be repeated twice. *Cf.* ABSOLUTION 1, BLESS 1.

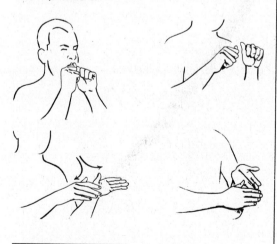

[F–224]

FORGIVE 2, *v.* (A wiped-off and cleaned slate.) The right hand wipes off the left palm several times. *Cf.*

APOLOGIZE 2, APOLOGY 2, EXCUSE, PARDON, PAROLE.

[F–225]

FORK (fôrk), *n.*, *v.*, FORKED, FORKING. (The natural sign.) The downturned fingertips of the right "V" hand are thrust repeatedly into the upturned left palm.

[F–226]

FORM (fôrm), *n.* (Contours are indicated or outlined.) Both "A" hands, held about a foot apart before the face, with palms facing each other, move down simultaneously in a wavy, undulating motion. *Cf.* FIGURE 2, IMAGE, SCULPT, SCULPTURE, SHAPE 1, STATUE.

[F–227]

FORMERLY (fôr′ mər lĭ), *adv.* (Something past, behind.) The upraised right hand, in the "5" position with palm facing the body, is held just above the right shoulder and is thrown back over it. *Cf.* AGO, ONCE UPON A TIME, PAST, PREVIOUS, PREVIOUSLY, WAS, WERE.

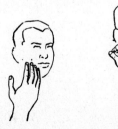

[F-228]

FORNICATE (fôr′ nə kāt′), *v.,* -CATED, -CATING. (The motions of the legs during the sexual act.) The upturned left "V" hand remains motionless, while the downturned right "V" hand comes down repeatedly on the left. *Cf.* COPULATE, SEXUAL INTERCOURSE.

[F-229]

FORSAKE 1 (fôr sāk′), *v.,* -SOOK, -SAKEN, -SAKING. (Pulling away.) The downturned open hands are held in a line, with fingers pointing to the left, the right hand behind the left. Both hands move in unison toward the right. As they do so, they assume the "A" position. *Cf.* DEPART, EVACUATE, GRADUATE 2, LEAVE 1, RETIRE 1, WITHDRAW 1.

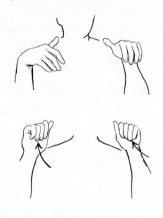

[F-230]

FORSAKE 2, *v.,* (Wiping knowledge from the mind.) The right hand, fingers pointing left, rests on the forehead. It moves off to the right, assuming the "A" position, thumb up and palm facing the signer's rear. *Cf.* FORGET 1.

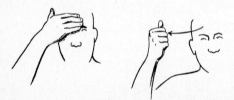

[F-231]

FORSAKE 3, *v.* (To throw something aside.) Both "S" hands are held with palms facing at chest level and then thrown down and to the left, opening into the "5" position. *Cf.* ABANDON 1, CAST OFF, DEPOSIT 2, DISCARD 1, LEAVE 2, LET ALONE, NEGLECT.

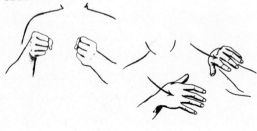

[F-232]

FORTIFY (fôr′ tə fī′), *v.,* -FIED, -FYING. (Hold down firmly; cover and strengthen.) The "S" hands, downturned, are held side by side in front of the body, the arms almost horizontal, and the left hand in front of the right. Both arms move a short distance forward and slightly downward. *Cf.* DEFEND, DEFENSE, GUARD, PROTECT, PROTECTION, SHIELD 1.

[F-233]

FORTITUDE (fôr′ tə tūd′, -tōōd′), *n.* (Strength emanating from the body.) Both "5" hands are placed palms against the chest. They move out and away, forcefully, closing and assuming the "S" position. *Cf.* BRAVE, BRAVERY, COURAGE, COURAGEOUS, HALE, HEALTH, HEALTHY, MIGHTY 2, STRENGTH, STRONG 2, WELL 2.

[F–234]

FORWARD (fôr′ wərd), *adv.* (Moving forward.) Both right-angle hands, palms facing each other and knuckles facing forward, move forward simultaneously. *Cf.* GO AHEAD, MOTION FORWARD, ONWARD, PROCEED, PROGRESS 2, RESUME.

[F–235]

FOUL (foul), *adj.* (A modification of the pig's snout groveling in a trough.) The downturned right hand is placed under the chin. Its fingers, pointing left, wiggle repeatedly. *Cf.* DIRTY, FILTHY, IMPURE, NASTY, SOIL 2, STAIN.

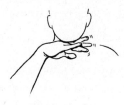

[F–236]

FOUND (found), *v.*, FOUNDED, FOUNDING. (To set up.) The right "A" hand, thumb up and palm facing left, comes down to rest on the back of the downturned left "S" hand. Before doing so, the right "A" hand may describe a clockwise circle above the left hand, but this is optional. *Cf.* ESTABLISH, FOUNDED.

[F–237]

FOUNDATION (foun dā′ shən), *n.* (The area below.) Both hands, in the "5" position, palms down, are held before the chest, the right under the left. The right hand moves under the left in a counterclock-

wise fashion. *Cf.* BACKGROUND, BASIS 2, BELOW 1, BOTTOM.

[F–238]

FOUNDED, *v.* See FOUND.

[F–239]

FOUNTAIN (foun′ tən), *n.* (Moving upward and flowing outward.) The right "AND" hand is moved up through the left "C" hand, which is held with thumb edge up and palm facing the body. As the fingers of the right hand emerge, they wiggle, to indicate a trickling of water. The action is usually repeated. *Cf.* SPRING 2.

[F–240]

FOUR (fōr), *adj.* (The natural sign.) Four fingers are displayed.

[F–241]

FOUR OF US, *n. phrase.* ("Four"; an encompassing movement.) The right "4" hand, palm facing the body, moves from the right shoulder to the left shoulder.

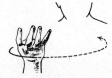

[F-242]

FOURTH (fōrth), *adj.* (The natural "one over four" sign.) The "1" hand drops down, assuming the "4" position. *Cf.* QUADRANT, QUARTER.

[F-243]

FOWL (foul), *n.* (The bill and the scratching.) The right index finger and thumb open and close as they are held pointing out from the mouth. (This is the root sign for any kind of bird.) The right "X" finger then scratches against the upturned left palm, as if scratching for food. The scratching is sometimes omitted. *Cf.* CHICKEN, HEN.

[F-244]

FOX (fŏks), *n.* (The letter "F"; the pointed snout.) The tip of the nose is placed in the circle formed by the right "F" hand, which swings back and forth a short distance. *Cf.* FOXY, SLY 1.

[F-245]

FOXY (fŏk' sĭ), *adj.* See FOX.

[F-246]

FRACTURE (frăk' chər), *n., v.,* -TURED, -TURING. (The natural sign.) The hands grasp an imaginary object and break it in two. *Cf.* BREAK.

[F-247]

FRAGRANT (frā' grənt), *adj.* (Bringing something up to the nose.) The upturned right hand moves slowly up to and past the nose, and the signer breathes in as the hand sweeps by. *Cf.* ODOR, SCENT, SMELL.

[F-248]

FRAIL (frāl), *adj.* (The knees buckle.) The right "V" hand is placed with fingertips resting in the upturned left palm. The knuckles of the "V" fingers buckle a bit. This motion may be repeated. *Cf.* FAINT 1, FEEBLE, WEAK, WEAKNESS.

[F-249]

FRAME (frām), *n., v.,* FRAMED, FRAMING. (The frame is outlined.) The downturned index finger and thumb of each hand outline the square shape of a frame. *Cf.* CHASE 2.

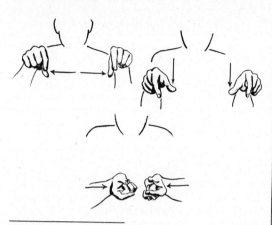

FRANCE (frăns), *n.* (The letter "F"; the French chef's gesture of approval in the kitchen.) The right "F" hand, held at about eye level, pivots back and forth. *Cf.* FRENCH, FRENCHMAN.

FRANK (frăngk), *adj.* (The letter "H," for HONEST; a straight and true path.) The index and middle fingers of the right "H" hand, whose palm faces left, move straight forward along the upturned left palm. *Cf.* HONEST, HONESTY, SINCERE 1.

FRANKFURTER (frăngk' fər tər), *n.* (The shape.) The "C" hands are held side by side, palms out,

thumbs and index fingers touching. They change to the "S" position as they are drawn apart. *Cf.* HOT DOG.

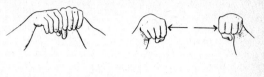

FRANKLY (frăngk' lĭ), *adv.* (Coming forth directly from the lips; true.) The index finger of the right "D" hand, palm facing left, is placed against the lips. It moves up an inch or two and then describes a small arc forward and away from the lips. *Cf.* ABSOLUTE, ABSOLUTELY, ACTUAL, ACTUALLY, AUTHENTIC, CERTAIN, CERTAINLY, FAITHFUL 3, FIDELITY, GENUINE, INDEED, POSITIVE 1, POSITIVELY, REAL, REALLY, SINCERE 2, SURE, SURELY, TRUE, TRULY, TRUTH, VALID, VERILY.

FRAUD (frôd), *n.* (Underhandedness.) The right hand, palm down, is held with index and little fingers pointing out. The left hand, in a similar position, is held above the right. The right hand moves forward repeatedly, each time emerging briefly from under the left hand. The positions may be reversed, with the left hand doing the movement, or both hands can move simultaneously. *Cf.* CHEAT 1, DECEIT, DECEIVE, DECEPTION, DEFRAUD, FRAUDULENT 1.

FRAUDULENT 1 (frô' jə lənt), *adj.* See FRAUD.

[F-256]

FRAUDULENT 2, *adj.* (Words diverted instead of coming straight, or truthfully, out.) The index finger of the right "D" hand, pointing to the left, moves along the lips from right to left. *Cf.* FALSE 1, FALSEHOOD, LIAR, LIE 1, PREVARICATE, UNTRUTH.

[F-257]

FREE 1 (frē), *adj., v.,* FREED, FREEING. (Breaking the bonds.) The "S" hands, crossed in front of the body, swing apart and face out. *Cf.* DELIVER 1, EMANCIPATE, INDEPENDENCE, INDEPENDENT, LIBERATION, REDEEM 1, RELIEF, RESCUE, SAFE, SALVATION, SAVE 1.

[F-258]

FREE 2, *adj., v.* (The letter "F.") The "F" hands make the same sign as in FREE 1.

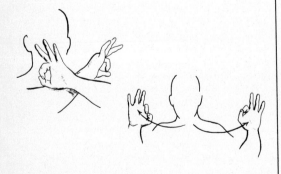

[F-259]

FREEDOM (frē' dəm), *n.* See FREE 1.

[F-260]

FREEZE (frēz), *v.,* FROZE, FROZEN, FREEZING. (The stiff fingers.) The fingers of the "5" hands, held palms down, stiffen and contract. *Cf.* FROZEN, ICE, RIGID.

[F-261]

FRENCH (frĕnch), *adj.* (The letter "F"; the French chef's gesture of approval in the kitchen.) The right "F" hand, held at about eye level, pivots back and forth. *Cf.* FRANCE, FRENCHMAN.

[F-262]

FRENCH FRIED POTATOES (frīd pə tā' tōz), *(colloq.).* (The letters "F," "F.") The right "F" hand, palm facing out or down, drops down an inch or two and moves in a short arc to the right.

[F-263]

FRENCHMAN (frĕnch' mən), *n.* See FRENCH. This is followed by the sign, MALE: The thumb and extended fingers of the right hand are brought up to grasp an imaginary cap brim.

[F–264]

FREQUENT (*adj.* frē' kwənt; *v.* frĭ kwĕnt'), -QUENTED, -QUENTING. The left hand, open in the "5" position, palm up, is held before the chest. The right hand, in the right-angle position, fingers pointing up, arches over and into the left palm. This is repeated several times. *Cf.* OFTEN.

[F–265]

FRESH 1 (frĕsh), *(colloq.), adj.* (A saucy and provoking gesture, similar to slapping one in the face with a glove.) The back of the right hand, moving up, slaps the open left palm, which is facing right. It continues its upward movement after the slap.

[F–266]

FRESH 2, *(colloq.), adj.* (The thoughts are directed downward toward someone, in an abrasive manner.) The curved right index finger rests on the right temple. The right hand is then thrown down so that the index finger, still curved, now points down. The right hand may then be raised slightly and flung down an inch or two again.

[F–267]

FRET (frĕt), *v.,* FRETTED, FRETTING, *n.* (A clouding over; a troubling.) Both "B" hands, palms facing each other, are rotated alternately before the fore-

head. *Cf.* ANNOY 2, ANNOYANCE 2, ANXIOUS 2, BOTHER 2, CONCERN 1, PROBLEM 1, TROUBLE, WORRIED, WORRY 1.

[F–268]

FRIDAY (frī' dĭ), *n.* (The letter "F.") The right "F" hand, palm out, describes a small clockwise circle.

[F–269]

FRIEND (frĕnd), *n.* (Locked together in friendship.) The right and left hands are interlocked at the index fingers. The hands separate, change their relative positions, and come together again as before. *Cf.* FRIENDSHIP.

[F–270]

FRIENDLY (frĕnd' lĭ), *adj.* (A crinkling-up of the face.) Both hands, in the "5" position, palms facing back, are placed on either side of the face. The fingers wiggle back and forth, while a pleasant, happy expression is worn. *Cf.* AMIABLE, CHEERFUL, CORDIAL, JOLLY, PLEASANT.

[F-271]

FRIENDSHIP (frĕnd′ ship), *n*. See FRIEND.

[F-272]

FRIGHT (frīt), *n*. (The heart is suddenly covered with fear.) Both hands, fingers together, are placed side by side, palms facing the chest. They quickly open and come together over the heart, one on top of the other. *Cf.* AFRAID, COWARD, FEAR 1, FRIGHTEN, SCARE(D), TERROR 1.

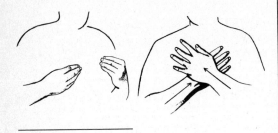

[F-273]

FRIGHTEN (frī′ tən), *v.*, -TENED, -TENING. See FRIGHT.

[F-274]

FRIGID (frĭj′ ĭd), *adj*. (The trembling from cold.) Both "S" hands, palms facing, are placed at the sides of the body. In this position the arms and hands shiver. *Cf.* CHILLY, COLD 1, SHIVER 1, WINTER 1.

[F-275]

FRIVOLOUS (frĭv′ ə ləs), *adj*. (Light thoughts.) The right index finger touches mid-forehead, as in THINK, *q.v.* The upturned open hands then move lightly up and down, as if carrying a light object.

[F-276]

FROCK (frŏk), *n*. (Draping the clothes on the body.) With fingertips resting on the chest, both hands move down simultaneously. The action is repeated. *Cf.* CLOTHES, CLOTHING, DRESS, GARMENT, GOWN, SHIRT, SUIT, WEAR 1.

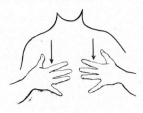

[F-277]

FROG 1 (frŏg), *n*. (The emission of the frog's croak.) The curved index and middle fingers of the right "V" hand, palm facing the body, are placed at the throat. The hand moves out and away from the throat as the "V" fingers open a bit. The palm may also face out from the body.

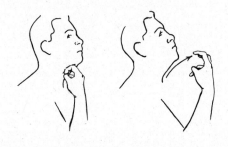

[F-278]

FROG 2, *n*. (The croaking and the action of the legs in leaping.) The right "V" hand is placed at the throat, as in FROG 1. Then the downturned "V" hands, fingers bent at the knuckles and the left behind the right, "leap" forward simultaneously, and the curved fingers open as they do.

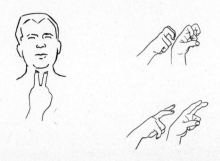

[F–279]

FROLIC (frŏl' ĭk), *v.,* -ICKED, -ICKING (Shaking tambourines.) The "Y" hands, held aloft, are shaken back and forth, pivoted at the wrists. *Cf.* PLAY 1, RECREATION.

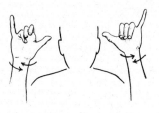

[F–280]

FROM (frŏm), *prep.* (The "away from" action is indicated.) The knuckle of the right "X" finger is placed against the base of the left "D" or "X" finger, and then moved away in a slight curve toward the body.

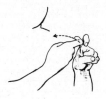

[F–281]

FROM THEN ON, *adv. phrase.* (From a point forward.) The right-angle hands are held before the chest, palms facing the body, the right hand resting against the back of the left. The right hand moves straight forward several inches. *Cf.* THENCEFORTH.

[F–282]

FRONT (frŭnt), *n.* (The front of the hand is indicated.) The right "5" hand is held palm facing out,

and the left index finger is placed in it. The hand positions may be reversed.

[F–283]

FROWN (froun), *n., v.,* FROWNED, FROWNING. (The features, and the dropping of the head.) The right hand is held palm in front of the face, fingers somewhat curved and pointing to the face. A frowning expression is assumed, as the hand moves forward and down a bit, and the head drops slightly.

[F–284]

FROZEN (frō' zən), *adj.* (The stiff fingers.) The fingers of the "5" hands, held palms down, stiffen and contract. *Cf.* FREEZE, ICE, RIGID.

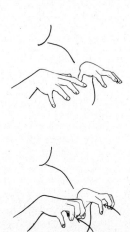

[F–285]

FRUIT (frōōt), *n.* (The growth and the shape.) The sign for GROW is made: The right hand, palm facing the body and fingers touching the thumb, is thrust up through the closed left hand, opening into the "5" position as it emerges. The right hand is then placed over the left "O" hand, whose fingers point to the right. The right hand is drawn toward the right, closing into the "O" position.

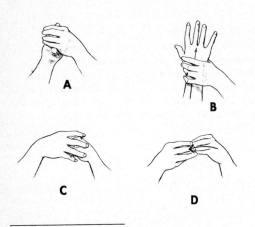

A

B

C

D

[F–286]

FRUSTRATED (frŭs′ trāt ĭd), *adj.* (Coming up against a wall; a door is slammed in the face.) The open right hand is brought up sharply, and its back strikes the mouth and nose. The head moves back a bit at the same time. *Cf.* DISAPPOINTED 2.

[F–287]

FRY (frī), *v.,* FRIED, FRYING. (The frying pan is held and its contents turned over.) The left hand holds the handle of an imaginary frying pan. The open right hand, held palm up on the same level as the left hand and representing a spatula, turns over.

[F–288]

FULL 1 (fŏŏl), *adj.* (Wiping off the top of a container, to indicate its condition of fullness.) The downturned open right hand wipes across the index finger edge of the left "S" hand, whose palm faces right. The movement of the right hand is toward the body. *Cf.* COMPLETE 2, FILL.

[F–289]

FULL 2, *adj., adv.* (Full—up to the chin.) The downturned open right hand moves up until its back comes into contact with the underside of the chin. The signer assumes an expression of annoyance. *Cf.* FED UP.

[F–290]

FUN (fŭn), *n.* (The wrinkled nose—indicative of laughter or fun.) The index and middle fingers of the right "U" hand, whose palm faces the body, are placed on the nose. The right hand swings down in an arc and, palm down, the "U" fingers strike their left counterparts on the downturned left "U" hand, and either stop at that point or continue on.

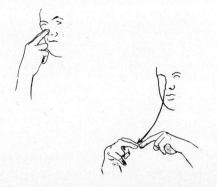

[F-291]

FUNCTION (fŭngk' shən), *n., v.,* -TIONED, -TION-ING. (The letter "F"; sharpening through usage.) The base of the right "F" hand moves back and forth along the outstretched, left index finger, describing a short arc as it moves.

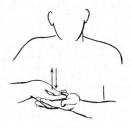

[F-292]

FUNDS (fŭndz), *n. pl.* (Slapping of paper money in the palm.) The upturned right hand, grasping some imaginary bills, is brought down into the upturned left palm a number of times. *Cf.* CAPITAL 2, CURRENCY, FINANCES, MONEY 1.

[F-293]

FUNERAL (fū' nər əl), *n.* (Rows of people marching behind the hearse.) Both "V" hands, palms out and the left behind the right, move forward in unison, in a series of short upward-arced motions. *Cf.* PARADE 1, PROCESSION.

[F-294]

FUNNY (fŭn' ĭ), *adj.* (The nose wrinkles in laughter.) The tips of the right index and middle fingers brush repeatedly off the tip of the nose. *Cf.* COMIC, COMICAL, HUMOR, HUMOROUS.

[F-295]

FURTHER 1 (fûr' thər), *comparative adj. and adv.* The sign for FAR is made: The "A" hands are held together, thumbs pointing away from the body. The right hand moves straight ahead in a slight arc. The left hand does not move. This is followed by the sign for the comparative suffix -ER: The "A" hand, thumb extended upward, is raised slightly. *Cf.* FARTHER.

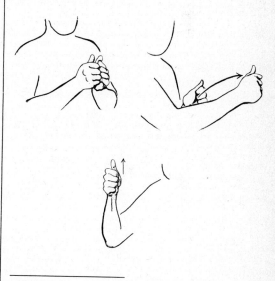

[F-296]

FURTHER 2, *comparative adv. and adj., v.* (One hand is added to the other; an addition.) Both hands, palms facing, are held fingers together, the left a bit above the right. The right hand is brought up to the left until their fingertips touch. *Cf.* ADD 4, BESIDES, MORE, MOREOVER 2.

[F-297]

FURTHEST (fûr' thĭst), *superlative adj. and adv.*
The sign for FAR, as in FURTHER, is made. This
is followed by the sign for the superlative suffix,
-EST: The right "A" hand, thumb pointing up,
quickly moves straight upward, until it is above the
head. *Cf.* FARTHEST.

[F-298]

FURY (fyŏŏr' ĭ), *n.* (A violent welling-up of the
emotions.) The curved fingers of the right hand are
placed in the center of the chest, and fly up suddenly
and violently. An expression of anger is worn. *Cf.*

ANGER, ANGRY 2, ENRAGE, INDIGNANT, INDIGNA-
TION, IRE, MAD 1, RAGE.

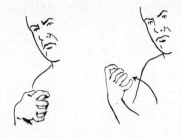

[F-299]

FUTURE (fū' chər), *n.* (Something ahead or in the
future.) The upright, open right hand, palm facing
left, moves straight out and slightly up from a position beside the right temple. *Cf.* BY AND BY, IN THE
FUTURE, LATER 2, LATER ON, SHALL, WILL 1,
WOULD.

G

GAGE (gāj), *(voc.)*, *n.* (The natural sign.) The curved index finger and thumb of the right "5" hand close carefully and deliberately against the edges of the left index finger, as if measuring its thickness. *Cf.* CALIPER, MICROMETER.

GAIETY 1 (gā' ə tǐ), *n.* (The heart is stirred; the spirits bubble up.) The open right hand, palm facing the body, strikes the heart repeatedly, moving up and off the heart after each strike. *CF.* DELIGHT, GAY, GLAD, HAPPINESS HAPPY, JOY, MERRY.

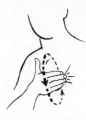

GAIETY 2, *n.* (The swinging of tambourines.) Both open hands, held somewhat above the head, are pivoted back and forth repeatedly, as if swinging a pair of tambourines. *Cf.* PARTY 1.

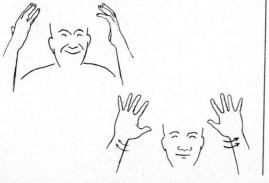

GAIN 1 (gān), *v.*, GAINED, GAINING. (Adding on.) The index and middle fingers of the right "H" hand, palm up, are swung up and over until they come to rest on the index and middle fingers of the left "H" hand, held palm down. *Cf.* ADD 3, ADDITION, EXTEND 1, EXTRA, INCREASE, ON TO, RAISE 2.

GAIN 2, *n.*, *v.* (To get a profit; a coin popped into the vest pocket.) The sign for GET is made: Both outstretched hands, held in a grasping "5" position, close into "S" positions, with the right on top of the left. At the same time both hands are drawn in to the body. The thumb and index finger of the right hand, holding an imaginary coin, are then popped into an imaginary vest or breast pocket. Note: the sign for GET is sometimes omitted. *Cf.* BENEFIT 2, PROFIT.

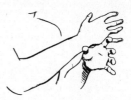

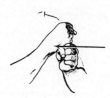

[G–6]

GALE (gāl), *n.* (The blowing back and forth of the wind.) The "5" hands, palms facing and held up before the body, sway gracefully back and forth, in unison. The cheeks meanwhile are puffed up and the breath is being expelled. The nature of the swaying movement—graceful and slow, fast and violent, etc.—determines the type of wind. The strength of exhalation is also a qualifying device. *Cf.* BLOW 1, BREEZE, STORM, WIND.

[G–7]

GALLAUDET, EDWARD MINER, *n.* (The sign for the first president of Gallaudet College.) The right "M" hand, palm facing the body and fingers pointing left, moves from the left shoulder to the right. *Cf.* MEMBER 2.

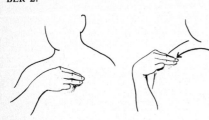

[G–8]

GALLAUDET, THOMAS HOPKINS, *n.* (The sign for the founder of the first permanent school for the deaf in the United States, after whom Gallaudet College was named. He wore eyeglasses and was the father of Edward Miner Gallaudet.) The thumb and index finger of the right hand, placed flat against the right temple, move back toward the right ear, tracing the line formed by the eyeglass frame. *Cf.* EYEGLASSES, GLASSES, SPECTACLES.

[G–9]

GALLEY (găl' ĭ), *(voc.), n.* (The shape of the galley or of the galley proof.) Both downturned open hands rest on the edges of an imaginary galley frame. The left hand moves forward, tracing the elongated shape of the frame.

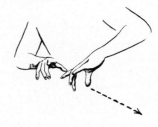

[G–10]

GAMBLE (găm' bəl), *n., v.,* -BLED, -BLING. (The shaking and throwing of the dice.) The upturned right "A" hand shakes a pair of imaginary dice and throws them out. *Cf.* DICE.

[G–11]

GAME (gām), *n., v.,* GAMED, GAMING. (Two individuals pitted against each other.) The hands are held in the "A" position, thumbs pointing straight up, palms facing the body. They come together forcefully, moving down a bit as they do, and the knuckles of one hand strike those of the other. *Cf.* CHALLENGE, OPPORTUNITY 2, VERSUS.

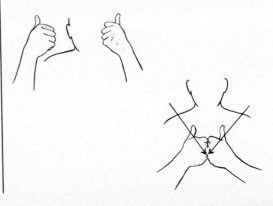

[G-12]

GANG (găng), *n.* (A grouping together.) Both "C" hands, palms facing, are held a few inches apart at chest height. They are swung around in unison, so that the palms now face the body. *Cf.* ASSOCIATION, AUDIENCE 1, CASTE, CIRCLE 2, CLASS, CLASSED 1, CLUB, COMPANY, FAMILY 2, GROUP 1, JOIN 2, ORGANIZATION 1.

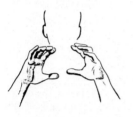

[G-13]

GARDEN (gär′ dən), *n.* (A fenced-in enclosure.) The "5" hands are held with palms facing the body and fingers interlocked but not curved. The hands separate, swinging first to either side of the body, and then moving in toward the body, tracing a circle and coming together palms out and bases touching. *Cf.* FIELD 2, YARD 2.

[G-14]

GARMENT (gär′ mənt), *n.* (Draping the clothes on the body.) With fingertips resting on the chest, both hands move down simultaneously. The action is repeated. *Cf.* CLOTHES, CLOTHING, DRESS, FROCK, GOWN, SHIRT, SUIT, WEAR 1.

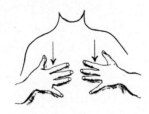

[G-15]

GAS 1 (găs), *n.* (The emission and the foul smell.) The upturned right index finger and thumb, in con-

tact with each other, move up through the hole formed by the left "F" hand. The right hand then grasps the tip of the nose. The signer assumes an appropriate expression to indicate the foulness of the odor. Another sign involves the left hand resting on top of the right, whose fingers open and close.

[G-16]

GAS 2, *n.* (The act of pouring gasoline into an automobile tank.) The thumb of the right "A" hand is placed into the hole formed by the left "O" hand. *Cf.* GASOLINE, POUR.

[G-17]

GASOLINE (găs′ ə lēn′, găs ə lēn′), *n.* See GAS 2.

[G-18]

GATE (gāt), *n.* (The natural sign.) The fingertips of both open hands touch each other before the body, palms toward the chest, thumbs pointing upward. Then the right fingers swing forward and back to their original position several times, imitating the movement of a gate opening and closing.

[G–19]

GATHER 1 (găth′ ər), v., -ERED, -ERING. (A gathering together.) The right "5" hand, fingers curved and palm facing left, sweeps across and over the upturned left palm, several times, in a circular movement. Cf. ACCUMULATE 2, GATHERING TOGETHER.

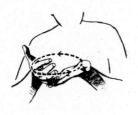

[G–20]

GATHER 2, v. (Assemble all together.) Both "5" hands, palms facing, are held with fingers pointing out from the body. With a sweeping motion they are brought in toward the chest, and all fingertips come together. This is repeated. Cf. ACCUMULATE 3, ASSEMBLE, ASSEMBLY, CONFERENCE, CONVENE, CONVENTION, GATHERING, MEETING 1.

[G–21]

GATHERING (găth′ ər ĭng), n. See GATHER 2.

[G–22]

GATHERING TOGETHER, phrase. See GATHER 1.

[G–23]

GAUGE (gāj), n., v., GAUGED, GAUGING. (The act of measuring a short distance.) Both "Y" hands, palms out, move alternately a short distance back and forth, away from and toward each other. Cf. MEASURE, SCALE 1.

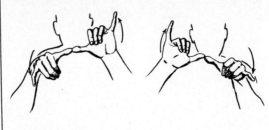

[G–24]

GAY (gā), adj. (The heart is stirred; the spirits bubble up.) The open right hand, palm facing the body, strikes the heart repeatedly, moving up and off the heart after each strike. Cf. DELIGHT, GAIETY 1, GLAD, HAPPINESS HAPPY, JOY, MERRY.

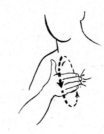

[G–25]

GAZE (gāz), v., GAZED, GAZING, n. (The vision is directed forward.) The tips of the right "V" fingers point to the eyes. The right hand is then swung around and forward a bit. Cf. LOOK AT, OBSERVE 1, WITNESS.

[G–26]

GENERATION (jĕn′ ə rā′ shən), n. (Persons descending, one after another, from an original or early person.) The downturned cupped hands are positioned one above the other at the right shoulder. They roll over each other as they move alternately downward and a bit away from the body. This sign is used only when talking about people.

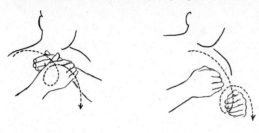

[G–27]

GENEROUS 1 (jĕn′ ər əs), *adj.* (The heart rolls out.) Both right-angle hands roll over each other as they move down and away from their initial position at the heart. *Cf.* BENEVOLENT, GENTLE 1, GENTLENESS, GRACIOUS, HUMANE, KIND 1, KINDNESS, MERCY 1, TENDER 3.

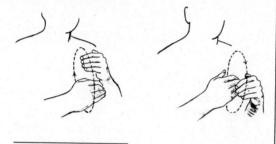

[G–28]

GENEROUS 2, *adj.* (The heart is encircled and its largeness indicated.) The right index finger traces a circle around the heart. The two "L" hands, held palms out and thumbs pointing at each other, then move apart from their initial position in front of the chest.

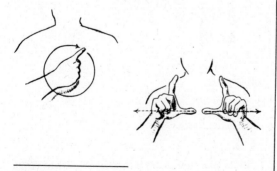

[G–29]

GENTILE (jĕn′ tīl), *n.* The sign for NOT 2 is made: The right "A" hand is placed with the tip of the

upturned thumb under the chin. The hand draws out and forward in a slight arc. This is followed by the sign for JEWISH: The fingers and thumb of each hand, are placed at the chin, and stroke an imaginary beard.

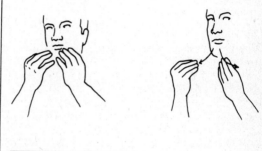

[G–30]

GENTLE 1 (jĕn′ təl), *adj.* See GENEROUS 1.

[G–31]

GENTLE 2, *(rare), adj.* (A gesture indicating peace and quiet.) The left index finger is held at the lips. The left right-angle hand then moves rather slowly down and under the right right-angle hand.

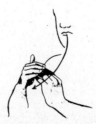

[G-32]

GENTLEMAN (jĕn' təl mən), *n.* (A fine or polite man.) The MALE prefix sign is made: The right hand grasps the edge of an imaginary cap. The sign for POLITE is then made: The thumb of the right "5" hand is placed slowly and deliberately on the right side of the chest.

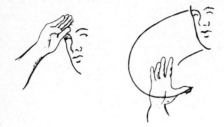

[G-33]

GENTLENESS (jĕn' təl nĭs), *n.* See GENEROUS 1.

[G-34]

GENUINE (jĕn' yŏo in), *adj.* (Coming forth directly from the lips; true.) The index finger of the right "D" hand, palm facing left, is placed against the lips. It moves up an inch or two and then describes a small arc forward and away from the lips. *Cf.* ABSOLUTE, ABSOLUTELY, ACTUAL, ACTUALLY, AUTHENTIC, CERTAIN, CERTAINLY, FAITHFUL 3, FIDELITY, FRANKLY, INDEED, POSITIVE 1, POSITIVELY, REAL, REALLY, SINCERE 2, SURE, SURELY, TRUE, TRULY, TRUTH, VALID, VERILY.

[G-35]

GEOGRAPHY (jĭ ŏg' rə ĭ), *n.* (The earth and its axis are indicated.) The downturned left "S" hand indicates the earth. The thumb and index finger of the downturned right "5" hand are placed at each edge of the left. In this position the right hand swings back and forth, while maintaining contact with the left. *Cf.* EARTH 1, GLOBE 1, PLANET.

[G-36]

GEOMETRY (jĭ ŏm' ə trĭ), *n.* (The "G" hands; multiplying or calculating.) The "G" hands, palms facing each other, are crossed at the wrists repeatedly.

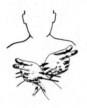

[G-37]

GERMAN (jûr' mən), *adj.* (The double eagle emblem of the old German empire.) The hands are held crossed at the wrists, with the right facing left and the left facing right. The fingers wiggle to indicate the ruffled feathers of the eagle. *Cf.* GERMANY.

[G-38]

GERMANY (jûr' mə nĭ), *n.* See GERMAN.

[G-39]

GET (gĕt), *v.,* GOT, GOTTEN, GETTING. (A grasping and bringing forward to oneself.) Both hands, in the "5" position, fingers curved, are crossed at the wrists, with the left palm facing right and the right palm facing left. They are brought in toward the

chest, while closing into a grasping "S" position. *Cf.*
ACQUIRE, OBTAIN, PROCURE, RECEIVE.

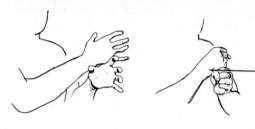

[G–40]

GET OFF (ôf, ŏf), *v. phrase.* (The legs are withdrawn
from a conveyance.) The curved index and middle
fingers of the right hand are withdrawn from the cup
formed by the left "O" hand.

[G–41]

GET READY (rĕd′ ĭ), *v. phrase.* (The "R" hands.)
The same sign as for READY 1, *q.v.,* is made, except
that the "R" hands are used. With palms facing
down, they move simultaneously from left to right.
Cf. READY 3.

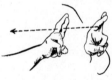

[G–42]

GET UP (ŭp), *v. phrase.* (Getting onto one's feet.)
The upturned index and middle fingers of the right
hand, representing the legs, are swung up and over
in an arc, coming to rest in the upturned left palm.
Cf. ARISE 2, ELEVATE, RAISE 1, RISE 1, STAND 2,
STAND UP.

[G–43]

GHOST (gōst), *n.* (Something thin and filmy, *i.e.,*
ephemeral.) The hands are held palms facing, with
one above the other and index fingers and thumbs
touching and almost connected. As the upper hand
moves straight up, the index fingers and thumbs of
both hands slowly come together, giving the impression of drawing out a thread or other thin substance.
Cf. SOUL, SPIRIT.

[G–44]

GIFT (gĭft), n. (A giving of something.) Both "A"
hands, with index fingers somewhat draped over the
tips of the thumbs, are held palms facing in front of
the chest. They are pivoted forward and down, in
unison, from the wrists. *Cf.* AWARD, BEQUEATH,
BESTOW, CONFER, CONSIGN, CONTRIBUTE, PRE-
SENT 2.

[G-45]

GIRAFFE (jə răf'), *n.* (The elongated neck.) Both hands grasp the neck, the left on top of the right, or vice versa. The upper hand moves up above the head, describing the long neck.

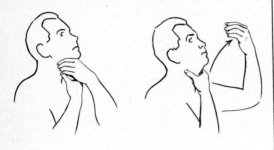

[G-46]

GIRL (gûrl), *n.* (A female who is small.) The FE-MALE root sign is given: The thumb of the right "A" hand moves down along the line of the right jaw, from ear almost to chin. This outlines the string used to tie ladies' bonnets in olden days. The down-turned open right hand is then held at waist level, indicating the short height of the female. *Cf.* MAIDEN.

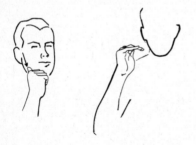

[G-47]

GIVE 1 (gĭv), *v.*, GAVE, GIVEN, GIVING. (The hands move forward and open.) Both hands are held palms up or down, about a foot apart, thumbs resting on fingertips. The hands are extended forward in a slight arc, opening to the "5" position as they do. *Cf.* EXTEND 2.

[G-48]

GIVE 2, *v.* (Holding something and extending it toward someone.) The right "O" hand is held before the right shoulder and then moved outward in an arc, away from the body.

[G-49]

GIVE ASSISTANCE (ə sĭs' təns), *v. phrase.* (Helping up; supporting.) The left "S" hand, thumb side up, rests in the open right palm. In this position the left hand is pushed up a short distance by the right. *Cf.* AID, ASSIST, ASSISTANCE, BENEFIT 1, BOOST, HELP.

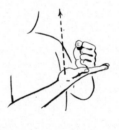

[G-50]

GIVE ATTENTION (TO) (ə tĕn' shən), *v. phrase.* (Directing one's attention forward; applying oneself; concentrating.) Both hands, fingers pointing up and together, are held at the sides of the face. They move straight out from the face. *Cf.* APPLY 2, ATTEND (TO), ATTENTION, CONCENTRATE, CONCENTRATION, FOCUS, MIND 2, PAY ATTENTION (TO).

[G–51]

GIVE ME (mē), *v. phrase.* (Extending the hand toward oneself.) This sign is a reversal of GIVE 2.

[G–52]

GIVE UP (gĭv ŭp′), *v. phrase.* (Throwing up the hands in a gesture of surrender.) Both "A" hands are held palms down before the chest and then thrown up in unison, ending in the "5" position. *Cf.* ABDICATE, CEDE, DISCOURAGE 1, FORFEIT, LOSE HOPE, RELINQUISH, RENOUNCE, RENUNCIATION, SURRENDER 1, YIELD.

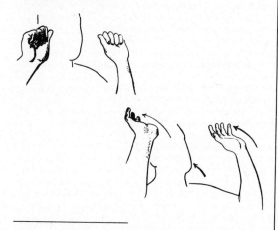

[G–53]

GLAD (glăd), *adj.* (The heart is stirred; the spirits bubble up.) The open right hand, palm facing the body, strikes the heart repeatedly, moving up and off the heart after each strike. *Cf.* DELIGHT, GAIETY 1, GAY, HAPPINESS, HAPPY, JOY, MERRY.

[G–54]

GLASS 1 (glăs, gläs), *n.* (The finger touches a brittle substance.) The index finger is brought up to touch the exposed front teeth. *Cf.* BONE, CHINA 2, DISH, PLATE, PORCELAIN.

[G–55]

GLASS 2, *n.* (The shape of a drinking glass.) The little finger edge of the right "C" hand rests in the upturned left palm. The right hand moves straight up a few inches, tracing the shape of a drinking glass.

[G–56]

GLASSES (glăs′ əs), *n. pl.* (The shape.) The thumb and index finger of the right hand, placed flat against the right temple, move back toward the right ear, tracing the line formed by the eyeglass frame. *Cf.* EYEGLASSES; GALLAUDET, THOMAS HOPKINS; SPECTACLES.

GLISTEN (glis′ ən), *v.*, -TENED, -TENING. (Reflected glistening of light rays.) The left hand, held supinely before the chest, palm down, represents the object from which the rays glisten. The right hand, in the "5" position, touches the back of the left lightly and moves up toward the right, pivoting slightly at the wrist, with fingers wiggling. *Cf.* BRIGHT 2, SHINE, SHINING.

GLOBE 1 (glōb), *n.* (The earth and its axes are indicated.) The downturned left "S" hand indicates the earth. The thumb and index finger of the downturned right "5" hand are placed at each edge of the left. In this position the right hand swings back and forth, while maintaining contact with the left. *Cf.* EARTH 1, GEOGRAPHY, PLANET.

GLOBE 2, *n.* (The letter "W," for WORLD, in orbit.) The right "W" hand makes a complete circle around the left "W" hand and comes to rest on the thumb edge of the left "W" hand. The left hand frequently assumes the "S" position instead of the "W," to represent the stationary sun. *Cf.* WORLD.

GLOOM (glōōm), *n.* (The facial features drop.) Both "5" hands, palms facing the eyes and fingers slightly curved, drop simultaneously to a level with the mouth. The head drops slightly as the hands move down, and an expression of sadness is assumed. *Cf.* DEJECTED, DEPRESSION, GLOOMY, GRAVE 3, GRIEF 1, MELANCHOLY, MOURNFUL, SAD, SORROWFUL 1.

GLOOMY (glōō′ mĭ), *adj.* See GLOOM.

GLORIOUS 1 (glōr′ ĭ əs), *adj.* See GLORY 1.

GLORIOUS 2, *adj.* (With glory.) The sign for WITH is made: Both "A" hands, knuckles together and thumbs up, are moved forward in unison, away from the chest. This is followed by the sign for GLORY 1.

GLORY 1 (glōr′ ĭ), *n.* (The letter "G"; scintillating or shining.) The right "G" hand moves in a clockwise circle, or is simply held stationary, above the downturned left "S" or "A" hand. The right hand then opens into the "5" position, palm facing the left

hand, and moves up in a deliberate wavy motion. *Cf.*
GLORIOUS 1.

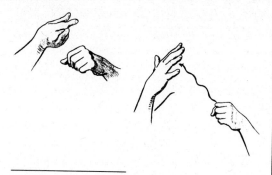

[G-65]

GLORY 2, *(rare), n.* (A modification of GLORY 1.)
The hands are clasped, and then both separate into
the "5" position, palms facing, with the right hand
moving up in a deliberate wavy motion, pivoted at
the wrist.

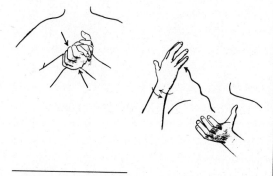

[G-66]

GLOVES (glŭvz), *n. pl.* (The natural sign.) The right
hand goes through the natural motions of smoothing
a glove over the left fingers.

[G-67]

GLUE (glōō), *n.* (The spreading and pressing together of the glued parts.) The index and middle
fingers of the right "U" hand spread imaginary glue

on the upturned left palm. Both hands, in the "5"
position, are then pressed firmly together.

[G-68]

GLUTTONY (glŭt' ə nĭ), *n.* (Stuffing the mouth with
both hands.) Both hands stuff the wide open mouth
simultaneously with imaginary food. The action is
repeated a number of times.

[G-69]

GO 1 (gō), *v.,* WENT, GONE, GOING. (Continuous
motion forward.) With palms facing each other, the
index fingers of the "D" hands revolve around each
other as both hands move forward.

[G-70]

GO 2, *interj., v.* (The natural sign.) The right index
finger is flung out, as a command to go. A stern
expression is usually assumed.

[G–71]

GO AHEAD (ə hĕd′), *v. phrase.* (Moving forward.) Both right-angle hands, palms facing each other and knuckles facing forward, move forward simultaneously. *Cf.* FORWARD, MOTION FORWARD, ONWARD, PROCEED, PROGRESS 2, RESUME.

[G–72]

GOAL (gōl), *n.* (A thought directed upward, toward a goal.) The left "D" hand, palm facing the body, is held above the head, to represent the goal. The index finger of the right "D" hand, after touching the forehead (modified sign for THINK, *q. v.*), moves slowly and deliberately up to the tip of the left index finger. *Cf.* AIM, AMBITION, ASPIRE, OBJECTIVE, PERSEVERE 4, PURPOSE 2.

[G–73]

GOAT (gōt), *n.* (The beard and horns.) The bent right "V" fingers rest at the chin, then move up to

the forehead. From there they move backward over the head a bit, to describe the sweep of the horns.

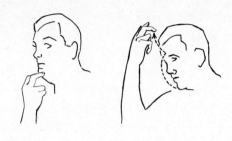

[G–74]

GO BY (bī), *v. phrase.* (One hand passes the other.) Both "A" hands, palms facing each other, are held before the body, the right behind the left. The right hand moves forward, its knuckles brushing those of the left, and continues forward a bit beyond the left. *Cf.* ELAPSE, PASS 1.

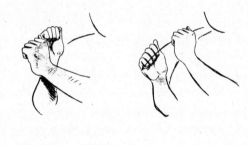

[G–75]

GOD (gŏd), *n.* (A motion indicating the One above.) The right open hand, palm facing left, swings up above the head, and is then moved down about an inch. The signer looks up while making the sign. *Cf.* LORD 2.

[G–76]

GODFATHER (gŏd′ fä′ t͟hər), *n.* (FATHER, RESPONSIBLE 1.) The sign for FATHER 1 is made:

The thumb and extended fingers of the right hand are brought up to grasp an imaginary cap brim, representing the tipping of caps by men in olden days. Both hands are then held open and palms facing up, as if holding a baby. This is followed by the sign for RESPONSIBLE 1: The fingertips of both hands, placed on the right shoulder, bear down.

[G–78]

GO DOWN, *v. phrase.* (The natural motion.) Both extended index fingers point downward as the hands move forward and down in an arc.

[G–79]

GOGGLES (gŏg′ əlz), *n. pl.* (The natural sign.) The "C" hands are held in front of the eyes. *Cf.* BINOCULARS, OPERA GLASSES.

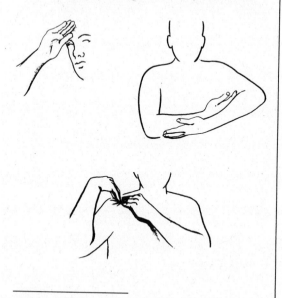

[G–77]

GODMOTHER (gŏd′ mŭth′ ər), *n.* (MOTHER, RESPONSIBLE 1.) The sign for MOTHER 1 is made: The thumb of the right "A" hand moves down along the line of the right jaw, from ear almost to chin. Both hands are then held open and palms facing up, as if holding a baby. This is followed by the sign for RESPONSIBLE 1: The fingertips of both hands, placed on the right shoulder, bear down.

[G–80]

GOLD (gōld), *n.* (Yellow earrings, *i.e.,* gold, which was discovered in California.) The earlobe is pinched, and then the sign for YELLOW is made: The "Y" hand, pivoted at the wrist, is shaken back and forth repeatedly. *Cf.* CALIFORNIA.

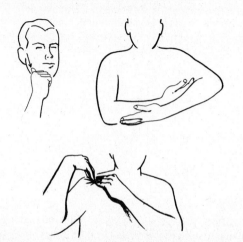

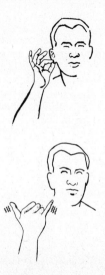

[G–81]

GOLF (gŏlf, gôlf), *n.* (The natural sign.) Holding an imaginary club, the signer goes through the deliberate motions of taking aim at the ball. The club may also be swung, but this is not necessary.

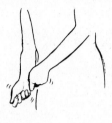

[G–82]

GONE 1 (gôn, gŏn), *adj.* (A disappearance.) The right open hand, palm facing the body, is held by the left hand and is drawn down and out, ending in a position with fingers drawn together. The left hand, meanwhile, may close into a position with fingers also drawn together. *Cf.* ABSENCE 1, ABSENT 1, DEPLETE, DISAPPEAR, EMPTY 1, EXTINCT, FADE AWAY, MISSING 1, OMISSION 1, OUT 3, OUT OF, VANISH.

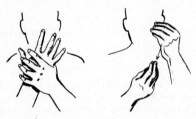

[G–83]

GONE 2, *adj.* (A wiping-off motion, to indicate a condition of no longer being present.) The little finger edge of the "5" hand, held palm facing the body, rests on the back of the downturned left hand. The right hand moves straight forward suddenly, closing into the "S" position, palm still facing the body. *Cf.* EXHAUSTED.

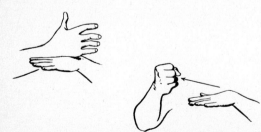

[G–84]

GONE 3, *(sl.)*, *adj.* (A modification of GONE 2, indicating a disappearance into the distance. The narrowing perspective is the main feature here.) The right "L" hand, resting on the back of the downturned left hand, moves straight forward suddenly. As it does, the index finger and thumb come together.

[G–85]

GOOD 1 (good), *adj.* (Tasting something, approving it, and offering it forward.) The fingertips of the right "5" hand are placed at the lips. The right hand then moves out and into a palm-up position on the upturned left palm. *Cf.* WELL 1.

[G–86]

GOOD 2, *(colloq.)*, *adj., interj.* (Thumbs up!) The right "A" hand is held with thumb pointing straight up. The right hand moves forward and out about an inch. This motion may be repeated.

[G–87]

GOODBYE 1 (good′ bī′), *interj., n.* (Words extended politely from the mouth.) The fingertips of the right

"5" hand are placed at the mouth. The hand moves away from the mouth to a palm-up position before the body. The signer meanwhile usually nods smilingly. *Cf.* FAREWELL 1, HELLO 1, THANKS, THANK YOU, YOU'RE WELCOME 1.

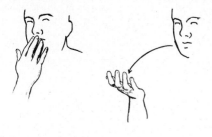

[G–88]

GOODBYE 2, *interj.* (A wave of the hand.) The right open hand waves back and forth several times. *Cf.* FAREWELL 2, HELLO 2, SO LONG.

[G–89]

GOOD ENOUGH (ĭ nŭf'), *adj. phrase.* (Just a quick touch or taste.) The tip of the middle finger of the right "5" hand, palm facing the body, is placed at the lips. The hand is then flung a few inches away from the mouth, into a position with palm facing left. *Cf.* MAKESHIFT.

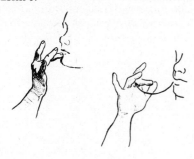

[G–90]

GO OFF THE TRACK, *v. phrase.* (The natural motion.) The "G" hands are held side by side and touching, palms down, index fingers pointing forward. Then the right hand moves forward, curving toward the right side as it does. *Cf.* DEFLECT, DEVIATE 2, STRAY, WANDER 1.

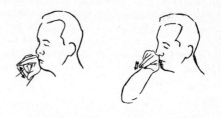

[G–91]

GOOSE (gōōs), *n.* (The broad bill.) The right hand is held with its back resting against the mouth. The thumb, index and middle fingers come together repeatedly, indicating the opening and closing of a broad bill. *Cf.* DUCK.

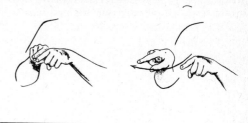

[G–92]

GOSPEL 1 (gŏs' pəl), *n.* (The unraveling or stretching out of words or sentences.) Both open hands are held close to each other, with fingers open and palms facing and almost touching. As the hands are drawn apart, the thumb and index finger of each hand come together to form circles. This is repeated several times. *Cf.* DESCRIBE 2, EXPLAIN 2, FABLE, FICTION, NARRATE, NARRATIVE, STORY 1, TALE, TELL ABOUT.

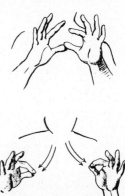

[G-93]

GOSPEL 2, *n.* (GOOD NEWS.) The sign for GOOD is made: The fingertips of the right "5" hand are placed at the lips. The right hand then moves out and into a palm-up position on the upturned left palm. This is followed by the sign for NEWS: With both hands held palms up before the body, the right hand sweeps in an arc into the left and continues up a bit.

[G-94]

GOSSIP (gŏs' əp), *n., v.,* -SIPED, -SIPING. (Mouths chattering.) Both hands are held before the face, their index fingers and thumbs extended. In this position the fingers open and close rapidly several times. The hands sometimes move back and forth.

[G-95]

GO STEADY (gō stĕd' ĭ), *(colloq.), v. phrase.* (The togetherness is emphasized.) Both "A" hands, knuckles together and thumbs up, move forward and backward in a slight shaking motion a number of times.

[G-96]

GO TO BED 1, *v. phrase.* (Laying the head on the pillow.) The head is placed on its side, in the open palm, and the eyes are closed.

[G-97]

GO TO BED 2, *(colloq.), v. phrase.* (Tucking the legs beneath the covers.) The index and middle fingers of the right "U" hand, held either palm down or palm up, are thrust into the downturned left "O" hand. *Cf.* RETIRE 2.

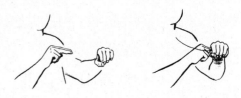

[G-98]

GOVERN (gŭv' ərn), *v.,* -ERNED, -ERNING. (Holding the reins over all.) The "A" hands, palms facing, move alternately back and forth, as if grasping and manipulating reins. The left "A" hand, still in position, swings over so that its palm now faces down. The right hand opens to the "5" position, palm down, and swings over the left which moves slightly to the right. *Cf.* AUTHORITY, CONTROL 1, DIRECT 1, MANAGE, MANAGEMENT, MANAGER, OPERATE, REGULATE, REIGN, RULE 1.

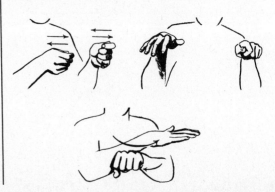

[G-99]

GOVERNMENT (gŭv′ ərn mənt, -ər-), *n.* (The head indicates the head or seat of government.) The right index finger, pointing toward the right temple, describes a small clockwise circle and comes to rest on the right temple. *Cf.* CAPITAL 1, ST. PAUL (Minn.).

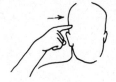

[G-100]

GOVERNOR (gŭv′ ər nər), *n.* The sign for GOVERNMENT is formed. This is followed by the sign for INDIVIDUAL: Both open hands, palms facing each other, move down the sides of the body, tracing its outline to the hips.

[G-101]

GOWN (goun), *n.* (Draping the clothes on the body.) With fingertips resting on the chest, both hands move down simultaneously. The action is repeated. *Cf.* CLOTHES, CLOTHING, DRESS, FROCK, GARMENT, SHIRT, SUIT, WEAR 1.

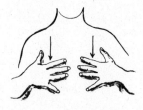

[G-102]

GRAB (grăb), *v.*, GRABBED, GRABBING, *n.* (Grasping something and holding it down.) Both hands,

palms down, quickly close into the "S" position, the right on top of the left. *Cf.* CAPTURE, CATCH 2, GRASP, SEIZE.

[G-103]

GRACE 1 (grās), *(eccles.), n.* (The blessing is bestowed on the head.) The right hand, fingers touching thumb, is held over the head. It opens to the "5" position as it comes down toward the head.

[G-104]

GRACE 2, *(eccles.), n.* (A helping grace; a shoring up.) The upturned open left hand is positioned under the little finger edge of the right "A" hand, whose palm faces the left. The left hand sweeps up, pushing the right hand up with it.

[G-105]

GRACIOUS (grā′ shəs), *adj*. (The heart rolls out.) Both right-angle hands roll over each other as they move down and away from their initial position at the heart. *Cf.* BENEVOLENT, GENEROUS 1, GENTLE 1, GENTLENESS, HUMANE, KIND 1, KINDNESS, MERCY 1, TENDER 3.

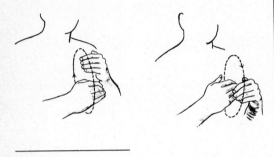

[G-106]

GRADUATE 1, (*n*. grăj′ ŏŏ ĭt; *v*. grăj′ ŏŏ āt′), -ATED, -ATING. (The letter "G"; the ribbon around the diploma.) The right "G" hand makes a single clockwise circle, and drops down into the upturned left palm.

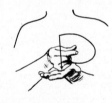

[G-107]

GRADUATE 2, (*loc.*), *adj., n., v.* (Pulling away.) The downturned open hands are held in a line, with fingers pointing to the left, the right hand behind the left. Both hands move in unison toward the right. As they do so, they assume the "A" position. *Cf.* DEPART, EVACUATE, FORSAKE 1, LEAVE 1, RETIRE 1, WITHDRAW 1.

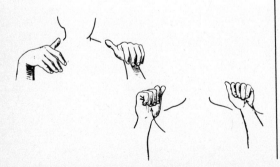

[G-108]

GRAIN (grān), *n*. The tips of the four right fingers move up and down simultaneously as they move along the left index finger from knuckle to tip. This sign is used generally for different grains. *Cf.* BEAN(S), OATMEAL, RICE.

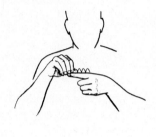

[G-109]

GRAND 1 (grănd), *adj*. (The hands gesture toward the heavens.) The "5" hands, palms out and arms raised rather high, are positioned somewhat above the line of vision. The arms move abruptly forward and up once or twice. An expression of pleasure or surprise is usually assumed. *Cf.* EXCELLENT, GREAT 3, MARVEL, MARVELOUS, MIRACLE, O!, SPLENDID 1, SWELL 1, WONDER 2, WONDERFUL 1.

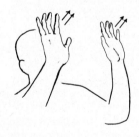

[G-110]

GRAND 2, *adj., interj.* (The feelings are titillated.) With the thumb resting on the upper part of the chest, the fingers are wiggled back and forth. *Cf.* ELEGANT, FINE 1, GREAT 4, SPLENDID 2, SWELL 2, WONDERFUL 2.

[G–111]

GRANDFATHER 1 (grănd′ fä′ ŧhər), *n.* (A male ba-by-holder; a predecessor.) The sign for **FATHER 2** is made: The thumbtip of the right "5" hand touches the right temple a number of times. Then both open hands, palms up, are extended in front of the chest, as if supporting a baby. From this position they sweep over the left shoulder. The whole sign is smooth and continuous.

[G–113]

GRANDMOTHER 1 (grănd′ mŭŧh′ ər), *n.* (Same ra-tionale as for GRANDFATHER 1.) The sign for **MOTHER 2** is made: The thumb of the right "5" hand rests on the right cheek or on the right chin bone. The rest of the sign follows that for GRAND-FATHER 1.

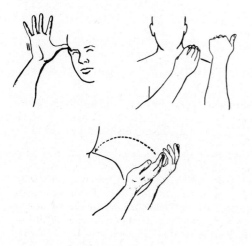

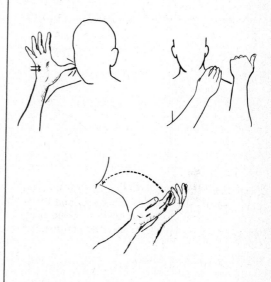

[G–112]

GRANDFATHER 2, *n.* (A variation of GRANDFA-THER 1. The "A" hands are held with the left in front of the right, and the right thumb positioned against the forehead. Both hands open into the "5" position, so that the right little finger touches or almost touches the left thumb. Both hands may, as they open, move forward an inch or two.

[G–114]

GRANDMOTHER 2, *n.* (A variation of GRAND-MOTHER 1.) The "A" hands are positioned as in GRANDFATHER 2 but with the right thumb on the right cheek. They open in the same manner as in GRANDFATHER 2.

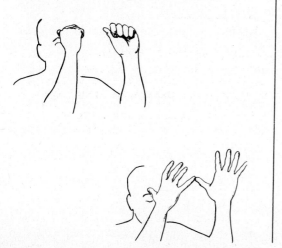

[G–115]

GRANT 1 (grănt, gränt), *v.*, GRANTED, GRANTING. (A permissive upswinging of the hands, as if giving in.) Both hands, palms facing and fingers pointing away from the body, are held at chest level, almost a foot apart. With an upward movement, using their wrists as pivots, the hands sweep up until the fingers point almost straight up. *Cf.* ALLOW, LET, LET'S, LET US, MAY 3, PERMISSION 1, PERMIT 1, TOLERATE 1.

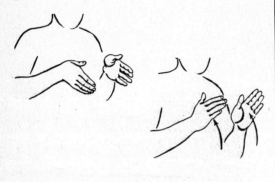

[G–116]

GRANT 2, *v.* The modified "O" hand, little finger edge down, moves forward and down in an arc before the body, as if giving something to someone.

[G–117]

GRAPES 1 (grāps), *n. pl.* (A clump of the fruit is outlined.) The curved right fingertips move along the back of the downturned open left hand, from wrist to knuckles, in a series of short, up-down, curved movements, outlining a clump of grapes.

[G–118]

GRAPES 2, *n pl.* (A variation of GRAPES 1.) The thumb and index fingers of the right "Q" hand execute the same movement as in GRAPES 1.

[G–119]

GRAPEVINE (grāp' vīn´), *n.* (The climbing and spreading of a vine.) The right "G" hand, palm out, with thumb and index finger pointing straight up, moves up in a wavy manner. Both "5" hands, palms out and thumbtips almost touching, then move up and apart. *Cf.* VINE.

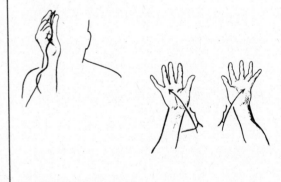

[G–120]

GRASP (grăsp, gräsp), *v.*, GRASPED, GRASPING. See GRAB.

[G–121]

GRASS (grăs), *n.* (GREEN; an expanse.) The right "G" hand makes the sign for GREEN: It pivots at the wrist a number of times. As it does so, it swings from left to right.

[G–122]

GRATEFUL (grāt' fəl), *adj.* (Expressions from the heart and mouth.) The open right hand is placed against the mouth, the open left hand against the heart. Both move forward, away from the body, simultaneously.

[G–123]

GRATIFY 1 (grăt' ə fī'), *v.,* -FIED, -FYING. (A pleasurable feeling on the heart.) The open right hand is circled on the chest, over the heart. *Cf.* APPRECIATE, ENJOY, ENJOYMENT, LIKE 3, PLEASE, PLEASURE, WILLING 2.

[G–124]

GRATIFY 2, *v.* (The inner feelings settle down.) Both "B" hands (or "5" hands, fingers together) are placed palms down against the chest, the right above the left. Both move down simultaneously a few inches. *Cf.* CONTENT, CONTENTED, SATISFACTION, SATISFIED, SATISFY 1.

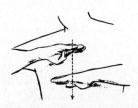

[G–125]

GRAVE 1 (grāv), *n.* (The mound of a grave.) The downturned open hands, slightly cupped, are held side by side. They describe an arc as they are drawn in toward the body. *Cf.* BURY, CEMETERY.

[G–126]

GRAVE 2, *adj.* (Tasting something, finding it unacceptable, and turning it down.) The tips of the right "B" hand are placed at the lips, and then the hand is thrown down. *Cf.* BAD 1, NAUGHTY, WICKED.

[G–127]

GRAVE 3, *adj.* (The facial features drop.) Both "5" hands, palms facing the eyes and fingers slightly curved, drop simultaneously to a level with the mouth. The head drops slightly as the hands move down, and an expression of sadness is assumed. *Cf.* DEJECTED, DEPRESSED, GLOOM, GLOOMY, GRIEF 1, MELANCHOLY, MOURNFUL, SAD, SORROWFUL 1.

[G-128]

GRAVY (grā′ vĭ), *n*. (The drippings from a fleshy, *i.e.*, animal, substance. Used, however, to indicate both organic and inorganic types of oil.) The right thumb and middle finger grasp the fleshy part of the open left hand. The right hand moves straight down. This is repeated once or twice. *Cf.* FAT 3, FATTY, GREASE, GREASY, OIL 2, OILY.

[G-129]

GRAY 1 (grā), *(rare), adj*. (Mixing of colors, in this case black and white, to produce the necessary shade.) The fingertips of the open right hand describe a continuous clockwise circle in the upturned left palm.

[G-130]

GRAY 2, *(rare), adj*. (Rationale unknown.) The right "R" hand, held with palm toward the face, swings around to the palm-out position.

[G-131]

GRAY 3, *(loc.), adj*. (Rationale unknown.) The right "O" hand traces an S-curve in the air as it moves down before the body.

[G-132]

GRAY 4, *adj*. (Intermingling of colors, in this case black and white.) The open "5" hands, fingers pointing to one another and palms facing the body, alternately swing in toward and out from the body. Each time they do so, the fingers of one hand pass through the spaces between the fingers of the other.

[G-133]

GREASE (*n*. grēs; *v*. grēs, grēz), *n., v.*, GREASED, GREASING. (The drippings from a fleshy, *i.e.*, animal, substance. Used, however, to indicate both organic and inorganic types of oil.) The right thumb and middle finger grasp the fleshy part of the open left hand. The right hand moves straight down. This is repeated once or twice. *Cf.* FAT 3, FATTY, GRAVY, GREASY, OIL 2, OILY.

[G-134]

GREASY (grē′ sĭ, -zĭ), *adj.* See GREASE.

[G-135]

GREAT 1 (grāt), *adj.* (A delineation of something big, modified by the letter "L," which stands for LARGE.) Both "L" hands, palms facing out, are placed before the face, and separate rather widely. *Cf.* BIG 1, ENORMOUS, HUGE, IMMENSE, LARGE.

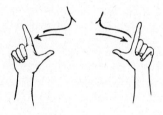

[G-136]

GREAT 2, *adj.* (A large amount.) The "5" hands face each other, fingers curved and touching. They move apart rather quickly. *Cf.* EXPAND, INFINITE, LOT, MUCH.

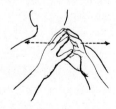

[G-137]

GREAT 3, *adj.* (The hands gesture toward the heavens.) The "5" hands, palms out and arms raised

rather high, are positioned somewhat above the line of vision. The arms move abruptly forward and up once or twice. An expression of pleasure or surprise is usually assumed. *Cf.* EXCELLENT, GRAND 1, MARVEL, MARVELOUS, MIRACLE, O!, SPLENDID 1, SWELL 1, WONDER 2, WONDERFUL 1.

[G-138]

GREAT 4, *adj., interj.* (The feelings are titillated.) With the thumb resting on the upper part of the chest, the fingers are wiggled back and forth. *Cf.* ELEGANT, FINE 1, GRAND 2, SPLENDID 2, SWELL 2, WONDERFUL 2.

[G-139]

GREAT BRITAIN (brĭt ən), *n.* (The English are supposed to be handshakers.) The right hand grasps and shakes the left. *Cf.* BRITAIN, BRITISH, ENGLAND, ENGLISH.

[G–140]

GREAT GRANDFATHER (grāt´ grănd´ fä´ ᵵhər), *n.* (A male holder of a baby, two predecessors removed.) The sign for GRANDFATHER 1, *q.v.*, is made, except that the hands swing over the left shoulder in two distinct steps.

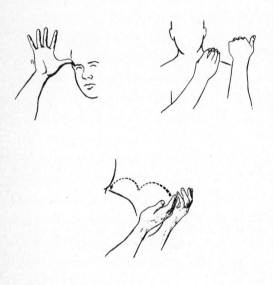

[G–141]

GREAT GRANDMOTHER (grāt´ grănd´ mŭᵵh´ ər), *n.* (Same rationale as for GREAT GRANDFATHER.) The sign for GRANDMOTHER 1, *q.v.*, is made, followed by the same end-sign as employed for GREAT GRANDFATHER.

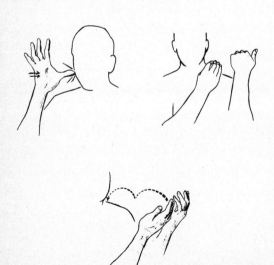

[G–142]

GREAT GRANDPARENTS, *n.* See GREAT GRANDFATHER.

[G–143]

GRECIAN (grē´ shən), *adj.* (The letter "G"; the profile, emphasizing the nose.) The thumb edge of either "G" hand moves down the line of the nose once or twice. *Cf.* GREECE, GREEK.

[G–144]

GREECE (grēs), *n.* See GRECIAN.

[G–145]

GREEDY 1 (grē´ dĭ), *adj.* (Pulling things toward oneself.) Both prone open or "V" hands are held in front of the body with fingers bent. The hands are then drawn quickly and forcefully inward, as if raking things toward oneself. *Cf.* SELFISH 1, STINGY 1, TIGHTWAD 1.

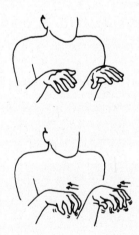

[G–146]

GREEDY 2, *adj.* (Scratching the palm in greed.) The right fingers scratch the upturned left palm several

times. A frowning expression is often used. *Cf.* AVA-
RICIOUS, SELFISH 2, STINGY 2, TIGHTWAD 2.

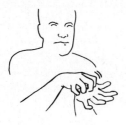

[G–147]

GREEDY 3, *adj.* (Scratching in greed.) The downturned "3" hands, held side by side, make a scratching motion as they move in toward the body. *Cf.*
SELFISH 3, STINGY 3.

[G–148]

GREEK (grēk), *adj.* See GRECIAN.

[G–149]

GREEN 1 (grēn), *adj.* (The letter "G.") The right
"G" hand is shaken slightly. The movement involves
a slight pivoting action at the wrist. *Cf.* GREENHORN
1, SALAD.

[G–150]

GREEN 2, *(colloq.)*, *adj.* (Clumsy in gait; all
thumbs.) The "3" hands, palms down, move alternately up and down before the body. *Cf.* AWK-
WARD, AWKWARDNESS, CLUMSINESS, CLUMSY 1,
GREENHORN 2, NAIVE.

[G–151]

GREENHORN 1 (grēn' hôrn´), *n.* See GREEN 1.

[G–152]

GREENHORN 2, *n.* See GREEN 2.

[G–153]

GRENADE (gri̇̆ nād´), *n.* (The natural sign.) The
signer, holding an imaginary grenade in the clenched
right hand, goes through the motions of pulling out
the pin with the teeth and then tossing the grenade
forward.

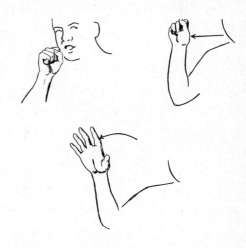

[G–154]

GREY (grā), *adj.* See GRAY.

[G–155]

GRIEF 1 (grēf), *n.* (The facial features drop.) Both "5" hands, palms facing the eyes and fingers slightly curved, drop simultaneously to a level with the mouth. The head drops slightly as the hands move down, and an expression of sadness is assumed. *Cf.* DEJECTED, DEPRESSED, GLOOM, GLOOMY, GRAVE 3, MELANCHOLY, MOURNFUL, SAD, SORROWFUL 1.

[G–156]

GRIEF 2, *n.* (Wringing the heart.) Both clenched hands, held at the heart with knuckles touching, go through back-and-forth wringing motions. A sad expression is usually assumed. *Cf.* GRIEVE, MOURN.

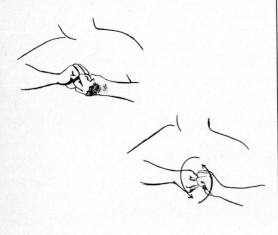

[G–157]

GRIEVE (grēv), *v.,* GRIEVED, GRIEVING. See GRIEF 2.

[G–158]

GRIMACE (grĭ mās′, grĭ′ məs), *n., v.,* -MACED, -MACING. (The facial features are distorted.) The "X" hands are moved alternately up and down in front of the face, whose features are distorted with

a pronounced frown. *Cf.* HOMELY 1, MAKE A FACE, UGLINESS 1, UGLY 1.

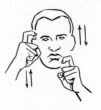

[G–159]

GRIND 1 (grīnd), *v.,* GROUND, GRINDING. (The natural sign.) The "A" hands, palms facing and the right held an inch above the left, move in concentric circles as if grinding something between the knuckles.

[G–160]

GRIND 2, *n.* (The nose is held to the grindstone, indicating a "grind," or boring, repetitious task.) The nose is touched with the right index finger. The thumb edge of the right "S" hand is then placed in the left palm, which is facing right. The right "S" hand, in this position, then moves in a continuous slow clockwise circle, always in contact with the left palm. *Cf.* MONOTONOUS 2.

[G–161]

GROCERIES (grō′ sə rĭz), *n. pl.* (Paying out money.) The right hand, palm up and all fingertips touching the thumb, is placed in the upturned left hand. From this position it moves forward and off the left hand a number of times. The right fingers usually remain against the thumb, but they may be opened very slightly each time the right hand moves forward. *Cf.* SHOP 1, SHOPPING.

[G-162]

GROTESQUE (grō těsk′), *adj.* (Something which distorts the vision.) The "C" hand describes a small arc in front of the face. *Cf.* CURIOUS 2, ODD, PECU-LIAR, QUEER 1, STRANGE 1, WEIRD.

[G-163]

GROUCHY (grou′ chǐ), *adj.* (A mean face.) The signer scratches at the face with all five fingers of the open hand and assumes an appropriately grouchy expression.

[G-164]

GROUND (ground), *n.* (Fingering the soil.) Both hands, held upright before the body, finger imaginary pinches of soil. *Cf.* DIRT, EARTH 2, SOIL 1.

[G-165]

GROUP 1 (gro͞op), *n.* (A grouping together.) Both "C" hands, palms facing, are held a few inches apart at chest height. They are swung around in unison, so that the palms now face the body. *Cf.* ASSOCIATION, AUDIENCE 1, CASTE, CIRCLE 2, CLASS, CLASSED 1, CLUB, COMPANY, FAMILY 2, GANG, JOIN 2, ORGANIZATION 1.

[G-166]

GROUP 2, *n.* (The letter "G.") The sign for GROUP 1 is made, using the "G" hands.

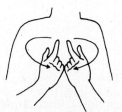

[G–167]

GROW (grō), *v.*, GREW, GROWN, GROWING. (Flowers or plants emerge from the ground.) The right fingers, pointing up, emerge from the closed left hand, and they spread open as they do. *Cf.* BLOOM, DEVELOP 1, GROWN, MATURE, PLANT 1, RAISE 3, REAR 2, SPRING 1.

[G–168]

GROWN (grōn), *adj.* See GROW.

[G–169]

GUARANTEE 1 (găr´ ən tē´), *n., v.*, -TEED, -TEEING. (The arm is raised.) The right index finger is placed at the lips. The right arm is then raised, palm out and elbow resting on the back of the left hand. *Cf.* LOYAL, OATH, PLEDGE, PROMISE 1, SWEAR 1, SWORN, TAKE OATH, VOW.

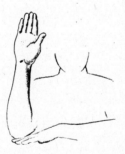

[G–170]

GUARANTEE 2, *(colloq.), n., v.* (The natural sign.) The right hand grasps an imaginary rubber stamp and presses it against the upturned left palm. *Cf.* SEAL 1, STAMP 2.

[G–171]

GUARD (gärd), *v.*, GUARDED, GUARDING. (Hold down firmly; cover and strengthen.) The "S" hands, downturned, are held side by side in front of the body, the arms almost horizontal, and the left hand in front of the right. Both arms move a short distance forward and slightly downward. *Cf.* DEFEND, DEFENSE, FORTIFY, PROTECT, PROTECTION, SHIELD 1.

[G–172]

GUESS 1 (gĕs), *n., v.*, GUESSED, GUESSING. (A thought comes into view.) The index finger of the right "D" hand is placed at mid-forehead, pointing straight up. The slightly cupped right hand, palm facing left, then swings around so that the palm is toward the face.

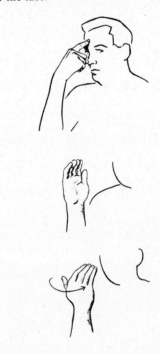

[G–173]

GUESS 2, *n., v.* (A thought is grasped.) The right fingertip touches the forehead; then the right hand makes a quick grasping movement in front of the head, ending in the "S" position.

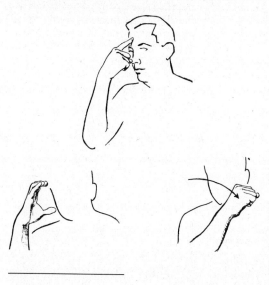

GUESS 3, *(rare), n., v.* (A typical gesture of hesitation or uncertainty.) The index fingertip of the right "V" hand is placed against the edge of the upper teeth. A look of slight puzzlement is sometimes assumed.

GUESS 4, *v.* (Weighing one thing against another.) The upturned open hands move alternately up and down. *Cf.* MAY 1, MAYBE, MIGHT 2, PERHAPS, POSSIBILITY, POSSIBLY, PROBABLE, PROBABLY, SUPPOSE.

 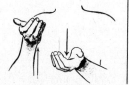

GUIDE (gīd), *n., v.,* GUIDED, GUIDING. (One hand leads the other.) The right hand grasps the tips of the left fingers and pulls the left hand forward. *Cf.* CONDUCT 2, LEAD 1.

GUILTY 1 (gĭl′ tĭ), *adj.* (The blame is firmly placed.) The right "A" hand, thumb pointing up, is brought down firmly against the back of the left hand, held palm down; the right thumb is then directed toward the person or object to blame. When personal blame is acknowledged, the thumb is brought in to the chest. *Cf.* ACCUSE 1, BLAME, FAULT 1.

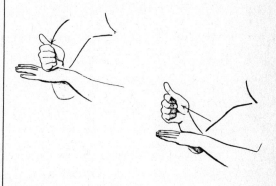

GUILTY 2, *adj.* (The "G" hand; a guilty heart.) The index finger edge of the right "G" hand taps the chest over the heart.

[G–179]

GUITAR (gǐ tär′), *n.* (The natural sign.) The signer plays an imaginary guitar.

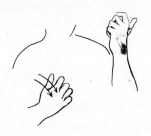

[G–180]

GULLIBLE (gul′ ə bəl), *adj.* (Fall for something, *i.e.*, swallowing the bait.) The right-angle hand is brought up toward the open mouth. *Cf.* CREDIBLE.

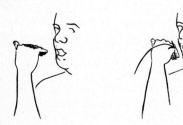

[G–181]

GUM (gŭm), *n.* (The chewing.) The side of the right "X" finger moves up and down on the right cheek. The mouth is held open, and may engage in a chewing motion, keeping time with the right "X" finger. *Cf.* RUBBER 1.

[G–182]

GUN (gŭn), *n.* (Shooting a gun.) The left "S" hand is held above the head as if holding a gun barrel. At the same time the right "L" hand is held below the left hand, its index finger moving back and forth, as if pulling a trigger. *Cf.* PISTOL, RIFLE, SHOOT 2, SHOT 2.

[G–183]

GYM (jǐm), *n.* (Typical calisthenic exercises.) The downturned "S" hands move back and forth simultaneously, and then up and down simultaneously. *Cf.* EXERCISE 1.

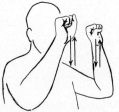

H

[H–1]

HABIT (hăb' ĭt), *n.* (Bound down to custom or habit.) Both "S" hands, palms down, are crossed and brought down in unison before the chest. *Cf.* ACCUSTOM, BOUND, CUSTOM, LOCKED, PRACTICE 3.

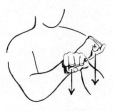

[H–2]

HAIL (hāl), *n.* (Frozen rain.) The sign for FREEZE is made: The fingers of the "5" hands, held palms down, stiffen and contract. This is followed by the sign for RAIN: Both "5" hands, palms down, move down simultaneously, with fingers wiggling.

[H–3]

HAIR (hâr), *n.* (The natural sign.) A lock of hair is grasped by the right index finger and thumb.

[H–4]

HAIRBRUSH (hâr' brŭsh´), *n.* (The natural sign.) Either hand, grasping an imaginary brush, brushes the hair. *Cf.* BRUSH 2.

[H–5]

HAIRDRESSER (hâr' drĕs´ ər), *n.* (Working on the hair.) The "S" hands, palms out, are positioned above the head. They move alternately toward and away from the head, as if pulling locks of hair. This sign is followed by the sign for INDIVIDUAL: Both open hands, palms facing each other, move down the sides of the body, tracing its outline to the hips. *Cf.* BEAUTY PARLOR.

[H–6]

HAIRPIN (hâr' pĭn´), *n.* (The natural sign.) The right "V" hand, palm down, is poised at the right side of the head. The index and middle fingers, held straight, are slipped under the hair.

[H-7]

HAIR RIBBON (rĭb' ən). (The natural sign; the letter "R.") The "R" hands, palms down and poised above the head, go through the natural motions of tying a bow in the hair.

[H-8]

HAIR'S-BREADTH (hârz' brĕdth´), (colloq.), n. (A single hair is indicated.) The right thumb and index finger grasp an imaginary hair at the head and move straight outward, as if slowly pulling the hair out.

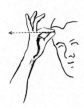

[H-9]

HAIRSPLITTING (hâr' splĭt´ ing), (colloq.), n., adj. The right index finger and thumb grasp an imaginary hair held by the left index finger and thumb. The right hand moves away from the left, as if pulling a hair. Cf. SPLIT HAIRS.

[H-10]

HALE (hāl), adj. (Strength emanating from the body.) Both "5" hands are placed palms against the chest. They move out and away, forcefully, closing and assuming the "S" position, Cf. BRAVE, BRAV-

ERY, COURAGE, COURAGEOUS, FORTITUDE, HEALTH, HEALTHY, MIGHTY 2, STRENGTH, STRONG 2, WELL 2.

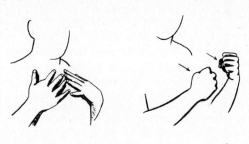

[H-11]

HALF 1 (hăf), n., adj. (The fraction, ½.) Using the same hand for each sign, first make the "1" sign, then drop the hand straight down a bit and make the "2" sign.

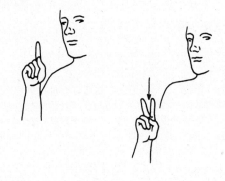

[H-12]

HALF 2, adj. (Half of the finger is indicated.) The right index finger is drawn across the midpoint of the left index finger, moving toward the body.

[H-13]

HALF-HOUR (hăf' our´), n. (The movement of the minute hand on a clock.) The thumb edge of the right "D" hand is placed against the palm of the left "5" hand, whose fingers point straight out. The right index finger, initially pointing straight up, executes a half-circle on the left palm, coming to a stop pointing straight down.

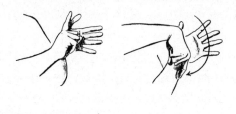

[H–14]

HALL (hôl), *n.* (The movement.) Both hands, palms facing and fingers together and extended straight out, move in unison away from the body, in a straight or winding manner. *Cf.* CORRIDOR, HALLWAY, MANNER 2, METHOD, OPPORTUNITY 3, PATH, ROAD, STREET, TRAIL, WAY 1.

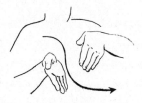

[H–15]

HALLELUJAH (hăl´ ə lōō´ yə), *(eccles.), interj.* (Clapping hands and waving flags.) The hands are clapped together once; then they separate, rise, grasp imaginary flag staffs, and wave them in the air in a circular manner. A happy expression is assumed. The clapping is often omitted.

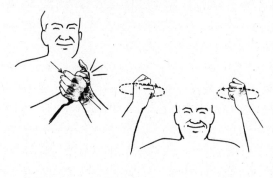

[H–16]

HALLOWED 1 (hăl´ ōd, hăl´ ō ĭd), *adj.* (Made holy.) The sign for MAKE is made: The right "S" hand,

palm facing left, is placed on top of its left counterpart, whose palm faces right. The hands are twisted back and forth, striking each other slightly after each twist. This is followed by the sign for HOLY: The right "H" hand makes a clockwise circular movement, and is then opened and wiped across the open left palm.

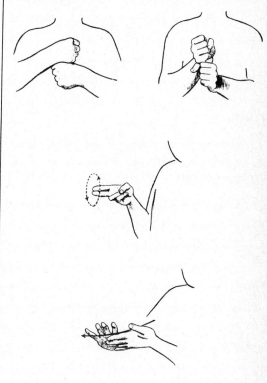

[H–17]

HALLOWED 2, *adj.* (The letter "H"; a gesture of respect.) The right "H" hand, palm facing left, swings down in an arc from its initial position in front of the forehead. The head bows slightly during this movement of the hand. *Cf.* HONOR 1, HONORARY.

[H–18]

HALLWAY (hôl´ wā´), *n.* See HALL.

[H–19]

HALT (hôlt), *v.*, HALTED, HALTING. (A stopping or cutting short.) The little finger edge of the right hand is thrust abruptly into the upturned left palm, indicating a cutting short. *Cf.* ARREST 2, CEASE, STOP.

[H–20]

HAMBURGER 1 (hăm' bûr' gər), *n.* (Making patties.) Both open hands go through the motions of forming patties.

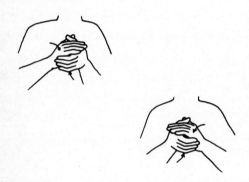

[H–21]

HAMBURGER 2, *n.* (Chopping meat.) The open hands face each other, little finger edges down. In this position both hands move up and down alternately, imitating chopping blades.

[H–22]

HAMMER (hăm' ər), *n.*, *v.*, -MERED, -MERING. (The natural sign.) The right hand, grasping an imaginary hammer, swings down toward the left fist, which represents the object being hammered. The right

hand does not touch the left, however. The action is usually repeated.

[H–23]

HAND 1 (hănd), *n.* (The natural sign.) The right index finger touches the back of the prone left hand.

[H–24]

HAND 2, *n.* (The natural sign.) The prone right hand is drawn over the back of the prone left hand. For the plural, the action is repeated with the hands switched. The little finger edge of the right hand may instead be drawn across the back of the left wrist, as if cutting off the left hand; and for the plural the action is repeated with the hands switched.

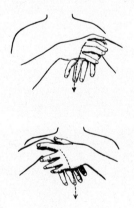

[H–25]

HANDKERCHIEF (hăng' kər chif, -chēf'), *n.* (Wiping the nose.) The signer makes the motions of wiping the nose several times with an imaginary handkerchief. This is the common cold. *Cf.* COLD 2.

[H-26]

HANDSAW (hănd' sô´), *(voc.), n.* (Act of holding a saw.) The right hand grasps an imaginary saw and moves back and forth over the downturned left hand. *Cf.* SAW 2.

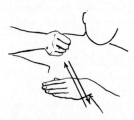

[H-27]

HAND SCRAPER (skrā' pər), *(voc.).* (The natural sign.) Both downturned hands, clasped over an imaginary scraper, work back and forth on a table or other convenient flat surface.

[H-28]

HANDSOME (hăn' səm), *adj.* (A nice face.) The sign for FACE 1 is made: The index finger outlines the face, without touching it. The sign for NICE is then made: The right hand slowly wipes the upturned left palm, from wrist to fingertips.

[H-29]

HANG 1 (hăng), *v.,* HUNG, HANGED, HANGING. (The natural sign.) The curved right index finger "hangs" on the extended left index finger. *Cf.* SUSPEND 1.

[H-30]

HANG 2, *v.* (Hanging by the throat.) The thumb of the "Y" hand is placed at the right side of the neck, and the head hangs toward the left, as if it were caught in a noose. *Cf.* SCAFFOLD.

[H-31]

HAPPEN 1 (hăp' ən), *v.,* -ENED, -ENING. (A befalling.) Both "D" hands, index fingers pointing away from the body, are simultaneously pivoted over so that the palms face down. *Cf.* ACCIDENT, BEFALL, CHANCE, COINCIDE 1, COINCIDENCE, EVENT, INCIDENT, OCCUR, OPPORTUNITY 4.

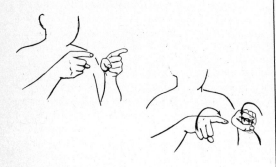

[H-32]

HAPPEN 2, *v.* The same sign as for HAPPEN 1 but the "H" hands are used.

[H-33]

HAPPINESS (hăp' ĭ nĭs), *n.* The sign for HAPPY is made. This is followed by the sign for the suffix, -NESS: The downturned right "N" hand moves down along the left palm, which is facing away from the body. *Cf.* DELIGHT, GAIETY 1, GAY, GLAD, HAPPY, JOY, MERRY.

[H-34]

HAPPY (hăp' ĭ), *adj.* (The heart is stirred; the spirits bubble up.) The open right hand, palm facing the body, strikes the heart repeatedly, moving up and off

the heart after each strike. *Cf.* DELIGHT, GAIETY 1, GAY, GLAD, HAPPINESS, JOY, MERRY.

[H-35]

HARBOR (här' bər), *n.* (A circle of water.) The sign for WATER 1 is formed: The right "W" hand, palm facing left, touches the lips a number of times. Then the outstretched right hand circles from right to left before the body.

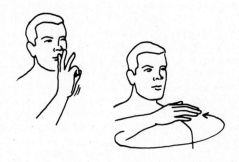

[H-36]

HARD 1 (härd), *adj.* (The knuckles are rubbed, to indicate a condition of being worn down.) The knuckles of the curved index and middle fingers of both hands are rubbed up and down against each other. Instead of the up-down rubbing, they may rub against each other in an alternate clockwise-counterclockwise manner. *Cf.* DIFFICULT 1, DIFFICULTY, HARDSHIP, POVERTY 2, PROBLEM 2.

[H-37]

HARD 2, *adj.* (Striking a hard object.) The curved index and middle fingers of the right hand, whose palm faces the body or the left, are brought down sharply against the back of the downturned left "S" hand. *Cf.* DIFFICULT 2, SOLID.

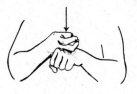

an alternate clockwise-counterclockwise motion, and in a somewhat more pronounced manner than that described in HARD 1.

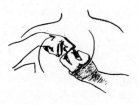

[H–38]

HARD-BOILED (härd' boild'), *(sl.), adj.* (A hard heart.) The index fingers trace a heart on the appropriate place on the chest. The knuckles of the downturned right "S" hand then come down sharply against the back of the left "S" hand. *Cf.* TOUGH 2.

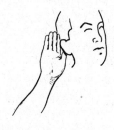

[H–42]

HARK (härk), *v.*, HARKED, HARKING. (Cupping the hand at the ear.) The right hand is placed, usually slightly cupped, behind the right ear. *Cf.* HEAR, HEARKEN, LISTEN.

[H–39]

HARD OF HEARING, *adj. phrase.* (The "H" is indicated twice.) The right "H" hand drops down an inch or so, rises, moves in a short arc to the right, and drops down an inch or so again.

[H–43]

HARLOT (här' lət), *n.* (The blood rushes up the cheek in shame—several times for emphasis.) The curved back of the right hand, placed against the right cheek, moves up and off the cheek several times. *Cf.* PROSTITUTE, STRUMPET, WHORE.

[H–40]

HARDSHIP (härd' shĭp), *n.* See HARD 1.

[H–41]

HARD TIMES (tīmz), *phrase.* (Same rationale as that of HARD 1.) The knuckles of the curved index and middle fingers of both hands are rubbed together in

[H–44]

HARM 1 (härm), *n.* (A stabbing pain.) The "D" hands, index fingers pointing to each other, are rotated in elliptical fashion before the chest—simultaneously but in opposite directions. *Cf.* ACHE, HURT 1, INJURE 1, INJURY, MAR 1, OFFEND, OFFENSE, PAIN, SIN, WOUND.

[H–45]

HARM 2 (härm), *v.*, HARMED, HARMING. (Striking down against.) Both "A" or "X" hands are held before the chest, the right above the left. The right hand strikes down and out, hitting the left thumb and knuckles with force. *Cf.* BACKBITE, BASE 3, CRUEL 1, HURT 2, MAR 2, MEAN 1, SPOIL.

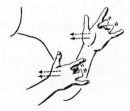

[H–46]

HARP (härp), *n.* (The natural sign.) The fingers, hands, and arms go through the natural motions of playing a harp.

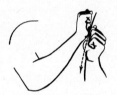

[H–47]

HARVEST 1 (här′ vĭst), *n.*, *v.*, -VESTED, -VESTING. (Cutting the stalks.) The left hand holds an imaginary bunch of stalks, and the right hand, holding an imaginary sickle, sweeps under the left as if cutting the stalks. *Cf.* REAP 1.

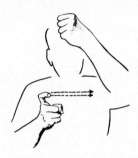

[H–48]

HARVEST 2, *v.* (Gathering in the harvest.) The right open hand sweeps across the upturned left palm and closes into the "A" position, as if gathering up some stalks. *Cf.* REAP 2.

[H–49]

HARVEST 3, *v.* (The cutting.) The left hand grasps the heads of imaginary wheat stalks. The upturned right hand, imitating a sickle blade, then swings in to cut the stalks. *Cf.* REAP 3.

[H–50]

HASTE (hāst), *n.* (Letter "H"; quick movements.) The "H" hands, palms facing each other and held about six inches apart, shake alternately up and

down. One hand alone may be used. *Cf.* HURRY,
HUSTLE.

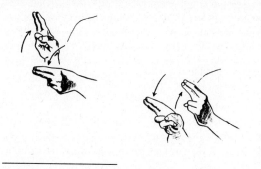

[H–51]

HAT (hăt), *n.* (The natural sign.) The right hand
pats the head.

[H–52]

HATE 1 (hāt), *n., v.,* HATED, HATING. (To push
away and recoil from; avoid.) The two open hands,
palms facing left, are pushed deliberately to the left,
as if pushing something away. An expression of disdain or disgust is worn. *Cf.* ABHOR, AVOID 2, DE-
SPISE 1, DETEST 1, LOATHE.

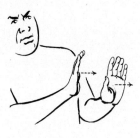

[H–53]

HATE 2, *v., n.* (The finger is flicked to indicate something petty, small; *i.e.,* to be scorned as inconsequential.) The right index finger and thumb are used to
press the lips down into an expression of contempt.
The right thumb is then flicked out from the closed
hand. The modern version of this sign omits pressing
down of the lips and includes only the flicking out

of the middle finger of one or both hands. *Cf.* CON-
TEMPT 2, DESPISE 2, DETEST 2, DISLIKE, SCORN 2.

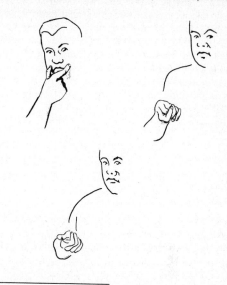

[H–54]

HAUGHTY (hô′ tĭ), *adj.* (The feelings rise up.) The
thumb of the right "A" hand, palm down, moves up
along the right side of the chest. A haughty expression is assumed. *Cf.* PRIDE, PROUD.

[H–55]

HAVE 1 (hăv), *v.,* HAS, HAD, HAVING. (The act of
bringing something over to oneself.) The right-angle
hands, palms facing and thumbs pointing up, are
swept toward the body until the fingertips come to
rest against the middle of the chest. *Cf.* POSSESS 2.

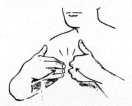

[H–56]

HAVE 2, *v.* (Bring to an end.) The left hand, fingers together and pointing forward, is held palm facing right. The right, palm down, fingers also together, moves along the top of the left, goes over the tip of the left index finger, and drops straight down, indicating a cutting off or a finishing. This sign is also used to indicate the past tense of a verb, in the sense of accomplishing an action or state of being. *Cf.* ACCOMPLISH 2, ACHIEVE 2, COMPLETE 1, CONCLUDE, DONE 1, END 4, EXPIRE 1, FINISH 1, TERMINATE

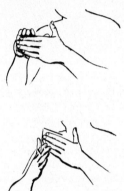

[H–57]

HAVE 3, *v.* (A modification of HAVE 1.) The hands are crossed over each other as they rest on the chest. *Cf.* POSSESS 1.

[H–58]

HAVE TO, *v. phrase.* (Being pinned down.) The right hand, in the "X" position, palm down, moves forcefully up and down once or twice. An expression of determination is frequently assumed. *Cf.* IMPERATIVE, MUST, NECESSARY 1, NECESSITY, NEED 1, OUGHT TO, SHOULD, VITAL 2.

[H–59]

HAVOC (hăv′ ək), *n.* (Wiping off.) The left "5" hand, palm up, is held slightly above the right "5" hand, held palm down. The right hand swings up, just brushing over the left palm. Both hands close into the "S" position, and the right is brought back with force to its initial position, striking a glancing blow against the left knuckles as it returns. *Cf.* ABOLISH 1, ANNIHILATE, CORRUPT, DEFACE, DEMOLISH, DESTROY, PERISH 2, REMOVE 3, RUIN.

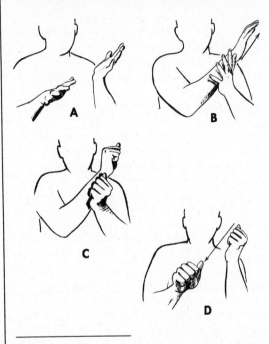

[H–60]

HAWAII (hə wī′ ē, -wä′ yə), *n.* (The dancing.) The hands and arms wave in the traditional undulating manner of the Hawaiian dance. *Cf.* HAWAIIAN.

[H–61]

HAWAIIAN (hə wī′ yən, -wä′-), *adj., n.* The sign for HAWAII is made. This is followed by the sign for INDIVIDUAL: Both open hands, palms facing each other, move down the sides of the body, tracing its outline to the hips. *Cf.* HAWAII.

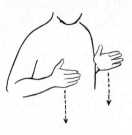

[H–62]

HAY (hā), *(rare), n.* (The stalks rise before the face.) The index finger of the right "4" hand, whose palm faces left, rests on the nose. The hand moves straight up.

[H–63]

HE (hē), *pron.* (Pointing at a male.) The MALE prefix sign is made: The right hand grasps an imaginary cap brim. The right index finger then points at an imaginary male. If in context the gender is clear, the prefix sign is usually omitted. *Cf.* HIM.

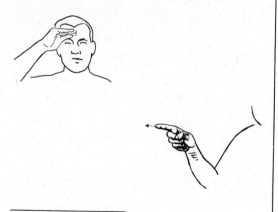

[H–64]

HEAD (hĕd), *n.* (The head is indicated.) The tips of the fingers of the right right-angle hand are placed

at the right temple, and then move down in an arc to the right jaw.

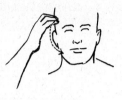

[H–65]

HEADACHE (hĕd′ āk′), *n.* (A stabbing pain in the head.) The index fingers, pointing to each other, move back and forth on the forehead.

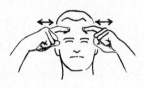

[H–66]

HEALTH (hĕlth), *n.* (Strength emanating from the body.) Both "5" hands are placed palms against the chest. They move out and away, forcefully, closing and assuming the "S" position. *Cf.* BRAVE, BRAVERY, COURAGE, COURAGEOUS, FORTITUDE, HALE, HEALTHY, MIGHTY 2, STRENGTH, STRONG 2, WELL 2.

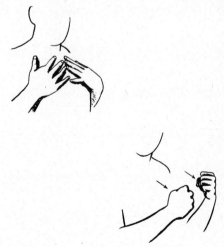

[H–67]

HEALTHY (hĕl′ thĭ), *adj.* See HEALTH.

[H–68]

HEAR (hǐr), *v.*, HEARD (hûrd), HEARING. (Cupping the hand at the ear.) The right hand is placed, usually slightly cupped, behind the right ear. *Cf.* HARK, HEARKEN, LISTEN.

[H–69]

HEARING (hǐr′ ing), *n., adj.* (Words tumbling from the mouth, indicating the old association of being able to hear with being able to speak.) The right index finger, pointing left, describes a continuous small circle in front of the mouth. *Cf.* BID 3, DIS-COURSE, MAINTAIN 2, MENTION, REMARK, SAID, SAY, SPEAK, SPEECH 1, STATE, STATEMENT, TALK 1, TELL, VERBAL 1.

[H–70]

HEARKEN (här′ kən), *v.*, -ENED, -ENING. See HEAR.

[H–71]

HEART 1 (härt), *n.* (The natural sign.) The index fingers trace a heart at the appropriate spot on the chest.

[H–72]

HEART 2, *n.* (The natural sign.) The middle fingers are used to trace a heart as in HEART 1.

[H–73]

HEART ATTACK (ə tăk′). (The heart is struck.) The sign for HEART 1 is made. Then the closed right fist strikes the open left palm, which faces right.

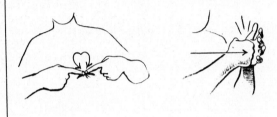

[H–74]

HEARTBEAT 1 (härt′ bēt′), *n.* (The opening and closing of a heart valve.) The middle finger of the right "5" hand touches the heart. The open right hand, fingers together, then moves rhythmically up and down on the thumb edge of the left "0" hand, in imitation of a valve alternately releasing and blocking the passage of blood in the heart.

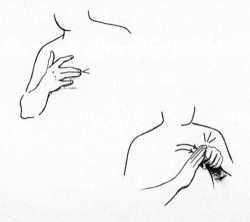

[H-75]

HEARTBEAT 2, *n.* (The natural sign.) The right fist beats rhythmically against the heart.

[H-76]

HEAT 1 (hēt), *n.*, *v.*, HEATED, HEATING. (The warmth of the breath is indicated.) The upturned cupped right hand is placed at the slightly open mouth. It moves up and away from the mouth, opening into the upturned "5" position, with fingers somewhat curved. *Cf.* WARM 1.

[H-77]

HEAT 2, *v.* (The action of flames under a pot or pan.) The upturned left hand is the pot. The fingers of the upturned right hand, held underneath the left hand, wiggle in imitation of the action of flames.

[H-78]

HEAVEN (hĕv' ən), *n.* (Entering heaven through a break in the clouds.) Both open hands, fingers

straight and pointing up, move upward in an arc on either side of the head. Just before they touch above the head, the right hand, palm down, sweeps under the left and moves up, its palm now facing out. *Cf.* SKY 1.

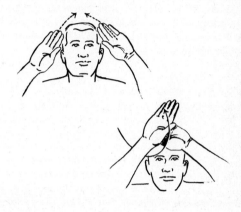

[H-79]

HEAVY (hĕv' ĭ), *adj.* (The hands drop under a weight.) The upturned "5" hands, held before the chest, suddenly drop a short distance. *Cf.* CRUSHING, WEIGHTY.

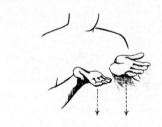

[H-80]

HEBREW (hē' brōō), *n.*, *adj.* (The beard of the old Jewish patriarchs.) The fingers and thumb of each hand are placed at the chin, and stroke an imaginary beard. *Cf.* ISRAELITE, JEW, JEWISH.

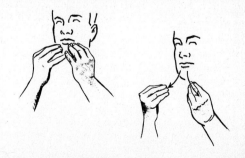

[H–81]

HEBREW BIBLE, *n.* (Literally: Hebrew book; the Old Testament.) The sign for HEBREW is formed. This is followed by the sign for BOOK: The open hands are held together, fingers pointing away from the body. They open with little fingers remaining in contact, as in the opening of a book. This sign is used by the Jews. *Cf.* BIBLE 3, HOLY SCRIPTURE, JEWISH BIBLE, TESTAMENT 3.

[H–82]

HEBREWS (hē′ brōōz), *(eccles.), n. pl.* (The Jewish people.) The sign for HEBREW is made. This is followed by the sign for PEOPLE: The "P" hands, side by side, are moved alternately in counterclockwise circles. *Cf.* ISRAEL, ISRAELITES.

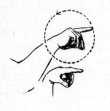

[H–83]

HEEDLESS (hēd′ lĭs), *adj.* (The vision is sidetracked, causing one to lose sight of the object in view.) The right "V" hand, representing the vision, is held in front of the face, palm facing left. The hand, pivoted at the wrist, moves back and forth a number of times. *Cf.* CARELESS, RECKLESS, THOUGHTLESS.

[H–84]

HEIGHT 1 (hīt), *n.* (The height is indicated.) The index finger of the right "D" hand moves straight up against the palm of the left "5" hand. *Cf.* TALL 1.

[H–85]

HEIGHT 2, *n.* (The height is indicated.) The right right-angle hand, palm facing the left, is held at the height the signer wishes to indicate. *Cf.* BIG 2, HIGH 3, TALL 2.

[H–86]

HELL 1 (hĕl), *n.* (The devil; pointing down.) The sign for DEVIL is made: With the thumbs resting on the temples, the index and middle fingers of both hands open and close repeatedly. The right index finger, pointing down, then moves straight down a few inches. The pointing may be omitted. *Cf.* DEMON, DEVIL, DEVILMENT, SATAN.

[H–87]

HELL 2, *n.* (The leaping of flames.) The "5" hands are held with palms facing the body. They move up and down alternately, while the fingers wiggle. *Cf.* BURN, FIRE 1, FLAME.

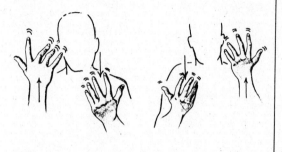

[H–88]

HELLO 1 (hĕ lō'), *interj., n.* (Words extended politely from the mouth.) The fingertips of the right "5" hand are placed at the mouth. The hand moves away from the mouth to a palm-up position before the body. The signer meanwhile usually nods smilingly. *Cf.* FAREWELL 1, GOODBYE 1, THANKS, THANK YOU, YOU'RE WELCOME 1.

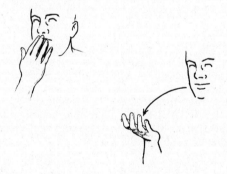

[H–89]

HELLO 2, *interj.* (A wave of the hand.) The right open hand waves back and forth several times. *Cf.* FAREWELL 2, GOODBYE 2, SO LONG.

[H–90]

HELP (hĕlp), *n., v.,* HELPED, HELPING. (Helping up; supporting.) The left "S" hand, thumb side up, rests in the open right palm. In this position the left hand is pushed up a short distance by the right. *Cf.* AID, ASSIST, ASSISTANCE, BENEFIT 1, BOOST, GIVE ASSISTANCE.

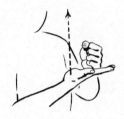

[H–91]

HEN (hĕn), *n.* (The bill and the scratching.) The right index finger and thumb open and close as they are held pointing out from the mouth. (This is the root sign for any kind of bird.) The right "X" finger then scratches against the upturned left palm, as if scratching for food. The scratching is sometimes omitted. *Cf.* CHICKEN, FOWL

[H–92]

HENCE (hĕns), *adv.* (In proportion.) Both "D" or "P" hands, palms facing down, are held before the body. They describe a short arc from right to left and, while unnecessary, they may return to their original position. *Cf.* PROPORTION, RATIO, THEREFORE 1, THUS.

[H-93]

HENPECK (hĕn′ pĕk′), v., -PECKED, -PECKING (The hen's beak pecks.) The index finger and thumb of the right hand, held together, are brought against the index finger of the left "D" hand a number of times. Cf. NAG, PECK, PICK ON.

 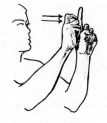

[H-94]

HER (hûr), pron. (Pointing at a female.) The FE-MALE prefix sign is made: The right "A" hand's thumb moves down along the line of the right jaw, from ear almost to chin. The right index finger then points at an imaginary female. If in context the gender is clear, the prefix sign is usually omitted. Cf. SHE. For the possessive sense of this pronoun, see HERS.

[H-95]

HERE (hĭr), adv. The open "5" hands, palms up and fingers slightly curved, move back and forth in front of the body, the right hand to the right and the left hand to the left. Cf. DIRECTION 2, WHERE 2.

[H-96]

HERESY (hĕr′ ə sĭ), n. (False faith.) The sign for FALSE 2 is made: The index finger of the right "D" hand, pointing to the left, moves along the lips from right to left. This is followed by the sign for FAITH: The "S" hands grasp and plant an imaginary flag-pole in the ground.

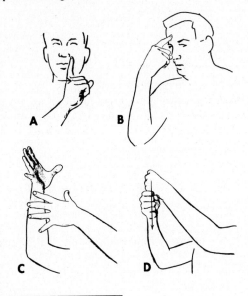

[H-97]

HERETIC (hĕr′ ə tĭk), n. (False believer.) The sign for FALSE 2, as in HERESY, is made. This is followed by the sign for BELIEVE: The index finger touches the middle of the forehead, and then both hands are clasped together. This is followed by the sign for INDIVIDUAL: Both open hands, palms facing each other, move down the sides of the body, tracing its outline to the hips.

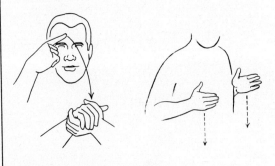

[H-98]

HERITAGE (hĕr′ ə tĭj), n. (The "H" hands; rolling down from the past into the present.) The "H" hands, palms down, are positioned over the shoulder, one atop the other, but not touching. They roll down over each other as they move down and forward. See also GENERATION.

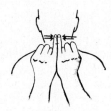

[H–99]

HERMIT (hûr′ mĭt), *(colloq.), n.* (A lone person with himself.) The "I" hands, palms facing the body, touch repeatedly along their little finger edges.

[H–100]

HERS (hûrz), *pron.* (Belonging to a female.) The FEMALE prefix sign is made. The open right hand, palm facing out, then moves straight forward a few inches. If in context the gender is clear, the prefix sign is usually omitted.

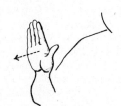

[H–101]

HERSELF (hər sĕlf′), *pron.* (The thumb indicates an individual who is stressed above others.) The FEMALE prefix sign is made. The right "A" hand, thumb upturned, then moves forward an inch or

two, either once or twice. If in context the gender is clear, the prefix sign is usually omitted.

[H–102]

HESITATE (hĕz′ ə tāt′), *v.,* -TATED, -TATING. (A faltering gesture.) The right "D" hand, palm facing left, moves forward in steps, an inch or so at a time. Each time it moves forward the head nods slightly.

[H–103]

HIDE (hīd), *v.,* HID, HIDDEN, HIDING. (One hand is hidden under the other.) The thumb of the right "A" hand, whose palm faces left, is placed against the lips. The hand then swings down and under the downturned left hand. The initial contact with the lips is sometimes omitted. *Cf.* COVER 4.

[H–104]

HIGH 1 (hī), *adj.* (Something high up.) Both hands, in the right angle position, are held before the face, about a foot apart, palms facing. They are raised abruptly about a foot, in a slight outward curving movement. *Cf.* ADVANCED, PROMOTE, PROMOTION.

[H–105]

HIGH 2, *adj.* (Indicating height.) The right "A" hand, held with thumb pointing upward, moves straight up above the right shoulder. *Cf.* PROMINENT 3, SUPERIOR.

[H–106]

HIGH 3, *adj.* (The height is indicated.) The right right-angle hand, palm facing the left, is held at the height the signer wishes to indicate. *Cf.* BIG 2, HEIGHT 2, TALL 2.

[H–107]

HIGH 4, *adj.* (The letter "H"; the natural movement.) The right "H" hand, palm facing the body, is moved up about a foot, to a position somewhat above the head.

[H–108]

HIGHBROW (hī' brou´), *(colloq.), n., adj.* (The natural sign.) The wide open right "C" hand is placed with thumb against the forehead, and palm facing left. The position of the hand thus indicates the height of the brow.

[H–109]

HIGH SCHOOL, (The letters "H" and "S.") The letters "H" and "S" are fingerspelled.

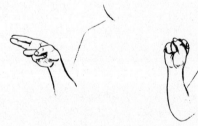

[H–110]

HILL (hĭl), *n.* (A rocky mound.) The sign for ROCK is made: The back of the right "S" hand is struck several times against the back of the left "S" hand. Both "5" hands, palms down, then move in a wavy, undulating manner either from left to right or from right to left. The sign for ROCK is frequently omitted.

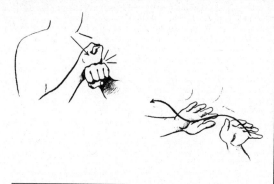

HIM (hĭm), *pron.* (Pointing at a male.) The MALE prefix sign is made: The right hand grasps an imaginary cap brim. The right index finger then points at an imaginary male. If in context the gender is clear, the prefix sign is usually omitted. *Cf.* HE.

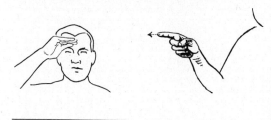

[H–112]

HIMSELF (hĭm sĕlf'), *pron.* (The thumb indicates an individual who is stressed above others.) The MALE prefix sign is made. The right "A" hand, thumb upturned, then moves forward an inch or two, either once or twice. If in context the gender is clear, the prefix sign is usually omitted.

[H–113]

HINDER (hĭn' dər), *v.,* -DERED, -DERING. (Obstruct, block.) The left hand, fingers together and palm flat, is held before the body, facing somewhat down. The little finger side of the right hand, held with palm

flat, makes one or several up-down chopping motions against the left hand, between its thumb and index finger. *Cf.* ANNOY 1, ANNOYANCE 1, BLOCK, BOTHER 1, CHECK 2, COME BETWEEN, DISRUPT, DISTURB, HINDRANCE, IMPEDE, INTERCEPT, INTERFERE, INTERFERENCE, INTERFERE WITH, INTERRUPT, MEDDLE 1, OBSTACLE, OBSTRUCT, PREVENT, PREVENTION.

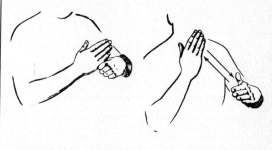

[H–114]

HINDRANCE (hĭn' drəns), *n.* See HINDER.

[H–115]

HINGE 1 (hĭnj), *n.* (The natural sign.) The hands are joined at the fingertips, and are positioned at right angles to each other, with the fingertips pointing away from the body. The hands come together and separate again, always with fingertips in contact. This imitates the action of a hinge.

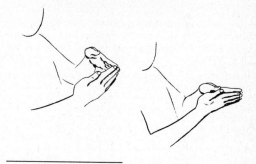

[H–116]

HINGE 2, *v.,* HINGED, HINGING. (Hanging onto.) With the right index finger resting across its left counterpart, both hands drop down a bit. *Cf.* DEPEND 1, DEPENDABLE, DEPENDENT, RELY 2.

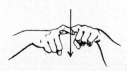

[H–117]

HIS (hĭz), *poss. pron.* (Belonging to a male.) The MALE prefix sign is made. The open right hand, palm facing out, then moves straight forward a few inches. If in context the gender is clear, the prefix sign is usually omitted.

[H–118]

HISTORY 1 (hĭs′ tə rĭ), *n.* (The letter "H"; moving down toward the present from the past.) The right "H" hand, palm facing left, swings down in an arc, from its initial position a bit above shoulder height.

[H–119]

HISTORY 2, *n.* (Occurrences or happenings coming down from the past and into the present.) The "D" hands, index fingers pointing ahead and palms facing each other, are initially poised near the right shoulder. They execute a series of downward movements, pivoted at the wrists. Each of these downward movements represents an event in history.

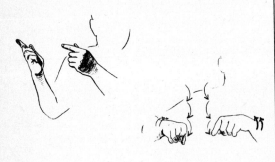

[H–120]

HIT 1 (hĭt), *n., v.,* HIT, HITTING. (The natural sign.) The right "S" hand strikes its knuckles forcefully

against the open left palm, which is held facing right. *Cf.* POUND 3, PUNCH 1, STRIKE 1.

[H–121]

HIT 2, *v.* (The natural sign.) The left "5" hand, palm facing the right, is the object hit. The right "S" hand swings down in an arc, its knuckles just missing the left palm.

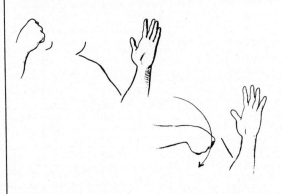

[H–122]

HIT 3, *n., v.* (Hit with a bullet.) The left "5" hand, palm facing right, is the object hit. The right hand, imitating a gun, "fires" an imaginary bullet at the left hand, and the projectile's path is traced until the right index finger strikes the left palm.

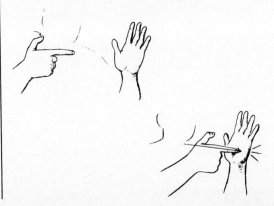

[H-123]

HITCH (hĭch), *n., v.,* HITCHED, HITCHING (Hooking on to something and pulling.) With index fingers interlocked, the right hand pulls the left hand from left to right. *Cf.* HOOK, PULL 2, TOW.

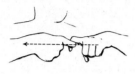

[H-124]

HITCHHIKE (hĭch' hīk´), *v.,* -HIKED, -HIKING. (The natural sign.) The right thumb makes the characteristic gesture used by hitchhikers.)

[H-125]

HOAX (hōks), *n.* (Pulling the nose.) The right "X" finger, resting on the nose, pulls the head with it as it moves down slightly. It does not leave its position on the nose. *Cf.* DOLL 1, FOOL 2, JOKE.

[H-126]

HOE (hō), *n., v.,* HOED, HOEING. (The natural sign.) The fingertips of the right right-angle hand are thrust repeatedly into the upturned left palm. The right hand is pulled back and a bit down before it is

thrust into the palm again. This is the characteristic motion of the hoe as it tills the soil.

[H-127]

HOG 1 (hŏg, hôg), *n.* (The snout digs into the trough.) The downturned right prone hand is placed under the chin, fingers pointing forward. The hand, in this position, swings alternately up and down. *Cf.* PIG 1.

[H-128]

HOG 2, *n.* (Same rationale as for PIG 1.) The sign for HOG 1, is repeated, except that the fingers point to the left. *Cf.* PIG 2.

[H-129]

HOLD (hōld), *n., v.*, HELD, HOLDING. (The gripping is emphasized.) Both "S" hands, one resting on the other, tremble slightly as they grip an imaginary object.

[H-130]

HOLDUP (hōld′ ŭp′), *(colloq.), n.* (The guns.) Both "L" hands, palms facing each other, thumbs pointing straight up, are thrown forward slightly, as if presenting a pair of revolvers. *Cf.* ROBBERY 2.

[H-131]

HOLE 1 (hōl), *n.* (A hole is traced.) Both index fingers, pointing down, are positioned side by side. They move in half circles toward the body until they come in contact with each other again. The right index finger then moves down a few inches, in the center of the imaginary circle just traced.

[H-132]

HOLE 2, *n.* (The natural sign.) The left index finger and thumb form a circle. The right index finger is placed on this circle and traces its outline.

[H-133]

HOLIDAY (hŏl′ ə dā′), *n.* (A position of idleness.) With thumbs tucked in the armpits, the remaining fingers of both hands wiggle. *Cf.* IDLE, LEISURE, RETIRE 3, VACATION.

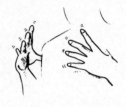

[H-134]

HOLLAND 1 (hŏl′ ənd), *n.* (The long pipe smoked by Netherlanders.) The right "Y" hand is held before the face, with thumbtip at the lips. It swings down and forward, outlining the shape of a long curved pipe. *Cf.* DUTCH 1, NETHERLANDS 1.

[H-135]

HOLLAND 2, *n.* (The hat worn by Netherlands women.) The hands, held open at either temple, grasp the points of the native female headgear. They swing upward a bit, as the fingers close over the thumbs. *Cf.* DUTCH 2, NETHERLANDS 2.

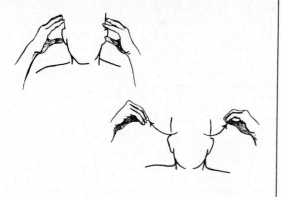

HOLY (hō′ lĭ), *adj.* (The letter "H"; cleanliness or purity.) The right "H" hand makes a clockwise circular movement, and is then opened and wiped across the open left palm.

HOLY COMMUNION 1, *n. phrase.* (The Blessed Sacrament.) The right thumb and index finger move as if placing the Sacred Host on the tip of the tongue; or they may trace a cross over the lips. *Cf.* EUCHARIST, COMMUNION (HOLY) 1.

HOLY COMMUNION 2, *n.* (Act of cutting a loaf of bread.) The left arm is held against the chest, representing a loaf of bread. The little finger edge of the right hand is drawn down over the back of the left hand several times, to indicate the cutting of slices. *Cf.* BREAD, COMMUNION (HOLY) 2, WINE 2.

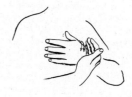

HOLY GHOST, *(eccles.).* The sign for HOLY is made, followed by the sign for GHOST: The hands are held palms facing, with one above the other and index fingers and thumbs touching and almost connected. As the upper hand moves straight up, the index fingers and thumbs of both hands slowly come together, giving the impression of drawing out a thread or other thin substance.

[H–140]

HOLY ORDERS, *(eccles.).* (Anointing of the hands.) The right "5" hand is held palm facing out. The thumb of the left "A" hand moves up along the edge of the right thumb to the tip of the right index finger, and then down again. This movement is repeated, with the left and right hands reversing their respective roles.

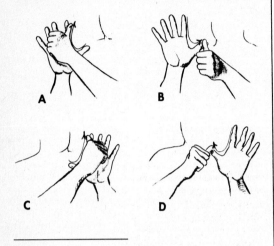

[H–141]

HOLY SCRIPTURE, *n.* (Literally: Jewish book; the Old Testament.) The sign for JEW is formed: The fingers and thumb of each hand are placed at the chin, and stroke an imaginary beard, as worn by the old Jewish patriarchs or Orthodox rabbis. The sign for BOOK is then formed: The open hands are held together, fingers pointing away from the body. They open with little fingers remaining in contact, as in the opening of a book. This sign is used by the Jews. *Cf.* BIBLE 3, HEBREW BIBLE, JEWISH BIBLE, TESTAMENT 3.

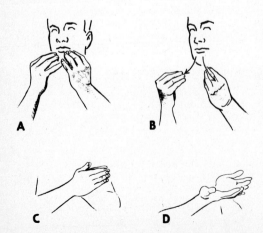

[H–142]

HOME (hōm), *n.* (A place where one eats and sleeps.) The closed fingers of the right hand are placed against the lips (the sign for EAT), and then, opening into a flat palm, against the right cheek (resting the head on a pillow, as in SLEEP). The head leans slightly to the right, as if going to sleep in the right palm, during this latter movement. *Cf.* ADDRESS 2, RESIDENCE 1.

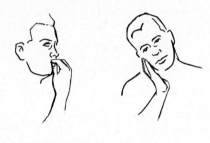

[H–143]

HOMELY 1 (hōm′ lĭ), *adj.* (The facial features are distorted.) The "X" hands are moved alternately up and down in front of the face, whose features are distorted with a pronounced frown. *Cf.* GRIMACE, MAKE A FACE, UGLINESS 1, UGLY 1.

[H–144]

HOMELY 2, *adj.* The "X" hands, palms down, move back and forth in a horizontal direction in front of the face, whose features are distorted with a pronounced frown. *Cf.* UGLINESS 2, UGLY 2.

[H–145]

HONEST (ŏn′ ĭst), *adj.* (The letter "H," for HONEST; a straight and true path.) The index and middle fingers of the right "H" hand, whose palm faces left, move straight forward along the upturned left palm. *Cf.* FRANK, HONESTY, SINCERE 1.

[H–146]

HONESTY (ŏn' ĭs tĭ), *n.* See HONEST.

[H–147]

HONOR 1 (ŏn' ər), *n., v.,* -ORED, -ORING. (The letter "H"; a gesture of respect.) The right "H" hand, palm facing left, swings down in an arc from its initial position in front of the forehead. The head bows slightly during this movement of the hand. *Cf.* HALLOWED 2, HONORARY.

[H–148]

HONOR 2, *n.* The right open hand faces the chest, with the thumb and index finger touching the mid-chest. The hand is drawn straight out and away, while the thumb and index finger come together and touch. The "H" position is next assumed and, with a sweeping motion, the index and middle fingers describe an arc directed inward to the forehead. *Cf.* ADMIRE 2.

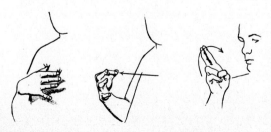

[H–149]

HONORARY (ŏn' ə rĕr´ ĭ), *adj.* See HONOR 1.

[H–150]

HOOK (ho͝ok), *n.* (Hooking on to something and pulling.) With index fingers interlocked, the right hand pulls the left hand from left to right. *Cf.* HITCH, PULL 2, TOW.

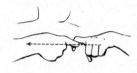

[H–151]

HOP 1 (hŏp), *v.,* HOPPED, HOPPING. (The natural sign.) The bent right index and middle fingers rest in the upturned left palm. The right hand rises suddenly, as if the fingers have jumped up. The fingers usually remain bent, but they may also straighten out as the hand rises. The motion may also be repeated. *Cf.* JUMP 1, LEAP.

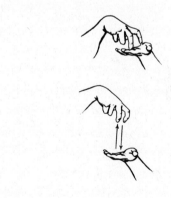

[H–152]

HOP 2, *v.* One finger is used here, the middle or the index, to represent a single leg. *Cf.* JUMP 2.

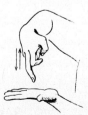

[H–153]

HOPE (hōp), *n., v.,* HOPED, HOPING. (A thought awaited.) The tip of the right index finger, held in the "D" position, palm facing the body, is placed on the forehead (modified THINK, *q. v.*). Both hands then assume right angle positions, fingers facing, with the left hand held above left shoulder level and the right before the right breast. Both hands, held thus, wave to each other several times. *Cf.* ANTICIPATE, ANTIC-IPATION, EXPECT.

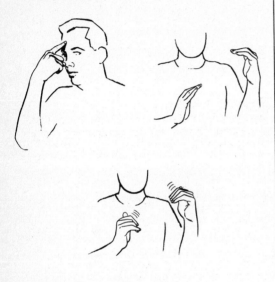

[H–154]

HOPELESSLY WEAK, *adj. phrase.* (The fingers collapse.) The little, ring, middle, and index fingers of the right hand, standing rigidly in the upturned left palm, suddenly bend at the knuckles and the right hand "crumples" into the left. *Cf.* WOEFULLY WEAK.

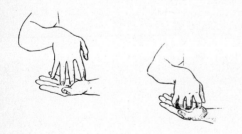

[H–155]

HORIZON (hə rī′ zən), *(rare), n.* (The natural sign.) The left arm, held horizontally a bit below eye level, with the left hand palm down, moves to the left

slowly and deliberately. The eyes look straight ahead, as if scanning the horizon. *Cf.* HORIZONTAL.

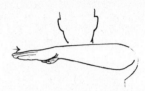

[H–156]

HORIZONTAL (hôr′ ə zŏn′ təl, hŏr′ -), *adj.* See HORI-ZON.

[H–157]

HORNS (hôrnz), *n. pl.* (The natural sign.) The "C" hands, held palms out at either temple, close over imaginary horns and move up a bit to either side, tracing the shape of the horns. *Cf.* PRESIDENT, SU-PERINTENDENT.

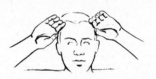

[H–158]

HORSE (hôrs), *n.* (The ears.) The "U" hands are placed palms out at either side of the head. The index and middle fingers move forward and back repeatedly, imitating the movement of a horse's ears.

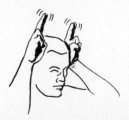

[H–159]

HORSEBACK (hôrs' băk´), *n.* (Mounted on horseback.) The right index and middle fingers straddle the left hand, which is held palm facing right. The left hand moves in a rhythmic up-down motion, carrying the right hand with it. *Cf.* RIDE.

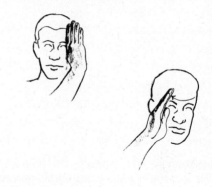

[H–160]

HOSE 1 (hōz), *n. pl.* (The knitting.) The index fingers, pointing forward, are rubbed back and forth against each other. *Cf.* KNIT, SOCK(S) 1, STOCKING(S) 1.

[H–161]

HOSE 2, *n. pl.* (Pulling on hose.) The downturned, open right hand grasps its left counterpart at the fingertips and slides over the back of the hand and up the arm, as if pulling on hose. *Cf.* SOCK(S) 2, STOCKING(S) 2.

[H–162]

HOSPITAL 1 (hŏs' pĭ təl), *n.* (The letter "H"; the red cross on the sleeve.) The index and middle fingers of the right "H" hand trace a cross on the upper part of the left arm. *Cf.* INFIRMARY 1.

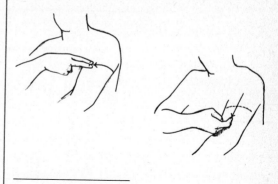

[H–163]

HOSPITAL 2, *n.* (The wide, bird-like hood worn by the French nursing sisters.) The right "B" hand, palm facing the left, swings over from the left side of the forehead to the right side.

[H–164]

HOT (hŏt), *adj.* (Removing hot food from the mouth.) The cupped hand, palm facing the body, moves up in front of the slightly open mouth. It is then flung down to the palm-down position.

[H-165]

HOT DOG, *(colloq.).* (The shape.) The "C" hands are held side by side, palms out, thumbs and index fingers touching. They change to the "S" position as they are drawn apart. *Cf.* FRANKFURTER.

[H-166]

HOTEL (hō tĕl′), *n.* (The letter "H"; the waving flag atop the building.) The right "H" hand is held upright with palm facing the body and fingertips pointing left. The right elbow rests on the downturned left hand. The right hand waves back and forth like a flag. *Cf.* INN.

[H-167]

HOT-HEADED (hŏt′ hĕd′ ĭd), *adj.* (The head is hot.) The sign for HOT is made: The cupped hand, palm facing the body, moves up in front of the slightly open mouth. It is then flung down to the palm-down position. The index finger then touches the forehead or the side of the head. The two signs are sometimes made in reverse order.

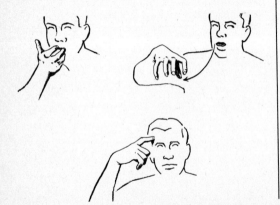

[H-168]

HOT-TEMPERED (tĕm′ pərd), *adj.* See HOT-HEADED.

[H-169]

HOT WEATHER. (Wiping the brow.) The down-turned right index finger, slightly curved, is drawn across the forehead from left to right. *Cf.* SUMMER.

[H-170]

HOUR (our), *n.* (The minute hand completes a circle around the clock's face.) The left "5" hand, palm facing right and fingers pointing forward or upward, is the clock's face. The right "D" hand is placed against it so that the right index finger points straight up. The right hand, always in contact with the left palm, executes a full clockwise circle, tracing the movement of the minute hand.

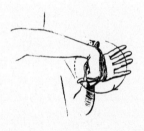

[H–171]

HOUSE (hous), *n.* (The shape of the house.) The open hands are held with fingertips touching, so that they form a pyramid a bit above eye level. From this position, the hands separate and move diagonally downward for a short distance; then they continue straight down a few inches. This movement traces the outline of a roof and walls. *Cf.* BARN, DOMICILE, RESIDENCE 2.

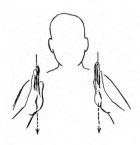

[H–172]

HOUSEKEEPER (hous' kēp' ər), *n.* The sign for HOUSE is made. This is followed by the sign for KEEP: The "K" hands are crossed, the right above the left, little finger edges down. The right hand is moved up and down a short distance. Then the sign for INDIVIDUAL is made: Both open hands, palms

facing each other, move down the sides of the body, tracing its outline to the hips.

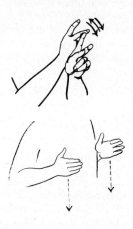

[H–173]

HOUSTON (hū' stən), *(loc.), n.* (The letter "H.") The index and middle finger of the right "H" hand, held upright and palm facing left, touch the right side of the face twice.

[H–174]

HOW (hou), *adv.* (The hands come into view, to reveal something.) The right-angle hands, palms down and knuckles touching, swing up and open to the palms-up position. *Cf.* MANNER 1.

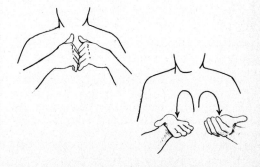

[H-175]

HOW ARE YOU?, *interrogative sent.* (The strength of the body; the inquisitive expression.) The "5" hands are placed on the chest rather forcefully. They then close into the "S" position, palms facing the body, as they leave the chest and move up a bit. In this terminal position they shake or tremble a bit. An inquisitive expression is all-important here.

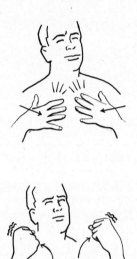

_____

[H-176]

HOWEVER 1 (hou ĕv′ ər), *conj.* (A divergence or a difference; the opposite of SAME.) The index fingers of both "D" hands, palms facing down, are crossed near their tips. The hands are drawn apart. *Cf.* ALTHOUGH, BUT, ON THE CONTRARY.

_____

[H-177]

HOWEVER 2, *conj.* Both hands, in the "5" position, are held before the chest, fingertips facing each other. With an alternate back-forth movement, the fingertips are made to strike each other. *Cf.* ANYHOW, ANYWAY, DESPITE, DOESN'T MATTER, INDIFFERENCE, INDIFFERENT, IN SPITE OF, MAKE NO DIF-

FERENCE, NEVERTHELESS, NO MATTER, WHEREVER.

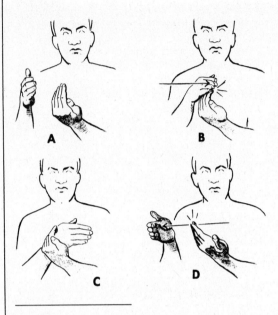

A   B

C   D

_____

[H-178]

HOW MANY?, *interrogative phrase.* (Throwing up a number of things before the eyes; a display of fingers to indicate a question of how many or how much.) The right hand, palm up, is held before the chest, all fingers touching the thumb. The hand is tossed straight up, while the fingers open to the "5" position. *Cf.* AMOUNT 2, HOW MUCH?, NUMBER 2.

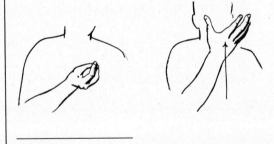

_____

[H-179]

HOW MUCH?, *interrogative phrase.* See HOW MANY?

_____

[H-180]

HOW MUCH MONEY?, *interrogative sent.* (Amount of money is indicated.) The sign for MONEY, is made: The upturned right hand, grasping some imaginary bills, is brought down into the upturned left palm a number of times. The right hand then moves straight up, opening into the "5" position, palm up. *Cf.* PRICE 1, WHAT IS THE PRICE?

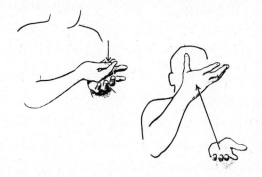

[H-181]

HOW OLD?, *interrogative phrase.* (AGE; HOW MUCH?) The sign for AGE or OLD is made: The right hand grasps an imaginary beard at the chin and pulls it downward. The same hand is then positioned with palm up and fingers touching the thumb. The hand is thrown up, opening into the palm-up "5" position. An inquisitive expression is assumed.

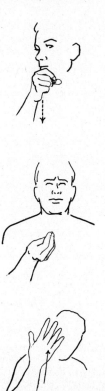

[H-182]

HUG (hŭg), *v.,* HUGGED, HUGGING, *n.* (The natural sign.) The arms clasp the body in a natural hugging position. *Cf.* EMBRACE.

[H-183]

HUGE (hūj), *adj.* (A delineation of something big, modified by the letter "L," which stands for LARGE.) Both "L" hands, palms facing out, are placed before the face, and separate rather widely. *Cf.* BIG 1, ENORMOUS, GREAT 1, IMMENSE, LARGE.

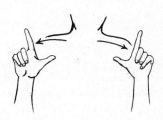

[H-184]

HUMAN (hū' mən), *adj.* (The man's cap.) The thumb and extended fingers of the right hand are brought up to grasp an imaginary cap brim, representing the tipping of caps by men in olden days. This is a root sign used to modify many others. As an alternative, the "H" hands are drawn up the sides of the chest. *Cf.* MALE, MAN, MANKIND.

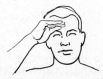

[H-185]

HUMANE (hū mān′), *adj.* (The heart rolls out.) Both right-angle hands roll over each other as they move down and away from their initial position at the heart. *Cf.* BENEVOLENT, GENEROUS 1, GENTLE 1, GENTLENESS, GRACIOUS, KIND 1, KINDNESS, MERCY 1, TENDER 3.

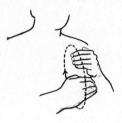

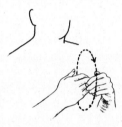

[H-186]

HUMANITY (hū măn′ ə tǐ), *n.* (People, indicated by the rotating "P" hands.) The "P" hands, side by side, are moved alternately in continuous counter-clockwise circles. *Cf.* AUDIENCE 2, PEOPLE, PUBLIC.

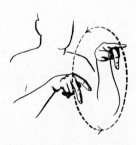

[H-187]

HUMBLE 1 (hŭm′ bəl, ŭm′-), *adj.* (The head bows; a turtle's head retreats into its shell; an act of humility.) The index finger edge of the right "B" hand, palm facing left, is placed at the lips. The right "B" hand is then brought down and under the down-

turned open left hand. The head, at the same time, bows. *Cf.* MEEK, MODEST.

[H-188]

HUMBLE 2, *adj.* Same as HUMBLE 1 but only the right hand is used.

[H-189]

HUMBLE 3, *adj.* (Dropping the hands and bowing the head; an act indicating humility.) The open hands, held with palms out or slightly facing each other, are dropped from their initial position before the head. As they drop the head bows.

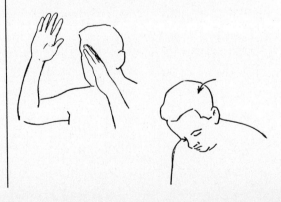

[H–190]

HUMBUG (hŭm′ bŭg), *n.* (A double face, *i.e.*, a mask covers the face.) The right hand is placed over the back of the left hand and pushes it down and a bit in toward the body. *Cf.* BLUFF, FAKE, HYPO-CRITE 1, IMPOSTOR.

[H–191]

HUMOR (hū′ mər, ū′-), *n.* (The nose wrinkles in laughter.) The tips of the right index and middle fingers brush repeatedly off the tip of the nose. *Cf.* COMIC, COMICAL, FUNNY, HUMOROUS.

[H–192]

HUMOROUS (hū′ mər əs, ū′-), *adj.* See HUMOR.

[H–193]

HUNDRED (hŭn′ drəd), *n., adj.* (The Roman "C," *centum,* for "hundred.") The letter "C" is formed. This is preceded by a "1" for a simple hundred, or by whatever number of hundreds one wishes to indicate.

[H–194]

HUNGARIAN (hŭng gâr′ ĭ ən), *adj., n.* (The upper alimentary tract is outlined.) The right "C" hand, palm facing the body, is placed with fingertips touching mid-chest. In this position it moves down a bit. The only rationale here is the phonetic similarity between HUNGARY and HUNGRY. *Cf.* APPETITE, CRAVE, DESIRE 2, FAMINE, HUNGARY, HUNGER, HUNGRY, STARVATION, STARVE, STARVED, WISH 2.

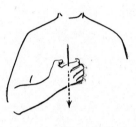

[H–195]

HUNGARY (hŭng′ gə ri), *n.* See HUNGARIAN.

[H–196]

HUNGER (hŭng′ gər), *n.* See HUNGARIAN.

[H–197]

HUNGRY (hŭng′ grĭ), *adj.* See HUNGARIAN.

[H–198]

HUNT (hŭnt), *n., v.,* HUNTED, HUNTING. (Firing a rifle.) The left hand grasps the barrel of an imaginary rifle, while the right hand grasps the base, its thumb extended upward to represent the sight, and index finger wiggling back and forth, as if pulling the trigger. At the same time, both hands make short back-and-forth movements, as if the rifle is firing.

[H–199]

HURRY (hûr′ i), *v.*, -RIED, -RYING. (Letter "H"; quick movements.) The "H" hands, palms facing each other and held about six inches apart, shake alternately up and down. One hand alone may be used. *Cf.* HASTE, HUSTLE.

[H–200]

HURT 1 (hûrt), *v.*, HURT, HURTING, *n.* (A stabbing pain.) The "D" hands, index fingers pointing to each other, are rotated in elliptical fashion before the chest—simultaneously but in opposite directions. *Cf.* ACHE, HARM 1, INJURE 1, INJURY, MAR 1, OFFEND, OFFENSE, PAIN, SIN, WOUND.

[H–201]

HURT 2, *v.*, *n.* (Striking down against.) Both "A" or "X" hands are held before the chest, the right above the left. The right hand strikes down and out, hitting the left thumb and knuckles with force. *Cf.* BACKBITE, BASE 3, CRUEL 1, HARM 2, MAR 2, MEAN 1, SPOIL.

[H–202]

HURT 3, *v.* (Silence; an avoidance of an outcry or impatience.) The index finger of the right "D" hand, palm facing left, is placed at the sealed lips. The head is held slightly bowed. *Cf.* PATIENCE 2, PATIENT 2.

[H–203]

HURT 4, *v.*, *n.* (The feelings are those which give pain, and cause the hand to be removed quickly from the source of the pain.) The sign for FEEL 2 is made: The right middle finger, touching the heart, moves up an inch or two a number of times. The right hand is then thrown down and out, opening into the downturned "5" position. *Cf.* FEEL HURT.

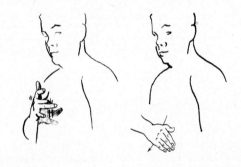

[H–204]

HUSBAND (hŭz′ bənd), *n.* (A male joined in marriage.) The MALE prefix sign is formed: The right hand grasps the brim of an imaginary cap. The hands are then clasped together.

[H–205]

HUSH (hŭsh), *n., interj., v.,* HUSHED, HUSHING. (The natural sign.) The index finger is brought up against the pursed lips. *Cf.* BE QUIET 1, CALM 2, NOISELESS, QUIET 1, SILENCE 1, SILENT, STILL 2.

[H–206]

HUSTLE (hŭs' əl), *v.,* -TLED, -TLING. (Letter "H"; quick movements.) The "H" hands, palms facing each other and held about six inches apart, shake alternately up and down. One hand alone may be used. *Cf.* HASTE, HURRY.

[H–207]

HYMN 1 (hĭm), *n.* (A rhythmic, wavy movement of the hand, to indicate a melody; the movement of a conductor's hand in directing a musical performance.) The right "5" hand, palm facing left, is waved back and forth over the downturned left hand, in a series of elongated figure-eights. *Cf.* CHANT, MELODY, MUSIC, SING, SONG.

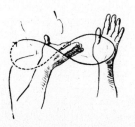

[H–208]

HYMN 2, *n.* (The letter "H.") The sign for HYMN 1 is made, but with the right "H" hand.

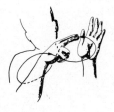

[H–209]

HYPOCRITE 1 (hĭp' ə krĭt), *n.* (A double face, *i.e.,* a mask covers the face.) The right hand is placed over the back of the left hand and pushes it down and a bit in toward the body. *Cf.* BLUFF, FAKE, HUMBUG, IMPOSTOR.

[H–210]

HYPOCRITE 2, *n.* (Covering the real face.) Both hands are held open, with palms down. The right hand, from a position above the left, swings out and under the left, and then moves straight out. *Cf.* FALSE-FACED, TWO-FACED, UNDERHAND.

[H–211]

| [H–212]

HYSTERICAL (hĭs tĕr′ ə kəl), *adj.* (The shaking of the stomach.) The cupped hands, held at stomach level, palms facing the body, move alternately up and down, describing short arcs. The signer meanwhile laughs. *Cf.* LAUGHTER 2.

HYSTERICAL LAUGH (Literally, rolling in the aisle.) With index and middle fingers bent to represent the doubled-up position, and its little finger edge resting on the upturned left palm, the right hand moves in a continuous counterclockwise circle in the left palm. An expression of glee is assumed. *Cf.* LAUGHTER 3.

[I-1]

I 1 (ī), *pron.* (The letter "I," held to the chest.) The right "I" hand is held with its thumb edge to the chest and little finger pointing up.

[I-2]

I 2, *pron.* (The natural sign.) The signer points to himself. *Cf.* ME.

[I-3]

ICE (īs), *n., v.,* ICED, ICING. (The stiff fingers.) The fingers of the "5" hands, held palms down, stiffen and contract. *Cf.* FREEZE, FROZEN, RIGID.

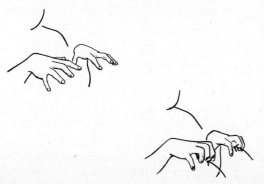

[I-4]

ICE CREAM 1 (crēm), *n.* (The eating action.) The upturned left palm represents a dish or plate. The curved index and middle fingers of the right hand represent the spoon. They are drawn up repeatedly from the left palm to the lips. *Cf.* SPOON.

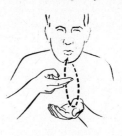

[I-5]

ICE CREAM 2, *n.* (The natural sign.) The signer goes through the act of licking an imaginary ice cream pop. *Cf.* LOLLIPOP.

[I-6]

ICE-SKATING (īs' skāt´ ing), *n.* (The natural sign.) The upturned "X" hands move gracefully back and forth. The index fingers here represent the upturned blades of the ice skates. *Cf.* SKATE.

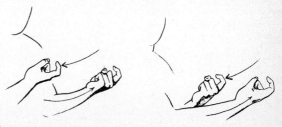

IDEA (ī dē′ ə), *n.* (A thought coming forward from the mind, modified by the letter "I" for "idea.") With the "I" position on the right hand, palm facing the body, touch the little finger to the forehead, and then move the hand up and away in a circular, clockwise motion. The hand may also be moved up and away without this circular motion. *Cf.* CONCEIVE 2, CONCEPT 1, CONCEPTION, FANCY 2, IMAGINATION, IMAGINE 1, JUST THINK OF IT!, NOTION, POLICY 2, THEORY, THOUGHT 2.

IDENTICAL (ī dĕn′ tə kəl), *adj.* (Matching fingers are brought together.) The outstretched index fingers are brought together, either once or several times. *Cf.* ALIKE, LIKE 2, SAME 1, SIMILAR, SUCH.

IDENTIFY (ī dĕn′ tə fī′), *v.,* -FIED, -FYING. (Gaze at intently and know.) With eyes fixed on an imaginary object, the head moves very slightly forward. The sign for KNOW is then made: The right fingers pat the forehead several times.

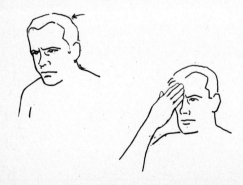

IDLE (ī′ dəl), *adj.* (A position of idleness.) With thumbs tucked in the armpits, the remaining fingers of both hands wiggle. *Cf.* HOLIDAY, LEISURE, RETIRE 3, VACATION.

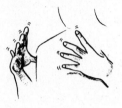

IDOL (ī′ dəl), *n.* (The "I" initials; the shape.) Both "I" hands move down simultaneously, in a wavy path, outlining the shape of an imaginary idol.

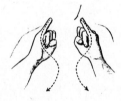

IF (ĭf), *conj.* (The scales move up and down.) The two "F" hands, palms facing each other, move alternately up and down. *Cf.* CONSIDER 3, COURT, EVALUATE 1, JUDGE 1, JUDGMENT, JUSTICE 1.

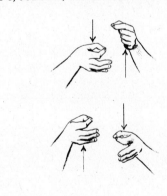

IGNORANT (ĭg′ nə rənt), *adj.* (The head is struck to emphasize its emptiness or lack of knowledge.) The back of the right "V" hand strikes the forehead once or twice. Two fingers represent prison bars across the mind—the mind is imprisoned.

IGNORE (ĭg nôr'), *v.,* -NORED, -NORING. (Thumbing the nose.) The index finger of the right "B" hand is placed under the tip of the nose. From this position the right hand moves straight forward, away from the face. *Cf.* DISREGARD.

ILL (ĭl), *adj., n., adv.* (The sick parts of the anatomy are indicated.) The right middle finger rests on the forehead, and its left counterpart is placed against the stomach. The signer assumes an expression of sadness or physical distress. *Cf.* DISEASE 1, ILLNESS, SICK, SICKNESS.

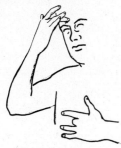

ILLNESS (ĭl' nĭs), *n.* See ILL. This is followed by the sign -NESS: The downturned right "N" hand

moves down along the left palm, which is facing away from the body.

ILL TEMPER (tĕm' pər). (Wrinkling the brow.) The "5" hand is held palm toward the face. The fingers open and close partly, several times, while an angry expression is worn on the face. *Cf.* ANGRY 1, CROSS 1, CROSSNESS, FIERCE, IRRITABLE.

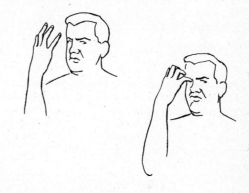

ILLUSTRATE (ĭl' ə strāt', ĭ lŭs' trāt), *v.,* -TRATED, -TRATING. (Directing the attention to something, and bringing it forward.) The right index finger points into the left palm, held facing out before the body. The left palm moves straight out. For the passive form of this verb, *i.e.,* BE SHOWN, the movement is reversed: The left hand, palm facing in, is moved in toward the body, while the right index finger remains pointing into the left palm. *Cf.* DEMONSTRATE, DISPLAY, EVIDENCE, EXAMPLE, EXHIBIT, EXHIBITION, INDICATE, INFLUENCE 3, PRODUCE 2, REPRESENT, SHOW 1, SIGNIFY 1.

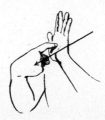

[I-19]

IMAGE (ĭm' ĭj), *n.* (Contours are indicated or outlined.) Both "A" hands, held about a foot apart before the face, with palms facing each other, move down simultaneously in a wavy, undulating motion. *Cf.* FIGURE 2, FORM, SCULPT, SCULPTURE, SHAPE 1, STATUE.

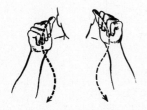

[I-20]

IMAGINATION (ĭ măj' ə nā' shən), *n.* (A thought coming forward from the mind, modified by the letter "I" for "idea.") With the "I" position on the right hand, palm facing the body, touch the little finger to the forehead, and then move the hand up and away in a circular, clockwise motion. The hand may also be moved up and away without this circular motion. *Cf.* CONCEIVE 2, CONCEPT 1, CONCEPTION, FANCY 2, IDEA, IMAGINE 1, JUST THINK OF IT!, NOTION, POLICY 2, THEORY, THOUGHT 2.

[I-21]

IMAGINE 1 (ĭ măj' ĭn), *v.,* -INED, -INING. See IMAGINATION.

[I-22]

IMAGINE 2, *v.* (Something emerges from the head and is grasped.) The index finger edge of the right "B" hand is placed in mid-forehead. The right hand moves straight up and then closes into the "S" position in front of the forehead, palm facing left. *Cf.* INVENT 2.

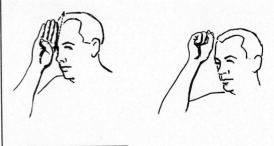

[I-23]

IMITATE (ĭm' ə tāt'), *v.,* -TATED, -TATING. (The natural sign.) The right fingers and thumb close together and move onto the upturned, open left hand, as if taking something from one place to another. *Cf.* COPY 1, DUPLICATE 1, MIMIC, MODEL.

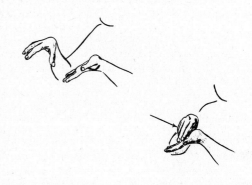

[I-24]

IMMACULATE (ĭ măk' yə lĭt), *adj.* (Everything is wiped off the hand, to emphasize an uncluttered or clean condition.) The right hand slowly wipes the upturned left palm, from wrist to fingertips. *Cf.* CLEAN 1, NEAT, NICE, PLAIN 2, PURE 1, PURITY, SIMPLE 2.

[I-25]

IMMACULATE CONCEPTION, *(eccles.)* (The halo; blamelessness, as indicated by the open hands.) The right index finger traces a halo around the head.

Both open hands are then dropped to the sides of the body.

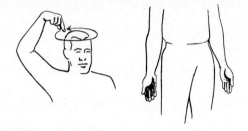

IMMEDIATE (ĭ mē′ dĭ ĭt), *adj.* (Something right in front of you.) The upturned right-angle hands drop down rather sharply. The "Y" hands may also be used. *Cf.* CURRENT, NOW, PRESENT 3.

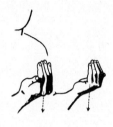

[I–27]

IMMEDIATELY (ĭ mē′ dĭ ĭt lĭ), *adv.* (A quick movement.) The thumbtip of the upright right hand is flicked quickly off the tip of the curved right index finger, as if shooting marbles. *Cf.* FAST 1, QUICK, QUICKNESS, RAPID, RATE 1, SPEED, SPEEDY, SWIFT.

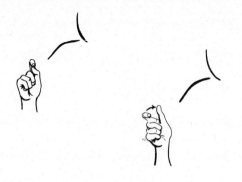

[I–28]

IMMENSE (i mĕns′), *adj.* (A delineation of something big, modified by the letter "L," which stands for LARGE.) Both "L" hands, palms facing out, are placed before the face, and separate rather widely. *Cf.* BIG 1, ENORMOUS, GREAT 1, HUGE, LARGE.

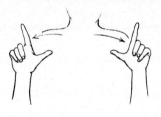

[I–29]

IMMODEST (ĭ mŏd′ ĭst), *adj.* (The color rises in the cheek; an attempt is made to hide the head.) The backs of the fingers of the right hand, held in the right angle position, are placed against the right cheek. The hand moves up along the cheek, pivoting at the wrist, so that the fingers finally point to the rear. *Cf.* ASHAMED 1, BASHFUL 1, IMMORAL, SHAME 1, SHAMEFUL, SHAME ON YOU, SHY 1.

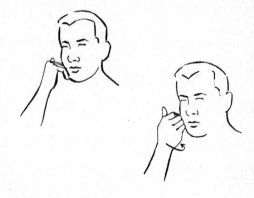

[I–30]

IMMORAL (ĭ môr′ əl, ĭ mŏr′-), *adj.* See IMMODEST.

[I–31]

IMPARTIAL (im pär′ shəl), *adj.* (Sameness is stressed.) The downturned "B" hands, held at chest height, are brought together repeatedly, so that the index finger edges or fingertips come into contact. *Cf.* EQUAL, EQUIVALENT, EVEN, FAIR 1, JUST 1, LEVEL.

[I–32]

IMPEDE (ĭm pēd′), *v.*, -PEDED, -PEDING. (Obstruct, block.) The left hand, fingers together and palm flat, is held before the body, facing somewhat down. The little finger side of the right hand, held with palm flat, makes one or several up-down chopping motions against the left hand, between its thumb and index finger. *Cf.* ANNOY 1, ANNOYANCE 1, BLOCK, BOTHER 1, CHECK 2, COME BETWEEN, DISRUPT, DISTURB, HINDER, HINDRANCE, INTERCEPT, INTERFERE, INTERFERENCE, INTERFERE WITH, INTERRUPT, MEDDLE 1, OBSTACLE, OBSTRUCT, PREVENT, PREVENTION.

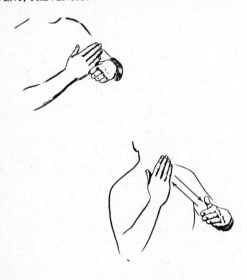

[I–33]

IMPEL 1 (ĭm pĕl′), *v.*, -PELLED, -PELLING. (Forcing the head to bow.) The right "C" hand pushes down on an imaginary neck. *Cf.* COERCE 1, COERCION 1, COMPEL 1, FORCE 1.

[I–34]

IMPEL 2, *v.* (Pushing something forward.) The open right hand is held palm down at chin level, fingers pointing left. From this position the hand turns to point forward, and moves forcefully forward and

away from the body, as if pushing something ahead of it. *Cf.* COERCE 2, COERCION 2, COMPEL 2, FORCE 2.

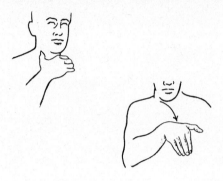

[I–35]

IMPERATIVE (ĭm pĕr′ ə tĭv), *adj.* (Being pinned down.) The right hand, in the "X" position, palm down, moves forcefully up and down once or twice. An expression of determination is frequently assumed. *Cf.* HAVE TO, MUST, NECESSARY 1, NECESSITY, NEED 1, OUGHT TO, SHOULD, VITAL 2.

[I–36]

IMPLORE (ĭm plōr′), *v.*, -PLORED, -PLORING. (An act of supplication.) With the right hand clasped over the left, both hands are shaken gently before the body. The eyes often are directed upward. *Cf.* BEG 2, BESEECH, ENTREAT, PLEA, PLEAD, SUPPLICATION.

[I–37]

IMPLY (ĭm plī′), *v.*, -PLIED, -PLYING. (Relative standing of one's thoughts.) A modified sign for THINK is made: The right index finger touches the middle of the forehead. The tips of the right "V" hand, palm down, are then thrust into the upturned left palm (as in STAND, *q.v.*). The right "V" hand is then re-thrust into the upturned left palm, with right palm now facing the body. *Cf.* CONNOTE, IN-TEND, INTENT 1, INTENTION, MEAN 2, MEANING, MOTIVE 3, PURPOSE 1, SIGNIFICANCE 2, SIGNIFY 2, SUBSTANCE 2.

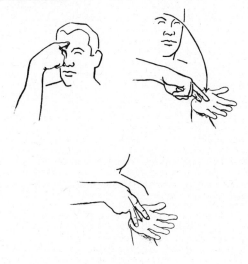

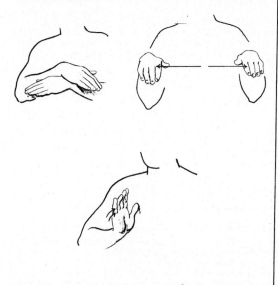

[I–38]

IMPOLITE (ĭm′ pə līt′), *adj.* (Not polite.) The sign for NOT is made. The downturned open hands are crossed. They are drawn apart rather quickly. The sign for POLITE is then made: The thumb of the right "5" hand touches the right side of the chest a number of times.

[I–39]

IMPORTANT 1 (ĭm pôr′ tənt), *adj.* Both "F" hands, palms facing each other, move apart, up, and together in a smooth elliptical fashion, coming together at the tips of the thumbs and index fingers of both hands. *Cf.* DESERVE, ESSENTIAL, MAIN, MERIT, PRECIOUS, PROMINENT 2, SIGNIFICANCE 1, SIGNIFICANT, VALUABLE, VALUE, VITAL 1, WORTH, WORTHWHILE, WORTHY.

[I–40]

IMPORTANT 2, *(arch.)*, *(rare)*, *adj.* (The letter "I" is brought up to a position of prominence.) The base of the right "I" hand rests on the back of the down-turned left "S" hand. The left hand moves straight up, carrying the right with it.

[I–41]

IMPOSSIBLE 1 (ĭm pŏs′ ə bəl), *adj.* (One finger en-counters an unyielding quality in striking another.) The right index finger strikes the left and continues moving down. The left index finger remains in place. *Cf.* CANNOT 1, CAN'T, UNABLE.

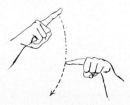

[I–42]

IMPOSSIBLE 2, *(loc.)*, *adj.* The downturned right "Y" hand is placed in the upturned left palm a number of times. The up-down movement is very slight.

[I–43]

IMPOST (ĭm′ pōst), *n.* (Nicking into one.) The knuckle of the right "X" finger is nicked against the palm of the left hand, held in the "5" position, palm facing right. *Cf.* ADMISSION 2, CHARGE 1, COST, DUTY 2, EXCISE, EXPENSE, FEE, FINE 2, PENALTY 3, PRICE 2, TAX 1, TAXATION 1, TOLL.

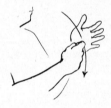

[I–44]

IMPOSTOR (ĭm pŏs′ tər), *n.* (A double face, *i.e.,* a mask covers the face.) The right hand is placed over the back of the left hand and pushes it down and a bit in toward the body. *Cf.* BLUFF, FAKE, HUMBUG, HYPOCRITE 1.

[I–45]

IMPREGNATE (ĭm prĕg′ nāt), *(sl.)*, *(vulg.)*, *v.,* -NATED, -NATING. (The uterus is locked, and the

seed is trapped.) The "5" hands, palms facing, swing together in an arc, so that the fingers interlock.

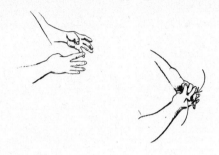

[I–46]

IMPRESS (ĭm prĕs′), *v.,* -PRESSED, -PRESSING. (Making an impression with the thumb.) The thumbtip is pressed into the upturned left palm. *Cf.* IMPRESSION.

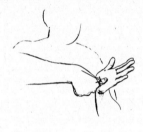

[I–47]

IMPRESSED (ĭm prĕst′), *adj.* (The impression is made on one.) As the sign for IMPRESS is made, both hands move an inch toward the body.

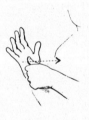

[I–48]

IMPRESSION (ĭm prĕsh′ ən), *n.* See IMPRESS 1.

[I–49]

IMPRISON (ĭm prĭz′ ən), *v.,* -PRISONED, -PRISON-ING. (The crossed bars.) The "4" hands, palms facing the body, are crossed at the fingers. *Cf.* JAIL, PENITENTIARY, PRISON.

[I-50]

IMPROVE (ĭm prōov'), *v.,* -PROVED, -PROVING. (Moving up.) The little finger edge of the right hand rests on the back of the downturned left hand. It moves up the left arm in successive stages, indicating improvement or upward movement. *Cf.* MEND 2.

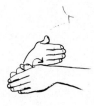

[I-51]

IMPURE (ĭm pyŏor'), *adj.* (A modification of the pig's snout groveling in a trough.) The downturned right hand is placed under the chin. Its fingers, pointing left, wiggle repeatedly. *Cf.* DIRTY, FILTHY, FOUL, NASTY, SOIL 2, STAIN.

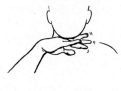

[I-52]

IN (ĭn), *prep., adv., adj.* (The natural sign.) The fingers of the right hand are thrust into the left. *Cf.* INSIDE, INTO, WITHIN.

[I-53]

IN A FEW DAYS, *adv. phrase.* (Several TOMOR-ROWS ahead.) The thumb of the right "A" hand is positioned on the right cheek. One by one, the remaining fingers appear, starting with the index finger. Usually, when all five fingers have been presented, the hand moves forward a few inches, to signify the concept of the future.

[I-54]

IN A FEW MONTHS, *adv. phrase.* (Few, month, future.) The sign for FEW is made: The right "A" hand is held palm facing up. One by one the fingers open, beginning with the index finger and ending with the little finger. This is followed by the sign for MONTH: The extended right index finger moves down along the upturned, extended left index finger. Finally, the sign for FUTURE, is made: The upright, open right hand, palm facing left, moves straight out and slightly up from a position beside the right temple.

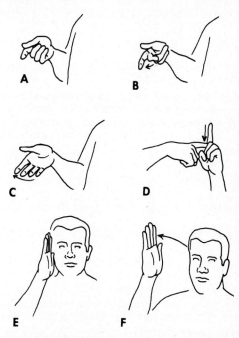

A   B

C   D

E   F

[I–55]

IN A FEW YEARS, *adv. phrase.* (Few, years, future.) The sign for FEW, as in IN A FEW MONTHS, is made. This is followed by the sign for YEAR: The right "S" hand, palm facing left, is positioned atop the left "S" hand, whose palm faces right. The right "S" hand describes a complete circle around the left and comes to rest in its original position. Finally, the sign for FUTURE, as in IN A FEW MONTHS, is made.

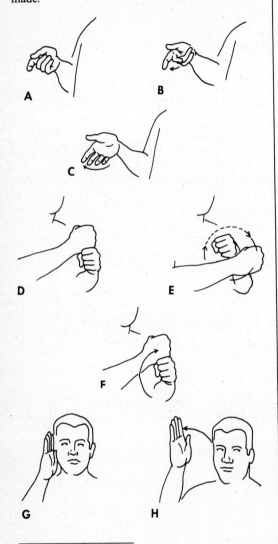

A   B

C

D   E

F

G   H

[I–56]

IN A WEEK, *adv. phrase.* (A week around the corner.) The upright, right "D" hand is placed palm-to-palm against the left "5" hand, whose palm faces right. The right "D" hand moves along the left palm

from base to fingertips and then curves to the left, around the left fingertips.

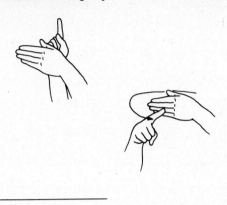

[I–57]

INCH 1 (ĭnch), *n.* (A small part of a sentence, *i.e.,* a word.) The tips of the right index finger and thumb, about an inch apart, are placed on the side of the outstretched left index finger, which represents the length of a sentence. *Cf.* VERBAL 2, WORD.

[I–58]

INCH 2, *n.* (The length of the thumb's first joint.) The upturned left thumb is crooked. The thumb and index finger of the right hand rest on the tip and first joint of the left thumb, to indicate its length.

[I–59]

INCIDENT (ĭn′ sə dənt), *n.* (A befalling.) Both "D" hands, index fingers pointing away from the body, are simultaneously pivoted over so that the palms face down. *Cf.* ACCIDENT, BEFALL, CHANCE, COIN-

CIDE 1, COINCIDENCE, EVENT, HAPPEN 1, OCCUR, OPPORTUNITY 4.

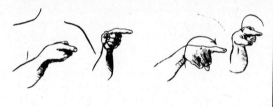

[I–60]

INCLINATION (ĭn´ klə nā′ shən), *n.* (The feelings of the heart move toward a specific object.) The tip of the right middle finger touches the heart. The open right hand, palm facing the body, then moves away from the heart toward the palm of the open left hand. *Cf.* DISPOSE, DISPOSED TO, DISPOSITION, IN-CLINE, INCLINED, TEND, TENDENCY.

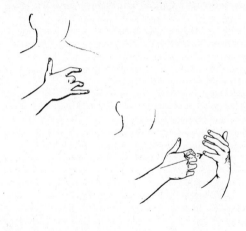

[I–61]

INCLINE (ĭn klīn′), *v.,* -CLINED, -CLINING. See IN-CLINATION.

[I–62]

INCLINED (ĭn klīnd′), *adj.* See INCLINATION.

[I–63]

INCLUDE (ĭn klōōd′), *v.,* -CLUDED, -CLUDING. (All; the whole.) The left hand is held in the "C" position, fingers pointing right. The right hand, in the "5" position, fingers facing out from the body, palm down, is held above the left. With a horizontal swing to the right, the right hand describes an arc, as the fingers close and are thrust into the left "C" hand,

which closes over it. *Cf.* ALL 2, ALTOGETHER, IN-CLUSIVE, WHOLE (THE).

[I–64]

INCLUSIVE (ĭn klōō′ sĭv), *adj.* See INCLUDE.

[I–65]

INCOME (ĭn′ kŭm), *n.* (A regular taking in.) The outstretched open left hand, held palm facing right, moves in toward the body, assuming the "A" posi-tion, palm still facing right. This is repeated several times. *Cf.* DIVIDEND, INTEREST 4, SUBSCRIBE, SUB-SCRIPTION.

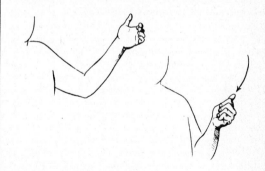

[I–66]

INCREASE (*n.* ĭn′ krēs; *v.* ĭn krēs′) -CREASED, -CREASING. (Adding on.) The index and middle fingers of the right "H" hand, palm up, are swung up and over until they come to rest on the index and middle fingers of the left "H" hand, held palm down. *Cf.* ADD 3, ADDITION, EXTEND 1, EXTRA, GAIN 1, ON TO, RAISE 2.

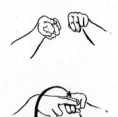

[I-67]

INCREDULITY (ĭn´ krə dū´ lə tĭ, -dо̄о̄´-), *n.* (The nose is wrinkled in disbelief.) The right "V" hand faces the nose. The index and middle fingers bend as a cynical expression is assumed. *Cf.* CYNIC, CYNICAL, DISBELIEF 1, DON'T BELIEVE, DOUBT 1, SKEPTIC 1, SKEPTICAL 1.

[I-68]

INDECISION (ĭn´ dĭ sĭzh´ ən), *n.* (On a fence.) The index and middle fingers of the right hand, palm down, straddle the index finger edge of the left "B" hand, which is held palm facing right. In this position the right hand rocks deliberately back and forth, from left to right. *Cf.* UNCERTAIN.

[I-69]

INDEED (ĭn dēd´), *adv., interj.* (Coming forth directly from the lips; true.) The index finger of the right "D" hand, palm facing left, is placed against the lips. It moves up an inch or two and then describes a small arc forward and away from the lips. *Cf.* ABSOLUTE, ABSOLUTELY, ACTUAL, ACTUALLY, AUTHENTIC, CERTAIN, CERTAINLY, FAITHFUL 3, FIDELITY, FRANKLY, GENUINE, POSITIVE 1, POSITIVELY, REAL, REALLY, SINCERE 2, SURE, SURELY, TRUE, TRULY, TRUTH, VALID, VERILY.

[I-70]

INDEPENDENCE (ĭn´ dĭ pĕn´ dəns), *n.* (Breaking the bonds.) The "S" hands, crossed in front of the body, swing apart and face out. *Cf.* DELIVER 1, EMANCIPATE, FREE 1, INDEPENDENT, LIBERATION, REDEEM 1, RELIEF, RESCUE, SAFE, SALVATION, SAVE 1.

[I-71]

INDEPENDENT (ĭn´ dĭ pĕn´ dənt), *adj.* See INDEPENDENCE.

[I-72]

INDIAN 1 (ĭn´ dĭ ən), *n., adj.* (The feathered headdress.) The right thumb and index fingers, holding an imaginary feather, are placed first on the tip of the nose and then under the right ear or on the right side of the head.

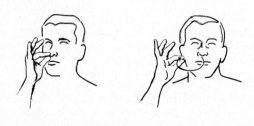

[I-73]

INDIAN 2, *n., adj.* (The characteristic motions during dancing.) The right "5" hand is placed behind the head, fingers pointing upward to indicate the feathers. The left hand touches the open lips repeatedly.

[I-74]

INDICATE (ĭn' də kāt'), v., -CATED, -CATING. (Directing the attention to something, and bringing it forward.) The right index finger points into the left palm, held facing out before the body. The left palm moves straight out. For the passive form of this verb, *i.e.*, BE SHOWN, the movement is reversed: The left hand, palm facing in, is moved in toward the body, while the right index finger remains pointing into the left palm. *Cf.* DEMONSTRATE, DISPLAY, EVIDENCE, EXAMPLE, EXHIBIT, EXHIBITION, ILLUSTRATE, INFLUENCE 3, PRODUCE 2, REPRESENT, SHOW 1, SIGNIFY 1.

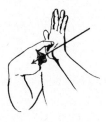

[I-75]

INDIFFERENCE (ĭn dĭf' ər əns), *n.* Both hands, in the "5" position, are held before the chest, fingertips facing each other. With an alternate back-forth movement, the fingertips are made to strike each other. *Cf.* ANYHOW, ANYWAY, DESPITE, DOESN'T MATTER, HOWEVER 2, INDIFFERENT, IN SPITE OF, MAKE NO DIFFERENCE, NEVERTHELESS, NO MATTER, WHEREVER.

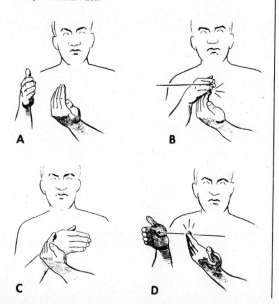

A   B

C   D

[I-76]

INDIFFERENT (ĭn dĭf' ər ənt), *adj.* See INDIFFERENCE.

[I-77]

INDIGNANT (ĭn dĭg' nənt), *adj.* (A violent welling-up of the emotions.) The curved fingers of the right hand are placed in the center of the chest, and fly up suddenly and violently. An expression of anger is worn. *Cf.* ANGER, ANGRY 2, ENRAGE, FURY, INDIGNATION, IRE, MAD 1, RAGE.

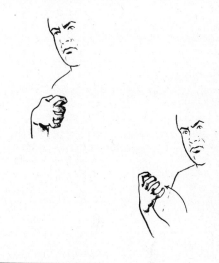

[I-78]

INDIGNATION (ĭn' dĭg nā' shən), *n.* See INDIGNANT.

[I-79]

INDIVIDUAL 1 (ĭn' də vĭj' ŏo əl), *n.* (The shape of an individual.) Both open hands, palms facing each other, move down the sides of the body, tracing its outline to the hips. This is an important suffix sign, that changes a verb to a noun. *E.g.*, TEACH, *v.*, becomes TEACHER, *n.*, by the addition of this sign.

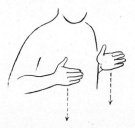

[I-80]

INDIVIDUAL 2, *n.* (The "I" hands; the outline of a person.) The "I" hands, palms facing and little fingers pointing out, are held before the body. They are drawn down a few inches, outlining the shape of an imaginary person standing before the signer.

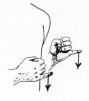

[I-81]

INDOCTRINATE (ĭn dŏk′ trĭ nāt′), *v.,* -NATED, -NATING. (Giving forth from the mind.) The fingertips of each hand are placed on the temples. They then swing out and into the "5" position. *Cf.* EDUCATE, INDOCTRINATION, INSTRUCT, INSTRUCTION, TEACH.

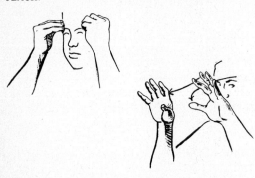

[I-82]

INDOCTRINATION *n.* See INDOCTRINATE.

[I-83]

INDORSE 1 (ĭn dôrs′), *v.,* -DORSED, -DORSING. (Holding up.) The right "S" hand pushes up the left "S" hand. *Cf.* ENDORSE 1, FAVOR, MAINTENANCE, SUPPORT 1, SUSTAIN, SUSTENANCE, UPHOLD, UPLIFT.

[I-84]

INDORSE 2, *v.* (One hand upholds the other.) Both hands, in the "S" position, are held palms facing the body, the right under the left. The right hand pushes up the left in a gesture of support. Essentially similar to INDORSE 1. *Cf.* ADVOCATE, ENDORSE 2, SUPPORT 2.

[I-85]

INDORSE 3, *v.* ("Second"—two fingers.) The right "L" hand, held somewhat above the head, index finger pointing straight up, pivots forward a bit, so that the index finger now points forward. Used in parliamentary procedure. *Cf.* ENDORSE 3, SECOND 2, SUPPORT 3.

[I-86]

INDUCE (ĭn dūs′, -dōōs′), *v.,* -DUCED, -DUCING. (Shaking someone, to implant one's will into another.) Both "A" hands, palms facing, are held before the chest, the left slightly in front of the right. In this position the hands move back and forth a short distance. *Cf.* COAX, CONVINCE, PERSUADE, PERSUASION, PROD, URGE 2.

[I–87]

INDULGENCE (ĭn dŭl′ jəns), *(eccles.)*, *n.* (The "P" refers to "Purgatory.") The tip of the middle finger of the right "P" hand executes a continuous clockwise circle on the upturned left palm.

[I–88]

INDUSTRIOUS (ĭn dŭs′ trĭ əs), *adj.* (Rubbing the hands together in zeal or ambition.) The open hands are rubbed vigorously back and forth against each other. *Cf.* AMBITIOUS 1, ANXIOUS 1, ARDENT, DILIGENCE 1, DILIGENT, EAGER, EAGERNESS, EARNEST, ENTHUSIASM, ENTHUSIASTIC, METHODIST, ZEAL, ZEALOUS.

[I–89]

INEXPENSIVE (ĭn′ ĭk spĕn′ sĭv), *adj.* (A small amount of money.) The sign for **MONEY** is made: The upturned right hand, grasping some imaginary bills, is brought down into the upturned left palm a number of times. The downturned cupped right hand is then positioned over the upturned cupped left hand. The right hand descends a short distance but does not touch the left. *Cf.* CHEAP 1.

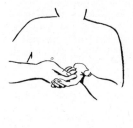
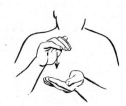

[I–90]

INFANT (ĭn′ fənt), *n.* (The rocking of the baby.) The arms are held with one resting on the other, as if cradling a baby. They rock from side to side. *Cf.* BABY, DOLL 2.

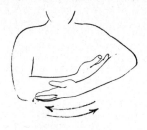

[I–91]

INFILTRATE (ĭn fĭl′ trāt), *v.,* -TRATED, -TRATING. (The threads are interwoven.) Both "5" hands, palms down, are brought slowly together, with the right sliding over the left. As they move together, the fingers wiggle. *Cf.* DARN, WEAVE.

[I–92]

INFINITE (ĭn′ fə nĭt), *adj.* (A large amount.) The "5" hands face each other, fingers curved and touching. They move apart rather quickly. *Cf.* EXPAND, GREAT 2, LOT, MUCH.

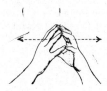

[I–93]

INFIRMARY 1 (ĭn fûr′ mə rĭ), *n.* (The letter "H"; the red cross on the sleeve.) The index and middle fingers of the right "H" hand trace a cross on the upper part of the left arm. *Cf.* HOSPITAL 1.

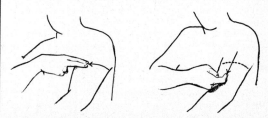

[I-94]

INFIRMARY 2 *n.* (The letter "I"; the red cross on the sleeve.) The little finger of the right "I" hand traces a cross on the upper part of the left arm.

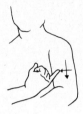

[I-95]

INFLUENCE 1 (ĭn' floŏ əns), *n., v.,* -ENCED, -ENCING. (Swaying one to one's side.) The "A" hands, palms facing each other and the right positioned above the left, swing over simultaneously to the left side of the body. *Cf.* EFFECT 2.

[I-96]

INFLUENCE 2, *n., v.* (Rays of influence emanating from a given source.) All the right fingertips, including the thumb, are positioned on the tip of the upturned thumb of the left "A" hand. The right hand, opening into the downturned "5" position, moves forward from its initial position. Instead of its initial position on the left thumb, the right hand is frequently placed on the back of the downturned left "S" hand, moving forward as described above. *Cf.* BASIS 1, CAUSE, EFFECT 1, INTENT 2, LOGIC, PRODUCE 4, REASON 2.

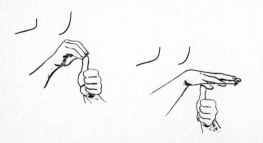

[I-97]

INFLUENCE 3, *n., v.* (Directing the attention to something, and bringing it forward.) The right index finger points into the left palm, held facing out before the body. The left palm moves straight out. For the passive form of this verb, *i.e.,* BE SHOWN, the movement is reversed: The left hand, palm facing in, is moved in toward the body, while the right index finger remains pointing into the left palm. *Cf.* DEMONSTRATE, DISPLAY, EVIDENCE, EXAMPLE, EXHIBIT, EXHIBITION, ILLUSTRATE, INDICATE, PRODUCE 2, REPRESENT, SHOW 1, SIGNIFY 1.

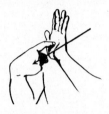

[I-98]

INFLUENCE 4, *n., v.* (Take something, *influence,* and disseminate it.) The left hand, held limp in front of the body, has its fingers pointing down. The fingers of the right hand, held all together, are placed on the top of the left hand, and then move forward, off the left hand, assuming a "5" position, palm down. Essentially similar to second part of INFLUENCE 2. *Cf.* ADVICE, ADVISE, COUNSEL, COUNSELOR.

[I-99]

INFORM 1 (ĭn fôrm'), *v.,* -FORMED, -FORMING. (Taking knowledge from the mind and giving it out to all.) The fingertips are positioned on either side of the forehead. Both hands then swing down and out, opening into the upturned "5" position. *Cf.* INFORMATION 1, LET KNOW 1, NOTIFY 1.

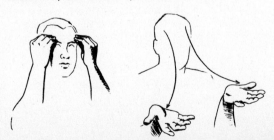

[I–100]

INFORM 2, *v*. The fingertips of the right "5" hand are positioned on the forehead. Both hands then swing forward and up, opening into the upturned "5" position. *Cf.* INFORMATION 2, LET KNOW 2, NOTIFY 2.

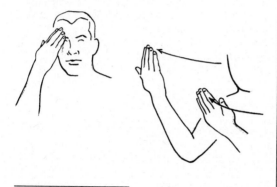

[I–101]

INFORMATION 1 (ĭn fər mā′ shən), *n*. See INFORM 1.

[I–102]

INFORMATION 2, *n*. See INFORM 2.

[I–103]

-ING, *progressive verb suffix*. The right "I" hand moves to the right.

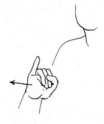

[I–104]

INITIAL (ĭ nĭsh′ əl), *adj., n., v.,* -TIALED, -TIALING. (The first finger is indicated.) The right index finger touches the upturned left thumb. *Cf.* FIRST 1, ORIGIN 2, PRIMARY.

[I–105]

INITIATE (*adj., n.* ĭ nĭsh′ ĭ ĭt, -āt′; *v.* ĭ nĭsh′ ĭ āt′), -ATED, -ATING. (Turning a key to open up a new venture.) The right index finger, resting between the left index and middle fingers, executes a half turn, once or twice. *Cf.* BEGIN, COMMENCE, INSTITUTE 2, ORIGIN 1, ORIGINATE 1, START.

[I–106]

INJECTION (in jĕk′ shən), *n*. (The natural sign.) The right hand goes through the motions of injecting a substance into the upper left arm. *Cf.* SHOT 1, SHOT IN THE ARM.

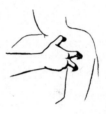

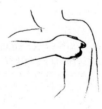

[I–107]

INJURE 1 (ĭn′ jər), *v.,* -JURED, -JURING. (A stabbing pain.) The "D" hands, index fingers pointing to each other, are rotated in elliptical fashion before the chest—simultaneously but in opposite directions. *Cf.* ACHE, HARM 1, HURT 1, INJURY, MAR 1, OFFEND, OFFENSE, PAIN, SIN, WOUND.

[I–108]

INJURE 2, v. (An encroachment; parrying a knife thrust.) The left "A" hand is held palm toward the body, knuckles facing right. The extended thumb of the right "A" hand is brought sharply over the back of the left. *Cf.* DANGER 2, DANGEROUS 2, PERIL, TRESPASS, VIOLATE.

[I–109]

INJURY (ĭn′ jə rĭ), n. See INJURE 1.

[I–110]

INJUSTICE (ĭn jŭs′ tĭs), n. (Not, justice.) The sign for NOT 1 is made: The downturned open hands are crossed. They are drawn apart rather quickly. This is followed by the sign for JUSTICE: The two "F" hands, palms facing each other, move alternately up and down.

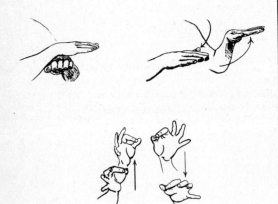

[I–111]

INK 1 (ĭngk), n. (The letter "I"; dipping the pen and shaking off the excess ink.) The little finger of the right "I" hand is dipped into the hole formed by the left "O" hand, held thumb side up. The right hand

then emerges and shakes off the imaginary ink from the little finger.

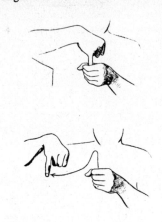

[I–112]

INK 2, n. (The letter "I"; dipping the pen; writing.) The little finger of the right "I" hand is drawn along the right eyebrow, from left to right. This is a modified sign for BLACK, *q.v.* The same finger is then "dipped into the inkwell," as explained in INK 1. Finally the right hand, holding an imaginary pen, writes on the upturned left palm.

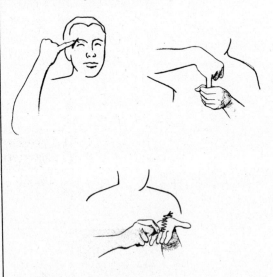

[I–113]

IN-LAW (ĭn′ lô′), n. (See material pertaining to each word.) The sign for IN is made: The fingers of the right hand are thrust into the left. This is followed by the sign for LAW: The upright right "L" hand, resting palm against palm on the upright left "5" hand, moves down in an arc a short distance, coming to rest on the base of the left palm.

brought in to the chest. The two signs are sometimes presented in reverse order. *Cf.* INNOCENT.

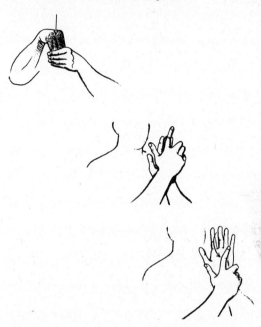

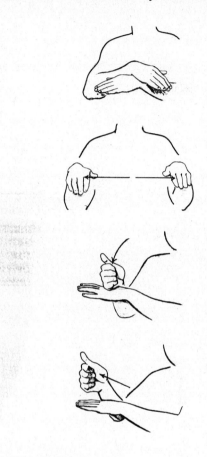

[I-114]

INN (ĭn), *n.* (The letter "H"; the waving flag atop the building.) The right "H" hand is held upright with palm facing the body and fingertips pointing left. The right elbow rests on the downturned left hand. The right hand waves back and forth like a flag. *Cf.* HOTEL.

[I-116]

INNOCENT (ĭn' ə sənt), *adj.* See INNOCENCE.

[I-117]

INOCULATE (ĭ nŏk' yə lāt´), *(colloq.),* *v.,* -LATED, -LATING. (A shot in the arm.) The right index finger is thrust into the left upper arm and the thumb wiggles back and forth a number of times, as if implanting a shot in the arm. *Cf.* COCA-COLA, COKE, DOPE, MORPHINE, NARCOTICS.

[I-115]

INNOCENCE (ĭn' ə səns), *n.* (Not to blame.) The sign for NOT is made: The downturned open hands are crossed at the wrists. They are drawn apart rather quickly. This is followed by the sign for BLAME: The right "A" hand, thumb pointing up, is brought down firmly against the back of the left hand, held palm down; the right thumb is then directed toward the person or object to blame. When personal blame is acknowledged, the thumb is

[I–118]

INQUIRE 1 (ĭn kwīr′), *v.,* -QUIRED, -QUIRING. (Pray tell.) Both hands, held upright about a foot in front of the chest, with palms facing and fingers pointing straight up, are positioned about a foot apart. Moving toward the chest, they come together until they touch, as if in prayer. *Cf.* ASK 1, CONSULT, REQUEST 1.

[I–119]

INQUIRE 2, *(colloq.), v.* (Fire a question.) The right hand, held in a modified "S" position with palm facing out, assumes a position with the thumb resting on the fingernail of the index finger. The index finger is flicked out and forward, usually directed at the person being asked a question. *Cf.* ASK 2, EXAMINATION 2, INTERROGATE 2, INTERROGATION 2, QUERY 2, QUESTION 2, QUIZ 2.

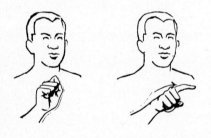

[I–120]

INQUIRE 3, *v.* (Firing questions.) The index fingers of both "D" hands repeatedly curve and straighten out as the hands are alternately flung forward and back, as if firing questions. *Cf.* ASK 3, EXAMINATION 3, INTERROGATE 1, INTERROGATION 1, QUERY 1, QUESTION 3, QUIZ 3.

[I–121]

INSANE (ĭn sān′), *adj.* (Turning of wheels in the head.) The open right hand is held palm down before the face, fingers spread, bent, and pointing toward the forehead. The fingers move in circles before the forehead. *Cf.* CRAZY 1, INSANITY, MAD 2, NUTS 1.

[I–122]

INSANITY (ĭn săn′ ə tĭ), *n.* See INSANE.

[I–123]

INSECT 1 (ĭn′ sĕkt), *n.* (The moving legs.) The downturned hands are crossed and interlocked at the little fingers. As they move forward, the fingers wiggle. *Cf.* SPIDER.

[I–124]

INSECT 2, *(sl.), n.* (The quivering antennae.) The thumb of the "3" hand rests against the nose, and the index and middle fingers bend slightly and straighten again a number of times. *Cf.* BUG.

[I–125]

INSENSATE (ĭn sĕn′ sāt), *adj.* (The slapping indicates the feelings of the heart are being tested.) The right hand rests on the heart. It then swings off and down, palm upturned, its fingertips slapping against the left palm as it moves down. An expression of contempt is often assumed.

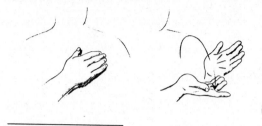

[I-126]

INSIDE (*prep., adv.* ĭn´ sīd´; *adj.* ĭn´ sīd´). (The natural sign.) The fingers of the right hand are thrust into the left. *Cf.* IN, INTO, WITHIN.

[I-127]

INSIST (ĭn sĭst´), *v.,* -SISTED, -SISTING. (Something specific is moved in toward oneself.) The palm of the left "5" hand faces right. The right index finger is thrust into the left palm, and both hands are drawn sharply in toward the chest. *Cf.* DEMAND, REQUEST 2, REQUIRE.

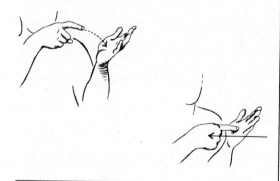

[I-128]

INSPECT (ĭn spĕkt´), *v.,* -SPECTED, -SPECTING. (The eye is directed in a probing operation.) The right index finger is placed just below the right eye. With palm down, the same finger then moves slowly and deliberately along the upturned left palm, from its base to its fingertips. Instead of the slow, deliberate movement, the finger may move along the left

palm in a series of short, stabbing motions. *Cf.* INVESTIGATE 2.

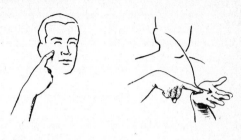

[I-129]

IN SPITE OF (spīt), *prep. phrase.* Both hands, in the "5" position, are held before the chest, fingertips facing each other. With an alternate back-forth movement, the fingertips are made to strike each other. *Cf.* ANYHOW, ANYWAY, DESPITE, DOESN'T MATTER, HOWEVER 2, INDIFFERENCE, INDIFFERENT, MAKE NO DIFFERENCE, NEVERTHELESS, NO MATTER, WHEREVER.

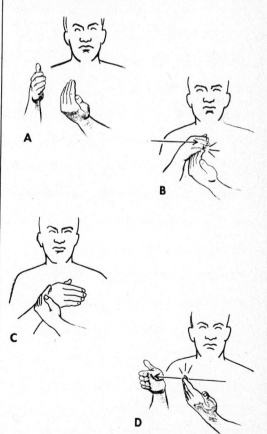

A

B

C

D

[I–130]

INSTALL (ĭn stôl′), *v.,* -STALLED, -STALLING. (Placing into.) The right hand, fingers touching the thumb, is placed into the left "C" hand, whose palm faces out or toward the right.

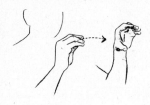

[I–131]

INSTEAD OF 1 (ĭn stĕd′), *prep. phrase.* (Exchanging places.) The right "A" hand, positioned above the left "A" hand, swings down and under the left, coming up a bit in front of it. *Cf.* EXCHANGE, REPLACE, SUBSTITUTE, TRADE.

[I–132]

INSTEAD OF 2, *prep. phrase.* This is the same sign as for INSTEAD OF 1, except that the "F" hands are used.

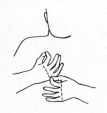
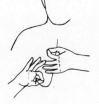

[I–133]

INSTITUTE 1 (ĭn′ stə tūt′, -to͞ot′), *n.* (The letter "I"; establishment on a firm base.) The right "I" hand is placed so that its base rests on the back of the downturned left "S" hand.

The movement is repeated, involving a slight up-down motion. Sometimes the right hand executes a small clockwise circle before coming to rest on the left. In this case the motion is not repeated. *Cf.* INSTITUTION.

[I–134]

INSTITUTE 2, *v.* -TUTED, -TUTING (Turning a key to open up a new venture.) The right index finger, resting between the left index and middle fingers, executes a half turn, once or twice. *Cf.* BEGIN, COMMENCE, INITIATE, ORIGIN 1, ORIGINATE 1, START.

[I–135]

INSTITUTION (ĭn′ stə tū′ shən), *n.* See INSTITUTE 1.

[I–136]

INSTRUCT (ĭn strŭkt′), *v.,* -STRUCTED, -STRUCTING. (Giving forth from the mind.) The fingertips of each hand are placed on the temples. They then swing out and open into the "5" position. *Cf.* EDUCATE, INDOCTRINATE, INDOCTRINATION, INSTRUCTION, TEACH.

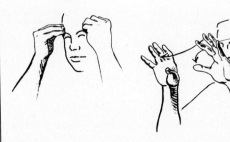

[I–137]

INSTRUCTION (ĭn strŭk′ shən), *n.* See INSTRUCT.

[I–138]

INSTRUCTOR (ĭn strŭk′ tər), *n.* The sign for IN-STRUCT is made. This is followed by the sign for INDIVIDUAL: Both open hands, palms facing each other, move down the sides of the body, tracing its outline to the hips. *Cf.* EDUCATOR, TEACHER.

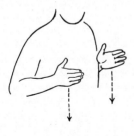

[I–139]

INSTRUMENT (ĭn′ strə mənt), *n.* (Something shown in the hand.) The outstretched right hand, palm up and held before the chest, is dropped slightly and brought over a bit to the right. *Cf.* ANYTHING, AP-PARATUS, MATTER, OBJECT 1, SUBSTANCE 1, THING.

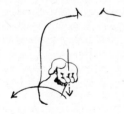

[I–140]

INSULT 1 (*n.* ĭn′ sŭlt; *v.* ĭn sŭlt′) -SULTED, -SULT-ING. (A puncturing.) The right index finger is thrust quickly and deliberately between the index and mid-dle fingers of the left "V" hand, which is held palm facing right.

[I–141]

INSULT 2, *v.* (A slap in the face.) The right hand slaps the back of the left a glancing blow, and its

momentum continues it beyond the left hand. *Cf.* BANISH.

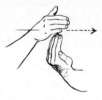

[I–142]

INSULT 3, *n., v.* (The thrust of a foil or épée.) The right index finger is thrust quickly forward and a bit up, in imitation of a fencing maneuver. *Cf.* RIPOSTE.

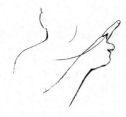

[I–143]

INSURANCE (ĭn shoõr′ əns), *n.* (The letter "I.") The right "I" hand, palm out, is shaken slightly.

[I–144]

INTELLECT (ĭn′ tə lekt′), *n.* (Patting the head to indicate something of value inside.) The right fingers pat the forehead several times. *Cf.* INTELLIGENCE, MENTAL, MIND 1, SENSE 1.

[I–145]

INTELLECTUAL (ĭn´ tə lek´ chŏo əl), *adj.* (Measuring the depth of the mind.) The downturned "X" finger moves up and down a short distance as it rests on mid-forehead. *Cf.* WISDOM, WISE.

[I–146]

INTELLIGENCE (ĭn tĕl´ ə jəns), *n.* See INTELLECT.

[I–147]

INTELLIGENT (ĭn tĕl´ ə jənt), *adj.* (The mind is bright.) The middle finger is placed at the forehead, and then the hand, with an outward flick, turns around so that the palm faces outward. This indicates a brightness flowing from the mind. *Cf.* BRIGHT 3, BRILLIANT 1, CLEVER 1, SMART.

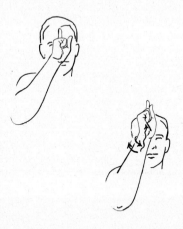

[I–148]

INTEND (ĭn tĕnd´), *v.,* -TENDED, -TENDING. (Relative standing of one's thoughts.) A modified sign for THINK is made: The right index finger touches the middle of the forehead. The tips of the right "V" hand, palm down, are then thrust into the upturned left palm (as in STAND, *q.v.*). The right "V" hand is then re-thrust into the upturned left palm, with right palm now facing the body. *Cf.* CONNOTE, IMPLY, INTENT 1, INTENTION, MEAN 2, MEANING,

MOTIVE 3, PURPOSE 1, SIGNIFICANCE 2, SIGNIFY 2, SUBSTANCE 2.

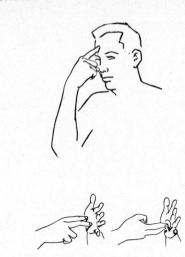

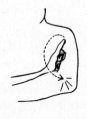

[I–149]

INTENSITY (ĭn tĕn´ sə tĭ), *n.* (The letter "I"; the strength or power, as indicated by the shape of the biceps.) The right "I" hand describes an arc as it moves down from a point on the left shoulder to the crook of the left elbow.

[I–150]

INTENT 1 (ĭn tĕnt´), *n.* See INTEND.

[I–151]

INTENT 2, *n.* (Rays of influence emanating from a given source.) All the right fingertips, including the thumb, are positioned on the tip of the upturned thumb of the left "A" hand. The right hand, opening into the downturned "5" position, moves forward from its initial position. Instead of its initial position on the left thumb the right hand is frequently placed on the back of the downturned left "S" hand, moving forward as described above. *Cf.* BASIS 1, CAUSE,

EFFECT 1, INFLUENCE 2, LOGIC, PRODUCE 4, REA-
SON 2.

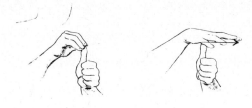

[I–152]

INTENTION (ĭn tĕn′ shən), *n.* See INTEND.

[I–153]

INTERCEPT (ĭn′ tər sĕpt′), *v.*, -CEPTED, -CEPTING.
(Obstruct, block.) The left hand, fingers together
and palm flat, is held before the body, facing somewhat down. The little finger side of the right hand,
held with palm flat, makes one or several up-down
chopping motions against the left hand, between its
thumb and index finger. *Cf.* ANNOY 1, ANNOYANCE
1, BLOCK, BOTHER 1, CHECK 2, COME BETWEEN,
DISRUPT, DISTURB, HINDER, HINDRANCE, IMPEDE,
INTERFERE, INTERFERENCE, INTERFERE WITH, IN-
TERRUPT, MEDDLE 1, OBSTACLE, OBSTRUCT, PRE-
VENT, PREVENTION.

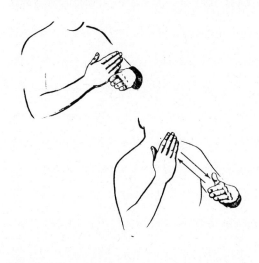

[I–154]

INTERCHANGE (ĭn′ tər chānj′), *v.*, -CHANGED,
-CHANGING. (The back-and-forth motion.) The "A"
hands, palms facing, swing alternately toward and

away from the body, passing each other as they do
so.

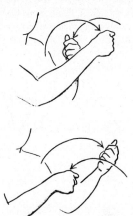

[I–155]

INTEREST 1 (ĭn′ tər ĭst, -trĭst), *n., v.*, -ESTED,
-ESTING. (Drawing one out.) The index and middle
fingers of both hands, one above the other, are
placed on the middle part of the chest. Both hands
move forward simultaneously. As they do, the index
and middle fingers of each hand come together. *Cf.*
FASCINATE 1, INTERESTED 1, INTERESTING 1.

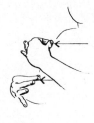

[I–156]

INTEREST 2, *n.* (A modification of INTEREST 1.)
The same movements are employed, except that one
of the hands is positioned in front of the mouth. *Cf.*
ENGROSS, FASCINATE 2.

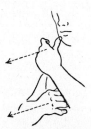

[I–157]

INTEREST 3, *n., v.* (The tongue is pulled out, causing the mouth to gape.) The curved open right hand is placed at the mouth, with index finger and thumb poised as if to grasp the tongue. The hand moves straight out, assuming the "A" position. *Cf.* INTERESTED 2, INTERESTING 2.

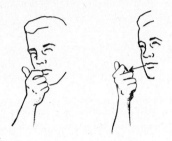

[I–158]

INTEREST 4, *n.* (A regular taking in.) The outstretched open left hand, held palm facing right, moves in toward the body, assuming the "A" position, palm still facing right. This is repeated several times. *Cf.* DIVIDEND, INCOME, SUBSCRIBE, SUBSCRIPTION.

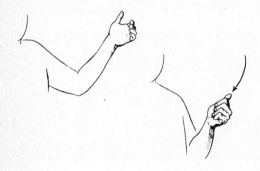

[I–159]

INTEREST 5, *n.* (The letter "I"; same rationale as for EARN.) The little finger edge of the right "I" hand rests on the upturned left palm. The right hand sweeps in an arc across the left palm, from right to left.

[I–160]

INTERESTED 1 (ĭn′ tər ĭs tĭd, -trĭs tĭd, -tə rĕs′ tĭd), *adj.* See INTEREST 1.

[I–161]

INTERESTED 2, *adj.* See INTEREST 3.

[I–162]

INTERESTING 1 (ĭn′ tər ĭs tĭng, -trĭs tĭng, -tə rĕs′ tĭng), *adj.* See INTEREST 1.

[I–163]

INTERESTING 2, *adj.* See INTEREST 3.

[I–164]

INTERFERE (ĭn′ tər fĭr′), *v.*, -FERED, -FERING. (Obstruct, block.) The left hand, fingers together and palm flat, is held before the body, facing somewhat down. The little finger side of the right hand, held with palm flat, makes one or several up-down chopping motions against the left hand, between its thumb and index finger. *Cf.* ANNOY 1, ANNOYANCE 1, BLOCK, BOTHER 1, CHECK 2, COME BETWEEN, DISRUPT, DISTURB, HINDER, HINDRANCE, IMPEDE, INTERCEPT, INTERFERENCE, INTERFERE WITH, INTERRUPT, MEDDLE 1, OBSTACLE, OBSTRUCT, PREVENT, PREVENTION.

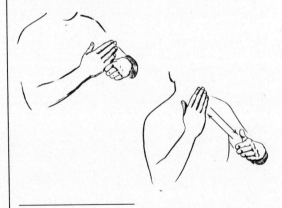

[I–165]

INTERFERENCE (ĭn′ tər fĭr′ əns), *n.* See INTERFERE.

[I–166]

INTERFERE WITH *v. phrase.* See INTERFERE.

[I-167]

INTERNATIONAL (ĭn tər năsh' ən əl), *adj.* (The letters, "I" and "N.") The right "I" hand makes a circle in the air and then moves straight down to rest on the back of the downturned left "S" hand. The right "N" hand then goes through the same motions.

[I-168]

INTERPRET (ĭn tûr' prĭt), *v.*, -PRETED, -PRETING. (Changing one language to another.) The "F" hands are held palms facing and thumbs and index fingers in contact with each other. The hands swing around each other, reversing their relative positions.

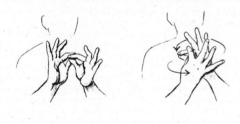

[I-169]

INTERROGATE 1 (ĭn tĕr' ə gāt'), *v.*, -GATED, -GATING. (Firing questions.) The index fingers of both "D" hands repeatedly curve and straighten out as the hands are alternately flung forward and back, as if firing questions. *Cf.* ASK 3, EXAMINATION 3, INQUIRE 3, INTERROGATION 1, QUERY 1, QUESTION 3, QUIZ 3.

[I-170]

INTERROGATE 2, *(colloq.)*, *v.* (Fire a question.) The right hand, held in a modified "S" position with palm facing out, assumes a position with the thumb resting on the fingernail of the index finger. The index finger is flicked out and forward, usually directed at the person being asked a question. *Cf.* ASK 2, EXAMINATION 2, INQUIRE 2, INTERROGATION 2, QUERY 2, QUESTION 2, QUIZ 2.

[I-171]

INTERROGATION 1 (ĭn tĕr' ə gā' shən), *n.* See INTERROGATE 1.

[I-172]

INTERROGATION 2, *(colloq.)*, *n.* See INTERROGATE 2.

[I-173]

INTERRUPT (ĭn' tə rŭpt'), *v.*, -RUPTED, -RUPTING. (Obstruct, block.) The left hand, fingers together and palm flat, is held before the body, facing somewhat down. The little finger side of the right hand, held with palm flat, makes one or several up-down chopping motions against the left hand, between its thumb and index finger. *Cf.* ANNOY 1, ANNOYANCE 1, BLOCK, BOTHER 1, CHECK 2, COME BETWEEN, DISRUPT, DISTURB, HINDER, HINDRANCE, IMPEDE, INTERCEPT, INTERFERE, INTERFERENCE, INTERFERE WITH, MEDDLE 1, OBSTACLE, OBSTRUCT, PREVENT, PREVENTION.

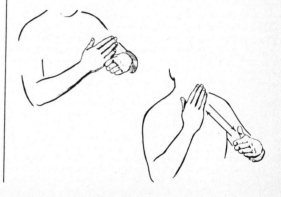

[I-174]

INTERSECT (ĭn′ tər sĕkt′), v., -SECTED, -SECTING. (Intersecting lines.) The extended index fingers move toward each other at right angles and cross. Cf. CROSS 4, CROSSING, INTERSECTION.

[I-175]

INTERSECTION (ĭn′ tər sĕk shən), n. See INTERSECT.

[I-176]

IN THE FIELD OF, prep. phrase. (A straight, i.e., special, path.) The hands are held in the "B" position, one above the other, with left palm facing right and right palm facing left. The little finger edge of the right hand moves straight forward along the index finger edge of the left. Cf. FIELD 3, SPECIALIZE, SPECIALTY.

[I-177]

IN THE FUTURE, adv. phrase. (Something ahead or in the future.) The upright, open right hand, palm facing left, moves straight out and slightly up from a position beside the right temple. Cf. BY AND BY, FUTURE, LATER 2, LATER ON, SHALL, WILL 1, WOULD.

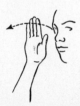

[I-178]

IN THE MEANTIME, adv. phrase. (Parallel time.) Both "D" hands, palms down, move forward in unison, away from the body. They may move straight forward or may follow a slight upward arc. Cf. DURING, IN THE PROCESS OF, MEANTIME, WHILE.

[I-179]

IN THE PROCESS OF, prep. phrase. See IN THE MEANTIME.

[I-180]

INTO (ĭn′ tōō), prep. (The natural sign.) The fingers of the right hand are thrust into the left. Cf. IN, INSIDE, WITHIN.

[I-181]

INTOXICATE (ĭn tŏk′ sə kāt′), v., -CATED, -CATING. (The act of drinking.) The thumbtip of the right "Y" hand is tilted toward the mouth, as if it were a drinking glass or bottle. The signer tilts his head back slightly, as if drinking. Cf. DRINK 2, DRUNK, DRUNKARD, DRUNKENNESS, INTOXICATION, LIQUOR 2.

[I-182]

INTOXICATION (ĭn tŏk′ sə ka′ shən), n. See INTOXICATE.

[I–183]

INTRODUCE (ĭn´ trə dūs´), v., -DUCED, -DUCING. (A bringing together.) Both upturned open hands swing in toward each other, stopping just before the fingertips touch. *Cf.* INTRODUCTION.

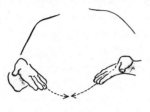

[I–184]

INTRODUCTION (ĭn´ trə dŭk´ shən), n. See INTRO-DUCE.

[I–185]

INTROSPECTION (ĭn´ trə spĕk´ shən), n. The sign for THINK is formed: The index finger makes a small circle on the forehead. This is followed by the sign for IN: The fingers of the right hand are thrust into the left.

[I–186]

IN TWO WEEKS, *adv. phrase.* (In a week, two.) The upright, right "2" hand is placed palm-to-palm against the left "5" hand, whose palm faces left. The right hand moves along the left palm from base to fingertips and then curves to the left, around the left fingertips. (This is the same sign as for IN A WEEK except the "2" hand is used here.)

[I–187]

INVENT 1 (ĭn vĕnt´), v., -VENTED, -VENTING. (First to be grasped from the mind.) The right "D" hand moves straight up against the forehead, and then closes into the "S" position, still against the fore-head. *Cf.* ORIGIN 3, ORIGINAL 1, ORIGINATE 2.

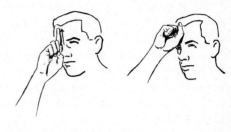

[I–188]

INVENT 2, v. (Something emerges from the head and is grasped.) The index finger edge of the right "B" hand is placed in mid-forehead. The right hand moves straight up and then closes into the "S" posi-tion in front of the forehead, palm facing left. *Cf.* IMAGINE 2.

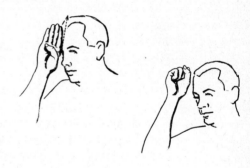

[I–189]

INVENTOR (ĭn vĕn´ tər), n. See INVENT 1. This is followed by the sign for INDIVIDUAL: Both open hands, palms facing each other, move down the sides of the body, tracing its outline to the hips.

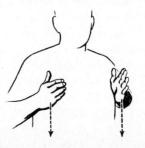

[I–190]

INVEST (ĭn vĕst′), v., -VESTED, -VESTING. (Stacking piles of chips or bills.) The "C" hands, holding imaginary stacks of chips or bills, move forward alternately, as if placing them on shelves of different heights.

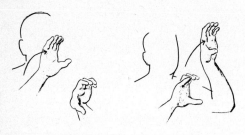

[I–191]

INVESTIGATE 1 (in vĕs′ tə gāt′), v., -GATED, -GATING. (Directing the vision from place to place.) The right "C" hand, palm facing left, moves from right to left across the line of vision, in a series of counterclockwise circles. The signer's gaze remains concentrated and his head turns slowly from right to left. Cf. CURIOUS 1, EXAMINE, LOOK FOR, PROBE 1, QUEST, SEARCH, SEEK.

[I–192]

INVESTIGATE 2, v. (The eye is directed in a probing operation.) The right index finger is placed just below the right eye. With palm down, the same finger then moves slowly and deliberately along the upturned left palm, from its base to its fingertips. Instead of the slow, deliberate movement, the finger may move along the left palm in a series of short, stabbing motions. Cf. INSPECT.

[I–193]

INVESTIGATOR (in vĕs′ tə gāt′ ər), n. See INVESTIGATE 1. This is followed by the sign for INDIVIDUAL: Both open hands, palms facing each other, move down the sides of the body, tracing its outline to the hips.

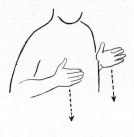

[I–194]

INVITATION (in′ və tā′ shən), n. (Opening or leading the way toward something.) The open right hand, held up before the body, sweeps down in an arc and over toward the left side of the chest, ending in the palm-up position. Cf. ADMIT 2, INVITE, INVITED, USHER, WELCOME.

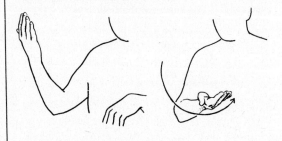

[I–195]

INVITE (in vīt′), v., -VITED, -VITING. (Opening or leading the way toward something.) The open right hand, held up before the body, sweeps down in an arc and over toward the left side of the chest, ending in the palm-up position. Reversing the movement gives the passive form of the verb, except that the hand does not arc upward but rather simply moves outward in a small arc from the body. Cf. ADMIT 2, INVITATION, INVITED, USHER, WELCOME.

[I–196]

INVITED, *passive voice of the verb* INVITE. The upturned right hand, touching the chest, moves straight forward and away from the body.

[I–197]

INVOLVE (ĭn vŏlv′), *v.,* -VOLVED, -VOLVING. (Immersed in something.) The downturned right "5" hand moves in a clockwise circle above the cupped left "C" hand. Then the right fingers are thrust into the cupped left "C" hand, which closes over the right fingers.

[I–198]

IRE (īr), *n.* (A violent welling-up of the emotions.) The curved fingers of the right hand are placed in the center of the chest, and fly up suddenly and violently. An expression of anger is worn. *Cf.* ANGER, ANGRY 2, ENRAGE, FURY, INDIGNANT, INDIGNATION, MAD 1, RAGE.

[I–199]

IRELAND (īr′ lənd), *n.* (A modified version of the sign for POTATO, *i.e.,* IRISH potato.) The down-

turned right "V" hand, poised over the downturned left "S" hand, executes a clockwise circle; then the "V" fingers stab the back of the left "S" hand. *Cf.* IRISH.

[I–200]

IRISH (ī′ rĭsh), *n., adj.* See IRELAND.

[I–201]

IRON 1 (ī′ ərn), *n.* (Striking an anvil with a hammer.) The left index finger, pointing forward from the body, represents the anvil. The right hand, grasping an imaginary hammer, swings down against the left index finger and glances off. This may be repeated. *Cf.* BLACKSMITH, STEEL.

[I–202]

IRON 2, *v.,* IRONED, IRONING. (The act of pressing with an iron.) The right hand goes through the motion of swinging an iron back and forth over the upturned left palm. *Cf.* FLATIRON, PRESS 1.

[I–203]

IRRESPONSIBLE 1 (ĭr′ ĭ spŏn′ sə bəl), *adj.* (The shoulder is not burdened.) The sign for NOT is made: The downturned open hands are crossed. They are drawn apart rather quickly. The fingertips of both downturned hands then press down on one shoulder.

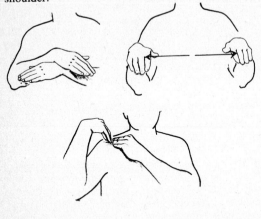

[I–204]

IRRESPONSIBLE 2, *(sl.)*, *adj.* (Responsibility is flicked off the shoulder.) The right hand flicks an imaginary grain of dust from the left shoulder.

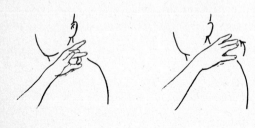

[I–205]

IRRITABLE (ĭr′ ə tə bəl), *adj.* (Wrinkling the brow.) The "5" hand is held palm toward the face. The fingers open and close partly, several times, while an angry expression is worn on the face. *Cf.* ANGRY 1, CROSS 1, CROSSNESS, FIERCE, ILL TEMPER.

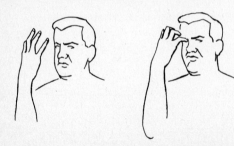

[I–206]

IS 1 (ĭz), *v.* (Part of the verb to BE.) The tip of the right index finger, held in the "D" position, palm facing left, is held at the lips, and the hand moves straight out and away from the lips. *Cf.* AM 1, ARE 1, BE 1.

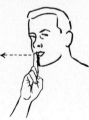

[I–207]

IS 2, *v.* (The letter "I.") The little finger of the upturned right "I" hand moves out from the lips. This is a modification of IS 1.

[I–208]

I SEE, (The up-down motion represents the nodding of the head in sudden recognition.) The right "Y" hand moves up and down a number of times. The signer usually nods slightly, keeping time with the hand. The mouth may be held open a little, and the eyes are usually wide open, as if in surprise. *Cf.* OH, I SEE, THAT'S IT.

[I–209]

ISLAND 1 (ī′ lənd), *n.* (The letter "I"; an encircling to outline an island.) The "I" hands, little fingers in contact and palms facing the body, separate, tracing a circle as they move in toward the body and resume their original position, closer to the body. The "I" hands may point down instead.

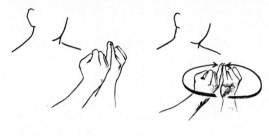

[I-210]

ISLAND 2, *n.* (The letter "I"; the island is traced.) The tip of the downturned right "I" finger traces a clockwise circle on the back of the downturned left hand.

[I-211]

ISRAEL (ĭz' rĭ əl), *n.* (The Jewish people.) The sign for HEBREW, ISRAELITE, or JEW is made: The fingers and thumb of each hand are placed at the chin, and stroke an imaginary beard. This is followed by the sign for PEOPLE: The "P" hands, held a few inches apart and palms facing, rotate in toward the body in alternate counterclockwise circles. *Cf.* HEBREWS, ISRAELITES. Also ISRAELI.

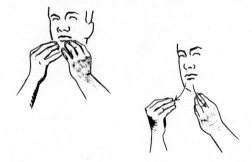

[I-212]

ISRAELITE (ĭz' rĭ ə līt´), *n.* See ISRAEL. Also ISRA-ELI.

[I-213]

ISRAELITES (ĭz' rĭ ə līts´), *(eccles.), n. pl.* (The Jewish people.) The sign for ISRAELITE, above, is made. This is followed by the sign for PEOPLE: The "P" hands, side by side, are moved alternately in counterclockwise circles. *Cf.* HEBREWS, ISRAEL. Also ISRAELI.

[I-214]

IT 1 (ĭt), *pron.* (A simple pointing.) The right index finger points at an object, either imaginary or real. This sign is understood mainly in context.

[I-215]

IT 2, *pron.* (Something specific.) The downturned right "Y" hand is placed on the upturned left palm. *Cf.* THAT 1, THESE, THIS, THOSE, WHICH 2.

[I–216]

IT 3, *(rare), pron.* (The letter "I.") The right "I" hand wiggles slightly as it moves from left to right.

[I–217]

ITALIAN (ĭ tăl' yən), *n., adj.* The sign for ITALY 1 is made, followed by the sign for INDIVIDUAL: Both open hands, palms facing each other, move down the sides of the body, tracing its outline to the hips. *Cf.* ITALY 1.

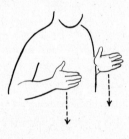

[I–218]

ITALY 1 (ĭt' ə lĭ), *n.* (The letter "I"; the cross, signifying the Vatican.) The right "I" finger traces a small cross on the forehead. See ITALIAN.

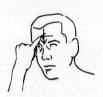

[I–219]

ITALY 2, *(loc.), n.* (A characteristic Italian gesture.) The thumb and index finger of the right "F" hand are placed against the right cheek, while the hand trembles.

[I–220]

ITS (ĭts), *pron.* (Belonging to it.) The open right hand, palm facing out, moves straight out from the body. This sign is understood mainly in context.

[I–221]

ITSELF (ĭt sĕlf'), *pron.* (The thumb indicates the individual, *i.e.,* self.) The right "A" hand, thumb pointing up, moves straight forward a number of times. This sign is understood mainly in context.

J

JAIL (jāl), *n., v.,* JAILED, JAILING. (The crossed bars.) The "4" hands, palms facing the body, are crossed at the fingers. *Cf.* IMPRISON, PENITENTIARY, PRISON.

JAM (jăm), *n.* (Spreading the letter "J.") The little finger of the right "J" hand moves twice across the upturned left palm, toward the base of the left hand. *Cf.* JELLY.

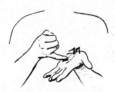

JAPAN (jə păn′), *n.* (The letter "J"; the slanting eyes.) The right little finger is placed at the corner of the right eye, pulling it back slightly into a slant. Both little fingers may also be used, involving both eyes. *Cf.* JAPANESE.

JAPANESE (jăp′ ə nēz′, -nēs′), *adj., n.* The sign for JAPAN is made. This is followed by the sign for INDIVIDUAL: Both open hands, palms facing each other, move down the sides of the body, tracing its outline to the hips. *Cf.* JAPAN.

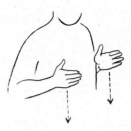

JEALOUS (jĕl′ əs), *adj.* (Biting the finger to suppress the feelings.) The tip of the index finger is bitten. The tip of the little finger is sometimes used. *Cf.* COVET 2, ENVIOUS, ENVY, JEALOUSY.

JEALOUSY (jĕl′ ə sĭ), *n.* See JEALOUS.

JELLY (jĕl′ ĭ), *n.* See JAM.

[J–8]

JERUSALEM (jĭ rōō′ sə ləm), *(eccles.), (rare), n.* (The holy city.) The sign for HOLY is made: The right "H" hand moves in a small clockwise circle several times. The right palm then wipes the up-turned left palm. This is followed by the sign for CITY: The fingertips of both hands are joined, the hands and arms forming a pyramid. The fingertips separate and rejoin a number of times. Both arms may move a bit from left to right each time the fingertips separate and rejoin.

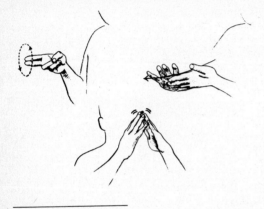

[J–9]

JESUIT (jĕzh′ ŏŏ it, jĕz′ yŏŏ-), *(eccles.), n.* (The initials of the Society of Jesus.) The letters "S" and "J" are fingerspelled.

[J–10]

JESUS (jē′ zəs), *n.* (The marks of the crucifixion.) Both "5" hands are used. The left middle finger touches the right palm, and then the right middle finger touches the left palm.

[J–11]

JET (jĕt), *n.* (The exhaust.) The right "S" hand, palm down, is positioned under the left elbow. The right fingers suddenly snap open, to indicate the escape of the jet's exhaust.

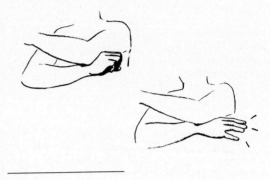

[J–12]

JEW (jōō), *n.* (The beard of the old Jewish patriarchs.) The fingers and thumb of each hand are placed at the chin, and stroke an imaginary beard. *Cf.* HEBREW, ISRAELITE, JEWISH.

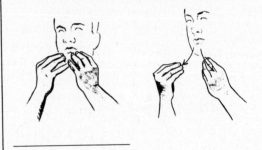

[J–13]

JEWISH (jōō′ ish), *adj.* See JEW.

[J–14]

JEWISH BIBLE, *n.* (Literally: Jewish book; the Old Testament.) The sign for JEW is formed. Then the sign for BOOK is made: The open hands are held together, fingers pointing away from the body. They open with little fingers remaining in contact, as in the opening of a book. This sign is used by the Jews. *Cf.* BIBLE 3, HEBREW BIBLE, HOLY SCRIPTURE, TESTAMENT 3.

[J-15]

JIG SAW (jĭg′ sô′), *(voc.), n.* (The natural sign.) The downturned "5" hands move forward in undulating curves, as if guiding a piece of wood through the saw and fashioning an elaborate series of curves.

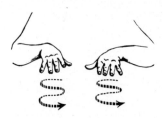

[J-16]

JOB (jŏb), *n.* (Striking an anvil.) Both "S" hands are held palms down. The right hand strikes against the back of the left a number of times. *Cf.* LABOR, OCCUPATION, TASK, TOIL, TRAVAIL, VOCATION, WORK.

[J-17]

JOIN 1 (join), *v.,* JOINED, JOINING. (Joining together.) Both hands, held in the modified "5" position, palms out, move toward each other. The thumbs and index fingers of both hands then connect. *Cf.* AFFILIATE 1, ANNEX, ASSOCIATE 2, ATTACH, BELONG, COMMUNION OF SAINTS, CONCERN 2, CONNECT, ENLIST, ENROLL, PARTICIPATE, RELATIVE 2, UNION, UNITE.

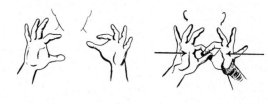

[J-18]

JOIN 2, *v.* (A grouping together.) Both "C" hands, palms facing, are held a few inches apart at chest height. They are swung around in unison, so that the palms now face the body. *Cf.* ASSOCIATION, AUDIENCE 1, CASTE, CIRCLE 2, CLASS, CLASSED 1, CLUB,

COMPANY, FAMILY 2, GANG, GROUP 1, ORGANIZATION 1.

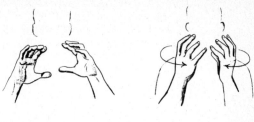

[J-19]

JOIN 3, *v.* (To enter into.) The index and middle fingers of the right "U" hand are thrust into the hole formed by the left "O" hand, held palm out. The two fingers represent the legs.

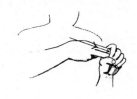

[J-20]

JOIN TO, *(rare), v. phrase.* (The connecting.) The "5" hands are thrust together and the fingers interlock.

[J-21]

JOINER (joi′ nər), *n.* The sign for JOIN 1 is made. This is followed by the sign for INDIVIDUAL: Both open hands, palms facing each other, move down the sides of the body, tracing its outline to the hips.

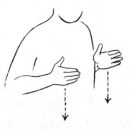

[J–22]

JOKE (jōk), *n., v.*, JOKED, JOKING. (Pulling the nose.) The right "X" finger, resting on the nose, pulls the head with it as it moves down slightly. It does not leave its position on the nose. *Cf.* DOLL 1, FOOL 2, HOAX.

[J–23]

JOLLY (jŏl′ ĭ), *adj.* (A crinkling-up of the face.) Both hands, in the "5" position, palms facing back, are placed on either side of the face. The fingers wiggle back and forth, while a pleasant, happy expression is worn. *Cf.* AMIABLE, CHEERFUL, CORDIAL, FRIENDLY, PLEASANT.

[J–24]

JOLT (jōlt), *v.*, JOLTED, JOLTING. (The mind is frozen; the thought is frozen.) The index finger of the right "D" hand, palm facing the body, touches the forehead (modified THINK sign, *q.v.*). Both hands, in the "5" position, palms down, are then suddenly and deliberately dropped down in front of the body. A look of surprise is assumed at this point, and the head jerks back slightly. *Cf.* AT A LOSS, DUMFOUNDED 1, SHOCKED 1, STUMPED.

[J–25]

JOURNEY 1 (jûr′ nĭ), *n., v.*, -NEYED, -NEYING. (Moving around from place to place.) Both "D" hands are held palms facing, the index fingers pointing to each other. In this position the hands describe a series of small counterclockwise circles as they move in random fashion from right to left. *Cf.* TRAVEL 1, TRIP 1.

[J–26]

JOURNEY 2, *n., v.* A variation of JOURNEY 1, but using only the right hand. *Cf.* TRAVEL 2, TRIP 2.

[J–27]

JOURNEY 3, *n., v.* A variation of JOURNEY 1 and JOURNEY 2, but using the downturned curved "V" fingers. *Cf.* TRANSIENT, TRAVEL 3, TRIP 3.

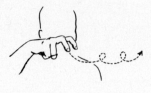

[J–28]

JOY (joi), *n.* (The heart is stirred; the spirits bubble up.) The open right hand, palm facing the body, strikes the heart repeatedly, moving up and off the heart after each strike. *Cf.* DELIGHT, GAIETY 1, GAY, GLAD, HAPPINESS, HAPPY, MERRY.

[J–29]

JUDAISM (joo′ dĭ ĭz′ əm), *n.* (Jew, religion.) The sign for JEW, *q.v.*, is made: The fingers and thumb of each hand are placed at the chin, and stroke an imaginary beard. This is followed by the sign for RELIGION: The right "R" hand is placed palm against the heart. It swings out, around, and up, in an arc.

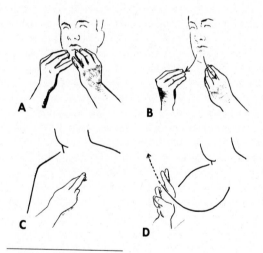

[J–30]

JUDGE 1 (jŭj), *n., v.,* JUDGED, JUDGING. (The scales move up and down.) The two "F" hands, palms facing each other, move alternately up and down. *Cf.* CONSIDER 3, COURT, EVALUATE 1, IF, JUDGMENT, JUSTICE 1.

[J–31]

JUDGE 2, *n.* (Judge, individual.) The sign for JUDGE 1 is made. This is followed by the sign for INDIVIDUAL: Both open hands, palms facing each other, move down the sides of the body, tracing its outline to the hips. *Cf.* REFEREE, UMPIRE.

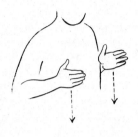

[J–32]

JUDGMENT (jŭj′ mənt), *n.* See JUDGE 1.

[J–33]

JUMP 1 (jŭmp), *v.,* JUMPED, JUMPING. (The natural sign.) The bent right index and middle fingers rest on the upturned left palm. The right hand rises suddenly, as if the fingers have jumped up. The fingers usually remain bent, but they may also straighten out as the hand rises. The motion may also be repeated. *Cf.* HOP 1, LEAP.

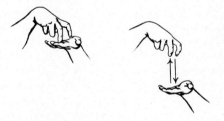

[J–34]

JUMP 2, *v.* One finger is used here, the middle or the index, to represent a single leg. *Cf.* HOP 2.

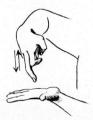

[J-35]

JUST 1 (jŭst), *adj., adv.* (Sameness is stressed.) The downturned "B" hands, held at chest height, are brought together repeatedly, so that the index finger edges or fingertips come into contact. *Cf.* EQUAL, EQUIVALENT, EVEN, FAIR 1, IMPARTIAL, LEVEL.

[J-36]

JUST 2, *adj., adv.* The right index finger, held above the left index finger, comes down rather forcefully so that the bottom of the right hand comes to rest on top of the left thumb joint. *Cf.* ACCURATE 2, CORRECT 1, DECENT, EXACT 2, PROPER, RIGHT 3, SUITABLE.

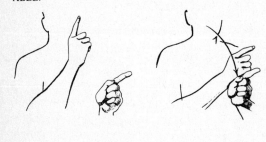

[J-37]

JUST A MOMENT AGO, *adv. phrase.* (Time moved backward a bit.) The right "D" hand, palm facing the body, is placed in the palm of the left hand, which is facing right. The right hand swings back a bit toward the body, with the index finger describing an arc. *Cf.* FEW SECONDS AGO, WHILE AGO, A 3.

[J-38]

JUSTICE 1 (jŭs′ tĭs), *n.* (The scales move up and down.) The two "F" hands, palms facing each other,

move alternately up and down. *Cf.* CONSIDER 3, COURT, EVALUATE 1, IF, JUDGE 1, JUDGMENT.

[J-39]

JUSTICE 2, *n.* (Fairness or equality; the scales of justice.) The hands are held palms facing and fingers pointing straight forward. The thumb and index finger of each hand form circles, and the hands move together until these circles touch.

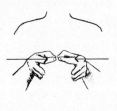

[J-40]

JUST NOW 1, *adv. phrase.* (A slight amount of time in the past.) The thumbtip of the closed right hand flicks off the tip of the curved right index finger. The hand then opens into the "5" position, palm facing the body, and swings back over the right shoulder. *Cf.* WHILE AGO, A 1.

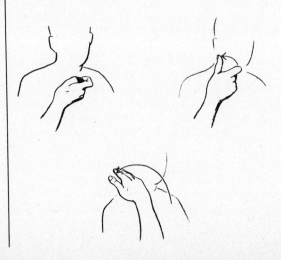

[J–41]

JUST NOW 2, *adv. phrase* (The slight movement represents a slight amount of time.) With the closed right hand held with knuckles against the right cheek, the thumbtip flicks off the tip of the curved index finger a number of times. The eyes squint a bit and the lips are drawn out in a slight smile. The hand remains against the cheek during the flicking movement. Sometimes, instead of the flicking movement, the tip of the curved index finger scratches slightly up and down against the cheek. In this case, the palm faces back toward the shoulder. The same expression is used as in the flicking movement. *Cf.* RECENT, RECENTLY, WHILE AGO, A 2.

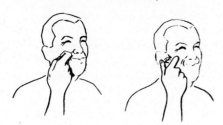

[J–42]

JUST THINK OF IT!, *(colloq.).* (A thought coming forward from the mind, modified by the letter "I" for "idea.") With the "I" position on the right hand, palm facing the body, touch the little finger to the forehead, and then move the hand up and away in a circular, clockwise motion. The hand may also be moved up and away without this circular motion. *Cf.* CONCEIVE 2, CONCEPT 1, CONCEPTION, FANCY 2, IDEA, IMAGINATION, IMAGINE 1, NOTION, POLICY 2, THEORY, THOUGHT 2.

K

KEEP (kēp), *v.*, KEPT, KEEPING. (Slow, careful movement.) The "K" hands are crossed, the right above the left, little finger edges down. In this position the hands are moved up and down a short distance. *Cf.* CARE 2, CAREFUL 2, MAINTAIN 1, MIND 3, PRESERVE, RESERVE 2, TAKE CARE OF 2.

[K–2]

KEEP QUIET 1, *v. phrase.* (The natural sign.) The index finger is placed forcefully against the closed lips. The signer frowns or looks stern. *Cf.* KEEP STILL 1.

[K–3]

KEEP QUIET 2, *v. phrase.* (The mouth is sealed; the sign for QUIET.) The downturned open hands are crossed at the lips with the left in front of the right. Both hands are drawn apart and down rather forcefully, while the signer frowns or looks stern. *Cf.* KEEP STILL 2.

[K–4]

KEEP STILL 1, *v. phrase.* See KEEP QUIET 1.

[K–5]

KEEP STILL 2, *v. phrase.* See KEEP QUIET 2.

[K–6]

KEY (kē), *n.* (The turning of the key.) The right hand, holding an imaginary key, twists it in the open left palm, which is facing right. *Cf.* LOCK 1.

[K–7]

KICK 1 (kĭk), *n., v.*, KICKED, KICKING. (The natural sign.) The right "B" hand, palm facing the body and fingers pointing down, swings in an arc to the left, striking the side of the left "S" hand, held palm facing up. *Cf.* KICK OUT, SOCCER.

[K–8]

KICK 2, *(sl.)*, *v.* (Kicking.) Both "S" hands are held before the chest. Then the hands move sharply to the side, opening into a modified "V" position, palms down, as if "kicking." *Cf.* COMPLAIN 2, OBJECT 3.

[K–9]

KICK OUT, *v. phrase.* See KICK 1.

[K–10]

KID 1 (kĭd), *(colloq.), n.* (The running nose.) The index and little fingers of the right hand, held palm down, are extended, pointing to the left. The index finger is placed under the nose and the hand trembles somewhat.

[K–11]

KID 2, *v.,* KIDDED, KIDDING. The knuckles of the right "X" hand move sharply forward along the thumb edge of the left "X" hand. *Cf.* TEASE 2.

[K–12]

KIDNAP (kĭd′ năp), *v.,* -NAPED, -NAPING. (The hand, partly concealed, takes something surreptitiously.) The index and middle fingers of the right hand, somewhat curved, are placed under the left elbow. As they move slowly along the left forearm toward the left wrist, they close a bit. *Cf.* ABDUCT, EMBEZZLE, EMBEZZLEMENT, ROB 1, ROBBERY 1, STEAL 1, SWIPE, THEFT 1, THIEF 1, THIEVERY.

[K–13]

KILL (kĭl), *v.,* KILLED, KILLING. (Thrusting a dagger and twisting it.) The outstretched right index finger is passed under the downturned left hand. As it moves under the left hand, the right wrist twists in a clockwise direction. *Cf.* MURDER, SLAY.

[K–14]

KIN (kĭn), *n.* (Touching one another, as members of a family.) The "D" hands, palms facing the body and index fingers pointing toward each other, swing alternately up and down. Each time they pass each other, the index fingertips come into mutual contact. *Cf.* RELATIVE 1.

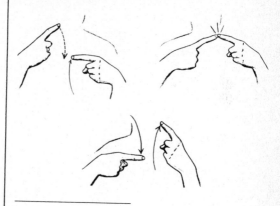

[K–15]

KIND 1 (kīnd), *adj.* (The heart rolls out.) Both right-angle hands roll over each other as they move down and away from their initial position at the heart. *Cf.* BENEVOLENT, GENEROUS 1, GENTLE 1, GENTLENESS, GRACIOUS, HUMANE, KINDNESS, MERCY 1, TENDER 3.

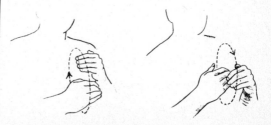

[K–16]

KIND 2, *n.* (The letter "K"; the wholeness or global characteristic.) The right "K" hand revolves once around the left "K" hand. This is used to describe a class or group.

[K–17]

KINDLE (kĭn' dəl), *v.,* -DLED, -DLING. (The natural sign.) The right hand, grasping an imaginary match, strikes it against the open left palm, which is facing right. *Cf.* MATCH.

[K–18]

KINDNESS (kīnd' nĭs), *n.* The sign for KIND 1 is made, followed by the sign for -NESS: The downturned right "N" hand moves down along the left palm, which is facing away from the body.

[K–19]

KING (kĭng), *n.* (The letter "K"; the royal sash.) The right "K" hand moves from the left shoulder to the right hip.

[K–20]

KINGDOM (kĭng' dəm), *n.* (Handling the reins over all.) The sign for KING is made. Then the hands, holding imaginary reins, move alternately back and forth. The downturned open right hand then swings from right to left over the downturned left "A" or "S" hand.

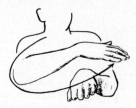

[K–21]

KISS 1 (kĭs), *n., v.,* KISSED, KISSING. (The natural sign.) The right fingertips are placed on the lips, and then on the right cheek. This latter movement is often omitted.

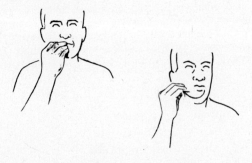

[K–22]

KISS 2, *n., v.* (The natural sign.) The right "A" hand, palm facing the body, is placed on the mouth so that the backs of the fingers rest against the lips. The hand, in this same position, is then placed on the right cheek, although this latter movement is often omitted.

[K–23]

KISS 3, *n., v.* (Lips touch lips.) With fingers touching their thumbs, both hands are brought together. They tremble slightly, indicating the degree of intensity of the kiss.

[K–24]

KITCHEN 1 (kĭch′ ən), *n.* (Turning over a pancake.) The open right hand rests on the upturned left palm. The right hand flips over and comes to rest with its back on the left palm. This is the action of turning over a pancake. Then the sign for ROOM is made: The open hands, palms facing and fingers pointing out, are dropped an inch or two simultaneously. They then shift their relative positions so that both palms face the body, with one hand in front of the other. In this new position they again drop an inch or two simultaneously. *Cf.* CHEF, COOK, PANCAKE.

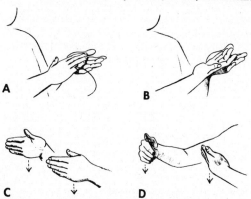

A

B

C

D

[K–25]

KITCHEN 2, *n.* (The letter "K.") The right "K" hand is placed palm down on the upturned left palm. It flips over to the palm-up position, and comes to rest again on the upturned left palm, as if flipping over a pancake.

[K–26]

KNEEL (nēl), *v.,* KNELT or KNEELED, KNEELING. (Kneeling in church.) The knuckles of the right index and middle fingers are placed in the upturned left palm. The action may be repeated. *Cf.* PROTESTANT.

[K–27]

KNIFE 1 (nīf), *n.* (Shaving or paring.) The edge of the right "H" hand, resting on the edge of its left counterpart, moves forward several times, as if shaving layers of flesh.

[K–28]

KNIFE 2, *n.* (A variation of KNIFE 1.) The index fingers are used here, in the same manner as above.

[K-29]

KNIFE 3, *n.* (The cutting.) The right index finger cuts back and forth across the midpoint of its left counterpart.

[K-30]

KNIT (nĭt), *n., v.,* KNITTED or KNIT, KNITTING. (The knitting.) The index fingers, pointing forward, are rubbed back and forth against each other. *Cf.* HOSE 1, SOCK(S) 1, STOCKING(S) 1.

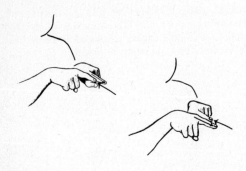

[K-31]

KNOCK (nŏk), *v.,* KNOCKED, KNOCKING. (The natural sign.) The right knuckles knock against the palm of the left hand, which is facing right. *Cf.* RAP.

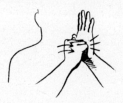

[K-32]

KNOCK DOWN (doun), *v. phrase.* (The natural sign.) The right "S" hand strikes the upturned left index finger. The right "V" hand, palm up and fingers pointing to the left, then slides along the upturned left palm, from its base to its fingertips. This indicates the striking of an upright individual

and his subsequent position on the floor. *Cf.* KNOCK OUT.

[K-33]

KNOCK OUT (out), *v. phrase.* See KNOCK DOWN.

[K-34]

KNOT (nŏt), *n., v.,* KNOTTED, KNOTTING. (The act of tying.) Both hands, in the "A" position, go through the natural hand-over-hand motions of tying and drawing out a knot. *Cf.* BIND, FASTEN, TIE 1.

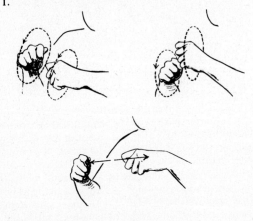

[K-35]

KNOW (nō), *v.,* KNEW, KNOWN, KNOWING. (Patting the head to indicate something of value inside.) The right fingers pat the forehead several times. *Cf.* INTELLIGENCE, KNOWLEDGE, RECOGNIZE.

[K–36]

KNOWING (nō′ ĭng), *adj.* See KNOW.

[K–37]

KNOWLEDGE (nŏl′ ĭj), *n.* See KNOW.

[K–38]

KNOW NOTHING (nuth′ ĭng), *(colloq.), v. phrase.* (KNOW and ZERO.) The sign for KNOW is made. The little finger edge of the right "O" hand is brought sharply into the upturned left palm, emphasizing the "nothingness." This is an emphatic sign, indicating a complete lack of knowledge.

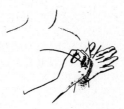

[K–39]

KOREA (kō rē′ ə), *n.* The fingertips of the right-angle hands move down either side of the head from the temples, and curve outward and up at the shoulders.

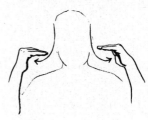

L

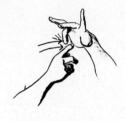

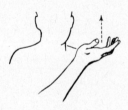

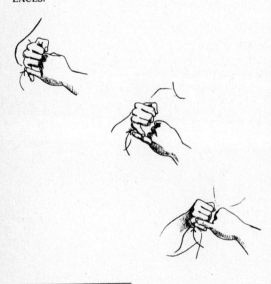

LABOR (lā′ bər), *n.*, *v.*, -BORED, -BORING. (Striking an anvil.) Both "S" hands are held palms down. The right hand strikes against the back of the left a number of times. *Cf.* JOB, OCCUPATION, TASK, TOIL, TRAVAIL, VOCATION, WORK.

[L-2]

LACE (lās), *n.*, *v.*, LACED, LACING. (The crisscross pattern.) The little fingers of both downturned "I" hands cross each other several times, with one alternately on top of the other. At the same time the hands are drawn in toward the body. *Cf.* SHOE-LACES.

[L-3]

LACK (lăk), *n.*, *v.*, LACKED, LACKING. The extended right index finger strikes against the down-turned middle finger of the left hand, which is held

with palm down and other fingers pointing right. *Cf.* DEARTH, MISSING.

[L-4]

LAD (lăd), *n.* (A modification of the MALE root sign; the familiar sign for BOY 1.) The right hand, palm down, is held at the forehead. The fingers open and close once or twice. *Cf.* BOY 2.

[L-5]

LADDER (lăd′ ər), *n.* (Rising.) The right open hand, palm up, moves slowly up. *Cf.* ASCEND, CLIMB 2.

[L-6]

LADY (lā′ dĭ), *n.* (A female with a ruffled bodice; *i.e.*, an elegantly dressed woman, a lady.) The FE-MALE root sign is made: The thumb of the right "A" hand moves down along the right jaw, from ear almost to chin. The thumbtip of the right "5" hand, palm facing left, is then placed on the chest, with the other fingers pointing up. Pivoted at the thumb, the hand swings down a bit, so that the other fingers are now pointing out somewhat. *Cf.* MADAM.

[L-7]

LAG (lăg), *n., v.,* LAGGED, LAGGING. (One hand falls behind the other.) The "A" hands, thumbs up, are positioned knuckle to knuckle in front of the chest. The right "A" hand moves slowly and deliberately toward the chest, as close as possible to the left arm. *Cf.* FALL BEHIND, RETARD.

[L-8]

LAKE (lāk), *n.* (An enclosed body of water.) The sign for WATER is made: The right "W" hand, palm facing out, is shaken slightly. The right index finger, pointing down, then describes a counterclockwise circle.

[L-9]

LAMB (lăm), *n.* (A small sheep.) The sign for SMALL is made: The cupped hands, right palm facing left and left palm facing right, move back and forth or toward each other and back in a series of small motions. They do not touch, however. The sign for SHEEP is then made: The left arm holds an imaginary sheep against the chest, while the right

hand, in the "V" position, palm up, moves up along the left arm. The "V" fingers open and close repeatedly, in imitation of scissors shearing the sheep.

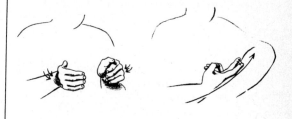

[L-10]

LAME (lām), *adj.* (The uneven movement of the legs.) The downturned index fingers move alternately up and down. The body sways to and fro a little, keeping time with the movement of the fingers. *Cf.* CRIPPLE.

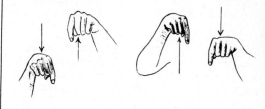

[L-11]

LAND 1 (lănd), *n.* (An expanse of ground.) The sign for SOIL 1 is made: Both hands, held upright before the body, finger imaginary pinches of soil. The downturned open right "5" hand then sweeps in an arc from right to left. *Cf.* FIELD 1.

[L-12]

LAND 2, *n.* (An established area.) The right "N" hand, palm down, executes a clockwise circle above the downturned prone left hand. The tips of the "N" fingers then move straight down and come to rest on the back of the left hand. *Cf.* COUNTRY 2, NATION.

[L-13]

LANGUAGE 1 (lăng' gwĭj), *n.* (A series of letters spelled out on the printed page.) The downturned "F" hands are positioned with thumbs and index fingertips touching. The hands move straight apart to either side in a wavy motion. *Cf.* SENTENCE.

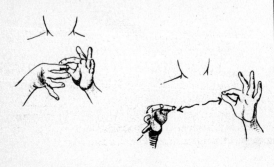

[L-14]

LANGUAGE 2, *n.* (The letter "L.") The sign for LANGUAGE 1 is made, but with the "L" hands.

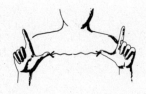

[L-15]

LANGUAGE OF SIGNS, *n.* (LANGUAGE 1 and hand/arm movements.) The "D" hands, palms facing and index fingers pointing back toward the face, describe a series of continuous counterclockwise circles toward and away from the face, imitating the foot motions in bicycling. This is followed by the sign for LANGUAGE 1. *Cf.* SIGN LANGUAGE, SIGNS.

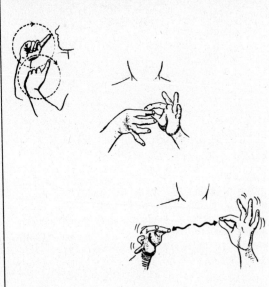

[L-16]

LARGE (lärj), *adj.* (A delineation of something big, modified by the letter "L," which stands for LARGE.) Both "L" hands, palms facing out, are placed before the face, and separate rather widely. *Cf.* BIG 1, ENORMOUS, GREAT 1, HUGE, IMMENSE.

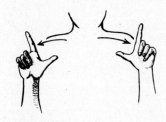

[L-17]

LAST 1 (lăst), *adj.* (The little, *i.e.,* LAST, fingers are indicated.) With the hands in the "I" position, the tip of the right little finger strikes the tip of its left counterpart. The right index finger may be used instead of the right little finger. *Cf.* END 1, EVENTUALLY, FINAL 1, FINALLY 1, ULTIMATE, ULTIMATELY.

[L–18]

LAST 2, *adj.* (A single little, *i.e.,* LAST, finger is indicated.) The tip of the index finger of the right "D" hand strikes the tip of the little finger of the left "I" hand. *Cf.* END 2, FINAL 2, FINALLY 2.

[L–19]

LAST 3, *v.* (Steady, uninterrupted movement.) The "A" hands are held with palms out, thumbs extended and touching, the right behind the left. In this position the hands move forward in a straight, steady line. *Cf.* CONTINUE 1, ENDURE 2, EVER 1, LASTING, PERMANENT, PERPETUAL, PERSEVERE 3, PERSIST 2, REMAIN, STAY 1, STAY STILL.

[L–20]

LASTING (lăs′ tĭng), *adj.* See LAST 3.

[L–21]

LASTLY (lăst′ lĭ), *adv.* See LAST 1 or 2.

[L–22]

LAST MONTH, *n. phrase.* The sign for AGO is made: The upright right hand, in the "5" position with palm facing the body, is held just above the right shoulder and is thrown back over it. This is followed by the sign for MONTH: The extended, right index finger moves down along the upturned, extended left index finger. The two signs may be reversed.

[L–23]

LAST NIGHT, *n. phrase.* The sign for AGO, as in LAST MONTH, is formed. This is followed by the sign for NIGHT: The left hand, palm down, is positioned at chest height. The downturned right hand, held an inch or so above the left, moves over the left hand in an arc. The two signs may be reversed.

[L–24]

LAST WEEK, *n. phrase.* The sign for AGO, as in LAST MONTH, is formed. This is followed by the sign for WEEK: The upright right "D" hand is placed palm-to-palm against the left "5" hand, whose palm is facing right. The right "D" hand then moves along the left palm from base to fingertips. The two signs may be reversed.

[L–25]

LAST YEAR, *adv. phrase* (A YEAR in the past.) The sign for YEAR is made: The little finger edge of the right "S" hand, representing the earth, rests on the thumb edge of the left "S" hand, representing the sun. The right hand describes a clockwise circle around the left, coming to rest in its original position. The right hand, changing into the "D" position, is then thrown over the right shoulder, palm facing back.

[L-26]

LATE (lāt), *adj.* (Hanging back.) The "5" hand and forearm, hanging loosely and straight down from the elbow, move back and forth under the armpit. *Cf.* BEHIND TIME, NOT DONE, NOT YET, TARDY.

[L-27]

LATE AT NIGHT (nīt), *adv. phrase.* (The sun, having set over the horizon, continues around the other side of the earth, until it reaches the opposite horizon.) The left arm is held before the chest, hand extended, fingers together, palm down. The right arm rests on the back of the left hand, with palm down, fingers extended and together. The right hand, pivoted at its wrist, describes a sweeping downward arc until it comes to a stop near the left elbow. *Cf.* ALL NIGHT.

[L-28]

LATER 1, *adj.* (A moving on of the minute hand of the clock.) The right "L" hand, its thumb thrust into the palm of the left and acting as a pivot, moves forward a short distance. *Cf.* AFTER A WHILE, AFTERWARD, SUBSEQUENT, SUBSEQUENTLY.

[L-29]

LATER 2, *adj., adv.* (Something ahead or in the future.) The upright, open right hand, palm facing left, moves straight out and slightly up from a position beside the right temple. *Cf.* BY AND BY, FUTURE, IN THE FUTURE, LATER ON, SHALL, WILL 1, WOULD.

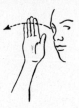

[L-30]

LATER ON, *adv. phrase.* See LATER 2.

[L-31]

LATIN 1 (lăt' ən), *n., adj.* (The Roman nose.) The index and middle fingertips of the right "N" hand, palm facing the body, move down in an arc from the bridge of the nose to its tip. *Cf.* ROMAN, ROME.

[L-32]

LATIN 2, *(rare), n., adj.* (Same rationale as in LATIN 1 with the "L" initial.) The thumbtip of the right "L" hand, palm facing left, moves down in an arc from mid-forehead to the tip of the nose.

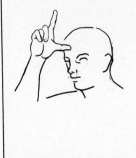

[L-33]

LAUGH (lăf), *n., v.,* LAUGHED, LAUGHING. (The natural sign.) The fingers of both "D" hands move repeatedly up along the jawline, or up from the corners of the mouth. The signer meanwhile laughs. *Cf.* LAUGHTER 1.

[L-34]

LAUGHTER 1 (lăf' tər), *n.* See LAUGH.

[L-35]

LAUGHTER 2, *(colloq.), n.* (The shaking of the stomach.) The cupped hands, held at stomach level, palms facing the body, move alternately up and down, describing short arcs. The signer meanwhile laughs. *Cf.* HYSTERICAL.

[L-36]

LAUGHTER 3, *(colloq.), n.* (Literally, rolling in the aisles; the legs are doubled up and the body rolls on the floor.) With index and middle fingers crooked, and its little finger edge or back resting on the upturned left palm, the right hand moves in a continuous counterclockwise circle in the left palm. The signer meanwhile laughs. *Cf.* HYSTERICAL LAUGH.

[L-37]

LAW (lô), *n.* (A series of LAWS as they appear on the printed page.) The upright right "L" hand, resting palm against palm on the upright left "5" hand, moves down in an arc a short distance, coming to rest on the base of the left palm. *Cf.* DECREE 2, LAWYER, LEGAL, PRECEPT.

[L-38]

LAWN MOWER, *n.* (The natural sign.) The "S" hands, palms down, hold the handles of an imaginary lawn mower. They move back and forth in unison, as if mowing a lawn. *Cf.* MOW 2, MOWER.

[L-39]

LAWYER (lô' yər), *n.* The sign for LAW is made. The sign for INDIVIDUAL is then added: Both hands, fingers together, are placed at either side of the chest and are moved down to waist level.

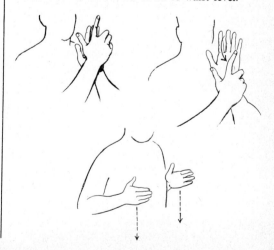

[L–40]

LAZINESS (lā' zǐ nǐs), *n*. (The initial "L" rests against the body; the concept of inactivity.) The right "L" hand is placed against the left shoulder once or a number of times. The palm faces the body. *Cf.* LAZY 1, SLOTH.

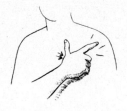

[L–41]

LAZY 1 (lā' zǐ), *adj*. See LAZINESS.

[L–42]

LAZY 2, *(rare), adj*. The thumbtip of the right "L" hand rests against the left shoulder, palm facing the body. The hand moves in a wavy manner down across the chest, from the left shoulder to the right side of the body.

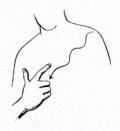

[L–43]

LEAD 1 (lēd), *v*., LED, LEADING, *n*. (One hand leads the other.) The right hand grasps the tips of the left fingers and pulls the left hand forward. *Cf.* CONDUCT 2, GUIDE.

[L–44]

LEAD 2 (lěd), *n*. (Heavy and hard substance.) The sign for HEAVY is made: The upturned "5" hands,

held before the chest, suddenly drop a short distance. The back of the downturned right "S" hand then strikes he underside of the chin a number of times.

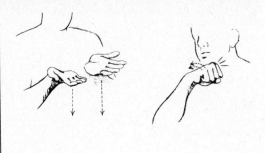

[L–45]

LEADER (lē' dər), *n*. (One who leads.) The sign for LEAD 1 is made, followed by the sign for INDIVIDUAL: Both open hands, palms facing each other, move down the sides of the body, tracing its outline to the hips.

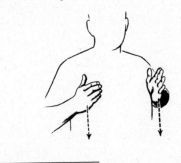

[L–46]

LEAF 1 (lēf), *n*. (The rustling.) This sign is used for the leaf of a tree. The right "5" hand, held straight up, represents the tree. The fingertips of the left hand are placed on the right wrist, and the right fingertips wiggle slightly.

[L–47]

LEAF 2, *n*. (The edge of the leaf of a book.) The sign for BOOK is made: The open hands, palms touching, open in imitation of the opening of a book. The right fingertips then run along the index finger edge of the left "B" hand, which is held with fingers pointing to the right.

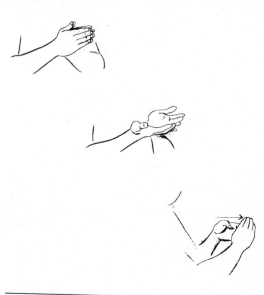

LEAK (lēk), *n., v.*, LEAKED, LEAKING. (The natural sign.) The right "4" hand, palm facing the body and fingers pointing left, moves down repeatedly from its position below the right "S" hand, whose palm faces the body with thumb edge up. *Cf.* DRIP.

LEAN 1 (lēn), *adj.* (The drawn face.) The thumb and index finger run down the cheeks, which are drawn in. *Cf.* POOR 2, THIN 1.

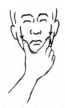

LEAN 2, *adj.* (The sunken cheeks.) The fingertips of both hands run down either side of the face. The cheeks meanwhile are sucked in a bit.

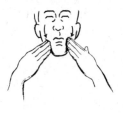

LEAP (lēp), *v.*, LEAPED, LEAPING. (The natural sign.) The bent right index and middle fingers rest in the upturned left palm. The right hand rises suddenly, as if the fingers have jumped up. The fingers usually remain bent, but they may also straighten out as the hand rises. The motion may also be repeated. *Cf.* HOP 1, JUMP 1.

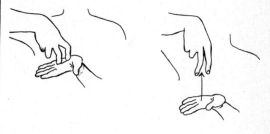

LEARN (lûrn), *v.*, LEARNED, LEARNING. (Taking knowledge from a book and placing it in the head.) The downturned fingers of the right hand are placed on the upturned left palm. They close, and then the hand rises and the right fingertips are placed on the forehead. *Cf.* EDUCATION.

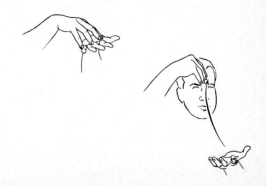

[L-53]

LEARNER (lûrn' ər), *n.* (One who learns.) The sign for LEARN is made. This is followed by the sign for INDIVIDUAL: Both open hands, palms facing each other, move down the sides of the body, tracing its outline to the hips. *Cf.* PUPIL 1, SCHOLAR, STUDENT 1.

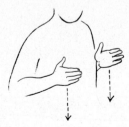

[L-54]

LEAST (lēst), *adj., n.* The sign for LESS is made: With palms facing, the right hand is held above the left. The right hand moves slowly down toward the left, but does not touch it. This is followed by the sign for FIRST: The right index finger touches the upturned left thumb. Instead of the sign for FIRST, the right thumb may be drawn straight up, to a position above the head. *Cf.* SMALLEST.

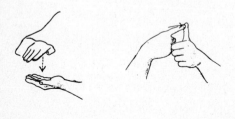

[L-55]

LEAVE 1 (lēv), *v.,* LEFT, LEAVING. (Pulling away.) The downturned open hands are held in a line, with fingers pointing to the left, the right hand behind the left. Both hands move in unison toward the right. As they do so, they assume the "A" position. *Cf.* DEPART, EVACUATE, FORSAKE 1, GRADUATE 2, RETIRE 1, WITHDRAW 1.

[L-56]

LEAVE 2, *v.* (To throw something aside.) Both "S" hands are held with palms facing at chest level and then thrown down and to the left, opening into the "5" position. *Cf.* ABANDON 1, CAST OFF, DEPOSIT 2, DISCARD 1, FORSAKE 3, LET ALONE, NEGLECT.

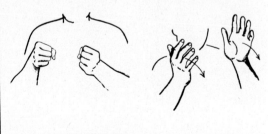

[L-57]

LEAVE CLANDESTINELY 1 (klăn dĕs' tĭn lĭ), *v. phrase.* (The underhandedness is stressed.) The left arm is held horizontally against the chest, palm down. The right "D" hand, palm facing the body and index finger pointing left, moves along the lower edge of the left arm from right to left.

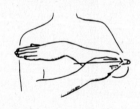

[L-58]

LEAVE CLANDESTINELY 2, *v. phrase.* (Slipping out and away.) The right index finger is held pointing upward between the index and middle fingers of the prone left hand. From this position the right index finger moves to the right, slipping out of the grasp of the left fingers and away from the left hand. *Cf.* RUN AWAY, SLIP AWAY.

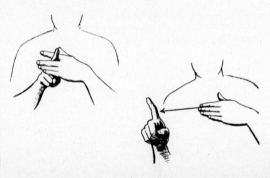

[L–59]

LECTURE (lek′ chər), *n., v.,* -TURED, -TURING. (A gesture of an orator.) The right open hand, palm facing left, is held above and to the right of the head. It pivots on the wrist, forward and backward, several times. *Cf.* ADDRESS 1, ORATE, SPEECH 2, TALK 2, TESTIMONY.

[L–60]

LEECH (lēch), *n., v.,* LEECHED, LEECHING. (Attaching to something and tugging on it.) The extended right thumb, index, and middle fingers grasp the extended left index and middle fingers. In this position the right hand pulls at the left several times. *Cf.* MOOCH, MOOCHER, PARASITE, TAKE ADVANTAGE OF 2.

[L–61]

LEFT 1 (lĕft), *adj., adv.* (The letter "L"; to the left side.) The left "L" hand, palm out, moves to the left.

[L–62]

LEFT 2, *adj.* (The remainder is left behind.) The "5" hands, palms facing each other and fingers pointing forward, are dropped simultaneously a few inches,

as if dropping something on the table. *Cf.* REMAINDER, RESERVE 4, REST 3.

[L–63]

LEG (lĕg), *n.* (The natural sign.) The right hand is placed on the right leg.

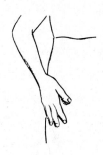

[L–64]

LEGAL (lē′ gəl), *adj.* (A series of LAWS as they appear on the printed page.) The upright right "L" hand, resting palm against palm on the upright left "5" hand, moves down in an arc, a short distance, coming to rest on the base of the left palm. *Cf.* DECREE 2, LAW, LAWYER, PRECEPT.

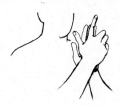

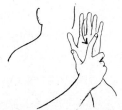

[L-65]

LEGISLATURE (lĕj′ ĭs lā′ chər), *n.* (The letter "L"; possibly the Roman toga.) The thumb of the right "L" hand moves from the left shoulder to the right shoulder.

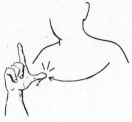

[L-66]

LEISURE (lē′ zhər, lĕzh′ ər), *n.* (A position of idleness.) With thumbs tucked in the armpits, the remaining fingers of both hands wiggle. *Cf.* HOLIDAY, IDLE, RETIRE 3, VACATION.

[L-67]

LEMON 1 (lĕm′ ən), *n.* (Yellow and sour.) The sign for YELLOW, is made: The right "Y" hand shakes back and forth, pivoted at the wrist. The sign for SOUR is then made: The right index finger is brought sharply up against the lips, while the mouth is puckered up as if tasting something sour. *Cf.* ACID, BITTER, DISAPPOINTED 1, SOUR.

[L-68]

LEMON 2, *n.* (Sucking the lemon.) The right hand, grasping an imaginary lemon, is placed at the lips. It may rotate slightly. A sour expression is assumed.

[L-69]

LEMON 3, *n.* (The letter "L"; sour.) The index finger (or thumb) of the right "L" hand is placed on the lips, which are puckered. A sour expression is assumed.

[L-70]

LEND 1 (lĕnd), *v.,* LENT, LENDING. (Something kept, *i.e.,* in one's custody, is moved forward to other, temporary, ownership.) The crossed "K" hands, for KEEP, *q.v.,* are moved forward simultaneously, in a short arc. *Cf.* LOAN 1.

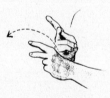

[L-71]

LEND 2, *v.* The side of the right index finger is brought up against the right side of the nose. *Cf.* LOAN 2.

[L-72]

LENT (lĕnt), *(eccles.)*, *n.* (The letter "L"; the lips are sealed as in fasting.) The thumb of the right "L" hand, palm out, is drawn across the lips, from left to right.

[L-73]

LEOPARD (lĕp' ərd), *n.* (The whiskers and the spots, *i.e.,* a spotted cat.) The sign for CAT is made: The thumb and index fingers of both hands stroke the whiskers of an imaginary cat. The curved fingers of the "5" hands are then placed on the chest again and again, each time moving down a little, as if placing spots on the body.

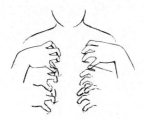

[L-74]

LEPROSY (lĕp' rə sĭ), *(arch.)*, *n.* (A sickness characterized by white spots, *i.e.,* pustules.) The sign for SICK is made: The right middle finger rests on the forehead, and its left counterpart is placed against the stomach. The sign for WHITE is then made: The right fingertips gently pull imaginary swan's down from the chest. Finally the curved fingers of the

downturned right "5" hand make a series of spots on top of the downturned open left hand.

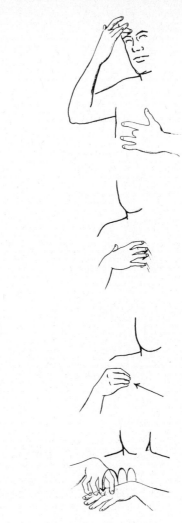

[L-75]

LESS 1 (lĕs), *adj.* (The diminishing size or amount.) With palms facing, the right hand is held above the left. The right hand moves slowly down toward the left, but does not touch it. *Cf.* DECREASE, REDUCE.

[L–76]

LESS 2, *adv.* (Removing.) The right "A" hand, resting in the palm of the left "5" hand, moves slightly up and away, describing a small arc. It is then cast downward, opening into the "5" position, palm down, as if removing something from the left hand and casting it down. *Cf.* ABOLISH 2, ABSENCE 2, ABSENT 2, ABSTAIN, CHEAT 2, DEDUCT, DEFICIENCY, DELETE 1, MINUS 3, OUT 2, REMOVE 1, SUBTRACT, SUBTRACTION, TAKE AWAY FROM, WITHDRAW 2.

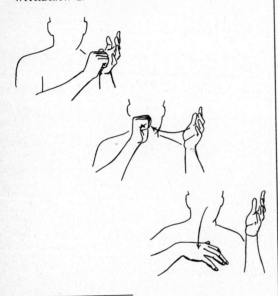

[L–77]

LESSON (lĕs' ən), *n.* (A section of a page.) The upturned open left hand represents the page. The little finger edge of the right-angle hand is placed on the left palm near the fingertips. It moves up and over, in an arc, to the base of the left palm. *Cf.* EXERCISE 2.

[L–78]

LET (lĕt), *v.,* LET, LETTING, *n.* (A permissive upswinging of the hands, as if giving in.) Both hands, palms facing and fingers pointing away from the body, are held at chest level, almost a foot apart. With an upward movement, using their wrists as pivots, the hands sweep up until the fingers point almost straight up. *Cf.* ALLOW, GRANT 1, LET'S, LET US, MAY 3, PERMISSION 1, PERMIT 1, TOLERATE 1.

[L–79]

LET ALONE, *v. phrase.* (To throw something aside.) Both "S" hands are held with palms facing at chest level and then thrown down and to the left, opening into the "5" position. *Cf.* ABANDON 1, CAST OFF, DEPOSIT 2, DISCARD 1, FORSAKE 3, LEAVE 2, NEGLECT.

[L–80]

LET KNOW 1, *v. phrase.* (Taking knowledge from the mind and giving it out to all.) The fingertips are positioned on either side of the forehead. Both hands then swing down and out, opening into the upturned "5" position. *Cf.* INFORM 1, INFORMATION 1, NOTIFY 1.

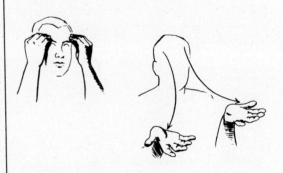

[L–81]

LET KNOW 2, *v. phrase.* The fingertips of the right "5" hand are positioned on the forehead. Both hands then swing forward and up, opening into the upturned "5" position. *Cf.* INFORM 2, INFORMATION 2, NOTIFY 2.

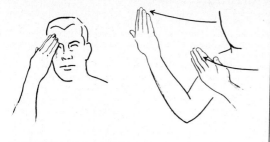

[L-82]

LET'S (lĕts); **LET US,** *v. phrase.* See LET.

[L-83]

LETTER (lĕt' ər), *n.* (The stamp is affixed.) The right thumb is placed on the tongue, and is then pressed into the open left palm. *Cf.* EPISTLE, MAIL 1.

[L-84]

LETTUCE 1 (lĕt' ĭs), *n.* (A "head" of lettuce; the upturned fingers represent the leaves.) The base of the right "5" hand strikes the right side of the head a number of times.

[L-85]

LETTUCE 2, *(rare), n.* (The downturned leaves.) The prone right hand is draped over the prone left.

The right hand moves slightly back and forth, fingers hanging down.

[L-86]

LEVEL (lĕv' əl), *adj., n., v.,* -ELED, -ELING. (Sameness is stressed.) The downturned "B" hands, held at chest height, are brought together repeatedly, so that the index finger edges or fingertips come into contact. *Cf.* EQUAL, EQUIVALENT, EVEN, FAIR 1, IMPARTIAL, JUST 1.

[L-87]

LIAR (lī' ər), *n.* (Words diverted instead of coming straight, or truthfully, out.) The index finger of the right "D" hand, pointing to the left, moves along the lips from the right to left. *Cf.* FALSE, FALSEHOOD, FRAUDULENT 2, LIE 1, PREVARICATE, UNTRUTH.

[L-88]

LIBERATION (lĭb' ər ā' shən), *n.* (Breaking the bonds.) The "S" hands, crossed in front of the body, swing apart and face out. *Cf.* DELIVER 1, EMANCIPATE, FREE 1, INDEPENDENCE, INDEPENDENT, REDEEM 1, RELIEF, RESCUE, SAFE, SALVATION, SAVE 1.

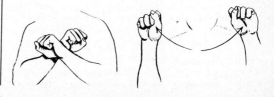

[L–89]

LIBERTY (lĭb′ ər tĭ), *n.* (The initial "L," followed by LIBERATION.) The right "L" hand, palm out, describes a small clockwise circle. The sign for LIBERATION is then made.

[L–90]

LIBRARY (lī′ brĕr´ ĭ), *n.* (The initial "L.") The right "L" hand, palm out, describes a small clockwise circle, as in LIBERTY.

[L–91]

LICENSE 1 (lī′ səns), *n., v.,* -CENSED, -CENSING. (Affixing a seal.) The little finger edge of the right "S" hand strikes the palm of the upturned left "5" hand.

[L–92]

LICENSE 2, *(loc.), n.* (The "L" hands outline the dimensions of the license form.) The "L" hands, palms out, touch at the thumbtips several times.

[L–93]

LID (lĭd), *n.* (The natural sign.) The open right hand lies over the upturned thumb edge of the left "S" hand. In this position the right hand turns in a clockwise direction several times, as if screwing on a lid. *Cf.* COVER 2.

[L–94]

LIE 1 (lī), *n., v.,* LIED, LYING. (Words diverted instead of coming straight, or truthfully, out.) The index finger of the right "D" hand, pointing to the left, moves along the lips from right to left. *Cf.* FALSE 1, FALSEHOOD, FRAUDULENT 2, LIAR, PREVARICATE, UNTRUTH.

[L–95]

LIE 2, *n., v.* (Same rationale as in LIE 1 but more emphatic, as indicated by several fingers.) The index finger edge of the downturned "B" hand moves along the lips (or under the chin) from right to left.

[L–96]

LIE 3, *v.,* LAY, LAIN, LYING. (The prone position of the legs, in lying down.) The index and middle fingers of the right "V" hand, palm facing up, are placed in the upturned left palm. *Cf.* LIE DOWN, RECLINE.

[L-97]

LIE DOWN, *v. phrase.* See LIE 3.

[L-98]

LIFE 1 (līf), *n.* (The fountain [of LIFE] wells up from within the body.) The upturned thumbs of the "A" hands move in unison up the chest. *Cf.* ADDRESS 3, ALIVE, DWELL, EXIST, LIVE 1, LIVING, MORTAL, RESIDE.

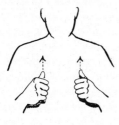

[L-99]

LIFE 2, *n.* (Same rationale as for LIFE 1 with the initials "L.") The upturned thumbs of the "L" hands move in unison up the chest.

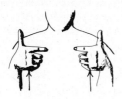

[L-100]

LIGHT 1 (līt), *n.* (The candle flame and the rays of light.) The index finger of the "D" hand is placed on the pursed lips, as if blowing out a candle. The right hand is then raised above the head, with the fingertips and thumbtip touching, and palm facing out. The hand then moves down and a bit forward, opening into the "5" position, palm down. (The "candle"

part of this sign is frequently omitted.) *Cf.* EPIPHANY, RAY.

[L-101]

LIGHT 2, *adj.* (Easily lifted.) The open hands, palms up, move up and down together in front of the body, as if lifting something very light.

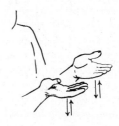

[L-102]

LIGHTNING (līt' nǐng), *n.* (The zigzag movement.) The right index finger traces a sharp and quick zigzag pattern in front of the body, from left to right, or down to chest level from a position above the head.

[L-103]

LIKE 1 (līk), *v.*, LIKED, LIKING. (Drawing out the feelings.) The thumb and index finger of the right open hand, held an inch or two apart, are placed at mid-chest. As the hand moves straight out from the chest the two fingers come together. *Cf.* ADMIRE 1, REVERE 1.

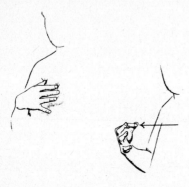

[L-104]

LIKE 2, *adj., n.* (Matching fingers are brought together.) The outstretched index fingers are brought together, either once or several times. *Cf.* ALIKE, IDENTICAL, SAME 1, SIMILAR, SUCH.

[L-105]

LIKE 3, *v.* (A pleasurable feeling on the heart.) The open right hand is circled on the chest, over the heart. *Cf.* APPRECIATE, ENJOY, ENJOYMENT, GRATIFY 1, PLEASE, PLEASURE, WILLING 2.

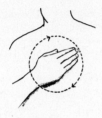

[L-106]

LIMBO (lĭm' bō), *n.* (The folded arms, a position of rest.) With palms facing the body, the arms are folded across the chest. *Cf.* RELAX 1, REST 1, RESTFUL 1.

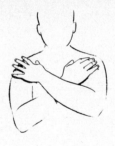

[L-107]

LIMIT (lĭm' ĭt), *n., v.*, LIMITED, LIMITING. (The upper and lower limits are defined.) The right-angle hands, palms facing, are held before the body, the right above the left. They swing out 45 degrees simultaneously, pivoted from their wrists. *Cf.* CAPACITY, QUANTITY 1, RESTRICT.

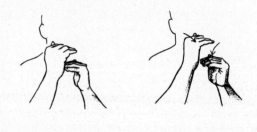

[L-108]

LIMOUSINE (lĭm' ə zēn´), *n.* (The elongated chassis.) The "C" hands, left palm facing right and right palm facing left, are joined as if holding a telescope, with the right hand in front of the left. The right hand moves straight forward about 6 inches. The left hand remains in position. Sometimes both hands close into the "S" position as the right hand moves forward.

[L-109]

LINCOLN (lĭng′ kən), *n.* (The initial "L" at the head, probably to denote the head of the country—the President.) The right "L" hand, palm facing out, is placed with the thumbtip resting on the right temple.

[L-110]

LINE (līn), *n.* (The natural sign.) The tip of the little finger of the right "I" hand moves straight down the palm of the open left hand, from fingertips to base of the palm.

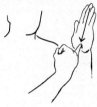

[L-111]

LINE-UP (līn′ ŭp′), *n.* (The fingers indicate a row of people, all in a line.) Both "5" hands are held before the chest with both palms facing left, and little fingertips touching. The right hand moves straight back from the left a short distance. The same sign may also be made with right hand facing left and left hand facing right, and the initial position involving the right little finger touching the tip of the left index finger. *Cf.* QUEUE, SINGLE FILE.

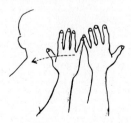

[L-112]

LINOTYPE (lī′ nə tīp), *(voc.)*, *n.* (The natural sign.) Both "5" hands, palms down, the left somewhat behind the right, go through the motions of operating a linotype keyboard. It is important that the fingers wiggle only very slightly, and remain quite straight.

[L-113]

LION (lī′ ən), *n.* (The mane.) The downturned "C" hand (or "5" hand with fingers somewhat curved) moves straight back over the head in a wavy motion.

[L-114]

LIPREADING (lĭp′ rēd′ ing) *n.* (Reading the lips—the lines of vision, represented by the two fingers, scan the lips.) The right "V" hand, palm facing the body, is placed in front of the face, with slightly curved index and middle fingers directly in front of the lips. The right hand moves in a small counter-clockwise circle around the lips. *Cf.* ORAL, READ LIPS, SPEECHREADING.

[L-115]

LIPSTICK (lĭp′ stĭk′), *n.* (The natural sign.) The outstretched thumb of the right "A" hand goes through the natural motions of applying lipstick to the lips.

[L–116]

LIQUID (lĭk′ wĭd), *adj., n.* (The letter "W.") The right "W" hand, palm facing out, is shaken slightly, as in the rippling of water. This sign is used as a prefix for different bodies of water. *Cf.* WATER 2.

[L–117]

LIQUOR 1 (lĭk′ ər), *n.* (The size of the jigger is indicated.) The right hand, with index and little fingers extended and the remaining fingers held against the palm by the thumb, strikes the back of the down-turned "S" hand several times. *Cf.* WHISKEY 1.

[L–118]

LIQUOR 2, *n.,* (The act of drinking.) The thumbtip of the right "Y" hand is tilted toward the mouth, as if it were a drinking glass or bottle. The signer tilts his head back slightly, as if drinking. *Cf.* DRINK 2, DRUNK, DRUNKARD, DRUNKENNESS, INTOXICATE, INTOXICATION.

[L–119]

LIST 1 (lĭst), *n.* (A series of items on a page.) The right hand is held in the right angle position; its little finger edge is placed in the open left palm, which is facing right. The right hand moves down the left palm in a series of short drops, from the tips of the fingers to the base of the palm.

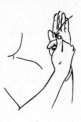

[L–120]

LIST 2, *(rare), n., v.,* LISTED, LISTING. (Writing a list and affixing it to paper.) The right hand goes through the motions of writing across the open left palm, which is facing right. The backs of the right fingers are then brought sharply against the left palm.

[L–121]

LISTEN (lĭs′ ən), *v.,* -TENED, -TENING. (Cupping the hand at the ear.) The right hand is placed, usually slightly cupped, behind the right ear. *Cf.* HARK, HEAR, HEARKEN.

[L–122]

LITTLE 1 (lĭt′ əl), *adj.* (Indicating a small size or amount.) The open hands are held facing each other, one facing down and the other facing up. In this position the top hand moves down toward the bottom hand but does not quite touch it. The space between the hands shows the small size or amount.

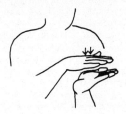

[L–123]

LITTLE 2, *adj., adv., n.* (A small or tiny movement.) The right thumbtip is flicked off the index finger several times, as if shooting marbles, although the movement is not so pronounced. *Cf.* MINUTE 2, TINY 1.

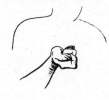

[L–124]

LIVE 1 (lĭv), *v.*, LIVED, LIVING. (The fountain [of LIFE] wells up from within the body.) The upturned thumbs of the "A" hands move in unison up the chest. *Cf.* ADDRESS 3, ALIVE, DWELL, EXIST, LIFE 1, LIVING, MORTAL, RESIDE.

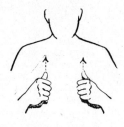

[L–125]

LIVE 2, *v.* See LIFE 2.

[L–126]

LIVER (lĭv' ər), *n.* (The liver is indicated.) The middle finger of the right "5" hand, palm facing the

body, is brought against the body, in the area of the liver, a number of times.

[L–127]

LIVING (lĭv' ĭng), *adj.* See LIVE 1.

[L–128]

LIVING ROOM, *n.* (Life, room.) The sign for LIFE 2 is made: The upturned thumbs of the "L" hands move in unison up the chest. This is followed by the sign for ROOM: The "R" hands, palms facing and fingers pointing forward, are dropped an inch or two simultaneously. Then they shift positions so that both palms face the body, with one hand in front of the other. In this new position they again drop an inch or two, simultaneously.

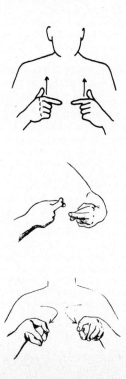

[L-129]

LOAN 1 (lōn), *n.* (Something kept, *i.e.,* in one's custody, is moved forward to other, temporary, ownership.) The crossed "K" hands, for KEEP, *q.v.,* are moved forward simultaneously, in a short arc. *Cf.* LEND 1.

[L-130]

LOAN 2, *(loc.), (colloq.), n., v.,* LOANED, LOANING. The side of the right index finger is brought up against the right side of the nose. *Cf.* LEND 2.

[L-131]

LOATHE (lōth), *v.,* LOATHED, LOATHING. (To push away and recoil from; avoid.) The two open hands, palms facing left, are pushed deliberately to the left, as if pushing something away. An expression of disdain or disgust is worn. *Cf.* ABHOR, AVOID 2, DESPISE 1, DETEST 1, HATE 1.

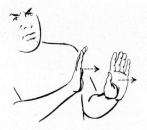

[L-132]

LOBSTER (lŏb' stər), *n.* (The claws.) The index and middle fingers of both "V" hands, pointing out from the sides of the body, open and shut repeatedly, imitating the opening and shutting of a lobster's claws.

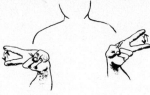

[L-133]

LOCATION (lō kā' shən), *n.* (The letter "P"; a circle or square is indicated, to show the locale or place.) The "P" hands are held side by side before the body, with middle fingertips touching. From this position, the hands separate and outline a circle (or a square), before coming together again closer to the body. *Cf.* PLACE 1, POSITION 1, SCENE, SITE.

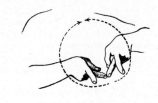

[L-134]

LOCK 1 (lŏk), *n., v.,* LOCKED, LOCKING. (The turning of the key.) The right hand, holding an imaginary key, twists it in the open left palm, which is facing right. *Cf.* KEY.

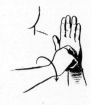

[L-135]

LOCK 2, *(loc.), v.* (Bind down.) The right "S" hand, palm down, makes a clockwise circle and comes down on the back of the left "S" hand, also held palm down.

[L–136]

LOCKED, *(loc.), adj.* (Bound down to custom or habit.) Both "S" hands, palms down, are crossed and brought down in unison before the chest. *Cf.* ACCUSTOM, BOUND, CUSTOM, HABIT, PRACTICE 3.

[L–137]

LOCOMOTIVE (lō´ kə mō´ tiv), *n.* (The natural movements of the wheels on the railroad track.) The sign for RAILROAD is made: The right "V" fingers move over the backs of the downturned left "V" fingers from base to tips. Both "S" hands, thumb sides facing up, the left in front of the right, then go through a series of simultaneous circular motions in imitation of the shafts which connect and drive the large locomotive wheels. The sign for RAILROAD is sometimes omitted.

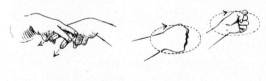

[L–138]

LOG (lôg, lŏg), *n.* (The sawing of wood; the shape of a log.) The sign for WOOD is made: The little finger edge of the open right hand moves back and forth in a sawing motion over the back of the downturned left hand. Both "C" hands, palms facing down and thumb edges touching, move straight apart to indicate the shape and length of a log.

[L–139]

LOGIC (lŏj´ ĭk), *n.* (Rays of influence emanating from a given source.) All the right fingertips, including the thumb, are positioned on the tip of the upturned thumb of the left "A" hand. The right hand, opening into the downturned "5" position, moves forward from its initial position. Instead of its initial position on the left thumb, the right hand is frequently placed on the back of the downturned left "S" hand, moving forward as described above. *Cf.* BASIS 1, CAUSE, EFFECT 1, INFLUENCE 2, INTENT 2, PRODUCE 4, REASON 2.

[L–140]

LOLLIPOP (lŏl´ ĭ pŏp´), *n.* (The natural sign.) The signer goes through the act of licking an imaginary lollipop. *Cf.* ICE CREAM 2.

[L–141]

LONE (lōn), *adj.* (One, wandering around in a circle.) The index finger, pointing straight up, palm facing the body (the number *one*), is rotated before the face in a counterclockwise direction. *Cf.* ALONE, ONE 2, ONLY, SOLE, UNITY.

[L-142]

LONELY 1 (lōn′ lĭ), *adj.* ("Oneness"; quietness.) The index finger of the right "1" hand moves straight down across the lips once or twice. *Cf.* LONESOME.

[L-143]

LONELY 2, *(colloq.), adj.* ("I" signs; *i.e.,* alone with oneself.) Both "I" hands are held facing the body, the little fingers upright and held an inch or two apart. The little fingers come together and separate repeatedly.

[L-144]

LONESOME (lōn′ səm), *adj.* See LONELY 1.

[L-145]

LONG 1 (lông, lŏng), *adj. n., adv.* (The distance is traced.) The right index finger traces a long line along the upturned left arm from wrist almost to shoulder.

[L-146]

LONG 2, *v.,* LONGED, LONGING. (Grasping something and pulling it in.) The upturned "5" hands, held side by side before the chest, close slightly into a grasping position as they move in toward the body.

Cf. COVET 1, DESIRE 1, NEED 2, WANT, WILL 2, WISH 1.

[L-147]

LONG AGO, *adv. phrase.* (A long time in the past, *i.e.,* behind one.) The sign for LONG 1 is made. The sign for AGO is then made: The right "5" hand, palm facing the body, swings over the right shoulder.

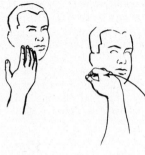

[L-148]

LONG LIST (lĭst). (The natural sign.) The left "5" hand is held up before the body, palm facing right. The little finger edge of the right right-angle hand executes a series of downward movements, beginning on the left palm and continuing along the inside of the left arm.

[L-149]

LOOK 1 (lŏŏk), *v.,* LOOKED, LOOKING. (The eyesight is directed forward.) The right "V" hand, palm facing the body, is placed so that the fingertips are just under the eyes. The hand swings around and out, so that the fingertips are now pointing forward.

Cf. PERCEIVE 1, PERCEPTION, SEE, SIGHT, WATCH 2.

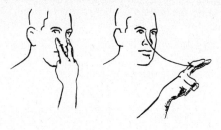

below the eyes, or stop just short of doing so. A rather stern expression is sometimes assumed.

[L-150]

LOOK 2 (lŏok), *v.* (Something presented before the eyes.) The open right hand, palm flat and facing out, with fingers together and pointing up, is positioned at shoulder level. Pivoting from the wrist, the hand is swung around so that the palm now faces the eyes. Sometimes the eyes glance at the newly presented palm. *Cf.* APPARENT, APPARENTLY, APPEAR 1, SEEM.

[L-153]

LOOK BACK, *v. phrase.* (Directing the vision backward, *i.e.,* toward the past.) The right "V" hand, palm facing the body, is placed so that the tips of the index and middle fingers are just under the eyes. The right hand, in the same "V" position, then sweeps back over the right shoulder, palm facing back.

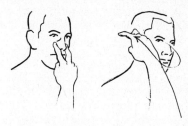

[L-151]

LOOK AT, *v. phrase.* (The vision is directed forward.) The tips of the right "V" fingers point to the eyes. The right hand is then swung around and forward a bit. *Cf.* GAZE, OBSERVE 1, WITNESS.

[L-154]

LOOK DOWN, *v. phrase.* (The gaze is cast downward.) Both "V" hands, side by side and palms facing out, are swept downward so that the fingertips now point down. A haughty expression, or one of mild contempt, is sometimes assumed. *Cf.* CONTEMPT 1, SCORN 1.

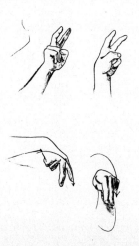

[L-152]

LOOK AT ME. (Directing the vision toward oneself.) The right "V" hand, palm facing the body, moves quickly toward the face, until the tips of the index and middle fingers either touch the face just

[L-155]

LOOK FOR, *v. phrase.* (Directing the vision from place to place; the French *chercher*.) The right "C" hand, palm facing left, moves from right to left across the line of vision, in a series of counterclockwise circles. The signer's gaze remains concentrated and his head turns slowly from right to left. *Cf.* CURIOUS 1, EXAMINE, INVESTIGATE 1, PROBE 1, QUEST, SEARCH, SEEK.

[L-156]

LOOKING GLASS. (A glass object through which one views oneself.) The sign for GLASS is made: The tip of the right index finger is brought up against the exposed front teeth. The open curved right hand is then held palm opposite the face. The hand, pivoting from the wrist, moves back and forth a bit, as if focusing the facial image in its center. Meanwhile, the eyes are directed to the center of the palm. (The sign for GLASS is frequently omitted.) *Cf.* MIRROR.

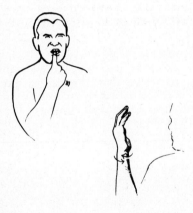

[L-157]

LOOSE (lōōs), *adj.* (Easily moved.) The left index finger is grasped by the right thumb and index finger and is worked up and down slightly a number of times.

[L-158]

LORD 1 (lôrd), *n.* (The ribbon worn across the chest by nobles; the initial "L.") The right "L" hand, palm facing out, moves down across the chest from left shoulder to right hip.

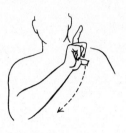

[L-159]

LORD 2, *n.* (A motion indicating the One above.) The right open hand, palm facing left, swings up above the head, and is then moved down about an inch. The signer looks up while making the sign. *Cf.* GOD.

[L-160]

LOS ANGELES (lŏs ăng′ gə ləs, an′ jə ləs, -lēz′), *n.* The letters "L" and "A" are fingerspelled.

[L-161]

LOSE (lōōz), *v.,* LOST, LOSING. (Dropping something.) Both hands, with fingers touching their respective thumbs, are held palms up and with the backs of the fingers almost touching or in contact with one another. The hands drop into an open position, with fingers pointing down. *Cf.* LOST.

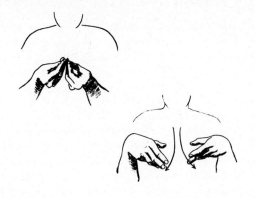

[L-162]

LOSE HOPE, *v. phrase.* (Throwing up the hands in a gesture of surrender.) Both "A" hands are held palms down before the chest and then thrown up in unison, ending in the "5" position. *Cf.* ABDICATE, CEDE, DISCOURAGE 1, FORFEIT, GIVE UP, RELINQUISH, RENOUNCE, RENUNCIATION, SURRENDER 1, YIELD.

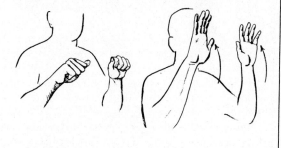

[L-163]

LOST (lôst, lŏst), *adj.* See LOSE.

[L-164]

LOT (lŏt), *n.* (A large amount.) The "5" hands face each other, fingers curved and touching. They move apart rather quickly. *Cf.* EXPAND, GREAT 2, INFINITE, MUCH.

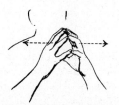

[L-165]

LOUD (loud), *adj.* (Something heard which shakes the surrounding area.) The right index finger touches the ear. The "5" hands, palms down, then move sharply in front of the body, in quick alternate motions, first away from and then back to the body. *Cf.* LOUDLY, LOUD NOISE.

[L-166]

LOUDLY (loud' lĭ), *adv.* See LOUD.

[L-167]

LOUD NOISE, *n. phrase.* See LOUD.

[L-168]

LOUSY (lou' zĭ), *(sl.), adj.* (A modification of the sign for spitting or thumbing the nose.) The right "3" hand is held with thumbtip against the nose. Then it is thrown sharply forward, and an expression of contempt is assumed. *Cf.* ROTTEN.

[L-169]

LOVE (lŭv), *n., v.,* LOVED, LOVING. (Clasping the heart.) The "5" hands are held one atop the other over the heart. Sometimes the "S" hands are used, in which case they are crossed at the wrists. *Cf.* BELOVED, CHARITY, DEVOTION, REVERE 2.

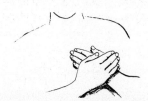

[L-170]

LOVER (lŭv' ər), *(colloq.), n.* (Heads nodding toward each other.) The "A" hands are placed together before the body with thumbs up. The thumbs wiggle up and down. *Cf.* BEAU, COURTING, COURTSHIP, MAKE LOVE 1, SWEETHEART 1.

[L-171]

LOW 1 (lō), *adj.* (Motion downward.) The "A" hand is held in front of the body, thumb pointing upward. The hand then moves straight downward several inches. Both hands may be used. *Cf.* BASE 1.

[L-172]

LOW 2, *adj., n.* (Motion downward.) The right-angle hands are held up before the head, fingertips pointing toward each other. From this position, the hands move down in an arc. *Cf.* BASE 2, DEMOTE, LOWER.

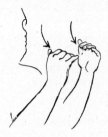

[L-173]

LOWBROW (lō' brou´), *(sl.), n., adj.* (The natural sign.) The right hand is placed on the forehead, with thumb and other fingers a short distance apart, denoting a small portion of the brow. Sometimes only

thumb and index fingers are used instead of the whole hand.

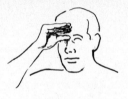

[L-174]

LOWER (lō' ər), *v.,* -ERED, -ERING. See LOW 2.

[L-175]

LOYAL (loi' əl), *adj.* (The arm is raised.) The right index finger is placed at the lips. The right arm is then raised, palm out and elbow resting on the back of the left hand. *Cf.* GUARANTEE 1, OATH, PLEDGE, PROMISE 1, SWEAR 1, SWORN, TAKE OATH, VOW.

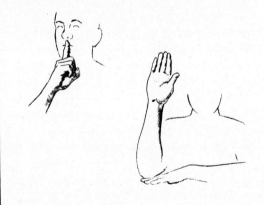

[L-176]

LUGGAGE (lŭg' ij), *n.* (The natural sign.) The downturned right "S" hand grasps an imaginary piece of luggage and shakes it up and down slightly, as if testing its weight. *Cf.* BAGGAGE, SUITCASE, VALISE.

[L-177]

LUMBER 1 (lŭm′ bər), *n.* (The sawing of wood.) The little finger edge of the open right hand moves back and forth in a sawing motion over the back of the downturned left hand. *Cf.* SAW 1, WOOD.

[L-178]

LUMBER 2, *n.* (The rotary blade's teeth sticking up through the wood.) The outstretched fingers of the right hand pass alternately back and forth between the index and middle fingers of the downturned left hand. *Cf.* SAWMILL.

[L-179]

LUNGS (lŭngz), *n. pl.* (The natural sign.) The fingertips of the "5" hands, palms facing the body, move alternately up and down on either side of the chest to denote the position of the lungs. *Cf.* PNEUMONIA.

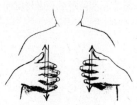

[L-180]

LUST (lŭst), *n., v.,* LUSTED, LUSTING. (The alimentary canal—the area of hunger and hunger gratification—is indicated.) The fingertips of the right "C" hand move slowly and deliberately down the middle of the chest once or twice. The eyes are usually narrowed and the teeth clenched. *Cf.* PASSION 1.

[L-181]

LUTHER (lōō′ thər), *(eccles.), n.* (The letter "L" for LUTHER; the action of Luther's nailing of the 95 theses to the church door.) The thumbtip of the right "L" hand, palm out, is thrust repeatedly into the palm of the left hand, which is facing right. *Cf.* LUTHERAN.

[L-182]

LUTHERAN (lōō′ thər ən), *adj.* See LUTHER.

M

MACHINE (mə shēn'), *n*. (The meshing gears.) With the knuckles of both hands interlocked, the hands pivot up and down, imitating the meshing of gear teeth. *Cf.* ENGINE, FACTORY, MACHINERY, MECHANIC 1, MECHANISM, MOTOR.

MACHINE GUN. (The natural sign.) Both hands grasp an imaginary machine gun. The signer takes aim, and then his arms tremble violently as if a hail of bullets is leaving the weapon.

MACHINERY (mə shē' nə rĭ), *n*. (The meshing gears.) With the knuckles of both hands interlocked, the hands pivot up and down, imitating the meshing of gear teeth. *Cf.* ENGINE, FACTORY, MACHINE, MECHANIC 1, MECHANISM, MOTOR.

MAD 1 (măd), *adj*. (A violent welling-up of the emotions.) The curved fingers of the right hand are placed in the center of the chest, and fly up suddenly and violently. An expression of anger is worn. *Cf.* ANGER, ANGRY 2, ENRAGE, FURY, INDIGNANT, INDIGNATION, IRE, RAGE.

MAD 2, *adj*. (Turning of wheels in the head.) The open right hand is held palm down before the face, fingers spread, bent, and pointing toward the forehead. The fingers move in circles before the forehead. *Cf.* CRAZY 1, INSANE, INSANITY, NUTS 1.

MADAM (măd' əm) *n*. (A female with a ruffled bodice; *i.e.*, an elegantly dressed woman, a lady.) The FEMALE root sign is made: The thumb of the right "A" hand moves down along the right jaw, from ear almost to chin. The thumbtip of the right "5" hand, palm facing left, is then placed on the chest, with the other fingers pointing up. Pivoted at the thumb, the hand swings down a bit, so that the other fingers are now pointing out somewhat. *Cf.* LADY.

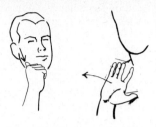

[M-7]

MAGAZINE (măg′ ə zēn′, măg′ ə zēn′), *n.* (A book with a narrow spine.) The left hand, fingers together, is held upright, palm facing right. The right hand wraps around the lower edge of the left and travels up to the little finger. This denotes a narrow object. The sign for **BOOK** is then made: The hands are placed together, palm to palm, and then opened, as if opening a book. Sometimes this latter sign is omitted. *Cf.* BOOKLET, CATALOG, MANUAL, PAMPHLET.

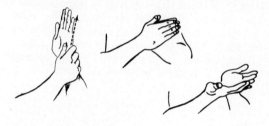

[M-8]

MAGIC (măj′ ĭk), *n., adj.* (The flourish of the magician's hands.) Both hands, palms out, are held before the body, with fingertips touching their respective thumbs. The hands are thrust forward, either straight or with a flourish, opening somewhat as they do so.

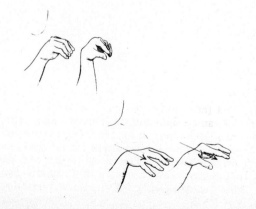

[M-9]

MAGICIAN (mə jĭsh′ ən), *n.* The sign for **MAGIC** is made, followed by the sign for **INDIVIDUAL**: Both open hands, palms facing each other, move down the sides of the body, tracing its outline to the hips.

[M-10]

MAGNANIMOUS (măg năn′ ə məs), *adj.* (The heart is opened.) The right hand is placed over the heart. It swings quickly away to a position in front of the body with palm facing left. *Cf.* WILLING 3.

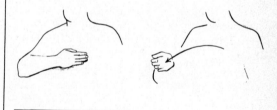

[M-11]

MAGNET (măg′ nĭt), *n.* (The attraction is indicated.) The left "5" hand, somewhat downturned, is the MAGNET. The open right hand, palm facing down, is held in front of the left. The back of the right hand is brought into sudden and sharp contact with the left palm as the right fingers are simultaneously brought together with the right thumb.

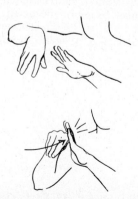

[M-12]

MAGNIFICENT (măg nif' ə sənt), *adj.* (The feelings are titillated.) The thumbtips of both "5" hands, palms facing, are placed on the chest near the armpits. Both hands move up and away from the body, with the fingers wiggling. A pleased expression is assumed.

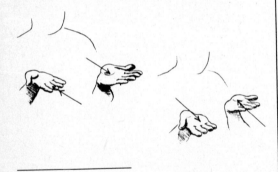

[M-13]

MAID (mād), *n.* (Passing the dishes, one by one.) The upturned "5" hands move alternately toward and away from the chest. *Cf.* SERVANT, SERVE 2, SERVICE, WAITER 2, WAIT ON 2, WAITRESS 2.

[M-14]

MAIDEN (mā' dən), *n.* (A female who is small.) The FEMALE root sign is given: The thumb of the right "A" hand moves down along the line of the right jaw, from ear almost to chin. This outlines the string used to tie ladies' bonnets in olden days. The downturned open right hand then indicates the short height of the female by being held at waist level. *Cf.* GIRL.

[M-15]

MAIL 1 (māl), *n.* (The stamp is affixed.) The right thumb is placed on the tongue, and is then pressed into the open left palm. *Cf.* EPISTLE, LETTER.

[M-16]

MAIL 2, *v.,* MAILED, MAILING. (Sending a letter.) The sign for LETTER is made: The right thumbtip is licked and placed against the upturned left palm. The right hand, palm out and fingers touching thumb, is then thrown forward, opening into the "5" position, palm out. *Cf.* POST.

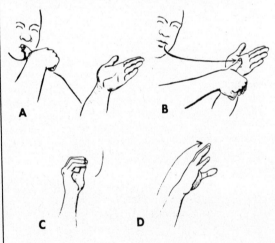

A　　　　**B**

C　　　　**D**

[M-17]

MAIN (mān), *adj.* Both "F" hands, palms facing each other, move apart, up, and together in a smooth elliptical fashion, coming together at the tips of the thumbs and index fingers of both hands. *Cf.* DESERVE, ESSENTIAL, IMPORTANT 1, MERIT, PRECIOUS, PROMINENT 2, SIGNIFICANCE 1, SIGNIFI-

CANT, VALUABLE, VALUE, VITAL 1, WORTH, WORTHWHILE, WORTHY.

[M–18]

MAINLY (mān' lǐ), *adv.* (The largest or greatest amount.) The sign for MUCH is made: The "5" hands, palms facing, fingers curved and thumbs pointing up, draw apart. The sign for the superlative suffix, "-EST," is then made: The right "A" hand, thumb pointing up, quickly moves straight upward, until it is above the head. *Cf.* CHIEF, MOST, MOST OF ALL, PRINCIPAL 2.

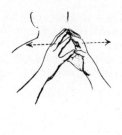 

[M–19]

MAINTAIN 1 (mān tān'), *v.*, -TAINED, -TAINING. (Slow, careful movement.) The "K" hands are crossed, the right above the left, little finger edges down. In this position the hands are moved up and down a short distance. *Cf.* CARE 2, CAREFUL 2, KEEP, MIND 3, PRESERVE, RESERVE 2, TAKE CARE OF 2.

[M–20]

MAINTAIN 2, *v.* (Words tumbling from the mouth.) The right index finger, pointing left, describes a continuous small circle in front of the mouth. *Cf.* BID 3, DISCOURSE, HEARING, MENTION, REMARK, SAID, SAY, SPEAK, SPEECH 1, STATE, STATEMENT, TALK 1, TELL, VERBAL 1.

[M–21]

MAINTENANCE (mān' tə nəns), *n.* (Holding up.) The right "S" hand pushes up the left "S" hand. *Cf.* ENDORSE 1, FAVOR, INDORSE 1, SUPPORT 1, SUSTAIN, SUSTENANCE, UPHOLD, UPLIFT.

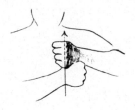

[M–22]

MAJESTY (măj' is tǐ), *n.* (The letter "M"; the highness.) Both "M" hands, facing each other, move up in an arc simultaneously, from their initial position at chest height.

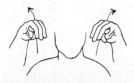

[M–23]

MAKE (māk), *v.*, MADE, MAKING, *n.* (Fashioning something with the hands.) The right "S" hand, palm facing left, is placed on top of its left counterpart, whose palm faces right. The hands are twisted back and forth, striking each other slightly after each twist. *Cf.* COMPOSE, CONSTITUTE, CONSTRUCT 2, CREATE, DEVISE 2, FABRICATE, FASHION, FIX, MANUFACTURE, MEND 1, PRODUCE 3, RENDER 1, REPAIR.

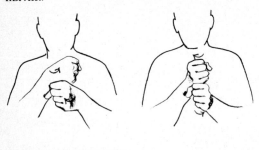

[M–24]

MAKE A FACE, *v. phrase.* (The facial features are distorted.) The "X" hands are moved alternately up and down in front of the face, whose features are distorted with a pronounced frown. *Cf.* GRIMACE, HOMELY 1, UGLINESS 1, UGLY 1.

[M–25]

MAKE BRIEF, *v. phrase.* (To squeeze or condense into a small space.) The "C" hands face each other, with the right hand nearer to the body than the left. Both hands draw together and close deliberately, squeezing an imaginary object. *Cf.* ABBREVIATE 1, BRIEF 2, CONDENSE, SUMMARIZE 1, SUMMARY 1.

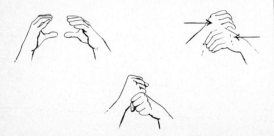

[M–26]

MAKE FUN OF, *v. phrase.* (Derision; poking or prodding.) Both hands are held closed except for index and little fingers, which extend straight out from the body. The right hand is brought up and its index fingertip pulls the right corner of the mouth into a slight smile. Both hands then move forward simultaneously in a series of short jabbing motions, the right somewhat behind the left. An expression of disdain is assumed during this sign. The first part of the sign, pulling the mouth into a smile, is frequently omitted. *Cf.* MOCK, RIDICULE.

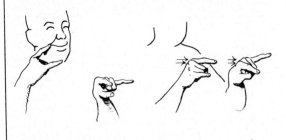

[M–27]

MAKE HALLOWED, *(eccles.)*, *v. phrase.* (MAKE and HOLY.) The sign for MAKE is made; and then the sign for HOLY is made: The right "H" hand makes a clockwise circle, and then opens into the downturned "5" position, wiping off the upturned left palm.

[M–28]

MAKE KNOWN, *v. phrase.* (An issuance from the mouth.) Both index fingers are placed at the lips, with palms facing the body. They are rotated once and swung out in arcs, until the left index finger points somewhat to the left and the right index somewhat to the right. Sometimes the rotation of the fingers is omitted in favor of a simple swinging out from the lips. *Cf.* ACCLAIM 1, ACCLAMATION, AN-

NOUNCE, ANNOUNCEMENT, DECLARE, PROCLAIM, PROCLAMATION.

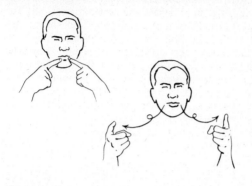

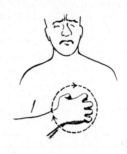

describe a continuous circle on the stomach. The signer assumes an exaggerated expression of disgust. *Cf.* DISGUST, DISGUSTED, DISGUSTING, DISPLEASED, MAKE ME SICK, NAUSEA, NAUSEATE, NAUSEOUS, OBNOXIOUS, REVOLTING.

[M-29]

MAKE LOVE 1, *(colloq.), v. phrase.* (Heads nodding toward each other.) The "A" hands are placed together before the body with thumbs up. The thumbs wiggle up and down. *Cf.* BEAU, COURTING, COURTSHIP, LOVER, SWEETHEART 1.

[M-30]

MAKE LOVE 2, *(sl.), v. phrase.* (Necks interlocked.) The "S" hands, palms facing, are crossed at the wrists. They swing up and down while the wrists remain in contact. *Cf.* NECKING, PETTING.

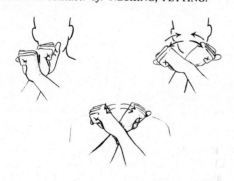

[M-31]

MAKE ME DISGUSTED, *v. phrase.* (Turning the stomach.) The fingertips of the curved right hand

[M-32]

MAKE ME SICK, *v. phrase.* See MAKE ME DISGUSTED.

[M-33]

MAKE NO DIFFERENCE, *v. phrase.* Both hands, in the "5" position, are held before the chest, fingertips facing each other. With an alternate back-forth movement, the fingertips are made to strike each other. *Cf.* ANYHOW, ANYWAY, DESPITE, DOESN'T MATTER, HOWEVER 2, INDIFFERENCE, INDIFFERENT, IN SPITE OF, NEVERTHELESS, NO MATTER, WHEREVER.

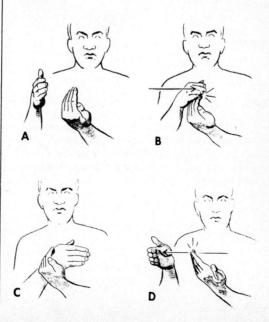

[M–34]

MAKE RESPONSE, *v. phrase.* (Directing a reply from the mouth to someone.) The tip of the right index finger, held in the "D" position, palm facing the body, is placed on the lips, while the left "D" hand, palm also facing the body, is held about a foot in front of the right hand. The right index finger, swinging around, moves toward and stops in a pointing position a few inches from the left index finger-tip. *Cf.* ANSWER 1, REPLY 1, RESPOND, RESPONSE 1.

[M–35]

MAKESHIFT (māk' shĭft'), *(colloq.), adj.* (Just a quick touch or taste.) The tip of the middle finger of the right "5" hand, palm facing the body, is placed at the lips. The hand is then flung a few inches away from the mouth, into a position with palm facing left. *Cf.* GOOD ENOUGH.

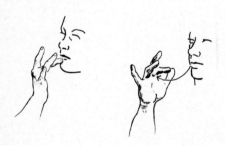

[M–36]

MAKE-UP (māk' ŭp), *n.* (Applying something to the face.) The thumbtip and fingertips of each hand are held together and rotated in small counterclockwise circles on both cheeks simultaneously. *Cf.* COSMETICS.

[M–37]

MAKE UP ONE'S MIND, *v. phrase.* (The mind stops wavering, and the pros and cons are resolved.) The right index finger touches the forehead, the sign for THINK, *q.v.* Both "F" hands, palms facing each other and fingers pointing straight out, then drop down simultaneously. The sign for JUDGE, *q.v.,* explains the rationale behind the movement of the two hands here. *Cf.* DECIDE, DECISION, DECREE 1, DETERMINE, MIND 5, RENDER JUDGMENT, RESOLVE, VERDICT.

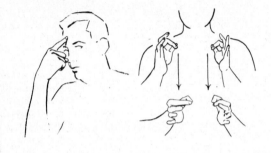

[M–38]

MALE (māl), *n., adj.* (The man's cap.) The thumb and extended fingers of the right hand are brought up to grasp an imaginary cap brim, representing the tipping of caps by men in olden days. This is a root sign used to modify many others. *Viz.* MALE plus BABY: SON; MALE plus SAME: BROTHER; etc. *Cf.* HUMAN, MAN, MANKIND.

[M–39]

MAMA (mä' mə), *n.* (Familiar derivation of the more formal MOTHER, *q.v.*) The thumb of the right "5" hand touches the right cheek repeatedly.

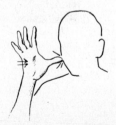

[M-40]

MAN (măn), *n.* See MALE.

[M-41]

MANAGE (măn' ĭj), *v.,* -AGED, -AGING. (Holding the reins over all.) The "A" hands, palms facing, move alternately back and forth, as if grasping and manipulating reins. The left "A" hand, still in position, swings over so that its palm now faces down. The right hand opens to the "5" position, palm down, and swings over the left which moves slightly to the right. *Cf.* AUTHORITY, CONTROL 1, DIRECT 1, GOVERN, MANAGEMENT, MANAGER, OPERATE, REGULATE, REIGN, RULE 1.

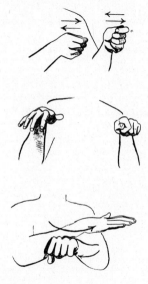

[M-42]

MANAGEMENT (măn' ĭj mənt), *n.* The sign for MANAGE is made. This is followed by the sign for -MENT: The downturned right "M" hand moves down along the left palm, which is facing away from the body.

[M-43]

MANAGER (măn' ĭj ər), *n.* The sign for MANAGE, *q.v.,* is made. This is followed by the sign for INDI-

VIDUAL: Both open hands, palms facing each other, move down the sides of the body, tracing its outline to the hips.

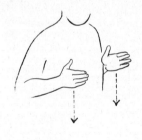

[M-44]

MANKIND (măn' kīnd'), *n.* See MALE.

[M-45]

MANNER 1 (măn' ər), *n.* (The hands come into view, to reveal the "how" of something.) The right-angle hands, palms down and knuckles touching, swing up and open to the palms-up position. *Cf.* HOW.

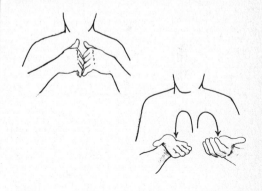

[M-46]

MANNER 2, *n.* (The movement.) Both hands, palms facing and fingers together and extended straight out, move in unison away from the body, in a straight or winding manner. *Cf.* CORRIDOR, HALL, HALLWAY, METHOD, OPPORTUNITY 3, PATH, ROAD, STREET, TRAIL, WAY 1.

[M–47]

MANUAL (măn′ yŏŏ əl), *n.* (A book with a narrow spine.) The left hand, fingers together, is held upright, palm facing right. The right hand wraps around the lower edge of the left and travels up to the little finger. This denotes a narrow object. The sign for BOOK is then made: The hands are placed together, palm to palm, and then opened, as if opening a book. Sometimes this latter sign is omitted. *Cf.* BOOKLET, CATALOG, MAGAZINE, PAMPHLET.

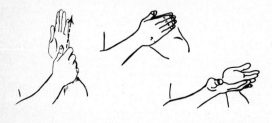

[M–48]

MANUAL ALPHABET. (The movement of the fingers in fingerspelling.) The right hand, palm out, is moved from left to right, with the fingers wriggling up and down. *Cf.* ALPHABET, DACTYLOLOGY, FINGERSPELLING, SPELL, SPELLING.

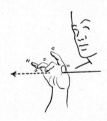

[M–49]

MANUFACTURE (măn′ yə făk′ chər), *n., v.,* -TURED, -TURING. (Fashioning something with the hands.) The right "S" hand, palm facing left, is placed on top of its left counterpart, whose palm faces right. The hands are twisted back and forth, striking each other slightly after each twist. *Cf.* COMPOSE, CONSTITUTE, CONSTRUCT 2, CREATE, DEVISE 2, FABRICATE, FASHION, FIX, MAKE, MEND 1, PRODUCE 3, RENDER 1, REPAIR.

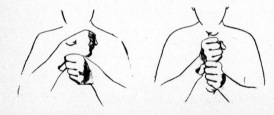

[M–50]

MANY (mĕn′ ĭ), *adj.* (*Many* fingers are indicated.) The upturned "S" hands are thrown up, opening into the "5" position, palms up. This may be repeated. *Cf.* MULTIPLE, NUMEROUS, PLURAL, QUANTITY 2.

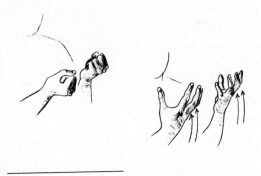

[M–51]

MAP (măp), *n., v.,* MAPPED, MAPPING. (Drawing on the hand.) The little finger of the right hand, representing a pencil, traces a curved line in the upturned left palm. *Cf.* ART, DRAW 1.

[M–52]

MAR 1 (mär), *v.,* MARRED, MARRING. (A stabbing pain.) The "D" hands, index fingers pointing to each other, are rotated in elliptical fashion before the chest—simultaneously but in opposite directions. *Cf.* ACHE, HARM 1, HURT 1, INJURE 1, INJURY, OFFEND, OFFENSE, PAIN, SIN, WOUND.

[M–53]

MAR 2, *v.* (Striking down against.) Both "A" or "X" hands are held before the chest, the right above the left. The right hand strikes down and out, hitting the left thumb and knuckles with force. *Cf.* BACK-

BITE, BASE 3, CRUEL 1, HARM 2, HURT 2, MEAN 1, SPOIL.

[M–54]

MARCH 1 (märch), *v.*, MARCHED, MARCHING. (A column of marchers, one behind the other.) The downturned open hands, fingers pointing down, are held one behind the other. Pivoted from the wrists, they move rhythmically forward and back in unison. *Cf.* PARADE 2.

[M–55]

MARCH 2, *n.* The same sign as MARCH 1 except that the downturned "V" hands are used.

[M–56]

MARK (märk), *n.*, *v.*, MARKED, MARKING. (Making a mark.) The hand, holding an imaginary writing implement, makes a small "mark" in the air.

[M–57]

MARRIAGE (măr′ ĭj), *n.* (A clasping of hands, as during the wedding ceremony.) The hands are clasped together, the right on top of the left. *Cf.* MARRY.

[M–58]

MARRY (măr′ ĭ), *v.*, -RIED, -RYING. See MARRIAGE.

[M–59]

MARTYR (mär′ tər), (eccles.), *n.* (A beheaded Catholic.) The sign for CATHOLIC, is made: The upright right "H" hand describes a cross in front of the face. The open right hand, forming an imaginary axe blade, then swings by the neck as if cutting off the head.

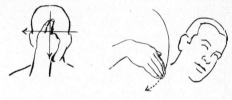

[M–60]

MARVEL (mär′ vəl), *n.* (The hands gesture toward the heavens.) The "5" hands, palms out and arms raised rather high, are positioned somewhat above the line of vision. The arms move abruptly forward and up once or twice. An expression of pleasure or surprise is usually assumed. *Cf.* EXCELLENT, GRAND 1, GREAT 3, MARVELOUS, MIRACLE, O!, SPLENDID 1, SWELL 1, WONDER 2, WONDERFUL 1.

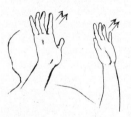

[M–61]

MARVELOUS (mär′ vəl əs), *adj.* See MARVEL.

[M–62]

MARY (mâr ĭ), *(eccles.), n.* (The veil.) The right "W" hand is held with fingers pointing down over the left ear. From this position the hand circles back over the forehead toward the right ear, the three extended fingers wiggling back and forth as it does. The "M" hand may also be used, without the wiggling.

[M–63]

MASH 1 (măsh), *n.* (The movement of the pestle in the mortar.) The little finger edge of the right "S" hand describes a circle, either clockwise or counterclockwise, as it presses against the upturned left palm.

[M–64]

MASH 2, *v.,* MASHED, MASHING. (The natural movement.) The balls of both open "5" hands are pressed together, with the right hand above the left. The right hand describes a circle, either clockwise or counterclockwise, as it remains pressed against the left.

[M–65]

MASS (măs), *(eccles.), n.* (A table for Mass.) The sign for ALTAR 1 is made; then the two "F" hands, palms out, are drawn up and together, so that the thumbs and index fingers of both hands touch before the face (bringing the Host to the lips in Roman

Catholic practice). The sign for ALTAR 1 is often omitted. *Cf.* ALTAR 2.

[M–66]

MASTICATE (măs′ tə kāt′), *v.,* -CATED, -CATING. (The grinding of teeth.) The knuckles of the downturned right "A" hand are placed against those of the upturned left "A" hand. The two hands "grind" against each other, in opposite directions. *Cf.* CHEW.

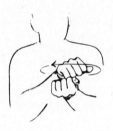

[M–67]

MATCH (măch), *n.* (The natural sign.) The right hand, grasping an imaginary match, strikes it against the open left palm, which is facing right. *Cf.* KINDLE.

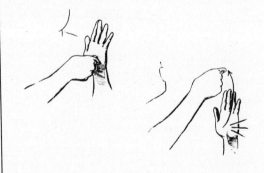

[M–68]

MATHEMATICS (măth′ ə măt′ ĭks), *n.* (Calculation; the "X" movement, with the letter "M.") Both "M"

hands, fingertips facing and palms facing the body, are crossed repeatedly.

against the right shoulder. *Cf.* CRACKER 1, PASS-OVER.

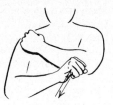

[M–69]

MATTER (măt′ ər), *n.* (Something shown in the hand.) The outstretched right hand, palm up and held before the chest, is dropped slightly and brought over a bit to the right. *Cf.* ANYTHING, APPARATUS, INSTRUMENT, OBJECT 1, SUBSTANCE 1, THING.

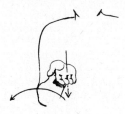

[M–70]

MATURE (mə tyŏŏr′, -tŏŏr′), *v.,* -TURED, -TURING. (Flowers or plants emerge from the ground.) The right fingers, pointing up, emerge from the closed left hand, and they spread open as they do. *Cf.* BLOOM, DEVELOP 1, GROW, GROWN, PLANT 1, RAISE 3, REAR 2, SPRING 1.

[M–71]

MATZOTH (mät′ sōth), *n. pl.* The thumb edge of the right fist strikes several times against the left elbow, while the left arm is bent so that the left fist is held

[M–72]

MAY 1 (mā), *v.* (Weighing one thing against another.) The upturned open hands move alternately up and down. *Cf.* GUESS 4, MAYBE, MIGHT 2, PERHAPS, POSSIBILITY, POSSIBLY, PROBABLE, PROBABLY, SUPPOSE.

[M–73]

MAY 2, *v.* (An affirmative movement of the hands, likened to a nodding of the head, to indicate ability or power to accomplish something.) Both "A" hands, held palms down, move down in unison a short distance before the chest. *Cf.* ABILITY, ABLE, CAN 1, CAPABLE, COMPETENT, COULD, FACULTY, POSSIBLE.

[M-74]

MAY 3, *v.* (A permissive upswinging of the hands, as if giving in.) Both hands, palms facing and fingers pointing away from the body, are held at chest level, almost a foot apart. With an upward movement, using their wrists as pivots, the hands sweep up until the fingers point almost straight up. *Cf.* ALLOW, GRANT 1, LET, LET'S, LET US, PERMISSION 1, PERMIT 1, TOLERATE 1.

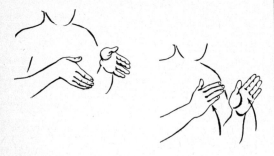

[M-75]

MAYBE (mā' bǐ, -bē), *adv.* See MAY 1.

[M-76]

ME (mē; *unstressed* mǐ), *pron.* (The natural sign.) The signer points to himself. *Cf.* I 2.

[M-77]

MEAL (mēl), *n.* (The natural sign.) The closed right hand goes through the natural motion of placing food in the mouth. This movement is repeated. *Cf.* CONSUME 1, CONSUMPTION, DEVOUR, DINE, EAT, FEED 1, FOOD 1.

[M-78]

MEAN 1 (mēn), *adj.* (Striking down against.) Both "A" or "X" hands are held before the chest, the right above the left. The right hand strikes down and out, hitting the left thumb and knuckles with force. *Cf.* BACKBITE, BASE 3, CRUEL 1, HARM 2, HURT 2, MAR 2, SPOIL.

[M-79]

MEAN 2, *v.,* MEANT, MEANING. (Relative standing of one's thoughts.) A modified sign for THINK is made: The right index finger touches the middle of the forehead. The tips of the right "V" hand, palm down, are then thrust into the upturned left palm (as in STAND, *q.v.*). The right "V" hand is then re-thrust into the upturned left palm, with right palm now facing the body. *Cf.* CONNOTE, IMPLY, INTEND, INTENT 1, INTENTION, MEANING, MOTIVE 3, PURPOSE 1, SIGNIFICANCE 2, SIGNIFY 2, SUBSTANCE 2.

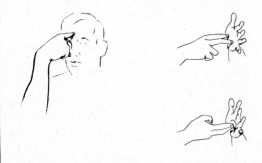

[M-80]

MEAN 3, *n., adj.* (Halfway between top and bottom.) The right open hand, held upright, palm facing left, rests its little finger edge across the index finger edge of the downturned, open left hand. In this position the right hand moves back and forth several times, rubbing the base of the little finger along the edge of the left hand. *Cf.* AVERAGE.

[M–81]

MEANING (mē′ nǐng), *n.* See MEAN 2.

[M–82]

MEANTIME (mēn′ tīm′), *n., adv.* (Parallel time.) Both "D" hands, palms down, move forward in unison, away from the body. They may move straight forward or may follow a slight upward arc. *Cf.* DURING, IN THE MEANTIME, IN THE PROCESS OF, WHILE.

[M–83]

MEASLES (mē′ zəlz), *n.* (The facial blotches are indicated.) The fingertips of the open right hand are brought repeatedly against the right cheek.

[M–84]

MEASURE (mězh′ ər), *n., v.,* -URED, -URING. (The act of measuring a short distance.) Both "Y" hands, palms out, move alternately a short distance back and forth, away from and toward each other. *Cf.* GAUGE, SCALE 1.

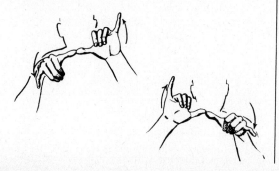

[M–85]

MEAT (mēt), *n.* (The fleshy part of the hand.) The right index finger and thumb squeeze the fleshy part of the open left hand, between thumb and index finger. *Cf.* BEEF, FLESH.

[M–86]

MECHANIC 1 (mə kăn′ ĭk), *n.* (The meshing gears.) With the knuckles of both hands interlocked, the hands pivot up and down, imitating the meshing of gear teeth. This may be followed by the sign for INDIVIDUAL 1, *q.v. Cf.* ENGINE, FACTORY, MACHINE, MACHINERY, MECHANISM, MOTOR.

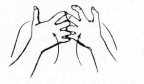

[M–87]

MECHANIC 2, *n.* (The natural movement.) The index finger of the right hand is grasped by the outstretched index and middle fingers of the left hand. The left hand executes a series of up-and-down movements, as if manipulating a wrench. This is followed by the sign for INDIVIDUAL: Both open hands, palms facing each other, move down the sides of the body, tracing its outline to the hips. *Cf.* PIPEFITTING, PLUMBER, STEAM FITTER, WRENCH.

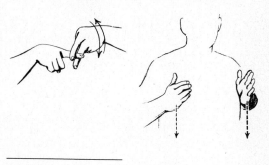

[M–88]

MECHANISM (měk′ ə nǐz′ əm), *n.* See MECHANIC 1.

[M-89]

MEDAL (mĕd' əl), *n.* (The medal hanging from the left side of the chest.) The right index and middle fingers, held together and pointing straight down, are brought against the left side of the chest, either once or twice.

[M-90]

MEDDLE 1 (mĕd' əl), *v.,* -DLED, -DLING. (Obstruct, block.) The left hand, fingers together and palm flat, is held before the body, facing somewhat down. The little finger side of the right hand, held with palm flat, makes one or several up-down chopping motions against the left hand, between its thumb and index finger. *Cf.* ANNOY 1, ANNOYANCE 1, BLOCK, BOTHER 1, CHECK 2, COME BETWEEN, DISRUPT, DISTURB, HINDER, HINDRANCE, IMPEDE, INTERCEPT, INTERFERE, INTERFERENCE, INTERFERE WITH, INTERRUPT, OBSTACLE, OBSTRUCT, PREVENT, PREVENTION.

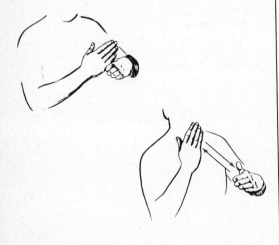

[M-91]

MEDDLE 2 (med' 'l), *v.* (The nose is poked into something.) The sign for NOSE is formed by touching the tip of the nose with the index finger. The sign for IN, INTO follows: The right hand, fingertips touching the thumb, is thrust into the left "C" hand,

which closes a bit over the right fingers as they enter. *Cf.* BUTT IN.

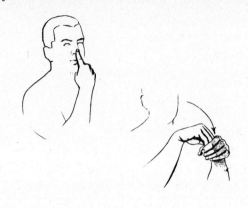

[M-92]

MEDIAN (mē' dĭ ən), *n., adj.* (The midpoint, with the letter "M.") The right hand is held in a modified "M" position, palm facing down. The edge of the right middle finger is placed at the midpoint of the upturned left index finger. In this position the right hand moves very slightly up and down.

[M-93]

MEDICINE (mĕd' ə sən), *n.* (Mixing of medicine; rolling a pill.) The ball of the middle fingertip of the right "5" hand describes a small counterclockwise circle in the upturned left palm. *Cf.* DRUG, POISON 1, PRESCRIPTION.

[M-94]

MEDITATE (mĕd' ə tāt'), *v.,* -TATED, -TATING. (Thinking, and holding the brow.) The sign for THINK is made: The right index finger describes a small counterclockwise circle in mid-forehead. The open right hand is then placed at the brow, holding it as if in deep thought. *Cf.* MEDITATION.

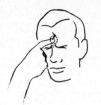

[M-95]

MEDITATION (mĕd′ ə tā′ shən), *n.* See MEDITATE.

[M-96]

MEDIUM (mē′ dĭ əm), *adj.* (The midpoint is emphasized.) The little finger edge of the open right hand, palm facing left, comes down against the middle of the index finger edge of the open left hand, whose palm faces the body. This movement may be repeated. *Cf.* MIDWAY, NEUTRAL.

[M-97]

MEEK (mēk), *adj.* (The head bows; a turtle's head retreats into its shell; an act of humility.) The index finger edge of the right "B" hand, palm facing left, is placed at the lips. The right "B" hand is then brought down and under the downturned open left hand. The head, at the same time, bows. *Cf.* HUMBLE 1, MODEST.

[M-98]

MEET (mēt), *v.,* MET, MEETING. (A coming together of two persons.) Both "D" hands, palms facing each other, are brought together. *Cf.* ENCOUNTER.

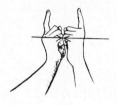

[M-99]

MEETING 1 (mē′ tǐng), *n.* (Assemble all together.) Both "5" hands, palms facing, are held with fingers pointing out from the body. With a sweeping motion they are brought in toward the chest, and all fingertips come together. This is repeated. *Cf.* ACCUMULATE 3, ASSEMBLE, ASSEMBLY, CONFERENCE, CONVENE, CONVENTION, GATHER 2, GATHERING.

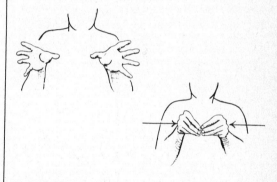

[M-100]

MEETING 2, *(loc.), n.* (A random coming together of different persons.) The "D" hands, facing each other and touching at the thumbs, are held with right palm facing the body and left palm facing away from the body. They pivot around so that their relative positions are now reversed. This may be done several times. In addition, the hands may be separated slightly during the pivoting, but they must come together at the end of this movement.

[M-101]

MELANCHOLY (mĕl′ ən kŏl′ ĭ), *n.* (The facial features drop.) Both "5" hands, palms facing the eyes and fingers slightly curved, drop simultaneously to a level with the mouth. The head drops slightly as the hands move down, and an expression of sadness is assumed. *Cf.* DEJECTED, DEPRESSED, GLOOM, GLOOMY, GRAVE 3, GRIEF 1, MOURNFUL, SAD, SORROWFUL 1.

[M-102]

MELODY (mĕl′ ə dĭ), *n.* (A rhythmic, wavy movement of the hand, to indicate a melody; the movement of a conductor's hand in directing a musical performance.) The right "5" hand, palm facing left, is waved back and forth over the downturned left hand, in a series of elongated figure-eights. *Cf.* CHANT, HYMN 1, MUSIC, SING, SONG.

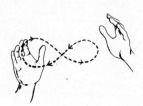

[M-103]

MELON (mĕl′ ən), *n.* (Sounding for ripeness.) The right middle finger is flicked once or twice against the back of the downturned left hand.

[M-104]

MELT (mĕlt), *v.,* MELTED, MELTING. (Fingering the small pieces resulting from the breaking up of something.) The thumbs rub slowly across the fingertips of the upturned hands, from the little fingers to the index fingers, and then continue to the "A" position, palms up. *Cf.* DECAY, DIE OUT, DISSOLVE, FADE, ROT.

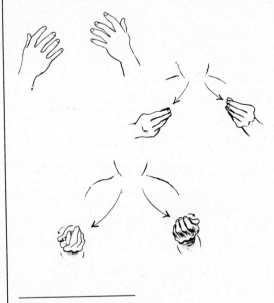

[M-105]

MEMBER 1 (mĕm′ bər), *n.* (Linked together.) The sign for JOIN is made: Both hands, held in the modified "5" position, palms out, move toward each other. The thumbs and index fingers of both hands then connect. This is followed by the sign for INDIVIDUAL: Both open hands, palms facing each other, move down the sides of the body, tracing its outline to the hips.

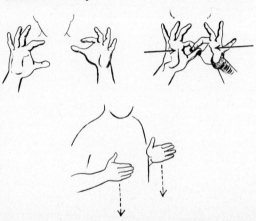

[M–106]

MEMBER 2, *n.* The right "M" hand, palm facing the body and fingers pointing left, moves from the left shoulder to the right. *Cf.* GALLAUDET, EDWARD MINER.

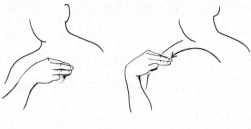

[M–107]

MEMORIZE 1 (měm' ə rīz´), *v.,* -RIZED, -RIZING. (Holding on to knowledge.) The open right hand is placed on the forehead. Then as it is removed straight forward, it is clenched into a fist.

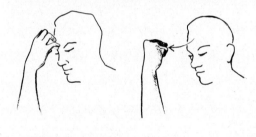

[M–108]

MEMORIZE 2, *v.* (Grasping a thought.) The index fingertip of the right hand touches the forehead, as in THINK, *q.v.* The right hand then swings outward from the forehead, opening as it does. Finally, the right hand closes into the "S" position before the face, as if grasping something.

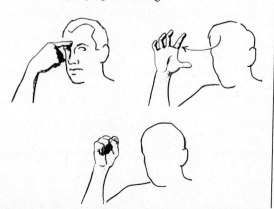

[M–109]

MEMORY (měm' ə rĭ), *n.* (Knowledge which remains.) The sign for KNOW is made: The right fingertips are placed on the forehead. The sign for REMAIN then follows: The "A" hands are held with palms toward the body, thumbs extended and touching, the right behind the left. In this position the hands move forward in a straight, steady line, or straight down. *Cf.* RECALL 2, RECOLLECT 2, REMEMBER.

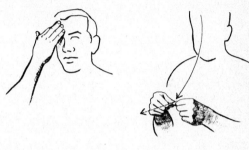

[M–110]

MEND 1 (měnd), *v.,* MENDED, MENDING. (Fashioning something with the hands.) The right "S" hand, palm facing left, is placed on top of its left counterpart, whose palm faces right. The hands are twisted back and forth, striking each other slightly after each twist. *Cf.* COMPOSE, CONSTITUTE, CONSTRUCT 2, CREATE, DEVISE 2, FABRICATE, FASHION, FIX, MAKE, MANUFACTURE, PRODUCE 3, RENDER 1, REPAIR.

[M–111]

MEND 2, *v.* (Moving up.) The little finger edge of the right hand rests on the back of the downturned left hand. It moves up the left arm in successive stages, indicating improvement or upward movement. The implication here is "mending one's ways." *Cf.* IMPROVE.

[M–112]

MENORAH (mə nôr' ə), *(eccles.), n.* (The eight candles.) The upturned right index finger is placed at the pursed lips (a candle). The "4" hands, side by side, palms out before the face, separate slowly, making a total of eight candles, the symbol of the Jewish festival of Chanukah. *Cf.* CHANUKAH.

[M–113]

MENSTRUATE (měn' strŏo āt´), *v.,* -ATED, -ATING. (Blotting the brow.) The knuckle edge of the right "A" hand is pressed twice against the right cheek.

[M–114]

-MENT, *condition. suffix.* The downturned right "M" hand moves down along the left palm, which is facing away from the body.

[M–115]

MENTAL (měn' təl), *adj.* (Patting the head to indicate something of value inside.) The right fingers pat the forehead several times. *Cf.* INTELLECT, INTELLIGENCE, MIND 1, SENSE 1.

[M–116]

MENTAL BREAKDOWN. (The mind caves in or collapses.) The forehead is touched, and then both hands, fingertips touching and forming a pyramid, "collapse" and crumble down and inward, back to back.

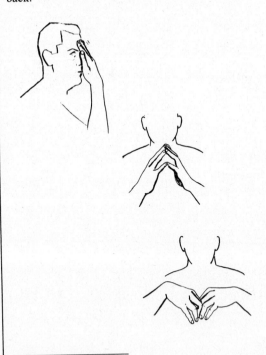

[M–117]

MENTALLY UNBALANCED 1, *adj. phrase.* (Mind, topsy-turvy.) The sign for MIND 1 is made: The right fingertips pat the forehead several times. Then the open hands, slightly curved, are held facing each other, the right above the left. From this position the right hand swings down and the left up, ending with the left palm facing down over the upturned right palm.

then traces a zigzag path on the upturned left palm. *Cf.* CRACKED IN THE HEAD.

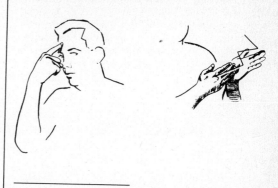

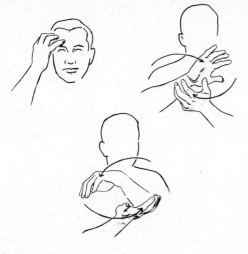

[M–118]

MENTALLY UNBALANCED 2, *(sl.), adj. phrase.* (The thoughts move away from a straight path.) The right fingertip touches the forehead (a modification of THINK, *q.v.*). The little finger edge of the open right hand is then placed in the upturned left palm. The right hand moves straight over the palm a short distance, then curves and moves off the palm toward the left. *Cf.* OFF THE BEAM.

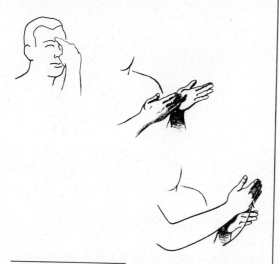

[M–119]

MENTALLY UNBALANCED 3, *adj. phrase.* (The mind is cracked.) The forehead is touched with the index finger. The little finger edge of the right hand

[M–120]

MENTALLY UNBALANCED 4, *adj. phrase.* (The mind is strange.) The forehead is touched with the index finger. The sign for STRANGE is made: The right "C" hand, palm facing left, sweeps from right to left across the face.

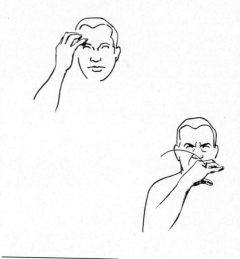

[M–121]

MENTALLY UNBALANCED 5, *adj. phrase.* (The natural sign.) The forehead is tapped repeatedly by the index finger. The signer frowns.

[M-122]

MENTION (měn' shən), *v.,* -TIONED, -TIONING. (Words tumbling from the mouth.) The right index finger, pointing left, describes a continuous small circle in front of the mouth. *Cf.* BID 3, DISCOURSE, HEARING, MAINTAIN 2, REMARK, SAID, SAY, SPEAK, SPEECH 1, STATE, STATEMENT, TALK 1, TELL, VERBAL 1.

[M-123]

MERCHANT (mûr' chənt), *n.* (Transferring ownership.) The sign for SALE is formed: The downturned hands, each with fingers grasping an imaginary object, pivot out from the wrists, away from the body. The sign for INDIVIDUAL is then made: Both open hands, palms facing each other, move down the sides of the body, tracing its outline to the hips. *Cf.* SALESMAN, SELLER, VENDER.

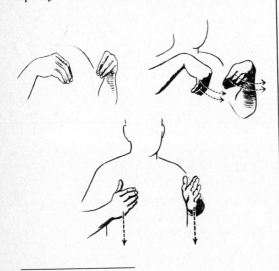

[M-124]

MERCY 1 (mûr' sĭ), *n.* (The heart rolls out.) Both right-angle hands roll over each other as they move down and away from their initial position at the heart. *Cf.* BENEVOLENT, GENEROUS 1, GENTLE 1, GENTLENESS, GRACIOUS, HUMANE, KIND 1, KINDNESS, TENDER 3.

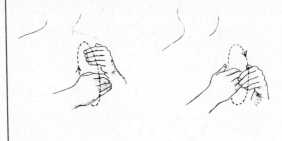

[M-125]

MERCY 2, *n.* (Feelings from the heart, conferred on others.) The middle fingertip of the open right hand touches the chest over the heart. The same open hand then moves in a small, clockwise circle before the right shoulder, with palm facing forward and fingers pointing up. *Cf.* PITY, POOR 3, SYMPATHY 2.

[M-126]

MERGE (mûrj), *v.,* MERGED, MERGING. (The natural sign.) Both open hands are held with palms toward the chest, fingertips pointing toward each other, thumbs pointing up. The hands then move toward each other until their fingers "merge."

[M-127]

MERIT (měr' ĭt), *n.* Both "F" hands, palms facing each other, move apart, up, and together in a smooth elliptical fashion, coming together at the tips of the thumbs and index fingers of both hands. *Cf.* DESERVE, ESSENTIAL, IMPORTANT 1, MAIN, PRECIOUS, PROMINENT 2, SIGNIFICANCE 1, SIGNIFICANT, VAL-

UABLE, VALUE, VITAL 1, WORTH, WORTHWHILE, WORTHY.

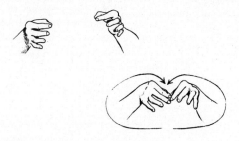

[M-128]

MERRY (mĕr' ĭ), *adj.* (The heart is stirred; the spirits bubble up.) The open right hand, palm facing the body, strikes the heart repeatedly, moving up and off the heart after each strike. *Cf.* DELIGHT, GAIETY 1, GAY, GLAD, HAPPINESS, HAPPY, JOY.

[M-129]

MESSAGE (mĕs' ĭj), *(rare), n.* (Word, carry.) The sign for WORD is formed: The right index fingertip and thumbtip are held about an inch apart and placed on the side of the outstretched left index finger, which represents the length of a sentence. This is followed by the sign for CARRY: Both open hands, palms up, move in an arc from left to right, as if carrying something from one point to another.

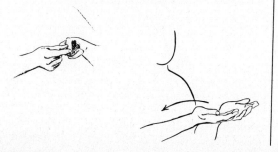

[M-130]

METAL 1 (mĕt' əl), *n.* (Hammering on metal.) The little finger edge of the right "S" hand is brought down forcefully against the back of the prone, open left hand several times.

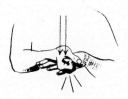

[M-131]

METAL 2, *n.* (A hard substance.) The right "S" hand moves up from the chest to strike the bottom of the chin several times, and continues forward in a short arc after each blow.

[M-132]

METHOD (mĕth' əd), *n.* (The movement.) Both hands, palms facing and fingers together and extended straight out, move in unison away from the body, in a straight or winding manner. *Cf.* CORRIDOR, HALL, HALLWAY, MANNER 2, OPPORTUNITY 3, PATH, ROAD, STREET, TRAIL, WAY 1.

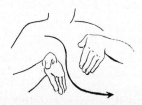

[M-133]

METHODIST (mĕth′ əd ĭst), *n., adj.* (Rubbing the hands together in zeal or ambition.) The open hands are rubbed vigorously back and forth against each other. *Cf.* AMBITIOUS 1, ANXIOUS 1, ARDENT, DILIGENCE 1, DILIGENT, EAGER, EAGERNESS, EARNEST, ENTHUSIASM, ENTHUSIASTIC, INDUSTRIOUS, ZEAL, ZEALOUS.

[M-134]

ME TOO, *(colloq.).* (Two figures are compared, back and forth.) The right "Y" hand, palm facing left, is moved alternately toward and away from the body. *Cf.* SAME 2.

[M-135]

MEXICAN (mĕk′ sə kən), *adj., n.* (The letter "M"; the characteristic moustache.) The fingertips of the "M" hands trace a rather large moustache on the upper lip. One hand only may be used. This is followed by the sign for INDIVIDUAL: Both open hands, palms facing each other, move down the sides of the body, tracing its outline to the hips. *Cf.* MEXICO.

[M-136]

MEXICO (mĕk′ sə kō′), *n.* See MEXICAN. The sign for INDIVIDUAL, however, is omitted.

[M-137]

MEZUZAH (mĕ zōō′ zä), *(eccles.), n.* (The mezuzah is traced on the doorpost.) The tips of the right thumb and index finger, held closely together as in the letter "G," trace the shape of the mezuzah against the upright left palm, representing the doorpost.

[M-138]

MICROMETER (mī krŏm′ ə tər), *(voc.), n.* (The natural sign.) The curved index finger and thumb of the right "5" hand close carefully and deliberately against the edges of the left index finger, as if measuring its thickness. *Cf.* CALIPER, GAGE.

[M-139]

MIDDAY (mĭd′ dā′), *n.* (The sun is directly overhead.) The right "B" hand, palm facing left, is held upright in a vertical position, its elbow resting on the back of the open left hand. *Cf.* NOON.

[M-140]

MIDDLE (mĭd′ əl), *adj.* (The natural sign.) The downturned right fingers describe a small clockwise circle and come to rest in the center of the upturned left palm. *Cf.* CENTER, CENTRAL.

[M-141]

MIDNIGHT (mĭd′ nīt′), *n.* (The sun is directly opposite the NOON position, *q.v.*) The right "B" hand is held fingers pointing straight down and palm facing left. The left hand, representing the horizon, is held open and fingers together, palm down, its little finger edge resting against the right arm near the crook of the elbow.

[M-142]

MIDST (mĭdst), *n.* (Wandering in and out.) The right index finger weaves its way in and out between the outstretched fingers of the left hand. *Cf.* AMID, AMIDST, AMONG.

[M-143]

MIDWAY (mĭd′ wā′), *adv., adj.* (The midpoint is emphasized.) The little finger edge of the open right hand, palm facing left, comes down against the middle of the index finger edge of the open left hand,

whose palm faces the body. This movement may be repeated. *Cf.* MEDIUM, NEUTRAL.

[M-144]

MIGHT 1 (mīt), *n.* (Flexing the muscles.) With fists clenched, palms facing back, the signer raises both arms and shakes them once, with force. *Cf.* MIGHTY 1, POWER 1, POWERFUL 1, STRONG 1, STURDY, TOUGH 1.

[M-145]

MIGHT 2, *v.* (Weighing one thing against another.) The upturned open hands move alternately up and down. *Cf.* GUESS 4, MAY 1, MAYBE, PERHAPS, POSSIBILITY, POSSIBLY, PROBABLE, PROBABLY, SUPPOSE.

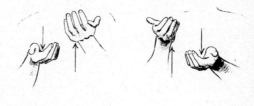

[M-146]

MIGHT 3, *n.* (The curve of the flexed biceps is indicated.) The left hand, clenched into a fist, is held up, palm facing the body. The index finger of the right "D" hand moves in an arc over the left biceps muscle, from shoulder to crook of the elbow. *Cf.* POWER 2, POWERFUL 2.

[M-147]

MIGHTY 1 (mī′ tĭ), *adj.* See MIGHT 1.

[M-148]

MIGHTY 2, *adj.* (Strength emanating from the body.) Both "5" hands are placed palms against the chest. They move out and away, forcefully, closing and assuming the "S" position. *Cf.* BRAVE, BRAVERY, COURAGE, COURAGEOUS, FORTITUDE, HALE, HEALTH, HEALTHY, STRENGTH, STRONG 2, WELL 2.

[M-149]

MIGRATE (mī′ grāt), *v.*, -GRATED, -GRATING. (Moving from one place to another.) The downturned hands, fingers touching their respective thumbs, move in unison from left to right. *Cf.* MOVE, PLACE 3, PUT, REMOVE 2, TRANSFER 2.

[M-150]

MILD (mīld), *adj.* (A neutral, *i.e.,* neither one way nor the other, movement.) The base of the open right "5" hand is held either just above or in the palm of the left "5" hand, which is facing either up or somewhat to the right. The right hand, in this position, moves slightly back and forth over the left palm a number of times.

[M-151]

MILE (mīl), *n.* (A measuring of distance, in equal portions.) The right hand, in the right-angle position, palm facing left, moves forward from the body in a series of equally spaced arcs. (This sign can be ambiguous and should be used only when clear in context.) *Cf.* MILEAGE.

[M-152]

MILEAGE (mī′ lĭj), *n.* See MILE.

[M-153]

MILITARY (mĭl′ ə tĕr′ ĭ), *adj.* (A group of armsbearers or soldiers.) The sign for ARMS, *q.v.,* is made. The "C" hands, palms facing each other, then pivot around on their wrists so that the palms now face the body (a class or category, all together as one unit). *Cf.* ARMY.

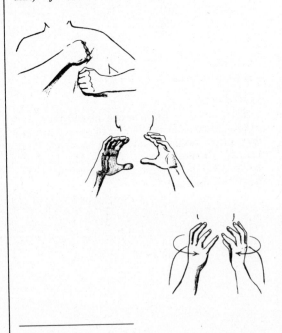

[M-154]

MILK (mĭlk), *n., v.,* MILKED, MILKING. (The act of milking a cow.) Both hands, alternately grasping and releasing imaginary teats, move alternately up and down before the body.

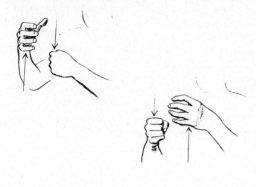

[M–155]

MILLION (mĭl′ yən), *n., adj.* (A thousand thousands.) The fingertips of the right "M" hand, palm down, are thrust twice into the upturned left palm, first at the base of the palm and then near the base of the left fingers. (The "M" stands for *mille,* the Latin word for *thousand.*)

[M–156]

MILWAUKEE (mĭl wô′ kĭ), *(loc.), n.* (Exact origin unclear, but believed to have had its genesis as a name sign for a deaf Milwaukee resident who lied a great deal. See LIE 1. Also, wiping beer foam from the lips.) The index finger of the right "D" hand, pointing left, moves back and forth an inch or two in its position on the chin.

[M–157]

MIMEOGRAPH (mĭm′ ĭ ə grăf, -gräf), *n., v.,* -GRAPHED, -GRAPHING. (The natural movement.) The right hand, grasping an imaginary handle, ro-

tates in a continuous clockwise manner as if manipulating the drum of a mimeograph machine.

[M–158]

MIMIC (mĭm′ ĭk), *v.,* -ICKED, -ICKING, *n.* (The natural sign.) The right fingers and thumb close together and move onto the upturned, open left hand, as if taking something from one place to another. *Cf.* COPY 1, DUPLICATE 1, IMITATE, MODEL.

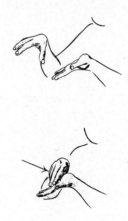

[M–159]

MIND 1 (mīnd), *n.* (Patting the head to indicate something of value inside.) The right fingers pat the forehead several times. *Cf.* INTELLECT, INTELLIGENCE, MENTAL, SENSE 1.

[M–160]

MIND 2, *n.* (Directing one's attention forward; applying oneself; concentrating.) Both hands, fingers pointing up and together, are held at the sides of the face. They move straight out from the face. *Cf.* APPLY 2, ATTEND (TO), ATTENTION, CONCENTRATE, CONCENTRATION, FOCUS, GIVE ATTENTION (TO), PAY ATTENTION (TO).

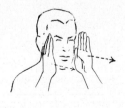

[M–161]

MIND 3, *v.* (Slow, careful movement.) The "K" hands are crossed, the right above the left, little finger edges down. In this position the hands are moved up and down a short distance. *Cf.* CARE 2, CAREFUL 2, KEEP, MAINTAIN 1, PRESERVE, RESERVE 2, TAKE CARE OF 2.

[M–162]

MIND 4, *v.,* MINDED, MINDING. (The hands are thrown open as an act of obeisance.) Both "A" hands, palms facing, are positioned at either side of the head. They are thrown open and out, ending in the "5" position, palms up. The head is bowed slightly at the same time. *Cf.* OBEDIENCE, OBEDIENT, OBEY.

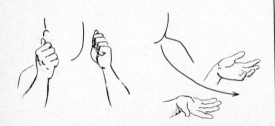

[M–163]

MIND 5, *n.* (The mind stops wavering, and the pros and cons are resolved.) The right index finger touches the forehead, the sign for THINK, *q.v.* Both "F" hands, palms facing each other and fingers pointing straight out, then drop down simultaneously. The sign for JUDGE, *q.v.,* explains the rationale behind the movement of the two hands here. *Cf.* DECIDE, DECISION, DECREE 1, DETERMINE, MAKE UP ONE'S MIND, RENDER JUDGMENT, RESOLVE, VERDICT.

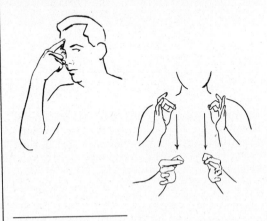

[M–164]

MINE 1 (mīn), *pron.* (Pressing something to one's bosom.) The "5" hand is brought up against the chest. *Cf.* MY, OWN.

[M–165]

MINE 2, *n.* (The action of a pick on the mine wall.) The right "X" finger "digs" repeatedly against the left palm, which faces right.

[M–166]

MINER (mī′ nər), *n.* The sign for MINE 2 is made, followed by the sign for INDIVIDUAL: Both open hands, palms facing each other, move down the sides of the body, tracing its outline to the hips.

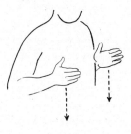

[M–167]

MINGLE 1 (mĭng′ gəl), *v.,* -GLED, -GLING. (Scrambling or mixing up.) The downturned right hand is positioned above the upturned left. The fingers of both are curved. Both hands move in opposite horizontal circles. *Cf.* CLUTTER, COMPLICATE, CONFUSE, CONFUSED, CONFUSION, DISORDER, MIX, MIXED, MIX UP, SCRAMBLE.

[M–168]

MINGLE 2, *v.* (Mingling with.) Both hands are held in modified "A" positions, thumbs out. The left hand is positioned with its thumb pointing straight up, and the right hand, with its thumb pointing down, revolves above the left thumb in a counter-clockwise direction. *Cf.* ASSOCIATE 1, EACH OTHER, FELLOWSHIP, MUTUAL 1, ONE ANOTHER.

[M–169]

MINISTER (mĭn′ ĭs tər), *n.* (Placing morsels of wisdom, or food for thought, into the mind.) The right hand, palm out, with thumb and index finger touching, is moved forward and slightly downward a number of times from its initial position near the right temple. This is followed by the sign for INDIVIDUAL: Both open hands, palms facing each other, move down the sides of the body, tracing its outline to the hips. *Cf.* PASTOR, PREACHER.

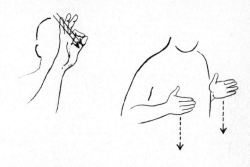

[M–170]

MINOR (mī′ nər), *adj., n.* (A shortness of height is indicated.) The right hand, in right-angle position, pats an imaginary head at approximately chest level. *Cf.* SHORT 2, SMALL 2.

[M–171]

MINUS 1 (mī′ nəs), *n., prep., adj.* (The minus sign.) The downturned right "D" hand is placed so that the side of the right index finger (representing the MINUS sign) rests in the open left palm, which is facing right.

[M-172]

MINUS 2, *prep.* (The hands fall away from the WITH position.) The sign for **WITH** is formed. The hands then drop down, open, and part, ending in the palms-down position. *Cf.* WITHOUT.

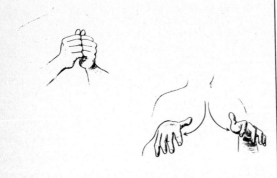

[M-173]

MINUS 3, *n., prep., adj.* (Removing.) The right "A" hand, resting in the palm of the left "5" hand, moves slightly up and away, describing a small arc. It is then cast downward, opening into the "5" position, palm down, as if removing something from the left hand and casting it down. *Cf.* ABOLISH 2, ABSENCE 2, ABSENT 2, ABSTAIN, CHEAT 2, DEDUCT, DEFICIENCY, DELETE 1, LESS 2, OUT 2, REMOVE 1, SUBTRACT, SUBTRACTION, TAKE AWAY FROM, WITHDRAW 2.

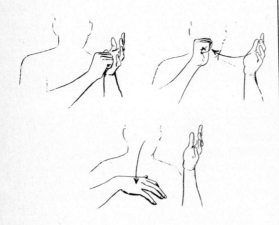

[M-174]

MINUTE 1 (mĭn' ĭt), *n.* (The minute hand of a clock.) The right "D" hand is held with its index finger edge against the palm of the left "5" hand,

which faces right. The right index finger moves forward in a short arc. *Cf.* MOMENT.

[M-175]

MINUTE 2, *adj.* (A small or tiny movement.) The right thumbtip is flicked off the index finger several times, as if shooting marbles, although the movement is not so pronounced. *Cf.* LITTLE 2, TINY 1.

[M-176]

MIRACLE (mĭr' ə kəl), *n.* (Wonderful work.) The sign for **WONDERFUL** is made: Both "5" hands, facing out from the body, are moved briefly and sharply up and forward from an initial position on either side of the face. This is followed by the sign for **WORK**: The ball of the right "S" hand is brought down sharply against the back of the downturned left "S" hand several times. *Cf.* EXCELLENT, GRAND 1, GREAT 3, MARVEL, MARVELOUS, O!, SPLENDID 1, SWELL 1, WONDER 2, WONDERFUL 1.

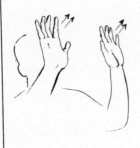

[M–177]

MIRROR (mĭr′ ər), *n*. (A glass object through which one views oneself.) The sign for GLASS is made: The tip of the right index finger is brought up against the exposed front teeth. The open curved right hand is then held palm opposite the face. The hand, pivoting from the wrist, moves back and forth a bit, as if focusing the facial image in its center. Meanwhile, the eyes are directed to the center of the palm. (The sign for GLASS is frequently omitted.) *Cf*. LOOKING GLASS.

[M–178]

MISCARRIAGE (mĭs kăr′ ĭj), *n*. (The fetus drops out of the womb and is lost.) Both hands, in the right-angle position, palms up, are placed so that the fingertips rest against the center of the waist. The hands drop down simultaneously into the "5" position, palms down.

[M–179]

MISS (mĭs), *n., v.,* MISSED, MISSING. (The nose is missed as an attempt is made to grasp it.) The right "C" hand, palm facing left, is positioned in front of the face. It moves quickly across the face, curving downward slightly, and ending in the downturned "S" position.

[M–180]

MISSILE (mĭs′ əl), *n*. (A rocket takes off from its pad.) The downturned right "R" hand (for ROCKET) is placed so that its index and middle fingers rest on the back of the downturned left "S" hand. The right hand moves quickly forward off the left hand. The "R" hand may also point up and move off the left hand from this position. *Cf*. ROCKET.

[M–181]

MISSING 1 (mĭs′ ĭng), *adj*. (A disappearance.) The right open hand, palm facing the body, is held by the left hand and is drawn down and out, ending in a position with fingers drawn together. The left hand, meanwhile, may close into a position with fingers also drawn together. *Cf*. ABSENCE 1, ABSENT 1, DEPLETE, DISAPPEAR, EMPTY 1, EXTINCT, FADE AWAY, GONE 1, OMISSION 1, OUT 3, OUT OF, VANISH.

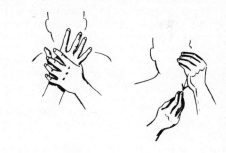

[M–182]

MISSING 2, *adj*. The extended right index finger strikes against the downturned middle finger of the left hand, which is held with palm down and other fingers pointing right. *Cf*. DEARTH, LACK.

[M-183]

MISSION 1 (mǐsh′ ən), *(eccles.), n.* (The letter "M" at the heart; God.) The right "M" hand, palm facing the body, is brought up against the heart. The sign for GOD is then made: The open right hand, palm facing left, swings up above the head, and is then moved down about an inch. The signer looks up while making the sign. *Cf.* MISSIONARY 1.

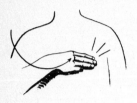

[M-184]

MISSION 2, *(eccles.), n.* (The letter "M"; set up or established.) The right "M" hand moves in a small clockwise circle and comes down to rest on the back of the downturned left "A" or "S" hand. *Cf.* MISSIONARY 2.

[M-185]

MISSIONARY 1 (mǐsh′ ə nər′ ǐ), *n.* See MISSION 1.

[M-186]

MISSIONARY 2, *n.* See MISSION 2.

[M-187]

MISTAKE (mǐs tāk′), *n.* (Rationale obscure; the thumb and little finger are said to represent, respectively, right and wrong, with the head poised between the two.) The right "Y" hand, palm facing the body, is brought up to the chin. *Cf.* ERROR, FAULT 2, SACRILEGIOUS, WRONG 1.

[M-188]

MISUNDERSTAND (mǐs′ ŭn dər stănd′), *v.,* -STOOD, -STANDING. (The thought is twisted around.) The right "V" hand is positioned with index and middle fingers touching the right side of the forehead. The hand swings around so that the palm now faces out, with the two fingers still on the forehead.

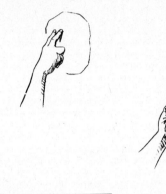

[M-189]

MITRE (mī′ tər), *(eccles.), n.* (The shape.) The downturned open hands, fingers together, move up from either side of the head, and the fingertips come together, forming an arch over the head, to describe the bishop's mitre. *Cf.* BISHOP 2.

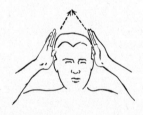

[M-190]

MITRE SAW (mī′ tər sô), *(voc.), n.* (The natural sign.) The open right hand, fingers together and pointing straight out, is the saw. It moves back and forth against the fingertips of the downturned left hand, which are held at right angles to it.

[M-191]

MIX (mĭks), *n., v.,* MIXED, MIXING. (Scrambling or mixing up.) The downturned right hand is positioned above the upturned left. The fingers of both are curved. Both hands move in opposite horizontal circles. *Cf.* CLUTTER, COMPLICATE, CONFUSE, CONFUSED, CONFUSION, DISORDER, MINGLE 1, MIXED, MIX UP, SCRAMBLE.

[M-192]

MIXED (mĭkst), *adj.* See MIX.

[M-193]

MIXED UP, *adj. phrase.* See MIX.

[M-194]

MIX-UP (mĭks' ŭp´), *n.* See MIX.

[M-195]

MOCK (mŏk), *v.,* MOCKED, MOCKING. (Derision; poking or prodding.) Both hands are held closed except for index and little fingers, which extend straight out from the body. The right hand is brought up and its index fingertip pulls the right corner of the mouth into a slight smile. Both hands then move forward simultaneously in a series of short jabbing motions, the right somewhat behind the left. An expression of disdain is assumed during this sign. The first part of the sign, pulling the mouth into a smile, is frequently omitted. *Cf.* MAKE FUN OF, RIDICULE.

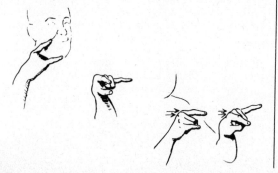

[M-196]

MODEL (mŏd' əl), *n., adj., v.,* -ELED, -ELING. (The natural sign.) The right fingers and thumb close together and move onto the upturned, open left hand, as if taking something from one place to another. *Cf.* COPY 1, DUPLICATE 1, IMITATE, MIMIC.

[M-197]

MODEST (mŏd' ĭst), *adj.* (The head bows; a turtle's head retreats into its shell; an act of humility.) The index finger edge of the right "B" hand, palm facing left, is placed at the lips. The right "B" hand is then brought down and under the downturned open left hand. The head, at the same time, bows. *Cf.* HUMBLE 1, MEEK.

[M-198]

MODIFY (mŏd' ə fī´), *v.,* -FIED, -FYING. (To change positions.) Both "A" hands, thumbs up, are held before the chest, several inches apart. The left hand is pivoted over so that its thumb points to the right. Simultaneously, the right hand is moved up and over the left, describing a small arc, with its thumb pointing to the left. *Cf.* ADJUST, ALTER, ALTERATION, CHANGE 1, CONVERT, REVERSE 2, TRANSFER 1.

[M-199]

MOIST (moist), *adj.* (The wetness.) The right finger-tips touch the lips, and then the fingers of both hands open and close against the thumbs a number of times. *Cf.* CERAMICS, CLAY, DAMP, WET.

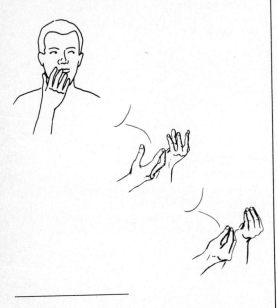

[M-200]

MOLASSES (mə lăs′ ĭz), *n.* (Wiping it from the lips.) The upturned right index finger moves across the lips from left to right. *Cf.* SYRUP.

[M-201]

MOMENT (mō′ mənt), *n.* (The minute hand of a clock.) The right "D" hand is held with its index finger edge against the palm of the left "5" hand, which faces right. The right index finger moves forward in a short arc. *Cf.* MINUTE 1.

[M-202]

MONDAY (mŭn′ dĭ), *n.* (The letter "M.") The right "M" hand moves in a small clockwise circle.

[M-203]

MONEY 1 (mŭn′ ĭ), *n.* (Slapping of paper money in the palm.) The upturned right hand, grasping some imaginary bills, is brought down into the upturned left palm a number of times. *Cf.* CAPITAL 2, CURRENCY, FINANCES, FUNDS.

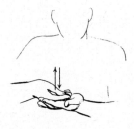

[M-204]

MONEY 2, *(rare)*, *n.* (Jiggling coins.) The cupped hands jiggle imaginary coins.

[M-205]

MONEY 3, *n.* (Fingering the money.) The thumb rubs over the index and middle fingers of the up-turned hand, as if fingering money.

[M–206]

MONKEY (mŭng′ kǐ), *n.* (The scratching of apes.) Both hands go through the natural motion of scratching the sides of the chest. *Cf.* APE.

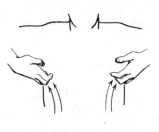

[M–207]

MONOTONOUS 1 (mə nŏt′ ə nəs), *adj.* (The nose is pressed, as if to a grindstone wheel.) The right index finger touches the tip of the nose, as a bored expression is assumed. The right hand is sometimes pivoted back and forth slightly, as the fingertip remains against the nose. *Cf.* BORING, TEDIOUS.

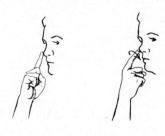

[M–208]

MONOTONOUS 2, *adj.* (The grindstone wheel is indicated here.) The sign for MONOTONOUS 1 is made. The thumb edge of the right "S" hand is then placed in the left palm, which is facing right. The right hand describes a rather slow, continuous clockwise circle in the left palm. *Cf.* GRIND 2.

[M–209]

MONOTONOUS 3, *adj.* (Identical hand positions, indicating sameness, emphasized over and over again.) Both downturned "Y" hands simultaneously describe small ellipses, the right hand in a counterclockwise and the left in a clockwise direction. Emphasis is given to the downward portions of the movements.

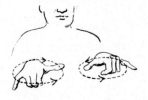

[M–210]

MONTH (mŭnth), *n.* (The tip and three joints represent the four weeks of a month.) The extended right index finger moves down along the upturned, extended left index finger.

[M–211]

MONTHLY (mŭnth′ lǐ), *adj., adv.* (Month after month.) The sign for MONTH is made several times.

[M–212]

MOOCH (mo͞och), *(sl.),* *v.,* MOOCHED, MOOCHING. (Attaching to something and tugging on it.) The extended right thumb, index, and middle fingers grasp the extended left index and middle fingers. In this position the right hand pulls at the left several times. *Cf.* LEECH, MOOCHER, PARASITE, TAKE ADVANTAGE OF 2.

[M-213]

MOOCHER (mōōch′ ər), *(sl.)*, *n.*, The sign for
MOOCH is made. This is followed by the sign for
INDIVIDUAL: Both open hands, palms facing
each other, move down the sides of the body, tracing
its outline to the hips.

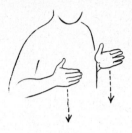

[M-214]

MOON 1 (mōōn), *n.* (The face in the moon; the
rays.) The right "C" hand is placed over the right
side of the face. The right fingers then close over the
thumb as the hand is raised above the head, palm
out. The hand moves down and out, opening into the
"5" position as it does.

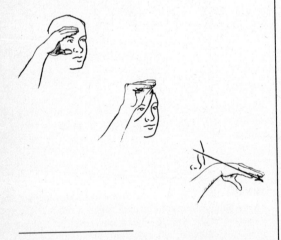

[M-215]

MOON 2, *n.* (The face only.) The right "C" hand
indicates the face of the moon, as in MOON 1. The
second part of the sign, however, is omitted.

[M-216]

MOOSE (mōōs), *n.* (The branching of the antlers
from the head.) Both hands, in the "5" position,
palms up, are placed at the head, thumbs resting on
the head above the temples. *Cf.* ANTLERS, DEER,
ELK.

[M-217]

MOP (mŏp), *n., v.,* MOPPED, MOPPING. (The natural
sign.) The hands, grasping an imaginary mop handle, imitate the mopping of a floor.

[M-218]

MORE (mōr), *adj., n., adv.* (One hand is added to
the other; an addition.) Both hands, palms facing,
are held fingers together, the left a bit above the
right. The right hand is brought up to the left until
their fingertips touch. *Cf.* ADD 4, BESIDES, FURTHER
2, MOREOVER 2.

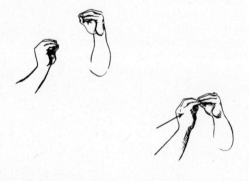

[M-219]

MOREOVER 1 (mōr ō′ vər), *adv.* The right "5"
hand, palm facing the body, fingers facing left,

moves from left to right, meanwhile closing until all its fingers touch around its thumb. *Cf.* ALSO 2, AND.

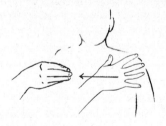

[M-220]

MOREOVER 2, *adv.* See MORE.

[M-221]

MORMON (môr′ mən), *n., adj.* The thumbtip and fingertips of the right hand are held against the right temple. The hand then moves to the right side, away from the temple, closing into the "AND" position as it does.

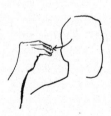

[M-222]

MORNING (môr′ nĭng), *n.* (The sun comes over the horizon.) The little finger edge of the left hand rests in the crook of the right elbow. The left arm, held horizontally, represents the horizon. The open right hand, fingers together and pointing up, with palm facing the body, rises slowly to an almost upright angle. *Cf.* FORENOON.

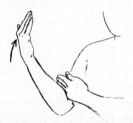

[M-223]

MORON (mōr′ ŏn), *(colloq.), n.* (The thickness of the skull is indicated, to stress intellectual density.) With the thumb of the right "C" hand grasped by the closed left hand, the right hand is swung in toward the body, describing a small arc as it moves. The space between the curved right fingers and the closed left hand indicates the thickness of the skull. *Cf.* CLUMSY 2, DUMB 2, STUPID 2, THICK-SKULLED, UNSKILLED.

[M-224]

MORPHINE (môr′ fēn), *n.* (A shot in the arm) The right index finger is thrust into the left upper arm and the thumb wiggles back and forth a number of times, as if implanting a shot in the arm. *Cf.* COCA-COLA, COKE, DOPE, INOCULATE, NARCOTICS.

[M-225]

MORTAL (môr′ təl), *adj.* (The fountain [of LIFE] wells up from within the body.) The upturned thumbs of the "A" hands move in unison up the chest. *Cf.* ADDRESS 3, ALIVE, DWELL, EXIST, LIFE 1, LIVE 1, LIVING, RESIDE.

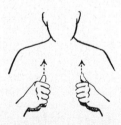

[M-226]

MORTIFICATION (môr´ tə fə kā´ shən), *n.* (The red rises in the cheeks.) The sign for RED is made: The tip of the right index finger of the "D" hand moves down over the lips, which are red. Both hands are then placed palms facing the cheeks, and move up along the face, to indicate the rise of color. *Cf.* BLUSH, EMBARRASS, EMBARRASSED, FLUSH.

[M-227]

MOST (mōst), *adv., adj.* (The largest or greatest amount.) The sign for MUCH is made: The "5" hands, palms facing, fingers curved and thumbs pointing up, draw apart. The sign for the superlative suffix, "-EST," is then made: The right "A" hand, thumb pointing up, quickly moves straight upward, until it is above the head. *Cf.* CHIEF, MAINLY, MOST OF ALL, PRINCIPAL 2.

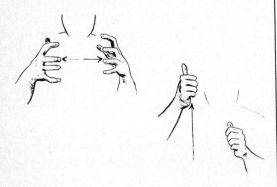

[M-228]

MOST OF ALL, *adv. phrase.* See MOST.

[M-229]

MOTHER 1 (mŭth´ ər), *n.* (A female who carries a baby.) The FEMALE root sign is made: The thumb of the right "A" hand moves down along the line of the right jaw, from ear almost to chin. Both hands

are then held open and palms facing up, as if holding a baby. This is the formal sign.

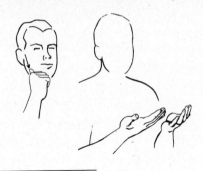

[M-230]

MOTHER 2, *(colloq.), n.* (Derived from the FE-MALE root sign.) The thumb of the right "5" hand rests on the right cheek or on the right chin bone. The other fingers wiggle slightly. Or the thumb is thrust repeatedly into the right side of the face, and the rest of the hand remains open and in the "5" position, palm facing out. This latter modification is used for MAMA.

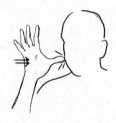

[M-231]

MOTHER-IN-LAW, *n.* The sign for MOTHER is made. This is followed by the sign for LAW: The upright right "L" hand, resting palm against palm on the upright left "5" hand, moves down in an arc a short distance, coming to rest on the base of the left palm.

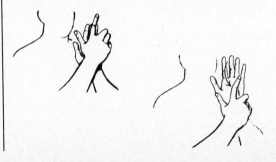

[M-232]

MOTION 1 (mō′ shən), *n.* (An offering; a presenting.) Both hands, slightly cupped, palms up, are held close to the chest. They move up and out in unison, describing a very slight arc. *Cf.* BID 2, OFFER 1, OFFERING 1, PRESENT 1, PROPOSE, SUGGEST, TENDER 2.

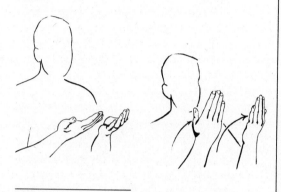

[M-233]

MOTION 2, *n.* (Continuous movement.) The downturned right index finger moves in a continuous clockwise direction.

[M-234]

MOTION FORWARD, *n. phrase.* (Moving forward.) Both right-angle hands, palms facing each other and knuckles facing forward, move forward simultaneously. *Cf.* FORWARD, GO AHEAD, ONWARD, PROCEED, PROGRESS 2, RESUME.

[M-235]

MOTION PICTURE. (The frames of the film speeding through the projector.) The left "5" hand, palm fac-

ing right and thumb pointing up, is the projector. The right "5" hand is placed against the left, and moves back and forth quickly. *Cf.* CINEMA, FILM, MOVIE(S), MOVING PICTURE.

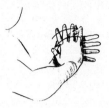

[M-236]

MOTIVATE (mō′ tə vāt′), *v.,* -VATED, -VATING. (Pushing forward.) Both "5" hands are held, palms out, the right fingers facing right and the left fingers left. The hands move straight forward in a series of short movements. *Cf.* ENCOURAGE, MOTIVATION, URGE 1.

[M-237]

MOTIVATION (mō′ tə vā′ shən), *n.* See MOTIVATE.

[M-238]

MOTIVE 1 (mō′ tĭv), *n.* (A thought is turned over in the mind.) The index finger makes a small circle on the forehead. *Cf.* CONSIDER 1, RECKON, SPECULATE 1, SPECULATION 1, THINK, THOUGHT 1, THOUGHTFUL.

[M-239]

MOTIVE 2, *n., adj.* (The welling up of feelings or emotions in the heart.) The right middle finger, touching the heart, moves up an inch or two a number of times. *Cf.* EMOTION 1, FEEL 2, FEELING, SENSATION, SENSE 2.

[M-240]

MOTIVE 3, *n., adj.* (Relative standing of one's thoughts.) A modified sign for THINK is made: The right index finger touches the middle of the forehead. The tips of the right "V" hand, palm down, are then thrust into the upturned left palm (as in STAND, *q.v.*). The right "V" hand is then re-thrust into the upturned left palm, with right palm now facing the body. *Cf.* CONNOTE, IMPLY, INTEND, INTENT 1, INTENTION, MEAN 2, MEANING, PURPOSE 1, SIGNIFICANCE 2, SIGNIFY 2, SUBSTANCE 2.

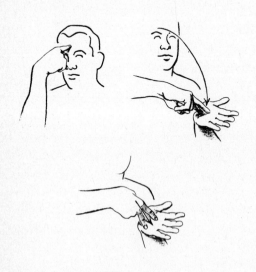

[M-241]

MOTOR (mō′ tər), *n.* (The meshing gears.) With the knuckles of both hands interlocked, the hands pivot

up and down, imitating the meshing of gear teeth. *Cf.* ENGINE, FACTORY, MACHINE, MACHINERY, MECHANIC 1, MECHANISM.

[M-242]

MOTORCYCLE (mō′ tər sī′ kəl), *n.* (Manipulating the handles.) The "S" hands, spread apart, grasp and manipulate the handle bars of an imaginary motorcycle.

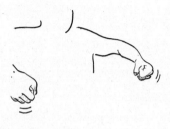

[M-243]

MOUNTAIN (moun′ tən), *n.* (An undulating pile of rocks.) The sign for ROCK is made: The back of the upturned right "S" hand strikes the back of the downturned left "S" hand twice. The downturned "5" hands then move from left to right in wavy, up-down movements.

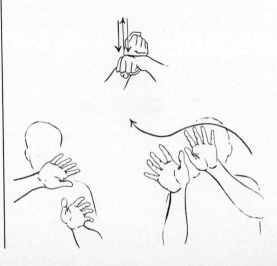

[M-244]

MOURN (mōrn), *v.,* MOURNED, MOURNING. (Wringing the heart.) Both clenched hands, held at the heart with knuckles touching, go through back-and-forth wringing motions. A sad expression is usually assumed. *Cf.* GRIEF 2, GRIEVE.

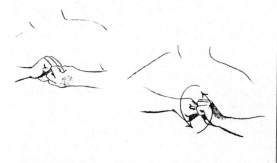

[M-245]

MOURNFUL (mōrn' fəl), *adj.* (The facial features drop.) Both "5" hands, palms facing the eyes and fingers slightly curved, drop simultaneously to a level with the mouth. The head drops slightly as the hands move down, and an expression of sadness is assumed. *Cf.* DEJECTED, DEPRESSED, GLOOM, GLOOMY, GRAVE 3, GRIEF 1, MELANCHOLY, SAD, SORROWFUL 1.

[M-246]

MOUSE 1 (mous), *n.* (The twitching nose.) The index finger brushes across the tip of the nose several times.

[M-247]

MOUSE 2, *n.* (A variation of MOUSE 1.) Both index fingers simultaneously brush the tip of the nose.

[M-248]

MOUTH (mouth), *n.* (The natural sign.) The index finger outlines the mouth.

[M-249]

MOVE (mōōv), *n., v.,* MOVED, MOVING. (Moving from one place to another.) The downturned hands, fingers touching their respective thumbs, move in unison from left to right. *Cf.* MIGRATE, PLACE 3, PUT, REMOVE 2, TRANSFER 2.

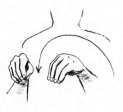

[M-250]

MOVIE(S) (mōō' vĭ), *n.* (The frames of the film speeding through the projector.) The left "5" hand, palm facing right and thumb pointing up, is the projector. The right "5" hand is placed against the left, and moves back and forth quickly. *Cf.* CINEMA, FILM, MOTION PICTURE, MOVING PICTURE.

[M–251]

MOVING PICTURE. See MOVIE(S).

[M–252]

MOW 1 (mō) *v.,* MOWED, MOWING. (Threshing by hand.) The signer manipulates an imaginary scythe with both hands. *Cf.* SCYTHE.

[M–253]

MOW 2, *v.* (The natural sign.) The "S" hands, palms down, hold the handles of an imaginary lawn mower. They move back and forth in unison, as if mowing a lawn. *Cf.* LAWN MOWER, MOWER.

[M–254]

MOWER (mō′ ĕr), *n.* See MOW 2.

[M–255]

MUCH (mŭch), *adj., adv.* (A large amount.) The "5" hands face each other, fingers curved and touching. They move apart rather quickly. *Cf.* EXPAND, GREAT 2, INFINITE, LOT.

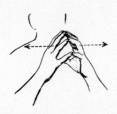

[M–256]

MUDDY (mŭd′ i), *adj.* (The fingers feel the mud.) The downturned hands open and close slowly a number of times, as if fingering mud. An expression of disgust is assumed.

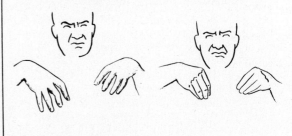

[M–257]

MUFFIN (mŭf′ ĭn), *n.* (Act of cutting biscuits with a cookie mold.) The right hand, in the "C" position, palm down, is placed into the open left palm. It then rises a bit, swings or twists around a little, and in this new position is placed again in the open left palm. *Cf.* BISCUIT, COOKIE.

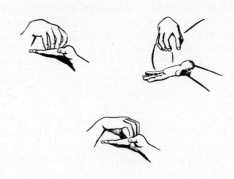

[M–258]

MULE (mūl), *n.* (The donkey's broad ear; the animal is traditionally a stubborn one.) The open hand, or the "B" hand, is placed at the side of the head, with palm out and fingers pointing straight up. The hand moves forward and back, pivoting at the wrist, as in the case of a donkey's ears flapping. Both hands may also be used, at either side of the head. *Cf.* DONKEY, MULISH, OBSTINATE, STUBBORN.

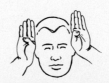

[M–259]

MULISH (mū′ lĭsh), *adj.* See MULE.

[M–260]

MULTIPLE (mŭl′ tə pəl), *adj.* (Many fingers are indicated.) The upturned "S" hands are thrown up, opening into the "5" position, palms up. This may be repeated. *Cf.* MANY, NUMEROUS, PLURAL, QUANTITY 2.

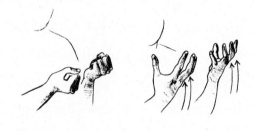

[M–261]

MULTIPLY 1 (mŭl′ tə plī′), *v.*, -PLIED, -PLYING. (A multiplying.) The "V" hands, palms facing the body, alternately cross and separate, several times. *Cf.* ARITHMETIC, CALCULATE, ESTIMATE, FIGURE 1.

[M–262]

MULTIPLY 2, *v.* (A variation of MULTIPLY 1.) The same sign as MULTIPLY 1 except that the index fingers are used instead of the "V" fingers. *Cf.* TIMES.

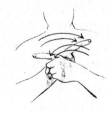

[M–263]

MUMPS (mŭmps), *n.* (The natural sign.) The cupped hands are placed at the sides of the neck to indicate the swelling of the glands. The cheeks are blown out a bit for emphasis.

[M–264]

MURDER (mûr′ dər), *n.* (Thrusting a dagger and twisting it.) The outstretched right index finger is passed under the downturned left hand. As it moves under the left hand, the right wrist twists in a clockwise direction. *Cf.* KILL, SLAY.

[M–265]

MUSCLE-BOUND (mŭs′ əl bound′), *(colloq.), adj.* (The muscles are felt.) The right hand feels the left biceps, and then the left hand feels the right biceps.

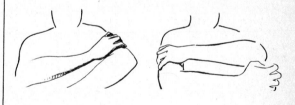

[M–266]

MUSIC (mū′ zĭk), *n.* (A rhythmic, wavy movement of the hand, to indicate a melody; the movement of a conductor's hand in directing a musical performance.) The right "5" hand, palm facing left, is waved back and forth over the downturned left hand, in a series of elongated figure-eights. *Cf.* CHANT, HYMN 1, MELODY, SING, SONG.

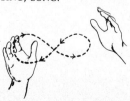

[M–267]

MUSKMELON (mŭsk′ mĕl′ ən), *n.* (Thumping to test the ripeness; the striped rind.) The right middle finger flicks against the back of the downturned left "S" hand, and then the right thumb and index fingers trace the stripes along the back of the left "S" hand, from the wrist to the knuckles.

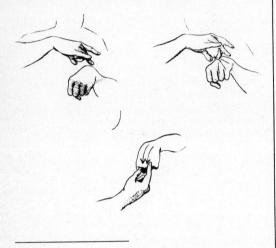

[M–268]

MUST (mŭst), *aux. v.* (Being pinned down.) The right hand, in the "X" position, palm down, moves forcefully up and down once or twice. An expression of determination is frequently assumed. *Cf.* HAVE TO, IMPERATIVE, NECESSARY 1, NECESSITY, NEED 1, OUGHT TO, SHOULD, VITAL 2.

[M–269]

MUTE (mūt), *n., adj.* (The lips are closed in silence.) The index finger is placed on the closed lips.

[M–270]

MUTUAL 1 (mū′ chŏo əl), *adj.* (Mingling with.) Both hands are held in modified "A" positions, thumbs out. The left hand is positioned with its thumb pointing straight up, and the right hand, with its thumb pointing down, revolves above the left thumb in a counterclockwise direction. *Cf.* ASSOCIATE 1, EACH OTHER, FELLOWSHIP, MINGLE 2, ONE ANOTHER.

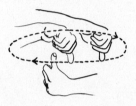

[M–271]

MUTUAL 2, *adj.* (The fingers are drawn together.) The right "2" hand, palm facing the body, is drawn down through the left "C" hand. As it does, the right index and middle fingers come together. *Cf.* BOTH, PAIR.

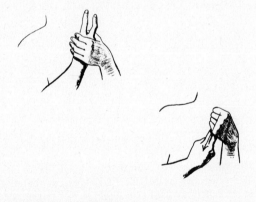

[M–272]

MY (mī), *pron.* (Pressing something to one's bosom.) The "5" hand is brought up against the chest. *Cf.* MINE 1, OWN.

[M–273]

MYSELF (mī sĕlf'), *pron.* (The thumb represents the self.) The upturned thumb of the right "A" hand is brought up against the chest.

[M–274]

MYSTERY (mĭs' tə rĭ), *n.* (A hidden secret.) The right index finger is placed against the closed lips.

The thumb of the right "A" hand is then placed on the closed lips, and the right "A" hand swings down and under the downturned left palm.

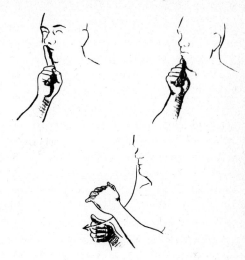

N

NAG (năg), *v.*, NAGGED, NAGGING. (The hen's beak pecks.) The index finger and thumb of the right hand, held together, are brought against the index finger of the left "D" hand a number of times. *Cf.* HENPECK, PECK, PICK ON.

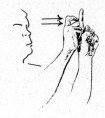

[N–2]

NAIL (nāl), *n.* (The shape; the act of driving a nail with a hammer.) The right thumb and index finger, held together, rest on the third knuckle of the index finger of the downturned left hand, to indicate the head of a nail. This is followed by the swinging of an imaginary hammer with the right hand. (The hammer sign, however, is sometimes omitted.)

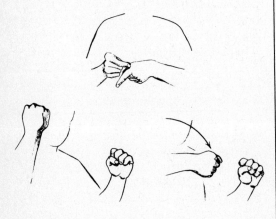

[N–3]

NAIL POLISH (pŏl′ ĭsh), *n.* (The natural sign.) The fingertips of the right "U" hand, held palm down,

are brushed repeatedly over the fingernail of the left middle or index finger.

[N–4]

NAIVE (nä ēv′), *adj.* (Clumsy in gait; all thumbs.) The "3" hands, palms down, move alternately up and down before the body. *Cf.* AWKWARD, AWKWARDNESS, CLUMSINESS, CLUMSY 1, GREEN 2, GREENHORN 2.

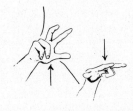

[N–5]

NAKED (nā′ kĭd), *adj.* (Devoid of everything on the surface.) The middle finger of the downturned right "5" hand sweeps over the back of the downturned left "A" or "S" hand, from wrist to knuckles, and continues beyond a bit. *Cf.* BARE 2, EMPTY 2, NUDE, OMISSION 2, VACANCY, VACANT, VOID.

[N–6]

NAME (nām), *n.*, *v.*, NAMED, NAMING. (The "X" used by illiterates in writing their names. This sign is indicative of widespread illiteracy when the language of signs first began to evolve as an instructional medium in deaf education.) The right "H" hand, palm facing left, is brought down on the left "H" hand, palm facing right.

[N–7]

NAMED, *v.* (NAME, indicating who is named.) The sign for NAME is made: The right "H" hand, palm facing left, is brought down on the left "H" hand, palm facing right. The hands, in this position, move forward a few inches. *Cf.* CALLED.

[N–8]

NAP (năp), *v.,* NAPPED, NAPPING, *n.* (The eyes are closed.) The fingers of the right open hand, facing the forehead, are placed on the forehead. The hand moves down and away from the head, with the fingers closing so that they all touch. The eyes meanwhile close, and the head bows slightly, as in sleep. *Cf.* ASLEEP, DOZE, SLEEP 1.

[N–9]

NAPKIN (năp′ kĭn), *n.* (The natural sign.) The fingertips of the right hand, palm facing the body, either pat the lips or rotate around them.

[N–10]

NARCOTICS (när kŏt′ iks), *(colloq.), n. pl.* (A shot in the arm.) The right index finger is thrust into the left upper arm and the thumb wiggles back and forth a number of times, as if implanting a shot in the arm. *Cf.* COCA-COLA, COKE, DOPE, INOCULATE, MORPHINE.

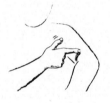

[N–11]

NARRATE (nă rāt′, năr′, āt), *v.,* -RATED, -RATING. (The unraveling or stretching out of words or sentences.) Both open hands are held close to each other, with fingers open and palms facing and almost touching. As the hands are drawn apart, the thumb and index finger of each hand come together to form circles. This is repeated several times. *Cf.* DESCRIBE 2, EXPLAIN 2, FABLE, FICTION, GOSPEL 1, NARRATIVE, STORY 1, TALE, TELL ABOUT.

[N–12]

NARRATIVE (năr′ ə tĭv), *n.* See NARRATE.

[N–13]

NARROW (năr′ ō), *adj., v.,* NARROWED, NARROW-ING. (The natural sign.) Both open hands are held before the body, with palms facing each other and fingers pointing forward. From this position the hands move slowly toward each other, indicating a narrow space.

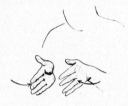

[N–14]

NARROW-MINDED (năr′ ō mīn′ dĭd), *adj.* (The thought processes are "narrow.") The sign for THINK is made: The right index finger describes a small counterclockwise circle in mid-forehead. The open hands, fingers together and palms facing, with fingertips pointing away from the body, are then moved forward, slowly coming together.

[N–15]

NASTY (năs′ tĭ), *adj.* (A modification of the pig's snout groveling in a trough.) The downturned right hand is placed under the chin. Its fingers, pointing left, wiggle repeatedly. *Cf.* DIRTY, FILTHY, FOUL, IMPURE, SOIL 2, STAIN.

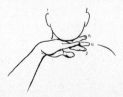

[N–16]

NATION (nā′ shən), *n.* (An established area.) The right "N" hand, palm down, executes a clockwise circle above the downturned prone left hand. The tips of the "N" fingers then move straight down and come to rest on the back of the left hand. *Cf.* COUNTRY 2, LAND 2.

[N–17]

NATURAL (năch′ ə rəl), *(loc.), adj.* The fingers of the downturned right "N" hand are grasped in the downturned left hand. The right hand moves out of the left, and the "N" fingers come to rest on the back of the left hand. *Cf.* NORMAL.

[N–18]

NAUGHT 1 (nôt), *n.* (The zeros.) Both "O" hands, palms facing, are thrown out and down into the "5" position. *Cf.* NONE 1, NOTHING 1.

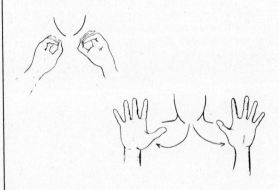

[N–19]

NAUGHT 2, *n.* (The zeros.) Both "0" hands, palms facing, move back and forth a number of times, the right hand to the right and the left hand to the left. *Cf.* NOTHING 2.

[N–20]

NAUGHT 3, *(sl.)*, *n.* (An emphatic movement of the "0," *i.e.*, ZERO hand.) The little finger edge of the right "0" hand is brought sharply into the upturned left palm. *Cf.* NONE 4, NOTHING 4, ZERO 1.

[N–21]

NAUGHTY (nô′ tĭ), *adj.* (Tasting something, finding it unacceptable, and turning it down.) The tips of the right "B" hand are placed at the lips, and then the hand is thrown down. *Cf.* BAD 1, GRAVE 2, WICKED.

[N–22]

NAUSEA (nô′ shə, -shĭ ə, -sĭ ə), *n.* (Turning the stomach.) The fingertips of the curved right hand describe a continuous circle on the stomach. The signer assumes an exaggerated expression of disgust. *Cf.* DISGUST, DISGUSTED, DISGUSTING, DIS-

PLEASED, MAKE ME DISGUSTED, MAKE ME SICK, NAUSEATE, NAUSEOUS, OBNOXIOUS, REVOLTING.

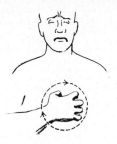

[N–23]

NAUSEATE, *v.*, -ATED, -ATING. See NAUSEA.

[N–24]

NAUSEOUS (nô′ shəs, -shĭ əs), *adj.* See NAUSEA.

[N–25]

NAZI (nä′ tsĭ, năt′ sĭ), *n.*, *adj.* (The Nazi salute.) The right arm is raised before the right shoulder, with hand held open, palm facing forward, fingers together and pointing upward.

[N–26]

NEAR 1 (nĭr), *adv.*, *prep.* (One hand is near the other.) The left hand, cupped, fingers together, is held before the chest, palm facing the body. The right hand, also cupped, fingers together, moves a very short distance back and forth, as it is held in front of the left. *Cf.* ADJACENT, BESIDE, BY 1, CLOSE (TO) 2, NEIGHBOR, NEIGHBORHOOD, VICINITY.

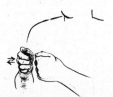

[N–27]

NEAR 2, *adv., prep.* (Coming close to.) Both hands are held in the right angle position, fingers facing each other, with the right hand held between the left hand and the chest. The right hand slowly moves toward the left. *Cf.* APPROACH, TOWARD 2.

[N–28]

NEARLY (nǐr′ lǐ), *adv.* The left hand is held at chest level in the right angle position, with fingers pointing up and the back of the hand facing right. The right fingers are swept up along the back of the left hand. *Cf.* ABOUT 2, ALMOST.

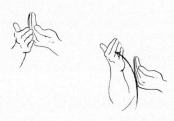

[N–29]

NEAT (nēt), *adj.* (Everything is wiped off the hand, to emphasize an uncluttered or clean condition.) The right hand slowly wipes the upturned left palm, from wrist to fingertips. *Cf.* CLEAN 1, IMMACULATE, NICE, PLAIN 2, PURE 1, PURITY, SIMPLE 2.

[N–30]

NECESSARY 1 (nĕs′ ə sĕr′ ĭ), *adj.* (Being pinned down.) The right hand, in the "X" position, palm down, moves forcefully up and down once or twice. An expression of determination is frequently as-

sumed. *Cf.* HAVE TO, IMPERATIVE, MUST, NECESSITY, NEED 1, OUGHT TO, SHOULD, VITAL 2.

[N–31]

NECESSARY 2, *adj.* (The letter "N"; a forceful movement of the hand.) The "N" hand is thrust straight down a few inches.

[N–32]

NECESSITY (nə sĕs′ ə tǐ), *n.* See NECESSARY 1.

[N–33]

NECKING (nĕk′ ĭng), *(sl.), n.* (Necks interlocked.) The "S" hands, palms facing, are crossed at the wrists. They swing up and down while the wrists remain in contact. *Cf.* MAKE LOVE 2, PETTING.

[N–34]

NECKLACE (nĕk′ lĭs), *n.* (The natural sign.) The index fingers move around the neck, from front to rear.

[N–35]

NECKTIE (nĕk′ tī′), *n.* (The natural motion.) The "H" hands go through the natural hand-over-hand motions of tying a knot in a necktie at the throat. The right "H" hand then moves down the front of the chest to indicate the fall of the tie. *Cf.* TIE 2.

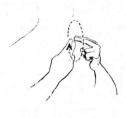

[N–36]

NEE (nā), *adj.* (Presenting the baby from womb to hand; a coming out from the womb to the waiting hand. Referring to birth name.) The upturned right hand is brought forward from the stomach to the upturned left palm. *Cf.* BIRTH 1, BORN 1.

[N–37]

NEED 1 (nēd), *n., v.,* NEEDED, NEEDING. (Being pinned down.) The right hand, in the "X" position, palm down, moves forcefully up and down once or twice. An expression of determination is frequently assumed. *Cf.* HAVE TO, IMPERATIVE, MUST, NECESSARY 1, NECESSITY, OUGHT TO, SHOULD, VITAL 2.

[N–38]

NEED 2, *n.* (Grasping something and pulling it in.) The upturned "5" hands, held side by side before the chest, close slightly into a grasping position as they move in toward the body. *Cf.* COVET 1, DESIRE 1, LONG 2, WANT, WILL 2, WISH 1.

[N–39]

NEED 3, *n., v.* (The letter "N"; a forceful movement of the hand.) The "N" hand is twice thrust down a few inches.

[N–40]

NEEDLE (nē′ dəl), *n.* (The sewing; the length is indicated.) The sign for SEW is made: The right hand, grasping an imaginary needle, goes through the natural motion of hand-stitching on the open left palm. The thumb and index finger of the right hand are then placed on the side of the left index finger, at the tip and third knuckle, to indicate the length of the needle.

[N–41]

NEGATION (nĭ gā′ shən), *n*. The right "A" hand is placed with the tip of the upturned thumb under the chin. The hand draws out and forward in a slight arc. *Cf.* NEGATIVE 2, NOT 2.

[N–42]

NEGATIVE 1 (nĕg′ ə tĭv), *adj., n.* (The crossed hands.) The downturned open hands are crossed at the wrists. They draw apart either once or twice. *Cf.* NOT 1, UN-.

[N–43]

NEGATIVE 2, *adj.* See NEGATION.

[N–44]

NEGLECT (nĭ glĕkt′), *v.*, -GLECTED, -GLECTING. (To throw something aside.) Both "S" hands are held with palms facing at chest level and then thrown down and to the left, opening into the "5" position. *Cf.* ABANDON 1, CAST OFF, DEPOSIT 2, DISCARD 1, FORSAKE 3, LEAVE 2, LET ALONE.

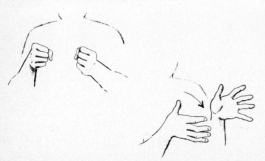

[N–45]

NEGRO 1 (nē′ grō), *(vulg.), n., adj.* (A flattened nose; the initial "N.") The fingertips of the right "N" hand are placed on the nose; there they either rock back and forth or describe a small, counterclockwise circle. (This sign is considered highly offensive and is never used in polite society. Instead the word is spelled out with the fingers, or the sign for BLACK, *q.v.,* is made. It is included here for the sake of comprehensiveness.)

[N–46]

NEGRO 2, *n., adj.* (A flattened nose.) The middle finger, after touching the tip of the nose, revolves in a counterclockwise direction around the face and comes to rest on the tip of the nose again. (This sign is considered somewhat improper and offensive.) *Cf.* AFRICA.

[N–47]

NEIGHBOR (nā′ bər), *n.* (One who is near.) The sign for NEAR is made: The left hand, cupped, fingers together, is held before the chest, palm facing the body. The right hand, also cupped, fingers together, moves a very short distance back and forth, as it is held in front of the left. This is followed by the sign for INDIVIDUAL: Both open hands, palms facing each other, move down the sides of the body, tracing its outline to the hips.

[N–48]

NEIGHBORHOOD (nā′ bər hŏod′), *n.* See NEIGH-
BOR. The sign is repeated on both sides of the body,
and the sign for INDIVIDUAL 1 is omitted.

[N–49]

NEITHER (nēth′ ər), *conj.* (Not either.) The sign for
NOT is made: The downturned open hands are
crossed. They are drawn apart rather quickly. This
is followed by the sign for EITHER: The left "V"
hand faces the body. The right thumb and index
finger close first over the left index fingertip and then
over the left middle fingertip. *Cf.* NOR.

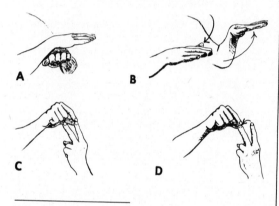

[N–50]

NEPHEW (něf′ ū), *n.* (The initial "N;" the upper or
masculine portion of the head.) The right "N" hand,
held near the right temple, shakes slightly or pivots
at the wrist.

[N–51]

NERVE (nûrv), *(colloq.), n.* (The cheek is indicated.)
The knuckles of the right index and middle fingers
are thrust or twisted against the right cheek. *Cf.*
CHEEK, NERVY.

[N–52]

NERVOUS (nûr′ vəs), *adj.* (The trembling fingers.)
Both "5" hands, held palm down, tremble notice-
ably.

[N–53]

NERVY (nûr′ vĭ), *adj.* See NERVE.

[N–54]

-NESS, *condition. suffix.* The downturned right
"N" hand moves down along the left palm, which is
facing away from the body.

[N–55]

NEST (nĕst), *n.* (The natural sign.) The upturned
cupped hands form an imaginary nest. They separate and swing in toward the body, outlining the
contours of the nest.

[N–56]

NETHERLANDS 1 (něth′ ər ləndz), *n.* (The long pipe smoked by Netherlanders.) The right "Y" hand is held before the face, with thumbtip at the lips. It swings down and forward, outlining the shape of a long curved pipe. *Cf.* DUTCH 1, HOLLAND 1.

[N–57]

NETHERLANDS 2, *n.* (The hat worn by Netherlands women.) The hands, held open at either temple, grasp the points of the native female headgear. They swing upward a bit, as the fingers close over the thumbs. *Cf.* DUTCH 2, HOLLAND 2.

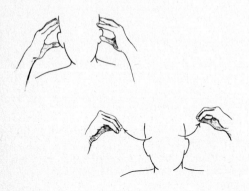

[N–58]

NEUTRAL (nū′ trəl, noo′ -), *adj.* (The midpoint is emphasized.) The little finger edge of the open right hand, palm facing left, comes down against the middle of the index finger edge of the open left hand, whose palm faces the body. This movement may be repeated. *Cf.* MEDIUM, MIDWAY.

[N–59]

NEVER (něv′ ər), *adv.* The open right hand, fingers together and palm facing out, moves in a short arc from left to right, and then straight down. The movement is likened to forming a question mark or an "S" in the air.

[N–60]

NEVER AGAIN, *(colloq.), adv. phrase.* (Refusal to touch.) The right hand is held in the "5" position. The right middle finger is thrust repeatedly into the upturned left palm. The signer frowns.

[N–61]

NEVERTHELESS (něv′ ər thə lĕs′), *adv.* Both hands, in the "5" position, are held before the chest, fingertips facing each other. With an alternate back-forth movement, the fingertips are made to strike each other. *Cf.* ANYHOW, ANYWAY, DESPITE, DOESN'T MATTER, HOWEVER 2, INDIFFERENCE, INDIFFERENT, IN SPITE OF, MAKE NO DIFFERENCE, NO MATTER, WHEREVER.

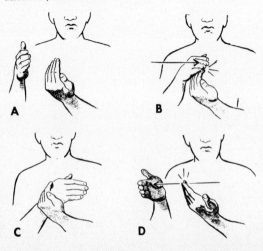

[N–62]

NEW (nū, nōō), *adj.* (Turning over a new leaf.) With both hands held palm up before the body, the right hand sweeps in an arc into the left, and continues up a bit. *Cf.* NEWS, NOVELTY, ORIGINAL 2, TIDINGS.

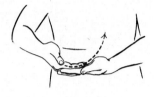

[N–63]

NEW ENGLAND, *(loc., rare).* The knuckles of the downturned right "E" hand move forward across the upturned open left palm, from wrist to fingertips. This is a modified sign for NEW.

[N–64]

NEW JERSEY (jûr′ zĭ), *(loc.)* (The letter "J"; a modified sign for NEW, *q.v.*) The little finger of the right "J" hand brushes the upturned open left palm, from the base of the fingers toward the wrist.

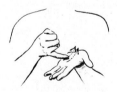

[N–65]

NEW ORLEANS (ôr′ lĭ ənz; *older:* ôr lēnz′), *n.* (The letter "O"; a modified sign for NEW, *q.v.*) The thumb side of the downturned right "O" hand brushes down twice across the left palm which is facing right.

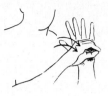

[N–66]

NEWS (nūz, nōōz), *n.* See NEW.

[N–67]

NEWSPAPER (nūz′ pā′ pər, nōōz′ -, nŭs,′- nōōs′ -), *n.* (The action of the press.) The right "5" hand, held palm down, fingers pointing left, is brought down twice against the upturned left "5" hand, whose fingers point right. *Cf.* PAPER, PUBLISH 1.

[N–68]

NEW TESTAMENT 1, *(eccles.),* *n.* The sign for BIBLE is formed: The middle finger of the open left hand is placed in the open right palm, and then the same motion is made with the right middle finger in the open left palm. Then the hands are placed together, palm to palm, and opened, as if opening a book. The letters "N" and "T" are then often fingerspelled.

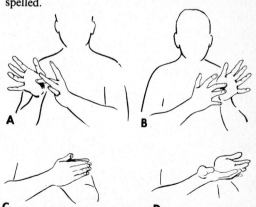

[N–69]

NEW TESTAMENT 2, *(eccles.)*, *n.* The sign for NEW is formed: With both hands held palm up before the body, the right hand sweeps in an arc into the left, and continues up a bit. This is followed by the sign for PART: The little finger edge of the open right hand moves straight down the middle of the upturned left palm. Then the sign for BIBLE, as in NEW TESTAMENT 1, is made.

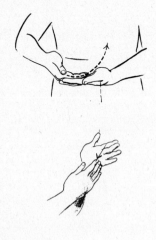

[N–70]

NEW TESTAMENT 3, *(eccles.)*, *n.* The sign for NEW, as in NEW TESTAMENT 2, is made. This is followed by the sign for HOLY: The right "H" hand makes a clockwise circular movement, and is then opened and wiped across the open left palm. Then the sign for BIBLE, as in NEW TESTAMENT 1, is made.

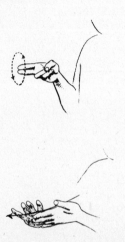

[N–71]

NEW YEAR (yĭr), *(eccles.)*, *n.* (The New Year.) The sign for NEW is made: With both hands held palm up before the body, the right hands sweeps in an arc into the left, and continues up a bit. This is followed by the sign for YEAR: The right "S" hand, palm facing left, represents the earth. It is positioned atop the left "S" hand, whose palm faces right, and represents the sun. The right "S" hand describes a clockwise circle around the left, coming to rest in its original position. *Cf.* ROSH HASHANAH.

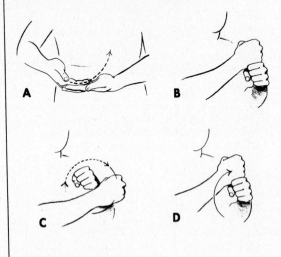

[N–72]

NEW YORK, *n.* (The letter "Y"; a modified sign for NEW, *q.v.*) The downturned right "Y" hand, fingers pointing left, brushes twice over the upturned left palm, from the ball of the left hand to its fingertips. (It is more correct to do it the other way, from fingertips to ball of the left hand, but it is more common to do it as described.)

[N–73]

NEXT 1 (nĕkst), *adj.* The index finger of the right hand is placed across the index finger of the left "L" hand. The right hand then flips over, around the tip of the left index finger and up against its underside. *Cf.* SERIES, THENCE.

 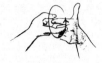

NEXT 2, *adj.* The extended right index finger is placed across the back of the thumb of the left "L" hand. The right hand then moves up over the left thumb and curves down, ending with its index fingertip touching the left index fingertip.

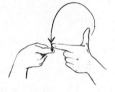

NEXT 3, *adj., adv.* The left hand is lifted over the right and placed down in front of the right palm.

NEXT 4, *adj, v.* The right open hand is held with palm toward the body, fingers pointing left. In this position the right hand moves forward and back against the back of the left open hand, which is also held with palm toward the body, fingers pointing right.

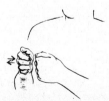

NEXT MONTH, *n. phrase.* The sign for FUTURE, is formed: The upturned, open right hand, palm facing left, moves straight out and slightly up from a position beside the right temple. This is followed by the sign for MONTH: The extended right index finger moves down along the upturned, extended left index finger. The two signs may be reversed.

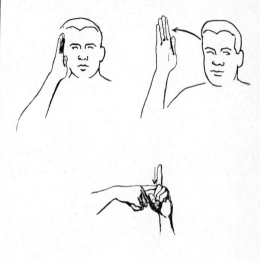

NEXT WEEK 1, *adv. phrase.* The right "L" hand is placed against the base of the open left palm, which faces right, fingers pointing forward. The right hand moves forward toward the left fingertips, its thumb and index finger coming together as it goes. Finally, the right index finger is extended, as the hand curves to the left, around the left fingertips.

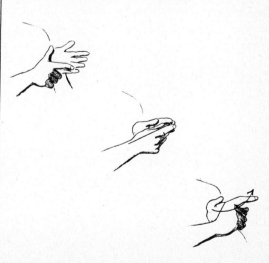

[N–79]

NEXT WEEK 2, *adv. phrase.* (A modification of NEXT WEEK 1.) The upright, right "D" hand is placed palm-to-palm against the left "5" hand, whose palm faces right. The right "D" hand moves along the left palm from base to fingertips and then beyond in an arc. *Cf.* WEEK 2.

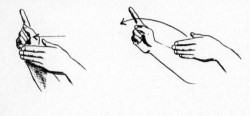

[N–80]

NEXT YEAR, *adv. phrase.* (A year in the future.) The right "S" hand, palm facing left, is brought forcefully down to rest on the upturned thumb edge of the left "S" hand, which is held with palm facing right. (*Cf.* YEAR.) From this position the right hand moves forward with index finger extended and pointing ahead.

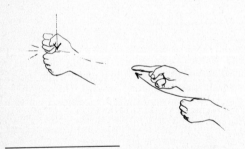

[N–81]

NICE (nīs), *adj.* (Everything is wiped off the hand, to emphasize an uncluttered or clean condition.) The right hand slowly wipes the upturned left palm, from wrist to fingertips. *Cf.* CLEAN 1, IMMACULATE, NEAT, PLAIN 2, PURE 1, PURITY, SIMPLE 2.

[N–82]

NIECE (nēs), *n.* (The initial "N"; the lower or feminine portion of the head.) The right "N" hand, held

near the right side of the jaw, shakes slightly, or pivots at the wrist.

[N–83]

NIGHT (nīt), *n.* (The sun drops beneath the horizon.) The left hand, palm down, is positioned at chest height. The downturned right hand, held an inch or so above the left, moves over the left hand in an arc, as the sun setting beneath the horizon. *Cf.* EVENING.

[N–84]

NINE (nīn), *n., adj.* The thumbtip and index fingertip touch, while the other fingers point straight up. The palm faces out from the body.

[N–85]

NINE OF US, *n. phrase.* The right "9" hand describes an arc as it moves from the right shoulder to the left.

[N–86]

NO 1 (nō), *adv., adj.* (The letter "O.") Both "O" hands are held facing each other in front of the face. They are then drawn apart slowly, the right hand moving to the right and the left hand moving to the left.

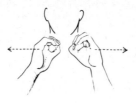

[N–87]

NO 2, *interj.* (The letters "N" and "O.") The index and middle fingers of the right "N" hand are held raised, and are then lowered against the extended right thumb, in a modified "O" position.

[N–88]

NOBLE (nō′ bəl), *adj.* (The letter "N" at the heart.) The right "N" hand swings with a flourish to the heart, and the right index and middle fingers touch the heart twice.

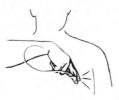

[N–89]

NOD (nŏd), *n., v.,* NODDED, NODDING. (The natural motion.) The right "S" hand is held upright, the forearm resting against the downturned open left hand. The "S" hand "nods" up and down, imitating the head. This sign is frequently used to indicate one is paying attention but not really heeding the signer.

[N–90]

NO GOOD 1, *(colloq.), phrase.* The letters "N" and "G" are fingerspelled. The signer frowns while doing so.

[N–91]

NO GOOD 2, *adj. phrase.* (Of no worth.) The "F" hands face each other, the right above the left. The right hand swings down in an arc, passing the left. As it does so, the thumb and index finger of the right hand strike the corresponding fingers of the left rather sharply. An expression of disdain is assumed. *Cf.* WORTHLESS 2.

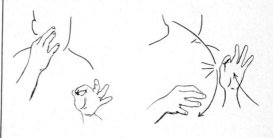

[N–92]

NOISE (noiz), *n.* (A shaking which disturbs the ear.) After placing the index finger on the ear, both hands assume the "S" position, palms down. They move alternately back and forth, forcefully. *Cf.* DIN, NOISY, RACKET, SOUND, THUNDER.

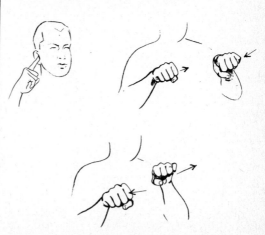

[N–93]

NOISELESS (noiz' lĭs), *adj.* (The natural sign.) The index finger is brought up against the pursed lips. *Cf.* BE QUIET 1, CALM 2, HUSH, QUIET 1, SILENCE 1, SILENT, STILL 2.

[N–94]

NOISY (noi' zĭ), *adj.* See NOISE.

[N–95]

NO MATTER, *phrase.* Both hands, in the "5" position, are held before the chest, fingertips facing each other. With an alternate back-forth movement, the fingertips are made to strike each other. *Cf.* ANY-HOW, ANYWAY, DESPITE, DOESN'T MATTER, HOW-EVER 2, INDIFFERENCE, INDIFFERENT, IN SPITE OF, MAKE NO DIFFERENCE, NEVERTHELESS, WHER-EVER.

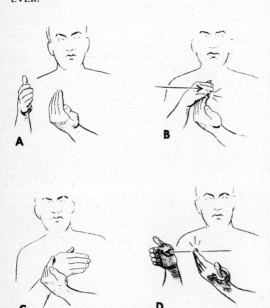

[N–96]

NONE 1 (nŭn), *adj.* (The zeros.) Both "O" hands, palms facing, are thrown out and down into the "5" position. *Cf.* NAUGHT 1, NOTHING 1.

[N–97]

NONE 2, *adj.* (The "O" hands.) Both "O" hands are crossed at the wrists before the chest, thumb edges toward the body. From this position the hands draw apart, the right hand moving to the right and the left hand to the left.

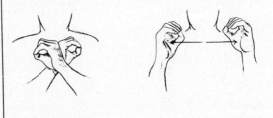

[N–98]

NONE 3, *n., adj.* (Blowing away.) The thumb and index finger of each hand come together to form circles in front of the mouth, as if holding something. The signer then blows on the hands, whereupon they move abruptly away from the face and open into the "5" position, palms out, showing that whatever they held is gone.

[N–99]

NONE 4, *(sl.), pron.* (An emphatic movement of the "O," *i.e.,* ZERO hand.) The little finger edge of the right "O" hand is brought sharply into the upturned left palm. *Cf.* NAUGHT 3, NOTHING 4, ZERO 1.

[N-100]

NONSENSE (nŏn' sĕns), *n.* (Thoughts flickering back and forth.) The right "Y" hand, thumb almost touching the forehead, is shaken back and forth across the forehead several times. *Cf.* ABSURD, DAFT, FOLLY, FOOLISH, RIDICULOUS, SILLY, TRIFLING.

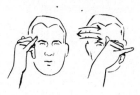

[N-101]

NOON (noōn), *n.* (The sun is directly overhead.) The right "B" hand, palm facing left, is held upright in a vertical position, its elbow resting on the back of the open left hand. *Cf.* MIDDAY.

[N-102]

NOR (nôr), *conj.* (Not either.) The sign for NOT is made: The downturned open hands are crossed. They are drawn apart rather quickly. This is followed by the sign for EITHER: The left "V" hand faces the body. The right thumb and index fingers

close first over the left index fingertip and then over the left middle fingertip. *Cf.* NEITHER.

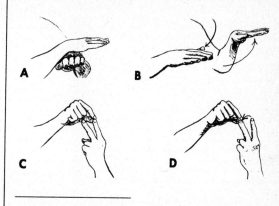

[N-103]

NORMAL (nôr' məl), *adj.* The fingers of the downturned right "N" hand are grasped in the downturned left hand. The right hand moves out of the left, and the "N" fingers come to rest on the back of the left hand. *Cf.* NATURAL.

[N-104]

NORTH (nôrth), *n., adj., adv.* (The letter "N"; the direction.) The "N" hand, held palm out before the body, moves straight up a few inches, the equivalent of north on a map.

[N-105]

NORTH AMERICA, *n.* (The initials "N" and "A.") The signer describes two small circles before him, first with the "N" hand then with the "A" hand.

[N-106]

NORTHEAST (nôrth′ ēst′), *adv., n., adj.* (The "N" and the "E.") The sign for NORTH is made, followed by the sign for EAST: The right "E" hand, held palm out before the body, moves toward the right.

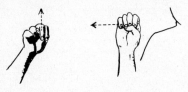

[N-107]

NORTHWEST (nôrth′ wĕst′), *adv., n., adj.* (The "N" and the "W.") The sign for NORTH, above, is made, followed by the sign for WEST: The right "W" hand, palm out, moves from left to right. The movement may also be from right to left.

[N-108]

NORWAY (nôr′ wā), *n.* (The letter "N"; the upper or "northern" part of the head indicates the geographical location of the country, *i.e.,* in the northern part of Europe.) The right "N" hand, palm down, describes a small counterclockwise circle on the forehead. *Cf.* NORWEGIAN.

[N-109]

NORWEGIAN (nôr wē′ jən), *adj.* The sign for NORWAY is made, followed by the sign for INDIVIDUAL: Both open hands, palms facing each other,

move down the sides of the body, tracing its outline to the hips. *Cf.* NORWAY.

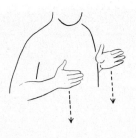

[N-110]

NOSE (nōz), *n.* (The nose is indicated.) The index finger touches the tip of the nose once.

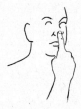

[N-111]

NOSY 1 (nō′ zĭ), *(sl.), adj.* (A big nose.) The right index finger, after resting on the tip of the nose, moves forward and then back to the nose, in an oval, as if tracing a long extension of the nose.

[N-112]

NOSY 2, *(sl.), adj.* (An elongated nose.) The index finger and thumb, held slightly apart, rest on the tip of the nose. As they move forward from the nose they come together.

[N-113]

NOSY 3, *(sl.)*, *adj.* (The nose is emphasized.) The index finger taps the tip of the nose a number of times.

[N-114]

NOT 1 (not), *adv.* (Crossing the hands—a negative gesture.) The downturned open hands are crossed. They are drawn apart rather quickly. *Cf.* NEGATIVE 1, UN-.

[N-115]

NOT 2, *adv.* The right "A" hand is placed with the tip of the upturned thumb under the chin. The hand draws out and forward in a slight arc. *Cf.* NEGATION, NEGATIVE 2.

[N-116]

NO TASTE FOR, *(colloq.)*, *phrase.* (Tasting something, removing it from the mouth, and throwing it away.) The index finger is brought to the lips, as if the signer were tasting something. Then the right "S" hand moves back away from the lips, as if removing something from the mouth. The hand then opens, palm down, and moves forcefully away from the mouth and downward, as if throwing something away.

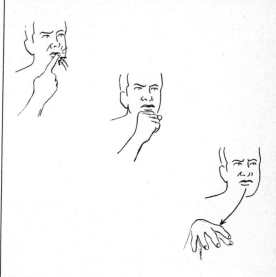

[N-117]

NOT DONE, *phrase.* (Hanging back.) The "5" hand and forearm, hanging loosely and straight down from the elbow, move back and forth under the armpit. *Cf.* BEHIND TIME, LATE, NOT YET, TARDY.

[N-118]

NOTE (nōt), *n., v.,* NOTED, NOTING. (The eye is directed to something specific.) The right index finger touches the base of the right eye, and is then thrust into the upturned left palm. *Cf.* DETECT, NOTICE, OBSERVE 2.

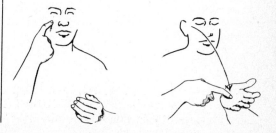

[N–119]

NOTHING 1 (nŭth' ĭng), *n.* (The zeros.) Both "O" hands, palms facing, are thrown out and down into the "5" position. *Cf.* NAUGHT 1, NONE 1.

[N–120]

NOTHING 2, *n.* (The zeros.) Both "O" hands, palms facing, move back and forth a number of times, the right hand to the right and the left hand to the left. *Cf.* NAUGHT 2.

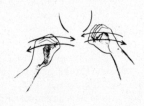

[N–121]

NOTHING 3, *(sl.), adv.* (Blowing something away so that it no longer remains.) The signer blows into the upturned palm. *Cf.* BLOW AWAY.

[N–122]

NOTHING 4, *(sl.), n.* (An emphatic movement of the "0," *i.e.,* ZERO hand.) The little finger edge of the right "O" hand is brought sharply into the upturned left palm. *Cf.* NAUGHT 3, NONE 4, ZERO 1.

[N–123]

NOTICE (nō' tĭs), *n., v.,* -TICED, -TICING. See NOTE.

[N–124]

NOTIFY 1 (nō' tə fī), *v.,* -FIED, -FYING. (Taking knowledge from the mind and giving it out to all.) The fingertips are positioned on either side of the forehead. Both hands then swing down and out, opening into the upturned "5" position. *Cf.* INFORM 1, INFORMATION 1, LET KNOW 1.

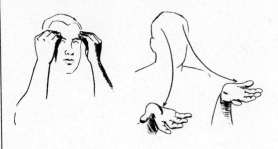

[N–125]

NOTIFY 2, *v.* The fingertips of the right "5" hand are positioned on the forehead. Both hands then swing forward and up, opening into the upturned "5" position. *Cf.* INFORM 2, INFORMATION 2, LET KNOW 2.

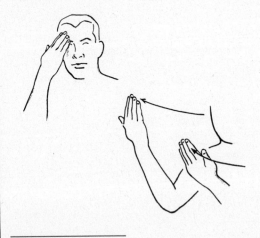

[N–126]

NOT IMPROVE, *phrase.* (Going down step by step.) The little finger edge of the open right hand is placed on the upper side of the extended left arm, which is held with the open left hand palm down. The right hand moves down along the left arm in a series of short movements. This is the opposite of IM-

PROVE, *q.v.* *Cf.* DECLINE 2, DETERIORATE, DETERIORATION.

NOTION (nō′ shən), *n.* (A thought coming forward from the mind, modified by the letter "I" for "idea.") With the "I" position on the right hand, palm facing the body, touch the little finger to the forehead, and then move the hand up and away in a circular, counterclockwise motion. The hand may also be moved up and away without this circular motion. *Cf.* CONCEIVE 2, CONCEPT 1, CONCEPTION, FANCY 2, IDEA, IMAGINATION, IMAGINE 1, JUST THINK OF IT!, POLICY 2, THEORY, THOUGHT 2.

NOT YET, *phrase.* (Hanging back.) The "5" hand and forearm, hanging loosely and straight down from the elbow, move back and forth under the armpit. *Cf.* BEHIND TIME, LATE, NOT DONE, TARDY.

NOVELTY (nŏv′ əl tĭ), *n.* (Turning over a new leaf.) With both hands held palm up before the body, the

right hand sweeps in an arc into the left, and continues up a bit. *Cf.* NEW, NEWS, ORIGINAL 2, TIDINGS.

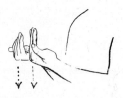

NOW (nou), *adv.* (Something right in front of you.) The upturned right-angle hands drop down rather sharply. The "Y" hands may also be used. *Cf.* CURRENT, IMMEDIATE, PRESENT 3.

NUDE (nūd, nōōd), *adj.* (Devoid of everything on the surface.) The middle finger of the downturned right "5" hand sweeps over the back of the downturned left "A" or "S" hand, from wrist to knuckles, and continues beyond a bit. *Cf.* BARE 2, EMPTY 2, NAKED, OMISSION 2, VACANCY, VACANT, VOID.

NUMBER 1 (nŭm′ bər), *n.* The "AND" hands touch each other at the fingertips, the right palm facing upward, the left palm facing down. Then the hands twist to reverse positions, so that the right hand faces down, the left up.

[N-133]

NUMBER 2, *n.* (Throwing up a number of things before the eyes; a display of fingers to indicate a question of how many or how much.) The right hand, palm up, is held before the chest, all fingers touching the thumb. The hand is tossed straight up, while the fingers open to the "5" position. *Cf.* AMOUNT 2, HOW MANY?, HOW MUCH?.

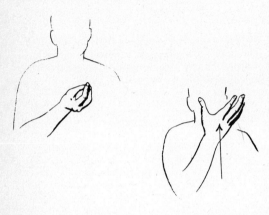

[N-134]

NUMEROUS (nū′ mər əs, nōō′ -), *adj.* (Many fingers are indicated.) The upturned "S" hands are thrown up, opening into the "5" position, palms up. This may be repeated. *Cf.* MANY, MULTIPLE, PLURAL, QUANTITY 2.

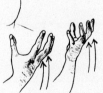

[N-135]

NUN (nŭn), *n.* (The veil.) Both open hands, palms facing the head and fingers pointing up, are moved down along either side of the head, as if tracing the outline of a nun's hood. *Cf.* SISTER 2.

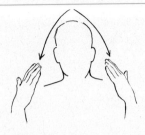

[N-136]

NURSE (nûrs), *n.* (The letter "N"; taking the pulse.) The index and middle fingers of the right "N" hand are placed against the upturned left wrist.

[N-137]

NUT (nŭt), *n.* (The thumbtip, representing a nut or acorn, is bitten.) The right thumbtip is placed between the teeth. It is sometimes moved out from the mouth after being placed in it, but this is optional. *Cf.* ACORN.

[N-138]

NUTS 1 (nŭts), *(sl.)*, *adj.* (Turning of wheels in the head.) The open right hand is held palm down before the face, fingers spread, bent, and pointing toward the forehead. The fingers move in circles before the forehead. *Cf.* CRAZY 1, INSANE, INSANITY, MAD 2.

[N–139]

NUTS 2, *(sl.), adj.* (Wheels in the head.) The sign for THINK is made. Then both index fingers, positioned one on top of the other and pointing to each other, spin around. *Cf.* CRAZY 2.

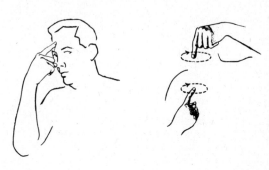

[N–140]

NUTS 3, *(sl.), adj.* (Turning of wheels in the head.) The right index finger revolves in a clockwise circle at the right temple. *Cf.* CRAZY 3.

O

O! (ō), *interj.* (The hands gesture toward the heavens.) The "5" hands, palms out and arms raised rather high, are positioned somewhat above the line of vision. The arms move abruptly forward and up once or twice. An expression of pleasure or surprise is usually assumed. *Cf.* EXCELLENT, GRAND 1, GREAT 3, MARVEL, MARVELOUS, MIRACLE, SPLENDID 1, SWELL 1, WONDER 2, WONDERFUL 1.

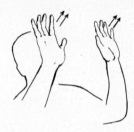

[O–2]

OATH (ōth), *n.* (The arm is raised.) The right index finger is placed at the lips. The right arm is then raised, palm out and elbow resting on the back of the left hand. *Cf.* GUARANTEE 1, LOYAL, PLEDGE, PROMISE 1, SWEAR 1, SWORN, TAKE OATH, VOW.

[O–3]

OATMEAL (ōt′ mēl′, ōt′ mēl′), *n.* The tips of the four right fingers move up and down simultaneously as they move along the left index finger from knuckle to tip. This sign is used generally for different grains. *Cf.* BEAN(S), GRAIN, RICE.

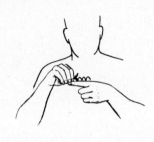

[O–4]

OBEDIENCE (ō bē′ dĭ əns), *n.* (The hands are thrown open as an act of obeisance.) Both "A" hands, palms facing, are positioned at either side of the head. They are thrown open and out, ending in the "5" position, palms up. The head is bowed slightly at the same time. *Cf.* MIND 4, OBEY, OBEDIENT.

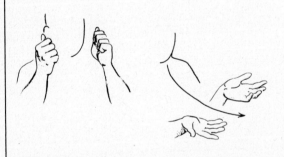

[O–5]

OBEDIENT (ō bē′ dĭ ənt), *adj.* See OBEDIENCE.

[O–6]

OBESE (ō bēs′), *(colloq.), adj.* (The legs are spread wide to accommodate a wide torso.) The downturned right "Y" hand is placed in the upturned left palm, so that the right little finger supports the right hand. The right hand pivots forward on the little finger until the right thumb comes to rest on the left palm. The right hand then pivots forward again until the little finger comes to rest again on the left palm.

The action is similar to the manipulation of a pair of dividers. *Cf.* FAT 2.

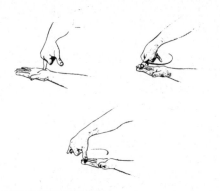

[O-7]

OBEY (ō bā'), *v.*, OBEYING, OBEYED. See OBEDIENT.

[O-8]

OBJECT 1 (ŏb' jĭkt), *n.* (Something shown in the hand.) The outstretched right hand, palm up and held before the chest, is dropped slightly and brought over a bit to the right. *Cf.* ANYTHING, APPARATUS, INSTRUMENT, MATTER, SUBSTANCE 1, THING.

[O-9]

OBJECT 2 (əb jĕk'), *v.*, -JECTED, -JECTING. (The hand is thrust into the chest to force a complaint out.) The curved fingers of the right hand are thrust forcefully into the chest. *Cf.* COMPLAIN 1, COMPLAINT, OBJECTION, PROTEST.

[O-10]

OBJECT 3, *(sl.)*, *v.* (Kicking.) Both "S" hands are held before the chest. Then the hands move sharply to the side, opening into a modified "V" position, palms down, as if "kicking." *Cf.* COMPLAIN 2, KICK 2.

[O-11]

OBJECTION (əb jĕk' shən), *n.* See OBJECT 2.

[O-12]

OBJECTIVE (əb jĕk' tĭv), *n.* (A thought directed upward, toward a goal.) The left "D" hand, palm facing the body, is held above the head, to represent the goal. The index finger of the right "D" hand, after touching the forehead (modified sign for THINK, *q.v.*), moves slowly and deliberately up to the tip of the left index finger. *Cf.* AIM, AMBITION, ASPIRE, GOAL, PERSEVERE 4, PURPOSE 2.

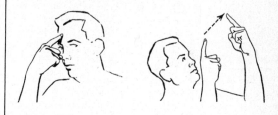

[O-13]

OBLATION (ŏb lā' shən), *(eccles.)*, *n.* (Offering upward.) The upturned hands, led by the right, move up and forward in unison, as the signer looks upward. *Cf.* OFFERING 2.

[O–14]

OBLIGATION 1 (ŏb′ lə gā′ shən), *n*. (Something which weighs down or burdens one with responsibility.) The fingertips of both hands, placed on the right shoulder, bear down. *Cf.* ATTRIBUTE 1, BEAR 4, BURDEN, RELY 1, RESPONSIBILITY 1, RESPONSIBLE 1.

[O–15]

OBLIGATION 2, *n*. (The letter "D"; bound down.) The base of the right "D" hand repeatedly strikes the back of the downturned left "S" hand. *Cf.* DUTY 1.

[O–16]

OBLIGATION 3, *n*. (Pointing to the palm, where the money should be placed.) The index finger of one hand is thrust into the upturned palm of the other several times. *Cf.* ARREARS, DEBIT, DEBT, DUE, OWE.

[O–17]

OBNOXIOUS (əb nŏk′ shəs), *adj*. (Turning the stomach.) The fingertips of the curved right hand describe a continuous circle on the stomach. The signer assumes an exaggerated expression of disgust. *Cf.*

DISGUST, DISGUSTED, DISGUSTING, DISPLEASED, MAKE ME DISGUSTED, MAKE ME SICK, NAUSEA, NAUSEATE, NAUSEOUS, REVOLTING.

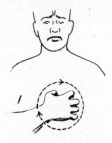

[O–18]

OBSCURE (əb skyŏŏr′), *adj., v.,* -SCURED, -SCURING. (The object is blurred.) The "5" hands are held palm to palm. The right hand circles over the left palm, in a counterclockwise manner.

[O–19]

OBSERVE 1 (əb zûrv′), *v.,* -SERVED, -SERVING. (The vision is directed forward.) The tips of the right "V" fingers point to the eyes. The right hand is then swung around and forward a bit. *Cf.* GAZE, LOOK AT, WITNESS.

[O–20]

OBSERVE 2, *v*. (The eye is directed to something specific.) The right index finger touches the base of the right eye, and is then thrust into the upturned left palm. *Cf.* DETECT, NOTE, NOTICE.

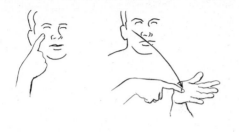

OBSTACLE (ŏb′ stə kəl), *n.* (Obstruct, block.) The left hand, fingers together and palm flat, is held before the body, facing somewhat down. The little finger side of the right hand, held with palm flat, makes one or several up-down chopping motions against the left hand, between its thumb and index finger. *Cf.* ANNOY 1, ANNOYANCE 1, BLOCK, BOTHER 1, CHECK 2, COME BETWEEN, DISRUPT, DISTURB, HINDER, HINDRANCE, IMPEDE, INTERCEPT, INTERFERE, INTERFERENCE, INTERFERE WITH, INTERRUPT, MEDDLE 1, OBSTRUCT, PREVENT, PREVENTION.

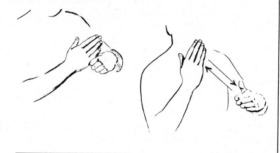

OBSTINATE (ŏb′ stə nĭt), *adj.* (The donkey's broad ear; the animal is traditionally a stubborn one.) The open hand, or the "B" hand, is placed at the side of the head, with palm out and fingers pointing straight up. The hand moves forward and back, pivoting at the wrist, as in the case of a donkey's ears flapping. Both hands may also be used, at either side of the head. *Cf.* DONKEY, MULE, MULISH, STUBBORN.

OBSTRUCT (əb strŭkt′), *v.,* -STRUCTED, -STRUCTING. See OBSTACLE.

OBTAIN (əb tān′), *v.,* -TAINED, -TAINING. (A grasping and bringing forward to oneself.) Both hands, in the "5" position, fingers curved, are crossed at the wrists, with the left palm facing right and the right palm facing left. They are brought in toward the chest, while closing into a grasping "S" position. *Cf.* ACQUIRE, GET, PROCURE, RECEIVE.

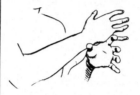

OBVIOUS (ŏb′ vĭ əs), *adj.* (Rays of light clearing the way.) Both hands are held at chest height, palms out, all fingertips together. They open into the "5" position in unison, the right hand moving toward the right and the left toward the left. The palms of both hands remain facing out. *Cf.* BRIGHT 1, BRILLIANCE 1, BRILLIANT 2, CLEAR, EXPLICIT 2, PLAIN 1.

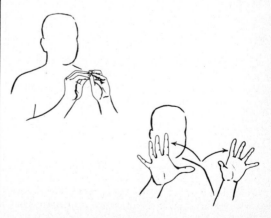

[O–26]

OCCASION (ə kā′ zhən), *n.* (A presenting.) Both hands, slightly cupped, palms up, are held close to the chest. They move up and out in unison, describing an arc. *Cf.* OPPORTUNITY 1, TIME 4.

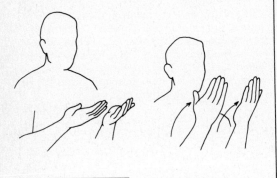

[O–27]

OCCASIONAL (ə kā′ zhən əl), *adj.* (The "1" finger is brought up very slowly.) The right index finger, resting in the open left palm, which is facing right, swings up slowly from its position to one in which it is pointing straight up. The movement is repeated slowly, after a pause. *Cf.* OCCASIONALLY, ONCE IN A WHILE, SELDOM, SOMETIME(S).

[O–28]

OCCASIONALLY (ə kā′ zhən ə lĭ), *adv.* See OCCASIONAL.

[O–29]

OCCUPATION (ŏk′ yə pā′ shən), *n.* (Striking an anvil.) Both "S" hands are held palms down. The right hand strikes against the back of the left a number of times. *Cf.* JOB, LABOR, TASK, TOIL, TRAVAIL, VOCATION, WORK.

[O–30]

OCCUR (ə kûr′), *v.,* -CURRED, -CURRING. (A befalling.) Both "D" hands, index fingers pointing away from the body, are simultaneously pivoted over so that the palms face down. *Cf.* ACCIDENT, BEFALL, CHANCE, COINCIDE 1, COINCIDENCE, EVENT, HAPPEN 1, INCIDENT, OPPORTUNITY 4.

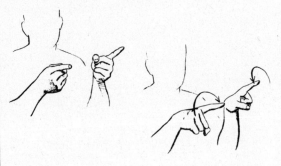

[O–31]

OCEAN 1 (ō′ shən), *n.* (The undulating waves) The sign for WATER is made: The right "W" hand, palm facing out, is shaken very slightly. Then both downturned "5" hands, side by side, execute a series of wavy, undulating movements from left to right. The "W" may be omitted. *Cf.* SEA.

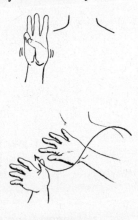

[O–32]

OCEAN 2, *(arch.), n.* (Water, wave, far.) The sign for WATER is made: The right "W" hand, palm facing left, touches the lips a number of times. This is followed by the sign for WAVE: Both "5" hands, held palms out before the chest, move in unison in a wavy, undulating manner, from left to right. Then the sign for FAR is made: The "A" hands are held together, thumbs pointing up or away from the body. The right hand moves straight ahead in a slight arc. The left hand does not move.

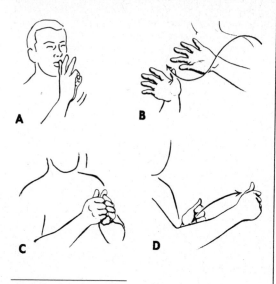

A   **B**

C   **D**

[O–33]

OCTOPUS (ŏk′ tə pəs), *n.* (The natural sign.) The downturned "5" hands, crossed at the arms, writhe and wiggle in imitation of the random movements of an octopus.

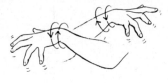

[O–34]

OCULIST (ŏk′ yə lĭst), *n.* (The natural sign.) The right index finger points to the right eye. The sign for DOCTOR is then made: The fingertips of the downturned right "M" hand are placed against the upturned left wrist.

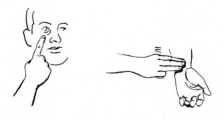

[O–35]

ODD (ŏd), *adj.* (Something which distorts the vision.) The "C" hand describes a small arc in front of the face. *Cf.* CURIOUS 2, GROTESQUE, PECULIAR, QUEER 1, STRANGE 1, WEIRD.

[O–36]

ODOR (ō′ dər), *n.* (Bringing something up to the nose.) The upturned right hand moves slowly up to and past the nose, and the signer breathes in as the hand sweeps by. *Cf.* FRAGRANT, SCENT, SMELL.

[O–37]

OF (ŏv, ŭv; *unstressed* əv), *prep.* (Revolving about.) The left hand is held at chest height, all fingers extended and touching the thumb, and all pointing to the right. The right index finger circles about the left fingers several times. *Cf.* ABOUT 1, CONCERNING, ELECTRIC MOTOR.

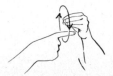

[O–38]

OFF 1 (ôf), *adv., prep.* The fingers of the down-turned, open right hand rest on the back of the fingers of the downturned, open left hand. Then the right hand moves up and forward, turning so that its palm faces the body. *Cf.* AWAY.

[O–39]

OFF 2, *adv.* (Moving beyond, *i.e.,* the concept of distance or "farness.") The "A" hands are held together, thumbs pointing up or away from the body. The right hand moves straight ahead in a slight arc. The left hand does not move. *Cf.* DISTANCE, DISTANT, FAR, REMOTE.

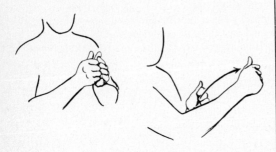

[O–40]

OFFEND (ə fĕnd'), *v.,* -FENDED, -FENDING. (A stabbing pain.) The "D" hands, index fingers pointing to each other, are rotated in elliptical fashion before the chest—simultaneously but in opposite directions. *Cf.* ACHE, HARM 1, HURT 1, INJURE 1, INJURY, MAR 1, OFFENSE, PAIN, SIN, WOUND.

[O–41]

OFFENSE (ə fĕns'), *n.* See OFFEND.

[O–42]

OFFER 1 (ôf' ər), *v.,* -FERED, -FERING. (An offering; a presenting.) Both hands, slightly cupped, palms up, are held close to the chest. They move up and out in unison, describing a very slight arc. *Cf.* BID 2, MOTION 1, OFFERING 1, PRESENT 1, PROPOSE, SUGGEST, TENDER 2.

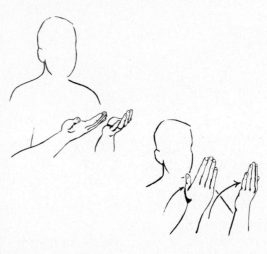

[O–43]

OFFER 2, *v., n.* (Bringing oneself forward.) The right index finger and thumb grasp the clothing near the right shoulder (often the lapel of a suit or the collar of a dress) and tug it up and down gently several times. Sometimes one tug only is used. *Cf.* APPLY 1, CANDIDATE, RUN FOR OFFICE, VOLUNTEER.

[O–44]

OFFERING 1 (ôf' ər ĭng), *n.* See OFFER 1.

[O–45]

OFFERING 2, *(eccles.), n.* (Offering upward.) The upturned hands, led by the right, move up and for-

ward in unison, as the signer looks upward. *Cf.*
OBLATION.

[O–46]

OFFICE 1 (ôf´ ĭs; ŏf´-), *n.* (A room.) The "R" hands,
palms facing and fingers pointing out, are dropped
an inch or two simultaneously. They then shift their
relative positions so that both palms face the body,
with one hand in front of the other. In this new
position they again drop an inch or two simultaneously. *Cf.* ROOM 2.

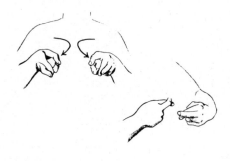

[O–47]

OFFICE 2 (ôf´ ĭs), *n.* (The letter "O"; the shape of
the room.) With the "O" hands, the sign for OF-
FICE 1 is made..

[O–48]

OFFICER (ôf´ ə sər, ŏf´ ə-), *n.* (The epaulets.) The
fingertips of the downturned right "5" hand strike
the right shoulder twice. *Cf.* CAPTAIN.

[O–49]

OFFSPRING (ôf´ sprĭng´, ŏf´-), *n.* (Succeeding generations.) The downturned open left hand is held
near the right shoulder, on which rest the fingertips
of the right hand. The right hand swings over the
back of the left, which then swings in turn over the
back of the right. This movement may continue a
number of times. *Cf.* DESCENDANT.

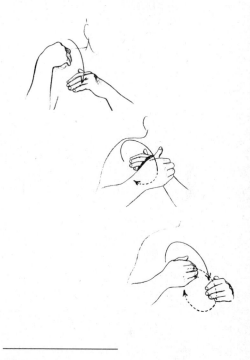

[O–50]

OFF THE BEAM, *(sl. term).* (The thoughts move
away from a straight path.) The right fingertip
touches the forehead (a modification of THINK, *q.v.*).
The little finger edge of the open right hand is then
placed in the upturned left palm. The right hand
moves straight over the palm a short distance, then
curves and moves off the palm toward the left. *Cf.*
MENTALLY UNBALANCED 2.

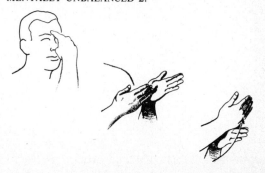

[O–51]

OFTEN (ôf′ ən, ŏf′ ən), *adv.* The left hand, open in the "5" position, palm up, is held before the chest. The right hand, in the right-angle position, fingers pointing up, arches over and into the left palm. This is repeated several times. *Cf.* FREQUENT.

[O–52]

OH (ō), *(rare), interj.* The right "O" hand, palm facing left, moves in front of the face, from left to right.

[O–53]

OH, I SEE, *phrase.* (The up-down motion represents the nodding of the head in sudden recognition.) The right "Y" hand moves up and down a number of times. The signer usually nods slightly, keeping time with the hand. The mouth may be held open a little, and the eyes are usually wide open, as if in surprise. *Cf.* I SEE, THAT'S IT.

[O–54]

OIL 1 (oil), *(colloq.), v.,* OILED, OILING. (The oil can.) The curved right "V" fingers grasp the crown of an imaginary oil can, and the right thumb moves

in and out repeatedly, as if pressing the bottom of the can.

[O–55]

OIL 2, *n.* (The drippings from a fleshy, *i.e.,* animal, substance. Used, however, to indicate both organic and inorganic types of oil.) The right thumb and middle finger grasp the fleshy part of the open left hand. The right hand moves straight down. This is repeated once or twice. *Cf.* FAT 3, FATTY, GRAVY, GREASE, GREASY, OILY.

[O–56]

OILY (oi′ lĭ), *adj.* See OIL 2.

[O–57]

O.K. 1 (ō′ kā′), *adj., adv.* (A straightening out.) The right hand, fingers together and palm facing left, is placed in the upturned left palm, whose fingers point away from the body. The right hand slides straight out along the left palm, over the left fingers, and stops with its heel resting on the left fingertips. *Cf.* ALL RIGHT, PRIVILEGE, RIGHT 1, RIGHTEOUS 1, YOU'RE WELCOME 2.

[O–58]

O.K. 2 (*adj., adv.* ō´ kā´; *v., n.* ō´ kā´), (*colloq.*), *phrase.* The letters "O" and "K" are fingerspelled.

[O–59]

OLD (ōld), *adj.* (The beard of an old man.) The right hand grasps an imaginary beard at the chin and pulls it downward. *Cf.* AGE 1, ANTIQUE.

[O–60]

OLDER, *adj., comparative degree.* The sign for OLD is made, followed by the comparative degree sign: The upturned right thumb moves up to a position in line with the right temple. *Cf.* ELDER.

[O–61]

OLDEST, *adj., superlative degree.* The sign for OLD is made, followed by the superlative degree sign: The upturned right thumb moves up to a position above the level of the head. *Cf.* ELDEST.

[O–62]

OLD TESTAMENT 1, (*eccles.*), *n.* The sign for BIBLE is made: The middle finger of the open right hand is placed in the open left palm and then the same motion is made with the left middle finger in the open right palm. Then the hands are placed together, palm to palm, and opened, as if opening a book. The letters, "O" and "I" are sometimes fingerspelled after this.

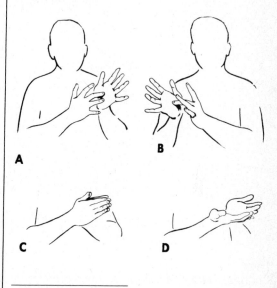

[O–63]

OLD TESTAMENT 2, (*eccles.*), *n.* The sign for OLD is made: The right hand grasps an imaginary beard at the chin and pulls it downward. This is followed by the sign for PART: The little finger edge of the open right hand moves straight down the middle of the upturned left palm. Then the sign for BOOK is made.

[O–64]

OLD TESTAMENT 3, *(eccles.), n.* The sign for JEW-
ISH is formed: The fingers of both hands are placed
at the chin, and stroke an imaginary beard. This is
followed by the sign for BOOK.

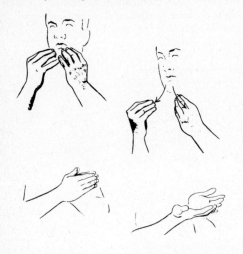

[O–65]

OLD TESTAMENT 4, *(eccles.), n.* The sign for OLD,
as in OLD TESTAMENT 2, is formed. This is followed by the sign for HOLY: The right "H" hand
moves in a small, clockwise circle several times. The
right palm then wipes the upturned left palm. Then
the sign for BOOK is made.

[O–66]

OMISSION 1 (ō mǐsh′ ən), *n.* (A disappearance.)
The right open hand, palm facing the body, is held
by the left hand and is drawn down and out, ending
in a position with fingers drawn together. The left
hand, meanwhile, may close into a position with
fingers also drawn together. *Cf.* ABSENCE 1, ABSENT

1, DEPLETE, DISAPPEAR, EMPTY 1, EXTINCT, FADE
AWAY, GONE 1, MISSING 1, OUT 3, OUT OF, VANISH.

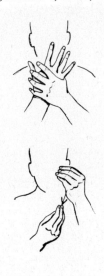

[O–67]

OMISSION 2, *n.* (Devoid of everything on the surface.) The middle finger of the downturned right "5"
hand sweeps over the back of the downturned left
"A" or "S" hand, from wrist to knuckles, and continues beyond a bit. *Cf.* BARE 2, EMPTY 2, NAKED,
NUDE, VACANCY, VACANT, VOID.

[O–68]

ON (ŏn, ôn), *prep.* (Placing one hand on the other.)
The right hand is placed on the back of the downturned left hand.

[O–69]

ONCE (wŭns), *adv.* (The "1" finger jumps up.) The
right index finger (the "1" finger) touches the left

palm, which is facing right. It is then brought up sharply, so that it points straight up.

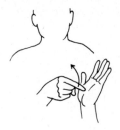

ONCE IN A WHILE, *adv. phrase.* (The "1" finger is brought up very slowly.) The right index finger, resting in the open left palm, which is facing right, swings up slowly from its position to one in which it is pointing straight up. The movement is repeated slowly, after a pause. *Cf.* OCCASIONAL, OCCASIONALLY, SELDOM, SOMETIME(S).

ONCE UPON A TIME, *adv. phrase.* (Something past, behind.) The upraised right hand, in the "5" position with palm facing the body, is held just above the right shoulder and is thrown back over it. *Cf.* AGO, FORMERLY, PAST, PREVIOUS, PREVIOUSLY, WAS, WERE.

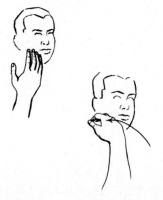

ONE 1 (wŭn), *adj.* (The natural sign.) The "1" finger is held up.

ONE 2, *adj.* (One, wandering around in a circle.) The index finger, pointing straight up, palm facing the body (the number *one*), is rotated before the face in a counterclockwise direction. *Cf.* ALONE, LONE, ONLY, SOLE, UNITY.

ONE ANOTHER, *pron. phrase.* (Mingling with.) Both hands are held in modified "A" positions, thumbs out. The left hand is positioned with its thumb pointing straight up, and the right hand, with its thumb pointing down, revolves above the left thumb in a counterclockwise direction. *Cf.* ASSOCIATE 1, EACH OTHER, FELLOWSHIP, MINGLE 2, MUTUAL 1.

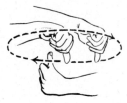

ONE-HALF (wŭn hăf', -häf'), *adj.* (The fraction ½.) After making the "1" sign, the hand drops down a bit as it assumes the "2" position.

[O–76]

ONE HUNDRED, *adj.* (The Latin "C" for *centum,* "hundred.") The "1" sign is made, followed by the manual letter "C."

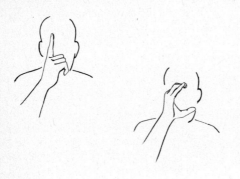

[O–77]

ONE HUNDRED YEARS, *n. pl.* (One hundred years.) The sign for ONE HUNDRED is made: ONE and "C." This is followed by the sign for YEAR: The right "S" hand, palm facing left, represents the earth. It is positioned atop the left "S" hand, whose palm faces right, and represents the sun. The right "S" hand describes a complete circle around the left, and comes to rest in its original position. *Cf.* CENTURY.

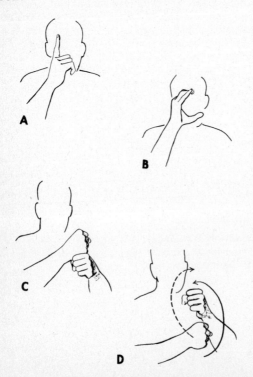

A

B

C

D

[O–78]

ONE-THIRD, *adj.* (The fraction ⅓.) After making the "1" sign, the right hand is dropped a bit and changes to the "3" sign. *Cf.* THIRD 3.

[O–79]

ONE-TO-ONE, *phrase.* (The natural sign.) The "D" hands, palms facing, are brought together a number of times.

[O–80]

ONION 1 (ŭn′ yən), *n.* (The rubbing of the eye, which is irritated by the onion.) The knuckle of the right "X" finger is placed just beside the right eye. The right hand pivots back and forth at the wrist.

[O–81]

ONION 2, *n.* (Same rationale as in ONION 1.) The knuckles of the right "S" hand, positioned as in ONION 1, execute the same pivoting movement.

[O–82]

ONLY (ōn' lĭ), *adv.* (One, wandering around in a circle.) The index finger, pointing straight up, palm facing the body (the number *one*), is rotated before the face in a counterclockwise direction. *Cf.* ALONE, LONE, ONE 2, SOLE, UNITY.

[O–83]

ONLY ONE *phrase.* (Emphasizing the "1" finger.) The "1" hand, palm out, swings around emphatically, moving slightly upward at the same time.

[O–84]

ON THE CONTRARY, *adv. phrase.* (A divergence or a difference; the opposite of SAME.) The index fingers of both "D" hands, palms facing down, are crossed near their tips. The hands are drawn apart. *Cf.* ALTHOUGH, BUT, HOWEVER 1.

[O–85]

ON THE SLY, *adv. phrase.* The index finger edge of the right "B" hand moves slowly up along the right cheek and arcs forward. The same hand, held palm down, then slips slowly under the downturned left hand.

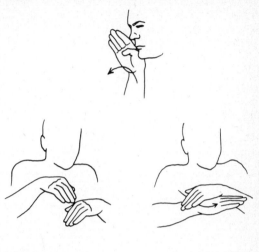

[O–86]

ON TO (tōō), *phrase.* (Adding on.) The index and middle fingers of the right "H" hand, palm up, are swung up and over until they come to rest on the index and middle fingers of the left "H" hand, held palm down. *Cf.* ADD 3, ADDITION, EXTEND 1, EXTRA, GAIN 1, INCREASE, RAISE 2.

[O–87]

ONWARD (ŏn' wərd), *adv.* (Moving forward.) Both right-angle hands, palms facing each other and knuckles facing forward, move forward simultaneously. *Cf.* FORWARD, GO AHEAD, MOTION FORWARD, PROCEED, PROGRESS 2, RESUME.

[O–88]

OPEN 1 (ō′ pən), *adj., v.*, OPENED, OPENING. (The natural sign.) The "B" hands, palms out, are held with index finger edges touching. They swing apart so that the palms now face each other.

[O–89]

OPEN 2, *adj., v.* (The natural sign.) Here the "B" hands move straight apart, with palms still facing out. See OPEN 1.

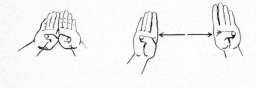

[O–90]

OPEN-EYED (ō′ pən īd′), *(colloq.)*, *adj.* (The eyes pop open.) The "S" hands, palms facing each other, are held before the eyes. They suddenly open into the "C" position, with the eyes wide open. *Cf.* SHOCKED 2, SURPRISED.

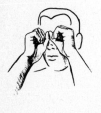

[O–91]

OPEN-MOUTHED (ō′ pən mouthd′, -moutht′), *(colloq.)*, *adj.* (The mouth drops open.) The fingertips of both "V" hands are held curved and touching before the body, one hand above the other. Then the hands are suddenly drawn apart, and at the same instant the mouth drops open and the eyes open wide. *Cf.*

DUMFOUNDED 2, FLABBERGASTED, SPEECHLESS, SURPRISE 2.

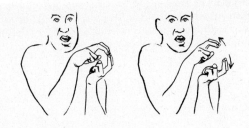

[O–92]

OPEN THE DOOR, *v. phrase.* (The opening and closing of the door.) The "B" hands, palms out and edges touching, are drawn apart and then come together again. *Cf.* DOOR, DOORWAY.

[O–93]

OPEN THE WINDOW, *phrase.* (The opening of the window.) With both palms facing the body, the little finger edge of the right hand rests atop the index finger edge of the left hand. The right hand then moves straight up. *Cf.* WINDOW.

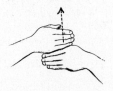

[O–94]

OPERA GLASSES, *n. pl.* (The natural sign.) The "C" hands are held in front of the eyes. *Cf.* BINOCULARS, GOGGLES.

[O-95]

OPERATE (ŏp' ə rāt´), *v.,* -ATED, -ATING. (Holding the reins over all.) The "A" hands, palms facing, move alternately back and forth, as if grasping and manipulating reins. The left "A" hand, still in position, swings over so that its palm now faces down. The right hand opens to the "5" position, palm down, and swings over the left which moves slightly to the right. *Cf.* AUTHORITY, CONTROL 1, DIRECT 1, GOVERN, MANAGE, MANAGEMENT, MANAGER, REGULATE, REIGN, RULE 1.

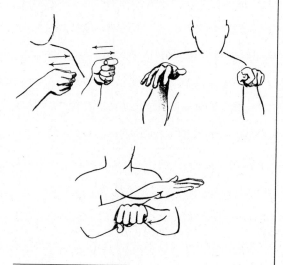

[O-96]

OPERATION 1 (ŏp' ə rā' shən), *n.* (The action of the scalpel.) The thumb of the right "A" hand is drawn straight down across the upright left palm. *Cf.* SURGERY.

[O-97]

OPERATION 2, *n.* (The action of a scalpel.) The thumbtip of the right "A" hand, palm facing down, moves a short distance across the lower chest or stomach region.

[O-98]

OPINION (ə pĭn' yən), *n.* (The "O" hand, circling in the head.) The right "O" hand circles before the forehead several times.

[O-99]

OPPONENT (ə pō' nənt), *n.* (At sword's point.) The two index fingers, after pointing to each other, are drawn sharply apart. This is followed by the sign for INDIVIDUAL: Both open hands, palms facing each other, move down the sides of the body, tracing its outline to the hips. *Cf.* ENEMY, FOE, RIVAL 1.

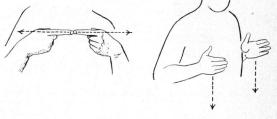

[O-100]

OPPORTUNITY 1 (ŏp' ər tū' nə tǐ), *n.* Both hands, slightly cupped, palms up, are held close to the chest. They move up and out in unison, describing an arc. *Cf.* OCCASION, TIME 4.

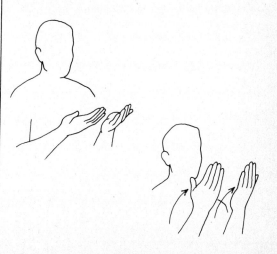

[O–101]

OPPORTUNITY 2, *n.* (Two individuals pitted against each other.) The hands are held in the "A" position, thumbs pointing straight up, palms facing the body. They come together forcefully, moving down a bit as they do, and the knuckles of one hand strike those of the other. *Cf.* CHALLENGE, GAME 1, VERSUS.

[O–102]

OPPORTUNITY 3, *n.* (The movement.) Both hands, palms facing and fingers together and extended straight out, move in unison away from the body, in a straight or winding manner. *Cf.* CORRIDOR, HALL, HALLWAY, MANNER 2, METHOD, PATH, ROAD, STREET, TRAIL, WAY 1.

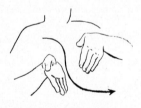

[O–103]

OPPORTUNITY 4, *n.* (A befalling.) Both "D" hands, index fingers pointing away from the body, are simultaneously pivoted over so that the palms face down. *Cf.* ACCIDENT, BEFALL, CHANCE, COINCIDE 1, COINCIDENCE, EVENT, HAPPEN 1, INCIDENT, OCCUR.

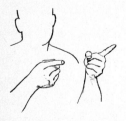

[O–104]

OPPORTUNITY 5, *n.* (The letters "O" and "P"; pushing through.) Both "O" hands are held palms down, side by side. They swing up a bit as they assume the "P" position.

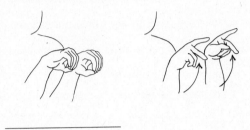

[O–105]

OPPOSE (ə' pōz), *v.*, OPPOSED, OPPOSING. (Opposed to; restraint.) The tips of the right fingers, held together, are thrust purposefully into the open left palm, whose fingers are also together and pointing forward. *Cf.* AGAINST.

[O–106]

OPPOSITE (ŏp' ə zĭt), *adj., n.* (Separateness.) The tips of the extended index fingers touch before the chest, the right finger pointing left and the left finger pointing right. The fingers then draw apart sharply to either side. *Cf.* CONTRAST 2, REVERSE 1.

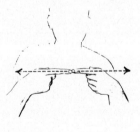

[O–107]

OR 1 (ôr; *unstressed* ər), *conj.* (Selection between two or among multiple choices.) The left "L" hand is held palm facing the body and thumb pointing straight up. The right index finger touches the left thumbtip and then the left index fingertip. *Cf.* EITHER 1.

[O-108]

OR 2, *conj.* (Considering one thing against another.) The "A" hands, palms facing and thumbs pointing straight up, move alternately up and down before the chest. *Cf.* EITHER 3, WHETHER, WHICH 1.

[O-109]

ORAL (ōr' əl), *adj.* (Reading the lips—the lines of vision, represented by the two fingers, scan the lips.) The right "V" hand, palm facing the body, is placed in front of the face, with slightly curved index and middle fingers directly in front of the lips. The right hand moves in a small counterclockwise circle around the lips. *Cf.* LIPREADING, READ LIPS, SPEECHREADING.

[O-110]

ORANGE 1 (ôr' ĭnj, ŏr'-), *n., adj.* (The action of squeezing an orange to get its juice into the mouth.) The right "C" hand is held at the mouth. It opens and closes deliberately, as if squeezing an orange.

[O-111]

ORANGE 2, *n.* (The peeling of the fruit.) The thumbtip of the right "Y" hand moves over the back of the left "S" hand, which is held palm down or palm facing the body.

[O-112]

ORANGE 3, *n., adj.* Both "Y" hands are held before the body, palms facing each other. In this position the hands alternate in drawing imaginary circles in the air with the little fingers. This sign is used for both the color and the fruit.

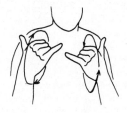

[O-113]

ORATE (ō rāt', ōr' āt), *v.,* ORATED, ORATING. (A gesture of an orator.) The right open hand, palm facing left, is held above and to the right of the head. It pivots on the wrist, forward and backward, several times. *Cf.* ADDRESS 1, LECTURE, SPEECH 2, TALK 2, TESTIMONY.

[O–114]

ORATOR (ôr′ ə tər, ŏr′ -), *n.* (The characteristic waving of the speaker's hand as he makes his point.) The sign for ORATE is made. This is followed by the sign for INDIVIDUAL: Both open hands, palms facing each other, move down the sides of the body, tracing its outline to the hips. *Cf.* SPEAKER.

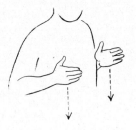

[O–115]

ORB (ôrb), *n.* (The shape.) The curved open hands are held with fingertips touching, as if holding a ball. *Cf.* BALL 2, ROUND 1, SPHERE.

[O–116]

ORBIT 1 (ôr′ bĭt), *n., v.,* -BITED, -BITING. (Encircling the planet.) The left hand, in the "S" position, knuckles facing right, is encircled by the right index finger, which travels in a clockwise direction. It makes one revolution and comes to rest atop the left hand. *Cf.* ALL YEAR, ALL YEAR 'ROUND, AROUND THE WORLD.

[O–117]

ORBIT 2, *n., v.* The same movement as in ORBIT 1, except that the right "O" hand (for "orbit") is used.

[O–118]

ORDAIN (ôr dān′), *(eccles.), adj., v.,* -DAINED, -DAINING. (Placing the hand on the head in the act of ordination.) The downturned left hand is held horizontally before the chest. The open right hand is placed on the head, and then moves down to rest on the back of the left hand. *Cf.* ORDINATION.

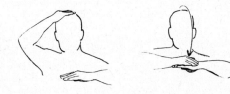

[O–119]

ORDER 1 (ôr′ dər), *n., v.,* -DERED, -DERING. (An issuance from the mouth.) The tip of the index finger of the "D" hand, palm facing the body, is placed at the closed lips. It moves around and out, rather forcefully. *Cf.* BID 1, COMMAND, DIRECT 2.

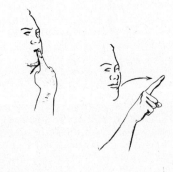

[O–120]

ORDER 2, *(rare), n.* (Something you write and give to someone.) The sign for WRITE is made: The right index finger and thumb, grasping an imaginary pen, write across the open left palm. This is followed by the sign for GIVE: Both hands are held palms down, about a foot apart, thumbs resting on finger-tips. The hands are extended forward in a slight arc, opening to the "5" position as they do.

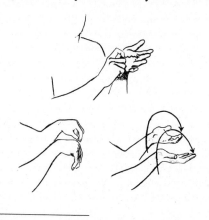

[O–121]

ORDER 3, *n., v.* (Placing things in order.) The hands, palms facing, fingers together and pointing away from the body, are positioned at the left side and held about a foot apart. With a slight up-down motion, as if describing waves, the hands travel in unison from left to right. *Cf.* ARRANGE, ARRANGE-MENT, CLASSED 2, DEVISE 1, PLAN 1, POLICY 1, PREPARE 1, PROGRAM 1, PROVIDE 1, PUT IN ORDER, READY 1, SCHEME, SYSTEM.

[O–122]

ORDERLY (ôr′ dər lĭ), *adj.* (In order, *i.e.*, equally spaced or arranged.) Both open hands, palms facing each other and fingers pointing away from the body, move in unison, in a series of short arcs, from left to right. This is essentially the same as ORDER 3.

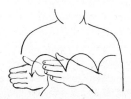

[O–123]

ORDINATION (ôr′ də nā′ shən), *(eccles.), n.* See OR-DAIN.

[O–124]

ORGANIZATION 1 (ôr′ gən ə zā′ shən), *n.* (A group-ing together.) Both "C" hands, palms facing, are held a few inches apart at chest height. They are swung around in unison, so that the palms now face the body. *Cf.* ASSOCIATION, AUDIENCE 1, CASTE, CIRCLE 2, CLASS, CLASSED 1, CLUB, COMPANY, FAM-ILY 2, GANG, GROUP 1, JOIN 2.

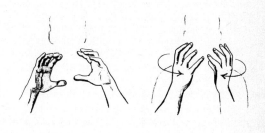

[O–125]

ORGANIZATION 2, *n.* (The letter "O"; a group or class.) Both "O" hands are held with palms facing out and thumb edges touching. The hands swing apart, around, and come together again with little finger edges touching.

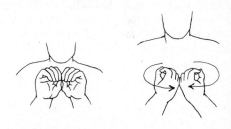

[O–126]

ORIENTAL (ōr′ ĭ ĕn′ təl), *adj.* (Slanting eyes.) The index fingers draw back the corners of the eyes, caus-ing them to slant. *Cf.* ASIA, CHINA 1, CHINESE.

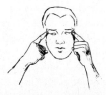

[O–127]

ORIENTATION (ōr´ ĭ ĕn tā′ shən), *n.* (The letter "O"; polishing up.) The fingertips of the right "O" hand brush back and forth over the left index finger. This is a modification of the sign for PRACTICE 1, *q. v.*

[O–128]

ORIGIN 1 (ôr′ ə jĭn, ŏr′ -), *n.* (Turning a key to open up a new venture.) The right index finger, resting between the left index and middle fingers, executes a half turn, once or twice. *Cf.* BEGIN, COMMENCE, INITIATE, INSTITUTE 2, ORIGINATE 1, START.

[O–129]

ORIGIN 2, *n.* (The first finger is indicated.) The right index finger touches the upturned left thumb. *Cf.* FIRST 1, INITIAL, PRIMARY.

[O–130]

ORIGIN 3, *n.* (First to be grasped from the mind.) The right "D" hand moves straight up against the forehead, and then closes into the "S" position, still against the forehead. *Cf.* INVENT 1, ORIGINAL 1, ORIGINATE 2.

[O–131]

ORIGINAL 1 (ə rĭj′ ə nəl), *adj.* See ORIGIN 3.

[O–132]

ORIGINAL 2, *adj.* (Turning over a new leaf.) With both hands held palm up before the body, the right hand sweeps in an arc into the left, and continues up a bit. *Cf.* NEW, NEWS, NOVELTY, TIDINGS.

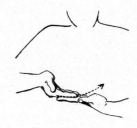

[O–133]

ORIGINATE 1 (ə rĭj′ ə nāt′), *v.*, -NATED, -NATING. See ORIGIN 1.

[O–134]

ORIGINATE 2, *v.* See ORIGIN 3.

[O–135]

ORNAMENT 1 (*n.* ôr′ nə mənt; *v.* ôr′ nə mĕnt′), -MENTED, -MENTING. (The hands describe the flounces of draperies.) Both "C" hands, palms out, are held somewhat above the head. They move out and down in a series of successive arcs. *Cf.* ADORN, DECORATE 1, TRIM 1.

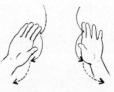

[O–136]

ORNAMENT 2, *n., v.* (Embellishing; adding to.) Both "O" hands, palms facing each other, move alternately back and forth in a curving up and down direction. The fingertips come in contact each time the hands pass each other. *Cf.* DECORATE 2, TRIM 2.

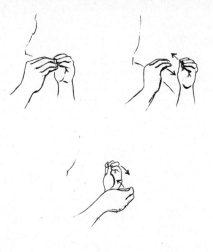

OTHER (ŭ*th*′ ər), *adj.* (Moving over to another position.) The right "A" hand, thumb up, is pivoted from the wrist and swung over to the right, so that the thumb now points to the right. *Cf.* ANOTHER.

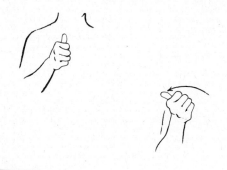

OUGHT TO (ôt), *v. aux.* (Being pinned down.) The right hand, in the "X" position, palm down, moves forcefully up and down once or twice. An expression of determination is frequently assumed. *Cf.* HAVE TO, IMPERATIVE, MUST, NECESSARY 1, NECESSITY, NEED 1, SHOULD, VITAL 2.

OUR (our), *pron.* (An encompassing, including oneself and others.) The right "C" hand, palm facing left, is placed at the right shoulder. It swings around to the left shoulder, its palm now facing right.

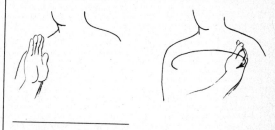

OURSELVES (our sĕlvz′), *pron. pl.* (An encompassing; the thumb representing *self*, *i.e.*, oneness.) The right "A" hand, thumb held straight up, is placed at the right shoulder. It executes the same movement as in OUR.

OUT 1 (out), *adv.* (The natural motion of withdrawing, *i.e.*, taking *out,* of the hand.) The downturned open right hand, grasped loosely by the left, is drawn up and out of the left hand's grasp. As it does so, the fingers come together with the thumb. The left hand, meanwhile, closes into the "O" position, palm facing right. *Cf.* EXIT.

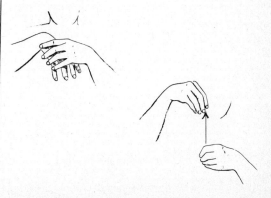

[O-142]

OUT 2, *adv.* (Removing.) The right "A" hand, resting in the palm of the left "5" hand, moves slightly up and away, describing a small arc. It is then cast downward, opening into the "5" position, palm down, as if removing something from the left hand and casting it down. *Cf.* ABOLISH 2, ABSENCE 2, ABSENT 2, ABSTAIN, CHEAT 2, DEDUCT, DEFICIENCY, DELETE 1, LESS 2, MINUS 3, REMOVE 1, SUBTRACT, SUBTRACTION, TAKE AWAY FROM, WITHDRAW 2.

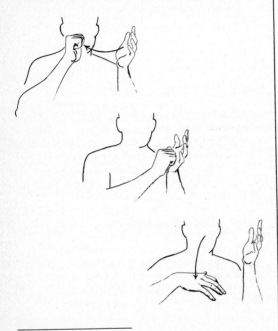

[O-143]

OUT 3, *adv.* (A disappearance.) The right open hand, palm facing the body, is held by the left hand and is drawn down and out, ending in a position with fingers drawn together. The left hand, meanwhile, may close into a position with fingers also drawn together. *Cf.* ABSENCE 1, ABSENT 1, DEPLETE, DISAPPEAR, EMPTY 1, EXTINCT, FADE AWAY, GONE 1, MISSING 1, OMISSION 1, OUT OF, VANISH.

[O-144]

OUT OF, *prep. phrase.* See OUT 3.

[O-145]

OVEN (ŭv′ ən), *n.* (Placing the bread in the oven.) The downturned right "B" hand, representing the bread, is thrust slowly forward under the downturned left hand, representing the oven. *Cf.* BAKE.

[O-146]

OVER 1 (ō′ vər), *prep.* (One hand moves above the other.) Both hands, palms flat and facing down, are held before the chest. The right hand circles horizontally above the left in a counterclockwise direction. *Cf.* ABOVE.

[O-147]

OVER 2, *prep.* (A crossing over.) The left hand is held before the chest, palm down and fingers together. The right hand, fingers together, glides over the left, with the right little finger touching the top of the left hand. *Cf.* ACROSS, CROSS 3.

[O–148]

OVERCOAT (ō′ vər kōt′), *n.* (The lapels are out-lined.) The tips of the "A" thumbs outline the lapels of the overcoat. *Cf.* CLOAK, COAT.

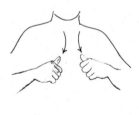

[O–149]

OVERCOME (ō′ vər kŭm′), *v.,* -CAME, -COME, -COM-ING. (Forcing the head into a bowed position.) The right "S" hand, placed across the left "S" hand, moves over and down a bit. *Cf.* BEAT 2, CONQUER, DEFEAT, SUBDUE.

[O–150]

OVERFLOW (*n.* ō′ vər flō′; *v.* ō′ vər flō′), *n., v.,* -FLOWED, -FLOWN, -FLOWING. (Running over the top.) The left "S" hand is held up before the chest. The right fingertips, pointing up, move upward along the thumb edge of the left hand and continue over the top of the hand, imitating the flow of water. *Cf.* RUN OVER.

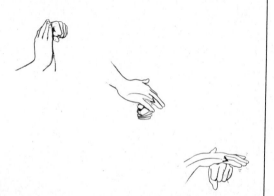

[O–151]

OVERSHOES (ō′ vər shoo′ z), *(rare), n. pl.* (The hardness is indicated by the teeth; the outline of the sole is made.) The thumb of the right "A" hand, placed under the upper teeth, is drawn out sharply. It then draws an outline around the edge of the upturned open left hand.

[O–152]

OVERSLEEP (ō′ vər slēp′), *(colloq.), v.,* -SLEPT, -SLEEPING. (The eyes remain shut while the sun rises.) The sign for SLEEP is made: The open right hand, palm facing the body, is held before the eyes. The hand moves down and away from the eyes, as the fingers close around the thumb. The eyes, at the same time, close, and the head drops forward slightly. The sign for SUNRISE is then made: The left "O" hand, palm facing right, represents the hori-zon. The right "F" hand, palm facing left, moves slowly up in front of the left. The left hand, instead of assuming the "O" position, may instead be held in a prone position; and the right may be held in the "O" position instead of the "F" position. The SLEEP part of this sign is sometimes omitted alto-gether.

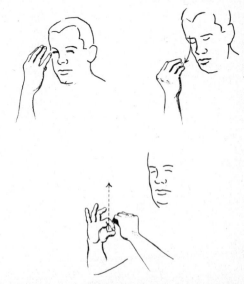

[O–153]

OVERTIME (ō′ vər tīm′), *n., adv., adj.* (Working after dark.) The sign for WORK is made: The base of the right "S" hand is struck repeatedly against the back of the downturned left "S" hand. The right hand then opens into a prone position and moves over and down, to a position almost under the down-turned left "S" hand, to indicate the sun setting under the horizon. The WORK sign is sometimes omitted.

[O–154]

OWE (ō), *v.*, OWED, OWING. (Pointing to the palm, where the money should be placed.) The index finger of one hand is thrust into the upturned palm of the other several times. *Cf.* ARREARS, DEBIT, DEBT, DUE, OBLIGATION 3.

[O–155]

OWL (oul), *n.* (The eyes are indicated.) The "O" hands are pivoted repeatedly in front of the eyes, to outline them.

[O–156]

OWN (ōn), *adj.* (Pressing something to one's bosom.) The "5" hand is brought up against the chest. *Cf.* MINE 1, MY.

[O–157]

OYSTER (ois′ tər), *n.* (The shucking action.) The open hands, palms facing, are held with right above left. The right hand swings down into sharp contact with the left palm and continues downward, as if having split open the shell.

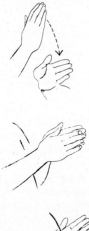

P

PACE (pās), *n., v.,* PACED, PACING. (The movement of the feet.) The downturned "5" hands move alternately toward and away from the chest. Cf. STEP 1, WALK.

PACKAGE (păk' ĭj), *n., v.,* -AGED, -AGING. (The dimensions are indicated.) The open hands, palms facing and fingers pointing out, are dropped an inch or two simultaneously. They then shift their relative positions so that both palms face the body, with one hand in front of the other. In this new position they again drop an inch or two simultaneously. Cf. BOX 1, ROOM 1, SQUARE 1, TRUNK.

PADDLE (păd' əl), *n., v.,* -DLED, -DLING. (The natural sign.) The hands, grasping an imaginary paddle, go through the motions of paddling a canoe. Cf. CANOEING.

PAGE (pāj), *n.* (Act of turning over a page.) The right "F" hand, grasping an imaginary page, goes through the motion of turning it over.

PAIN (pān), *n.* (A stabbing pain.) The "D" hands, index fingers pointing to each other, are rotated in elliptical fashion before the chest—simultaneously but in opposite directions. Cf. ACHE, HARM 1, HURT 1, INJURE 1, INJURY, MAR 1, OFFEND, OFFENSE, SIN, WOUND.

PAINT 1 (pānt), *n., v.,* PAINTED, PAINTING. (The action of the brush.) The hands are held open with palms facing each other. The right hand, representing a wide brush, sweeps back and forth over the left palm, as if spreading paint on it. (This sign is used in the sense of painting a large area such as a wall.)

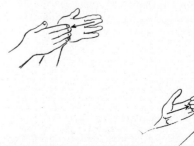

[P-7]

PAINT 2, *n., v.* (The action of a small brush.) The tips of the fingers of the right "H" hand are swept back and forth repeatedly over the left palm, as if spreading paint on it with a small or narrow brush. (This sign is used in reference to fine art painting.)

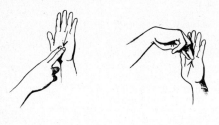

[P-8]

PAINTER 1 (pān' tər), *n.* The sign for PAINT 1 is made, followed by the sign for INDIVIDUAL: Both open hands, palms facing each other, move down the sides of the body, tracing its outline to the hips.

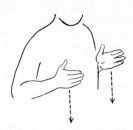

[P-9]

PAINTER 2, *n.* The sign for PAINT 2 is made, followed by the sign for INDIVIDUAL, as in PAINTER 1.

[P-10]

PAIR (pâr), *n. pl., v.,* PAIRED, PAIRING. (Two fingers are drawn together.) The right "2" hand, palm facing the body, is drawn down through the left "C" hand. As it does, the right index and middle fingers come together. *Cf.* BOTH, MUTUAL 2.

[P-11]

PALE (pāl) *adj., v.,* PALED, PALING. The sign for WHITE is made: The fingertips of the "5" hand are placed against the chest. The hand moves straight out from the chest, while the fingers and thumb all come together. Then both hands, fingers spread, rise up and over the cheeks.

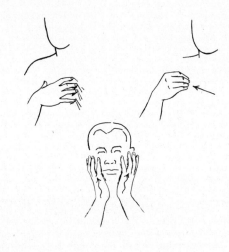

[P-12]

PAMPHLET (pam' flit), *n.* (A book with a narrow spine.) The left hand, fingers together, is held upright, palm facing right. The right hand wraps around the lower edge of the left and travels up to the little finger. This denotes a narrow object. The sign for BOOK is then made: The hands are placed together, palm to palm, and then opened, as if opening a book. Sometimes this latter sign is omitted. *Cf.* BOOKLET, CATALOG, MAGAZINE, MANUAL.

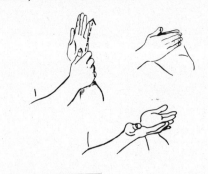

[P-13]

PANCAKE (păn' kāk'), *n.* (Turning over a pancake.) The open right hand rests on the upturned left palm. The right hand flips over and comes to rest with its back on the left palm. This is the action of turning over a pancake. *Cf.* CHEF, COOK, KITCHEN 1.

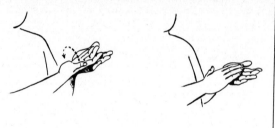

[P-14]

PANHANDLER (păn' hăn' dəl ər), *n.* (An individual who begs.) The right open hand, palm up and fingers slightly cupped, is moved up and down by the left hand, positioned under it. It is followed by the sign for INDIVIDUAL: Both hands, fingers together, are placed at either side of the chest and are moved down to waist level. *Cf.* ASK ALMS, BEG 1, BEGGAR.

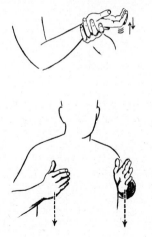

[P-15]

PANTS (pănts), *n. pl.* (The natural sign.) The open hands are drawn up along the thighs, starting at the knees. *Cf.* TROUSERS.

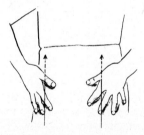

[P-16]

PAPA (pä' pə), *n.* (Derived from the formal sign for FATHER 1, *q.v.*) The thumbtip of the right "5" hand touches the right temple a number of times. The other fingers may also wiggle. *Cf.* DAD, DADDY, FATHER 2, POP 2.

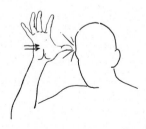

[P-17]

PAPAL (pā' pəl), *adj.* (The triple crown.) The cupped hands are held at the sides of the head. The fingertips come together three times as the hands move up in successive stages. *Cf.* PONTIFF, POPE.

[P-18]

PAPER (pā' pər), *n.* (The action of the press.) The right "5" hand, held palm down, fingers pointing left, is brought down twice against the upturned left "5" hand, whose fingers point right. *Cf.* NEWSPAPER, PUBLISH 1.

[P–19]

PAPER CLIP (pā′ pər klĭp), *n.* (The natural sign.) The right thumb, index, and middle fingers are clamped over the middle of the index and middle fingers of the left "U" hand, whose palm faces right. The right fingers may also be slipped over the left fingers instead of being clamped over them.

[P–20]

PAPER CUTTER (pā′ pər kŭt′ ər), *(voc.), n.* (The action of the blade.) The open left hand, palm facing right, is held before the body. The little finger edge of the open right hand is swung down against the left fingertips, and continues beyond a bit.

[P–21]

PAPER PAD (pā′ pər păd′), *n.* (The shape of the pad.) The sign for PAPER is made. Then the right thumb and index fingers, spread rather widely apart, move down across the open left palm from index finger edge to little finger edge.

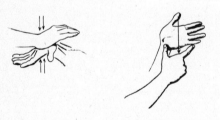

[P–22]

PARACHUTE (păr′ ə shōōt′), *n., v.,* -CHUTED, -CHUTING. (The natural sign.) The open right hand, palm facing down and fingers open and curved to

form a cup, is positioned above the left "D" hand. Both hands move straight down in unison.

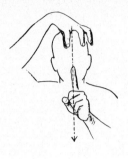

[P–23]

PARADE 1 (pə rād′), *n., v.,* -RADED, -RADING. (Rows of people marching.) Both "V" hands, palms out and the left behind the right, move forward in unison, in a series of short upward-arced motions. *Cf.* FUNERAL, PROCESSION.

[P–24]

PARADE 2, *n., v.* (A column of marchers, one behind the other.) The downturned open hands, fingers pointing down, are held one behind the other. Pivoted from the wrists, they move rhythmically forward and back in unison. *Cf.* MARCH 1.

[P–25]

PARAGRAPH (păr′ ə grăf′, -gräf′), *n.* (A portion of a page.) The thumb and fingertips of the right "C" hand, held rather closely together, are brought against the palm of the left "5" hand.

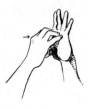

[P–26]

PARALLEL (păr′ ə lĕl′), *adj.* (Moving side by side.) Both index fingers, pointing straight out from the body and held an inch or two apart, move in unison away from the body.

[P–27]

PARASITE (păr′ ə sīt′), *n.* (Attaching to something and tugging on it.) The extended right thumb, index, and middle fingers grasp the extended left index and middle fingers. In this position the right hand pulls at the left several times. *Cf.* LEECH, MOOCH, MOOCHER, TAKE ADVANTAGE OF 2.

[P–28]

PARDON (păr′ dən), *n.* (A wiped-off and cleaned slate.) The right hand wipes off the left palm several

times. *Cf.* APOLOGIZE 2, APOLOGY 2, EXCUSE, FORGIVE 2, PAROLE.

[P–29]

PARE (pâr), *v.*, PARED, PARING. (The natural motion.) The extended right thumb scrapes forward across the upturned thumb edge of the left "O" hand. *Cf.* PEEL 1.

[P–30]

PARK (pärk), *v.*, PARKED, PARKING. (A vehicle is brought to a distinct stop.) The right "3" hand, palm facing left, moves down an inch or two in front of the body. It may also, in so doing, be placed in the upturned open left palm.

[P–31]

PAROLE (pə rōl′), *n.*, *v.*, -ROLED, -ROLING. See PARDON.

[P–32]

PART 1 (pärt), *n.*, *adj.* (Cutting off or designating a part.) The little finger edge of the open right hand moves straight down the middle of the upturned left palm. *Cf.* PIECE, PORTION, SECTION, SHARE 1, SOME.

[P–33]

PART 2, *n., adj.* (Separating to classify.) Both hands, in the right angle position, are placed palms down before the body, knuckles to knuckles. They pull apart or separate, once or a number of times. *Cf.* ASSORT, SEPARATE 2.

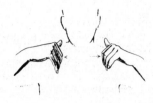

[P–34]

PART 3, *n., adj.* (The hands are moved apart.) Both hands, in the "A" position, thumbs up, are held together, with knuckles touching. With a deliberate movement they come apart. *Cf.* APART, DIVORCE 1, SEPARATE 1.

[P–35]

PART 4, *n.* (The letter "P.") This is the same sign as for PART 1, except that the middle finger of the right "P" hand touches the upturned left palm as the sign is made.

[P–36]

PART FROM, *v. phrase.* (An unlocking.) With thumbs and index fingers interlocked initially (the

links of a chain), the hands draw apart, showing the break in the chain. *Cf.* DETACH, DISCONNECT.

[P–37]

PARTICIPATE (pär tĭs′ ə pāt′), *v.,* -PATED, -PATING. (Joining together.) Both hands, held in the modified "5" position, palms out, move toward each other. The thumbs and index fingers of both hands then connect. *Cf.* AFFILIATE 1, ANNEX, ASSOCIATE 2, ATTACH, BELONG, COMMUNION OF SAINTS, CONCERN 2, CONNECT, ENLIST, ENROLL, JOIN 1, RELATIVE 2, UNION, UNITE.

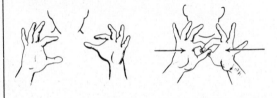

[P–38]

PARTY 1 (pär′ tĭ), *n.* (The swinging of tambourines.) Both open hands, held somewhat above the head, are pivoted back and forth repeatedly, as if swinging a pair of tambourines. *Cf.* GAIETY 2.

[P–39]

PARTY 2, *n.* (The rhythmic swaying of the feet.) The downturned index and middle fingers of the right "V" hand swing rhythmically back and forth over the upturned left palm. *Cf.* BALL 1, DANCE.

[P–40]

PARTY 3, *(loc.), n.* The right "O" hand, palm facing the rear, is placed with knuckles touching the right cheek. The hand is thrown out and down a bit, into the palm-down "5" position. Both hands, placed at either cheek, may also be used.

[P–41]

PASS 1 (păs), *v.,* PASSED, PASSING. (One hand passes the other.) Both "A" hands, palms facing each other, are held before the body, the right behind the left. The right hand moves forward, its knuckles brushing those of the left, and continues forward a bit beyond the left. *Cf.* ELAPSE, GO BY.

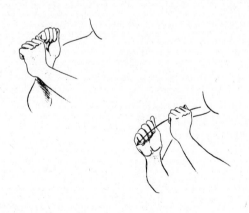

[P–42]

PASS 2, *(sports), v.* (The action of passing a football.) The left hand goes through the natural motion

of passing an imaginary football. (The right hand may also be used.)

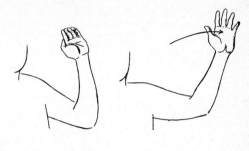

[P–43]

PASS BY (păs bī), *v. phrase.* (The fingers pass each other.) The right "D" hand, palm facing away from the body, moves forward a bit. At the same time the left "D" hand, palm facing the body, moves toward the body a bit. The action involves both hands passing each other as they move in opposite directions.

[P–44]

PASSETH (păs əth), *(eccles.) v.* (Rising above something.) Both hands, in the right-angle position, are held before the chest, with the right atop the left. The right hand arcs upward to a position about eight inches above the left. *Cf.* EXCEED, EXCESSIVE, SURPASS.

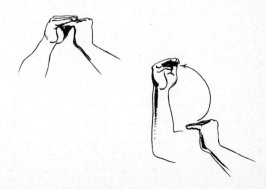

[P-45]

PASSION 1 (păsh' ən), *n.* (The alimentary canal—the area of hunger and hunger gratification—is indicated.) The fingertips of the right "C" hand move slowly and deliberately down the middle of the chest once or twice. The eyes are usually narrowed and the teeth clenched. *Cf.* LUST.

[P-46]

PASSION 2, *v.* (A clenching of the fists; the rise and fall of pain.) Both "S" hands, tightly clenched, revolve about each other, slowly and deliberately, while a pained expression is worn. *Cf.* AGONY, BEAR 3, DIFFICULT 3, ENDURE 1, SUFFER 1, TOLERATE 2.

[P-47]

PASS OUT, *v. phrase.* (An animal's legs sticking up in the air, in death.) Both hands are held with palms facing each other, and curved index and middle fingers presented. The hands pivot up a bit, simultaneously, assuming the "V" position as they do. *Cf.* DEAD 2, DIE 2.

[P-48]

PASSOVER (păs' ṓ vər), *n.* The thumb edge of the right fist strikes several times against the left elbow, while the left arm is bent so that the left fist is held against the right shoulder. *Cf.* CRACKER 1, MATZOTH.

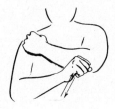

[P-49]

PAST (păst), *adj., n., adv.* (Something past, behind.) The upraised right hand, in the "5" position with palm facing the body, is held just above the right shoulder and is thrown back over it. *Cf.* AGO, FORMERLY, ONCE UPON A TIME, PREVIOUS, PREVIOUSLY, WAS, WERE.

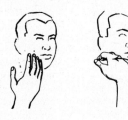

[P-50]

PASTOR (păs' tər), *n.* (Placing morsels of wisdom, or food for thought, into the mind.) The right hand, palm out, with thumb and index finger touching, is moved forward and slightly downward a number of times from its initial position near the right temple. This is followed by the sign for INDIVIDUAL: Both open hands, palms facing each other, move down the sides of the body, tracing its outline to the hips. *Cf.* MINISTER, PREACHER.

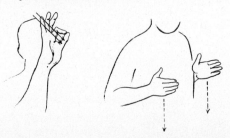

[P–51]

PATH (păth), *n.* (The winding movement.) Both hands, palms facing and fingers together and extended straight out, move in unison away from the body, in a winding manner. *Cf.* CORRIDOR, HALL, HALLWAY, MANNER 2, METHOD, OPPORTUNITY 3, ROAD, STREET, TRAIL, WAY 1.

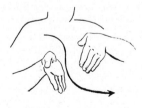

[P–52]

PATIENCE 1 (pā' shəns), *n.* The thumb of the right "A" hand is drawn down across the lips. This is frequently followed by the sign for SUFFER 1: Both "S" hands, tightly clenched, revolve about each other, slowly and deliberately, while a pained expression is worn. *Cf.* PATIENT 1.

[P–53]

PATIENCE 2, *n.* (Silence; an avoidance of an outcry or impatience.) The index finger of the right "D" hand, palm facing left, is placed at the sealed lips. The head is held slightly bowed. *Cf.* HURT 3, PATIENT 2.

[P–54]

PATIENT 1 (pā' shənt), *n.* See PATIENCE 1.

[P–55]

PATIENT 2, *adj.* See PATIENCE 2.

[P–56]

PATIENT 3, *n.* (The letter "P"; the red cross on the hospital gown's sleeve.) The thumb and middle fingers of the right "P" hand trace a small cross on the upper left arm.

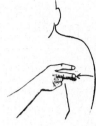

[P–57]

PAY 1 (pā), *v.*, PAID, PAYING. (Giving forth of money.) The right index finger, resting in the upturned left palm, swings forward and up a bit.

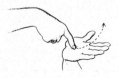

[P–58]

PAY 2, *v.* (Releasing coins from the grasp.) The right hand, palm up, holds some imaginary coins, with the thumb resting on the tips of the fingers. The hand moves forward, and the thumb meanwhile glides over the fingertips and assumes the "A" position, palm still up.

[P–59]

PAY 3, *v.* (A modification of PAY 1, with the letter "P.") The middle finger of the right "P" hand is placed in the upturned left palm, and the right "P" hand executes the same movement as in PAY 1.

[P–60]

PAY ATTENTION (TO), *v. phrase.* (Directing one's attention forward; applying oneself; concentrating.) Both hands, fingers pointing up and together, are held at the sides of the face. They move straight out from the face. *Cf.* APPLY 2, ATTEND (TO), ATTENTION, CONCENTRATE, CONCENTRATION, FOCUS, GIVE ATTENTION (TO), MIND 2.

[P–61]

PEACE (pēs), *n.* (The hands are clasped as a gesture of harmony or *peace;* the opening signifies quiet or calmness.) The hands are clasped both ways, and then open and separate, assuming the "5" position, palms down.

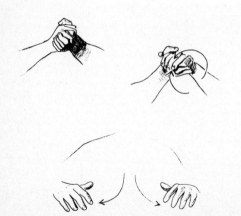

[P–62]

PEACE OF MIND, *(colloq.), n. phrase.* (The thoughts are reduced, *i.e.,* the pressure on the mind is reduced.) The sign for **THINK** is made: The right index finger touches mid-forehead. Both cupped hands are then held, palms facing, the right above the left. The right hand moves slowly and deliberately down until it stops an inch or so above the left. The breath may be exhaled as the right hand moves down, with the lips deliberately pursed, as if breathing, "whew!"

[P–63]

PEACH 1 (pēch), *n.* (The breaking of the fruit.) Both hands, palms up and thumbs resting on their respective fingertips, are held touching each other. The hands move upward as if breaking open a peach.

[P–64]

PEACH 2, *n.* (The fuzz of the peach.) The open right hand is placed on the right cheek, and moves off and away to the right, closing into the "O" position, palm facing back.

[P–65]

PEACH 3, *n.* (The fuzz is indicated, on the cheek.) The three fingers of the right "M" hand, palm facing the body, are placed on the right cheek. The right hand describes a small counterclockwise circle on the cheek.

[P-66]

PEAK (pēk), *n.* (Hard rock, shape of mountain.) The right "S" hand is brought down sharply against the back of the downturned left "S" hand. Then the open hands, palms down, move upward from either side, to meet at a point just above the head.

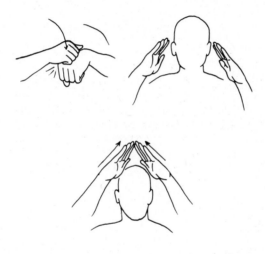

[P-67]

PEANUT (pē′ nŭt′), *n.* (Cracking a hard substance with the teeth; squeezing and breaking the nut.) The sign for NUT is made: The right thumbtip is placed between the teeth. The right thumb and index finger then grasp the tip of the left index finger and, pivoting at the wrist, the right hand manipulates the left index finger back and forth, while squeezing it as if cracking a peanut. The sign for NUT may be omitted.

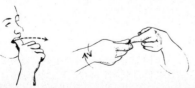

[P-68]

PEAR (pâr), *n.* (The shape and stem.) The fingers of the right hand grasp the closed left hand. The right hand moves slowly to the right, its fingers sliding off the left hand and coming together. The fingers of the left hand then grasp the tip of the right index finger as if holding the stem of a pear. This latter part of the sign is frequently omitted.

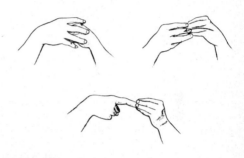

[P-69]

PEAS (pēz), *n. pl.* (Scraping peas from the pod.) The extended left index finger points forward, representing the pod, while the right thumb and index finger rub back and forth along the finger, as if scraping off peas.

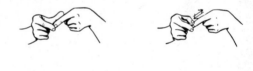

[P-70]

PECK (pĕk), *v.*, PECKED, PECKING. (The hen's beak pecks.) The index finger and thumb of the right hand, held together, are brought against the index finger of the left "D" hand a number of times. *Cf.* HENPECK, NAG, PICK ON.

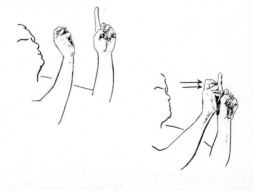

[P-71]

PECULIAR (pǐ kūl′ yər), *adj.* (Something which distorts the vision.) The "C" hand describes a small arc in front of the face. *Cf.* CURIOUS 2, GROTESQUE, ODD, QUEER 1, STRANGE 1, WEIRD.

[P-72]

PEDAL (pĕd′ əl), *n., v.,* -ALED, -ALING. (The motion of the feet on the pedals.) Both hands, in the "S" position, rotate alternately before the chest. *Cf.* BICYCLE, TRICYCLE.

[P-73]

PEEK 1 (pēk), *v.,* PEEKED, PEEKING. (The eye is alternately hidden and uncovered.) The right "B" hand, palm facing left, is held against the face so that it covers the right eye. The hand moves alternately an inch to the left and right, covering and uncovering the right eye. *Cf.* SPY 1.

[P-74]

PEEK 2, *n., v.* (The eye looks through a narrow aperture.) The right "V" hand, palm facing out, is held at the face, with the right eye looking out between the index and middle fingers. *Cf.* SPY 2.

[P-75]

PEEL 1 (pēl), *v.,* PEELED, PEELING. (The natural motion.) The extended right thumb scrapes forward across the upturned thumb edge of the left "O" hand. *Cf.* PARE.

[P-76]

PEEL 2, *v.* (The natural sign.) The tips of the right thumb and index finger rest on the back of the downturned left "S" hand. The right hand goes through the natural motion of *peeling* off a piece of skin.

[P-77]

PEEP (pēp), *v.,* PEEPED, PEEPING. (The natural sign.) The index and middle fingers of one hand are spread and held before the eyes. The signer "peeps" through the hand.

[P-78]

PEER (pĭr), *n.* (Equal in height or status.) The right-angle hands, palms down, are held at about eye level, one in front of the other. The hand in front moves straight forward a short distance, away from the face, while the other hand remains stationary. This sign is used to indicate an equal, never a member of the nobility.

[P-79]

PEN (pĕn), *n., v.,* PENNED, PENNING. (The natural movement.) The right index finger and thumb, grasping an imaginary pen, write across the open left palm. *Cf.* SIGN, WRITE.

[P-80]

PENALTY 1 (pĕn' əl tĭ), *n.* (A striking movement.) The right index finger makes a striking movement below the left "S" hand, which is held up, as if grasping a culprit. *Cf.* DISCIPLINE 3, PUNISH 1.

[P-81]

PENALTY 2, *n.* (A modification of the striking movement.) The right index finger strikes the left elbow with a glancing blow. *Cf.* DISCIPLINE 2, PENANCE 1, PUNISH 3.

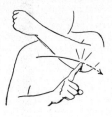

[P-82]

PENALTY 3, *n.* (Nicking into one.) The knuckle of the right "X" finger is nicked against the palm of the left hand, held in the "5" position, palm facing right. *Cf.* ADMISSION 2, CHARGE 1, COST, DUTY 2, EXCISE, EXPENSE, FEE, FINE 2, IMPOST, PRICE 2, TAX 1, TAXATION 1, TOLL.

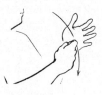

[P-83]

PENANCE 1 (pĕn' əns), *n.* (A modification of the striking movement.) The right index finger strikes the left elbow with a glancing blow. *Cf.* DISCIPLINE 2, PENALTY 2, PUNISH 3.

[P-84]

PENANCE 2, *(eccles.), n.* (The grating through which confession is heard.) The fingers of the right open hand are spread slightly and placed with their backs resting diagonally across the front of the spread fingers of the left open hand, so as to form a grid held just to the side of the face, palms toward the face. *Cf.* CONFESSION 2, CONFESSIONAL.

[P–85]

PENCIL (pĕn′ səl), *n.* (The natural sign.) The right index finger and thumb, grasping an imaginary pencil, bring its tip to the tongue, as if wetting it. Still holding the "pencil," the right hand then goes through the natural motion of writing on the upturned left palm.

[P–86]

PENDING (pĕn′ dĭng), *prep., adj.* (The fingers wiggle with impatience.) The upturned "5" hands are positioned with the right behind the left. The fingers of both hands wiggle. *Cf.* WAIT.

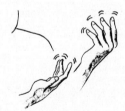

[P–87]

PENETRATE (pĕn′ ə trāt′), *v.,* -TRATED, -TRATING. (The natural sign.) The index finger of the right "1" hand is thrust between the middle and ring fingers of the left open hand, which is held with palm facing right, fingers held together and pointing upward. *Cf.* PIERCE.

[P–88]

PENIS (pē′ nĭs), *n.* (The shape is indicated.) Both "C" hands, palms up, are held in front of the body, the little finger edge of the right hand touching the index finger edge of the left. The right hand

moves forward a short distance, in a slight arc, while the left remains stationary.

[P–89]

PENITENT (pĕn′ ə tənt), *adj.* (The heart is circled, to indicate feeling, modified by the letter "S," for SORRY.) The right "S" hand, palm facing the body, is rotated several times over the area of the heart. *Cf.* APOLOGIZE 1, APOLOGY 1, CONTRITION, REGRET, REGRETFUL, REPENT, REPENTANT, RUE, SORROW, SORROWFUL 2, SORRY.

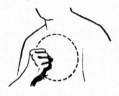

[P–90]

PENITENTIARY (pĕn′ ə tĕn′ shə rĭ), *n.* (The crossed bars.) The "4" hands, palms facing the body, are crossed at the fingers. *Cf.* IMPRISON, JAIL, PRISON.

[P–91]

PENNY (pĕn′ ĭ), *n.* (The Lincoln head.) The right index finger touches the right temple and moves up and away quickly. This is "one cent." For two cents, the "2" hand is used, etc. *Cf.* CENT, CENTS.

[P-92]

PEOPLE (pē′ pəl), *n. pl.* (The letter "P" in continuous motion, to indicate plurality.) The "P" hands, side by side, are moved alternately in continuous counterclockwise circles. *Cf.* AUDIENCE 2, HUMANITY, PUBLIC.

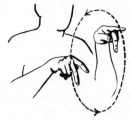

[P-93]

PEPPER (pĕp′ ər), *n.* (Something black which is shaken on food.) The sign for BLACK is made: The right index finger is drawn over the right eyebrow, from left to right. The right hand, grasping an imaginary shaker, then shakes the pepper on some unseen food. The sign for BLACK is frequently omitted.

[P-94]

PERCEIVE 1 (pər sēv′), *v.,* -CEIVED, -CEIVING. (The eyesight is directed forward.) The right "V" hand, palm facing the body, is placed so that the fingertips are just under the eyes. The hand swings around and out, so that the fingertips are now pointing forward. *Cf.* LOOK 1, PERCEPTION, SEE, SIGHT, WATCH 2.

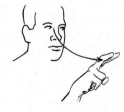

[P-95]

PERCEIVE 2, *v.* (The vision is directed forward, into the distance.) The right "V" fingertips are placed under the eyes, with palm facing the body. The hand is then swung around and forward, moving under the downturned prone left hand and continuing forward and upward. *Cf.* FORECAST, FORESEE, FORETELL, PREDICT, PROPHECY, PROPHESY, PROPHET, VISION 2.

[P-96]

PERCENT (pər sĕnt′), *n.* (Drawing a *percent* symbol in the air.) The right "O" hand traces the *percent* symbol (%) in the air. *Cf.* RATE 2.

[P-97]

PERCEPTION (pər sĕp′ shən), *n.* See PERCEIVE 1.

[P-98]

PERCH (pûrch), *n., v.,* PERCHED, PERCHING. (The bird's claws are draped over a perch.) The right index and middle fingers are draped over the left index finger. As this is done both hands may move down an inch or two, although this is optional.

[P–99]

PERFECT (*adj., n.* pûr' fĭkt; *v.* pər fĕkt'), -FECTED, -FECTING. (The letter "P"; the hands come into precise contact.) The "P" hands face each other. The right executes a clockwise circle above the stationary left, and then moves down so that the thumb and middle fingers of each hand come into precise contact.

[P–100]

PERFORM 1 (pər fôrm'), *v.*, -FORMED, -FORMING. (An activity.) Both open hands, palms down, are swung right and left before the chest. *Cf.* ACT 2, ACTION, ACTIVE, ACTIVITY, BUSY 2, CONDUCT 1, DEED, DO, PERFORMANCE 1, RENDER 2.

[P–101]

PERFORM 2, *v.* (Motion or movement, modified by the letter "A" for "act.") Both "A" hands, palms out, are held at shoulder height and rotate alternately toward the head. *Cf.* ACT 1, ACTOR, ACTRESS, DRAMA, PERFORMANCE 2, PLAY 2, SHOW 2.

[P–102]

PERFORMANCE 1 (pər fôr' məns), *n.* See PERFORM 1.

[P–103]

PERFORMANCE 2, *n.* See PERFORM 2.

[P–104]

PERFUME (pûr' fūm, pər fūm'), *n.,* (Act of smelling and pouring.) The right "A" hand, holding the neck of an imaginary bottle, is placed at the nose. The hand is then tipped over slightly against the chest. *Cf.* COLOGNE.

[P–105]

PERHAPS (pər hăps'), *adv.* (Weighing one thing against another.) The upturned open hands move alternately up and down. *Cf.* GUESS 4, MAY 1, MAYBE, MIGHT 2, POSSIBILITY, POSSIBLY, PROBABLE, PROBABLY, SUPPOSE.

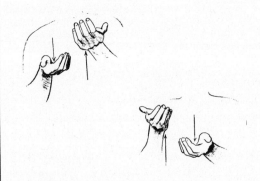

[P–106]

PERIL (pĕr' əl), *n.* (An encroachment; parrying a knife thrust.) The left "A" hand is held palm toward the body, knuckles facing right. The extended thumb of the right "A" hand is brought sharply over the back of the left. *Cf.* DANGER 2, DANGEROUS 2, IN-JURE 2, TRESPASS, VIOLATE.

[P-107]

PERIOD 1 (pǐr′ ǐ əd), *n.* (The natural motion of making a period in the air.) The right hand, holding an imaginary pencil, makes a dot in the air.

[P-108]

PERIOD 2, *n.* (Time in the abstract, indicated by the rotating of the "T" hand on the face of a clock.) The right "T" hand is placed palm to palm in the open left hand. It describes a clockwise circle and comes to rest again in the left palm. *Cf.* AGE 2, EPOCH, ERA, SEASON, TIME 2.

[P-109]

PERISH 1 (pěr′ ǐsh), *v.,* -ISHED, -ISHING. (Turning over on one's side.) The open hands, fingers pointing ahead, are held side by side, with the right palm down and the left palm up. The two hands reverse their relative positions as they move from the left to the right. *Cf.* DEAD 1, DEATH, DIE 1, DYING, EXPIRE 2.

[P-110]

PERISH 2, *v.* (Wiping off.) The left "5" hand, palm up, is held slightly above the right "5" hand, held palm down. The right hand swings up, just brushing over the left palm. Both hands close into the "S" position, and the right is brought back with force to its initial position, striking a glancing blow against the left knuckles as it returns. *Cf.* ABOLISH 1, ANNIHILATE, CORRUPT, DEFACE, DEMOLISH, DESTROY, HAVOC, REMOVE 3, RUIN.

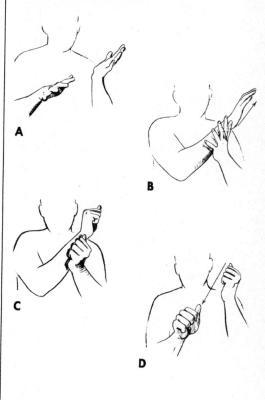

[P-111]

PERMANENT (pûr′ mə nənt), *adj.* (Steady, uninterrupted movement.) The "A" hands are held with palms out, thumbs extended and touching, the right behind the left. In this position the hands move forward in a straight, steady line. *Cf.* CONTINUE 1, ENDURE 2, EVER 1, LAST 3, LASTING, PERPETUAL, PERSEVERE 3, PERSIST 2, REMAIN, STAY 1, STAY STILL.

[P-112]

PERMISSION 1 (pər mĭsh′ ən), *n.* (A permissive upswinging of the hands, as if giving in.) Both hands, palms facing and fingers pointing away from the body, are held at chest level, almost a foot apart. With an upward movement, using their wrists as pivots, the hands sweep up until the fingers point almost straight up. *Cf.* ALLOW, GRANT 1, LET, LET'S, LET US, MAY 3, PERMIT 1, TOLERATE 1.

[P-113]

PERMISSION 2, *n.* (The "P" hands are used.) The same sign as in PERMISSION 1 is used, except with the "P" hands. *Cf.* PERMIT 2.

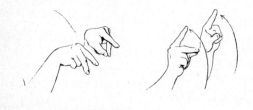

[P-114]

PERMIT 1 (pər mit′), *v.*, -MITTED, -MITTING. See PERMISSION 1.

[P-115]

PERMIT 2, *n.*, *v.* See PERMISSION 2.

[P-116]

PERPETUAL (pər pĕch′ o͞o əl), *adj.* (Steady, uninterrupted movement.) The "A" hands are held with palms out, thumbs extended and touching, the right behind the left. In this position the hands move forward in a straight, steady line. *Cf.* CONTINUE 1, ENDURE 2, EVER 1, LAST 3, LASTING, PERMANENT, PERSEVERE 3, PERSIST 2, REMAIN, STAY 1, STAY STILL.

[P-117]

PERSECUTE (pûr′ sə kūt′), *v.*, -CUTED, -CUTING. (Striking against one.) The knuckles of the right "A" hand move sharply forward along the thumb edge of the left "A" hand. The "X" hands may also be used. *Cf.* TEASE 1, TORMENT.

[P-118]

PERSEVERE 1 (pûr′ sə vĭr′), *v.*, -VERED, -VERING. (Trying to push through.) The "A" hands, palms facing before the body, are swung around and a bit down, so that the palms now face out. The movement indicates an attempt to push through a barrier. *Cf.* ATTEMPT 1, EFFORT 1, ENDEAVOR, PERSIST 1, TRY 1.

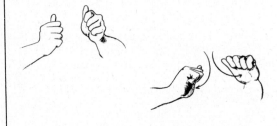

[P-119]

PERSEVERE 2, *v.* (Trying to push through, using the "T" hands, for "try.") This is the same sign as PERSEVERE 1, except that the "T" hands are employed. *Cf.* ATTEMPT 2, EFFORT 2, TRY 2.

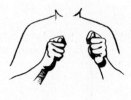

[P-120]

PERSEVERE 3, *v.* (Steady, uninterrupted movement.) The "A" hands are held with palms out, thumbs extended and touching, the right behind the left. In this position the hands move forward in a straight, steady line. Cf. CONTINUE 1, ENDURE 2, EVER 1, LAST 3, LASTING, PERMANENT, PERPETUAL, PERSIST 2, REMAIN, STAY 1, STAY STILL.

steady line. Cf. CONTINUE 1, ENDURE 2, EVER 1, LAST 3, LASTING, PERMANENT, PERPETUAL, PERSEVERE 3, REMAIN, STAY 1, STAY STILL.

[P-121]

PERSEVERE 4, v. (A thought directed upward, toward a goal.) The left "D" hand, palm facing the body, is held above the head, to represent the goal. The index finger of the right "D" hand, after touching the forehead (modified sign for THINK, q.v.), moves slowly and deliberately up to the tip of the left index finger. Cf. AIM, AMBITION, ASPIRE, GOAL, OBJECTIVE, PURPOSE 2.

[P-124]

PERSON (pûr' sən), n. (The letter "P"; an individual is indicated.) The "P" hands, side by side, move straight down a short distance, as if outlining the sides of an unseen individual.

[P-125]

PERSONALITY (pûr' sə nǎl' ə tǐ), n. (The letter "P"; the heart, i.e., character, is indicated.) The right "P" hand, palm down, executes a small counterclockwise circle against the heart.

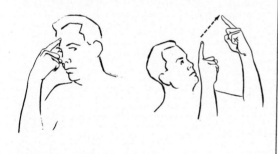

[P-122]

PERSIST 1 (pər sǐst', -zǐst'), v., -SISTED, -SISTING. (Trying to push through.) The "A" hands, palms facing before the body, are swung around and a bit down, so that the palms now face out. The movement indicates an attempt to push through a barrier. Cf. ATTEMPT 1, EFFORT 1, ENDEAVOR, PERSEVERE 1, TRY 1.

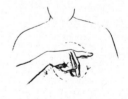

[P-126]

"PERSON" ENDING. Both open hands, palms facing each other, move down the sides of the body, tracing its outline to the hips.

[P-123]

PERSIST 2, v. (Steady, uninterrupted movement.) The "A" hands are held with palms out, thumbs extended and touching, the right behind the left. In this position the hands move forward in a straight,

[P–127]

PERSPIRATION 1 (pûr´ spə rā´ shən), *n*. See PER-SPIRE 1.

[P–128]

PERSPIRATION 2, *n*. See PERSPIRE 2.

[P–129]

PERSPIRE 1 (pər spīr´), *v*., -SPIRED, -SPIRING. (Wiping the brow.) The bent right index finger is drawn across the forehead from left to right and then shaken to the side, as if getting rid of the sweat. *Cf.* PERSPIRATION 1, SWEAT 1.

[P–130]

PERSPIRE 2, *v*. (Perspiration dripping from the brow.) The index finger edge of the open right hand wipes across the brow, and the same open hand then continues forcefully downward off the brow, its fingers wiggling, as if shaking off the perspiration gathered. *Cf.* PERSPIRATION 2, SWEAT 2.

[P–131]

PERSUADE (pər swād´), *v*., -SUADED, -SUADING. (Shaking someone, to implant one's will into another.) Both "A" hands, palms facing, are held before the chest, the left slightly in front of the right. In this position the hands move back and forth a short distance. *Cf.* COAX, CONVINCE, INDUCE, PERSUASION, PROD, URGE 2.

[P–132]

PERSUASION (pər swā´ zhən), *n*. See PERSUADE.

[P–133]

PEST (pĕst), *(colloq.), n*. (Spitting out, in an attempt to drive away an annoyance.) The thumb of the right "5" hand rests under the chin, with palm facing left. The hand moves forward sharply. An expression of annoyance is assumed throughout.

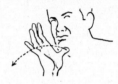

[P–134]

PET (pĕt), *n., adj., v.,* PETTED, PETTING. (Stroking a person or the head of a pet.) The right hand strokes the back of the left several times. *Cf.* DEAR 1, FOND 1, STROKE 2, TAME.

[P–135]

PETTING (pĕt´ ĭng), *(sl.), v*. (Necks interlocked.) The "S" hands, palms facing, are crossed at the wrists. They swing up and down while the wrists remain in contact. *Cf.* MAKE LOVE 2, NECKING.

[P-136]

PETTY (pĕt′ ĭ), *adj.* (Indicating a small mass.) The extended right thumb and index finger are held slightly spread. They are then moved slowly toward each other until they almost touch. *Cf.* SLIGHT, SMALL 1, TINY 2.

[P-137]

PHILADELPHIA (fĭl′ ə dĕl′ fĭ ə), *n.* The right "P" hand moves down in a quick, curved, right-left-right manner.

[P-138]

PHILOSOPHY (fĭ lŏs′ ə fĭ), *n.* (The letter "P"; the mind is measured for its depth.) The right "P" hand, palm facing left, is held at the middle of the forehead. It moves alternately up and down a short distance.

[P-139]

PHOENIX (fē′ nĭks), *(loc.), n.* The right "X" hand is shaken slightly back and forth.

[P-140]

PHONE 1 (fōn), *n., v.,* PHONED, PHONING. (The natural sign.) The left "S" hand represents the mouthpiece and is placed at the mouth, with palm facing right. Its right counterpart represents the earpiece and is placed at the right ear, with palm facing forward. This is the old fashioned two-piece telephone. *Cf.* TELEPHONE 1.

[P-141]

PHONE 2, *n., v.* (The natural sign.) The right "Y" hand is placed at the right side of the head with the thumb touching the ear and the little finger touching the lips. This is the more modern telephone receiver. *Cf.* TELEPHONE 2.

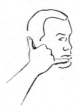

[P-142]

PHOTOCOPY (fō′ tə kŏp′ ĭ), *n.* (Taking up an image.) The prone open right hand is held about a foot below the prone open left hand. The right hand moves up into sharp contact with the left, closing into the "0" position. *Cf.* PHOTOSTAT.

[P–143]

PHOTOGRAPH 1 (fō′ tə grăf′), *n.*, *v.*, -GRAPHED, -GRAPHING. (Recording an image.) The right "C" hand is held in front of the face, with thumb edge near the face and palm facing left. The hand is then brought sharply around in front of the open left hand and is struck firmly against the left palm, which is held facing forward with fingers pointing up. *Cf.* PICTURE 1.

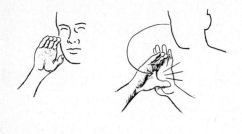

[P–144]

PHOTOGRAPH 2, *n.* (Recording an image.) The right "C" hand or crooked index finger is drawn down over the face. The hand is then brought sharply around in front of the open left hand and is struck firmly against the left palm, which is held facing forward with fingers pointing up. (In Step 1, the right "C" hand or index finger may simply touch the bridge of the nose instead of moving down over the face.) *Cf.* PICTURE 2.

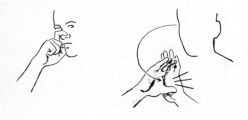

[P–145]

PHOTOGRAPH 3, *v.* (Capturing an image) Both open hands are held before the body, fingers pointing upward, the right hand positioned in front of the left. The right hand then moves forcefully backward against the left palm, closing into the "AND" position as it does. *Cf.* TAKE A PICTURE.

[P–146]

PHOTOSTAT (fō′ tə stăt′), *n.* See PHOTOCOPY.

[P–147]

PHYLACTERIES (fə lăk′ tə rĭz), *(eccles.)*, *n. pl.* (The items are described.) The fingertips of the open right hand are placed in mid-forehead, and are then placed against the left biceps. The right hand, holding the imaginary thongs, winds around the lower left arm a number of times. *Cf.* TEFILLIN.

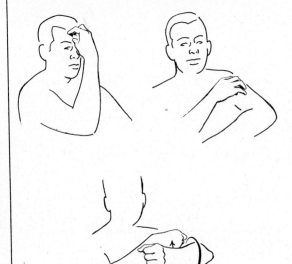

[P–148]

PHYSICAL (fĭz′ ə kəl), *adj.* (The body is indicated.) One or both hands are placed against the chest and then are removed and replaced at a point a bit below the first. *Cf.* BODY.

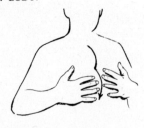

[P–149]

PHYSICAL BREAKDOWN, *n. phrase.* (The body collapses.) The sign for BODY is made: One or both hands are placed against the chest and then are removed and replaced at a point a bit below the first. Then the sign for BREAKDOWN is made: Both "5" hands, fingertips joined before the chest, swing down so that the fingertips face down.

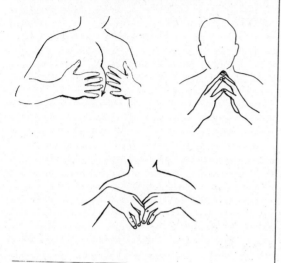

[P–152]

PIANO (pǐ ăn′ ō), *n.* (The natural sign.) The downturned hands go through the natural movements involved in manipulating a piano keyboard.

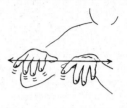

[P–153]

PICK 1 (pǐk), *v.*, PICKED, PICKING. (The natural motion of selecting something from the hand.) The thumb and index fingers of the outstretched right hand grasp an imaginary object on the upturned left palm. The right hand then moves straight up. *Cf.* CHOOSE 2, DISCOVER, FIND, SELECT 1.

[P–150]

PHYSICS (fǐz′ ǐks), *n.* (The points of the electrodes.) The "X" hands are held palms facing the body, thumb edges up. The knuckles of the index fingers touch each other repeatedly. *Cf.* ELECTRIC, ELECTRICITY.

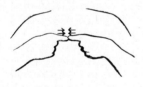

[P–151]

PIANIST (pǐ ăn′ ǐst, pē′ ə nǐst), *n.* The sign for PIANO is made, followed by the sign for INDIVIDUAL: Both open hands, palms facing each other, move down the sides of the body, tracing its outline to the hips.

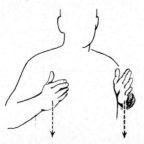

[P–154]

PICK 2, *v.* (The natural sign.) The fingertips and thumbtip of the downturned open right hand come together, and the hand moves up a short distance, as if picking something. *Cf.* PICK UP 2, SELECT 3.

[P-155]

PICKET (pĭk′ ĭt), *v.,* -ETED, -ETING. (Holding a picket's sign.) Both upright hands grasp the stick of an imaginary display sign. The hands move forward and back repeatedly against the chest. This movement represents the walking back and forth of a striker or picket. *Cf.* STRIKE 2.

[P-156]

PICKLE (pĭk′ əl), *n., v.* -LED, -LING. (Something sour or bitter.) The right index finger is brought sharply up against the lips, while the mouth is puckered up as if tasting something sour. The thumb and index finger may then indicate the length of the pickle. *Cf.* ACID, BITTER, DISAPPOINTED 1, LEMON 1, SOUR.

[P-157]

PICK ON (pĭk), *v., phrase.* (The hen's beak pecks.) The index finger and thumb of the right hand, held together, are brought against the index finger of the left "D" hand a number of times. *Cf.* HENPECK, NAG, PECK.

 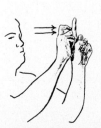

[P-158]

PICK OUT, *v. phrase.* (The natural sign.) The palm of the left "5" hand faces the body. The right thumb and index finger move toward one of the fingers of the left hand, close, and move back toward the body. They do not, however, touch the finger they select.

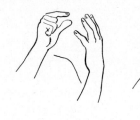

[P-159]

PICK UP 1, *v. phrase.* (To take up.) Both hands, held palms down in the "5" position, are at chest level. With a grasping upward movement, both close into "S" positions before the face. *Cf.* ASSUME, TAKE UP.

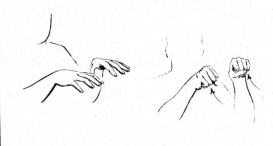

[P-160]

PICK UP 2, *v. phrase.* See PICK 2.

[P-161]

PICNIC 1 (pĭk′ nĭk), *(rare), n., v.,* -NICKED, -NICKING. (Holding a gun—because cadets led the picnic crowd.) Both fists are struck against the left side of the chest, with the left hand positioned above the right, as if holding a rifle over the shoulder.

[P-162]

PICNIC 2, *n.* (Playing a fife.) The thumbs and fingers of both hands grasp an imaginary fife and hold it to the mouth. The fingers move up and down, as if playing the instrument, and the signer purses his lips as if blowing. *Cf.* FIFE.

[P-163]

PICTURE 1 (pĭk′ chər), *n.*, *v.*, -TURED, -TURING. (Recording an image.) The right "C" hand is held in front of the face, with thumb edge near the face and palm facing left. The hand is then brought sharply around in front of the open left hand and is struck firmly against the left palm, which is held facing forward with fingers pointing up. *Cf.* PHOTOGRAPH 1.

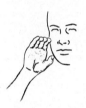 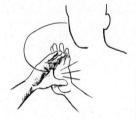

[P-164]

PICTURE 2, *n.* (Recording an image.) The right "C" hand or crooked index finger is drawn down over the face. The hand is then brought sharply around in front of the open left hand and is struck firmly against the left palm, which is held facing forward with fingers pointing up. (In Step 1, the right "C" hand or index finger may simply touch the bridge of the nose instead of moving down over the face.) *Cf.* PHOTOGRAPH 2.

[P-165]

PIE 1 (pī), *n.* (Slicing a wedge-shaped piece of pie.) The upturned left hand represents the pie. The little finger edge of the open right hand goes through the motions of slicing a wedge-shaped piece from the pie.

[P-166]

PIE 2, *(loc.), n.* (The letter "K," the last initial of an instructor of baking at a school for the deaf.) The middle finger of the right "K" hand touches the right cheek twice. *Cf.* CAKE 2.

[P-167]

PIECE (pēs), *n.*, *v.*, PIECED, PIECING. (Cutting off or designating a part.) The little finger edge of the open right hand moves straight down the middle of the upturned left palm. *Cf.* PART 1, PORTION, SECTION, SHARE 1, SOME.

[P-168]

PIERCE (pĭrs), *v.*, PIERCED, PIERCING. (The natural sign.) The index finger of the right "1" hand is thrust between the middle and ring fingers of the left open hand, which is held with palm facing right, fingers held together and pointing upward. *Cf.* PENETRATE.

[P-169]

PIG 1 (pĭg), *n.* (The snout digs into the trough.) The downturned right prone hand is placed under the chin, fingers pointing forward. The hand, in this position, swings alternately up and down. *Cf.* HOG 1.

[P-170]

PIG 2, *n.* (Same rationale as for PIG 1.) The sign for PIG 1 is repeated, except that the fingers point to the left. *Cf.* HOG 2.

[P-171]

PIGEON (pĭj′ ən), *n.* (The beak and puffed-out breast.) The sign for BIRD is made: The right thumb and index finger are placed against the mouth, pointing straight out. They open and close, imitating the beak. Then the open right hand is placed beside the

right cheek. It swings down in a curving arc, coming to rest with the fingertips at the right breast.

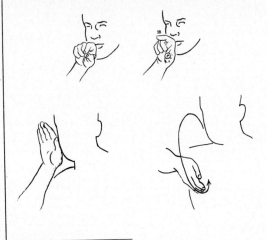

[P-172]

PILE OF MONEY, *(colloq.), n. phrase.* (The height of the pile is indicated.) The sign for MONEY 1 is made: The fingertips of the right hand, palm up, touch the right thumb, and the back of the right hand, in this position, is brought down into the up-turned left palm. The hands then open, with palms facing each other and fingers curved. The right hand moves straight up from the left, which remains stationary.

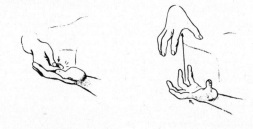

[P-173]

PILL (pĭl), *n.* (The natural sign.) The right thumb and index finger go through the motion of popping an imaginary pill into the open mouth. *Cf.* TAKE A PILL.

[P-174]

PILOT (pī′ lət), *n.* (An individual who flies a plane.) The sign for either AIRPLANE 1 or AIRPLANE 2 is made, and this is followed by the sign for INDI-VIDUAL: Both open hands, palms facing each other, move down the sides of the body, tracing its outline to the hips. *Cf.* AVIATOR, FLIER.

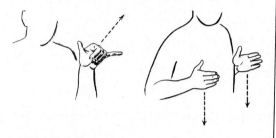

[P-175]

PIN 1 (pĭn), *n., v.,* PINNED, PINNING. (The natural sign.) The right thumb and index finger go through the motion of pushing a pin down into the clothing, just above the heart.

[P-176]

PIN 2, *n., v.* (The shape and location of the item.) The thumb and index finger of one hand form a circle, and are placed against the chest. The hand then moves down an inch. *Cf.* BROOCH.

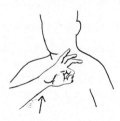

[P-177]

PIN 3, *(sports), v.* (Pinning one's opponent in wres-tling.) Both "A" or "S" hands, extended before the body, palms facing each other or held slightly to the side, move down forcefully an inch or two, as if

grasping someone by the ankles and forcing his shoulders to touch the ground. *Cf.* THROW 3.

[P-178]

PING-PONG (pĭng′ pŏng′), *n.* (The natural sign.) The signer goes through the actions involved in play-ing table tennis or Ping-Pong. *Cf.* TABLE TENNIS.

[P-179]

PINK (pĭngk), *adj.* (The letter "P," at the lips, which are red or pink.) The middle finger of the right "P" hand moves down over the lips a number of times.

[P-180]

PIOUS (pī′ əs), *adj.* (Worshiping.) The hands are clasped together, with the left cupped over the right. Both are brought in toward the body, while the eyes are shut and the head is bowed slightly. *Cf.* ADORE, AMEN, DEVOUT, WORSHIP.

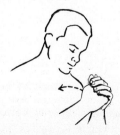

[P-181]

PIPE 1 (pīp), *n.* (The stem and bowl are held at the lips.) The right "Y" hand is held with thumb touching the lips.

[P-182]

PIPE 2, *n.* (The natural sign.) The thumbtips and index fingertips of the both open hands are held together, forming two circles side by side before the body, palms facing out. From this position the hands move apart to either side, outlining a straight rod. *Cf.* ROD.

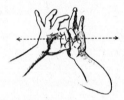

[P-183]

PIPE-FITTING, *(voc.), n.* (The natural movement.) The index finger of the right hand is grasped by the outstretched index and middle fingers of the left hand. The left hand executes a series of up-and-down movements, as if manipulating a wrench. *Cf.* MECHANIC 2, PLUMBER, STEAM FITTER, WRENCH.

[P-184]

PISTOL (pis' təl), *n.* (Shooting a gun.) The right "L" hand is held before the body, its index finger

moving back and forth, as if pulling a trigger. *Cf.* GUN, RIFLE, SHOOT 2, SHOT 2.

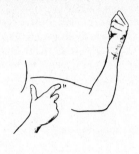

[P-185]

PITCH (pĭch), *v.,* PITCHED, PITCHING. (The natural sign.) The signer goes through the natural motions of throwing a ball. *Cf.* THROW 1.

[P-186]

PITTSBURGH (pĭts' bûrg), *n.* The right "F" hand, palm facing down, is moved up and down against the left breast.

[P-187]

PITY (pĭt' ĭ), *n., v.,* PITIED, PITYING. (Feelings from the heart, conferred on others.) The middle fingertip of the open right hand touches the chest over the heart. The same open hand then moves in a small, clockwise circle before the right shoulder, with palm facing forward and fingers pointing up. *Cf.* MERCY 2, POOR 3, SYMPATHY 2.

[P-188]

PLACE 1 (plās), *n.* (The letter "P"; a circle or square is indicated, to show the locale or place.) The "P" hands are held side by side before the body, with middle fingertips touching. From this position, the hands separate and outline a circle (or a square), before coming together again closer to the body. *Cf.* LOCATION, POSITION 1, SCENE, SITE.

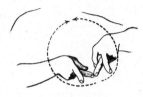

[P-189]

PLACE 2, *n.* (An area is outlined.) With the "I" hands held palms up and the tips of the little fingers touching, the hands separate as they move in toward the body. As they do, the tips of the little fingers come together again. *Cf.* POSITION 2.

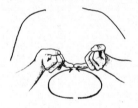

[P-190]

PLACE 3, *v.*, PLACED, PLACING. (Moving from one place to another.) The downturned hands, fingers touching their respective thumbs, move in unison from left to right. *Cf.* MIGRATE, MOVE, PUT, REMOVE 2, TRANSFER 2.

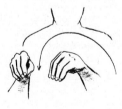

[P-191]

PLAIN 1 (plān), *adj.* (Rays of light clearing the way.) Both hands are held at chest height, palms out, all fingertips together. They open into the "5" position in unison, the right hand moving toward the right and the left toward the left. The palms of both hands remain facing out. *Cf.* BRIGHT 1, BRILLIANCE 1, BRILLIANT 2, CLEAR, EXPLICIT 2, OBVIOUS.

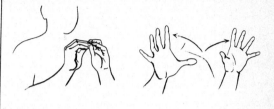

[P-192]

PLAIN 2, *adj.* (Everything is wiped off the hand, to emphasize an uncluttered or clean condition.) The right hand slowly wipes the upturned left palm, from wrist to fingertips. *Cf.* CLEAN 1, IMMACULATE, NEAT, NICE, PURE 1, PURITY, SIMPLE 2.

[P-193]

PLAN 1 (plăn), *n., v.,* PLANNED, PLANNING. (Placing things in order.) The hands, palms facing, fingers together and pointing away from the body, are positioned at the left side and held about a foot apart. With a slight up-down motion, as if describing waves, the hands travel in unison from left to right. *Cf.* ARRANGE, ARRANGEMENT, CLASSED 2, DEVISE 1, ORDER 3, POLICY 1, PREPARE 1, PROGRAM 1, PROVIDE 1, PUT IN ORDER, READY 1, SCHEME, SYSTEM.

[P-194]

PLAN 2, *n., v.* (The initial "P.") PLAN 1 is repeated, except with the "P" hands, palms down.

[P-195]

PLANE 1 (plān), *n*. (The wings of the airplane.) The "Y" hand, palm down and drawn up near the shoulder, moves forward, up and away from the body. Either hand may be used. *Cf.* AIRPLANE 1, FLY 1.

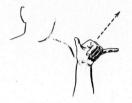

[P-196]

PLANE 2, *n*. (The wings and fuselage of the airplane.) The hand assumes the same position as in PLANE 1, but the index finger is also extended, to represent the fuselage of the airplane. Either hand may be used, and the movement is the same as in PLANE 1. *Cf.* AIRPLANE 2, FLY 2.

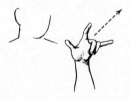

[P-197]

PLANE 3, *(voc.)*, *n.*, *v.*, PLANED, PLANING. (The natural motion.) The left "S" hand moves forward forcefully over the open right palm, from wrist to fingertips. The movement is repeated. This is the carpenter's plane.

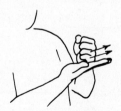

[P-198]

PLANET (plăn′ĭt), *n*. (The earth and its axes are indicated.) The downturned left "S" hand indicates the earth. The thumb and index finger of the downturned right "5" hand are placed at each edge of the left. In this position the right hand swings back and forth, while maintaining contact with the left. *Cf.* EARTH 1, GEOGRAPHY, GLOBE 1.

[P-199]

PLANT 1 (plănt), *n*. (Flowers or plants emerge from the ground.) The right fingers, pointing up, emerge from the closed left hand, and they spread open as they do. *Cf.* BLOOM, DEVELOP 1, GROW, GROWN, MATURE, RAISE 3, REAR 2, SPRING 1.

[P-200]

PLANT 2, *v.*, PLANTED, PLANTING. (Placing the seed into the ground.) The right hand, holding some imaginary seeds, is thrust into the cupped left hand.

[P–201]

PLATE (plāt), *n.* (The material and shape.) The sign for GLASS or PORCELAIN is made: The index finger is brought up to touch the exposed front teeth. The downturned index fingers then describe the circular shape of the plate.

[P–202]

PLAY 1 (plā), *v.,* PLAYED, PLAYING. (Shaking tambourines.) The "Y" hands, held aloft, are shaken back and forth, pivoted at the wrists. *Cf.* FROLIC, RECREATION.

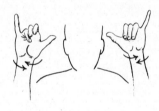

[P–203]

PLAY 2, *n.* (Motion or movement, modified by the letter "A" for "act.") Both "A" hands, palms out, are held at shoulder height and rotate alternately toward the head. *Cf.* ACT 1, ACTOR, ACTRESS, DRAMA, PERFORM 2, PERFORMANCE 2, SHOW 2.

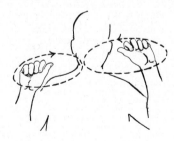

[P–204]

PLAYER (plā' ər), *n.* The sign for PLAY 1 is made, followed by the sign for INDIVIDUAL: Both open hands, palms facing each other, move down the sides of the body, tracing its outline to the hips.

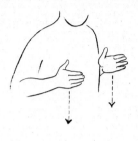

[P–205]

PLAYING CARDS, *n. pl.* (The action of dealing out cards.) The signer goes through the motions of dealing out imaginary playing cards. *Cf.* CARD PLAYING, CARDS, DISTRIBUTE 2.

[P–206]

PLEA (plē), *n.* (An act of supplication.) With the right hand clasped over the left, both hands are shaken gently before the body. The eyes often are directed upward. *Cf.* BEG 2, BESEECH, ENTREAT, IMPLORE, PLEAD, SUPPLICATION.

[P-207]

PLEAD (plēd), *v.*, PLEADED, PLEADING. See PLEA.

[P-208]

PLEASANT (plĕz' ənt), *adj.* (A crinkling-up of the face.) Both hands, in the "5" position, palms facing back, are placed on either side of the face. The fingers wiggle back and forth, while a pleasant, happy expression is worn. *Cf.* AMIABLE, CHEERFUL, CORDIAL, FRIENDLY, JOLLY.

[P-209]

PLEASE (plēz), *v.*, PLEASED, PLEASING. (A pleasurable feeling on the heart.) The open right hand is circled on the chest, over the heart. *Cf.* APPRECIATE, ENJOY, ENJOYMENT, GRATIFY 1, LIKE 3, PLEASURE, WILLING 2.

[P-210]

PLEASURE (plĕzh' ər), *n.* See PLEASE.

[P-211]

PLEDGE (plĕj), *n., v.*, PLEDGED, PLEDGING. (The arm is raised.) The right index finger is placed at the lips. The right arm is then raised, palm out and elbow resting on the back of the left hand. *Cf.* GUARANTEE 1, LOYAL, OATH, PROMISE 1, SWEAR 1, SWORN, TAKE OATH, VOW.

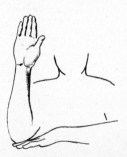

[P-212]

PLENTY (plĕn' tĭ), *n., adj., adv.* (A full cup.) The left hand, in the "S" position, is held palm facing right. The right "5" hand, palm down, is brushed outward several times over the top of the left, indicating a wiping off of the top of a cup. *Cf.* ABUNDANCE, ABUNDANT, ADEQUATE, AMPLE, ENOUGH, SUBSTANTIAL, SUFFICIENT.

[P-213]

PLIERS (plī' ərs), *(voc.), n., pl.* (The natural sign.) The right hand, opening and closing forcefully, goes through the natural motion of manipulating a pair of pliers. *Cf.* SHEARS 1, SNIPS.

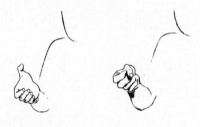

[P-214]

PLOW (plou), *n.* (The action of the plow's blade in making a furrow.) The open right hand is placed upright in a perpendicular position on the upturned left palm, with the little finger edge resting in the palm. The right hand moves forward along the left palm. As it does so, it swings over to a palm-down position, and moves off a bit to the right. *Cf.* FARM 1.

[P–215]

PLOWER (plou′ ər), *n.* The sign for PLOW is made. This is followed by the sign for INDIVIDUAL: Both open hands, palms facing each other, move down the sides of the body, tracing its outline to the hips.

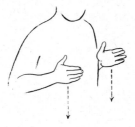

[P–216]

PLUMBER (plŭm′ ər), *n.* (The natural movement.) The index finger of the right hand is grasped by the outstretched index and middle fingers of the left hand. The left hand executes a series of up-and-down movements, as if manipulating a wrench. This is followed by the sign for INDIVIDUAL: Both open hands, palms facing each other, move down the sides of the body, tracing its outline to the hips. *Cf.* MECHANIC 2, PIPE-FITTING, STEAM FITTER, WRENCH.

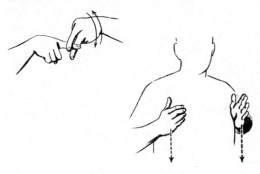

[P–217]

PLUNGE (plŭnj), *(sports), v.,* PLUNGED, PLUNGING. (Plunging through the line, in football.) The right "S" hand is thrust forcefully through the upturned left "C" hand.

[P–218]

PLURAL (plŏŏr′ əl), *adj.* (Many fingers are indicated.) The upturned "S" hands are thrown up, opening into the "5" position, palms up. This may be repeated. *Cf.* MANY, MULTIPLE, NUMEROUS, QUANTITY 2.

[P–219]

PLUS (plŭs), *prep., n.* (A mathematical symbol.) The two index fingers are crossed at right angles. *Cf.* ADD 2, ADDITION, POSITIVE 2.

[P–220]

PNEUMONIA (nū mō′ nyə), *n.* (The natural sign.) The fingertips of the "5" hands, palms facing the body, move alternately up and down on either side of the chest to denote the position of the lungs. *Cf.* LUNGS.

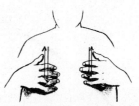

[P–221]

POCKET (pŏk' ĭt), *n., v.,* -ETED, -ETING. (The natural sign.) The hand is thrust into a pocket.

[P–222]

POEM (pō' ĭm), *n.* (The letter "P"; the waving hand denotes rhythm.) The right "P" hand swings back and forth rhythmically over the open left hand, whose palm faces the body. The right hand may also describe a figure-eight movement instead of the back-and-forth movement. *Cf.* POETRY, PSALM.

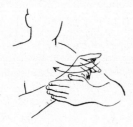

[P–223]

POETRY (pō' ĭt rĭ), *n.* See POEM.

[P–224]

POINT 1 (point), *v.,* POINTED, POINTING. (The natural sign.) The index finger of either hand makes a simple pointing motion.

[P–225]

POINT 2, *n.* (A tapering or sharp point is indicated.) The index finger and thumb of the left hand grasp the tip of the index finger of the right "D" hand. The left hand then moves away a short distance, and its index finger and thumb come together. *Cf.* SHARP 2, TIP.

[P–226]

POINT 3, *n.* (A jutting piece of land.) The sign for LAND is made: Both hands, held upright before the body, finger imaginary pinches of soil. The open hands, fingers outstretched and palms facing, then move forward, coming together at the fingertips, as if describing the point of a triangle.

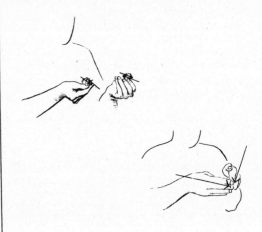

[P–227]

POISON 1 (poi' zən), *n.* (Mixing of medicine; rolling a pill.) The ball of the middle fingertip of the right "5" hand describes a small counterclockwise circle in the upturned left palm. *Cf.* DRUG, MEDICINE, PRESCRIPTION.

[P-228]

POISON 2, *n.* (The letter "P"; something taken by mouth.) The middle finger and thumb of the right "P" hand touch the lips repeatedly.

[P-229]

POLAND (pō' lənd), *n.* (The upturned nose, said to be a common characteristic of Poles.) The thumbtip of the right "A" hand moves up off the nose a number of times. *Cf.* POLE, POLISH 2.

[P-230]

POLE (pōl), *n.* See POLAND.

[P-231]

POLICE (pə lēs'), *n., v.,* -LICED, -LICING. (The letter "C" for "cop"; the shape and position of the badge.) The right "C" hand, palm facing left, is placed against the heart. *Cf.* COP, POLICEMAN, SHERIFF.

[P-232]

POLICEMAN (pə lēs' mən), *n.* See POLICE.

[P-233]

POLICY 1 (pŏl' ə sĭ), *n.* (Placing things in order.) The hands, palms facing, fingers together and pointing away from the body, are positioned at the left side and held about a foot apart. With a slight up-down motion, as if describing waves, the hands travel in unison from left to right. *Cf.* ARRANGE, ARRANGEMENT, CLASSED 2, DEVISE 1, ORDER 3, PLAN 1, PREPARE 1, PROGRAM 1, PROVIDE 1, PUT IN ORDER, READY 1, SCHEME, SYSTEM.

[P-234]

POLICY 2, *n.* (A thought coming forward from the mind, modified by the letter "I" for "idea.") With the "I" position on the right hand, palm facing the body, touch the little finger to the forehead, and then move the hand up and away in a circular, clockwise motion. The hand may also be moved up and away without this circular motion. *Cf.* CONCEIVE 2, CONCEPT 1, CONCEPTION, FANCY 2, IDEA, IMAGINATION, IMAGINE 1, JUST THINK OF IT!, NOTION, THEORY, THOUGHT 2.

[P-235]

POLISH 1 (pŏl' ĭsh), *(voc.), n., v.,* -ISHED, -ISHING. (The act of rubbing.) The right knuckles rub briskly against the outstretched left palm. *Cf.* RUB, SANDPAPER, SHINE SHOES.

[P-236]

POLISH 2 (pō′ lĭsh), *adj.* See POLAND.

[P-237]

POLITE (pə līt′), *adj.* (The ruffled shirt front of a gentleman of old.) The thumb of the right "5" hand is thrust into the chest. The hand then pivots down, with thumb remaining in place. This latter part of the sign, however, is optional. *Cf.* COURTEOUS, COURTESY, FINE 4.

[P-238]

PONDER (pŏn′ dər), *v.,* -DERED, -DERING. (Turning thoughts over in the mind.) Both index fingers, pointing to the forehead, describe continuous alternating circles. *Cf.* CONSIDER 2, CONTEMPLATE, SPECULATE 2, SPECULATION 2, WEIGH 2, WONDER 1.

[P-239]

PONTIFF (pŏn′ tĭf), *n.* (The triple crown.) The cupped hands are held at the sides of the head. The fingertips come together three times as the hands move up in successive stages. *Cf.* PAPAL, POPE.

[P-240]

POOL (pōōl), *v.,* POOLED, POOLING. (Paying in.) The "AND" hands are held about a foot apart in front of the body, with fingertips facing each other and palms toward the chest. From this position the hands move downward and toward each other in an arc. At the same time, both thumbs slide forward along the index fingers. *Cf.* CHIP IN.

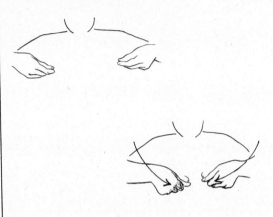

[P-241]

POOR 1 (pōōr), *adj.* (Ragged elbows.) The open right hand is placed at the left elbow. It moves down and off, closing into the "O" position. *Cf.* POVERTY 1.

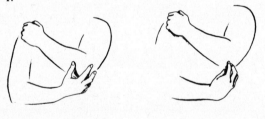

[P-242]

POOR 2, *adj.* (The drawn face.) The thumb and index finger run down the cheeks, which are drawn in. *Cf.* LEAN 1, THIN 1.

[P-243]

POOR 3, *adj.* (Feelings from the heart, conferred on others.) The middle fingertip of the open right hand touches the chest over the heart. The same open hand then moves in a small, clockwise circle before the right shoulder, with palm facing forward and fingers pointing up. *Cf.* MERCY 2, PITY, SYMPATHY 2.

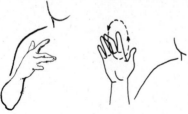

[P-244]

POP 1 (pŏp), *n.* (Corking a bottle.) The left "O" hand is held with thumb edge up, representing a bottle. The thumb and index finger of the right "5" hand represent a cork, and are inserted into the circle formed by the "O" hand. The palm of the open right hand then strikes down on the upturned edge of the "O" hand, as if forcing the cork into the bottle. *Cf.* SODA POP, SODA WATER.

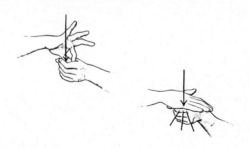

[P-245]

POP 2, (*informal*), *n.* (Derived from the formal sign for FATHER 1, *q.v.*) The thumbtip of the right "5" hand touches the right temple a number of times. The other fingers may also wiggle. *Cf.* DAD, DADDY, FATHER 2, PAPA.

[P-246]

POPE (pōp), *n.* (The triple crown.) The cupped hands are held at the sides of the head. The fingertips come together three times as the hands move up in successive stages. *Cf.* PAPAL, PONTIFF.

[P-247]

POPULATION (pŏp′ yə lā′ shən), *n.* (The letter "P"; an encompassing movement.) The "P" hands are held side by side, palms facing out. They swing out and around, describing a circle, and come together with little finger edges touching.

[P-248]

POP UP, (*colloq.*), *v.* (Popping up before the eyes.) The right index finger, pointing up, pops up between the index and middle fingers of the left hand, whose palm faces down. *Cf.* APPEAR 2, RISE 2.

[P-249]

PORCELAIN (pōr′ sə lĭn, pōrs′ lĭn), *n*. (The finger touches a brittle substance.) The index finger is brought up to touch the exposed front teeth. *Cf.* BONE, CHINA 2, DISH, GLASS 1, PLATE.

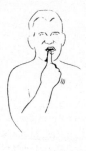

[P-250]

PORTION (pōr′ shən), *n*. (Cutting off or designating a part.) The little finger edge of the open right hand moves straight down the middle of the upturned left palm. *Cf.* PART 1, PIECE, SECTION, SHARE 1, SOME.

[P-251]

POSITION 1 (pə zĭsh′ ən), *n*. (The letter "P"; a circle or square is indicated, to show the locale or place.) The "P" hands are held side by side before the body, with middle fingertips touching. From this position, the hands separate and outline a circle (or a square), before coming together again closer to the body. *Cf.* LOCATION, PLACE 1, SCENE, SITE.

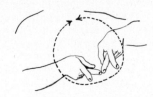

[P-252]

POSITION 2, *n*. (An area is outlined.) With the "I" hands held palms up and the tips of the little fingers

touching, the hands separate as they move in toward the body. As they do, the tips of the little fingers come together again. *Cf.* PLACE 2.

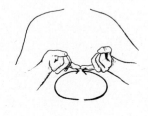

[P-253]

POSITION 3, *n*. (The feet planted on the ground.) The downturned right "V" fingers are thrust into the upturned left palm. *Cf.* STAND 1, STANDING.

[P-254]

POSITIVE 1 (pŏz′ ə tĭv), *adj*. (Coming forth directly from the lips; true.) The index finger of the right "D" hand, palm facing left, is placed against the lips. It moves up an inch or two and then describes a small arc forward and away from the lips. *Cf.* ABSOLUTE, ABSOLUTELY, ACTUAL, ACTUALLY, AUTHENTIC, CERTAIN, CERTAINLY, FAITHFUL 3, FIDELITY, FRANKLY, GENUINE, INDEED, POSITIVELY, REAL, REALLY, SINCERE 2, SURE, SURELY, TRUE, TRULY, TRUTH, VALID, VERILY.

[P-255]

POSITIVE 2, *adj.* (A mathematical symbol.) The two index fingers are crossed at right angles in the sign for PLUS. *Cf.* ADD 2, ADDITION, PLUS.

[P-256]

POSITIVELY, *adv.* See POSITIVE 1.

[P-257]

POSSESS 1 (pə zĕs'), *v.*, -SESSED, -SESSING. (A modification of HAVE 1.) The hands are crossed over each other as they rest on the chest. *Cf.* HAVE 3.

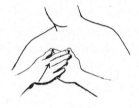

[P-258]

POSSESS 2, *v.* (The act of bringing something over to oneself.) The right-angle hands, palms facing and thumbs pointing up, are swept toward the body until the fingertips come to rest against the middle of the chest. *Cf.* HAVE 1.

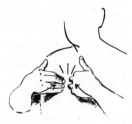

[P-259]

POSSIBILITY (pŏs' ə bĭl' ə tĭ), n. (Weighing one thing against another.) The upturned open hands move alternately up and down. *Cf.* GUESS 4, MAY 1, MAYBE, MIGHT 2, PERHAPS, POSSIBLY, PROBABLE, PROBABLY, SUPPOSE.

[P-260]

POSSIBLE (pŏs' ə bəl), *adj.* (An affirmative movement of the hands, likened to a nodding of the head, to indicate ability or power to accomplish something.) Both "A" hands, held palms down, move down in unison a short distance before the chest. *Cf.* ABILITY, ABLE, CAN 1, CAPABLE, COMPETENT, COULD, FACULTY, MAY 2.

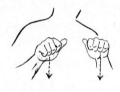

[P-261]

POSSIBLY (pŏs' ə blĭ), *adv.* See POSSIBILITY.

[P-262]

POST (pōst), *n.* (Sending a letter.) The sign for LETTER is made: The right thumbtip is licked and placed against the upturned left palm. The right hand, palm out and fingers touching thumb, is then thrown forward, opening into the "5" position, palm out. *Cf.* MAIL 2.

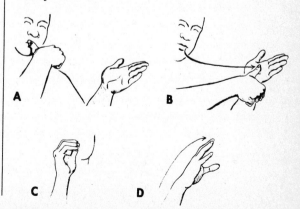

[P–263]

POSTPONE (pōst pōn′), *v.*, -PONED, -PONING. (Putting off; moving things forward repeatedly.) The "F" hands, palms facing and fingers pointing out from the body, are moved forward simultaneously in a series of short movements. *Cf.* DEFER, DELAY, PROCRASTINATE, PUT OFF.

[P–264]

POT (pŏt), *n.* (The natural shape.) The cupped hands form a bowl and move up a bit to indicate the height. *Cf.* BOWL 1.

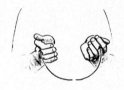

[P–265]

POTATO (pə tā′ tō), *n.* (The fork is thrust into the potato.) The downturned left "S" hand represents the potato. The slightly bent fingers of the right "V" hand are thrust repeatedly against the back of the left hand.

[P–266]

POUND 1 (pound), *n.* (The balancing of the scale is described.) The fingers of the right "H" hand are centered on the left index finger and rocked back and forth. *Cf.* SCALE 2, WEIGH 1, WEIGHT.

[P–267]

POUND 2, *(rare)*, *n.* (A small amount of weight.) The slightly curved right index finger exerts a small amount of downward pressure as it rests on the downturned left index finger.

[P–268]

POUND 3, *v.*, POUNDED, POUNDING. (The natural sign.) The right "S" hand strikes its knuckles forcefully against the open left palm, which is held facing right. *Cf.* HIT 1, PUNCH 1, STRIKE 1.

[P–269]

POUR (pōr), *v.*, POURED, POURING. (The act of pouring.) The thumb of the right "A" hand is placed into the hole formed by the left "O" hand. *Cf.* GAS 2, GASOLINE.

[P–270]

POVERTY 1 (pŏv′ ər tĭ), *n.* (Ragged elbows.) The open right hand is placed at the left elbow. It moves down and off, closing into the "O" position. *Cf.* POOR 1.

[P–271]

POVERTY 2, *n*. (The knuckles are rubbed, to indicate a condition of being worn down.) The knuckles of the curved index and middle fingers of both hands are rubbed up and down against each other. Instead of the up-down rubbing, they may rub against each other in an alternate clockwise-counterclockwise manner. *Cf.* DIFFICULT 1, DIFFICULTY, HARD 1, HARDSHIP, PROBLEM 2.

[P–272]

POWDER 1 (pou' dər), *n. v.,* -DERED, -DERING. (The natural sign.) The open right hand pats the right cheek several times, as if applying face powder.

[P–273]

POWDER 2, *n*. (White material blown off the hand.) The sign for WHITE is made: The fingertips of the "5" hand are placed against the chest. The hand moves straight out from the chest, while the fingers and thumb all come together. The right fingertips then feel the texture of an imaginary pinch of powder. The right hand is then opened and brought up to the mouth, which blows the powder away. The sign for WHITE is often omitted.

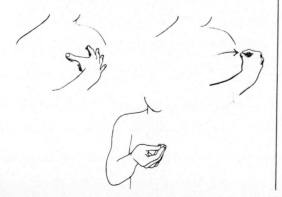

[P–274]

POWER 1 (pou' ər), *n*. (Flexing the muscles.) With fists clenched, palms facing back, the signer raises both arms and shakes them once, with force. *Cf.* MIGHT 1, MIGHTY 1, POWERFUL 1, STRONG 1, STURDY, TOUGH 1.

[P–275]

POWER 2, *n*. (The curve of the flexed biceps is indicated.) The left hand, clenched into a fist, is held up, palm facing the body. The index finger of the right "D" hand moves in an arc over the left biceps muscle, from shoulder to crook of the elbow. *Cf.* MIGHT 3, POWERFUL 2.

[P–276]

POWERFUL 1 (pou' ər fəl), *adj*. See POWER 1.

[P–277]

POWERFUL 2, *adj*. See POWER 2.

[P–278]

PRACTICE 1 (prăk' tĭs), *n., v.,* -TICED, -TICING. (Polishing or sharpening up.) The knuckles of the downturned right "A" hand are rubbed briskly back and forth over the side of the hand and index finger of the left "D" hand. *Cf.* DISCIPLINE 1, DRILL 3, TRAIN 2, TRAINING 1.

[P–279]

PRACTICE 2, *(rare), v.* (Same rationale as for PRACTICE 1.) The knuckles of both "A" hands, palms facing, sweep past each other repeatedly, coming in contact each time they do.

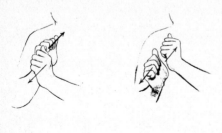

[P–280]

PRACTICE 3, *n., v.* (Bound down to custom or habit.) Both "S" hands, palms down, are crossed and brought down in unison before the chest. *Cf.* ACCUSTOM, BOUND, CUSTOM, HABIT, LOCKED.

[P–281]

PRACTICE WHAT YOU PREACH, *(expression).* (Preaching to oneself as one preaches to others.) The "F" hands are held upright, palms facing, the left facing toward the body and the right facing out. They swing back and forth repeatedly, always maintaining their relative position. See PREACH.

[P–282]

PRAISE (prāz), *n., v.,* PRAISED, PRAISING. (Good words coming from the mouth; clapping hands.) The fingertips of the right hand, palm flat and facing the body, are brought up to the lips so that they touch (part of the sign for GOOD, *q.v.*). The hands are then clapped together several times. *Cf.* ACCLAIM 2, APPLAUD, APPLAUSE, APPROBATION, APPROVAL, APPROVE, CLAP, COMMEND, CONGRATULATE 1, CONGRATULATIONS 1.

[P–283]

PRAY (prā), *v.,* PRAYED, PRAYING. The hands are held palm to palm and drawn toward the body, as the head is bowed slightly. *Cf.* PRAYER.

[P–284]

PRAYER (prâr), *n.* See PRAY.

[P–285]

PREACH (prēch), *v.,* PREACHED, PREACHING. (Placing morsels of wisdom, or food for thought, into the mind.) The right hand, palm out, with thumb and index finger touching, is moved forward and slightly downward a number of times from its initial position near the right temple. *Cf.* SERMON.

[P-286]

PREACHER (prē' chər), *n*. The sign for PREACH is made. This is followed by the sign for INDIVIDUAL: Both open hands, palms facing each other, move down the sides of the body, tracing its outline to the hips. *Cf.* MINISTER, PASTOR.

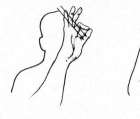

[P-287]

PRECEPT (prē' sĕpt), *n*. (A series of laws as they appear on the printed page.) The upright right "L" hand, resting palm against palm on the upright left "5" hand, moves down in an arc, a short distance, coming to rest on the base of the left palm. *Cf.* DECREE 2, LAW, LAWYER, LEGAL.

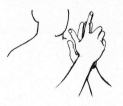
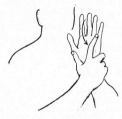

[P-288]

PRECIOUS (prĕsh' əs), *adj*. Both "F" hands, palms facing each other, move apart, up, and together in a smooth elliptical fashion, coming together at the tips of the thumbs and index fingers of both hands. *Cf.* DESERVE, ESSENTIAL, IMPORTANT 1, MAIN, MERIT, PROMINENT 2, SIGNIFICANCE 1, SIGNIFICANT, VALUABLE, VALUE, VITAL 1, WORTH, WORTHWHILE, WORTHY.

[P-289]

PRECISE (prĭ sīs'), *adj*. (The fingers come together precisely.) The thumb and index finger of each hand, palms facing, the right above the left, form circles. They are brought together with a deliberate movement, so that the fingers and thumbs now touch. Sometimes the right hand, before coming together with the left, executes a slow clockwise circle above the left. *Cf.* ACCURATE 1, EXACT 1, EXACTLY, EXPLICIT 1, SPECIFIC.

[P-290]

PREDICT (prĭ dĭkt'), *v.*, -DICTED, -DICTING. (The vision is directed forward, into the distance.) The right "V" fingertips are placed under the eyes, with palm facing the body. The hand is then swung around and forward, moving under the downturned prone left hand and continuing forward and upward. *Cf.* FORECAST, FORESEE, FORETELL, PERCEIVE 2, PROPHECY, PROPHESY, PROPHET, VISION 2.

[P-291]

PREFER (prĭ fûr'), *v.*, -FERRED, -FERRING. (More good.) The fingertips of one hand are placed at the lips, as if tasting something (*vide,* GOOD). Then the hand is moved up to a position just above the head, where it assumes the "A" position, thumb up. *Cf.* BETTER.

[P–292]

PREPARE 1 (prĭ pâr′), *v.*, -PARED, -PARING. (Placing things in order.) The hands, palms facing, fingers together and pointing away from the body, are positioned at the left side and held about a foot apart. With a slight up-down motion, as if describing waves, the hands travel in unison from left to right. *Cf.* ARRANGE, ARRANGEMENT, CLASSED 2, DEVISE 1, ORDER 3, PLAN 1, POLICY 1, PROGRAM 1, PROVIDE 1, PUT IN ORDER, READY 1, SCHEME, SYSTEM.

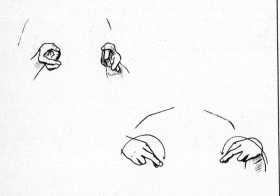

[P–293]

PREPARE 2, *v.* (The "R" hands, for READY.) The "R" hands are held side by side before the body, palms up and fingers pointing outward. The hands then turn toward each other and over, so that the palms face down and fingers point toward each other. *Cf.* READY 2.

[P–294]

PREPARE 3, *v.* (Set out.) The "A" hands are crossed, with the right resting on top of the left. The right palm faces left and the left palm faces right. Both hands suddenly open and swing apart to the palm-down position. *Cf.* READY 4.

[P–295]

PRESBYTERIAN (prĕz′ bə tir′ ĭ ən, prĕs′-), *(eccles.)*, *n., adj.* (The act of standing and singing in church.) The tips of the downturned, right "V" fingers are placed in the upturned left palm.

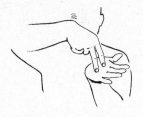

[P–296]

PRESCRIPTION (prĭ skrĭp′ shən), *n.* (Mixing of medicine; rolling a pill.) The ball of the middle fingertip of the right "5" hand describes a small counterclockwise circle in the upturned left palm. *Cf.* DRUG, MEDICINE, POISON 1.

[P–297]

PRESENCE (prĕz′ əns), *n.* (Face to face.) The left hand, fingers together, palm flat and facing the eyes, is held a bit above eye level. The right hand, fingers also together, is held in front of the mouth, with palm facing the left hand. With a sweeping upward movement the right hand moves toward the left, which moves straight up an inch or two at the same time. *Cf.* APPEAR 3, APPEARANCE, BEFORE 3, CONFRONT, FACE 2, FACE TO FACE.

[P–298]

PRESENCE OF GOD, *(eccles. phrase).* (God looking down.) The sign for GOD is made: The right open hand, palm facing left, swings up above the head, and is then moved down about an inch. The signer looks up while making the sign. Then the sign for LOOK DOWN is made: Both "V" hands, side by side and palms facing out, are swept downward so that the fingertips now point down.

[P–299]

PRESENT 1 (prĕz' ənt), *n.* (An offering; a presenting.) Both hands, slightly cupped, palms up, are held close to the chest. They move up and out in unison, describing a very slight arc. *Cf.* BID 2, MOTION 1, OFFER 1, OFFERING 1, PROPOSE, SUGGEST, TENDER 2.

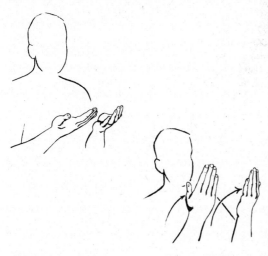

[P–300]

PRESENT 2 (*n.* prĕz' ənt; *v.* pri zĕnt'), -SENTED, -SENTING. (A giving of something.) Both "A" hands, with index fingers somewhat draped over the tips of the thumbs, are held palms facing in front of the chest. They are pivoted forward and down in

unison, from the wrists. *Cf.* AWARD, BEQUEATH, BESTOW, CONFER, CONSIGN, CONTRIBUTE, GIFT.

[P–301]

PRESENT 3, *adj.* (Something right in front of you.) The upturned right-angle hands drop down rather sharply. The "Y" hands may also be used. *Cf.* CURRENT, IMMEDIATE, NOW.

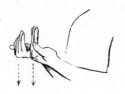

[P–302]

PRESERVE (pri zûrv'), *v.,* -SERVED, -SERVING. (Slow, careful movement.) The "K" hands are crossed, the right above the left, little finger edges down. In this position the hands are moved up and down a short distance. *Cf.* CARE 2, CAREFUL 2, KEEP, MAINTAIN 1, MIND 3, RESERVE 2, TAKE CARE OF 2.

[P–303]

PRESIDENT (prĕz' ə dənt), *n.* The "C" hands, held palms out at either temple, close over imaginary horns and move up a bit to either side, tracing the shape of the horns. *Cf.* HORNS, SUPERINTENDENT.

[P-304]

PRESS 1 (prĕs), *v.*, PRESSED, PRESSING. (The act of pressing with an iron.) The right hand goes through the motion of swinging an iron back and forth over the upturned left palm. *Cf.* FLATIRON, IRON 2.

[P-305]

PRESS 2, *v.* (The act of pressing clothes.) The downturned "S" hands swing down in unison, as if manipulating a tailor's steam press.

[P-306]

PRESS 3, *v.* (The act of pressing something together with the hands.) The ball of the right "5" hand is pressed against the upturned left palm. The right hand may turn back and forth, maintaining its pressure against the left. *Cf.* SQUASH 2.

[P-307]

PRETTY (prĭt' ĭ), *adj.* (Literally, a good face.) The right hand, fingers closed over the thumb, is placed at or just below the lips (indicating a tasting of some-

thing GOOD, *q. v.*). It then describes a counterclockwise circle around the face, opening into the "5" position, to indicate the whole face. At the completion of the circling movement the hand comes to rest in its initial position, at or just below the lips. *Cf.* ATTRACTIVE 2, BEAUTIFUL, BEAUTY, EXQUISITE, SPLENDID 3.

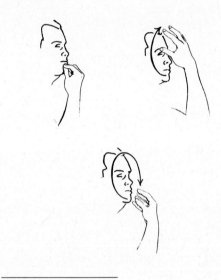

[P-308]

PREVARICATE (prĭ văr' ə kāt´), *v.*, -CATED, -CATING. (Words diverted instead of coming straight, or truthfully, out.) The index finger of the right "D" hand, pointing to the left, moves along the lips from right to left. *Cf.* FALSE 1, FALSEHOOD, FRAUDULENT 2, LIAR, LIE 1, UNTRUTH.

[P-309]

PREVENT (prĭ vĕnt'), *v.*, -VENTED, -VENTING. (Obstruct, block.) The left hand, fingers together and palm flat, is held before the body, facing somewhat down. The little finger side of the right hand, held with palm flat, makes one or several up-down chopping motions against the left hand, between its thumb and index finger. *Cf.* ANNOY 1, ANNOYANCE

1, BLOCK, BOTHER 1, CHECK 2, COME BETWEEN, DISRUPT, DISTURB, HINDER, HINDRANCE, IMPEDE, INTERCEPT, INTERFERE, INTERFERENCE, INTERFERE WITH, INTERRUPT, MEDDLE 1, OBSTACLE, OBSTRUCT, PREVENTION.

[P–310]

PREVENTION (prĭ vĕn′ shən), *n.* See PREVENT.

[P–311]

PREVIOUS (prē′ vĭ əs), *adj.* (Something past, behind.) The upraised right hand, in the "5" position with palm facing the body, is held just above the right shoulder and is thrown back over it. *Cf.* AGO, FORMERLY, ONCE UPON A TIME, PAST, PREVIOUSLY, WAS, WERE.

[P–312]

PREVIOUSLY, *adv.* See PREVIOUS.

[P–313]

PRICE 1 (prīs), *n., v.,* PRICED, PRICING. (Amount of money is indicated.) The sign for MONEY is made: The upturned right hand, grasping some imaginary bills, is brought down into the upturned left palm a number of times. The right hand then moves straight up, opening into the "5" position, palm up. *Cf.* HOW MUCH MONEY?, WHAT IS THE PRICE?

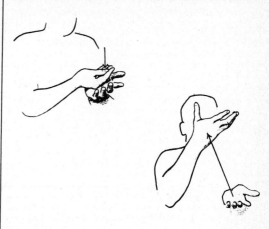

[P–314]

PRICE 2, *n., v.* (Nicking into one.) The knuckle of the right "X" finger is nicked against the palm of the left hand, held in the "5" position, palm facing right. *Cf.* ADMISSION 2, CHARGE 1, COST, DUTY 2, EXCISE, EXPENSE, FEE, FINE 2, IMPOST, PENALTY 3, TAX 1, TAXATION 1, TOLL.

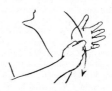

[P–315]

PRIDE (prīd), *n., v.,* PRIDED, PRIDING. (The feelings rise up.) The thumb of the right "A" hand, palm down, moves up along the right side of the chest. A haughty expression is assumed. *Cf.* HAUGHTY, PROUD.

[P–316]

PRIEST 1 (prēst), *n.* (The ecclesiastical collar.) The thumbs and index fingers of both hands indicate the shape of the collar as they move around the neck, coming together in front of the throat. Sometimes only one hand is used. *Cf.* FATHER 3.

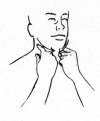

[P–317]

PRIEST 2, *n.* (The breastplate worn by the priests of the Old Testament.) The index fingers, placed on the chest, describe the shape of the breastplate.

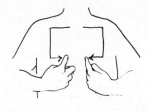

[P–318]

PRIEST 3, *n.* (Modified sign of the cross.) The right "4" hand, palm facing the body, is drawn down the middle of the chest, almost to the waist. The same hand is then drawn across the chest, from the left shoulder to the right shoulder.

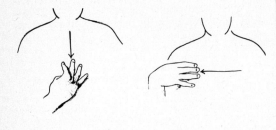

[P–319]

PRIEST 4, *n.* (The sign of the Oremus at Mass.) The "F" hands, palms facing and thumb sides facing up, are joined at their respective fingertips. They sepa-

rate, move apart and toward the body in half circles, and come together again in their initial position, closer to the body than before. *Cf.* RECTOR, REVEREND.

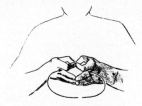

[P–320]

PRIMARY (prī′ měr′ ĭ, -məri), *adj., n.* (The first finger is indicated.) The right index finger touches the upturned left thumb. *Cf.* FIRST 1, INITIAL, ORIGIN 2.

[P–321]

PRINCE (prĭns), *n.* (The letter "P"; the sash worn by royalty.) The MALE root sign is made: The thumb and extended fingers of the right hand are brought up to grasp an imaginary cap brim, representing the tipping of caps by men in olden days. The right "P" hand then moves from the left shoulder to the right waist.

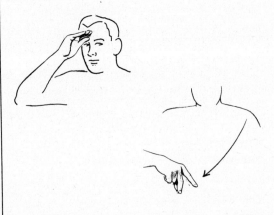

[P–322]

PRINCESS (prĭn′ sĭs), *n.* (The letter "P"; the sash worn by royalty.) The FEMALE root sign is made:

The thumb of the right "A" hand moves down along the line of the right jaw, from ear almost to chin. The right "P" hand then moves from the left shoulder to the right waist.

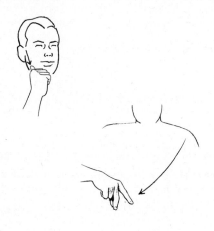

[P-323]

PRINCIPAL 1 (prĭn' sə pəl), *n.* (The letter "P"; one who rules over others.) The downturned, right "P" hand is swung from right to left over the back of the prone left hand.

[P-324]

PRINCIPAL 2, *adj.* (The largest or greatest amount.) The sign for MUCH is made: The "5" hands, palms facing, fingers curved and thumbs pointing up, draw apart. The sign for the superlative suffix, "-EST," is then made: The right "A" hand, thumb pointing up, quickly moves straight upward, until it is above the head. The MUCH sign may be omitted. *Cf.* CHIEF, MAINLY, MOST, MOST OF ALL.

[P-325]

PRINCIPLE (prĭn' sə pəl), *n.* (A collection or listing is indicated by the open palm, representing a page.) The right "P" hand is placed against the upper part of the open left hand, which faces right, fingers pointing upward. The right "P" hand swings down to the lower part of the left palm. *Cf.* DOCTRINE 1.

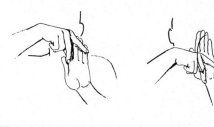

[P-326]

PRINT (prĭnt), *v.*, PRINTED, PRINTING. (Placing type in a printer's stick.) The upturned, left "5" hand represents the printer's stick. The right index finger and thumb close over an imaginary piece of type and place it in the left palm. *Cf.* PUBLISH 2.

[P-327]

PRINTER, *n.* (An individual who prints.) The sign for PRINT is made, followed by the sign for INDIVIDUAL: Both open hands, palms facing each other, move down the sides of the body, tracing its outline to the hips.

[P–328]

PRINTSHOP (prĭnt′ shŏp), *n.* (Print place.) The sign for PRINT is made followed by the sign for PLACE 1: The "P" hands are held side by side before the body, with middle fingertips touching. From this position the hands separate and outline a circle (or a square), before coming together again closer to the body.

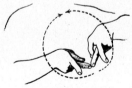

[P–329]

PRISON (prĭz′ ən), *n.* (The crossed bars.) The "4" hands, palms facing the body, are crossed at the fingers. *Cf.* IMPRISON, JAIL, PENITENTIARY.

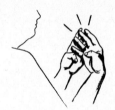

[P–330]

PRIVACY (prī′ və sĭ), *n.* (The sealing of the lips; keeping the words back.) The back of the thumb of the right "A" hand is placed firmly against the closed lips. The thumb, in this position, may move off the lips slightly and return again to the lips. As an optional addition, the thumb may swing down under the downturned cupped left hand, after being placed on the lips as above. *Cf.* DON'T TELL, PRIVATE 1, SECRET.

[P–331]

PRIVATE 1 (prī′ vĭt), *adj.* See PRIVACY.

[P–332]

PRIVATE 2, *(colloq.), adj.* (Closed.) Both open hands are held before the body, fingers pointing out, right palm facing left and left facing right. The right hand, held above the left, comes down against the index finger edge of the left a number of times.

[P–333]

PRIVATE 3, *n.* (The stripe on the uniform sleeve.) The right index finger traces the shape of the private's stripe on the left sleeve.

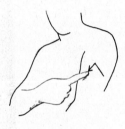

[P–334]

PRIVATE CONVERSATION, *(colloq. phrase).* (Small give-and-take from the mouth.) The index and middle fingers of the right or left "V" hand move alternately back and forth on the lips.

[P–335]

PRIVILEGE (prĭv′ ə lĭj), *n.* (A straightening out.) The right hand, fingers together and palm facing left, is placed in the upturned left palm, whose fingers point away from the body. The right hand slides straight out along the left palm, over the left fingers, and stops with its heel resting on the left fingertips. *Cf.* ALL RIGHT, O.K. 1, RIGHT 1, RIGHTEOUS 1, YOU'RE WELCOME 2.

[P–336]

PROBABLE (prŏb′ ə bəl), *adj.* (Weighing one thing against another.) The upturned open hands move alternately up and down. *Cf.* GUESS 4, MAY 1, MAYBE, MIGHT 2, PERHAPS, POSSIBILITY, POSSIBLY, PROBABLY, SUPPOSE.

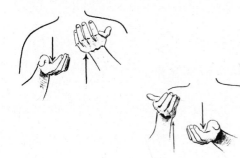

[P–337]

PROBABLY (prŏ′ ə blĭ), *adv.* See PROBABLE.

[P–338]

PROBE 1 (prōb), *v.*, PROBED, PROBING, *n.* (Directing the vision from place to place.) The right "C" hand, palm facing left, moves from right to left across the line of vision, in a series of counterclockwise circles. The signer's gaze remains concentrated and his head turns slowly from right to left. *Cf.* CURIOUS 1, EXAMINE, INVESTIGATE 1, LOOK FOR, QUEST, SEARCH, SEEK.

[P–339]

PROBE 2, *v.* (Drilling.) The "S" hands revolve around each other in front of the chest, as if drilling a hole with a hand brace. *Cf.* PRY, PUMP 2.

[P–340]

PROBLEM 1 (prŏb′ ləm), *n.* (A clouding over; a troubling.) Both "B" hands, palms facing each other, are rotated alternately before the forehead. *Cf.* ANNOY 2, ANNOYANCE 2, ANXIOUS 2, BOTHER 2, CONCERN 1, FRET, TROUBLE, WORRIED, WORRY 1.

[P–341]

PROBLEM 2, *n.* (The knuckles are rubbed, to indicate a condition of being worn down.) The knuckles of the curved index and middle fingers of both hands are rubbed up and down against each other. Instead of the up-down rubbing, they may rub against each other in an alternate clockwise-counterclockwise manner. *Cf.* DIFFICULT 1, DIFFICULTY, HARD 1, HARDSHIP, POVERTY 2.

[P–342]

PROBLEM 3, *n.* (Coming to grips.) The curved index and middle fingers of both hands, palms facing the body, are brought sharply into an interlocking position. The action may be repeated, this time with the wrists first twisted slightly in opposite directions.

[P–343]

PROCEED (prə sēd'), *v.,* -CEEDED, -CEEDING. (Moving forward.) Both right-angle hands, palms facing each other and knuckles facing forward, move forward simultaneously. *Cf.* FORWARD, GO AHEAD, MOTION FORWARD, ONWARD, PROGRESS 2, RESUME.

[P–344]

PROCESSION (prə sĕsh' ən), *n.* (Rows of people marching.) Both "V" hands, palms out and the left behind the right, move forward in unison, in a series of short upward-arced motions. *Cf.* FUNERAL, PARADE 1.

[P–345]

PROCLAIM (prō klām'), *v.,* -CLAIMED, -CLAIMING. (An issuance from the mouth.) Both index fingers are placed at the lips, with palms facing the body.

They are rotated once and swung out in arcs, until the left index finger points somewhat to the left and the right index somewhat to the right. Sometimes the rotation of the fingers is omitted in favor of a simple swinging out from the lips. *Cf.* ACCLAIM 1, ACCLAMATION, ANNOUNCE, ANNOUNCEMENT, DECLARE, MAKE KNOWN, PROCLAMATION.

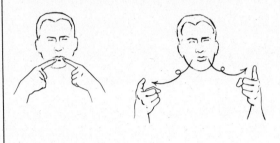

[P–346]

PROCLAMATION (prŏk' lə mā' shən), *n.* See PROCLAIM.

[P–347]

PROCRASTINATE (prō krăs' tə nāt'), *v.,* -NATED, -NATING. (Putting off; moving things forward repeatedly.) The "F" hands, palms facing and fingers pointing out from the body, are moved forward simultaneously in a series of short movements. *Cf.* DEFER, DELAY, POSTPONE, PUT OFF.

[P–348]

PROCURE (prō kyŏŏr'), *v.,* -CURED, -CURING. (A grasping and bringing forward to oneself.) Both hands, in the "5" position, fingers curved, are crossed at the wrists, with the left palm facing right and the right palm facing left. They are brought in toward the chest, while closing into a grasping "S" position. *Cf.* ACQUIRE, GET, OBTAIN, RECEIVE.

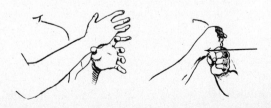

[P–349]

PROD (prŏd), *v.*, PRODDED, PRODDING. (Shaking someone, to implant one's will into another.) Both "A" hands, palms facing, are held before the chest, the left slightly in front of the right. In this position the hands move back and forth a short distance. *Cf.* COAX, CONVINCE, INDUCE, PERSUADE, PERSUASION, URGE 2.

[P–350]

PRODUCE 1 (*n.* prŏd′ ūs; *v.* prə dūs′), -DUCED, -DUCING. (Carrying something over.) Both open hands, palms up, move in an arc from left to right, as if carrying something from one point to another. *Cf.* BRING, CARRY 2, DELIVER 2, FETCH, TRANSPORT.

[P–351]

PRODUCE 2, *v., n.* (Directing the attention to something, and bringing it forward.) The right index finger points into the left palm, held facing out before the body. The left palm moves straight out. For the passive form of this verb, *i.e.,* BE SHOWN, the movement is reversed: The left hand, palm facing in, is moved in toward the body, while the right index finger remains pointing into the left palm. *Cf.* DEMONSTRATE, DISPLAY, EVIDENCE, EXAMPLE, EXHIBIT, EXHIBITION, ILLUSTRATE, INDICATE, INFLUENCE 3, REPRESENT, SHOW 1, SIGNIFY 1.

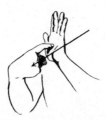

[P–352]

PRODUCE 3, *v.* (Fashioning something with the hands.) The right "S" hand, palm facing left, is placed on top of its left counterpart, whose palm faces right. The hands are twisted back and forth, striking each other slightly after each twist. *Cf.* COMPOSE, CONSTITUTE, CONSTRUCT 2, CREATE, DEVISE 2, FABRICATE, FASHION, FIX, MAKE, MANUFACTURE, MEND 1, RENDER 1, REPAIR.

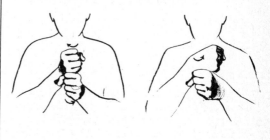

[P–353]

PRODUCE 4, *v., n.* (Rays of influence emanating from a given source.) All the right fingertips, including the thumb, are positioned on the tip of the upturned thumb of the left "A" hand. The right hand, opening into the downturned "5" position, moves forward from its initial position. Instead of its initial position on the left thumb, the right hand is frequently placed on the back of the downturned left "S" hand, moving forward as described above. *Cf.* BASIS 1, CAUSE, EFFECT 1, INFLUENCE 2, INTENT 2, LOGIC, REASON 2.

[P–354]

PROFESSION 1 (prə fĕsh′ ən), *n.* (The letter "F" for FIELD; straight line denotes a specific "line" or area of pursuit.) The thumb edge of the right "F" hand moves forward along the outstretched left index finger. *Cf.* FIELD 4.

[P-355]

PROFESSION 2 (prə fĕsh′ ən), *n.* (The letter "P"; the field or line.) The middle finger of the right "P" hand moves forward along the line of the outstretched, left index finger.

[P-356]

PROFIT (prŏf′ ĭt), *n., v.,* -FITED, -FITING. (To get a profit; a coin popped into the vest pocket.) The sign for GET is made: Both outstretched hands, held in a grasping "5" position, close into "S" positions, with the right on top of the left. At the same time both hands are drawn in to the body. The thumb and index finger of the right hand, holding an imaginary coin, are then popped into an imaginary vest or breast pocket. *Note:* the sign for GET is sometimes omitted. *Cf.* BENEFIT 2, GAIN 2.

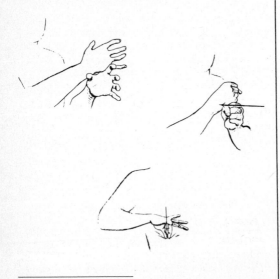

[P-357]

PROGRAM 1 (prō′ grăm, -grəm), *n.* (Placing things in order.) The hands, palms facing, fingers together and pointing away from the body, are positioned at the left side and held about a foot apart. With a slight up-down motion, as if describing waves, the hands travel in unison from left to right. *Cf.* AR-RANGE, ARRANGEMENT, CLASSED 2, DEVISE 1,

ORDER 3, PLAN 1, POLICY 1, PREPARE 1, PROVIDE 1, PUT IN ORDER, READY 1, SCHEME, SYSTEM.

[P-358]

PROGRAM 2, *n.* (The letter "P"; a listing on both sides of the page.) The thumb side of the right "P" hand is placed against the palm of the open left hand, which is facing right. The right "P" hand moves down the left palm. The left hand then swings around so that its palm faces the body. The right "P" hand then moves down the back of the left hand.

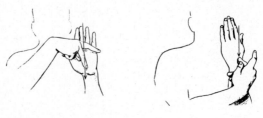

[P-359]

PROGRESS 1 (*n.* prŏg′ rĕs; *v.* prə grĕs′), -GRESSED, -GRESSING. (Moving forward, step by step.) Both hands, in the right angle position, palms facing, are held before the chest, a few inches apart, with the right hand slightly behind the left. The right hand is brought up, over and forward, so that it is now ahead of the left. The left hand then follows suit, so that it is now ahead of the right. *Cf.* AD-VANCE.

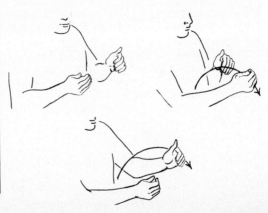

[P-360]

PROGRESS 2, *n.* See PROCEED.

[P-361]

PROHIBIT (prō hĭb′ ĭt), *v.*, -ITED, -ITING. (A modification of LAW, *q.v.;* "against the law.") The downturned right "D" or "L" hand is thrust forcefully into the left palm. *Cf.* BAN, FORBID 1, FORBIDDEN 1.

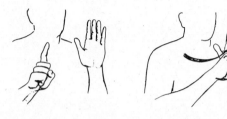

[P-362]

PROMINENT 1 (prŏm′ ə nənt), *adj.* (One's fame radiates far and wide.) The extended index fingers rest on the lips (or on the temples). Moving in small, continuous spirals, they move up and to either side of the head. *Cf.* CELEBRATED, FAME, FAMOUS, RENOWNED.

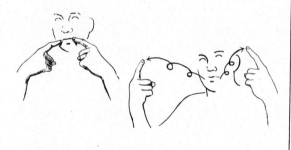

[P-363]

PROMINENT 2, *adj.* Both "F" hands, palms facing each other, move apart, up, and together in a smooth elliptical fashion, coming together at the tips of the thumbs and index fingers of both hands. *Cf.* DESERVE, ESSENTIAL, IMPORTANT 1, MAIN, MERIT, PRECIOUS, SIGNIFICANCE 1, SIGNIFICANT, VALUABLE, VALUE, VITAL 1, WORTH, WORTHWHILE, WORTHY.

[P-364]

PROMINENT 3, *adj.* (Indicating height.) The right "A" hand, held with thumb pointing upward, moves straight up above the right shoulder. *Cf.* HIGH 2, SUPERIOR.

[P-365]

PROMISE 1 (prŏm′ ĭs), *n., v.,* -ISED, -ISING. (The arm is raised.) The right index finger is placed at the lips. The right arm is then raised, palm out and elbow resting on the back of the left hand. *Cf.* GUARANTEE 1, LOYAL, OATH, PLEDGE, SWEAR 1, SWORN, TAKE OATH, VOW.

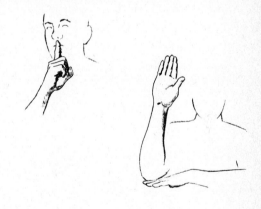

[P-366]

PROMISE 2, *n., v.* (Sealing the word.) The right index finger is placed at the lips, as in PROMISE 1. The open right hand is then brought down against the upturned left hand.

[P–367]

PROMISE 3, *n., v.* (A variation of PROMISE 2.) The right index finger is placed at the lips, as in PROMISE 1. The open right hand is then brought down against the thumb side of the left "S" hand.

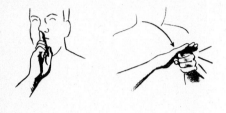

[P–368]

PROMOTE (prə mōt'), *v.,* -MOTED, -MOTING. (Something high up.) Both hands, in the right angle position, are held before the face, about a foot apart, palms facing. They are raised abruptly about a foot, in a slight outward curving movement. *Cf.* ADVANCED, HIGH 1, PROMOTION.

[P–369]

PROMOTION (prə mō' shən), *n.* See PROMOTE.

[P–370]

PROOF (pro͞of), *n.* (Laying out the proof for all to see.) The back of the open right hand is placed with a flourish on the open left palm. The index finger may first touch the lips. *Cf.* PROVE.

[P–371]

PROPER (prŏp' ər), *adj.* The right index finger, held above the left index finger, comes down rather forcefully so that the bottom of the right hand comes to rest on top of the left thumb joint. *Cf.* ACCURATE 2, CORRECT 1, DECENT, EXACT 2, JUST 2, RIGHT 3, SUITABLE.

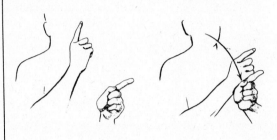

[P–372]

PROPHECY (prŏf' ə sĭ), *n.* (The vision is directed forward, into the distance.) The right "V" fingertips are placed under the eyes, with palm facing the body. The hand is then swung around and forward, moving under the downturned prone left hand and continuing forward and upward. *Cf.* FORECAST, FORESEE, FORETELL, PERCEIVE 2, PREDICT, PROPHESY, PROPHET, VISION 2.

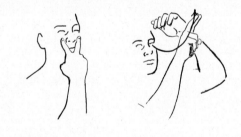

[P–373]

PROPHESY (prŏf' ə sī), *v.,* -SIED, -SYING. See PROPHECY.

[P–374]

PROPHET (prŏf' ĭt), *n.* See PROPHECY.

[P–375]

PROPITIATION (prə pĭsh´ ĭ ā' shən), *(eccles.), n.* (An exchange.) The "F" hands, fingers pointing out and palms facing each other, are held with the left in front of the right. They gracefully reverse their positions, with the right moving forward in a downward arc and the left moving back in an upward arc.

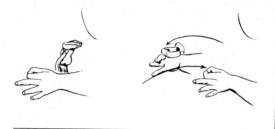

[P–376]

PROPORTION (prə pōr' shən), *n.* (In proportion.) Both "D" or "P" hands, palms facing down, are held before the body. They describe a short arc from right to left and, while unnecessary, they may return to their original position. *Cf.* HENCE, RATIO, THERE-FORE 1, THUS.

[P–377]

PROPOSE (prə pōz'), *v.*, -POSED, -POSING. (An offering; a presenting.) Both hands, slightly cupped, palms up, are held close to the chest. They move up and out in unison, describing a very slight arc. *Cf.* BID 2, MOTION 1, OFFER 1, OFFERING 1, PRESENT 1, SUGGEST, TENDER 2.

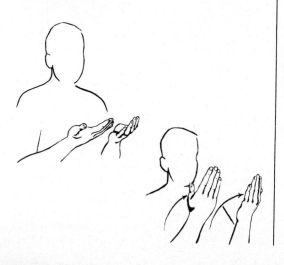

[P–378]

PROSPER (prŏs' pər), *v.*, -PERED, -PERING. (Penetrating the heights.) The "D" hands, palms back, are held at each side of the head, near the temples. With a pivoting motion of the wrists, the hands swing up and around, simultaneously, to a position above the head, with palms facing out. *Cf.* ACCOMPLISH 1, ACHIEVE 1, ATTAIN, SUCCEED, SUCCESS, SUCCESS-FUL, TRIUMPH 2.

[P–379]

PROSTITUTE (prŏs' tə tūt´), *n.* (The blood rushes up the cheek in shame—several times for emphasis.) The curved back of the right hand, placed against the right cheek, moves up and off the cheek several times. *Cf.* HARLOT, STRUMPET, WHORE.

[P–380]

PROTECT (prə tĕkt'), *v.*, -TECTED, -TECTING. (Hold down firmly; cover and strengthen.) The "S" hands, downturned, are held side by side in front of the body, the arms almost horizontal, and the left hand in front of the right. Both arms move a short distance forward and slightly downward. *Cf.* DE-FEND, DEFENSE, FORTIFY, GUARD, PROTECTION, SHIELD 1.

[P-381]

PROTECTION (prə těk′ shən), *n.* See PROTECT.

[P-382]

PROTEST (*n.* prō′ těst; *v.* prə těst′), -TESTED, -TESTING. (The hand is thrust into the chest to force a complaint out.) The curved fingers of the right hand are thrust forcefully into the chest. *Cf.* COMPLAIN 1, COMPLAINT, OBJECT 2, OBJECTION.

[P-383]

PROTESTANT (prŏt′ ĭs tənt), *n., adj.* (Kneeling in church.) The knuckles of the right index and middle fingers are placed in the upturned left palm. The action may be repeated. *Cf.* KNEEL.

[P-384]

PROUD (proud), *adj.* (The feelings rise up.) The thumb of the right "A" hand, palm down, moves up along the right side of the chest. A haughty expression is assumed. *Cf.* HAUGHTY, PRIDE.

[P-385]

PROVE (proov), *v.,* PROVED, PROVEN, PROVING. See PROOF.

[P-386]

PROVIDE 1 (prə vīd′), *v.,* -VIDED, -VIDING. (Placing things in order.) The hands, palms facing, fingers together and pointing away from the body, are positioned at the left side and held about a foot apart. With a slight up-down motion, as if describing waves, the hands travel in unison from left to right. *Cf.* ARRANGE, ARRANGEMENT, CLASSED 2, DEVISE 1, ORDER 3, PLAN 1, POLICY 1, PREPARE 1, PROGRAM 1, PUT IN ORDER, READY 1, SCHEME, SYSTEM.

[P-387]

PROVIDE 2, *v.* (Handing over.) The "AND" hands are held upright with palms toward the body. From this position they swing forward and down, opening up as if giving something out.

[P-388]

PRUNE (proon), *(loc.), n.* (The shape.) The "Q" hands, palms facing each other, are held before the body, respective thumbs and index fingers in contact. The hands then draw apart a few inches, and their thumbs and index fingers come together.

[P–389]

PRY (prī), *v.*, PRIED, PRYING. (Drilling.) The "S" hands revolve around each other in front of the chest, as if drilling a hole with a hand brace. *Cf.* PROBE 2, PUMP 2.

[P–390]

PSALM (säm), *n.* (The letter "P"; the waving hand denotes rhythm.) The right "P" hand swings back and forth rhythmically over the open left hand, whose palm faces the body. The right hand may also describe a figure-eight movement instead of the back-and-forth movement. *Cf.* POEM, POETRY.

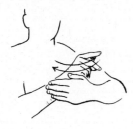

[P–391]

PSYCHIATRIST (sī kī' ə trist), *n.* (The letter "P"; the pulse, which the doctor feels.) The thumb and middle finger of the right "P" hand twice touch the pulse of the upturned left hand.

[P–392]

PSYCHOLOGY 1 (sī kŏl' ə jĭ), *n.* (The Greek letter Ψ, "psi," symbol of psychology.) The little finger edge of the open right hand is thrust into the open left hand, between thumb and index finger. The action is usually repeated.

[P–393]

PSYCHOLOGY 2, *n.* (The letter "P"; the mind.) The thumb and middle finger of the right "P" hand twice tap the right temple.

[P–394]

PUBLIC (pŭb' lĭk), *adj., n.* (People, indicated by the rotating "P" hands.) The "P" hands, side by side, are moved alternately in continuous counterclockwise circles. *Cf.* AUDIENCE 2, HUMANITY, PEOPLE.

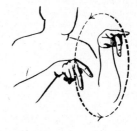

[P–395]

PUBLISH 1 (pŭb' lĭsh), *v.*, -LISHED, -LISHING. (The action of the press.) The right "5" hand, held palm down, fingers pointing left, is brought down twice against the upturned left "5" hand, whose fingers point right. *Cf.* NEWSPAPER, PAPER.

[P-396]

PUBLISH 2, *v.* (Placing type in a printer's stick.) The upturned, left "5" hand represents the printer's stick. The right index finger and thumb close over an imaginary piece of type and place it in the left palm. *Cf.* PRINT.

[P-397]

PULL 1 (pŏŏl), *v.*, PULLED, PULLING. (The natural action.) Both open hands, the right palm up and the left palm down, grasp an imaginary pole and pull it toward the body. *Cf.* DRAG, DRAW 2.

[P-398]

PULL 2, *v.* (Hooking on to something and pulling.) With index fingers interlocked, the right hand pulls the left hand from left to right. *Cf.* HITCH, HOOK, TOW.

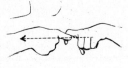

[P-399]

PULSE (pŭls), *n.* (The natural action of feeling the pulse.) The right fingertips are placed against the left pulse.

[P-400]

PUMP 1 (pŭmp), *n., v.,* PUMPED, PUMPING. (The natural action.) The downturned "S" hands manipulate the handles of an imaginary pump by moving up and down in unison a number of times.

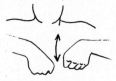

[P-401]

PUMP 2, *v.* (Drilling.) The "S" hands revolve around each other in front of the chest, as if drilling a hole with a hand brace. *Cf.* PROBE 2, PRY.

[P-402]

PUMPKIN 1 (pŭmp' kĭn), *n.* (Thumping a yellow sphere.) The sign for YELLOW is made: The right "Y" hand, palm facing the body, shakes slightly, pivoting at the wrist. The downturned, left "S" hand represents the pumpkin. The middle finger of the right hand is then flicked against the back of the left. *Cf.* SQUASH 1.

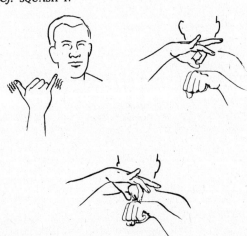

[P–403]

PUMPKIN 2, *n.* (The yellow object is defined.) The sign for YELLOW, as in PUMPKIN 1, *q.v.*, is made. Then the open "5" hands, fingers curved and palms facing, are held before the body to define the shape of the pumpkin.

[P–404]

PUNCH 1 (pŭnch), *n., v.*, PUNCHED, PUNCHING. (The natural sign.) The right "S" hand strikes its knuckles forcefully against the open left palm, which is held facing right. *Cf.* HIT 1, POUND 3, STRIKE 1.

[P–405]

PUNCH 2, *n., v.* (The natural sign.) The right fist strikes the chin.

[P–406]

PUNCH PRESS (pŭnch' prĕs), *(voc.), n.* (The natural motion.) The upturned, open left hand represents the platform of the machine. The right "S" hand, grasping an imaginary handle, moves up and down repeatedly above the left.

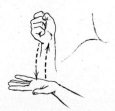

[P–407]

PUNISH 1 (pŭn' ĭsh), *v.*, -ISHED, -ISHING. (A striking movement.) The right index finger makes a striking movement below the left "S" hand, which is held up, as if grasping a culprit. *Cf.* DISCIPLINE 3, PENALTY 1.

[P–408]

PUNISH 2, *v.* (The natural sign.) The left hand is held in a fist before the face, as if grasping something or someone. The right hand, at the same time, is held as if grasping a stick or whip; it strikes repeatedly at the imaginary object or person dangling from the left hand. *Cf.* BEAT 1, WHIP.

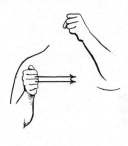

[P–409]

PUNISH 3, *v.* (A modification of the striking movement.) The right index finger strikes the left elbow with a glancing blow. *Cf.* DISCIPLINE 2, PENALTY 2, PENANCE 1.

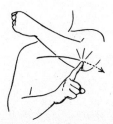

[P-410]

PUPIL 1 (pū′ pəl), *n.* (One who learns.) The sign for LEARN is made: The downturned fingers of the right hand are placed on the upturned left palm. They close, and then the hand rises and the right fingertips are placed on the forehead. This is followed by the sign for INDIVIDUAL: Both open hands, palms facing each other, move down the sides of the body, tracing its outline to the hips. *Cf.* LEARNER, SCHOLAR, STUDENT 1.

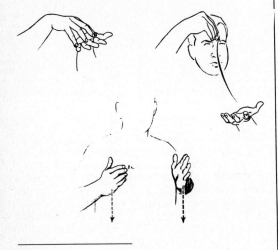

[P-411]

PUPIL 2, *n.* (One who studies.) The sign for STUDY is made: The upturned left hand represents a page. The right fingers wiggle as they move back and forth a short distance above the left hand. This is followed by the sign for INDIVIDUAL, as in PUPIL 1.

[P-412]

PUPIL 3, *n.* (The letter "P.") The middle finger of the right "P" hand is placed in the upturned left palm and moved from little finger edge to thumb edge a number of times.

[P-413]

PURCHASE (pûr′ chəs), *n., v.,* -CHASED, -CHASING. (Giving out money.) The sign for MONEY is made: The upturned right hand, grasping some imaginary bills, is brought down into the upturned left palm, and then the right hand moves forward and up in a small arc, opening up as it does. *Cf.* BUY.

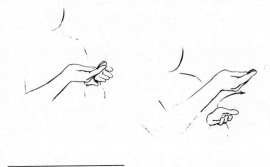

[P-414]

PURE 1 (pyŏŏr), *adj.* (Everything is wiped off the hand, to emphasize an uncluttered or clean condition.) The right hand slowly wipes the upturned left palm, from wrist to fingertips. *Cf.* CLEAN 1, IMMACULATE, NEAT, NICE, PLAIN 2, PURITY, SIMPLE 2.

[P-415]

PURE 2, *n.* (The letter "P," for PURE, passed over the palm to denote CLEAN.) The right "P" hand moves forward along the palm of the upturned left hand, which is held flat, with fingers pointing forward. *Cf.* CHASTITY.

[P-416]

PURGATORY (pûr′ gə tōr´ i), *(eccles.), n.* (The letter "P.") The middle finger of the right "P" hand is placed in the upturned left palm, where it describes a continuous, small, counterclockwise circle.

[P–417]

PURITY (pyŏŏr′ ə tĭ), *n.* See PURE 1.

[P–418]

PURPLE (pûr′ pəl), *adj.* (The letter "P.") The right "P" hand is shaken slightly, pivoting at the wrist.

[P–419]

PURPOSE 1 (pûr′ pəs), *n.* (Relative standing of one's thoughts.) A modified sign for THINK is made: The right index finger touches the middle of the forehead. The tips of the right "V" hand, palm down, are then thrust into the upturned left palm (as in STAND, *q.v.*). The right "V" hand is then re-thrust into the upturned left palm, with right palm now facing the body. *Cf.* CONNOTE, IMPLY, INTEND, INTENT 1, INTENTION, MEAN 2, MEANING, MOTIVE 3, SIGNIFICANCE 2, SIGNIFY 2, SUBSTANCE 2.

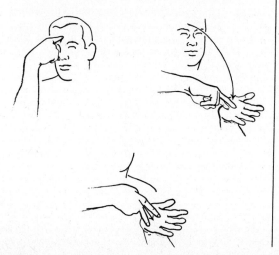

[P–420]

PURPOSE 2, *n.* (A thought directed upward, toward a goal.) The left "D" hand, palm facing the body, is held above the head, to represent the goal. The index finger of the right "D" hand, after touching the forehead (modified sign for THINK, as in PURPOSE 1), moves slowly and deliberately up to the tip of the left index finger. *Cf.* AIM, AMBITION, ASPIRE, GOAL, OBJECTIVE, PERSEVERE 4.

[P–421]

PURPOSE 3, *n.* (The letter "P"; the mind, seat of thought.) The middle finger of the right "P" hand describes a small, counterclockwise circle on the middle of the forehead.

[P–422]

PURSUE (pər sōō′), *v.,* -SUED, -SUING. (The natural sign.) The "A" hands are held in front of the body, with the thumbs facing forward, the right palm facing left and the left palm facing right. The left hand is held slightly ahead of the right; it then moves forward in a straight line while the right hand follows after, executing a circular motion or swerving back and forth, as if in pursuit. *Cf.* CHASE 1.

[P-423]

PUSH (poŏsh), *n., v.,* PUSHED, PUSHING. (The natural motion.) The outstretched "5" hands push an imaginary object.

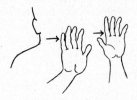

[P-424]

PUT (poŏt), *v.,* PUT, PUTTING. (Moving from one place to another.) The downturned hands, fingers touching their respective thumbs, move in unison from left to right. *Cf.* MIGRATE, MOVE, PLACE 3, REMOVE 2, TRANSFER 2.

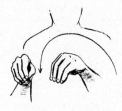

[P-425]

PUT DOWN, *v. phrase.* (The natural motion.) The downturned "O" hands are brought down and to the left simultaneously from an initial side-by-side position near the right shoulder. *Cf.* DEPOSIT 1.

[P-426]

PUT IN ORDER, *v. phrase.* (Placing things in order.) The hands, palms facing, fingers together and pointing away from the body, are positioned at the left side and held about a foot apart. With a slight up-down motion, as if describing waves, the hands travel in unison from left to right. *Cf.* ARRANGE, ARRANGEMENT, CLASSED 2, DEVISE 1, ORDER 3, PLAN 1, POLICY 1, PREPARE 1, PROGRAM 1, PROVIDE 1, READY 1, SCHEME, SYSTEM.

[P-427]

PUT OFF, *v. phrase.* (Putting off; moving things forward repeatedly.) The "F" hands, palms facing and fingers pointing out from the body, are moved forward simultaneously in a series of short movements. *Cf.* DEFER, DELAY, POSTPONE, PROCRASTINATE.

[P-428]

PUTTY (pŭt′ĭ), *n.* (The natural motion.) The thumb of the right "A" hand goes through the motion of pressing putty into an imaginary crack in the left palm. The action is repeated several times.

Q

QUADRANT (kwŏd′ rənt), *n.* (The natural "one over four" sign.) The "1" hand drops down, assuming the "4" position. *Cf.* FOURTH, QUARTER.

[Q–2]

QUAIL 1 (kwāl), *(rare), n.* The sign for BIRD is made: The right thumb and index finger are placed against the mouth, pointing straight out. They open and close, to represent the beak. The extended right index fingertip is then placed against the right side of the neck, and the hand is pivoted at the wrist a number of times.

[Q–3]

QUAIL 2, (rare), *n.* (The stripe at the neck.) The sign for BIRD, as in QUAIL 1, is made. The down-turned, right index finger then traces a line along the

right side of the neck, moving up toward the back of the right ear.

[Q–4]

QUAKE (kwāk), *(colloq.), v.,* QUAKED, QUAKING. (The legs tremble.) Both "D" hands, index fingers pointing down, are held side by side to represent the legs. The hands tremble.

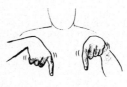

[Q–5]

QUAKER (kwā′ kər), *n.* (Twiddling the thumbs in church.) With hands clasped, the thumbs rotate around each other a number of times.

[Q–6]

QUANTITY 1 (kwŏn′ tə tĭ), *n.* (The upper and lower limits are defined.) The right-angle hands, palms facing, are held before the body, the right above the left. They swing out 45 degrees simultaneously, pivoted from their wrists. *Cf.* CAPACITY, LIMIT, RESTRICT.

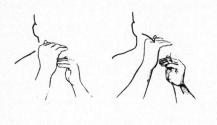

[Q–7]

QUANTITY 2, *n.* (Many fingers are indicated.) The upturned "S" hands are thrown up, opening into the "5" position, palms up. This may be repeated. *Cf.* MANY, MULTIPLE, NUMEROUS, PLURAL.

[Q–8]

QUARREL (kwôr′ əl, kwŏr′ -), *n., v.* -RELED, -RELING. (Repeated rejoinders.) Both "D" hands are held with index fingers pointing toward each other. The hands move up and down alternately, each pivoting in turn at the wrist. *Cf.* ROW 2.

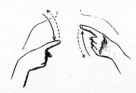

[Q–9]

QUARTER (kwôr′ tər), *n.* (The natural "one over four" sign.) The "1" hand drops down, assuming the "4" position. *Cf.* FOURTH, QUADRANT.

[Q–10]

QUARTER-HOUR, *n.* (The movement of the minute hand.) The thumb edge of the right "D" hand is placed against the left palm, which is facing right. From its initial position pointing straight up, the right index finger, pivoting at the wrist, swings down 90 degrees. Contact is maintained with the left palm at all times.

[Q–11]

QUEEN (kwēn), *n.* (The letter "Q"; the royal sash.) The right "Q" hand, palm down, moves from left shoulder to right hip, tracing the sash worn by royalty.

[Q–12]

QUEER 1 (kwĭr), *adj.* (Something which distorts the vision.) The "C" hand describes a small arc in front of the face. *Cf.* CURIOUS 2, GROTESQUE, ODD, PECULIAR, STRANGE 1, WEIRD.

[Q–13]

QUEER 2, *(sl.)*, *adj.* (An effeminate gesture.) The right fingertips slap the back of the limply held left wrist.

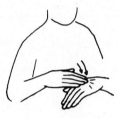

[Q–14]

QUERY 1 (kwĭr′ ĭ), *n.*, *v.*, -RIED, -RYING. (Firing questions.) The index fingers of both "D" hands repeatedly curve and straighten out as the hands are alternately flung forward and back, as if firing questions. *Cf.* ASK 3, EXAMINATION 3, INQUIRE 3, INTERROGATE 1, INTERROGATION 1, QUESTION 3, QUIZ 3.

[Q–15]

QUERY 2, *(colloq.)*, *n.* (Fire a question.) The right hand, held in a modified "S" position with palm facing out, assumes a position with the thumb resting on the fingernail of the index finger. The index finger is flicked out and forward, usually directed at the person being asked a question. *Cf.* ASK 2, EXAM-

INATION 2, INQUIRE 2, INTERROGATE 2, INTERROGATION 2, QUESTION 2, QUIZ 2.

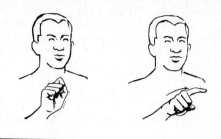

[Q–16]

QUEST (kwĕst), *n.* (Directing the vision from place to place.) The right "C" hand, palm facing left, moves from right to left across the line of vision, in a series of counterclockwise circles. The signer's gaze remains concentrated and his head turns slowly from right to left. *Cf.* CURIOUS 1, EXAMINE, INVESTIGATE 1, LOOK FOR, PROBE 1, SEARCH, SEEK.

[Q–17]

QUESTION 1 (kwĕs′ chən), *n.* (The natural sign.) The right index finger draws a question mark in the air. *Cf.* QUESTION MARK.

[Q–18]

QUESTION 2, *n.* See QUERY 2.

[Q–19]

QUESTION 3, *n.* See QUERY 1.

[Q–20]

QUESTION MARK, *n.* See QUESTION 1.

[Q–21]

QUESTIONNAIRE (kwĕs´ chə nâr´), *n.* (A list of questions on a sheet of paper.) The sign for EXAMINATION is made: Both "D" hands, palms down, simultaneously execute a simple circle, the right hand moving in a clockwise direction and the left in a counterclockwise direction. Upon completion of the circle, both hands open into the "5" position and move straight down a short distance. (The hands actually draw question marks in the air.) The index fingers then describe the outlines of a sheet of paper.

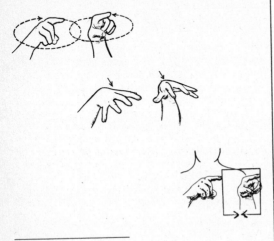

[Q–22]

QUEUE (kū), *n., v.,* QUEUED, QUEUING. (The fingers indicate a row of people, all in a line.) Both "5" hands are held before the chest, with both palms facing left and little fingertips touching. The right hand moves straight back from the left a short distance. The same sign may also be made with right hand facing left and left hand facing right, and the initial position involving the right little fingertip touching the tip of the left index finger. *Cf.* LINE-UP, SINGLE FILE.

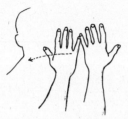

[Q–23]

QUICK (kwĭk), *adj.* (A quick movement.) The thumbtip of the upright right hand is flicked quickly

off the tip of the curved right index finger, as if shooting marbles. *Cf.* FAST 1, IMMEDIATELY, QUICKNESS, RAPID, RATE 1, SPEED, SPEEDY, SWIFT.

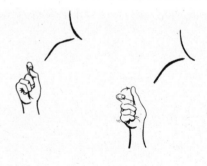

[Q–24]

QUICKNESS, *n.* See QUICK.

[Q–25]

QUIET 1 (kwī´ ət), *n., adj., interj., v.,* QUIETED, QUIETING. (The natural sign.) The index finger is brought up against the pursed lips. *Cf.* BE QUIET 1, CALM 2, HUSH, NOISELESS, SILENCE 1, SILENT, STILL 2.

[Q–26]

QUIET 2, *n., adj., interj., v.* (Quiet and peace.) The open hands are crossed before the mouth, the right palm facing left, left facing right. Then both hands, held palms down, move down from the mouth, curving outward to either side of the body. *Cf.* BE QUIET 2, BE STILL, CALM 1, SILENCE 2.

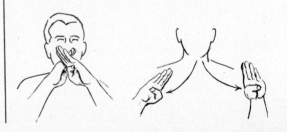

[Q–27]

QUIT (kwĭt), *v.*, QUIT, QUITTING. (Pulling out.) The index and middle fingers of the right "H" hand are grasped by the left hand. The right hand pulls out of the left. *Cf.* RESIGN, WITHDRAW 3.

[Q–28]

QUIZ 1 (kwĭz), *v.*, QUIZZED, QUIZZING, *n.* (A series of questions, spread out on a page.) Both "D" hands, palms down, simultaneously execute a single circle, the right hand moving in a clockwise direction and the left in a counterclockwise direction. Upon completion of the circle, both hands open into the "5" position and move straight down a short distance. (The hands actually draw question marks in the air.) *Cf.* EXAMINATION 1, TEST.

[Q–29]

QUIZ 2, *(colloq.), n. v.,* (Fire a question.) The right hand, held in a modified "S" position with palm facing out, assumes a position with the thumb resting on the fingernail of the index finger. The index finger is flicked out and forward, usually directed at the person being asked a question. *Cf.* ASK 2, EXAMINATION 2, INQUIRE 2, INTERROGATE 2, INTERROGATION 2, QUERY 2, QUESTION 2.

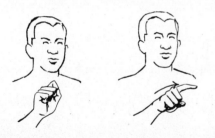

[Q–30]

QUIZ 3, *v., n.* (Firing questions.) The index fingers of both "D" hands repeatedly curve and straighten out as the hands are alternately flung forward and back, as if firing questions. *Cf.* ASK 3, EXAMINATION 3, INQUIRE 3, INTERROGATE 1, INTERROGATION 1, QUERY 1, QUESTION 3.

[Q–31]

QUOTATION (kwō tā′ shən), *n.* (The quotation marks are indicated.) The curved index and middle fingers of both hands, held palms out, move slightly to either side of the body, as if drawing quotation marks in the air. *Cf.* CAPTION, CITE, QUOTE, SO-CALLED, SUBJECT, THEME, TITLE, TOPIC.

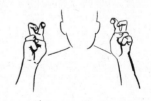

[Q–32]

QUOTE (kwōt), *n., v.,* QUOTED, QUOTING. See QUOTATION.

R

RABBI 1 (răb′ ĭ), *n.* (A Jewish minister or preacher.) The sign for JEW is made: The fingers and thumb of each hand are placed at the chin, and stroke an imaginary beard. This is followed by the sign for MINISTER or PREACHER: The right hand, palm out, with thumb and index finger touching, is moved forward and slightly downward a number of times from its initial position near the right temple. This is followed by the sign for INDIVIDUAL: Both open hands, palms facing each other, move down the sides of the body, tracing its outline to the hips.

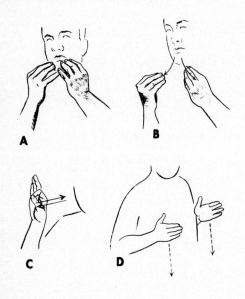

RABBI 2, *n.* (The letter "R"; the prayer shawl or talis.) Both upright "R" hands trace the fall of the shawl down the sides of the chest.

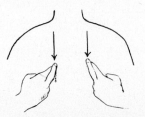

RABBIT 1 (răb′ ĭt), *n.* (The movement of the ears.) Both "U" hands are placed at either side of the head, palms facing back. The index and middle fingers, joined together, move forward and back repeatedly, imitating a rabbit's ears.

RABBIT 2, *n.* (Same rationale as for RABBIT 1.) The "H" hands are crossed at the wrists, palms facing the body. The index and middle fingers of both hands move up and down repeatedly.

RACCOON (ră kōōn′), *n.* (The stripes on the face.) The fingertips of the "V" hands, palms facing the body, are drawn across either side of the face, from below the eyes to just above the jaw.

[R–6]

RACE 1 (rās), *n., v.,* RACED, RACING. (Two opponents come together.) Both hands are closed, with thumbs pointing straight up and palms facing the body. From their initial position about a foot apart, the hands are brought together sharply, so that the knuckles strike. The hands, as they are drawn together, also move down a bit, so that they describe a "V." *Cf.* COMPETE 1, COMPETITION 1, CONTEND 1, CONTEST 1, RIVAL 2, RIVALRY 1, VIE 1.

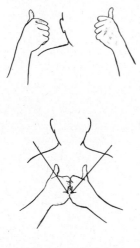

[R–7]

RACE 2, *n., v.* (Opposing objects.) The "A" hands are held side by side before the chest, palms facing each other and thumbs pointing forward. In this position the hands move alternately back and forth, toward and away from the body. *Cf.* COMPETE 2, COMPETITION 2, CONTEND 2, CONTEST 2, RIVAL 3, RIVALRY 2, VIE 2.

[R–8]

RACE 3, *n., v.,* (The changing fortunes of competitors.) The "A" hands are held facing each other, thumbs pointing up in front of the body. Both hands are moved alternately backward and forward past each other several times. *Cf.* COMPETE 3, COMPETITION 3, CONTEND 3, CONTEST 3, RIVAL 4, RIVALRY 3, VIE 3.

[R–9]

RACKET (răk' ĭt), *n.* (A shaking which disturbs the ear.) After placing the index finger on the ear, both hands assume the "S" position, palms down. They move alternately back and forth, forcefully. *Cf.* DIN, NOISE, NOISY, SOUND, THUNDER, VIBRATION.

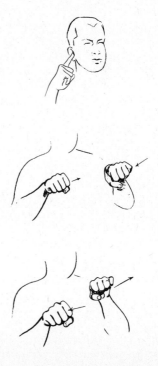

[R-10]

RADIO 1 (rā′ dĭ ō′), *n.* (The old-fashioned earphones.) The cupped hands are placed over the ears.

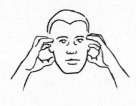

[R-11]

RADIO 2, *n.* (The earphone and dials.) One or both hands are cupped over the ears, and then the fingers manipulate a set of imaginary dials.

[R-12]

RADISH (răd′ ĭsh), *n.* (The color and the shape.) The sign for RED is made: The tip of the right index finger moves down across the lips. The right hand, palm facing left, is held with thumb and index finger touching. The left index finger rests on the tip of its right counterpart, then swings up in a small arc, coming to rest on the right thumb. This outlines the shape of the radish.

[R-13]

RAGE (rāj), *n., v.,* RAGED, RAGING. (A violent welling-up of the emotions.) The curved fingers of the

right hand are placed in the center of the chest, and fly up suddenly and violently. An expression of anger is worn. *Cf.* ANGER, ANGRY 2, ENRAGE, FURY, INDIGNANT, INDIGNATION, IRE, MAD 1.

[R-14]

RAILROAD 1 (rāl′ rōd′), *n.* (Running along the tracks.) The "V" hands are held palms down. The right "V" fingers move over the backs of the downturned left "V" fingers from base to tips. *Cf.* CARS, TRAIN 1.

[R-15]

RAILROAD 2, *n.* (The letter "R.") The right "R" hand, palm down, moves down an inch or two, and moves to the right in a small arc.

[R-16]

RAILROAD TRACK (rāl′ rōd trăk), *n. phrase.* The extended index and middle fingers of the downturned right hand move back and forth crosswise over the same two fingers of the downturned left hand. Both "G" hands, held side by side, then move forward. *Cf.* TRACK 1.

[R-17]

RAIN (rān), *n., v.,* RAINED, RAINING. (The falling of the raindrops.) Both "5" hands, palms down, move down simultaneously, with fingers wiggling. The sign is sometimes preceded by the sign for WATER 1: The right "W" hand, palm facing left, touches the lips a number of times.

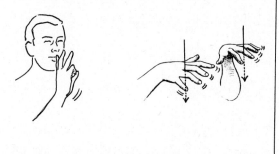

[R-18]

RAISE 1 (rāz), *v.,* RAISED, RAISING, *n.* (Getting onto one's feet.) The upturned index and middle fingers of the right hand, representing the legs, are swung up and over in an arc, coming to rest in the upturned left palm. *Cf.* ARISE 2, ELEVATE, GET UP, RISE 1, STAND 2, STAND UP.

[R-19]

RAISE 2, *n., v.* (Adding on.) The index and middle fingers of the right "H" hand, palm up, are swung up and over until they come to rest on the index and middle fingers of the left "H" hand, held palm down. *Cf.* ADD 3, ADDITION, EXTEND 1, EXTRA, GAIN 1, INCREASE, ON TO.

[R-20]

RAISE 3, *n., v.* (Flowers or plants emerge from the ground.) The right fingers, pointing up, emerge from the closed left hand, and they spread open as they do. *Cf.* BLOOM, DEVELOP 1, GROW, GROWN, MATURE, PLANT 1, REAR 2, SPRING 1.

[R-21]

RAISE 4, *v.* (To bring up, say, a child.) The downturned, open left hand slowly rises straight up, indicating the growth of a child. The right hand may also be used.

[R-22]

RAKE (rāk), *n., v.,* RAKED, RAKING. (The natural sign.) The downturned right hand scratches the upturned, open left palm, moving toward the base of the left hand as it does. The movement is usually repeated.

[R-23]

RAP (răp), *n., v.,* RAPPED, RAPPING. (The natural sign.) The right knuckles knock against the palm of the left hand, which is facing right. *Cf.* KNOCK.

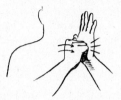

[R-24]

RAPID (răp′ĭd), *adj.* (A quick movement.) The thumbtip of the upright right hand is flicked quickly off the tip of the curved right index finger, as if shooting marbles. *Cf.* FAST 1, IMMEDIATELY, QUICK, QUICKNESS, RATE 1, SPEED, SPEEDY, SWIFT.

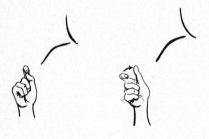

[R-25]

RARE (râr), *adj.* (The fingers are presented in order, to convey the concept of "several.") The right "A" hand is held palm facing up. One by one the fingers open, beginning with the index finger and ending with the little finger. Some use only the index and middle fingers. *Cf.* FEW, SCARCE, SEVERAL, SUNDRY.

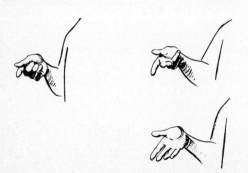

[R-26]

RAT (răt), *n.* (The twitching nose.) The tips of the right "R" fingers brush the tip of the nose several times.

[R-27]

RATE 1 (rāt), *n., v.,* RATED, RATING. See RAPID.

[R-28]

RATE 2, *n., v.* (Drawing a percent symbol in the air.) The right "O" hand traces the percent symbol (%) in the air. *Cf.* PERCENT.

[R-29]

RATHER (răth′ər, räth′ər), *adv.* (Derived from BETTER, the comparative degree of GOOD, *q.v.*) The tips of the right "5" hand touch the lips repeatedly.

[R–30]

RATIO (rā′ shō, -shǐ ō′), *n.* (In proportion.) Both "D" or "P" hands, palms facing down, are held before the body. They describe a short arc from right to left and, while unnecessary, they may return to their original position. *Cf.* HENCE, PROPORTION, THEREFORE 1, THUS.

[R–31]

RATTLESNAKE (răt′ əl snāk′), *n.* (The characteristic shaking of the snake's rattles.) The right "D" hand is held upright, with the right elbow resting on the downturned left hand. The right index finger, held rigid, trembles slightly. The "R" hand may be used instead of the "D."

[R–32]

RAY (rā), *n.* (The candle flame and the rays of light.) The index finger of the "D" hand is placed on the pursed lips, as if blowing out a candle. The right hand is then raised above the head, with the fingertips and thumbtip touching, and palm facing out. The hand then moves down and a bit forward, opening into the "5" position, palm down. (The "candle"

part of this sign is frequently omitted.) *Cf.* EPIPHANY, LIGHT 1.

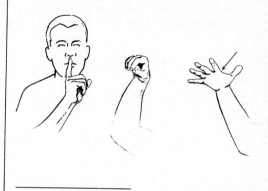

[R–33]

RAZOR (rā′ zər), *n.* (The natural sign.) The right "Y" hand represents an opened straight razor. The right thumb is drawn down the side of the right cheek. *Cf.* SHAVE.

[R–34]

REACH (rēch), *v.,* REACHED, REACHING. (Arrival at a designated place.) The right hand, palm facing the body and fingers pointing up, is brought forward from a position near the right shoulder and placed in the upturned palm of the left hand (the designated place). *Cf.* ARRIVAL, ARRIVE.

[R-35]

REACTION (rĭ ăk′ shən), *n.* (The letter "R"; coming out of the mouth.) Both "R" hands are held before the face, with the right "R" hand at the lips and behind the left "R" hand. Both hands move forward simultaneously, describing a small upward arc. *Cf.* ANSWER 2, REPLY 2, REPORT, RESPONSE 2.

[R-36]

READ 1 (rēd), *v.*, READ, READING. (The eyes scan the page.) The left hand is held before the body, palm up and fingers pointing to the right. This represents the page. The right "V" hand then moves down as if scanning the page.

[R-37]

READ 2, *v.* (The eyes scan a page.) The index and middle fingers of the right "V" hand represent the eyes and follow imaginary lines on the left palm, which represents the page of a book.

[R-38]

READ 3, *v.* (Reading a book.) The open hands support an imaginary book. The signer, looking at the book, moves his head repeatedly from left to right as if reading.

[R-39]

READ LIPS, *v. phrase.* (Reading the lips—the lines of vision, represented by the two fingers, scan the lips.) The right "V" hand, palm facing the body, is placed in front of the face, with slightly curved index and middle fingers directly in front of the lips. The right hand moves in a small counterclockwise circle around the lips. *Cf.* LIPREADING, ORAL, SPEECH-READING.

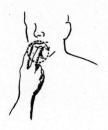

[R-40]

READY 1 (rĕd′ ĭ), *adj., v.*, READIED, READYING. (Placing things in order.) The hands, palms facing, fingers together and pointing away from the body, are positioned at the left side and held about a foot apart. With a slight up-down motion, as if describing waves, the hands travel in unison from left to right. *Cf.* ARRANGE, ARRANGEMENT, CLASSED 2, DEVISE 1, ORDER 3, PLAN 1, POLICY 1, PREPARE 1, PROGRAM 1, PROVIDE 1, PUT IN ORDER, SCHEME, SYSTEM.

[R-41]

READY 2, *adj.* (The "R" hands.) The "R" hands are held side by side before the body, palms up and fingers pointing outward. The hands then turn toward each other and over, so that the palms face down and fingers point toward each other. *Cf.* PREPARE 2.

[R–42]

READY 3, *adj., adv.* (The "R" hands.) The same sign as for READY 1, *q.v.,* is made, except that the "R" hands are used. With palms facing down, they move simultaneously from left to right. *Cf.* GET READY.

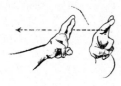

[R–43]

READY 4, *adj., v.* (Set out.) The "A" hands are crossed, with the right resting on top of the left. The right palm faces left and the left palm faces right. Both hands suddenly open and swing apart to the palm-down position. *Cf.* PREPARE 3.

[R–44]

REAL (rē' əl, rēl), *adj.* (Coming forth directly from the lips; true.) The index finger of the right "D" hand, palm facing left, is placed against the lips. It moves up an inch or two and then describes a small arc forward and away from the lips. *Cf.* ABSOLUTE, ABSOLUTELY, ACTUAL, ACTUALLY, AUTHENTIC, CERTAIN, CERTAINLY, FAITHFUL 3, FIDELITY, FRANKLY, GENUINE, INDEED, POSITIVE 1, POSITIVELY, REALLY, SINCERE 2, SURE, SURELY, TRUE, TRULY, TRUTH, VALID, VERILY.

[R–45]

REALIZE (rē' ə līz'), *v.,* -IZED, -IZING. (Knowing and understanding.) The sign for KNOW is made: The right fingers pat the forehead several times. This is followed by the sign for UNDERSTAND: The curved index finger of the right hand, palm facing the body, is placed with the fingernail resting on the middle of the forehead. It suddenly flicks up into the "D" position.

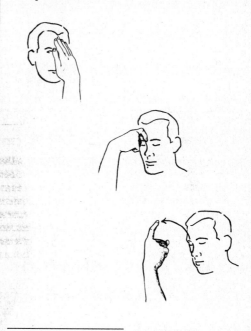

[R–46]

REALLY (rē' ə lĭ, rē' lĭ), *adv.* See REAL.

[R–47]

REAP 1 (rēp), *v.,* REAPED, REAPING. (Cutting the stalks.) The left hand holds an imaginary bunch of stalks, and the right hand, holding an imaginary sickle, sweeps under the left as if cutting the stalks. The right "X" hand may also be used. Here the curved finger represents the blade. *Cf.* HARVEST 1.

[R–48]

REAP 2, *v.* (Gathering in the harvest.) The right open hand sweeps across the upturned left palm and closes into the "A" position, as if gathering up some stalks. *Cf.* HARVEST 2.

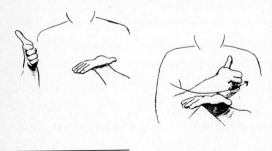

[R–49]

REAP 3, *v.* (The cutting.) The left hand grasps the heads of imaginary wheat stalks. The upturned right hand, imitating a sickle blade, then swings in to cut the stalks. *Cf.* HARVEST 3.

[R–50]

REAR 1 (rĭr), *n.* (The natural sign.) The right hand moves over the right shoulder to tap the back. *Cf.* BACK 2.

[R–51]

REAR 2, *v.* (Flowers or plants emerge from the ground.) The right fingers, pointing up, emerge from the closed left hand, and they spread open as they

do. *Cf.* BLOOM, DEVELOP 1, GROW, GROWN, MATURE, PLANT 1, RAISE 3, SPRING 1.

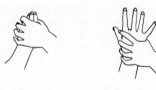

[R–52]

REASON 1 (rē′ zən), *n.* (The letter "R"; the thought.) The fingertips of the right "R" hand describe a small counterclockwise circle in the middle of the forehead.

[R–53]

REASON 2, *n.* (Rays of influence emanating from a given source.) All the right fingertips, including the thumb, are positioned on the tip of the upturned thumb of the left "A" hand. The right hand, opening into the downturned "5" position, moves forward from its initial position. Instead of its initial position on the left thumb, the right hand is frequently placed on the back of the downturned left "S" hand, moving forward as described above. *Cf.* BASIS 1, CAUSE, EFFECT 1, INFLUENCE 2, INTENT 2, LOGIC, PRODUCE 4.

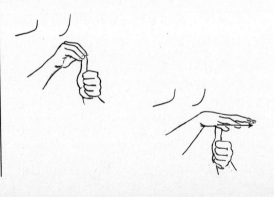

[R-54]

REBEL (*adj., n.* rĕb' əl; *v.* rĭ bĕl'), -BELLED, -BELL-ING. (Turning the head.) The right "S" hand, held up with its palm facing the body, swings sharply around to the palm-out position. The head meanwhile moves slightly toward the left. *Cf.* DISOBEDI-ENCE, DISOBEY.

[R-55]

RECALL 1 (rĭ kôl'), *v.,* -CALLED, -CALLING. (Bringing something back from the past.) The right open hand reaches back over the right shoulder as if to grasp something, and then brings the imaginary thing before the face with the closed "AND" hand. *Cf.* RECOLLECT 1.

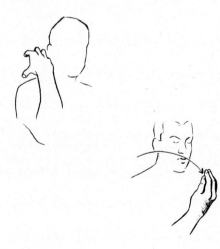

[R-56]

RECALL 2, *v.* (Knowledge which remains.) The sign for KNOW is made: The right fingertips are placed on the forehead. The sign for REMAIN then follows: The "A" hands are held with palms toward the body, thumbs extended and touching, the right behind the left. In this position the hands move for-

ward in a straight, steady line, or straight down. *Cf.* MEMORY, RECOLLECT 2, REMEMBER.

[R-57]

RECEIVE (rĭ sēv'), *v.,* -CEIVED, -CEIVING. (A grasping and bringing forward to oneself.) Both hands, in the "5" position, fingers curved, are crossed at the wrists, with the left palm facing right and the right palm facing left. They are brought in toward the chest, while closing into a grasping "S" position. *Cf.* ACQUIRE, GET, OBTAIN, PROCURE.

[R-58]

RECENT (rē' sənt), *adj.* (The slight movement represents a slight amount of time.) With the closed right hand held with knuckles against the right cheek, the thumbtip flicks off the tip of the curved index finger a number of times. The eyes squint a bit and the lips are drawn out in a slight smile. The hand remains against the cheek during the flicking movement. Sometimes, instead of the flicking movement, the tip of the curved index finger scratches slightly up and down against the cheek. In this case, the palm faces back toward the shoulder. The same expression is used as in the flicking movement. *Cf.* JUST NOW 2, RECENTLY, WHILE AGO, A 2.

[R–59]

RECENTLY, *adv.* See RECENT.

[R–60]

RECITATION (rĕs´ ə tā´ shən), *n.* (Studying back and forth.) This sign is derived from the sign for STUDY, *q.v.* The right-angle hands face each other, with the right hand facing left and the left hand facing right. They move alternately forward and back, with fingers wiggling.

[R–61]

RECKLESS (rĕk´ lĭs), *adj.* (The vision is side-tracked, causing one to lose sight of the object in view.) The right "V" hand, representing the vision, is held in front of the face, palm facing left. The hand, pivoted at the wrist, moves back and forth a number of times. *Cf.* CARELESS, HEEDLESS, THOUGHTLESS.

[R–62]

RECKON (rĕk´ ən), *v.,* -ONED, -ONING. (A thought is turned over in the mind.) The index finger makes a small circle on the forehead. *Cf.* CONSIDER 1, MOTIVE 1, SPECULATE 1, SPECULATION 1, THINK, THOUGHT 1, THOUGHTFUL.

[R–63]

RECLINE (rĭ klīn´), *v.,* -CLINED, -CLINING. (The prone position of the legs, in lying down.) The index and middle fingers of the right "V" hand, palm facing up, are placed in the upturned left palm. *Cf.* LIE 3, LIE DOWN.

[R–64]

RECOGNIZE (rĕk´ əg nīz´), *v.,* -NIZED, -NIZING. (Patting the head to indicate something of value inside.) The right fingers pat the forehead several times. *Cf.* INTELLIGENCE, KNOW, KNOWLEDGE.

[R–65]

RECOLLECT 1 (rĕk ə lĕkt´), *v.,* -LECTED, -LECTING. (Bringing something back from the past.) The right open hand reaches back over the right shoulder as if to grasp something, and then brings the imaginary thing before the face with the closed "AND" hand. *Cf.* RECALL 1.

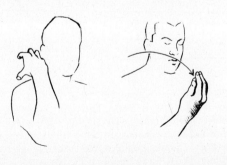

[R–66]

RECOLLECT 2, *v.* (Knowledge which remains.) The sign for KNOW is made: The right fingertips are placed on the forehead. The sign for REMAIN then follows: The "A" hands are held with palms toward the body, thumbs extended and touching, the right behind the left. In this position the hands move forward in a straight, steady line, or straight down. *Cf.* MEMORY, RECALL 2, REMEMBER.

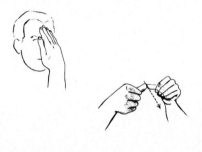

[R–67]

RECREATION (rĕk´ ri ā´ shən), *n.* (Shaking tambourines.) The "Y" hands, held aloft, are shaken back and forth, pivoted at the wrists. *Cf.* FROLIC, PLAY 1.

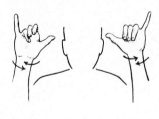

[R–68]

RECTOR (rĕk´ tər), *n.* (The sign of the Oremus at Mass.) The "F" hands, palms facing and thumb sides facing up, are joined at their respective fingertips. They separate, move apart and toward the body in half circles, and come together again in their initial position, closer to the body than before. *Cf.* PRIEST 4, REVEREND.

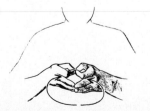

[R–69]

RED (rĕd), *adj., n.* (The lips, which are red, are indicated.) The tip of the right index finger moves down across the lips. The "R" hand may also be used.

[R–70]

REDEDICATE (rē dĕd ə kāt´), *v.,* -CATED, -CATING. (Grasping something and giving it over, again.) Both open hands are held palms facing inward before the body, the right hand slightly above the left, thumb edges up. In this position the hands close into the "S" position; then they open and turn over, to lie side by side before the body, palms up, fingers pointing forward. Finally, the sign for AGAIN is made: The left hand, open in the "5" position, palm up, is held before the chest. The right hand, in the right-angle position, fingers pointing up, arches over and into the left palm.

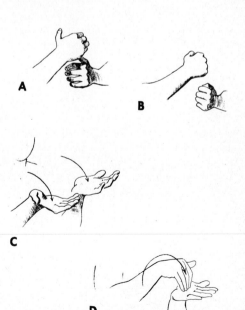

[R–71]

REDEEM 1 (rĭ dēm′), v., -DEEMED, -DEEMING. (Breaking the bonds.) The "S" hands, crossed in front of the body, swing apart and face out. Cf. DELIVER 1, EMANCIPATE, FREE 1, INDEPENDENCE, INDEPENDENT, LIBERATION, RELIEF, RESCUE, SAFE, SALVATION, SAVE 1.

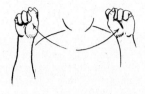

[R–72]

REDEEM 2, v. (The "R" hands.) The sign for REDEEM 1 is made with the "R" hands.

[R–73]

REDEEMER (rĭ dē′ mər), n. (One who redeems.) The sign for REDEEM 1 or 2 is made. This is followed by the sign for INDIVIDUAL: Both open hands, palms facing each other, move down the sides of the body, tracing its outline to the hips.

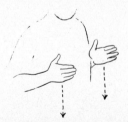

[R–74]

REDUCE (rĭ dūs′, -dōōs′), v., -DUCED, -DUCING. (The diminishing size or amount.) With palms facing, the right hand is held above the left. The right hand moves slowly down toward the left, but does not touch it. Cf. DECREASE, LESS 1.

[R–75]

REFER (rĭ fûr′), v., -FERRED, -FERRING. (The letter "R," transferring.) The fingertips of the right "R" hand touch the palm of the open left hand, which is held with palm facing right, fingers pointing upward. From this position the right hand moves backward, off the left palm.

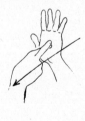

[R–76]

REFEREE (rĕf ə rē′), n. (Judge, individual.) The sign for JUDGE is formed: The two "F" hands, palms facing each other, move alternately up and down. This is followed by the sign for INDIVIDUAL: Both open hands, palms facing each other, move down the sides of the body, tracing its outline to the hips. Cf. JUDGE 2, UMPIRE.

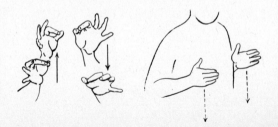

[R–77]

REFUGE (rĕf' ūj), *n.* (A shield.) The "S" hands are held before the chest, the left behind the right, and are pushed slightly away from the body. Then the right hand opens, palm facing out, and moves clockwise as if shielding the left fist. *Cf.* SHELTER, SHIELD 2.

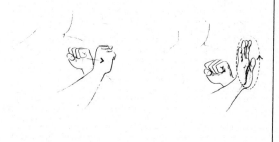

[R–78]

REFUSE (rĭ fūz'), *v.,* -FUSED, -FUSING. (Holding back.) The right "A" hand, palm facing left, moves up sharply to a position above the right shoulder. *Cf.* WON'T.

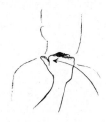

[R–79]

REGRET (rĭ grĕt'), *v.,* -GRETTED, -GRETTING, *n.* (The heart is circled, to indicate feeling, modified by the letter "S," for SORRY.) The right "S" hand, palm facing the body, is rotated several times over the area of the heart. *Cf.* APOLOGIZE 1, APOLOGY 1, CONTRITION, PENITENT, REGRETFUL, REPENT, REPENTANT, RUE, SORROW, SORROWFUL 2, SORRY.

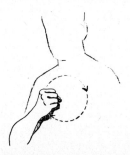

[R–80]

REGRETFUL (rĭ grĕt' fəl), *adj.* See REGRET.

[R–81]

REGULAR (rĕg' yə lər), *adj.* (Coming together with regular frequency.) Both "D" hands are held with index fingers pointing forward, the right hand above the left. The right "D" hand is brought down on the left several times in rhythmic succession as both hands move forward. *Cf.* CONSISTENT, FAITHFUL 1.

[R–82]

REGULATE (rĕg' yə lāt'), *v.,* -LATED, -LATING. (Holding the reins over all.) The "A" hands, palms facing, move alternately back and forth, as if grasping and manipulating reins. The left "A" hand, still in position, swings over so that its palm now faces down. The right hand opens to the "5" position, palm down, and swings over the left which moves slightly to the right. *Cf.* AUTHORITY, CONTROL 1, DIRECT 1, GOVERN, MANAGE, MANAGEMENT, MANAGER, OPERATE, REIGN, RULE 1.

[R–83]

REGULATION(S) (rĕg´ yə lā´ shən), *n.* (The letter "R"; the listing.) The upright, open left hand, fingers together and palm facing out, represents a piece of paper on which are listed the rules or regulations. The right "R" hand is placed upright against the tips of the left fingers, and then it moves down in an arc to a position against the base of the left hand. *Cf.* RULE(S) 2.

___

[R–84]

REHABILITATION (rē´ hə bĭl´ ə tā´ shən), *n.* (The letter "R"; one hand helps or supports the other.) The right "R" hand rests with its base or side in the upturned left palm. The left hand pushes up the right a short distance.

___

[R–85]

REIGN (rān), *n.* See REGULATE.

___

[R–86]

REINFORCE (rē´ in fōrs´), *v.,* -FORCED, -FORCING. (The letter "R"; pushing up, *i.e.,* assisting or reinforcing.) The right "R" hand, palm facing down, pushes up the left "S" hand, which is facing right.

[R–87]

REINS (rānz), *n. pl.* (Holding the reins.) The hands grasp and manipulate imaginary reins.

___

[R–88]

REJECT (*n.* rē´ jĕkt; *v.* ri jĕkt´), -JECTED, -JECTING. (The act of rejecting or sending off.) The downturned, right right-angle hand is positioned just above the base of the upturned, open left hand. The right hand sweeps forward in an arc over the left, and its fingertips brush sharply against the left palm. *Cf.* REJECTION.

___

[R–89]

REJECTION (ri jĕk´ shən), *n.* See REJECT.

___

[R–90]

REJOICE (ri jois´), *v.,* -JOICED, -JOICING. (Waving of flags.) Both upright hands, grasping imaginary flags, wave them in small circles. *Cf.* CELEBRATE, CELEBRATION, CHEER, VICTORY 1, WIN 1.

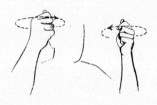

___

[R–91]

RELAPSE (ri lăps´), *n., v.,* -LAPSED, -LAPSING. (Going down.) The little finger edge of the open right hand is placed at the elbow of the downturned left arm. The right hand travels down the left arm in one sweeping movement, or in short stages. This is the opposite of IMPROVE, *q.v.*

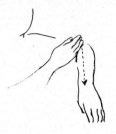

[R–92]

RELATION (rǐ lā' shən), *(rare), n.* (A variation of the COUSIN sign, *q.v.*) The right "C" hand, held near the right temple, wiggles down to shoulder level.

[R–93]

RELATIONSHIP 1 (rǐ lā' shən shǐp'), *n.* (The fingers are connected.) The index fingers and thumbs of both hands interlock, and the hands move back and forth from right to left. *Cf.* CONNECTION.

[R–94]

RELATIONSHIP 2, *n.* (The "R" hands.) The fingertips of the "R" hands move toward each other and touch. This is followed by the -SHIP suffix sign: The

downturned right "S" hand moves down along the left palm, which is facing away from the body.

[R–95]

RELATIVE 1 (rěl' ə tǐv), *n.* (Touching one another, as members of a family.) The "D" hands, palms facing the body and index fingers pointing toward each other, swing alternately up and down. Each time they pass each other, the index fingertips come into mutual contact. *Cf.* KIN.

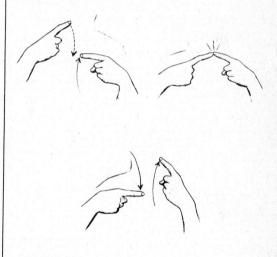

[R–96]

RELATIVE 2, *adj.* (Joining together.) Both hands, held in the modified "5" position, palms out, move toward each other. The thumbs and index fingers of both hands then connect. *Cf.* AFFILIATE 1, ANNEX, ASSOCIATE 2, ATTACH, BELONG, COMMUNION OF SAINTS, CONCERN 2, CONNECT, ENLIST, ENROLL, JOIN 1, PARTICIPATE, UNION, UNITE.

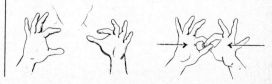

[R-97]

RELAX 1 (rĭ lăks′), *v.*, -LAXED, -LAXING. (The folded arms; a position of rest.) With palms facing the body, the arms are folded across the chest. *Cf.* LIMBO, REST 1, RESTFUL 1.

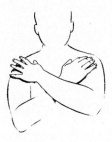

[R-98]

RELAX 2, *n.* (The "R" hands.) The sign for REST 1, *q.v.,* is made, but with the crossed "R" hands. *Cf.* REST 2, RESTFUL 2.

[R-99]

RELIEF (rĭ lēf′), *n.* (Breaking the bonds.) The "S" hands, crossed in front of the body, swing apart and face out. *Cf.* DELIVER 1, EMANCIPATE, FREE 1, INDEPENDENCE, INDEPENDENT, LIBERATION, REDEEM 1, RESCUE, SAFE, SALVATION, SAVE 1.

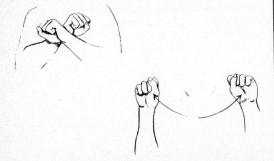

[R-100]

RELIGION (rĭ lĭj′ ən), *n.* (The letter "R"; directing the heart upward, toward God.) The right "R" hand is placed palm against the heart. It swings out, around, and up, in an arc.

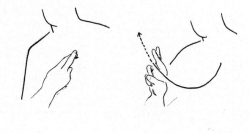

[R-101]

RELINQUISH (rĭ lĭng′ kwĭsh), *v.,* -QUISHED, -QUISHING. (Throwing up the hands in a gesture of surrender.) Both "A" hands are held palms down before the chest and then thrown up in unison, ending in the "5" position. *Cf.* ABDICATE, CEDE, DISCOURAGE 1, FORFEIT, GIVE UP, LOSE HOPE, RENOUNCE, RENUNCIATION, SURRENDER 1, YIELD 1.

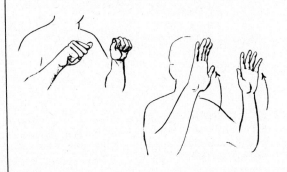

[R-102]

RELY 1 (rĭ lī′), *v.,* -LIED, -LYING. (Something which weighs down or burdens one with responsibility.) The fingertips of both hands, placed on the right shoulder, bear down. *Cf.* ATTRIBUTE 1, BEAR 4, BURDEN, OBLIGATION 1, RESPONSIBILITY 1, RESPONSIBLE 1.

[R-103]

RELY 2, *v.* (Hanging on to.) With the right index finger resting across its left counterpart, both hands drop down a bit. *Cf.* DEPEND 1, DEPENDABLE, DEPENDENT, HINGE 2.

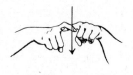

[R-104]

REMAIN (rĭ mān′), *v.*, -MAINED, -MAINING. (Steady, uninterrupted movement.) The "A" hands are held with palms out, thumbs extended and touching, the right behind the left. In this position the hands move forward in a straight, steady line, or down. *Cf.* CONTINUE 1, ENDURE 2, EVER 1, LAST 3, LASTING, PERMANENT, PERPETUAL, PERSEVERE 3, PERSIST 2, STAY 1, STAY STILL.

[R-105]

REMAINDER (rĭ mān′ dər), *n.* (The remainder is left behind.) The "5" hands, palms facing each other and fingers pointing forward, are dropped simultaneously a few inches, as if dropping something on the table. *Cf.* LEFT 2, RESERVE 4, REST 3.

[R-106]

REMARK (rĭ märk′), *v.*, -MARKED, -MARKING. (Words tumbling from the mouth.) The right index finger, pointing left, describes a continuous small circle in front of the mouth. *Cf.* BID 3, DISCOURSE,

HEARING, MAINTAIN 2, MENTION, SAID, SAY, SPEAK, SPEECH 1, STATE, STATEMENT, TALK 1, TELL, VERBAL 1.

[R-107]

REMEMBER (rĭ mĕm′ bər), *v.*, -BERED, -BERING. (Knowledge which remains.) The sign for KNOW is made: The right fingertips are placed on the forehead. The sign for REMAIN then follows: The "A" hands are held with palms toward the body, thumbs extended and touching, the right behind the left. In this position the hands move forward in a straight, steady line, or straight down. *Cf.* MEMORY, RECALL 2, RECOLLECT 2.

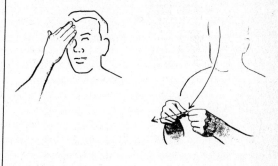

[R-108]

REMIND (rĭ mīnd′), *(colloq.) v.*, -MINDED, -MINDING. (Bring up to mind.) The index finger swings up quickly to the forehead. As it touches the forehead, the head tilts back. The eyes are sometimes opened wide for emphasis.

[R-109]

REMOTE (rĭ mōt'), *adj.* (Moving beyond, *i.e.,* the concept of distance or "farness.") The "A" hands are held together, thumbs pointing away from the body. The right hand moves straight ahead in a slight arc. The left hand does not move. *Cf.* DISTANCE, DISTANT, FAR, OFF 2.

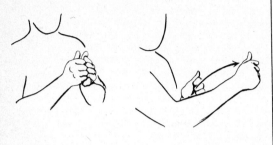

[R-110]

REMOVE 1 (rĭ mŏŏv'), *v.,* -MOVED, -MOVING. (Removing.) The right "A" hand, resting in the palm of the left "5" hand, moves slightly up and away, describing a small arc. It is then cast downward, opening into the "5" position, palm down, as if removing something from the left hand and casting it down. *Cf.* ABOLISH 2, ABSENCE 2, ABSENT 2, ABSTAIN, CHEAT 2, DEDUCT, DEFICIENCY, DELETE 1, LESS 2, MINUS 3, OUT 2, SUBTRACT, SUBTRACTION, TAKE AWAY FROM, WITHDRAW 2.

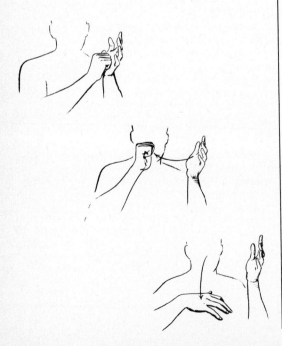

[R-111]

REMOVE 2, *v.* (Moving from one place to another.) The downturned hands, fingers touching their respective thumbs, move in unison from left to right. *Cf.* MIGRATE, MOVE, PLACE 3, PUT, TRANSFER 2.

[R-112]

REMOVE 3, *v.* (Wiping off.) The left "5" hand, palm up, is held slightly below the right "5" hand, held palm down. The right hand swings up, just brushing over the left palm. Both hands close into the "S" position, and the right is brought back with force to its initial position, striking a glancing blow against the left knuckles as it returns. *Cf.* ABOLISH 1, ANNIHILATE, CORRUPT, DEFACE, DEMOLISH, DESTROY, HAVOC, PERISH 2, RUIN.

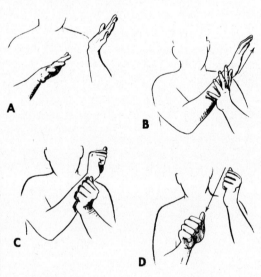

A   B

C   D

[R-113]

REND (rĕnd), *v.,* RENT, RENDING. (The natural motion.) Both "A" hands, held palms down before the body, grasp an imaginary object; then they move forcefully apart, as if tearing the object. *Cf.* RIP 1, TEAR 1.

[R–114]

RENDER 1, *v.*, -DERED, -DERING. (Fashioning something with the hands.) The right "S" hand, palm facing left, is placed on top of its left counterpart, whose palm faces right. The hands are twisted back and forth, striking each other slightly after each twist. *Cf.* COMPOSE, CONSTITUTE, CONSTRUCT 2, CREATE, DEVISE 2, FABRICATE, FASHION, FIX, MAKE, MANUFACTURE, MEND 1, PRODUCE 3, REPAIR.

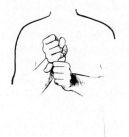 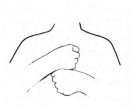

[R–115]

RENDER 2, *v.* (An activity.) Both open hands, palms down, are swung right and left before the chest. *Cf.* ACT 2, ACTION, ACTIVE, ACTIVITY, BUSY 2, CONDUCT 1, DEED, DO, PERFORM 1, PERFORMANCE 1.

[R–116]

RENDER JUDGMENT, *v. phrase.* (The mind stops wavering, and the pros and cons are resolved.) The right index finger touches the forehead, the sign for THINK, *q.v.* Both "F" hands, palms facing each other and fingers pointing straight out, then move up and down simultaneously. The sign for JUDGE,

q.v., explains the rationale behind the movement of the two hands here. *Cf.* DECIDE, DECISION, DECREE 1, DETERMINE, MAKE UP ONE'S MIND, MIND 5, RESOLVE, VERDICT.

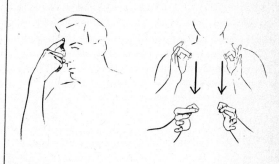

[R–117]

RENOUNCE (rĭ nouns'), *v.*, -NOUNCED, -NOUNCING. (Throwing up the hands in a gesture of surrender.) Both "A" hands are held palms down before the chest and then thrown up in unison, ending in the "5" position. *Cf.* ABDICATE, CEDE, DISCOURAGE 1, FORFEIT, GIVE UP, LOSE HOPE, RELINQUISH, RENUNCIATION, SURRENDER 1, YIELD.

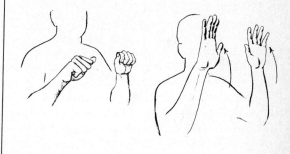

[R–118]

RENOWNED (rĭ nound'), *adj.* (One's fame radiates far and wide.) The extended index fingers rest on the lips (or on the temples). Moving in small, continuous spirals, they move up and to either side of the head. *Cf.* CELEBRATED, FAME, FAMOUS, PROMINENT 1.

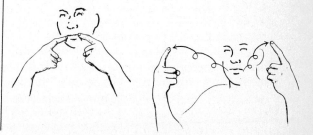

[R-119]

RENUNCIATION (rĭ nŭn′ sĭ ā′ shən, -shĭ-), *n.* See RENOUNCE.

[R-120]

REPAIR (rĭ pâr′), *v.*, -PAIRED, -PAIRING. (Fashioning something with the hands.) The right "S" hand, palm facing left, is placed on top of its counterpart, whose palm faces right. The hands are twisted back and forth, striking each other slightly after each twist. *Cf.* COMPOSE, CONSTITUTE, CONSTRUCT 2, CREATE, DEVISE 2, FABRICATE, FASHION, FIX, MAKE, MANUFACTURE, MEND 1, PRODUCE 3, RENDER 1.

[R-121]

REPEAT (rĭ pēt′), *v.*, -PEATED, -PEATING. The left hand, open in the "5" position, palm up, is held before the chest. The right hand, in the right angle position, fingers pointing up, arches over and into the left palm. *Cf.* AGAIN, ENCORE.

[R-122]

REPEATEDLY, *adv.* (Repeating over and over again.) The sign for REPEAT is made several times.

[R-123]

REPENT (rĭ pĕnt′), *v.*, -PENTED, -PENTING. (The heart is circled, to indicate feeling, modified by the letter "S," for SORRY.) The right "S" hand, palm

facing the body, is rotated several times over the area of the heart. *Cf.* APOLOGIZE 1, APOLOGY 1, CONTRITION, PENITENT, REGRET, REGRETFUL, REPENTANT, RUE, SORROW, SORROWFUL 2, SORRY.

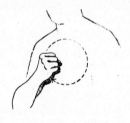

[R-124]

REPENTANT (rĭ pĕn′ tənt), *adj.* See REPENT.

[R-125]

REPLACE (rĭ plās′), *v.*, -PLACED, -PLACING. (Exchanging places.) The right "A" hand, positioned above the left "A" hand, swings down and under the left, coming up a bit in front of it. *Cf.* EXCHANGE, INSTEAD OF 1, SUBSTITUTE, TRADE.

[R-126]

REPLY 1 (rĭ plī′), *n., v.*, -PLIED, -PLYING. (Directing a reply from the mouth to someone.) The tip of the right index finger, held in the "D" position, palm facing the body, is placed on the lips, while the left "D" hand, palm also facing the body, is held about a foot in front of the right hand. The right index finger, swinging around, moves toward and stops in a pointing position a few inches from the left index fingertip. *Cf.* ANSWER 1, MAKE RESPONSE, RESPOND, RESPONSE 1.

[R-127]

REPLY 2, *v.* (The letter "R"; coming out of the mouth.) Both "R" hands are held before the face, with the right "R" hand at the lips and behind the left "R" hand. Both hands move forward simultaneously, describing a small upward arc. *Cf.* ANSWER 2, REACTION, REPORT, RESPONSE 2.

[R-128]

REPORT (rĭ pōrt'), *v.*, -PORTED, -PORTING. See REPLY 2.

[R-129]

REPRESENT (rĕp´ rĭ zĕnt'), *v.*, -SENTED, -SENTING. (Directing the attention to something, and bringing it forward.) The right index finger points into the left palm, held facing out before the body. The left palm moves straight out. For the passive form of this verb, *i.e.,* BE SHOWN, the movement is reversed: The left hand, palm facing in, is moved in toward the body, while the right index finger remains pointing into the left palm. *Cf.* DEMONSTRATE, DISPLAY, EVIDENCE, EXAMPLE, EXHIBIT, EXHIBITION, ILLUSTRATE, INDICATE, INFLUENCE 3, PRODUCE 2, SHOW 1, SIGNIFY 1.

[R-130]

REPRESENTATIVE (rĕp´ rĭ zĕn' tə tĭv), *n.* (The letter "R"; perhaps the drape of the Roman toga about the shoulders.) The right "R" hand, palm facing left, swings from the right shoulder to the left shoulder.

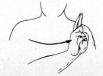

[R-131]

REPRIMAND (rĕp´ rə mănd´), *n., v.,* -MANDED, -MANDING. (A scolding with the finger.) The right index finger shakes back and forth in a natural scolding movement. *Cf.* ADMONISH 2, REPROVE, SCOLD 1.

[R-132]

REPROVE (rĭ prōōv'), *v.*, -PROVED, -PROVING. See REPRIMAND.

[R-133]

REPUBLICAN (rĭ pŭb´ lə kən), *n., adj.* (The letter "R.") The right "R" hand, palm facing out, is shaken slightly.

[R-134]

REQUEST 1 (rĭ kwĕst'), *n., v.,* -QUESTED, -QUESTING. (Pray tell.) Both hands, held upright about a foot in front of the chest, with palms facing and fingers pointing straight up, are positioned about a foot apart. Moving toward the chest, they come together until they touch, as if in prayer. *Cf.* ASK 1, CONSULT, INQUIRE 1.

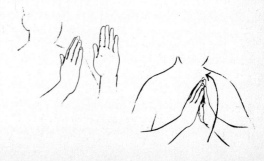

[R-135]

REQUEST 2, *n., v.* (Something specific is moved in toward oneself.) The palm of the left "5" hand faces right. The right index finger is thrust into the left palm, and both hands are drawn sharply in toward the chest. *Cf.* DEMAND, INSIST, REQUIRE.

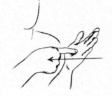

[R-136]

REQUIRE (rĭ kwīr'), *v.,* -QUIRED, -QUIRING. See RE-QUEST 2.

[R-137]

RESCUE (rĕs' kū), *v.,* -CUED, -CUING, *n.* (Breaking the bonds.) The "S" hands, crossed in front of the body, swing apart and face out. *Cf.* DELIVER 1, EMANCIPATE, FREE 1, INDEPENDENCE, INDEPENDENT, LIBERATION, REDEEM 1, RELIEF, SAFE, SALVATION, SAVE 1.

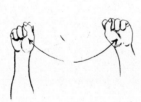

[R-138]

RESEARCH (rĭ sûrch', rē' sûrch), *n., v.,* -SEARCHED, -SEARCHING. (The letter "R"; digging or probing.) The right "R" hand moves in a series of short forward movements along the upturned left palm.

[R-139]

RESERVATION (rĕz' ər vā' shən), *n.* (Binding the hands down.) The downturned, right "S" hand makes a single, clockwise circle and comes down to rest on the back of the downturned, left "S" hand. *Cf.* RESERVE 1

[R-140]

RESERVE 1 (rĭ zûrv'), *v.* -SERVED, -SERVING. See RESERVATION.

[R-141]

RESERVE 2, *v.* (Slow, careful movement.) The "K" hands are crossed, the right above the left, little finger edges down. In this position the hands are moved up and down a short distance. *Cf.* CARE 2, CAREFUL 2, KEEP, MAINTAIN 1, MIND 3, PRESERVE, TAKE CARE OF 2.

[R-142]

RESERVE 3, *v.* (Holding back.) The right "V" fingers are tapped once or twice across the back of their left counterparts. Both palms face the chest. *Cf.* SAVE 2, STORE 2.

[R-143]

RESERVE 4, *n.* (The remainder is left behind.) The "5" hands, palms facing each other and fingers pointing forward, are dropped simultaneously a few inches, as if dropping something on the table. *Cf.* LEFT 2, REMAINDER, REST 3.

[R-144]

RESIDE (rĭ zīd′), *v.* -SIDED, -SIDING. (A place where one lives.) The "A" hands, thumbs up, are placed on either side of the body, at waist level. They slide up the body in unison, to chest level. This is the sign for LIFE or LIVE, indicating an upsurging of life. *Cf.* ADDRESS 3, ALIVE, DWELL, EXIST, LIFE 1, LIVE 1, LIVING, MORTAL.

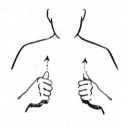

[R-145]

RESIDENCE 1 (rĕz′ ə dəns), *n.* (A place where one eats and sleeps.) The closed fingers of the right hand are placed against the lips (the sign for EAT), and then, opening into a flat palm, against the right cheek (resting the head on a pillow, as in SLEEP). The head leans slightly to the right, as if going to sleep in the right palm, during this latter movement. *Cf.* ADDRESS 2, HOME.

[R-146]

RESIDENCE 2, *n.* (The shape of the building.) The open hands are held with fingertips touching, so that they form a pyramid a bit above eye level. From this position, the hands separate and move diagonally downward for a short distance; then they continue straight down a few inches. This movement traces the outline of a roof and walls. *Cf.* BARN, DOMICILE, HOUSE.

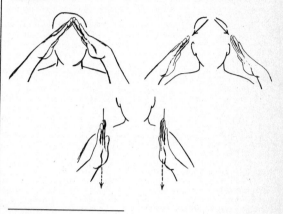

[R-147]

RESIGN (rĭ zīn′), *v.,* -SIGNED, -SIGNING. (Pulling out.) The index and middle fingers of the right "H" hand are grasped by the left hand. The right hand pulls out of the left. *Cf.* QUIT, WITHDRAW 3.

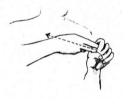

[R-148]

RESIST (rĭ zĭst′), *v.,* -SISTED, -SISTING. (Fending off.) The downturned, left "S" hand, held at waist level, moves back and forth toward the left a number of times. Each time the hand moves toward the left, the head tilts back slightly, as if the body is assuming a posture of resistance.

[R-149]

RESOLVE (rĭ zŏlv′), v., -SOLVED, -SOLVING, n. (The mind stops wavering, and the pros and cons are resolved.) The right index finger touches the forehead, the sign for THINK, q.v. Both "F" hands, palms facing each other and fingers pointing straight out, then drop down simultaneously. The sign for JUDGE, q.v., explains the rationale behind the movement of the two hands here. Cf. DECIDE, DECISION, DECREE 1, DETERMINE, MAKE UP ONE'S MIND, MIND 5, RENDER JUDGMENT, VERDICT.

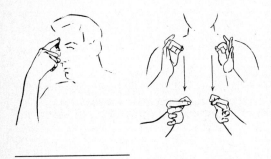

[R-150]

RESPECT (rĭ spĕkt′), n., v., -SPECTED, -SPECTING. (The letter "R"; bowing the head.) The right "R" hand swings up in an arc toward the head, which bows somewhat as the hand moves up toward it. The hand's movement is sometimes reversed, moving down and away from the head in an arc, while the head bows.

[R-151]

RESPIRATION (rĕs′ pə rā′ shən), n. (The rise and fall of the chest in respiration.) The hands, folded over the chest, move forward and back to the chest, to indicate the breathing. Cf. BREATH, BREATHE.

[R-152]

RESPOND (rĭ spŏnd′), v., -PONDED, -PONDING. (Directing a reply from the mouth to someone.) The tip of the right index finger, held in the "D" position, palm facing the body, is placed on the lips, while the left "D" hand, palm also facing the body, is held about a foot in front of the right hand. The right index finger, swinging around, moves toward and stops in a pointing position a few inches from the left index fingertip. Cf. ANSWER 1, MAKE RESPONSE, REPLY 1, RESPONSE 1.

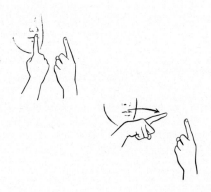

[R-153]

RESPONSE 1 (rĭ spŏns′), n. See RESPOND.

[R-154]

RESPONSE 2, n. (The letter "R"; coming out of the mouth.) Both "R" hands are held before the face, with the right "R" hand at the lips and behind the left "R" hand. Both hands move forward simultaneously, describing a small upward arc. Cf. ANSWER 2, REACTION, REPLY 2, REPORT.

[R-155]

RESPONSIBILITY 1 (rĭ spŏn′ sə bĭl′ ə tĭ), n. (Something which weighs down or burdens one with responsibility.) The fingertips of both hands, placed on the right shoulder, bear down. Cf. ATTRIBUTE 1,

BEAR 4, BURDEN, OBLIGATION 1, RELY 1, RESPONSIBLE 1.

[R-156]

RESPONSIBILITY 2, *n.* (Something which weighs down or burdens, modified by the letter "R," for "responsibility.") The "R" hands bear down on the right shoulder, in the same manner as RESPONSIBILITY 1. *Cf.* ATTRIBUTE 2, RESPONSIBLE 2.

[R-157]

RESPONSIBLE 1 (rĭ spŏn′ sə bəl), *adj.* See RESPONSIBILITY 1.

[R-158]

RESPONSIBLE 2, *adj.* See RESPONSIBILITY 2.

[R-159]

REST 1 (rĕst), *n.* (The folded arms; a position of rest.) With palms facing the body, the arms are folded across the chest. *Cf.* LIMBO, RELAX 1, RESTFUL 1.

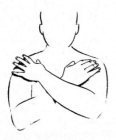

[R-160]

REST 2, *n.* (The "R" hands.) The sign for REST 1 is made, but with the crossed "R" hands. *Cf.* RELAX 2, RESTFUL 2.

[R-161]

REST 3, *n.* (The remainder is left behind.) The "5" hands, palms facing each other and fingers pointing forward, are dropped simultaneously a few inches, as if dropping something on the table. *Cf.* LEFT 2, REMAINDER, RESERVE 4.

[R-162]

REST 4, *n.* (Dropping something left over.) Both open hands, fingers pointing down and palms facing each other, are dropped slightly, as if releasing something. This sign is used to indicate "the remainder."

[R-163]

RESTFUL 1 (rĕst′ fəl), *adj.* See REST 1.

[R-164]

RESTFUL 2, *adj.* See REST 2.

[R-165]

RESTLESS (rĕst′ lĭs), *adj.* (Tossing and turning in bed.) The right hand, curved index and middle fingers representing the legs, is placed in the upturned left palm. The right hand, pivoted at the wrist, swings back and forth on the left palm. *Cf.* RESTLESSNESS.

[R-166]

RESTLESSNESS, *n.* See RESTLESS.

[R-167]

RESTRICT (rĭ strĭkt′), *v.,* -STRICTED, -STRICTING. (The upper and lower limits are defined.) The right-angle hands, palms facing, are held before the body, the right above the left. They swing out 45 degrees simultaneously, pivoted from their wrists. *Cf.* CAPACITY, LIMIT, QUANTITY 1.

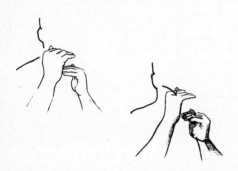

[R-168]

RESUME (rĭ zōōm′), *v.,* -SUMED, -SUMING. (Moving forward.) Both right-angle hands, palms facing each other and knuckles facing forward, move forward simultaneously. *Cf.* FORWARD, GO AHEAD, MOTION FORWARD, ONWARD, PROCEED, PROGRESS 2.

[R-169]

RESURRECTION (rĕz′ ə rĕk′ shən), *n.* (A rising.) The right index and middle fingers, representing the legs, are positioned in the upturned left palm. The right hand moves slowly up and off the left. *Note:* This sign is considered vulgar by some; it is at best used in a colloquial sense. *Cf.* ASCENSION, EASTER 2.

[R-170]

RETALIATE 1 (rĭ tăl′ ĭ āt′), *v.,* -ATED, -ATING. (Birds pecking back and forth at each other.) The right index finger and thumb, pressed together, strike their counterparts with force. *Cf.* RETALIATION 1, REVENGE.

[R-171]

RETALIATE 2, *v.* (An exchange.) The downturned "O" hands are positioned one in front of the other. They then exchange places. *Cf.* RETALIATION 2.

[R-172]

RETALIATION 1 (rĭ tăl′ ĭ ā′ shən), *n.* See RETALIATE 1.

[R-173]

RETALIATION 2, *n.* See RETALIATE 2.

[R–174]

RETARD (rĭ tärd'), *v.*, -TARDED, -TARDING. (One hand falls behind the other.) The "A" hands, thumbs up, are positioned knuckle to knuckle in front of the chest. The right "A" hand moves slowly and deliberately toward the chest, as close as possible to the left arm. *Cf.* FALL BEHIND, LAG.

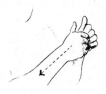

[R–175]

RETIRE 1 (rĭ tīr'), *v.*, -TIRED, -TIRING. (Pulling away.) The downturned open hands are held in a line, with fingers pointing to the left, the right hand behind the left. Both hands move in unison toward the right. As they do so, they assume the "A" position. *Cf.* DEPART, EVACUATE, FORSAKE 1, GRADUATE 2, LEAVE 1, WITHDRAW 1.

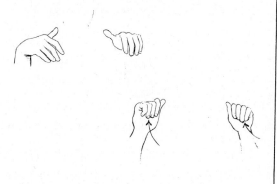

[R–176]

RETIRE 2, *(colloq.)*, *v.* (Tucking the legs beneath the covers.) The index and middle fingers of the right "U" hand, held either palm down or palm up, are thrust into the downturned left "O" hand. *Cf.* GO TO BED 2.

[R–177]

RETIRE 3, *v.* (A position of idleness.) With thumbs tucked in the armpits, the remaining fingers of both hands wiggle. *Cf.* HOLIDAY, IDLE, LEISURE, VACATION.

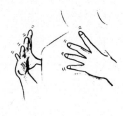

[R–178]

RETREAT (rĭ trēt'), *(eccles.)*, *n.* (The letter "R.") The right "R" hand, palm facing left, is placed on the forehead, and then swings down to the lips.

[R–179]

RETROSPECTION (rĕt′ rə spĕk′ shən), *n.* (Thinking and looking back.) The sign for THINK, *q.v.*, is made: The right index finger is placed on the forehead. The right "V" hand, palm facing back, then swings slowly over the right shoulder.

[R–180]

RETURN (rĭ tûrn′), *v.*, -TURNED, -TURNING. (To come again.) The sign for COME, *q.v.*, is made: The index fingers, pointing to each other, are rolled in toward the body. This is followed by the sign for AGAIN, *q.v.:* The left hand, open in the "5" position, palm up, is held before the chest. The right hand, in the right-angle position, fingers pointing up, arches over and into the left palm.

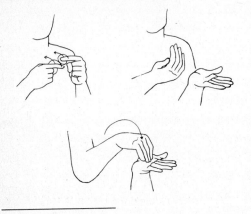

[R–181]

REVENGE (rĭ vĕnj′), *n.*, *v.*, -VENGED, -VENGING. (Birds pecking back and forth at each other.) The right index finger and thumb, pressed together, strike their left counterparts with force. *Cf.* RETALI-ATE 1, RETALIATION 1.

[R–182]

REVERE 1 (rĭ vir′), *v.*, -VERED, -VERING. (Drawing out the feelings.) The thumb and index finger of the right open hand, held an inch or two apart, are placed at mid-chest. As the hand moves straight out from the chest the two fingers come together. *Cf.* ADMIRE 1, REVERE 1.

[R–183]

REVERE 2, *v.* (Clasping the heart.) The "5" hands are held one atop the other over the heart. Sometimes the "S" hands are used, in which case they are crossed at the wrists. *Cf.* BELOVED, CHARITY, DE-VOTION, LOVE.

[R–184]

REVEREND (rĕv′ ər ənd), *adj.* (The sign of the Oremus at Mass.) The "F" hands, palms facing and thumb sides facing up, are joined at their respective fingertips. They separate, move apart and toward the body in half circles, and come together again in their initial position, closer to the body than before. *Cf.* PRIEST 4, RECTOR.

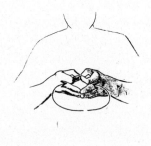

[R–185]

REVERSE 1 (rĭ vûrs′), *adj., n., v.,* -VERSED, -VERS-ING. (Separateness.) The tips of the extended index fingers touch before the chest, the right finger pointing left and the left finger pointing right. The fingers then draw apart sharply to either side. *Cf.* CON-TRAST 2, OPPOSITE.

[R–186]

REVERSE 2, *adj., n., v.* (To change positions.) Both "A" hands, thumbs up, are held before the chest, several inches apart. The left hand is pivoted over so that its thumb points to the right. Simultaneously, the right hand is moved up and over the left, describing a small arc, with its thumb pointing to the left. *Cf.* ADJUST, ALTER, ALTERATION, CHANGE 1, CONVERT, MODIFY, TRANSFER 1.

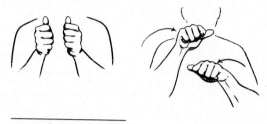

[R–187]

REVIVE (rĭ vīv'), *(rare), v.,* -VIVED, -VIVING. (Bringing back to the present, *i.e.,* to life.) Both open hands, positioned behind the shoulders, close into the "S" position as they swing forward, ending in the upturned "S" position.

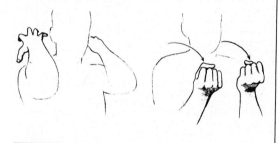

[R–188]

REVOKE (rĭ vōk'), *v.,* -VOKED, -VOKING. (A canceling out.) The right index finger makes a cross on the open left palm. *Cf.* ANNUL, CANCEL, CHECK 1, CORRECT 2, CRITICISM, CRITICIZE, FIND FAULT 1.

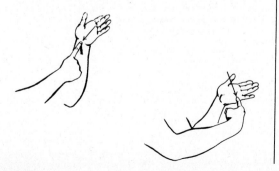

[R–189]

REVOLTING (rĭ vōl' tĭng), *adj.* (Turning the stomach.) The fingertips of the curved right hand describe a continuous circle on the stomach. The signer assumes an exaggerated expression of disgust. *Cf.* DISGUST, DISGUSTED, DISGUSTING, DISPLEASED, MAKE ME DISGUSTED, MAKE ME SICK, NAUSEA, NAUSEATE, NAUSEOUS, OBNOXIOUS.

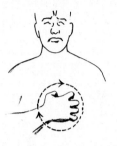

[R–190]

RICE (rīs), *n.* The tips of the four right fingers move up and down simultaneously as they move along the left index finger from knuckle to tip. This sign is used generally for different grains. *Cf.* BEAN(S), GRAIN, OATMEAL.

[R–191]

RICH (rĭch), *adj.* (A pile of money.) The sign for MONEY is made: The back of the upturned right hand, whose thumb and fingertips are all touching, is placed in the upturned left palm. The right hand then moves straight up, as it opens into the "5" position, palm facing down and fingers somewhat curved. *Cf.* WEALTH, WEALTHY.

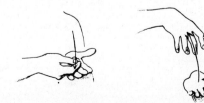

[R-192]

RIDE (rīd), *v.*, RODE, RIDDEN, RIDING. (Mounted on horseback.) The right index and middle fingers straddle the left hand, which is held palm facing right. The left hand moves in a rhythmic up-down motion, carrying the right hand with it. *Cf.* HORSEBACK.

[R-193]

RIDICULE (rĭd′ ə kūl′), *n., v,* -CULED, -CULING. (Derision; poking or prodding.) Both hands are held closed except for index and little fingers, which extend straight out from the body. The right hand is brought up and its index fingertip pulls the right corner of the mouth into a slight smile. Both hands then move forward simultaneously in a series of short jabbing motions, the right somewhat behind the left. An expression of disdain is assumed during this sign. The first part of the sign, pulling the mouth into a smile, is frequently omitted. *Cf.* MAKE FUN OF, MOCK.

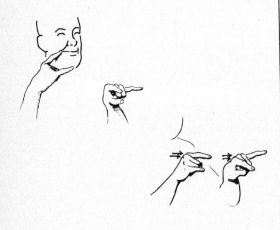

[R-194]

RIDICULOUS (rĭ dĭk′ yə ləs), *adj.* (Thoughts flickering back and forth.) The right "Y" hand, thumb almost touching the forehead, is shaken back and forth across the forehead several times. *Cf.* ABSURD,

DAFT, FOLLY, FOOLISH, NONSENSE, SILLY, TRIFLING.

[R-195]

RIFLE (rī′ fəl), *n.* (Shooting a gun.) The left "S" hand is held above the head as if holding a gun barrel. At the same time the right "L" hand is held below the left hand, its index finger moving back and forth, as if pulling a trigger. *Cf.* GUN, PISTOL, SHOOT 2, SHOT 2.

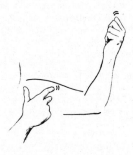

[R-196]

RIGHT 1 (rīt), *adj.* (A straightening out.) The right hand, fingers together and palm facing left, is placed in the upturned left palm, whose fingers point away from the body. The right hand slides straight out along the left palm, over the left fingers, and stops with its heel resting on the left fingertips. *Cf.* ALL RIGHT, O.K. 1, PRIVILEGE, RIGHTEOUS 1, YOU'RE WELCOME 2.

[R–197]

RIGHT 2, *adj., adv.* (The letter "R"; the movement.) The right "R" hand moves toward the right. *Cf.* RIGHT-HAND.

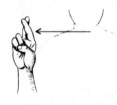

[R–198]

RIGHT 3, *adj., adv.* The right index finger, held above the left index finger, comes down rather forcefully so that the bottom of the right hand comes to rest on top of the left thumb joint. *Cf.* ACCURATE 2, CORRECT 1, DECENT, EXACT 2, JUST 2, PROPER, SUITABLE.

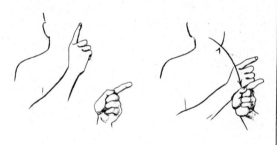

[R–199]

RIGHTEOUS 1 (rī′ chəs), *adj.* See RIGHT 1.

[R–200]

RIGHTEOUS 2, *adj.* (The letter "R"; the wiping signifies cleanliness or purity.) The right "R" hand moves in a small, clockwise circle, and then the right palm wipes across its upturned left counterpart.

[R–201]

RIGHT-HAND (rīt′ hănd′), *adj.* See RIGHT 2.

[R–202]

RIGID (rij′ id), *adj.* (The stiff fingers.) The fingers of the "5" hands, held palms down, stiffen and contract. *Cf.* FREEZE, FROZEN, ICE.

[R–203]

RING 1 (ring), *n.* (The natural sign.) The index finger and thumb of the open right hand go through the motions of slipping a ring on the left ring finger.

[R–204]

RING 2, *n., v.*, RANG, RUNG, RINGING. (The bell's reverberations.) The right fist strikes the front of the left hand, and then opens and moves away from the left in an undulating manner, to indicate the sound waves. *Cf.* BELL 1.

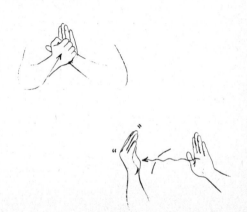

[R–205]

RING BINDER 1, *n.* The sign for BOOK is formed: The open hands are held together, fingers pointing away from the body. They open with little fingers remaining in contact, as in the opening of a book. Then the extended right thumb and index finger move up along the little finger edge of the upright open left hand, from the wrist toward the fingertips.

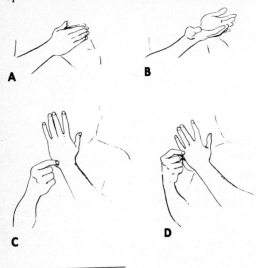

A   B

C   D

[R–206]

RING BINDER 2, *n.* The sign for BOOK, as in RING BINDER 1, is made. This is followed by the same movement as in RING BINDER 1, except that all of the right fingers are used.

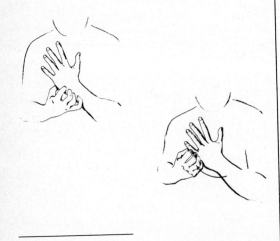

[R–207]

RIOT (rī′ ət), *n., v.,* RIOTED, RIOTING. (The violent movement causes the dust to swirl.) The "5" hands,

positioned one above the other, with fingers somewhat curved, move rapidly in opposing circles.

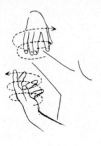

[R–208]

RIP 1 (rĭp), *n., v.,* RIPPED, RIPPING. (The natural motion.) Both "A" hands, held palms down before the body, grasp an imaginary object; then they move forcefully apart, as if tearing the object. *Cf.* REND, TEAR 1.

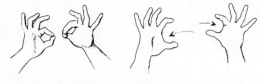

[R–209]

RIP 2, *n., v.* (Stitches coming apart.) The "F" hands face each other about an inch apart. As they draw apart, they open to the "5" position. The sign is usually repeated.

[R–210]

RIPE (rīp), *adj.* (Squeezing for softness.) The hands slowly and deliberately squeeze an imaginary object or substance. *Cf.* SOFT, TENDER 1.

[R-211]

RIPOSTE (rĭ pōst′), *n., v.,* -POSTED, -POSTING. (The thrust of a foil or épée.) The right index finger is thrust quickly forward and a bit up, in imitation of a fencing maneuver. *Cf.* INSULT 3.

[R-212]

RISE 1 (rīz), *v.,* ROSE, RISEN, RISING, *n.* (Getting onto one's feet.) The upturned index and middle fingers of the right hand, representing the legs, are swung up and over in an arc, coming to rest in the upturned left palm. *Cf.* ARISE 2, ELEVATE, GET UP, RAISE 1, STAND 2, STAND UP.

[R-213]

RISE 2, *v., n.* (Popping up before the eyes.) The right index finger, pointing up, pops up between the index and middle fingers of the left hand, whose palm faces down. *Cf.* APPEAR 2, POP UP.

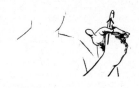

[R-214]

RISE 3, *v., n.* (Rising up.) Both upturned hands, held at chest level, rise in unison, to about shoulder height. *Cf.* ARISE 1, STAND 3.

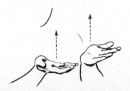

[R-215]

RIVAL 1 (rī′ vəl), *n., adj., v.,* -VALED, -VALING. (At sword's point.) The two index fingers, after pointing to each other, are drawn sharply apart. This is followed by the sign for INDIVIDUAL: Both open hands, palms facing each other, move down the sides of the body, tracing its outline to the hips. *Cf.* ENEMY, FOE, OPPONENT.

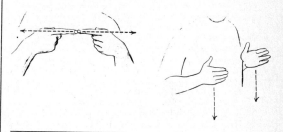

[R-216]

RIVAL 2, *v.* (Two opponents come together.) Both hands are closed, with thumbs pointing straight up and palms facing the body. From their initial position about a foot apart, the hands are brought together sharply, so that the knuckles strike. The hands, as they are drawn together, also move down a bit, so that they describe a "V." *Cf.* COMPETE 1, COMPETITION 1, CONTEND 1, CONTEST 1, RACE 1, RIVALRY 1, VIE 1.

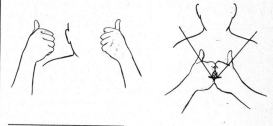

[R-217]

RIVAL 3, *n., v.* (Opposing objects.) The "A" hands are held side by side before the chest, palms facing each other and thumbs pointing forward. In this position the hands move alternately back and forth, toward and away from the body. *Cf.* COMPETE 2, COMPETITION 2, CONTEND 2, CONTEST 2, RACE 2, RIVALRY 2, VIE 2.

[R–218]

RIVAL 4, *n., v.* (The changing fortunes of competitors.) The "A" hands are held facing each other, thumbs pointing up in front of the body. Both hands are moved alternately backward and forward past each other several times. *Cf.* COMPETE 3, COMPETITION 3, CONTEND 3, CONTEST 3, RACE 3, RIVALRY 3, VIE 3.

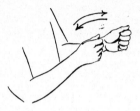

[R–219]

RIVALRY 1 (rī' vəl rĭ), *n.* See RIVAL 2.

[R–220]

RIVALRY 2, *n.* See RIVAL 3.

[R–221]

RIVALRY 3, *n.* See RIVAL 4.

[R–222]

RIVER 1 (rĭv' ər), *n.* (A meandering stream of water.) The sign for WATER 2 is made: The right "W" hand, palm facing out, is shaken slightly. The open hands, palms facing each other and fingers pointing away from the body, then move forward in unison, describing a series of parallel curves.

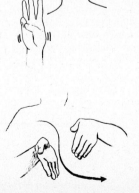

[R–223]

RIVER 2, *n.* (The rippling water.) The WATER prefix sign of RIVER 1 is made. The downturned "5" hands, fingers wiggling, then move from right to left.

[R–224]

RIVER 3, *n.* (The letter "R.") This is the same sign as for RIVER 1, except that the "R" hands are used.

[R–225]

ROAD (rōd), *n.* (The winding movement.) Both hands, palms facing and fingers together and extended straight out, move in unison away from the body, in a winding manner. *Cf.* CORRIDOR, HALL, HALLWAY, MANNER 2, METHOD, OPPORTUNITY 3, PATH, STREET, TRAIL, WAY 1.

[R–226]

ROAM (rōm), *v.,* ROAMED, ROAMING. (Random movement.) The right "D" hand, palm facing left, moves to and fro from right to left. *Cf.* WANDER 2.

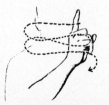

[R-227]

ROB 1 (rŏb), *v.*, ROBBED, ROBBING. (The hand, partly concealed, takes something surreptitiously.) The index and middle fingers of the right hand, somewhat curved, are placed under the left elbow. As they move slowly along the left forearm toward the left wrist, they close a bit. *Cf.* ABDUCT, EMBEZZLE, EMBEZZLEMENT, KIDNAP, ROBBERY 1, STEAL 1, SWIPE, THEFT 1, THIEF 1, THIEVERY.

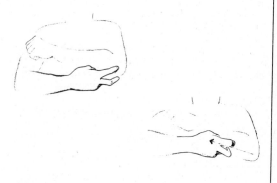

[R-228]

ROB 2, *(colloq.), v.* (A sly, underhanded movement.) The right open hand, palm down, is held a bit behind the body at waist level. Beginning with the little finger, the hand closes finger by finger into the "A" position, as if wrapping itself around something. *Cf.* ROBBERY 1, STEAL 2, THEFT 2.

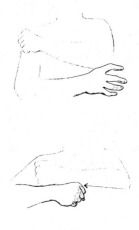

[R-229]

ROB 3, *v.* (A mustachioed thief.) The fingertips of both "H" hands, palms facing the body, are placed above the lips and are drawn slowly apart, describing a mustache. Sometimes one hand only is used. *Cf.* BANDIT, BURGLAR, BURGLARY, CROOK, ROBBER 1, ROBBERY 1, STEAL 3, THEFT 3, THIEF 2.

[R-230]

ROBBER 1 (rŏb' ər), *n.* See ROB 3. This is followed by the sign for INDIVIDUAL: Both open hands, palms facing each other, move down the sides of the body, tracing its outline to the hips.

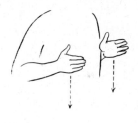

[R-231]

ROBBER 2, *n.* The sign, ROB 1, 2, or 3 is used. It is followed by the sign, INDIVIDUAL, as in ROBBER 1.

[R-232]

ROBBERY 1 (rŏb' ə rĭ), *n.* See ROB 1, 2, 3.

[R-233]

ROBBERY 2, *(colloq.), n.* (The guns.) Both "L" hands, palms facing each other, thumbs pointing straight up, are thrown forward slightly, as if presenting a pair of revolvers. *Cf.* HOLDUP.

[R-234]

ROBIN (rŏb′ ĭn), *n.* (Bird with a red breast.) The sign for BIRD is made: The right thumb and index finger are placed against the mouth, pointing straight out, to indicate the beak. The sign for RED is then made: The tip of the right index finger moves down across the lips. The right open hand, held with palm facing the body and fingers pointing left, then indicates the breast, moving downward over it in an arc. The whole sign may also be combined in the beak movement, using the "R" hand.

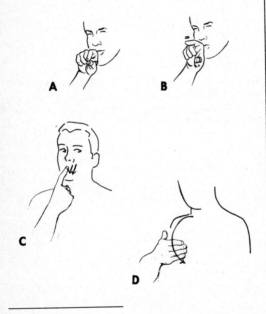

[R-235]

ROCK 1 (rŏk), *n.* (The hardness is indicated by the striking of the fists.) The back of the right "S" hand is struck several times against the back of the left "S" hand. *Cf.* STONE 1.

[R-236]

ROCK 2, *n.* (A hard object.) The right "S" hand swings downward before the body, striking its knuckles against the knuckle of the index finger of the left "S" hand, which is held palm down. The

right hand continues downward and away from the body in a short curve. *Cf.* ROCKY, STONE 2.

[R-237]

ROCKET (rŏk′ ĭt), *n.* (A rocket takes off from its pad.) The downturned right "R" hand (for ROCKET) is placed so that its index and middle fingers rest on the back of the downturned left "S" hand. The right hand moves quickly forward off the left hand. The "R" hand may also point up and move off the left hand from this position. *Cf.* MISSILE.

[R-238]

ROCKING CHAIR 1, *n.* (A rocking chair.) The "L" hands, palms facing each other and about two feet apart, are held before the chest. They arc up and down toward the shoulders a number of times. The body is sometimes rocked back and forth in time with the movement of the hands. *Cf.* CHAIR 3.

[R-239]

ROCKING CHAIR 2, (The natural sign.) The extended left index and middle fingers are draped over the thumb of the right "C" hand. In this position, both hands rock alternately forward and back a number of times, in imitation of the motion of the rocking chair. The body may also swing forward and back, to emphasize the motion.

[R-240]

ROCKY (rŏk ĭ), *adj.* See ROCK 2.

[R-241]

ROD (rŏd), *n.* (The natural sign.) The thumbtips and index fingertips of both open hands are held together, forming two circles side by side before the body, palms facing out. From this position the hands move apart to either side, outlining a straight rod. *Cf.* PIPE 2.

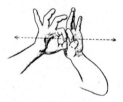

[R-242]

ROLL 1 (rōl), *v.*, ROLLED, ROLLING. (The natural sign.) The two index fingers "roll" around one another.

[R-243]

ROLL 2, *v.* (The letter "R," pivoted on the open palm.) The right "R" hand is held with palm facing

left and with its thumb extended and resting on the palm of the open left hand, which is held facing right with fingers pointing forward. In this position the right hand pivots on its thumb, moving forward and down.

[R-244]

ROLLER SKATING, *n. phrase.* (The natural motion.) Both "V" hands are held before the chest, one behind the other, with palms up and fingers curved to represent skate wheels. In this position, the hands move back and forth as if skating.

[R-245]

ROMAN (rō′ mən), *n., adj.* (The Roman nose.) The index and middle fingertips of the right "N" hand, palm facing the body, move down in an arc from the bridge of the nose to its tip. *Cf.* LATIN 1, ROME.

[R-246]

ROME (rōm), *n.* See ROMAN.

[R–247]

ROOF (ro͞of, roͦof), *n.* (A slant.) Both open hands are held up with palms toward the face, the right fingers pointing left and the left fingers pointing right, and with the left hand held above the right, its little finger edge resting on the index finger edge of the right hand. In this position both hands move diagonally forward and down, indicating a slanting roof.

[R–248]

ROOM 1 (ro͞om, roͦom), *n.* (The dimensions are indicated.) The open hands, palms facing and fingers pointing out, are dropped an inch or two simultaneously. They then shift their relative positions so that both palms face the body, with one hand in front of the other. In this new position they again drop an inch or two simultaneously. *Cf.* BOX 1, PACKAGE, SQUARE 1, TRUNK.

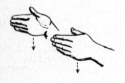

[R–249]

ROOM 2, *n.* (The "R" hands.) This is the same sign as for ROOM 1, except that the "R" hands are used. *Cf.* OFFICE 1.

[R–250]

ROOSTER (ro͞os′ tər), *n.* (The pecking beak and the comb of the cock.) The "Q" hand's back is placed against the lips, and the thumb and index fingers open and close, representing a beak. The thumb of the right "3" hand is then thrust against the forehead a couple of times, representing the comb. *Cf.* COCK.

[R–251]

ROOT (ro͞ot, roͦot), *n., v.,* ROOTED, ROOTING. (The natural sign.) The right "AND" hand is pushed down through the left "C" hand. As the fingers come through, they spread out like roots.

[R–252]

ROPE 1 (rōp), *n.* (The letter "R," indicating a length of rope.) The fingertips of the "R" hands are placed together and then drawn apart with a slight wavy motion.

[R–253]

ROPE 2, *n.* (Rationale same as for ROPE 1.) The index and middle fingers of the right "R" hand grasp the little finger of the left "I" hand. From this position, the "R" hand moves straight away from the "I" hand, to indicate a length of rope.

[R-254]

ROSARY 1 (rō′ zə rĭ), *n.* (Fingering prayer beads.) The upright open hands are held with the index fingers and thumbs touching each other in front of the body, palms facing forward. From this position the two hands separate and circle away from the body, until they meet again. As the two hands circle, their thumbs and index fingers open and close repeatedly, as if counting rosary beads.

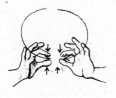

[R-255]

ROSARY 2, *n.* Both hands, their thumbs and index fingers touching, meet and are then drawn apart horizontally, while the thumbs and index fingers open and close, imitating the counting of the beads.

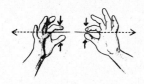

[R-256]

ROSH HASHANAH (rŏsh hə shä′ nə, rōsh), *(eccles.)*, *n.* (The New Year.) The sign for NEW is made: With both hands held palm up before the body, the right hand sweeps in an arc into the left, and continues up a bit. This is followed by the sign for YEAR: The right "S" hand, palm facing left, represents the earth. It is positioned atop the left "S" hand, whose palm faces right, and represents the sun. The right "S" hand describes a clockwise circle around the

left, coming to rest in its original position. *Cf.* NEW YEAR.

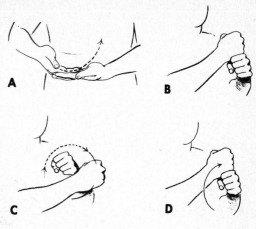

[R-257]

ROT (rŏt), *v.,* ROTTED, ROTTING, *n.* (Fingering the small pieces resulting from the breaking up of something.) The thumbs rub slowly across the fingertips of the upturned hands, from the little fingers to the index fingers, and then continue to the "A" position, palms up. *Cf.* DECAY, DIE OUT, DISSOLVE, FADE, MELT.

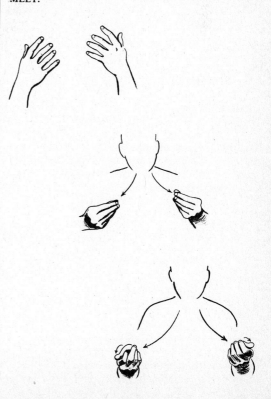

[R–258]

ROTTEN (rŏt′ ən), *adj.* (A modification of the sign for spitting or thumbing the nose.) The right "3" hand is held with thumbtip against the nose. Then it is thrown sharply forward, and an expression of contempt is assumed. *Cf.* LOUSY.

[R–259]

ROUGH 1 (rŭf), *adj.* (The "roughness," in the form of ridges, described.) The tips of the curved right fingers trace imaginary ridges over the upright left palm, from the base of the hand to the fingertips. The action is repeated several times. *Cf.* ROUGHNESS, RUDE 1, SCOLD 2.

[R–260]

ROUGH 2, *adj.* (Same rationale as for ROUGH 1.) The little finger edge of the open right hand passes along the back of the downturned, open left hand, from wrist to fingertips, making a waving motion, as if it were passing over a rough surface.

[R–261]

ROUGH 3, *adj.* (Rationale the same as for ROUGH 1.) The right palm is placed against the left palm and

moved forward with a wavy motion, as if moving over a rough surface. *Cf.* RUGGED.

[R–262]

ROUGHNESS, *n.* The sign for ROUGH 1 is made, followed by the sign for -NESS: The downturned right "N" hand moves down along the left palm, which is facing away from the body.

[R–263]

ROUND 1 (round), *adj.* (The shape.) The curved open hands are held with fingertips touching, as if holding a ball. *Cf.* BALL 2, ORB, SPHERE.

[R–264]

ROUND 2, *adj.* (The circle is described.) The index finger, pointing down or out, describes a circle. *Cf.* CIRCLE 1.

[R–265]

ROW 1 (rō), v., ROWED, ROWING. (The natural sign.) The signer manipulates a pair of imaginary oars, as if rowing a boat.

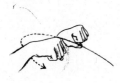

[R–266]

ROW 2 (rou), n. (Repeated rejoinders.) Both "D" hands are held with index fingers pointing toward each other. The hands move up and down alternately, each pivoting in turn at the wrist. *Cf.* QUARREL.

[R–267]

RUB (rŭb), v., RUBBED, RUBBING. (The act of rubbing.) The right knuckles rub briskly against the outstretched left palm. *Cf.* POLISH 1, SANDPAPER, SHINE SHOES.

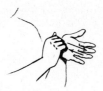

[R–268]

RUBBER 1 (rŭb′ ər), n. (The pliability.) The side of the right "X" finger moves up and down on the right cheek. The mouth is held open, and may engage in a chewing motion, keeping time with the right "X" finger. *Cf.* GUM.

[R–269]

RUBBER 2, n. (Snapping a rubber band.) The thumbtip of the right "A" hand is placed behind the tips of the upper front teeth, and is then "snapped" out and forward, away from the mouth.

[R–270]

RUBBER 3, n. (Snapping and stretching a rubber band.) The sign for RUBBER 2 is made. Then both "A" hands are held before the body, palms down and knuckles facing forward. The hands move apart slowly, as if grasping the ends of a rubber band and stretching it.

[R–271]

RUBBERNECK 1 (rŭb′ ər nĕk′), (sl.), n., v., -NECKED, -NECKING. (The natural movement.) The right "S" hand is held before the right shoulder, with the right arm bent at the elbow, while the left hand grasps the right forearm. The right "S" hand then rotates back and forth several times.

[R-272]

RUBBERNECK 2, *(sl.), n., v.* (Indicating the neck.) The thumb and index finger of the right "O" hand rub downward against the right side of the neck several times.

[R-273]

RUDE 1 (ro͞od), *adj.* (The "roughness," of words is described.) The tips of the curved right fingers trace imaginary ridges over the upright left palm, from the base of the hand to the fingertips. The action is repeated several times. *Cf.* ROUGH 1, ROUGHNESS, SCOLD 2.

[R-274]

RUDE 2, *adj.* The left hand is held palm down, with index finger pointing forward. The right hand is held in the same way, but slightly above, and to the right of, the left hand. The right hand then moves down and forward repeatedly, striking against the base of the left index finger at each pass. *Cf.* RUDENESS.

[R-275]

RUDENESS (ro͞od′ nĭs), *n.* See RUDE 2.

[R-276]

RUE (ro͞o), *v.,* RUED, RUING, *n.* (The heart is circled, to indicate feeling, modified by the letter "S," for SORRY.) The right "S" hand, palm facing the

body, is rotated several times over the area of the heart. *Cf.* APOLOGIZE 1, APOLOGY 1, CONTRITION, PENITENT, REGRET, REGRETFUL. REPENT, REPENTANT, SORROW, SORROWFUL 2, SORRY.

[R-277]

RUGGED (rŭg′ ĭd), *adj.* The right palm is placed against the left palm and moved forward with a wavy motion, as if moving over a rough surface. *Cf.* ROUGH 3.

[R-278]

RUIN (ro͞o′ ĭn), *n.* (Wiping off.) The left "5" hand, palm up, is held slightly below the right "5" hand, held palm down. The right hand swings up, just brushing over the left palm. Both hands close into the "S" position, and the right is brought back with force to its initial position, striking a glancing blow against the left knuckles as it returns. *Cf.* ABOLISH 1, ANNIHILATE, CORRUPT, DEFACE, DEMOLISH, DESTROY, HAVOC, PERISH 2, REMOVE 3.

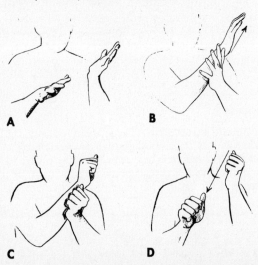

[R–279]

RULE 1 (rōol), *n., v.,* RULED, RULING. (Holding the reins over all.) The "A" hands, palms facing, move alternately back and forth, as if grasping and manipulating reins. The left "A" hand, still in position, swings over so that its palm now faces down. The right hand opens to the "5" position, palm down, and swings over the left which moves slightly to the right. *Cf.* AUTHORITY, CONTROL 1, DIRECT 1, GOVERN, MANAGE, MANAGEMENT, MANAGER, OPERATE, REGULATE, REIGN.

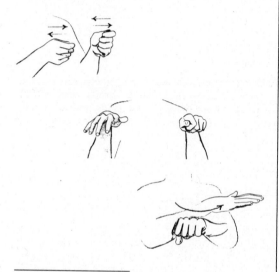

[R–280]

RULE(S) 2, *n.* (The letter "R;" the listing.) The upright, open left hand, fingers together and palm facing out, represents a piece of paper on which are listed the rules or regulations. The right "R" hand is placed upright against the tips of the left fingers, and then it moves down in an arc to a position against the base of the left hand. *Cf.* REGULATION(S).

[R–281]

RUN 1 (rŭn), *v.,* RAN, RUN, RUNNING. The open left hand is held pointing out, palm down. The open right hand is held beneath it, facing up. The right

hand is thrown forward rather quickly so the palm brushes repeatedly across the palm of the left.

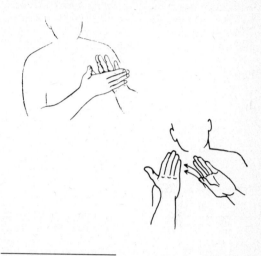

[R–282]

RUN 2, *v.* The "L" hands are held side by side, palms down. The left index finger rests across the right thumb, and in this position the two index fingers wiggle back and forth. The hands may move forward simultaneously.

[R–283]

RUN 3, *v.* (A turning wheel, as in a machine that is running.) The upturned, open right hand moves in a counterclockwise circle on the palm of the downturned, open left hand.

[R-284]

RUN AWAY, *v. phrase*. (Slipping out and away.) The right index finger is held pointing upward between the index and middle fingers of the prone left hand. From this position the right index finger moves to the right, slipping out of the grasp of the left fingers and away from the left hand. *Cf.* LEAVE CLANDESTINELY 2, SLIP AWAY.

[R-285]

RUN FOR OFFICE, *v. phrase*. (Bringing oneself forward.) The right index finger and thumb grasp the clothing near the right shoulder (often the lapel of a suit or the collar of a dress) and tug it up and down gently several times. Sometimes one tug only is used. *Cf.* APPLY 1, CANDIDATE, OFFER 2, VOLUNTEER.

[R-286]

RUN OVER, *v. phrase*. (Running over the top.) The left "S" hand is held up before the chest. The right fingertips, pointing up, move upward along the thumb edge of the left hand and continue over the top of the hand, imitating the flow of water. *Cf.* OVERFLOW.

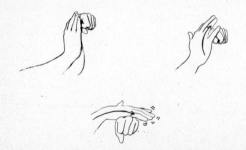

[R-287]

RUN UP AGAINST, *(colloq.), v.* (The natural movement.) The fists come together with force. *Cf.* COLLIDE 1, COLLISION 1, CRASH, WRECK.

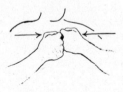

[R-288]

RUSSIA (rŭsh′ ə), *n.* (The characteristic Cossack dance.) The downturned "5" hands swing repeatedly in toward the hips. The hands come in contact with the hips at the midpoints between thumbs and index fingers. *Cf.* RUSSIAN.

[R-289]

RUSSIAN (rŭsh′ ən), *adj.* The sign for RUSSIA is made, followed by the sign for INDIVIDUAL: Both open hands, palms facing each other, move down the sides of the body, tracing its outline to the hips. The latter sign may be omitted.

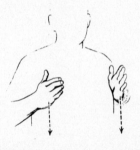

S

'S (An ending marking the possessive singular or plural of nouns, as in *girl's* and *girls'.*) The "S" hand is twisted clockwise.

SABBATH 1 (săb′ əth), *n.* (Day of rest.) The sign for REST 1 is made: With palms facing the body, the arms are folded across the chest. This is followed by the sign for DAY: The left arm, held horizontally, palm down, represents the horizon. The right elbow rests on the back of the left hand, with the right arm in a perpendicular position. The right "D" hand, palm facing left, moves in an arc to the left until it is just above the left elbow. This latter movement may be reversed.

SABBATH 2, *n.* (A day of quiet, of rest.) The "5" hands, held side by side and palms out before the body, move straight down a short distance. They may also move slightly outward as they move down. *Cf.* SUNDAY 1.

SABBATH 3, *n.* (The letter "S.") The right "S" hand, palm facing out, moves straight down a few inches.

SACRAMENT (săk′ rə mənt), *(eccles.), n.* (The blessing placed on the head.) The right hand, fingers together and palm facing down, assumes a position just above the head. The fingers open and the hand comes down atop the head.

[S–6]

SACRIFICE (săk′ rə fīs′), *n., v.,* -FICED, -FICING. (An offering.) The outstretched hands, palms up, move upward gracefully. The head turns upward at the same time.

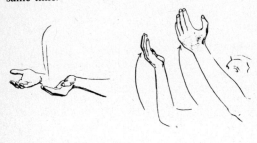

[S–7]

SACRILEGIOUS (săk′ rə lij′ əs), *adj.* (Rationale obscure; the thumb and little finger are said to represent, respectively, right and wrong, with the head poised between the two.) The right "Y" hand, palm facing the body, is brought up to the chin. *Cf.* ERROR, FAULT 2, MISTAKE, WRONG 1.

[S–8]

SAD (săd), *adj.* (The facial features drop.) Both "5" hands, palms facing the eyes and fingers slightly curved, drop simultaneously to a level with the mouth. The head drops slightly as the hands move down, and an expression of sadness is assumed. *Cf.* DEJECTED, DEPRESSED, GLOOM, GLOOMY, GRAVE 3, GRIEF 1, MELANCHOLY, MOURNFUL, SORROWFUL 1.

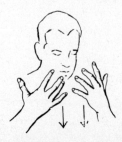

[S–9]

SAFE (sāf), *adj., n.* (Breaking the bonds.) The "S" hands, crossed in front of the body, swing apart and face out. *Cf.* DELIVER 1, EMANCIPATE, FREE 1, INDEPENDENCE, INDEPENDENT, LIBERATION, REDEEM 1, RELIEF, RESCUE, SALVATION, SAVE 1.

[S–10]

SAID (sĕd), *v.* (Words tumbling from the mouth.) The right index finger, pointing left, describes a continuous small circle in front of the mouth. *Cf.* BID 3, DISCOURSE, HEARING, MAINTAIN 2, MENTION, REMARK, SAY, SPEAK, SPEECH 1, STATE, STATEMENT, TALK 1, TELL, VERBAL 1.

[S–11]

SAILBOAT (sāl′ bōt), *n.* (The rocking of the masts.) The right "3" hand, palm facing left, rocks back and forth. *Cf.* SAILING.

[S–12]

SAILING (sā′ lĭng), *n.* See SAILBOAT.

[S–13]

SAILOR 1 (sā′ lər), *n.* (The three stripes on the sailor's blouse.) The middle finger of the right "3" hand brushes against the right shoulder several times. *Cf.* SEAMAN.

[S–14]

SAILOR 2, *n.* (An individual who sails on a ship.) The sign for BOAT is made: Both hands are cupped together to form the hull of a boat. They move forward in a bobbing motion. This is followed by the sign for INDIVIDUAL: Both open hands, palms facing each other, move down the sides of the body, tracing its outline to the hips.

[S–15]

SAINT 1 (sānt), *(eccles.), n.* (Cleanliness or purity, defined by the letter "S.") The right hand wipes off the left palm. As it moves across the left palm, it assumes the "S" position.

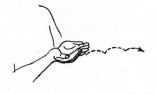

[S–16]

SAINT 2, *(eccles.), n.* (See SAINT 1 for rationale.) The right "S" hand is wiped across the open left palm.

[S–17]

SAINT JOHN (sānt jŏn′), *(eccles.).* The sign for SAINT 1 or 2 is formed. Then the little finger of the right "I" hand traces a "J" on the back of the down-turned left hand.

[S–18]

SAINT JOSEPH (jō′ zəf), *(eccles.)* The sign for SAINT 1 or SAINT 2 is formed. The right "J" finger then comes down and touches the upturned left palm.

[S–19]

SAINTS (sānts), *(eccles.), n. pl.* (Holy people.) The sign for HOLY is made: The right "H" hand moves in a small, clockwise circle several times. The right palm then wipes the upturned left palm. This is followed by the sign for PEOPLE: The "P" hands, side by side, are moved alternately in continuous counterclockwise circles.

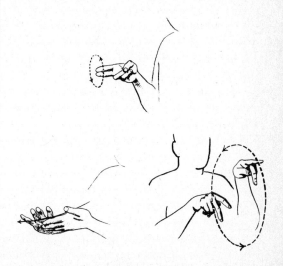

[S-20]

SALAD (săl′ əd), *n.* (The letter "G.") The right "G" hand is shaken slightly. The movement involves a slight pivoting action at the wrist. The hands may also go through the motions of tossing a salad. *Cf.* GREEN 1, GREENHORN 1.

[S-21]

SALARY (săl′ ə rĭ), *n.* (Gathering in.) The right "5" hand, its little finger edge touching the upturned left palm, is drawn in an arc toward the body, closing into the "S" position as it sweeps over the base of the left hand. *Cf.* ACCUMULATE 1, COLLECT, EARN, WAGES.

[S-22]

SALE (sāl), *n.* (Transferring ownership of an object.) Both "AND" hands, fingers touching their respective thumbs, are held palms down before the body. The hands are pivoted simultaneously outward and away from the body, once or several times. *Cf.* SELL, VEND.

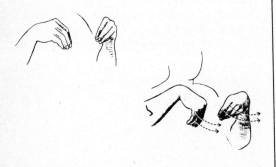

[S-23]

SALESMAN (sālz′ mən), *n.* (Transferring ownership.) The sign for SALE is formed. The sign for

INDIVIDUAL is then made: Both open hands, palms facing each other, move down the sides of the body, tracing its outline to the hips. *Cf.* MERCHANT, SELLER, VENDER.

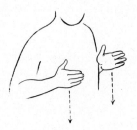

[S-24]

SALT 1 (sôlt), *n.* (The act of tapping the salt from a knife edge.) Both "H" hands, palms down, are held before the chest. The fingers of the right "H" hand tap those of the left several times.

[S-25]

SALT 2, *n.* (Tasting the salt.) The tips of the right "H" hand are placed against the lips. The rest of this sign is exactly like SALT 1.

[S-26]

SALVATION (săl vā′ shən), *n.* (Breaking the bonds.) The "S" hands, crossed in front of the body, swing apart and face out. *Cf.* DELIVER 1, EMANCIPATE, FREE 1, INDEPENDENCE, INDEPENDENT, LIBERATION, REDEEM 1, RELIEF, RESCUE, SAFE, SAVE 1.

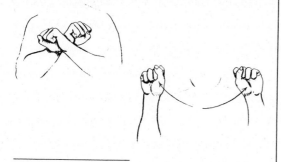

[S–27]

SAME 1 (săm), *adj.* (Matching fingers are brought together.) The outstretched index fingers are brought together, either once or several times. *Cf.* ALIKE, IDENTICAL, LIKE 2, SIMILAR, SUCH.

[S–28]

SAME 2, *(colloq.), adj.* (Two figures are compared, back and forth.) The right "Y" hand, palm facing left, is moved alternately toward and away from the body. *Cf.* ME TOO.

[S–29]

SAME 3, *adj.* (Parallel movement.) Both downturned "Y" hands, held a few inches apart, move simultaneously from left to right. *Cf.* UNIFORM, UNIFORMLY.

[S–30]

SAME AS, *phrase.* (A likeness; a sameness.) Both index fingers, held together at one side of the body near waist level, point forward. As they travel to the other side of the body they separate an inch or two and come together again. *Cf.* ACCORDING (TO), ALSO 1, AS, DUPLICATE 2, TOO.

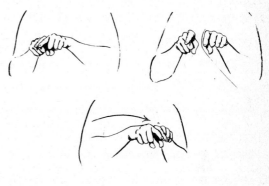

[S–31]

SAMPLE (săm′ pəl), *n.* (The letter "S"; something shown or pushed forward.) The left "5" hand pushes the right "S" hand forward.

[S–32]

SANCTIFY (săngk′ tə fī′), *(eccles.), v.,* -FIED, -FYING. (Make holy.) The sign for MAKE is made: The right "S" hand, palm facing left, is placed on top of its left counterpart, whose palm faces right. The hands are twisted back and forth, striking each other slightly after each twist. This is followed by the sign for HOLY: The right "H" hand moves in a small, clockwise circle several times. The right palm then wipes the upturned left palm.

[S–33]

SANDALS (săn′ dəls), *n. pl.* (The thong between the toes.) The left "5" hand is held palm down. The index finger traces the course of an imaginary thong between the left index and middle fingers.

[S–34]

SANDPAPER (sănd′ pā′ pər), *(voc.), n.* (The act of rubbing.) The right knuckles rub briskly against the outstretched left palm. *Cf.* POLISH 1, RUB, SHINE SHOES.

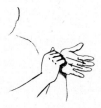

[S–35]

SANDWICH (sănd′ wĭch, săn′ -), *n.* (The two pieces of bread.) With the fingertips of both hands facing the body, one hand is placed atop the other and both are brought up to the mouth, which opens slightly.

[S–36]

SAN FRANCISCO (săn′ frən sĭs′ kō.) The initials "S" and "F" are formed. During the formation of the "F," the hand may be moved slightly to the right.

[S–37]

SATAN (sā′ tən), *n.* (The horns.) With the thumbs resting on the temples, the index and middle fingers of both hands open and close repeatedly. *Cf.* DEMON, DEVIL, DEVILMENT, HELL 1.

[S–38]

SATELLITE (săt′ ə lĭt′), *n.* (A rotating body, identified by the letter "S.") The right "S" hand circles around the left, which represents a planet in space.

[S–39]

SATISFACTION (săt′ ĭs făk′ shən), *n.* (The inner feelings settle down.) Both "B" hands (or "5" hands, fingers together) are placed palms down against the chest, the right above the left. Both move down simultaneously a few inches. *Cf.* CONTENT, CONTENTED, GRATIFY 2, SATISFIED, SATISFY 1.

[S–40]

SATISFIED, *adj.* See SATISFACTION.

[S–41]

SATISFY 1 (săt′ ĭs fī), *v.,* -FIED, -FYING. See SATISFACTION.

[S–42]

SATISFY 2, *v.* This is the same sign as for SATISFY 1 but with only one hand used.

[S–43]

SATURDAY (săt′ ər dĭ), *n.* The "S" hand, held before the body, is rotated clockwise.

[S–44]

SAUCY (sô′ sĭ), *(rare), adj.* The "A" hands, thumbs up, are alternately moved up and down from chest to shoulder level. An expression of haughtiness is assumed.

[S–45]

SAVE 1 (sāv), *v.,* SAVED, SAVING. (Breaking the bonds.) The "S" hands, crossed in front of the body, swing apart and face out. *Cf.* DELIVER 1, EMANCIPATE, FREE 1, INDEPENDENCE, INDEPENDENT, LIBERATION, REDEEM 1, RELIEF, RESCUE, SAFE, SALVATION.

[S–46]

SAVE 2, *v.* (Holding back.) The right "V" fingers are tapped once or twice across the back of their left

counterparts. Both palms face the chest. *Cf.* RESERVE 3, STORE 2.

[S–47]

SAVIOR (sāv′ yər), *(eccles.), n.* (One who saves.) The sign for SAVE 1 is made. This is followed by the sign for INDIVIDUAL: Both open hands, palms facing each other, move down the sides of the body, tracing its outline to the hips.

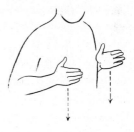

[S–48]

SAVORY (sā′ və rĭ), *adj.* (The salivary glands are indicated.) The right index finger touches the side of the throat. A sour expression is assumed. *Cf.* TART.

[S–49]

SAW 1 (sô), *n., v.,* SAWED, SAWN, SAWING. (The sawing of wood.) The little finger edge of the open right hand moves back and forth in a sawing motion over the back of the downturned left hand. *Cf.* LUMBER 1, WOOD.

[S–50]

SAW 2, *(voc.)*, *n.*, *v.* (Act of holding a saw.) The right hand grasps an imaginary saw and moves back and forth over the downturned left hand. *Cf.* HAND-SAW.

[S–51]

SAWMILL (sô′ mĭl′), *n.* (The rotary blade's teeth cutting through the wood.) The outstretched fingers of the right hand pass alternately back and forth between the index and middle fingers of the downturned left hand. *Cf.* LUMBER 2.

[S–52]

SAY (sā), *v.*, SAID, SAYING. (Words tumbling from the mouth.) The right index finger, pointing left, describes a continuous small circle in front of the mouth. *Cf.* BID 3, DISCOURSE, HEARING, MAINTAIN 2, MENTION, REMARK, SAID, SPEAK, SPEECH 1, STATE, STATEMENT, TALK 1, TELL, VERBAL 1.

[S–53]

SCAFFOLD (skăf′ əld, -ōld), *n.* (Hanging by the throat.) The thumb of the right "Y" hand is placed

at the right side of the neck, and the head hangs toward the left, as if it were caught in a noose. *Cf.* HANG 2.

[S–54]

SCALE 1 (skāl), *(voc.)*, *n.* (The act of measuring a short distance.) Both "Y" hands, held side by side palms out, move alternately a short distance back and forth, away from and toward each other. *Cf.* GAUGE, MEASURE.

[S–55]

SCALE 2, *n.* (The balancing of the scale is described.) The fingers of the right "H" hand are centered on the left index finger and rocked back and forth. *Cf.* POUND 1, WEIGH 1, WEIGHT.

[S–56]

SCALE 3, *n.*, *v.* (The scales.) Both open hands, held palms down in front of the body, move alternately up and down, imitating a pair of scales. *Cf.* BALANCE 2.

[S–57]

SCAPULAR (skăp′ yələr), *(eccles.)*, *n.* (The garment is described.) The index fingers are drawn from the shoulders to a point where they come together at the center of the chest.

[S–58]

SCARCE (skârs), *adj.* (The fingers are presented in order, to convey the concept of "several.") The right "A" hand is held palm facing up. One by one the fingers open, beginning with the index finger and ending with the little finger. Some use only the index and middle fingers. *Cf.* FEW, RARE, SEVERAL, SUNDRY.

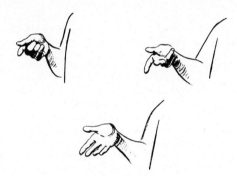

[S–59]

SCARE(D) (skâr), *v.*, SCARED, SCARING, *n.* (The heart is suddenly covered with fear.) Both hands, fingers together, are placed side by side, palms facing the chest. They quickly open and come together over the heart, one on top of the other. *Cf.* AFRAID, COWARD, FEAR 1, FRIGHT, FRIGHTEN, TERROR 1.

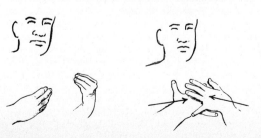

[S–60]

SCATTER (skăt′ ər), *v.*, -TERED, -TERING. (Scattering apart.) Both "AND" hands are held before the body, palms down. They are then directed forward and toward each side, while the fingers open out. *Cf.* SPREAD 1.

[S–61]

SCENE (sēn), *n.* (The letter "P"; a circle or square is indicated, to show the locale or place.) The "P" hands are held side by side before the body, with middle fingertips touching. From this position, the hands separate and outline a circle (or a square), before coming together again closer to the body. *Cf.* LOCATION, PLACE 1, POSITION 1, SITE.

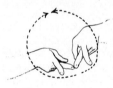

[S–62]

SCENT (sĕnt), *n.* (Bringing something up to the nose.) The upturned right hand moves slowly up to and past the nose, and the signer breathes in as the hand sweeps by. *Cf.* FRAGRANT, ODOR, SMELL.

[S–63]

SCHEME (skēm), *n., v.,* SCHEMED, SCHEMING. (Placing things in order.) The hands, palms facing, fingers together and pointing away from the body, are positioned at the left side and held about a foot apart. With a slight up-down motion, as if describing waves, the hands travel in unison from left to right. *Cf.* ARRANGE, ARRANGEMENT, CLASSED 2, DEVISE 1, ORDER 3, PLAN 1, POLICY 1, PREPARE 1, PROGRAM 1, PROVIDE 1, PUT IN ORDER, READY 1, SYSTEM.

[S–64]

SCHOLAR (skŏl′ ər), *n.* (One who learns.) The sign for LEARN is made: The downturned fingers of the right hand are placed on the upturned left palm. They close, and then the hand rises and the right fingertips are placed on the forehead. This is followed by the sign for INDIVIDUAL: Both open hands, palms facing each other, move down the sides of the body, tracing its outline to the hips. *Cf.* LEARNER, PUPIL 1, STUDENT 1.

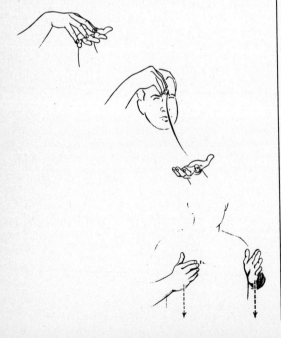

[S–65]

SCHOOL (skōōl), *n.* (The teacher's hands are clapped for attention.) The hands are clapped together several times.

[S–66]

SCIENCE 1 (sī′ əns), *n.* (Deep wisdom.) The right index fingertip touches the forehead, and is then moved down and thrust between the extended and loosely parted fingers of the downturned left hand, to indicate that wisdom goes deep.

[S–67]

SCIENCE 2, *n.* (Pouring alternately from test tubes.) The upright thumbs of both "A" hands swing over alternately, as if pouring out the contents of a pair of test tubes. *Cf.* CHEMISTRY.

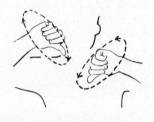

[S–68]

SCISSORS (sĭz′ ərz), *n., pl.* or *sing.* (The natural sign.) The index and middle fingers, forming a "V," open and close like scissors.

[S–69]

SCOLD 1 (skōld), *v.*, SCOLDED, SCOLDING. (A scolding with the finger.) The right index finger shakes back and forth in a natural scolding movement. *Cf.* ADMONISH 2, REPRIMAND, REPROVE.

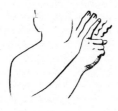

[S–70]

SCOLD 2, *(colloq.), v.* (Rough language.) The tips of the curved right fingers trace imaginary ridges over the upright left palm, from the base of the hand to the fingertips. The action is repeated several times. *Cf.* ROUGH 1, ROUGHNESS, RUDE 1.

[S–71]

SCOLD 3, *(sl.), v.* (The opening and closing of the barking dog's mouth.) The hands are positioned palm against palm before the body, with the fingertips pointing forward. With the bases of the hands always touching and serving as a hinge, the hands open and close repeatedly, with the stress on the opening movement, which is sudden and abrupt. *Cf.* BARK.

[S–72]

SCOLD 4, *(sl.), v.* (Big, i.e. curse, words tumble out.) The right "Y" hand moves forward in a wavy manner along the left index finger, which is pointing forward. The action is repeated several times. The wide space between the thumb and little finger of the "Y" hand represents the length of the words, and the forward movement the tumbling out of the words in anger.

[S–73]

SCORE (skōr), *(colloq.), v.*, SCORED, SCORING. (A basketball dropping into a basket.) The index finger of the right "X" hand drops into a circle formed by the thumb and index finger of the left hand.

[S–74]

SCORN 1 (skôrn), *n.* (The gaze is cast downward.) Both "V" hands, side by side and palms facing out, are swept downward so that the fingertips now point down. A haughty expression, or one of mild contempt, is sometimes assumed. *Cf.* CONTEMPT 1, LOOK DOWN.

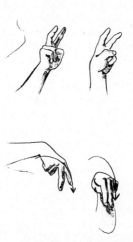

[S–75]

SCORN 2, *(rare), n., v.,* SCORNED, SCORNING. (The finger is flicked to indicate something petty, small; *i.e.,* to be scorned as inconsequential.) The right index finger and thumb are used to press the lips down into an expression of contempt. The right thumb is then flicked out from the closed hand. *Cf.* CONTEMPT 2, DESPISE 2, DETEST 2, DISLIKE, HATE 2.

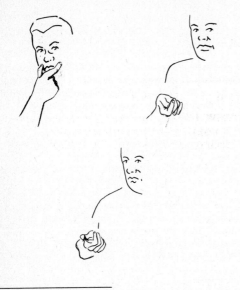

[S–76]

SCOT 1 (skŏt), *n.* (The crossing of the plaid pattern is indicated on the hand.) The outstretched fingers of the open right hand, palm down, are brought over the back of the downturned left hand, from the little finger side to the thumb side. The right hand then turns to the palm-up position and is drawn along the left hand, back to back, from wrist to fingertips. *Cf.* SCOTCH 1, SCOTLAND 1, SCOTTISH 1.

[S–77]

SCOT 2, *n.* (The plaid.) The "5" hands are held with palms toward the chest, the right fingers resting across the back of the left fingers, to represent "plaid." The hands then drop away toward either side. *Cf.* SCOTCH 2, SCOTLAND 2, SCOTTISH 2.

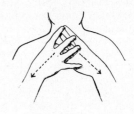

[S–78]

SCOT 3, *n.* (Plaid.) The four fingers of the right "B" hand, held slightly spread, trace a set of imaginary parallel lines across the left arm just below the shoulder. The hand is then turned over, and the backs of the fingers trace another set of parallel lines downward across the first set, completing an imaginary plaid pattern. *Cf.* SCOTCH 3, SCOTLAND 3, SCOTTISH 3.

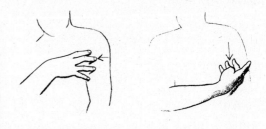

[S–79]

SCOTCH 1 (skŏch), *n., adj.* See SCOT 1.

[S–80]

SCOTCH 2, *n., adj.* See SCOT 2.

[S–81]

SCOTCH 3, *n., adj.* See SCOT 3.

[S–82]

SCOTLAND 1 (skŏt' lənd), *n.* See SCOT 1.

[S–83]

SCOTLAND 2, *n.* See SCOT 2.

[S–84]

SCOTLAND 3, *n.* See SCOT 3.

[S–85]

SCOTTISH 1 (skŏt' ish), *adj.* See SCOT 1.

[S–86]

SCOTTISH 2, *adj.* See SCOT 2.

[S–87]

SCOTTISH 3, *adj.* See SCOT 3.

[S–88]

SCRAMBLE (skrăm' bəl), *v.,* -BLED, -BLING. (Scrambling or mixing up.) The downturned right hand is positioned above the upturned left. The fingers of both are curved. Both hands move in opposite horizontal circles. *Cf.* CLUTTER, COMPLICATE, CONFUSE, CONFUSED, CONFUSION, DISORDER, MINGLE 1, MIX, MIXED, MIX UP.

[S–89]

SCRAPE (skrāp), *(voc.), v.,* SCRAPED, SCRAPING, *n.* (The natural motion of using a scraper.) The tips of the right "B" hand move along the upturned left palm, from mid-palm to fingertips. The motion is repeated several times.

[S–90]

SCREAM (skrēm), *v.,* SCREAMED, SCREAMING. (Harsh words thrown out.) The right hand, as in

CURSE 1, appears to claw words out of the mouth. This time, however, it turns and throws them out, ending in the "5" position. *Cf.* BLASPHEME 2, CALL OUT, CRY 3, CRY OUT, CURSE 2, SHOUT, SUMMON 1, SWEAR 3.

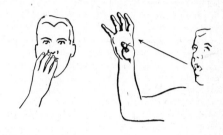

[S–91]

SCREW 1 (skrōō), *n.* (The length of the screw is indicated.) The thumb and index finger are held up an inch or two apart, to indicate the length of the screw.

[S–92]

SCREW 2, *n.* (The length of the screw is indicated.) The thumb and index finger of the right hand, held an inch or two apart, are placed on the left index finger to indicate the length of the screw.

[S–93]

SCREWDRIVER 1 (skrōō drī' vər) *n.* (The act of driving a screw.) The sign for SCREW 1 is made, and then the tips of the fingers of the right "H" hand are placed in the open left palm and twisted around several times.

[S-94]

SCREWDRIVER 2, *n*. The same as SCREW-
DRIVER 1, except that the sign for SCREW 2 is
used instead.

[S-95]

SCRIBER (skrī′ bər), *(voc.), n*. (A writing implement of metal or steel.) The sign for METAL or
STEEL is made: The right "S" hand, palm facing
left, is passed sharply over the extended left index
finger several times. The sign for WRITE is then
made: The right hand, grasping an imaginary pencil,
writes across the upturned left palm.

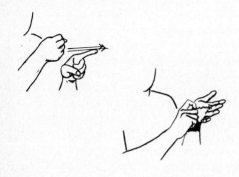

[S-96]

SCULPT (skŭlpt), *v.*, SCULPTED, SCULPTING. (Contours are indicated or outlined.) Both "A" hands,
held about a foot apart before the face, with palms
facing each other, move down simultaneously in a
wavy, undulating motion. *Cf.* FIGURE 2, FORM,
IMAGE, SCULPTURE, SHAPE 1, STATUE.

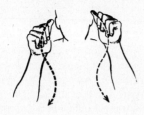

[S-97]

SCULPTOR (skŭlp′ tər), *n*. (An individual who
carves.) The thumb of the right "A" hand, placed in
the upturned left palm, is twisted up and down several times, as if gouging out material from the left
palm. This is followed by the sign for INDIVID-
UAL: Both open hands, palms facing each other,

move down the sides of the body, tracing its outline
to the hips.

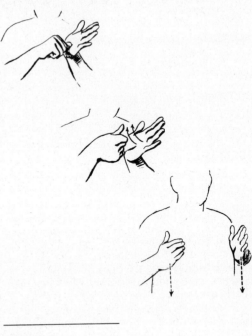

[S-98]

SCULPTURE (skŭlp′ chər), *n., v.*, -TURED, -TURING.
See SCULPT.

[S-99]

SCYTHE (sīth), *n., v.*, SCYTHED, SCYTHING.
(Threshing by hand.) The signer manipulates an
imaginary scythe with both hands. *Cf.* MOW 1.

[S-100]

SEA (sē), *n*. (The undulating waves.) The sign for
WATER 2 is made: The right "W" hand, palm facing out, is shaken very slightly. Then both downturned "5" hands, side by side, execute a series of

wavy, undulating movements from left to right. *Cf.* OCEAN 1.

SEAL 1 (sēl), *n.* (The natural sign.) The right hand grasps an imaginary rubber stamp and presses it against the upturned left palm. *Cf.* GUARANTEE 2, STAMP 2.

SEAL 2, *n.* (Squeezing the embossing seal.) The right hand grips the arms of an imaginary seal held at the little finger edge of the upturned left hand. The right hand squeezes the seal once or twice.

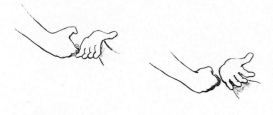

SEAMAN (sē' mən), *n.* (The three stripes on the sailor's blouse.) The middle finger of the right "3" hand brushes against the right shoulder several times. *Cf.* SAILOR 1.

SEARCH (sûrch), *v.,* SEARCHED, SEARCHING. (Directing the vision from place to place.) The right "C" hand (the French *chercher*), palm facing left, moves from right to left across the line of vision, in a series of counterclockwise circles. The signer's gaze remains concentrated and his head turns slowly from right to left. *Cf.* CURIOUS 1, EXAMINE, INVESTIGATE 1, LOOK FOR, PROBE 1, QUEST, SEEK.

SEASIDE (sē' sīd´), *n.* (Near the sea.) The sign for NEAR is made: The left hand, cupped, fingers together, is held before the chest, palm facing the body. The right hand, also cupped, fingers together, moves a very short distance back and forth, as it is held in front of the left. This is followed by the sign for SEA, *q.v.*

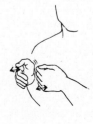

SEASON (sē' zən), *n.* The right "T" hand is placed palm to palm in the open left hand. It describes a clockwise circle and comes to rest again in the left palm. *Cf.* AGE 2, EPOCH, ERA, PERIOD 2, TIME 2.

[S-107]

SEAT (sēt), *n., v.,* SEATED, SEATING. (The act of sitting.) The extended right index and middle fingers are draped across the back of the same two fingers of the downturned left hand. The hands then move straight downward a short distance. *Cf.* BE SEATED, CHAIR 1, SIT 1.

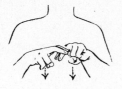

[S-108]

SECOND 1 (sĕk' ənd), *adj.* (The second finger is indicated.) The tip of the index finger of the right "D" hand is placed on the tip of the middle finger of the left "V" hand. The right hand then executes a short pivotal movement in a clockwise direction. The left "L" hand may be substituted for the left "V" hand, with the right index fingertip placed on the left index fingertip. *Cf.* SECONDARY, SECONDLY.

[S-109]

SECOND 2, *v.,* -ONDED, -ONDING. ("Second"—two fingers.) The right "L" hand, held somewhat above the head, index finger pointing straight up, pivots forward a bit, so that the index finger now points forward. Used in parliamentary procedure. *Cf.* ENDORSE 3, INDORSE 3, SUPPORT 3.

[S-110]

SECOND 3, *n.* (The ticking off of seconds on the clock.) The index finger of the right "D" hand exe-

cutes a series of very short movements in a clockwise manner as it rests against the left "S" hand, which is facing right.

[S-111]

SECONDARY (sĕk' ən dĕr´ ĭ), *adj.* See SECOND 1.

[S-112]

SECONDLY (sĕk' ənd lĭ), *adv.* See SECOND 1.

[S-113]

SECRET (sē' krĭt), *n., adj.* (The sealing of the lips; keeping the words back.) The back of the thumb of the right "A" hand is placed firmly against the closed lips. The thumb, in this position, may move off the lips slightly and return again to the lips. As an optional addition, the thumb may swing down under the downturned cupped left hand, after being placed on the lips as above. *Cf.* DON'T TELL, PRIVACY, PRIVATE 1.

[S-114]

SECRETARY (sĕk' rə tĕr´ ĭ), *n.* (Taking a pencil from behind the ear.) An imaginary pencil is taken from the right ear and then is used to go through the motions of writing on the upturned left palm.

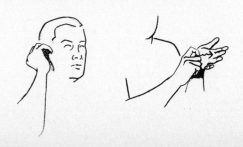

[S-115]

SECTION (sĕk′ shən), *n*. (Cutting off or designating a part.) The little finger edge of the open right hand moves straight down the middle of the upturned left palm. *Cf.* PART 1, PIECE, PORTION, SHARE 1, SOME.

[S-116]

SEE (sē), *v.*, SAW, SEEN, SEEING. (The eyesight is directed forward.) The right "V" hand (the French *voir*), palm facing the body, is placed so that the fingertips are just under the eyes. The hand swings around and out, so that the fingertips are now pointing forward. The hand often moves straight out, without turning around. *Cf.* LOOK 1, PERCEIVE 1, PERCEPTION, SIGHT, WATCH 2.

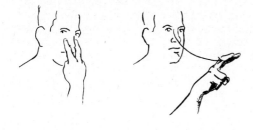

[S-117]

SEED 1 (sēd), *n*. (A tiny thing is indicated.) The thumb and index finger of the right hand pinch the tip of the little finger of the left hand.

[S-118]

SEED 2, *n., v.,* SEEDED, SEEDING. (The act of sprinkling seed.) The thumb and index finger of either hand go through the natural motions of sprinkling seeds. *Cf.* SOW.

[S-119]

SEED 3, *n., v.* (Seeds in a pod are indicated, and then sown.) The tips of the thumb and index finger of the right hand are placed together, and move up and down along the outstretched index finger of the left hand, from knuckle to tip. The right hand then goes through the motions of sprinkling seed at random.

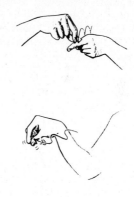

[S-120]

SEEK (sēk), *v.,* SOUGHT, SEEKING. (Directing the vision from place to place.) The right "C" hand (the French *chercher*), palm facing left, moves from right to left across the line of vision, in a series of counterclockwise circles. The signer's gaze remains concentrated and his head turns slowly from right to left. *Cf.* CURIOUS 1, EXAMINE, INVESTIGATE 1, LOOK FOR, PROBE 1, QUEST, SEARCH.

[S–121]

SEEM (sēm), *v.*, SEEMED, SEEMING. (Something presented before the eyes.) The open right hand, palm flat and facing out, with fingers together and pointing up, is positioned at shoulder level. Pivoting from the wrist, the hand is swung around so that the palm now faces the eyes. Sometimes the eyes glance at the newly presented palm. *Cf.* APPARENT, APPARENTLY, APPEAR 1, LOOK 2.

[S–122]

SEIZE (sēz), *v.*, SEIZED, SEIZING. (Grasping something and holding it down.) Both hands, palms down, quickly close into the "S" position, the right on top of the left. *Cf.* CAPTURE, CATCH 2, GRAB, GRASP.

[S–123]

SELDOM (sĕl′ dəm), *adv.* (The "1" finger is brought up very slowly.) The right index finger, resting in the open left palm, which is facing right, swings up slowly from its position to one in which it is pointing straight up. The movement is repeated slowly, after a pause. *Cf.* OCCASIONAL, OCCASIONALLY, ONCE IN A WHILE, SOMETIME(S).

[S–124]

SELECT 1 (sĭ lĕkt′), *v.*, -LECTED, -LECTING. (The natural motion of selecting something from the hand.) The thumb and index fingers of the outstretched right hand grasp an imaginary object on the upturned left palm. The right hand then moves straight up. *Cf.* CHOOSE 2, DISCOVER, FIND, PICK 1.

[S–125]

SELECT 2, *v.* (Taking unto oneself.) The right hand, palm out, is extended before the chest, index finger and thumb in an open position, the other fingers separated and pointing up. The hand is drawn in toward the chest, and the index and thumb close at the same time, indicating something taken to oneself. *Cf.* ADOPT, APPOINT, CHOOSE 1, TAKE.

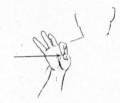

[S–126]

SELECT 3, *v.* (The natural sign.) The fingertips and thumbtip of the downturned open right hand come together, and the hand moves up a short distance, as if picking something. *Cf.* PICK 2, PICK UP 2.

[S–127]

-SELF 1 (sĕlf), *n. used with a gender prefix as a reflexive and intensive pronoun; adj.* (The individual is indicated with the thumb.) The right hand, held in the "A" position, thumb up, moves several times in the direction of the person indicated: *myself, yourself, himself, herself, itself, oneself, ourselves, yourselves, themselves.*

[S–128]

SELF 2, *n.* (The self is carried uppermost.) The right "A" hand, thumb up, is brought up against the chest, from waist to breast. *Cf.* AMBITIOUS 2, EGOTISM 1.

[S–129]

SELFISH 1 (sĕl' fĭsh), *adj.* (Pulling things toward oneself.) Both prone open or "V" hands are held in front of the body with fingers bent. The hands are then drawn quickly and forcefully inward, as if raking things toward oneself. *Cf.* GREEDY 1, STINGY 1, TIGHTWAD 1.

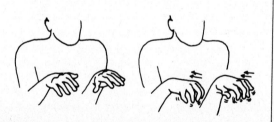

[S–130]

SELFISH 2, *adj.* (Scratching the palm in greed.) The right fingers scratch the upturned left palm several times. A frowning expression is often used. *Cf.* AVARICIOUS, GREEDY 2, STINGY 2, TIGHTWAD 2.

[S–131]

SELFISH 3, *adj.* (Scratching in greed.) The downturned "3" hands, held side by side, make a scratching motion as they move in toward the body. *Cf.* GREEDY 3, STINGY 3.

[S–132]

SELL (sĕl), *v.,* SOLD, SELLING. (Transferring ownership of an object.) Both "AND" hands, fingers touching their respective thumbs, are held palms down before the body. The hands are pivoted simultaneously outward and away from the body, once or several times. *Cf.* SALE, VEND.

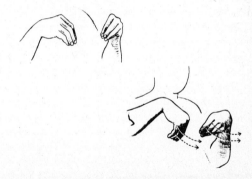

[S–133]

SELLER (sĕl' ər), *n.* (Transferring ownership.) The sign for SELL is formed. The sign for INDIVID-UAL is then made: Both open hands, palms facing each other, move down the sides of the body, tracing its outline to the hips. *Cf.* MERCHANT, SALESMAN, VENDER.

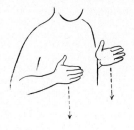

[S–134]

SEMICOLON (sĕm' i kō' lən), *n.* (The natural motion of making a semicolon in the air.) The thumb and index finger, held together, draw a semicolon in the air.

[S–135]

SEMINARY 1 (sĕm' ə nĕr´ i), *(eccles.), n.* (A college dedicated to Christianity.) The sign for JESUS is made: Both "5" hands are used. The left middle finger touches the right palm, and then the right middle finger touches the left palm. This is followed by the sign for COLLEGE: The sign for SCHOOL, *q.v.,* is made, but without the clapping of hands. The upper hand swings up in an arc above the lower. The upper hand may form a "C," instead of assuming a clapping position.

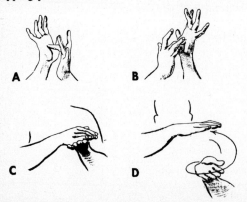

A   B

C   D

[S–136]

SEMINARY 2, *n.* (The letter "S"; a college.) The downturned, right "S" hand rests on the upturned left palm. The right hand moves up toward the right and then over toward the left, describing an arc, as in COLLEGE, *q.v.*

[S–137]

SENATE (sĕn' ĭt), *n.* (The letter "S"; perhaps the drape of the Roman toga about the shoulders.) The right "S" hand, palm facing left, swings from one shoulder to the other.

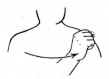

[S–138]

SENATOR (sĕn' ə tər), *n.* (An individual member of the SENATE.) The sign for SENATE is followed by the sign for INDIVIDUAL: Both open hands, palms facing each other, move down the sides of the body, tracing its outline to the hips.

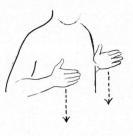

[S–139]

SEND 1 (sĕnd), *v.,* SENT, SENDING. (Sending away from.) The right fingertips tap the back of the downturned, left "S" hand and then swing forward, away from the hand.

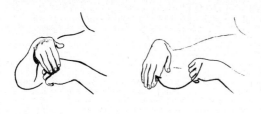

[S-140]

SEND 2, *v.* (Sending something forth.) The right "AND" hand is held palm out. It then opens and moves forcefully outward, in a throwing motion.

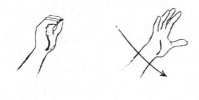

[S-141]

SEND AWAY 1, *v. phrase.* (Moving away from.) The fingertips of the right hand move off the top of the left hand. *Cf.* DISPATCH.

[S-142]

SEND AWAY 2, *v. phrase.* (Forcing something away.) The left open hand is held with fingers pointing forward. The extended right index finger points forward. In this position the right index finger moves forcefully across the left palm, from wrist to fingertips, and continues upward in an arc. The left hand may be omitted.

[S-143]

SEND TO ME, *v. phrase.* (Pulling something toward one.) The index finger of the right "D" hand moves up to strike the fingertips of the open left hand, which is held before the body with palm facing right and fingers pointing forward. The right hand then moves quickly downward and back toward the body, pivoting at the wrist.

[S-144]

SENSATION (sĕn sā′ shən), *n.* (The welling up of feelings or emotions in the heart.) The right middle finger, touching the heart, moves up an inch or two a number of times. *Cf.* EMOTION 1, FEEL 2, FEELING, MOTIVE 2, SENSE 2.

[S-145]

SENSE 1 (sĕns), *n.* (Patting the head to indicate something of value inside.) The right fingers pat the forehead several times. *Cf.* INTELLECT, INTELLIGENCE, MENTAL, MIND 1.

[S–146]

SENSE 2, *n., v.,* SENSED, SENSING. See SENSATION.

[S–147]

SENSITIVE (sĕn′ sə tǐv), *adj.* (A nimble touch.) The middle finger of the right hand touches the chest over the heart very briefly and lightly, and is then flicked off. *Cf.* SENSITIVITY.

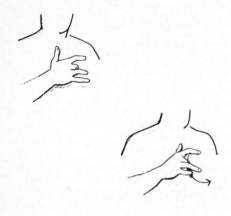

[S–148]

SENSITIVITY (sĕn′ sə tǐv′ ə tǐ), *n.* See SENSITIVE.

[S–149]

SENTENCE (sĕn′ təns), *n., v.,* -TENCED, -TENCING. (A series of letters spelled out on the printed page.) The downturned "F" hands are positioned with thumbs and index fingertips touching. The hands move straight apart to either side in a wavy or straight motion. *Cf.* LANGUAGE.

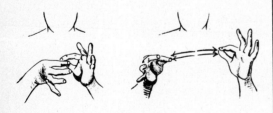

[S–150]

SEPARATE 1 (*v.* sĕp′ ə rāt′; *adj., n.* sĕp′ ə rĭt), -RATED, -RATING. (The hands are moved apart.) Both hands, in the "A" position, thumbs up, are held together, with knuckles touching. With a delib-

erate movement they come apart. *Cf.* APART, DIVORCE 1, PART 3.

[S–151]

SEPARATE 2, *v., adj., n.* (Separating to classify.) Both hands, in the right angle position, are placed palms down before the body, knuckles to knuckles. They pull apart or separate, once or a number of times. *Cf.* ASSORT, PART 2.

[S–152]

SEQUEL (sē′ kwəl), *n.* (One hand follows the other.) The "A" hands are used, thumbs pointing up. The right is positioned a few inches behind the left. The left hand moves straight forward, while the right follows behind in a series of wavy movements. *Cf.* CONSECUTIVE, FOLLOW, FOLLOWING.

[S–153]

SERGEANT (sär′ jənt), *n.* (The three stripes on the sleeve.) The fingertips of the right "W" hand trace the three stripes of a sergeant on the upper part of the left sleeve.

[S–154]

SERIES (sĭr′ ĭz), *n.* The index finger of the right hand is placed across the index finger of the left "L" hand. The right hand then flips over, around the tip of the left index finger and up against its underside. *Cf.* NEXT 1, THENCE.

[S–155]

SERMON (sûr′ mən), *n.* (Placing morsels of wisdom, or food for thought, into the mind.) The right hand, palm out, with thumb and index finger touching, is moved forward and slightly downward a number of times from its initial position near the right temple. *Cf.* PREACH.

[S–156]

SERVANT (sûr′ vənt), *n.* (Passing the dishes, one by one.) The upturned "5" hands move alternately toward and away from the chest. This may be followed by the INDIVIDUAL 1 sign, *q.v. Cf.* MAID, SERVE 2, SERVICE, WAITER 2, WAIT ON 2, WAITRESS 2.

[S–157]

SERVE 1 (sûrv), *v.,* SERVED, SERVING, *n.* (Passing out dishes of food, one by one.) The upturned hands are held before the chest, as if bearing dishes of food. The left moves alternately to the left and back to the right, as if extending the dishes to a diner. *Cf.* WAIT ON 1.

[S–158]

SERVE 2, *v.* See SERVANT.

[S–159]

SERVICE (sûr′ vĭs), *n., v.,* -VICED, -VICING. See SERVANT.

[S–160]

SEVEN (sĕv′ ən), *n., adj.* The thumbtip and ring fingertip touch, while the other fingers point straight up. The palm faces out from the body.

[S–161]

SEVEN OF US, *n. phrase* The right "7" hand describes an arc as it moves from the right shoulder to the left.

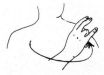

[S-162]

SEVERAL (sĕv' ər əl), *adj.* (The fingers are presented in order, to convey the concept of "several.") The right "A" hand is held palm facing up. One by one the fingers open, beginning with the index finger and ending with the little finger. Some use only the index and middle fingers. *Cf.* FEW, RARE, SCARCE, SUNDRY.

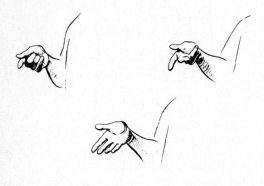

[S-163]

SEW (sō), *v.,* SEWED, SEWED or SEWN, SEWING. (The natural sign.) The right thumb and index finger grasp an imaginary needle and go through the motions of sewing stitches along the upturned left palm, from the base of the fingers to the base of the hand.

[S-164]

SEWER (sō' ər), *n.* (One who sews.) The sign for SEW is made, followed by the sign for INDIVIDUAL: Both open hands, palms facing each other, move down the sides of the body, tracing its outline to the hips. *Cf.* TAILOR.

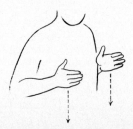

[S-165]

SEXUAL INTERCOURSE, *n. phrase.* (The motions of the legs during the sexual act.) The upturned left "V" hand remains motionless, while the downturned right "V" hand comes down repeatedly on the left. *Cf.* COPULATE, FORNICATE.

[S-166]

SHADOW (shăd' ō), *n.* (A darkness cast over something.) The sign for BLACK is made: The tip of the right index finger moves across the right eyebrow, from left to right. The right "S" hand, palm facing down, then makes a sweeping movement from right to left over the upturned left hand. Note: The left hand may also be downturned.

[S-167]

SHAKE (shāk), *v.,* SHAKEN, SHAKING. (The natural sign.) Both "5" hands, grasping an imaginary object, go through the motions of shaking it several times.

[S-168]

SHALL (shăl, *unstressed* shəl), *v., future tense of the verb* TO BE. (Something ahead or in the future.) The upright, open right hand, palm facing left, moves straight out and slightly up from a position beside the right temple. *Cf.* BY AND BY, FUTURE, IN THE FUTURE, LATER 2, LATER ON, WILL 1, WOULD.

SHALLOW (shăl' ō), *adj.* (The depth is small.) The downturned left palm is held in front of the body, with fingers extended and loosely parted. The right index fingertip is moved down and thrust between the fingers of the left hand, to indicate depth. Then the open hands are held facing each other, one facing down, the other facing up. In this position the top hand moves down toward the bottom hand but does not quite touch it. The space between the hands represents the small depth.

SHAME 1 (shām), *n., v.,* SHAMED, SHAMING. (The color rises in the cheek; an attempt is made to hide the head.) The backs of the fingers of the right hand, held in the right angle position, are placed against the right cheek. The hand moves up along the cheek, pivoting at the wrist, so that the fingers finally point to the rear. *Cf.* ASHAMED 1, BASHFUL 1, IMMODEST, IMMORAL, SHAMEFUL, SHAME ON YOU, SHY 1.

SHAME 2, *n.* Similar to SHAME 1, but both hands are used, at either cheek. *Cf.* ASHAMED 2, BASHFUL 2, SHY 2.

SHAMEFUL (shām' fəl), *adj.* See SHAME 1.

SHAME ON YOU, *phrase.* See SHAME 1.

SHAPE 1 (shāp), *n., v.,* SHAPED, SHAPING. (Contours are indicated or outlined.) Both "A" hands, held about a foot apart before the face, with palms facing each other, move down simultaneously in a wavy, undulating motion. *Cf.* FIGURE 2, FORM, IMAGE, SCULPT, SCULPTURE, STATUE.

SHAPE 2, *(voc.),* *v.* The downturned, open right hand rubs across the back of the downturned, left "S" hand, from wrist to knuckles.

[S-176]

SHARE 1 (shâr), *n.*, *v.*, SHARED, SHARING. (Cutting off or designating a part.) The little finger edge of the open right hand moves straight down the middle of the upturned left palm. *Cf.* PART 1, PIECE, PORTION, SECTION, SOME.

[S-177]

SHARE 2, *n.*, *v.* (A splitting apart or dividing.) The two hands are crossed, with the right little finger resting on the left index finger. Both hands are dropped down and separated simultaneously, so that the palms face down. *Cf.* APPORTION, DIVIDE 1.

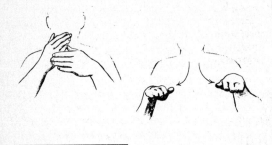

[S-178]

SHARP 1 (shärp), *adj.* (The finger feels a sharp edge.) The index finger of the right "D" hand, palm facing down, moves quickly over the index finger of the left "D" hand, striking a glancing blow on it.

[S-179]

SHARP 2, *adj.* (A tapering or sharp point is indicated.) The index finger and thumb of the left hand grasp the tip of the index finger of the right "D"

hand. The left hand then moves away a short distance, and its index finger and thumb come together. *Cf.* POINT 2, TIP.

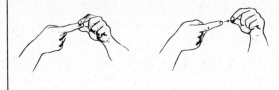

[S-180]

SHARP 3, *adj.* (The mind is bright.) The right "5" hand, palm facing the signer, is placed with the tip of the middle finger touching the forehead. The hand swings quickly out and around, moving up an inch or two as it does so. *Cf.* CLEVER 2.

[S-181]

SHARP 4, *adj.* (A sharp-edged hand.) The right hand grasps the little finger edge of the left firmly. As it leaves this position, moving down and out, it assumes the "A" position, palm facing left. *Cf.* ADEPT, EXPERIENCE 1, EXPERT, SHREWD, SKILL, SKILLFUL.

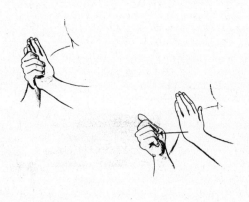

[S-182]

SHAVE (shāv), *v.*, SHAVED or SHAVEN, SHAVING. (The natural sign.) The right "Y" hand represents an opened straight razor. The right thumb is drawn down the side of the right cheek. *Cf.* RAZOR.

[S-183]

SHE (shē), *pron.* (Pointing at a female.) The FE-MALE prefix sign is made: The right "A" hand's thumb moves down along the line of the right jaw, from ear almost to chin. The right index finger then points at an imaginary female. If in context the gender is clear, the prefix sign is usually omitted. *Cf.* HER.

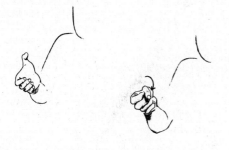

[S-184]

SHEARS 1 (shĭrz), *(voc.), n. pl.* (The natural sign.) The right hand, opening and closing forcefully, goes through the natural motion of manipulating a pair of shears. *Cf.* PLIERS, SNIPS.

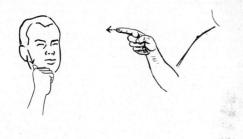

[S-185]

SHEARS 2, *(voc.), n. pl.* (The natural sign.) The index and middle fingers of the right hand go

through the natural open-and-close movements involved in "cutting off" the left fingertips.

[S-186]

SHEEP (shēp), *n.* (The shearing of the sheep.) The left arm is held close to the body, as if restraining an imaginary sheep. The right index and middle fingers go through the natural open-and-close cutting movements as they travel up along the left arm.

[S-187]

SHELF (shĕlf), *n.* (A flat piece of wood.) The sign for WOOD is made: The little finger edge of the open right hand moves back and forth in a sawing motion over the back of the downturned left hand. Both "B" hands, placed side by side and touching, with palms facing down, are drawn sharply apart, indicating the shape and length of the shelf. *Note:* The sign for WOOD is often omitted, especially in the case of a non-wooden shelf.

[S-188]

SHELTER (shĕl′ tər), *n.* (A shield.) The "S" hands are held before the chest, the left behind the right, and are pushed slightly away from the body. Then the right hand opens, palm facing out, and moves clockwise as if shielding the left fist. *Cf.* REFUGE, SHIELD 2.

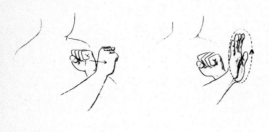

[S-189]

SHEPHERD (shĕp′ ərd), *n.* (A sheep keeper.) The sign for SHEEP is made. This is followed by the sign for KEEP: Both "K" hands are crossed, the right above the left, little finger edges down. In this position the hands are moved up and down a short distance. The sign for INDIVIDUAL then follows: Both open hands, palms facing each other, move down the sides of the body, tracing its outline to the hips.

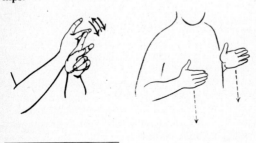

[S-190]

SHERIFF (shĕr′ ĭf), *n.* (The letter "C" for "cop"; the shape and position of the badge.) The right "C" hand, palm facing left, is placed against the heart. *Cf.* COP, POLICE, POLICEMAN.

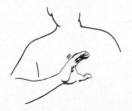

[S-191]

SHIELD 1 (shēld), *n., v.,* SHIELDED, SHIELDING. (Hold down firmly; cover and strengthen.) The "S" hands, downturned, are held side by side in front of the body, the arms almost horizontal, and the left hand in front of the right. Both arms move a short distance forward and slightly downward. *Cf.* DEFEND, DEFENSE, FORTIFY, GUARD, PROTECT, PROTECTION.

[S-192]

SHIELD 2, *n., v.* See SHELTER.

[S-193]

SHIELD 3, *n., v.* (Warding off danger; the shape.) The sign for SHIELD 1 is made. The thumbs then trace the outline of an imaginary shield.

[S-194]

SHINE (shīn), *v.,* SHINED, SHINING, SHONE. (Reflected glistening of light rays.) The left hand, held supinely before the chest, palm down, represents the object from which the rays glisten. The right hand, in the "5" position, touches the back of the left lightly and moves up toward the right, pivoting slightly at the wrist, with fingers wiggling. *Cf.* BRIGHT 2, GLISTEN, SHINING.

[S–195]

SHINE SHOES, *v. phrase.* (The act of rubbing.) The right knuckles rub briskly against the outstretched left palm. *Cf.* POLISH 1, RUB, SANDPAPER.

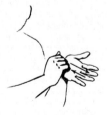

[S–196]

SHINING, *adj.* See SHINE.

[S–197]

SHIP (shĭp), *n.* (The ship is transported over the waves; its masts are indicated.) The right "3" hand, palm facing left and resting on the upturned left palm, is moved forward by the left hand, in a series of undulating movements.

[S–198]

-SHIP, *suffix.* The downturned right "S" hand moves down along the left palm, which is facing away from the body.

[S–199]

SHIRK (shûrk), *v.*, SHIRKED, SHIRKING. (Ducking back and forth, away from something.) Both "A"

hands, thumbs pointing straight up, are held some distance before the chest, with the left hand in front of the right. The right hand, swinging back and forth, moves away from the left and toward the chest. *Cf.* AVOID 1, EVADE, EVASION, SHUN.

[S–200]

SHIRT (shûrt), *n.* (Draping the clothes on the body.) With fingertips resting on the chest, both hands move down simultaneously. The action is repeated. *Cf.* CLOTHES, CLOTHING, DRESS, FROCK, GARMENT, GOWN, SUIT, WEAR 1.

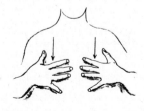

[S–201]

SHIVER 1 (shĭv′ ər), *v.*, -ERED, -ERING. (The trembling from cold.) Both "S" hands, palms facing, are placed at the sides of the body. In this position the arms and hands shiver. *Cf.* CHILLY, COLD 1, FRIGID, WINTER 1.

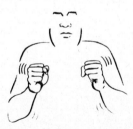

[S–202]

SHIVER 2, *(colloq.), v., n.* (The chattering of the teeth.) The extended and curved index and middle fingers of both hands are placed together, almost touching, with the right hand above the left, palms facing. Both hands shake back and forth in opposing directions a number of times.

[S–203]

SHOCKED 1 (shŏkt), *v.* (The mind is frozen; the thought is frozen.) The index finger of the right "D" hand, palm facing the body, touches the forehead (modified THINK sign, *q. v.*). Both hands, in the "5" position, palms down, are then suddenly and deliberately dropped down in front of the body. A look of surprise is assumed at this point, and the head jerks back slightly. *Cf.* AT A LOSS, DUMFOUNDED 1, JOLT, STUMPED.

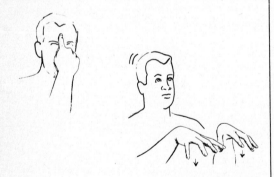

[S–204]

SHOCKED 2, *(colloq.), adj.* (The eyes pop open.) The "S" hands, palms facing each other, are held before the eyes. They suddenly open into the "C" position, with the eyes wide open. *Cf.* OPEN-EYED, SURPRISED.

[S–205]

SHOE(S) 1 (sho͞o), *n.* Both "S" hands, palms facing down, are brought together sharply twice.

[S–206]

SHOE(S) 2, *n.* (Slipping the foot into the shoe.) The downturned right "B" hand is slipped into the upturned left "C" hand.

[S–207]

SHOEBRUSH (sho͞o′ brŭsh′), *n.* (The natural motion.) The right hand, grasping an imaginary brush, "brushes" the back of the downturned open left hand several times.

[S–208]

SHOELACES (sho͞o′ lās′as), *n. pl.* (The crisscross pattern.) The little fingers of both downturned "I" hands cross each other several times, with one alternately on top of the other. At the same time the hands are drawn in toward the body. *Cf.* LACE.

[S–209]

SHOEMAKER (shōō'mā´ kar), *n.* (The stitching action of the sewing machine.) Both "D" hands, palms facing each other, are alternately crossed and pulled apart a number of times. Each time they come apart, the index fingers close tightly into the "X" position. The sign for INDIVIDUAL is then made: Both open hands, palms facing each other, move down the sides of the body, tracing its outline to the hips. *Cf.* COBBLER, COBBLING, SHOEMAKING, SHOE REPAIR.

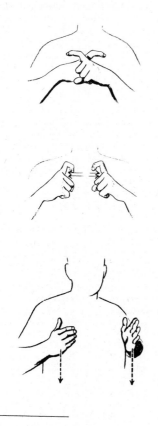

[S–210]

SHOEMAKING, *n.* See SHOEMAKER. The sign for INDIVIDUAL, however, is omitted.

[S–211]

SHOE REPAIR, *n. phrase.* See SHOEMAKER. The sign for INDIVIDUAL, however, is omitted.

[S–212]

SHOOT 1 (shōōt), *v.,* SHOT, SHOOTING. (Firing a gun.) The right "L" hand is pointed forward, palm facing left. The right thumb is then moved down, as in the movement of the pistol's hammer. The index or trigger finger may also move.

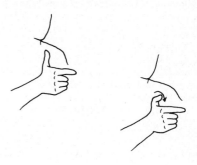

[S–213]

SHOOT 2, *v.* (Shooting a gun.) The left "S" hand is held above the head as if holding a gun barrel. At the same time the right "L" hand is held below the left hand, its index finger moving back and forth, as if pulling a trigger. *Cf.* GUN, PISTOL, RIFLE, SHOT 2.

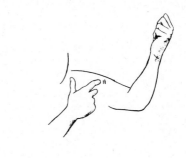

[S–214]

SHOP 1 (shŏp), *n., v.,* SHOPPED, SHOPPING. (Paying out money.) The right hand, palm up and all fingertips touching the thumb, is placed in the upturned left hand. From this position it moves forward and off the left hand a number of times. The right fingers usually remain against the thumb, but they may be opened very slightly each time the right hand moves forward. *Cf.* GROCERIES, SHOPPING.

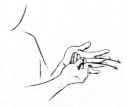

[S-215]

SHOP 2, *n.* (A house where things are sold.) The sign for SELL is made: Both "AND" hands, fingertips touching their respective thumbs, are held palms down before the body. The hands are pivoted outward and away from the body once or several times. This is followed by the sign for HOUSE: The hands form a pyramid a bit above eye level and then separate, moving diagonally downward and then straight down a few inches. It may also be followed by the sign for PLACE: The "P" hands are held side by side before the body, with middle fingertips touching. From this position the hands separate and outline a circle (or a square), before coming together again closer to the body. *Cf.* STORE 1.

[S-216]

SHOPPING (shŏp' ing), *n.* See SHOP 1.

[S-217]

SHORE (shōr), *n.* (Describing the undulating shoreline.) The left hand, representing the land, is held with palm facing the chest and fingers pointing right. The right hand, representing the water, is placed against the back of the left hand, with fingers pointing left. In this position both hands describe an arc as they move in unison from right to left. As they do so, the right hand taps the back of the left a number of times.

[S-218]

SHORT 1 (shôrt), *adj.* (To make short; to measure off a short space.) The index and middle fingers of the right "H" hand are placed across the top of the index and middle fingers of the left "H" hand, and move a short distance back and forth, along the length of the left index finger. *Cf.* ABBREVIATE 2, BRIEF 1, SHORTEN.

[S-219]

SHORT 2, *adj.* (A shortness of height is indicated.) The right hand, in right-angle position, pats an imaginary head at approximately chest level. *Cf.* MINOR, SMALL 2.

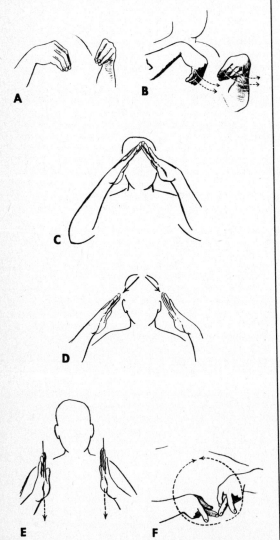

A

B

C

D

E

F

[S–220]

SHORTEN (shôr′ tən), *v.*, -ENED, -ENING. See SHORT 1.

[S–221]

SHOT 1 (shŏt), *(colloq.)*, *n.* (The natural sign.) The right hand goes through the motions of injecting a substance into the upper left arm. *Cf.* INJECTION, SHOT IN THE ARM.

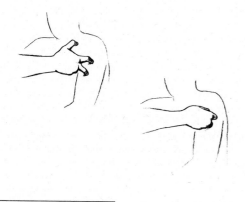

[S–222]

SHOT 2, *n.* (Shooting a gun.) The left "S" hand is held above the head as if holding a gun barrel. At the same time the right "L" hand is held below the left hand, its index finger moving back and forth, as if pulling a trigger. *Cf.* GUN, PISTOL, RIFLE, SHOOT 2.

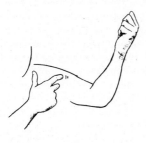

[S–223]

SHOT IN THE ARM, *(sl.)*, *n. phrase.* See SHOT 1.

[S–224]

SHOULD (shŏŏd), *v.* (Being pinned down.) The right hand, in the "X" position, palm down, moves forcefully up and down once or twice. An expression of determination is frequently assumed. *Cf.* HAVE TO, IMPERATIVE, MUST, NECESSARY 1, NECESSITY, NEED 1, OUGHT TO, VITAL 2.

[S–225]

SHOUT (shout), *v.,* SHOUTED, SHOUTING. (Harsh words thrown out.) The right hand, as in CURSE 1, appears to claw words out of the mouth. This time, however, it turns and throws them out, ending in the "5" position. *Cf.* BLASPHEME 2, CALL OUT, CRY 3, CRY OUT, CURSE 2, SCREAM, SUMMON 1, SWEAR 3.

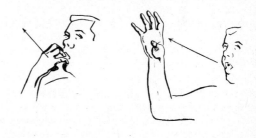

[S–226]

SHOVEL (shŭv′ əl), *n., v.,* -ELED, -ELING. (The natural motion.) Both hands, in the "A" position, right hand facing up and left hand facing down, grasp an imaginary shovel. They go through the natural movements of shoveling earth—first digging in and then tossing the earth aside. *Cf.* DIG 2, SPADE.

[S-227]

SHOW 1 (shō), *n., v.,* SHOWED, SHOWN, SHOWING. (Directing the attention to something, and bringing it forward.) The right index finger points into the left palm, held facing out before the body. The left palm moves straight out. For the passive form of this verb, *i.e.,* BE SHOWN, the movement is reversed: The left hand, palm facing in, is moved in toward the body, while the right index finger remains pointing into the left palm. *Cf.* DEMONSTRATE, DISPLAY, EVIDENCE, EXAMPLE, EXHIBIT, EXHIBITION, ILLUSTRATE, INDICATE, INFLUENCE 3, PRODUCE 2, REPRESENT, SIGNIFY 1.

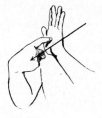

[S-228]

SHOW 2, *n.* (Motion or movement, modified by the letter "A" for "act.") Both "A" hands, palms out, are held at shoulder height and rotate alternately toward the head. *Cf.* ACT 1, ACTOR, ACTRESS, DRAMA, PERFORM 2, PERFORMANCE 2, PLAY 2.

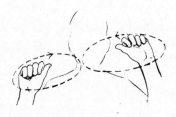

[S-229]

SHOWER (shou' ər), *n.* (The sprinkling of water on the head.) The right hand sprinkles imaginary water on the head. *Cf.* BAPTISM.

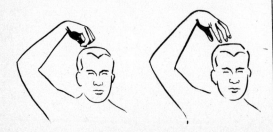

[S-230]

SHOW OFF 1 (shō ôf'), *v.* (Indicating the self, repeatedly.) The thumbs of both "A" hands are alternately thrust into the chest a number of times. *Cf.* BOAST, BRAG.

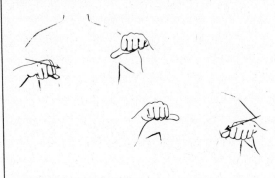

[S-231]

SHOW-OFF 2, *(loc.), n.* The right "P" hand, palm facing down, is swung several times into the open left hand, whose palm is facing right.

[S-232]

SHREWD (shrōōd), *adj.* (A sharp-edged hand.) The right hand grasps the little finger edge of the left firmly. As it leaves this position, moving down and out, it assumes the "A" position, palm facing left. *Cf.* ADEPT, EXPERIENCE 1, EXPERT, SHARP 4, SKILL, SKILLFUL.

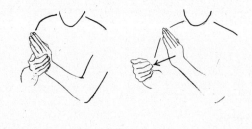

[S-233]

SHUN (shŭn), *v.,* SHUNNED, SHUNNING. (Ducking back and forth, away from something.) Both "A" hands, thumbs pointing straight up, are held some distance before the chest, with the left hand in front of the right. The right hand, swinging back and forth, moves away from the left and toward the chest. *Cf.* AVOID 1, EVADE, EVASION, SHIRK.

brought up forcefully against the lips. An angry expression is assumed.

[S–234]

SHUT (shŭt), *adj., v.,* SHUT, SHUTTING. (The act of closing.) Both "B" hands, held palms out before the body, come together with some force. *Cf.* CLOSE 1.

[S–235]

SHUT UP 1 (shŭt ŭp′), *interj.* (Closing of the mouth.) The open right hand, fingers together and pointing left, palm toward the face, is placed so that the back of the thumb rests against the lips. The hand snaps shut so that all fingers now also rest on the lips. An angry expression is assumed.

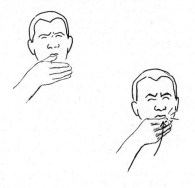

[S–236]

SHUT UP 2, *interj.* (The natural motion of "shushing.") The index finger of the right "D" hand is

[S–237]

SHY 1 (shī), *adj.* (The color rises in the cheek; an attempt is made to hide the head.) The backs of the fingers of the right hand, held in the right angle position, are placed against the right cheek. The hand moves up along the cheek, pivoting at the wrist, so that the fingers finally point to the rear. *Cf.* ASHAMED 1, BASHFUL 1, IMMODEST, IMMORAL, SHAME 1, SHAMEFUL, SHAME ON YOU.

[S–238]

SHY 2, *adj.* Similar to SHY 1, but both hands are used, at either cheek. *Cf.* ASHAMED 2, BASHFUL 2, SHAME 2.

[S–239]

SICK (sĭk), *adj., adv.* (The sick parts of the anatomy are indicated.) The right middle finger rests on the forehead, and its left counterpart is placed against the stomach. The signer assumes an expression of sadness or physical distress. *Cf.* DISEASE 1, ILL, ILLNESS, SICKNESS.

[S-240]

SICKNESS (sĭk′ nĭs), *n.* See SICK. This is followed by the sign -NESS: The downturned right "N" hand moves down along the left palm, which is facing away from the body.

[S-241]

SICK OF IT, *(colloq.), phrase.* (A more emphatic expression of the sign for SICK.) The right middle fingertip rests on the forehead. The right hand, pivoting on the middle finger, twists quickly in a counterclockwise direction. The signer assumes an expression of utter and exaggerated disgust.

[S-242]

SIDE (sīd), *n.* The right open hand is placed in front of the left, both palms facing the body. The right hand is drawn in slightly, so that it closes up to the left. The hands do not touch.

[S-243]

SIDE BY SIDE, *adv. phrase.* (The natural sign.) The "A" hands are held side by side before the body with palms facing each other and thumbs pointing outward.

[S-244]

SIDETRACK (sīd′ trăk′), *v.,* -TRACKED, -TRACKING. (The natural movement.) Both prone index fingers are held side by side and pointing forward before the body. The right hand is moved forward along the left and then diverted to the right.

[S-245]

SIGHT (sīt), *n.,* SAW, SEEN, SEEING. (The eyesight is directed forward.) The right "V" hand, palm facing the body, is placed so that the fingertips are just under the eyes. The hand swings around and out, so that the fingertips are now pointing forward. *Cf.* LOOK 1, PERCEIVE 1, PERCEPTION, SEE, WATCH 2.

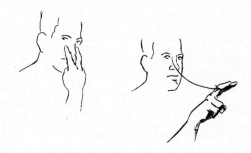

[S-246]

SIGN (sīn), *v.,* SIGNED, SIGNING. (The natural movement.) The right index finger and thumb, grasping an imaginary pen, write across the open left palm. The index and middle fingers of the right hand may instead be slapped into the open left palm. *Cf.* PEN, SIGNATURE, WRITE.

[S–247]

SIGNATURE (sig′ nə chər), *n.* See SIGN.

[S–248]

SIGNIFICANCE 1 (sĭg nĭf′ ə kəns), *n.* Both "F" hands, palms facing each other, move apart, up, and together in a smooth elliptical fashion, coming together at the tips of the thumbs and index fingers of both hands. *Cf.* DESERVE, ESSENTIAL, IMPORTANT 1, MAIN, MERIT, PRECIOUS, PROMINENT 2, SIGNIFICANT, VALUABLE, VALUE, VITAL 1, WORTH, WORTHWHILE, WORTHY.

[S–249]

SIGNIFICANCE 2, *n.* (Relative standing of one's thoughts.) A modified sign for THINK is made: The right index finger touches the middle of the forehead. The tips of the right "V" hand, palm down, are then thrust into the upturned left palm (as in STAND, *q.v.*). The right "V" hand is then re-thrust into the upturned left palm, with right palm now facing the body. *Cf.* CONNOTE, IMPLY, INTEND, INTENT 1, INTENTION, MEAN 2, MEANING, MOTIVE 3, PURPOSE 1, SIGNIFY 2, SUBSTANCE 2.

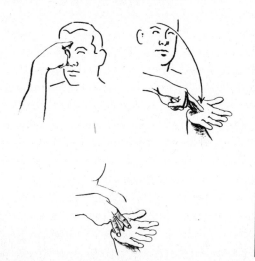

[S–250]

SIGNIFICANT (sĭg nĭf′ ə kənt), *adj.* See SIGNIFICANCE 1.

[S–251]

SIGNIFY 1 (sĭg′ nə fī′), *v.*, -FIED, -FYING. (Directing the attention to something, and bringing it forward.) The right index finger points into the left palm, held facing out before the body. The left palm moves straight out. For the passive form of this verb, *i.e.*, BE SHOWN, the movement is reversed: The left hand, palm facing in, is moved in toward the body, while the right index finger remains pointing into the left palm. *Cf.* DEMONSTRATION, DISPLAY, EVIDENCE, EXAMPLE, EXHIBIT, EXHIBITION, ILLUSTRATE, INDICATE, INFLUENCE 3, PRODUCE 2, REPRESENT, SHOW 1.

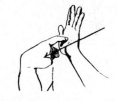

[S–252]

SIGNIFY 2, *n.* See SIGNIFICANCE 2.

[S–253]

SIGN LANGUAGE, *n.* (LANGUAGE 1, *q.v.*, and hand/arm movements.) The "D" hands, palms facing and index fingers pointing back toward the face, describe a series of continuous counterclockwise circles toward and away from the face, imitating the foot motions in bicycling. This is followed by the sign for LANGUAGE: The downturned "F" hands are positioned with thumbs and index fingertips touching. The hands move straight apart to either side in a wavy motion. The LANGUAGE part is often omitted. *Cf.* LANGUAGE OF SIGNS, SIGNS.

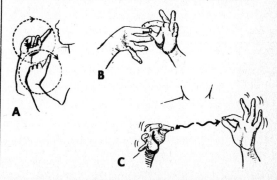

[S–254]

SIGNS (sīnz), *n. pl.* See SIGN LANGUAGE.

[S–255]

SILENCE 1 (sī′ lᵊns), *interj., n., v.,* -LENCED, -LENC-ING. (The natural sign.) The index finger is brought up against the pursed lips. *Cf.* BE QUIET 1, CALM 2, HUSH, NOISELESS, QUIET 1, SILENT, STILL 2.

[S–256]

SILENCE 2, *n., interj., v.* (Quiet and peace.) The open hands are crossed before the mouth, the right palm facing left, left facing right. Then both hands, held palms down, move down from the mouth, curv-ing outward to either side of the body. *Cf.* BE QUIET 2, BE STILL, CALM 1, QUIET 2.

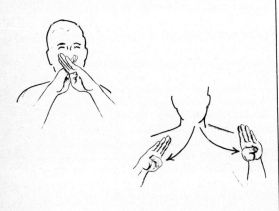

[S–257]

SILENT (sī′ lᵊnt), *adj.* See SILENCE 1.

[S–258]

SILLY (sil′ ĭ), *adj.* (Thoughts flickering back and forth.) The right "Y" hand, thumb almost touching the forehead, is shaken back and forth across the forehead several times. *Cf.* ABSURD, DAFT, FOLLY, FOOLISH, NONSENSE, RIDICULOUS, TRIFLING.

[S–259]

SILVER 1 (sil′ vᵊr), (*rare*), *n.* (Jiggling coins.) The sign for WHITE is formed: The fingertips of the "5" hand are placed against the chest. The hand moves straight out from the chest, while the fingers and thumb all come together. Then the left open hand grasps the right fingers and shakes them several times. The sign for WHITE is often omitted.

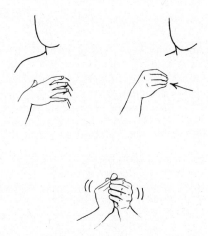

[S–260]

SILVER 2, *(loc.), n., adj.* Both "5" hands are held before the face with palms facing each other, thumb edges up, and fingers somewhat bent. From this po-sition, the hands turn palms downward and move away from each other to either side.

[S-261]

SIMILAR (sĭm′ ĭ lər), *adj.* (Matching fingers are brought together.) The outstretched index fingers are brought together, either once or several times. *Cf.* ALIKE, IDENTICAL, LIKE 2, SAME 1, SUCH.

[S-262]

SIMPLE 1 (sĭm′ pəl), *adj.* (The fingertips are easily moved.) The right fingertips brush repeatedly over their upturned left counterparts, causing them to move. *Cf.* EASY 1, FACILITATE.

[S-263]

SIMPLE 2, *adj.* (Everything is wiped off the hand, to emphasize an uncluttered or clean condition.) The right hand slowly wipes the upturned left palm, from wrist to fingertips. *Cf.* CLEAN 1, IMMACULATE, NEAT, NICE, PLAIN 2, PURE 1, PURITY.

[S-264]

SIN (sĭn), *n., v.,* SINNED, SINNING. (A stabbing.) The "D" hands, index fingers pointing to each other, are rotated in elliptical fashion before the chest—simultaneously but in opposite directions. *Cf.* ACHE,

HARM 1, HURT 1, INJURE 1, INJURY, MAR 1, OFFEND, OFFENSE, PAIN, WOUND.

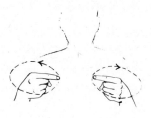

[S-265]

SINCE (sĭns), *adv., prep., conj.* (From a point up and over.) In the "D" position, palms down, both index fingers touch the right shoulder and then are brought up and over, ending in a palm-up position, pointing straight ahead of the body. *Cf.* ALL ALONG, ALL THE TIME, EVER SINCE, SO FAR, THUS FAR.

[S-266]

SINCERE 1 (sĭn sîr′), *adj.* (The letter "H," for HONEST; a straight and true path.) The index and middle fingers of the right "H" hand, whose palm faces left, move straight forward along the upturned left palm. *Cf.* FRANK, HONEST, HONESTY.

[S-267]

SINCERE 2, *adj.* (Coming forth directly from the lips; true.) The index finger of the right "D" hand, palm facing left, is placed against the lips. It moves up an inch or two and then describes a small arc forward and away from the lips. *Cf.* ABSOLUTE, ABSOLUTELY, ACTUAL, ACTUALLY, AUTHENTIC, CERTAIN, CERTAINLY, FAITHFUL 3, FIDELITY, FRANKLY, GENUINE, INDEED, POSITIVE 1, POSITIVELY, REAL, REALLY, SURE, SURELY, TRUE, TRULY, TRUTH, VALID, VERILY.

[S-268]

SING (sĭng), *n.*, *v.*, SANG or SUNG, SUNG, SINGING, (A rhythmic, wavy movement of the hand, to indicate a melody; the movement of a conductor's hand in directing a musical performance.) The right "5" hand, palm facing left, is waved back and forth near the open left hand, in a series of elongated figure-eights. *Cf.* CHANT, HYMN 1, MELODY, MUSIC, SONG.

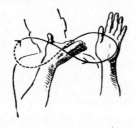

[S-269]

SINGLE FILE, *phrase.* (The fingers indicate a row of people, all in a line.) Both "5" hands are held before the chest with both palms facing left, and little fingertips touching. The right hand moves straight back from the left a short distance. The same sign may also be made with right hand facing left and left hand facing right, and the initial position involving the right little fingertip touching the tip of the left index finger. *Cf.* LINE-UP, QUEUE.

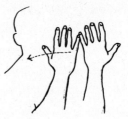

[S-270]

SINK 1 (sĭngk), *v.*, SANK or SUNK, SUNK or SUNKEN, SINKING. (The natural sign.) The thumb of the right "3" hand protrudes upward between the index and middle fingers of the downturned left hand. The right hand then slips out from between the left fingers and moves straight downward.

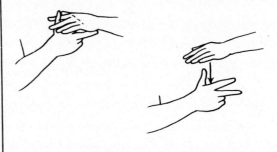

[S-271]

SINK 2, *v.* (Movement downward.) The index and middle fingers of the right "V" hand, held pointing down, move downward through the spread middle and ring fingers of the downturned open left hand.

[S-272]

SISTER 1 (sĭs' tər), *n.* (Female root sign; SAME. Meaning a female from the same family.) The FEMALE root sign is made: The thumb of the right "A" hand moves down along the right jawbone, almost to the chin. This is followed by the sign for

SAME: The outstretched index fingers are brought together, either once or several times.

SISTER 2, *n.* (The hood.) Both open hands, palms facing the head and fingers pointing up, are moved down along either side of the head, as if tracing the outline of a nun's hood. *Cf.* NUN.

SISTER-IN-LAW (sĭs′ tər ĭn lô′), *n.* (The three pertinent signs are made.) The sign for SISTER 1 is made. This is followed by the sign for IN: The fingers of the right hand are thrust into the left. The sign for LAW then follows: The upright right "L" hand, resting palm against palm on the upright left "5" hand, moves down in an arc a short distance, coming to rest on the base of the left palm.

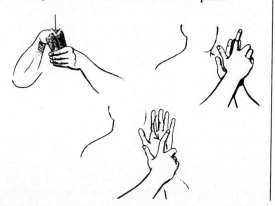

SIT 1 (sĭt), *v.*, SAT, SITTING. (The act of sitting.) The extended right index and middle fingers are draped across the back of the same two fingers of the downturned left hand. The hands then move straight downward a short distance. The movement is repeated. *Cf.* BE SEATED, CHAIR 1, SEAT.

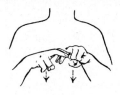

SIT 2, *v.*, (Act of sitting down; the legs of the chair.) Both hands, palms down, are held before the chest, and they move down a short distance in unison. The downturned index fingers are then thrust downward a few inches, moved in toward the body, and thrust downward once again, to represent the four legs of the chair. *Cf.* CHAIR 2.

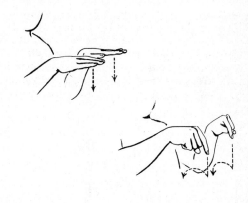

SIT DOWN, *v. phrase.* (Act of sitting down.) Both open hands are held palms down and fingers pointing forward before the chest. The hands then move straight down a short distance.

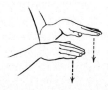

[S-278]

SITE (sīt), *n.* (The letter "P"; a circle or square is indicated, to show the locale or place.) The "P" hands are held side by side before the body, with middle fingertips touching. From this position, the hands separate and outline a circle (or a square), before coming together again closer to the body. *Cf.* LOCATION, PLACE 1, POSITION 1, SCENE.

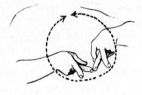

[S-279]

SIX (sĭks), *n., adj.* The thumbtip and little fingertip touch, while the other fingers point straight up. The palm faces out from the body.

[S-280]

SIX OF US, *n. phrase.* The "6" hand circles from right to left before the body, palm facing the chest.

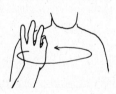

[S-281]

SKATE (skāt), *n., v.,* SKATED, SKATING. (The natural sign.) The upturned "X" hands move gracefully back and forth. The index fingers here represent the upturned blades of the ice skates. *Cf.* ICE-SKATING.

[S-282]

SKEPTIC 1 (skĕp' tĭk), *n.* (The nose is wrinkled in disbelief.) The right "V" hand faces the nose. The index and middle fingers bend as a cynical expression is assumed. This is followed by the sign for INDIVIDUAL: Both open hands, palms facing each other, move down the sides of the body, tracing its outline to the hips. *Cf.* CYNIC, CYNICAL, DISBELIEF 1, DON'T BELIEVE, DOUBT 1, INCREDULITY, SKEPTICAL 1.

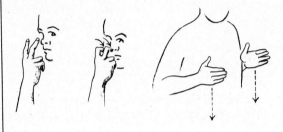

[S-283]

SKEPTIC 2, *n.* (Warding off.) The sign for SKEPTICAL 2 is formed. This is followed by the sign for INDIVIDUAL, as in SKEPTIC 1.

[S-284]

SKEPTICAL 1 (skĕp' tə kəl), *adj.* See SKEPTIC 1.

[S-285]

SKEPTICAL 2, *adj.* (Warding off.) The right "S" hand is held before the right shoulder, elbow bent out to the side. The hand is then thrown forward several times, as if striking at someone. *Cf.* SUSPICION 3.

[S-286]

SKID (skĭd), *n., v.,* SKIDDED, SKIDDING. (The natural movement.) The sign for STAND is made: The downturned right "V" fingers are thrust into the upturned left palm. The fingers then "skid" forward across the left palm, from wrist to fingertips.

[S-287]

SKILL (skĭl), *n.* (A sharp-edged hand.) The right hand grasps the little finger edge of the left firmly. As it leaves this position, moving down and out, it assumes the "A" position, palm facing left. *Cf.* ADEPT, EXPERIENCE 1, EXPERT, SHARP 4, SHREWD, SKILLFUL.

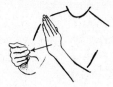

[S-288]

SKILLFUL (skĭl' fəl), *adj.* See SKILL.

[S-289]

SKIN 1 (skĭn), *n.* (Feeling the texture of the skin.) The right fingers move slowly over the back of the left hand.

[S-290]

SKIN 2, *n.* (Pinching the skin.) The right hand pinches the skin of the back of the left hand.

[S-291]

SKINNY (skĭn' ĭ), *(sl.), adj.* (A thin, tapering object is described with the little fingers, the thinnest of all.) The tips of the little fingers, touching, one above the other, are drawn apart. The cheeks may also be drawn in for emphasis. *Cf.* BEANPOLE, THIN 2.

[S-292]

SKIRT 1 (skûrt), *n.* (The drape of the skirt.) The downturned "5" hands are positioned at the hips, and trace the fall of a skirt.

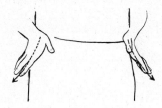

[S-293]

SKIRT 2, *n.* (Pulling the skirt.) The hands grasp and pull down the sides of an imaginary skirt.

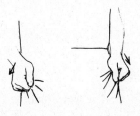

[S-294]

SKUNK (skŭngk), *n.* (The smell and the striped pattern.) The right thumb and index finger pinch the nose, and then the two open fingers trace the line of an imaginary stripe up the forehead and over and down the back of the head.

[S-295]

SKY 1 (skī), *n.* (Entering heaven through a break in the clouds.) Both open hands, fingers straight and pointing up, move upward in an arc on either side of the head. Just before they touch above the head, the right hand, palm down, sweeps under the left and moves up, its palm now facing out. *Cf.* HEAVEN.

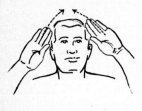

[S-296]

SKY 2, *n.* (Blue overhead.) The "B" hand is drawn in a wavy motion over the head.

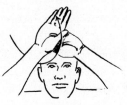

[S-297]

SLAP (slăp), *n., v.,* SLAPPED, SLAPPING. (The natural sign.) The open right hand SLAPS the back of the open left hand, which is held before the body with palm facing inward; the right hand then contin-

ues upward and outward, curving away from the left hand.

[S-298]

SLATE (slāt), *n.* (Black, hard, write.) The sign for BLACK is made: The tip of the index finger moves along the eyebrow. This is followed by the sign for HARD: The bent right index and middle fingers strike the back of the left fist. Then the sign for WRITE is made: The right index finger and thumb, grasping an imaginary piece of chalk, write across the open left palm. *Cf.* BLACKBOARD.

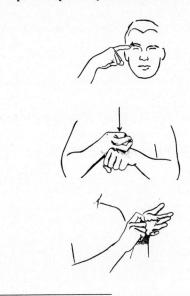

[S-299]

SLAVE (slāv), *n.* (Shackled hands.) The "S" hands, held palms down before the body, are crossed at the wrists. In this position they move up and down a short distance several times.

[S-300]

SLAY (slā), *v.*, SLEW, SLAIN, SLAYING. (Thrusting a dagger and twisting it.) The outstretched right index finger is passed under the downturned left hand. As it moves under the left hand, the right wrist twists in a clockwise direction. *Cf.* KILL, MURDER.

[S-301]

SLEEP 1 (slēp), *v.*, SLEPT, SLEEPING, *n.* (The eyes are closed.) The fingers of the right open hand, facing the forehead, are placed on the forehead. The hand moves down and away from the head, with the fingers closing so that they all touch. The eyes meanwhile close, and the head bows slightly, as in sleep. *Cf.* ASLEEP, DOZE, NAP.

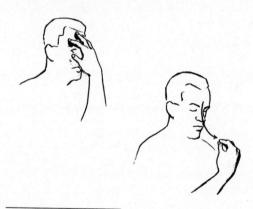

[S-302]

SLEEP 2, *n.*, *v.* (The natural sign.) The signer's head leans to the right and rests in the upturned palm of the open right hand.

[S-303]

SLEEP SOUNDLY, *v. phrase.* (Sleep hard.) The sign for SLEEP 1 is formed. Then the right "A" hand sweeps down to strike its knuckles forcefully against the knuckles of the upturned left "A" hand, or the back of the closed left hand.

[S-304]

SLEEPY (slē' pĭ), *adj.* (Drooping eyelids.) The right fingers are wiggled in front of the face, and the head is bowed forward.

[S-305]

SLENDER (slĕn' dər), *adj.* (A slender figure.) Both open hands, held with palms facing each other, move in a curve down the sides of the body, tracing its outline to the hips. *Cf.* SLIM.

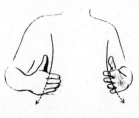

[S-306]

SLICE (slīs), *n., v.,* SLICED, SLICING. (The natural sign.) Both open hands are held before the body, palms facing each other, fingers together and pointing forward. In this position both hands move in alternate clockwise circles past each other, imitating slicing blades. The right hand alone may do the slicing.

[S-307]

SLIDE 1 (slīd), *v.,* SLID, SLIDING. (The natural sign.) The right crooked "V" hand slides forward on the upturned left palm.

[S-308]

SLIDE 2, *n., v.* (The natural sign.) The index and middle fingertips of the downturned, right "V" hand slide forward over the upturned left palm, from wrist to fingertips.

[S-309]

SLIGHT (slīt), *adj.* (Indicating a small mass.) The extended right thumb and index finger are held slightly spread. They are then moved slowly toward each other until they almost touch. *Cf.* PETTY, SMALL 1, TINY 2.

[S-310]

SLIM (slĭm), *adj.* (A slim figure.) Both open hands, held with palms facing each other, move in a curve down the sides of the body, tracing its outline to the hips. *Cf.* SLENDER.

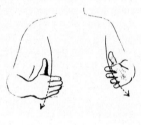

[S-311]

SLIP AWAY, *v. phrase.* (Slipping out and away.) The right index finger is held pointing upward between the index and middle fingers of the prone left hand. From this position the right index finger moves to the right, slipping out of the grasp of the left fingers and away from the left hand. *Cf.* LEAVE CLANDESTINELY 2, RUN AWAY.

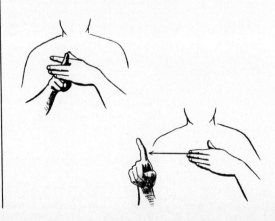

[S-312]

SLIPPER (slĭp' ər), *n.* The downturned right open hand moves back and forth across the upturned cupped left palm.

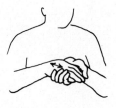

[S-313]

SLOTH (slōth, slôth), *n.* (The initial "L," for LAZY, rests against the body; the concept of inactivity.) The right "L" hand is placed against the left shoulder once or a number of times. The palm faces the body. *Cf.* LAZINESS, LAZY 1.

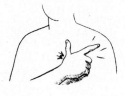

[S-314]

SLOW (slō), *adj.* (The movement indicates the slowness.) The right hand is drawn slowly over the back of the downturned left hand, from fingertips to wrist.

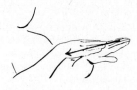

[S-315]

SLY 1 (slī), *adj.* (The letter "F"; the pointed snout for FOX.) The tip of the nose is placed in the circle formed by the right "F" hand, which swings back and forth a short distance. *Cf.* FOX, FOXY.

[S-316]

SLY 2, *adj.* The right "B" hand, held with thumb edge against the chin and fingers pointing upward, moves up along the chin and then curves forward. *Cf.* SNEAK.

[S-317]

SLY 3, *(arch., sl.), adj.* Both open hands face each other, fingers curved slightly, the right held palm down a little above the left, which is held palm up. Then, in a quick movement, thumbs and index fingers of both hands come together and the hands move away from each other, the right hand moving upward and the left downward.

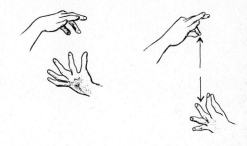

[S-318]

SMACK (smăk), *(colloq.), n., v.,* SMACKED, SMACKING. (Lips touch lips.) The right "AND" hand is held with fingertips touching the mouth. Then the fingertips of both "AND" hands are brought together forcefully.

[S–319]

SMALL 1 (smôl), *adj.* (Indicating a small mass.) The extended right thumb and index finger are held slightly spread. They are then moved slowly toward each other until they almost touch. *Cf.* PETTY, SLIGHT, TINY 2.

[S–320]

SMALL 2, *adj.* (A shortness of height is indicated.) The right hand, in right-angle position, pats an imaginary head at approximately chest level. *Cf.* MINOR, SHORT 2.

[S–321]

SMALLEST (smôl′ ĭst), *superlative adj.* The sign for LESS is made: With palms facing, the right hand is held above the left. The right hand moves slowly down toward the left, but does not touch it. This is followed by the sign for FIRST: The right index finger touches the upturned left thumb. Instead of the sign for FIRST, the right thumb may be drawn straight up, to a position above the head. *Cf.* LEAST.

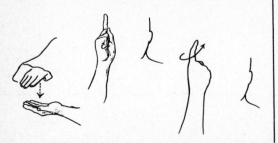

[S–322]

SMALLPOX (smôl′ pŏks′), *n.* (The pock-marked face.) The right index fingertip digs into the cheek. The sign may be repeated at another spot on the cheek.

[S–323]

SMART (smärt), *adj.* (The mind is bright.) The middle finger is placed at the forehead, and then the hand, with an outward flick, turns around so that the palm faces outward. This indicates a brightness flowing from the mind. *Cf.* BRIGHT 3, BRILLIANT 1, CLEVER 1, INTELLIGENT.

[S–324]

SMELL (smĕl), *v.,* SMELLED, SMELLING, *n.* (Bringing something up to the nose.) The upturned right hand moves slowly up to and past the nose, and the signer breathes in as the hand sweeps by. *Cf.* FRAGRANT, ODOR, SCENT.

[S-325]

SMILE (smīl), *v.*, SMILED, SMILING, *n.* (Drawing the lips into a smile.) The right index finger is drawn back over the lips, toward the ear. As the finger moves back, the signer breaks into a smile. (Both index fingers may also be used.)

[S-326]

SMOKE 1 (smōk), *v.*, SMOKED, SMOKING. (The natural sign.) The right "V" hand touches the lips twice, as if bringing a cigarette to the mouth.

[S-327]

SMOKE 2, *n.* (The spiraling motion.) The sign for BLACK is made: The right index finger is drawn over the eyebrow. The downturned, right index finger then spirals upward.

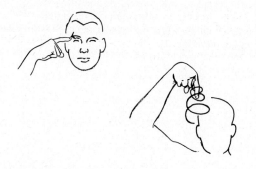

[S-328]

SMOKE CIGAR, *v. phrase.* (The natural sign.) The right "V" hand is held before the face with palm

toward the body, as if holding a cigar. The signer moves his lips as if smoking.

[S-329]

SMOKE CIGARETTE, *v. phrase.* (The natural motion.) The signer holds the extended right index and middle fingers together near the mouth, as if smoking a cigarette.

[S-330]

SMOOTH (smo͞oŧh), *adj.* (Feeling the quality of smoothness with the fingers.) The right thumb slowly glides over the fingertips of the upturned right hand, from the little finger to the index finger. Both hands may be used simultaneously.

[S–331]

SNAKE 1 (snāk), *n.* (The movement.) The left hand is held up with palm down. The right index finger imitates the weaving movement of a snake, as it passes under the left palm.

[S–332]

SNAKE 2, *n.* (The slithering movement.) The right index finger, pointing outward, moves in a cork-screw motion along the outer left forearm, from wrist to elbow, while the left arm is held against the chest and the left hand assumes the "S" position, palm down.

[S–333]

SNAKE 3, *n.* (The movement.) The right "G" hand, palm facing left, is held with its elbow resting on the upturned open left palm. In this position the hand spirals forward.

[S–334]

SNAKE 4, *n.* (The head and fangs gyrating.) The right elbow rests on the palm of the left hand, while the right hand gyrates in imitation of a snake's head,

the thumb and first two fingers extended forward to represent fangs.

[S–335]

SNAKE 5, *n.* (The fangs and the slithering movement.) The right "V" hand is held palm forward before the face, with the index and middle fingers bending forward in imitation of fangs. The right elbow then rests on the palm of the left hand, while the right forearm and "G" hand move forward in a wavy movement, imitating a SNAKE.

[S–336]

SNAKE 6, *n.* (The fangs and forward movement.) The backs of the right index and middle fingers are held to the mouth. In this position, the fingers are drawn in and extended quickly, in imitation of a snake's fangs. Then the fingers move forward in a rapid, spiraling motion.

[S-337]

SNEAK (snēk), *v.*, SNEAKED, SNEAKING. The right
"B" hand, held with thumb edge against the chin
and fingers pointing upward, moves up along the
chin and then curves forward. *Cf.* SLY 2.

[S-338]

SNEER (snĭr), *n.*, *v.*, SNEERED, SNEERING. (The
natural expression.) The extended right index finger
is drawn along the face in a small arc, from the right
corner of the mouth and up to the middle of the right
cheek. The signer assumes a sneering expression.

[S-339]

SNEEZE (snēz), *n.*, *v.*, SNEEZED, SNEEZING. (The
natural motion.) The signer goes through the motions of covering his nose and sneezing: The head is
tossed back while the thumb and index finger are
placed over the nose. The head then moves abruptly
forward and down, the hand still covering the nose.

[S-340]

SNIPS (snĭps), *(voc.)*, *n. pl.* (The natural sign.) The
right hand, opening and closing forcefully, goes
through the natural motion of manipulating a pair
of snips. *Cf.* PLIERS, SHEARS 1.

[S-341]

SNOB (snŏb), *n.* (Turning up the nose.) The tip of
the extended right index finger is held against the
right side of the nose. The signer raises his chin and
assumes a haughty air.

[S-342]

SNOW (snō), *n.*, *v.*, SNOWED, SNOWING. (A white
substance falling.) The sign for WHITE is made:
The fingertips of the "5" hand are placed against the
chest. The hand moves straight out from the chest,
while the fingers and thumb all come together. The
downturned "5" hands then move down simultaneously, usually with fingers wiggling.

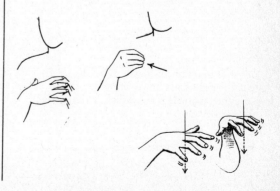

[S–343]

SNUB (snŭb), *n., v.,* SNUBBED, SNUBBING. (Turning up the nose.) The signer grasps the tip of the nose between the extended right thumb and index finger, and then moves the hand quickly forward and up in an arc. At the same time, the signer raises his chin and assumes a haughty air.

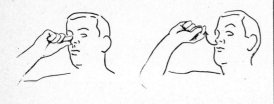

[S–344]

SOAP 1 (sōp), *n., v.,* SOAPED, SOAPING. (Working up a lather in the hand.) The fingertips of the right hand move back and forth on the upturned left palm, in small downturned arcs.

[S–345]

SOAP 2, *n., v.* (Same rationale as for SOAP 1.) The fingertips of the right hand move straight back and forth across the upturned left palm.

[S–346]

SOAP 3, *n., v.* (Same rationale as for SOAP 1.) The base of the right hand moves around in small circles against the open left palm, which is facing right.

[S–347]

SOAP 4, *n., v.* (Same rationale as for SOAP 1.) The fingertips of the right hand move straight up and down against the upturned left palm.

[S–348]

SO-CALLED (sō′ kôld′), *adj.* (The quotation marks are indicated.) The curved index and middle fingers of both hands, held palms out, move slightly to either side of the body, as if drawing quotation marks in the air. *Cf.* CAPTION, CITE, QUOTATION, QUOTE, SUBJECT, THEME, TITLE, TOPIC.

[S–349]

SOCCER (sŏk′ ər), *n.* (The natural sign.) The right "B" hand, palm facing the body and fingers pointing down, swings in an arc to the left, striking the side of the left "S" hand, held palm facing up. *Cf.* KICK 1, KICK OUT.

[S–350]

SOCKET (sŏk′ ĭt), *n.* (Plugging in.) Both "V" hands, palms facing each other, are held before the body. The right "V" hand, representing the prongs of a plug, is brought into an interlocking position with the left. *Cf.* ELECTRIC OUTLET, ELECTRIC PLUG.

Then the right thumb and index finger are joined and placed on the chest to indicate a medal.

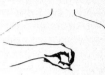

[S–351]

SOCK(S) 1 (sŏk), *n.* (The knitting.) The index fingers, pointing forward, are rubbed back and forth against each other. *Cf.* HOSE 1, KNIT, STOCKING(S) 1.

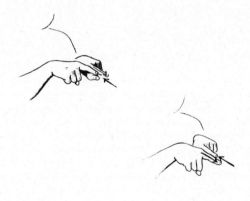

[S–354]

SODA POP, *n.* (Corking a bottle.) The left "O" hand is held with thumb edge up, representing a bottle. The thumb and index finger of the right "5" hand represent a cork, and are inserted into the circle formed by the "O" hand. The palm of the open right hand then strikes down on the upturned edge of the "O" hand, as if forcing the cork into the bottle. *Cf.* POP 1, SODA WATER.

[S–352]

SOCK(S) 2, *n.* (Pulling on hose.) The downturned, open right hand grasps its left counterpart at the fingertips and slides over the back of the hand and up the arm, as if pulling on hose. *Cf.* HOSE 2, STOCKING(S) 2.

[S–355]

SODA WATER, *n. phrase.* See SODA POP.

[S–356]

SO FAR, *adv. phrase.* (From a point up and over.) In the "D" position, palms down, both index fingers touch the right shoulder and then are brought up and over, ending in a palm-up position, pointing straight ahead of the body. *Cf.* ALL ALONG, ALL THE TIME, EVER SINCE, SINCE, THUS FAR.

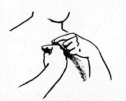

[S–353]

SODALITY (sō dăl′ ə tǐ), *(eccles.), n.* (The ribbon and medal of the fellowship.) The fingertips of each hand are placed on either shoulder. The hands then pass down the sides of the chest to indicate ribbons.

[S–357]

SO FORTH, *phrase.* (A continuing line.) The index fingers of both "L" hands touch each other before the body, with palms facing inward and thumbs pointing up. From this position the fingers move away from each other and draw wavy lines in the air as they do—the right hand moving to the right and the left hand to the left. *Cf.* ET CETERA (ETC.).

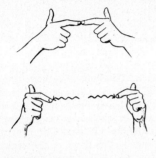

[S–358]

SOFT (sôft, sŏft), *adj.* (Squeezing for softness.) The hands slowly and deliberately squeeze an imaginary object or substance. *Cf.* RIPE, TENDER 1.

[S–359]

SOFT-HEARTED (sôft′ här′ tĭd, sŏft′ -), *adj. phrase.* (The heart is squeezed to emphasize its softness.) Both hands are held directly in front of the heart, with palms facing the body. They open and close repeatedly, as if squeezing the heart.

[S–360]

SOIL 1 (soil), *n.* (Fingering the soil.) Both hands, held upright before the body, finger imaginary pinches of soil. *Cf.* DIRT, EARTH 2, GROUND.

[S–361]

SOIL 2, *v.,* SOILED, SOILING. (A modification of the pig's snout groveling in a trough.) The downturned right hand is placed under the chin. Its fingers, pointing left, wiggle repeatedly. *Cf.* DIRTY, FILTHY, FOUL, IMPURE, NASTY, STAIN.

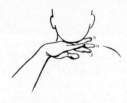

[S–362]

SOLDIER (sōl′ jər), *n.* (Bearing arms.) Both "A" hands, palms facing the body, are placed at the left breast, with the right hand above the left, as if holding a rifle against the body. The sign for INDIVIDUAL follows: Both open hands, palms facing each other, move down the sides of the body, tracing its outline to the hips. *Cf.* ARMS.

[S-363]

SOLE, (sōl), *adj.* (One, wandering around in a circle.) The index finger, pointing straight up, palm facing the body (the number *one*), is rotated before the face in a counterclockwise direction. *Cf.* ALONE, LONE, ONE 2, ONLY, UNITY.

[S-364]

SOLID (sŏl' ĭd), *adj.* (Striking a hard object.) The curved index and middle fingers of the right hand, whose palm faces the body or the left, are brought down sharply against the back of the downturned left "S" hand. *Cf.* DIFFICULT 2, HARD 2.

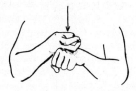

[S-365]

SO LONG, *interj.* (A wave of the hand.) The right open hand waves back and forth several times. *Cf.* FAREWELL 2, GOODBYE 2, HELLO 2.

[S-366]

SOME (sŭm; *unstressed* sǝm), *adj.* (Cutting off or designating a part.) The little finger edge of the open right hand moves straight down the middle of the upturned left palm. *Cf.* PART 1, PIECE, PORTION, SECTION, SHARE 1.

[S-367]

SOMEONE (sŭm' wŭn´, -wǝn), *pron.* (The "1" hand, circling.) The right index finger, held pointing upward, moves in a small counterclockwise circle. *Cf.* SOMETHING.

[S-368]

SOMETHING (sŭm thĭng), *n.* See SOMEONE.

[S-369]

SOMETIME(S) (sŭm' tīmz´), *adv.* (The "1" finger is brought up very slowly.) The right index finger, resting in the open left palm, which is facing right, swings up slowly from its position to one in which it is pointing straight up. The movement is repeated slowly, after a pause. *Cf.* OCCASIONAL, OCCASIONALLY, ONCE IN A WHILE, SELDOM.

[S–370]

SON (sŭn), *n.* (Male, baby.) The sign for MALE is made: The thumb and extended fingers of the right hand are brought up to grasp an imaginary cap brim. This is followed by the sign for BABY: The arms are held with one resting on the other, as if cradling a baby.

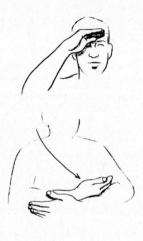

[S–371]

SONG (sông, sŏng), *n.* (A rhythmic, wavy movement of the hand, to indicate a melody; the movement of a conductor's hand in directing a musical performance.) The right "5" hand, palm facing left, is waved back and forth near the open left hand, in a series of elongated figure-eights. *Cf.* CHANT, HYMN 1, MELODY, MUSIC, SING.

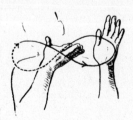

[S–372]

SON-IN-LAW (sŭn' in lô'), *n.* (The three pertinent signs are made.) The sign for SON, *q.v.,* is made. This is followed by the sign for IN: The fingers of the right hand are thrust into the left. The sign for LAW, then follows: The upright right "L" hand, resting palm against palm on the upright left "5"

hand, moves down in an arc a short distance, coming to rest on the base of the left palm.

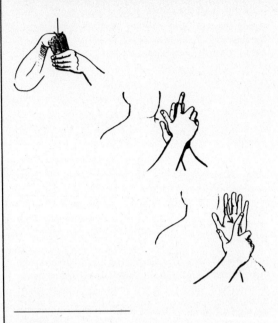

[S–373]

SORROW (sŏr' ō, sôr' ō), *n.* (The heart is circled, to indicate feeling, modified by the letter "S," for SORRY.) The right "S" hand, palm facing the body, is rotated several times over the area of the heart. *Cf.* APOLOGIZE 1, APOLOGY 1, CONTRITION, PENITENT, REGRET, REGRETFUL, REPENT, REPENTANT, RUE, SORROWFUL 2, SORRY.

[S–374]

SORROWFUL 1 (sŏr' ə fəl, sôr' -), *adj.* (The facial features drop.) Both "5" hands, palms facing the eyes and fingers slightly curved, drop simultaneously to a level with the mouth. The head drops slightly as the hands move down, and an expression of sadness is assumed. *Cf.* DEJECTED, DEPRESSED,

GLOOM, GLOOMY, GRAVE 3, GRIEF 1, MELAN-CHOLY, MOURNFUL, SAD.

[S–375]

SORROWFUL 2, *adj.* See SORROW.

[S–376]

SORRY (sŏr′ ĭ, sôr′ ĭ), *adj.* See SORROW.

[S–377]

SOUL (sōl), *n.* (Something thin and filmy, *i.e.,* ephemeral.) The hands are held palms facing, with one above the other and index fingers and thumbs touching and almost connected. As the upper hand moves straight up, the index fingers and thumbs of both hands slowly come together, giving the impression of drawing out a thread or other thin substance. *Cf.* GHOST, SPIRIT.

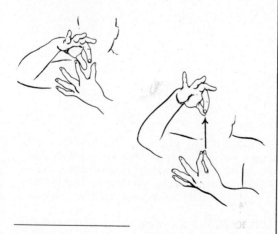

[S–378]

SOUND (sound), *n.* (A shaking which disturbs the ear.) After placing the index finger on the ear, both hands assume the "S" position, palms down. They move alternately back and forth, forcefully. *Cf.* DIN, NOISE, NOISY, RACKET, THUNDER, VIBRATION.

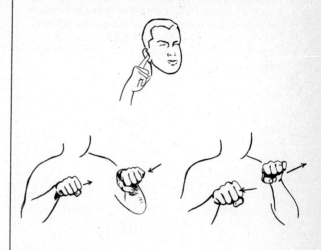

[S–379]

SOUP (so͞op), *n.* (The natural sign.) The upturned open left hand represents the bowl of soup. The index and middle fingers of the right "H" hand form a small scoop to represent the spoon, and move from the left palm to the lips. The movement is usually repeated.

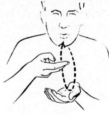

[S–380]

SOUR (sour), *adj.* (Something sour or bitter.) The right index finger is brought sharply up against the lips, while the mouth is puckered up as if tasting something sour. *Cf.* ACID, BITTER, DISAPPOINTED 1, LEMON 1, PICKLE.

[S-381]

SOUTH (south), *n., adv.* (The letter "S"; the direction.) The right "S" hand, palm facing left, moves straight down, the equivalent of south on a map.

[S-382]

SOUTH AMERICA 1. ("S," "A.") The signer describes a small circle with the "S" hand and then does the same with the "A" hand.

[S-383]

SOUTH AMERICA 2. The sign for SOUTH is made. This is followed by the sign for AMERICA: The extended fingers of both hands are interlocked, and are swept in an arc from left to right as if encompassing an imaginary house or stockade.

[S-384]

SOW (sō), *v.*, SOWED, SOWN, SOWING. (The act of sprinkling seed.) The thumb and index finger of either hand go through the natural motions of sprinkling seeds. *Cf.* SEED 2.

[S-385]

SPACE (spās), *n.* (Area high above earth.) The sign for EARTH 1 is made: The thumb and index finger of the downturned right "5" hand are placed at each edge of the downturned left "S" hand. In this position the right hand swings back and forth. Then the open right hand, held upright with palm out, moves in an upward arc from left to right above the head, indicating an area high overhead.

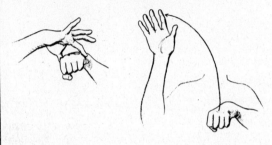

[S-386]

SPADE (spād), *n., v.*, SPADED, SPADING. (The natural motion.) Both hands, in the "A" position, right hand facing up and left hand facing down, grasp an imaginary spade. They go through the natural movements of shoveling earth—first digging in and then tossing the earth aside. *Cf.* DIG 2, SHOVEL.

[S-387]

SPAGHETTI (spə gĕt' ĭ), *n.* (Unraveling a thin string, as indicated by the little fingers.) With palms facing the body, the tips of the extended little fingers touch. As they are drawn slowly apart, they describe very small spirals. *Cf.* STRING, THREAD, TWINE.

[S-388]

SPAIN (spān), *n.* (The bullfighter's cape fastened across the chest.) The curved index fingers touch the shoulders and then draw together and interlock. A variation of this sign involves moving the curved right index finger from the right shoulder to the left. *Cf.* SPANIARD, SPANISH.

[S-389]

SPANIARD (spăn′ yərd), *n.* See SPAIN. The sign is followed by the sign for INDIVIDUAL: Both open hands, palms facing each other, move down the sides of the body, tracing its outline to the hips. *Cf.* SPAIN, SPANISH.

[S-390]

SPANISH (spăn′ ĭsh), *adj.* See SPAIN.

[S-391]

SPANK (spăngk), *n., v.,* SPANKED, SPANKING. (The natural motion.) The left "S" hand is held up before the face, as if grasping a culprit; while the upturned open left hand swings back and forth beneath it, as if spanking someone.

[S-392]

SPEAK (spēk), *v.,* SPOKE, SPOKEN, SPEAKING. (Words tumbling from the mouth.) The right index finger, pointing left, describes a continuous small circle in front of the mouth. *Cf.* BID 3, DISCOURSE, HEARING, MAINTAIN 2, MENTION, REMARK, SAID, SAY, SPEECH 1, STATE, STATEMENT, TALK 1, TELL, VERBAL 1.

[S-393]

SPEAKER (spē′ kər), *n.* (The characteristic waving of the speaker's hand as he makes his point.) The right hand is held above the head, palm facing left. The hand, pivoting at the wrist, swings forward and back repeatedly. This is followed by the sign for INDIVIDUAL: Both open hands, palms facing each other, move down the sides of the body, tracing its outline to the hips. *Cf.* ORATOR.

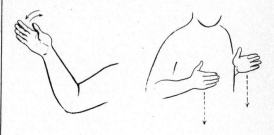

[S-394]

SPEAK PRIVATELY, *v. phrase.* (The mouth is covered.) The signer leans to one side, covers one side of his mouth, and whispers. *Cf.* WHISPER.

[S-395]

SPECIAL (spĕsh′ əl), *adj.* (Selecting a particular item from among several.) The index finger and thumb of the right hand grasp and pull up the left index finger. *Cf.* ESPECIAL, EXCEPT, EXCEPTION.

[S-396]

SPECIALIZE (spĕsh′ ə līz′), *v.*, -IZED, -IZING. (A straight, *i.e.*, special, path.) The hands are held in the "B" position, one above the other, with left palm facing right and right palm facing left. The little finger edge of the right hand moves straight forward along the index finger edge of the left. *Cf.* FIELD 3, IN THE FIELD OF, SPECIALTY.

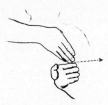

[S-397]

SPECIALTY (spĕsh′ əl tĭ), *n., pl.* -TIES. See SPECIALIZE.

[S-398]

SPECIFIC (spĭ sif′ ĭk), *adj.* (The fingers come together precisely.) The thumb and index finger of each hand, palms facing, the right above the left, form circles. They are brought together with a deliberate movement, so that the fingers and thumbs now touch. Sometimes the right hand, before coming together with the left, executes a slow clockwise circle above the left. *Cf.* ACCURATE 1, EXACT 1, EXACTLY, EXPLICIT 1, PRECISE.

[S-399]

SPECTACLES (spĕk′ tə kəlz), *n., pl.* (The shape.) The thumb and index finger of the right hand, placed flat against the right temple, move back toward the right ear, tracing the line formed by the eyeglass frame. *Cf.* EYEGLASSES; GALLAUDET, THOMAS HOPKINS; GLASSES.

[S-400]

SPECULATE 1 (spĕk′ yə lāt′), *v.*, -LATED, -LATING. (A thought is turned over in the mind.) The index finger makes a small circle on the forehead. *Cf.* CONSIDER 1, MOTIVE 1, RECKON, SPECULATION 1, THINK, THOUGHT 1, THOUGHTFUL.

[S-401]

SPECULATE 2, *v.* (Turning thoughts over in the mind.) Both index fingers, pointing to the forehead, describe continuous alternating circles. *Cf.* CONSIDER 2, CONTEMPLATE, PONDER, SPECULATION 2, WEIGH 2, WONDER 1.

[S-402]

SPECULATION 1 (spĕk′ yə lā′ shən), *n.* See SPECULATE 1.

[S–403]

SPECULATION 2, *n.* See SPECULATE 2.

[S–404]

SPEECH 1 (spēch), *n.* (Words tumbling from the mouth.) The right index finger, pointing left, describes a continuous small circle in front of the mouth. *Cf.* BID 3, DISCOURSE, HEARING, MAINTAIN 2, MENTION, REMARK, SAID, SAY, SPEAK, STATE, STATEMENT, TALK 1, TELL, VERBAL 1.

[S–405]

SPEECH 2 *n.* (A gesture of an orator.) The right open hand, palm facing left, is held above and to the right of the head. It pivots, forward and backward, on the wrist several times. *Cf.* ADDRESS 1, LECTURE, ORATE, TALK 2, TESTIMONY.

[S–406]

SPEECHLESS (spēch' lĭs), *(colloq.), adj.* (The mouth drops open.) The fingertips of both "V" hands are held curved and touching before the body, one hand above the other. Then the hands are suddenly drawn apart, and at the same instant the mouth drops open and the eyes open wide. *Cf.* DUM-

FOUNDED 2, FLABBERGASTED, OPEN-MOUTHED, SURPRISE 2.

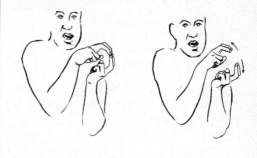

[S–407]

SPEECHREADING, *n.* (Reading the lips—the lines of vision, represented by the two fingers, scan the lips.) The right "V" hand, palm facing the body, is placed in front of the face, with slightly curved index and middle fingers directly in front of the lips. The right hand moves in a small counterclockwise circle around the lips. *Cf.* LIPREADING, ORAL, READ LIPS.

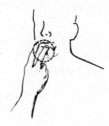

[S–408]

SPEED (spēd), *n., v.,* SPED, or SPEEDED, SPEEDING. (A quick movement.) The thumbtip of the upright right hand is flicked quickly off the tip of the curved right index finger, as if shooting marbles. *Cf.* FAST 1, IMMEDIATELY, QUICK, QUICKNESS, RAPID, RATE 1, SPEEDY, SWIFT.

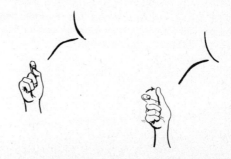

[S–409]

SPEEDY (spē' di), *adj.* See SPEED.

[S–410]

SPELL (spĕl), *v.,* SPELLED or SPELT, SPELLING. (The movement of the fingers in fingerspelling.) The right hand, palm out, is moved from left to right, with the fingers wriggling up and down. *Cf.* ALPHABET, DACTYLOLOGY, FINGERSPELLING, MANUAL ALPHABET, SPELLING.

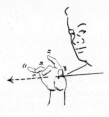

[S–411]

SPELLING (spĕl' ing), *n.* See SPELL.

[S–412]

SPEND (spĕnd), *v.,* SPENT, SPENDING. (Repeated giving forth.) The back of the upturned right hand, thumb touching fingertips, is placed in the upturned left palm. The right hand moves off and away from the left once or several times, each time opening into the "5" position, palm up. *Cf.* EXTRAVAGANT, SQUANDER, WASTE 1.

[S–413]

SPHERE (sfīr), *n.* (The shape.) The curved open hands are held with fingertips touching, as if holding a ball. *Cf.* BALL 2, ORB, ROUND 1.

[S–414]

SPIDER (spī' dər), *n.* (The moving legs.) The down-turned hands are crossed and interlocked at the little fingers. As they move forward, the fingers wiggle. *Cf.* INSECT 1.

[S–415]

SPIN (spin), *n., v.,* SPUN, SPINNING. (The natural sign.) The extended right index finger is held pointing downward in front of the face, while the extended left index finger is held pointing upward toward its right counterpart. In this position both index fingers simultaneously trace small opposing circles before the body. *Cf.* TORNADO.

[S–416]

SPIRIT (spir' it), *n.* (Something thin and filmy, *i.e.,* ephemeral.) The hands are held palms facing, with one above the other and index fingers and thumbs touching and almost connected. As the upper hand moves straight up, the index fingers and thumbs of both hands slowly come together, giving the impression of drawing out a thread or other thin substance. *Cf.* GHOST, SOUL.

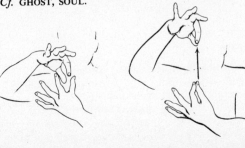

[S–417]

SPIT (spĭt), *v.*, SPAT or SPIT, SPITTING, *n.* (The flinging out of saliva.) The thumb and index finger, forming a circle, are placed at the lips. The index finger suddenly flicks open and away from the mouth. *Cf.* EXPECTORATE.

[S–418]

SPLENDID 1 (splĕn' dĭd), *adj.* (The hands gesture toward the heavens.) The "5" hands, palms out and arms raised rather high, are positioned somewhat above the line of vision. The arms move abruptly forward and up once or twice. An expression of pleasure or surprise is usually assumed. *Cf.* EXCELLENT, GRAND 1, GREAT 3, MARVEL, MARVELOUS, MIRACLE, O!, SWELL 1, WONDER 2, WONDERFUL 1.

[S–419]

SPLENDID 2, *adj., interj.* (The feelings are titillated.) With the thumb resting on the upper part of the chest, the fingers are wiggled back and forth. *Cf.* ELEGANT, FINE 1, GRAND 2, GREAT 4, SWELL 2, WONDERFUL 2.

[S–420]

SPLENDID 3, *adj.* (Literally, a good face.) The right hand, fingers closed over the thumb, is placed at or just below the lips (indicating a tasting of something GOOD, *q.v.*). It then describes a counterclockwise circle around the face, opening into the "5" position, to indicate the whole face. At the completion of the circling movement the hand comes to rest in its initial position, at or just below the lips. *Cf.* ATTRACTIVE 2, BEAUTIFUL, BEAUTY, EXQUISITE, PRETTY.

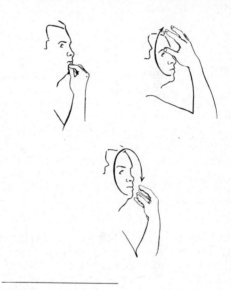

[S–421]

SPLICE (splīs), *v.*, SPLICED, SPLICING, *n.* (Placing a strip of film on top of another strip.) The tips of the downturned right index and middle fingers are placed carefully on top of their downturned left counterparts. This sign is used only in reference to splicing film, not rope or wire.

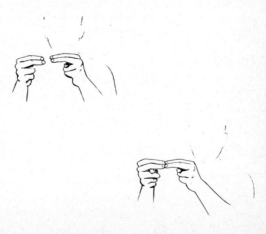

[S-422]

SPLIT HAIRS, *(colloq.), v. phrase*. The right index finger and thumb grasp an imaginary hair held by the left index finger and thumb. The right hand moves away from the left, as if pulling a hair. *Cf.* HAIRSPLITTING.

[S-423]

SPOIL (spoil), *n., v.,* SPOILED, SPOILING, (Striking down against.) Both "A" or "X" hands are held before the chest, the right above the left. The right hand strikes down and out, hitting the left thumb and knuckles with force. *Cf.* BACKBITE, BASE 3, CRUEL 1, HARM 2, HURT 2, MAR 2, MEAN 1.

[S-424]

SPONGE (spŭnj), *n.* (The natural sign.) The fingers of one hand are pressed together repeatedly, as if squeezing a sponge. The signer looks beneath the hand, as if watching water trickle.

[S-425]

SPOON (spōon), *n., v.,* SPOONED, SPOONING. (The shape and action.) The upturned left palm represents

a dish or plate. The curved index and middle fingers of the right hand represent the spoon. They are drawn up repeatedly from the left palm to the lips. *Cf.* ICE CREAM 1.

[S-426]

SPRAIN (sprān), *n., v.,* SPRAINED, SPRAINING. (A twisting of muscles.) The knuckles of both "S" or curved "V" hands are held near each other, and the hands are twisted in opposite directions.

[S-427]

SPRAY (sprā), *(voc.), n., v.,* SPRAYED, SPRAYING. (The action of a spray gun.) The index finger of the right "L" hand is pointed at the upright left palm. The right hand moves in a small clockwise circle, as if spraying the left.

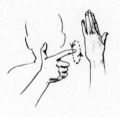

[S-428]

SPREAD 1 (sprĕd), *v.,* SPREAD, SPREADING. (Spreading apart.) Both "AND" hands are held before the body, palms down. They are then directed forward and toward each side, while the fingers open out. *Cf.* SCATTER.

[S–429]

SPREAD 2, *n.* (The natural motion.) The fingers of the downturned open right hand sweep across the upturned open left hand several times, from fingertips to wrist. The right hand may also move in a circle.

[S–430]

SPRING 1 (spring), *n.* (Flowers or plants emerge from the ground.) The right fingers, pointing up, emerge from the closed left hand, and they spread open as they do. The action may be repeated. *Cf.* BLOOM, DEVELOP 1, GROW, GROWN, MATURE, PLANT 1, RAISE 3, REAR 2.

[S–431]

SPRING 2, *n.* (Moving upward and flowing outward.) The right "AND" hand is moved up through the left "C" hand, which is held with thumb edge up and palm facing the body. As the fingers of the right hand emerge, they wiggle, to indicate a trickling of water. The action is usually repeated. *Cf.* FOUNTAIN.

[S–432]

SPRINKLE (sprĭng' kəl), *v.*, -KLED, -KLING. The "AND" hands touch each other at the thumbtips, palms out. The hands then separate, open, and sweep upward and to the sides several times, with fingers spread.

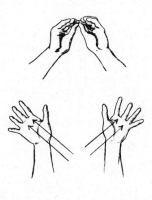

[S–433]

SPY 1 (spī), *n., v.*, SPIED, SPYING. (The eye is alternately hidden and uncovered.) The right "B" hand, palm facing left, is held against the face so that it covers the right eye. The hand moves alternately an inch to the left and right, covering and uncovering the right eye. *Cf.* PEEK 1.

[S–434]

SPY 2, *n., v.* (The eye looks through a narrow aperture.) The right "V" hand, palm facing out, is held at the face, with the right eye looking out between the index and middle fingers. *Cf.* PEEK 2.

[S-435]

SPY 3, *(arch.)*, *n.* The end of the index finger of the "V" hand is placed under and against the front teeth; then, without moving the arms, the ends of the fingers are thrown outward, the index finger slipping away from the teeth. *Cf.* SUSPECT 2, SUSPICION 2.

[S-436]

SQUANDER (skwŏn' dər) *v.*, -DERED, -DERING. (Repeated giving forth.) The back of the upturned right hand, thumb touching fingertips, is placed in the upturned left palm. The right hand moves off and away from the left once or several times, each time opening into the "5" position, palm up. *Cf.* EXTRAVAGANT, SPEND, WASTE 1.

[S-437]

SQUARE 1 (skwâr), *n., v.*, SQUARED, SQUARING, *adj., adv.* (The dimensions are indicated.) The open hands, palms facing and fingers pointing out, are dropped an inch or two simultaneously. They then shift their relative positions so that both palms face the body, with one hand in front of the other. In this new position they again drop an inch or two simultaneously. *Cf.* BOX 1, PACKAGE, ROOM 1, TRUNK.

[S-438]

SQUARE 2, *(sl.)*, *adj., n.* (A square face, *i.e.*, person.) The "B" hands outline a square in front of the face. Used to indicate an unsophisticated or naive person.

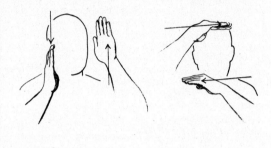

[S-439]

SQUASH 1 (skwŏsh), *n.* (Thumping a yellow sphere.) The sign for YELLOW is made: The right "Y" hand, palm facing the body, shakes slightly, pivoting at the wrist. The downturned, left "S" hand represents the squash. The middle finger of the right hand is then flicked against the back of the left. *Cf.* PUMPKIN 1.

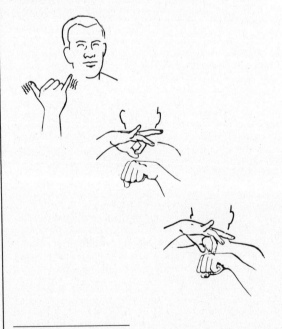

[S-440]

SQUASH 2, *v.* (The act of pressing something together with the hands.) The ball of the right "5" hand is pressed against the upturned left palm. The right hand may turn back and forth, maintaining its pressure against the left. *Cf.* PRESS 3.

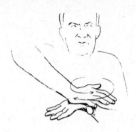

SQUEAL (skwēl), *(sl.), n.* (A word escapes from the mouth.) The base of the "S" hand rests against the lips. The index finger suddenly flicks out, as the hand jumps away from the mouth and to the side an inch or two. *Cf.* TIP OFF.

SQUIRREL (skwûr′ əl), *n.* (The squirrel's teeth in a nut.) The curved "V" fingers of both hands, held upright with palms facing, strike each other several times. The upright position of the hands represents the upright position of the rodent when chewing.

STAGE (stāj), *n.* (The letter "S"; the flat surface.) The right "S" hand is drawn over the back of the

downturned left hand, from the wrist to the finger-tips.

STAIN (stān), *n.* (A modification of the pig's snout groveling in a trough.) The downturned right hand is placed under the chin. Its fingers, pointing left, wiggle repeatedly. *Cf.* DIRTY, FILTHY, FOUL, IMPURE, NASTY, SOIL 2.

STAIR(S) 1 (stâr), *n.* (The natural sign.) The downturned open hands, fingers pointing forward, move in alternate upward "steps" before the body. *Cf.* STEP(S) 2.

STAIR(S) 2, *n.* (The natural sign.) The right open hand, palm facing left or down, traces a series of "steps" upward. *Cf.* STEP(S) 3.

[S–447]

STAMP 1 (stămp), *n.* (Licking the stamp.) The tips of the right index and middle fingers are licked with the tongue, and then the fingers are pressed against the upturned left palm, as if affixing a stamp to an envelope.

[S–448]

STAMP 2, *n., v.* (The natural sign.) The right hand grasps an imaginary rubber stamp and presses it against the upturned left palm. *Cf.* GUARANTEE 2, SEAL 1.

[S–449]

STAND 1 (stănd), *v.,* STOOD, STANDING, *n.* (The feet planted on the ground.) The downturned right "V" fingers are thrust into the upturned left palm. *Cf.* POSITION 3, STANDING.

[S–450]

STAND 2, *n., v.* (Getting onto one's feet.) The upturned index and middle fingers of the right hand, representing the legs, are swung up and over in an arc, coming to rest in the upturned left palm. *Cf.*

ARISE 2, ELEVATE, GET UP, RAISE 1, RISE 1, STAND UP.

[S–451]

STAND 3, *v., n.* (Rising up.) Both upturned hands, held at chest level, rise in unison, to about shoulder height. *Cf.* ARISE 1, RISE 3.

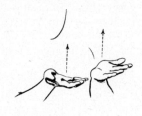

[S–452]

STANDING (stăn′ dĭng), *n.* See STAND 1.

[S–453]

STAND UP, *v. phrase.* See STAND 2.

[S–454]

STAR (stär), *n., adj., v.,* STARRED, STARRING. (Striking flints to draw twinkling sparks or stars.) The index fingers, pointing forward, alternately strike glancing blows off each other and move forward and upward a bit.

[S–455]

START (stärt), *v.*, STARTED, STARTING. (Turning a key to open up a new venture.) The right index finger, resting between the left index and middle fingers, executes a half turn, once or twice. *Cf.* BEGIN, COMMENCE, INITIATE, INSTITUTE 2, ORIGIN 1, ORIGINATE 1.

[S–456]

STARVATION (stär vā' shən), *n.* (The upper alimentary tract is outlined.) The right "C" hand, palm facing the body, is placed with fingertips touching mid-chest. In this position it moves down a bit. *Cf.* APPETITE, CRAVE, DESIRE 2, FAMINE, HUNGARIAN, HUNGARY, HUNGER, HUNGRY, STARVE, STARVED, WISH 2.

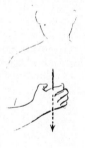

[S–457]

STARVE (stärv), *v.*, STARVED, STARVING. See STARVATION.

[S–458]

STARVED *v.* See STARVATION.

[S–459]

STATE (stāt), *v.*, STATED, STATING. (Words tumbling from the mouth.) The right index finger, pointing left, describes a continuous small circle in front of the mouth. *Cf.* BID 3, DISCOURSE, HEARING, MAINTAIN 2, MENTION, REMARK, SAID, SAY,

SPEAK, SPEECH 1, STATEMENT, TALK 1, TELL, VERBAL 1.

[S–460]

STATEMENT (stāt' mənt), *n.* The sign for STATE is made. This is followed by the sign for -MENT: The downturned right "M" hand moves down along the left palm, which is facing away from the body.

[S–461]

STATION (stā' shən), *n.* (A house for trains.) The sign for RAILROAD is made: The "V" hands are held palms down, the right fingers placed across the left. The right "V" fingers move back and forth across the left "V" fingers. This is followed by the sign for HOUSE: The open hands, forming a pyramid a bit above eye level, move down as they separate, and then continue straight down a few inches.

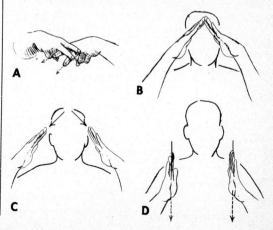

[S–462]

STATUE (stăch′ ōō), *n.* (Contours are indicated or outlined.) Both "A" hands, held about a foot apart before the face, with palms facing each other, move down simultaneously in a wavy, undulating motion. *Cf.* FIGURE 2, FORM, IMAGE, SCULPT, SCULPTURE, SHAPE 1.

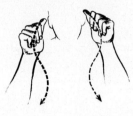

[S–463]

STATUTE (stăch′ ŏot), *n.* (The letter "S"; a set of statutes or laws on a page.) The open left hand, palm out, represents the page. The right "S" hand, palm facing left, is placed against the upper part of the left palm, and then moves down in a small arc to the lower part of the left palm. This is similar to the sign for LAW, *q.v.*

[S–464]

STAY 1 (stā), *n., v.,* STAYED, STAYING. (Steady, uninterrupted movement.) The "A" hands are held with palms out, thumbs extended and touching, the right behind the left. In this position the hands move forward in a straight, steady line. *Cf.* CONTINUE 1, ENDURE 2, EVER 1, LAST 3, LASTING, PERMANENT, PERPETUAL, PERSEVERE 3, PERSIST 2, REMAIN, STAY STILL.

[S–465]

STAY 2, *n., v.,* STAYED, STAYING. (Duration of movement from past to present.) The right "Y"

hand is held palm down in front of the right shoulder and is then moved slowly down and forward in a smooth curve. *Cf.* CONTINUE 2, STILL 1, YET 1.

[S–466]

STAY 3, *v.* (Remaining in place.) One "Y" hand, held palm down, drops down a few inches.

[S–467]

STAY 4, *v.* (A firm, steadying motion.) The down-turned open right hand is held before the right shoulder and moved down a short distance.

[S–468]

STAY STILL, *v. phrase.* See STAY 1.

[S–469]

STEAL 1 (stēl), *n., v.,* STOLE, STOLEN, STEALING. (The hand, partly concealed, takes something surreptitiously.) The index and middle fingers of the right hand, somewhat curved, are placed under the left elbow. As they move slowly along the left forearm toward the left wrist, they close a bit. *Cf.* AB-

DUCT, EMBEZZLE, EMBEZZLEMENT, KIDNAP, ROB 1, ROBBERY 1, SWIPE, THEFT 1, THIEF 1, THIEVERY.

open hands, palms facing each other, move down the sides of the body, tracing its outline to the hips.

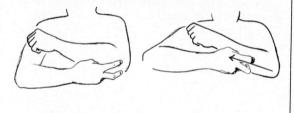

[S–470]

STEAL 2, *(colloq.), v.* (A sly, underhanded movement). The right open hand, palm down, is held a bit behind the body at waist level. Beginning with the little finger, the hand closes finger by finger into the "A" position, as if wrapping itself around something. *Cf.* ROB 2, ROBBERY 1, THEFT 2.

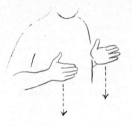

[S–473]

STEAM (stēm), *n.* (Water, hot.) The sign for WATER is made: The right "W" hand, palm facing left, touches the lips a number of times. This is followed by the sign for HOT: The cupped hand, palm facing the body, moves up in front of the slightly open mouth. It is then flung down to the palm-down position, while the signer puffs out his cheeks as if blowing out vapor.

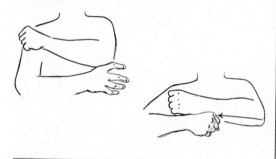

[S–471]

STEAL 3, *v.* (A mustachioed thief.) The fingertips of both "H" hands, palms facing the body, are placed above the lips and are drawn slowly apart, describing a mustache. Sometimes one hand only is used. *Cf.* BANDIT, BURGLAR, BURGLARY, CROOK, ROB 3, ROBBER 1, THEFT 3, THIEF 2.

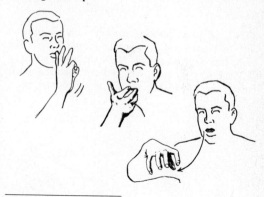

[S–474]

STEAMER (stē′ mər), *n.* (A boat, and wheels turning.) The sign for BOAT is made: Both cupped hands are held palms up before the body, with index finger edges touching, representing the hull of a boat. In this position both hands bob forward, as if riding over waves. Both "B" hands then face the body and revolve in two separate circles, one behind the other, representing engine wheels.

[S–472]

STEALER, *n.* The sign for STEAL 1, 2, or 3 is made. It is followed by the sign for INDIVIDUAL: Both

[S–475]

STEAM FITTER, *n.* (The natural sign.) The index finger of the right hand is grasped by the outstretched index and middle fingers of the left hand. The left hand executes a series of up-and-down movements, as if manipulating a wrench. This is followed by the sign for INDIVIDUAL: Both open hands, palms facing each other, move down the sides of the body, tracing its outline to the hips. *Cf.* MECHANIC 2, PIPE-FITTING, PLUMBER, WRENCH.

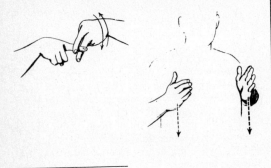

[S–476]

STEEL (stēl), *n.* (Striking an anvil with a hammer.) The left index finger, pointing forward from the body, represents the anvil. The right hand, grasping an imaginary hammer, swings down against the left index finger and glances off. *Cf.* BLACKSMITH, IRON 1.

[S–477]

STEM (stĕm), *n.* (Green, the natural sign.) The sign for GREEN is made: The right "G" hand is shaken slightly, pivoted at the wrist. Then the right "F" hand, palm down, moves straight upward, indicating an imaginary stem.

[S–478]

STEP 1 (stĕp), *n., v.,* STEPPED, STEPPING. (The movement of the feet.) The downturned "5" hands move alternately toward and away from the chest. *Cf.* PACE, WALK.

[S–479]

STEP(S) 2, *n.* (The natural sign.) The downturned open hands, fingers pointing forward, move in alternate upward "steps" before the body. *Cf.* STAIR(S) 1.

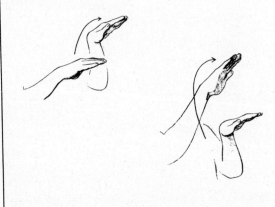

[S–480]

STEP(S) 3, *n.* (The natural sign.) The right open hand, palm facing left or down, traces a series of "steps" upward. *Cf.* STAIR(S) 2.

[S–481]

STEPFATHER (stĕp′ fä′ t͟hər), *n.* (Father, once removed.) The right "L" hand is held with its thumbtip at the right temple; its index finger moves back and forth several times.

[S–482]

STEPMOTHER (stĕp′ mŭ*th*′ ər), *n.* (Mother, once removed.) The index finger of the right "L" hand pivots back and forth on the right thumbtip, which is held against the right side of the chin.

[S–483]

STICK 1 (stĭk), *v.*, STUCK, STICKING. (The natural sign.) The right thumb and index finger touch each other and move away several times in quick succession, as if they were sticky. Then the open hands, palm-to-palm, one atop the other, touch and move away several times in the same manner. *Cf.* STICKY.

[S–484]

STICK 2, *n.* (Wood, straight.) The sign for WOOD is made: The little finger edge of the open right hand moves back and forth in a sawing motion over the back of the downturned left hand. Then the modified "O" hands are held with thumb edges touching before the body. From this position the hands separate

and move in straight lines to either side, outlining an imaginary stick.

[S–485]

STICKY (stĭk′ ĭ), *adj.* See STICK 1.

[S–486]

STILL 1 (stĭl), *adv., conj.* (Duration of movement from past to present.) The right "Y" hand is held palm down in front of the right shoulder and is then moved slowly down and forward in a smooth curve. *Cf.* CONTINUE 2, STAY 2, YET 1.

[S–487]

STILL 2, *adj.* (The natural sign.) The index finger is brought up against the pursed lips. *Cf.* BE QUIET 1, CALM 2, HUSH, NOISELESS, QUIET 1, SILENCE 1, SILENT.

[S–488]

STINGY 1 (stĭn' jĭ), *adj.* (Pulling things toward one-self.) Both prone open or "V" hands are held in front of the body with fingers bent. The hands are then drawn quickly and forcefully inward, as if raking things toward oneself. *Cf.* GREEDY 1, SELFISH 1, TIGHTWAD 1.

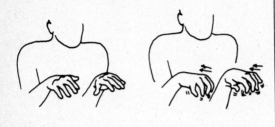

[S–489]

STINGY 2, *adj.* (Scratching the palm in greed.) The right fingers scratch the upturned left palm several times. A frowning expression is often used. *Cf.* AVA-RICIOUS, GREEDY 2, SELFISH 2, TIGHTWAD 2.

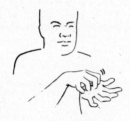

[S–490]

STINGY 3, *adj.* (Scratching in greed.) The down-turned "3" hands, held side by side, make a scratch-ing motion as they move in toward the body. *Cf.* GREEDY 3, SELFISH 3.

[S–491]

STITCH (stĭch), *n., v.,* STITCHED, STITCHING. (The natural movement.) The thumb and index finger of the right "F" hand move as if taking stitches on the upturned left palm.

[S–492]

STOCKING(S) 1, (stŏk' ing), *n.* (The knitting.) The index fingers, pointing forward, are rubbed back and forth against each other. *Cf.* HOSE 1, KNIT, SOCK(S) 1.

[S–493]

STOCKING(S) 2, *n.* (Pulling on hose.) The down-turned, open right hand grasps its left counterpart at the fingertips and slides over the back of the hand and up the arm, as if pulling on hose. *Cf.* HOSE 2, SOCK(S) 2.

[S–494]

STONE 1 (stōn), *n.* (The hardness is indicated by the striking of the fists.) The back of the right "S" hand is struck several times against the back of the left "S" hand. *Cf.* ROCK 1.

STONE 2, *n.* (A hard object.) The right "S" hand swings downward before the body, striking its knuckles against the knuckle of the index finger of the left "S" hand, which is held palm down. The right hand continues downward and away from the body in a short curve. *Cf.* ROCK 2, ROCKY.

STOOPED (sto͞opt), *adj.* (The natural motion.) The signer stoops his shoulders and moves the extended, crooked right index finger forward in a series of short, upward-arcing curves.

STOP (stŏp), *v.,* STOPPED, STOPPING, *n.* (A stopping or cutting short.) The little finger edge of the right hand is thrust abruptly into the upturned left palm, indicating a cutting short. *Cf.* ARREST 2, CEASE, HALT.

STORE 1 (stōr), *n.* (A house where things are sold.) The sign for SELL, is made: Both "AND" hands, fingertips touching their respective thumbs, are held palms down before the body. The hands are pivoted outward and away from the body once or several times. This is followed by the sign for HOUSE: The hands form a pyramid a bit above eye level and then separate, moving diagonally downward and then straight down a few inches. It may also be followed by the sign for PLACE: The "P" hands are held side by side before the body, with middle fingertips touching. From this position the hands separate and outline a circle (or a square), before coming together again closer to the body. *Cf.* SHOP 2.

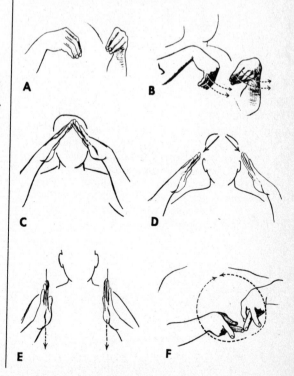

A   B
C   D
E   F

[S–499]

STORE 2, *v.* (Holding back.) The right "V" fingers are tapped once or twice across the back of their left counterparts. Both palms face the chest. *Cf.* RE-SERVE 3, SAVE 2.

[S–500]

STORE 3, *(rare), n., v.* (The shape.) The left arm is held horizontally, the right index finger describes an arc under it, from wrist to elbow, representing the shape of a basket as it hangs on the left arm. *Cf.* BASKET, EPISCOPAL, EPISCOPALIAN.

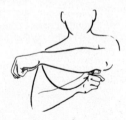

[S–501]

STORM (stôrm), *n.* (The blowing back and forth of the wind.) The "5" hands, palms facing and held up before the body, sway gracefully back and forth, in unison. The cheeks meanwhile are puffed up and the breath is being expelled. The nature of the swaying movement—graceful and slow, fast and violent, etc. —determines the type of wind. The strength of exhalation is also a classifier. *Cf.* BLOW 1, BREEZE, GALE, WIND.

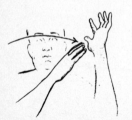 

[S–502]

STORY 1 (stōr' ĭ), *n.* (The unraveling or stretching out of words or sentences.) Both open hands are held close to each other, with fingers open and palms facing and almost touching. As the hands are drawn apart, the thumb and index finger of each hand come together to form circles. This is repeated several times. *Cf.* DESCRIBE 2, EXPLAIN 2, FABLE, FICTION, GOSPEL 1, NARRATE, NARRATIVE, TALE, TELL ABOUT.

[S–503]

STORY 2, *n.* (A level surface.) The downturned "B" hands are held side by side, with index fingers touching. Then they move apart several inches. This action is usually repeated, with the hands held somewhat higher, indicating a higher story in a building. The sign is somewhat similar to FLOOR, *q.v.*

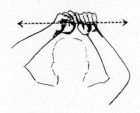

[S–504]

STOUT (stout), *adj.* (The swollen cheeks.) The cheeks are puffed out and the open "C" hands, positioned at either cheek, move away to their respective sides. *Cf.* FAT 1.

[S–505]

STRAIGHT (strāt), *adj.* (The natural sign.) Both open hands are held with fingers pointing out from the body, the right above the left, the right palm facing left and left palm facing right. The right hand moves its little finger edge along the thumb edge of the left hand, in a straight line outward.

[S–506]

STRANDED (strănd∂d), *adj.* (Impaled on a stick, as a snake's head.) The "V" fingers are thrust into the throat. *Cf.* CAUGHT IN THE ACT 2, CHOKE 2, STUCK 2, TRAP.

[S–507]

STRANGE 1 (strānj), *adj.* (Something which distorts the vision.) The "C" hand describes a small arc in front of the face. *Cf.* CURIOUS 2, GROTESQUE, ODD, PECULIAR, QUEER 1, WEIRD.

[S–508]

STRANGE 2, *(rare), adj.* The open hands are held in front of the body, palms up, and are lifted with an apparent effort, as if they held a load.

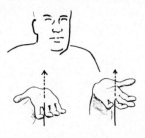

[S–509]

STRAWBERRY (strô′bĕr´ĭ), *n.* (Indicating a small, round object.) The right thumb and fingers grasp the index fingertip or thumb of the left "1" hand. In this position the right hand twists back and forth at the wrist.

[S–510]

STRAY (strā), *v.*, STRAYED, STRAYING. (The natural motion.) The "G" hands are held side by side and touching, palms down, index fingers pointing forward. Then the right hand moves forward, curving toward the right side as it does. *Cf.* DEFLECT, DEVIATE 2, GO OFF THE TRACK, WANDER 1.

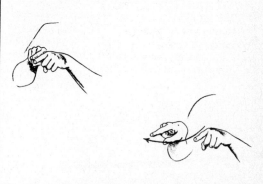

[S–511]

STREET (strēt), *n.* (The path.) Both hands, palms facing and fingers together and extended straight out, move in unison away from the body, in a straight or winding manner. *Cf.* CORRIDOR, HALL, HALLWAY, MANNER 2, METHOD, OPPORTUNITY 3, PATH, ROAD, TRAIL, WAY 1.

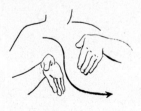

[S–512]

STRENGTH (strĕngkth, strĕngth), *n.* (Strength emanating from the body.) Both "5" hands are placed palms against the chest. They move out and away, forcefully, closing and assuming the "S" position. *Cf.* BRAVE, BRAVERY, COURAGE, COURAGEOUS, FORTITUDE, HALE, HEALTH, HEALTHY, MIGHTY 2, STRONG 2, WELL 2.

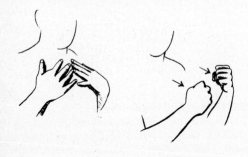

[S–513]

STRESS (strĕs), *n., v.,* STRESSED, STRESSING. (Pressing down to emphasize.) The right thumb is pressed down deliberately against the upturned left palm. Both hands move forward a bit. *Cf.* EMPHASIS, EMPHASIZE, EMPHATIC.

[S–514]

STRETCH (strĕch), *v.,* STRETCHED, STRETCHING. (Pulling apart.) Both "S" hands are pulled apart once or twice slowly, as if stretching something they are holding. *Cf.* ELASTIC.

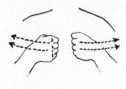

[S–515]

STRICT 1 (strĭkt), *adj.* (A sharp quality, indicated by pointing and jabbing.) The prone left open hand is held with fingers pointing forward and upward. Meanwhile, the extended right index finger is pushed and twisted slowly and steadily leftward under the left palm.

[S–516]

STRICT 2, *(colloq.), adj.* The extended right index and middle fingers are bent and brought up sharply, so that the edge of the index finger strikes the bridge of the nose.

[S–517]

STRIKE 1 (strīk), *v.,* STRUCK, STRIKING. (The natural sign.) The right "S" hand strikes its knuckles forcefully against the open left palm, which is held facing right. *Cf.* HIT 1, POUND 3, PUNCH 1.

[S–518]

STRIKE 2, *n., v.* (Holding a picket's sign.) Both upright hands grasp the stick of an imaginary display sign. The hands move forward and back repeatedly against the chest. This movement represents the walking back and forth of a striker or picket. *Cf.* PICKET.

[S–519]

STRING (strĭng), *n., v.* STRUNG, STRINGING. (Unraveling a thin string, as indicated by the little fingers.) With palms facing the body, the tips of the extended little fingers touch. As they are drawn slowly apart, they describe very small spirals. *Cf.* SPAGHETTI, THREAD, TWINE.

[S–520]

STRIPED (strīpt, strī′ pĭd), *adj.* (The shape of the stripes.) The right thumb and index finger are drawn down the chest several times, each time a bit more to the left.

[S–521]

STROKE 1 (strōk), *n.* (A blow or accident inside the head.) The right fingertips touch the forehead or the side of the head, and then the right hand forms a fist which strikes the left palm. This sign is used only for a cardiovascular accident.

[S–522]

STROKE 2, *v., n.* (Stroking a person or the head of a pet.) The right hand strokes the back of the left several times. *Cf.* DEAR 1, FOND 1, PET, TAME.

[S–523]

STRONG 1 (strông, strŏng), *adj.* (Flexing the muscles.) With fists clenched, palms facing down or back, the signer raises both arms and shakes them once, with force. *Cf.* MIGHT 1, MIGHTY 1, POWER 1, POWERFUL 1, STURDY, TOUGH 1.

[S–524]

STRONG 2, *adj.* (Strength emanating from the body.) Both "5" hands are placed palms against the chest. They move out and away, forcefully, closing and assuming the "S" position. *Cf.* BRAVE, BRAVERY, COURAGE, COURAGEOUS, FORTITUDE, HALE, HEALTH, HEALTHY, MIGHTY 2, STRENGTH, WELL 2.

[S-525]

STRONG-MINDED (strông´ mīnd´ dĭd, strŏng´ -), *adj.* (A strong head or mind.) The right index finger touches the right temple; then the right hand closes into the "S" position and is held upright near the head. *Cf.* WILL POWER.

[S-526]

STRUGGLE (strŭg´ əl), *n., v.,* -GLED, -GLING. (Two opposing forces.) Both "S" hands, held knuckle to knuckle before the body, move alternately up and down, the knuckles striking against each other as the hands pass.

[S-527]

STRUMPET (strŭm´ pĭt), *n.* (The blood rushes up the cheek in shame—several times for emphasis.) The curved back of the right hand, placed against the right cheek, moves up and off the cheek several times. *Cf.* HARLOT, PROSTITUTE, WHORE.

[S-528]

STUBBORN (stŭb´ ərn), *adj.* (The donkey's broad ear; the animal is traditionally a stubborn one.) The open hand, or the "B" hand, is placed at the side of the head, with palm out and fingers pointing straight up. The hand moves forward and back, pivoting at

the wrist, as in the case of a donkey's ears flapping. Both hands may also be used, at either side of the head. *Cf.* DONKEY, MULE, MULISH, OBSTINATE.

[S-529]

STUCK 1 (stŭk), *adj.* (Catching one by the throat.) The right hand makes a natural movement of grabbing the throat. *Cf.* CHOKE 1.

[S-530]

STUCK 2, *adj.* (Impaled on a stick, as a snake's head.) The "V" fingers are thrust into the throat. *Cf.* CAUGHT IN THE ACT 2, CHOKE 2, STRANDED, TRAP.

[S-531]

STUDENT 1 (stū´ dənt, stōō´ -), *n.* (One who learns.) The sign for LEARN is made: The downturned fingers of the right hand are placed on the upturned left palm. They close, and then the hand rises and the right fingertips are placed on the forehead. This is followed by the sign for INDIVIDUAL: Both open hands, palms facing each other, move down the sides of the body, tracing its outline to the hips. *Cf.* LEARNER, PUPIL 1, SCHOLAR.

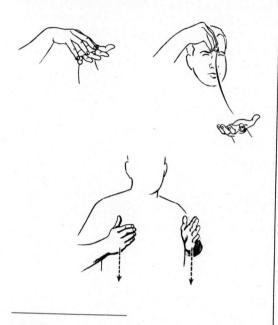

back slightly. *Cf.* AT A LOSS, DUMFOUNDED 1, JOLT, SHOCKED 1.

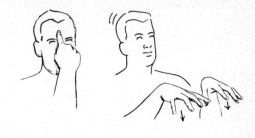

[S-535]

STUPID 1 (stū′ pĭd, stoo′ -), *adj.* (Knocking the head to indicate its empty state.) The "S" hand, palm facing the body, knocks against the forehead. *Cf.* DULL 1, DUMB 1, DUNCE.

[S-532]

STUDENT 2, *n.* (One who studies.) The sign for STUDY is made. This is followed by the sign for INDIVIDUAL, as in STUDENT 1.

[S-533]

STUDY (stŭd′ ĭ), *n., v.,* STUDIED, STUDYING. (The eyes scan the page thoroughly.) The upturned left hand represents a page. The right fingers wiggle as they move back and forth a short distance above the left hand.

[S-534]

STUMPED (stŭmpt), *v.* (The mind is frozen; the thought is frozen.) The index finger of the right "D" hand, palm facing the body, touches the forehead (modified THINK sign, *q.v.*). Both hands, in the "5" position, palms down, are then suddenly and deliberately dropped down in front of the body. A look of surprise is assumed at this point, and the head jerks

[S-536]

STUPID 2, *(colloq.), adj.* (The thickness of the skull is indicated, to stress intellectual density.) With the thumb of the right "C" hand grasped by the closed left hand, the right hand is swung in toward the body, describing a small arc as it moves. The space between the curved right fingers and the closed left hand indicates the thickness of the skull. *Cf.* CLUMSY 2, DUMB 2, MORON, THICK-SKULLED, UN-SKILLED.

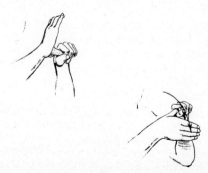

[S–537]

STURDY (stûr′ dĭ), *adj.* (Flexing the muscles.) With fists clenched, palms facing down or back, the signer raises both arms and shakes them once, with force. *Cf.* MIGHT 1, MIGHTY 1, POWER 1, POWERFUL 1, STRONG 1, TOUGH 1.

[S–538]

STYLISH (stī′ lĭsh), *adj.* (Embellishment.) Both hands, initially in the "O" position, palms out, are held with the fingertips in contact. Alternately, each hand opens into the "5" position, describes a small circle (the right clockwise and the left counterclockwise), and returns to its original position. *Cf.* FASHIONABLE.

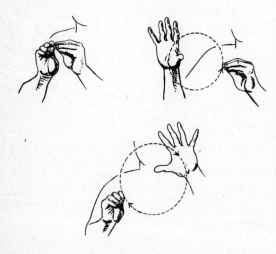

[S–539]

SUBDUE (səb dū′, -dōō′), *v.*, -DUED, -DUING. (Forcing the head into a bowed position.) The right "S" hand, placed across the left "S" hand, moves over and down a bit. *Cf.* BEAT 2, CONQUER, DEFEAT, OVERCOME.

[S–540]

SUBJECT (sŭb′ jĭkt), *n.* (The quotation marks are indicated.) The curved index and middle fingers of both hands, held palms out, move slightly to either side of the body, as if drawing quotation marks in the air. *Cf.* CAPTION, CITE, QUOTATION, QUOTE, SO-CALLED, THEME, TITLE, TOPIC.

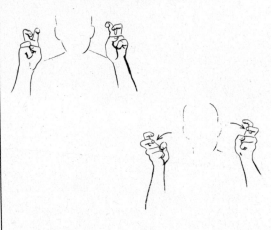

[S–541]

SUBSCRIBE (səb skrīb′), *v.*, -SCRIBED, -SCRIBING. (A regular taking in.) The outstretched open left hand, held palm facing right, moves in toward the body, assuming the "A" position, palm still facing right. This is repeated several times. *Cf.* DIVIDEND, INCOME, INTEREST 4, SUBSCRIPTION.

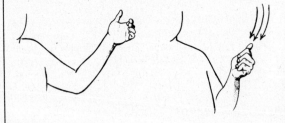

[S–542]

SUBSCRIPTION (səb skrip′ shən), *n.* See SUB-SCRIBE.

[S–543]

SUBSEQUENT (sub′ sə kwənt), *adj.* (A moving on of the minute hand of the clock.) The right "L" hand, its thumb thrust into the palm of the left and acting as a pivot, moves forward a short distance.

Cf. AFTER A WHILE, AFTERWARD, LATER 1, SUBSE-
QUENTLY.

[S–544]

SUBSEQUENTLY (sub' sə kwənt ly), *adv.* See SUB-
SEQUENT.

[S–545]

SUBSTANCE 1 (sŭb' stəns), *n.* (Something shown in
the hand.) The outstretched right hand, palm up and
held before the chest, is dropped slightly and
brought over a bit to the right. *Cf.* ANYTHING, AP-
PARATUS, INSTRUMENT, MATTER, OBJECT 1,
THING.

[S–546]

SUBSTANCE 2, *n.* (Relative standing of one's
thoughts.) A modified sign for THINK is made: The
right index finger touches the middle of the forehead. The tips of the right "V" hand, palm down, are
then thrust into the upturned left palm (as in
STAND, *q.v.*). The right "V" hand is then re-thrust
into the upturned left palm, with right palm now
facing the body. *Cf.* CONNOTE, IMPLY, INTEND, IN-
TENT 1, INTENTION, MEAN 2, MEANING, MOTIVE 3,
PURPOSE 1, SIGNIFICANCE 2, SIGNIFY 2.

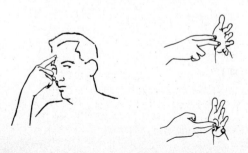

[S–547]

SUBSTANTIAL (səb stăn' shəl), *adj.* (A full cup.)
The left hand, in the "S" position, is held palm
facing right. The right "5" hand, palm down, is
brushed outward several times over the top of the
left, indicating a wiping off of the top of a cup. *Cf.*
ABUNDANCE, ABUNDANT, ADEQUATE, AMPLE,
ENOUGH, PLENTY, SUFFICIENT.

[S–548]

SUBSTITUTE (sŭb' stə tūt´), *n., v.,* -TUTED, -TUT-
ING. (Exchanging places.) The right "A" hand, positioned above the left "A" hand, swings down and
under the left, coming up a bit in front of it. *Cf.*
EXCHANGE, INSTEAD OF 1, REPLACE, TRADE.

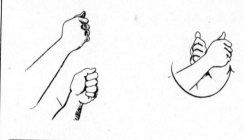

[S–549]

SUBTRACT (səb trăkt'), *v.,* -TRACTED, -TRACTING.
(Removing.) The right "A" hand, resting in the
palm of the left "5" hand, moves slightly up and
away, describing a small arc. It is then cast downward, opening into the "5" position, palm down, as
if removing something from the left hand and casting it down. *Cf.* ABOLISH 2, ABSENCE 2, ABSENT 2,
ABSTAIN, CHEAT 2, DEDUCT, DEFICIENCY, DELETE
1, LESS 2, MINUS 3, OUT 2, REMOVE 1, SUBTRAC-
TION, TAKE AWAY FROM, WITHDRAW 2.

[S–550]

SUBTRACTION (səb trăk′ shən), *n.* See SUBTRACT.

[S–551]

SUCCEED (sək sēd′), *v.*, -CEEDED, -CEEDING. (Penetrating the heights.) The "D" hands, palms back, are held at each side of the head, near the temples. With a pivoting motion of the wrists, the hands swing up and around, simultaneously, to a position above the head, with palms facing out. *Cf.* ACCOMPLISH 1, ACHIEVE 1, ATTAIN, PROSPER, SUCCESS, SUCCESSFUL, TRIUMPH 2.

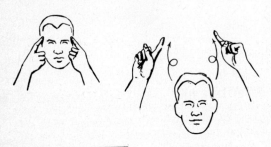

[S–552]

SUCCESS (sək sĕs′), *n.* See SUCCEED.

[S–553]

SUCCESSFUL (sək sĕs′ fəl), *adj.* See SUCCEED.

[S–554]

SUCCOTH (soo′ kawth), *(eccles.)*, *n.* (Shaking the *lulav* and *etrog,* the traditional Jewish symbols of this holiday.) One hand is clasped over the other, thumbs parallel and touching and pointing straight forward. In this position, both hands are shaken up and down several times. *Cf.* TABERNACLES, FEAST OF.

[S–555]

SUCH (sŭch), *adj.* (Matching fingers are brought together.) The outstretched index fingers are

brought together, either once or several times. *Cf.* ALIKE, IDENTICAL, LIKE 2, SAME 1, SIMILAR.

[S–556]

SUCKER (sŭk′ ər), *(colloq.)*, *n.* (Knocking someone.) The knuckles of the right "S" hand repeatedly strike the fingertips of the left right-angle hand. *Cf.* TAKE ADVANTAGE OF 1.

[S–557]

SUFFER 1 (sŭf′ ər), *v.*, -FERED, -FERING. (A clenching of the fists; the rise and fall of pain.) Both "S" hands, tightly clenched, revolve about each other, slowly and deliberately, while a pained expression is worn. *Cf.* AGONY, BEAR 3, DIFFICULT 3, ENDURE 1, PASSION 2, TOLERATE 2.

[S–558]

SUFFER 2, *v.* (Patience, suffering.) The sign for PATIENCE is made: The thumb of the right "A" hand is drawn down across the lips. This is followed by the sign for SUFFER 1.

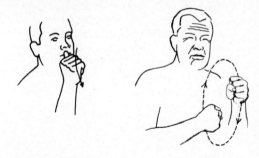

[S-559]

SUFFER 3, *(rare), v.* (Carrying a burden and keeping the lips sealed.) The thumb or index finger is pressed against the closed lips. Both "S" hands are then placed before the stooped left shoulder, as if holding on to a heavy bag draped over the shoulder.

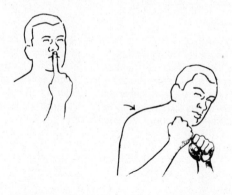

[S-560]

SUFFICIENT (sə fish' ənt), *adj.* (A full cup.) The left hand, in the "S" position, is held palm facing right. The right "5" hand, palm down, is brushed outward several times over the top of the left, indicating a wiping off of the top of a cup. *Cf.* ABUNDANCE, ABUNDANT, ADEQUATE, AMPLE, ENOUGH, PLENTY, SUBSTANTIAL.

[S-561]

SUGAR (shŏŏg' ər), *n.* (Titillating to the taste.) The fingertips of the right "U" hand, palm facing the body, brush against the chin a number of times beginning at the lips. *Cf.* CANDY 1, CUTE 1, SWEET.

[S-562]

SUGGEST (səg jĕst'), *v.,* -GESTED, -GESTING. (An offering; a presenting.) Both hands, slightly cupped, palms up, are held close to the chest. They move up and out in unison, describing a very slight arc. *Cf.* BID 2, MOTION 1, OFFER 1, OFFERING 1, PRESENT 1, PROPOSE, TENDER 2.

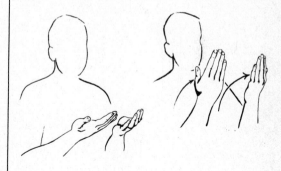

[S-563]

SUIT (sŏŏt), *n.* (Draping the clothes on the body.) With fingertips resting on the chest, both hands move down simultaneously. The action is repeated. *Cf.* CLOTHES, CLOTHING, DRESS, FROCK, GARMENT, GOWN, SHIRT, WEAR 1.

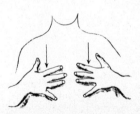

[S–564]

SUITABLE (so͞o′ tə bəl), *adj.* The right index finger, held above the left index finger, comes down rather forcefully so that the bottom of the right hand comes to rest on top of the left thumb joint. *Cf.* ACCURATE 2, CORRECT 1, DECENT, EXACT 2, JUST 2, PROPER, RIGHT 3.

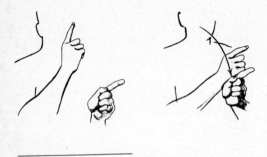

[S–565]

SUITCASE (so͞ot′ kās′), *n.* (The natural sign.) The downturned right "S" hand grasps an imaginary piece of luggage and shakes it up and down slightly, as if testing its weight. *Cf.* BAGGAGE, LUGGAGE, VALISE.

[S–566]

SUIT YOURSELF, *(colloq.), v. phrase.* (The thought is your own.) The right index finger touches the forehead in the modified THINK sign. Then the right "A" hand, with thumb pointing straight up, moves forward toward the person spoken to. See SELF. *Cf.* UP TO YOU.

[S–567]

SUM (sŭm), *n., v.,* SUMMED, SUMMING. (To bring up all together.) The two open hands, palms and fingers facing each other, with the left hand above the right, are brought together, with all fingers closing simultaneously. This sign is used mainly in the sense of adding up figures or items. *Cf.* ADD 1, ADDITION, AMOUNT 1, SUMMARIZE 2, SUMMARY 2, SUM UP, TOTAL.

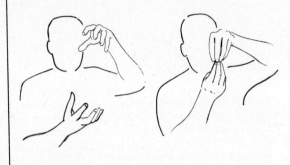

[S–568]

SUMMARIZE 1 (sŭm′ ə rīz′), *v.,* -RIZED, -RIZING. (To squeeze or condense into a small space.) The "C" hands face each other, with the right hand nearer to the body than the left. Both hands draw together and close deliberately, squeezing an imaginary object. *Cf.* ABBREVIATE 1, BRIEF 2, CONDENSE, MAKE BRIEF, SUMMARY 1.

[S–569]

SUMMARIZE 2, *v.* See SUM.

[S–570]

SUMMARY 1 (sŭm′ ə ri), *n., adj.* See SUMMARIZE 1.

[S–571]

SUMMARY 2, *n.* See SUM.

[S–572]

SUMMER (sŭm' ər), *n.* (Wiping the brow.) The downturned right index finger, slightly curved, is drawn across the forehead from left to right. *Cf.* HOT WEATHER.

[S–573]

SUMMON 1 (sŭm' ən), *v.,* -MONED, -MONING, (Harsh words thrown out.) The right hand appears to claw words out of the mouth as in CURSE 1. This time, however, it turns and throws them out, ending in the "5" position. *Cf.* BLASPHEME 2, CALL OUT, CRY 3, CRY OUT, CURSE 2, SCREAM, SHOUT, SWEAR 3.

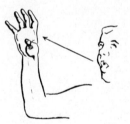

[S–574]

SUMMON 2, *v.* (To tap someone for attention.) The right hand is placed upon the back of the left, held palm down. The right hand then moves up and in toward the body, assuming the "A" position. As an optional addition, the right hand may then assume a beckoning movement. *Cf.* CALL 1.

[S–575]

SUM UP, *v. phrase.* See SUM.

[S–576]

SUN (sŭn), *n., v.,* SUNNED, SUNNING. (The round shape and the rays.) The right index finger, pointing forward and held above the face, describes a small clockwise circle. The right hand, all fingers touching the thumb, then drops down and forward from its position above the head. As it does so, the fingers open to the "5" position. *Cf.* SUNSHINE.

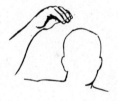

[S–577]

SUNDAY 1 (sŭn' dĭ), *n.* (A day of quiet, of rest.) The "5" hands, held side by side and palms out before the body, move straight down a short distance. They may also move slightly outward as they move down. *Cf.* SABBATH 2.

[S–578]

SUNDAY 2, *(loc.), n.* The thumb side of the right "S" hand is brought sharply into the palm of the left "5" hand, which is facing right.

[S–579]

SUNDRY (sŭn′ drĭ), *adj.* (The fingers are presented in order, to convey the concept of "several.") The right "A" hand is held palm facing up. One by one the fingers open, beginning with the index finger and ending with the little finger. Some use only the index and middle fingers. *Cf.* FEW, RARE, SCARCE, SEVERAL.

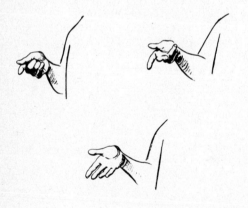

[S–580]

SUNRISE (sŭn′ rīz′), *n.* (The natural sign.) The downturned left arm, held horizontally, represents the horizon. The right thumb and index finger form a circle, and this circle is drawn up from a position in front of the downturned left hand.

[S–581]

SUNSET (sŭn′ sĕt′), *n.* (The natural sign.) The movement described in SUNRISE is reversed, with the right hand moving down below the downturned left hand.

[S–582]

SUNSHINE (sŭn′ shīn′), *n.* See SUN.

[S–583]

SUPERINTENDENT (sōō′ pər in tĕn′ dənt, sōō′ prin-), *n.* The "C" hands, held palms out at either temple, close over imaginary horns and move up a bit to either side, tracing the shape of the horns. *Cf.* HORNS, PRESIDENT.

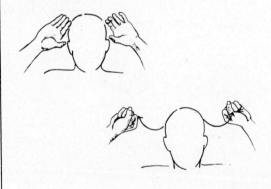

[S–584]

SUPERIOR (sə pir′ i ər, sōō-), *adj.* (Indicating height.) The right "A" hand, held with thumb pointing upward, moves straight up above the right shoulder. *Cf.* HIGH 2, PROMINENT 3.

[S–585]

SUPERLATIVE (sə pûr′ lə tĭv, soo-), *adj.* (The uppermost.) The upturned thumb of the right "A" hand moves sharply up to a position above the right side of the head.

[S–586]

SUPERNATURAL (soo pər năch′ ə rəl), *adj.* The sign for FROM is formed: The knuckle of the right "X" finger is placed against the base of the left "D" or "X" finger, and then moved away in a slight curve toward the body. This is followed by the sign for HEAVEN: Both open hands, fingers straight and pointing up, move upward in an arc on either side of the head. Just before they touch above the head, the right hand, palm down, sweeps under the left and moves up, its palm now facing out.

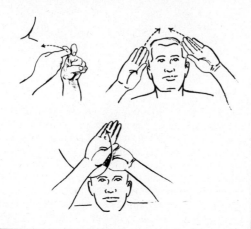

[S–587]

SUPERVISE (soo′ pər vīz′), *v.*, -VISED, -VISING. (The eyes sweep back and forth.) The "V" hands, held crossed, describe a counterclockwise circle before the chest.

[S–588]

SUPERVISOR (soo′ pər vī′ zər), *n.* The sign for SUPERVISE is made, followed by the sign for INDIVIDUAL: Both open hands, palms facing each other, move down the sides of the body, tracing its outline to the hips. *Cf.* FOREMAN.

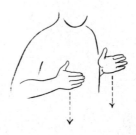

[S–589]

SUPPER (sŭp′ ər), *n.* (An evening or night meal.) The sign for NIGHT is made: The left hand, palm down, is positioned at chest height. The downturned right hand, held an inch or so above the left, moves over the left hand in an arc, the sun setting beneath the horizon. This is followed by the sign for EAT: The closed right hand goes through the natural motion of placing food in the mouth. This latter movement is repeated. The NIGHT and EAT signs may be reversed.

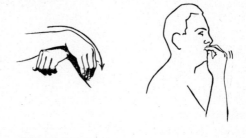

[S–590]

SUPPLICATION (sŭp′ lə kā′ shən), *n.* (An act of supplication.) With the right hand clasped over the left, both hands are shaken gently before the body. The eyes often are directed upward. *Cf.* BEG 2, BESEECH, ENTREAT, IMPLORE, PLEA, PLEAD.

[S-591]

SUPPORT 1 (sə pōrt′), *n., v.* -PORTED, -PORTING. (Holding up.) The right "S" hand pushes up the left "S" hand. *Cf.* ENDORSE 1, FAVOR, INDORSE 1, MAINTENANCE, SUSTAIN, SUSTENANCE, UPHOLD, UPLIFT.

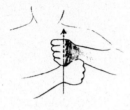

[S-592]

SUPPORT 2, *n., v.* (One hand upholds the other.) Both hands, in the "S" position, are held palms facing the body, the right under the left. The right hand pushes up the left in a gesture of support. *Cf.* ADVOCATE, ENDORSE 2, INDORSE 2.

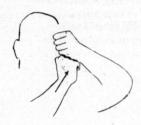

[S-593]

SUPPORT 3, *(rare), n., v.* ("Second"—two fingers.) The right "L" hand, held somewhat above the head, index finger pointing straight up, pivots forward a bit, so that the index finger now points forward. Used in parliamentary procedure. *Cf.* ENDORSE 3, INDORSE 3, SECOND 2.

[S-594]

SUPPOSE (sə pōz′), *v.,* -POSED, -POSING. (Weighing one thing against another.) The upturned open hands move alternately up and down. *Cf.* GUESS 4, MAY 1, MAYBE, MIGHT 2, PERHAPS, POSSIBILITY, POSSIBLY, PROBABLE, PROBABLY.

[S-595]

SUPPRESS FEELINGS, *v. phrase.* (Keeping the feelings down.) The curved fingertips of both hands are placed against the chest. The hands slowly move down as the fingers close into the "S" position. One hand only may also be used. *Cf.* CONTROL 2.

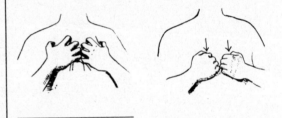

[S-596]

SURE (shŏŏr), *adj., adv.* (Coming forth directly from the lips; true.) The index finger of the right "D" hand, palm facing left, is placed against the lips. It moves up an inch or two and then describes a small arc forward and away from the lips. *Cf.* ABSOLUTE, ABSOLUTELY, ACTUAL, ACTUALLY, AUTHENTIC, CERTAIN, CERTAINLY, FAITHFUL 3, FIDELITY, FRANKLY, GENUINE, INDEED, POSITIVE 1, POSITIVELY, REAL, REALLY, SINCERE 2, SURELY, TRUE, TRULY, TRUTH, VALID, VERILY.

[S–597]

SURELY (shŏor' lĭ), *adv.* See SURE.

[S–598]

SURGEON (sur' jən), *n.* (The letter "M," from "M.D."; feeling the pulse.) The fingertips of the right "M" hand lightly tap the left pulse a number of times. The right "D" hand may also be used, in which case the thumb and fingertips tap the left pulse. *Cf.* DOCTOR.

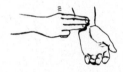

[S–599]

SURGERY (sûr' jə rĭ), *n.* (The action of the scalpel.) The thumb of the right "A" hand is drawn straight down across the upright left palm. *Cf.* OPERATION 1.

[S–600]

SURPASS (sər păs'), *v.*, -PASSED, -PASSING. (Rising above something.) Both hands, in the right-angle position, are held before the chest, with the right atop the left. The right hand arcs upward to a position about eight inches above the left. *Cf.* EXCEED, EXCESSIVE, PASSETH.

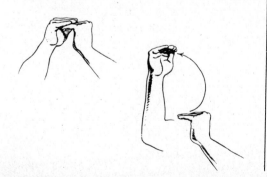

[S–601]

SURPRISE 1 (sər prīz'), *v.*, -PRISED, -PRISING, *n.* (The eyes pop open in amazement.) Both hands are held in modified "O" positions with thumb and index fingers of each hand near the eyes. These fingers suddenly flick open, and the eyes simultaneously pop open wide. *Cf.* AMAZE, AMAZEMENT, ASTONISH, ASTONISHED, ASTONISHMENT, ASTOUND.

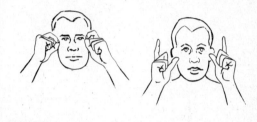

[S–602]

SURPRISE 2, *(colloq.), adj.* (The mouth drops open.) The fingertips of both "V" hands are held curved and touching before the body, one hand above the other. Then the hands are suddenly drawn apart, and at the same instant the mouth drops open and the eyes open wide. *Cf.* DUMFOUNDED 2, FLABBERGASTED, OPEN-MOUTHED, SPEECHLESS.

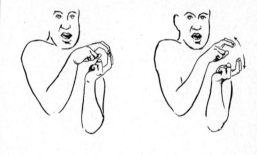

[S–603]

SURPRISED, *(colloq.), adj.* (The eyes pop open.) The "S" hands, palms facing each other, are held before the eyes. They suddenly open into the "C" position, with the eyes wide open. *Cf.* OPEN-EYED, SHOCKED 2.

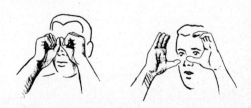

[S-604]

SURRENDER 1 (sə rĕn' dər), *v.*, -DERED, -DERING. (Throwing up the hands in a gesture of surrender.) Both "A" hands are held palms down before the chest and then thrown up in unison, ending in the "5" position. *Cf.* ABDICATE, CEDE, DISCOURAGE 1, FORFEIT, GIVE UP, LOSE HOPE, RELINQUISH, RENOUNCE, RENUNCIATION, YIELD.

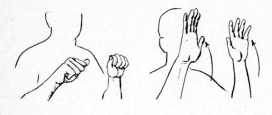

[S-605]

SURRENDER 2, *v.* (Grasping something and giving it over.) Both open hands are held palms facing inward before the body, the right hand slightly above the left, thumb edges up. In this position the hands close into the "S" position. Then they open and turn over, to lie side by side before the body, palms up, fingers pointing forward.

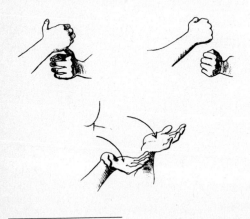

[S-606]

SURROUND (sə round'), *v.*, -ROUNDED, -ROUNDING. (The natural movement.) The open right hand, held with palm toward the body and fingers pointing up, circles around the extended left index finger, which is held pointing up.

[S-607]

SURVEYOR (sər vā' ər), *n.* (Using a surveying instrument.) The hands are held in front of the body as if adjusting a surveyor's instrument, making motions of sighting and measuring. The -ER suffix sign is then made: Both open hands, palms facing each other, move down the sides of the body, tracing its outline to the hips.

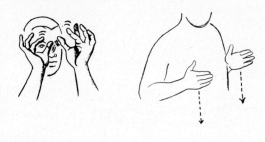

[S-608]

SUSPECT 1 (sə spĕkt'), *v.*, -PECTED, -PECTING. (Digging into the mind.) The right index finger scratches at the right temple several times. *Cf.* SUSPICION 1.

[S-609]

SUSPECT 2, *(arch.)*, *n.* The end of the index finger of the "V" hand is placed under and against the front teeth; then, without moving the arms, the ends of the fingers are thrown outward, the index finger slipping away from the teeth. *Cf.* SPY 3, SUSPICION 2.

[S–610]

SUSPEND 1 (sə spĕnd′), *v.,* -PENDED, -PENDING. (The natural sign.) The curved right index finger "hangs" on the extended left index finger. *Cf.* HANG 1.

[S–611]

SUSPEND 2, *v.* (The natural sign.) The extended index fingers are hooked together, with the left hand thus suspended from the right. *Cf.* SUSPENSION.

[S–612]

SUSPENSION (sə spĕn′ shən), *n.* See SUSPEND 2.

[S–613]

SUSPICION 1 (sə spish′ ən). *n.* See SUSPECT 1.

[S–614]

SUSPICION 2, *n.* See SUSPECT 2.

[S–615]

SUSPICION 3, *n.* (Warding off.) The right "S" hand is held before the right shoulder, elbow bent out to the side. The hand is then thrown forward several times, as if striking at someone. *Cf.* SKEPTICAL 2.

[S–616]

SUSTAIN (sə stān′), *v.,* -TAINED, -TAINING. (Holding up.) The right "S" hand pushes up the left "S" hand. *Cf.* ENDORSE 1, FAVOR, INDORSE 1, MAINTENANCE, SUPPORT 1, SUSTENANCE, UPHOLD, UPLIFT.

[S–617]

SUSTENANCE (sŭs′ tə nəns), *n.* See SUSTAIN.

[S–618]

SWALLOW 1 (swŏl′ ō), *v.,* -LOWED, -LOWING. (The movement.) The index finger moves down the throat a short distance. *Cf.* THIRST, THIRSTY.

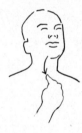

[S–619]

SWALLOW 2, *v.* (Downward movement.) The extended right index finger is drawn downward along the open left palm, which is held toward the face with fingers pointing right.

[S-620]

SWAN (swŏn), *n.* (The natural sign.) The right elbow is bent, and the right thumb, index and middle fingers are extended before the face, palm facing forward, representing the swan's long neck and beak. In this position the extended thumb and first two fingers open and close several times.

[S-621]

SWEAR 1 (swâr), *v.* SWORE, SWORN, SWEARING. (The arm is raised.) The right index finger is placed at the lips. The right arm is then raised, palm out and elbow resting on the back of the left hand. *Cf.* GUARANTEE 1, LOYAL, OATH, PLEDGE, PROMISE 1, SWORN, TAKE OATH, VOW.

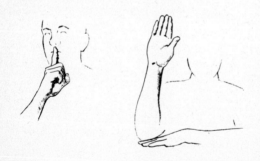

[S-622]

SWEAR 2, *v.* (Harsh words and a threatening hand.) The right hand appears to claw words out of the mouth. It ends in the "S" position, above the head, shaking back and forth in a threatening manner. *Cf.* BLASPHEME 1, CURSE 1.

[S-623]

SWEAR 3, *v.* (Harsh words thrown out.) The right hand as in SWEAR 2, appears to claw words out of the mouth. This time, however, it turns and throws them out, ending in the "5" position. *Cf.* BLASPHEME 2, CALL OUT, CRY 3, CRY OUT, CURSE 2, SCREAM, SHOUT, SUMMON 1.

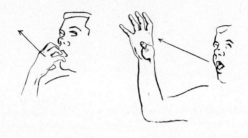

[S-624]

SWEAR 4, *(sl.), v.* (Curlicues, as one finds in cartoon-type swear words.) The right "Y" hand, palm down, pivots at the wrist along the left "G" hand, from the wrist to the tip of the finger. *Cf.* BLASPHEME 3, CURSE 3.

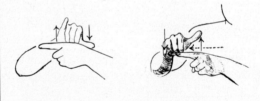

[S-625]

SWEAT 1 (swĕt), *n., v.,* SWEAT or SWEATED, SWEATING. (Wiping the brow.) The bent right index finger is drawn across the forehead from left to right and then shaken to the side, as if getting rid of the sweat. *Cf.* PERSPIRATION 1, PERSPIRE 1.

[S-626]

SWEAT 2, *n., v.* (Perspiration dripping from the brow.) The index finger edge of the open right hand wipes across the brow, and the same open hand then continues forcefully downward off the brow, its fingers wiggling, as if shaking off the perspiration gathered. *Cf.* PERSPIRATION 2, PERSPIRE 2.

[S-627]

SWEATER (swĕt′ ər), *n.* (The neck of the garment is indicated.) The open "C" hand, held at the throat, moves up and down a short distance. The signer may also mime pulling a sweater over the head.

[S-628]

SWEDE (swēd), *n.* The right "S" hand, palm facing left, describes a small circle on the forehead. (All the Scandinavian—northern—countries are indicated at the forehead, the topmost part of the body.) *Cf.* SWEDEN, SWEDISH.

[S-629]

SWEDEN (Swē′ dən), *n.* See SWEDE.

[S-630]

SWEDISH (Swē′ dĭsh), *adj.* See SWEDE.

[S-631]

SWEEP (swēp), *v.,* SWEPT, SWEEPING, *n.* (The natural sign.) The hands grasp and manipulate an imaginary broom. *Cf.* BROOM.

[S-632]

SWEET (swēt), *adj., n.* (Titillating to the taste.) The fingertips of the right "U" hand, palm facing the body, brush against the chin a number of times beginning at the lips. *Cf.* CANDY 1, CUTE 1, SUGAR.

[S-633]

SWEETHEART 1 (swēt′ härt′), *(colloq.), n.* (Heads nodding toward each other.) The "A" hands are placed together before the body with thumbs up. The thumbs wiggle up and down. *Cf.* BEAU, COURTING, COURTSHIP, LOVER, MAKE LOVE 1.

[S–634]

SWEETHEART 2, *(colloq.), n.* (Locked together.) With little fingers interlocked and palms facing the body, the thumbs of both hands wiggle back and forth.

[S–635]

SWELL 1 (swĕl), *adj.* (The hands gesture toward the heavens.) The "5" hands, palms out and arms raised rather high, are positioned somewhat above the line of vision. The arms move abruptly forward and up once or twice. An expression of pleasure or surprise is usually assumed. *Cf.* EXCELLENT, GRAND 1, GREAT 3, MARVEL, MARVELOUS, MIRACLE, O!, SPLENDID 1, WONDER 2, WONDERFUL 1.

[S–636]

SWELL 2, *adj., interj.* (The feelings are titillated.) With the thumb resting on the upper part of the chest, the fingers are wiggled back and forth. *Cf.* ELEGANT, FINE 1, GRAND 2, GREAT 4, SPLENDID 2, WONDERFUL 2.

[S–637]

SWELL 3, *v., SWELLED, SWELLING.* (A swelling.) The palm of the right hand is placed on the back of the downturned left hand. Then the right hand is raised slowly off the left, indicating a swelling.

[S–638]

SWELL-HEADED, *(colloq.), adj.* (The natural sign.) Both downturned "L" hands are positioned with index fingers at the temples. They move away from the head rather slowly, indicating the size or growth of the head. The head is often moved slightly back and forth as the hands move away. An expression of superiority is assumed. *Cf.* BIG-HEADED, CONCEITED, BIG SHOT.

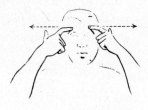

[S–639]

SWIFT (swĭft), *adj.* (A quick movement.) The thumbtip of the upright right hand is flicked quickly off the tip of the curved right index finger, as if shooting marbles. *Cf.* FAST 1, IMMEDIATELY, QUICK, QUICKNESS, RAPID, RATE 1, SPEED, SPEEDY.

[S–640]

SWIM (swĭm), *v.,* SWAM, SWUM, SWIMMING, *n.* (The natural sign.) The signer's arms go through the actions of swimming, using the breast stroke.

[S-641]

SWIMMER (swĭm′ ər), *n.* The sign for SWIM is made, followed by the sign for INDIVIDUAL: Both open hands, palms facing each other, move down the sides of the body, tracing its outline to the hips.

[S-642]

SWING (swĭng), *n., v.,* SWUNG, SWINGING. (A swinging seat.) The sign for SEAT is made: The extended index and middle fingers of the down-turned right hand are draped across the same two fingers of the downturned left hand. In this position the hands swing together from side to side, or forward and back.

[S-643]

SWIPE (swīp), *n., v.,* SWIPED, SWIPING. (The hand, partly concealed, takes something surreptitiously.) The index and middle fingers of the right hand, somewhat curved, are placed under the left elbow. As they move slowly along the left forearm toward the left wrist, they close a bit. *Cf.* ABDUCT, EMBEZ-ZLE, EMBEZZLEMENT, KIDNAP, ROB 1, ROBBERY 1, STEAL 1, THEFT 1, THIEF 1, THIEVERY.

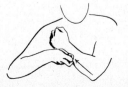

[S-644]

SWORD (sōrd), *n.* (The natural sign.) An imaginary sword is drawn and presented.

[S-645]

SWORN (swōrn), *adj.* (The arm is raised.) The right index finger is placed at the lips. The right arm is then raised, palm out and elbow resting on the back of the left hand. *Cf.* GUARANTEE 1, LOYAL, OATH, PLEDGE, PROMISE 1, SWEAR 1, TAKE OATH, VOW.

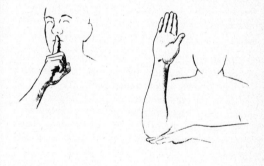

[S-646]

SYMPATHETIC (sĭm′ pə thĕt′ ĭk), *adj.* (Feeling with.) The tip of the right middle finger, touching the heart, moves up an inch or two on the chest. The sign for WITH is then made: Both "A" hands come together, so that the thumbs are side by side. *Cf.* SYMPATHY 1.

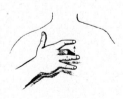

[S-647]

SYMPATHY 1 (sǐm′ pə thǐ), *n.* See SYMPATHETIC.

[S-648]

SYMPATHY 2, *n.* (Feelings from the heart, conferred on others.) The middle fingertip of the open right hand touches the chest over the heart. The same open hand then moves in a small, clockwise circle before the right shoulder, with palm facing forward and fingers pointing up. *Cf.* MERCY 2, PITY, POOR 3.

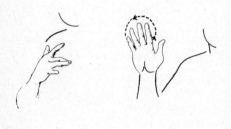

[S-649]

SYNONYM (sǐn′ ə nǐm), *n.* (A similar word.) The sign for WORD is made: The tips of the right index finger and thumb, about an inch apart, are placed on the side of the outstretched left index finger, which represents the length of a sentence. This is followed by the sign for SAME: The outstretched index fingers are brought together, either once or several times.

[S-650]

SYRUP (sǐr′ əp, sûr′ -), *n.* (Wiping it from the lips.) The upturned right index finger moves across the lips from left to right. *Cf.* MOLASSES.

[S-651]

SYSTEM (sǐs′ təm), *n.* (Placing things in order.) The hands, palms facing, fingers together and pointing away from the body, are positioned at the left side and held about a foot apart. With a slight up-down motion, as if describing waves, the hands travel in unison from left to right. *Cf.* ARRANGE, ARRANGEMENT, CLASSED 2, DEVISE 1, ORDER 3, PLAN 1, POLICY 1, PREPARE 1, PROGRAM 1, PROVIDE 1, PUT IN ORDER, READY 1, SCHEME.

T

TABERNACLES, FEAST OF (tăb′ ər năk´ əls), *(eccles.), n. phrase.* (Shaking the *lulav* and *etrog,* the traditional Jewish symbols of this holiday.) One hand is clasped over the other, thumbs parallel and touching and pointing straight forward. In this position, both hands are shaken up and down several times. *Cf.* SUCCOTH.

TABLE 1 (tā′ bəl), *n.* (The shape and the legs.) The downturned open hands are held together before the chest, fingers pointing forward. From this position the hands separate and move in a straight line to either side, indicating the table top. Then the downturned index fingers are thrust downward simultaneously, moved in toward the body, and again thrust downward. These motions indicate the legs.

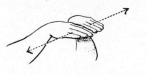

TABLE 2, *v.* (Shelving a motion or proposal.) The right "V" hand is brought down over the upturned left index finger.

TABLECLOTH (tā′ bəl klôth´), *n.* (Laying the cloth on the table.) The closed hands go through the natural motions of flinging the cloth in the air and guiding its descent on the table. This sign may be preceded by the sign for WHITE, *q.v.*

TABLE TENNIS, *n. phrase.* (The natural sign.) The signer goes through the actions involved in playing table tennis or Ping-Pong. *Cf.* PING-PONG.

TACKLE (tăk′ əl), *(sports), n.* (The natural motion.) The right open hand closes forcefully over the extended index and middle fingers of the downturned left hand.

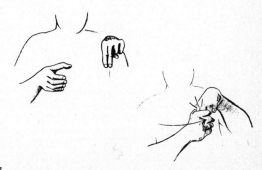

[T-7]

TAIL (tāl), *n.* (The shape.) The extended right thumb and index finger come together, and the hand moves away from the body in a downward arc, outlining an imaginary tail.

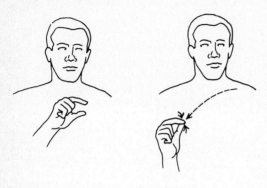

[T-8]

TAILOR (tā' lər), *n.* (One who sews.) The sign for SEW is made: The right thumb and index finger grasp an imaginary needle and go through the motions of sewing stitches along the upturned left palm, from the base of the fingers to the base of the hand. The sign for INDIVIDUAL is then made: Both open hands, palms facing each other, move down the sides of the body, tracing its outline to the hips. *Cf.* SEWER.

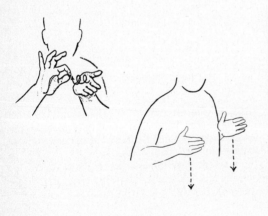

[T-9]

TAKE (tāk), *v.* TOOK, TAKEN, TAKING, *n.* (Taking unto oneself.) The right hand, palm out, is extended before the chest, index finger and thumb in an open position, the other fingers separated and pointing up. The hand is drawn in toward the chest, and the index and thumb close at the same time, indicating

something taken to oneself. *Cf.* ADOPT, APPOINT, CHOOSE 1, SELECT 2.

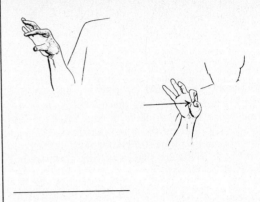

[T-10]

TAKE ADVANTAGE OF 1, *(colloq.), v. phrase.* (Knocking someone.) The knuckles of the right "S" hand repeatedly strike the fingertips of the left right-angle hand. Cf. SUCKER.

[T-11]

TAKE ADVANTAGE OF 2, *v. phrase.* (Attaching to something and tugging on it.) The extended right thumb, index, and middle fingers grasp the extended left index and middle fingers. In this position the right hand pulls at the left several times. *Cf.* LEECH, MOOCH, MOOCHER, PARASITE.

[T-12]

TAKE A PICTURE, *v. phrase.* (Capturing an image.) Both open hands are held before the body, fingers pointing upward, the right hand positioned in front of the left. The right hand then moves forcefully backward against the left palm, closing into the "AND" position as it does. *Cf.* PHOTOGRAPH 3.

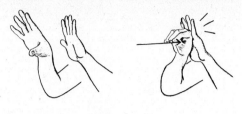

[T–13]

TAKE A PILL, *(colloq.), v. phrase.* (The natural sign.) The right thumb and index finger go through the motion of popping an imaginary pill into the open mouth. *Cf.* PILL.

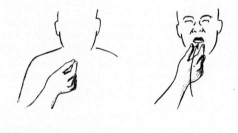

[T–14]

TAKE AWAY FROM, *v. phrase.* (Removing.) The right "A" hand, resting in the palm of the left "5" hand, moves slightly up and away, describing a small arc. It is then cast downward, opening into the "5" position, palm down, as if removing something from the left hand and casting it down. *Cf.* ABOLISH 2, ABSENCE 2, ABSENT 2, ABSTAIN, CHEAT 2, DEDUCT, DEFICIENCY, DELETE 1, LESS 2, MINUS 3, OUT 2, REMOVE 1, SUBTRACT, SUBTRACTION, WITHDRAW 2.

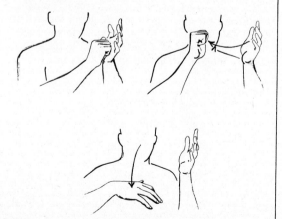

[T–15]

TAKE CARE OF 1, *v. phrase.* (The "K" for *keep* in the sense of *keeping carefully.*) Both "K" hands are crossed, the right atop the left. The right hand moves up and down a very short distance, several times, each time coming to rest on top of the left. *Cf.* BE CAREFUL, CAREFUL 3.

[T–16]

TAKE CARE OF 2, *v. phrase.* (Slow, careful movement.) The "K" hands are crossed, the right above the left, little finger edges down. In this position the hands are moved up and down a short distance. *Cf.* CARE 2, CAREFUL 2, KEEP, MAINTAIN 1, MIND 3, PRESERVE, RESERVE 2.

[T–17]

TAKE CARE OF 3, *v. phrase.* (Slow, careful movement.) The "K" hands are crossed, the right above the left, little finger edges down. In this position they describe a small counterclockwise circle in front of the chest. *Cf.* CARE 1, CARE FOR, CAREFUL 1.

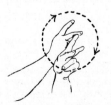

[T–18]

TAKE OATH (ōth), *v. phrase.* (The arm is raised.) The right index finger is placed at the lips. The right arm is then raised, palm out and elbow resting on the back of the left hand. *Cf.* GUARANTEE 1, LOYAL, OATH, PLEDGE, PROMISE 1, SWEAR 1, SWORN, VOW.

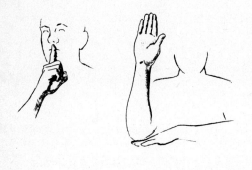

[T–19]

TAKE UP, *v. phrase.* (Responsibility.) Both hands, held palms down in the "5" position, are at chest level. With a grasping upward movement, both close into "S" positions before the face. *Cf.* ASSUME, PICK UP 1.

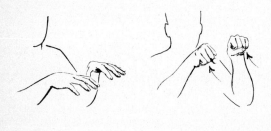

[T–20]

TALE (tāl), *n.* (The unraveling or stretching out of words or sentences.) Both open hands are held close to each other, with fingers open and palms facing and almost touching. As the hands are drawn apart, the thumb and index finger of each hand come together to form circles. This is repeated several times. *Cf.* DESCRIBE 2, EXPLAIN 2, FABLE, FICTION, GOSPEL 1, NARRATE, NARRATIVE, STORY 1, TELL ABOUT.

[T–21]

TALIS (tä' lĭs), *(eccles.), n.* (The drape of the Jewish prayer shawl.) Both "T" hands are brought down along either side of the chest.

[T–22]

TALK 1 (tôk), *v.,* TALKED, TALKING. (Words tumbling from the mouth.) The right index finger, pointing left, describes a continuous small circle in front of the mouth. *Cf.* BID 3, DISCOURSE, HEARING, MAINTAIN 2, MENTION, REMARK, SAID, SAY, SPEAK, SPEECH 1, STATE, STATEMENT, TELL, VERBAL 1.

[T–23]

TALK 2, *n., v.* (A gesture of an orator.) The right open hand, palm facing left, is held above and to the right of the head. It pivots on the wrist, forward and backward, several times. *Cf.* ADDRESS 1, LECTURE, ORATE, SPEECH 2, TESTIMONY.

[T-24]

TALK 3, *n., v.* (Movement forward from, and back to, the mouth.) The tips of both index fingers, held pointing up, move alternately forward from, and back to, the lips. *Cf.* COMMUNICATE WITH, CONVERSATION 1, CONVERSE.

[T-25]

TALL 1 (tôl), *adj.* (The height is indicated.) The index finger of the right "D" hand moves straight up against the palm of the left "5" hand. *Cf.* HEIGHT 1.

[T-26]

TALL 2, *adj.* (The height is indicated.) The right right-angle hand, palm facing the left, is held at the height the signer wishes to indicate. *Cf.* BIG 2, HEIGHT 2, HIGH 3.

[T-27]

TALL 3, *(loc.), adj.* (The stooped position.) The curved index finger of the right "D" hand, held up before the body, moves forward, away from the body, in a series of small bobbing motions. The head may be stooped and may also bob slightly in cadence with the hand.

[T-28]

TAME (tām), *adj., v.,* TAMED, TAMING. (Stroking a person or the head of a pet.) The right hand strokes the back of the left several times. *Cf.* DEAR 1, FOND 1, PET, STROKE 2.

[T-29]

TAN (tăn), *adj., n.* (The letter "T"; a tanned complexion.) The right "T" hand, palm facing out from the body, moves down the right side of the face.

[T-30]

TAPE (tāp), *n., v.,* TAPED, TAPING. (The positioning and stretching out of the tape.) The "A" hands, palms facing down, touch at the thumbtips. They move apart a short distance.

[T-31]

TARDY (tär′ dĭ), *adj.* (Hanging back.) The "5" hand and forearm, hanging loosely and straight down from the elbow, move back and forth under the armpit. *Cf.* BEHIND TIME, LATE, NOT DONE, NOT YET.

[T-32]

TART (tärt), *adj.* (The salivary glands are indicated.) The right index finger touches the side of the throat. A sour expression is assumed. *Cf.* SAVORY.

[T-33]

TASK (tăsk), *n.* (Striking an anvil.) Both "S" hands are held palms down. The right hand strikes against the back of the left a number of times. *Cf.* JOB, LABOR, OCCUPATION, TOIL, TRAVAIL, VOCATION, WORK.

[T-34]

TASTE (tāst), *n., v.,* TASTED, TASTING. (The natural motion.) The index fingertip or middle finger touches the tip of the tongue.

[T-35]

TATTLE 1 (tăt′ əl), *v.,* -TLED, -TLING. (Words moving outward from the mouth.) The right hand is held with index and middle fingertips touching the thumbtip, and with its thumb edge at the mouth. The hand then moves outward from the mouth, with its extended thumb and first two fingers alternately opening and closing. *Cf.* TATTLETALE 1, TELLTALE 1.

[T-36]

TATTLE 2, *v.* (Words shooting out from the mouth.) The right "S" hand is held palm out before the mouth, with the knuckle of the index finger touching the lips. From this position the hand moves forward, away from the mouth. At the same time the index finger straightens and points forward. *Cf.* TATTLETALE 2, TELLTALE 2.

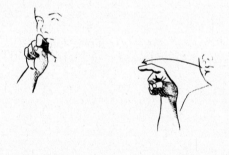

[T-37]

TATTLETALE 1 (tăt′ əl tāl′), *n.* See TATTLE 1.

[T-38]

TATTLETALE 2, *n.* See TATTLE 2.

[T-39]

TAX 1 (tăks), *n., v.,* TAXED, TAXING. (Nicking into one.) The knuckle of the right "X" finger is nicked against the palm of the left hand, held in the "5" position, palm facing right. *Cf.* ADMISSION 2, CHARGE 1, COST, DUTY 2, EXCISE, EXPENSE, FEE,

FINE 2, IMPOST, PENALTY 3, PRICE 2, TAXATION 1, TOLL.

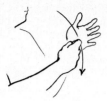

[T–40]

TAX 2, *n., v.* (Making a nick, as in "nicking the pocketbook.") The tip of the right index finger, moving downward in an arc, makes a nick in the open left palm, which is facing right. *Cf.* TAXATION 2.

[T–41]

TAXATION 1 (tăks ā' shən), *n.* See TAX 1.

[T–42]

TAXATION 2, *n.* See TAX 2.

[T–43]

TAXI (tăk' sĭ), *n.* (The letter "T"; the act of driving.) The "T" hands go through the motion of manipulating a steering wheel.

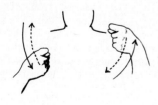

[T–44]

TEA 1 (tē), *n.* (Dipping the teabag.) The right index finger and thumb raise and lower an imaginary tea-

bag into a "cup" formed by the left "C" or "O" hand, held thumb side up.

[T–45]

TEA 2, *n.* (Stirring the teabag.) The hand positions in TEA 1 are assumed, but the right hand executes a circular, stirring motion instead.

[T–46]

TEACH (tēch), *v.,* TAUGHT, TEACHING. (Giving forth from the mind.) The fingertips of each hand are placed on the temples. They then swing out and open into the "5" position. *Cf.* EDUCATE, INDOCTRINATE, INDOCTRINATION, INSTRUCT, INSTRUCTION.

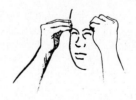

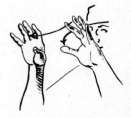

[T–47]

TEACHER (tē′ chər), *n.* The sign for TEACH is made. This is followed by the sign for INDIVID-UAL: Both open hands, palms facing each other, move down the sides of the body, tracing its outline to the hips. *Cf.* EDUCATOR, INSTRUCTOR.

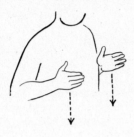

[T–48]

TEAR 1 (târ), *n., v.,* TORE, TORN, TEARING. (The natural motion.) Both "A" hands, held palms down before the body, grasp an imaginary object; then they move forcefully apart, as if tearing the object. *Cf.* REND, RIP 1.

[T–49]

TEAR 2, *n.* (Tears streaming down the cheeks.) Both index fingers, in the "D" position, move down the cheeks, either once or several times. Sometimes one finger only is used. *Cf.* BAWL 1, CRY 1, TEAR-DROP, WEEP 1.

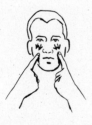

[T–50]

TEARDROP (tĭr′ drŏp′), *n.* See TEAR 2.

[T–51]

TEASE 1 (tēz), *n., v.,* TEASED, TEASING. (Striking against one.) The knuckles of the right "A" hand move sharply forward along the thumb edge of the left "A" hand. *Cf.* PERSECUTE, TORMENT.

[T–52]

TEASE 2, *n., v.* The movements in TEASE 1 are duplicated, except that the "X" hands are used. *Cf.* KID 2.

[T–53]

TEASE 3, *n., v.* The movements in TEASE 1 are duplicated, except that the "G" hands are used. *Cf.* CRUEL 3.

[T–54]

TEDIOUS (tē′ dĭ əs, tē′ jəs), *adj.* (The nose is pressed, as if to a grindstone wheel.) The right index finger touches the tip of the nose, as a bored expression is assumed. The right hand is sometimes pivoted back and forth slightly, as the fingertip remains against the nose. *Cf.* BORING, MONOTONOUS 1.

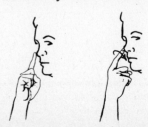

[T–55]

TEETH (tēth), *n. pl.* (The natural sign.) The extended right index finger passes over the exposed teeth.

[T–56]

TEFILLIN (tə fĭ′ lĭn), *(eccles.), n.* (The items are described.) The fingertips of the open right hand are placed in mid-forehead, and are then placed against the left biceps. The right hand, holding the imaginary thongs, winds around the lower left arm a number of times. *Cf.* PHYLACTERIES.

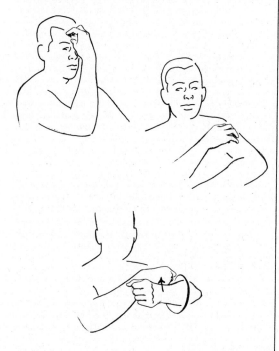

[T–57]

TELEGRAM 1 (tĕl′ ə grăm′), *n.* (The tapping of the telegraph key.) The curved right index finger taps repeatedly against the outstretched left index finger as it moves from the base to the tip, as if making

impressions on telegraph tape. *Cf.* TELEGRAPH 1, WIRE 1.

[T–58]

TELEGRAM 2, *n.* The right middle finger moves outward across the open left palm, from wrist to fingertips. *Cf.* TELEGRAPH 2, WIRE 2.

[T–59]

TELEGRAPH 1 (tĕl′ ə grăf′), *n.* See TELEGRAM 1.

[T–60]

TELEGRAPH 2, *n.* See TELEGRAM 2.

[T–61]

TELEPHONE 1 (tĕl′ ə fōn′), *n., v.,* -PHONED, -PHONING. (The natural sign.) The left "S" hand represents the mouthpiece and is placed at the mouth, with palm facing right. Its right counterpart represents the earpiece and is placed at the right ear, with palm facing forward. This is the old fashioned two-piece telephone. *Cf.* PHONE 1.

[T–62]

TELEPHONE 2, *n., v.* (The natural sign.) The right "Y" hand is placed at the right side of the head with the thumb touching the ear and the little finger touching the lips. This is the more modern telephone receiver. *Cf.* PHONE 2.

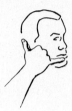

[T–63]

TELEVISION (tĕl′ ə vĭzh′ ən), *n.* (The letters "T" and "V.") The letters "T" and "V" are fingerspelled. *Cf.* TV.

[T–64]

TELL (tĕl), *v.,* TOLD, TELLING. (Words tumbling from the mouth.) The right index finger, pointing left, describes a continuous small circle in front of the mouth. *Cf.* BID 3, DISCOURSE, HEARING, MAINTAIN 2, MENTION, REMARK, SAID, SAY, SPEAK, SPEECH 1, STATE, STATEMENT, TALK 1, VERBAL 1.

[T–65]

TELL ABOUT, *v. phrase.* (The unraveling or stretching out of words or sentences.) Both open hands are

held close to each other, with fingers open and palms facing and almost touching. As the hands are drawn apart, the thumb and index finger of each hand come together to form circles. This is repeated several times. *Cf.* DESCRIBE 2, EXPLAIN 2, FABLE, FICTION, GOSPEL 1, NARRATE, NARRATIVE, STORY 1, TALE.

[T–66]

TELL ME, *phrase.* (The natural sign.) The tip of the index finger of the right "D" hand, palm facing the body, is first placed at the lips and then moves down to touch the chest.

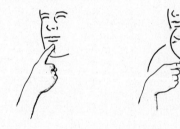

[T–67]

TELLTALE 1 (tĕl′ tāl′), *n.,* (Words moving outward from the mouth.) The right hand is held with index and middle fingertips touching the thumbtip, and with its thumb edge at the mouth. The hand then moves outward from the mouth, with its extended thumb and first two fingers alternately opening and closing. *Cf.* TATTLE 1, TATTLETALE 1.

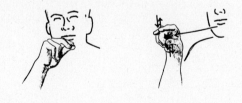

[T–68]

TELLTALE 2, *n.* (Words shooting out from the mouth.) The right "S" hand is held palm out before the mouth, with the knuckle of the index finger touching the lips. From this position the hand moves forward, away from the mouth. At the same time the index finger straightens and points forward. *Cf.* TATTLE 2, TATTLETALE 2.

[T-69]

TEMPERANCE (tĕm' pər əns), *n.* (A middle path.) The little finger edge of the right "5" hand is brought down repeatedly between the middle and third fingers of the left "5" hand, which is facing the body. Both open hands, held about a foot apart with palms facing and fingers pointing straight out, then move forward simultaneously, tracing a slightly curved path.

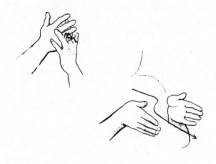

[T-70]

TEMPERATE (tĕm' pər ĭt), *adj.* (In between.) The little finger edge of the right "5" hand is placed between the thumb and index finger of the left "C" hand, whose palm faces the body. The right hand moves back and forth.

[T-71]

TEMPERATURE (tĕm' pər ə chər, -prə chər), *n.* (The rise and fall of the mercury in the thermometer.) The index finger of the right "D" hand, pointing left, moves slowly up and down the index finger of the left "D" hand, which is held pointing up. *Cf.* FEVER, THERMOMETER.

[T-72]

TEMPLE (tĕm' pəl), *n.* (The letter "T"; an establishment, *i.e.,* something placed upon a foundation.) The base of the right "T" hand comes down against the back of the downturned left "S" hand. The action is repeated.

[T-73]

TEMPT (tĕmpt), *v.,* TEMPTED, TEMPTING. (Tapping one surreptitiously at a concealed place.) With the left arm held palm down before the chest, the curved right index finger taps the left elbow a number of times. *Cf.* ENTICE, TEMPTATION.

[T-74]

TEMPTATION (tĕmp tā' shən), *n.* See TEMPT.

[T-75]

TEN (tĕn), *adj.* (Five over five.) The right "A" hand, thumb pointing straight up and palm facing left, pivots over a bit, in a clockwise direction.

[T-76]

TEND (tĕnd), *v.,* TENDED, TENDING. (The feelings of the heart move toward a specific object.) The tip of the right middle finger touches the heart. The open right hand, palm facing the body, then moves away from the heart toward the palm of the open left hand. *Cf.* DISPOSE, DISPOSED TO, DISPOSITION, INCLINATION, INCLINE, INCLINED, TENDENCY.

[T-77]

TENDENCY (tĕn′ dən sĭ), *n.* See TEND.

[T-78]

TENDER 1 (tĕn′ dər), *adj.* (Squeezing for softness.) The hands slowly and deliberately squeeze an imaginary object or substance. *Cf.* RIPE, SOFT.

[T-79]

TENDER 2, *v.,* -DERED, -DERING. (An offering; a presenting.) Both hands, slightly cupped, palms up, are held close to the chest. They move up and out in unison, describing a very slight arc. *Cf.* BID 2, MOTION 1, OFFER 1, OFFERING 1, PRESENT 1, PROPOSE, SUGGEST.

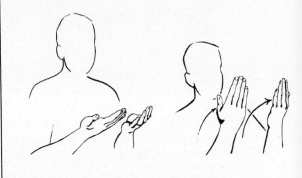

[T-80]

TENDER 3, *adj.* (The heart rolls out.) Both right-angle hands roll over each other as they move down and away from their initial position at the heart. *Cf.* BENEVOLENT, GENEROUS 1, GENTLE 1, GENTLENESS, GRACIOUS, HUMANE, KIND 1, KINDNESS, MERCY 1.

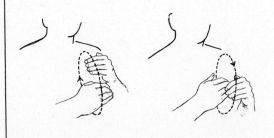

[T-81]

TENNIS (tĕn′ ĭs), *n.* (The natural sign.) The signer goes through the action of striking a ball a number of times with a tennis racquet. The ball is struck in a left-right-left manner, to illustrate the back-and-forth action of the ball.

[T–82]

TENT (tĕnt), *n.* (The sloping shape.) The tips of the index and middle fingers of both "V" hands are placed in contact. The hands move down, separating as they do. This describes the slanting top of a tent.

[T–83]

TERMINATE (tûr' mə nāt'), *v.*, -NATED, -NATING. (Bring to an end.) The left hand, fingers together and pointing forward, is held palm facing right. The right, palm down, fingers also together, moves along the top of the left, goes over the tip of the left index finger, and drops straight down, indicating a cutting off or a finishing. This sign is also used to indicate the past tense of a verb, in the sense of terminating an action or state of being. *Cf.* ACCOMPLISH 2, ACHIEVE 2, COMPLETE 1, CONCLUDE, DONE 1, END 4, EXPIRE 1, FINISH 1, HAVE 2.

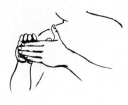

[T–84]

TERRIBLE (tĕr' ə bəl), *adj.* (Throwing out the hands.) Both hands, their fingertips touching their respective thumbs, are held, palms facing each other, near the temples. They are thrown out before the face, assuming "5" positions, palms still facing. *Cf.*

AWFUL, CALAMITOUS, CATASTROPHIC, DANGER 1, DANGEROUS 1, DREADFUL, FEARFUL, TRAGEDY, TRAGIC.

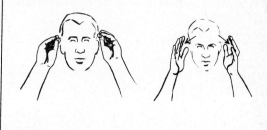

[T–85]

TERROR 1 (tĕr' ər), *n.* (The heart is suddenly covered with fear.) Both hands, fingers together, are placed side by side, palms facing the chest. They quickly open and come together over the heart, one on top of the other. *Cf.* AFRAID, COWARD, FEAR 1, FRIGHT, FRIGHTEN, SCARE(D).

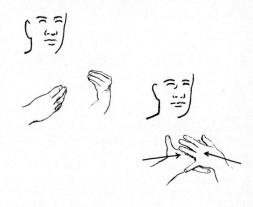

[T–86]

TERROR 2, *n.* (The hands attempt to ward off something which causes fear.) The "5" hands, right behind left, move downward before the body, in a wavy motion. *Cf.* DREAD, FEAR 2, TIMID.

[T–87]

TERTIARY 1 (tûr′ shĭ ĕr′ ĭ, tûr′ shə rĭ), *adj., n.* (The third finger is indicated.) The right index finger touches and twists on the tip of the left middle finger. *Cf.* THIRD 1.

[T–88]

TERTIARY 2, *adj., n.* (The "3" sign is emphasized.) The right "3" hand is pivoted a bit to the left. *Cf.* THIRD 2.

[T–89]

TEST (tĕst), *n., v.,* TESTED, TESTING. (A series of questions, spread out on a page.) Both "D" hands, palms down, simultaneously execute a single circle, the right hand moving in a clockwise direction and the left in a counterclockwise direction. Upon completion of the circle, both hands open into the "5" position and move straight down a short distance. (The hands actually draw question marks in the air.) *Cf.* EXAMINATION 1, QUIZ 1.

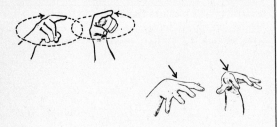

[T–90]

TESTAMENT 1 (tĕs′ tə mənt), *n.* (Literally: Jesus, book.) The sign for JESUS is made: The left middle finger touches the right palm, and then the right middle finger touches the left palm (the crucifixion marks). The sign for BOOK, is then made: The open hands are held together, fingers pointing away from the body. They open with little fingers remaining in contact, as in the opening of a book. This BIBLE sign signifies the Christian Bible. *Cf.* BIBLE 1.

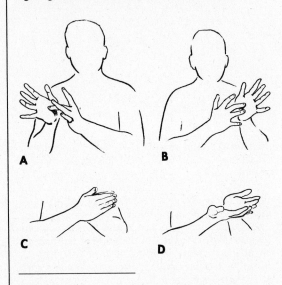

[T–91]

TESTAMENT 2, *n.* (Literally: Holy, book.) The right "H" hand makes a clockwise circular movement, and is then opened and wiped across the open left palm (something nice or clean with an "H," *i.e.,* HOLY). The sign for BOOK, as in TESTAMENT 1, is then made. This sign may be used by all religious faiths. *Cf.* BIBLE 2.

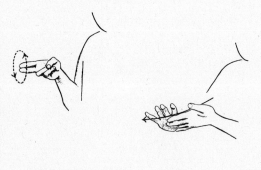

[T–92]

TESTAMENT 3, *n.* (Literally: Jewish book; the Old Testament.) The sign for JEW is formed: The fingers and thumb of each hand are placed at the chin, and stroke an imaginary beard, as worn by the old Jewish patriarchs or Orthodox rabbis. The sign for BOOK, as in TESTAMENT 1, is then made. This sign is used by the Jews. *Cf.* BIBLE 3, HEBREW BIBLE, HOLY SCRIPTURE, JEWISH BIBLE.

[T–93]

TESTIMONY (tĕs′ tə mō´ nĭ), *n.* (A gesture of an orator.) The right open hand, palm facing left, is held above and to the right of the head. It pivots on the wrist, forward and backward, several times. *Cf.* ADDRESS 1, LECTURE, ORATE, SPEECH 2, TALK 2.

[T–94]

TEXAS (tĕk′ səs), *(loc.), n.* (The "X" finger, part of the word. Also the stooped position of a very tall person—Texans are supposed to be tall.) The right "X" hand is held in front of the head. It is moved to the right a bit and then dropped downward.

[T–95]

TEXTBOOK (tĕkst′ boŏk´), *n.* (Opening a book.) The open hands are held together, fingers pointing

away from the body. They open with little fingers remaining in contact, as in the opening of a book. *Cf.* BOOK, VOLUME.

[T–96]

THAN (ᵺan, *unstressed* ᵺən), *conj.* The right prone hand is brought down against the left prone hand, so that its fingertips strike the back of the hand. The right hand then continues its downward movement a few inches.

[T–97]

THANKS (thăngks), *n. pl., interj.* See THANK YOU.

[T–98]

THANKSGIVING (thăngks´ gĭv´ ĭng), *n.* (An offering of thanks.) The sign for THANK YOU is made, but without the smile and nod. Both upturned open hands then move upward simultaneously, with the signer looking up.

[T–99]

THANK YOU, *phrase.* (Words extended politely from the mouth.) The fingertips of the right "5" hand are placed at the mouth. The hand moves away from the mouth to a palm-up position before the body. The signer meanwhile usually nods smilingly. *Cf.* FAREWELL 1, GOODBYE 1, HELLO 1, THANKS, YOU'RE WELCOME 1.

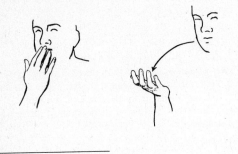

[T–100]

THAT 1 (*that, unstressed* thət), *pron.* (Something specific.) The downturned right "Y" hand is placed on the upturned left palm. *Cf.* IT 2, THESE, THIS, THOSE, WHICH 2.

[T–101]

THAT 2, *pron.* (Indicating a specific item.) The right index finger touches the tip of the index finger of the left "L" hand, which is held thumb pointing up and palm facing right.

[T–102]

THAT 3, *pron.* (The concept of alternateness, *i.e.,* "this or *that.*") The extended right index finger

touches the tip of its left counterpart, and then moves over to the extended left thumbtip, describing a small arc as it does so.

[T–103]

THAT'S IT, *(colloq.), phrase.* (The up-down motion represents the nodding of the head in sudden recognition.) The right "Y" hand moves up and down a number of times. The signer usually nods slightly, keeping time with the hand. The mouth may be held open a little, and the eyes are usually wide open, as if in surprise. *Cf.* I SEE; OH, I SEE.

[T–104]

THE (thē, *unstressed* thə *or* thi), *def. art., (rare).* (Pointing to something specific.) The right index finger points at an imaginary object.

[T–105]

THEATRE (thē' ə tər), *n.* (A house of drama.) The sign for DRAMA is made: Both "A" hands, palms out, are held at shoulder height and rotate alternately toward the head. This is followed by the sign for HOUSE: The hands, forming a pyramid a bit above eye level, move down as they separate, and then continue straight down a few inches. This movement traces the outlines of a roof and walls.

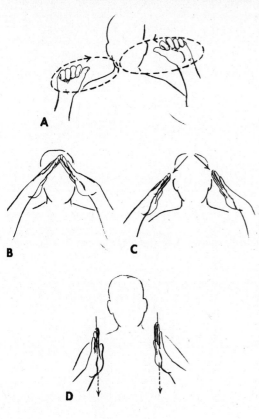

A

B   **C**

D

[T-106]

THEE (t͟hē), *(eccles.), pron.* (Indicating God.) The signer points his extended index finger upward before the face. *Cf.* THOU.

[T-107]

THEFT 1 (thĕft), *n.* (The hand, partly concealed, takes something surreptitiously.) The index and middle fingers of the right hand, somewhat curved, are placed under the left elbow. As they move slowly along the left forearm toward the left wrist, they close a bit. *Cf.* ABDUCT, EMBEZZLE, EMBEZZLE-MENT, KIDNAP, ROB 1, ROBBERY 1, STEAL 1, SWIPE, THIEF 1, THIEVERY.

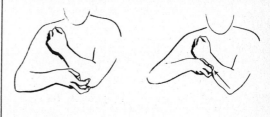

[T-108]

THEFT 2, *(colloq.), n.* (A sly, underhanded movement.) The right open hand, palm down, is held a bit behind the body at waist level. Beginning with the little finger, the hand closes finger by finger into the "A" position, as if wrapping itself around something. *Cf.* ROB 2, ROBBERY 1, STEAL 2.

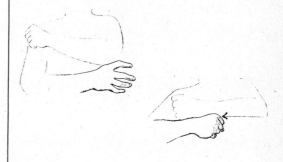

[T-109]

THEFT 3, *n.* (A mustachioed thief.) The fingertips of both "H" hands, palms facing the body, are placed above the lips and are drawn slowly apart, describing a mustache. Sometimes one hand only is used. *Cf.* BANDIT, BURGLAR, BURGLARY, CROOK, ROB 3, ROBBER 1, STEAL 3, THIEF 2.

[T-110]

THEIR(S) (*th̯âr*, *unstressed th̯ər*), *pron.* (Belonging to; pushed toward.) The open right hand, palm facing out and fingers together and pointing up, moves out a short distance from the body. This is repeated several times, with the hand moving an inch or two toward the right each time. The hand may also be swept in a short left-to-right arc in this position.

[T-111]

THEM (*th̯ĕm*, *unstressed th̯əm*), *pron.* (The natural sign.) The right index finger points in turn to a number of imaginary persons or objects. *Cf.* THEY.

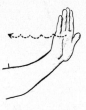

[T-112]

THEME (*th̯ēm*), *n.* (The quotation marks are indicated.) The curved index and middle fingers of both hands, held palms out, move slightly to either side of the body, as if drawing quotation marks in the air. *Cf.* CAPTION, CITE, QUOTATION, QUOTE, SO-CALLED, SUBJECT, TITLE, TOPIC.

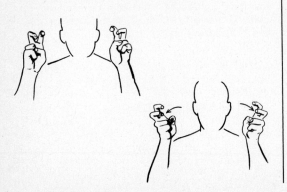

[T-113]

THEMSELVES (*th̯əm sĕlvz'*), *pron. pl.* (The thumb indicates an individual, *i.e.,* a *self;* several are indicated.) The right hand, in the "A" position with thumb pointing up, makes a series of short forward movements as it sweeps either from right to left, or from left to right.

[T-114]

THEN 1 (*th̯ĕn*), *adv.* (Going from one specific point in time to another.) The left "L" hand is held palm facing right and thumb pointing left. The right index finger, positioned behind the left thumb, moves in an arc over the left thumb and comes to rest on the tip of the left index finger.

[T-115]

THEN 2, *adv.* (Same basic rationale as for THEN 1, but modified to incorporate the concept of nearness, *i.e.,* NEXT. The sign, then, is "one point [in time] to the next.") The left hand is held as in THEN 1. The extended right index finger rests on the ball of the thumb. The right hand then opens and arcs over, coming to rest on the back of the left hand, whose index finger has now closed.

[T-116]

THENCE (ŧhĕns), *adv.* The index finger of the right hand is placed across the index finger of the left "L" hand. The right hand then flips over, around the tip of the left index finger and up against its underside. *Cf.* NEXT 1, SERIES.

[T-117]

THENCEFORTH (ŧhĕns´ fōrth´, ŧhĕns´ fōrth´), *adv.* (From a point forward.) The right-angle hands are held before the chest, palms facing the body, the right hand resting against the back of the left. The right hand moves straight forward several inches. *Cf.* FROM THEN ON.

[T-118]

THEORY (thē´ ə rĭ, thĭr´ ĭ), *n.* (A thought coming forward from the mind, modified by the letter "I"for "idea.") With the "I" position on the right hand, palm facing the body, touch the little finger to the forehead, and then move the hand up and away in a circular, clockwise motion. The hand may also be moved up and away without this circular motion. The "T" hand may be substituted. *Cf.* CONCEIVE 2, CONCEPT 1, CONCEPTION, FANCY 2, IDEA, IMAGINATION, IMAGINE 1, JUST THINK OF IT!, NOTION, POLICY 2, THOUGHT 2.

[T-119]

THERE 1 (ŧhâr), *adv.* (The natural sign.) The right index finger points to an imaginary object, usually at or slightly above eye level, *i.e.*, "yonder."

[T-120]

THERE 2, *adv.* (Something brought to the attention.) The right hand is brought forward, simultaneously opening into the palm-up position.

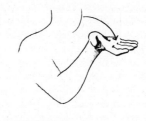

[T-121]

THEREFORE 1 (ŧhâr´ fōr´), *adv.* (In proportion.) Both "D" or "P" hands, palms facing down, are held before the body. They describe a short arc from right to left and, while unnecessary, they may return to their original position. *Cf.* HENCE, PROPORTION, RATIO, THUS.

[T-122]

THEREFORE 2, *adv.* (The mathematical symbol.) The index finger describes three dots in the air, in pyramidal arrangement. This is used in the mathematical context.

[T-123]

THEREFORE 3, *adv.* (A natural sign.) Both hands simultaneously open into a supine position on either side of the body. As they do so, the head nods slightly and the shoulders sink slightly.

[T-124]

THERMOMETER (thər mŏm′ ə tər), *n.* (The rise and fall of the mercury in the thermometer.) The index finger of the right "D" hand, pointing left, moves slowly up and down the index finger of the left "D" hand, which is held pointing up. *Cf.* FEVER, TEMPERATURE.

[T-125]

THESE (*ŧ*hēz), *pron., adj.* (Something specific.) The downturned right "Y" hand is placed on the upturned left palm. *Cf.* IT 2, THAT 1, THIS, THOSE, WHICH 2.

[T-126]

THEY (*ŧ*hā), *pron.* (The natural sign.) The right index finger points in turn to a number of imaginary persons or objects. *Cf.* THEM.

[T-127]

THICK (thĭk), *adj.* (A thickness is indicated.) The curved right thumb and index finger indicate a thickness. *Cf.* THICKNESS.

[T-128]

THICKNESS (thĭk′ nĭs), *n.* The sign for THICK is made. This is followed by the sign for -NESS: The downturned right "N" hand moves down along the left palm, which is facing away from the body.

[T-129]

THICK-SKULLED, *(colloq.), adj.* (The thickness of the skull is indicated, to stress intellectual density.) With the thumb of the right "C" hand grasped by the closed left hand, the right hand is swung in toward the body, describing a small arc as it moves. The space between the curved right fingers and the closed left hand indicates the thickness of the skull. *Cf.* CLUMSY 2, DUMB 2, MORON, STUPID 2, UNSKILLED.

[T-130]

THIEF 1 (thēf), *n.* (The hand, partly concealed, takes something surreptitiously.) The index and middle fingers of the right hand, somewhat curved, are placed under the left elbow. As they move slowly along the left forearm toward the left wrist, they close a bit. This is followed by INDIVIDUAL, as in THIEF 2. *Cf.* ABDUCT, EMBEZZLE, EMBEZZLE-MENT, KIDNAP, ROB 1, ROBBERY 1, STEAL 1, SWIPE, THEFT 1, THIEVERY.

[T-131]

THIEF 2, *n.* (A mustachioed thief.) The fingertips of both "H" hands, palms facing the body, are placed above the lips and are drawn slowly apart, describing a mustache. Sometimes one hand only is used. This is followed by the sign for INDIVIDUAL: Both open hands, palms facing each other, move down the sides of the body, tracing its outline to the hips. *Cf.* BANDIT, BURGLAR, BURGLARY, CROOK, ROB 3, ROBBER 1, STEAL 3, THEFT 3.

[T-132]

THIEVERY (thē′və rĭ), *n.* See THIEF 1 or 2.

[T-133]

THIMBLE (thĭm′ bəl), *n.* (The natural sign.) An imaginary thimble is placed on the middle finger.

[T-134]

THIN 1 (thĭn), *adj.* (The drawn face.) The thumb and index finger run down the cheeks, which are drawn in. *Cf.* LEAN 1, POOR 2.

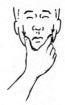

[T-135]

THIN 2, *(sl.), adj.* (A thin, tapering object is described with the little fingers, the thinnest of all.) The tips of the little fingers, touching, one above the other, are drawn apart. The cheeks may also be drawn in for emphasis. *Cf.* BEANPOLE, SKINNY.

[T-136]

THINE (th̄in), *(eccles.), pron.* (The natural sign.) The right "5" hand, palm facing up, moves upward. The signer also looks upward.

[T–137]

THING (thǐng), *n.* (Something shown in the hand.) The outstretched right hand, palm up and held before the chest, is dropped slightly and brought over a bit to the right. *Cf.* ANYTHING, APPARATUS, INSTRUMENT, MATTER, OBJECT 1, SUBSTANCE 1.

[T–138]

THINK (thǐngk), *v.,* THOUGHT, THINKING. (A thought is turned over in the mind.) The index finger makes a small circle on the forehead. *Cf.* CONSIDER 1, MOTIVE 1, RECKON, SPECULATE 1, SPECULATION 1, THOUGHT 1, THOUGHTFUL.

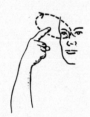

[T–139]

THIRD 1 (thûrd), *adj.* (The third finger is indicated.) The right index finger touches and twists on the tip of the left middle finger. *Cf.* TERTIARY 1.

[T–140]

THIRD 2, *adj.* (The "3" sign is emphasized.) The right "3" hand is pivoted a bit to the left. *Cf.* TERTIARY 2.

[T–141]

THIRD 3, *adj.* (The fraction ⅓.) After making the "1" sign, the right hand is dropped a bit and changes to the "3" sign. *Cf.* ONE-THIRD.

[T–142]

THIRST (thûrst), *n.* (The parched throat.) The index finger moves down the throat a short distance. *Cf.* SWALLOW 1, THIRSTY.

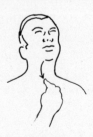

[T–143]

THIRSTY (thûrs' tǐ), *adj.* See THIRST.

[T–144]

THIRTY (thûr' tǐ), *adj.* (Three and zero.) The right "3" hand moves slightly to the right, closing into a modified "0" position.

[T–145]

THIS (*th*is), *pron., adj.* (Something specific.) The downturned right "Y" hand is placed on the upturned left palm. *Cf.* IT 2, THAT 1, THESE, THOSE, WHICH 2.

[T–146]

THIS MONTH, *phrase.* (Now, month.) The sign for NOW is made: The upturned right-angle hands drop down rather sharply. The "Y" hands may also be used. This is followed by the sign for MONTH: The extended right index finger moves down along the upturned, extended left index finger. The two signs are sometimes given in reverse order.

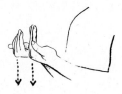

[T–147]

THORN (thôrn), *n.* (The natural motion of the pricking of a thorn, its removal, and the rubbing of the wound.) The right index finger, representing a thorn, jabs into the back of the prone left hand. It

then moves away quickly, as in a sudden extraction, and finally the right fingertips rub the back of the left hand in a circular fashion.

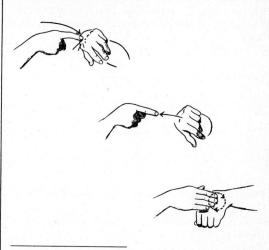

[T–148]

THOSE (*th*ōz), *pron., adj.* (Something specific.) The downturned right "Y" hand is placed on the upturned left palm. *Cf.* IT 2, THAT 1, THESE, THIS, WHICH 2.

[T–149]

THOU (*th*ou), *(eccles.), pron.* (Indicating God.) The signer points his extended index finger upward before the face. *Cf.* THEE.

[T-150]

THOUGHT 1 (thôt), *n*. (A thought is turned over in the mind.) The index finger makes a small circle on the forehead. *Cf*. CONSIDER 1, MOTIVE 1, RECKON, SPECULATE 1, SPECULATION 1, THINK, THOUGHT-FUL.

[T-151]

THOUGHT 2, *n*. (A thought coming forward from the mind, modified by the letter "I" for "idea.") With the "I" position on the right hand, palm facing the body, touch the little finger to the forehead, and then move the hand up and away in a circular, clockwise motion. The hand may also be moved up and away without this circular motion *Cf*. CONCEIVE 2, CONCEPT 1, CONCEPTION, FANCY 2, IDEA, IMAGINATION, IMAGINE 1, JUST THINK OF IT!, NOTION, POLICY 2, THEORY.

[T-152]

THOUGHTFUL (thôt′ fəl), *adj*. See THOUGHT 1.

[T-153]

THOUGHTLESS (thôt′ lĭs), *adj*. (The vision is sidetracked, causing one to lose sight of the object in view.) The right "V" hand, representing the vision, is held in front of the face, palm facing left. The hand, pivoted at the wrist, moves back and forth a number of times. *Cf*. CARELESS, HEEDLESS, RECKLESS.

[T-154]

THOUSAND (thou′ zənd), *n*. ("M" for the Latin *mille*, thousand.) The tips of the right "M" hand are thrust into the upturned left palm.

[T-155]

THREAD (thrĕd), *n*. (Unraveling a thin string, as indicated by the little fingers.) With palms facing the body, the tips of the extended little fingers touch. As they are drawn slowly apart, they describe very small spirals. *Cf*. SPAGHETTI, STRING, TWINE.

[T-156]

THREE (thrē), *adj*. The thumb, index, and middle fingers are held up.

[T-157]

THREE-FOURTHS, *adj*. (The fraction ¾.) After making the "3" sign, the hand drops down a bit as it assumes the "4" position.

[T-158]

THREE OF US, *phrase.* (Three all around.) The right "3" hand, palm facing the body, moves in a half circle from right shoulder to left shoulder.

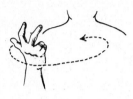

[T-159]

THREE-QUARTERS OF AN HOUR, *phrase.* (Movement of the minute hand of a timepiece.) The left "5" hand, facing right, represents the face of a clock. The extended right index finger, held upright against the left palm, represents the "12" position of the minute hand. The right index finger, always in contact with the left palm, moves in a 270-degree arc to the "9" position on the left palm.

[T-160]

THREE TIMES, *phrase.* (The "3" hand; once up, *i.e.,* thrice.) The middle finger of the right "3" hand rests against the open left palm. The right hand moves up a short distance. *Cf.* THRICE.

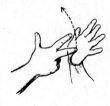

[T-161]

THREE WEEKS, *phrase.* (A combination of "3" and WEEK 2.) The right "3" hand is placed palm-to-

palm against the open left hand, whose fingers point forward in front of the body. The right hand moves forward along the left palm, from its base to its fingertips.

[T-162]

THRICE (thrīs), *adv.* See THREE TIMES.

[T-163]

THRILL 1 (thrĭl), *n., v.,* THRILLED, THRILLING. (The heart beats violently.) Both middle fingers move up alternately to strike the heart sharply. *Cf.* EXCITE, EXCITEMENT, EXCITING.

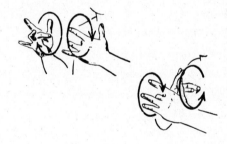

[T-164]

THRILL 2, *(colloq.), n., v.* (The feelings well up and come out.) The open hands are placed near the chest, with middle fingers resting on the chest. Both hands move up and out simultaneously. A happy expression is assumed. *Cf.* WHAT'S NEW?, WHAT'S UP?

[T-165]

THROB (thrŏb), *n., v.,* THROBBED, THROBBING. (The pounding.) The sign for HURT is made: The "D" hands, index fingers pointing to each other, are rotated in elliptical fashion before the chest—simultaneously but in opposite directions. The knuckles of the right fist are then thrust rhythmically into the open left hand a number of times.

[T-166]

THROUGH (thrōō), *adv., prep., adj.* (The natural movement.) The open right hand is pushed between either the middle and index or the middle and third fingers of the open left hand.

[T-167]

THROW 1 (thrō), *v.,* THREW, THROWN, THROWING, *n.* (The natural sign.) The signer goes through the natural motions of throwing a ball. *Cf.* PITCH.

[T-168]

THROW 2, *v.* (The natural movement.) The right "S" hand is thrown forward and up a bit, as it opens into the "5" position. *Cf.* TOSS.

[T-169]

THROW 3, *(sports), v.* (Pinning one's opponent in wrestling.) Both "A" or "S" hands, extended before the body, palms facing each other or held slightly to the side, move down forcefully an inch or two, as if grasping someone by the ankles and forcing his shoulders to touch the ground. *Cf.* PIN 3.

[T-170]

THROW(N) OUT, *phrase.* (Represents a striking as in a vehicular accident, and the hurtling of the human body. This sign is used only in describing this type of occurrence.) The right fist strikes the palm of the open left hand. The right "V" hand, palm facing the body, then spirals upward, to represent the body hurtling up feet first.

[T–171]

THUMB (thŭm), *n.* (The natural indication of the thumb.) The extended thumb is held up.

[T–172]

THUNDER (thŭn′ dər), *n.* (A shaking which disturbs the ear.) After placing the index finger on the ear, both hands assume the "S" position, palms down. They move alternately back and forth, forcefully. *Cf.* DIN, NOISE, NOISY, RACKET, SOUND, VIBRATION.

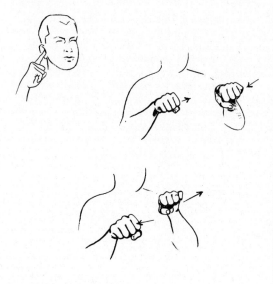

[T–173]

THURSDAY (thûrz′ dĭ), *n.* (The "H," from Thursday, is indicated.) The "H" hand, palm facing out from the body, is rotated clockwise. The "T" and "H" may also be used, with or without the rotation.

[T–174]

THUS (thŭs), *adv.* (In proportion.) Both "D" or "P" hands, palms facing down, are held before the body. They describe a short arc from right to left and, while unnecessary, they may return to their original position. *Cf.* HENCE, PROPORTION, RATIO, THEREFORE 1.

[T–175]

THUS FAR, *adv. phrase.* (From a point up and over.) In the "D" position, palms down, both index fingers touch the right shoulder and then are brought up and over, ending in a palm-up position, pointing straight ahead of the body. *Cf.* ALL ALONG, ALL THE TIME, EVER SINCE, SINCE, SO FAR.

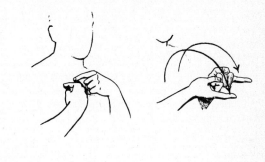

[T–176]

TICKET 1 (tĭk′ ĭt), *n.* (The natural sign.) The sides of the ticket are outlined with the thumb and index finger of each hand. *Cf.* CARD.

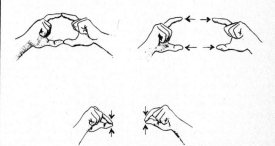

[T–177]

TICKET 2, *n.* (A baggage check or ticket.) The sign for TICKET 1 is made. Then the middle knuckles of the second and third fingers of the right hand squeeze the outer edge of the left palm, as a conductor's ticket punch. *Cf.* CHECK 4.

[T–178]

TIDINGS (tī′ dĭngz), *n. pl.* (Turning over a new leaf.) With both hands held palm up before the body, the right hand sweeps in an arc into the left, and continues up a bit. *Cf.* NEW, NEWS, NOVELTY, ORIGINAL 2.

[T–179]

TIE 1 (tī), *v.,* TIED, TYING. (The act of tying.) Both hands, in the "A" position, go through the natural hand-over-hand motions of tying and drawing out a knot. *Cf.* BIND, FASTEN, KNOT.

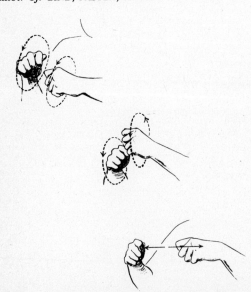

[T–180]

TIE 2, *n.* (The natural motion.) The "H" hands go through the natural hand-over-hand motions of tying a knot in a necktie at the throat. The right "H" hand then moves down the front of the chest to indicate the fall of the tie. *Cf.* NECKTIE.

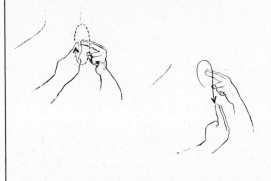

[T–181]

TIGER (tī′ gər), *n,* (A striped cat.) The sign for CAT is made: The thumbs and index fingers of both hands stroke an imaginary pair of whiskers at either side of the face. The right thumb and index finger, held an inch apart, then trace a series of stripes down the chest, moving left with each stripe. Both hands may also be used, moving either toward or away from each other with each successive stripe. The bent fingers of both hands may also trace stripes across the face, from the edges of the mouth to the ears. The stripes on the chest are then omitted.

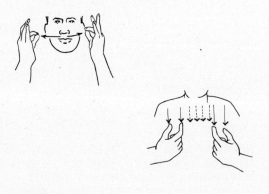

[T–182]

TIGHTWAD 1 (tīt′ wŏd′), *n.* (Pulling things toward oneself.) Both prone open or "V" hands are held in front of the body with fingers bent. The hands are then drawn quickly and forcefully inward, as if raking things toward oneself. *Cf.* GREEDY 1, SELFISH 1, STINGY 1.

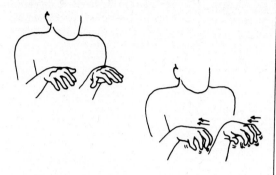

[T–183]

TIGHTWAD 2, *n.* (Scratching the palm in greed.) The right fingers scratch the upturned left palm several times. A frowning expression is often used. *Cf.* AVARICIOUS, GREEDY 2, SELFISH 2, STINGY 2.

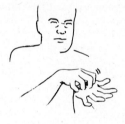

[T–184]

TIGHTWAD 3, *(colloq.), n.* (Holding tightly to money.) The "S" hand, tightly clenched, is held up, and trembles a bit. A frowning expression is frequently assumed for emphasis.

[T–185]

TILL (tĭl), *prep.* (From one point to the next.) The extended right index finger moves forward slowly and comes to rest on the tip of the extended, up-

turned left index finger. *Cf.* TO 1, TOWARD 1, UNTIL, UNTO, UP TO, UP TO NOW.

[T–186]

TIME 1 (tīm), *n.* (Time by the clock, indicated by the ticking of the clock or watch.) The curved right index finger taps the back of the left wrist several times. *Cf.* CLOCK, WATCH 3.

[T–187]

TIME 2, *n.* (Time in the abstract, indicated by the rotating of the "T" hand on the face of a clock.) The right "T" hand is placed palm to palm in the open left hand. It describes a clockwise circle and comes to rest again in the left palm. *Cf.* AGE 2, EPOCH, ERA, PERIOD 2, SEASON.

[T–188]

TIME 3, *(sports), n.* (The gesture employed in sports.) The fingertips of the right hand, pointing up, are thrust into the open left hand, whose palm is facing down. A "T" is thus formed. This movement may be repeated. *Cf.* TIME OUT.

[T-189]

TIME 4, *n.* Both hands, slightly cupped, palms up, are held close to the chest. They move up and out in unison, describing an arc. *Cf.* OCCASION, OPPORTUNITY 1.

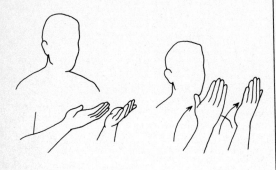

[T-190]

TIME OUT, *(sports), phrase.* See TIME 3.

[T-191]

TIMES (tīmz), *n. pl.* (A multiplying.) The "D" or "V" hands, palms facing the body, alternately cross and separate, several times.

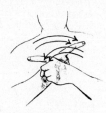

[T-192]

TIMID (tĭm'ĭd), *adj.* (The hands attempt to ward off something which causes fear.) The "5" hands, right behind left, move downward before the body, in a wavy motion. *Cf.* DREAD, FEAR 2, TERROR 2.

[T-193]

TIN (tĭn), *n.* (A hard, yet flexible, substance.) The back of the right "S" hand strikes under the chin. Then the fingers of the right hand grasp the end of the open left hand and turn it downward, as if bending tin.

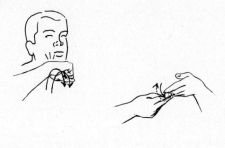

[T-194]

TINY 1 (tī'ni), *adj.* (A small or tiny movement.) The right thumbtip is flicked off the index finger several times, as if shooting marbles, although the movement is not so pronounced. *Cf.* LITTLE 2, MINUTE 2.

[T-195]

TINY 2, *adj.* (Indicating a small mass.) The extended right thumb and index finger are held slightly spread. They are then moved slowly toward each other until they almost touch. *Cf.* PETTY, SLIGHT, SMALL 1.

[T-196]

TIP (tĭp), *n., v.,* TIPPED, TIPPING. (A tapering or sharp point is indicated.) The index finger and thumb of the left hand grasp the tip of the index finger of the right "D" hand. The left hand then moves away a short distance, and its index finger and thumb come together. *Cf.* POINT 2, SHARP 2.

[T–197]

TIP OFF, *(sl.)*, *v. phrase*. (A word escapes from the mouth.) The base of the "S" hand rests against the lips. The index finger suddenly flicks out, as the hand jumps away from the mouth and to the side an inch or two. *Cf.* SQUEAL.

[T–198]

TIRE (tīr), *v.*, TIRED, TIRING. (The hands collapse in exhaustion.) Both "C" hands are placed either on the lower chest or at the waist. The palms face the body. They fall away into a palms-up position. At the same time, the shoulders suddenly sag in a very pronounced fashion. An expression of weariness may be used for emphasis. *Cf.* DISCOURAGE 2, EXHAUST, FATIGUE, TIRED, WEARY.

[T–199]

TIRED (tīrd), *adj.* See TIRE.

[T–200]

TITHE (tīth), *(eccles.)*, *n.*, *v.*, TITHED, TITHING. (One-tenth.) The "1" hand is held upright, and drops down as it forms a "10."

[T–201]

TITLE (tī' təl), *n.* (The quotation marks are indicated.) The curved index and middle fingers of both hands, held palms out, move slightly to either side of the body, as if drawing quotation marks in the air. *Cf.* CAPTION, CITE, QUOTATION, QUOTE, SO-CALLED, SUBJECT, THEME, TOPIC.

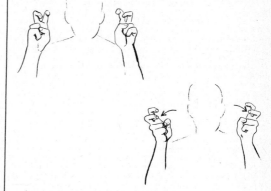

[T–202]

TO 1 (too), *prep.* (From one point to the next.) The extended right index finger moves forward slowly and comes to rest on the tip of the extended, up-turned left index finger. This sign should never be used for an infinitive; it is simply omitted in that case. *Cf.* TILL, TOWARD 1, UNTIL, UNTO, UP TO, UP TO NOW.

[T–203]

TO 2, *prep.* (The thoughts are directed outward, toward a specific goal or purpose.) The right index finger, resting on the right temple, leaves its position and moves straight out in front of the face. *Cf.* FOR 1, TOWARD 3.

[T–204]

TOAST 1 (tōst), *n., v.,* TOASTED, TOASTING. (The fork is thrust into each side of the toast, to turn it around.) With the left hand held upright, the tips of the right "V" fingers are thrust into the open left palm and then into the back of the same hand.

[T–205]

TOAST 2, *n., v.* (Bringing the glasses together.) Both hands, holding imaginary glasses, come together knuckle-to-knuckle, with a flourish.

[T–206]

TOBACCO (tə băk′ ō), *n.* (Chewing tobacco.) Three or four fingertips of the right hand rest on the right cheek. The hand pivots at the wrist, first one way

and then the other, as if the tobacco is being ground by the teeth.

[T–207]

TODAY (tə dā′), *n.* (Now, day.) The sign for NOW is made: The upturned right-angle hands drop down rather sharply. The "Y" hands may also be used. This is followed by the sign for DAY: The left arm, held horizontally, palm down, represents the horizon. The right elbow rests on the back of the left hand, with the right arm in a perpendicular position. The right "D" hand, palm facing left, moves in an arc to the left until it is just above the left elbow. The two signs may be reversed.

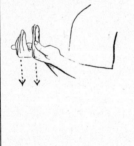

[T–208]

TOE (tō), *n.* (The wiggling and pointing.) The extended thumb is wiggled, and then the signer points to his foot. The signs may also be reversed.

[T–209]

TOGETHER (tŏŏ gĕth′ ər), *adv.* (To go along with.) Both "A" hands, knuckles together and thumbs up, are moved forward in unison, away from the chest. *Cf.* ACCOMPANY, WANDER AROUND WITH, WITH.

[T–210]

TOIL (toil), *n., v.,* TOILED, TOILING. (Striking an anvil.) Both "S" hands are held palms down. The right hand strikes against the back of the left a number of times. *Cf.* JOB, LABOR, OCCUPATION, TASK, TRAVAIL, VOCATION, WORK.

[T–211]

TOILET (toi′ lĭt), *n.* (The letter "T.") The right "T" hand is shaken slightly.

[T–212]

TOLERATE 1 (tŏl′ ə rāt′), *v.,* -ATED, -ATING. (A permissive upswinging of the hands, as if giving in.) Both hands, palms facing and fingers pointing away from the body, are held at chest level, almost a foot apart. With an upward movement, using their wrists as pivots, the hands sweep up until the fingers point almost straight up. *Cf.* ALLOW, GRANT 1, LET, LET'S, LET US, MAY 3, PERMISSION 1, PERMIT 1.

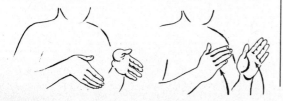

[T–213]

TOLERATE 2, *v.* (A clenching of the fists; the rise and fall of pain.) Both "S" hands, tightly clenched, revolve about each other, slowly and deliberately, while a pained expression is worn. *Cf.* AGONY, BEAR 3, DIFFICULT 3, ENDURE 1, PASSION 2, SUFFER 1.

[T–214]

TOLL (tōl), *n.* (Nicking into one.) The knuckle of the right "X" finger is nicked against the palm of the left hand, held in the "5" position, palm facing right. *Cf.* ADMISSION 2, CHARGE 1, COST, DUTY 2, EXCISE, EXPENSE, FEE, FINE 2, IMPOST, PENALTY 3, PRICE 2, TAX 1, TAXATION 1.

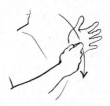

[T–215]

TOMATO 1 (tə mā′ tō), *n.* (The slicing is indicated.) The sign for RED is made: The tip of the right index finger moves down across the lips. The open right hand, palm facing left, is then brought down against the thumb side of the downturned left "S" hand in a slicing movement. This latter movement is repeated a number of times. The slicing may also be done with the index finger.

[T–216]

TOMATO 2, *(rare), n.* (The peeling is indicated.) After the sign for RED is made, as in TOMATO 1, the thumbtip of the right "A" hand is drawn over the back of the left "S" hand a number of times.

[T–217]

TOMORROW (tə môr′ ō, -mŏr′ ō), *n., adv.* (A single step ahead, *i.e.,* into the future.) The thumb of the right "A" hand, placed on the right cheek, moves straight out from the face, describing an arc.

[T–218]

TONGUE (tŭng), *n.* (The natural sign.) The index finger points to the slightly extended tongue.

[T–219]

TONIGHT (tə nīt′), *n.* (Now, night.) The sign for NOW is made: The upturned right-angle hands drop down rather sharply. The "Y" hands may also be used. This is followed by the sign for NIGHT: The left hand, palm down, is positioned at chest height. The downturned right hand, held an inch or so

above the left, moves over the left hand in an arc, as the sun setting beneath the horizon. The two signs may be reversed.

[T–220]

TONSILLECTOMY (tŏn′ sə lĕk′ tə mǐ), *n.* (The extraction is indicated.) The curved "V" fingers, placed close to the open mouth, are drawn up and out. *Cf.* TONSILS.

[T–221]

TONSILS (tŏn′ səls), *n. pl.* See TONSILLECTOMY.

[T–222]

TOO (to͞o), *adv.* (A likeness; a sameness.) Both index fingers, held together at one side of the body near waist level, point forward. As they travel to the other side of the body they separate an inch or two and come together again. *Cf.* ACCORDING (TO), ALSO 1, AS, DUPLICATE 2, SAME AS.

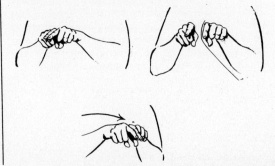

[T-223]

TOOTH (tōōth), *n.* (The natural sign.) The extended index fingertip is tapped against the teeth.

[T-224]

TOOTHACHE (tōōth' āk´), *n.* (A stabbing pain in the tooth.) Both index fingers, positioned at the side of the open mouth, jab toward each other twice. The signer usually assumes a pained expression.

[T-225]

TOOTHBRUSH (tōōth' brŭsh´), *n.* (The natural sign.) The index finger is thrust back and forth in front of the exposed teeth. *Cf.* BRUSH 4.

[T-226]

TOP (tŏp), *n.* (A spinning toy.) One extended index finger points downward and imitates the revolving motion of a top.

[T-227]

TOPIC (tŏp' ĭk), *n.* (The quotation marks are indicated.) The curved index and middle fingers of both hands, held palms out, move slightly to either side of the body, as if drawing quotation marks in the air. *Cf.* CAPTION, CITE, QUOTATION, QUOTE, SO-CALLED, SUBJECT, THEME, TITLE.

[T-228]

TORAH (tōr' ə), *(eccles.)*, *n.* (The opening and holding of the Jewish scroll.) The "S" hands, held a bit above the head, palms facing, are swung around so that the palms now face out. After repeating this movement, the hands and arms assume the natural position of holding a large object to the chest.

[T-229]

TORMENT (*n.* tôr′ mĕnt; *v.* tôr mĕnt′), -MENTED, -MENTING. (Striking against one.) The knuckles of the right "A" hand move sharply forward along the thumb edge of the left "A" hand. *Cf.* PERSE-CUTE, TEASE 1.

[T-230]

TORNADO (tôr nā′ dō), *n.* (The natural sign.) The extended right index finger is held pointing downward in front of the face, while the extended left index finger is held pointing upward toward its right counterpart. In this position both index fingers simultaneously trace small opposing circles before the body. *Cf.* SPIN.

[T-231]

TORTOISE (tôr′ təs), *n.* (The neck.) The downturned left hand is draped over the downturned right "A" hand, whose thumb emerges from under the left hand and wiggles back and forth. *Cf.* TURTLE.

[T-232]

TOSS (tôs, tŏs), *n., v.,* TOSSED, TOSSING. (The natural movement.) The right "S" hand is thrown for-

ward and up a bit, as it opens into the "5" position. *Cf.* THROW 2.

[T-233]

TOTAL (tō′ təl), *adj., n., v.,* -TALED, -TALING. (To bring up all together.) The two open hands, palms and fingers facing each other, with the left hand above the right, are brought together, with all fingers closing simultaneously. This sign is used mainly in the sense of adding up figures or items. *Cf.* ADD 1, ADDITION, AMOUNT 1, SUM, SUMMARIZE 2, SUM-MARY 2, SUM UP.

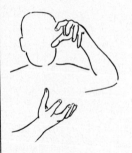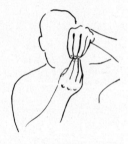

[T-234]

TOUCH (tŭch), *n., v.,* TOUCHED, TOUCHING. (The natural movement of touching.) The tip of the middle finger of the downturned right "5" hand touches the back of the left hand a number of times. *Cf.* CONTACT 1, FEEL 1, TOUCHDOWN.

[T-235]

TOUCHDOWN (tŭch′ doun′), *(sports), n.* See TOUCH.

[T-236]

TOUCHED (tŭcht), *adj.* (A piercing of the heart.) The tip of the middle finger of the right "5" hand is thrust against the heart. The head, at the same time, moves abruptly back a very slight distance. *Cf.* FEEL TOUCHED, TOUCHING.

[T-237]

TOUCHING (toŭch' ing), *adj.* See TOUCHED.

[T-238]

TOUGH 1 (tŭf), *adj.* (Flexing the muscles.) With fists clenched, palms facing back, the signer raises both arms and shakes them once, with force. *Cf.* MIGHT 1, MIGHTY 1, POWER 1, POWERFUL 1, STRONG 1, STURDY.

[T-239]

TOUGH 2, *(sl.)*, *adj.* (A hard heart.) The index fingers trace a heart on the appropriate place on the chest. The knuckles of the downturned right "S" hand then come down sharply against the back of the left "S" hand. *Cf.* HARD-BOILED.

[T-240]

TOUGH 3, *(sl.)*, *adj.* (Striking the chest to indicate toughness, *i.e.*, a "tough guy.") The little finger edge of the upturned right "S" hand strikes the chest repeatedly.

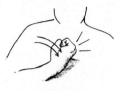

[T-241]

TOW (tō), *n., v.*, TOWED, TOWING. (Hooking on to something and pulling.) With index fingers interlocked, the right hand pulls the left hand from left to right. *Cf.* HITCH, HOOK, PULL 2.

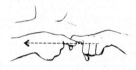

[T-242]

TOWARD 1 (tōrd, tə wôrd'), *prep.* (From one point to the next.) The extended right index finger moves forward slowly and comes to rest on the tip of the extended, upturned left index finger. *Cf.* TILL, TO 1, UNTIL, UNTO, UP TO, UP TO NOW.

[T-243]

TOWARD 2, *prep.* (Coming close to.) Both hands are held in the right angle position, fingers facing each other, with the right hand held between the left hand and the chest. The right hand slowly moves toward the left. *Cf.* APPROACH, NEAR 2.

[T-244]

TOWARD 3, *prep.* (The thoughts are directed outward, toward a specific goal or purpose.) The right index finger, resting on the right temple, leaves its position and moves straight out in front of the face. *Cf.* FOR 1, TO 2.

[T-245]

TOWEL (tou' əl), *n.* (The natural sign.) The signer goes through the motions of wiping his face with a towel. *Cf.* WASH 2.

[T-246]

TOWER (tŏw' ər), *n., v.,* -ERED, -ERING. (The natural sign.) Both "A" or "T" hands are held up, thumb edges facing back toward either temple. From this position both hands move up and toward each other until they meet over the head.

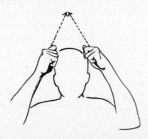

[T-247]

TOWN (toun), *n.* (A collection of rooftops.) The fingertips of both hands are joined, the hands and arms forming a pyramid. The fingertips separate and rejoin a number of times. Both arms may move a bit from left to right each time the fingertips separate and rejoin. *Cf.* CITY, COMMUNITY 2.

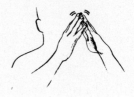

[T-248]

TRACK 1 (trăk), *n.* The extended index and middle fingers of the downturned right hand move back and forth crosswise over the same two fingers of the downturned left hand. Both "G" hands, held side by side, then move forward. *Cf.* RAILROAD TRACK.

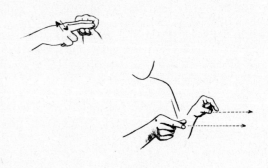

[T-249]

TRACK 2, *n.* (The impressions left by the feet.) The downturned "5" hands move out from the body, alternately and step by step.

[T-250]

TRADE (trād), *n., v.,* TRADED, TRADING. (Exchanging places.) The right "A" hand, positioned above the left "A" hand, swings down and under the left,

coming up a bit in front of it. *Cf.* EXCHANGE, IN-
STEAD OF 1, REPLACE, SUBSTITUTE.

[T–251]

TRADITION (trə dĭsh′ ən), *n.* (The letter "T"; bound
down to habit.) The base of the right "T" hand rests
on the back of the downturned left "T" hand, and
pushes it down an inch or two.

[T–252]

TRAFFIC (trăf′ ĭk), *n.* (The traffic pattern.) The
upright fingers of the "4" hands represent motor or
pedestrian traffic. One hand faces forward, the other
faces the body. The hands pass each other repeatedly
as they move back and forth.

[T–253]

TRAGEDY (trăj′ ə dĭ), *n.* (Throwing out the hands.)
Both hands, their fingertips touching their respective
thumbs, are held, palms facing each other, near the
temples. They are thrown out before the face, assuming "5" positions, palms still facing. *Cf.* AWFUL,
CALAMITOUS, CATASTROPHIC, DANGER 1, DANGER-
OUS 1, DREADFUL, FEARFUL, TERRIBLE, TRAGIC.

[T–254]

TRAGIC (trăj′ ĭk), *adj.* See TRAGEDY.

[T–255]

TRAIL (trāl), *n.* (The winding movement.) Both
hands, palms facing and fingers together and extended straight out, move in unison away from the
body, in a winding manner. *Cf.* CORRIDOR, HALL,
HALLWAY, MANNER 2, METHOD, OPPORTUNITY 3,
PATH, ROAD, STREET, WAY 1.

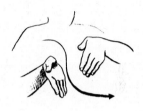

[T–256]

TRAIN 1 (trān), *n.* (Running along the tracks.) The
"V" hands are held palms down. The right "V"
moves back and forth over the left "V." *Cf.* CARS,
RAILROAD 1.

[T–257]

TRAIN 2, *v.,* TRAINED, TRAINING. (Polishing or
sharpening up.) The knuckles of the downturned
right "A" hand are rubbed briskly back and forth
over the side of the hand and index finger of the left
"D" hand. *Cf.* DISCIPLINE 1, DRILL 3, PRACTICE 1,
TRAINING 1.

[T–258]

TRAIN 3, *v.* The same movement as in TRAIN 2 is executed, but the right hand is held in the "T" position instead, for the initial letter in TRAIN. *Cf.* TRAINING 2.

[T–259]

TRAINING 1, *n.* See TRAIN 2.

[T–260]

TRAINING 2, *n.* See TRAIN 3.

[T–261]

TRANSFER 1 (*n.* trăns' fər; *v.* trăns fûr'), -FERRED, -FERRING. (To change positions.) Both "A" hands, thumbs up, are held before the chest, several inches apart. The left hand is pivoted over so that its thumb points to the right. Simultaneously, the right hand is moved up and over the left, describing a small arc, with its thumb pointing to the left. *Cf.* ADJUST, ALTER, ALTERATION, CHANGE 1, CONVERT, MODIFY, REVERSE 2.

[T–262]

TRANSFER 2, *n., v.* (Moving from one place to another.) The downturned hands, fingers touching their respective thumbs, move in unison from left to right. *Cf.* MIGRATE, MOVE, PLACE 3, PUT, REMOVE 2.

[T–263]

TRANSIENT (trăn' shənt), *adj.* A variation of TRAVEL 1 and TRAVEL 2, but using the downturned curved "V" fingers. *Cf.* JOURNEY 3, TRAVEL 3, TRIP 3.

[T–264]

TRANSPORT (*n.* trăns' pōrt; *v.* trăns pōrt'), -PORTED, -PORTING. (Carrying something over.) Both open hands, palms up, move in an arc from left to right, as if carrying something from one point to another. *Cf.* BRING, CARRY 2, DELIVER 2, FETCH, PRODUCE 1.

[T–265]

TRANSPORTATION (trăns' pər tā' shən), *n.* (The natural sign.) The right "A" hand, palm facing left and thumb held straight up, moves back and forth repeatedly from left to right. *Cf.* BACK AND FORTH.

[T–266]

TRAP (trăp), *n., v.*, TRAPPED, TRAPPING. (Impaled on a stick, as a snake's head.) The "V" fingers are thrust into the throat. *Cf.* CAUGHT IN THE ACT 2, CHOKE 2, STRANDED, STUCK 2.

[T-267]

TRAVAIL (trăv′ ăl), *n.* (Striking an anvil.) Both "S" hands are held palms down. The right hand strikes against the back of the left a number of times. *Cf.* JOB, LABOR, OCCUPATION, TASK, TOIL, VOCATION, WORK.

[T-268]

TRAVEL 1 (trăv′ əl), *n., v.,* -ELED, -ELING. (Moving around from place to place.) Both "D" hands are held palms facing, the index fingers pointing to each other. In this position the hands describe a series of small counterclockwise circles as they move in random fashion from right to left. *Cf.* JOURNEY 1, TRIP 1.

[T-269]

TRAVEL 2, *n., v.* A variation of TRAVEL 1, but using only the right hand. *Cf.* JOURNEY 2, TRIP 2.

[T-270]

TRAVEL 3, *n., v.* A variation of TRAVEL 1 and TRAVEL 2, but using the downturned curved "V" fingers. *Cf.* JOURNEY 3, TRANSIENT, TRIP 3.

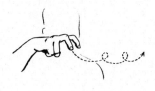

[T-271]

TRAY (trā), *n.* (The shape and function.) The extended index fingers outline the shape of a tray before the body. The signer then makes a motion as if carrying a tray.

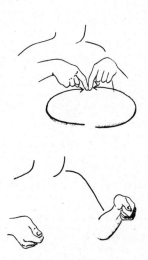

[T-272]

TREASURER (trĕzh′ ər ər), *n*. (A keeper of money.) The sign for MONEY is made: The upturned right hand, grasping some imaginary bills, is brought down into the upturned left palm a number of times. The sign for KEEP is then formed: The "K" hands are crossed, the right above the left, little finger edges down. In this position the hands are moved up and down a short distance. Finally the sign for INDIVIDUAL is made: Both open hands, palms facing each other, move down the sides of the body, tracing its outline to the hips.

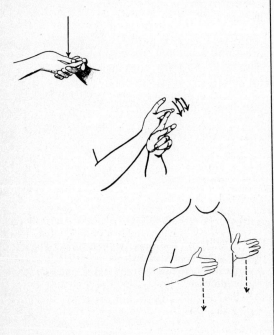

[T-273]

TREE (trē), *n*. (The shape.) The elbow of the upright right arm rests on the palm of the upturned left hand. This is the trunk. The right "5" fingers wiggle to imitate the movement of the branches and leaves. *Cf.* BRANCH.

[T-274]

TRESPASS (trĕs′ pəs), *n., v.,* -PASSED, -PASSING. (An encroachment.) The left "A" hand is held palm toward the body, knuckles facing right. The extended thumb of the right "A" hand is brought sharply over the back of the left. *Cf.* DANGER 2, DANGEROUS 2, INJURE 2, PERIL, VIOLATE.

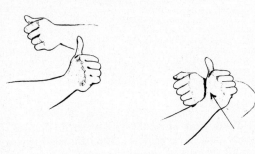

[T-275]

TRIANGLE (trī′ ăng′ gəl), *n*. (The shape.) The index finger traces a triangle in the air. Both index fingers may also be used.

[T-276]

TRICYCLE, (trī′ sĭk əl), *n*. (The motion of the feet on the pedals.) Both hands, in the "S" position, rotate alternately before the chest. *Cf.* BICYCLE, PEDAL.

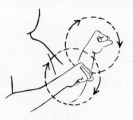

[T-277]

TRIFLING (trī′ flĭng), *adj*. (Thoughts flickering back and forth.) The right "Y" hand, thumb almost touching the forehead, is shaken back and forth across the forehead several times. *Cf.* ABSURD, DAFT, FOLLY, FOOLISH, NONSENSE, RIDICULOUS, SILLY.

[T–278]

TRIGONOMETRY (trĭg′ ə nŏm′ ə trĭ), *n.* (The "T" hands; multiplying or calculating.) The "T" hands, palms facing each other, are crossed at the wrists repeatedly.

[T–279]

TRIM 1 (trĭm), *v.*, TRIMMED, TRIMMING. (The hands describe the flounces of draperies.) Both "C" hands, palms out, are held somewhat above the head. They move out and down in a series of successive arcs. *Cf.* ADORN, DECORATE 1, ORNAMENT 1.

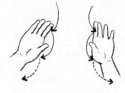

[T–280]

TRIM 2 *v., n., adj.* (Embellishing; adding to.) Both "O" hands, palms facing each other, move alternately back and forth in a curving up-and-down direction. The fingertips come in contact each time

the hands pass each other. *Cf.* DECORATE 2, ORNAMENT 2.

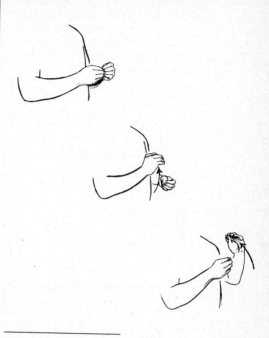

[T–281]

TRINITY (trĭn′ ə tĭ), *(eccles.), n.* (The doctrine of the Trinity; three in one, *i.e.*, the Father, the Son, and the Holy Spirit.) The right "3" hand, palm facing the body, is drawn down through the left "C" hand, palm also facing the body. As the "3" hand disappears into the left hand, its fingers come together, and the left hand assumes the "1" position, palm still facing the body.

[T-282]

TRIP 1 (trĭp), *n.* (Moving around from place to place.) Both "D" hands are held palms facing, the index fingers pointing to each other. In this position the hands describe a series of small counterclockwise circles as they move in random fashion from right to left. *Cf.* JOURNEY 1, TRAVEL 1.

[T-283]

TRIP 2, *n.* A variation of TRIP 1, but using only the right hand. *Cf.* JOURNEY 2, TRAVEL 2.

[T-284]

TRIP 3, *n.* A variation of TRIP 1 and TRIP 2, but using the downturned curved "V" fingers. *Cf.* JOURNEY 3, TRANSIENT, TRAVEL 3.

[T-285]

TRIUMPH 1 (trī' əmf), *n., v.,* -UMPHED, -UMPHING. (Waving a flag.) The right "A" hand goes through the natural movement of waving a flag in circular fashion. Preceding this, the right hand may go

through the motion of grabbing the flagstaff out of the left hand. *Cf.* EXULTATION, VICTORY 2, WIN 2.

[T-286]

TRIUMPH 2, *n.* (Penetrating the heights.) The "D" hands, palms back, are held at each side of the head, near the temples. With a pivoting motion of the wrists, the hands swing up and around, simultaneously, to a position above the head, with palms facing out. *Cf.* ACCOMPLISH 1, ACHIEVE 1, ATTAIN, PROSPER, SUCCEED, SUCCESS, SUCCESSFUL.

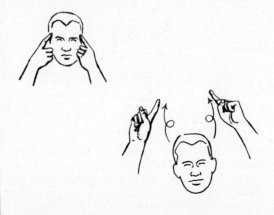

[T-287]

TROLLEY CAR 1 (trŏl' ĭ), *n.* (Running along the overhead cable.) The extended index finger of the downturned left "D" hand represents the overhead cable. The knuckles of the curved right index and middle fingers, grasping the left index finger, move along its length, from base to tip.

[T-288]

TROLLEY CAR 2, *n.* (The overhead cable.) The right "E" hand is drawn along the outstretched left index finger, from its base to its fingertip, as if riding along a cable. This sign is also used for "el," an elevated railway.

[T-289]

TROMBONE (trŏm′ bōn, trŏm bōn′), *n.* (The natural sign.) The signer goes through the natural motions of playing a trombone.

[T-290]

TROUBLE (trŭb′ əl), *n., v.,* -BLED, -BLING. (A clouding over; a troubling.) Both "B" hands, palms facing each other, are rotated alternately before the forehead. *Cf.* ANNOY 2, ANNOYANCE 2, ANXIOUS 2, BOTHER 2, CONCERN 1, FRET, PROBLEM 1, WORRIED, WORRY 1.

[T-291]

TROUSERS (trou′ zərz), *n. pl.* (The natural sign.) The open hands are drawn up along the thighs, starting at the knees. *Cf.* PANTS.

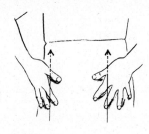

[T-292]

TRUE (trōō), *adj.* (Coming forth directly from the lips; true.) The index finger of the right "D" hand, palm facing left, is placed against the lips. It moves up an inch or two and then describes a small arc forward and away from the lips. *Cf.* ABSOLUTE, ABSOLUTELY, ACTUAL, ACTUALLY, AUTHENTIC, CERTAIN, CERTAINLY, FAITHFUL 3, FIDELITY, FRANKLY, GENUINE, INDEED, POSITIVE 1, POSITIVELY, REAL, REALLY, SINCERE 2, SURE, SURELY, TRULY, TRUTH, VALID, VERILY.

[T-293]

TRULY (trōō′ lĭ), *adv.* See TRUE.

[T-294]

TRUNK (trŭngk), *n.* (The dimensions are indicated.) The open hands, palms facing and fingers pointing out, are dropped an inch or two simultaneously. They then shift their relative positions so that both palms face the body, with one hand in front of the other. In this new position they again drop an inch or two simultaneously. *Cf.* BOX 1, PACKAGE, ROOM 1, SQUARE 1.

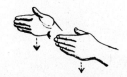

[T–295]

TRUST (trŭst), *n., v.,* TRUSTED, TRUSTING. (Planting a flagpole, *i.e.,* planting one's trust.) The "S" hands grasp and plant an imaginary flagpole in the ground. This sign may be preceded by the extended index finger placed against the forehead. *Cf.* CONFIDENCE, FAITH.

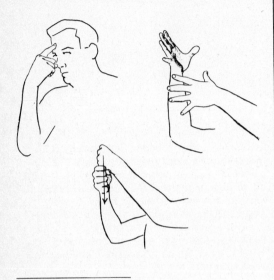

[T–296]

TRUTH (trōͦth), *n.* See TRUE.

[T–297]

TRY 1 (trī), *n., v.,* TRIED, TRYING. (Trying to push through.) The "A" hands, palms facing before the body, are swung around and a bit down, so that the palms now face out. The movement indicates an attempt to push through a barrier. *Cf.* ATTEMPT 1, EFFORT 1, ENDEAVOR, PERSEVERE 1, PERSIST 1.

[T–298]

TRY 2, *v., n.* (Trying to push through, using the "T" hands, for "try.") This is the same sign as TRY 1, except that the "T" hands are employed. *Cf.* ATTEMPT 2, EFFORT 2, PERSEVERE 2.

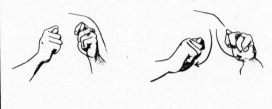

[T–299]

T SQUARE, *(voc.), n.* (The natural sign.) The fingertips of the right hand, pointing up, are thrust into the open left hand, whose palm is facing down. Both hands then form a modified "C" position, palms down and thumb edges touching; then they are drawn apart, the right hand moving straight up and to the side, tracing a right angle.

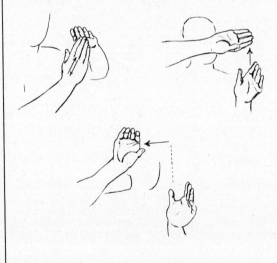

[T–300]

TUESDAY (tūz′ dǐ, tōͦz′-), *n.* The "T" hand, facing out, is moved in a small clockwise circle.

[T–301]

TURKEY 1 (tûr' kǐ), *n.* (The wattle shakes.) The "G" hand, palm down, is shaken before the nose or under the chin.

[T–302]

TURKEY 2, *n.* A variation of TURKEY 1. The "9" hand shakes as it moves straight down from the tip of the nose.

[T–303]

TURKEY 3, *n.* (The crescent on the Turkish flag is indicated.) The "C" hand is placed against the upper part of the forehead.

[T–304]

TURMOIL (tûr' moil), *n.* (The thoughts are topsy-turvy.) The THINK sign is made: The index finger touches the middle of the forehead. The open "5" hands, palms facing and fingers somewhat curved,

swing over each other so that first the right and then the left is on top.

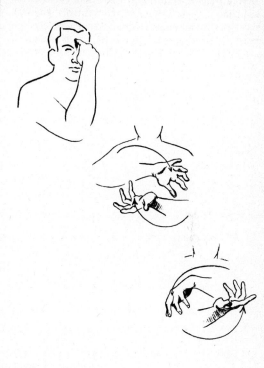

[T–305]

TURN (tûrn) *n., v.,* TURNED, TURNING. (The natural motion.) The outstretched right index finger swings around the upturned left index finger, executing a 90-degree turn to the left.

[T–306]

TURNIP (tûr' nəp), *n.* The nail side of the thumb of the right "A" hand is rubbed in the center of the open left palm.

[T–307]

TURTLE (tûr′ təl), *n.* (The neck.) The downturned left hand is draped over the downturned right "A" hand, whose thumb emerges from under the left hand and wiggles back and forth. *Cf.* TORTOISE.

[T–308]

TV (tē′ vē′), *n.* (The letters "T" and "V.") The letters "T" and "V" are fingerspelled. *Cf.* TELEVISION.

[T–309]

TWICE (twīs), *adv.* (Two fingers are brought up.) The right "V" fingers rest in the open left palm, and are then swung in an arc to an upright position. *Cf.* DOUBLE.

[T–310]

TWILIGHT (twī′ līt), *n.* (Shutting out the light.) Both open hands are held in front of the face, the right palm over the right eye and the left palm over the left eye. The hands then move toward each other and slightly downward in a short arc, coming to rest

one behind the other so that they hide the face. *Cf.* DARK(NESS).

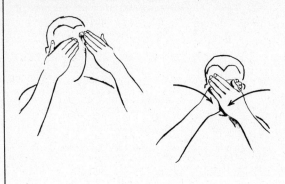

[T–311]

TWINE (twīn), *n., v.,* TWINED, TWINING. (Unraveling a thin string, as indicated by the little fingers.) With palms facing the body, the tips of the extended little fingers touch. As they are drawn slowly apart, they describe very small spirals. *Cf.* SPAGHETTI, STRING, THREAD.

[T–312]

TWO (tōō), *n., adj.* (The natural sign.) The index and middle fingers are held up, with the palm facing in or out. The thumb rests against the third and little fingers, which are bent back against the palm.

[T–313]

TWO-FACED (tōō′ fāst′), *adj.* (Covering the real face.) Both hands are held open, with palms down. The right hand, from a position above the left, swings out and under the left, and then moves straight out. *Cf.* FALSE-FACED, HYPOCRITE 2, UNDERHAND.

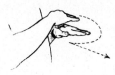

TWO OF US, *n. phrase.* (Two; an encompassing movement.) The right "2" hand, palm facing out or twisted to the right, is positioned at the right shoulder. There it moves forward and back several times.

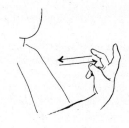

TWO WEEKS, *n. phrase.* ("2"; week.) The base of the right "2" hand is drawn across the upturned left palm, from its base to its fingertips. See WEEK 2.

TYPE (tīp), *n., v.,* TYPED, TYPING. (The natural sign.) The fingers punch an imaginary typewriter keyboard. *Cf.* TYPEWRITER.

TYPIST (tī′ pĭst), *n.* (An individual who types.) The sign for TYPE is made. This is followed by the sign for INDIVIDUAL: Both open hands, palms facing each other, move down the sides of the body, tracing its outline to the hips.

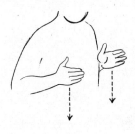

TYPEWRITER (tīp′ rī′ tər), *n.* See TYPE.

U

[U–1]

UGLINESS 1 (ŭg′ lǐ nəs), *n.* (The facial features are distorted.) The "X" hands are moved alternately up and down in front of the face, whose features are distorted with a pronounced frown. *Cf.* GRIMACE, HOMELY 1, MAKE A FACE, UGLY 1.

[U–2]

UGLINESS 2, *n.* The "X" hands, palms down, move back and forth in a horizontal direction in front of the face whose features are distorted with a pronounced frown. *Cf.* HOMELY 2, UGLY 2.

[U–3]

UGLINESS 3, *n.* The "X" hands, crossed in front of the face, alternately move apart and recross. The facial features are distorted with a pronounced frown. *Cf.* UGLY 3.

 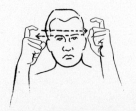

[U–4]

UGLY 1 (ŭg′ lǐ), *adj.* See UGLINESS 1.

[U–5]

UGLY 2, *adj.* See UGLINESS 2.

[U–6]

UGLY 3, *adj.* See UGLINESS 3.

[U–7]

ULTIMATE (ŭl′ tə mǐt), *adj.* (The little, *i.e.,* LAST, fingers are indicated.) With the hands in the "I" position, the tip of the right little finger strikes the tip of its left counterpart. The right index finger may be used instead of the right little finger. *Cf.* END 1, EVENTUALLY, FINAL 1, FINALLY 1, LAST 1, ULTIMATELY.

[U–8]

ULTIMATELY, *adv.* See ULTIMATE.

[U–9]

UMBRELLA (ŭm brĕl′ ə), *n.* (The natural sign.) The signer goes through the motions of opening an umbrella.

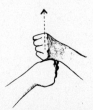

[U–10]

UMPIRE (ŭm′ pīr), *n.* (Judge, individual.) The sign for JUDGE is formed: The two "F" hands, palms facing each other, move alternately up and down. This is followed by the sign for INDIVIDUAL: Both open hands, palms facing each other, move down the sides of the body, tracing its outline to the hips. *Cf.* JUDGE 2, REFEREE.

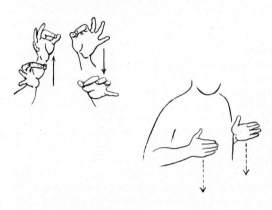

[U–11]

UN-, *prefix.* (Crossing the hands—a negative gesture.) The downturned open hands are crossed at the wrists. They are drawn apart rather quickly. *Cf.* NEGATIVE 1, NOT 1.

[U–12]

UNABLE (ŭn ā′ bəl), *adj.* (One finger encounters an unyielding quality in striking another.) The right index finger strikes the left and continues moving down. The left index finger remains in place. *Cf.* CANNOT, CAN'T, IMPOSSIBLE 1.

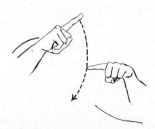

[U–13]

UNCERTAIN (ŭn sûr′ tən), *adj.* (On a fence.) The index and middle fingers of the right hand, palm down, straddle the index finger edge of the left "B" hand, which is held palm facing right. In this position the right hand rocks deliberately back and forth, from left to right. *Cf.* INDECISION.

[U–14]

UNCLE (ŭng′ kəl), *n.* (The letter "U"; the "male" or upper portion of the head.) The right "U" hand is held near the right temple and is shaken slightly.

[U–15]

UNCLEAR, *adj.* (One hand obscures the other.) The "5" hands are held up palm against palm in front of the body. The right hand moves in a slow, continuous clockwise circle over the left palm, as the signer tries to see between the fingers. *Cf.* BLURRY, VAGUE.

[U-16]

UNDER 1 (ŭn′ dər), *prep.* (Underneath something.) The right hand, in the "A" position, thumb pointing straight up, moves down under the left hand, held outstretched, fingers together, palm down. *Cf.* BELOW 2, BENEATH 1, UNDERNEATH.

[U-17]

UNDER 2, *prep.* (The area below.) The right "A" hand, thumb pointing up, moves in a counterclockwise fashion under the downturned left hand. *Cf.* BELOW 3, BENEATH 2.

[U-18]

UNDERHAND (ŭn′ dər hănd′), *adj.* (Covering the real face.) Both hands are held open, with palms down. The right hand, from a position above the left, swings out and under the left, and then moves straight out. *Cf.* FALSE-FACED, HYPOCRITE 2, TWO-FACED.

[U-19]

UNDERNEATH (ŭn′ dər nēth′, -nĕth), *prep.* See UNDER 1.

[U-20]

UNDERSTAND 1 (ŭn′ dər stănd′), *v.,* -STOOD, -STANDING. (An awakening of the mind.) The right "S" hand is placed on the forehead, palm facing the body. The index finger suddenly flicks up into the "D" position.

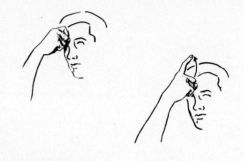

[U-21]

UNDERSTAND 2, *v.* (See rationale for UNDERSTAND 1.) The curved index finger of the right hand, palm facing the body, is placed with the fingernail resting on the middle of the forehead. It suddenly flicks up into the "D" position. *Cf.* COMPREHEND, UNDERSTANDING, UNDERSTOOD.

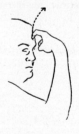

[U-22]

UNDERSTANDING (ŭn′ dər stăn′ dĭng), *n.* See UNDERSTAND 2.

[U-23]

UNDERSTOOD (ŭn′ dər sto͝od′), *v., adj.* See UNDERSTAND 2.

[U-24]

UNDERWEAR (ŭn′ dər wâr′), *n.* (Indicating an undergarment.) Both open hands are held in front of the chest, palms facing the body and fingers pointing to either side, with the right hand nearer the chest and the left held just in front of the right. While the left hand remains stationary in this position, the extended thumb of the right hand rubs downward on the chest a short distance several times.

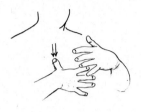

UNFAIR 1 (ŭn fâr'), *adj.* (NOT, EQUAL.) The sign for the prefix UN- is made: The downturned open hands are crossed at the wrists. They are drawn apart rather quickly. This is followed by the sign for EQUAL: The downturned "B" hands, held at chest height, are brought together repeatedly, so that the index finger edges come into contact.

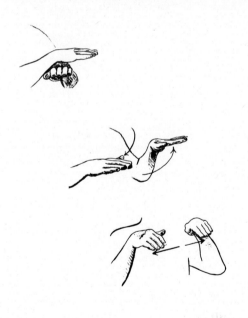

UNFAIR 2, *adj.* (Nicking into one.) The "AND" hands are held one above the other, palms toward the body, the right fingers pointing left, the left

fingers pointing right. The upper hand then moves forcefully downward, striking its fingertips across those of the lower hand as it passes by. The "F" hands may also be used. *Cf.* UNJUST, UNJUSTIFIED.

UNFORGIVABLE, *adj.* (NOT, FORGIVE.) The sign for the prefix UN-, as in UNFAIR 1, is made. This is followed by the sign for FORGIVE: The right hand, palm flat, facing down, is brushed over the left hand, held palm flat and facing up. This action may be repeated twice.

UNGRATEFUL (ŭn grāt' fəl), *adj.* (NOT, GRATE-FUL.) The sign for the prefix UN-, as in UNFAIR 1, is made. This is followed by the sign for GRATE-FUL: The open right hand is placed against the mouth, the open left hand against the heart. Both move forward, away from the body, simultaneously.

[U-29]

UNHAPPY (ŭn hăp' ĭ), *adj.* (NOT, HAPPY.) The sign for the prefix UN-, as in UNFAIR 1, is made. This is followed by the sign for HAPPY: The open right hand, palm facing the body, strikes the heart repeatedly, moving up and off the heart after each strike.

[U-30]

UNIFORM (ū' nə fôrm′), *adj.* (Parallel movement.) Both downturned "Y" hands, held a few inches apart, move simultaneously from left to right or toward and away from each other. *Cf.* SAME 3, UNIFORMLY.

[U-31]

UNIFORMLY, *adv.* See UNIFORM.

[U-32]

UNION (ūn' yən), *n.* (Joining together.) Both hands, held in the modified "5" position, palms out, move toward each other. The thumbs and index fingers of both hands then connect. *Cf.* AFFILIATE 1, ANNEX, ASSOCIATE 2, ATTACH, BELONG, COMMUNION OF SAINTS, CONCERN 2, CONNECT, ENLIST, ENROLL, JOIN 1, PARTICIPATE, RELATIVE 2, UNITE.

[U-33]

UNION, THE, *n.* (The fences built by the early settlers as protection against the Indians.) The extended fingers of both hands are interlocked, and are swept in an arc from left to right as if encompassing an imaginary house or stockade. *Cf.* AMERICA.

[U-34]

UNITE (ū nīt′), *v.,* UNITED, UNITING. See UNION.

[U-35]

UNITED STATES. ("U," "S.") The manual letters "U" and "S" are made. With each letter, the hand makes a small clockwise circle.

[U-36]

UNITY (ū' nə tĭ), *n.* (One, wandering around in a circle.) The index finger, pointing straight up, palm facing the body (the number *one*), is rotated before the face in a counterclockwise direction. *Cf.* ALONE, LONE, ONE 2, ONLY, SOLE.

[U-37]

UNIVERSAL (ū′ nə vûr′ səl), *adj.* (Encompassing; a gathering together.) Both hands are held in the right angle position, palms facing the body, and the right hand in front of the left. The right hand makes a sweeping outward movement around the left, and comes to rest with the back of the right hand resting in the left palm. *Cf.* ALL, ENTIRE, WHOLE.

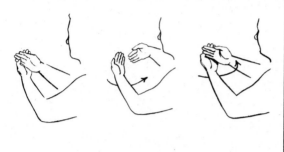

[U–38]

UNIVERSITY 1 (ū´ nə vûr´ sə tĭ), *n.* (The letter "U.") The right "U" hand, palm facing out, rotates in a small clockwise circle.

[U–39]

UNIVERSITY 2, *n.* (The letter "U"; set up on a solid base; the concept of establishment of an institution.) The right "U" hand, palm facing out, rotates in a clockwise circle, and its base then comes down firmly on the back of the downturned left "S" hand.

[U–40]

UNIVERSITY 3, *n.* (The letter "U"; a higher school.) The base of the right "U" hand rests in the upturned left palm. It swings to the left a bit and up a few inches, describing an arc. See also COLLEGE, SCHOOL.

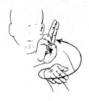

[U–41]

UNJUST (ŭn jŭst´), *adj.* (Nicking into one.) The "AND" hands are held one above the other, palms toward the body, the right fingers pointing left, the left fingers pointing right. The upper hand then moves forcefully downward, striking its fingertips across those of the lower hand as it passes by. The "F" hands may also be used. *Cf.* UNFAIR 2, UNJUSTIFIED.

[U–42]

UNJUSTIFIED (ŭn jŭs´ tĭ fīd), *adj.* See UNJUST.

[U–43]

UNLESS (ŭn lĕs´), *conj.* (If, not.) The sign for IF is made: The two "F" hands, palms facing each other, move alternately up and down. This is followed by the sign for NOT: The downturned open hands are crossed at the wrists. They are drawn apart either once or twice.

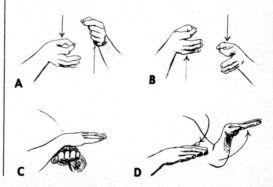

[U-44]

UNLIKE (ŭn līk′), *adj.* (Separated; different.) The "D" hands, palms down, are crossed at the index fingers or are held side by side. They separate once or a number of times. *Cf.* ASSORTED, DIFFERENCE, DIFFERENT, DIVERSE 1, DIVERSITY 1, VARIED.

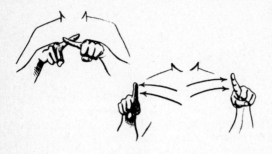

[U-45]

UNNECESSARY 1 (ŭn nĕs′ ə sĕr′ i), *adj.* (NOT and NECESSARY.) The sign for NOT as in UNLESS, is made. This is followed by the sign for NECESSARY: The right hand, in the "X" position, palm down, moves forcefully up and down a number of times.

[U-46]

UNNECESSARY 2, *(colloq.)*, *adj.* (Without necessity.) The sign for NECESSARY, as in UNNECESSARY is made. After the downward movement of the "X" hand, the hand turns over gracefully, opening into the "5" position, palm facing up.

[U-47]

UNSKILLED (ŭn skĭld′), *(colloq.)*, *adj.* (The thickness of the skull is indicated, to stress intellectual density.) With the thumb of the right "C" hand grasped by the closed left hand, the right hand is swung in toward the body, describing a small arc as it moves. The space between the curved right fingers and the closed left hand indicates the thickness of the skull. *Cf.* CLUMSY 2, DUMB 2, MORON, STUPID 2, THICK-SKULLED.

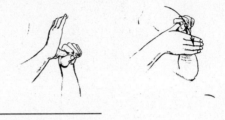

[U-48]

UNTIL (ŭn tĭl′), *prep.* (From one point to the next.) The extended right index finger moves forward slowly and comes to rest on the tip of the extended, upturned left index finger. *Cf.* TILL, TO 1, TOWARD 1, UNTO, UP TO, UP TO NOW.

[U-49]

UNTO (ŭn′ tōō), *prep.* See UNTIL.

[U-50]

UNTRUE (ŭn trōō′), *adj.* (Not, true.) The sign for the prefix UN-, as in UNLESS, is made. This is followed by the sign for TRUE: The index finger of the right "D" hand, palm facing left, is placed against the lips. It moves up an inch or two, and then describes a small arc forward and away from the lips.

[U–51]

UNTRUTH (ŭn trōōth′), *n.* (Words diverted instead of coming straight, or truthfully, out.) The index finger of the right "D" hand, pointing to the left, moves along the lips from right to left. *Cf.* FALSE 1, FALSEHOOD, FRAUDULENT 2, LIAR, LIE 1, PREVARICATE.

[U–52]

UP (ŭp), *prep.* (The natural sign.) The right index finger, pointing straight up, moves up a short distance.

[U–53]

UPHOLD (ŭp hōld′), *v.,* -HELD, -HOLDING. (Holding up.) The right "S" hand pushes up the left "S" hand. *Cf.* ENDORSE 1, FAVOR, INDORSE 1, MAINTENANCE, SUPPORT 1, SUSTAIN, SUSTENANCE, UPLIFT.

[U–54]

UPHOLSTERY (ŭp hōl′ stə ri, -strĭ), *(voc.), n.* (Hammering tacks.) The left hand grasps an imaginary tack, and the right, holding an imaginary uphol-

sterer's hammer, strikes the tack with a series of rather dainty taps.

[U–55]

UPLIFT (ŭp lĭft′), *v.,* -LIFTED, -LIFTING. See UPHOLD.

[U–56]

UPON (ə pŏn′, ə pôn′), *prep.* (The natural sign.) The downturned right hand is placed deliberately on the back of the downturned left hand, describing an arc as it does so.

[U–57]

UP TO, *prep. phrase.* (From one point to the next.) The extended right index finger moves forward slowly and comes to rest on the tip of the extended, upturned left index finger. *Cf.* TILL, TO 1, TOWARD 1, UNTIL, UNTO, UP TO NOW.

[U–58]

UP TO NOW, *adv. phrase.* See UP TO.

[U–59]

UP TO YOU, *phrase.* (The thought is your own.) The right index finger touches the forehead in the modified THINK sign. Then the right "A" hand, with thumb pointing straight up, moves forward toward the person spoken to. See SELF. *Cf.* SUIT YOURSELF.

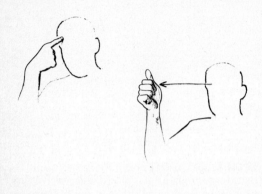

[U–60]

URGE 1 (ûrj), *v.,* URGED, URGING, *n.* (Pushing forward.) Both "5" hands are held, palms out, the right fingers facing right and the left fingers left. The hands move straight forward in a series of short movements. *Cf.* ENCOURAGE, MOTIVATE, MOTIVATION.

[U–61]

URGE 2, *v.* (Shaking someone, to implant one's will into another.) Both "A" hands, palms facing, are held before the chest, the left slightly in front of the right. In this position the hands move back and forth a short distance. *Cf.* COAX, CONVINCE, INDUCE, PERSUADE, PERSUASION, PROD.

[U–62]

URINE (yŏŏr' ĭn), *(loc.), (vulg.), n.* (The slang term, "pee.") The tips of the thumb and middle finger of either "P" hand brush the tip of the nose a number of times.

[U–63]

US (ŭs), *pron.* (The letter "U"; an encompassing gesture.) The right "U" hand, palm facing the body, swings from right shoulder to left shoulder.

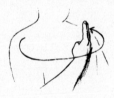

[U–64]

USE (*n.* ūs; *v.* ūz), USED, USING. (The letter "U.") The right "U" hand describes a small clockwise circle. *Cf.* CONSUME 2, USED, USEFUL, UTILIZE, WEAR 2.

[U–65]

USED (ūzd), *v.* See USE.

[U–66]

USEFUL (ūs' fəl), *adj.* See USE.

[U–67]

USHER (ŭsh′ ər), *v.*, -ERED, -ERING. (Opening or leading the way toward something.) The open right hand, held up before the body, sweeps down in an arc and over toward the left side of the chest, ending in the palm-up position. Reversing the movement gives the passive form of the verb, except that the hand does not arc upward but rather simply moves outward in a small arc from the body. *Cf.* ADMIT 2, INVITATION, INVITE, INVITED, WELCOME.

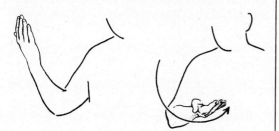

[U–68]

UTILIZE (ū′ tə līz′), *v.*, -LIZED, -LIZING. See USE.

VACANCY (vā′ kən sǐ), *n.* (Devoid of everything on the surface.) The middle finger of the downturned right "5" hand sweeps over the back of the downturned left hand, from wrist to knuckles, and continues beyond a bit. *Cf.* BARE 2, EMPTY 2, NAKED, NUDE, OMISSION 2, VACANT, VOID.

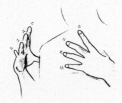

VACANT (vā′ kənt), *adj.* See VACANCY.

VACATION (vā kā′ shən), *n.* (A position of idleness.) With thumbs tucked in the armpits, the remaining fingers of both hands wiggle. *Cf.* HOLIDAY, IDLE, LEISURE, RETIRE 3.

VACCINATION (văk′ sə nā′ shən), *n.* (The natural sign.) The right hand, holding an imaginary needle, prods the upper left arm several times.

VAGINA (və jī′ nə), *n.* (The shape of the vagina.) The extended thumbtips and index fingertips touch each other to form a triangle, with palms facing the body and index fingers pointing downward.

VAGUE (vāg), *adj.* (One hand obscures the other.) The "5" hands are held up, palm against palm in front of the body. The right hand moves in a slow, continuous clockwise circle over the left palm, as the signer tries to see between the fingers. *Cf.* BLURRY, UNCLEAR.

VAIN (vān), *adj.* (All eyes upon oneself.) The "V" hands, held on either side of the face with palms facing the body, swing back and forth simultaneously, pivoting at the wrists. *Cf.* VAINLY, VANITY.

VAINLY (vān′ lǐ), *adv.* See VAIN.

[V–9]

VALE (vāl), *n.* (The natural shape of a depression in the landscape.) Both "5" hands, palms down, are held about two feet apart above eye level. They dip down simultaneously, describing the sides of an imaginary vale or valley, and come together side by side. *Cf.* VALLEY.

[V–10]

VALID (văl' ĭd), *adj.* (Coming forth directly from the lips; true.) The index finger of the right "D" hand, palm facing left, is placed against the lips. It moves up an inch or two and then describes a small arc forward and away from the lips. *Cf.* ABSOLUTE, ABSOLUTELY, ACTUAL, ACTUALLY, AUTHENTIC, CERTAIN, CERTAINLY, FAITHFUL 3, FIDELITY, FRANKLY, GENUINE, INDEED, POSITIVE 1, POSITIVELY, REAL, REALLY, SINCERE 2, SURE, SURELY, TRUE, TRULY, TRUTH, VERILY.

[V–11]

VALISE (və lēs'), *n.* (The natural sign.) The downturned right "S" hand grasps an imaginary piece of luggage and shakes it up and down slightly, as if testing its weight. Cf. BAGGAGE, LUGGAGE, SUITCASE.

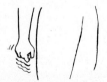

[V–12]

VALLEY (văl' ĭ), *n.* See VALE.

[V–13]

VALUABLE (văl' yōo ə bəl, văl' yə bəl), *adj.* Both "F" hands, palms facing each other, move apart, up, and together in a smooth elliptical fashion, coming together at the tips of the thumbs and index fingers of both hands. *Cf.* DESERVE, ESSENTIAL, IMPORTANT 1, MAIN, MERIT, PRECIOUS, PROMINENT 2, SIGNIFICANCE 1, SIGNIFICANT, VALUE, VITAL 1, WORTH, WORTHWHILE, WORTHY.

[V–14]

VALUE (văl' ū), *n.* See VALUABLE.

[V–15]

VANISH (văn' ĭsh), *v.,* -ISHED, -ISHING. (A disappearance.) The right open hand, palm facing the body, is held by the left hand and is drawn down and out, ending in a position with fingers drawn together. The left hand, meanwhile, may close into a position with fingers also drawn together. *Cf.* ABSENCE 1, ABSENT 1, DEPLETE, DISAPPEAR, EMPTY 1, EXTINCT, FADE AWAY, GONE 1, MISSING 1, OMISSION 1, OUT 3, OUT OF.

[V-16]

VANITY (văn′ ə tĭ), *n*. (All eyes upon oneself.) The "V" hands, held on either side of the face with palms facing the body, swing back and forth simultaneously, pivoting at the wrists. *Cf.* VAIN, VAINLY.

[V-17]

VARIED (vâr′ ĭd), *adj*. (Separated many times; different.) The "D" hands, palms down, are crossed at the index fingers or are held side by side. They separate and return to their initial position a number of times. *Cf.* ASSORTED, DIFFERENCE, DIFFERENT, DIVERSE 1, DIVERSITY 1, UNLIKE.

[V-18]

VARIOUS (vâr′ ĭ əs), *adj*. (The fingertips indicate many things.) Both hands, in the "D" position, palms out and index fingertips touching, are drawn apart. As they move apart, the index fingers wiggle up and down. *Cf.* DIFFERENT OBJECTS, DIVERSE 2, DIVERSITY 2, VARY.

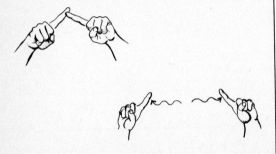

[V-19]

VARY (vâr′ ĭ), *v.*, VARIED, VARYING. See VARIOUS.

[V-20]

VEIL (vāl), *n*. (The letter "V"; the natural drape of the veil.) Both "V" hands, palms facing each other, move down the respective sides of the head.

[V-21]

VEND (věnd), *v.*, VENDED, VENDING. (Transferring ownership of an object.) Both "AND" hands, fingers touching their respective thumbs, are held palms down before the body. The hands are pivoted simultaneously outward and away from the body, once or several times. *Cf.* SALE, SELL.

[V-22]

VENDER (věn′ dər), *n*. (Transferring ownership.) The sign for VEND is formed. The sign for INDIVIDUAL is then made: Both open hands, palms facing each other, move down the sides of the body, tracing its outline to the hips. *Cf.* MERCHANT, SALESMAN, SELLER.

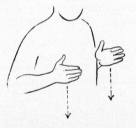

[V–23]

VERBAL 1 (vûr′ bəl), *adj.* (Words tumbling from the mouth.) The right index finger, pointing left, describes a continuous small circle in front of the mouth. *Cf.* BID 3, DISCOURSE, HEARING, MAINTAIN 2, MENTION, REMARK, SAID, SAY, SPEAK, SPEECH 1, STATE, STATEMENT, TALK 1, TELL.

[V–24]

VERBAL 2, *adj.* (A small part of a sentence, *i.e.,* a word.) The tips of the right index finger and thumb, about an inch apart, are placed on the side of the outstretched left index finger, which represents the length of a sentence. *Cf.* INCH 1, WORD.

[V–25]

VERDICT (vûr′ dĭkt), *n.* (The mind stops wavering, and the pros and cons are resolved.) The right index finger touches the forehead, the sign for THINK, *q.v.* Both "F" hands, palms facing each other and fingers pointing straight out, then drop down simultaneously. The sign for JUDGE, *q.v.,* explains the rationale behind the movement of the two hands here. *Cf.* DECIDE, DECISION, DECREE 1, DETERMINE, MAKE UP ONE'S MIND, MIND 5, RENDER JUDGMENT, RESOLVE.

[V–26]

VERILY (vĕr′ ə lĭ), *adv.* (Coming forth directly from the lips; true.) The index finger of the right "D" hand, palm facing left, is placed against the lips. It moves up an inch or two and then describes a small arc forward and away from the lips. *Cf.* ABSOLUTE, ABSOLUTELY, ACTUAL, ACTUALLY, AUTHENTIC, CERTAIN, CERTAINLY, FAITHFUL 3, FIDELITY, FRANKLY, GENUINE, INDEED, POSITIVE 1, POSITIVELY, REAL, REALLY, SINCERE 2, SURE, SURELY, TRUE, TRULY, TRUTH, VALID.

[V–27]

VERSE (vûrs), *(eccles.), n.* (A portion of the page.) The open left hand, palm facing right and fingertips pointing forward, represents the page. The fingertips of the "C" hand, held so that thumb and other fingers are only an inch apart, move across the left palm from its base to its fingertips.

[V–28]

VERSUS (vûr′ səs), *prep.* (Two individuals pitted against each other.) The hands are held in the "A" position, thumbs pointing straight up, palms facing the body. They come together forcefully, moving down a bit as they do, and the knuckles of one hand strike those of the other. *Cf.* CHALLENGE, GAME 1, OPPORTUNITY 2.

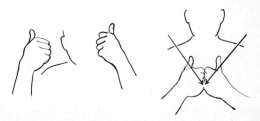

[V–29]

VERTICAL PRESS (vûr′ tə kəl), *(voc.), n.* (The movement of the press.) The open hands, palms facing, move alternately up and down.

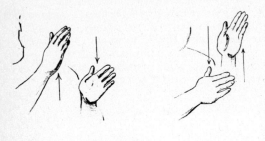

[V–30]

VERY (vĕr′ ĭ), *adv.* (The "V" hands, with the sign for MUCH.) The fingertips of the "V" hands are placed together, and then moved apart.

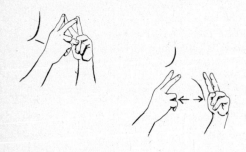

[V–31]

VEST (vĕst), *n.* (The "V" hand on the chest.) The right "V" hand, palm facing the body, moves a short distance up the middle of the chest a number of times.

[V–32]

VESTIBULAR (vĕs tĭb′ yə lər), *adj.* (The letter "V," on the outside.) The right "V" hand, held before the body with palm out, touches its index fingertip against the little fingertip of the open left hand, which is held with palm facing the body and fingers

pointing up. This sign, essentially a local one, describes a prefreshman college program.

[V–33]

VIBRATION (vī brā′ shən), *n.* (A shaking which disturbs the ear.) After placing the index finger on the ear, both hands assume the "S" position, palms down. They move alternately back and forth, forcefully. *Cf.* DIN, NOISE, NOISY, RACKET, SOUND, THUNDER.

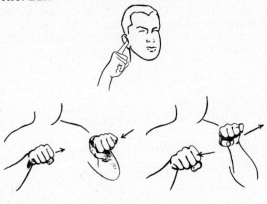

[V–34]

VICE-PRESIDENT 1 (vīs′ prĕz′ ə dənt), *n.* (The second one after the president.) The sign for PRESIDENT is made: The "C" hands, held at either side of the head with fingers slightly curved, move out and up a bit, closing into the "S" position. The sign for SECOND, is then made: The "2" hand, palm facing down and index and middle fingers pointing left, pivots around so that the palm faces the body.

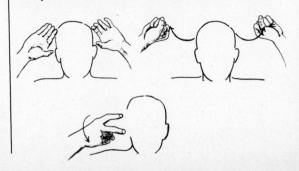

[V–35]

VICE-PRESIDENT 2, *n*. (The letters "V" and "P.") The letters "V" and "P" are made with the right hand.

[V–36]

VICINITY (vĭ sin′ ə tĭ), *n*. (One hand is near the other.) The left hand, cupped, fingers together, is held before the chest, palm facing the body. The right hand, also cupped, fingers together, moves a very short distance back and forth, as it is held in front of the left. *Cf.* ADJACENT, BESIDE, BY 1, CLOSE (TO) 2, NEAR 1, NEIGHBOR, NEIGHBORHOOD.

[V–37]

VICTORY 1 (vĭk′ tə rĭ), *n*. (Waving of flags.) Both upright hands, grasping imaginary flags, wave them in small circles. *Cf.* CELEBRATE, CELEBRATION, CHEER, REJOICE, WIN 1.

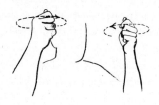

[V–38]

VICTORY 2, *n*. (Waving a flag.) The right "A" hand goes through the natural movement of waving a flag

in circular fashion. Preceding this, the right hand may go through the motion of grabbing the flagstaff out of the left hand. *Cf.* EXULTATION, TRIUMPH 1, WIN 2.

[V–39]

VIE 1 (vī), *v.*, VIED, VYING. (Two opponents come together.) Both hands are closed, with thumbs pointing straight up and palms facing the body. From their initial position about a foot apart, the hands are brought together sharply, so that the knuckles strike. The hands, as they are drawn together, also move down a bit, so that they describe a "V." *Cf.* COMPETE 1, COMPETITION 1, CONTEND 1, CONTEST 1, RACE 1, RIVAL 2, RIVALRY 1.

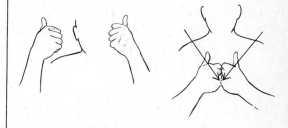

[V–40]

VIE 2, *v.* (Opposing objects.) The "A" hands are held side by side before the chest, palms facing each other and thumbs pointing forward. In this position the hands move alternately back and forth, toward and away from the body. *Cf.* COMPETE 2, COMPETITION 2, CONTEND 2, CONTEST 2, RACE 2, RIVAL 3, RIVALRY 2.

[V–41]

VIE 3, *v.* (The changing fortunes of competitors.) The "A" hands are held facing each other, thumbs pointing up in front of the body. Both hands are moved alternately backward and forward past each other several times. *Cf.* COMPETE 3, COMPETITION 3, CONTEND 3, CONTEST 3, RACE 3, RIVAL 4, RIVALRY 3.

[V–42]

VIEW (vū), *n., v.,* VIEWED, VIEWING. (Look around.) The sign for LOOK is made: The right "V" hand, palm facing the body, is placed so that the fingertips are just under the eyes. Then both "V" hands are held with palms down and fingers pointing forward in front of the body. In this position the hands move simultaneously from side to side several times. *Cf.* VISION 1.

[V–43]

VILLAGE (vil' ij), *n.* (The letter "V"; a collection of slanting rooftops.) The tips of the index and middle fingers of both "V" hands come together repeatedly, as both hands move from right to left.

[V–44]

VINE (vīn), *n.* (The climbing and spreading of a vine.) The right "G" hand, palm out, with thumb and index finger pointing straight up, moves up in a wavy manner. Both "5" hands, palms out and thumbtips almost touching, then move up and apart. *Cf.* GRAPEVINE.

[V–45]

VINEGAR (vĭn' ə gər), *n.* (The "V" at the mouth.) The right "V" hand is held palm facing right and index fingertip touching the lips. The hand moves back and forth a very slight distance to and from the mouth. The lips may be puckered.

[V–46]

VIOLATE (vī' ə lāt'), *v.,* -LATED, -LATING. (An encroachment; parrying a knife thrust.) The left "A" hand is held palm toward the body, knuckles facing right. The extended thumb of the right "A" hand is brought sharply over the back of the left. *Cf.* DANGER 2, DANGEROUS 2, INJURE 2, PERIL, TRESPASS.

[V–47]

VIOLIN (vī′ ə lǐn′), *n.* (The natural movement.) The hands and arms go through the natural motions of playing a violin. *Cf.* FIDDLE.

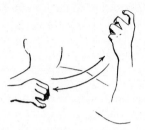

[V–48]

VIRGIN (vûr′ jǐn), *n.* (The "V" describes a halo.) The right "V" hand moves over the head in an arc from left side to right side.

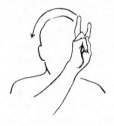

[V–49]

VIRGIN MARY, *(eccles.), n.* (The "V" and a halo.) The right "V" fingers are pointed over the left shoulder and then moved up over the forehead and down to a position pointing over the right shoulder.

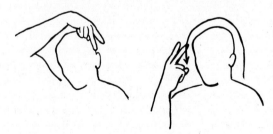

[V–50]

VISIBLE (vǐz′ ə bəl), *adj.* (Able to see.) The sign for ABLE or CAN is made: Both "A" hands, held palms down, move down in unison a short distance before the chest. This is followed by the sign for SEE: The right "V" hand, palm facing the body, is placed so that the fingertips are just under the eyes. The hand swings around and out, so that the fingertips are now pointing forward.

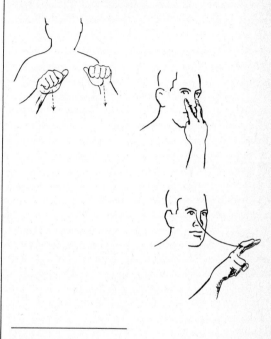

[V–51]

VISION 1 (vǐzh′ ən), *n.* (Look around.) The sign for LOOK is made: The right "V" hand, palm facing the body, is placed so that the fingertips are just under the eyes. Then both "V" hands are held with palms down and fingers pointing forward in front of the body. In this position the hands move simultaneously from side to side several times. *Cf.* VIEW.

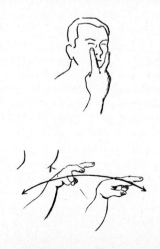

[V-52]

VISION 2, *n.* (The vision is directed forward, into the distance.) The right "V" fingertips are placed under the eyes, with palm facing the body. The hand is then swung around and forward, moving under the downturned prone left hand and continuing forward and upward. *Cf.* FORECAST, FORESEE, FORETELL, PERCEIVE 2, PREDICT, PROPHECY, PROPHESY, PROPHET.

[V-53]

VISIT (vĭz′ ĭt), *n., v.,* -ITED, -ITING. (The letter "V"; random movement, *i.e.,* moving around as in visiting.) The "V" hands, palms facing, move alternately in clockwise circles out from the chest.

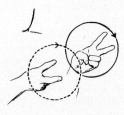

[V-54]

VITAL 1 (vī′ təl), *adj.* Both "F" hands, palms facing each other, move apart, up, and together in a smooth elliptical fashion, coming together at the tips of the thumbs and index fingers of both hands. *Cf.* DESERVE, ESSENTIAL, IMPORTANT 1, MAIN, MERIT, PRECIOUS, PROMINENT 2, SIGNIFICANCE 1, SIGNIFICANT, VALUABLE, VALUE, WORTH, WORTHWHILE, WORTHY.

[V-55]

VITAL 2, *adj,* (Being pinned down.) The right hand, in the "X" position, palm down, moves forcefully up and down once or twice. An expression of determination is frequently assumed. *Cf.* HAVE TO, IMPERATIVE, MUST, NECESSARY 1, NECESSITY, NEED 1, OUGHT TO, SHOULD.

[V-56]

VOCATION (vō kā′ shən), *n.* (Striking an anvil.) Both "S" hands are held palms down. The right hand strikes against the back of the left a number of times. *Cf.* JOB, LABOR, OCCUPATION, TASK, TOIL, TRAVAIL, WORK.

[V-57]

VOICE (vois), *n.* (The letter "V"; an emission from the throat.) The fingertips of the right "V" hand move up along the front of the throat.

[V-58]

VOID (void), *adj., n.* (Devoid of everything on the surface.) The middle finger of the downturned right "5" hand sweeps over the back of the downturned left "A" or "S" hand, from wrist to knuckles, and continues beyond a bit. *Cf.* BARE 2, EMPTY 2, NAKED, NUDE, OMISSION 2, VACANCY, VACANT.

VOLCANO (vŏl kā′ nō), *n.* (The shape; the upward explosion.) The sign for MOUNTAIN is made: The back of the upturned right "S" hand strikes the back of the downturned left "S" hand twice. The downturned "5" hands then move from left to right in wavy, up-down movements. This is followed by the sign for ERUPT: The left hand forms a cup, palm facing right. The right hand, fingertips together, shoots upward suddenly from its position within the left hand. As it emerges, the fingers open quickly. The sign is repeated. The ERUPT sign alone may be used. *Cf.* ERUPT.

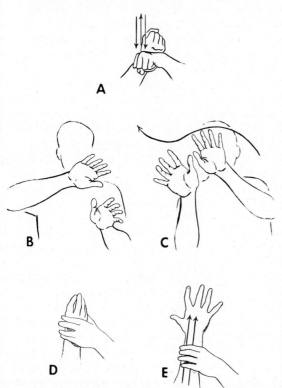

[V–60]

VOLLEYBALL (vŏl′ ĭ bôl′), *n.* (The natural sign.) The upturned hands boost an imaginary volleyball over the net. The letters "V" and "B" are sometimes substituted for this sign.

[V–61]

VOLUME (vŏl′ ūm, -yəm), *n.* (Opening a book.) The open hands are held together, fingers pointing away from the body. They open with little fingers remaining in contact, as in the opening of a book. *Cf.* BOOK, TEXTBOOK.

[V–62]

VOLUNTEER (vŏl′ ən tîr′), *n., v.,* -TEERED, -TEERING. (Bringing oneself forward.) The right index finger and thumb grasp the clothing near the right shoulder (often the lapel of a suit or the collar of a dress) and tug it up and down gently several times. Sometimes one tug only is used. *Cf.* APPLY 1, CANDIDATE, OFFER 2, RUN FOR OFFICE.

[V-63]

VOMIT (vŏm' ĭt), *n., v.,* -ITED, -ITING. (The natural sign.) The mouth is held open, with tongue hanging slightly out. The right "5" hand, initially held against the chest, moves up and forward in an arc. The head may move slightly forward simultaneously.

[V-65]

VOW (vou), *v.,* VOWED, VOWING. (The arm is raised.) The right index finger is placed at the lips. The right arm is then raised, palm out and elbow resting on the back of the left hand. *Cf.* GUARANTEE 1, LOYAL, OATH, PLEDGE, PROMISE 1, SWEAR 1, SWORN, TAKE OATH.

[V-64]

VOTE (vōt), *n., v.,* VOTED, VOTING. (Placing a ballot in a box.) The right hand, holding an imaginary ballot between the thumb and index finger, places it into an imaginary box formed by the left "O" hand, palm facing right. *Cf.* ELECT, ELECTION.

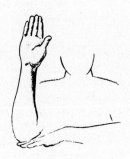

W

[W–1]

WAGER (wā′ jər), *n.* (The placing or slamming down of bets by two parties.) Both open hands, palms up, are suddenly swung over in unison, to the palms-down position. Sometimes they are swung over one at a time. *Cf.* BET.

[W–2]

WAGE(S) (wāj), *n.* (Gathering in.) The right "5" hand, its little finger edge touching the upturned left palm, is drawn in an arc toward the body, closing into the "S" position as it sweeps over the base of the left hand. *Cf.* ACCUMULATE 1, COLLECT, EARN, SALARY.

[W–3]

WAGE WAR, *v. phrase.* (The contending armies.) The "4," "W," or "5" hands face each other, and move simultaneously from side to side, representing the successive advance and retreat of contending armed forces. *Cf.* WAR.

[W–4]

WAGON (wăg′ ən), *n.* (The wheels.) With index fingers facing each other and arms held quite close to the chest, the hands describe small continuous clockwise circles. The arms then extend forward a few inches, and the hands repeat their earlier movement.

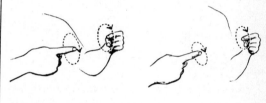

[W–5]

WAIT (wāt), *n., v.,* WAITED, WAITING. (The fingers wiggle with impatience.) The upturned "5" hands are positioned with the right behind the left. The fingers of both hands wiggle. *Cf.* PENDING.

[W–6]

WAITER 1 (wā′ tər), *n.* (An individual who waits on someone.) The sign for WAITER 2 is made. This is followed by the sign for INDIVIDUAL: Both open hands, palms facing each other, move down the sides of the body, tracing its outline to the hips. *Cf.* WAITRESS 1.

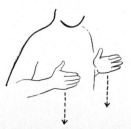

[W-7]

WAITER 2, *n.* (Passing the dishes, one by one.) The upturned "5" hands move alternately toward and away from the chest. *Cf.* MAID, SERVANT, SERVE 2, SERVICE, WAIT ON 2, WAITRESS 2.

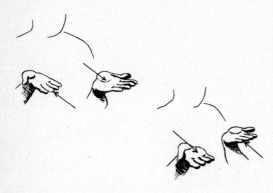

[W-8]

WAIT ON 1, *v. phrase.* (Passing out dishes of food, one by one.) The upturned hands are held before the chest, as if bearing dishes of food. They move alternately forward and back, as if extending the dishes to a diner. *Cf.* SERVE 1.

[W-9]

WAIT ON 2, *v.* See WAITER 2.

[W-10]

WAITRESS 1 (wā' trĭs), *n.* See WAITER 1.

[W-11]

WAITRESS 2, *n.* See WAITER 2.

[W-12]

WAKE UP (wāk), *v. phrase.* (Opening the eyes.) Both hands are closed, with thumb and index finger of each hand held together, extended, and placed at the corners of the closed eyes. Slowly they separate, and the eyes open. *Cf.* AROUSE, AWAKE, AWAKEN.

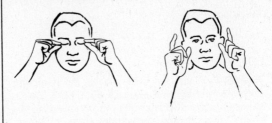

[W-13]

WALK (wôk), *n., v.,* WALKED, WALKING. (The movement of the feet.) The downturned "5" hands move alternately toward and away from the chest. *Cf.* PACE, STEP 1.

[W-14]

WALL 1 (wôl), *n.* (The shape.) The upright hands, fingers straight and palms facing, move apart from their initial edge-against-edge position, the right hand moving forward and the left toward the body.

[W–15]

WALL 2, *n.* (The natural shape.) The upright open hands, palms facing each other, move straight up, as if outlining a pair of walls.

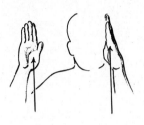

[W–16]

WANDER 1 (wŏn′ dər), *v.*, -DERED, -DERING. (The natural motion.) The "G" hands are held side by side and touching, palms down, index fingers pointing forward. Then the right hand moves forward, curving toward the right side as it does. *Cf.* DEFLECT, DEVIATE 2, GO OFF THE TRACK, STRAY.

[W–17]

WANDER 2, *v.* (Random movement.) The right "D" hand, palm facing left, moves to and fro from right to left. *Cf.* ROAM.

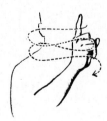

[W–18]

WANDER AROUND WITH, *v. phrase.* (To go along with.) Both "A" hands, knuckles together and thumbs up, are moved forward in unison, away from the chest. *Cf.* ACCOMPANY, TOGETHER, WITH.

[W–19]

WANT (wŏnt, wônt), *v.*, WANTED, WANTING. (Grasping something and pulling it in.) The upturned "5" hands, held side by side before the chest, close slightly into a grasping position as they move in toward the body. *Cf.* COVET 1, DESIRE 1, LONG 2, NEED 2, WILL 2, WISH 1.

[W–20]

WAR (wôr), *n., v.*, WARRED, WARRING. (The contending armies.) The "4", "W" or "5" hands face each other, and move simultaneously from side to side, representing the successive advance and retreat of contending armed forces. *Cf.* WAGE WAR.

[W–21]

WARM 1 (wôrm), *adj., v.*, WARMED, WARMING. (The warmth of the breath is indicated.) The upturned cupped right hand is placed at the slightly open mouth. It moves up and away from the mouth, opening into the upturned "5" position, with fingers somewhat curved. *Cf.* HEAT 1.

[W-22]

WARM 2, *adj.* (Wiping off perspiration.) The extended, bent, right index finger is drawn across the forehead from left to right.

[W-23]

WARN (wôrn), *v.,* WARNED, WARNING. (Tapping one to draw attention to danger.) The right hand taps the back of the left several times. *Cf.* ADMONISH 1, CAUTION, FOREWARN.

[W-24]

WAS (wŏz, wŭz; *unstressed* wəz), *v.* (Something past, behind.) The upraised right hand, in the "5" position with palm facing the body, is held just above the right shoulder and is thrown back over it. *Cf.* AGO, FORMERLY, ONCE UPON A TIME, PAST, PREVIOUS, PREVIOUSLY, WERE.

[W-25]

WASH 1 (wŏsh, wôsh), *n., v.,* WASHED, WASHING. (Rubbing the clothes.) The knuckles of the "A"

hands rub against one another, in circles. *Cf.* CLEAN 2.

[W-26]

WASH 2, *v.* (The natural sign.) The signer goes through the motions of wiping his face with a towel. *Cf.* TOWEL.

[W-27]

WASH 3, *v.* (The natural sign.) The closed hands move up and down against the chest as if scrubbing it. *Cf.* BATH, BATHE.

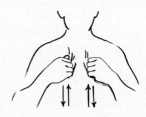

[W-28]

WASHCLOTH (wŏsh′ klôth′), *n.* (Washing the face, the square shape.) The upright open hands move up and down over the face, as if washing it. The extended index fingers then outline a square shape before the body.

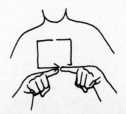

[W–29]

WASH DISHES, *v. phrase.* (The natural sign.) The downturned right "5" hand describes a clockwise circle as it moves over the upturned left "5" hand. *Cf.* DISHWASHING.

[W–30]

WASHING MACHINE, *n.* (The clothes are tumbled around.) The cupped, open hands, palms facing and one above the other, execute opposing circular movements.

[W–31]

WASHINGTON 1 (wŏsh′ ĭng tən, wôsh′ -), *n.* (The letter "W"; the epaulets on the uniform.) The right "W" hand, resting on the right shoulder, moves up a short distance and executes a counterclockwise circle. *Cf.* WASHINGTON, D.C.

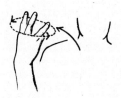

[W–32]

WASHINGTON 2, *n.* (The long hair; the letter "W.") The right "W" hand, palm facing out, executes a wavy downward movement along the right side of the head.

[W–33]

WASHINGTON, D.C. See WASHINGTON 1.

[W–34]

WASTE 1 (wāst), *n., v.,* WASTED, WASTING. (Repeated giving forth.) The back of the upturned right hand, thumb touching fingertips, is placed in the upturned left palm. The right hand moves off and away from the left once or several times, each time opening into the "5" position, palm up. *Cf.* EXTRAVAGANT, SPEND, SQUANDER.

[W–35]

WASTE 2, *n., v.* (The "W" is indicated.) The same movement as in WASTE 1 is used, except that the right hand assumes the "W" position and keeps it.

[W–36]

WATCH 1 (wŏch), *v.*, WATCHED, WATCHING. (Careful, constant vision.) The downturned, left "V" hand sweeps back and forth from side to side beneath the downturned, right "V" hand, which remains stationary and pointing forward.

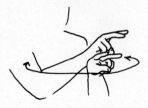

[W–37]

WATCH 2, *n., v.* (The eyesight is directed forward.) The right "V" hand, palm facing the body, is placed so that the fingertips are just under the eyes. The hand swings around and out, so that the fingertips are now pointing forward. *Cf.* LOOK 1, PERCEIVE 1, PERCEPTION, SEE, SIGHT.

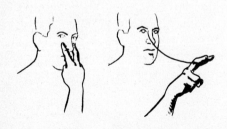

[W–38]

WATCH 3, *n.* (Time by the clock, indicated by the ticking of the clock or watch.) The curved right index finger taps the back of the left wrist several times. *Cf.* CLOCK, TIME 1.

[W–39]

WATCH 4, *n.* (The shape of the wristwatch.) The thumb and index finger of the right hand, forming

a circle, are placed on the back of the left wrist. *Cf.* WRISTWATCH.

[W–40]

WATER 1 (wô' tər, wŏt' ər), *n.* (The letter "W" at the mouth, as in drinking water.) The right "W" hand, palm facing left, touches the lips a number of times.

[W–41]

WATER 2, *n.* (The letter "W.") The right "W" hand, palm facing out, is shaken slightly, as in the rippling of water. This sign is used as a prefix for different bodies of water, *Cf.* LIQUID.

[W–42]

WATERCOLOR, *n.* (Mixing the colors.) The sign for WATER 1 is made. The right fingertips, moving in a small counterclockwise circle, then go through the motions of mixing imaginary colors in the upturned left palm.

[W–43]

WATER HOSE *n.* (The natural sign.) The upturned right hand, grasping an imaginary hose nozzle, swings back and forth repeatedly, from left to right.

[W–44]

WATERMELON (wô′ tər mĕl′ ən, wŏt′ ər-), *n.* (The green skin; the thumping of the melon to see if it is ripe.) The sign for GREEN is made: The right "G" hand is shaken slightly. The movement involves a slight pivoting action at the wrist. The right middle finger then flicks against the back of the left hand, once or twice.

[W–45]

WAVE 1 (wāv), *n.* (The undulating motion.) Both "5" hands, held palms down before the chest, move in unison in a wavy, undulating manner, from left to right.

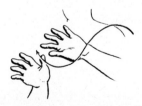

[W–46]

WAVE 2, *v.,* WAVED, WAVING. (The natural motion.) The right hand goes through the natural motion of waving, as if saying goodbye.

[W–47]

WAVER 1 (wā′ vər), *v.,* -VERED, -VERING. (On a fence; uncertain.) The downturned right "V" hand straddles the index finger edge of the left "B" hand, whose palm faces right. The right hand sways slightly back and forth, from left to right.

[W–48]

WAVER 2, *v.* (The wavering.) The downturned "S" hands swing alternately up and down. *Cf.* DISBELIEF 2, DOUBT 2, DOUBTFUL.

[W–49]

WAY 1 (wā), *n.* (The winding movement.) Both hands, palms facing and fingers together and extended straight out, move in unison away from the body, in a winding manner. *Cf.* CORRIDOR, HALL, HALLWAY, MANNER 2, METHOD, OPPORTUNITY 3, PATH, ROAD, STREET, TRAIL.

[W–50]

WAY 2, *n.* (The letter "W.") The sign for WAY 1 is made, but with the "W" hands.

[W–51]

WE 1 (wē; *unstressed* wǐ), *pron.* (An encompassing movement.) The right index finger points down as it swings over from the right shoulder to the left shoulder.

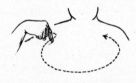

[W–52]

WE 2, *pron.* (The letter "W.") The right "W" hand, fingers pointing up, goes through the same motion as in WE 1.

[W–53]

WEAK (wēk), *adj.* (The knees buckle.) The right "V" hand is placed with fingertips resting in the upturned left palm. The knuckles of the "V" fingers buckle a bit. This motion may be repeated. *Cf.* FAINT 1, FEEBLE, FRAIL, WEAKNESS.

[W–54]

WEAK-MINDED (wēk' mīn' dǐd), *adj.* (Weakness at the mind.) The fingers of the right "V" hand, placed at the right temple, collapse. The movement may be repeated. *Cf.* FEEBLE-MINDED.

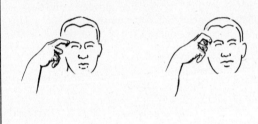

[W–55]

WEAKNESS (wēk' nǐs), *n.* See WEAK.

[W–56]

WEALTH (wĕlth), *n.* (A pile of money.) The sign for MONEY is made: The back of the upturned right hand, whose thumb and fingertips are all touching, is placed in the upturned left palm. The right hand then moves straight up, as it opens into the "5" position, palm facing down and fingers somewhat curved. *Cf.* RICH, WEALTHY.

[W–57]

WEALTHY (wĕl' thǐ), *adj.* See WEALTH.

[W-58]

WEAR 1 (wâr), *n., v.,* WORE, WORN, WEARING. (Draping the clothes on the body.) With fingertips resting on the chest, both hands move down simultaneously. The action is repeated. *Cf.* CLOTHES, CLOTHING, DRESS, FROCK, GARMENT, GOWN, SHIRT, SUIT.

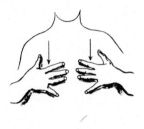

[W-59]

WEAR 2, *v.* (To use; the letter "U.") The right "U" hand describes a small clockwise circle. *Cf.* CONSUME 2, USE, USED, USEFUL, UTILIZE.

[W-60]

WEARY (wĭr' ĭ), *adj.* (The hands collapse in exhaustion.) Both "C" hands are placed either on the lower chest or at the waist. The palms face the body. They fall away into a palms-up position. At the same time, the shoulders suddenly sag in a very pronounced fashion. An expression of weariness may be used for emphasis. *Cf.* DISCOURAGE 2, EXHAUST, FATIGUE, TIRE, TIRED.

[W-61]

WEAVE (wēv), *v.,* WOVE, WOVEN, WEAVING. (The threads are interwoven.) Both "5" hands, palms down, are brought slowly together, with the right sliding over the left. As they move together, the fingers wiggle. *Cf.* DARN, INFILTRATE.

[W-62]

WEDDING (wĕd' ĭng), *n.* (A joining of hands.) The downturned "B" hands are joined together with a flourish.

[W-63]

WEDNESDAY (wĕnz' dĭ), *n.* (The letter "W.") The upright "W" hand moves in a small clockwise circle.

[W-64]

WEEK 1 (wēk), *n.* (Seven fingers, *i.e.,* days, are brought together.) The downturned right "L" hand is placed on the upturned left "5" hand, near the base. The right hand moves forward toward the left fingertips, and the left hand begins to close, so that, in the final position, the fingertips of the left hand are closed and touching the tips of the right thumb and index finger.

[W-65]

WEEK 2, *(vern.), n.* (A modification of WEEK 1.) The upright, right "D" hand is placed palm-to-palm against the left "5" hand, whose palm faces right. The right "D" hand moves along the left palm from base to fingertips. *Cf.* NEXT WEEK 2.

[W-66]

WEEK AGO, A, *phrase.* (A week in the past.) After beginning the sign for WEEK 2, the right index finger is thrown back over the right shoulder.

[W-67]

WEEKLY (wēk' lǐ), *adj., adv., n.* (Week after week.) The sign for WEEK 2 is made several times.

[W-68]

WEEP 1 (wēp), *v.,* WEPT, WEEPING. (Tears streaming down the cheeks.) Both index fingers, in the "D"

position, move down the cheeks, either once or several times. Sometimes one finger only is used. *Cf.* BAWL 1, CRY 1, TEAR 2, TEARDROP.

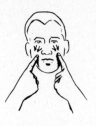

[W-69]

WEEP 2, *v.* (Tears gushing from the eyes.) Both "B" hands are held before the face, palms facing forward, with the backs of the index fingertips touching the face just below the eyes. From this position both hands move forward and over in an arc, to indicate a flow of tears. *Cf.* BAWL 2, CRY 2.

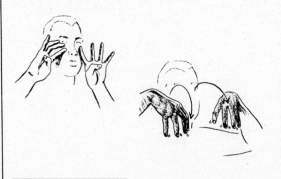

[W-70]

WEIGH 1 (wā), *v.,* WEIGHED, WEIGHING. (The balancing of the scale is described.) The fingers of the right "H" hand are centered on the left index finger or "H" hand and rocked back and forth. *Cf.* POUND 1, SCALE 2, WEIGHT.

[W-71]

WEIGH 2, *v.* (Turning thoughts over in the mind.) Both index fingers, pointing to the forehead, describe continuous alternating circles. *Cf.* CONSIDER 2,

CONTEMPLATE, PONDER, SPECULATE 2, SPECULA-TION 2, WONDER 1.

[W–72]

WEIGHT (wāt), *n.* See WEIGH 1.

[W–73]

WEIGHTY (wā′ tĭ), *adj.* (The hands drop under a weight.) The upturned "5" hands, held before the chest, suddenly drop a short distance. *Cf.* CRUSH-ING, HEAVY.

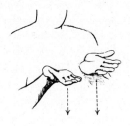

[W–74]

WEIRD (wĭrd), *adj.* (Something which distorts the vision.) The "C" hand describes a small arc in front of the face. *Cf.* CURIOUS 2, GROTESQUE, ODD, PECU-LIAR, QUEER 1, STRANGE 1.

[W–75]

WELCOME (wĕl′ kəm), *n., v.,* -COMED, -COMING. (Opening or leading the way toward something.)

The open right hand, held up before the body, sweeps down in an arc and over toward the left side of the chest, ending in the palm-up position. Revers-ing the movement gives the passive form of the verb, except that the hand does not arc upward but rather simply moves outward in a small arc from the body. *Cf.* ADMIT 2, INVITATION, INVITE, INVITED, USHER.

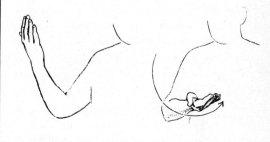

[W–76]

WELL 1 (wĕl), *adv.* (Tasting something, approving it, and offering it forward.) The fingertips of the right "5" hand are placed at the lips. The right hand then moves out and into a palm-up position on the up-turned left palm. *Cf.* GOOD 1.

[W–77]

WELL 2, *adj.* (Strength emanating from the body.) Both "5" hands are placed palms against the chest. They move out and away, forcefully, closing and assuming the "S" position. *Cf.* BRAVE, BRAVERY, COURAGE, COURAGEOUS, FORTITUDE, HALE, HEALTH, HEALTHY, MIGHTY 2, STRENGTH, STRONG 2.

[W-78]

WELL 3, *n.* (Water in a hole.) The sign for WATER 1 or WATER 2, *q.v.,* is made. Then the right index finger, pointing down, traces a clockwise circle in the air, after which it drops straight down a few inches into the left "C" hand, whose palm faces right.

[W-79]

WERE (wûr, *unstressed* wər), *v.* (Something past, behind.) The upraised right hand, in the "5" position with palm facing the body, is held just above the right shoulder and is thrown back over it. *Cf.* AGO, FORMERLY, ONCE UPON A TIME, PAST, PREVIOUS, PREVIOUSLY, WAS.

[W-80]

WEST (wĕst), *n., adj.* (The letter "W"; the direction.) The right "W" hand, palm out, moves from left to right before the right shoulder.

[W-81]

WET (wĕt), *adj., n., v.,* WET or WETTED, WETTING. (The wetness.) The right fingertips touch the lips,

and then the fingers of both hands open and close against the thumbs a number of times. *Cf.* CERAMICS, CLAY, DAMP, MOIST.

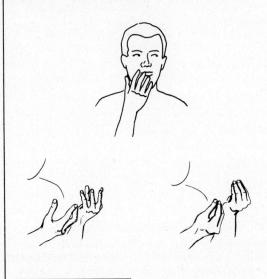

[W-82]

WHALE (hwāl), *(rare), n.* (The spouting.) The index fingers of the "D" hands, placed at the sides of the nose, move up simultaneously, to describe the spouting above the whale's head.

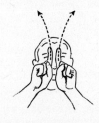

[W-83]

WHAT (hwŏt, hwŭt; *unstressed* hwət), *pron., adj., adv., interj., conj.* (The finger passes over several specifics to bring out the concept of "which one?") The right index finger passes over the fingers of the upturned left "5" hand, from index to little finger.

[W–84]

WHATEVER (hwŏt ĕv′ ər), *pron.* (WHAT, ANY.) The sign for WHAT is made. This is followed by the sign for ANY: The "A" hand, palm out, moves down in an S-shaped curve to a point a bit above waist level.

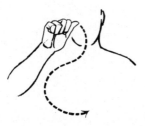

[W–85]

WHAT IS THE PRICE? (Amount of money is indicated.) The sign for MONEY is made: The upturned right hand, grasping some imaginary bills, is brought down into the upturned left palm a number of times. The right hand then moves straight up, opening into the "5" position, palm up. *Cf.* HOW MUCH MONEY?, PRICE 1.

[W–86]

WHAT'S NEW? (The feelings well up and come out.) The open hands are placed near the chest, with middle fingers resting on the chest. Both hands move up and out simultaneously. A happy expression is assumed. *Cf.* THRILL 2, WHAT'S UP?

[W–87]

WHAT'S UP? See WHAT'S NEW?

[W–88]

WHEEL (hwēl) *n.* (The natural sign.) The right index finger, pointing left, describes a clockwise circle in front of the body.

[W–89]

WHEN (hwĕn), *adv., conj., n.* (Fixing a point in time.) The left "D" hand is held upright, palm facing the body. The right index finger describes a clockwise circle around the left, coming to rest on the left index fingertip.

[W–90]

WHENEVER (hwĕn ĕv′ ər), *conj.* (A place in time; of no matter or import.) The sign for WHEN is made, followed by the sign for WHEREVER, *q.v.*

[W–91]

WHERE 1 (hwâr), *adv.* (Alternate directions are indicated.) The right "D" hand, with palm out and index finger straight or slightly curved, moves a short distance back and forth, from left to right. *Cf.* DIRECTION 1.

[W-92]

WHERE 2, *adv.* The open "5" hands, palms up and fingers slightly curved, move back and forth in front of the body, the right hand to the right and the left hand to the left. *Cf.* DIRECTION 2, HERE.

and thumbs pointing straight up, move alternately up and down before the chest. *Cf.* EITHER 3, OR 2, WHICH 1.

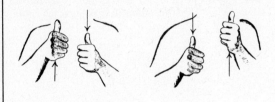

[W-95]

WHICH 1 (hwĭch), *pron. (esp. interrog. pron.), adj.* See WHETHER.

[W-93]

WHEREVER (hwâr ĕv′ ər), *conj.* Both hands, in the "5" position, are held before the chest, fingertips facing each other. With an alternate back-forth movement, the fingertips are made to strike each other. *Cf.* ANYHOW, ANYWAY, DESPITE, DOESN'T MATTER, HOWEVER 2, INDIFFERENCE, INDIFFERENT, IN SPITE OF, MAKE NO DIFFERENCE, NEVERTHELESS, NO MATTER.

[W-96]

WHICH 2, *pron.* (Something specific.) The downturned right "Y" hand is placed on the upturned left palm. *Cf.* IT 2, THAT 1, THESE, THIS, THOSE.

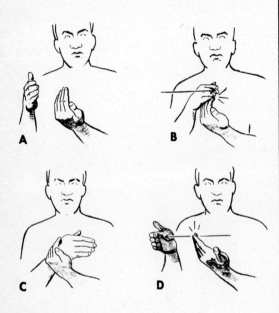

A

B

C

D

[W-97]

WHILE (hwīl), *conj. only.* (Parallel time.) Both "D" hands, palms down, move forward in unison, away from the body. They may move straight forward or may follow a slight upward arc. *Cf.* DURING, IN THE MEANTIME, IN THE PROCESS OF, MEANTIME.

[W-94]

WHETHER (hwĕ*th*′ ər), *conj.* (Considering one thing against another.) The "A" hands, palms facing

[W-98]

WHILE AGO, A 1, *phrase.* (A slight amount of time in the past.) The thumbtip of the closed right hand flicks off the tip of the curved right index finger. The hand then opens into the "5" position, palm facing the body, and swings back over the right shoulder. *Cf.* JUST NOW 1.

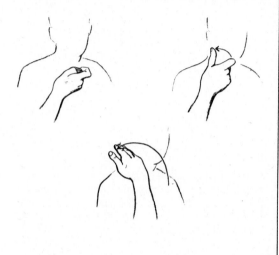

[W-99]

WHILE AGO, A 2, *phrase.* (The slight movement represents a slight amount of time.) With the closed right hand held with knuckles against the right cheek, the thumbtip flicks off the tip of the curved index finger a number of times. The eyes squint a bit and the lips are drawn out in a slight smile. The hand remains against the cheek during the flicking movement. Sometimes, instead of the flicking movement, the tip of the curved index finger scratches slightly up and down against the cheek. In this case, the palm faces back toward the shoulder. The same expression is used as in the flicking movement. *Cf.* JUST NOW 2, RECENT, RECENTLY.

[W-100]

WHILE AGO, A 3, *phrase.* (Time moved backward a bit.) The right "D" hand, palm facing the body, is placed in the palm of the left hand, which is facing

right. The right hand swings back a bit toward the body, with the index finger describing an arc. *Cf.* FEW SECONDS AGO, JUST A MOMENT AGO.

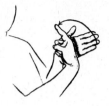

[W-101]

WHIP (hwĭp), *n., v.,* WHIPPED, WHIPPING. (The natural sign.) The left hand is held in a fist before the face, as if grasping something or someone. The right hand, at the same time, is held as if grasping a stick or whip; it strikes repeatedly at the imaginary object or person dangling from the left hand. *Cf.* BEAT 1, PUNISH 2.

[W-102]

WHISKEY 1 (hwĭs′ kĭ), *n.* (The size of the jigger is indicated.) The right hand, with index and little fingers extended and the remaining fingers held against the palm by the thumb, strikes the back of the downturned "S" hand several times. *Cf.* LIQUOR 1.

[W–103]

WHISKEY 2, *(arch.)*, *n.* (Literally, strong wine, indicated by "W" making the color rise in the face.) The right "W" hand is placed, palm facing, against the face. It moves straight up the cheek. Both hands then close into the "S" position, palms facing, and drop down forcefully a short distance in front of the chest.

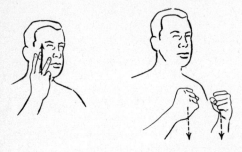

[W–104]

WHISPER (hwĭs′ pər), *n., v.,* -PERED, -PERING. (The mouth is covered.) The signer leans to one side, covers one side of his mouth, and whispers. *Cf.* SPEAK PRIVATELY.

[W–105]

WHISTLE 1 (hwĭs′ əl, wĭs′ əl), *n., v.,* -TLED, -TLING. (The natural sign.) The index and middle fingers hold an imaginary whistle at the lips, and the signer purses his lips as if blowing the whistle.

[W–106]

WHISTLE 2, *v.* (The sound.) The extended right index fingertip moves in a wavy line out from the right ear. The lips are pursed.

[W–107]

WHITE (hwīt), *adj.* (The *white,* downy breast of a swan is fingered.) The fingertips of the "5" hand are placed against the chest. The hand moves straight out from the chest, while the fingers and thumb all come together.

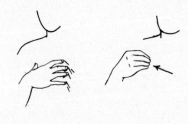

[W–108]

WHO (ho͞o), *pron.* (The pursed lips are indicated.) The right index finger traces a small counterclockwise circle in front of the lips, which are pursed in the enunciation of the word. *Cf.* WHOM.

[W–109]

WHOEVER (ho͞o ĕv′ ər), *pron.* The sign for WHO is made, followed by the sign for ANY: The "A" hand, palm out, moves down in an S-shaped curve to a

point a bit above waist level. *Cf.* WHOMEVER, WHO-
SOEVER.

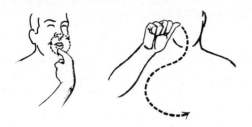

[W–110]

WHOLE (hōl), *adj., n.* (Encompassing; a gathering
together.) Both hands are held in the right angle
position, palms facing the body, and the right hand
in front of the left. The right hand makes a sweeping
outward movement around the left, and comes to
rest with the back of the right hand resting in the left
palm. *Cf.* ALL, ENTIRE, UNIVERSAL.

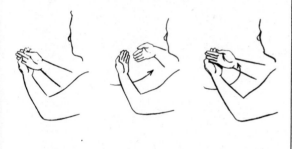

[W–111]

WHOLE (THE), *n.* (An inclusion, in the sense of a
total number.) The left hand is held in the "C" position, fingers pointing right. The right hand, in the
"5" position, fingers facing out from the body, palm
down, is held above the left. With a horizontal swing
to the right, the right hand describes an arc, as the
fingers close and are thrust into the left "C" hand,
which closes over it. *Cf.* ALL 2, ALTOGETHER, IN-
CLUDE, INCLUSIVE.

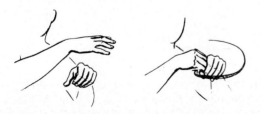

[W–112]

WHOM (hōom), *pron.* See WHO.

[W–113]

WHOMEVER (hōom ĕv' ər), *pron.* See WHOEVER.

[W–114]

WHORE (hōr), *n.* (The blood rushes up the cheek in
shame—several times for emphasis.) The curved
back of the right hand, placed against the right
cheek, moves up and off the cheek several times. *Cf.*
HARLOT, PROSTITUTE, STRUMPET.

[W–115]

WHOSE (hōoz), *pron.* (Who; outstretched open
hand signifies possession, as if pressing an item
against the chest of the person spoken to.) The sign
for WHO is made: The right index finger traces a
small counterclockwise circle in front of the lips,
which are pursed in the enunciation of the word.
Then the right "5" hand, palm facing out, moves
straight out toward the person spoken to or about.

[W–116]

WHOSOEVER (hōo sō ĕv' ər), *pron.* See WHOEVER.

[W–117]

WHY (hwī), *adv., n., interj.* (Reason—coming from the mind—modified by the letter "Y," the phonetic equivalent of WHY.) The fingertips of the right hand, palm facing the body, are placed against the forehead. The right hand then moves down and away from the forehead, assuming the "Y" position, palm still facing the body. Expression is an important indicator of the context in which this sign is used. Thus, as an interjection, a severe expression is assumed; while as an adverb or a noun, the expression is blank or inquisitive.

[W–118]

WICKED (wĭk′ ĭd), *adj.* (Tasting something, finding it unacceptable, and turning it down.) The tips of the right "B" hand are placed at the lips, and then the hand is thrown down. *Cf.* BAD 1, GRAVE 2, NAUGHTY.

[W–119]

WIDE (wīd), *adj.* (The width is indicated.) The open hands, fingers pointing out and palms facing each other, separate from their initial position an inch or two apart. *Cf.* BROAD, WIDTH.

[W–120]

WIDE AWAKE, *phrase.* (The natural sign.) The right index finger and thumb, held before the right eye, separate deliberately as the eyes open wide.

[W–121]

WIDESPREAD (wīd′ sprĕd′), *adj.* (The natural sign.) Both open hands are held palms down and fingers together before the body, with index finger edges touching. From this position the hands separate and move to either side, thumbs and fingers spreading as they do. Then, with both hands still held palms down, the right hand circles around the left fingertips and may come to rest on the back of the downturned left hand.

[W–122]

WIDTH (wĭdth), *n.* See WIDE.

[W–123]

WIFE (wīf), *n.* (A female whose hand is clasped in marriage.) The FEMALE root sign is made: The thumb of the right "A" hand moves down along the right jawbone, almost to the chin. The hands are then clasped together, right above left.

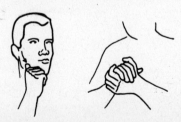

[W-124]

WILD 1 (wīld), *adj.* (Wild movements of the hands.) The "5" hands, held on either side of the head, twist in opposing circles as they move up from the head.

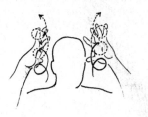

[W-125]

WILD 2, *adj.* (The "W" hands, with the same movements as in WILD 1.) Both "W" hands, palms facing out, are placed so that the index fingertips of each hand touch the respective temples. The same movement as in WILD 1 is then used, except that the hands remain in the "W" position.

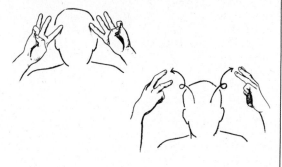

[W-126]

WILL 1 (wĭl), *v.* (Something ahead or in the future.) The upright, open right hand, palm facing left, moves straight out and slightly up from a position beside the right temple. *Cf.* BY AND BY, FUTURE, IN THE FUTURE, LATER 2, LATER ON, SHALL, WOULD.

[W-127]

WILL 2, *n.* (Grasping something and pulling it in.) The upturned "5" hands, held side by side before the chest, close slightly into a grasping position as they move in toward the body. *Cf.* COVET 1, DESIRE 1, LONG 2, NEED 2, WANT, WISH 1.

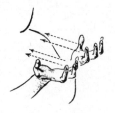

[W-128]

WILLFUL (wĭl′ fəl), *(rare), adj.* (Pushing oneself forward, and thumping the chest.) With the thumb of the right "A" hand pointing up, the right hand is brought up smartly several times against the right side of the chest. Each time contact is made, the head and shoulders move forward a bit.

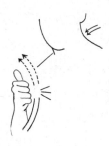

[W-129]

WILLING 1 (wĭl′ ing), *adj.* (A taking of something unto oneself.) Both open hands, palms down, are held in front of the chest. They move in unison toward the chest, where they come to rest, all fingers closed. *Cf.* ACCEPT.

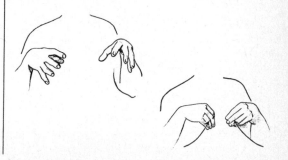

[W-130]

WILLING 2, *adj.* (A pleasurable feeling on the heart.) The open right hand is circled on the chest, over the heart. *Cf.* APPRECIATE, ENJOY, ENJOYMENT, GRATIFY 1, LIKE 3, PLEASE, PLEASURE.

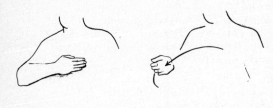

[W-131]

WILLING 3, *adj.* (The heart is opened.) The right hand is placed over the heart. It swings quickly away to a position in front of the body with palm facing left. *Cf.* MAGNANIMOUS.

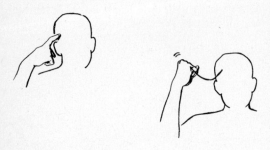

[W-132]

WILL POWER, *n.* (A strong head or mind.) The right index finger touches the right temple; then the right hand closes into the "S" position and is held upright near the head. *Cf.* STRONG-MINDED.

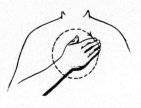

[W-133]

WIN 1 (wĭn), *v.,* WON, WINNING, *n.* (Waving of flags.) Both upright hands, grasping imaginary flags,

wave them in small circles. *Cf.* CELEBRATE, CELEBRATION, CHEER, REJOICE, VICTORY 1.

[W-134]

WIN 2, *v., n.* (Waving a flag.) The right "A" hand goes through the natural movement of waving a flag in circular fashion. Preceding this, the right hand may go through the motion of grabbing the flagstaff out of the left hand. *Cf.* EXULTATION, TRIUMPH 1, VICTORY 2.

[W-135]

WIND (wĭnd), *n.* (The blowing back and forth of the wind.) The "5" hands, palms facing and held up before the body, sway gracefully back and forth, in unison. The cheeks meanwhile are puffed up and the breath is being expelled. The nature of the swaying movement—graceful and slow, fast and violent, etc.—determines the type of wind. The strength of exhalation is also a classifier. *Cf.* BLOW 1, BREEZE, GALE, STORM.

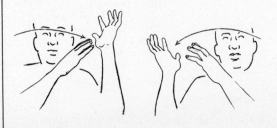

[W-136]

WINDOW (wĭn' dō), *n.* (The opening of the window.) With both palms facing the body, the little finger edge of the right hand rests atop the index finger edge of the left hand. The right hand then moves straight up and down. *Cf.* OPEN THE WINDOW.

[W-137]

WINE 1 (wīn), *n.* (The "W" hand indicates a flushed cheek.) The right "W" hand, palm facing the face, rotates at the right cheek, in either a clockwise or a counterclockwise direction.

[W-138]

WINE 2, *(eccles.)*, *n.* (Act of cutting a loaf of bread.) The left arm is held against the chest, representing a loaf of bread. The little finger edge of the right hand is drawn down over the back of the left hand several times, to indicate the cutting of slices. *Cf.* BREAD, COMMUNION (HOLY) 2, HOLY COMMUNION 2.

[W-139]

WINGS (wĭngz), *n. pl.* (The natural sign.) The fingertips of both open hands are placed on the shoulders. From this position the hands move forward off the shoulders and the fingertips turn outward to either side.

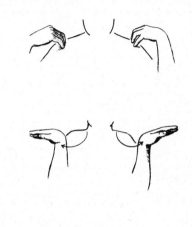

[W-140]

WINK (wĭngk), *n., v.,* WINKED, WINKING. (The natural movement.) The right thumb and index finger come together in front of the right eye, which closes at the same time.

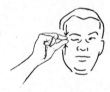

[W-141]

WINTER 1 (wĭn' tər), *n.* (The trembling from cold.) Both "S" or "W" hands, palms facing, are placed at the sides of the body. In this position the arms and hands shiver. *Cf.* CHILLY, COLD 1, FRIGID, SHIVER 1.

[W-142]

WINTER 2, *n.* (The letter "W.") The upright "W" hands, palms facing or forward, are brought together forcefully before the body one or two times.

[W-143]

WIRE 1 (wīr), *n., adj., v.,* WIRED, WIRING. (The tapping of the telegraph key.) The curved right index finger taps repeatedly against the outstretched left index finger as it moves from the base to the tip, as if making impressions on telegraph tape. *Cf.* TELEGRAM 1, TELEGRAPH 1.

[W-144]

WIRE 2, *n.,* The right middle finger moves outward across the open left palm, from wrist to fingertips. *Cf.* TELEGRAM 2, TELEGRAPH 2.

[W-145]

WISDOM (wĭz' dəm), *n.* (Measuring the depth of the mind.) The downturned "X" finger moves up and down a short distance as it rests on mid-forehead. *Cf.* INTELLECTUAL, WISE.

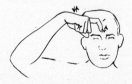

[W-146]

WISE (wīz), *adj.* See WISDOM.

[W-147]

WISH 1 (wĭsh), *v.,* WISHED, WISHING. (Grasping something and pulling it in.) The upturned "5" hands, held side by side before the chest, close slightly into a grasping position as they move in toward the body. *Cf.* COVET 1, DESIRE 1, LONG 2, NEED 2, WANT, WILL 2.

[W-148]

WISH 2, *v., n.* (The upper alimentary tract is outlined.) The right "C" hand, palm facing the body, is placed with fingertips touching mid-chest. In this position it moves down a bit. *Cf.* APPETITE, CRAVE, DESIRE 2, FAMINE, HUNGARIAN, HUNGARY, HUNGER, HUNGRY, STARVATION, STARVE, STARVED.

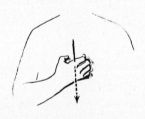

[W-149]

WISHY-WASHY (wĭsh' ĭ wŏsh´ ĭ, -wôsh´ ĭ), *(sl.), adj.* (Changing again and again.) The "5" hands, fingers curved and palms facing, swing in unison, in alternate, clockwise and counterclockwise directions, with the left and right hands alternating in front of each other. *Cf.* CHANGEABLE.

[W-150]

WITH (wĭth), *prep.* (The two hands are together, *i.e.*, WITH each other.) Both "A" hands, knuckles together and thumbs up, are moved forward in unison, away from the chest. They may also remain stationary. *Cf.* ACCOMPANY, TOGETHER, WANDER AROUND WITH.

[W-151]

WITHDRAW 1 (wĭth drô', wĭth-), *v.*, -DREW, -DRAWN, -DRAWING. (Pulling away.) The down-turned open hands are held in a line, with fingers pointing to the left, the right hand behind the left. Both hands move in unison toward the right. As they do so, they assume the "A" position. *Cf.* DEPART, EVACUATE, FORSAKE 1, GRADUATE 2, LEAVE 1, RETIRE 1.

[W-152]

WITHDRAW 2, *v.* (Removing.) The right "A" hand, resting in the palm of the left "5" hand, moves slightly up and away, describing a small arc. It is then cast downward, opening into the "5" position, palm down, as if removing something from the left hand and casting it down. *Cf.* ABOLISH 2, ABSENCE 2, ABSENT 2, ABSTAIN, CHEAT 2, DEDUCT, DEFICIENCY, DELETE 1, LESS 2, MINUS 3, OUT 2, RE-

MOVE 1, SUBTRACT, SUBTRACTION, TAKE AWAY FROM.

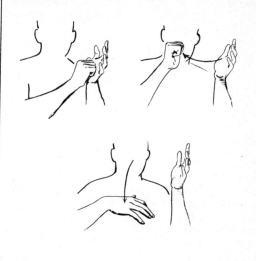

[W-153]

WITHDRAW 3, *v.* (Pulling out.) The index and middle fingers of the right "H" hand are grasped by the left hand. The right hand pulls out of the left. *Cf.* QUIT, RESIGN.

[W-154]

WITHDRAW 4, *v.* (Withdraw a resolution by pulling it off the agenda.) Both hands, facing forward, close and are pulled down.

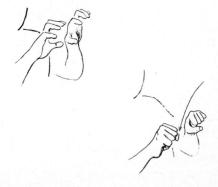

[W–155]

WITHIN (wĭth ĭn', wĭth-), *adv., prep.* (The natural sign.) The fingers of the right hand are thrust into the left. *Cf.* IN, INSIDE, INTO.

[W–156]

WITHOUT (wĭth out', wĭth-), *prep., adv.* (The hands fall away from the WITH position.) The sign for WITH is formed. The hands then drop down, open, and part, ending in the palms-down position. *Cf.* MINUS 2.

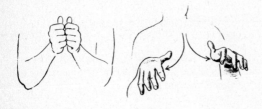

[W–157]

WITNESS (wĭt' nĭs), *v.*, -NESSED, -NESSING. (The vision is directed forward.) The tips of the right "V" fingers point to the eyes. The right hand is then swung around and forward a bit. *Cf.* GAZE, LOOK AT, OBSERVE 1.

[W–158]

WOEFULLY WEAK, *adj. phrase.* (The fingers collapse.) The little, ring, middle, and index fingers of the right hand, standing rigidly in the upturned left palm, suddenly bend at the knuckles and the right

hand "crumples" into the left. *Cf.* HOPELESSLY WEAK.

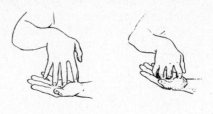

[W–159]

WOLF (wŏŏlf), *n.* (The pointed muzzle or snout.) The fingers grasp the nose, and then the hand is drawn away from the face as the fingertips come together with the thumb.

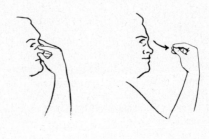

[W–160]

WOMAN (wŏŏm' ən), *n.* (A big female.) The FE-MALE prefix sign is made: The thumb of the right "A" hand moves down along the line of the right jaw, from ear almost to chin. This outlines the string used to tie ladies' bonnets in olden days. This is a root sign to modify many others. The downturned right hand then moves up to a point above the head, to indicate the relative height.

[W–161]

WONDER 1 (wŭn' dər), *v.*, -DERED, -DERING. (Turning thoughts over in the mind.) Both index fingers, pointing to the forehead, describe continuous alternating circles. *Cf.* CONSIDER 2, CONTEMPLATE, PONDER, SPECULATE 2, SPECULATION 2, WEIGH 2.

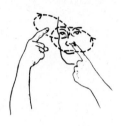

[W-162]

WONDER 2, *n.* (The hands gesture toward the heavens.) The "5" hands, palms out and arms raised rather high, are positioned somewhat above the line of vision. The arms move abruptly forward and up once or twice. An expression of pleasure or surprise is usually assumed. *Cf.* EXCELLENT, GRAND 1, GREAT 3, MARVEL, MARVELOUS, MIRACLE, O!, SPLENDID 1, SWELL 1, WONDERFUL 1.

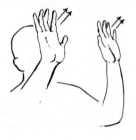

[W-163]

WONDER 3, *v.* (The letter "W.") The sign for WONDER 1 is made, using the right "W" hand.

[W-164]

WONDERFUL 1 (wŭn' dər fəl), *adj.* See WONDER 2.

[W-165]

WONDERFUL 2, *adj., interj.* (The feelings are titillated.) With the thumb resting on the upper part of the chest, the fingers are wiggled back and forth. *Cf.* ELEGANT, FINE 1, GRAND 2, GREAT 4, SPLENDID 2, SWELL 2.

[W-166]

WON'T (wōnt, wŭnt), *v.* Contraction of *will not.* (Holding back.) The right "A" hand, palm facing left, moves up sharply to a position above the right shoulder. *Cf.* REFUSE.

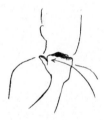

[W-167]

WOOD (wŏŏd), *n.* (The sawing of wood.) The little finger edge of the open right hand moves back and forth in a sawing motion over the back of the downturned left hand. *Cf.* LUMBER 1, SAW 1.

[W–168]

WOODS (woŏdz), *n. pl.* (A series of trees.) The open right "5" hand is raised, with elbow resting on the back of the left hand, as in TREE, *q.v.* As the right hand swings around and back a number of times, pivoting at the wrist, the left arm carries the right arm from left to right. *Cf.* FOREST.

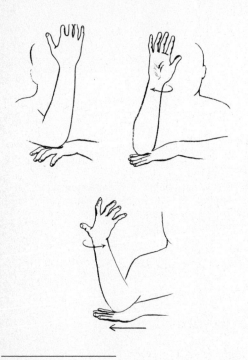

[W–169]

WOOL (woŏl), *n.* (Plucking wool.) The right "A" hand is held palm down on the left forearm. The hand then moves quickly away from the arm, as if plucking wool from an animal. The action may be repeated.

[W–170]

WORD (wûrd), *n.* (A small part of a sentence, *i.e.,* a word.) The tips of the right index finger and thumb, about an inch apart, are placed on the side

of the outstretched left index finger, which represents the length of a sentence. *Cf.* INCH 1, VERBAL 2.

[W–171]

WORK (wûrk), *n., v.,* WORKED, WORKING. (Striking an anvil.) Both "S" hands are held palms down. The right hand strikes against the back of the left a number of times. *Cf.* JOB, LABOR, OCCUPATION, TASK, TOIL, TRAVAIL, VOCATION.

[W–172]

WORKER (wûr′ kər), *n.* See WORK. This is followed by the sign for INDIVIDUAL: Both open hands, palms facing each other, move down the sides of the body, tracing its outline to the hips.

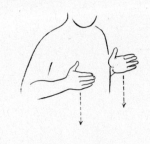

[W–173]

WORKSHOP (wûrk′ shŏp′), *n.* (A collection of people together in a group; the letters "W" and "S.") The "W" hands, palms out, touch at the tips of the index fingers or at the base of the thumbs. They swing around describing a circle, ending in the "S" position, palms facing the body and little finger edges touching. (This sign is used only in the sense of a seminar or conference and never as a place where things are manufactured or repaired.)

[W–174]

WORLD (wûrld), *n.* (The letter "W" in orbit.) The right "W" hand makes a complete circle around the left "W" hand and comes to rest on the thumb edge of the left "W" hand. The left hand frequently assumes the "S" position instead of the "W," to represent the stationary sun. *Cf.* GLOBE 2.

[W–175]

WORM (wûrm), *n.* (The natural motion.) The index finger of the right "X" hand, placed against the left palm, which is facing right, wiggles up and down as it moves along the left palm from base to fingertips.

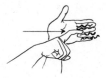

[W–176]

WORN 1 (wōrn), *adj.* (Friction causing wear.) The right fingertips move in a counterclockwise circle as they rub against the upturned left palm.

[W–177]

WORN 2, *adj.* Both "A" hands are held knuckle to knuckle before the body, thumb edges up. From this position both hands turn over to either side, opening as they do, and ending palms up and side by side, fingers spread and pointing forward. *Cf.* WORN OUT.

[W–178]

WORN OUT, *adj. phrase.* See WORN 2.

[W–179]

WORRIED, *v.* (A clouding over; a troubling.) Both "B" hands, palms facing each other, are rotated alternately before the forehead. *Cf.* ANNOY 2, ANNOYANCE 2, ANXIOUS 2, BOTHER 2, CONCERN 1, FRET, PROBLEM 1, TROUBLE, WORRY 1.

[W–180]

WORRY 1 (wûr' ĭ), *v.,* -RIED, -RYING. See WORRIED.

[W–181]

WORRY 2, *v., n.* (Drumming at the forehead, to represent many worries making inroads on the thinking process.) The right fingertips drum against the forehead. The signer frowns somewhat, or looks very concerned.

[W–182]

WORRY 3, *v. n.* (The "W" hands.) The sign for WORRY 1 is made, but with the "W" hands.

[W–183]

WORRY 4, *v., n.* (Making inroads on one's emotional equilibrium.) The middle fingers are thrust alternately and rhythmically against the chest. The signer frowns somewhat or looks concerned.

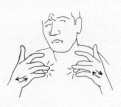

[W–184]

WORSE 1 (wûrs), *adj.* The "V" hands, palms facing the body, cross quickly. The comparative degree suffix sign -ER is often used after this sign: The upright thumb of the right "A" hand is brought

sharply up to a level opposite the right ear. *Cf.* WORST 1.

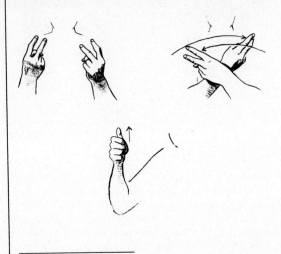

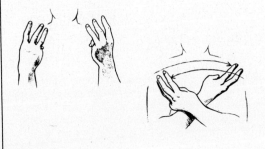

[W–185]

WORSE 2, *adj.* The same movements as in WORSE 1 are used, except that the "W" hands are employed. The comparative degree suffix sign may likewise follow. *Cf.* WORST 2.

[W–186]

WORSE 3, *(rare), adj.* The "A" hands face each other, the right poised somewhat above the left. The right hand swings down in an arc, passing the stationary left hand. As it does so, the bases of both hands, or their knuckles, come into brief contact. *Cf.* WORST 3.

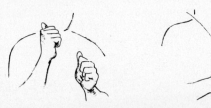

[W–187]

WORSHIP (wûr′ shĭp), *n., v.,* -SHIPED, -SHIPING. (Worshiping.) The hands are clasped together, with the left cupped over the right. Both are brought in toward the body, while the eyes are shut and the head is bowed slightly. *Cf.* ADORE, AMEN, DEVOUT, PIOUS.

[W–188]

WORST 1 (wûrst), *adj.* The sign for WORSE 1 is made. This is followed by the superlative degree suffix -EST: The upright thumb of the right "A" hand is brought sharply up to a level a bit above the right side of the head. *Cf.* WORSE 1.

[W–189]

WORST 2, *adj.* The sign for WORSE 2 is repeated, followed by the superlative degree suffix sign, as in WORST 1. *Cf.* WORSE 2.

[W–190]

WORST 3, *(rare), adj.* The sign for WORSE 3 is repeated, followed by the superlative degree suffix sign, as in WORST 1. *Cf.* WORSE 3.

[W–191]

WORTH (wûrth), *adj., n.* Both "F" hands, palms facing each other, move apart, up, and together in a smooth elliptical fashion, coming together at the tips of the thumbs and index fingers of both hands. *Cf.* DESERVE, ESSENTIAL, IMPORTANT 1, MAIN, MERIT, PRECIOUS, PROMINENT 2, SIGNIFICANCE 1, SIGNIFICANT, VALUABLE, VALUE, VITAL 1, WORTHWHILE, WORTHY.

[W–192]

WORTHLESS 1 (wûrth′ lĭs), *adj.* (The hands are thrown out from the sign for WORTH.) The "F" hands, palms down and held side by side or touching, close into the "S" or "E" position, palms still down. They are then thrown out and apart, opening into the "5" position, palms still down.

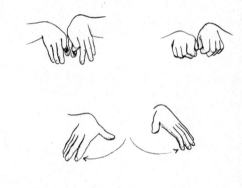

[W–193]

WORTHLESS 2, *(vern.), adj.* (A modification of WORTHLESS 1.) The "F" hands face each other, the right above the left. The right hand swings down in an arc, passing the left. As it does so, the thumb and index finger of the right hand strike the corresponding fingers of the left rather sharply. An expression of disdain is assumed. *Cf.* NO GOOD 2.

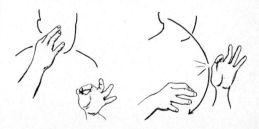

[W–194]

WORTHWHILE (wûrth′ hwīl′), *adj.* See WORTH.

[W–195]

WORTHY (wûr′ thǐ), *adj.* See WORTH.

[W–196]

WOULD (wŏŏd, *unstressed* wəd), *v.* (Something ahead or in the future.) The upright, open right hand, palm facing left, moves straight out and slightly up from a position beside the right temple. *Cf.* BY AND BY, FUTURE, IN THE FUTURE, LATER 2, LATER ON, SHALL, WILL 1.

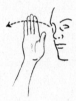

[W–197]

WOUND (wŏŏnd), *n.* (A stabbing pain.) The "D" hands, index fingers pointing to each other, are rotated in elliptical fashion before the chest—simultaneously but in opposite directions. *Cf.* ACHE, HARM 1, HURT 1, INJURE 1, INJURY, MAR 1, OFFEND, OFFENSE, PAIN, SIN.

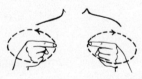

[W–198]

WOW! (wou), *(colloq.), interj.* (This is a universal gesture.) The prone right hand is shaken up and down. An appropriate expression is assumed.

[W–199]

WREATH (rēth), *n.* (The shape.) The right "C" hand, palm facing out, describes an arc from left to right. *Cf.* CHRISTMAS 1.

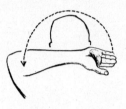

[W–200]

WRECK (rĕk), *n.* The fists come together with force. *Cf.* COLLIDE 1, COLLISION 1, CRASH, RUN UP AGAINST.

[W–201]

WRENCH (rĕnch), *n.* (The natural movement.) The index finger of the right hand is grasped by the outstretched index and middle fingers of the left hand. The left hand executes a series of up-and-down movements, as if manipulating a wrench. *Cf.* MECHANIC 2, PIPE-FITTING, PLUMBER, STEAM FITTER.

[W–202]

WRESTLING (rĕs′ lǐng), *n.* (Locked in combat.) The open "5" hands, fingers interlocked, move forward and back in front of the chest.

[W–203]

WRIST (rĭst), *n.* (The natural act of indicating the wrist.) The right hand grasps the left wrist.

[W–204]

WRISTWATCH, *n.* (The shape of the wristwatch.) The thumb and index finger of the right hand, forming a circle, are placed on the back of the left wrist. *Cf.* WATCH 4.

[W–205]

WRITE (rīt), *v.,* WROTE, WRITTEN, WRITING. (The natural movement.) The right index finger and thumb, grasping an imaginary pen, write across the open left palm. *Cf.* PEN, SIGN, SIGNATURE.

[W–206]

WRITER (rī′ tər), *n.* (An individual who writes.) The sign for WRITE is made. This is followed by the

sign for INDIVIDUAL: Both open hands, palms facing each other, move down the sides of the body, tracing its outline to the hips.

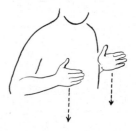

[W–207]

WRONG 1 (rông, rŏng), *adj., n.* (Rationale obscure; the thumb and little finger are said to represent, respectively, right and wrong, with the head poised between the two.) The right "Y" hand, palm facing the body, is brought up to the chin. *Cf.* ERROR, FAULT 2, MISTAKE, SACRILEGIOUS.

[W–208]

WRONG 2, *adj., n.* (Going astray.) The open right hand, palm facing left, is placed with its little finger edge resting on the upturned left palm. The right hand curves rather sharply to the left as it moves across the palm. *Cf.* DEVIATE 1.

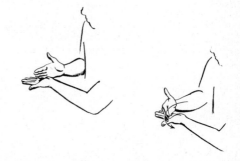

X

XEROX (zǐr′ ŏks), *n.* (The letter "X;" the movement of the light as it moves under the item to be copied.) The "X" finger moves back and forth rather rapidly under the downturned hand.

[X–2]

XMAS, *n.* See CHRISTMAS.

[X–3]

X-RAY (ĕks′ rā′), *n.* (The opening and closing of the camera shutter.) The outstretched fingers, resting against the thumb, are pointed at the area of the body to be photographed. The hand opens and closes rapidly. For a chest X-ray, the "B" hands, facing down, are positioned so that they outline the upper and lower limits of the chest.

[X–4]

XYLOPHONE (zī′ lə fōn′, zǐl′ ə-), *n.* (The natural motion.) The closed hands, holding imaginary sticks, go through the motions of tapping out a tune on the instrument.

Y

[Y–1]

YARD 1 (yärd), *n.* (A measuring off.) Both modified "O" hands are held before the face, palms facing each other. Then the right hand moves straight away to the right side, while the left hand keeps its original position.

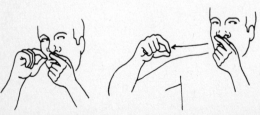

[Y–2]

YARD 2, *n.* (A fenced-in enclosure.) The "5" hands are held with palms facing the body and fingers interlocked but not curved. The hands separate, swinging first to either side of the body, and then moving in toward the body, tracing a circle and coming together palms out and bases touching. *Cf.* FIELD 2, GARDEN.

[Y-3]

YEAR (yĭr), *n.* (A circumference around the sun.) The right "S" hand, palm facing left, represents the earth. It is positioned atop the left "S" hand, whose palm faces right, and represents the sun. The right "S" hand describes a clockwise circle around the left, coming to rest in its original position.

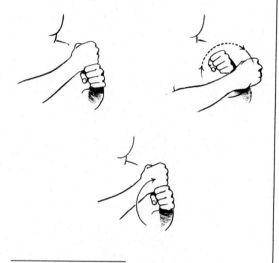

[Y-4]

YEARLY (yĭr′ lĭ, yûr′-), *adj., adv., n.* (Several years brought forward.) This sign is actually a modification of the sign for YEAR, *q.v.* The ball of the right "S" hand, moving straight out from the body, palm facing left, glances over the thumb side of the left "S" hand, which is held palm facing right. As this contact is made, the right index finger is flung straight out, and the right hand, in this new position, continues forward. This is repeated several times, to indicate several years. *Cf.* ANNUAL, EVERY YEAR.

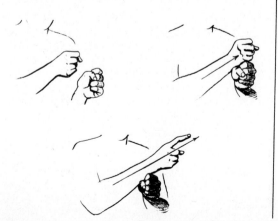

[Y-5]

YEARS (yĭrs), *n. pl.* The sign for YEAR is made twice.

[Y-6]

YELL (yĕl), *v.,* YELLED, YELLING. (Sound escapes from the lips.) The right "C" hand is held to the mouth and is then drawn away in a continuous motion, as if a sound is being drawn out of the mouth. The motion is done quickly and forcefully.

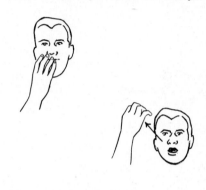

[Y-7]

YELLOW (yĕl′ ō), *adj.* (The letter "Y.") The "Y" hand, pivoted at the wrist, is shaken back and forth repeatedly.

[Y-8]

YELLOW RACE, *n. phrase.* (YELLOW, SKIN.) The sign for YELLOW is made. The signer then pinches the skin of the back of the left hand.

[Y-9]

YES (yĕs), *(colloq.), adv., n.* (The nodding.) The right "S" hand, imitating the head, "nods" up and down.

[Y-10]

YESTERDAY (yĕs′ tər dǐ, -dā′), *adv., n.* (A short distance into the past.) The thumbtip of the right "A" or "Y" hand, palm facing left, rests on the right cheek. It then moves back a short distance.

[Y-11]

YET 1 (yĕt), *adv., conj.* (Duration of movement from past to present.) The right "Y" hand is held palm down in front of the right shoulder and is then moved slowly down and forward in a smooth curve. *Cf.* CONTINUE 2, STAY 2, STILL 1.

[Y-12]

YET 2, *(arch.), adv.* The fingertips of the down-turned right "5" hand execute a series of small

jumps as they move forward along the upturned left palm, from its base to the left fingertips.

[Y-13]

YIELD (yēld), *v.,* YIELDED, YIELDING. (Throwing up the hands in a gesture of surrender.) Both "A" hands are held palms down before the chest and then thrown up in unison, ending in the "5" position. *Cf.* ABDICATE, CEDE, DISCOURAGE 1, FORFEIT, GIVE UP, LOSE HOPE, RELINQUISH, RENOUNCE, RENUNCIATION, SURRENDER 1.

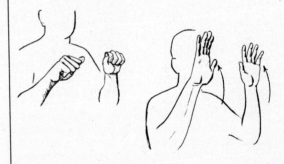

[Y-14]

YOKE (yōk), *n.* (Pressing down on the neck.) The right hand grasps the right side of the neck and pushes the head down a bit.

[Y-15]

YOM KIPPUR (yŏm kǐp′ ər; *Heb.* yŏm kǐp′ o͞ɑr), *(eccles.), n.* (Day of Atonement, *i.e.,* Sorrow.) The sign for DAY is made: The right "D" hand, palm facing left, is held high, with the right elbow resting in the palm or on the back of the left hand. The right arm describes a 45-degree arc as it moves from right to left. The sign for SORROW or SORROW is then made: The right "S" hand, palm facing the body, is rotated several times over the area of the heart. The "S" hand may instead strike the heart. *Cf.* DAY OF ATONEMENT.

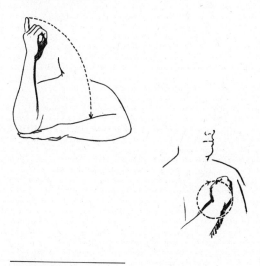

shoulders. This is repeated several times. *Cf.* ADO-LESCENCE, ADOLESCENT, YOUTH, YOUTHFUL.

[Y-19]

YOUR (yŏor), *pron., adj.* (The outstretched open hand indicates possession, as if pressing an item against the chest of the person spoken to.) The right "5" hand, palm facing out, moves straight out toward the person spoken to. This sign is also used for YOURS.

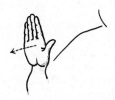

[Y-16]

YOU 1 (ŭ), *pron. sing.* (The natural sign.) The signer points to the person he is addressing.

[Y-17]

YOU 2, *pron. pl.* (The natural sign.) The signer points to several persons before him, or swings his index finger in an arc from left to right.

[Y-18]

YOUNG (yŭng), *adj.* (The spirits bubbling up.) The fingertips of both open hands, placed on either side of the chest just below the shoulders, move up and off the chest, in unison, to a point just above the

---

[Y-20]

YOU'RE WELCOME 1. (Words extended politely from the mouth.) The fingertips of the right "5" hand are placed at the mouth. The hand moves away from the mouth to a palm-up position before the body. The signer meanwhile usually nods smilingly. *Cf.* FAREWELL 1, GOODBYE 1, HELLO 1, THANKS, THANK YOU.

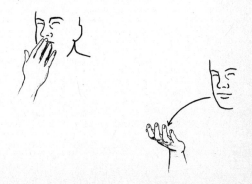

[Y–21]

YOU'RE WELCOME 2, *phrase*. (A straightening out.) The right hand, fingers together and palm facing left, is placed in the upturned left palm, whose fingers point away from the body. The right hand slides straight out along the left palm, over the left fingers, and stops with its heel resting on the left fingertips. *Cf.* ALL RIGHT, O.K. 1, PRIVILEGE, RIGHT 1, RIGHTEOUS 1.

[Y–22]

YOURS (yŏŏrz, yôrz), *pron.* See YOUR.

[Y–23]

YOURSELF (yŏŏr sĕlf'), *pron.* The signer moves his upright thumb in the direction of the person spoken to. See SELF.

[Y–24]

YOURSELVES (yŏŏr sĕlvz'), *pron. pl.* The signer moves his upright thumb toward several people before him, in a series of small forward movements from left to right.

[Y–25]

YOUTH (ūth), *n.* See YOUNG.

[Y–26]

YOUTHFUL (ūth' fəl), *adj.* See YOUTH.

[Y–27]

YUGOSLAVIA (ū´ gō slä' vĭ ə), *n.* (Part of the native costume.) The right "5" hand, palm facing the body, is drawn across the chest from the left shoulder to the right side of the waist. The "Y" hand is used more frequently today.

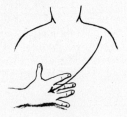

Z

[Z–1]

ZEAL (zēl), *n.* (Rubbing the hands together in zeal or ambition.) The open hands are rubbed vigorously back and forth against each other. *Cf.* AMBITIOUS 1, ANXIOUS 1, ARDENT, DILIGENCE 1, DILIGENT, EAGER, EAGERNESS, EARNEST, ENTHUSIASM, EN-THUSIASTIC, INDUSTRIOUS, METHODIST, ZEALOUS.

[Z–2]

ZEALOUS (zĕl′ əs), *adj.* See ZEAL.

[Z–3]

ZEBRA (zē brə), *n.* (A striped horse.) The sign for HORSE is made: The "U" hands are placed palms out at either side of the head. The index and middle fingers move forward and back repeatedly, imitating the movement of a horse's ears. The signer, using his thumbs and index fingers, then traces a series of stripes across the chest.

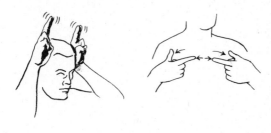

[Z–4]

ZERO 1 (zĭr′ ō), *(colloq.), n.* (An emphatic movement of the "O," *i.e.,* ZERO hand.) The little finger edge of the right "O" hand is brought sharply into the upturned left palm. *Cf.* NAUGHT 3, NONE 4, NOTHING 4.

[Z–5]

ZERO 2, *n.* (The natural sign.) The right "O" hand, palm facing left, is held in front of the face. It then moves an inch or two toward the right.

[Z–6]

ZOOM OFF (zo͞om), *(colloq.), v. phrase.* (The natural movement of vanishing in the distance.) The back of the thumb of the right "L" hand rests on the back of the prone left hand. The right hand suddenly and quickly leaves this position, moving off into the distance. As it does so, the tips of the thumb and index finger come together.

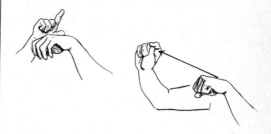

Bibliography

1 *A basic course in fingerspelling and sign language: a guide for teaching the course.* Austin, Tex.: Texas School for the Deaf, 1973.

2 Abbott, C. "Encodedness and sign language." *Sign lang. studies* 7 (1975), 109–120.

3 Abelson, B. R. *Alpha-Hands flash cards* and teacher-parent manual. Buffalo, N.Y.: Kenworthy Educational Service, 1969.

4 Abernethy, E. "An historical sketch of the manual alphabets." *Amer. ann. deaf* 104:2 (March 1959), 232–240.

5 Abrams, P. *Simultaneous language program for non-verbal preschool children.* Chicago, Ill.: Dysfunctioning Child Center, Michael Reese Medical Center, 1975.

6 Adler, E. *Grammatical language and the language of signs.* Paper delivered to the international research seminar on the vocational rehabilitation of deaf persons, Washington, D.C., 1968.

7 Affolter, F. "Sensory deprivation and the development of serial pattern perception: a comparison study of hearing, deaf, and blind children." In F. B. Crammatte, and A. B. Crammatte (eds.), *VII world congress of the world federation of the deaf.* Silver Spring, Md.: National Assoc. of the Deaf, 1976, 125–127.

8 Ahlgren, I. *Early linguistic cognitive development in the deaf and severely hard of hearing.* Paper presented at the national symposium on sign language research and teaching, Chicago, Ill., 1977.

9 Ahlgren, M. *Teaching English as a second language to a young deaf girl.* Working paper, available for consultation in LRL.

10 Akerly, S. "Observations on the language of signs . . ." *Am. j. of science and arts* 8:2 (August 1824), 348–358.

11 "All hands on deck: playing cards depicting gesture language." *UNESCO Courier* 27 (1974).

12 Amon, A. *Talking hands. How to use Indian sign language.* Garden City, N.Y.: Doubleday, 1968.

13 Anderson, J. "The language of gesture." *Folklore* 31 (1970), 70–71.

14 Anderson, L. B. *Towards a grammar of the American sign language on a comparative-typological basis.* Boulder, Colo.: 1977.

15 Anderson, L. B. "Historical change and stability of American sign language." Working paper, Gallaudet College, linguistics research laboratory, Washington, D.C., 1978.

16 Anderson, L. B. "Perceptual space vs. articulatory features." Working paper, Gallaudet College, linguistics research laboratory, Washington, D.C., 1978.

17 Anderson, L. B. "Phonological processes in sign languages." Working paper, Gallaudet College, linguistics research laboratory, Washington, D.C., 1978.

18 Anderson, L. B. *A comparison of some American, English, and Swedish signs: evidence on historical change in signs and some family relationships of sign languages.* Washington, D.C.: Gallaudet College, 1979.

19 Anderson, L. B. *Handshape changes in the history of fingerspelling.* Washington, D.C.: Gallaudet College, 1979.

20 Anderson, L. B., et al. "The grammar of noun-classification in spoken and signed languages." Working paper, Gallaudet College, linguistics research laboratory, Washington, D.C., 1979.

21 Anderson, T. "What of the sign language?" *Amer. ann. deaf* 83:2 (1938), 120–130.

22 Andreas, J. *Let your fingers do the talking: a teaching manual for use with non-verbal retardates.* Sonyea, N.Y.: Dept. of Communication Disorders and Education and Teaching, Craig Developmental Center, 1975.

23 Anthony, D. A. "Handy ways to teach English." *Hearing and speech news,* 41:6, 8–9, 22.

24 Anthony, D. A. *Seeing essential English.* Unpub. thesis, Eastern Michigan Univ., 1966.

25 Anthony, D. A. (ed.) *Seeing essential English manual.* Greeley, Colo.: Univ. of Northern Colo., 1971.

26 Anthony, D. A. *Book I: the seeing essential English codebreaker.* Greeley, Colo.: Univ. of Northern Colo., 1974.

27 Anthony, D., & Assocs. *Seeing essential English.* Anaheim, Calif.: Educational Services Div., Anaheim Union High School District, 1971. (2 vols.)

28 Anthony, D. A., et al. *Seeing essential English codebreaker.* (Rev. ed.), Boulder, Colo.: Pruett Publ. Co., 1979.

29 Anthony, D. A., et al. *Seeing essential English: elementary dictionary.* Boulder, Colo.: Pruett Publ. Co., 1979.

30 Argila, C. A. *Computer generation and recognition of sign language.* Copy available for consultation in the LRL summary.

31 Arnason, J. *Dactylismus ecclesiasticus.* Iceland: Utgefid af P. Jonssyni, Kaupmannahøfn, 1838.

32 Asher, J. *Learning another language through actions: the complete teacher's guide book.* Los Gatos, Calif.: Sky Oaks Productions, 1977.

33 Athey, J. *Measuring rate in signing.* La Jolla, Calif.: Salk Institute for Biological Studies, 1976.

34 Aungier, G. J. *A history of antiquities of Lyon monastery in the parish of Isleworth.* London, 1840.

35 Australian Catholic Schools for the Deaf. *How to converse with the deaf.* Waratah and Castle Hill. New South Wales: Australian Schools for the Deaf, 1942.

36 Babbini, B. E. "American manual alphabet." Training films series, captioned films for the deaf, Graphic Film Corp., n.d.

37 Babbini, B. E. *An introductory course in manual communication.* Northridge, Calif.: San Fernando Valley State College, 1965.

38 Babbini, B. E. *Manual communication: a course of study outline for instructors.* Urbana, Ill.: University of Illinois Press, 1973.

39 Babbini, B. E. *Manual communication: a course of study outline for students.* Urbana, Ill.: University of Illinois Press, 1973.

40 Babbini, B. E. *Manual Communication: fingerspelling and the language of signs.* Urbana, Ill.: University of Illinois Press, 1974.

41 Bacon, A. *A manual of gesture.* Chicago, Ill., 1873.

42 Baker, C. *Eye-openers in ASL.* Paper presented at Calif. linguistics assoc. conference, San Diego, 1976.

43 Baker, C. *What's not on the other hand in American sign language.* Paper presented at the 12th regional meeting of the Chicago linguistics society, 1976.

44 Baker, C. "Regulators and turn-taking in American sign language discourse." In L. Friedman (ed.), *On the other hand: new perspectives on American sign language.* New York: Academic Press, 1977, 215–236.

45 Baker, C., and D. Cokely. *Learning American sign language: a text based on linguistic research.* Silver Spring, Md.: T. J. Publishers, 1980.

46 Baker, C., and A. DeMatteo. *Toward understanding the structure of Ameslan.* Berkeley: Univ. of Calif. Press, 1974.

47 Baker, C., and C. Padden. *Studying American sign language as a multi-channel communication system.* Paper presented at the conference of sign language and neurolinguistics, Rochester, N.Y., 1976.

48 Baker, C., and C. Padden. *American sign language: a look at its history, structure, and community.* Silver Spring, Md.: T. J. Publishers, 1978.

49 Baker, C., and C. Padden. "Focusing on the non-manual components of American sign language." In P. Siple (ed.), *Understanding language through sign language research.* New York: Academic Press, 1978, 27–57.

50 Ballin, A. *The deaf mute howls.* Los Angeles, Calif.: Grafton Publishing Co., 1930.

51 Ballingall, P. *The sign language of deaf children in New Zealand.* Unpub. thesis, Univ. of Auckland, New Zealand, 1972.

52 Barakat, R. A. "Gesture systems." *Keystone folklore quarterly,* 1969, 105–121.

53 Barakat, R. *Cistercian sign language—a study in non-verbal communication.* Kalamazoo, Mich.: Cistercian Publications, 1975.

54 Barakat, R. "On ambiguity in the Cistercian sign language." *Sign lang. studies* 8 (1975), 275–289.

55 Barnes, S. *The use of sign language as a technique for language acquisition in autistic children: an applied model bridging verbal and non-verbal theoretical systems.* Unpub. dissertation, Calif. School of Professional Psy., 1973.

56 Baron, N. S. *Functional range in speech, writing, and sign: an integrative analysis.* Providence, R.I.: Brown Univ., 1977.

57 Baron, N. S. "Trade jargons and pidgins: a functionalist approach." *J. of creole studies* 1:1 (1977), 5–28.

58 Baron, N. S., and L. M. Isensee. *Effectiveness of manual versus spoken language with an autistic child.* Unpub. paper, Providence, R.I.: Brown Univ., 1976.

59 Baron, N. S., and L. M. Isensee. *A functional analysis of iconicity in language.* Washington, D.C.: Gallaudet College, 1977.

60 Barrois, J. *Dactylologie et langage primitif.* Paris, France, 1850.

61 Battison, R. *Language divided: two modes.* La Jolla, Calif.: Univ. of Calif., 1971.

62 Battison, R. *Some observations on sign languages, semantics and aphasia.* La Jolla, Calif.: Univ. of Calif., 1972.

63 Battison, R. *Gesture in aphasic rehabilitation and*

the lateralization of sign language. La Jolla, Calif.: Univ. of Calif., 1973.

64 Battison, R. "Phonological deletion in American sign language." *Sign lang. studies* 5 (1974), 1–19.

65 Battison, R. *Fingerspelled loan words in American sign language: evidence for restructuring.* Paper presented at the conference of sign language and neurolinguistics, Rochester, N.Y., 1976.

66 Battison, R. *Lexical borrowing in American sign language.* La Jolla, Calif.: Univ. of Calif., 1977.

67 Battison, R. *Lexical borrowing in American sign language.* Silver Spring, Md.: Linstock Press, 1978.

68 Battison, R., and C. Erting. *The hand is faster than the brain: errors in ASL.* Paper presented at the summer meeting of the linguistic society of America, Amherst, Mass., 1974.

69 Battison, R., and I. K. Jordan. "Communication with foreign signers: fact and fancy." *Sign lang. studies* 10 (1976), 53–68.

70 Battison, R., H. Markowicz, and J. Woodward. "A good rule of thumb: variable phonology in American sign language." In R. Shuy and R. Fasold (eds.), *New ways of analyzing variation in English, vol. 2.* Washington, D.C.: Georgetown Univ. Press, 1976.

71 Battison, R., and C. Padden. *Sign language aphasia: a case study.* Paper presented at the 49th annual meeting of the linguistic society of America, N.Y., 1974.

72 Baur, S. "First message from the planet of the apes." *New York* magazine 8:8 (1975), 30–37.

73 Bayne, H. L. *Basic signs.* Available in Gallaudet College library.

74 Bearden, C. E. *A handbook for religious interpreters for the deaf.* Atlanta, Ga.: Home Mission Board of the Southern Baptist Convention, 1975.

75 Bearden, C., and J. Potter. *A manual of religious signs.* Atlanta, Ga.: Home Mission Board of the Southern Baptist Convention, 1973.

76 Becker, V. "The universal language." *Lion* magazine, 1953, 26–28.

77 Becker, V. "Sign language." *Silent worker* 8:7 (1956), 4–7.

78 Becker, V. *Underwater sign language,* catalog no. 1919. Write author: Supervisor of physically handicapped, public school system, San Francisco, Calif.

79 Beirne, H. *Total communication: handbook.* Anchorage, AL.: Alaska Treatment Center for Crippled Children & Adults, 1972.

80 Belcher, J. *110 school survival signs.* Northridge, Calif.: Joyce Media, 1977.

81 Bell, A. G. "Utility of signs." *The educator,* 1894.

82 Bellugi, U. "Review of Joanne Greenberg, in this sign." *Psychology today* 4 (1971), 10–11.

83 Bellugi, U. *The language of signs and the signs of language.* Paper presented to the 3rd annual Michigan conference on applied linguistics, Ann Arbor, Mich. 1971.

84 Bellugi, U. "Studies in sign language." In T. J. O'Rourke (ed.), *Psycholinguistics and total communication.* Washington, D.C.: *Amer. ann. deaf,* 1972, 68–83.

85 Bellugi, U. *The study of sign language: book review of Dr. W. C. Stokoe's book by this title.* La Jolla, Calif.: Salk Institute for Biological Studies, 1972.

86 Bellugi, U. "Some aspects of language acquisition." In T. A. Sebeok (ed.), *Trends in linguistics.* The Hague: Mouton, 1974, 1135–1158.

87 Bellugi, U. *Attitudes toward sign language: is there need for a change?* San Diego, Calif.: Salk Institute for Biological Studies, 1975.

88 Bellugi, U. "Interview for the deaf American." *The deaf Amer.* 27(9) (1975), 12–14.

89 Bellugi, U. *On the creation of lexical items by compounding.* Unpub. MS. La Jolla, Calif.: Salk Institute for Biological Studies, 1975.

90 Bellugi, U. "Attitudes toward sign language." In A. B. Crammate and F. B. Crammate (eds.), *Proceedings of the 7th world federation of the deaf.* Silver Spring, Md.: National Association of the Deaf, 1976, 266–273.

91 Bellugi, U. "Attitudes toward sign language: is there need for a change?" *British deaf news* 10:11 (1976), 333–337.

92 Bellugi, U. "Formal devices for creating new signs in ASL." *Proceedings of the national symposium on sign language research and teaching.* Chicago, 1977.

93 Bellugi, U. *The signs of language.* Paper presented at the national symposium on sign language research and teaching, Chicago, 1977.

94 Bellugi, U., and S. Fischer. "A comparison of sign language and spoken language: rate and grammatical mechanisms." *Cognition* 1:3 (1972), 173–200.

95 Bellugi, U., and E. Klima. "The roots of language in the sign talk of the deaf." *Psychology Today* 14:7 (December 1970), 32–35, 66.

96 Bellugi, U., P. Siple, and E. Klima. "The roots of language in the sign talk of the deaf." *Psychology today* 6 (1972), 60–64, 76.

97 Bellugi, U., E. Klima, and P. Siple. "Remembering in signs." *Cognition: international j. of cognitive psy.* 3:2 (1975), 93–125.

98 Bellugi, U., and E. S. Klima. "Aspects of sign language and its structure." In J. Kavanagh and J. E. Cutting (eds.), *Role of speech in language.* Cambridge, Mass.: MIT Press, 1975, 171–205.

99 Bellugi, U., and E. Klima. "Two faces of sign: iconic and abstract." In S. Harnad (ed.), *Origins and evolution of language and speech.* New York: N.Y. Academy of Sciences, 280 (1976), 514–538.

100 Bellugi, U., and E. S. Klima. "Language: perspectives from another modality." Proceedings of the CIBA foundation symposium: *Brain and Mind.* London, Eng., 1978.

101 Bellugi, U., and E. S. Klima. "Le langage gestuel des sourds." *La recherche* 11 (95), (1978), 1083–1091.

102 Bellugi, U., and E. S. Klima. "Structural properties of American sign language." In L. Liben (ed.), *Deaf children: developmental perspectives.* New York: Academic Press, 1978, 43–67.

103 Bellugi, U., and D. Newkirk. "Formal devices for creating new signs in American sign language." In Wm. Stokoe (ed.), *Proceedings of the national symposium on sign language research and teaching.* In press.

104 Bellugi, U., and P. Siple. "Remembering with and without words." In F. Bresson (ed.), *Current problems in psycholinguistics.* Paris: Centre National de la Recherche Scientifique, 1974, 215–236.

105 Bellugi, U., and P. Siple. *Remembering with and without words.* San Diego, Calif.: Salk Institute for Biological Studies, 1975.

106 Benaroya, S. "Sign language and multisensory input training of children with communication and related developmental disorders." *J. of autism and childhood schizophrenia* 7:1 (1977), 23–31.

107 Bender, R. *Conquest of deafness.* Cleveland, Ohio: Case Western Reserve U., 1970.

108 Benson, E. *The language of signs.* Unpub. MS., mimeographed. Washington, D.C., 1960.

109 Benson, E. *Sign language: course outline.* Washington, D.C.: Gallaudet College; outline of course in sign language given to new faculty from 1954–1964.

110 Benson, E. *Sign language.* St. Paul, Minn.: St. Paul Technical Vocational Institute, 1964.

111 Benson, E. *Suggestions relative to the mastery of the language of signs.* Unpublished manual used in teaching sign language at Gallaudet College. (n.d.)

112 Benthall, J., and T. Polhemus. *The body as a medium of expression.* New York: Dutton, 1975.

113 Bergman, B. *Teckensprakets lingvistiska status.* Stockholm: Stockholm Univ., report no. 4, 1975.

114 Bergman, E. "Autonomous and unique features of American sign language." *Amer. ann. deaf* 117:1 (1972), 1, 20–24.

115 Berndt, R. "Notes on the sign language of the Jaralde tribe of the lower river Murray, South Australia." *Royal society of South Australia. Transactions and proceedings and report* 64 (1940), 267–272.

116 Birdwhistell, R. L. *Kinesics & context; essays on body motion communication.* Philadelphia, Pa.: Univ. of Penn. Press, 1970.

117 Bjurgate, A. M. *Teckensprak for dova-illus-trerad ordbok svenska techenspraket.* Stockholm: So-forlaget, 1968.

118 Blanton, B. "Some psycholinguistic aspects of sign language." In Schlesinger and Namir (eds.), *Sign language of the deaf: psychological, linguistic and sociological perspectives.* New York: Academic Press, 1978, 243–269.

119 Blanton, R. L., et al. *Symbolic and linguistic processes in the deaf.* Nashville, Tenn.: Vanderbilt Univ., 1971.

120 Blasdell, R. *Preliminaries to the model of manual and simultaneous communications.* Washington, D.C.: Gallaudet College, 1977.

121 Blasdell, R., and F. Caccamise. *Factors influencing the reception of fingerspelling.* Houston, Tex.: American Speech and Hearing Assoc., 1976.

122 Blasdell, R., and F. Caccamise. *The effects of viewing angle on the reception of fingerspelling.* Unpub. MS. Rochester, N.Y.: National Technical Institute for the Deaf, 1976.

123 Blasdell, R., and W. Clymer. *An empirical study of cipher, phonological and syntactic models of fingerspelling production.* Rochester, N.Y.: National Technical Institute for the Deaf, 1977.

124 Boatner, M.T. *Voice of the deaf: A biography of Edward Miner Gallaudet.* Washington, D.C.: Public Affairs Press, 1959.

125 Bode, L. "Communication of agent, object, and indirect object in signed and spoken languages." *Perceptual and motor skills* 39 (1974), 1151–1158.

126 Boese, R. *Native sign language and the problem of meaning.* Unpub. doctoral dissertation. Santa Barbara, Calif.: Univ. of Calif., 1971.

127 Bonet, J. P. *Reducción de las letras y para enseñar a ablar los mudos.* Madrid, 1620.

128 Bonvillian, J., and V. Charrow. *Psycholinguistic implication of deafness: a review.* Technical report, 188. Stanford, Calif.: Institute for Mathematical Studies in the Social Sciences, 1972.

129 Bonvillian, J. D., V. R. Charrow, and K. Nelson. "Psycholinguistic and educational implications of deafness." *Human development* 16 (1973), 321–345.

130 Bonvillian, J., and R. J. Friedman. "Language development in another mode: the acquisition of signs by a brain-damaged adult." *Sign lang. studies* 19 (1978), 111–120.

131 Bonvillian, J., and K. Nelson. "Sign language acquisition in a mute autistic boy." *J. speech & hearing dis.* 41:3 (August 1976), 339–347.

132 Bonvillian, J. D., and K. E. Nelson. "Development of sign language in autistic children and other language-handicapped individuals." In P. Siple (ed.), *Understanding language through sign language research.* New York: Academic Press, 1978, 187–212.

133 Bonvillian, J.D., K. Nelson, and V. Charrow. "Languages and language-related skills in deaf and hearing children." *Sign lang. studies* 12 (1976), 189–210.

134 Bornstein, H. *An experimental film for teaching the manual alphabet.* Washington, D.C.: Gallaudet College, 1963.

135 Bornstein, H. *Reading the manual alphabet.* Washington, D.C.: Gallaudet College Press, 1965.

136 Bornstein, H. *Recent national dictionaries of signs.* Washington, D.C.: Gallaudet College, 1971.

137 Bornstein, H. "A description of some current sign systems designed to represent English." *Amer. ann. deaf* 118:3 (1973), 454–463.

138 Bornstein, H. *Intercultural sign language.* Washington, D.C.: Gallaudet College, 1973.

139 Bornstein, H. *Further developments in international sign language.* Washington, D.C.: Gallaudet College, 1974.

140 Bornstein, H. *New developments in international sign language.* Washington, D.C.: Gallaudet College, 1974.

141 Bornstein, H. "Signed English: a manual approach to English language development." *J. speech & hearing dis.* 39:3 (1974), 330–343.

142 Bornstein, H. "Sign language in the education of the deaf." In Schlesinger and Namir (eds.), *Sign language of the deaf: psychological, linguistic, and sociological perspectives.* New York: Academic Press, 1978, 333–361.

143 Bornstein, H. "Systems of sign." In L. Bradford and W. Hardy (eds.), *Hearing and hearing impairment.* New York: Grune and Stratton, 1980.

144 Bornstein, H., et al. *Basic preschool signed English dictionary.* Washington, D.C.: Gallaudet College Press, 1973.

145 Bornstein, H., et al. *Signed English dictionary for preschool and elementary levels.* Washington, D.C.: Gallaudet College Press, 1975.

146 Bornstein, H., et al. "A guide to the selection and use of the teaching aids in the signed English system." *Teaching English to the deaf* 3:1 (1976), 15–19.

147 Bornstein, H., et al. *A guide to the selection and use of the teaching aids of the signed English system.* Washington, D.C.: Gallaudet College Press, 1976.

148 Bornstein, H., B. Hamilton, and B. Kannapell, *Signs for instructional purposes.* Washington, D.C.: Gallaudet College Press, 1969.

149 Bornstein, H., and L. Hamilton. "National dictionaries of signs." *Sign lang. studies* 1 (1972), 42–63.

150 Bornstein, H., and B. Kannapell. "Report on new signs for instructional purposes." *Office of educ. report 6-1924,* 1969.

151 Bowling, W. "The introduction of signs and fingerspelling to a deaf-blind child." *Ed. of the visually handicapped* 2:3 (October 1970), 89–90.

152 Boyes, P. *An initial report: work in progress on a developmental phonology of American sign language.* Working paper. La Jolla, Calif.: Salk Institute for Biological Studies, 1973.

153 Boyes, P. *A study of the acquisition of dez in American sign language.* Working paper. La Jolla, Calif.: Salk Institute for Biological Studies, 1973.

154 Boyes-Braem, P. *The acquisition of handshape in American sign language.* Unpub. MS. La Jolla, Calif.: Salk Institute for Biological Studies, 1973.

155 Bragg, B. "Ameslish—our American heritage: a testimony." *Amer. ann. deaf* 118:6 (1973), 672–674.

156 *Bragg, Bernard series.* Southern Regional Media Center for the Deaf, 1814 Lake Ave., Knoxville, Tenn. 37916.

157 Brasel, B. B. "The component skills of interpreting as viewed by interpreters." *J. of rehab. of deaf* 7 (January 1974).

158 Brault, G. J. "Kinesics in the classroom: some typical French gestures." *French review* (1963), 374–382.

159 Breger, I. "Perception of sign language of the deaf." *Perceptual and motor skills* 31:2 (1970), 426.

160 Brennan, M. "Can deaf children acquire language? An evaluation of linguistic principles in deaf education." *Amer. ann. deaf* 120 (1975), 463–479.

161 Bricker, D. D. "Imitative sign training as a facilitator of word-object association with low-functioning children." *Amer. j. of mental deficiency* 76 (1972), 509–516.

162 Briggs, T. *Sign language in alingual retardates.* Paper presented to the Amer. assoc. of mental deficiency, Toronto, Canada, 1974.

163 Brill, E. "Traveler, say it with signs." *Rotarian magazine* 93 (1958), 16–17.

164 British deaf and dumb assoc. *The language of the silent world.* Oxford, Eng.: Church Army Press, 1960.

165 Bronowski, J., and U. Bellugi. "Language, name, and concept." *Science* 168 (1970), 669–673.

166 Brookner, S., and N. Murphy. "The use of a total communication approach with a non-deaf child: a case study." *Lang., speech, and hearing services in schools* 6:3 (July 1975), 131–139.

167 Brown, J. *A vocabulary of mute signs.* Baton Rouge, La.: Morning Comet Office, 1856.

168 Brown, R. "Why are signed languages easier to learn than spoken languages?" In Wm. Stokoe (ed.), *Proceedings of the national symposium on sign language research and teaching,* Chicago, 1977.

169 Browne, L. E. *The future of the deaf and dumb vernacular.* Address delivered at Queens College, Cambridge, to the Ely diocesan assoc. for work among the deaf, 1917.

170 Brun, T. *The international dictionary of sign language.* London: Wolfe Publishing, 1969.

171 Buyssens, E. "Le langage par gestes chez les moines: the language through gestures in the house of the monks." *Revue de l'institut de sociologie* 29 (1956), 537–545.

172 Cabiedas, J. L. M. *El lenguaje mímico.* Madrid: Federación National de S.S.E., 1975.

173 Caccamise, F. *Selection, standardization, and development of technical signs and fingerspelled words.* Rochester, N.Y.: National Technical Institute for the Deaf, 1978.

174 Caccamise, F. "Sign language and simultaneous communication: linguistic, psychological and instructional ramifications." *Amer. ann. deaf* 123:7 (1978).

175 Caccamise, F., et al. "A project for standardization and development of technical signs." *Amer. ann. deaf* 122:1 (1977), 44–49.

176 Caccamise, F., et al. *Signs and manual communication systems: selection, standardization and development.* Rochester, N.Y.: National Technical Institute for the Deaf, 1977.

177 Caccamise, F., et al. *The American sign language lexicon and guidelines for the standardization and development of technical signs.* Rochester, N.Y.: National Technical Institute for the Deaf, 1977.

178 Caccamise, F., et al. *Update of a process for selection, standardization, and development of signs and fingerspelled words.* Rochester, N.Y.: National Technical Institute for the Deaf, 1978.

179 Caccamise, F., and R. Blasdell. "Reception of sentences under oral-manual interpreted and simultaneous test conditions." *Amer. ann. deaf* 122 (August 1977).

180 Caccamise, F., and C. Norris, *Code book #1: general signs for messages to and from deaf people.* Eureka, Calif.: Alinda Press, n.d.

181 Caccamise, F., and C. Norris. *Animals in signs.* Eureka, Calif.: Alinda Press, 1973.

182 Caccamise, F., and C. Norris. *Community in signs.* Eureka, Calif.: Alinda Press, 1973.

183 Caccamise, F., and C. Norris. *Food in signs.* Eureka, Calif.: Alinda Press, 1973.

184 Caccamise, F., and C. Norris. *Home in signs.* Eureka, Calif.: Alinda Press, 1973.

185 CAID parent's section. *Coloring books in sign language—animals and home.* Silver Spring, Md.: Parents' Section, CAID, 1975.

186 Carmel, S. J. *International hand alphabet charts.* Published by author: 10500 Rockville Pike, Apt. 405, Rockville, Md. 20852, 1975.

187 Carmel, S. J. *Study of precise facial expressions in the context of sign language by the deaf and non-verbal signs by the hearing in Israel.* Washington, D.C.: American Univ., 1978, 1–19.

188 Carmel, S. *International number charts.* (In press by author.)

189 Carr, E. G. "Teaching autistic children to use sign language: some research issues." *J. autism and developmental disorders* 9:4 (1979), 345–359.

190 Carr, E. G. "A program for establishing sign language in developmentally disabled children." In O.I. Lovaas et al., *The me book: teaching manual for parents and teachers of developmentally disabled children.* Baltimore: University Park Press, 1980.

191 Carr, E. G., et al. "Acquisition of sign language by autistic children. I: Expressive labelling." *J. applied behavior analysis* 11:4 (Winter 1978), 489–501.

192 Carr, E. G., and E. Kologinsky. *Teaching psychotic children to use sign language: development of descriptive generative sentences.* Paper presented at 87th Annual Meeting, APA, New York City, 1979.

193 Carter, S. M., and R. Lauritsen. "Interpreter recruitment, selection and training." *J. of rehab. of deaf* 7 (January 1974).

194 Cassirer, E. *Philosophie des symbolischen formen: die sprache.* Berlin, Federal Republic of Germany: Bruno Cassirer, 1923. [English translation: New Haven, Conn.: Yale Univ. Press, 1953.]

195 Charlip, R., Mary Beth, and G. Ancona. *Handtalk.* New York: Parents' Magazine Press, 1974.

196 Charrow, V. R. "Manual English—a linguist's viewpoint." In Crammatte, et al. (eds.), *Proceedings of the VII world congress of the world federation of the deaf.* Silver Spring, Md.: National Assoc. of the Deaf, 1976, 78–82.

197 Charrow, V. R., and J. D. Fletcher. *English as the second language of deaf students.* Stanford, Calif.: Stanford Univ., technical report no. 208, 1973.

198 Chaves, T., and J. Soler. "Pedro Ponce de León, first teacher of the deaf." *Sign lang. studies* 5 (1974), 48–63.

199 Chaves, T., and J. Soler. "Manuel Ramirez de Carrion (1579–1652?) and his secret method of teaching the deaf." *Sign lang. studies* 8 (1975), 235–248.

200 Chen, L. Y. "Manual communication by combined alphabet and gestures." *Archives of physical medicine and rehab.* 52 (1971).

201 *Children's playing cards.* Silver Spring, Md.: National Assoc. of the Deaf, n.d.

202 Chinchor, N. *The syllable in American sign language: sequential and simultaneous phonology.* Providence, R. I.: Brown Univ., 1978.

203 Christopher, D. A. *Manual communication: a basic text and workbook with practical exercises.* Baltimore: University Park Press, 1976.

204 Cicourel, A. "Gestural sign language and the study of nonverbal communication." *Sign lang. studies* 4 (1974), 35–76.

205 Cicourel, A. V. *Sociolinguistic aspects of the use of sign language.* La Jolla, Calif.: Univ. of Calif., 1974.

206 Cicourel, A. V. "Gestural-sign language and the study of non-verbal communication." In J. Benthall and T. Polhemus (eds.), *The body as a medium of expression: an anthology.* New York: Dutton, 1975, 195–232.

207 Cicourel, A. V. "Sociolinguistic aspects of the use of sign language." In I. M. Schlesinger and L. Namir (eds.), *Sign language of the deaf.* New York: Academic Press, 1978, 243–269.

208 Cicourel, A. V., and R. J. Boese. *Sign language acquisition and the teaching of deaf children.* La Jolla, Calif.: Univ. of Calif., 1970.

209 Cicourel, A. V., and R. J. Boese. *The acquisition of manual sign language and generative semantics.* La Jolla, Calif.: Univ. of Calif., 1970.

210 Cicourel, A. V., and R. J. Boese. "Sign language acquisition and the teaching of deaf children." *Amer. ann. deaf* 117(1), (1972), 27–33, Part 1; 117(3), (1972), 403–411, Part II.

211 Cicourel, A.V., and R. Boese. "Sign language acquisition and the teaching of deaf children." In C. Cazden, V. John, and D. Hymes (eds.), *Functions of language in the classroom.* New York: Teachers College Press, 1972, 32–62.

212 Cicourel, A. V., and R. Boese. "The acquisition of manual sign language and generative semantics." *Semiotica* 5:3 (1972).

213 Ciolek, T. M. "Materials for alchemy of gestures." *Etnografia polska* 17:2 (1973), 59–79.

214 Ciolek, T. M. "Human communicational behavior: a bibliography." *Sign lang. studies* 6 (1975), 1–64.

215 Ciolek, T. M., et al. "Selected references to coenetics. The study of behavioral organization of face-to-face interactions." *Sign lang. studies* 22 (1979), 23–72.

216 Cissna, R. *Introduction to the sign language.* Jefferson City, Mo.: Missouri Baptist Convention, 1961 (?).

217 Cissna, R.L. *Basic sign language.* Jefferson City, Mo.: Missouri Baptist Press, 1963.

218 Clark, M. *The William Terry touch alphabet for use by the deaf and by the deaf-blind.* n.p. 1916.

219 Clark, W. P. *Indian sign language.* n.p. 1885.

220 Clarke, B. R., and D. Ling. "The effects of using cued speech: a follow-up study." *Volta review* 78 (1976), 23–34.

221 Clerc, L. *The diary of Laurent Clerc's voyage from France to America in 1816.* West Hartford, Conn.: Amer. School for the Deaf, 1952.

222 Cliffe, P. "One-hand alphabet." *Hearing* 25 (1970), 232–233.

223 Coats, G. "Characteristics of communication methods." *Amer. ann. deaf* 95:5 (1950), 489–490.

224 Cochrane, W. "Methodical signs instead of colloquial." *Amer. ann. deaf and dumb* 16:1 (1871), 11–17.

225 Cody, Iron Eyes. *Indian talk: hand signals of the American Indians.* Healdsburg, Calif.: Naturegraph, n.d.

226 Cogen, C. "On three aspects of time expression in American sign language." In L. Friedman (ed.), *On the other hand: new perspectives on American sign language.* New York: Academic Press, 1977, 197–214.

227 Cohen, E., L. Namir, and I. M. Schlesinger. *A new dictionary of sign language.* The Hague: Mouton, 1977.

228 Cokely, D. *Instructor's manual for Kendall demonstration elementary school family sign program.* Washington, D.C.: Gallaudet College, 1973.

229 Cokely, D. R. *A discussion of assessment needs in manual communication for pre-college students.* Washington, D.C.: Model Secondary School for the Deaf, 1978.

230 Cokely, D., and C. Baker. *Manual for sign language teachers.* Silver Spring, Md: T. J. Publishers, 1980.

231 Cokely, D. R., and R. Gawlik. *Options: a position paper on the relationship between manual English and sign.* Washington, D.C.: Kendall Demonstration Elementary School for the Deaf, 1973.

232 Cokely, D., and R. Gawlik. "Options: a position paper on the relationship between manual English and sign." *The deaf Amer.* 25:9 (1973), 7–11.

233 Cokely, D. R., and R. Gawlik. "Childrenese as pidgin." *Sign lang. studies* 5 (1974), 72–81.

234 Cokely, D., and R. Gawlik. "Options II: childrenese as pidgin." *The deaf Amer.* 26:8 (1974), 5–6.

235 Collins-Ahlgren, M. "Language development of two deaf children." *Amer. ann. deaf* 120:6 (1975), 524–539.

236 Collins-Ahlgren, M. "Teaching English as a second language to young deaf children: a case study." *J. of speech and hearing disorders* 39:4 (1975), 524–539.

237 *Communications: devices and methods.* Sands Point, N.Y.: Helen Keller Nat'l. Center for Deaf-Blind Youths and Adults, n.d.

238 Condon, W. S. "An analysis of behavioral organization." *Sign lang. studies* 13 (1976), 285–318.

239 Conrad, R. *Towards a definition of oral success.* R.W.I.D. educ. meeting, October 1976.

240 "Conversations with a chimp." *Life* magazine 72 (1972), 55–56.

241 Cooper, J. A., and J. Nunier. *Talking in silence.* Unpub. paper. Staten Island, N.Y.: Mission Deaf Ministry, 1968.

242 Cornett, R. O. *Cued speech: a new aid in the education of hearing impaired children.* Washington, D.C.: Gallaudet College, 1966.

243 Cornett, R. O. "Cued speech." *Amer. ann. deaf* 112:1 (1967), 3–13.

244 Cornett, R. O. "A study of the readability of cued speech." In R. O. Cornett, *Cued speech parent training and follow up program, final report.* Washington, D.C.: Govt. Printing Office, 1972, 45–52.

245 Cornett, R. O. "Effects of cued speech upon speechreading." In Fant, Gunnar (eds.), *International symposium on speech communication ability and profound deafness.* Washington, D.C.: Alexander Graham Bell Assoc. for the Deaf, 1972, 223–230.

246 Corson, H. *Comparing deaf children of oral deaf parents and deaf parents using manual communication with deaf children of hearing parents on academic, social, and communicative functioning.* Unpub. doctoral dissertation, Univ. of Cinn., 1973.

247 Cosma-Rossellio, R. P. F. C. *Thesaurus artificiosae memoriae.* Venice, 1579.

248 Costello, E. *Appraising certain linguistic structures in the receptive-signing competence of deaf children.* Syracuse, N.Y.: Syracuse Univ., 1974.

249 Coulter, G. *American sign language pantomime.* Manuscript. La Jolla, Calif.: Salk Institute for Biological Studies, 1975.

250 Coulter, G. R. "American sign language relative clauses." Working paper, Salk Institute for Biological Studies, 1978.

251 Coulter, G. R. "On the linguistic relevance of the sign space." Working paper, Salk Institute for Biological Studies, 1978.

252 Coulter, G. R. "Raised eyebrows and wrinkled noses: the grammatical function of facial expression in relative clauses." Paper presented at the 2nd national symposium on sign language research and teaching, 1978.

253 Coulter, G. R. "Continuous representation." In Wm. Stokoe (ed.), *Proceedings of the national symposium on sign language research and teaching.* In press.

254 Council for Exceptional Children. *Aurally handicapped research: a selective bibliography. Exceptional children series no. 625.* Arlington, Va., 1972.

255 Council for Exceptional Children. *Exceptional children conference papers: education of the trainable mentally handicapped.* Arlington, Va.: by author, 1973.

256 Covington, V. "Features of stress in American sign language." *Sign lang. studies* 2 (1973), 39–50.

257 Covington, V. "Juncture in American sign language." *Sign lang. studies* 2 (1973), 29–38.

258 Covington, V. "Problems for a sign language planning agency." *Linguistics—an international review* 189 (1977), 85–106.

259 Craig, E. *The Paget-Gorman sign system: a reference book for parents and teachers, no. 1.* London: The Spastics Society, 1971.

260 Craig, E. "The Paget-Gorman sign system." *Deaf welfare* (United Kingdom), 6:6 (1972), 90–92.

261 Craig, E. *The Paget-Gorman sign system: a report of the research project 1970–1973.* Reading, Eng.: Univ. of Reading, 1973.

262 Craig, E., and D. Crystal. *Systematic sign language.* Reading, Eng.: Univ. of Reading, n.d.

263 Crandall, K. E. *A comparison of sign used by mothers and deaf children during early childhood.* Rochester, N.Y.: National Technical Institute for the Deaf, 1975.

264 Creedon, M. *Language development in non-verbal autistic children using simultaneous communication systems.* Chicago, Ill.: Dysfunctioning Child Center, 1973.

265 Creedon, M. (ed.). *Appropriate behavior through communication: a new program in simultaneous language.* Chicago, Ill.: Dysfunctioning Child Center, 1975.

266 Creedon, M. (ed.). *The David school: a simultaneous communication model.* Speech given at annual conference of the nat. society for autistic children, June 1976.

267 Creider, C. A. "Towards a description of East African gestures." *Sign lang. studies* 14 (1977), 1–20.

268 Criswell, E. C., and N. L. Higgs. *A manual of signed English (two volumes).* Dallas, Tex.: World Center, 1975.

269 Critchley, M. *The language of gesture.* London: Edward Arnold and Co., 1939.

270 Crittenden, J. B. "Categorization of cheremic errors in sign language reception." *Sign lang. studies* 5 (1974), 64–71.

271 Crittenden, J. S. "Psychology of deafness: some implications for the interpreter." *J. of rehab. of deaf* 8, 1974.

272 Croneberg, C. G. "Sign language dialects." In Stokoe, Casterline, Croneberg (eds.), *A dictionary of American sign language.* Washington, D.C.: Gallaudet College Press, 1965, 313–319.

273 Cross, J. W. "Sign language and second-language teaching." *Sign lang. studies* 16 (1977), 269–282.

274 Crystal, D., and E. Craig. "Contrived sign language." In Schlesinger and Namir (eds.), *Sign language of the deaf: psychological, linguistic, and sociological perspectives.* New York: Academic Press, 1978, 141–168.

275 Curtiss, S. *Genie: a psycholinguistic study of a modern-day "wild child."* New York: Academic Press, 1977.

276 Custer, D., et al. *Index to American sign language.* St. Paul, Minn.: St. Paul Technical Vocational Institute, 1976.

277 Dalgleisch, B. "Systematically inflected vs. grapheme modified signing: an educational viewpoint." *Exceptional child* 24:2 (1977), 73–78.

278 Darwin, C. *The expression of emotions in man and animals.* London: John Murray, 1872. [Republished in Chicago, Ill.: Univ. of Chicago Press, 1965.]

279 Davidson, L. "Some current folk gestures and sign language." *Amer. speech* 25 (1950), 3–9.

280 Davis, A. *The language of signs.* New York: Conference of church workers among the deaf, executive council of the Episcopal church in the United States, 1966.

281 Davis, M. *Understanding body movement: an annotated bibliography.* New York: Arno Press, 1972.

282 "Deafness is no barrier to these employees." *Nation's business* 60:14 (1972).

283 Decroo, K. L. *A clarification of some misconceptions surrounding the American sign language.* Riverside, Calif.: Univ. of Calif., 1972, 1–35.

284 Decroo, L. C. *An analysis of the hand configurations used in the manual alphabet.* Riverside, Calif.: Univ. of Calif., 1973.

285 DeGering, E. *Gallaudet: friend of the deaf.* New York: David McKay Co., 1964.

286 DeHaerne, Msgr. "The natural language of signs—I." *Amer. ann. deaf and dumb* 20:2 (1875), 73–87.

287 DeHaerne, Msgr. "The natural language of signs—II." *Amer. ann. deaf and dumb* 20:3 (1875), 37–53.

288 DeHaerne, Msgr. "The natural language of signs—III." *Amer. ann. deaf and dumb* 20:4 (1875), 216–228.

289 deJorio, A. *La mimica.* Naples, Italy, 1832.

290 DeLaney, T. *Sing unto the lord, a hymnal for the deaf.* Ephetha conference of Lutheran pastors for the deaf, 1959.

291 De la Torre, T. "Trilingualism: Spanish-sign-English." In Crammatte, et al. (eds.), *VII world congress of the world federation of the deaf.* Silver Spring, Md.: National Assoc. of the Deaf, 1976, 87–89.

292 Deleau, N. *Exposé d'une nouvelle dactylologie alphabétique et syllabique.* Cambrai, France: A. F. Hurz, 1830.

293 De l'Épée, C. M. Abbé, "The true method of educating the deaf and dumb: confirmed by long experience." *Amer. ann. deaf* 12:2 (1860), 61–132.

294 De l'Épée, C. M. Abbé. "Extracts from the institution des sourds et muets of the Abbé de l'Épée." *Amer. ann. deaf and dumb* 8:1 (March 1861), 8–29.

295 de Mas-Latrie, L. "Dactylographie." *Dictionnaire de paléographie* 27, n.d.

296 De Matteo, A. "Analogue grammar in the American sign language." In H. Thompson, et al. (eds.), *Proceedings of the 2nd annual meeting of the Berkeley linguistic society.* Berkeley, Calif.: 1976, 149–157.

297 De Matteo, A. "Visual imagery and visual analogues in American sign language." In L. Friedman (ed.), *On the other hand: new perspectives on American sign language.* New York: Academic Press, 1977, 109–136.

298 Denton, D. M. "A rationale for total communication." In T. J. O'Rourke (ed.), *Psycholinguistics and total communication: the state of the art.* Washington, D.C.: *Amer. ann. deaf,* 1972, 53–61.

299 Deuchar, M. *A selected bibliography on sign language studies. CAL-ERIC/CLL series on language and linguistics no. 34.* Arlington, Va.: ERIC Clearing House on Language and Linguistics, n.d.

300 Deuchar, M. "Sign language diglossia in a British deaf community." *Sign lang. studies* 17 (1977), 347–356.

301 Deuchar, M. *Diglossia in British sign language.* Stanford, Calif.: Stanford Univ., 1978.

302 *De wonderlyke gebarentaal der Indianen.* Uitgegeven door chocolaterie, n.d.

303 Dicker, L. "Intensive interpreter training." *Amer. ann. deaf* 123, June 1976.

304 Dicker, L. *Facilitating manual communication for teachers, students and interpreters.* Registry of interpreters for the deaf, 1978.

305 *Digiti-lingua.* London: P. Buck, 1698.

306 Dinsmore, A. "The alphabet glove." *Methods of communication with deaf-blind people.* New York: American Foundation for the Blind, 1953.

307 DiPietro, L. (ed.). *Proceedings of the first convention of the registry of interpreters for the deaf.* Silver Spring, Md.: Registry of interpreters for the deaf, 1970.

308 Dixie-Hawes, M., and J. L. Danhauer. "Perceptual features of the manual alphabet." *Amer. ann. deaf* 123:4 (1978), 464–474.

309 Doctor, P. *Communication with the deaf.* Lancaster, Pa.: Intelligence Printing Co., 1963.

310 Domingue, R., and B. Ingram. "Sign language interpretation: the state of the art." In D. Gerver and H. W. Sinaiko (eds.), *Language interpretation*

and communication. New York: Plenum Press, 1978.

311 Dominican Nuns. *How to converse with the deaf in sign language.* Castle Hill, New South Wales, Australia: Christian Brothers, n.d.

312 Dores, P. A., and E. Carr. *Sign language comprehension by autistic children following simultaneous communication training.* Paper presented at 87th Annual Convention, APA, New York City, 1979.

313 Drake, H. "The American manual alphabet." *Silent worker* 11:8 (1959), 9–10.

314 Dross, J. "Sign language and second-language teaching." *Sign lang. studies* 16 (1977), 269–282.

315 DuChamp, M. "The national institution for the deaf and dumb at Paris." *Amer. ann. deaf* 22:1 (1877), 1–10.

316 Dudesert, P. *Mémoire sur l'education des sourds-muets.* Paris, France: Imprimerie de Monnoyer, 1834.

317 Dumas, A. "Use of the language of signs by the Sicilians." *Amer. ann. deaf and dumb* 11:2 (April 1859), 124–126.

318 Duncan, J. L., and F. H. Silverman. "Impacts of learning American Indian sign language on mentally retarded children: a preliminary report." *Perceptual motor skills* 44:3 (1977), 1138.

319 Duquin, L. H. "Ameslan—sexist language?" *Arise* 2:8 (June 1979), 29–30.

320 Dyer, E. "Sign language agglutination: a brief look at ASL and Turkish." *Sign lang. studies* 11 (1976), 133–148.

321 Eastman, G. *Sign me Alice.* Washington, D.C.: Gallaudet College Press, 1974.

322 Eastman, G. *Non-verbal communication as a sign language base.* Unpub. paper. Washington, D.C.: Gallaudet College, 1976.

323 Edge, V., and L. Hermann. "Verbs and the determination of subject in American sign language." In L. Friedman (ed.), *On the other hand: new perspectives on American sign language.* New York: Academic Press, 1977, 137–179.

324 Ekman, P. "Biological and cultural contributions to body and facial movement." In J. Blacking (ed.), *A.S.A. monograph: the anthropology of the body.* London: Academic Press, 1977.

325 Ekman, P., and W. V. Friesen. *The repertoire of nonverbal behavior-categories, origins, usage, and coding.* San Francisco: Univ. of Calif. Medical Center, 1971.

326 Ekman, P., and W. V. Friesen. *Unmasking the face.* Englewood Cliffs, N.J.: Prentice-Hall, 1975.

327 Ellenberger, R. *The model auxiliary systems of American sign language and English.* Research report 96. Minneapolis: Univ. of Minnesota, 1975.

328 Ellenberger, R., D. Moores, and R. Hoffmeister.

"Early stages in the acquisition of negation by a deaf child of deaf parents." Research report no. 94. Minneapolis: Univ. of Minnesota, August 1975.

329 Ellenberger, R., and M. Steyaert. *A child's representation of action in American sign language.* Minneapolis: Univ. of Minnesota, 1976.

330 Ellenberger, R. L., and M. Steyaert. "Child's representation of action in American sign language." In P. Siple (ed.), *Understanding language through sign language research.* New York: Academic Press, 1978, 261–269.

331 Ellsworth, S., and R. Kotkin. "If only Jimmy could speak." *Hearing & speech action* 43:6 (November–December 1975), 6–8, 10.

332 *Episcopal Church training films (8 mm cartridge).* Audio-visual library, The Episcopal Church Center, 815 Second Ave., New York, N.Y. 10017.

333 Erting, C. *Language socialization in the classroom.* Paper presented at the Gallaudet College sign language conference, Washington, D.C., 1974.

334 Erting, C. "Language policy and deaf ethnicity in the U.S." *Sign lang. studies* 19 (1978), 139–152.

335 Erting, C., and J. Woodward. *Sign language and the deaf community: a sociolinguistic profile.* Washington, D.C.: Gallaudet College, 1974, 1–30.

336 Eschbach, A., and W. Rader. *Semiotik—bibliographi I* 26 (1976). Frankfurt-am-Main: Syndikat.

337 Eshkol, N. *The hand book: a detailed notation of hand and finger movements and forms.* Tel Aviv: The movement notation society, 1971.

338 Evans, E. *A manual alphabet for the deaf-blind.* London: Royal National Institution for the Deaf-Blind, 224-6-8 Great Portland St., W.l. n.d.

339 Falberg, R. *Learning the language of signs.* Wichita, Kan.: Wichita social services for the deaf, 1962.

340 Falberg, R. *The language of silence.* Wichita, Kan.: Wichita social services for the deaf, 1963.

341 Falberg, R. *A psycholinguistic view of the evolution, nature, and value of the sign language of the deaf.* Master's thesis. Wichita, Kan.: Wichita State Univ., 1964.

342 Fant, L. *Why Ameslan?* Unpub. paper. Write to author: Program for the deaf, Calif. State Univ., Northridge, Calif., n.d.

343 Fant, L. J. *A description of some characteristics of Ameslan.* Copy available in the LRL.

344 Fant, L. *A tentative description of the grammar of Ameslan.* Copy available for consultation in the LRL.

345 Fant, L. *Beginning Ameslan.* Copy available for consultation in the LRL.

346 Fant, L. *Enough of imitations.* Copy available for consultation in the LRL.

347 Fant, L. *Practice sentences (Ameslan).* Copy available for consultation in the LRL.

348 Fant, L. *Signs for expressing negatives.* Copy available for consultation in the LRL.

349 Fant, L. *Some preliminary observations on the grammar of Ameslan.* Graduate colloquium, Gallaudet College; copy available for consultation in the LRL.

350 Fant, L. *Say it with hands.* Washington, D.C.: Gallaudet College Press, 1964.

351 Fant, L. "Enough of imitations . . ." *The deaf Amer.* 23:5 (1971), 14–15.

352 Fant, L., *Ameslan: an introduction to sign language.* Northridge, Calif.: Joyce Motion Picture Co., 1972.

353 Fant, L. *Ameslan: an introduction to American sign language.* Silver Spring, Md.: National Association of the Deaf, 1972.

354 Fant, L. *Ameslan: an introduction to American sign language—teacher's guide.* Silver Spring, Md.: National Association of the Deaf, 1972.

355 Fant, L. *Some preliminary observations on the grammar of Ameslan.* Unpub. paper, 1972.

356 Fant, L. *Sign language.* Northridge, Calif.: Joyce Media, 1977.

357 Fant, L. *Where do we go from here?* Paper presented at the national symposium on sign language research and teaching, Chicago, 1977.

358 Fant, L. *Admonition and waiver of rights in American sign language.* Northridge, Calif.: Joyce Motion Picture Co., in press.

359 Fauth, B. L., and W. W. Fauth. "A study of the proceedings of the convention of American instructors of the deaf 1850–1949, IV. The manual alphabet." *Amer. ann. deaf* 96 (1951), 292–296.

360 Fauth, B. L., and W. W. Fauth. "Sign language." *Amer. ann. deaf* 100 (1955), 253–263.

361 Fay, G. "The sign language: the basis of instruction for deaf-mutes." *Amer. ann. deaf* 27:3 (1882), 208–211.

362 Feldman, S. S. *Mannerisms of speech and gestures in everyday life.* New York: Int'l. Universities Press, Inc., 1973.

363 Fenn, G. *The development of language through signing in children with severe auditory impairments.* Cambridge, Eng.: Univ. of Cambridge, report to the social science research council, 1974–75.

364 Fenn, G. "Development of language in profoundly deaf children through the medium of manual signs." *Sign lang. studies* 11 (1976), 109–120.

365 Fenn, G., and J. Rome. "An experiment in manual communication." *Brit. j. disorders of communication* 10:1 (1975), 3–16.

366 Ferry, P., and J. Cooper. "Sign language in communication disorders of childhood." *J. of pediatrics* 93:4 (1978), 547–552.

367 *Fingerspelling films.* (8mm cartridge). Washington, D.C.: U.S. Office of Education, Media Services and Captioned Films.

368 Finlayson, K. *You can communicate.* Filang, 1978.

369 Finnestad, K. L. *A basic sign language vocabulary for Western Canada.* Luther theological seminary, thesis, 1961.

370 Fischer, C. "Fingerspelling intelligibility." *Amer. ann. deaf* 118:4 (1973), 508–510.

371 Fischer, S. D. *Two processes of reduplication in the American sign language.* La Jolla, Calif.: Salk Institute for Biological Studies, 1972.

372 Fischer, S. "Two processes of reduplication in the American sign language." *Foundations of lang.* 9 (1973), 469–480.

373 Fischer, S. "Sign language and linguistic universals." In T. Rohrer and N. Ruwet (eds.), *Actes de colloque Franco-Allemand de grammarie transformationelle, band II: études de semantique et autres.* Tubingen: Max Neimeyer Verlang, 1974, 187–204.

374 Fischer, S. *Some differences between sign language and spoken language.* Working paper. La Jolla, Calif.: Salk Institute for Biological Studies, 1974.

375 Fischer, S. "Influences on word-order change in American sign language." In C. N. Li (ed.), *Word order and word order change.* Austin, Tex.: Univ. of Texas Press, 1975.

376 Fischer, S. "The ontogenetic development of language." In E. Strauss (ed.), *Language and language disturbances: fifth Lexington conference on phenomenology.* Pittsburgh, Pa.: Duquesne Univ. Press, 1975, 22–43.

377 Fischer, S. D. "Sign language and creoles." In P. Siple (ed.), *Understanding language through sign language research.* New York: Academic Press, 1978, 309–311.

378 Fischer, S., and B. Gough. *Some unfinished thoughts on FINISH.* Unpub. MS. La Jolla, Calif.: Salk Institute for Biological Studies, 1972.

379 Fischer, S., and B. Gough. "Verbs in American sign language." *Sign lang. studies* 18 (1978), 14–48.

380 Fischer, S., and B. Gough. "Verbs in American sign language." In E. Klima and U. Bellugi, *The signs of language.* Cambridge, Mass.: Harvard Univ. Press, 1979.

381 Fitzgerald, E. *Signs and pure oralism.* Circular no. 3 of the national assoc. of the deaf. Berkeley, Calif.: National Assoc. of the Deaf, n.d.

382 Fitzgerald, E. *Straight language for the deaf.* Washington, D.C.: Volta Bureau, 1965.

383 Fleischer, L. *Bring sign language out of the dark ages.* Paper presented at the national symposium on sign language research and teaching, Chicago, 1977.

384 Fleischer, L. *Sign language bibliography.* Chicago, Ill.: National Symposium on Sign Language Research and Teaching, 1977.

385 Fleischer, L., and M. Cottrell. "Sign language interpretation under four interpreting conditions." In H. Murphy (ed.), *Selected readings in the integration of postsecondary deaf students at CSUN: center on deafness publication series no. 1.* Northridge, Calif.: Calif. State Univ., 1976.

386 Fleming, J. "Field report: the state of the apes." *Psychology today,* (1974).

387 Fondelius, E. *Teckenørdbok.* Sweden: Sveriges Döves Riksförbund, 1971.

388 Ford, B. "How they taught a chimp to talk." *Science digest magazine* 67:5 (1970), 10–17.

389 Foret, A., and M. Petrowska. *A manual and dictionary of legal terms for interpreting for the deaf.* Detroit, Mich.: Center for the Administration of Justice, Wayne State Univ., 1976.

390 Fouts, R. S. *The use of guidance in teaching sign language to a chimpanzee.* Unpub. dissertation, Univ. of Nevada, 1971.

391 Fouts, R. *Acquisition and testing of gestural signs in four young chimpanzees.* Norman: Univ. of Oklahoma, 1972.

392 Fouts, R. S. "Use of guidance in teaching sign language to a chimpanzee." *J. of comparative and physiological psy.* 80:3 (1972), 515–522.

393 Fouts, R. S. "Acquisition and testing of gestural sign in four young chimpanzees." *Science* 180 (1973), 978–980.

394 Fouts, R. S. "Language: origins, definitions and chimpanzees." *J. of human evolution* 3 (1974), 475–482.

395 Fouts, R. S. "Capacities for language in great apes." In R. Tuttle (ed.), *Socioecology and psychology of primates.* The Hague: Mouton Press, 1975.

396 Fouts, R. S. "Communication with chimpanzees." In E. Eibl-Eibesfeldt and G. North (eds.), *Hominisation und verhalten.* Stuttgart, Federal Republic of Germany: Gustav Fischer Verlag, 1975.

397 Fouts, R. S. "Field report: the state of the apes." *Psychology today* 7:8 (1975), 31–54.

398 Fouts, R. S., et al. *Comprehension and production of American sign language by a chimpanzee.* Paper presented to the 21st int'l. congress of psychology in Paris, France, 1976.

399 Fouts, R. S., et al. "Transfer of signed responses in American sign language from vocal English stimuli to physical object stimuli by a chimpanzee." *Learning & motivation* 7 (1976), 458–475.

400 Fouts, R. S., and R. L. Mellgren. "Language, signs, and cognition in the chimpanzee." *Sign lang. studies* 13 (1976), 319–346.

401 Fouts, R. S., and R. L. Rigby. "Man-chimpanzee communication." In T. Sebeok (ed.), *How animals communicate.* Bloomington: Indiana Univ. Press, 1975.

402 Friedman, I. A. *Zero derivation and how it grew* (in English and in ASL) *synchronically.* Berkeley: Univ. of Calif., 1972.

403 Friedman, L. *A comparative analysis of oral and visual phonology.* Unpub. MS. Berkeley: Univ. of Calif., 1972.

404 Friedman, L. A. *On the physical manifestation of stress in American sign language.* Unpub. MS. Berkeley: Univ. of Calif., 1974.

405 Friedman, L. *On the semantics of space, and person reference in American sign language.* Master's thesis. Berkeley: Univ. of Calif., 1974.

406 Friedman, L. "Phonological processes in the American sign language." *Proceedings of the 1st annual meeting of the Berkeley linguistics society.* Berkeley: Univ. of Calif., 1975, 147–154.

407 Friedman, L. "Space, time and person reference in American sign language." *Language* 51:4 (1975), 940–961.

408 Friedman, L. "On the physical manifestation of stress in American sign language." *Language* 51:4 (1976).

409 Friedman, L. *Phonology of a soundless language: phonological structure of American sign language.* Unpub. doctoral dissertation, Berkeley: Univ. of Calif., 1976.

410 Friedman, L. "The manifestation of subject, object, and topic in ASL." In C. N. Li (ed.), *Subject and topic.* New York: Academic Press, 1976.

411 Friedman, L. "Formational properties of American sign language." In L. Friedman (ed.), *On the other hand: new perspectives on American sign language.* New York: Academic Press, 1977, 13–56.

412 Friedman, L. (ed.). *On the other hand: new perspectives on American sign language.* New York: Academic Press, 1977.

413 Friedman, L. "Phonological processes in ASL." In L. Friedman (ed.), *On the other hand: new perspectives on American sign language.* New York: Academic Press, 1977.

414 Friedman, L. "The manifestation of subject, object, and topic in ASL." In L. Friedman (ed.), *On the other hand: new perspectives on American sign language.* New York: Academic Press, 1977.

415 Friedman, L. A., and R. Battison. *Phonological structures in American sign language.* N.E.H. report AY 8218 73 136, 1973.

416 Frishberg, N. *A brief history of sign language.* La Jolla, Calif.: Univ. of Calif., 1971.

417 Frishberg, N. *Sharp and soft: two aspects of movement in sign.* Working paper. San Diego: Univ. of Calif., 1972.

418 Frishberg, N. *The case of the missing length.* Paper presented at the 49th annual meeting of the

linguistic society of America, New York, 1974.

419 Frishberg, N. "Arbitrariness and iconicity: historical change in American sign language." *Language* 51 (1975), 696–719.

420 Frishberg, N. *The case of the missing length.* Rochester, N.Y.: National Technical Institute for the Deaf, 1975.

421 Frishberg, N. *A linguist looks at sign language teaching.* Paper presented at the national symposium on sign language research and teaching, Chicago, 1977.

422 Frishberg, N. "Culture and code." Paper presented to *American association for the advancement of science.* Denver, Colo., 1977.

423 Frishberg, N. "Some aspects of historical change in American sign language." Doctoral dissertation, Univ. of Calif., San Diego, 1976. *Dissertation abstracts international,* 1977.

424 Frishberg, N., and B. Gough. *Time on our hands.* Paper presented to the 3rd annual May California linguistics meeting, Stanford, Calif., 1973.

425 Frishberg, N., and B. Gough. *Morphology in American sign language.* Working paper. La Jolla, Calif.: Salk Institute for Biological Studies, 1974.

426 Fristoe, M. *Language intervention systems for the retarded.* State of Alabama Dept. of Educ., 1976.

427 Fristoe, M., and L. L. Lloyd. "Manual communication for the retarded and others with severe communication impairment: a resource list." *Mental retardation* 15:5 (1977), 18–21.

428 Fristoe, M. and L. L. Lloyd. "Signs used in manual communication training with persons having severe communication impairment." *AAESPH review* 4:4 (1979), 364–373.

429 Fristoe, M. and L. L. Lloyd. "Planning an initial expressive sign lexicon for persons with severe communicative impairment." *J. spch. & hear. dis.,* February 1980.

430 Fulwiler, R., and R. Fouts. "Acquisition of American sign language by a non-communicating autistic child." *J. autism & childhood schizophrenia* 6:1 (March 1976), 43–51.

431 Funderburg, R. S. *The relationship of short term visual memory and intelligence to the manual communication skills of profoundly deaf children.* Unpub. thesis, Univ. of Arizona, 1975.

432 Furth, H. G. *Thinking without language.* New York: Free Press, 1966.

433 Furth, H. G. "Linguistic deficiency and thinking: research with deaf subjects, 1964–69." *Psycholinguistics bulletin* 76:1 (1971), 58–72.

434 Furth, H. G. *Deafness and learning: a psychosocial approach.* Belmont, Calif.: Wadsworth Pub., 1973.

435 Furth, H. G., and J. Youniss. "Formal operation and language: a comparison of deaf and hearing adolescents." *International j. of psych.* 6 (1971), 49–64.

436 Fusfeld, I. "How the deaf communicate—manual language." *Amer. ann. deaf* 103:2 (1958), 264–282.

437 Gadlin, D., et al. *Lift your hands.* Washington, D.C.: The National Grange, 1976.

438 Gallaudet, E. "Is the sign language used to excess in teaching deaf-mutes?" *Amer. ann. deaf* 16:1 (1871), 26–33.

439 Gallaudet, E. "The value of the sign language to the deaf." *Amer. ann. deaf* 32:3 (1887), 141–147.

440 Gallaudet, T. "On the natural language of signs and its value and uses in the instruction of the deaf and dumb." *Amer. ann. deaf* 1:1 (1847), 55–60 (part I); 1:2 (1848), 79–93 (part II).

441 Gallaudet College. *New signs for instruction in library science.* Washington, D.C.: Gallaudet College, 1967 (?).

442 Gama, F. *Iconographia dos signaes dos surdos-mudos.* Rio de Janeiro: E. & H. Laemmert, 1875.

443 Gardner, B. T., and R. A. Gardner. "Teaching sign language to a chimpanzee." *Science* 165 (1969), 664–672.

444 Gardner, B. T., and R. A. Gardner. "Two-way communication with an infant chimpanzee." In A. Schrier and F. Stollnitz (eds.), *Behavior of nonhuman primates.* New York: Academic Press, 4 (1971), 117–183.

445 Gardner, B. T., and R. A. Gardner. *Measuring the vocabulary of very young primates.* Paper presented to the eastern psychological meeting, Philadelphia, Pa., 1974.

446 Gardner, R. A., and B. T. Gardner. "Comparing the early utterances of child and chimpanzee." *Minn. symposium of child psy.,* n.d.

447 Gardner, R. A., and B. T. Gardner. *Development of behavior in a young chimp: 7th summary of Washoe's diary—6.23.68–10.19.68.* Reno: Univ. of Nevada, 1969.

448 Gardner, R. A., and B. T. Gardner. *Development of behavior in a young chimp—8th summary of Washoe's diary–10.20.68.* Reno: Univ. of Nevada, 1969.

449 Gardner, R. A., and B. T. Gardner. "Communication with a young chimpanzee." In R. Chauvin (ed.), *Modèles animaux du comportement humain.* Paris, France: Centre National de la Recherche Scientifique, 1972.

450 Gardner, R. A., and B. T. Gardner. *Psychobiology of two-way communication.* Reno: Univ. of Nevada, 1972.

451 Gardner, R. A., and B. T. Gardner. "Teaching sign language to the chimp, Washoe bulletin." *D'audio phonologie* 4:5 (1974).

452 Gardner, R. A., and B. T. Gardner. *Use of order in Washoe's sign combinations.* Paper presented to the meeting of the psychonomic society, 1974.

453 Gardner, R. A., and B. T. Gardner. "Early signs of language in child and chimpanzee." *Science* 187 (1975), 752–753.

454 Gardner, R. A., and B. T. Gardner. "Teaching sign language to a chimp." *Science* 187 (1975).

455 Gardner, R. A., and B. T. Gardner. *Comparative psychology and language acquisition.* Reno: Univ. of Nevada, 1977.

456 Gardner, R. A., and B. T. Gardner. "Comparative psychology and language acquisition." *Ann. of NY academy of sciences* 308 (1978), 37–76.

457 Garnett, C. *The exchange of letters between Samuel Heinicke and Abbé Charles Michel de l'Épée.* New York: Vantage, 1968.

458 Gerland, G. *Die zeichensprache der Indianer.* Berlin: Gebruder Paeteli, 1883.

459 Geylman, I. F. *The manual alphabet and the signs of the deaf and dumb.* Moscow: Usesojuznoe Kooperativnoe Izdatel'stvo, 1957.

460 Gisholt, T. *Tegnsprak—durs 3.* Norway: Norges Døveforbund, 1976.

461 Godin, L. "Professions for deaf citizens in the USSR." *Amer. ann. deaf* 112, September 1967.

462 Godsave, B. F. *Fingerspelling's distinctive features.* Geneseo, N.Y.: State Univ. College, n.d.

463 Gold, M. W., and R. K. Rittenhouse. "Task analysis for teaching eight practical signs to deaf-blind individuals." *Teaching exceptional children* 10:2 (1978), 34–37.

464 Goldberg, P. J. "Adult second-language development: reasonable expectations and what it takes to achieve them." *Teaching English to the deaf* 4:1 (1971), 22–25.

465 Goldin-Meadow, S. J. *The representation of semantic representation in a manual language.* Philadelphia: Univ. of Penn., technical report 26: the acquisition of linguistic structure, 1975.

466 Goldin-Meadow, S. *Semantic relations in a manual language created by deaf children of hearing parents.* Paper presented at the conference of sign lang. and neurolinguistics, Rochester, N. Y., 1976.

467 Goldin-Meadow, S., and H. Feldman. "The creation of a communication system: a study of deaf children of hearing parents." *Sign lang. studies* 8, (1975), 225–234.

468 Goldin-Meadow, S., and H. Feldman. "The development of language-like communication without a language model." *Science* 197 (1977), 401–403.

469 Goodstadt, R. *Speaking with signs.* Hong Kong: Government Printer, 1970.

470 Gorman, P., and G. Paget. *A systematic sign language.* Unpub. paper. London, 1964.

471 Gougard, L. "The language of the silent." *Dix-neuvième année* 19:74 (1929), 93–100.

472 Grecco, R. V. *Results of a manual language program for non-verbal hearing and hearing impaired retarded.* Paper presented to the Conn. speech and hearing convention, 1974.

473 Greenberg, J. *In this sign.* New York: Holt, Rinehart & Winston, 1970.

474 Greenlee, D. "Peirce's concept of sign." In T. A. Sebeok (ed.), *Approaches to semiotics paperback series.* The Hague: Mouton, 1973.

475 Grinnell, M., et al. "Sign it successful: manual English encourages expressive communication." *Teaching exceptional children* 8:3 (Spring 1976), 123–124.

476 Grobsmith, E. S. *Nonverbal modes of learning: Dakota sign language and gestures and communication.* n.p., 1973.

477 Grosjean, F. *A study of timing in a manual and a spoken language: American sign language and English.* Boston: Northeastern Univ., 1977.

478 Grosjean, F. "The perception of rate in spoken and sign languages." *Perception and psychophysics* 22:4 (1977), 408–413.

479 Grosjean, F., et al. *The patterns of silence: performance structures in sentence production.* Boston: Northeastern Univ., 1978.

480 Grosjean, F., and H. Lane. *Pauses and structure in American sign language.* Paper presented at the conference of sign language and neurolinguistics, Rochester, N.Y., 1976.

481 Grosjean, F., and H. Lane. "Pauses and syntax in American sign language." *Cognition* 5:2 (1977), 101–117.

482 Grosjean, F., H. Teuber, and H. Lane. "When is a sign a sign? The on-line processing of gated signs in American sign language." Working paper. Boston: Northeastern Univ., Psych. dept., 1978.

483 Grow, C. *The language of signs.* Master's thesis. Washington, D.C.: Gallaudet College, 1924.

484 *Guidelines on interpreting for deaf-blind persons,* Washington, D.C.: Public Service Programs, Gallaudet College, 1978.

485 Guillory, L. *Expressive and receptive fingerspelling for hearing adults.* Baton Rouge, La.: Claitor's Book Store, 1966.

486 Gustason, G. "The language of communication." *J. of rehab. of deaf* III (1973), 83–93.

487 Gustason, G., et al. *Signing exact English. Supplement I.* Rossmoor, Calif.: Modern Sign Press, 1973.

488 Gustason, G., et al. "The rationale of signing exact English." *The deaf amer.* 27:1 (1974), 5–6.

489 Gustason, G., et al. *Signing exact English. Supplement II.* Rossmoor, Calif.: Modern Sign Press, 1975.

490 Gustason, G., D. Pfetzing, and E. Zawolkow,

Signing exact English. Seeing instead of hearing. Rossmoor, Calif.: Modern Sign Press, 1972.

491 Gustason, G., and R. Rosen. "The deaf child's right to communicate." In F. B. Crammatte, et al. (eds.), *VII world congress of the world federation of the deaf.* Silver Spring, Md.: National Assoc. of the Deaf, 1976, 450–453.

492 Gustason, G., and J. Woodward (eds.). *Recent developments in manual English.* Washington, D.C.: Gallaudet College Press, 1973.

493 Habig, M. "The first manual alphabet." *Catholic Ed. Rev.* 34:5 (May 1936). Washington, D.C.: Catholic Ed. Press, Catholic Univ. of America.

494 Haddon, A. "The gesture language of the eastern islanders of Torres Straits." *Cambridge anthropological expedition to Torres Straits, reports* 3 (1907), 261–262.

495 Hadley, L. *Indian sign talk.* Chicago, 1893.

496 Hahn, E. "A reporter at large—Washoese." *The New Yorker* 47:43 (1971), 54–98.

497 Hahn, E. *Look who's talking.* New York: Crowell, 1978.

498 Hale, K., et al. *Transcription and comments on a tape of Warlpiri sign language: spoken and sign.* Cambridge, Mass.: M.I.T., 1976, 1–24.

499 Hall, E. T. *The silent language.* New York: Doubleday, 1959.

500 Hall, S. "Evaluation of a manual approach to programming for deaf retarded." *Am. j. of mental deficiency* 75:3 (November 1970), 378–380.

501 Hamanaka, T., and H. Ohashi. " 'Aphasia' in pantomimic sign language." *Studia phono.* 8 (1974), 23–35.

502 Hammond, A., and J. Burns. *Teaching sign language to the multiple handicapped deaf person.* Paper presented to the annual convention of the council for exceptional children, Chicago, 1976.

503 Hansen, B. "Varieties in Danish sign language and grammatical features of the original sign language." *Sign lang. studies* 8 (1975), 249–256.

504 Hanson, O. *Superintendents defend the sign language.* Circular no. 4 of the national assoc. of the deaf. Berkeley, Calif.: National Assoc. of the Deaf.

505 Harrington, J. "American Indian sign language." *Indians at work,* 1938.

506 Harris, J. C. *Hand signs for ideas should not be used in the education of the deaf.* Cave Spring, Ga.: Georgia School for the Deaf, 1925.

507 Hayes, F. "Should we have a dictionary of gestures?" *Southern folklore quarterly* 4 (1940), 239–245.

508 Hayes, F. "Gestures: a working bibliography." *Southern folklore quarterly* 21 (1957), 218–317.

509 Hayes, F. "Gesture." *Encyclopedia Americana* 12 (1966), 627a–d.

510 Hayes, H. "The pursuit of reason." *New York Times Magazine,* 1977.

511 Heiman, G. *The intelligibility and comprehension of time compressed American sign language.* Unpub. thesis, Bowling Green State Univ., 1976.

512 Heiman, G. W., and R. D. Tweney. *The intelligibility of temporally interrupted ASL as a function of linguistic organization.* Bowling Green, Ohio: Bowling Green State Univ., 1975.

513 Hester, M. "Manual communication." *Proceedings of the international congress on education of the deaf and of the 41st meeting of the convention of American instructors of the deaf.* Washington, D.C.: Gallaudet College, 1963, 211–221.

514 Hewes, G. W. "An explicity formulation of the relationship between tool-using, tool-making, and the emergence of visible language." *Language* 8:2 (1973), 101–127.

515 Hewes, G. W. "Primate communication and the gestural origin of language." *Current anthropology* 14:1–2 (1973), 5–24.

516 Hewes, G. W. "Gesture language in culture contact." *Sign lang. studies* 4 (1974), 1–34.

517 Hewes, G. W. *The current status of the gestural theory of language origin.* Boulder: Univ. of Colorado, 1975.

518 Hewes, G. W. *The evolutionary significance of pongid sign language acquisition.* Boulder: Univ. of Colorado, 1975.

519 Hewes, G. W. "A model for language evolution." *Sign lang. studies* 15 (1977), 97–168.

520 Hewes, G. W. "The phylogeny of sign language." In Schlesinger and Namir (eds.), *Sign language of the deaf: psychological, linguistic, and sociological perspectives.* New York: Academic Press, 1978, 11–56.

521 Higgins, D. C., C. Ss. R. *How to talk to the deaf.* Chicago: J. S. Paluch, 1942.

522 Higgins, D. *How to talk to the deaf.* Newark, N.J.: Mt. Carmel Guild, 1959.

523 Higgins, E. "An analysis of the comprehensibility of three communication methods used with hearing impaired students." *Amer. ann. deaf* 118:1 (1973), 46–49.

524 Hill, J. H. "Apes, wolves, birds, and humans: toward a comparative foundation for a functional theory of language evolution." *Sign lang. studies* 14 (1977), 21–58.

525 Hinkle, C. *We have hands: a teaching manual for those concerned with our deaf.* Greenville, Tenn.: Green Valley Developmental Center, 1974.

526 Hobson, P., and P. Duncan. "Sign learning and profoundly retarded people." *Mental Retardation* (February 1979), 33–37.

527 Hodges, M., and L. McGehoe. *Total communication: a manual for parents and friends of the deaf.*

Houston, Tex.: Developmental Education Services, 1977.

528 Hoemann, H. W. *Proceedings: better techniques of communication for severely language-handicapped deaf people.* Washington, D.C.: Health, Education and Welfare, Report of Training Grant 67–10, 1967.

529 Hoemann, H. W. "The sign language's new look." *Rehab. record,* 1968, 5–8.

530 Hoemann, H. *Improved techniques of communication: a training manual for use with severely handicapped deaf clients.* Bowling Green, Ohio: Bowling Green State Univ., 1970.

531 Hoemann, H. *The development of communication skills in deaf and hearing children.* Bowling Green, Ohio: Bowling Green State Univ., 1971.

532 Hoemann, H. W. "Children's use of fingerspelling vs. sign language to label pictures." *Exceptional children* 39 (1972), 161–162.

533 Hoemann, H. "Communication accuracy in a sign language interpretation of a group test." *J. of rehab. of deaf* 5 (1972), 40–43.

534 Hoemann, H. W. "Deaf children's use of fingerspelling to label pictures of common objects: a followup study." *Exceptional children* 40 (1974), 519–520.

535 Hoemann, H. W. "The communicative behavior of preverbal deaf children." *Proceedings from the eastern psychological assoc.,* 1974.

536 Hoemann, H. *American sign language: lexical and grammatical notes with translation exercises.* Silver Spring, Md.: National Association of the Deaf, 1975.

537 Hoemann, H. *Order constraints in American sign language: the effects of sentence structure on short term memory for anomalous sign language sentences.* Bowling Green, Ohio: Bowling Green State Univ., 1975.

538 Hoemann, H. "The transparency of meaning in sign language gestures." *Sign lang. studies* 7 (1975), 151–161.

539 Hoemann, H. *Teaching American sign language: a rationale.* Paper presented at the national symposium on sign language research and teaching, Chicago, 1977.

540 Hoemann, H. W. "Categorical coding of sign and English in short term memory by deaf and hearing subjects." In P. Siple (ed.), *Understanding language through sign language research.* New York: Academic Press, 1978, 289–305.

541 Hoemann, H. *Communicating with deaf people: a resource manual for teachers and students of American sign language.* Baltimore: Univ. Park Press, 1978.

542 Hoemann, H., et al. "Categorical encoding in short-term memory by deaf and hearing children." *J. of speech and hearing research* 17 (1974), 426–431.

543 Hoemann, H. W., et al. *The spelling proficiency of deaf children taught by the Rochester method.* Bowling Green, Ohio: Bowling Green State Univ., 1974.

544 Hoemann, H., and V. Florian. "Order constraints in American sign language." *Sign lang. studies* 11 (1976), 121–132.

545 Hoemann, H., and V. A. Florian. "Order constraints in American sign language: the effects of structure on judgments of meaningfulness and an immediate recall of anomalous sign sequences." *Sign lang. studies* 11 (1976), 121–132.

546 Hoemann, H., V. Florian, and S. Hoemann. "A computer simulation of American sign language." *Amer. j. of computational linguistics* 13 (1976). AJCL microfiche 37.

547 Hoemann, H., and S. Hoemann. *Sign language flash cards.* Silver Spring, Md.: National Association of the Deaf, 1973.

548 Hoemann, H., and R. Tweney. "Back translation: a method for the analysis of manual languages." *Sign lang. studies* 2 (1973), 51–80.

549 Hoemann, H., and R. Tweney. "Is the sign language of the deaf an adequate communication channel?" *Proceedings of the 81st convention American psychological association* 11 (1973), 801–802.

550 Hoffmeister, R. J. "An analysis of possessive constructions in the ASL of a young deaf child of deaf parents." *J. of communication and cognition.* Temple Univ., 1977.

551 Hoffmeister, R. *The parameters of sign language defined: translation and definition rules.* Research report no. 83. Minneapolis: Univ. of Minnesota, 1975.

552 Hoffmeister, R. *The influence of pointing in American sign language development.* Paper presented at the national symposium on sign language research and teaching, Chicago, 1977.

553 Hoffmeister, R. J. "The influential point." In Wm. Stokoe (ed.), *Proceedings of the national symposium on sign language research and teaching,* Chicago, 1977.

554 Hoffmeister, R. J. "The development of demonstrative pronouns, locatives and personal pronouns in the acquisition of American sign language by deaf children of deaf parents." Unpub. diss., Univ. of Minnesota, 1978.

555 Hoffmeister, R., et al. *The acquisition of sign language in deaf children of deaf parents: progress report.* Research report no. 65. Minneapolis: Univ. of Minnesota, June 1974.

556 Hoffmeister, R. J., et al. "Some procedural guidelines for the study of the acquisition of sign language." *Sign lang. studies* 7 (1975), 121–137.

557 Hoffmeister, R., et al. *The parameters of sign language defined: translation and definition rules.* Research report no. 83. Minneapolis: Univ. of Minnesota, 1975.

558 Hoffmeister, R., and A. Farmer. "The development of manual sign language in mentally retarded deaf individuals." *J. of rehab. of deaf* 6:1 (1972), 19–26.

559 Hoffmeister, R., and D. Moores. *The acquisition of specific reference in the linguistic system of a deaf child of deaf parents.* Research report no. 53. Minneapolis: Univ. of Minnesota, August 1973.

560 Hollister, H. "The manual alphabet." *Amer. ann. deaf and dumb* 15:2 (1870), 88–92.

561 Hood, M., and L. Searle. "Hand signals for safety: directing machinery." *Successful farming* 71:2 (1973), 16–17.

562 Hovland C. R. "Literature can live through signs." *Amer. ann. deaf* 120:6 (1975), 558–563.

563 "How a chimp says tickle." *Newsweek* magazine, 82:69 (1973).

564 Howe, C. *The deaf mutes of Canada: a history of their education with an account of the deaf mute institutions of the dominion and a description of all known finger and sign alphabets.* Toronto: C. J. Howe, 1888.

565 Howse, J., and J. Fitch. "Effects of parent orientation in sign language on communication skills of preschool children." *Amer. ann. deaf* 117:4 (1972), 459–462.

566 Huffman, J., *et al. Talk with me: communication with the multi-handicapped deaf.* Northridge, Calif. Joyce Motion Picture Co., 1975.

567 Hughes, J. "Acquisition of non-verbal 'language' by aphasic children." *Cognition* 3 (1974/75), 41–56.

568 Hughes, R. M. *La meri: the gesture language of the Hindu dance.* New York: Benjamin Bloom, 1964.

569 Humphreys, B. *The visionary.* Fresno, Calif.: by author, 1979.

570 Humphries, T. "Report: national symposium on sign language research and teaching." *Teaching English to the deaf* 78:4 (1977), 4–5.

571 Hutcheson, S. *The elements of the universal sign language and universal sign language phonetic alphabet.* Toronto: Univ. of Toronto Press, 1935.

572 Hutt, C. "Examination of a corpus: dictionary of the manual language in the house of the monks." *Languages* 10 (1968), 107–118.

573 Huttenlocher, J. "Encoding information in American sign language." In J. F. Kavanagh and J. E. Cutting (eds.), *The role of speech in language.* Cambridge, Mass.: M.I.T. Press, 1975, 229–240.

574 Hutton, G. *Specimens of a dictionary of natural signs for the deaf and dumb.* Washington, D.C., n.p., n.d.

575 Hyett, R. "The art of dactylology and signs." *Hearing* 24:9 (1970), 264–267.

576 Industrial home for the blind. *Guidelines for the helper of deaf-blind persons.* Write to I.H.B., 57 Willoughby St., Brooklyn, N.Y. 11201.

577 Industrial home for the blind. *The LORM alphabet.* Write to I.H.B., 57 Willoughby St., Brooklyn, N.Y. 11201.

578 Industrial home for the blind. *Recommended international standard manual alphabet for communicating with deaf-blind persons,* 1958. Write to I.H.B., 57 Willoughby St., Brooklyn, N.Y. 11201.

579 Ingram, R. M. *Iconism in American sign language.* Washington, D.C.: Gallaudet College, 1972.

580 Ingram, R. M. *A model of sociolinguistic variation in sign language forms.* Paper presented to the summer meeting, linguistic society of America, Ann Arbor, Mich., 1973.

581 Ingram, R. M. "A communication model of the interpreting process." *J. of rehab. of deaf* 7, January 1974.

582 Ingram, R. M. "Concepts of employment of interpreters for the deaf." *Deaf Amer.* 27, 1975.

583 Ingram, R. M. *Tabula restriction in American sign language: implications from synchrony to diachrony.* Providence, R.I.: Brown Univ., 1976.

584 Ingram, R. M., *On the inequality of signed and spoken languages.* Paper presented to the Linguistic Circle of Copenhagen. Copenhagen, Denmark, 1977.

585 Ingram, R. *Principles and procedures of teaching sign language.* Carlisle, Eng.: Unpub. paper, 1977.

586 Ingram, R. M. "Sign language interpretation and general theories of language, interpretation, and communication." In D. Gerver and H. W. Sinaiko (eds.), *Language interpretation and communication.* New York: Plenum Press, 1978.

587 Ingram, R. M. "Theme, rheme, topic and comment in the syntax of American sign language." *Sign lang. studies* 20 (1978), 193–218.

588 Ingram, R. M., and B. Ingram (eds.). *Hands across the sea: proceedings of the first international conference on interpreting.* Registry of interpreters for the deaf, 1975.

589 Institut regional des jeunes sourds. *Communication and the hearing impaired.* Marseille, France: Institute Regional des jeunes sourds, 3, Rue Abbe Dassy-13007, 1978.

590 *Internationale zeitschrift für allgemeine sprachwissenschaft.* Vol. 47, 1933.

591 Isaacs, M. "A natural approach to technical sign construction." *J. of rehab. of deaf* 7:1 (1973), 11–14.

592 Jacobs, J. "The methodical signs for 'and' and the verb 'to be'." *Amer. ann. deaf and dumb* 8:3 (1856), 185–186.

593 Jacobs, J. "The relation of written words to signs, the same as their relation to spoken words." *Amer. ann. deaf* 11:2 (1859), 65–78.

594 Jacobs, J. (chairperson). *SOS standardization of signs.* Austin, Tex.: Statewide Project for the Deaf, Fall 1973.

595 Jacobs, J. *Preferred signs for instructional purposes.* Austin, Tex.: Standardization of Signs Committee for the Schools for the Deaf, 1974.

596 Jacobs, L. R. "The efficiency of interpreting input for processing lecture information by deaf college students." *J. of rehab. of deaf* 11, 1977.

597 James, W. "Thought before language: a deaf-mute's recollections." *Philosophical review* 1 (1892), 613–624.

598 Jameson, S. *122 work survival signs—a mini dictionary.* Northridge, Calif.: Joyce Media, Inc., n.d.

599 Jarrow, J. E. "Signing for communication in hearing youngsters: further support." *Deaf Amer.* 30:8 (1978), 13.

600 Jennings, A., and W. E. Clayton. *Some candid opinions of the sign language.* Boston: Hermann Schulz & Co., 1910.

601 Johnson, R. E. "A comparison of the phonological structures of two northwest sawmill sign languages." *Communication and cognition,* 1977.

602 Johnson, R. E. "An extension of Oregon sawmill sign language." *Current anthropology* 18:2 (1977), 353–354.

603 Johnson, R. E. "A phonological comparison of extended Oregon sawmill sign language and American sign language." In R. W. Shuy (ed.), *New ways of analyzing variation in English.* Washington, D.C.: Georgetown Univ. Press, 1977.

604 Jones, H. *Sign language.* London: English Univ. Press, 1968.

605 Jones, N. *On expressing plurality in American sign language.* Unpub. master's thesis, Univ. of Calif., Berkeley, 1975.

606 Jordan, F. *Lesson outlines for teaching and the study of dactylology.* Hampton, Va.: Christian deaf fellowship, 75 Brogden Lane, n.d.

607 Jordan, I. K. "A referential communication study of signers and speakers using realistic referents." *Sign lang. studies* 6 (1975), 65–103.

608 Jordan, I. K., and R. Battison. "A referential communication experiment with foreign sign languages." *Sign lang. studies* 10 (1976), 69–80.

609 Jorgensen, J. *De døvstummes haandalfabet og 280 af de almindeligste tegn.* Copenhagen: Alfred Jacobsens Grafiske Etablissement, 1907.

610 Jorgensen, J. *Ordbog de døvstummes tegnsprog; udgivet af døvstumme-raadet; udgivet med under-* *støttelse fra staten.* Copenhagen: Herm. Rolsteds Bogrr., 1926.

611 Joyce Media, Inc. *133 library survival signs—a mini dictionary.* Northridge, Calif.: by author, n.d.

612 Joyce Media, Inc. *Various children's books in sign language.* Northridge, Calif.: Joyce Media, Inc., n.d.

613 Joyce Media, Inc. *100 medical survival signs—a mini dictionary.* Northridge, Calif.: by author, 1978.

614 Julesz, B., and I. Hirsh. "Visual and auditory perception: an essay of comparison." In E. E. David and P. B. Denes (eds.), *Human communication: a unified view.* New York: McGraw-Hill, 1972, 283–340.

615 Kahn, J. "A comparison of manual and oral language training with mute retarded children." *Mental retardation* 15:3 (1977), 21–23.

616 Kakumasu, J. "Urubu sign language." *Intl. j. of Amer. linguistics* 34:4 (1968), 275–281.

617 Kannapell, B. *Bilingualism: a new direction in the education of the deaf.* Washington, D.C.: Gallaudet College, 1973.

618 Kannapell, B. "Bilingualism: a new direction in the education of the deaf." *The deaf Amer.* 26:10 (1974), 9–15.

619 Kannapell, B. *Bilingualism: a new direction in the education of the deaf.* Washington, D.C.: Deafpride Inc., 1976.

620 Kannapell, B. Response to "social-psychological aspects of the use of sign language." In *Deafpride Papers: perspectives and options.* Washington, D.C.: Deafpride Inc., 1976, 31–35.

621 Kannapell, B. M. *The deaf person as a teacher of American sign language: unifying and separatist functions of American sign language.* Paper presented at the national symposium on sign language research and teaching, Chicago, 1977.

622 Kannapell, B. M., L. B. Hamilton, and H. Bornstein. *Signs for instructional purposes.* Washington, D.C.: Gallaudet College Press, 1969.

623 Kantor, R. M. "The acquisition of classifiers in American sign language." Paper presented at the 2nd annual Boston Univ. language development conference, 1977.

624 Kark, C. *Path of life sign language manual.* Port Crane, N.Y.: Path of Life Summer Camp, n.d.

625 Keep, J. "The language of signs." *Amer. ann. deaf and dumb* 14:2 (1869), 89–95.

626 Keep, J. "Natural signs—shall they be abandoned?" *Amer. ann. deaf* 16:1 (1871), 17–25.

627 Keep, J. "The sign language." *Amer. ann. deaf and dumb* 16:4 (1871), 221–234.

628 *Keep quiet.* Sign language crossword cubes game. Northridge, Calif.: Sign Language Store, n.d.

629 Kegl, J. *Relational grammar and American sign language.* Unpub. MS. Cambridge, Mass.: Mass. Institute of Tech., 1976.

630 Kegl, J. A., and N. Chinchor. "A frame analysis of American sign language." In T. Diller (ed.), *Proceedings of the 13th annual meeting, association for computational linguistics.* Amer. j. of computational linguistics microfiche 35. St. Paul, Minn.: Sperry-Univac, 1975.

631 Kegl, J., and G. Nigrosh. *Sign language and pictographs. A comparison of the signs and picture writing of the North American plains Indians.* Unpub. MS. Providence, R.I.: Brown Univ., 1975.

632 Kegl, J., and R. Wilbur. "When does structure stop and style begin? Syntax, morphology, and phonology vs. stylistic variation in American sign language." In S. Hufwene, C. Walker, and S. Streeven (eds.), *Papers from the 12th regional meeting of the Chicago linguistics society.* Chicago, Ill., 1976.

633 Kendon, A. "Gesticulation, speech, and the gesture theory of language origins." *Sign lang. studies* 9 (1975), 349–373.

634 Kendon, A. "Some emerging features of face-to-face interaction." *Sign lang. studies* 22 (1979), 7–22.

635 Kesert, S. M. *A checklist of the Charles Baker collection of the Gallaudet college library.* Unpub. thesis, Gallaudet College, 1948.

636 Key, M. R. *Nonverbal communication: a research guide and bibliography.* Metuchen, N.J.: Scarecrow Press, 1977.

637 Kiernan, C. "Alternatives to speech: a review of research on manual and other forms of communication with the mentally handicapped and other non-communicating populations." *British j. of mental subnormality* 23 (1977), 6–28.

638 Kimura, D. "The neural basis of language qua gesture." *Studies in neurolinguistics* 2 (1976), 145–156.

639 Kimura, D., et al. "Impairment of nonlinguistic hand movements in a deaf aphasic." *Brain and lang.* 3 (1976), 566–571.

640 Kinchla, S. *Silent speech.* Redding, Calif.: by author, 1977.

641 King, W. "Hand gestures." *Western folklore* 8 (1949), 263–264.

642 Kirchner, C. *Professional or amateur.* San Fernando, Calif.: Southern Calif. Registry of Interpreters for the Deaf, 1969.

643 Kirchner, C. *Project LEARN.* San Fernando, Calif.: Southern Calif. Registry of Interpreters for the Deaf, 1970.

644 Kirchner, S. L. *Play it by sign: games in sign language.* Northridge, Calif.: Joyce Motion Picture Co., 1974.

645 Kirchner, S. *Signs for all seasons.* Northridge, Calif.: Joyce Media, Inc., 1977.

646 Kirschner, A., et al. Manual communication systems: a comparison and its implications. *Education and Training of the Mentally Retarded* (February 1979), 5–10.

647 Kjaer-Sorensen, R., and B. Hansen. *The sign language of deaf children in Denmark: a pilot-study.* Copenhagen: The School for the Deaf, Kasterlsvej 58, 1976.

648 Klima, E. S. "Sound and its absence in the linguistic symbol." In L. Kavanagh and J. Cutting (eds.), *The role of speech in language.* Cambridge, Mass.: M.I.T. Press, 1975, 249–270.

649 Klima, E. S., and U. Bellugi. *Teaching apes to communicate.* La Jolla, Calif.: Univ. of Calif. and Salk Institute for Biological Studies, 1971.

650 Klima, E., and U. Bellugi. "The signs of language in child and chimpanzee." In T. Alloway, and P. Plinear (eds.), *Communication and affect: the comparative approach.* New York: Academic Press, 1972.

651 Klima, E., and U. Bellugi. "Language in another mode." *Neurosciences research program bulletin* 12 (1974), 539–550.

652 Klima, E. S., and U. Bellugi. "Language in another mode." In E. Lenneberg (ed.), *Language and the brain, developmental aspects. Neurosciences research program bulletin* 12 (1974), 539–550.

653 Klima, E., and U. Bellugi. *Perception and production in a visually based language.* Paper presented to the conference on psycholinguistic and communication disorders, New York Academy of Sciences, 1975.

654 Klima, E. S., and U. Bellugi. "Perception and production in a visually based language." In D. Aaronson and R. W. Rieber (eds.), *Developmental psycholinguistics and communication disorders.* New York: New York Academy of Sciences, 1975, 225–235.

655 Klima, E., and U. Bellugi. "Wit and poetry in American sign language." *Sign lang. studies* 8 (1975), 203–224.

656 Klima, E. S., and U. Bellugi. "Poetry and song in a language without sound." *Cognition* 4:1 (1976), 45–97.

657 Klima, E. S., and U. Bellugi. "Poetry without sound." *Human nature* 1(10), (1978), 74–83.

658 Klima, E. S., and U. Bellugi. "Propriétés des symboles dans un langage sans parole." In H. Hecaen and M. Jeannerod (eds.), *Du controle moteur a l'organisation du geste.* Paris: Masson, 1978, 398–423.

659 Klima, E. S., and U. Bellugi. *The signs of language.* Cambridge, Mass.: Harvard Univ. Press, 1979.

660 Klopping, H. "Language understanding of deaf

students under three auditory-visual conditions." *Amer. ann. deaf* 117:3 (1972), 389–392.

661 Knast, J. F. *The acquisition of a manual system of communication by nonverbal retardates.* New Brunswick, N.J.: Rutgers College, 1973.

662 Kohl, F. L., et al. "Effects of pairing manual signs with verbal cues upon the acquisition of instruction-following behaviors and the generalization to expressive language with severely handicapped students." *AAESPH review* 4:3 (1979), 291–300.

663 Kohl, H. *Language and education of the deaf.* New York: Center for Urban Ed., 1966.

664 Konstantareas, M. M. "Simultaneous communication: an alternative to speech training with autistic children." *J. of practical approaches to developmental handicaps* 1:1 (1977), 15–21.

665 Konstantareas, M. M., et al. "Simultaneous communication with non-verbal children: an alternative to speech with autistic and other severely dysfunctional non-verbal children." *J. of comm. disorders* 10 (1977), 267–271.

666 Kopchick, G. "A total communication environment in an institution." *Mental retardation* 13:3 (June 1975), 22–23.

667 Kosche, M. *Hymns for signing and singing.* Write to author: 116 Walnut St., Delavan, Wis. 53115.

668 Krairiksh, K. *Why manual language is necessary for the Thai deaf.* Bangkok, 1956 (?).

669 Kuschel, R. "The silent inventor: the creation of a sign language by the only deaf mute on a Polynesian island." *Sign lang. studies* 3 (1973), 1–28.

670 Kuschel, R. *A lexicon of signs from a Polynesian outliner island.* Copenhagen: Kobenhavns Univ., 8 (1974).

671 Labarta de Chaves, T., and J. L. Soler. "Pedro Ponce de León, first teacher of the deaf." *Sign lang. studies,* 5 (1974), 48–63. [See Chaves, T.]

672 Lacy, R. "Putting some of the syntax back into semantics." Paper presented at the 49th annual meeting, linguistic society of America, 1974.

673 Lacy, R. *Noun-verb agreement in American sign language.* Unpub. MS. San Diego: Univ. of Calif., 1977.

674 Lacy, R. *Pronouns in American sign language as 'indexic pronouns.'* Unpub. MS. San Diego: Univ. of Calif., 1977.

675 La Fin. *Sermo mirabilis, or The silent language.* London, 1692.

676 Laird, C. "A non-human being can learn language." *College composition and communication* 23:2 (1972), 142–154.

677 Lake, S. J. *The handbook. A guide to manual communication for the multiple handicapped.* Tucson, Ariz.: Communication Skill Builders, 1976.

678 Lamb, B. *Symbology, English, vocabulary.* Miami, Fla.: Dade County Public Schools, 1971.

679 Landes, R. *Approaches: a digest of methods in learning the language of signs.* Richmond, Va., 1968.

680 Lane, H. *The wild boy of Aveyron.* Cambridge, Mass.: Harvard Univ. Press, 1976.

681 Lane, H. "Notes for a psycho-history of American sign language." *The deaf Amer.* 30:1 (1977), 3–7.

682 Lane, H., et al. "Preliminaries to a distinctive feature analysis of handshapes in American sign language." *Cognitive Psy.* 8:2 (April 1976), 263–289.

683 Lane, H., and R. Battison. "The role of oral language in the evolution of manual language." Working paper. Northeastern Univ., psych. dept., 1978.

684 Lange, P. "Lange surveys the foreign scene." *Silent worker* 2:12 (1950), 11.

685 "Language of signs." *Science digest* 72 (1972), 32–33.

686 LaPlace, V., and S. Livingston. *Manual communication guide.* New York: School for the Deaf—JHS47M, 1977.

687 Larson, T. *Communication for the non-verbal child.* Johnstown, Pa.: Mafex Assoc., 1975.

688 Laura, Sister M. *Let's talk.* Port-au-Prince, Haiti: École St. Vincent, 1970.

689 Lauritsen, R. R. "The national interpreter training consortium." In F. B. Crammatte and A. B. Crammatte (eds.), *VII world congress of the world federation of the deaf.* Silver Spring, Md.: National Assoc. of the Deaf, 1976, 89–92.

690 Lawrence, E. D. *Sign language made simple.* Springfield, Mo.: Gospel Publishing House, 1975.

691 Layall, A. "Italian sign language." *Twentieth century magazine* 159 (1956).

692 Lebeis, S., and R. Lebeis. "The use of signed communication with the normal hearing, non-verbal mental retarded." *Bureau memo.* 17:1 (February 1975), 28–30.

693 Leibovitz, S. *Sign versus speech in the imitation learning of a mute autistic child.* Unpub. thesis, McGill Univ., 1976.

694 Lenneberg, E. H. *The biological foundations of language.* New York: John Wiley & Sons, 1967.

695 Lentz, E. *Informing the deaf about the structure of ASL.* Paper presented at the national symposium on sign language research and teaching, Chicago, 1977.

696 "Letter to Prof. John R. Keep." *Amer. ann. deaf* 14:2 (1869), 89–95.

697 Levett, L. "A method of communication for non-speaking severely subnormal children—trial results." *British j. of disorders of comm.,* 125–128.

698 Levett, L. "Discovering how mime can help." *Special educ.* 60:1 (1971), 17–19.

699 Lewis, M. *The education of deaf children: the possible place of fingerspelling and signing.* London: Her Majesty's Stationery Office, 1968.

700 Liddell, S. K. *The acquisition of some American sign language grammatical processes.* Unpub. MS. La Jolla, Calif.: Salk Institute for Biological Studies, n.d.

701 Liddell, S. *Restrictive relative clauses in American sign language.* Unpub. MS. La Jolla, Calif.: Salk Institute for Biological Studies, 1975.

702 Liddell, S. K. *Non-manual signals and relative clauses in American sign language.* Paper presented to the conference of sign language and neurolinguistics, Rochester, N.Y., 1976.

703 Liddell, S. K. "An investigation into the syntatic structure of American sign language." Unpub. diss., Univ. of Calif., San Diego, 1977.

704 Liddell, S. *Non-manual signals in American sign language: a many layered system.* Paper presented at the national symposium on sign language research and teaching, Chicago, 1977.

705 Liddell, S. K. "The role of facial expression in American sign language." In Wm. Stokoe (ed.), *Proceedings of the national symposium on sign language research and teaching,* Chicago, 1977.

706 Liddell, S. K. "Non-manual signals and relative clauses in American sign language." In P. Siple (ed.), *Understanding language through sign language research.* New York: Academic Press, 1978, 59–90.

707 Linville, S. "Signed English: a language teaching technique with totally non-verbal severely mentally retarded adolescents." *Lang., speech and hearing services in schools* 8:3 (1977), 170–175.

708 Lively, E. *Phonetical alphabet for the deaf.* Albuquerque, N.M., 1976.

709 Livingston, S. *The structure of American sign language.* Unpub. MS. New York: New York Univ., 1973.

710 Livingston, S. *Manual communication guide.* New York: JHS47M, 1977.

711 Ljung, M. "Principles of a stratificational analysis of the plains Indian sign language." *Int'l. j. of linguistics* 31 (1965), 119–127.

712 Lloyd, G. (ed.). "Special issue concerning interpreting." *J. rehab. of deaf* 7:3 (January 1974).

713 Long, J. S. *The sign language: a manual of signs.* Iowa City, Iowa: Athens Press, 1918.

714 Long, J. S. *The sign language: a manual of signs,* 2nd ed. Washington, D.C.: Gallaudet College, 1961.

715 Long, S. H. "The Indian language of signs." *Expedition to the Rocky Mountains* 1, 378–407.

716 Loomis, S. F. "Sign language of truck drivers." *Western folklore* 5, 205–206.

717 Lucas, T. *Chyrology; or, the art of reading, spelling, and ciphering by the fingers, designed for the benefit of the deaf, and for the instruction and amusement of youth.* London: Harrison and Leigh, 1812.

718 MacLeod, C. "A deafman's sign language—its nature and position relative to spoken languages." *York papers on linguistics,* York, Eng.: Univ. of York. n.d.

719 Madsen, W. *Conversational sign language II: an intermediate-advanced manual* (rev. ed.). Washington, D.C.: Gallaudet College, 1972.

720 Madsen, W. J. "Sign language as a means of increasing fluency in English." *Teaching English to the deaf* 1:2 (1973/74), 16–22.

721 Madsen, W. J. "Report on the international dictionary of sign language." In F. B. Crammatte, et al. (eds.), *VII world congress of the world federation of the deaf.* Silver Spring, Md.: National Assoc. of the Deaf, 1976, 71–74.

722 Madsen, W. J. "The teaching of sign language to hearing adults." In F. B. Crammatte and A. B. Crammatte (eds.), *VII world congress of the world federation of the deaf.* Silver Spring, Md.: National Assoc. of the Deaf, 1976.

723 Magarotto, C. "Towards an international language of gestures." *UNESCO courier,* 1974, 20–21.

724 Magarotto, C., and D. Vukotic. *First contribution to the international dictionary of sign language.* Rome, Italy: Ecole Professionelle de l'E.N.S., 1959.

725 Mallery, G. "A collection of gesture signs and signals of the North American Indians with some comparisons." *Bureau of American ethnology,* miscellaneous publication, 1, 1880.

726 Mallery, G. "Sign language among North American Indians." In J. W. Powell (ed.), *First annual report of the bureau of ethnology* 1 (1881), 263–552.

727 Mandel, M. "Iconic devices in American sign language." In L. Friedman (ed.), *On the other hand: new perspectives on American sign language.* New York: Academic Press, 1977, 57–107.

728 Mandel, M. *Iconicity of signs and their learnability by non-signers.* Paper presented at the national symposium on sign language research and teaching, Chicago, 1977.

729 Mandel, M. A. *Morphophonology of American sign language.* Berkeley: Univ. of Calif., 1978.

730 *(The) Manual alphabet with one hand, for the deaf and dumb.* Memphis, Tenn.: Price, Jones & Co., 1870.

731 Markowicz, H. "Aphasia and deafness." *Sign lang. studies* 3 (1973), 61–71.

732 Markowicz, H. "Some sociolinguistic considera-

tions of American sign language." *Sign lang. studies* 1 (1973), 15–41.

733 Markowicz, H. "What language do deaf children acquire? A review article." *Sign lang. studies* 3 (1973), 72–78.

734 Markowicz, H. "Book review: psycholinguistics and total communication: the state of the art," T. O'Rourke (ed.), *Sign lang. studies* 5 (1974), 82–91.

735 Markowicz, H. "Are sign languages primitive?" Washington, D.C.: Gallaudet College, Buff and Blue newspaper, 1975.

736 Markowicz, H. *Sign language: a universal language?* Washington, D.C.: Gallaudet College, Buff and Blue newspaper, Oct. 9, 1975.

737 Markowicz, H. *Signs as glorified gestures.* Washington, D.C.: Gallaudet College, Buff and Blue newspaper, Oct. 23, 1975.

738 Markowicz, H. *The myth about the Abbé de L'Épée and sign language.* Washington, D.C.: Gallaudet College, Buff and Blue newspaper, Sept. 25, 1975.

739 Markowicz, H. *Three misconceptions of ASL.* Washington, D.C.: Gallaudet College, Buff and Blue newspaper, Nov. 6, 1975.

740 Markowicz, H. *Touch finish anyone?* Washington, D.C.: Gallaudet College, Buff and Blue newspaper, Dec. 11, 1975.

741 Markowicz, H. *American sign language: fact and fancy.* Washington, D.C.: Gallaudet College, 1976.

742 Markowicz, H. "De l'Épée's methodical signs revisited." In C. Williams (ed.), *Language and communication research problems.* Washington, D.C.: Gallaudet College Press, 1976, 73–78.

743 Markowicz, H. *Fact and fancy.* Washington, D.C.: Gallaudet College Press, 1977.

744 Markowicz, H., and J. Woodward. *Language and the maintenance of ethnic boundaries in the deaf community.* Paper presented at the conference on culture and communication, Philadelphia, Pa.: Temple Univ., 1975.

745 Marmor, G. S., and L. A. Petitto. *Simultaneous communication: a psycholinguistic analysis.* Ithaca, N.Y.: Cornell Univ., Dept. of Human Development and Family Studies. *Sign lang. studies* 23 (1979).

746 Martsinovskaia, E. "O daktil'noirechi." *Defektologiia* 5 (1969), 19–26.

747 Masagatani, G. "Hand-gesturing behavior in psychotic children." *Amer. j. of occupational therapy* 27:1 (1973), 24–29.

748 Mattingly, I. G. "Speech cues and sign stimuli." *American scientist* 60 (1972), 327–337.

749 Maxwell, M. "A child's garden of lexical gaps." Working paper. Salk Institute and Univ. of Arizona, 1977.

750 Mayberry, R. I. "Manual communication." In H. Davis and S. R. Silverman (eds.), *Hearing and deafness,* 4th ed., New York: Holt, Rinehart, and Winston, 1970.

751 Mayberry, R. "An assessment of some oral and manual-language skills of hearing children of deaf parents." *Amer. ann. deaf,* 1976, 507–512.

752 Mayberry, R. "If a chimp can learn sign language, surely my nonverbal client can too." *Asha* 18:4 (1976), 223–228.

753 Mayberry, R. *Facial expression, noise, and shadowing in American sign language.* Paper presented to the national symposium on sign language research and teaching, Chicago, 1977.

754 Mayberry, R. I. "French Canadian sign language: a study of inter-sign language comprehension." In P. Siple (ed.), *Understanding language through sign language research.* New York: Academic Press, 1978, 349–373.

755 McCall, E. *A generative grammar of sign.* Unpub. master's thesis, Univ. of Iowa, 1965.

756 McCarr, D. *Self-instructional basic vocabulary study cards.* Lake Oswego, Ore.: Dormac Publishing Co., n.d.

757 McIntire, M. "Language acquisition in a different mode." Master's thesis, Calif. State Univ. at Northridge, 1973.

758 McIntire, M. L. *A modified model for the description of language acquisition in a deaf child.* Northridge, Calif.: Calif. State Univ., 1974.

759 McIntire, M. "The acquisition of American sign language hand configurations." *Sign lang. studies* 16 (1977), 247–266.

760 McIntire, M., and J. Yamada. "Visual shadowing: an experiment in American sign language." Ling. society of America, Philadelphia, Pa., 1976.

761 McIntire, M. L., and J. E. Yamada. *Shadowing in another modality.* Los Angeles, Calif.: Univ. of Calif., 1977.

762 McKeever, W., et al. "Evidence of minimal cerebral asymmetries for the processing of English words and American sign language in the congenitally deaf." *Neurologia* 14 (1976), 413–423.

763 Meadow, K. P. "Early manual communication in relation to the deaf child's intellectual, social, and communicative functioning. *Amer. ann. deaf* 113 (1968), 29–41.

764 Meadow, K. *Sociolinguistics, sign language, and the deaf subculture.* Unpub. MS. Univ. of Calif. at San Francisco: Langley Porter Neuropsychiatric Institute, 1971.

765 Meadow, K. "Sociolinguistics, sign language and the deaf sub-culture." In T. J. O'Rourke (ed.), *Psycholinguistics and total communication.* Silver Spring, Md.: *Amer. ann. deaf,* 1972, 19–33.

766 Meadow, K. "The deaf subculture." *Hearing and speech action* 43:4 (1975), 16–18.

767 Meadow, K. "Name signs as identity symbols in

the deaf community." *Sign lang. studies* 17 (1977), 237–246.

768 Meier, R. "Verbs of motion in American sign language." Working paper. Salk Institute for Biological Studies, 1978.

769 Meissner, M., and S. B. Philpott. "A dictionary of sawmill workers' signs." *Sign lang. studies* 9 (1975), 309–347.

770 Meissner, M., and S. Philpott. "The sign language of sawmill workers in British Columbia." *Sign lang. studies* 9 (1975), 291–347.

771 Mendelson, J. H., et al. "The language of signs and symbolic behavior of the deaf." In D. M. Rioch and E. Weinstein (eds.), *Disorders of communication*. Baltimore: Williams and Wilkins Co., 1964, 151–170.

772 Mergitt, M. "Sign language among the Walbiri of Central Australia." *Oceania* 25 (1954), 2–16.

773 Michaels, J.W. *A handbook of the sign language of the deaf*. Atlanta, Ga.: Home Mission Board, Southern Baptist Convention, 1923.

774 Miles, D. *Gestures: poetry in sign language*. Northridge, Calif.: Joyce Motion Picture Co., 1976.

775 Miller, A. "Cognitive developmental training with elevated boards and sign language." *J. of autism and childhood schizophrenia* 3:1 (1973), 65–85.

776 Miller, L. *Attitudes toward deafness, motivation and expectations of students enrolled in manual communication classes*. Unpub. dissertation, Brigham Young Univ., 1976.

777 Miller, W. R. *Bibliography of Australian sign language*. Washington, D.C.: Gallaudet College, 1971.

778 Millham, J., et al. "A program for mentally retarded deaf children and their families." *J. of rehab. of deaf* 8:1 (1974), 43–58.

779 Mitchell, M., et al. *Signs for technical vocational education*. St. Paul, Minn.: St. Paul Technical Vocational Institute, 1976.

780 Moores, D. F. "Communication psycholinguistics and deafness: II parts." Part I in the *proceedings of the teacher institute*. Frederick, Md.: Council of organizations serving the deaf, 1969, 4–15. Part II in the *Md. Bulletin* 90:3 (1969).

781 Moores, D. F. "Cued speech: some practical and theoretical considerations." *Amer. ann. deaf* 114 (1969), 23–27.

782 Moores, D. F. "Psycholinguistics and deafness." *Amer. ann. deaf* 115:1 (1970), 37–48.

783 Moores, D. F. *Recent research on manual communication*. Washington, D.C.: Dept. of Health, Educ., and Welfare, U.S. Office of Educ., 1971.

784 Moores, D. *Communication—some unanswered questions and some unquestioned answers*. Minneapolis: Univ. of Minnesota, 1972.

785 Moores, D. F. "Communication—some unanswered questions and some unquestioned answers." In T. O'Rourke (ed.), *Psycholinguistics and total communication: the state of the art*. Silver Spring, Md.: *Amer. ann. deaf*, 1972, 1–10.

786 Moores, D. F. "Non vocal systems of verbal behavior." In K. Schiefelbusch and L. Lloyds (eds.), *Language perspectives: acquisition, retardation and prevention*. Baltimore: University Park Press, 1974.

787 Moores, D. F. *Issues in the utilization of manual communication*. Washington, D.C.: Gallaudet College, 1977.

788 Moores, D. F. *Educating the deaf: psychology, principles, and practices*. Boston: Houghton Mifflin, 1978.

789 Moores, D. F., et al. "Gestures, signs, and speech in the evaluation of programs for hearing impaired children." *Sign lang. studies* 2 (1973), 9–28.

790 Morgan, S. M. "Interpreting as an interpreter sees it." *J. of rehab. of deaf* 7 (January 1974).

791 Morris, C. *Signs, language and behavior*. New York: Prentice-Hall, Inc., 1964.

792 Morton, M. *International language game in thirty-six languages*. Seattle: World Wings Int'l., n.d.

793 Moser, H. *Hand signals: fingerspelling*. Technical note 49. Columbus, Ohio: Ohio State Univ., 1958.

794 Moser, H., et al. "Historical aspects of manual communication." *J. speech & hear. dis.* 25:2 (May 1960).

795 Mossel, M. "Manually speaking." *Silent worker* 8:9 (1956), 7.

796 Mounford, C. "Gesture language of the Ngada tribe of the Warburton Ranges, Western Australia." *Oceania* 9 (1938), 152–155.

797 Mounin, G. "Language, communication, chimpanzees." *Current anthropology* 17:1 (1976), 1–23.

798 Murphy, H., and L. Fleischer. "The effects of Ameslan versus Siglish upon test scores." In H. Murphy (ed.), *Selected readings in the integration of postsecondary deaf students at CSUN: center on deafness publication series no. 1*. Northridge, Calif.: Calif. State Univ., 1976, 27–28.

799 Murphy, H., and L. Fleischer. "The effects of Ameslan vs. Siglish upon test scores." *J. of rehab. of deaf* 11:2 (1977), 15–18.

800 Murphy, H. J. "Research in sign language interpreting at California State University, Northridge." In D. Gerver and H. W. Sinaiko (eds.), *Language interpretation and communication*. New York: Plenum Press, 1978.

801 Myers, L. J. *The law and the deaf*. Washington, D.C.: Vocational Rehabilitation Administration, Dept. of Health, Education, and Welfare, 1964.

802 Nakanishi, K. *Watashitachi no shuwa (four vols.).* Kyoto City, Japan: Kyoto School for the Deaf, 1970.

803 Namir, L., et al. *Dictionary of sign language of the deaf in Israel.* Jerusalem: Ministry of Social Welfare, in cooperation with the Association of the Deaf in Israel, 1977.

804 Namir, L., and I. M. Schlesinger. "The grammar of sign language." In Schlesinger and Namir (eds.), *Sign language of the deaf: psychological, linguistic, and sociological perspectives.* New York: Academic Press, 1978, 97–140.

805 Nash, A. "Negotiated interaction in the classroom." In J. E. Nash and J. P. Spradley (eds.), *Sociology: a descriptive approach.* Chicago, Ill.: Rand McNally, 1976, 388–403.

806 Nash, J. E. "Cues or signs: a case study in language acquisition." *Sign lang. studies* 3 (1973), 79–92.

807 Nash, K. *Manual communications handbook.* Technical series vol. 1. Rochester, N.Y.: National Technical Institute for the Deaf, 1973.

808 National Assoc. of the Deaf. "Methods of education of the deaf and opinions about the sign language." Circular no. 9., n.d.

809 National Swedish Board of Educ. *The linguistic status of sign language.* Stockholm: by author, 1974.

810 Neesam, R. F. "Rating forms and checklists for interpreters." *J. of rehab. of deaf* 2, 1968.

811 Neville, H. J. *Asymmetries in normal and congenitally deaf signers and nonsigners.* Paper presented at the conference of sign language and neurolinguistics, Rochester, N.Y., 1976.

812 Neville, H. J., and U. Bellugi. "Patterns of cerebral specialization in congenitally deaf adults." In P. Siple (ed.), *Understanding language through sign language research.* New York: Academic Press, 1978, 239–257.

813 Newell, L. E. *A stratificational view of plains Indian sign language.* Buffalo, N.Y.: Summer institute of linguistics, 1971.

814 Newkirk, D. *Outline for a proposed orthography for American sign language.* Working paper. La Jolla, Calif.: Salk Institute for Biological Studies, 1975.

815 Newkirk, D. *Some phonological distinctions between citation form signing and free pantomime.* MS. La Jolla, Calif.: Salk Institute for Biological Studies, 1975.

816 Newkirk, D. *On determining base handshapes in American sign language.* Working paper. La Jolla, Calif.: Salk Institute for Biological Studies, 1978.

817 Newkirk, D., et al. "Linguistic evidence from slips of the hand." In V. Fromkin (ed.), *Slips of the tongue, ear, pen and hands.* New York: Academic Press, 1977.

818 Newkirk, D., and C. Pedersen. *Interferences between sequentially produced signs in American sign language.* Unpub. MS. La Jolla, Calif.: Salk Institute for Biological Studies, 1975.

819 Newport, E. L. "Task specificity in language learning? Evidence from speech perception and American sign language." Paper presented at the Univ. of Penn. conference on language acquisition, 1978.

820 Newport, E., and E. Ashbrook. *The emergence of semantic relations in American sign language.* Paper presented to the Stanford child language research forum, Stanford, Calif., 1977.

821 Newport, E., and U. Bellugi. "Linguistic expression of category levels in a visual-gestural language." In E. Rosch and B. B. Lloyd (eds.), *Cognition and categorization.* Hillsdale, N.J.: Erlbaum, 1978, 49–71.

822 *New signs for instruction in library science.* Washington, D.C.: Gallaudet College, 1967.

823 Niedzielski, H. *The silent language of France: French culture through French gestures adapted to individualized instruction.* Dubuque, Iowa: Educational Research Associates, 1975.

824 Nietupski, J., and S. Hamre-Nietupski. "Teaching auxiliary communication skills to severely handicapped students." *AAESPH review* 4:2 (1979), 107–124.

825 Noble, E. "By this sign . . ." *Hearing* 25:11 (1970), 338–339.

826 Norges Døveforbund. *Moren og det høselschemmede barnet.* Bergen, Norway: Norges Døveforbund, 1977.

827 Norske Døves Landsforbund. *Jørgen Clevin: Hei, klaer!* Bergen, Norway: Norske Døves Landsforbund, Møllendalsveien 17, n.d.

828 Northcott, W. "The oral interpreter: a necessary support specialist for the hearing impaired." *Volta review* 79 (April 1977).

829 "No thank you, said the ape." *Newsweek* magazine, 78:101 (1971).

830 Nowell, R. F., and E. R. Stuckless. "An interpreter training program." *J. of rehab. of deaf* 7 (January 1974).

831 Oates, E., C. Ss. R., *Linguagem das mãos.* Rio de Janeiro: Gráfica Editôra Livro s a, 1969.

832 Oates, E., C.Ss.R., *No silêncio da fé.* Rio de Janeiro: Oficina Gráfica Editôra Santuário de Aparecida, C. Ss. R., 1971.

833 *Officer, I can't hear you.* City of Freemont, Calif., Police dept., 1977.

834 Offir, C. "Visual speech: their fingers do the talking." *Psychology today* 10:1 (June 1976), 72–78.

835 Oléron, P. *Éléments de répertoire du langage gestuel des sourds-muets.* Paris: Éditions du Centre National de la Recherche Scientifique, 1974.

836 Oléron, P. *Some ideas on the syntax of the manual language of the deaf.* Paris: Université René Descartes, 1977, 1–50.

837 Oléron, P. *Communication and syntax in the sign language of the deaf.* Paris: Université René Descartes, 1978, 1–94.

838 Oléron, P. *The manual language of the deaf, syntax and communication.* Paris: Éditions du Centre National de la Recherche Scientifique, 1978.

839 Olson, J. "A case study for the use of sign language to stimulate language development during the critical period for learning in a congenitally deaf child." *Amer. ann. deaf* 117:3 (1972), 397–400.

840 Oregon State School for the Deaf. *Communication with the hearing impaired.* By author: Salem, Ore., 1974.

841 Oregon State School for the Deaf. *Oregon sign language dictionary.* Salem, Ore.: by author, 1976.

842 O'Rourke, T. "The report on the CAL conference on sign languages" by W. Stokoe. *The linguistic reporter* 12:2 (1970), 5–8.

843 O'Rourke, T. *Psycholinguistics and total communication: the state of the art.* Washington, D.C.: *Amer. ann. deaf* (special pub.), 1972.

844 O'Rourke, T. *A basic course in manual communication.* Silver Spring, Md.: National Association of the Deaf, 1973.

845 O'Rourke, T. *Curso básico en comunicación manual.* Transl. by Frances Parsons, with introduction and index by M.L.A. Sternberg. Washington, D.C.: National Association of the Deaf, 1974.

846 O'Rourke, T. *The way we are.* Paper presented at the national symposium on sign language research and teaching, Chicago, 1977.

847 O'Rourke, T. *A basic vocabulary: American sign language for parents and children.* Silver Spring, Md.: T. J. Publishers, 1977.

848 Orrdingwall, W. *The evolution of human communication systems.* College Park, Md.: Univ. of Md., 1977.

849 Österberg, O. *Över det av sveriges dóvstumm använda atbords-spráket.* Uppsala, Sweden: P. Alfr. Persons Förlag, n.d.

850 Österberg, O. *Teckenspráket, med rikt illusterad ordbok.* Uppsala, Sweden: P. Alfr. Persons Förlag, n.d.

851 Overmann, S., and M. Brown. *Signing for social workers.* Wagon Road Camp, The Children's Aid Society, n.d. 4 pp. (mimeo.).

852 Owens, M., and B. Harper. *Sign language: a teaching manual for cottage parents of non-verbal retardates.* Pineville, La.:Pinecrest State School,1971.

853 Owrid, H. "Studies in manual communication with hearing impaired children." *Volta review* 73:7 (1971), 428–438.

854 Oxman, J., et al. *The possible function of sign language in facilitating verbal communication in severely dysfunctional children.* Paper presented to the Univ. of Louisville interdisciplinary linguistics conference, Louisville, Ky., 1976.

855 Oxman, J., et al. "The perception and processing of information by severely dysfunctional nonverbal children: a rationale for the use of manual communication." *Sign lang. studies* 21 (1978), 289–316.

856 Padden, C. "The new signs on the market: are they better?" *Teaching English to the deaf* 4:1 (1971), 18–21.

857 Padden, C. "The eyes have it: linguistic function of the eye in American sign language." In C. Williams (ed.), *Language and communication.* Washington, D.C.: Gallaudet College Press, 1976.

858 Padden, C. *Some contributions of research in American sign language toward a linguistic awareness of ASL.* Paper presented at the national symposium on sign language research and teaching, Chicago, 1977.

859 Padden, C., and C. Baker. *American sign language, a look at its history, structure, and community.* Silver Spring, Md.: T. J. Publishers, 1978.

860 Padden, C., and H. Markowicz. "Cultural conflicts between hearing and deaf communities." Working paper. Gallaudet College, linguistics research laboratory, Washington, D.C., n.d.

861 Padden, C., and H. Markowicz. *Crossing cultural group boundaries into the deaf community.* Paper presented at the conference on culture and communication. Philadelphia, Pa.: Temple Univ., 1975.

862 Paget, R. *The development of a systematic sign language.* Copy available for consultation in the LRL.

863 Paget, R. *The new sign language.* London: Wellcome Foundation, 1951.

864 Paget, R. *The children's vocabulary of the new sign language: notes for teachers.* London: Wellcome Foundation, 1958 (?).

865 Palmer, J. (ed.). *Proceedings of the second national workshop/convention of the registry of interpreters for deaf people.* Long Beach, Calif., 1972.

866 Palmer, J. "The interpreting scene." *Proceedings of the 2nd national workshop and convention of the registry of interpreters for the deaf.* Northridge, Calif.: Joyce Media, Inc., 1974.

867 Patterson, F. *Sign language acquisition by an infant gorilla: some preliminary data.* Unpub. MS, Stanford, Calif.: Stanford Univ., 1974.

868 Patterson, F. "Conversations with a gorilla." *National geographic magazine* 154:4 (1978), 438–465.

869 Patterson, P. "The gestures of a gorilla: language acquisition in another Pongid species." *Brain and language* 5:1 (1978), 72–97.

870 Paul, E. *American sign language and deaf persons.* Washington, D.C.: Deafpride Inc., 1976, 13–23.

871 Pedersen, C. C. "Verb modulations in American sign language." In Wm. Stokoe (ed.), *Proceedings of the national symposium on sign language research and teaching,* Chicago, 1977.

872 Peet, E. "The philology of the sign language," (reprint). The buff and blue. Washington, D.C.: Gallaudet College, March 1921.

873 Peet, E. Untitled manuscript on sign language, based on a partial list from *Basic English words* (somewhat modified), from the *Pocket book of basic English,* by I. A. Richards, 1945 ed.

874 Peet, H. P. "Analysis of Bonet's treatise on the art of teaching the dumb to speak." *Amer. ann. deaf* 3:4 (1851).

875 Peet, H. "Words not 'representatives' of signs, but of ideas." *Amer. ann. deaf* 11:1 (1859), 1–8.

876 Peet, H. P. "Elements of the language of signs." (Reprint). *Rocky mountain leader* 40:6. Great Falls, Mont.: Montana School for the Deaf, March 1941.

877 Peet, I. "Initial signs." *Amer. ann. deaf* 13 (1861), 171–184.

878 Peled, T. *A system of notation for the sign language of the deaf.* Working paper no. 3, MS. Jerusalem: Hebrew Univ. of Jerusalem, 1966(?).

879 Peng, F. "On the nature of language." n.d., n.p.

880 Peng, F. *The deaf and their acquisition of the various systems of communication: a speculation against innatism.* Tokyo: Intl. Christian Univ., 197?.

881 Peng, F. "Kinship sign in Japanese sign language." *Sign lang. studies* 5 (1974), 31–47.

882 Peng, F. "On the fallacy of language innatism." *Lang. sciences* 37 (October 1975), 13–16.

883 Penna, D., and F. Caccamise. "Communication instruction with hearing-impaired college students within the manual/simultaneous communication dept., NTID." *Amer. ann. deaf* 123:5 (1978), 572–579.

884 Perry, F. *An experimental investigation of visual, cognitive and linguistic factors underlying the comprehension of fingerspelling.* Unpub. dissertation, Monash Univ., Australia, 1973.

885 Personen, J. *Phoneme communication of the deaf: theory and elementary visio-oral verbal education by means of individualized visiophonemes.* Helsinki: Annales academiae scientiarum fennicae, series B, 151,2. 1968.

886 Peters, L. J. "Sign language stimulus in vocabulary learning of a brain injured child." *Sign lang. studies* 3 (1973), 116–118.

887 Petitto, L. *A notational system for the transcription of American sign language.* La Jolla, Calif.: Salk Institute for Biological Studies, 1977.

888 Petitto, L., and M. S. Seidenberg. "On the evidence for language abilities in apes." *Brain and language,* 1978.

889 Petitto, L., and M. S. Seidenberg. *What do signing chimpanzees have to say to linguists?* Paper presented to the 14th regional meeting of the Chicago linguistic society, Chicago, 1978.

890 Petrinovich, L. "Communication and language: an evolutionary view." *Sign lang. studies* 13 (1976), 347–376.

891 Phillips, G. *An analysis of the results of a sign language training program on selected aphasic children: as a function of degree of aphasia, chronological age and intelligence.* Unpub. paper, Washington, D.C.: Amer. Univ., 1973.

892 Phillott, D. "A note on the mercantile sign language of India." *J. and proceedings, royal Asiatic society of Bengal* 5:3 (1906), 333–334.

893 Phillott, D. "A note of sign, gesture, code and secret language etc., amongst the Persians." *J. and proceedings, royal Asiatic society of Bengal* 3 (1907), 619–622.

894 Pickett, J. M. "Sign alternates for learning English: a discussion of Sherreck's paper." In J. Davanagh and W. Strange (eds.), *Speech and language in the laboratory, school, and clinic.* Cambridge, Mass.: MIT Press, 1978, 199–208.

895 Pimentel, A. T. "Interpreting services for deaf people." *J. of rehab. of deaf* 3 (1969).

896 Plum, O. M. *Handbóg i tegnsprog.* København: Danske Døves Landsforbund, 1967.

897 Poizner, H. "Cerebral asymmetry in the perception of American sign language." Unpub. diss., Boston: Northeastern Univ., 1977.

898 Poizner, H., and R. Battison. "Cerebral asymmetry for sign language: clinical and experimental evidence." MS., Salk Institute for Biological Studies, n.d.

899 Poizner, H., R. Battison, and H. Laue, *Cerebral asymmetry for perception of American sign language: the effects of moving stimuli.* Washington, D.C.: Gallaudet College, 1978.

900 Poizner H., U. Bellugi, and R. Tweney. "Short-term encoding of formational, semantic and iconic information of signs from American sign language." Working paper. Salk Institute and Bowling Green Univ., n.d.

901 Poizner, H., and H. Lane. "Discrimination of location in American sign language." In P. Siple (ed.), *Understanding language through sign language research.* New York: Academic Press, 1978, 271–286.

902 *Policies, procedures, and guidelines for the implementation of the National Interpreter for the Deaf Training Act of 1978.* Registry of Interpreters for the Deaf, 1978.

903 Porta, J. B. *De furtivis literarum notis, vulgo de ziferis.* Napoli, Italy, 1563.

904 Powells, W. "Sign language." In *Wanderings in a wild country,* 1883. (Signs used by primitive peoples.) n.p.

905 *Preferred signs for instructional purposes.* Developed by the standardization of signs committee for the schools for the deaf in Texas. Austin: 1976.

906 Presneau, J. R. *Rise and decline of an educational practice: manual method in the 18th and 19th centuries.* Washington, D.C.: Gallaudet College, 1978.

907 *Professional or amateur.* Northridge, Calif.: Joyce Media, Inc., 1970.

908 *Project learn.* Joyce Media, Inc., 1970.

909 Propp, G. *Sign by design, and instructional guide for teachers of manual communication for use in conjunction with a basic course in manual communication.* Silver Spring, Md.: Communicative Skills Program, National Assoc. of the Deaf, n.d.

910 Prouolo, A. *Manuale per la scuola dei sordi-muti di Verona.* Verona, Italy: Coi Tipi di Paolo Libanti, 1840.

911 Quigley, S. P. *The influence of fingerspelling on the development of language, communication, and educational achievement in deaf children.* Urbana: University of Illinois, n.d.

912 Quigley, S. (ed.). *Interpreting for deaf people: report of a workshop on interpreting.* Portland, Maine: Governor Baxter State School for the Deaf, 1964.

913 Quigley, S. "The influence of fingerspelling on the development of language, communication, and educational achievement of deaf children." *Proceedings of the 42nd meeting of the convention of Amer. instructors of the deaf.* Flint, Mich., 1964.

914 Quigley, S. (ed.). *Interpreting for deaf people.* Washington, D.C.: U.S. Government Printing Office, 1969.

915 Quigley, S. *Educational implications of research on manual communication.* Paper presented at the 49th international council of exceptional children convention, Miami Beach, Fl., 1971.

916 Quigley, S., B. Brasel, and R. Wilbur. "A survey of interpreters for deaf people in the state of Illinois." *J. of rehab. of deaf* 6 (1972).

917 Quigley, S., and J. P. Youngs (eds.). *Interpreting for deaf people.* Washington, D.C.: Vocational Rehabilitation Administration, Dept. of Health, Education, and Welfare, 1966.

918 Rand, L. W. *An annotated bibliography of the sign language of the deaf.* Unpub. thesis, Univ. of Washington, 1962.

919 *Readings for sign instructors' guidance network certification.* Silver Spring, Md.: Communicative Skills Program, National Assoc. of the Deaf, 1978.

920 Recoing, J. *Syllabaire dactylologique.* Paris: Imprimerie de Chaignieau Jeune, 1823.

921 Reich, P. "Visible distinctive features." In A. Makkai, and V. Makkai (eds.), *The first LACUS forum.* Columbia, S. C.: Hornbean Press, 1974.

922 Reich, P. *Variables affecting the comprehension of visible English.* Unpub. MS. Toronto: Univ. of Toronto, 1976.

923 Reich, P., and M. Bick. *An empirical investigation of some claims made in support of visible English.* Unpub. MS. Toronto: Univ. of Toronto, 1975.

924 Reich, P. A., and M. Bick. "How visible is visible English?" *Sign lang. studies* 14 (1977), 59–72.

925 Reich, P. A., and C. M. Reich. "Communications patterns of adult deaf." *Canadian j. of behavioral science* 8:1 (1976), 56–67.

926 Reilly, J., and M. L. McIntire. *ASL and PSE: what's the difference?* Los Angeles, Calif.: Univ. of Calif., 1978.

927 *Reverse interpreting practice package.* Silver Spring, Md.: National Assoc. of the Deaf, n.d.

928 Ricci Bitti, P. E. "Communication by gestures in south and northern Italians." *Giornale italiano di psicologia* 3:1 (1976), 117–125.

929 Rice, C. *Sign language for everyone.* Nashville, Tenn.: Thomas Nelson, Publishers, 1977.

930 Richardin, C. *Dactylologie.* Nancy, France: Institut des Sourds-Muets, 1852.

931 Richardson, P. *Signs for everyday, book 1.* Elwyn, Pa.: Elwyn Institute, n.d.

932 Richardson, P. *Signs for everyday, book 2.* Elwyn, Pa.: Elwyn Institute, n.d.

933 Richardson, T. *Sign language as a means of communication for the institutionalized mentally retarded.* Unpub. paper, Southbury, Conn.: Southbury Training School, 1974.

934 Richardson, T. "Sign language for the SMR and PMR." *Mental retardation* 13:3 (1975), 17.

935 Richardson, T. *The third year of the gestural language program at Southbury training school, 1974–75.* Unpub. paper, Southbury, Conn.: Southbury Training School, 1975.

936 Riekehof, L. *Talk to the deaf.* Springfield, Mo.: Gospel Publishing House, 1963.

937 Riekehof, L. "Factors relating to interpreter proficiency." *Language and communication research problems: proceedings of the second Gallaudet symposium on research in deafness,* 1975.

938 Riekehof, L. *The joy of signing.* Springfield, Mo.: Gospel Publishing House, 1978.

939 Rimland, B. "Where does research lead?" *Proceedings of the 1975 annual meeting of the national society for autistic children.* Albany, N.Y.: National Society for Autistic Children, 1975.

940 Robbins, N. *Perkins sign language dictionary: a*

sign dictionary for use with multi-handicapped deaf children in school. Watertown, Mass.: Perkins School for the Blind, 1975.

941 Roberts, L. C. L. Effectiveness of programmed instruction for teaching manual communication (fingerspelling and signing) to hearing adults. Unpub. dissertation, Univ. of Texas, 1973.

942 Roddy, A. J. Elementary observations concerning the structure of the language of signs. Unpub. paper, Missouri Baptist Convention, n.d.

943 Roddy, A. Introducing the language of signs. Atlanta, Ga.: Southern Baptist Convention, 1966.

944 Romeo, L. "For a medieval history of gesture communication." Sign lang. studies 21 (1978), 353–380.

945 Rosenfeld, J. Communication techniques with the adult deaf-blind. Speech presented to the prevocational and vocational services for the deaf-blind workshop, Oklahoma City, Okla., 1975.

946 Roth, S. D. A book of basic signs used by the deaf. Frederick, Md.: Maryland School for the Deaf Press, 1948.

947 Roth, S. D., A book of basic signs used by the deaf. Fulton, Mo.: Missouri School for the Deaf, 1948.

948 Royster, M. Games and activities in sign language. Silver Spring, Md.: National Assoc. of the Deaf, n.d.

949 Rubino, F., and A. Hayhurst. Second contribution to the international dictionary of sign language. Rome: World Federation of the Deaf, 1971.

950 Rusman, G., et al. "Medical interpreting for hearing impaired patients." J. of Amer. medical assoc. 237:22 (1977).

951 Sabatino, L. "What if your patient is also deaf?" Registered nurse, 1976.

952 St. Paul Technical Vocational Institute. Index to American sign language. St. Paul, Minn.: Career Media for the Handicapped, in press.

953 Saitz, R., and E. Cervenka. Hand book of gestures. The Hague: Mouton Press, 1972.

954 Salisbury, C., C. Wambold, and G. Walter. "Manual communication for the severely handicapped: an assessment and instructional strategy." Education and training of the mentally retarded 13 (1978), 393–397.

955 Sallagoity, P. "The sign language of southern France." Sign lang. studies 7 (1975), 181–202.

956 Sallop, M. "Language acquisition: pantomine and gesture to signed English." Sign lang. studies 3 (1973), 29–38.

957 Salvin, A., et al. "Acquisition of modified Amer. sign language by a mute autistic child." J. of autism and childhood schizophrenia 7:4 (1977), 359–371.

958 Sanborn, D., et al. "Teaching sign language by interactive television." Amer. ann. deaf 120:1 (February 1975), 58–62.

959 Sanders, J. (ed.). The ABC's of sign language. Tulsa, Okla.: Manca Press, 1968.

960 San Se Kasin. Julkaisija: Kuurojen Liitto R.Y., 1974. (310 word vocabulary)

961 Sarles, H. B. "On the problem: the origin of language." Sign lang. studies 11 (1976), 149–181.

962 Savisaari, E., et al. Viittomakielen sanakirja. Helsinki: Suomen Kuurojen Liitto R.Y. 1965.

963 Savisaari, E., et al. Viittomakielen kuvasanakirja. Julkaisija: Kuurojen Liitto R.Y. 1973.

964 Savisaari, E., et al. Viittomakielen opas. Julkaisija: Kuurojen Liitto R.Y. 1974.

965 Say it with hands series. Southern Regional Media Center for the Deaf, n.d.

966 Schaeffer, B. "Teaching spontaneous sign language to nonverbal children." Sign lang. studies 21 (1978), 317–352.

967 Schaeffer, B., et al. Signed speech: a new treatment for autism. Paper presented at annual meeting of the national society for autistic children, San Diego, Calif., 1975.

968 Schaeffer, B., et al. "Spontaneous verbal language for autistic children through signed speech." Sign lang. studies 17 (1977), 287–328.

969 Schein, J. "Sign language: coming of age." Sign lang. studies 3 (1973), 113–115.

970 Schein, J. D. "Personality characteristics associated with interpreter proficiency." J. of rehab. of deaf 7 (January 1974).

971 Scherer, P., and S. Hayward. Effective learning, teacher's guide. A curriculum for teachers of signs and fingerspelling. Glenview, Ill.: Center on Deafness, 1974.

972 Schlesinger, H. "Language acquisition in four deaf children." Hearing and speech news, 1972, 4–7, 22–28.

973 Schlesinger, H. S. "Meaning and enjoyment: language acquisition of deaf children." In T. J. O'Rourke (ed.), Psycholinguistics and total communication. Washington, D.C.: Amer. ann. deaf, 1972, 92–102.

974 Schlesinger, H. S. "The acquisition of bimodal language." In Schlesinger and Namir (eds.), Sign language of the deaf: psychological, linguistic and sociological perspectives. New York: Academic Press, 1978, 57–140.

975 Schlesinger, H. S., and K. Meadow. "Interpreting for deaf persons: a contribution to mental health." Deaf Amer. 20 (July–August 1968).

976 Schlesinger, H., and K. Meadow. "Development of maturity in deaf children." Exceptional children, 1972.

977 Schlesinger, H., and K. Meadow. Sound and sign: childhood deafness and mental health. Berkeley: Univ. of Calif. Press, 1972.

978 Schlesinger, I. M. "The grammar of sign language and the problems of language universals." In J. Morton (ed.), *Biological and social factors in psycholinguistics.* Urbana: Univ. of Illinois Press, 1970, 98–121.

979 Schlesinger, I. M. *Dictionary of Israeli sign language.* The Hague: Mouton Press, 1979.

980 Schlesinger, I. M., et al. "Transfer of meaning in sign language." Working paper, no. 12. Jerusalem: Hebrew University of Jerusalem, 1970.

981 Schlesinger, I. M., and L. Namir. *The grammar of sign language.* Tel Aviv: Hebrew Univ., 1976.

982 Schlesinger, I. M., and L. Namir. *Sign language of the deaf: psychological, linguistic, and sociological perspectives.* New York: Academic Press, 1978.

983 Schlesinger, I., and L. Namir (eds.). *Current trends in the study of sign language.* The Hague: Mouton, 1978.

984 Schlesinger, I., and B. Presser. *Compound signs in sign language.* MS. Jerusalem: Hebrew Univ. of Jerusalem, 1970.

985 Schools at Waratah and Castle Hill, Australian Schools for the Deaf. *How to converse with the deaf.* Newcastle: Davies & Cannington Pty, Ltd., 1943.

986 Schowe, B. "What is the true sign language?" *The deaf Amer.* 28:11 (1975), 3–4.

987 Schroedel, J. G. *The not so silent revolution: adapting signs to English and speech.* New York: NYU, 1973.

988 Scott, M. "The sign language of the plains Indians of North America." *Archives of the int'l. folklore assoc.* 1 (1893), 1–26.

989 Scouten, E. *A revaluation of the Rochester method.* Rochester, N.Y.: Alumni Association of the Rochester School for the Deaf, 1942.

990 Scouten, E. L. "Manual alphabet as an instructional medium for deaf children."*Just once a month.* Washington, D.C.: The Kendall School, 1955.

991 Sebeok, T. A. "Iconicity." *Modern lang. notes* 91 (1976), 1427–1456.

992 Sebeok, T. A. *Native languages of the Americas: Vol. I.* New York: Plenum Press, 1976.

993 Sebeok, T. A. *Native languages of the Americas: Vol. II.* New York: Plenum Press, 1976.

994 *See n' sign.* Super 8 cartridges. Silver Spring, Md.: National Assoc. of the Deaf, n.d.

995 Seguin, E. *Jacob-Rodrigues Pereire etc. . . . . Notice sur sa vie et ses travaux et analyse raisonée de sa methode.* Paris, 1847. (On the Pereira method for the teaching of sign language.)

996–997 Seidenberg, M. S., and L. A. Petitto. *Signing behavior in apes: a critical review.* New York: Columbia Univ., 1978.

998 Seligmann, C. G., and A. Wilkin. "The gesture language of the western islanders." *Report of the Cambridge anthropological expedition to the Torres Straits* 3 (1907), 255–260.

999 Seton, E. *Sign talk.* Washington, D.C.: Gallaudet College Library, 1918.

1000 Shaffer, T., and H. Goehl. "The alinguistic child." *Mental retardation* 12:2 (1974), 3–6.

1001 Sherzer, J. "Verbal and nonverbal deixis: the pointed lip gesture among the Sen Blas Cura." *Lang. in society* 2:1 (1973), 117–131.

1002 Shields, J. "The Paget system at pathways." *Special ed.* 60:2 (June 1971), 11–14.

1003 Shunary, J. *Social background of the Israeli sign language.* Unpub. paper, Jerusalem: Univ. of Jerusalem, 1969.

1004 Sicard, R. A. C., Abbé. *Cours d'instruction d'un sourd-muet de naissance,* 2nd ed. Paris, 1803.

1005 Siegel, J.P. "The enlightenment and the evolution of a language of signs in France and England." *J. of the history of ideas* 30:1 (1969), 96–115.

1006 Siger, L. "Gestures, the language of signs, and human communication." *Amer. ann. deaf* 113:1 (January 1968), 11–28.

1007 Siger, L. *On the teaching of sign language.* Paper presented at the national symposium on sign language research and teaching, Chicago, 1977.

1008 *Signing exact English development kit.* Modern Signs Press, n.d.

1009 "Sign it." *Sesame street magazine,* 14243 (1977), 18–21.

1010 *Sign language.* Washington: U.S. Office of Ed., Media Services and Captioned Films, n.d.

1011 *Signs for technical vocational education.* 16 mm reel to reel or 8 mm film cartridges. St. Paul, Minn.: Technical Vocational Institute, n.d.

1012 "Signs go under the sea." *Silent worker* 8:5 (1956), 3–4.

1013 "(The) Silent language; underwater language for navy men." In *All hands. Bureau of naval personnel info. bulletin* 527, 1960.

1014 *Silent siren: a manual communication guide for field officers.* Eureka, Calif.: Alinda Press, n.d.

1015 *Single and double-handed alphabets of the deaf and dumb.* Boston, Mass.: M. J. Kiley, 1872.

1016 Siple, P. "Constraints for sign language from visual perception data." *Sign lang. studies* 19 (1978), 95–110.

1017 Siple, P. (ed.). *Understanding language through sign language research.* New York: Academic Press, 1978.

1018 Siple, P., S. Fischer, and U. Bellugi. "Memory for non-semantic attributes of American sign language signs and English words." *J. of verbal learning and verbal behavior* 16:5 (1977), 561–574.

1019 Skelly, M. "American Indian sign (amerind) as a facilitator of verbalization for the oral verbal apraxic." *J. speech and hearing disorders* 39:4 (1974).

1020 Skelly, M. "American Indian sign: a gestural communication system for the speechless." *Ar-*

chives of physical medicine and rehabilitation 56 (1975).

1021 Sklarewitz, N. " 'When they talk with their hands, what are they saying?' Industrial signs." *Popular mechanics magazine* 135 (1971), 72–73.

1022 Smeets, P. M. "Establishing generative performance and cross-modal generalization of the manual plural sign in a severely retarded girl." *British J. of disorders of communication* 13:1 (1978), 49–57.

1023 Smeets, P. M., and S. Striefel. "Acquisition and cross-modal generalization of receptive and expressive signing skills in a retarded deaf girl." *J. of mental deficiency research* 20:4 (1976), 251–260.

1024 Smelz, J. K. *Some sociological-linguistic aspects of the American sign language of the deaf.* Unpub. dissertation. Washington, D.C.: Georgetown Univ., 1976.

1025 Smith, J. M. (ed.). *Workshop on interpreting for the deaf.* Muncie, Ind.: Ball State Teachers College, 1964.

1026 Smith, M. T., et al. *Considerations in the design and development of interpreter education programs.* National Technical Institute for the Deaf, 1978.

1027 Smith, W. H. *Taiwan sign language.* Northridge, Calif.: Calif. State Univ., 1976, 1–29.

1028 Smith, W. H. *A comparison of the Chinese language with American sign language.* Northridge, Calif.: Calif. State Univ., 1977, 1–33.

1029 Smith, W. H. *A study of non-verbal signals in Taiwan sign language.* Northridge, Calif.: Calif. State Univ., 1977, 1–32.

1030 Smith, W. H. *History and development of deaf education and sign language in Taiwan.* Northridge, Calif.: Calif. State Univ., 1977.

1031 Snell, M. "Sign language and total communication." In L. R. Kent (ed.), *Language acquisition program for the severely retarded.* Champaign, Ill.: Research Press, 1974.

1032 Sorensen, R. K. "Indications of regular syntax in deaf Danish school children's sign language." *Sign lang. studies* 8 (1975), 257–263.

1033 Sparhawk, C. M. *Contrastive-identificational features of Persian gesture.* Washington, D.C.: Gallaudet College, 1976.

1034 Springer, C. J., C. Ss. R. *Talking with the deaf.* Baton Rouge, La.: Redemptorist Fathers, in association with International Catholic Deaf Association, 1961.

1035 Ssali, C. L. "Problems of deafness in Africa." In F. B. Crammatte and A. B. Crammatte (eds.), *VII world congress of the world federation of the deaf.* Silver Spring, Md.: National Assoc. of the Deaf, 1976, 169–171.

1036 Stangarone, J. E. "Interpreting in the seventies." *J. of rehab. of deaf* 4 (1971).

1037 Stark, R. E. *Visible speech for the deaf.* Balti-more: Johns Hopkins Univ. School of Medicine, 1967, 347–354.

1038 Statewide Project for the Deaf, Texas Education Agency. *Signs for instructional purposes.* Austin, Tex.: Texas Education Agency, 1976.

1039 Stein, S. P., and R. Weller. "Public speaking through total communication." In F. B. Crammatte, et al. (eds.), *VII world congress of the world federation of the deaf.* Silver Spring, Md.: National Assoc. of the Deaf, 1976, 455–458.

1040 Steinberg, D., et al. *Language acquisition of Japanese deaf children.* Washington, D.C.: Gallaudet College, 1976.

1041 Steklis, H. D., and M. J. Raleigh. *Chimpanzees and language evolution.* Berkeley: Univ. of Calif., 1972.

1042 Sternberg, M. L. A. A comprehensive dictionary of American sign language. In *Proceedings, VI World Congress of the Deaf,* Paris, 1971.

1043 Sternberg, M. L. A. "Brief, intensive training to develop interpreters." *J. of rehab. of deaf* 7 (1974).

1044 Sternberg, M. L. A., and C. Tipton. *Modified manual communication for deaf-blind children.* New York: New York University Deafness Research & Training Center, 1976.

1045 Sternberg, M. L. A., C. Tipton, and J. Schein, *Interpreter training: a curriculum guide.* New York: New York University Deafness Research & Training Center, 1973.

1046 Stevens, R. "Children's language should be learned and not taught." *Sign lang. studies* 11 (1976), 97–108.

1047 Steyaert, M., and R. Ellenberger. *The acquisition of action representations in American sign language.* Minneapolis: Univ. of Minnesota, 1977.

1048 Stoevesand, B. *Tausend taubstummengebärden.* Berlin, Federal Republic of Germany: Bernard Stoevesand, 1970.

1049 Stohr, P., and K. Van Hook. *Have hands—will sign.* Buckley, Washington: Ranier School, 1973.

1050 Stokoe, W. C. *Sign language structure: an outline of the visual communication systems of the American deaf.* Buffalo, N.Y.: Univ. of Buffalo, 1960.

1051 Stokoe, W. "Linguistic description of sign language." In F. P. Dinneen (ed.), *Monograph series on language and linguistics.* Washington, D.C.: Georgetown Univ., 1966, 243–250.

1052 Stokoe, W. C. *Two approaches to sign language syntax.* Washington, D.C.: Gallaudet College, 1966.

1053 Stokoe, W. C. *Learning the sound, sense, and shape of language.* Washington, D.C.: Gallaudet College, 1967.

1054 Stokoe, W. C. "Sign language diglossia." *Studies in linguistics* 21 (1969–70), 27–41.

1055 Stokoe, W. "CAL conference on sign languages." *Linguistic reporter* 12:2 (1970), 5–8.

1056 Stokoe, W. C. *Sign language and order in communication.* Washington, D.C.: Gallaudet College, 1971.

1057 Stokoe, W. C. *The study of sign language.* Arlington, Va.: Center for Applied Linguistics, 1971.

1058 Stokoe, W. *The study of sign language.* Rev. ed. Silver Spring, Md.: National Association of the Deaf, 1971.

1059 Stokoe, W. C. *Two-dimensional arrays and language relationships.* Washington, D.C.: Gallaudet College, 1971.

1060 Stokoe, W. "A classroom experiment in two languages." In T. O'Rourke (ed.), *Psycholinguistics and total communication: the state of the art.* Silver Spring, Md.: *Amer. ann. deaf,* 1972, 85–91.

1061 Stokoe, W. "Classification and description of sign language." In T. Sebeok (ed.), *Current trends in linguistics,* 12. The Hague: Mouton, 1972.

1062 Stokoe, W. C. *English from a sign base.* Washington, D.C.: Gallaudet College, 1972.

1063 Stokoe, W. C. *It takes two to total: sign and English.* Washington, D.C.: Gallaudet College, 1972.

1064 Stokoe, W. C. "Linguistic description of sign language." In T. Sebeok (ed.), *Monograph series on language and linguistics,* 12. The Hague: Mouton, 1972.

1065 Stokoe, W. C. *Linguistics, sign language, and total communication.* Washington, D.C.: Gallaudet College, 1972.

1066 Stokoe, W. C. *Review of research.* Washington, D.C.: Gallaudet College, 1972.

1067 Stokoe, W. *Semiotics and human sign languages.* The Hague: Mouton, 1972.

1068 Stokoe, W. C. *Bilingual research program.* Washington, D.C.: Gallaudet College, 1973.

1069 Stokoe, W. C. Comments on "Back translation." *Sign lang. studies* 2 (1973), 13–76.

1070 Stokoe, W. C. "Face to face interaction: signs to language." In A. Kendon, et al. (eds.), *Organization of behavior in face-to-face interaction.* Chicago: Aldine Pub. Co., 1973.

1071 Stokoe, W. "It takes two to total: sign and English." *Maryland Bulletin* 43:3 (1973), 41–43, 56.

1072 Stokoe, W. C. "Review: seeing essential English manual." *Sign lang. studies* 2 (1973), 84–93.

1073 Stokoe, W. "Sign language vs. spoken language." *Sign lang. studies* 18 (1978), 69–90.

1074 Stokoe, W. C. "Sign syntax and human language capacity." *Florida foreign language reporter: a J. of language and culture in educ.* 51 (1973), 3–6, 52–53.

1075 Stokoe, W. C. "The shape of soundless language." In J. F. Kavanagh and J. E. Cutting (eds.), *The role of speech in language.* Cambridge, Mass.: MIT Press, 1973, 207–246.

1076 Stokoe, W. C. "Appearances, words, and signs." In Hewes, Stokoe, and Wescott (eds.), *Language origins.* Silver Spring, Md.: Linstok Press, 1974, 51–68.

1077 Stokoe, W. C. "Motor signs as the first form of language." *Semiotica* 10:2 (1974), 117–130.

1078 Stokoe, W. "Seeing and signing language." *Hearing and speech news* 42:5 (1974), 32–37.

1079 Stokoe, W. C. *The ins and outs of in and out in sign.* Washington, D.C.: Gallaudet College, 1974.

1080 Stokoe, W. C. *Signing apes and evolving linguistics.* Washington, D.C.: Gallaudet College, 1975.

1081 Stokoe, W. C. *Sign language autonomy.* Washington, D.C.: Gallaudet College, 1975.

1082 Stokoe, W. C. *Signs of language in the linguistic communities of the deaf.* Washington, D.C.: Gallaudet College, 1975.

1083 Stokoe, W. C. *Social correlates of sign color terms.* Washington, D.C.: Gallaudet College, 1975.

1084 Stokoe, W. "The use of sign language in teaching English." *Amer. ann. deaf* 120:4 (1975), 417–421.

1085 Stokoe, W. C. *Sign language and the verbal/nonverbal distinction.* Unpub. paper, Gallaudet College, 1976.

1086 Stokoe, W. C. *Gestural signs in codes and languages: redefining "nonverbal."* Educational Resources Information Center, available in microfiche, E R I C #123918, 1976.

1087 Stokoe, W. C. *Sign codes and sign language: two orders of communication.* Washington, D.C.: Gallaudet College, 1976.

1088 Stokoe, W. C. *Sign languages and the verbal/nonverbal distinction.* Washington, D.C.: Gallaudet College, 1976.

1089 Stokoe, W. "The study and use of sign language." *Sign lang. studies* 10 (1976), 1–36.

1090 Stokoe, W. C. "Die 'Sprache' der taubstummen." In R. Posner, and H. P. Reinecke (eds.), *Zei chenprozesse, semiotische forschung, in den einzelwissenschafter.* West Berlin, 1977, 167–179.

1091 Stokoe, W. C. *What ever happened to the sign-English contrastive project?* Washington, D.C.: Gallaudet College, 1977.

1092 Stokoe, W. C. "Review: Charles K. Bliss, the book to the film 'Mr. symbol man'." *Sign lang. studies* 20 (1978), 275–285.

1093 Stokoe, W. C. "Sign codes and sign language: two orders of communication." *J. of communication disorders* 11:2–3 (1978), 187–192.

1094 Stokoe, W. C. *Sign language structures.* Rev. ed. Silver Spring, Md.: Linstok Press, 1978.

1095 Stokoe, W. C., and R. M. Battison. *Sign language, mental health, and satisfying interaction.*

866

Washington, D.C.: Gallaudet College, 1975.

1096 Stokoe, W., H. Bernard, and C. Padden. "An elite group in deaf society." *Sign lang. studies* 12 (1976), 189–210.

1097 Stokoe, W., D. Casterline, and C. Croneberg. *Dictionary: American sign language.* Washington, D.C.: Gallaudet College Press, 1965.

1098 Stokoe, W. C., D. Casterline, and S. C. Croneberg, *A dictionary of American sign language on linguistic principles.* Silver Spring, Md.: Linstok Press, 1976. (New ed.)

1099 Stoloff, L., and Z. G. Dennis. "Matthew." *Amer. ann. deaf* 123:4 (1978), 442–447.

1100 Streeter, S. *Let your hands speak.* International sign language for travelers. Washington, D.C.: American Tourist Assn., 1424 K. St. N.W. (Printed by Rand-McNally.)

1101 Stuckless, E., and J. Birch. "The influence of early manual communication on the linguistic development of deaf children." *Amer. ann. deaf* 111:2 (1966), 452–460 (part I); 111:3 (1966), 499–504 (part II).

1102 Stuckless, E. R., and G. Pollard. "Processing of fingerspelling and print by deaf students." *Amer. ann. deaf* 122:5 (1977), 475–479.

1103 Suomela, E. K. "A call for scientific thinking in manual communication methods," In F. B. Crammatte, et al. (eds.), *VII world congress of the world federation of the deaf.* Silver Spring, Md.: National Assoc. of the Deaf, 1976, 453–455.

1104 Supalla, T., and E. Newport. *Systems for modulating nouns and verbs in ASL.* Paper presented at the conference on sign language and neurolinguistics, Rochester, N.Y., 1976.

1105 Supalla, T. *Grammatical modulations of nouns in American sign language.* La Jolla, Calif.: Salk Institute for Biological Studies, 1977.

1106 Supalla, T. *The derivation of nouns from verbs in American sign language.* La Jolla, Calif.: Salk Institute for Biological Studies, 1977.

1107 Supalla, T. "Derivational morphology in ASL." Paper presented at the 2nd national symposium on sign language research and teaching, 1978.

1108 Supalla, T., and E. Newport. "How many seats in a chair? The derivation of nouns and verbs in American sign language." In P. Siple (ed.), *Understanding language through sign language research.* New York: Academic Press, 1978, 91–132.

1109 Sutcliffe, M. *Conversation with the deaf.* London: Royal National Institute for the Deaf, 1954.

1110 Sutcliffe, R. E. "Some characteristics in communication preference affecting relationships in a deaf community." In F. B. Crammatte and A. B. Crammatte (eds.), *VII world congress of the world federation of the deaf.* Silver Spring, Md.: National Assoc. of the Deaf, 1976, 173–176.

1111 Sutherland, G. "Teaching the mentally re-tarded sign language." *J. of rehab. of deaf* 2:4 (1969), 56–60.

1112 Sutton, V. *Sutton movement shorthand. Book one: the classical ballet key.* Irvine, Calif.: Movement Shorthand Society, 1973.

1113 Sutton, V. *Examples of notation of the Danish deaf sign language.* Irvine, Calif.: Movement Shorthand Society Press, 1976.

1114 Sutton, V. J. *Silent night.* Irvine, Calif.: Movement Shorthand Society Press, 1976.

1115 Sutton, V. J. *Sutton movement shorthand: a visual, easy-to-learn way to read and write deaf sign language—the American manual alphabet.* Irvine, Calif.: Movement Shorthand Society Press, 1976.

1116 Sutton, V. J. *The pledge of allegiance.* Irvine, Calif.: Movement Shorthand Society Press, 1976.

1117 Sutton, V. J. *Sutton movement shorthand writing tool for research.* Irvine, Calif.: Movement Shorthand Society, 1977.

1118 Sveriges dövas riksförbund. *Teckenordbok.* Borlänge: Sveriges dövas riksförbund, 1971.

1119 Szczepankowski, B. *System migowe-jezykowy na kursach jezyka migowego I stopnia.* Warsaw: Polish Assoc. of the Deaf, 1966.

1120 Szczepankowski, B. *Jezyk migowy.* Warsaw: Zaklan Wydawnictw C. R. S., 1970.

1121 Talkington, L., and S. Hall. *A manual communication system for the deaf retarded.* Austin, Tex.: Austin State School, 1970.

1122 Tanokami, T., et al. *On the nature of sign language.* (Japanese). Hiroshima: Bunka Hyoron Publishing Co., 1976.

1123 Taylor, A. R. "Nonverbal communications systems in native North America." *Semiotica* 13:4, 329–374.

1124 Taylor, E. F., et al. *Peer teaching of sign language among mentally retarded individuals.* Paper presented at 87th annual meeting, APA, New York City, 1979.

1125 Taylor, L. (ed.). *Proceedings of the registry of interpreters for the deaf: Workshop II.,* n.d.

1126 *Teaching the manual alphabet.* Washington, D.C.: Gallaudet College.

1127 Temerlin, M. "My daughter Lucy." *Psychology today* 9 (1975), 59–62.

1128 Tennenbaum, D. *Gestural communication with aphasics in a dyadic situation.* Unpub. paper, Ohio State Univ., 1966.

1129 Terrace, H. S., et al. *Project Nim, progress report 1.* New York: Columbia Univ., 1976.

1130 Terrace, H. S., et al. *Project Nim, progress report 2.* New York: Columbia Univ., 1976.

1131 Terrace, H., et al. *Project NIM, project report 3.* New York: Columbia Univ., 1978.

1132 Terrace, H., and T. Bever. "What might be learned from studying language in the chimpanzee? The importance of symbolizing oneself." *Ann. of New York Academy of Sciences* 280 (1976), 579–588.

1133 Tervoort, B. *Structurele analyse van visueel taalgegruik binnen een croe; dove kinderen. Deel I, deel II.* Amsterdam: N.V. Noord-Hollandische Uitgevers Maatschappij, 1953.

1134 Tervoort, B. T. *Research project on language of the deaf.* St. Michielsgestel, Netherlands: School for the Deaf, 1959.

1135 Tervoort, B. "Esoteric symbolism in the communication behavior of young deaf children." *Amer. ann. deaf* 106:5 (1961), 436–480.

1136 Tervoort, B. "You me downtown movie fun?" *Linqua* 21 (1968), 455–465.

1137 Tervoort, B. T. *Bilingual interference between acoustic and visual communication.* Amsterdam: Univ. of Amsterdam, 1975.

1138 Tervoort, B. "Could there be a human sign language?" *Semiotica* 9 (1975), 347–382.

1139 Tervoort, B. *Developmental features of visual communication.* Amsterdam: North-Holland Publishing Co., 1975.

1140 Tervoort, B. T. "Bilingual interference." In Schlesinger and Namir (eds.), *Sign language of the deaf: psychological, linguistic and sociological perspectives.* New York: Academic Press, 1978, 169–240.

1141 Tervoort, B. T., and A. J. Verberk. *Analysis of communicative structure patterns in deaf children.* Groningen, Netherlands: Project supported jointly by the vocational rehab. administration, Dept. H.E.W., and the Netherlands organisation for pure scientific research. Final report, 1967.

1142 Thompson, H. "The lack of subordination in American sign language." In L. Friedman (ed.), *On the other hand: new perspectives on American sign language.* New York: Academic Press, 1977, 181–195.

1143 Tipton, C. "Interpreting ethics." *J. of rehab. of deaf* 7 (January 1974).

1144 Todd, P. H. "A case of structural interference across sensory modalities in second-language learning." *Word* 27:1–3 (1971), 102–118.

1145 Todd, P. H. *From sign language to speech: delayed acquisition of English by a hearing child of deaf parents.* Berkeley: Univ. of Calif., 1975.

1146 Tomkins, W. *Universal Indian sign language of the plains Indians of North America.* San Diego, Calif.: William Tomkins and Neyenesch Printers, 1929.

1147 Tomkins, W. *Indian sign language.* New York: Dover Publications, 1969.

1148 Tomlinson-Keasey, C., and R. Kelly. "The development of thought processes in deaf children." *Amer. ann. deaf* 119:6 (1974), 693–700.

1149 Tomlinson-Keasey, C., and R. Kelly. "The deaf child's symbolic world." *Amer. ann. deaf* 123:4 (1978), 452–459.

1150 Topper, S. "Gesture language for a non-verbal severely retarded male." *Mental retardation* 13:1 (February 1975), 30–31.

1151 *Total communication (video tapes).* Anchorage, Alaska: Alaska Head Start.

1152 Turecheck, A. G. "The interpreter—a bridge between the deaf and hearing worlds." *Deaf American* 28 (1976).

1153 Tweney, R. D. "The development of semantic associations in profoundly deaf children." *J. of speech and hearing research* 16 (1973), 152–160.

1154 Tweney, R. "Sign language and psycholinguistic process: fact, hypothesis and implications for interpreting." In D. Gerver and H. W. Wallace (eds.), *Language interpretation and communication.* New York: Plenum Press, 1978.

1155 Tweney, R., et al. "Semantic organization in deaf and hearing subjects." *J. of psycholinguistic res.* 4:1 (1975), 61–73.

1156 Tweney, R. D., et al. "Psychological processing of sign language: the effects of visual disruption on sign intelligibility." *J. of experimental psych.,* in press.

1157 Tweney, R. D., and G. W. Heiman. "The effect of sign language grammatical structure on recall." *Bulletin of the psychonomic society* 16:4 (1977), 331–334.

1158 Tweney, R. D., G. W. Heiman, and H. W. Hoemann. "Psychological processing of sign language: the effects of visual disruption of sign intelligibility." *J. of experimental psych.* 106 (1977), 255–268.

1159 Tweney, R. D., and H. Hoemann. "Authors' rejoinder." *Sign lang. studies* 2 (1973), 77–80.

1160 Tweney, R. D., and H. W. Hoemann. "Back translation: a method for the analysis of manual languages." *Sign lang. studies* 2 (1973), 51–72.

1161 Tweney, R., and H. Hoemann. "Translation and sign language." In R. Brislin (ed.), *Translation: applications and research.* Honolulu: Univ. of Hawaii Press, 1976, 138–161.

1162 Tweney, R., S. K. Liddell, and U. Bellugi. "The perception of grammatical boundaries in ASL." MS. Salk Institute and Bowling Green Univ., n.d.

1163 Tyler, E. B. "The gesture language." *Studies in early history of mankind,* 1878.

1164 UdalRicus Cluniacensis Monachus: In subsequentem collectionem. In Mosne, J. R. (ed.), *Patrologial cursus completus, series latina,* vol. 149, p. 633, n.d. (oldest sign list, A. D. 1086.)

1165 Ueno, M. "The process of the introduction of the French method to the institutions for the deaf and dumb in America." *Bulletin of the faculty of educ.* 20 (1974), 111–117.

868

1166 Ukranian Society of the Deaf. *Mimicry-gesticulated speech.* Kiev, U.S.S.R.: Reklama Publishing House, 1969.

1167 Ulfsparre, S. *Teaching sign language to hearing parents with deaf children.* Paper presented at the national symposium on sign language research and teaching, Chicago, 1977.

1168 Umiker-Sebeok, D. J., and T. A. Sebeok. "Aboriginal sign 'languages' from a semiotic point of view." *Ars semiotica* 1:4 (1977), 69–99.

1169 Umiker-Sebeok, D. J., and T. A. Sebeok (eds.). *Aboriginal sign language of the Americas and Australia: North America classic comparative perspectives.* New York: Plenum Press, 1 (1978).

1170 Umiker-Sebeok, D. J., and T. A. Sebeok (eds.). *Aboriginal sign languages of the Americas and Australia: the Americas and Australia.* New York: Plenum Press, 2 (1978).

1171 Vail, J. L., and D. Spas. *A manual communication program for non-verbal retardates.* DeKalb, Ill.: NEWSEARCH—Title I, 1974.

1172 Valade, R. "The sign language in primitive times." *Amer. ann. deaf and dumb* 18:1 (January 1873), 27–41.

1173 Valade, Y. *Études sur la lexicologie et la grammaire du langage naturel des signes.* Paris: Librairie Philosophique Lagrange, 1854.

1174 Valentine, E. G. "Shall we abandon the English order?" *Amer. ann. deaf* 17:1 (1872), 33–47.

1175 Van Biervliet, A. "Establishing words and objects as functionally equivalent through manual sign training." *Amer. j. of mental deficiency* 82:2 (1977), 178–186.

1176 Ver Hoef, N., et al. *Fingerspelling.* Tucson, Ariz.: Communication Skill Builders, 1976.

1177 Verney, A. W. "Gestuno, international sign language of the deaf, a review of the book." *British deaf news,* 1975, 102–103.

1178 Vernon, M. *Non-linguistic aspects of sign language. Human feelings and thought processes.* Unpub. paper, Westminster, Md.: Western Maryland College, 1971.

1179 Vernon, M. "Non-linguistic aspects of sign language, human feelings and thought process." In T. J. O'Rourke (ed.), *Psycholinguistics and total communication: the state of the art.* Washington, D.C.: *Amer. ann. deaf,* 1972, 11–18.

1180 Vernon, M., et al. "The use of sign language in the reading-language development process." *Sign lang. studies* 22 (1979), 84–94.

1181 Vernon, M., and J. Coley. *The sign language of the deaf and the reading language development process.* Washington, D.C.: Gallaudet College Press, 1978.

1182 Vernon, M., and J. Coley. *Use of sign language with hearing students having severe reading problems.* Washington, D.C.: Gallaudet College Press, 1978.

1183 Vernon, M., and S. Koh. "Early manual communication and deaf children's achievement." *Amer. ann. deaf* 115:5 (1970), 527–536.

1184 Vernon, M., and S. Koh. "Effects of oral preschool compared to early manual communication on education and communication in deaf children." *Amer. ann. deaf* 115:6 (1971), 569–574.

1185 Vernon, M., and B. Makowsky. "Deafness and minority group dynamics." *The deaf amer.* 21:11 (1969), 3–6.

1186 Vilhjálmsson, V., and I. Jónsdóttir. *Táknmál.* Félagi heyrnarlausra og Foreldra-og styrktarfélagi heyrnardaufra, 1976.

1187 Voegelin, C. F. "Sign language analysis, on one level or on two?" *Int'l. j. of Amer. linguistics* 24 (1958), 71–77.

1188 Volterra, V., and T. Taeschner. "The organization and development of language by bilingual children." *J. child language* 5 (1977), 311–326.

1189 Von der Lieth, L. *Dansk dove-tegnsprog.* København: Academisk Forlag, 1967.

1190 Von der Lieth, L. "Le geste et la mimique dans la communication totale." *Bulletin de psychologie* 304:26 (1972), 5–9, 494–500.

1191 Von der Lieth, L. *Psykologisk skriftserie nr. 4—nonverbal kommunikation.* København: Københavns Univ., 1973.

1192 Von der Lieth, L. *Tekster om gestikulation.* Copenhagen: Univ. of Copenhagen, 1973.

1193 Von der Lieth, L. "The use of deaf sign language." In F. B. Crammatte, et al. (eds.), *VII world congress of the world federation of the deaf.* Silver Spring, Md.: National Assoc. of the Deaf, 1976, 316–327.

1194 Von der Lieth, L. "Social-psychological aspects of the use of sign language." In Schlesinger and Namir (eds.), *Sign language of the deaf: psychological, linguistic and sociological perspectives.* New York: Academic Press, 1978, 315–332.

1195 Von Raffler-Engel, W. "The correlation of gestures and verbalizations in first language acquisition." In Kendon, et al. *Organization of behavior in face-to-face interaction.* Chicago, Ill.: Aldine Publishing Co., 1973.

1196 Vuillemey, P. *La pensée et les signes autres que ceux de la langue.* Unpub. dissertation, Paris: Université de Paris, 1940.

1197 Vygotsky, L. S. *Thought and language.* Cambridge, Mass. M.I.T. Press, 1962.

1198 Wampler, D. W. *An introduction to the spatial symbol system as used in linguistics of visual English.* Santa Rosa, Calif.: Santa Rosa City Schools, 1971.

1199 Wampler, D. *Linguistics of visual English.*

Unpub. MS. Santa Rosa (Calif.) City Schools, 1971.

1200 Wampler, D. W. *Linguistics of visual English: morpheme list one.* Santa Rosa, Calif.: Santa Rosa City Schools, 1971.

1201 Waratah, New South Wales Deaf and Dumb Institute. *How to converse with the deaf in sign language (as used in the Australian Catholic schools for the deaf.)* Newcastle, Australia: Davies and Cannington Pty., 1943.

1202 Ward, J. *Signs n' synonyms.* Northridge, Calif.: Joyce Media, Inc., 1977.

1203 Ward, J. *Sign language thesaurus of useful signs and synonyms.* Northridge, Calif.: Joyce Media, Inc., 1978.

1204 Warren, K. "Aspect marking in American sign language." In P. Siple (ed.), *Understanding language through sign language research.* New York: Academic Press, 1978, 133–159.

1205 Washabaugh, W. "The iconic and the analog in sign." In W. Von Raffler-Engel and B. Hoffer (eds.), *Aspects of non-verbal communication,* 1977, 75–120.

1206 Washabaugh, W. *Aspects of the syntax of Providence Island sign language.* Milwaukee: Univ. of Wis., 1978.

1207 Washabaugh, W. *Review of I. M. Schlesinger and L. Namir (eds.), sign language of the deaf;* New York: Academic Press, 1978. Milwaukee: Univ. of Wis., 1978.

1208 Washabaugh, W., et al. *Providence Island sign language.* Paper presented to the annual meeting of the linguistic society of America, Philadelphia, Pa., 1976.

1209 Washabaugh, W., et al. "Providence Island: a context dependent language." *Anthropological linguistics* 20:3 (1978), 95–111.

1210 Washburn, A. *Seeing essential English.* Unpub. MS. Denver, Colo.: Community College of Denver, 1971.

1211 Washburn, A. *The SEE thesaurus: grouping of seeing essential English signs.* Dubuque, Iowa: Kendall/Hunt Co., 1973.

1212 Washington State School for the Deaf. *An introduction to manual English.* Vancouver, Wash.: Washington State School for the Deaf, 1972.

1213 Watson, D. O. *Talk with your hands.* Winneconne, Wis.: published by author, 1964.

1214 Watson, D. *Talk with your hands, vols. I and II.* Menasha, Wis.: George Banta Co., 1973.

1215 Waxman, J., et al. "The perception and processing of information by severely dysfunctional nonverbal children: a rationale for the use of manual communication." *Sign lang. studies* 21 (1978), 289–316.

1216 Webster, C. "Gestural training breaks communication barrier in child autism." *Special educ. in Canada* 48:1 (1973), 6–26.

1217 Webster, C., et al. "Communicating with an autistic boy by gestures." *J. of autism and childhood schizophrenia* 3:4 (1973), 337–346.

1218 Webster, C., et al. *Simultaneous communication with severely dysfunctional non-verbal children: an alternative to speech training.* Unpub. working paper, Univ. of Victoria, 1976.

1219 Wedell, J. R. "Acquisition of signed English by deaf preschoolers: concepts, context and constructions." *Dissertation abstracts int'l.* 37 (1976), 507–508.

1220 Weld, L. "Suggestions on certain varieties of the language of signs as used in the instruction of the deaf and dumb." *Amer. ann. deaf and dumb* 5:3 (1853), 149–158.

1221 Wells, J. "The Paget systematic sign language." *Teacher of the deaf* 70:411 (1972), 28–39.

1222 Wescott, R. W. "Linguistic iconism." *Language* 47:2 (1971), 416–428.

1223 West, L. *The sign language, an analysis.* Bloomington: Indiana Univ., 1960.

1224 Western Maryland College Laboratory. *Films of deafness and hearing loss.* Westminster, Md.: Total Communications Laboratory, Western Maryland College, n.d.

1225 Weyer, S. *Fingerspelling by computer.* Report # TR 212. Calif.: Stanford University, August 1973.

1226 Whipple, Z. *The Whipple natural alphabet.* Rochester, N.Y.: Institute for Deaf-Mutes, 1892.

1227 Wilbur, R. "The linguistics of manual language and manual systems." In L. Lloyd, (ed.), *Communication assessment and intervention strategies.* Baltimore: Univ. Park Press, 1976.

1228 Wilbur, R. *American sign language and sign systems: research and applications.* Baltimore: Univ. Park Press, 1978.

1229 Wilk, J. N. *Drama improvisations and sign language.* Silver Spring, Md.: National Assoc. of the Deaf, 1976.

1230 Wilkins, J. "Mercury of the secret and swift messenger." *Mathematical and philosophical works* 2 (1802).

1231 Williams, J. "Bilingual experiences of a deaf child." *Sign lang. studies* 10 (1976), 37–41.

1232 Willoughby, J. "The Georg Forchammer mouth-hand system." *Hearing* 29:9 (1974).

1233 Wilson, P. *Sign language as a means of communication for the mentally retarded.* Paper presented to the annual meeting of the eastern psychological assoc., Philadelphia, Pa., 1974.

1234 Wilson, P. *Manual language for the child without language: a behavioral approach for teaching the exceptional child.* Hartford, Conn.: Developmental Team, 1975.

1235 Wilson, P., et al. *Manual language dictionary: functional vocabulary for the retarded.* Mansfield Depot, Conn.: Mansfield Occupational Training Center, 1973.

1236 Winslow, L. *Learning to see a language. Development of the language of signs: a first language at a late age.* Unpub. thesis, Cambridge, Mass.: Harvard Univ., 1973.

1237 Wisconsin Department of Public Instruction. *Wisconsin instructional signs.* Illus. by D. O. Watson. Wisc. Dept. Public Instruction, 1978. (Write to D. O. Watson, Winneconne, Wis.)

1238 Wisher, P. *Use of the sign language in underwater communication,* n.d. Write to author: Gallaudet College, Washington, D.C. 20002.

1239 Woodward, J. C. *A transformational approach to the syntax of American sign language.* Washington, D.C.: Georgetown Univ., 1970.

1240 Woodward, J. C. *Personal pronominalization in American sign language.* Washington, D.C.: Georgetown Univ., 1970.

1241 Woodward, J. C. *Pidgin sign language English.* Washington, D.C.: Georgetown Univ., 1971.

1242 Woodward, J. "Implications for sociolinguistic research among the deaf." *Sign lang. studies* 1 (1972), 1–7.

1243 Woodward, J. C. "A program to prepare language specialists for work with the deaf." *Sign lang. studies* 2 (1973), 1–8.

1244 Woodward, J. "Deaf awareness." *Sign lang. studies* 3 (1973), 57–60.

1245 Woodward, J. *Implicational effects on the deaf diglossic continuum.* Unpub. dissertation, Washington, D.C.: Georgetown Univ., 1973.

1246 Woodward, J. C. *Implicational lects on the deaf diglossic continuum.* Washington, D.C.: Gallaudet College, 1973, 1–166.

1247 Woodward, J. "Inter-rule implication in American sign language." *Sign lang. studies* 3 (1973), 47–56.

1248 Woodward, J. "Language continuum, a different point of view." *Sign lang. studies* 2 (1973), 81–83.

1249 Woodward, J. "Linguistics and language teaching." *Teaching English to the deaf* 1 (1973), 2.

1250 Woodward, J. C. "Some characteristics of pidgin sign English." *Sign lang. studies* 3 (1973), 39–46.

1251 Woodward, J. "Some observations on sociolinguistics variation and American sign language." *Kansas j. of sociology* 9:2 (1973), 191–200.

1252 Woodward, J. C. "A report on Montana-Washington implicational research." *Sign lang. studies* 4 (1974), 77–101.

1253 Woodward, J. C. "ESL training for teachers of the deaf." *Teaching English to the deaf* 1:3 (1974), 3–4.

1254 Woodward, J. C. "Implicational variation in American sign language negative incorporation." *Sign lang. studies* 4 (1974), 20–30.

1255 Woodward, J. C. *Linguistics and sign language.* Washington, D.C.: Gallaudet College, 1974.

1256 Woodward, J. *Early creolization in American sign language.* Working paper, linguistics research laboratory. Unpub. MS. Washington, D.C.: Gallaudet College, 1975.

1257 Woodward, J. *How you gonna get to heaven if you can't talk with Jesus: the educational establishment vs. the deaf community.* Paper presented at the society for applied anthropology, Amsterdam, 1975.

1258 Woodward, J. C. "Variation in American sign language syntax." In R. W. Fasold and R. W. Shuy (eds.), *Analyzing variation in language.* Papers from the 2nd colloquium on new ways of analyzing variation, 1975, 303–311.

1259 Woodward, J. "Black Southern signing." *Lang. in society* 5:2 (August 1976), 211–218.

1260 Woodward, J. C. *Historical bases of American sign language.* Washington, D.C.: Gallaudet College, 1976, 1–22.

1261 Woodward, J. "Signs of change: historical variation in American sign language." *Sign lang. studies* 10 (Spring 1976), 81–94.

1262 Woodward, J. "Sex is definitely a problem: interpreters' knowledge of signs for sexual behavior." *Sign lang. studies* 14 (1977), 73–88.

1263 Woodward, J. "All in the family: kinship lexicalization across sign languages." *Sign lang. studies* 19 (1978), 121–138.

1264 Woodward, J. "Historical bases of American sign language." In P. Siple (ed.), *Understanding language through sign language research.* New York: Academic Press, 1978, 333–348.

1265 Woodward, J. *Signs of sexual behavior.* Silver Spring, Md.: T. J. Publishers, 1978.

1266 Woodward, J. *Beliefs about and attitudes toward Providence Island sign language: a final look.* Washington, D.C.: Gallaudet College, 1979.

1267 Woodward, J., and S. De Santis. *Negative incorporation in American sign language.* Paper presented at the linguistic society of America meeting, Philadelphia, Pa., 1976.

1268 Woodward, J., and S. De Santis. "Negative incorporation in French and American sign language." *Lang. in society* 6:3 (1977), 379–388.

1269 Woodward, J., and S. De Santis. "Two to one it happens: dynamic phonology in two sign languages." *Sign lang. studies* 17 (1977), 329–346.

1270 Woodward, J., and S. De Santis. *Co-occurence restrictions on handshape and location in PRO-*

VISL: face tabs. Washington, D.C.: Gallaudet College, 1979.

1271 Woodward, J. C., and C. Erting. "Synchronic variation and historical change in American sign language." *Lang. sciences* 37 (1975), 9–12.

1272 Woodward, J., C. Erting, and S. Oliver. "Facing and handling variation in American sign language phonology." *Sign lang. studies* 10 (1976), 43–51.

1273 Woodward, J. C., and H. Markowicz. "Some handy new ideas on pidgins and creoles: pidgin sign languages." Presented languages, Honolulu. MS. Washington, D.C.: Gallaudet College, 1975.

1274 World Federation of the Deaf. *Gestuno.* Carlisle, Eng.: British Deaf Association, 1975.

1275 Wundt, W. *The language of gestures.* The Hague: Mouton, 1973.

1276 Yamada, J., et al. *The use of simultaneous communication in a language intervention program for an autistic child: a case study.* Los Angeles, Calif.: Univ. of Calif., 1979.

1277 Yanulov, N., et al. *A short dictionary of sign language.* Sofia, Bulgaria: Narodna Prosveta, 1961.

1278 Yau, S.C. "Semiotic structure of signs in Chinese sign language." MS. Centre National de la Recherche Scientifique, Paris, France, 1975.

1279 Yau, S. C. *Element ordering in gestural languages and in archaic Chinese ideograms (preliminary version).* Paris: Centre de Recherches Linguistiques sur l'Asie Orientale, 1977.

1280 Yau, S. C. *The Chinese signs; lexicon of the standard sign language for the deaf in China.* Hong Kong: Chiu Ming Publishing Co., 1977.

1281 Young, R. "I see what you mean: the semantic environment of sign language." *ETC* 35:2 (1978).

1282 Youngs, J. P., Jr. "Interpreting for deaf clients." *J. of rehab. of deaf* 1 (1967).

1283 Zaitsyeva, G. "The syntax of the gestural language of the deaf." *Defektologiya* 3 (1974), 7–13.

1284 Zakia, R. *Fingerspelling as a visual sequential process.* Unpub. dissertation, Rochester, N.Y.: Univ. of Rochester, 1970.

1285 Zweiban, S. T. "Indicators of success in learning a manual communication mode." *Mental retardation* 15:2 (1977), 47–49.

Subject Index to Bibliography

LEARNING AND TEACHING OF SIGN LANGUAGE

Textbooks

35, 37, 38, 40, 73, 75, 79, 80, 109, 110, 149, 167, 203, 216, 217, 268, 280, 311, 340, 345, 347, 350, 352, 353, 356, 487, 489, 490, 521, 522, 538, 594, 595, 604, 610, 622, 624, 686, 690, 713, 714, 719, 772, 802, 826, 844, 845, 847, 850, 896, 905, 929, 931, 932, 935, 938, 946, 947, 959, 985, 999, 1004, 1034, 1038, 1109, 1118, 1192, 1197, 1210, 1212, 1213, 1214, 1237, 1274

Other curricular materials

Curriculum guides, teacher manuals, etc.

1, 3, 22, 32, 38, 45, 109, 111, 146, 147, 150, 228, 230, 259, 276, 339, 354, 525, 527, 530, 541, 565, 585, 606, 679, 710, 807, 852, 864, 909, 919, 952, 971, 1007, 1126, 1249

Foreign sign language materials

35, 60, 113, 117, 172, 186, 387, 442, 459, 460, 469, 564, 571, 604, 609, 610, 647, 724, 730, 802, 803, 826, 827, 831, 832, 834, 849, 850, 896, 910, 920, 930, 949, 960, 979, 985, 1108, 1118, 1166, 1177, 1189, 1201, 1277, 1280

Specialized vocabularies

75, 80, 144, 145, 148, 180, 181, 182, 183, 184, 185, 195, 369, 441, 598, 611, 613, 622, 779, 822, 832, 841, 845, 847, 851, 864, 1011, 1202, 1203, 1237, 1265

Nontext instructional materials, including audiovisual

3, 11, 36, 134, 156, 185, 195, 201, 290, 321, 332, 358, 367, 547, 628, 644, 645, 667, 756, 792, 927, 948, 958, 965, 994, 1008, 1010, 1011, 1151, 1202, 1203, 1224, 1225

Acquisition

American Sign Language (ASL) acquisition

8, 45, 83, 86, 95, 96, 111, 152, 153, 154, 160, 168, 208, 209, 210, 211, 212, 229, 231, 232, 233, 234, 235, 263, 322, 328, 329, 330, 430, 535, 552, 553, 554, 555, 556, 557, 559, 624, 700, 722, 728, 733, 749, 751, 757, 758, 759, 763, 764, 765, 776, 806, 819, 820, 839, 843, 853, 880, 1046, 1047, 1101, 1183, 1231, 1236

Acquisition of other signing systems

32, 51, 141, 143, 144, 145, 229, 231, 232, 233, 234, 248, 263, 363, 364, 365, 465, 466, 467, 468, 532, 565, 647, 707, 733, 789, 806, 853, 856, 880, 883, 972, 1133, 1134, 1135, 1141, 1219, 1229, 1231

Signed and spoken language

5, 79, 95, 168, 239, 245, 246, 265, 266, 273, 291, 299, 331, 363, 364, 365, 376, 381, 382, 529, 597, 613, 660, 693, 733, 745, 751, 762, 789, 823, 843, 880, 882, 894, 941, 972, 973, 974, 977, 987, 1032, 1038, 1040, 1060, 1091, 1138, 1139, 1140, 1144, 1145, 1167, 1180, 1181, 1195, 1231

Second language acquisition (including English as a Second Language [ESL] for deaf persons)

9, 23, 141, 197, 235, 236, 314, 464, 720, 883, 941, 1060, 1062, 1063, 1084, 1144, 1145, 1180, 1253

Manual representations of spoken language

Manual English and other contrived signing systems

24, 25, 26, 27, 28, 29, 137, 196, 197, 220, 224, 231, 242, 243, 244, 245, 259, 260, 261, 262, 274, 277, 292, 293, 475, 487, 488, 489, 490, 491, 591, 592, 646, 701, 707, 742, 781, 862, 863, 926, 987, 1002, 1008, 1072, 1177, 1197, 1198, 1200, 1210, 1211, 1212, 1219, 1221, 1232, 1274

French-English Index

A

à
à cheval
à côté de
à côté de
à droit
à jamais
à l'esprit étroit
à l'esprit large
à l'instant
à la mode
à mi-chemin
à moins que
à point
abandonné
abandonner
abattu
abattu
abdiquer
abeille
abhorrer
abolir
abondance
abondance
abondonner
abonner
aboyer
Abraham
abréger
abri
absence
absent
absent
absolu
absolution
absorber
abstinence
absurde
absurdité
abuser de

accent
accepter
accident
acclamer
accompagner

at   A-292
to   T-202, 203
horseback   H-159
next   N-73, 74, 75, 76
beside   B-126
right   R-196
forever   F-218
narrow-minded   N-14
broad minded   B-250
just now   J-40, 41
fashionable   F-59
midway   M-143
unless   U-43
medium   M-96
stranded   S-506
abandon   A-2, 3
dejected   D-73
depressed   D-102
abdicate   A-7
bee   B-87
abhor   A-9
abolish   A-12, 13
abundance   A-30
plenty   P-206
relinquish   R-101
subscribe   S-541
bark   B-35
Abraham   A-17
abbreviate   A-4, 5
shelter   S-188
absence   A-18, 19
away   A-327
out   O-141, 142, 143
absolute   A-23
absolution   A-25, 26
engross   E-105
abstinence   A-28
absurd   A-29
nonsense   N-100
take-advantage of
   T-10, 11
emphasis   E-74
accept   A-32
accident   A-33
acclaim   A-34, 35
accompany   A-37

accomplir
accord
accorder
accorder
accrocher
acculer
accumuler

accuser
acheter
acheter
achever
achever
acide
acier
acquérir
acquiescer
acteur
action
actrice
Adam
additionner
adepte
adieu
adjacent
admettre
administration
admirer
admission
admonester
adolescence
adopter
adoration
adorer
adresse
affaires
affilier
affreux
Afrique
âge
agir
agitation
agneau
agrafe
agréable
aider
aider
aigle

accomplish   A-38, 39
accord   A-40
bestow   B-130
grant   G-115, 116
hitch   H-123
corner   C-402, 403
accumulate   A-43, 44,
   45
accuse   A-48, 49
buy   B-285
purchase   P-413
complete   C-282, 283
terminate   T-83
acid   A-54
steel   S-476
acquire   A-58
acquiesce   A-56
actor   A-65
deed   D-55
actress   A-66
Adam   A-69
add   A-70, 71, 72, 73
adept   A-78
farewell   F-44, 45
adjacent   A-80
admit   A-87
government   G-99
admire   A-82, 83
admission   A-84
admonish   A-88, 89
adolescence   A-90
adopt   A-92
worship   W-187
adore   A-93
address   A-76, 77
business   B-276
affiliate   A-100, 101
dreadful   D-302
Africa   A-103
age   A-111
act   A-61
turmoil   T-304
lamb   L-9
paper clip   P-19
pleasant   P-208
help   H-90
aid   A-118
eagle   E-6

aigre	sour S-380	annihiler	annihilate A-180
aigrelet	tart T-32	annoncer	announce A-181
aigu	sharp S-180, 181	annuel	annual A-187
aiguille	needle N-40	annuel	yearly Y-4
aile	wing W-139	annuler	cancel C-28
aimable	nice N-81	annuler	annul A-188
aimable	amiable A-161	antérieur	previous P-304
aimant	fond F-193, 194	anticiper	anticipate A-194
aimant	magnet M-11	antique	antique A-196
aimer	like L-103, 105	apercevoir	perceive P-94, 95
aîné	elder E-47	apparaître	appear A-217, 218
aîné	eldest E-48	appareil	apparatus A-213
ainsi	thus T-174	appareil	
air	air A-120	photographique	camera C-21, 22
aire	area A-242	apparent	apparent A-214
ajouter	add A-70, 71, 72, 73	appartenir	belong B-106, 107
ajuster	adjust A-81	appeler	call C-12, 13
algèbre	algebra A-124	appelé	called C-14
aliéné	mentally unbalanced M-117, 118, 119, 120, 121	appétit	appetite A-220
		applaudir	applaud A-221
		applaudir	cheer C-134
		applaudir	clap C-179
alléluia	hallelujah H-15	apporter	bring B-246
Allemand	German G-37	apprécier	appreciate A-229
aller	go G-69, 70	apprendre	learn L-52
aller chercher	fetch F-101	apprendre par coeur	memorize M-107, 108
aller de l'avant	go ahead G-71	apprivoisé	tame T-28
allonger	extend E-229	approbation	approbation A-231
allumer	kindle K-17	approvisionner	store S-499, 500
allumette	match M-67	après	after A-104, 105
alors	then T-114, 115	après-demain	day after tomorrow D-18
alphabet	alphabet A-142		
alphabet manuel	manual alphabet M-48	après-midi	afternoon A-107
altercation	row R-265	araignée	spider S-414
amant	lover L-170	arbitre	umpire U-10
ambitieux	ambitious A-157, 158	arbitre	referee R-76
ambition	ambition A-156	arbre	tree T-273
âme	soul S-377	archevêque	archbishop A-237
améliorer	improve I-50	ardent	ardent A-239
amen	amen A-159	ardent	eager E-4
amende	fine F-135	ardoise	slate S-298
amer	bitter B-162	argent	silver S-259, 260
Amérique	America A-160	argent	money M-203, 204, 205
Amérique du Nord	North America N-105		
Amérique du Sud	South America S-382, 383	argumenter (oiscuter)	argue A-243
		aride	arid A-245
ami(e)	friend F-269	arithmétique	arithmetic A-248
amical	friendly F-270	armée	army A-251
amour	love L-169	armes	arms A-250
ample	ample A-167	armoire	closet C-199
amusant	amusing A-168	arpenteur	surveyor S-607
amusement	fun F-290	arranger	arrange A-255
an	year Y-3	arrérages	arrears A-257
ancêtres	ancestors A-169, 170	arrêt	stop S-497
andouillers	antlers A-197	arrêter	arrest A-258, 259
âne	donkey D-268	arrière	rear R-50
ange	angel A-172	(end) arrière	back B-3
Anglais	Englishman E-102	arrivée	arrival A-260
angle	angle A-174	arriver	befall B-90
angoisse	agony A-114	arriver	happen H-31, 32
animal	animal A-177, 178	arriver	occur O-30
année prochaine	next year N-80	arriver à	reach R-34
annexer	annex A-179		

arroser	baste B-50	authentique	genuine G-34
arroser	sprinkle S-432	automne	fall F-25, 26
art	art A-262	automne	autumn A-316, 317
artiste	artist A-263	automobile	automobile A-315
ascenseur	elevator E-61, 62	autorité	authority A-314
ascension	ascension A-266	autour de	around A-252
Asie	Asia A-270	autour du monde	around the world A-253
aspirer à	aspire A-276		
assembler	assemble A-277	autre	other O-137
assembler	collect C-233	autrefois	formerly F-227
assembler	convene C-377	aux épaules larges	broad shouldered B-251
asseyez-vous	be seated B-124		
assez	enough E-110	avaler	swallow S-618, 619
assiette	plate P-201	avance	advanced A-96
assister	give assistance G-49	avancer	advance A-95
assister	assist A-280	avant	before B-91, 92, 93
assister	attend A-299	avant-hier	day before yesterday D-19
associer	associate A-282, 283		
assorti	assorted A-286	avaricieux	avaricious A-318
assortir	assort A-285	avec	with W-150
assumer	assume A-287	avec ruse	on the sly O-85
assurance	insurance I-143	avenir	future F-299
atelier	workshop W-173	averse	shower S-229
attacher	attach A-294	aversion	dislike D-215
attacher	fasten F-62	avertir	caution C-83
attaque à main armée	holdup H-130	avertir	admonish A-88, 89
attaque d'apoplexie	stroke S-521	avertir	warn W-23
attaquer	tackle T-6	aveu	admission A-84
attaquer	attack A-295	aveugle	blind B-174
atteindre	attain A-296	aviateur	flier F-172
atteindre	achieve A-52, 53	aviateur	aviator A-320
attendre	wait W-5	avide	greedy G-145, 146, 147
attirer	attract A-303	avion	plane P-195, 196
attirer	entice E-116	avion	airplane A-121, 122
attitude	attitude A-301	avion à réaction	jet J-11
attraper	catch C-75, 76, 77	avocat	lawyer L-39
attrayant	attractive A-306	avocat	attorney A-302
attribuer	attribute A-307, 308	avoir	have H-55, 57
au contraire	on the contrary O-84	avoir l'intention	intend I-148
au lieu de	instead of I-131, 132	avoir peur	afraid A-102
au milieu de	amid A-162	avoir sommeil	sleepy S-304
au revoir	goodbye G-87, 88		
au sujet de	concerning C-300		
au sujet de	about A-14		**B**
au travers de	across A-59		
au travers de	through T-166	badauder	rubberneck R-271, 272
au-delà de	beyond B-134	bagage	baggage B-11
au-dessous de	beneath B-114, 115	bagages	luggage L-176
au-dessus	above A-16	bague	ring R-203
auberge	inn I-114	baguette	rod R-241
audience	hearing H-69	bain	bath B-52
auditoire	audience A-309, 310	baiser	kiss K-21, 22, 23
augmentation	raise R-19	balai	broom B-255
augmenter	increase I-66	balai à franges	mop M-217
augmenter	raise R-19	balance	scale S-54, 55, 56
aujourd'hui	today T-207	balayer	sweep S-631
au loin	off O-38, 39	baleine	whale W-82
aussi	too T-222	balle	ball B-17, 18
aussi	also A-143, 144	banane	banana B-21, 22
Australie	Australia A-312	banc	bench B-112
autel	altar A-145, 146	bandage	bandage B-23
authentique	authentic A-313	bande	gang G-12

bandit	bandit B-25	billets	bills B-148, 149
bannière	banner B-28	billion	billion B-147
bannir	banish B-26	bis	encore E-81
banquet	banquet B-29	bisaïeul	great grandfather G-140
baptême	baptism B-30		
baptiste	Baptist B-31	bisaïeule	great grandmother G-141
Bar Mitzvah	Bar Mitzvah B-36		
barbe	beard B-70, 71	biscuit	cracker C-445, 446
baril	barrel B-38	bizarre	curious C-488
bas	base B-39, 40, 41	bizarre	queer Q-12
bas	stocking S-492, 493	bizarre	odd O-35
bas	hose H-160, 161	blague	humbug H-190
bas	low L-171, 172	blaguer	kid K-11
base	basis B-45, 46	blâmer	blame B-167
baseball	baseball B-42	blanc	white W-107
baser	base B-39, 40, 41	blanc-bec	green G-150
basket (ball)	basketball B-48	blanchissage	wash W-25, 26, 27
bataille	battle B-56	blasphémer	blaspheme B-168, 169, 170
bâtard	bastard B-49		
bateau	boat B-190	blesser	injure I-107, 108
bateau à voiles	sailboat S-11	blessure	wound W-197
bâton de rouge	lipstick L-115	bleu	blue B-184
bâtonnet	stick S-484	bluffer	bluff B-185
batte	bat B-51	boeuf	beef B-88
battement	heartbeat H-74, 75	boire	drink D-309, 310
battre	beat B-72, 73, 74	boire à la santé	toast T-205
bavarder	gossip G-94	bois	wood W-167
bavarder	tattle T-35, 36	bois	woods W-168
beau	fine F-134	bois de charpente	lumber L-177, 178
beau	beautiful B-77	boisson alcoolique	liquor L-117, 118
beau	handsome H-28	boîte	can C-25
beau-père	stepfather S-481	boîte	box B-213
beaucoup	lot L-164	boiteux	lame L-10
beaucoup de	many M-50	bol	bowl B-211
beaucoup (de)	much M-255	bon	good G-85, 86
bébé	baby B-1	bon	kind K-15
bec	beak B-63	bon marché	cheap C-125, 126
bêche	spade S-386	bonbons	candy C-31, 32
becqueter	peck P-70	bondir	leap L-51
beignet	doughnut D-293	bonne	maid M-13
belle-mère	stepmother S-482	bord (de la mer)	seaside S-105
bénédiction	benediction B-116, 117	bosse	bump B-269
bénéfice	benefit B-118, 119	bouche	mouth M-248
bénir	bless B-172, 173	bouche bée	open-mouthed O-91
besoin	need N-37, 38, 39	bouchon	cork C-399
beurre	butter B-280	boucle d'oreille	earring E-12
Bible	Bible B-135, 136, 137	boucler	curl C-490
bibliothèque	library L-90	bouclier	shield S-191, 193
bicyclette	bicycle B-138	boueux	muddy M-256
bien	well W-76	boulanger	baker B-13
bien	well W-77	bousculade	scramble S-88
bien disposé (envers)	sympathetic S-646	boutique	shop S-215
bien éveillé	wide awake W-120	bouton	button B-283, 284
bien que	although A-149	boxer	box B-214
bien-aimée	sweetheart S-633, 634	Boy-Scout	Boy Scout B-217
bienfait	benefit B-118, 119	brailler	bawl B-57, 58
bientôt	by and by B-288	branche	branch B-222
bienveillant	benevolent B-120	bras	arm A-249
bienvenu	welcome W-75	bref	brief B-236, 237
bière	beer B-89	brillant	bright B-238, 239, 240, 241
biffer	delete D-75, 76, 77		
billet	ticket T-176, 177	briller	shine S-194

brise	breeze B-232	caractère	character C-115, 116
briser	break B-227	cardinal	cardinal C-50
broche	brooch B-254	carême	lent L-72
broche	pin P-176	caresser	petting P-135
brochure	pamphlet P-12	caresser	stroke S-522
bronze	tan T-29	carie	caries C-60
brosse à cheveux	hairbrush H-4	carré	square S-437
brosse à dents	toothbrush T-225	carte	card C-49
brosse à souliers	shoebrush S-207	carte	playing card P-205
brosse à vêtements	clothesbrush C-201	carte	map M-51
brosser	brush B-260, 261, 262, 263	casquette	cap C-39
		caste	caste C-69
bruit	noise N-92	catalogue	catalog C-73
brûler	burn B-273	catastrophique	catastrophic C-74
brun	brown B-259	catholique	Catholic C-79
bûche	log L-138	cause	cause C-82
buisson	bush B-275	causer	chat C-124
bureau	office O-46, 47	ce soir	tonight T-219
but	purpose P-419, 420, 421	ceci	this T-145
		céder	cede C-87
but	goal G-72	céder	give up G-52
but	aim A-119	cela	that T-100, 101, 102
		célèbre	celebrated C-89
		célébrer	celebrate C-88
C		célibataire	bachelor B-2
		cent	cent C-92
cabinet	toilet T-211	cent	hundred H-193
(se) cacher	hide H-103	centre	center C-93
cacahouète	peanut P-67	cependant	however H-176, 177
cadeau	present P-301	céramique	ceramics C-97
cadeau	gift G-44	cercle	circle C-174, 175
cadre	frame F-249	céréale	grain G-108
café	coffee C-222	cerf	deer D-57
cahot	jolt J-24	certain	certain C-98
caille	quail Q-2, 3	cerveau	brain B-221
cajoler	coax C-213	ces	those T-148
calamiteux	calamitous C-6	cesser(de)	cease C-86
calcul	calculus C-8	ceux	these T-125
calculer	calculate C-7	chacun(e)	each one E-2
calculer	figure F-119	chagrin	grief G-155, 156
calculer	reckon R-62	chaîne	chain C-100
Californie	California C-10	chair	flesh F-171
Calvaire	Calvary C-18, 19	chaise	chair C-101, 102, 103
camaraderie	fellowship F-96	chaise à bascule	rocking chair R-238, 239
cambrioleur	burglar B-271		
camp	camp C-23	chaleur	heat H-76, 77
campagne	country C-423	chameau	camel C-20
Canada	Canada C-26	champ	field C-111, 112
canard	duck D-323	champion	champion C-106
candidat	candidate C-29	chance	chance C-107
canoe	canoeing C-37	chandail	sweater S-627
canon	cannon C-33, 34	chandelle	candle C-30
caoutchouc	rubber R-268, 269, 270	changeant	changeable C-110
caoutchoucs	overshoes O-151	changer	change C-108, 109
cap	point P-224	changer	alter A-147
capable	capable C-40	changer de conduite	mend M-110, 111
capable	competent C-275	chanson	song S-371
capacité	capacity C-41	chant	chant C-111
capitaine	captain C-45	chanter	sing S-268
capital	capital C-42, 43	chapeau	hat H-51
capturer	capture C-47	chapelle	chapel C-113
car	for F-204, 205	chapitre	chapter C-114

comparer — compare C-268
compassion — compassion C-269
compassion — sympathy S-648
compatissant — soft-hearted S-359
complet — suit S-563
complètement — altogether A-150
compliquer — complicate C-284
composer — compose C-286
comprendre — comprehend C-287
comprendre — understand U-20, 21
comprendre — include I-63
compte — score S-73
compte — account A-42
compter — count C-422
concéder — grant G-115, 116
concéder — concede C-288
concentrer — concentrate C-293
concept — concept C-295, 296
conception immaculée — Immaculate Conception I-25
concevoir — conceive C-290, 291, 292
conclure — conclude C-301
concourir — compete C-273, 274
condenser — condense C-303
conduire — conduct C-304, 305
conduire — drive D-312
conduire — lead L-43
conférence — lecture L-59
conférence — conference C-307
conférence — talk T-22, 23, 24
conférer — confer C-306
confesser — confess C-308
confession — confession C-310
confiance — confidence C-312
confiance — trust T-295
confidentiel — private P-332
confirmation — confirmation C-313
confitures — jam J-2
confondre — confuse C-316
confort — comfort C-251
confortable — cozy C-442
confronter — confront C-315
congédier — fire F-147
congédier — discharge D-190, 191
conscience — conscience C-328, 329, 330
conscient — conscious C-331
conscient — aware of A-326
consécration — consecration C-333
consécutif — consecutive C-334
conseil — advice A-97
conseil d'administration — board B-188
conseiller — counsel C-420
consentir — consent C-335
considérer — consider C-336, 337, 338
consigner — consign C-339
consistant — consistent C-340
consoler — console C-341
consommer — consume C-348, 349

constituer — constitute C-342
construire — construct C-344, 345
construire — build B-266
consulter — consult C-347
consumer — consume C-348, 349
contact — contact C-351, 352
contagieux — contagious C-353
conte — tale T-20
contempler — contemplate C-355
content — content C-361
content — glad G-53
continuation — sequel S-152
continuer — proceed P-343
continuer — continue C-366, 367
contraindre — coerce C-218, 219
contraindre — compel C-270, 271
contraire — reverse R-185, 186
contraste — contrast C-370, 371
contre — against A-110
contre — versus V-28
contredire — contradict C-368
contremaître — foreman F-213
contribuer — contribute C-372
contrition — contrition C-373
controverse — controversy C-376
convaincre — convince C-387
convenable — suitable S-564
conversation — conversation C-379, 380
convertir — convert C-382
conviction — conviction C-384, 385, 386
convoiter — covet C-438, 439
convoiter — crave C-448
convoquer — summon S-573, 574
coopérer — cooperate C-391
copier — copy C-394, 395, 396
coq — cock C-217
coq — rooster R-250
corde — rope R-252, 253
corde — cord C-397
cordial — cordial C-398
cordonnier — shoemaker S-209
coriace — tough T-238, 239, 240
cornes — horns H-157
cornichon — pickle P-156
corporal — corporal C-407
corps — body B-191
corps législatif — legislature L-65
corpulent — stout S-504
correct — right R-192
correct — correct C-408, 409
corridor — hall H-14
corriger — correct C-408, 409
corrompre — bribe B-233
corrompu — corrupt C-412
cosmétiques — cosmetics C-413
côte — coast C-211
côté — side S-242
côté à côté — side by side S-243
coton — cotton C-416
coucher du soleil — sunset S-581

défendre	defend D-62	désoeuvré	idle I-10
défendre	forbid F-206, 207	désordre	disorder D-218
défendre	prohibit P-361	dessiner	draw D-298
déféquer	defecate D-61	détaché	loose L-157
défi	challenge C-105	détacher	detach D-121
défigurer	deface D-58	détective	detective D-123, 124
défilé	parade P-23, 24	déteindre	fade F-9
définir	define D-66, 67	détendre	relax R-97, 98
dégénération	degeneration D-72	détériorer	deteriorate D-125
dégonfler	deflate D-68	déterminer	determine D-127
dégoût	disgust D-208	détestable	obnoxious O-17
dégoûtant	revolting R-189	détester	loathe L-131
dégoutter	drip D-311	détester	detest D-128, 129
dehors	out O-141, 142, 143	détourner	deflect D-70
délaisser	forsake F-229, 230, 231	détourner	embezzle E-68
		Detroit	Detroit D-130
délassement	recreation R-67	détruire	destroy D-119
décevoir	disappoint D-181	dette	obligation O-14, 15, 16
délice	delight D-80	deux	two T-312
délicieux	delicious D-78, 79	deux fois	twice T-309
délivrer	deliver D-81	deux points	colon C-240
demain	tomorrow T-217	deuxième	second S-108
demander	ask A-271, 272, 273	devant	before B-91, 92, 93
demander	request R-134, 135	devant	front F-282
demander	inquire I-118, 119, 120	devenir	become B-83
demeurer	reside R-144	dévier	deviate D-135, 136
demeurer	dwell D-339	deviner	guess G-172, 173, 174, 175
demi	half H-11, 12		
demi-heure	half-hour H-13	devoir	exercise E-201
démissionner	resign R-147	devoir	duty D-337
démocrate	democrat D-84	devoir	have to H-58
démolir	demolish D-85	devoir	obligation O-14, 15, 16
démon	demon D-86	devoir	owe O-154
démontrer	demonstrate D-87	devoir	must M-268
dent	tooth T-223	dévorer	devour D-143
dentiste	dentist D-90	dévot	devout D-144
dents	teeth T-55	dévouement	devotion D-142
dépendre de	depend D-94, 95, 96	devrais	ought O-138
dépenser	spend S-412	diable	devil D-138
déposer	deposit D-100, 101	diacre	deacon D-23, 24
depression nerveuse	mental breakdown M-116	diamant	diamond D-145, 146, 147
depuis	ever since E-167	diarrhée	diarrhea D-148
depuis	since S-265	dictionnaire	dictionary D-150, 151
déranger	trouble T-290	Dieu	God G-75
déranger	bother B-204, 205	différence	difference D-156, 158
déranger	disturb D-237	différent	diverse D-240, 241
déraper	skid S-286	différer	disagree D-179
dernier	last L-17, 18	différer	defer D-64
derrière	behind B-98	différer	differ D-155
dès	dice D-149	difficile	difficult D-159, 160, 161
dès lors	from then on F-281		
dès lors	thenceforth T-117	difficile	hard H-36, 37
descendant	descendant D-106	diligence	diligence D-165, 166
descendre	descend D-104, 105	dimanche	Sunday S-577, 578
descendre	go down G-78	diminuer	decrease D-50
descendre	get off G-40	dinde	turkey T-301, 302
désespérer	lose hope L-162	dîner	dinner D-170
désirer	desire D-114, 115	dîner	dine D-169
désirer	wish W-147, 148	diocèse	diocese D-171
désireux	anxious A-199	dire	speak S-392
désobéir à	disobey D-217	dire	tell T-64

Grande-Bretagne	Great Britain G-139	hibou	owl O-155
grandiose	grand G-109, 110	hier	yesterday Y-10
gras (se)	fat F-63, 64	histoire	story S-502
gratter	scrape S-89	histoire	history H-118, 119
grave	grave G-125	hiver	winter W-141, 142
graver	engrave E-103	hollandais	Dutch D-335, 336
gravir	climb C-192, 193, 194	homard	lobster L-132
grec(que)	Grecian G-143	homosexuel	queer Q-13
grêle	hail H-2	homosexuel	fairy F-19
grenade	grenade G-153	hongrois	Hungarian H-194
grenouille	frog F-277, 278	honnête	honest H-145
grève	strike S-518	honneur	honor H-147, 148
grillade	toast T-204	honoraires	fee F-85
griller	broil B-252	honte	shame S-170, 171
grimace	grimace G-158	honteux	ashamed A-267, 268
grippe-sou	tightwad T-182, 183, 184	hôpital	hospital H-162, 163
		horizon	horizon H-155
gris	gray G-129, 130, 131, 132	hôtel	hotel H-166
		houe	hoe H-126
grognon	grouchy G-163	huile	oil O-54
gronder	scold S-69, 70, 71, 72	huiler	oil O-55
groseille	currant C-491	huissier	usher U-67
grossier	rough R-259, 260, 261	huit	eight E-38
grotesque	grotesque G-162	huitième	eighth E-39
groupe	group G-165, 166	huître	oyster O-157
guerre	war W-20	humain	human H-184
guider	guide G-176	humain	humane H-185
guirlande	wreath W-199	humanité	humanity H-186
guitare	guitar G-179	humble	humble H-187, 188, 189
gymnase	gym G-183		
gymnastique	exercise E-200	humide	damp D-7
		humour	humor H-191
		hurler	yell Y-6
H		hymne	hymn H-207, 208
		hypocrite	hypocrite H-209, 210
habile	clever C-188, 189	hystérique	hysterical H-211
habileté	skill S-287		
habitude	practice P-278, 279, 280		
		I	
habitude	habit H-1		
habituer	accustom A-50	ici	here H-95
haine	hate H-52, 53	idée	idea I-7
haleine	breath B-230	identifier	identify I-9
hamburger	hamburger H-20, 21	identique	identical I-8
haricot	bean B-64	idiot	moron M-223
harpe	harp H-46	idole	idol I-11
hâte	haste H-50	ignorant	ignorant I-13
haut	high H-104, 105, 106, 107	il	it I-214, 215, 216
		il	he H-63
haut	loud L-165	il fait chaud	hot weather H-169
haut	top T-226	il y a	ago A-113
hautain	haughty H-54	il y a quelques seconds	few seconds ago F-106
hauteur	height H-84, 85	il y a quelques jours	few days ago F-105
hébreu	Hebrew H-80	il y avait une fois	once upon a time O-71
hélas	alas A-123	île	island I-209, 210
herbe	grass G-121	illustrer	illustrate I-18
hérésie	heresy H-96	ils	they T-126
héritage	heritage H-98	image	image I-119
hésiter	hesitate H-102	imagination	imagination I-20
heure	hour H-170	imiter	imitate I-23
heureux	happy H-34	imiter	mimic M-158
heurter	run up against R-287	immaculé	immaculate I-24

Jesus	Jesus J-10	la Turquie	Turkey T-303
jeter	throw T-167, 168, 169	la Vierge	Mary M-62
jeu	game G-11	labeur	labor L-1
jeudi	Thursday T-173	lac	lake L-8
jeune	young Y-18	lacet	shoelace S-208
jeune fille	girl G-46	lâche	coward C-441
jeune fille	maiden M-14	laid	homely H-143, 144
jeune homme	lad L-4	laideur	ugliness U-1, 2, 3
joie	joy J-28	laine	wool W-169
joindre	join J-17, 18, 19	laisser	leave L-55
joli	pretty P-307	laisser tomber	drop D-313
jonction	connection C-324	lait	milk M-154
joue	cheek C-133	laitue	lettuce L-84, 85
jouer	act A-60	lampe de poche	flashlight F-159
jouer	gamble G-10	lancer	pitch P-185
jouer	play P-202	langue	language L-13, 14
jouer	perform P-100, 101	langue	tongue T-218
jouer au boules	bowl B-211	lapin	rabbit R-3, 4
jouer aux cartes	card playing C-51	large	wide W-119
jouir de	enjoy E-106	large	broad B-249
jour	day D-17	larme	tear T-49
jour de fête	holiday H-133	las	weary W-60
journal	newspaper N-67	latin	Latin L-31, 32
joyeux	jolly J-23	laver	wash W-25, 26, 27
judaïsme	Judaism J-29	laver la vaisselle	dish wash (ing) D-213
juger	judge J-30	le	the T-104
juif	Jew J-12	le Danemark	Denmark D-89
jumelle	binoculars B-151	le Japon	Japan J-3
jumelles	opera glasses O-94	le leur	their T-110
jupe	skirt S-292, 293	le long de	along A-141
juré	sworn S-645	le lui	him H-111
jurer	swear S-621	le même	same S-27, 28, 29
juron	oath O-2	le mien	mine M-164
jusqu'ici	thus far T-175	le moindre	least L-54
jusqu'ici	so far S-356	le seigneur	lord L-159
jusqu'à	till T-185	le sien	hers H-100
jusqu'à	up to U-53	leçon	lesson L-77
jusqu'à	until U-48	légal	legal L-64
juste	just J-35, 36	léger	slight S-309
juste	righteous R-200	léger	light L-101
juste	fair F-17	léguer	bequeath B-121
justice	justice J-38, 39	lentement	slow S-314
		léopard	leopard L-73
		lèpre	leprosy L-74
L		les	them T-111
		les États-Unis	United States U-35
l'Angleterre	England E-100	les îles Hawai	Hawaii H-60
l'Espagne	Spain S-388	lettre	letter L-83
l'Irlande	Ireland I-199	lever du soleil	sunrise S-580
l'Italie	Italy I-218, 219	libération	liberation L-88
l'un à l'autre	each other E-3	liberté	liberty L-89
l'un et l'autre	one another O-74	libre	free F-257, 258
là	there T-119, 120	lier	bind B-150
la Chine	China C-151	lier	tie T-179
la Corée	Korea K-39	ligne	line L-110
la France	France F-250	limbes	limbo L-106
la Grande-Bretagne	Britain B-247	lime	file F-121
la Hollande	Holland H-134, 135	limite	limit L-107
la Pâque (hebreue)	Passover P-48	limousine	limousine L-108
la plupart	most M-227	Lincoln	Lincoln L-109
la Pologne	Poland P-229	linge de toilette	washcloth W-28
la Russie	Russia R-288	Linotype	Linotype L-112

méditer meditate M-94
méfiance distrust D-236
meilleur better B-132
meilleur best B-128
mélancolie melancholy M-101
mélanger mix M-191
mélasse molasses M-200
mêler mingle M-167, 168
mélodie melody M-102
melon melon M-103
melon d'eau watermelon W-44
melon muscat muskmelon M-267
membre member M-105, 106
mémoire memory M-109
ménagère housekeeper H-172
mendiant panhandler P-14
mendier beg B-94, 95
mendier ask alms A-274
mener par le bout du
   nez henpeck H-93
menstruation menstruate M-113
mental mental M-115
menteur liar L-87
mentionner mention M-122
mentir lie L-94, 95
menton chin C-150
menu minute M-174
mépris scorn S-74, 75
mépris contempt C-356, 357
méprisable mean M-78
mépriser despise D-116, 117
mer sea S-100
merci thank you T-99
mercredi Wednesday W-63
mercredi des cendres Ash Wednesday A-269
mère mother M-229, 230
mérite merit M-127
mériter deserve D-113
merveille marvel M-60
merveille wonder W-162
merveilleux wonderful W-165
mesquin petty P-136
message message M-129
mesurer measure M-84
métal metal M-130, 131
méthode method M-132
méthodiste Methodist M-133
métier field F-113, 114
mettre put P-424
mettre à la poste mail M-15, 16
mettre au point focus F-187
meurtre murder M-264
mexicain Mexican M-135
micromètre micrometer M-138
midi midday M-139
midi noon N-101
mignon cute C-500, 501
milieu middle M-140
milieu midst M-142
militaire military M-153
mille mile M-151
mille thousand T-154

million million M-155
Milwaukee Milwaukee M-156
mince thin T-134, 135
mine mine M-165
mineur minor M-170
miniscule tiny T-194, 195
minuit midnight M-141
minute minute M-174
miracle miracle M-176
miroir mirror M-177
miroir looking glass L-156
miséricorde mercy M-124, 125
mission mission M-183, 184
mitrailleuse machine gun M-2
mitre mitre M-189
mode stylish S-538
modèle model M-196
modérer check C-129, 130
modeste modest M-197
modifier modify M-198
moi me M-76
moi aussi me too M-134
moi-même myself M-273
moindre less L-76
moins minus M-171, 172,
   173
mois month M-210
mois passé last month L-22
mois prochain next month N-77
moissonner reap R-47, 48, 49
moite moist M-199
moment moment M-201
mon my M-272
monde earth E-13
monde world W-174
monnaie currency C-492
monotone monotonous M-207,
   208, 209
montagne mountain M-243
monter ascend A-265
monter à cheval ride R-192
montre watch (timepiece)
   W-38, 39
montre bracelet wristwatch W-204
montrer show S-227
morceau piece P-161
mordre bite B-161
moribond dying D-341
mormon Mormon M-221
morphine morphine M-224
mort dead D-25, 26
mortel mortal M-225
mortification mortification M-226
mot word W-170
moteur motor M-241
moteur electric motor E-53
motif motive M-238, 239,
   240
motion motion M-233
motiver motivate M-236
motocyclette motorcycle M-242
mou soft S-358

O

o	oh O-52
o je vois	oh i see O-53
O.K.	O.K. O-57, 58
obéir à	mind M-162
obéissance	obedience O-4
obèse	obese O-6
objecter	object O-8, 9
objectif	objective O-12
objet	object O-10
oblation	oblation O-13
obligation	obligation O-14, 15, 16
oblige	bound B-207
obscur	obscure O-18
observation	remark R-106
observer	observe O-19, 20
observer	watch (observe) W-36, 37
obstacle	obstacle O-21
obstacle	block B-176
obstiné	obstinate O-22
obtenir	obtain O-24
obtenir	procure P-348
obtenir	get G-39
occasion	opportunity O-100, 101, 102, 103, 104
occasion	occasion O-26
occasionnel	occasional O-27
occupation	occupation O-29
occupé	busy B-277, 278
océan	ocean O-31, 32
oculiste	oculist O-34
odeur	odor O-35
odeur	scent S-62
oeil	eye E-236
oeuf	egg E-32
offrande	offering O-44, 45
offrir	offer O-42, 43
oh	oh O-52
oie	goose G-91
oignon	onion O-80, 81
oindre	anoint A-189, 190
oiseau	bird B-152
ombre	shadow S-166
omission	omission O-66, 67
oncle	uncle U-14
onde	wave W-46
ongle	fingernail F-139
ooh	wow W-198
opération	operation O-96, 97
opérer	operate O-95
opinion	opinion O-98
opportunité	opportunity O-100, 101, 102, 103, 104
opposant	opponent O-99
opposé	opposite O-106
opposer	oppose O-105
or	gold G-80
orage	storm S-501
oral	oral O-109
orange	orange O-110, 111, 112

orateur	orator O-114
orateur	speaker S-393
orbe	orb O-115
orbite	orbit O-116, 117
ordonnance	prescription P-289
ordonné	orderly O-122
ordonner	ordain O-118
ordonner	order O-119
ordonner	bid B-139, 141
ordre	order O-119
ordres sacrés	holy orders H-140
oreille	ear E-7
oreillons	mumps M-263
organisation	organization O-124, 125
orgueil	pride P-307
oriental	oriental O-126
orientation	orientation O-127
original	original O-131, 132
origine	origin O-128, 129, 130
ornement	ornament O-135, 136
orner	adorn A-94
os	bone B-192
ou	or O-107, 108
où	where W-91, 92
oublier	forget F-221, 222
ouest	west W-80
oui	yes Y-9
ours	bear B-66
ouvrez la fenêtre	open the window O-93
ouvrez la porte	open the door O-92
ouvrir	open O-88, 89

P

pagaie	paddle P-3
page	page P-4
pain	bread B-226
pair	peer P-78
paire	pair P-10
paire	yoke Y-14
paix	peace P-61
pâle	pale P-11
palper	feel F-91
palpiter	throb T-165
panier	basket B-47
panne	breakdown B-228
pantalon	trousers T-291
pantalon	pants P-15
pantoufle	slipper S-312
papa	papa P-16
papa	dad D-2
papal	papal P-17
pape	pope P-246
papier	paper P-18
papier de verre	sandpaper S-34
papillon	butterfly B-281
paquebot	steamer S-474
Pâques	Easter E-17, 18, 19
paquet	package P-2
par	by B-287

peu clair	unclear U-15	plonger	plunge P-217
peu de	few F-104	plonger	dive D-238, 239
peu importe	doesn't matter D-258	pluie	rain R-17
peu profond	shallow S-169	plume	pen P-79
peur	fear F-78, 79	pluriel	plural P-218
peut-être	perhaps P-105	plus	plus P-219
phénix	phoenix P-139	plus	more M-218
Philadelphie	Philadelphia P-137	plus loin	farther F-54
philosophie	philosophy P-138	plus tard	later L-28, 29
photocopier	photocopy P-142	plusieurs	several S-162
photographie	photograph P-143, 144, 145	plutôt	rather R-29
		pneumonie	pneumonia P-220
phrase	sentence S-149	poche	pocket P-221
phylactère	phylacteries P-147	poème	poem P-222
physique	physical P-148	poignet	wrist W-203
physique	physics P-150	point	stitch S-491
piano	piano P-152	point	period P-108
pièce	play P-203	point-virgule	semicolon S-134
pièce	room R-248, 249	pointe	point P-226
pièce de monnaie	coin C-223, 224	poire	pear P-68
pied	foot F-200	poison	poison P-227, 228
pieds	feet F-95	poisson	fish F-151, 152
piège	trap T-266	poitrine	chest C-140
pierre	stone S-494, 495	poivre	pepper P-93
pieuvre	octopus O-33	poli	polite P-237
pieux	pious P-180	police	police P-231
pigeon	pigeon P-171	polir	polish P-235
piler	pound P-268	politique	policy P-233, 234
pilote	pilot P-174	pomme	apple A-223
pilule	pill P-173	pomme de terre	potato P-265
pince à linge	clothespin C-202	pommes frites	French fried potatoes F-262
pinces	pliers P-213		
Ping-Pong	Ping-Pong P-178	pompe	pump P-400, 401
pipe	pipe P-181, 182	pompier	fireman F-148
pipe-line	pipe-fitting P-183	pont	bridge B-234, 235
pique-nique	picnic P-161, 162	pontife	pontiff P-239
piqûre	shot S-221	population	population P-247
pire	worse W-184, 185, 186	porcelaine	porcelain P-249
pistolet	pistol P-184	porcelaine	china C-152
pitié	pity P-187	port	harbor H-35
place	place P-188, 189	porte	gate G-18
place	seat S-107	porte	door D-284
placer	place P-190	porter	carry C-64, 65
placer (de l'argent)	invest I-190	porter	wear W-58
plaine	plain P-191, 192	portion	portion P-250
plaisanterie	joke J-22	(de) poser	put down P-425
plan	plan P-193, 194	poser sa candidature	
plancer	floor F-177	pour	run for office R-281
planète	planet P-198	positif	positive P-254, 255
planter	plant P-199, 200	position	position P-251, 252, 253
plat	dish D-211		
plat	flat F-160	posséder	possess P-257, 258
plat	even E-158	possibilité	possibility P-259
plateau	tray T-271	possible	possible P-260
plein	full F-288, 289	poste	mail M-15, 16
pleurer	cry C-479, 480	pot	pot P-264
pleurer	weep W-68, 69	potage	soup S-379
pleurer	mourn M-244	pouce	inch I-57, 58
plier	bend B-113	pouce	thumb T-171
plier	fold F-189	poudre	powder P-272, 273
plomb	lead L-44	poule	hen H-91
plombier	plumber P-216	poulet	chicken C-144

pouls	pulse P-399	preuve	proof P-370
poumons	lungs L-179	prévenir	forewarn F-219
poupée	doll D-261, 262	prier	ask A-271, 272, 273
pour	for F-204, 205	prier	pray P-283
pourboire	tip T-196	primaire	primary P-320
pourcent	percent P-96	prince	prince P-321
pourpre	purple P-418	princesse	princess P-322
pourquoi	why W-117	principal	principal P-323, 324
pourri	rotten R-258	principal	main M-17
pourrir	rot R-257	principal	chief C-146
pourrir	decay D-37	principe	principle P-325
poursuivre	pursue P-422	printemps	spring S-430
pourtant	nevertheless N-61	prise de courant	electric outlet E-54
pousser	impel I-33, 34	prison	prison P-329
pousser	prod P-349	prison	jail J-1
pousser	push P-423	privilège	privilege P-335
pousser	boost B-195	prix	price P-313, 314
pousser	grow G-167	prix	cost C-414
pouvoir	can C-24	prix	award A-325
pouvoir	power P-275, 276	prix	charge C-117, 118
pouvoir	may M-72, 73, 74	probable	probable P-336
pratiquer	practice P-278, 279, 280	problème	problem P-340, 341, 342
précepte	precept P-287	procession	procession P-344
prêcher	preach P-285	prochain	next N-73, 74, 75, 76
prêcher d'exemple	practice what you preach P-281	proclamer	proclaim P-345
précieux	precious P-288	produire	produce P-350, 351, 352, 353
précieux	valuable V-13	proéminent	prominent P-362, 363, 364
précis	precise P-289		
précis	just J-35, 36	profession	profession P-354, 355
prédire	predict P-290	profit	profit P-356
préférer	prefer P-291	profond	deep D-56
premier	first F-149, 150	profondeur	depth D-103
prendre sa revanche	retaliate R-170, 171	progéniture	offspring O-49
prendre	take T-9	programme	program P-357, 358
prendre soin de	care C-53, 54	progrès	progress P-359
prendre une photo	take a picture T-12	projectile	missile M-180
prendre une pilule	take a pill T-13	projet	scheme S-63
prenez garde	be careful B-80	promenade	walk W-13
préparer	prepare P-292, 293, 294	promesse	pledge P-211
		promesse	promise P-365, 366, 367
près	near N-26, 27		
près de	close C-197	promouvoir	promote P-368
près de	by B-286	pronostic	forecast F-212
presbytérien	Presbyterian P-295	prophétie	prophecy P-372
présence	presence P-291	propitiation	propitiation P-375
présent	present P-301	proportion	ratio R-30
présenter	present P-300	proportion	proportion P-376
présenter	introduce I-183	proposer	propose P-377
préserver	preserve P-302	propre	proper P-371
président	president P-303	propre	neat N-29
presque	nearly N-28	propre	clean C-185, 186
presque	about A-14	propre à soi	own O-156
presque	almost A-139	proscrire	ban B-20
presser	press P-304, 305, 306	prospérer	prosper P-378
presser	urge U-60, 61	prostituée	prostitute P-379
prêt	ready R-40, 41, 42, 43	prostituée	harlot H-43
prêter	lend L-70, 71	protéger	protect P-380
pretre	priest P-316, 317, 318, 319	protestant	Protestant P-383
prêtre	father F-68	protestation	protest P-322

prudent — careful C-58
pruneau — prune P-388
psaume — psalm P-390
psychiatre — psychiatrist P-391
psychologie — psychology P-392, P-393

public — public P-394
publier — publish P-395, 396
puce — flea F-167, 168, 169
puissance — might M-144, 146
puissant — mighty M-148
pulvériser — spray S-427
punir — punish P-407, 408, 409
punir — discipline D-193, 194, 195

pur — pure P-414, 415
purgatoire — purgatory P-416
putain — strumpet S-527
putain — whore W-114

Q

quadrant — quadrant Q-1
quaker — Quaker Q-5
quand — when W-89
quantité — quantity Q-6, 7
quart — quarter Q-9
quart d'heure — quarter hour Q-10
quatre — four F-240
quatrième — fourth F-242
que — what W-83
que — than T-96
quel age — how old H-181
quelqu'un — someone S-367
quelque temps après — after a while A-106
quelquefois — sometime(s) S-369
quelques — some S-366
querelle — quarrel Q-8
question — question Q-17
questionnaire — questionnaire Q-21
quête — quest Q-16
queue — queue Q-22
queue — line-up L-111
queue — tail T-7
qui — which W-96
qui — who W-108
quitter — quit Q-27
quoi de neuf? — what's new? W-86
quotidien — daily D-5

R

rabbin — rabbi R-1, 2
rabot — plane P-197
rabrouer — snub S-343
racheter — redeem R-71, 72
racine — root R-251
raconter — tell about T-65
radio — radio R-10, 11
radis — radish R-12

rage — rage R-13
raisin — grape G-117, 118
raison — reason R-52, 53
ramasser — pick up P-159, 160
ramasser — gather G-19, 20
ramer — row R-265
ranimer — revive R-187
rapide — rapid R-24
rapide — quick Q-23
rapide — fast F-60
rapide — swift S-639
rappel — recall R-55, 56
rappeler — remind R-108
rapports sexuels — sexual intercourse S-165

rare — scarce S-58
rare — rare R-25
rarement — seldom S-123
rasoir — razor R-33
rat — rat R-26
râteau — rake R-22
raton laveur — raccoon R-5
ravage — havoc H-59
rayé — striped S-580
rayon — ray R-32
rayon — shelf S-187
rayons x — X-ray X-3
récolte — harvest H-47, 48, 49
réaction — reaction R-35
réaliser — achieve A-52, 53
rebelle — rebel R-54
récent — recent R-58
réception — party P-38, 39, 40
recevoir — receive R-57
recherche — research R-138
recherché — far-fetched F-46
rechute — relapse R-91
récipient — container C-354
récitation — recitation R-60
recommander — advocate A-99
reconnaissant — grateful G-122
reconnaître — recognize R-64
recteur — rector R-68
réduire — restrict R-167
réduire — reduce R-74
réel — real R-44
référer — refer R-75
refuge — refuge R-77
refuser — refuse R-78
refuser — decline D-47
regarder — gaze G-25
regarder — look L-149
règlement — regulation R-83
regler — regulate R-82
regretter — regret R-79
regretter amèrement — rue R-276
régulier — regular R-81
réhabilitation — rehabilitation R-84
reine — queen Q-11
rejeter — reject R-88
rejeter — cast off C-70
relatif — relative R-96

relation	relation R-92	retarder	retard R-174
religion	religion R-100	retirer	withdraw W-151, 152, 153, 154
reluire	glisten G-57		
remettre	put off P-427	retourner	return R-180
remettre	postpone P-263	retraite	retreat R-178
remorquer	tow T-241	rétrospection	retrospection R-179
remplaçant	substitute S-548	réunion	meeting M-99, 100
remplacer	replace R-125	réussir	succeed S-561
remplir	fill F-123	rêve	dream D-303
renard	fox F-244	réveiller	arouse A-254
rencontre	meeting M-99, 100	revenant	ghost G-43
rencontrer	meet M-98	revenu	income I-65
recontrer	encounter E-82	révérence	bow B-209
rendez-vous	engagement E-98	révérend	reverend R-184
rendez-vous	appointment A-227	révérer	revere R-182, 183
rendre	render R-114, 115	rêverie	daydream D-20
rendre la pareille (à)	retaliate R-170, 171	révoquer	revoke R-188
rêne	rein R-87	revue	magazine M-7
renforcer	reinforce R-86	rhume	cold C-230
renommé	renowned R-118	ricaner	sneer S-338
renommée	fame F-36	riche	rich R-191
renoncer	renounce R-117	richesse	wealth W-56
renverser	reverse R-185, 186	rideau	curtain C-497
renverser	knock down K-32	ridicule	ridicule R-193
répandre	spread S-428, 429	rien	no N-86
réparer	mend M-110, 111	rien	nothing N-119, 120, 121, 122
réparer	repair R-120		
réparer	fix F-155	rien	naught N-18, 19, 20
repartir	apportion A-228	rigide	rigid R-202
repas	meal M-77	rire	laughter L-35, 36
repasser	iron I-202	rire	laugh L-33
répéter	repeat R-121	rivage	shore S-217
répondre	respond R-152	rival	rival R-215, 216, 217, 218
répondre	reply R-126, 127		
répondre	answer A-192, 193	rivaliser	contend C-358, 359, 360
réponse	response R-154		
repos	rest R-159, 160	rivaliser	vie V-38, 39, 40
reposer	recline R-63	riz	rice R-190
représentante	representative R-130	robe	dress D-304
représenter	represent R-129	robe	gown G-101
réprimande	reprimand R-131	robuste	hale H-10
repriser	darn D-15	robuste	sturdy S-537
républican	republican R-133	roche	rock R-235, 236
réserver	reserve R-141, 142	rocking-chair	rocking chair R-238, 239
résister	resist R-148		
résolu	strong-minded S-525	roi	king K-19
résoudre	resolve R-149	romain	Roman R-245
respecter	respect R-150	rond	round R-263, 264
respiration	respiration R-151	ronger	fret F-267
responsabilité	responsibility R-155, 156	rosaire	rosary R-254, 255
		rose	pink P-179
restant	left L-62	roue	wheel W-88
reste	rest R-161, 162	rouge	red R-69
rester	remainder R-105	rouge-gorge	robin R-234
rester	remain R-104	rougeole	measles M-83
rester	stay S-464, 465, 466, 467	rougir	flush F-182
		rougir	blush B-187
rester en arrière	fall behind F-29	rouler	roll R-242, 243
résumer	summarize S-568	route	road R-225
résumer	resume R-168	routine	grind G-159
résurrection	resurrection R-169	ruban	tape T-30
retard	delay D-74	rude	rugged R-277

son	its I-220	suffisant	swell-headed S-638
sonder	probe P-338, 339	suffisant	adequate A-79
sonner	ring R-203	suggérer	suggest S-562
sonnette	bell B-103, 104, 105	suis	am A-152, 153
sorte	kind K-16	suivre	follow F-190
sortie	exit E-207	sujet	topic T-227
sot	foolish F-199	sujet	subject S-540
sot	silly S-258	supérieur	superior S-584
sot (te)	dumb D-328	superlatif	superlative S-585
sou	penny P-91	supplication	supplication S-590
souci	concern C-298	supplier	entreat E-120
souci	worry W-181, 182, 183	supplier	beseech B-125
souffrir	suffer S-557, 558, 559	supporter	endure E-93, 94
souffrir	bear B-69	supposer	suppose S-594
souiller	soil S-361	sur	sure S-596
soûl	drunk D-319	sur	upon U-59
soulagement	relief R-99	sur	on O-68
soulier	shoe S-205, 206	sur	over O-146, 147
soupçon	suspicion S-615	surnaturel	supernatural S-586
soupçonner	suspect S-608, 609	surpasser	surpass S-600
souper	supper S-589	surprendre	surprise S-601, 602, 603
soupirer après	long L-146		
source	spring S-431	surveiller	supervise S-587
sourd	deaf D-27, 28	suspendre	suspend S-610, 611
sourire	smile S-325	svelte	slender S-305
souris	mouse M-246, 247	synonyme	synonym S-649
sournois	underhand U-18	système	system S-651
sous	under U-16, 17		
sous-vêtements	underwear U-24		
soustraire	subtract S-549		**T**
soutenir	support S-591, 592, 593		
soutenir	sustain S-616	tabac	tobacco T-206
soutenir	uphold U-56	table	table T-2, 3
soutenir	maintain M-20	tableau	picture P-163, 164
souvent	often O-51	tablier	apron A-234
spécial	special S-395	tache	stain S-444
spécialiser	specialize S-396	tâche	task T-33
spécifique	specific S-398	tailleur	tailor T-8
spectacle	show S-227	tais toi	shut up S-235, 236
spéculer	speculate S-400, 401	taler	cut-off C-502
sphère	sphere S-413	tambour	drum D-318
splendice	splendid S-418, 419, 420	tante	aunt A-311
		tape	slap S-297
stationner	park P-30	taper	type T-316
statue	statue S-462	tapisserie	upholstery U-57
statut	statute S-463	taquiner	tease T-51, 52, 53
strict	strict S-515, 516	tard	late L-26
stupéfait	dumfounded D-329, 330	tarte	pie P-165, 166
		tasse	cup C-484
stupéfiant	dope D-287	taureau	bull B-268
stupide	dull D-325	taxi	taxi T-43
stupide	stupid S-535, 536	teinture	dye D-340
subjuguer	subdue S-539	tel	such S-555
subséquent	subsequent S-543	télégramme	telegram T-57, 58
substance	substance S-545, 546	téléphone	telephone T-61, 62
substantiel	substantial S-547	téléphone	phone P-140, 141
sucre	sugar S-561	téléviseur	television T-63
sud	south S-381	témoignage	testimony T-93
suédois	Swede S-628	témoin	witness W-157
sueur	sweat S-625, 626	tempérance	temperance T-69
suffisant	sufficient S-560	température	temperature T-71
		tempéré	temperate T-70

trois fois	three times T-158	veille	eve E-157
trois semaines	three weeks T-159	vendre	sell S-132
troisième	third T-139, 140, 141	vendre	vend V-21
trombone	trombone T-289	vendredi	Friday F-268
tromper	cheat C-127, 128	vengeance	revenge R-181
tromperie	deceit D-38	venir	come C-246, 247, 248
trou	hole H-131, 132	vent	wind W-135
trouver	find F-131	vente	sale S-22
truque	fake F-24	ver	worm W-175
tu	thou T-149	verbal	verbal V-23, 24
tuer	slay S-300	verdict	verdict V-25
tuer	kill K-13	véritable	actual A-67
tuyau	pipe P-181, 182	vernis à ongles	nail polish N-3
tuyauter	tip off T-197	verre	glass G-54
		vers	toward T-242, 243, 244
U		vers	verse V-27
		verser	pour P-269
ultérieur	further F-295, 296	vert	green G-149
ultime	ultimate U-7	vertigineux	dizzy D-253
un	a A-1	veston	coat C-212
un	one O-73	vêtement	garment G-14
un autre	another A-191	vêtements	clothes C-200
une fois	once O-69	viande	meat M-85
uniforme	uniform U-30	vibration	vibration V-33
union	union U-32, 33	vice-président	vice president V-34, 35
unité	unity U-36	victoire	victory V-37, 38
universel	universal U-37	vide	void V-58
université	university U-38, 39, 40	vide	vacancy V-1
urine	urine U-62	vide	empty E-79, 80
usé	worn W-176, 177	vie	life L-98, 99
		vierge	virgin V-48
		vieux	old O-59
V		Vieux Testament	Old Testament O-62, 63, 64, 65
		vigilant	open-eyed O-90
vacances	vacation V-3	vigne	vine V-44
vacarme	racket R-9	village	village V-43
vacarme	din D-168	ville	town T-247
vaccination	vaccination V-4	ville	city C-178
vache	cow C-440	vin	wine W-137, 138
vaciller	waver W-47, 48	vinaigre	vinegar V-45
vagin	vagina V-5	violer	violate V-46
vague	vague V-6	violon	violin V-47
vain	vain V-7	violon	fiddle F-109
vaincre	defeat D-59	virgule	comma C-255
vaincre	conquer C-326	vis	screw S-91, 92
vaincre	beat B-72, 73, 74	visage	face F-3
vaincre	overcome O-149	viser	aim A-119
vaincu	beaten B-75	visible	visible V-50
vaincu	defeated D-60	vision	vision V-51, 52
valable	valid V-10	visite	visit V-53
valise	valise V-11	vital	vital V-54, 55
valise	suitcase S-565	vitesse	speed S-408
vallon	vale V-9	vivant	alive A-126
valoir	worth W-191	vivre	live L-124
vanité	vanity V-16	vocation	vocation V-56
vaniteux	conceited C-289	voeu	vow V-65
vapeur	steam S-473	voie	track T-248
varicelle	chickenpox C-145	voile	veil V-20
varié	varied V-17	voir	see S-116
variole	smallpox S-322	voisin	neighbor N-47
veau	calf C-9		

voisinage	vicinity V-36	vue	view V-42
voiture	car C-48	vue	sight S-245
voiture	carriage C-62, 63		
voix	voice V-57	**W**	
vol	theft T-107, 108, 109		
vol	robbery R-233	wagons	cars C-66
volaille	fowl F-243	Washington	Washington W-31, 32
volcan	volcano V-58	whisky	whiskey W-102, 103
voler	fly F-183, 184		
voler	steal S-469, 470, 471	**X**	
voler	rob R-227, 228, 229		
voleur	thief T-130, 131	Xerox	Xerox X-1
volley-ball	volleyball V-60	xylophone	xylophone X-4
volontaire	volunteer V-62		
volontaire	willful W-129	**Y**	
volonté	will W-127		
volume	volume V-61	y mettre son sou	chip in C-154
vomir	vomit V-63	yard	yard Y-1
voter	vote V-64	Yougoslavie	Yugoslavia Y-27
vôtre	your Y-19		
vouloir	want W-19	**Z**	
vouloir	will W-126		
vouloir dire	mean M-79	zèbre	zebra Z-3
vous	you Y-16, 17	zèle	zeal Z-1
voûte	arch A-236	zéro	zero Z-4, 5
voyage	trip T-282, 283, 284		
voyage	journey J-25, 26, 27		
voyager	travel T-268, 269, 270		
vrai	true T-292		

German-English Index

anflehen	beseech B-125	Armbanduhr	wristwatch W-204
anflehen	implore I-36	Armut	poverty P-270, 271
anfühlen	touch T-234	Art	kind K-16
anführen	cite C-176	Arznei	medicine M-93
angeben	state S-459	Arzneimittel	drug D-317
Angebot	bid B-140	Arzt	doctor D-255
Angel	hinge H-115, 116	Aschermittwoch	Ash Wednesday A-269
angenehm	pleasant P-208	Asien	asia A-270
angliedern	affiliate A-100, 101	Ast	branch B-222
angreifen	attack A-295	Atem	breath B-230
angreifen	tackle T-6	atmen	respiration R-151
Angst	anxiety A-198	ätzen	etch E-147
anhaken	hitch H-123	auch	also A-143, 144
anhängen	attach A-294	auch	too T-222
anhäufen	accumulate A-43, 44, 45	auf	upon U-56
		auf	on O-68
anheften	pin P-175	auf wiedersehen	goodbye G-87, 88
anklagen	accuse A-48, 49	aufbewahren	store S-499, 500
ankündigen	announce A-181	aufbrüllen	bawl out B-59
Ankunft	arrival A-260	aufeinanderfolgend	consecutive C-334
Anleihe	loan L-129, 130	Aufenthalt	stay S-464, 465, 466, 467
anliegend	adjacent A-80		
annehmen	adopt A-92	Auferstehung	resurrection R-169
annehmen	assume A-287	aufführen	perform P-100, 101
annehmen	accept A-32	Aufgabe	problem P-340, 341, 342
annektieren	annex A-179		
Anrede	address A-75	Aufgabe	task T-33
anschwellen	swell S-637	aufgeben	abandon A-2, 3
anständig	decent D-40	aufhalten	arrest A-258, 259
anstatt	instead of I-131, 132	aufhängen	suspend S-610, 611
ansteckend	contagious C-353	aufheben	annul A-188
anstellen	employ E-77	aufheben	cancel C-28
anstössig	obnoxious O-17	aufheben	pick up P-159
anstreichen	paint P-7	aufhören	cease C-86
Anteil	share S-176, 177	auflösen	dissolve D-230
antik	antique A-196	aufmerksam	open-eyed O-90
Antrag	motion M-233	aufnehmen	take a picture T-12
antreiben	impel I-33, 34	aufpassen	pay attention to P-60
Antwort	response R-154	aufpassen auf	mind M-161
antworten	respond R-152	aufrecht erhalten	uphold U-53
antworten	answer A-192, 193	aufrechterhalten	maintain M-19
anwerben	enlist E-108	Aufrechterhaltung	maintenance M-21
anzeigen	indicate I-74	aufregen	excite E-194
anziehen	attract A-303	aufrichtig	sincere S-266, 267
anziehend	attractive A-306	Aufruhr	turmoil T-304
Anzug	suit S-563	Aufruhr	riot R-207
anzünden	kindle K-17	aufrührerisch	revolting R-1189
Apfel	apple A-223	aufschieben	defer D-64
Apfelsine	orange O-110, 111, 112	Aufsichtsrat	board B-188
Appetit	appetite A-220	aufstehen	get up G-42
applaudieren	applaud A-221	aufstehen	arise A-246, 247
Arbeit	labor L-1	aufstehen	rise R-212, 213, 214
Arbeit	job J-16	aufstehen	stand S-449, 450, 451
Arbeit	work W-171	aufsteigen	ascend A-265
areal fläche (flaeche)	area A-242	Aufstieg	ascension A-266
ärgerlich	cross C-463	Aufwand	expense E-213
ärgern	fret F-267	aufziehen	kid K-11
ärgern	annoy A-183, 184	Auge	eye E-236
(be) argwöhen	suspect S-608	Augenarzt	oculist O-34
Arithmetik	arithmetic A-248	Augenblick	moment M-201
Arm	arm A-249	aus	out O-141, 142, 143
arm	poor P-241, 242, 243	aus	from F-200

ausbreiten	expand E-208	Bahnhof	station S-461
auslöschen	expunge E-227	Ball	ball B-17, 18
ausbessern	mend M-110, 111	Ball	orb O-113
ausbilden	educate E-24	Banane	banana B-21, 22
Ausbildung	education E-25	Band	tape T-30
ausbrechen	erupt E-139	Bande	gang G-12
ausdauern	persevere P-118, 119, 120, 121	Bandit	bandit B-25
		Bank	bench B-112
ausdehnen	extend E-229	Bankett	banquet B-29
Ausdruck	expression E-226	bankrott	bankrupt B-27
ausdrücklich	explicit E-222	bannen	ban B-20
ausdrücklich	explicit E-223	Banner	banner B-28
Ausflüchte machen	prevaricate P-309	Bär	bear B-66
Ausgang	exit E-207	Bar Mitzvah	Bar Mitzvah B-36
ausgeben	spend S-412	Barmherzigkeit	mercy M-124, 125
ausgelassen sein	frolic F-279	Bart	beard B-70, 71
ausgestorben	extinct E-231	Base	cousin C-432, 433
ausgezeichnet	excellent E-188	Baseball	baseball B-42
ausgleiten	skid S-286	Bastard	bastard B-49
ausharren	persist P-122, 123	bauen	build B-266
Auslassung	omission O-66, 67	Bauernhof	farm F-47, 48, 49
ausleeren	evacuate E-152	Baum	tree T-273
auslösen	redeem R-71, 72	Baumstamm	log L-138
ausmachen	constitute C-342	Baumwolle	cotton C-416
ausmessen	gauge G-23	beabsichtigen	intend I-148
ausnützen	take-advantage of T-10, 11	beben	quake Q-4
		bedauern	regret R-79
ausradieren	erase E-136	bedecken	cover C-434, 435, 436, 437
ausschliessen	exclude E-197		
ausser	except E-189	bedeuten	mean M-80
ausserdem	besides B-127	bedeuten	imply I-37
ausserdem	moreover M-219	bedeuten	signify S-251
Aussicht	view V-42	bedienen	wait on W-8
aussteigen	get off G-40	bedrücken	worry W-181, 182, 183
ausstellen	exhibit E-204	beeindrucken	impress I-46
ausstellung	display D-220	beenden	terminate T-83
ausstossen	expel E-211, 212	beendigen	finish F-142, 143
ausstrecken	extend E-229	befehlen	command C-256
ausstreichen	delete D-75, 76, 77	befehlen	order O-117
Austausch	trade T-250	befestigen	fortify F-232
Auster	oyster O-157	befestigen	fasten F-62
Australien	Australia A-312	befördern	forward F-234
austreiben	expel E-211, 212	befördern	convey C-383
auswählen	select S-124, 125, 126	befördern	transport T-264
ausweichen	evade E-153	beförderung	transportation T-265
ausweisen	evict E-173	befragung	quiz Q-28, 29, 30
auswendig lernen	memorize M-107, 108	befreien	deliver D-81
auswerfen	cast out C-71	befreiung	liberation L-88
authentisch	authentic A-313	befriedigen	gratify G-123, 124
Auto	automobile A-315	befühlen	feel F-91
Auto kraftwagen	car C-48	befürworten	advocate A-99
Autorität	authority A-314	begegnen	encounter E-82
Autostopp machen	hitchike H-124	begegnen	meet M-98
		Begegnung	meeting M-99, 100
		begehren	covet C-438, 439
		Begeisterung	enthusiasm E-114
	B	begierig	anxious A-199
		beginnen	commence C-258
backen	bake B-12	begleiten	accompany A-37
Bäcker	baker B-13	beglückwünschen	congratulate C-319, 320
Backofen	oven O-145		
Bad	bath B-52	begraben	bury B-274
Badezimmer	bathroom B-54		

bewundern	admire A-82, 83
bewusst	aware of A-326
bewusst	conscious C-331
bezahlen	pay P-57, 58, 59
bezaubern	fascinate F-56, 57
Bibel	Bible B-135, 136, 137
Bibliothek	library L-90
biegen	bend B-113
Biene	bee B-87
Bier	beer B-89
Bild	picture P-163, 164
Bildhauer	sculptor S-97
Bildsäule	statue S-462
billig	cheap C-125, 126
bin	am A-152, 153
binden	bind B-150
binden	tie T-179
Bindfaden	twine T-311
Birne	pear P-68
bis	till T-185
bis	until U-48
bis hierher	thus far T-175
bis zu	up to U-57
Bischof	bishop B-158, 159
bischöflich	episcopal E-127
Bischofsmütze	mitre M-189
bisher	so far S-356
bist seit	are A-240, 241
bitte	you're welcome Y-20, 21
bitte	please P-209
bitten	ask (for) A-271, 272, 273
bitter	bitter B-162
blass	pale P-11
Blatt	leaf L-46
blau	blue B-184
Blei	lead L-44
bleiben	remain R-104
bleiben	stay S-464, 465, 466, 467
Bleistift	pencil P-85
blenden	dazzle D-22
blind	blind B-174
Blitz	lightning L-102
blöde	daft D-4
blühen	bloom B-179
Blume	flower F-180
Blutegel	leech L-60
bluten	bleed B-171
Bockwurst	hotdog H-165
Boden	ground G-164
Boden	land L-11, 12
Boden	bottom B-206
Boden	dirt D-176
Boden	soil S-360
Bogen	arch A-236
Bogenschiessen	archery A-238
Bohne	bean B-64
Bohnenstange	beanpole B-65
bohren	bore B-197
bohren	drill D-306, 307

Boot	boat B-190
borgen entlehnen	borrow B-202
bös	evil E-175
böse	angry A-175
böse	wicked W-118
boxen	box B-214
braten	broil B-252
braten	fry F-287
bratkartoffeln	French fried potatoes F-262
Brauch	practice P-278, 279, 280
braun	brown B-259
brechen	break B-227
brechen	fracture F-246
breit	broad B-249
breit	wide W-119
breitschultrig	broad shouldered B-251
(ver) brennen	burn B-273
Brennpunkt	focus F-187
Brief	letter L-83
Briefmarke	stamp S-447, 448
Brille	spectacles S-399
Brille	glasses G-56
Brille	eyeglasses E-237
bringen	bring B-246
Brise	breeze B-232
Brosche	brooch B-254
Brosche	pin P-176
Broschüre	pamphlet P-12
Brot	bread B-226
Brücke	bridge B-234, 235
Bruder	brother B-256, 257
Brust	chest C-140
Buch	book B-193
Büchse	can C-25
buchstabieren	spell S-410
bügeln	iron I-201
bügeln	press P-304, 305, 306
Bühne	stage S-443
Bürger	citizen C-177
Büro	office O-46
bürsten	brush B-260, 261, 262, 263
Busch	bush B-275
Busse	penance P-83, 84
Butter	butter B-280

C

cent	cent C-92
Champion Meistersportler	champion C-106
Charakter	character C-115, 116
charakterschwach	weak-minded W-54
Chemie	chemistry C-139
Chicago	Chicago C-143
China	China C-151
Chirurg	surgeon S-598
Christ	Christian C-163

914

gehen arbeiten	function F-291	gerecht	just J-35, 36
Gehirn	brain B-221	Gerechtigkeit	justice J-38, 39
gehorchen	mind M-162	gerichtet sein	tend T-76
gehoren	belong B-106, 107	Gerichtshof	court C-427
Gehorsamkeit	obedience O-5	gering	slight S-309
Geige	fiddle F-109	Geringfügig	trifling T-277
Geige	violin V-47	geringst	least L-54
Geist	spirit S-416	gern haben	like L-103, 105
Geist	mind M-159, 160, 163	gern haben	fond F-193, 194
geistesgestört	mentally unbalanced M-117, 118, 119, 120, 121	Geruch	scent S-62
		Gesamtbetrag	total T-233
geistig	mental M-115	Gesang	chant C-111
geistlicher Stand	holy orders H-140	Geschäft	business B-276
Geizhals	tightwad T-182, 183, 184	Geschäft	shop S-215
		geschehen	happen H-31, 32
geizig	stingy S-488, 489, 490	gescheit	bright B-238, 239, 240, 241
geizig	avaricious A-318		
Gelächter	laughter L-35, 36	Geschenk	gift G-44
gelb	yellow Y-7	Geschenk	present P-300
Geld	money M-203, 204, 205	Geschichte	history H-118, 119
		Geschicklichkeit	skill S-287
Geldmittel	funds F-292	geschickt	adept A-78
Geldscheine	bills B-148, 149	geschlagen	defeated D-60
Geldstrafe	fine F-135	Geschmack	taste T-34
Geldstrafe	penalty P-80	geschwind	swift S-639
Gelegenheit	opportunity O-100, 101, 102, 103, 104	geschworen	sworn S-645
		Geschwindigkeit	speed S-408
Gelegenheit	occasion O-26	Geselligkeit	fellowship F-96
gelegentlich	once in a while O-70	Gesellschaft	company C-267
Gelehrte(r)	scholar S-64	Gesetz	law L-37
Geleise	track T-248	gesetzlich	legal L-64
geliebt	beloved B-108	Gesicht	face F-3
Geliebte	sweetheart S-633, 634	Gespenst	ghost G-43
Geliebte	lover L-170	Gespräch	conversation C-379, 380
gellen	yell Y-6		
gelten	worth W-191	Gespräch	discourse D-200
Gelübde	vow V-65	Gespräch	talk T-22, 23, 24
gemäss	according to A-41	gestern	yesterday Y-10
gemässigt	temperate T-70	gestreift	striped S-520
gemein	base B-39, 40, 41	Gesuch	plea P-206
gemein	mean M-80	Gesundheit	health H-66
Gemeinde	community C-265, 266	Getreide	grain G-108
gemeinsame Kasse	pool P-240	getrennt	apart A-207
gemischte	assorted A-286	gewähren	grant G-115, 116
genannt	named N-7	Gewand	garment G-14
genau	precise P-289	gewandt	smart S-323
genau	accurate A-46, 47	Gewehr	gun G-182
genau	exact E-176, 177	Gewehr	rifle R-195
Generation	generation G-26	Geweih	antlers A-197
geniessen	enjoy E-106	Gewinn	profit P-356
Gentleman Herr	gentleman G-32	gewinnen	gain G-4, 5
genug	enough E-110	gewinnen	win W-133, 134
genügend	adequate A-79	gewiss	certain C-98
genügend	sufficient S-560	Gewissen	conscience C-328, 329, 330
Genugtuung	satisfaction S-39		
Geometrie	geometry G-36	gewöhnen	accustom A-50
Gepäck	baggage B-11	Gewohnheit	habit H-1
Gepäck	luggage L-176	Gewohnheit	custom C-498
gerade	straight S-505	gib Acht	be careful B-80
Gerät	apparatus A-213	gierig	greedy G-145, 146, 147
geräuschlos	noiseless N-93	giessen	pour P-269
		Gift	poison P-227, 228

Giraffe	giraffe G-45	Gruppe	group G-165, 166
Gitarre	guitar G-179	Gruppe	circle C-174, 175
glänzend	bright B-238, 239, 240, 241	grüss Gott wie geht's	hello H-88, 89
		gucken	peep P-77
glänzend	splendid S-418, 419, 420	Gummi	rubber R-268, 269, 270
		Gummischuhe	overshoes O-151
Glas	glass G-54, 55	Günstling	favorite F-75, 76, 77
glatt	smooth S-330	Gusseisen	flatiron F-162
Glaube	faith F-20	gut	good G-85, 86
Glaube	belief B-101	gut	well W-76
glaubwürdig	credible C-455	gütig	kind K-15
gleich	equal E-131	gutmütig	soft-hearted S-359
gleich	alike A-125		
gleich	like L-104		
gleichförmig	uniform U-30		**H**
Gleichgewicht	balance B-14, 15		
Gleichgültigkeit	indifference I-75	Haar	hair H-3
gleiten	slide S-307, 308	Haarbürste	hairbrush H-4
glitzern	glisten G-57	Haaresbreite	hair's-breadth H-8
Glocke	bell B-103, 104, 105	Haarnadel	hairpin H-6
glücklich	happy H-34	Haarspalterei	hairsplitting H-9
Gnade	grace G-103, 104	Haarspalterei treiben	split hairs S-422
gnädige Frau	madam M-6	haben	have H-55, 56, 57
Gold	gold G-80	Hacke	hoe H-126
Golf	golf G-81	Hafen	harbor H-35
Gott	God G-75	Hafergrütze	oatmeal O-5
Gott der Herr	Lord L-159	Hagel	hail H-2
göttlich	divine D-247	Hahn	cock C-217
Götzenbild	idol I-11	Hahn	rooster R-250
Grab	grave G-125	häkeln	crochet C-460
Granate	grenade G-153	Haken	hook H-150
Gras	grass G-121	halb	half H-11, 12
grau	gray G-129, 130, 131, 132	halbe Stunde	half-hour H-13
		halber Weg	midway M-143
grausam	cruel C-475, 476, 477	halleluja	hallelujah H-15
graziös	gracious G-105	Halsband	necklace N-34
greifen	grab G-102	halt	stop S-497
grenze	limit L-107	halten	hold H-129
griechisch	grecian G-143	halten	halt H-19
Grimasse	grimace G-158	Haltung	attitude A-301
Grimassen schneiden	make a face M-24	Hamburger(am)	hamburger H-20, 21
grob	rude R-273, 274	Hammer	hammer H-22
gross	great G-135, 136	Hand	hand H-23, 24
Grösse	height H-84, 85	Handalphabet	manual alphabet M-48
gross	big B-142, 143	Handbuch	manual M-47
gross	large L-16	handeln	act A-60
gross	tall T-25, 26, 27	Handgelenk	wrist W-203
grossartig	grand G-109, 110	Handkoffer	suitcase S-65
Grossbritannien	Great Britain G-139	Handkoffer	valise V-11
Grossbritannien	Britain B-247	Handsäge	handsaw H-26
Grossmutter	grandmother G-113, 114	Handschuh	glove G-66
		Handtuch	towel T-245
Grossvater	grandfather G-111, 112	hangen	hang H-29
grosszügig	generous G-27, 28	Harfe	harp H-46
grosszügig	magnanimous M-10	Harke	rake R-22
grotesk	grotesque G-162	hart	hard H-36, 37
grübeln	speculate S-400, 401	hartherzig	hard-boiled H-38
grün	green G-149	hartnackig	stubborn S-528
gründen	found F-236	Hass	hate H-52, 53
gründen	base B-39, 40, 41	Hasslichkeit	ugliness U-1, 2, 3
Grundlage	basis B-45, 46	häufig	frequent F-264
Grünschnabel	green G-150	Hauptmann	captain C-45

hauptsächlich	main M-17	Hitze	heat H-76, 77
Hauptstadt	capital C-42	hitzkopfig	hot-headed H-167
Haus	house H-171	Hobel	plane P-197
Hausangestellte	maid M-13	hoch	high H-104, 105, 106,
Haushalterin	housekeeper H-172		107
Haut	skin S-289, 290	hochmütig	haughty H-54
Hawaii	hawaii H-60	Hochzeit	wedding W-62
hebräisch	hebrew H-80	Hof	yard Y-2
Heer	army A-251	hoffen	hope H-153
heften	baste B-50	höflich	polite P-237
Heftklammer	paper clip P-19	höflich	courteous C-428
heil	safe S-9	höher	superior S-584
heilig	holy H-136	Höhere Lehranstalt	college C-234
heilig	hallowed H-16, 17	Höhere Schule	high school H-109
Heilige (r)	saint S-15, 16	hohnlacheln	sneer S-338
Heilige Schrift	holy scriptures H-141	holen	fetch F-101
Heim	home H-142	Hölle	hell H-86, 87
Heirat	marriage M-57	Holz	wood W-167
heiss	hot H-164	Holz	lumber L-177, 178
heiss	ardent A-239	homosexuell	queer Q-13
heiter	cheerful C-135	homosexuell warmer	fairy F-19
helfen	help H-90	horch!	hark H-42
helfen	give assistance G-49	hören	hear H-68
helfen	aid A-118	Horizont	horizon H-155
Hemd	shirt S-200	Hörner	horns H-157
Hemmnis	check C-131, 132	Hosen	pants P-15
Henne	hen H-91	Hosen	trousers T-291
Herausforderung	challenge C-105	Hotel	hotel H-166
herausgeben	publish P-395, 396	hübsch	pretty P-307
Herbst	fall F-25, 26	Hufschmied	blacksmith B-166
Herbst	autumn A-316, 317	Hügel	hill H-110
hergeben	part from P-36	Hühnchen	chicken C-144
herrlich	magnificent M-12	human	humane H-185
herrlich	glorious G-63	Hummer	lobster L-132
herrlich	wonderful W-165	Humor	humor H-191
herrschen	rule R-279, 280	Hund	dog D-259, 260
herstellen	manufacture M-49	hundert	hundred H-193
herstellen	fabricate F-2	Hündin	bitch B-160
Herz	heart H-71, 72	Hungersnot	famine F-39
Herzanfall	heart attack H-73	Hungertod	starvation S-456
herzlich	cordial C-398	hüpfen	hop H-151, 152
Herzschlag	heartbeat H-74, 75	Hure	whore W-114
Heu	hay H-62	Hure	harlot H-43
Heuchler	hypocrite H-209, 210	husten	cough C-417, 418
heuchlerisch	false-faced F-34	Hut	hat H-51
heute	today T-207	Hymne	hymn H-207, 208
heute abend	tonight T-219	hysterisch	hysterical H-211
hier	here H-95		
Himmel	heaven H-78		
Himmel!	wow W-198		
Himmel	sky S-295, 296	**I**	
Himmelsraum	orbit O-114, 115		
hin und her	back and forth B-5	ich	I I-1, 2
hindern	hinder H-113	ich auch	me too M-134
Hindernis	obstacle O-21	ich selbst	myself M-273
Hindernis	block B-176	ich verstehe	oh i see O-53
hinter	behind B-98	ich verstehe	I see I-208
Hintergrund	background B-7	Idee	idea I-7
hinterher	behind time B-99	identifizieren	identify I-9
Hinterseite	rear R-52	identisch	identical I-8
hinzufügen	add A-70, 71, 72, 73	ignorieren	ignore I-14
Hirsch	deer D-57	ihr	her H-94
		Ihr	your Y-19

Kunsttischler	cabinetmaker C-2	leichtsinnig	frivolous F-275
Kürbis	squash S-439	leiden	suffer S-557, 558, 559
Kürbis	pumpkin P-402, 403	Leidenschaft	passion P-45, 46
kurz	short S-218, 219	leidlich	fair F-17
kurz	brief B-236, 237	leihen	lend L-70, 71
kurz danach	after a while A-106	Leim	glue G-67
Kuss	kiss K-21, 22, 23	leisten	perform P-100, 101
Kuste	coast C-211	leiten	conduct C-304, 305
		leiten	direct D-172, 173
		Leiter	ladder L-5
L		Leiter	superintendant S-583
		Leopard	leopard L-73
lächeln	smile S-325	Lepra	leprosy L-74
lachen	laugh L-33	lernen	learn L-52
lächerliches	ridicule R-193	lesen	read R-36, 37, 38
Laden	store S-498	letzt	last L-17, 18
Lage	location L-133	letzt	ultimate U-7
Lager	camp C-23	Leute	people P-92
lahm	lame L-10	Licht	light L-100
Lamm	lamb L-9	lieb	dear D-30
Land	land L-11, 12	Liebe	love L-169
Land	country C-423, 424	liebenswürdig	amiable A-161
Landkarte	map M-51	Liebkosen	petting P-135
Landspitze	point P-226	Lied	song S-371
lang	long L-145	liefern	deliver D-81
lange Liste	long list L-148	Limousine	limousine L-108
langsam	slow S-314	Lincoln	Lincoln L-109
langweilen	bore B-196	Linie	line L-110
langweilig	boring B-198	linke	left L-61
langweilig	tedious T-54	Lippenstift	lipstick L-115
Lärm	din D-168	Liste	list L-119, 120
Lärm	noise N-92	listig	cunning C-483
Lärm	racket R-9	Lizenz	license L-91, 92
lassen	let L-78	Lob	praise P-282
lastern	blaspheme B-168, 169, 170	loben	commend C-259
		Loch	hole H-131, 132
Latein	Latin L-31, 32	locker	loose L-157
laufen	run R-281, 282	lockern	relax R-97, 98
laut	loud L-165	Löffel	spoon S-425
laut	sound S-378	Logik	logic L-139
leben	live L-124	lohfarben	tan T-29
Leben	life L-98, 99	Lohn	wage(s) W-2
lebendig	alive A-126	Lokomotive	locomotive L-137
Lebensmittel	groceries G-161	Lord	lord L-158
lebenswichtig	vital V-54, 55	Los Angeles	Los Angeles L-160
Leber	liver L-126	Lossprechung	absolution A-25, 26
lebewohl	farewell F-44, 45	Löwe	lion L-113
lecken	leak L-48	Luft	air A-120
leer	empty E-79, 80	Lüge	fib F-107
leer	void V-58	lügen	lie L-94, 95
Leere	vacancy V-1	Lügner	liar L-87
lehnen	recline R-63	Lüngen	lungs L-179
Lehrbuch	textbook T-95	Lungenentzündung	pneumonia P-220
Lehre	lesson L-77	lustig	jolly J-23
Lehre	doctrine D-256, 257	lustig	gay G-24
lehren	teach T-46	Luther	Luther L-181
Leibesübung	exercise E-201		
Leibwasche	underwear U-24		
Leichenbegängnis	funeral F-293	**M**	
leicht	easy E-20, 21		
leicht	light L-101	mach das nicht	do not D-269, 270
leichtgläubig	gullible G-180	mach die Tur auf	open the door O-92

machen	make M-23	Melone	melon M-103
Macht	might M-144, 146	Menge	crowd C-468
Macht	power P-274, 275	Menschenraub	kidnap K-12
macht nichts	make no difference M-33	Menschheit	humanity H-186
		menschlich	human H-184
macht nichts	doesn't matter D-258	menstruieren	menstruate M-113
machtig	mighty M-148	messen	measure M-84
Mädchen	girl G-46	Messer	knife K-27, 28, 29
mager	skinny S-291	Metall	metal M-130, 131
mager	lean L-49, 50	Methode	method M-132
magisch	magic M-8	Methodist	Methodist M-133
Magnet	magnet M-11	mexikanisch	Mexican M-135
mähen	mow M-252, 253	mich	me M-76
Mahl	meal M-77	mich anekeln	make disgusted M-31
Mais	corn C-401	Mikrometer	micrometer M-138
Majestät	majesty M-22	Milch	milk M-154
malen	paint P-7	mild	mild M-150
Mama	mama M-39	militarisch	military M-153
manchmal	sometime(s) S-369	Milliarde	billion B-147
Mangel	lack L-3	Million	million M-155
Mangel	dearth D-32	Milwaukee	Milwaukee M-156
Mangel	deficiency D-65	minderjährig	minor M-170
mangeln	fail F-11, 12, 13	minus	less L-75, 76
Mann	husband H-204	Minute	minute M-174
Mann	male M-38	mischen	mingle M-167, 168
Mantel	overcoat O-148	mischen	mix M-191
Mantel	cloak C-195	Mission	mission M-183, 184
Märchen	fable F-1	misstrauen	distrust D-236
markieren	mark M-56	missverstehen	misunderstand M-188
Marmelade	jam J-2	mit	with W-150
marschieren	parade P-23, 24	mit aufgesperrtem	
marschieren	march M-54, 55	Munde	open-mouthed O-91
martern	torment T-229	mit der Post schicken	mail M-15, 16
Martyrer	martyr M-59	mit Muskelkater	muscle-bound M-265
Maschine	machine M-1	Mitglied	member M-105, 106
Maschine	engine E-99	Mitleid	pity P-187
Maschinen	machinery M-3	Mitleid	sympathy S-647
Maschinengewehr	machine gun M-2	Mitleid	compassion C-269
Masern	measles M-83	Mittag	noon N-101
Massigkeit	temperance T-69	Mittag	midday M-139
Mathematik	mathematics M-68	Mitte	middle M-140
Matrose	sailor S-13, 14	Mitte	midst M-142
Mauer	wall W-14, 15	mitteilen	communicate C-260
Maulschelle	slap S-297	Mitteilung	communication C-261
Maultier	mule M-258	Mitteilung	message M-129
Maus	mouse M-246, 247	mittelmassig	medium M-96
Mechaniker	mechanic M-86, 87	Mittelwert	median M-92
Meeresküste	seaside S-105	mitten in	amid A-162
Mehl	flour F-178, 179	Mitternacht	midnight M-141
mehr	more M-218	Mittwoch	Wednesday W-63
mehrere	several S-162	modisch	stylish S-538
meiden	shun S-233	Modell	model M-196
Meile	mile M-151	modifizieren	modify M-198
mein	my M-272	modisch	elegant E-58
Meinung	opinion O-98	modisch	fashionable F-59
meisseln	sculpt S-96	mögen	may M-72, 73, 74
meisseln	chisel C-155	möglich	possible P-260
melancholisch	melancholy M-101	Möglichkeit	possibility P-259
Melasse	molasses M-200	Möglichkeit	opportunity O-100, 101, 102, 103, 104
melden	notify N-124, 125		
Melodie	melody M-102	Monat	month M-210
Melone	muskmelon M-267	Mond	moon M-214, 215

monoton	monotonous M-207, 208, 209
Montag	Monday M-202
Mop	mop M-217
Mord	murder M-264
Morgen	morning M-222
Morgen	tomorrow T-217
Mormon	Mormon M-221
Morphium	morphine M-224
Mortifikation	mortification M-226
motivieren	motivate M-236
Motor	motor M-241
Motorrad	motorcycle M-242
müde	weary W-60
Mühe	effort E-29, 30, 31
multiplizieren	multiply M-261, 262
Mund	mouth M-248
Mund halten	shut up S-235, 236
mündlich	oral O-109
Münze	coin C-223, 224
mürrisch	grouchy G-163
Musik	music M-266
Müsse	leisure L-66
müssen	must M-268
müssen	have to H-58
müssig	idle I-10
Muster	sample S-31
Mut	courage C-425
Mutter	mother M-229, 230
Mütze	cap C-39

N

nach	after A-104, 105
nachahmen	mimic M-158
nachahmen	imitate I-23
Nachbar	neighbor N-47
nachdenken	meditate M-94
Nachdruck	emphasis E-74
nachgeben	give up G-52
nachgeben	yield Y-13
nachhelfen	boost B-195
Nachkomme	descendant D-106
Nachkömmling	offspring O-49
nachlässig	careless C-59
Nachmittag	afternoon A-107
Nachsicht	indulgence I-87
nächste Woche	next week N-78, 79
nächsten Monat	next month N-77
Nächstenliebe	charity C-120
nächstes Jahr	next year N-80
Nacht	night N-83
nackt	naked N-5
nackt	nude N-131
nackt	bare B-33, 34
Nadel	needle N-40
nagel	nail N-2
Nagellack	nail polish N-3
nähe	near N-26, 27
nähe	close (to) C-198
nähe	by B-286

Nähe	vicinity V-36
nähen	sew S-163
Nährung	food F-195, 196
naiv	naive N-4
Name	name N-6
narr	silly S-258
narren	fool F-197, 198
närrisch	foolish F-199
Nase	nose N-110
nass	wet W-81
Nation	nation N-16
natürlich	natural N-17
Nazi	Nazi N-25
neben	beside B-126
nebeneinander	side by side S-243
necken	tease T-51, 52, 53
Neffe	nephew N-50
negativ	negative N-42
Neger	Negro N-45, 46
nehmen	take T-9
neidisch	envious E-121
neigen	stoop (ed) S-496
Neigung	inclination I-60
nein	no N-87
Nerv	nerve N-51
Nervenzusammenbruch	mental breakdown M-116
nervös	nervous N-52
Nest	nest N-55
nett	nice N-81
neu	new N-62
neu	recent R-58
Neu York	New York N-72
Neues England	New England N-63
neugierig	nosy N-111, 112, 113
neugierig	curious C-487, 488, 489
Neuheit	novelty N-129
Neuigkeiten	tidings T-178
Neujahr	New Year N-71
neun	nine N-84
Neutral	neutral N-58
New Jersey	New Jersey N-64
New Orleans	New Orleans N-65
nicht	not N-114, 115
nicht beachten	disregard D-226
nicht bedürfen	don t want D-283
nicht bessern	not improve N-126
nicht daran kümmern	don't care D-274, 275, 276
nicht fertig	not done N-117
nicht gehorchen	disobey D-217
nicht glauben	don t believe D-273
nicht können	cannot C-35, 36
nicht mögen	don't care for D-277
nicht teuer	inexpensive I-89
nicht wissen	don't know D-279
Nichte	niece N-82
Nichtjüdisch	gentile G-29
Nichts	limbo L-106
nichts	nothing N-119, 120, 121, 122

nichts wissen	know nothing K-38	Onkel	uncle U-14
nichtsdestoweniger	nevertheless N-61	Operation	surgery S-599
nicken	nod N-89	Operation	operation O-96, 97
nie wieder	never again N-60	Opernglas	opera glasses O-94
niedergehen	descend D-104, 105	Opfer	oblation O-13
niedergeschlagen	depressed D-102	Opfer	sacrifice S-6
niedergeschlagen	dejected D-73	orange	orange O-110, 111, 112
Niederlande	Holland H-134, 135	Orden	medal M-89
Niederlande die	Netherlands N-56, 57	ordentlich	neat N-29
Niederländisch	Dutch D-335, 336	ordentlich	orderly O-122
niederschlagen	knock down K-32	ordinieren	ordain O-118
niedlich	cute C-500, 501	Ordnung	order O-119
niedrig	low L-171, 172	Organisation	organization O-124, 125
niemals	never N-59		
niessen	sneeze S-339	orientalisch	oriental O-126
noch	still S-486	Orientierung	orientation O-127
noch	yet Y-11, 12	Osten	east E-16
noch	nor N-102	Ostern	Easter E-17, 18, 19
noch nicht	not yet N-128	Ozean	ocean O-31, 32
Nonne	nun N-135		
nord	north N-104		
NordAmerika	North America N-105		
nordost	northeast N-106	**P**	
nordwest	northwest N-107		
nörgeln	kick K-8	Paar	pair P-10
nörgeln	nag N-1	Päckchen	package P-2
normal	normal N-103	Paddel	paddle P-3
Norwegen	Norway N-108	Pair	peer P-78
Not	need N-37, 38, 39	Panne	breakdown B-228
notbehelf	makeshift M-35	Pantoffel	slipper S-312
notieren	note N-119	Pantoffelheld	henpeck H-93
notwendig	necessary N-30, 31	Papa	dad D-2
null	naught N-18, 19, 20	Papier	paper P-18
null	zero Z-4, 5	Papst	pontiff P-246
Nummer	number N-132, 133	päpstlich	papal P-17
nun	now N-130	Parade	parade P-23, 24
Nuss	nut N-137	Paragraph	paragraph P-25
nutzen	benefit B-118, 119	parallel	parallel P-26
		Parfum	perfume P-104
		parken	park P-30
O		Passahfest	passover P-48
		passend	suitable S-564
		Pastor	pastor P-50
O.K.	O.K. O-57, 58	Pate	godfather G-76
ob	whether W-94	Pater	father F-66, 67
oben	up U-52	Patin	godmother G-77
oben	above A-16	Pedal	pedal P-72
oberer Teil	top T-226	Peitsche	whip W-101
obgleich	although A-149	Penis	penis P-88
Obst	fruit F-285	Penny	penny P-91
oder	or O-107, 108	Periode	period P-108
öffentlich	public P-394	Person	person P-124
Offizier	officer O-48	Persönlichkeit	personality P-125
öffne das Fenster	open the window O-93	Pest	pest P-133
öffnen	open O-88, 89	Pfad	path P-51
oft	often O-51	Pfad	trail T-255
ohne	minus M-171, 172, 173	Pfadfinder	Boy Scout B-217
ohnmachtig werden	pass out P-47	Pfand	pledge P-211
Ohr	ear E-7	Pfannkuchen	pancake P-13
ohrenschmerz	earache E-8	Pfannkuchen	doughnut D-293
Ohrring	earring E-12	Pfarrer	minister M-169
Öl	oil O-55	Pfeffer	pepper P-93
ölen	oil O-54	Pfeife	pipe P-181, 182

Rasiermesser	razor R-33	Religion	religion R-100
rastlos	restless R-165	reparieren	repair R-120
Rat	advice A-97	Repräsentant	representative R-130
raten	counsel C-420	Republikaner	republican R-133
raten	guess G-172, 173, 174, 175	reservieren	reserve R-141
		reservieren	reserve R-142
Ratte	rat R-26	Rest	remainder R-105
Raub	robbery R-233	Rest	rest R-161, 162
rauben	rob R-227, 228, 229	retten	rescue R-137
Rauch	smoke S-326, 327	retten	save S-45
rauchen	smoke S-328, 329	Rettich	radish R-12
rauh	rough R-259, 260, 261	reuen	rue R-276
rauh	rugged R-277	reuig	penitent P-89
Raum	space S-385	Revanche	revenge R-177
Rauschgift	narcotic N-10	Rezept	prescription P-296
Rauschgift	dope D-287	Rezitation	recitation R-60
Rebell	rebel R-54	richten	judge J-30
rechnen	reckon R-62	richtig	proper P-371
rechnen	figure F-119	richtig	right R-198
rechts	right R-196	richtig	correct C-408, 409
Rechtsanwalt	lawyer L-39	Richtung	direction D-174, 175
Rechtsanwalt	attorney A-302	riechen	smell S-324
rechtschaffen	righteous R-200	riesig	huge H-183
Rechtsgrundsatz	rule R-279, 280	Rindfleisch	beef B-81
Rede	speech S-404, 405	Ring	ring R-203
Rede halten	orate O-113	ringen	contend C-358, 359, 360
reden	talk T-22, 23, 24		
redlich	fair F-18	Ringkampf	wrestling W-202
Redner	orator O-114	Rivale	rival R-215, 216, 217, 218
Regal	shelf S-187		
regelmässig	regular R-81	Rock	skirt S-292, 293
regeln	regulate R-82	Rock	coat C-212
regen	rain R-17	Röhre	pipe P-181, 182
Regenschauer	shower S-229	Rohrlegen	pipe-fitting P-183
Regenschirm	umbrella U-9	rollen	roll R-242, 243
regieren	govern G-98	Rollschuh fahren	roller skating R-244
Regierung	government G-99	Römer	Roman R-245
Regulierung	regulations R-83	Röntgenstrahl	X-ray X-3
Rehabilitierung	rehabilitation R-84	rosa	pink P-179
reiben	rub R-267	Rosenkranz	rosary R-254, 255
reich	rich R-191	Rostbrot	toast T-204
reichlich	ample A-167	rot	red R-69
Reichtum	wealth W-56	Rotkehlchen	robin R-234
reif	ripe R-210	Rückblick	retrospection R-179
reif	mature M-70	Rücken	back B-3
Reihe	line-up L-111	Rückfall	relapse R-91
Reihe	series S-154	Rückwirkung	reaction R-35
rein	pure P-414, 415	Rückzug	retreat R-178
rein	clean C-185, 186	rudern	row R-265
Reis	rice R-190	rufen	call C-12, 13
Reise	journey J-25, 26, 27	ruhe	be quiet B-122, 123
Reise	trip T-282, 283, 284	ruhe	rest R-159, 160
reisen	travel T-268, 269, 270	ruhig	calm C-16, 17
reissen	tear T-48	Ruhm	fame F-36
reissen	rip R-208, 209	Ruhm	glory G-64, 65
(zer) reissen	rend R-113	Rührung	emotion E-71, 72
reiten	ride R-192	ruinieren	ruin R-278
reizbar	irritable I-203	rülpsen	belch B-100
reizlos	homely H-143, 144	rund	round R-263, 264
Rektor	rector R-68	Rundfunkgerät	radio R-10, 11
relativ	relative R-96		

Russland	Russia R-288	Schaufel	shovel S-226
Rute	rod R-241	Schaukelstuhl	rocking chair R-238, 239

S

		Schauspiel	play P-203
		Schauspiel	show S-228
		Schauspiel	drama D-297
Sabbat	Sabbath S-2, 3, 4	Schauspieler	actor A-65
säen	seed S-117, 118, 119	Schauspielerin	actress A-66
säen	sow S-384	Scheck	check C-131, 132
Säge	jig saw J-15	Scheide	vagina V-5
sage mir	tell me T-66	Scheidung	divorce D-249, 250, 251
Sägemühle	saw mill S-51		
sägen	saw S-49, 50	scheinbar	apparent A-214
sagen	say S-52	scheinen	appear A-216
sagen	tell T-64	scheinen	seem S-121
sagen Sie nicht	don't tell D-282	scheinen	shine S-194
Sahne	cream C-452	scheinen	look L-150
Saison	season S-106	schelten	snub S-343
Sakrament	sacrament S-5	Schema	scheme S-63
Sakrileg	sacrilegious S-7	Schere	scissors S-68
Salat	salad S-20	Scherz	joke J-22
Salat	lettuce L-84, 85	schieben	push P-423
salben	anoint A-189, 190	Schiedsrichter	referee R-76
Salz	salt S-24, 25	Schiedsrichter	umpire U-10
Salzgurke	pickle P-156	schiessen	shoot S-212, 213
Salzkeks	cracker C-445, 446	Schiff	ship S-197
Same	seed (n) S-117, 118, 119	Schild	shield S-191, 193
		Schildkröte	turtle T-307
sammeln	collect C-233	Schildkröte	tortoise T-231
sammeln	gather G-19, 20	Schlacht	battle B-56
Samstag	Saturday S-43	Schlaf	sleep S-301, 302
San Franzisko	San Francisco S-36	Schläfchen	nap N-8
Sandalen	sandals S-33	schlafen	sleep S-303
Sandpapier	sandpaper S-35	schlafen	asleep A-275
Sandwich	sandwich S-35	schläfrig sein	sleepy S-304
sanft	meek M-97	Schlag	smack S-318
sanft	gentle G-31	Schlag	punch P-404, 405
Satan	Satan S-37	Schlag	blow B-182
Satellit	satellite S-38	schlagen	beat B-72, 73, 74
Satz	sentence S-149	schlagen	rap R-23
sauer	sour S-380	schlagen	hit H-120, 121, 122
sauer	tart T-32	schlagen	strike S-517
Säugling	infant I-90	schlagen	swipe S-643
Säure	acid A-54	Schläger	batter B-55
schaben	scrape S-89	Schlagholz	bat B-51
Schachtel	box B-213	schlammig	muddy M-256
schaden	harm H-44, 45	Schlange	snake S-331, 332, 333, 334, 335, 336
schaden	hurt H-200, 201, 202, 203		
		Schlange	queue Q-22
Schaf	sheep S-186	schlank	slender S-305
(er) schaffen	create C-453	schlau	sly S-315, 316, 317
Schaffott	scaffold S-53	schlau	shrewd S-232
schälen	peel P-75, 76	schlecht	bad B-9, 10
schälen	pare P-29	schlecht gelaunt	ill temper I-17
Scham	shame S-170, 171	schlechte Zeiten	hard times H-41
scharf	sharp S-178, 179, 180, 181	schlechter	worse W-184, 185, 186
		schleichen	sneak S-337
Schatten	shadow S-166	Schleier	veil V-20
schätzen	rate R-28	Schleife	bow B-208
schätzen	estimate E-145	schleppen	tow T-241
Schatzmeister	treasurer T-272	schliessen	conclude C-301
schauen	look at L-151	schliessen	close C-197

German	English
schliessen	shut S-234
schliesslich	eventually E-162
Schlips	bow tie B-212
Schlittschuh laufen	skate S-281
Schlittschuhlaufen	ice-skating I-6
Schloss	lock L-134, 135
schlummern	doze D-295
Schlüssel	key K-6
Schmarotzer	parasite P-27
schmeicheln	flatter F-163, 164
schmelzen	melt M-104
Schmerz	pain P-5
Schmerz	ache A-51
schmerzen	hurt H-200, 201, 202, 203
Schmetterling	butterfly B-281
Schmiere	grease G-133
schminken	make-up M-36
Schmuck	ornament O-135, 136
schmücken	trim T-279, 280
schmutzig	nasty N-15
schmutzig	foul F-235
schmutzig	dirty D-177
Schnabel	beak B-63
Schnee	snow S-342
schneiden	reap R-47, 48, 49
schneiden	cut C-499
Schneider	tailor T-8
Schneiderin	dressmaker D-305
schnell	fast F-60
schnell	rapid R-24
schnell	quick Q-23
Schnitte	slice S-306
schnitzen	carve C-68
Schnur	cord C-397
Schnur	string S-519
Schnürsenkel	shoelace S-208
schockert	shocked S-203, 204
Schokolade	chocolate C-156
schön	handsome H-28
schön	beautiful B-77
Schönheitssalon	beauty parlor B-79
Schotte	soot S-76, 77, 78
Schraube	screw S-91, 92
Schraubenschlüssel	wrench W-201
Schraubenzieher	screwdriver S-93, 94
Schreck	fright F-272
schrecken	terror T-85, 86
schrecklich	terrible T-84
schreiben	write W-205
schreien	cry C-481
schreien	shout S-225
schreien	scream S-90
Schritt	pace P-1
Schritt	step S-478, 479, 480
Schublade	drawer D-300
Schüchtern	bashful B-43
Schüchtern	shy S-237, 238
Schuh	shoe S-205, 206
Schuh putzen	shine shoes S-195
Schuhmacher	shoemaker S-209
Schuhmacher	cobbler C-214
Schuld	fault F-72, 73
Schuld	obligation O-14, 15, 16
schulden	owe O-154
Schulden	arrears A-257
schuldig	guilty G-177, 178
Schule	school S-65
schulen	indoctrinate I-81
schulen	drill D-308
Schüler	pupil P-410, 411, 412
Schunbürste	shoebrush S-207
Schuppe	scale S-54, 55, 56
Schur	shears S-184, 185
Schürze	apron A-234
Schuss	shot S-222
Schüssel	bowl B-211
schütteln	shake S-167
Schutzbrille	goggles G-79
schützen	protect P-380
schwach	frail F-248
schwach	feeble F-86
schwach	weak W-53
schwachsinnig	feeble-minded F-87
Schwachsinniger	moron M-223
Schwamm	sponge S-424
Schwan	swan S-620
schwangern	impregnate I-45
schwanken	waver W-47, 48
Schwanz	tail T-7
schwarz	black B-164
schwatzen	tattle T-35, 36
Schwede	Swede S-628
schweigen	keep quiet K-2, 3
Schwein	hog H-127, 128
Schwein	pig P-169, 170
Schweiss	sweat S-625, 626
schwenken	wave W-46
schwer	difficult D-159, 160, 161
schwer	grave G-126
schwer	hard H-36, 37
schwer	heavy H-79
schwere Arbeit	toil T-210
schwerhörig	hard-of-hearing H-39
Schwert	sword S-644
Schwester	sister S-272, 273
schwimmen	swim S-640
schwimmen	float F-175
schwind(e)lig	dizzy D-252, 253
schwindel	humbug H-190
schwinden	vanish V-15
Schwindler	crook C-461
schwingen	swing S-642
Schwingung	vibration V-33
schwören	swear S-624
(be) schwören	take oath T-18
sechs	six S-279
See	sea S-100
See	lake L-8
Seele	soul S-377
Seelenfrieden	peace of mind P-62
seelische Stärke	fortitude F-233
Seemann	seaman S-103

spähen pry P-389
spähen peek P-73, 74
Spanien Spain S-388
Spannung stress S-513
sparen save S-45
spät late L-26
spät tardy T-31
Spaten spade S-386
später later L-28, 29
später by and by B-288
Spaziergang walk W-13
speisen dine D-169
speisen feed F-88, 89
spezialisieren specialize S-396
spezifisch specific S-398
Sphäre sphere S-413
Spiegel mirror M-177
Spiegel looking glass L-156
Spiel game G-11
spielen gamble G-10
spielen act A-60
spielen play P-202
Spielkarte playing cards P-205
Spinne spider S-414
spinnen spin S-415
Spion spy S-433, 434, 435
Spitze point P-224
Spitze peak P-66
spleisen splice S-421
spotten mock M-195
Sprache language L-13, 14
Sprache speech S-404, 405
sprachlos speechless S-406
sprechen speak S-392
Sprecher(in) speaker S-393
sprengen explode E-224
Springbrunnen fountain F-239
springen jump J-33, 34
springen leap L-51
spritzen sprinkle S-432
Spruch verdict V-25
Sprühregen spray S-427
Sprung crack C-443
spucken expectorate E-210
spucken spit S-417
Spur track T-249
Stadt town T-247
Stadt city C-178
Stahl steel S-476
Stamm stem S-477
Strange perch P-98
stark stout S-504
stark strong S-523, 524
starren gaze G-25
Statut statute S-463
stechen engrave E-103
Steckdose electric outlet E-54
stecken stuck S-529, 530
stehen stand 449, 450, 451
stehlen steal S-469, 470, 471
steif rigid R-202
Stein stone S-494, 495

stellen put P-424
stellen place P-190
Stellung position P-251, 252, 253
Stellvertreter substitute S-548
sterben die D-152, 153
sterbend dying D-341
sterblich mortal M-225
Stern star S-454
Steuer tax T-39, 40
Stich stitch S-491
Stiefmutter stepmother S-482
Stiefvater stepfather S-481
Stier bull B-268
still hush H-205
still quiet Q-25, 26
Stille silence S-255, 256
stille still S-487
Stimme voice V-57
stimmen vote V-64
stirnrunzeln frown F-282
Stock stick S-484
Stock story S-503
Stoff matter M-69
Stolz pride P-315
stolz proud P-384
stopfen darn D-15
stören disturb D-237
stören bother B-204, 205
stören trouble T-290
Stoss prod P-349
Stoss jolt J-24
stossen kick K-7
Strafe penalty P-82, 83
strafen punish P-407, 408, 409
Strahl ray R-32
strampeln scramble S-88
stranden stranded S-506
Strasse street S-511
Strasse road R-225
Strassenbahnwagen trolley car T-287, 288
streben aspire A-276
streben endeavor E-88
streicheln stroke S-522
Streichholz match M-67
Streik strike S-517
streiten argue A-243
Streitfrage controversy C-376
streng strict S-515, 516
Strichpunkt semicolon S-134
stricken knit K-30
Strom current C-493
Strumpf hose H-160, 161
Strumpf stocking S-492, 493
Stück piece P-167
Student student S-531, 532
Studium study S-533
Stufe step S-478, 479, 480
Stuhl chair C-101, 102, 103
Stuhl feces F-83
Stuhlgang haben defecate D-61
stumm dumb D-328

stumm	mute M-269	Teller	plate P-201
stumpf	thick-skulled T-129	Teller	dish D-211
Stunde	hour H-170	Tempel	temple T-72
Sturm	storm S-501	Temperatur	temperature T-71
Sturm	gale G-6	Tennis	tennis T-81
stützen	sustain S-616	Testament	testament T-90, 91, 92
Substanz	substance S-545, 546	teuer	dear D-31
subtrahieren	subtract S-549	teuer	costly C-415
Suche	quest Q-16	teuer	expensive E-214
suchen	seek S-120	Teufel	devil D-138
suchen	look for L-155	Theater	theatre T-105
Südamerika	South America S-382, 383	Thema	theme T-112
		Theorie	theory T-118
Süden	south S-381	Thermometer	thermometer T-124
Summe	sum S-567	tief	deep D-56
Sünde	sin S-264	Tiefe	depth D-103
sündigen	offend O-43	Tier	animal A-177, 178
superlatif	superlative S-585	Tiger	tiger T-181
Suppe	soup S-379	Tinte	ink I-111, 112
süss	sweet S-632	Tintenfisch	octopus O-33
Süssigkeiten	candy C-31, 32	tippen	type T-316
Synonym	synonym S-649	Tisch	table T-2, 3
System	system S-651	Tischtennis	Ping-Pong P-178
Szene	scene S-61	Tischtuch	tablecloth T-5
		Titel	title T-201
		Tochter	daughter D-16
	T	Toilette	toilet T-211
		tollkühn	reckless R-61
Tabak	tobacco T-206	Tomate	tomato T-215, 216
Tablett	tray T-271	Ton	clay C-184
Tadel	reprimand R-131	Topf	pot P-264
tadeln	scold S-69, 70, 71, 72	Tor	gate G-18
tadeln	blame B-167	Torheit	folly F-192
tadeln	find fault F-132, 133	Tornado	tornado T-230
Tag	day D-17	torte	pie P-165, 166
täglich	daily D-5	tot	dead D-25, 26
Tal	vale V-9	töten	kill K-13
Tante	aunt A-311	Tradition	tradition T-251
tanzen	dance D-8	tragen	wear W-58
tapfer	brave B-223	tragen	carry C-64, 65
Tasche	pocket P-221	Träne	tear T-49
Taschenlampe	flashlight F-159	Trauerspiel	tragedy T-253
Taschentuch	handkerchief H-25	trauervoll	mournful M-245
Tasse	cup C-484	Traum	dream D-303
Tat	deed D-55	Träumerei	daydream D-20
taub	deaf D-27, 28	traurig	sad S-8
Taube	pigeon P-171	traurig	sorrowful S-374
tauchen	dive D-238, 239	trennen	separate S-150, 151
Taufe	baptism B-30	trennen	part P-32, 33, 34, 35
Täufer	Baptist B-31	trennen	disjoin D-214
täuschen	bluff B-185	Treppe	stair(s) S-445, 446
Täuschung	deceit D-38	treu	loyal L-175
tausend	thousand T-154	treu	faithful F-21, 22, 23
Taxi	taxi T-43	Treue	fidelity F-110
Tee	tea T-44, 45	triftig	valid V-10
Teil	part P-32, 33, 34, 35	Trigonometrie	trigonometry T-278
Teil	portion P-250	trinken	drink D-309, 310
teilen	share S-176, 177	Trinkgeld	tip T-196
teilen	divide D-244, 245	Trinkspruch	toast T-205
teilnehmen	participate P-376	Triumph	triumph T-285, 286
Telephon	phone P-140, 141	trocken	dry D-322
Telephon	telephone T-61, 62	trocken	arid A-245

Trockenheit	drought D-314	um Rat fragen	consult C-347
Trommel	drum D-318	umarmen	embrace E-70
tropfen	drip D-311	umarmen	hug H-182
trösten	console C-341	umgeben	surround S-606
trotz	despite D-118	Umgebung	environment E-122,
trotz	in spite of I-129		123
Trübsinn	gloom G-60	umherstreifen	roam R-226
Truthahn	turkey T-301, 302	umherstreuen	clutter C-209
tue was du empfehlst	practice what you	Umkehrung	reverse R-185, 186
	preach P-281	umkommen	perish P-109, 110
tuen Sie es nicht	do not D-269, 270	unabhängigkeit	independence I-70
tun	do D-254	unartig	naughty N-21
Tür	door D-284	unaufhörlich	perpetual P-116
Türklingel	doorbell D-285	unbefleckt	immaculate I-24
Turm	tower T-246	unbefleckte	
Turnhalle	gym G-183	Empfängnis	Immaculate Conception
			I-25

U

Übelkeit	nausea N-22	unbescheiden	immodest I-29
üben	practice P-278, 279,	unbeständig	changeable C-110
	280	unbestimmt	vague V-6
über	over O-146, 147	unbrauchbar	no good N-90, 91
über	about A-14	und	and A-171
über hinaus	beyond B-134	und soweiter (usw)	et cetera (etc) E-146
überdrüssig	sick of S-241	undeutlich	obscure O-18
übereinstimmen	concur C-302	unehrlich	dishonest D-212
Übereinstimmung	accord A-40	uneinig sein	disagree D-179
Überfall	holdup H-130	unendlich	infinite I-92
überfliessen	run over R-286	unentbehrlich	essential E-142
überfluten	overflow O-150	Unentschlossenheit	indecision I-68
übergeblieben	left L-62	unermesslich	immense I-28
übermässig	enormous E-109	unfähig	unable U-12
übermorgen	day after tomorrow	Unfall	accident A-33
	D-18	ungarisch	Hungarian H-194
übernatürlich	supernatural S-586	ungehalten	displeased D-221
überqueren	cross C-464, 465	ungelernt	unskilled U-47
überraschen	surprise S-601, 602,	ungerecht	unjust U-41
	603	ungerecht	unfair U-25, 26
überreden	coax C-213	Ungerechtigkeit	injustice I-110
überreden	persuade P-131	Ungeschicklichkeit	clumsiness C-206
überreichen	present P-299	ungeschickt	clumsy C-208
übersenden	consign C-339	ungeschickt	awkward A-329
überspannt	extravagant E-233	Unglaube	disbelief D-185, 186
übersteigen	surpass S-600	Ungläubigkeit	incredulity I-67
übertrágen	transfer T-261, 262	ungleich	unlike U-44
übertreffen	exceed E-187	unheimlich	weird W-74
übertreiben	exaggerate E-179, 180	unhöflich	impolite I-38
Übertretung	trespass T-274	Union	union U-32
übertrieben	far-fetched F-46	Union	union U-33
überwachen	supervise S-587	universal	universal U-37
überwältigen	overcome O-149	Universität	university U-38, 39, 40
überzeugen	convince C-387	unklar	unclear U-15
Überzeugung	conviction C-384, 385,	unmittelbar	immediate I-26
	386	unmöglich	impossible I-41, 42
Übung	exercise E-201	unnötig	unnecessary U-45, 46
Ufer	shore S-217	Unordnung	disorder D-218
Uhr	clock C-196	unparteiisch	impartial I-31
Uhr	watch (timepiece)	unrein	impure I-51
	W-38, 39	uns	us U-63
um	around A-252	Unschuld	innocence I-115
		unser	our O-139
		unsicher	uncertain U-13
		Unsinn	nonsense N-100

unten	down D-294
unten	below B-109, 110, 111
unter	beneath B-114, 115
unter	under U-1617
unter der Hand	underhand U-18
unterbrechen	interrupt I-173
untergehen	go down G-78
unterrichten	instruct I-136
unterscheiden	differ D-155
Unterschied	difference D-156, 158
unterschlagen	embezzle E-68
unterschreiben	sign S-246
unterstützen	support S-591, 592, 593
Untersuchung	examination E-181, 182, 183
untertauchen	plunge P-217
unterweisen	train T-257, 258
unterwerfen	subdue S-539
unverantwortlich	irresponsible I-203, 204
unverschämt	saucy S-44
unwissend	ignorant I-13
Unzucht treiben	fornicate F-228
unzufrieden	discontented D-197
Unzufriedenheit	dissatisfaction D-228
Urgrossmutter	great grandmother G-141
Urgrossvater	great grandfather G-140
Urin	urine U-62
Ursache	cause C-82
Ursprung	origin O-128, 129, 130
ursprünglich	original O-132

V

Vater	father F-66, 67, 68
Vati	papa P-16
Verabredung	engagement E-98
Verabredung	appointment A-227
verabscheuen	abhor A-9
verabscheuen	detest D-128, 129
verabscheuen	loathe L-131
verachten	despise D-116, 117
Verachtung	contempt C-356, 357
Verachtung	scorn S-74, 75
verändern	change C-108, 109
Verantwortlichkeit	responsibility R-155, 156
Verband	bandage B-23
verbannen	banish B-26
(sich) verbergen	hide H-103
verbessern	improve I-50
Verbeugung	bow B-209
verbinden	associate A-282, 283
verbieten	forbid F-206, 207
verbieten	prohibit P-361
Verbindung	connection C-324
verblüfft	stumped S-534
verblüfft	dumbfounded D-329, 330

verbrauchen	consume C-348, 349
verbrechen	crime C-456
verbreiten	spread S-428, 429
Verdacht	suspicion S-615
verdammen	damn D-6
verderben	spoil S-423
verdienen	deserve D-113
verdienen	earn E-10
Verdienst	merit M-127
verdolmetschen	interpret I-168
verehren	revere R-182, 183
Verehrer	beau B-76
Verein	association A-284
Verein	club C-205
verfallen	decline D-45, 46
verfaulen	rot R-257
verfehlen	miss M-179
verfliessen	go by G-74
verfolgen	persecute P-117
verfolgen	pursue P-422
vergangenen Monat	last month L-22
Vergangenheit	past P-49
vergehen	elapse E-45
vergelten	retaliate R-170, 171
vergessen	forget F-221, 222
vergleichen	compare C-268
vergrössern	increase I-66
verhaften	arrest A-258, 259
Verhältnis	ratio R-30
Verhältnis	proportion P-376
verhauen	spank S-391
verhindern	prevent P-309
Verhör	hearing H-69
verhören	interrogate I-169, 170
Verkauf	sale S-22
verkaufen	sell S-132
verkaufen	vend V-21
Verkehr	traffic T-252
verkleinern	reduce R-74
verkünden	proclaim P-345
verlangen	demand D-83
verlassen	forsake F-229, 230, 231
verlassen	relinquish R-101
verlassen	quit Q-23
verlassen	leave L-55
verlassen	embarrass E-66
verlegen	confer C-306
verleihen	bestow B-130
verletzen	injure I-107, 108
verletzen	violate V-46
verleumden	backbite B-6
verlieren	lose L-161
verlobt	engaged E-96, 97
verlocken	entice E-116
verloschen	die out D-154
vermachen	bequeath B-121
vermeiden	avoid A-321, 322
vermuten	suppose S-594
vernachlässigen	neglect N-44
verneinen	deny D-91
verneinung	negation N-41

vorschlagen suggest S-562
vorschlagen propose P-377
Vorschrift precept P-287
vorstellen introduce I-183
Vortrag lecture L-59
vorübergehen pass by P-43
vorwärts onward O-87
vorwärtskommen go ahead G-71
vorziehen prefer P-291
vorzüglich exquisite E-228
Vulkan volcano V-59

W

wach awake A-323
wachsen grow G-167
Wachtel quail Q-2, 3
Waffen arms A-250
Wagen chariot C-119
Wagen cars C-66
Wagen carriage C-62, 63
Wagen wagon W-4
Wahl choice C-157
wählen choose C-160, 161
wählen elect E-49
wahnsinnig mad M-5
wahnsinnig insane I-121
wahr true T-292
während while W-97
während pending P-86
während during D-334
Wahrheit truth T-296
wahrnehmen perceive P-94, 95
wahrscheinlich probable P-336
Währung currency C-492
Wald forest F-216
Wald woods W-168
Walfisch whale W-82
wandern wander W-16, 17
wandern migrate M-149
Wandschrank closet C-199
Wange cheek C-133
wann when W-89
Wanze bug B-265
warm warm W-21, 22
warnen warn W-23
warnen caution C-83
warnen admonish A-88, 89
warten wait W-5
warum why W-117
was what W-83
was ist los? what's new? W-86
Waschbär raccoon R-5
Wäsche wash W-25, 26, 27
Wäscheklammer clothespin C-202
waschen wash W-25, 26, 27
Waschlappen washcloth W-28
Waschmaschine washing machine W-30
Washington Washington W-31, 32
Wasser water W-40, 41
Wassermelone watermelon W-44

weben weave W-61
wechseln exchange E-192
weg gone G-82, 83, 84
weg away A-327
Weg way W-49
wegblasen blow away B-183
wegnehmen take away from T-14
wegräumen remove R-110, 111, 112
wehen blow B-182
weiblich female F-97
weich soft S-358
weihen sanctify S-33
Weihnachten Christmas C-166, 167
Weihung consecration C-333
weil because B-81
Wein wine W-137, 138
weinen weep W-68, 69
weinen cry C-479, 480, 481
Weinstock grapevine G-119
Weinstock vine V-44
Weintraube grape G-117, 118
Weise manner M-45, 46
Weisheit wisdom W-145
weiss white W-107
weisse Rübe turnip T-306
weit far F-43
weit entfernt off O-38, 39
weiter farther F-54
weitherzig broad minded B-250
weitverbreitet widespread W-121
welcher which W-96
Welle wave W-45
Welt world W-174
Welt earth E-13
Wendung turn T-305
wenig little L-122, 123
wenige few F-104
weniger minus M-171, 172, 173
weniger less L-75, 76
wenn if I-12
wenn nicht unless U-43
wer who W-108
werden become B-83
werfen throw T-167, 168, 169
werfen pitch P-185
Werk factory F-7
Werkmeister foreman F-213
Werkstatt workshop W-173
Werkzeug instrument I-139
wertlos worthless W-192, 193
wertvoll valuable V-13
wesentlich substantial S-547
Weste vest V-31
Westen west W-80
Wette wager W-1
Wette bet B-131
wetteifern vie V-39, 40, 41
wettrennen race R-6, 7, 8
Whisky whiskey W-102, 103
wichtig important I-39, 40

(ge)wichtig	weighty W-73
widerrufen	revoke R-188
widersprechen	contradict C-368
widerstehen	resist R-148
Widmung	devotion D-142
wie	as A-264
wie	how H-174
wie alt	how old H-181
wie geht es Ihnen?	how are you? H-175
wieder	again A-109
wiederaufnehmen	resume R-168
wiederbeleben	revive R-187
wiederholen	repeat R-121
Wiege	scale S-54, 55, 56
wiegen	weigh W-70
wiegen	weigh W-71
wieviel	how many H-178
wieviel kostet	how much money H-180
wild	wild W-124, 125
wild	fierce F-115
wille	will W-127
willensstark	strong-minded S-525
willfahren	comply C-285
willkommen	welcome W-75
Wind	wind W-135
Windpocken	chickenpox C-145
Wink geben	tip off T-197
Winkel	angle A-174
winken	beckon B-82
Winter	winter W-141, 142
winzig	tiny T-194, 195
winzig	minute M-175
wir	we W-51, 52
wir neun	nine of us N-85
wir selbst	ourselves O-140
wirklich	real R-44
wirklich	actual A-67
Wirkung	effect E-27, 28
wissen	know K-35
wissen lassen	let know L-80, 81
Wissenschaft	science S-66, 67
Wissenschaftler	highbrow H-108
wo	where W-91, 92
Woche	week W-64, 65
wohl	well W-77
wohlgesinnt	sympathetic S-646
wohlriechend	fragrant F-247
Wohltat	benefit B-118, 119
wohlwollend	benevolent B-120
wohnen	dwell D-339
wohnen	reside R-144
Wohnort	domicile D-265
Wohnsitz	residence R-145, 146
Wohnzimmer	living room L-128
Wolf	wolf W-159
Wolke	cloud C-204
Wolle	wool W-169
wollen	want W-19
wollen	will W-126
Wollust	lust L-180
Wort	word W-170

Wörterbuch	dictionary D-150, 151
wörtlich	verbal V-23, 24
Wrack	wreck W-200
wühlen	dig D-163, 164
Wunde	wound W-197
Wunder	wonder W-162
Wunder	marvel M-60
Wunder	miracle M-176
wunderbar	great G-137, 138
wünschen	desire D-114, 115
wünschen	wish W-147, 148
würdigen	appreciate A-229
Würfel	dice D-149
Wurfgeschoss	missile M-180
Wurm	worm W-175
Würstchen	frankfurter F-252
Wurzel	root R-251
Wut	rage R-13
Wut	fury F-298

X

Xerox	Xerox X-1
Xylophon	xylophone X-4

Y

Yard	yard Y-1

Z

zähe	tough T-238, 239, 240
zählen	count C-422
zahlreich	numerous N-133
zahm	tame T-28
Zahn	tooth T-223
Zahnarzt	dentist D-90
Zahnbürste	toothbrush T-225
Zähne	teeth T-55
Zahnweh	toothache T-224
Zange	pliers P-213
Zank	quarrel Q-8
zärtlich	tender T-78, 79, 80
Zaun	fence F-98, 99
Zebra	zebra Z-3
Zehe	toe T-208
Zehn	ten T-75
zeichnen	draw D-298
zeigen	show S-227
zeigen	point P-225
Zeit	time T-186, 187, 188, 189
Zeitalter	age A-112
Zeitraum	epoch E-130
Zeitschrift	magazine M-7
Zeitung	newspaper N-67
Zelt	tent T-82
Zentrum	center C-93
Zerknirschung	contrition C-373

Italian-English Index

adirato	angry A-175	alterco	quarrel Q-8
adirato	mad M-4, 5	alternazione	interchange I-154
adolescenza	adolescence A-90	altezza	height H-84, 85
adorare	adore A-93	alto	high H-104, 105, 106, 107
adorazione	worship W-187		
adottare	adopt A-92	alto	loud L-165
adunarsi	assemble A-277	alto	tall T-25, 26, 27
aèreo	airplane A-121, 122	alto	top T-226
aèreo	plane P-195, 196	altro	other O-137
affari	business B-276	alunno	pupil P-410, 411, 412
affascinare	fascinate F-56, 57	alzarsi	arise A-246, 247
afferrare	catch C-75, 76, 77	alzarsi	get up G-42
afferrare	seize S-122	amabile	amiable A-161
affiliare	affiliate A-100, 101	amante	fond F-193, 194
affogarsi	drown D-315, 316	amante	lover L-170
affollato	crowded C-469	amaro	bitter B-162
affondare	sink S-270, 271	amato	beloved B-108
affrettare	hustle H-206	ambedue	both B-203
affrettarsi	hurry H-199	ambiente	environment E-122, 123
affrontare	face F-4		
affronto	snub S-343	ambizione	ambition A-156
Africa	Africa A-103	ambizioso	ambitious A-157, 158
agganciare	hitch H-123	amen	amen A-159
aggiungere	add A-70, 71, 72, 73	America	America A-160
aggiustare	adjust A-81	America del Nord	North America N-105
aggredire	attack A-295	amichevole	friendly F-270
agire	act A-60, 61	amico	friend F-269
agitarsi	fret F-267	ammalato	ill I-15
agnello	lamb L-9	ammalato	sick S-239
ago	needle N-40	ammettere	admit A-87
agognare	long L-146	ammiccare	wink W-140
agognare	covet C-438, 439	ammirare	admire A-82, 83
agrimensore	surveyor S-607	ammissione	admission A-84
agro	sour S-380	ammonire	admonish A-88, 89
agro	tart T-32	ammonire	caution C-83
ahimè	alas A-123	ammutolito	speechless S-406
aiutare	aid A-118	amore	love L-169
aiutare	help H-90	anche	too T-222
al contrario	on the contrary O-84	anche	also A-143, 144
al verde	broke B-253	anch'io	me too M-134
ali	wings W-139	ancora	yet Y-11, 12
albergo	hotel H-166	ancora	still S-486
albero	tree T-273	andare	go G-69, 70
alce	elk E-64	andare a letto	go to bed G-96, 97
alce americana	moose M-216	anello	ring R-203
alcuni giorni fa	few days ago F-105	angelo	angel A-172
alfabeto	alphabet A-142	angolo	angle A-174
alfabeto manuale	manual alphabet M-48	angolo	corner C-402, 403
algebra	algebra A-124	angoscia	agony A-114
alimentare	feed F-88, 89	anima	soul S-377
alimentari	groceries G-161	animale	animal A-177, 178
allegro	jolly J-23	anitra	duck D-323
allegro	merry M-128	annettere	annex A-179
allegro	cheerful C-135	annientare	annihilate A-180
alleluia	hallelujah H-15	anno	year Y-3
allevare	raise R-21	anno prossimo	next year N-80
allontanare	remove R-110, 111, 112	annoiare	bore B-196
		annuale	annual A-187
allora	then T-114, 115	annuale	yearly Y-4
almalgamarsi	merge M-126	annullare	annul A-188
altare	altar A-145, 146	annunziare	announce A-181
alterare	alter A-147	ansia	anxiety A-198

aver cura di | take care of T-15, 16, 17
avere | have H-55, 57
avere da | have to H-58
avere intenzione | intend I-148
avere paura | afraid A-102
avere sonno | sleepy S-304
avere vergogna | ashamed A-267, 268
aviatore | aviator A-320
aviatore | flier F-172
avido | eager E-4
avido | greedy G-145, 146, 147
aviogetto | jet J-11
avvenimento | event E-161
avversario | opponent O-99
avversità | hard times H-41
avvertire | warn W-23
avvicinarsi (a) | approach A-230
avvocato | attorney A-302
avvocato | lawyer L-39
azienda | concern C-299
azzurro | blue B-184

B

babbo | dad D-2
babbo | papa P-16
bacchetta | rod R-241
bacio | kiss K-21, 22, 23
badare a | mind M-161
bagagli | luggage L-176
bagaglio | baggage B-11
bagnato | wet W-81
bagno | bath B-52
balena | whale W-82
bambini | children C-148
bambino | child C-147
bambino | baby B-1
bambola | doll D-261
bambola | doll D-262
banana | banana B-21, 22
banchetto | banquet B-29
banco | bench B-112
bandiera | banner B-28
bandiera | flag F-157
bandire | banish B-26
bandire | ban B-20
bandito | bandit B-25
Bar Mitzvah | Bar Mitzvah B-36
barba | beard B-70, 71
barca a vela | sailboat S-11
barile | barrel B-38
basare | base B-39, 40, 41
base | basis B-45, 46
baseball | baseball B-42
basso | low L-171, 172
basso | short S-218, 219
bassofondo | shallow S-169
bastardo | bastard B-49
bastimento a vapore | steamer S-474
bastoncino | stick S-484

bastone | bat B-51
battaglia | battle B-56
battello | boat B-190
battere | beat B-72, 73, 74
battere | pound P-268
battere le mani | clap C-179
battesimo | baptism B-30
battista | Baptist B-31
baule | trunk T-294
beccare | peck P-70
becco | beak B-63
beffarsi di | mock M-195
bello | handsome H-28
bello | beautiful B-77
bello | fine F-134
ben disposto | sympathetic S-646
ben sveglio | wide awake W-120
benchè | although A-149
benda | bandage B-23
bene | well W-76, 77
benedire | bless B-172, 173
benedizione | benediction B-116, 117
beneficio | benefit B-118, 119
benevolo | benevolent B-120
benvenuto | welcome W-75
benzina | gas G-16
bere | drink D-309, 310
bernoccolo | bump B-269
berretto | cap C-39
bestemmiare | blaspheme B-168, 169, 170
bestemmiare | swear S-622, 623, 624
bevanda alcolica | liquor L-117, 118
biancheria personale | underwear U-24
bianco | white W-107
biasimare | blame B-167
bibbia | Bible B-135, 136, 137
biblioteca | library L-90
bicchiere | glass G-55
bicicletta | bicycle B-138
biglietti | bills B-148, 149
biglietto | ticket T-176, 177
bilancia | balance B-14, 15
bilancia | scale S-54, 55, 56
bilione | billion B-147
bimbo | kid K-10, 11
binario | track T-248
binocolo | binoculars B-151
binocolo di teatro | opera glasses O-94
birra | beer B-89
bis | encore E-81
bisnonna | great grandmother G-141
bisnonno | great grandfather G-140
bisbigliare | whisper W-104
biscotto | cookie C-389
biscotto | cracker C-445, 446
bisogno | need N-37, 38, 39
bizzarro | odd O-35
bizzarro | queer Q-12
blandire | coax C-213

bleffare	bluff B-185	camicia	shirt S-200
bocca	mouth M-248	cammello	camel C-20
bocca aperta	open-mouthed O-91	cammino	way W-49
bosco	woods W-168	campagna	country C-423, 424
bottone	button B-283, 284	campana	bell B-103, 104, 105
Boy Scout	Boy Scout B-217	campanello	doorbell D-285
braccio	arm A-249	campione	champion C-106
brama	lust L-180	campione	sample S-31
bramare	crave C-448	campo	field C-111, 112
breve	brief B-236, 237	Canadà	Canada C-26
brezza	breeze B-232	cancellare	erase E-136
brillante	bright B-238, 239, 240, 241	cancellare	cancel C-28
		cancellare	delete D-75, 76, 77
brillare	shine S-194	candela	candle C-30
brindare a	toast T-205	candidato	candidate C-29
brontolare	nag N-1	cane	dog D-259, 260
brontolare	kick K-8	cannone	cannon C-33, 34
bruciare	burn B-273	canoa	canoeing C-37
bruno	brown B-259	cantare	sing S-268
bruttezza	ugliness U-1, 2, 3	canto	chant C-111
brutto	homely H-143, 144	canzone	song S-371
bucato	wash W-25, 26, 27	capace	capable C-40
buco	hole H-131, 132	capacità	capacity C-41
bugiardo	liar L-87	capacità	ability A-10
buono	good G-85, 86	capelli	hair H-3
burro	butter B-280	capire	understand U-20, 21
bussare	knock K-31	capire dal moto delle	
bussare	rap R-23	labbia	lip read L-114
buttare	throw T-167, 168, 169	capitale	capital C-42, 43
		capitano	captain C-45
		capitolo	chapter C-114
C		capo	point P-225
		capo cuoco	chef C-137
c'era una volta	once upon a time O-71	capo operaio	foreman F-213
cacciare	hunt H-198	capodanno	new year N-71
cacciare	chase C-121, 122	caporale	corporal C-407
cacciavite	screwdriver S-93, 94	capovolgersi	capsize C-44
cadere	fall F-27, 28	cappella	chapel C-113
caffè	coffee C-222	cappello	hat H-51
cagna	bitch B-160	capra	goat G-73
calamita	magnet M-11	carattere	character C-115, 116
calamitoso	calamitous C-6	carbina	rifle R-195
calcio	football F-202, 203	carbone	coal C-210
calcio	soccer S-349	carcere	jail J-1
calcolare	figure F-119, 120	cardinale	cardinal C-50
calcolare	calculate C-7	carestia	famine F-39
calcolare	reckon R-62	carie	caries C-60
calcolo	calculus C-8	carino	pretty P-307
caldo	hot H-164	carino	nice N-81
caldo	warm W-21, 22	carità	charity C-120
California	California C-10	carne	flesh F-171
calore	heat H-76, 77	carne	meat M-85
Calvario	Calvary C-18, 19	caro	expensive E-214
calvo	bald B-16	caro	dear D-30, 31
calza	stocking S-492, 493	carro	chariot C-119
calze	hose H-160, 161	carrozzina per	
calzino (i)	sock(s) S-351, 352	bambina	carriage C-62, 63
calzolaio	shoemaker S-209	carta	map M-51
cambiare	change C-108, 109	carta	paper P-18
cameratismo	fellowship F-96	carta da giuoco	playing card P-205
cameriera	maid M-13	carta vetrata	sandpaper S-34
cameriere	waiter W-6, 7	cartolina	card C-49

colletto	collar C-232	conferenza	conference C-307
collina	hill H-110	conferire	confer C-306
collo di cigno	rubberneck R-271, 272	conferire	bestow B-130
collocare	place P-188, 189	conferma	confirmation C-313
colore	color C-241, 242, 243	confessare	confess C-308
colpa	fault F-72, 73	confessione	confession C-310
colpevole	guilty G-177, 178	confessione	admission A-84
colpire	hit H-120, 121	confidenza	confidence C-312
colpire	hit H-122	confidenziale	private P-331, 332, 333
colpire	shocked S-203, 204	confondere	confuse C-316
colpire	strike S-517, 518	confondere	stumped S-534
colpo	blow B-182	confrontare	confront C-315
coltello	knife K-27, 28, 29	confrontare	compare C-268
coltivare	raise R-20, 21	congedare	discharge D-190, 191
comandamenti	commandments C-257	congratularsi con	congratulate C-319, 320
comandare	command C-256		
combattere	combat C-245	coniglio	rabbit R-3, 4
combattere	fight F-117, 118	connotare	connote C-325
combriccola	gang G-12	consacrazione	consecration C-333
come	as A-264	conscio	conscious C-331
come	how H-174	conscio	aware of A-326
comico	comic C-253	consecutivo	consecutive C-334
comico	funny F-294	consegnare	deliver D-81
cominciare	begin B-97	consegnare	consign C-339
cominciare	commence C-258	consentire	consent C-335
cominciare	start S-455	conservare	preserve P-302
commerciante	merchant M-123	considerare	consider C-336, 337, 338
commuoversi	feel touched F-94		
comodo	cozy C-442	consigliare	counsel C-420
comodo	comfort C-251	consiglio	advice A-97
compagnia	company C-267	consiglio	
compassione	compassion C-269	d'amministrazione	board B-188
compassione	sympathy S-647, 648	consolare	console C-341
competente	competent C-275	consultare	consult C-347
competere	compete C-273, 274	consumare	consume C-348, 349
compitare	spell S-410	contagioso	contagious C-353
compito	task T-33	contare	count C-422
compito	exercise E-201	contatto	contact C-351, 352
completare	complete C-282, 283	contemplare	contemplate C-355
complicare	complicate C-284	contendere	contend C-358, 359, 360
comporre	compose C-286		
comprare	buy B-285	contento	content C-361
comprare	purchase P-413	continuare	continue C-366, 367
comprendere	include I-63	continuare	persist P-122, 123
comprendere	comprehend C-287	conto	account A-42
comunicare	communicate C-260	contraddire	contradict C-368
comunicazione	communication C-261	contraffazione	fake F-24
comunione	communion, holy H-262, 263	contrario	opposite O-106
		contrastare	contrast C-370, 371
comunità	community C-265, 266	contribuire	contribute C-372
comunque	anyhow A-203	contrizione	contrition C-373
con	with W-150	contro	against A-110
concedere	grant G-115, 116	contro	versus V-28
concedere	concede C-288	controllare	control C-374, 375
concentrare	concentrate C-293	controversia	controversy C-376
concepire	conceive C-290, 291, 292	conveniente	suitable S-564
		convenire	convene C-377
concetto	concept C-295, 296	conversazione	conversation C-379, 380
concludere	conclude C-301		
condurre	conduct C-304, 305	conversazione	talk T-22, 23, 24
condurre	lead L-43	convertire	convert C-382
conferenza	lecture L-59	convincere	convince C-387

decrepito	decrepit D-53
decretare	decree D-51, 52
dedurre	deduct D-54
defecare	defecate D-61
deficienza	deficiency D-65
definire	define D-66, 67
deflettere	deflect D-70
defraudare	embezzle E-68
defraudere	defraud D-71
degenerazione	degeneration D-72
degente	patient P-54
delizioso	delicious D-78, 79
deludere	disappoint D-181
deluso	disappointed D-182, 183
democratico	democrat D-84
demolire	demolish D-85
demonio	demon D-86
denaro	money M-203, 204, 205
denigrare	backbite B-6
dente	tooth T-223
denti	teeth T-55
dentista	dentist D-90
dentro	inside I-126
depositare	deposit D-100, 101
depresso	depressed D-102
descrivere	describe D-109, 110, 111
desiderare	desire D-114, 115
desiderare	wish W-147, 148
desideroso	anxious A-199
detective	detective D-123, 124
deteriorare	deteriorate D-125
determinare	determine D-127
detestare	detest D-128, 129
Detroit	Detroit D-130
devastazione	havoc H-59
deviare	deviate D-135, 136
devo	must M-268
devoto	devout D-144
devozione	devotion D-142
di	of O-37
di	than T-96
di idee ristrette	narrow-minded N-14
di moda	fashionable F-59
di nuovo	again A-109
di sotto	below B-109, 110, 111
diacono	deacon D-23, 24
diadema	coronet C-406
diamante	diamond D-145, 146, 147
diarrea	diarrhea D-148
diavolo	devil D-138
dibattimento	debate D-34
dichiarare	declare D-44
dichiarare	state S-459
dieci	ten T-75
dietro	behind B-98
difendere	defend D-62
differenza	difference D-156, 158
differire	differ D-155
differire	defer D-64
differire	postpone P-256
differire	put off P-427
difficile	hard H-36, 37
difficile	difficult D-159, 160, 161
diffuso	widespread W-121
diletto	delight D-80
diligenza	diligence D-165, 166
dimenticare	forget F-221, 222
dimettersi	resign R-147
diminuire	decrease D-50
dimostrare	demonstrate D-87
dio	god G-75
diocesi	diocese D-171
dipende da te	up to you U-59
dipendere	depend D-94, 95, 96
dipendere	hinge H-115, 116
dipingere	paint P-7
diramare	spread S-428, 429
dire	tell T-64
dire	say S-52
direzione	direction D-174, 175
dirigere	direct D-172, 173
dirigere	manage N-41
diritto	straight S-505
discendente	descendant D-106
discepolo	disciple D-192
disciplinare	discipline D-193, 194, 195
discorso	discourse D-200
discorso	address A-75
discorso	speech S-404, 405
discredito	disbelief D-185, 186
discussione	discussion D-205
discutere	discuss D-203
disegnare	draw D-298
disgiungere	disjoin D-214
disgusto	disgust D-208
disinnestare	disconnect D-196
disobbidire	disobey D-217
disoccupato	idle I-10
disonesto	dishonest D-212
disordine	disorder D-218
disperare	lose hope L-162
disperdere	scatter S-60
disporre	arrange A-255
disposto	willing W-129, 130, 131
disprezzare	despise D-116, 117
disprezzo	contempt C-356, 357
disprezzo	scorn S-74, 75
disputare	dispute D-225
disputare	argue A-243
dissentire	disagree D-179
dissimile	unlike U-44
dissipare	blow away B-183
dissolvere	dissolve D-230
distanza	distance D-231
distratto	absent-minded A-22
distrazione	distraction D-233
distribuire	distribute D-234

distribuire	apportion A-228	dovrei	ought to O-138
distruggere	destroy D-119	dramma	drama D-297
distruggere	perish P-109, 110	droga	drug D-317
distruzione	wreck W-200	dubitare	doubt D-289, 290, 291
disturbare	trouble T-290	due	two T-312
disturbare	disturb D-237	due punti	colon C-240
disturbare	bother B-204, 205	due volte	twice T-309
ditale	thimble T-133	duplicare	duplicate D-332, 333
dito	finger F-138	durante	during D-334
dito del piede	toe T-208	durare	wear W-59
diventare	become B-83	durare	last L-19
diversi	sundry S-579	duro	hard H-36, 37
diverso	diverse D-240, 241	duro d'orecchio	hard-of-hearing H-39
divertente	amusing A-168		
divertimento	fun F-290		
dividendo	dividend D-246	**E**	
dividere	divide D-244, 245		
divino	divine D-247	è	is I-206, 207
divorare	devour D-143	è	and A-171
divorzio	divorce D-249, 250, 251	ebanista	cabinetmaker C-2
dizino	tithe T-200	ebreo	Hebrew H-80
dizionario	dictionary D-150, 151	eccedere	exceed E-187
dolce	soft-hearted S-359	eccellente	excellent E-188
dolce	sweet S-632	eccentrico	eccentric E-23
dolci	candy C-31, 32	eccetera (ecc)	et cetera (etc.) E-146
dolere	hurt H-200, 201, 202, 203	eccetto	except E-189
dollaro	dollar D-263, 264	eccitabile	hot-headed H-167
dolore	ache A-51	eccitare	excite E-194
dolore	grief G-155, 156	edificio	building B-267
dolore	pain P-5	educare	educate E-24
dolore	sorrow S-373	educazione	education E-25
dolore di denti	toothache T-224	effetto	effect E-27, 28
doloroso	sorrowful S-374	egli	he H-63
doloroso	mournful M-245	egoista	selfish S-129, 130, 131
domanda	question Q-17	egotismo	egotism E-33, 34, 35
domandare	inquire I-118, 119, 120	elastico	elastic E-46
domandare	ask A-271, 272, 273	elastico	rubber R-268, 269, 270
domandarsi	wonder W-161, 163	elefante	elephant E-59
domani	tomorrow T-217	elegante	elegant E-58
domenica	Sunday S-577, 578	eleggere	elect E-49
domestico	servant S-156	elettrico	electric E-51
domicilio	residence R-145, 146	elevare	elevate E-60
domicilio	domicile D-265	eliminare	eliminate E-63
dominare (marito)	henpeck H-93	eliminare	remove R-110, 111, 112
donna	woman W-160	eloquio	speech S-404, 405
dopo	after A-104, 105	emancipare	emancipate E-65
dopo d'allora	from then on F-281	emendarsi	mend M-110, 111
dopo un po'	after a while A-106	emettere	throw out T-170
dopodomani	day after tomorrow D-18	emozione	emotion E-71, 72
doppio	double D-288	enfasi	emphasis E-74
dormire	sleep S-301, 302	enorme	enormous E-109
dormire troppo a lungo	oversleep O-152	enorme	huge H-183
dottore	doctor D-255	entrare	enter E-113
dottrina	doctrine D-256, 257	entusiasmo	enthusiasm E-114
dove	where W-91, 92	entusiasmo	zeal Z-1
dovere	duty D-337	episcopale	Episcopal E-127
dovere	owe O-154	epistola	epistle E-129
dovere	obligation O-14, 15, 16	epoca	epoch E-130
		era	age A-112
		erba	grass G-121
		eredità	heritage H-98

fuggire	flee F-170	giocare	play P-202
fuggire	run away R-284	giocare alle carte	card playing C-51
fulmine	lightning L-102	gioco	game G-11
fumare	smoke S-328, 329	gioco delle bocce	bowl B-211
funerale	funeral F-293	giogo	yoke Y-14
funzionare	function F-291	gioia	joy J-28
fuoco	focus F-187	giornale	newspaper N-67
fuoco	fire F-146	giorno	day D-17
fuori	out O-141, 142, 143	Giorno delle Ceneri	Ash Wednesday A-269
furgone	wagon W-4	giorno di festa	holiday H-133
furia	fury F-298	giovane	young Y-18
furto	theft T-107, 108, 109	giovedì	Thursday T-173
furto	robbery R-233	gioventù	youth Y-25
futuro	future F-299	giraffa	giraffe G-45
		giù	down D-294
		giudaismo	Judaism J-29
G		Giudeo	Jew J-12
		giudicare	judge J-30
gabinetto	toilet T-211	giuramento	oath O-2
gaiezza	gaiety G-2, 3	giurare	swear S-621, 622, 623
gaio	gay G-24	giurare	sworn S-645
galleggiare	float F-175	giustizia	justice J-38, 39
gallina	hen H-91	giusto	just J-35, 36
gallo	cock C-217	giusto	righteous R-200
gallo domestico	rooster R-250	giusto	fair F-17
gamba	leg L-63	Gli Stati Uniti	United States U-35
ganghero	hinge H-115, 116	globo	globe G-58, 59
garanzia	guarantee G-169, 170	gloria	glory G-64, 65
gareggiare	vie V-39, 40, 41	glorioso	glorious G-63
gas	gas G-15	gocciolare	drip D-311
gatto	cat C-72	godere	enjoy E-106
gazzarra	riot T-207	goffaggine	clumsiness C-206
gelare	freeze F-260	goffo	clumsy C-208
gelato	frozen F-284	golf	golf G-81
gelato	ice cream I-4, 5	gomma	rubber R-268, 269, 270
geloso	jealous J-5	gomma da masticare	gum G-181
generazione	generation G-26	gonfiare	swell S-637
genere	kind K-16	gonna	skirt S-292, 293
generoso	generous G-27, 28	governare	govern G-98
gente	people P-92	governare	rule R-279, 280
gentile	kind K-15	governo	government G-99
gentiluomo	gentleman G-32	gradazione	scale S-54, 55, 56
genuino	genuine G-34	gradino	step S-478, 479, 480
geografia	geography G-35	graffetta	paper clip P-19
geometria	geometry G-36	Gran Bretagna	Great Britain G-139
Gerusalemme	Jerusalem J-8	granata	grenade G-153
gesso	chalk C-104	grande	great G-135, 136
Gesù	Jesus J-10	grande	big B-142, 143
gesuita	Jesuit J-9	grande	large L-16
gettare	pitch P-185	grandine	hail H-2
ghiaccio	ice I-3	grandioso	grand G-109, 110
ghianda	acorn C-55	grandioso	swell S-635, 636
ghiottoneria	gluttony G-68	grano	grain G-108
ghirlanda	wreath W-199	granturco	corn C-401, 405
giacca	coat C-212	grasso	fat F-65
giacere	lie down L-97	grasso	fatty F-71
giallo	yellow Y-7	grasso	grease G-133
Giappone	Japan J-3	grato	grateful G-122
giapponese	Japanese J-4	grave	grave G-126
giardino	garden G-13	gravoso	weighty W-73
ginnastica	exercise E-200	grazia	grace G-103, 104
giocare	gamble G-10	grazie	thank you T-99

irritato	cross C-463	
isola	island I-209, 210	
ispezionare	inspect I-128	
isterico	hysterical H-211	
istituire	institute I-133, 134	
istruire	instruct I-136	
italiano	Italian I-217	

J

Jugoslavia	Yugoslavia Y-27	

L

l'Egitto	Egypt E-36
l'Inghilterra	England E-100
l'Olanda	Holland H-134, 135
l'un l'altro	each other E-3
l' uno e l' altro	one another O-74
la	there T-119, 120
la Cina	China C-151
la Danimarca	Denmark D-89
la Francia	France F-250
la Gran Bretagna	Britain B-247
la maggior parte	most M-227
la Polonia	Poland P-229
la Russia	Russia R-288
la Spagna	Spain S-388
la Turchia	Turkey T-303
la Vergine	Mary M-62
laccio	shoelace S-208
lacuna	void V-58
ladro	thief T-130, 131
ladro	burglar B-271
lago	lake L-8
lagrima	tear T-49
lamentarsi	complain C-279, 280
lampadina tascabile	flashlight F-159
lana	wool W-169
lapis	pencil P-85
largo	wide W-119
largo	broad B-249
lasciare	quit Q-27
lasciare	leave L-55
lasciar cadere	drop D-313
latino	Latin L-31, 32
lato	side S-242
latte	milk M-154
lattuga	lettuce L-84, 85
laurearsi	graduate G-106, 107
lavare	wash W-25, 26, 27
lavare piatti	dish wash (ing) D-213
lavorare a maglia	knit K-30
lavorare all'uncinetto	crochet C-460
lavoro	labor L-1
lavoro	toil T-210
lavoro	work W-171
leale	loyal L-175
lebbra	leprosy L-74
legale	legal L-64

legare	tie T-179
legare	bequeath B-121
legare	bind B-150
legge	law L-37
leggere	read R-36, 37, 38
leggero	light L-101
legislatura	legislature L-65
legname	lumber L-177, 178
legno	wood W-167
lei	you Y-16, 17
lei come sta?	how are you? H-175
leone	lion L-113
leopardo	leopard L-73
lettera	letter L-83
letto	bed B-85
levarsi	rise R-212, 213, 214
levarsi in piedi	stand S-449, 450, 451
levata del sole	sunrise S-580
lezione	lesson L-77
libbra	pound P-266, 267
liberare	deliver D-81
liberazione	liberation L-88
libero	free F-257, 258
libertà	liberty L-89
libro	book B-193
libro di testo	textbook T-95
licenza	license L-91, 92
licenziare	fire F-147
lieto	glad G-53
lima	file F-121
limbo	limbo L-106
limite	limit L-107
limone	lemon L-67, 68, 69
limousine	limousine L-108
Lincoln	Lincoln L-109
lindo	neat N-29
linea	line L-110
lingua	language L-13, 14
lingua	tongue T-218
linotipo	Linotype L-112
liquido	liquid L-116
liscio	smooth S-330
lista	list L-119, 120
lista lunga	long list L-148
livellato	level L-86
lo lui	him H-111
lo stesso	same S-27, 28, 29
locanda	inn I-114
locomotiva	locomotive L-137
lodare	commend C-259
lode	praise P-282
logica	logic L-139
logoro	worn W-176, 177
lontano	off O-38, 39
lontano	far F-43
loro	them T-111
Los Angeles	Los Angeles L-160
lotta	wrestling W-202
lottare	struggle S-526
luce	light L-100
lucidare	polish P-235
lucidare le scarpe	shine shoes S-195

messicano	Mexican M-135	momento	moment M-201
meta	goal G-72	monaca	nun N-135
metallo	metal M-130, 131	mondo	world W-174
metodista	Methodist M-133	mondo	earth E-13
metodo	method M-132	moneta	currency C-492
mettere	show off S-230, 231	moneta	coin C-223, 224
mettere	put P-424	monotono	monotonous M-207, 208, 209
mettere al corrente	tip off T-197		
mettere alle strette	corner C-403	montagna	mountain M-243
mezz'ora	half-hour H-13	montare	ride R-192
mezzanotte	midnight M-141	mordere	bite B-161
mezzo	middle M-140	morente	dying D-341
mezzo	midst M-142	morfina	morphine M-224
mezzo	half H-11, 12	morire	die D-152, 153
mezzodì	midday M-139	mormone	Mormon M-221
mezzogiorno	noon N-101	mortale	mortal M-225
mi dia	give me G-51	mortificazione	mortification M-226
mi dica	tell me T-66	morto	dead D-25, 26
mi disgusta	make me disgusted M-31	mosca	fly F-185
		mostrare	show S-227
micrometro	micrometer M-138	motivare	motivate M-236
mietere	reap R-47, 48, 49	motivo	motive M-238, 239-240
miglio	mile M-151	moto	motion M-232
migliorare	improve I-50	motocicletta	motorcycle M-242
migliore	best B-128	motore	motor M-241
migliore	better B-132	motore	electric motor E-53
migrare	migrate M-149	mozione	motion M-233
milione	million M-155	mulo	mule M-258
militare	military M-153	multa	penalty P-82
mille	thousand T-154	multa	fine F-135
Milwaukee	Milwaukee M-156	multiplo	multiple M-260
minestra	soup S-379	muover(e si)	move M-249
miniera	mine M-165	muro	wall W-14, 15
minimo	least L-54	musica	music M-266
minorenne	minor M-170	muslebound	muscle-bound M-265
minuscolo	tiny T-194, 195	mutevole	changeable C-110
minuto	minute M-174	muto	mute M-269
miracolo	miracle M-176	mutuo	mutual M-270, 271
mischia	scramble S-88		
misericordia	mercy M-124, 125		
missile	missile M-180		**N**
missione	mission M-183, 184		
mistero	mystery M-274	narcotico	narcotic N-10
misurare	measure M-84	narrare	narrate N-11
misurare	gauge G-23	nascere	born B-199, 200, 201
mite	gentle G-31	nascita	birth B-153, 154, 155
mite	meek M-97	nascondere	hide H-103
mite	mild M-150	naso	nose N-110
mitra	mitre M-189	nasone	nosy N-111, 112, 113
mitragliatrice	machine gun M-2	nastro	tape T-30
moda	stylish S-538	Natale	Christmas C-166, 167
modello	model M-196	nato	nee N-36
modesto	modest M-197	naturale	natural N-17
modificare	modify M-198	nausea	nausea N-22
moglie	wife W-123	nave	ship S-197
molestare	annoy A-183, 184	nazione	nation N-16
molletta	clothespin C-202	nazista	Nazi N-25
molti	many M-50	ne	neither N-49
moltiplicare	multiply M-261, 262	ne	nor N-102
molto	much M-255	necessario	necessary N-30, 31
molto	lot L-164	negare	deny D-91, 92
molto	very V-30	negativo	negative N-42

parallelo	parallel P-26	penalità	penalty P-80, 81, 82
parassita	parasite P-27	pendente	pending P-86
parecchi	several S-162	pene	penis P-88
pareggiare	pare P-29	penetrare	penetrate P-87
parente	kin K-14	penetrare	pierce P-168
parente	relative R-95	penitente	penitent P-89
parentela	relationship R-93, 94	penitenza	penance P-83, 84
parere	look L-149, 150	penitenziale	penitentiary P-90
parere	appear A-216	penna	pen P-79
pari	peer P-78	pensare	think T-138
parlare	speak S-392	pensiero	thought T-150, 151
parlare	talk T-22, 23, 24	pentirsi	rue R-276
parola	word W-170	pentirsi di	repent R-123
parroco	rector R-68	pentola	pot P-264
parrucchiere	hairdresser H-5	pepe	pepper P-93
parte	share S-176, 177	per	for F-204, 205
parte	part P-32, 33, 34, 35	per favore	please P-209
partecipare	participate P-37	per sempre	forever F-218
partire	leave L-55	per tutto l'anno	all year (round) A-137
partire	depart D-93	pera	pear P-68
partire		percento	percent P-96
clandestinamente	leave clandestinely	percepire	perceive P-94, 95
	L-57, 58	perché	because B-81
partorire	bear B-67, 68	perché	why W-117
Pasqua	Easter E-17, 18, 19	perciò	therefore T-121, 122,
Pasqua ebraica	Passover P-48		123
passare	pass P-41	perdere	lose L-161
passare	go by G-74	perdere	leak L-48
passare per	pass by P-43	perdere conoscenza	pass out P-47
passato	past P-49	perdere la pazienza	flip the lid F-173
passeggiata	walk W-13	perdersi	stray S-510
passione	passion P-45	perdonare	forgive F-223, 224
passione	passion P-46	perdono	pardon P-28
passo	pace P-1	perfetto	perfect P-99
passo	step S-478, 479, 480	perfido	false-faced F-34
pasto	meal M-77	pericolo	danger D-10, 11
pastore	pastor P-50	pericolo	peril P-106
pastore	minister M-169	periodo	period P-108
patata	potato P-265	perire	perish P-109, 110
patate fritte	French fried potatoes	permanente	permanent P-111
	F-262	permesso	permission P-112, 113
patrigno	stepfather S-481	permettere	let L-78
pattinare	skate S-281	permettere	allow A-134
pattinare	ice-skating I-6	perpetuo	perpetual P-116
pattino a rotelle	roller skating R-244	perquisire	search S-104
paura	fear F-78, 79	perseguire	pursue P-422
pavimento	floor F-177	perseguitare	persecute P-117
pazienza	patience P-52, 53	perseverare	persevere P-118, 119,
pazzo	mad M-4		120, 121
pazzo	insane I-121	persistere	persist P-122, 123
pazzo	nuts N-138, 139, 140	persona	person P-124
pazzo	off the beam O-50	personalità	personality P-125
pazzo	crazy C-449, 450, 451	persuadere	persuade P-131
peccato	sin S-264	pesante	heavy H-79
pecora	sheep S-186	pesare	weigh W-70, 71
peculiare	peculiar P-71	pesca	peach P-63, 64, 65
pedaggio	toll T-214	pescare	fish F-151, 152
pedalare	pedal P-72	peste	pest P-133
peggiore	worse W-184, 185, 186	pettegolare	gossip G-94
pegno	pledge P-211	pettinare	comb C-244
pelle	skin S-289, 290	pettirosso	robin R-234
pellirossa	Indian I-72, 73	petto	chest C-140

960

pezzo	piece P-167	pollo	chicken C-144
pezzo sagomato	pipe-fitting P-183	pollo	fowl F-242
piacere	like L-103, 105	polmoni	lungs L-179
piacevole	pleasant P-208	polmonite	pneumonia P-220
pialla	plane P-197	polso	pulse P-399
pianeta	planet P-198	polso	wrist W-203
piangere	mourn M-244	pomeriggio	afternoon A-107
piangere	cry C-479, 480	pomodoro	tomato T-215, 216
piangere	weep W-68, 69	pompa	pump P-400, 401
piano	story S-503	pompiere	fireman F-148
piano	even E-158	ponderare	ponder P-238
piano	slow S-314	ponte	bridge B-234, 235
piano	plan P-193, 194	pontefice	pontiff P-239
piano	piano P-152	popolazione	population P-246
pianta	plant P-199, 200	porcellana	porcelain P-249
pianura	plain P-191, 192	porcellana	china C-152
piatto	plate P-201	porco	pig P-169, 170
piatto	flat F-160	porgere	extend E-230
piatto	dish D-211	porporeo	purple P-418
piccione	pigeon P-171	porta	door D-284
piccolo	little L-122, 123	porta	gate G-18
piccolo	small S-319, 320	portalampada	socket S-350
picnic	picnic P-161, 162	portare	wear W-58
piede	foot F-200	portare	carry C-64, 65
piedi	feet F-95	portare	bring B-246
piegare	bend B-113	portare via	take away T-14
piegare	fold F-189	porto	harbor H-35
pieno	full F-288, 289	porzione	portion P-250
pietà	pity P-187	positivo	positive P-254, 255
pietra	stone S-494, 495	posizione	site S-278
piffero	fife F-116	posizione	location L-133
pigrizia	laziness L-40	posizione	position P-251, 252, 253
pigro	lazy L-42		
pillola	pill P-173	possedere	possess P-257, 258
pilota	pilot P-174	possibile	possible P-260
pinze	pliers P-213	possibilità	possibility P-259
pio	pious P-180	possibilità	opportunity O-100, 101, 102, 103, 104
pioggia	rain R-17		
piombo	lead L-44	posta	mail M-15, 16
pipa	pipe P-181, 182	posto	seat S-107
pisello	pea P-69	posto	place P-188, 189, 190
pistola	pistol P-184	potente	mighty M-148
più	more M-218	potenza	might M-144, 146
più lontano	farther F-54	potere	may M-72, 73, 74
più tardi	later L-28, 29	potere	power P-274, 275
piuttosto	rather R-29	potere	can C-24
plurale	plural P-218	povero	poor P-241, 242, 243
pochi	few F-104	povertà	poverty P-270, 271
pochi secondi fa	few seconds ago F-106	pranzare	dine D-169
poco	little L-122, 123	praticare	practice P-278, 279, 280
poco chiaro	unclear U-15		
poco costoso	inexpensive I-89	preavvertire	forewarn F-219
poco fa	while ago, a W-98, 99, 100	precetto	precept P-287
		preciso	precise P-289
poema	poem P-222	predicare	preach P-285
poichè	for F-204, 205	predire	predict P-290
polipo	octopus O-33	preferire	prefer P-291
politica	policy P-233, 234	pregare	pray P-283
polizia	police P-231	prego	you're welcome Y-20, 21
poliziotto	cop C-392		
pollice	inch I-57, 58	premio	aware A-325
pollice	thumb T-171	prendere	take T-9

prendere a prestito	borrow B-202	profitto	profit P-356
prendere in giro	kid K-11	profitto	benefit B-118, 119
prendere una pillola	take a pill T-13	profondità	depth D-103
prenotare	reserve R-141, 142	profondo	deep D-56
prenotazione	reservation R-139	profumo	perfume P-104
preparare	prepare P-292, 293, 294	progenie	offspring O-49
		programma	program P-357, 358
prepararsi	get ready G-41	progresso	progress P-359
presa elettrica	electric outlet E-54	proibire	prohibit P-361
presbiteriano	Presbyterian P-295	proibire	forbid F-206, 207
presentare	present P-300	promessa	promise P-365, 366, 367
presentare	introduce I-183		
presente	present P-301	prominente	prominent P-362, 363, 364
presenza	presence P-297		
presidente	president P-303	promuovere	promote P-368
pressare	press P-304, 305, 306	pronosticare	forecast F-212
pressione	stress S-513	pronto	ready R-40, 41, 42, 43
presso a	by B-286	propiziare	propitiation P-375
prestare	lend L-70, 71	proporre	propose P-377
prestare aiuto	give assistance G-49	proporzione	proportion P-376
prestare attenzione a	give attention to G-50	proporzione	ratio R-30
prestare un giuramento	take oath T-18	proprio	just J-35, 36
prestito	loan L-129, 130	proprio	own O-156
presto	early E-9	proprio	proper P-371
presuntuoso	swell-headed S-638	proseguire	go ahead G-71
prete	father F-68	prosperare	prosper P-378
prete	priest P-316, 317, 318, 319	prossimo	next N-73, 74, 75, 76
		prostituta	prostitute P-379
prevenire	prevent P-309	prostituta	strumpet S-527
prevenire	hinder H-113	proteggere	protect P-380
prezioso	precious P-288	protesta	protest P-382
prezioso	valuable V-13	protestante	Protestant P-383
prezzo	price P-313, 314	prova	proof P-370
prezzo	charge C-117, 118	provvedere	provide P-386, 387
prigione	prison P-329	prugna secca	prune P-388
prima	before B-91, 92, 93	psichiatra	psychiatrist P-391
prima	formerly F-227	psicologia	psychology P-392, 393
prima colazione	breakfast B-229	pubblicare	publish P-395, 396
prima di	ahead A-117	pubblico	public P-394
primato	primary P-320	pugno	punch P-404, 405
primavera	spring S-430	pulce	flea F-167, 168, 169
primo	first F-149, 150	pulire	clean C-185, 186
principale	chief C-146	pulsazione	heartbeat H-74, 75
principale	principal P-323, 324	punire	punish P-407, 408, 409
principale	main M-17	punta	point P-226
principe	prince P-321	puntare	pin P-175
principessa	princess P-322	punteggio	score S-73
principio	principle P-325	punto	query Q-14, 15
privilegio	privilege P-335	punto	period P-107
privo di	minus M-171, 172, 173	punto	stitch S-491
probabile	probable P-336	punto e virgola	semicolon S-134
problema	problem P-340, 341, 342	purgatorio	purgatory P-416
		puro	pure P-414, 415
procedere	proceed P-343	putrido	rotten R-258
processione	procession P-344	puttana	whore W-114
procione	raccoon R-5	puzzola	skunk S-294
proclamare	proclaim P-345		
produrre	produce P-350, 351, 352, 353		
			Q
professione	profession P-354, 355		
professione	field F-113, 114	quacquero	Quaker Q-5
profezia	prophecy P-372	quadrante	quadrant Q-1

riabilitazione	rehabilitation R-84
riassumere	summarize S-569
ribellarsi	rebel R-54
ribes	currant C-491
ricaduta	relapse R-91
ricchezza	wealth W-56
ricco	rich R-191
ricerca	research R-138
ricercato	far-fetched F-46
ricetta	prescription P-296
ricevere	receive R-57
richiamare	recall R-55, 56
richiedere	request R-134, 135
richiedere	apply A-224
riconoscere	recognize R-64
ricordare	recollect R-65, 66
ricordare	remind R-108
ricordarsi di	remember R-107
ricovero	refuge R-77
ricreazione	recreation R-67
ricuperare	redeem R-71, 72
ridere	laugh L-33
ridicolo	ridicule R-193
ridurre	reduce R-74
riempire	fill F-123
riferire	refer R-75
rifiutare	refuse R-78
rifiutare	decline D-47
rifugio	shelter S-188
rigido	rigid R-202
riguardo a	concerning C-300
rilassare	relax R-97, 98
rimandare	procrastinate P-347
rimanente	left L-62
rimanenza	remainder R-105
rimanere	remain R-104
rimorchiare	tow T-241
rimproverare	scold S-69, 70, 71, 72
rimprovero	reprimand R-131
rimuovere	remove R-110, 111, 112
rinforzare	reinforce R-86
rinomato	renowned R-118
rinunziare	renounce R-117
riparare	repair R-120
riparare	mend M-110, 111
riparare	fix F-155
ripetere	repeat R-121
riposo	rest R-161, 162
riprendere	resume R-168
riso	rice R-190
riso	laughter L-35, 36
risoluzione	resolve R-149
risparmiare	save S-46
rispettare	respect R-150
rispondere	reply R-126, 127
rispondere	respond R-152
rispondere	answer A-192, 193
risposta	response R-154
risurrezione	resurrection R-169
ritardare	retard R-174
ritardo	delay D-74

ritirare	retire R-175, 176, 177
ritirare	withdraw W-151, 152, 153, 154
ritirata	retreat R-178
ritornare	return R-180
riunione	meeting M-99, 100
riunirsi	gather G-19, 20
riuscire	succeed S-551
rivale	rival R-215, 216, 217, 218
riverenza	bow B-209
rivista	magazine M-7
rivoltante	revolting R-189
robusto	hale H-10
robusto	stout S-504
roccia	rock R-235, 236
romano	Roman R-245
rompere	break R-227
rosa	pink P-179
rosario	rosary R-254, 255
rosolia	measles M-83
rossetto	lipstick L-115
rosso	red R-69
rotazione	spin S-415
rotolare	roll R-242, 243
rotondo	round R-263, 264
rovescio	reverse R-185, 186
rovinare	ruin R-278
rubare	rob R-227, 228, 229
rubare	steal S-469, 470, 471
rumore	din D-168
ruota	wheel W-88
ruttare	belch B-100
ruvido	rugged R-277

S

sabato	Saturday S-43
sabato ebraico	Sabbath S-2, 3, 4
sacramento	sacrament S-5
sacre scritture	Holy Scriptures H-141
sacrificio	sacrifice S-6
sacrilego	sacrilegious S-7
sagace	shrewd S-232
saggezza	wisdom W-145
salario	wage(s) W-1
sale	salt S-24, 25
salire	ascend A-265
salmo	psalm P-390
salone di bellezza	beauty parlor B-79
salsiccia calda	hotdog H-165
saltare	hop H-151, 152
saltare	leap L-51
saltare	jump J-33, 34
salute	health H-66
salvare	save S-45
salvare	rescue R-137
salvezza	salvation S-26
salvo	safe S-9
San Francisco	San Francisco S-36
sanctificare	sanctify S-32

sandali	sandals S-33	schiocco	smack S-318
sanguinare	bleed B-171	schivare	shirk S-199
sanguisuga	leech L-60	scialacquare	squander S-436
santificato	hallowed H-16, 17	scienza	science S-66, 67
San Giovanni	Saint John S-17	scimmia	monkey M-206
San Giusseppe	Saint Joseph S-18	scimmia	ape A-208
santi	saints S-19	scintillare	glisten G-57
santo	holy H-136	sciocco	daft D-4
santo	saint S-15, 16	sciocco	dumb D-328
sapere	know K-35	sciocco	silly S-258
sapone	soap S-344, 345, 346, 347	sciolto	loose L-157
		sciopero	strike S-518
saporito	savory S-48	sciroppo	syrup S-650
sarta	dressmaker D-305	sciupare	waste W-34, 35
sarto	tailor T-8	scivolare	slide S-306, 307
Santana	Satan S-37	scivolare via	slip away S-311
satellite	satellite S-38	scodella	bowl B-211
sbagliare	miss M-179	scoiattolo	squirrel S-442
sbagliato	wrong W-207, 208	scolpire	sculpt S-96
sbalordire	flabbergasted F-156	scolpire	carve C-68
sbalordire	dumfounded D-329, 330	scommessa	bet B-131
		scommessa	wager W-1
sbandare	skid S-286	scomparso	missing M-181, 182
sbiadire	fade F-9	sconfiggere	defeat D-59
sbirciare	peek P-73, 74	sconfitto	defeated D-60
sbucciare	peel P-72, 73	scontento	discontented D-197
scaffale	shelf S-187	scontrarsi	collide C-235, 236
scala (e)	stair(s) S-445, 446	scontrino	check C-130
scala a piuoli	ladder L-5	scopa	broom B-255
scaltro	sly S-315, 316, 317	scopa di stracci	mop M-217
scambiare	exchange E-192	scopo	purpose P-419, 420, 421
scambio	trade T-250		
scapolo	bachelor B-2	scopo	aim A-119
scappare	escape E-140	scoprire	discover D-201
scarpa	shoe S-205, 206	scoprire	detect D-122
scarsezza	dearth D-32	scoraggiare	discourage D-198, 199
scarso	scarce S-58	scoraggiato	dejected D-73
scartare	discard D-187, 188, 189	scortese	impolite I-38
		scortese	rude R-273, 274
scartare	cast off C-70	scossa	jolt J-24
scatola	box B-213	scozzese	Scot S-76, 77, 78
scatola di latta	can C-25	scrivere	write W-205
scavare	dig D-163, 164	scudo	shield S-191, 193
scavare	pick P-153	sculacciare	spank S-391
scegliere	select S-124, 125, 126	scultore	sculptor S-97
scegliere	choose C-160, 161	scuola	school S-65
scelta	choice C-157	scuola media	high school H-109
scena	scene S-61	scuotere	shake S-167
scena	stage S-443	scuro	dark D-14
scendere	get off G-40	scusa	plea P-206
scendere	go down G-78	scusare	excuse E-199
scendere	descend D-104, 105, 106	scusarsi	apologize A-209, 210
		se	if I-12
sceriffo	sheriff S-190	se	whether W-94
scettico	skeptic S-282, 283	se stessa	herself H-101
schema	scheme S-63	se stesso	himself H-112
schermire	fence F-100	seccante	tedious T-54
scherzo	joke J-22	secco	dry D-322
schiacciare	squash S-439 or 440	secolo	century C-96
schiaffo	slap S-297	secondo	according to A-41
schiavo	slave S-299	secondo	second S-108
schiena	back B-3	secondo	second S-110

sedere sit S-275, 276
sedersi sit down S-277
sedia chair C-101, 102, 103
sedia a dondolo rocking chair R-238, 239
sega saw S-49, 50
sega a mano handsaw H-26
sega da intaglio jig saw J-15
segheria saw mill S-51
segretario secretary S-114
segreto secret S-113
segreto underhand U-18
seguire follow F-190
sei are A-240, 241
sei six S-279
selvaggio wild W-125, 125
sembrare seem S-121
seme seed (n) S-117, 118, 119
seminare sow S-384
seminare seed S-117, 118, 119
seminario seminary S-135, 136
semplice simple S-262, 263
semplice plain P-191, 192
sempre always A-151
senato senate S-137
sensazione sensation S-144
sensibile sensitive S-147
senso sense S-145
senta hark H-42
sentenza verdict V-25
sentiero trail T-255
sentiero path P-51
sentire feel F-91
separare part P-32, 33, 34, 35
separare separate S-150, 151
separarsi da part from P-36
separato apart A-207
seppellire bury B-274
sequela sequel S-152
sera evening E-159
sergente sergeant S-153
serie series S-154
serio earnest E-11
serio grave G-126
sermone sermon S-155
serpente snake S-331, 332, 333, 334, 335, 336
serpente a sonagli rattlesnake R-31
serratura lock L-134, 135
servire serve S-157
servire wait on W-8, 9
sete thirst T-142
sette seven S-160
settimana week W-64, 65
settimana prossima next week N-78, 79
sezione section S-115
sfera sphere S-413
sfida challenge C-105
sfiducia distrust D-236
sfilata parade P-23, 24
sforzarsi endeavor E-88

sforzo effort E-29, 30, 31
sfrattare evict E-173
sfregiare deface D-58
sgonfiare deflate D-68
sgridare bawl out B-59
sguardo retrospettivo retrospection R-179
si yes Y-9
si accomodi be seated B-124
siccità drought D-314
sicuro sure S-596
sigaretta cigarette C-172
sigaro cigar C-170, 171
sigillo seal S-101, 102
significare signify S-252
significato significance S-248, 249
signora lady L-6
signora madam M-6
signore lord L-158
silenzio silence S-255, 256
silenzio shut up S-235, 236
silenzio keep quiet K-2, 3
silenzio be quiet B-122, 123
silenzioso noiseless N-93
silenzioso quiet Q-25, 26
silofono xylophone X-4
simile like L-104
simile similar S-261
simile alike A-125
sin qui so far S-356
sincero sincere S-266, 267
sinistro left L-61
sinonimo synonym S-649
sistema system S-651
slealmente on the sly O-85
smalto nail polish N-3
smorfia grimace G-158
smorzarsi die out D-154
snello slender S-305
snob snob S-341
soda soda pop S-354
soddisfazione satisfaction S-39
soffiare blow B-181
soffice soft S-358
soffocare choke C-158, 159
soffrire suffer S-557, 558, 559
soggetto subject S-540
sogghignare sneer S-338
soggiorno stay S-464, 465, 466, 467
sogno dream D-303
solamente only O-82
solamente uno only one O-83
soldato soldier S-362
soldato semplice private P-333
sole sun S-576
sollevare rear R-50
solido solid S-364
solitario lonely L-142, 143
solitudine privacy P-330
sollecitare urge U-60, 61
sollievo relief R-99
solo lone L-141

966

steccone	beanpole B-65	
stella	star S-454	
stelo	stem S-477	
stimare	estimate E-145	
stimolare	prod P-349	
stipendio	salary S-21	
stirare	iron I-202	
stirare	press P-304, 305, 306	
stirarsi	stretch S-514	
stolto	foolish F-199	
storia	history H-118, 119	
storia	story S-502	
storpio	cripple C-457	
storta	sprain S-426	
strada	road R-225	
strano	curious C-488	
strano	strange S-507, 508	
strano	weird W-74	
strappare	tear T-48	
strappare	rip R-208, 209	
stravagante	extravagant E-233	
stretto	narrow N-13	
stretto	strict S-515, 516	
strillare	scream S-90	
strillare	squeal S-441	
striscia	striped S-580	
strisciare	sneak S-337	
strumento	instrument I-139	
stucco	putty P-428	
studente	student S-531, 532	
studio	study S-533	
studioso	scholar S-64	
stupefacente	dope D-287	
stupido	stupid S-535, 536	
stupire	amaze A-154	
stupire	astonish A-288	
stuzzicare	tease T-51, 52, 53	
su	up U-52	
su	over O-146, 147	
su	on O-67	
succedere	happen H-31, 32	
successivamente	thence T-116	
sud	south S-381	
Sud America	South America S-382, 383	
sudicio	nasty N-15	
sudicio	filthy F-125	
sudore	sweat S-625, 626	
sufficiente	sufficient S-560	
sufficiente	ample A-167	
suggerire	suggest S-562	
sugo di carne	gravy G-128	
suo	its I-220	
suolo	soil S-361	
suolo	dirt D-176	
suonare	ring R-204	
suono	sound S-378	
superare	overcome O-149	
superare	surpass S-600	
superbo	haughty H-54	
superiore	superior S-584	
superlativo	superlative S-585	

supplica	supplication S-590
supplicare	entreat E-120
supplicare	beseech B-125
supporre	suppose S-594
susseguente	subsequent S-543
svanire	vanish V-15
svanire	fade away F-10
svedese	Swede S-628
svegliare	arouse A-254
svegliarsi	wake up W-12
sveglio	awake A-323
svenire	faint F-15, 16
sventato	heedless H-83
sviare	sidetrack S-244
sviluppare	develop D-131, 132, 133

T

tabacco	tobacco T-206
tacchino	turkey T-303
tagliare	cut C-499
taguare a zero	mow M-252, 253
tale	such S-555
tamburo	drum D-318
tappezzeria	upholstery U-54
tappo	cork C-399
tardivo	tardy T-31
tardo	dull D-325
tardo	late T-26
tartaruga	tortoise T-231
tartaruga	turtle T-307
tasca	pocket P-221
tassì	taxi T-43
tastare	feel F-90
tatto	touch T-234
tavola	table T-2, 3
tazza	cup C-484
te	thee T-106
tè	tea T-44, 45
te stesso	yourself Y-23
teatro	theatre T-105
tedesco	German G-37
telefono	telephone T-61, 62
telefono	phone P-140, 141
telegramma	telegram T-57, 58
televisione	television T-63
tema	theme T-112
tema	topic T-227
temperanza	temperance T-69
temperato	temperate T-70
temperatura	temperature T-71
tempesta	storm S-501
tempesta	gale G-6
tempio	temple T-72
tempo	time T-186, 187, 188, 189
tenda	tent T-82
tenere	hold H-129
tenere	keep K-1
tenero	tender T-78, 79, 80

ufficiale	officer O-48
ufficio	office O-46
uguale	equal E-131
ulteriore	further F-295, 296
ultimo	last L-17, 18
ultimo	ultimate U-7
umanità	humanity H-186
umanitario	humane H-185
umano	human H-184
umido	damp D-7
umido	moist M-199
umile	humble H-187, 188, 189
umorismo	humor H-191
un	a A-1
un altro	another A-191
una volta	once O-69
uncino	hook H-150
ungere	anoint A-189, 190
ungherese	Hungarian H-194
unghia	fingernail F-139
unico	sole S-363
uniforme	uniform U-30
unione	union U-32, 33
unire	join J-17, 18, 19
unità	unity U-36
universale	universal U-37
università	university U-38, 39, 40
università	college C-234
uno	one O-72, 73
uomo	man M-40
uovo	egg E-32
urlare	bawl B-57, 58
usare	use U-64
uscita	exit E-207
utilizzare	utilize U-68
uva	grape G-117, 118

V

va bene	all right A-135
vacanza	vacancy V-1
vacanze	vacation V-3
vacca	cow C-440
vaccinazione	vaccination V-4
vagare	wander W-16, 17
vagare	roam R-226
vagina	vagina V-5
vago	vague V-6
vagoni	cars C-66
vaiolo	smallpox S-322
valere	worth W-191
valido	valid V-10
valigetta	valise V-11
valigia	suitcase S-565
valle	vale V-9
valutare	evaluate E-154, 155
vanga	spade S-386
vangelo	gospel G-92, 93
vanità	vanity V-16
vanitoso	conceited C-289

vano	vain V-7
vantare	brag B-219
vantarsi	boast B-189
vapore	steam S-473
vari	various V-18
varicella	chickenpox C-145
vario	varied V-17
vassoio	tray T-271
vecchio	old O-58
Vecchio Testamento	Old Testament O-62, 63, 64, 65
vedere	see S-116
veduta	view V-42
veleno	poison P-227, 228
velo	veil V-20
velocità	speed S-408
vendere	sell S-132
vendere	vend V-21
vendetta	revenge R-181
vendita	sale S-22
venerare	revere R-182, 183
venerdì	Friday F-268
venire	come C-246, 247, 248
vento	wind W-135
verbale	verbal V-23, 24
verde	green G-149
vergine	virgin V-48
vergine	maiden M-14
vergogna	shame S-170, 171
verità	truth T-296
verme	worm W-175
verniciare	paint P-6
vero	true T-292
vero	actual A-67
versare	pour P-269
versi	verse V-27
verso	toward T-242, 243, 244
vertiginoso	dizzy D-252, 253
vescovo	bishop B-158, 159
veste	gown G-101
vestiti	clothes C-200
vestito	frock F-276
vestito	garment G-14
vetro	glass G-54
vettura	car C-48
vettura	carriage C-62, 63
via	street S-511
viaggiare	travel T-268, 269, 270
viaggiare con l'autostop	hitchhike H-124
viaggio	trip T-282, 283, 284
viaggio	journey J-25, 26, 27
vibrazione	vibration V-33
vice presidente	vice president V-34, 35
vicinanza	vicinity V-36
vicino	near N-26, 27
vicino	neighbor N-47
vicino	close C-197
vigilia	eve E-157
vigoroso	sturdy S-537
villaggio	village V-43

Japanese-English Index

あ

ああ [ā]	alas! A-123
愛 [ai]	love L-169
哀願 [aigan]	supplication S-590
愛人 [aijin]	lover L-170
アイスクリーム [aisukurīmu]	ice cream I-4, 5
アイススケート [aisu-sukēto]	ice-skating I-6
合図する [aizu-suru]	beckon B-82
間 [aida]	while W-97
相等しい [aihitoshii]	equal E-131
愛撫 [aibu]	petting P-135
合間 [aima]	meantime M-82
あいまいな [aimaina]	obscure O-18
アイルランド [airurando]	Ireland I-199
アイロンをかける [airon-o-kakeru]	iron I-202
アイロンをかける [airon-o-kakeru]	press P-305
青い [aoi]	blue B-184
青ざめた [aozameta]	pale P-11
赤 [aka]	red R-69
赤らむ [akaramu]	flush F-182
赤ン坊 [akanbō]	baby B-1
秋 [aki]	autumn A-316, 317
秋 [aki]	fall F-25
明らかな [akiraka-na]	obvious O-25
あきらめる [akirameru]	forfeit F-220
悪魔 [akuma]	devil D-138
悪魔 [akuma]	Satan S-37
あけっぱなしの [akeppanashi-no]	frank F-251
上げる [ageru]	raise R-18, 19
上げる [ageru]	elevate E-60
あご [ago]	chin C-150
あごひげ [agohige]	beard B-70, 71
朝 [asa]	morning M-222
浅い [asai]	shallow S-169
あざ笑う [azawarau]	sneer S-338
足 [ashi]	feet F-95
足 [ashi]	foot F-200
足 [ashi]	leg L-63
味 [aji]	taste T-34
アジア [azia]	Asia A-270
足跡 [ashiato]	track T-249
足の指 [ashi-no-yubi]	toe T-208
足場 [ashiba]	scaffold S-53
明日 [asu]	tomorrow T-217
預ける [azukeru]	check C-132
汗 [ase]	sweat S-625, 626
あぜんとする [azen-to-suru]	dumfounded D-329, 330
遊び [asobi]	game G-11

洗う 〔arau〕	wash W-26, 27
洗う事 〔arau-koto〕	wash W-25
あらかじめ警告する 〔arakajime-keikoku-suru〕	forewarn F-219
嵐 〔arashi〕	storm S-501
争う 〔arasou〕	contend C-358, 360
競う 〔arasou〕	vie V-39, 40, 41
改める 〔aratameru〕	alter A-147
霰 〔arare〕	hail H-2
現われる 〔arawareru〕	appear A-217
ありがたく思わない 〔arigataku-omowanai〕	ungrateful U-28
ありがとう 〔arigatō〕	thank you T-90
ありそうな事 〔arisōna-koto〕	probable P-336
歩き回る 〔arukimawaru〕	roam R-226
歩き廻る 〔arukimawaru〕	wander W-16, 17
歩く 〔aruku〕	walk W-13
アルコール飲料 〔arukōru-inryō〕	liquor L-117, 118
アルファベット 〔arufabetto〕	alphabet A-142
合わせる 〔awaseru〕	join to J-20
憐み 〔awaremi〕	compassion C-269
憐み 〔awaremi〕	mercy M-124, 125
憐み 〔awaremi〕	pity P-187

い

いいえ 〔iie〕	no N-86, 87
言いまぎらす 〔iimagirasu〕	prevaricate P-308
言う 〔iu〕	say S-52
家 〔ie〕	house H-171
イエスキリスト 〔iesu-kirisuto〕	Jesus J-10
イエズス会の 〔iezusukai-no〕	Jesuit J-9
いかに…であろうとも 〔ikani～dearōtomo〕	however H-176, 177
怒り 〔ikari〕	anger A-173
怒り 〔ikari〕	ire I-198
生き返る 〔ikikaeru〕	revive R-187
生きている 〔ikiteiru〕	alive A-126
いきな 〔iki-na〕	stylish S-538
異教徒 〔ikyōto〕	heretic H-97
イギリス人 〔igirisu-jin〕	Englishman E-102
生きる 〔ikiru〕	live L-124
行く 〔iku〕	go G-69
いくつ 〔ikutsu〕	how old? H-181
いくつかの 〔ikutsuka-no〕	several S-162
いくら 〔ikura〕	how much money? H-180
行け 〔ike〕	go G-70
意見 〔iken〕	opinion O-98
以後 〔igo〕	since S-265
石 〔ishi〕	stone S-494, 495
意志 〔ishi〕	will W-126, 127
意志 〔ishi〕	intent I-151
維持 〔iji〕	maintenance M-21
意識 〔ishiki〕	conscience C-328, 330
意識 〔ishiki〕	consciousness C-332
いじくる 〔ijikuru〕	meddle M-90, 91
意地の悪い 〔iji-no-warui〕	nasty N-15
いじめる 〔ijimeru〕	tease T-51, 52, 53
意志力 〔ishi-ryoku〕	will power W-132
医者 〔isha〕	doctor D-255
移住する 〔ijū-suru〕	migrate M-149
衣装 〔ishō〕	garment G-14
いす 〔isu〕	chair C-101, 102, 103
泉 〔izumi〕	fountain F-239

イスラエル [isuraeru]	Israel I-211
イスラエル人 [isuraeru-jin]	Hebrew H-80
いずれかの [izurekano]	either E-41, 42, 43
遺贈する [izō-suru]	bequeath B-121
忙しい [isogashii]	busy B-277, 278
急ぎ [isogi]	haste H-48
急ぐ [isogu]	hustle H-206
急ぐ [isogu]	hurry H-199
いたずらな [itazura-na]	naughty N-21
痛み [itami]	ache A-51
痛めた [itameta]	hurt H-203
イタリア [itaria]	Italy I-218, 219
イタリアの [itaria-no]	Italian I-217
一 [ichi]	one O-72, 73
位置 [ichi]	location L-133
位置 [ichi]	position P-251, 252, 253
一群 [ichigun]	gang G-12
いちご [ichigo]	strawberry S-509
一度 [ichido]	once O-69
一日中 [ichinichijū]	all day A-131
一年中 [ichinenjū]	all year (round) A-137
一年の [ichinen-no]	annual A-187
一番悪い [ichiban-warui]	worst W-188
一部分 [ichibubun]	part P-32
一枚 [ichimai]	slice S-306
一覧表 [ichiran-hyō]	list L-119, 120
いつ [itsu]	when W-89
いつも [itsumo]	ever E-163, 164, 165
一週間で [isshūkan-de]	in a week I-56
一週間前 [isshūkanmae]	week ago, a W-66
一掃する [issō-suru]	banish B-26
一致 [itchi]	unity U-36
一致する [itchi-suru]	coincide C-225, 226
一杯にする [ippai-ni-suru]	fill F-123
一片 [ippen]	piece P-167
糸 [ito]	thread T-155
井戸 [ido]	well W-76
いとこ [itoko]	cousin (f) C-432
いとこ [itoko]	cousin (m) C-433
いとしい [itoshii]	beloved B-108
いない [inai]	out O-143
田舎 [inaka]	country C-423
犬 [inu]	dog D-259, 260
祈る [inoru]	pray P-283
衣服 [ifuku]	clothes C-200
異邦人 [ihōjin]	Gentile G-29
今 [ima]	now N-130
居間 [ima]	living room L-128
いまだに [imadani]	still S-486
今の [imano]	current C-493
意味 [imi]	significance S-248, 249
いや気 [iyake]	disgust D-208
卑しい心 [iyashii-kokoro]	dirty-minded D-178
いやで気持が悪くなる [iyade-kimochi-ga-warukunaru]	make me disgusted, sick M-31
いやな [iya-na]	revolting R-189
いやになる [iya-ni-naru]	fed up F-84
イヤリング [iyaringu]	earring E-12
いらいらする [irairasuru]	frustrated F-286
いら立たせる [iradataseru]	annoy A-183, 184
入口 [iriguchi]	entrance E-119
色 [iro]	color C-241, 242, 243
色々の [iroiro-no]	sundry S-579

岩 [iwa]　rock R-235, 236
祝う [iwau]　celebrate C-88
祝う [iwau]　congratulate C-319, 320
言わないで [iwanaide]　don't tell D-282
いわゆる [iwayuru]　so-called S-348
印 [in]　seal S-101, 102
陰気になる [inki-ni-naru]　gloom G-60
インク [inku]　ink I-111, 112
陰茎 [inkei]　penis P-88
印刷する [insatsu-suru]　print P-326
印刷屋 [insatsuya]　printer P-327
印刷屋 [insatsuya]　printshop P-328
印象づける [inshōzukeru]　impress I-46
インチ [inchi]　inch I-57, 58
院長 [inchō]　rector R-68
インテリの [interi-no]　highbrow H-108
インドの [indo-no]　Indian I-72, 73
隠とん者 [intonsha]　hermit H-99
引用 [inyō]　quotation Q-31
引用する [inyō-suru]　cite C-176

う

ウイスキー [uisukī]　whiskey W-102, 103
ウェイター [ueitā]　waiter W-6, 7
上に [ueni]　on O-68
植える [ueru]　plant P-200
浮く [uku]　float F-175
受付 [uketsuke]　usher U-67
受け取る [uketoru]　receive R-57
動き [ugoki]　motion M-232, 233
動く [ugoku]　move M-249
動く [ugoku]　run R-283
ウサギ [usagi]　rabbit R-3, 4
牛や馬の飼 [ushi-ya-uma-no-esa]　mash M-63
失う [ushinau]　lose L-161
後 [ushiro]　rear R-50
後ろへ [ushiro-e]　back B-3
うす明り [usuakari]　twilight T-310
淡紅色 [usubeniiro]　pink P-179
ウズラ [uzura]　quail Q-2, 3
うそつき [usotsuki]　liar L-87
うそをつく [uso-o-tsuku]　lie L-94, 95
歌 [uta]　song S-371
歌 [uta]　chant C-111
歌う [utau]　sing S-268
疑い [utagai]　doubt D-289, 290, 291
疑い [utagai]　suspicion S-615
疑い深い事 [utagaibukai-koto]　incredulity I-617
疑う [utagau]　doubt D-289, 290, 291
うたた寝する [utatane-suru]　doze D-295
打ち勝つ [uchikatsu]　overcome O-149
打ち砕く [uchikudaku]　pound P-268
打ち負かす [uchimakasu]　beat B-73
打つ [utsu]　beat B-72, 74
打つ [utsu]　strike S-517
打つ [utsu]　hit H-120, 121, 122
撃つ [utsu]　shoot S-212, 213
美しい [utsukushii]　beautiful B-77
写す [utsusu]　copy C-394, 395
移す [utsusu]　transfer T-261, 262

え

延期する [enki-suru] postpone P-263
延期する [enki-suru] put off P-427
円形 [enkei] circle C-174
エンジン [enjin] engine E-99
演ずる [enzuru] perform P-101
演説 [enzetsu] address A-75
演説 [enzetsu] speech S-405
演説する [enzetsu-suru] orate O-113
えんどう豆 [endōmame] peas P-69
鉛筆 [enpitsu] pencil P-85

お

甥 [oi] nephew N-50
追いかける [oikakeru] pursue P-422
おいしい [oishii] delicious D-78, 79
おいしい [oishii] savory S-48
老いた [oita] old O-59
追い出す [oidasu] cast out C-71
追い出す [oidasu] expel E-211, 212
追い払う [oiharau] send away S-141, 142
老いぼれの [oibore-no] decrepit D-53
追う [ou] chase C-121
雄牛 [oushi] bull B-268
終える [oeru] conclude C-301
終える [oeru] terminate T-83
終える [oeru] finish F-142, 143
王位についた [ōi-ni-tsuita] crowned C-472
おおかみ [ōkami] wolf W-159
大きい [ōkii] big B-142, 143
大きい [ōkii] great G-135
大きい [ōkii] large L-16
多くの [ōku-no] lot L-164
多くの [ōku-no] much M-255
大げさに言う [ōgesa-ni-yuu] exaggerate E-179, 180
大声で叫ぶ [ōgoe-de-sakebu] call out C-15
王国 [ōkoku] kingdom K-20
王様 [ōsama] king K-19
王子 [ōji] prince P-321
大鹿 [ōjika] elk E-64
大鹿 [ōjika] moose M-216
応じる [ōjiru] comply C-285
王女 [ōjo] princess P-322
黄色人種 [ōshoku-jinshu] yellow race Y-8
オーストラリア [ōsutoraria] Australia A-312
応答 [ōtō] response R-154
オートバイ [ōtobai] motorcycle M-242
オートミール [ōtomīru] oatmeal O-3
応募する [ōbo-suru] apply A-224
横領する [ōryō-suru] embezzle E-68
大笑い [ōwarai] hysterical laugh H-212
丘 [oka] hill H-110
お母さん [okāsan] mama M-39
お母さん [okāsan] mother M-229, 230
おかしい [okashii] funny F-294
おかしい [okashii] ridiculous R-194
犯す [okasu] violate V-46
お金 [okane] money M-203, 205
おきざりにする [okizari-ni-suru] leave L-56
起きた [okita] awake A-323
起きて [okite] commandments C-257

落とす [otosu]	drop D-313
一昨日 [ototoi]	day before yesterday D-19
音の大きい [oto-no-ōkii]	loud L-165
音のしない [oto-no-shinai]	noiseless N-93
衰える [otoroeru]	fade F-9
驚かす [odorokasu]	surprise S-601, 602
驚く [odoroku]	wonder W-161, 163
同じ [onaji]	same S-27, 28, 29
各々の [ono-ono-no]	each E-1
各々の [ono-ono-no]	every E-168
鬼 [oni]	demon D-86
おば [oba]	aunt A-311
お針女 [ohariko]	sewer S-164
オペラグラス [operagurasu]	opera glasses O-94
おぼれる [oboreru]	drown D-315, 316
お守り [omamori]	phylacteries P-147
重い [omoi]	heavy H-79
重い [omoi]	weighty W-73
思いあがった [omoi-agatta]	swell-headed S-638
思い出す [omoidasu]	recall R-55, 56
思い出す [omoidasu]	recollect R-65, 66
思い出す [omoidasu]	remember R-107
思い出させる [omoidasaseru]	remind R-108
思いつき [omoitsuki]	fancy F-42
おもしろい [omoshiroi]	amusing A-168
主な [omona]	main M-17
主に [omoni]	burden B-270
主に [omoni]	mainly M-18
おや [oya]	O! O-1
おや [oya]	oh O-52
親方 [oyakata]	foreman F-213
親指 [oyayubi]	thumb T-171
泳ぐ [oyogu]	swim S-640
オランダ [oranda]	Holland H-134, 135
オランダ [oranda]	Netherlands N-56, 57
オランダ人 [orandajin]	Dutch (people) D-335, 336
オランダの [oranda-no]	Dutch D-335, 336
降りる [oriru]	get off G-40
折る [oru]	break B-227
折る [oru]	fold F-189
織る [oru]	weave W-61
オレンヂ [orenji]	orange O-110, 111
愚かさ [orokasa]	folly F-192
疎かにする [orosokani-suru]	neglect N-44
終り [owari]	end E-84, 87
音楽 [ongaku]	music M-266
恩恵 [onkei]	benefit B-119
温暖な [ondan-na]	warm W-21, 22
恩ちょう [onchō]	grace G-103, 104
温度 [ondo]	temperature T-71
温度計 [ondokei]	thermometer T-124
雄鶏 [ondori]	cock C-217
おんどり [ondori]	rooster R-250
女の子 [onnanoko]	girl G-46
女の人 [onnanohito]	woman W-160
温和な [onwa-na]	mild M-150

か

カーテン [kāten]	curtain C-497
階 [kai]	story S-503

会員 [kaiin]	member M-105, 106
海岸 [kaigan]	coast C-211
海岸 [kaigan]	seaside S-105
会議 [kaigi]	conference C-307
懐疑的な [kaigiteki-na]	skeptical S-285
階級 [kaikyū]	class C-180
階級制度 [kaikyūseido]	caste C-69
懐疑論者 [kaigironja]	skeptic S-282
会計係り [kaikeigakari]	treasurer T-272
解決する [kaiketsu-suru]	resolve R-149
回顧 [kaiko]	retrospection R-179
会合 [kaigō]	meeting M-99, 100
会合する [kaigō-suru]	convene C-377
悔恨 [kaikon]	contrition C-373
開始する [kaishi-suru]	commence C-258
会社 [kaisha]	concern C-299
会社 [kaisha]	company C-267
改善する [kaizen-suru]	mend M-111
階段 [kaidan]	stair(s) S-445, 446
階段 [kaidan]	step(s) S-479, 480
害虫 [gaichū]	pest P-133
懐中電燈 [kaichūdentō]	flashlight F-159
回転する [kaiten-suru]	roll R-242, 243
外套 [gaitō]	cloak C-195
外套 [gaitō]	overcoat O-148
概念 [gainen]	concept C-295, 296
概念 [gainen]	notion N-127
解放 [kaihō]	liberation L-88
解放する [kaihō-suru]	deliver D-81
解放する [kaihō-suru]	emancipate E-65
かいま見る [kaimamiru]	peek P-73, 74
買い戻す [kaimodosu]	redeem R-71, 72
買戻し人 [kaimodoshi-nin]	redeemer R-73
買物する [kaimono-suru]	shop S-214
会話 [kaiwa]	conversation C-379, 380
買う [kau]	buy B-285
買う [kau]	purchase P-413
変える [kaeru]	change C-108, 109
変える [kaeru]	convert C-382
変える [kaeru]	frog F-277, 278
顔 [kao]	face F-3
香り [kaori]	odor O-36
画家 [gaka]	painter P-8
価格 [kakaku]	price P-313, 314
化学 [kagaku]	chemistry C-139
科学 [kagaku]	science S-66, 67
鏡 [kagami]	mirror M-177
鏡 [kagami]	looking glass L-156
輝かしい [kagayakashii]	glorious G-63
かがる [kagaru]	darn D-15
かき [kaki]	oyster O-157
鍵 [kagi]	key K-6
鍵がかかっている [kagi-ga-kakkatte-iru]	locked L-136
書き留める [kakitomeru]	note N-118
かぎ針編みをする [kagibariami-o-suru]	crochet C-460
かぎ棒 [kagibō]	hook H-150
かき乱す [kakimidasu]	disturb D-237
描く [kaku]	draw D-298
書く [kaku]	write W-205
家具 [kagu]	smell S-324
家具業 [kagugyō]	upholstery U-54
家具師 [kagushi]	cabinetmaker C-2

各自　[kakuji]　　　　　　　　　　each one　E-2
各自　[kakuji]　　　　　　　　　　individual　I-79, 80
確実な　[kakujitsu-na]　　　　　certain　C-98
確実な　[kakujitsu-na]　　　　　sure　S-596
学者　[gakusha]　　　　　　　　scholar　S-64
各種の　[kakushu-no]　　　　　various　V-18
学習　[gakushū]　　　　　　　　lesson　L-77
学習者　[gakushūsha]　　　　　learner　L-53
確信　[kakushin]　　　　　　　　conviction　C-384, 385, 386
隠す　[kakusu]　　　　　　　　　hide　H-103
学生　[gakusei]　　　　　　　　student　S-531
覚せい剤　[kakuseizai]　　　　dope　D-287
角度　[kakudo]　　　　　　　　angle　A-174
格闘　[kakutō]　　　　　　　　combat　C-245
獲得する　[kakutoku-suru]　　acquire　A-58
獲得する　[kakutoku-suru]　　obtain　O-24
獲得する　[kakutoku-suru]　　procure　P-348
確認　[kakunin]　　　　　　　　confirmation　C-313
確認する　[kakunin-suru]　　identify　I-9
隠れて　[kakurete]　　　　　　on the sly　O-85
かけ　[kake]　　　　　　　　　bet　B-131
賭　[kake]　　　　　　　　　　wager　W-1
影　[kage]　　　　　　　　　　shadow　S-166
陰口をきく　[kageguchi-o-kiku]　backbite　B-6
かけ事をする　[kakegoto-o-suru]　gamble　G-10
賭ける　[kakeru]　　　　　　　bet　B-131
掛ける　[kakeru]　　　　　　　multiply　M-262
過去　[kako]　　　　　　　　　past　P-49
かご　[kago]　　　　　　　　　basket　B-47
囲い　[kakoi]　　　　　　　　fence　F-98, 99
囲む　[kakomu]　　　　　　　surround　S-606
傘　[kasa]　　　　　　　　　　umbrella　U-9
飾る　[kazaru]　　　　　　　　adorn　A-94
飾る　[kazaru]　　　　　　　　decorate　D-48, 49
火山　[kazan]　　　　　　　　volcano　V-59
餓死　[gashi]　　　　　　　　starvation　S-456
賢い　[kashikoi]　　　　　　　shrewd　S-232
賢いこと　[kashikoikoto]　　wisdom　W-145
果実　[kajitsu]　　　　　　　fruit　F-285
貸付け　[kashitsuke]　　　　loan　L-129, 130
かじ屋　[kajiya]　　　　　　blacksmith　B-166
かしら　[kashira]　　　　　　chief　C-146
貸す　[kasu]　　　　　　　　lend　L-70, 71
風　[kaze]　　　　　　　　　wind　W-135
風邪　kaze]　　　　　　　　　cold　C-230
課税する　[kazei-suru]　　　excise　E-193
稼ぐ　[kasegu]　　　　　　　earn　E-10
数える　[kazoeru]　　　　　count　C-422
家族　[kazoku]　　　　　　　family　F-37, 38
ガソリン　[gasorin]　　　　　gas　G-16
堅い　[katai]　　　　　　　　hard　H-37
堅い　[katai]　　　　　　　　rigid　R-202
がたがた揺れる　[gata-gata-yureru]　jolt　J-24
固く締った　[katakushimatta]　fast　F-61
形　[katachi]　　　　　　　　form　F-226
形　[katachi]　　　　　　　　shape　S-174, 175
〜がたまる　[〜ga tamaru]　accumulate　A-43, 44, 45
固める　[katameru]　　　　　fortify　F-232
傾くこと　[katamuku-koto]　inclination　I-60
固湯での　[katayude-no]　　hardboiled　H-38
片寄らない　[katayoranai]　impartial　I-31
カタログ　[katarogu]　　　　catalog　C-73

982

勝気な [kachiki-na]	strong-minded S-525
価値のある [kachi-no-aru]	valuable V-13
価値のある [kachi-no-aru]	deserve D-113
価値のない [kachi-no-nai]	worthless W-192, 193
勝つ [katsu]	win W-133, 134
閣下 [kakka]	lord L-158
活気のない [kakki-no-nai]	depressed D-102
学校 [gakkō]	school S-65
かっさいする [kassai-suru]	acclaim A-34
合衆国 [gasshūkoku]	United States U-35
かっときやすい [katto-kiyasui]	hot-headed H-167
カップケーキ [kappu kēki]	muffin M-257
仮定する [katei-suru]	suppose S-594
角 [kado]	corner C-402
～かどうか [～kadōka]	whether W-94
カトリックの [katorikku-no]	Catholic C-79
悲しい [kanashii]	sad S-8
悲しみ [kanashimi]	sorrow S-373
悲しみに沈んだ [kanashimi-ni-shizunda]	mournful M-245
悲しむ [kanashimu]	sorrowful S-374
カナダ [kanada]	Canada C-26
カナダの [kanada-no]	Canadian C-27
金づち [kanazuchi]	hammer H-22
カヌーこぎ [kanū-kogi]	canoeing C-37
鐘 [kane]	bell B-104, 105
彼女 [kanojo]	her (pron) H-94
彼女 [kanojo]	she S-183
彼女自身 [kanojo-jishin]	herself H-101
彼女の [kanojo-no]	her (poss) H-94
彼女のもの [kanojo-no-mono]	hers H-100
可能性 [kanōsei]	possibility P-259
可能な [kanōna]	possible P-260
かぶら [kabura]	turnip T-306
壁 [kabe]	wall W-14, 15
貨幣 [kahei]	coin C-223, 224
貨幣 [kahei]	currency C-492
カボチャ [kabocha]	pumpkin P-402, 403
かぼちゃ [kabocha]	squash S-439
かまわない [kamawanai]	doesn't matter D-258
我慢する [gaman-suru]	persevere P-118, 119, 121
髪 [kami]	hair H-3
神 [kami]	God G-75
紙 [kami]	paper P-18
嚙みこなす [kamikonasu]	masticate M-66
神様 [kamisama]	Lord L-159
かみそり [kamisori]	razor R-33
雷 [kaminari]	lightning L-102
雷 [kaminari]	thunder T-172
～が身にふりかかる [～ga-mini-furikakaru]	befall B-90
神の [kamino]	divine D-247
紙ばさみ [kamibasami]	paper clip P-19
紙やすり [kamiyasuri]	sandpaper S-34
かむ [kamu]	bite B-161
かむ [kamu]	chew C-142
ガム [gamu]	gum G-181
亀 [kame]	tortoise T-231
仮面をかぶった [kamen-o-kabutta]	false-faced F-34
カメラ [kamera]	camera C-21, 22
かも [kamo]	duck D-323
火曜日 [kayōbi]	Tuesday T-300
～から [～kara]	from F-280
体 [karada]	body B-191

からかう　[karakau]　　　　　　　　　　kid　K-11
からかう　[karakau]　　　　　　　　　　make fun of　M-26
がらがらへび　[garagarahebi]　　　　　rattlesnake　R-31
ガラス　[garasu]　　　　　　　　　　　glass　G-54
空にする　[kara-ni-suru]　　　　　　　evacuate　E-152
空の　[kara-no]　　　　　　　　　　　empty　E-79, 80
空っぽの　[karappo-no]　　　　　　　　void　V-58
借り　[kari]　　　　　　　　　　　　　obligation　O-16
カリエス　[kariesu]　　　　　　　　　caries　C-60
借りがある　[karigaaru]　　　　　　　owe　O-154
借方　[karikata]　　　　　　　　　　　debit　D-35
かり立てる　[kari-tateru]　　　　　　urge　U-60, 61
刈り取る　[karitoru]　　　　　　　　　reap　P-47, 48, 49
仮縫いする　[karinui-suru]　　　　　　baste　B-50
カリフォルニア　[kariforunia]　　　　California　C-10
借りる　[kariru]　　　　　　　　　　　borrow　B-202
狩る　[karu]　　　　　　　　　　　　　hunt　H-198
軽い　[karui]　　　　　　　　　　　　light　L-101
彼　[kare]　　　　　　　　　　　　　　he　H-63
彼自身　[karejishin]　　　　　　　　　himself　H-112
彼の　[kare-no]　　　　　　　　　　　his (adj)　H-117
彼のもの　[kareno-mono]　　　　　　　his (pron)　H-117
彼ら　[karera]　　　　　　　　　　　they　T-126
彼ら自身　[karerajishin]　　　　　　　themselves　T-113
彼らの物　[karera-no-mono]　　　　　　their　T-110
彼らを(に)　[karera-o(ni)]　　　　　　them　T-111
彼を　[kare-o]　　　　　　　　　　　him　H-111
ガロデット，EM　[garodetto,E,M]　　　Gallaudet, E. M.　G-7
ガロデット，T.H　[garodetto,T.H]　　　Gallaudet, T. H.　G-8
川　[kawa]　　　　　　　　　　　　　river　R-222, 223, 224
かわいい　[kawaii]　　　　　　　　　　cute　C-500, 501
変りやすい　[kawariyasui]　　　　　　changeable　C-110
皮をむく　[kawa-o-muku]　　　　　　　peel　P-75, 76
カン(詰めにする)　[kan(zume-ni-suru)]　can(ning)　C-25
管　[kan]　　　　　　　　　　　　　　pipe　P-182
雁　[gan]　　　　　　　　　　　　　　goose　G-91
かんいんを行う　[kanin-o-okonau]　　fornicate　F-228
眼科医　[gankai]　　　　　　　　　　　oculist　O-34
考え込む　[kangaekomu]　　　　　　　speculate　S-400, 401
考える　[kangaeru]　　　　　　　　　conceive　C-290, 291
考える　[kangaeru]　　　　　　　　　think　T-138
感覚　[kankaku]　　　　　　　　　　　sense　S-145
歓喜　[kanki]　　　　　　　　　　　　exultation　E-235
喚起する　[kanki-suru]　　　　　　　arouse　A-254
環境　[kankyō]　　　　　　　　　　　environment　E-122, 123
関係　[kankei]　　　　　　　　　　　connection　C-324
関係　[kankei]　　　　　　　　　　　relation　R-92
歓迎する　[kangei-suru]　　　　　　　welcome　W-75
関係のある　[kankei-no-aru]　　　　　relative　R-96
勧告　[kankoku]　　　　　　　　　　　advice　A-97
看護婦　[kangofu]　　　　　　　　　　nurse　N-136
観察する　[kansatsu-suru]　　　　　　observe　O-19, 20
観察する　[kansatsu-suru]　　　　　　watch　W-36, 37
かんしゃくをおこす　[kanshaku-o-okosu]　flip the lid　F-173
感謝祭　[kanshasai]　　　　　　　　　Thanksgiving　T-98
感じやすい　[kanjiyasui]　　　　　　　sensitive　S-147
感謝する　[kansha-suru]　　　　　　　grateful　G-122
観衆　[kanshū]　　　　　　　　　　　audience　A-309, 310
感情　[kanjō]　　　　　　　　　　　　emotion　E-71, 72
干渉する　[kanshō-suru]　　　　　　　interfere　I-164
干渉する　[kanshō-suru]　　　　　　　butt in　B-282
感じる　[kanjiru]　　　　　　　　　　feel　F-91

感心する [kanshin-suru]	impressed I-47
歓声 [kansei]	cheer C-134
関税 [kanzei]	duty D-338
完全な [kanzen-na]	complete C-282, 283
完全な [kanzen-na]	perfect P-99
簡素な [kanso-na]	plain P-192
肝臓 [kanzō]	liver L-126
乾燥した [kansō-shita]	arid A-245
乾燥している [kansō-shiteiru]	dry D-322
寛大な [kandaina]	magnanimous M-10
寛大に取り扱う [kandai-ni-toriatsukau]	tolerate T-212, 213
簡単な [kantan-na]	brief B-236, 237
簡単な [kantan-na]	simple S-262, 263
簡単なテスト [kantan-na-tesuto]	quiz Q-28, 29, 30
貫通する [kantsū-suru]	penetrate P-87
感づく [kanzuku]	suspect S-608, 609
監督 [kantoku]	supervisor S-588
監督教 [kantoku-kyō]	Episcopal E-127
監督教会の [kantokukyōkai-no]	Episcopalian E-128
監督する [kantoku-suru]	supervise S-587
かんな [kañna]	plane P-197
乾杯 [kanpai]	toast T-205
かんばつ [kanbatsu]	drought D-314
完璧な [kanpeki-na]	immaculate I-24
冠 [kanmuri]	crown C-470, 471
寛容な [kanyō-na]	generous G-27, 28
肝要な [kanyō-na]	imperative I-35
管理者 [kanrisha]	superintendent S-583
管理する [kanri-suru]	operate O-95

<h2 style="text-align:center">き</h2>

木 [ki]	tree T-273
木 [ki]	wood W-167
黄色 [kiiro]	yellow Y-7
消える [kieru]	disappear D-180
消える [kieru]	vanish V-15
記憶 [kioku]	memory M-109
機会 [kikai]	chance C-107
機械 [kikai]	machine M-1
機会 [kikai]	opportunity O-100, 101, 102, 103, 104
機会 [kikai]	occasion O-26
危害 [kigai]	harm (n) H-44, 45
機械類 [kikairui]	machinery M-3
危害を加える [kigai-o-kuwaeru]	harm (v) H-44, 45
幾何学 [kikagaku]	geometry G-36
気が変な [ki-ga-henna]	cracked in the head C-444
期間 [kikan]	period P-108
機関車 [kikansha]	locomotive L-137
機関銃 [kikanjū]	machine gun M-2
戯曲 [gikyoku]	drama D-297
飢きん [kikin]	famine F-39
義兄 [gikei]	brother-in-law B-258
危険 [kiken]	danger D-10, 11
危険 [kiken]	peril P-106
起源 [kigen]	origin O-128, 129, 130
聞く [kiku]	hear H-68
聞く [kiku]	listen L-121
器具 [kigu]	instrument I-139
器具 [kigu]	apparatus A-213
岸 [kishi]	shore S-217

義姉妹　[gishimai]　　　　　　　　　　sister-in-law　S-274
汽車　[kisha]　　　　　　　　　　　　cars (railroad)　C-66
汽車　[kisha]　　　　　　　　　　　　train　T-256
キス　[kisu]　　　　　　　　　　　　kiss　K-21, 22, 23
傷つける　[kizutsukeru]　　　　　　　mar　M-52, 53
犠牲　[gisei]　　　　　　　　　　　　sacrifice　S-6
寄生動物　[kiseidōbutsu]　　　　　　　parasite　P-27
奇蹟　[kiseki]　　　　　　　　　　　miracle　M-176
季節　[kisetsu]　　　　　　　　　　　season　S-106
気絶する　[kizetsu-suru]　　　　　　　faint　F-15, 16
為善者　[gizensha]　　　　　　　　　hypocrite　H-209, 210
基礎　[kiso]　　　　　　　　　　　　basis　B-45, 46
規則　[kisoku]　　　　　　　　　　　rule　R-280
規則　[kisoku]　　　　　　　　　　　regulation　R-83
規則だてる　[kisokudateru]　　　　　　regulate　R-82
規則的な　[kisokuteki-na]　　　　　　regular　R-81
基礎とする　[kiso-to-suru]　　　　　　base　B-39, 40
基礎となる　[kiso-to-naru]　　　　　　base　B-41
北　[kita]　　　　　　　　　　　　　north　N-104
ギター　[gitā]　　　　　　　　　　　guitar　G-179
北アメリカ　[kita-amerika]　　　　　　North America　N-105
気体　[kitai]　　　　　　　　　　　　gas　G-15
期待する　[kitai-suru]　　　　　　　　expect　E-209
きたない　[kitanai]　　　　　　　　　foul　F-235
気違い　[kichigai]　　　　　　　　　nuts　N-139, 140
気違いじみた　[kichigaijimita]　　　　crazy　C-449, 450, 451
きちんとした　[kichintoshita]　　　　　proper　P-371
きつね　[kitsune]　　　　　　　　　　fox　F-244
切手　[kitte]　　　　　　　　　　　　stamp　S-447, 448
切符　[kippu]　　　　　　　　　　　ticket　T-176, 177
軌道　[kidō]　　　　　　　　　　　　orbit　O-116, 117
気にしない　[ki-ni-shinai]　　　　　　don't care　D-274, 275, 276
機能　[kinō]　　　　　　　　　　　　function　F-291
気の狂った　[ki-no-kurutta]　　　　　mad　M-5
気の狂った　[ki-no-kurutta]　　　　　off the beam　O-50
木の実　[kinomi]　　　　　　　　　　nut　N-137
気の弱い　[kinoyowai]　　　　　　　　weak-minded　W-54
寄付する　[kifu-suru]　　　　　　　　contribute　C-372
基本　[kihon]　　　　　　　　　　　foundation　F-237
気迷う　[kimayou]　　　　　　　　　waver　W-47, 48
奇妙な　[kimyō-na]　　　　　　　　　curious　C-488
奇妙な　[kimyō-na]　　　　　　　　　queer　Q-12
奇妙な　[kimyō-na]　　　　　　　　　strange　S-507, 508
義務　[gimu]　　　　　　　　　　　　duty　D-337
義務　[gimu]　　　　　　　　　　　　obligation　O-15
義務ずけられた　[gimuzukerareta]　　　bound　B-207
着物　[kimono]　　　　　　　　　　　dress　D-304
客　[kyaku]　　　　　　　　　　　　client　C-190, 191
虐待する　[gyakutai-suru]　　　　　　crucify　C-474
逆戻り　[gyakumodori]　　　　　　　relapse　R-91
キャッチャー　[kyatcher]　　　　　　catcher　C-78
キャベツ　[kyabetsu]　　　　　　　　cabbage　C-1
キャンプ　[kyampu]　　　　　　　　　camp　C-23
キャンディー　[kyandei]　　　　　　　candy　C-31, 32
九　[kyū]　　　　　　　　　　　　　nine　N-84
休暇　[kyūka]　　　　　　　　　　　vacation　V-3
休憩　[kyūkei]　　　　　　　　　　　rest　R-159, 160
救済　[kyūsai]　　　　　　　　　　　salvation　S-26
休日　[kyūjitsu]　　　　　　　　　　holiday　H-133
救出する　[kyūshutsu-suru]　　　　　　rescue　R-137
弓術　[kyūjutsu]　　　　　　　　　　archery　A-238
救助者　[kyūjyosha]　　　　　　　　　savior　S-47

きれいな	[kireina]	pretty P-307
きれいに	[kireini]	clean C-185
議論する	[giron-suru]	argue A-243
気を失う	[ki-o-ushinau]	pass out P-47
気を散らす	[ki-o-chirasu]	distraction D-233
金	[kin]	gold G-80
銀	[gin]	silver S-259, 260
銀行口座	[ginkō-kōza]	charge C-118
禁じる	[kinjiru]	forbid F-206, 207
禁止する	[kinshi-suru]	ban B-20
禁止する	[kinshi-suru]	prohibit P-361
近所	[kinjo]	vicinity V-36
均勢	[kinsei]	balance B-14, 15
金属	[kinzoku]	metal M-130, 131
勤勉	[kinben]	diligence D-165, 166
勤勉な	[kinben-na]	industrious I-88
金曜日	[kinyōbi]	Friday F-268
禁欲	[kinyoku]	abstinence A-28
禁欲	[kinyoku]	mortification M-226

く

食いしんぼう	[kuishinbō]	greedy G-145, 146, 147
クウェーカー	[kuwēkā]	Quaker Q-5
空間	[kūkan]	space S-385
空気	[kūki]	air A-120
空虚	[kūkyo]	vacancy V-1
空想	[kūso]	daydream D-20
偶像	[gūzō]	idol I-11
寓話	[gūwa]	fable F-1
茎	[kuki]	stem S-477
釘	[kugi]	nail N-2
釘づけにする	[kugizuke-ni-suru]	pin P-177
釘抜き金づち	[kuginuki-kanazuchi]	claw hammer C-183
草	[kusa]	grass G-121
草刈りがま	[kusakarigama]	scythe S-99
腐った	[kusatta]	rotten R-258
鎖	[kusari]	chain C-100
腐る	[kusaru]	decay D-37
腐る	[kusaru]	perish P-110
腐る	[kusaru]	rot R-257
草を刈る	[kusa-o-karu]	mow (v) M-252, 253
くじく	[kujiku]	sprain S-426
櫛でとかす	[kushi-de-tokasu]	comb C-244
くしゃみする	[kushami-suru]	sneeze S-339
鯨	[kujira]	whale W-82
薬	[kusuri]	medicine M-93
薬	[kusuri]	pill P-173
薬を飲む	[kusuri-o-nomu]	take a pill T-13
下さい	[kudasai]	give me G-51
くだらない	[kudaranai]	frivolous F-275
くだらない	[kudaranai]	trifling T-277
下る	[kudaru]	descend D-104, 105
下る	[kudaru]	go down G-78
口	[kuchi]	mouth M-248
口がふさがらない	[kuchi-ga-fusagaranai]	open-mouthed O-91
嘴	[kuchibashi]	beak B-63
嘴で突っつく	[kuchibashi-de-tsuttsuku]	peck P-70
口笛を吹く	[kuchibue-o-fuku]	whistle W-105, 106
口紅	[kuchibeni]	lipstick L-115
靴	[kutsu]	shoe(s) S-205, 206

苦痛 [kutsū]   agony A-114
苦痛 [kutsū]   pain P-5
くっついた [kuttsuita]   stuck S-529, 530
靴作り [kutsuzukuri]   shoemaking S-210
靴のひも [kutsu-no-himo]   lace L-2
靴ひも [kutsuhimo]   shoelaces S-208
靴ブラシ [kutsuburashi]   shoebrush S-207
靴屋 [kutsuya]   cobbler C-214
靴屋 [kutsuya]   shoemaker S-209
靴をみがく [kutsu-o-migaku]   shine shoes S-195
句点 [kuten]   comma C-255
愚鈍な [gudon-na]   thick-skulled T-129
国 [kuni]   country C-424
国 [kuni]   nation N-16
国 [kuni]   land L-12
首飾り [kubikazari]   necklace N-34
首にする [kubi-ni-suru]   discharge D-190, 191
首になる [kubi-ni-naru]   fire F-147
工夫する [kufū-suru]   devise D-140, 141
熊 [kuma]   bear B-66, 67
くま手 [kumade]   rake R-22
組合 [kumiai]   association A-284
組合 [kumiai]   sodality S-353
組合 [kumiai]   union U-32, 33
雲 [kumo]   cloud(s) C-204
蜘蛛 [kumo]   spider S-414
暗い [kurai]   dark(ness) D-14
クラッカー [kurakkā]   cracker C-445, 446
クラブ [kurabu]   club C-205
クランクのこぎり [kuranku-nokoḡiri]   jigsaw J-15
クリーム [kurīmu]   cream C-452
繰返す [kurikaesu]   repeat R-121
クリスマス [kurisumasu]   Christmas C-166, 167
クリスマス [kurisumasu]   Xmas X-2
来る [kuru]   come C-246, 247, 249
苦しい時 [kurushii-toki]   hard times H-41
苦しむ [kurushimu]   suffer S-557, 558, 559
車 [kuruma]   car C-48
黒い [kuroi]   black B-164
グロテスクな [gurotesuku-na]   grotesque G-162
鍬 [kuwa]   hoe H-126
加えて [kuwaete]   plus P-219
加える [kuwaeru]   add A-70, 71, 72, 73
加える [kuwaeru]   join J-17, 18, 19
群衆 [gunshū]   crowd C-468
勲章 [kunshō]   medal M-89
軍人 [gunjin]   soldier S-362
軍隊 [guntai]   army A-251
軍隊の [guntai-no]   military M-153
訓練する [kunren-suru]   discipline D-193
訓練する [kunren-suru]   train T-257, 258

け

経営 [kei-ei]   management M-42
計画 [keikaku]   scheme S-63
計画 [keikaku]   plan P-193, 194
経過する [keika-suru]   elapse E-45
経過する [keika-suru]   go by G-74
経過する [keika-suru]   slip away S-311
経験 [keiken]   experience E-215, 216

経験する　[keiken-suru]	experience (v)　E-215, 216
警告する　[keikoku-suru]	admonish　A-89
警察　[keisatsu]	police　P-231
計算する　[keisan-suru]	calculate　C-7
計算する　[keisan-suru]	figure　F-119
計算する　[keisan-suru]	reckon　R-62
芸術　[geijutsu]	art　A-262
芸術家　[geijutsuka]	artist　A-263
継続する　[keizoku-suru]	continue　C-366, 367
刑罰　[keibatsu]	penalty　P-80, 81
敬服する　[keifuku-suru]	admire　A-82, 83
軽蔑　[keibetsu]	scorn　S-74, 75
刑務所　[keimusho]	jail　J-1
刑務所　[keimusho]	penitentiary　P-90
刑務所　[keimusho]	prison　P-329
刑務所に入れる　[keimusho-ni-ireru]	imprison　I-49
ケーキ　[kēki]	cake　C-3, 4, 5
外科　[geka]	surgery　S-599
外科医　[gekai]	surgeon　S-598
けがき針　[kegakibari]	scriber　S-95
怪我する　[kega-suru]	injure　I-107, 108
怪我をした　[kega-o-shita]	hurt　H-200, 201
激怒　[gekido]	rage　R-13
激情　[gekijō]	fury　F-298
劇場　[gekijō]	theatre　T-105
景色　[keshiki]	sight　S-245
化粧　[keshō]	make-up　M-36
化粧品　[keshōhin]	cosmetics　C-413
消す　[kesu]	erase　E-136
消す　[kesu]	expunge　E-227
けち臭い　[kechikusai]	stingy　S-488, 489, 490
けちんぼう　[kechinbō]	tightwad　T-182, 183, 184
結局　[kekkyoku]	eventually　E-162
結婚　[kekkon]	marriage　M-57
結婚式　[kekkonshiki]	wedding　W-62
決して～しない　[kesshite～shinai]	never　N-59
決心する　[kesshin-suru]	make up one's mind　M-37
決定する　[kettei-suru]	decide　D-42
欠点　[ketten]	fault　F-72, 73
欠乏　[ketsubō]	lack　L-3
げっぷをする　[geppu-o-suru]	belch　B-100
毛ほどの幅　[ke-hodo-no-haba]	hair's-breadth　H-8
月曜日　[getsuyōbi]	Monday　M-202
憲法　[kenpō]	constitution　C-343
煙　[kemuri]	smoke　S-327
煙る　[kemuru]	smoke　S-326
ゲラ刷り　[gera-zuri]	galley　G-9
下痢　[geri]	diarrhea　D-148
ける　[keru]	kick　K-7
けれども　[keredomo]	although　A-149
券　[ken]	bill(s)　B-148, 149
剣　[ken]	sword　S-644
懸案中の　[kenanchū-no]	pending　P-86
原因　[genin]	cause　C-82
玄関の　[genkan-no]	vestibular　V-32
厳格な　[genkaku-na]	strict　S-515, 516
研究　[kenkyū]	research　R-138
顕現日　[kengenjitsu]	epiphany　E-126
言語　[gengo]	language　L-13, 14
言語　[gengo]	speech　S-404
健康　[kenkō]	health　H-66
げんこつで打つこと　[genkotsu-de-utsukoto]	punch　P-404, 405

検査 [kensa]　　examination　E-182, 183
現在の [genzai-no]　　present　P-301
献身 [kenshin]　　devotion　D-142
堅信礼 [kenshinrei]　　confirmation　C-314
剣術をする [kenjutsu-o-suru]　　fence　F-100
減少する [genshō-suru]　　decrease　D-50
現像する [genzō-suru]　　develop film　D-133
原則 [gensoku]　　principle　P-325
謙遜な [kenson-na]　　humble　H-187, 188, 189
減退する [gentai-suru]　　decline　D-45, 46
建築する [kenchiku-suru]　　build　B-266
拳闘する [kentō-suru]　　box　B-214
検討する [kentō-suru]　　discuss　D-203
現場をつかまる [genba-o-tsukamaru]　　caught in the act　C-80, 81
権力 [kenryoku]　　authority　A-314

こ

五 [go]　　five　F-153
恋人 [koibito]　　sweetheart　S-633, 634
恋人同士になる [koibitodōshi-ni-naru]　　go steady　G-95
恋をする [koi-o-suru]　　fall in love with　F-31
請う [kou]　　beg　B-94, 95
考案 [kōan]　　idea　I-7
行為 [kōi]　　act　A-61
行為 [kōi]　　deed　D-55
合意しない [gōi-shinai]　　disagree　D-179
光栄 [kōei]　　glory　G-64, 65
講演 [kōen]　　discourse　D-200
効果 [kōka]　　effect　E-27, 28
後悔 [kōkai]　　rue　R-276
後悔した [kōkaishita]　　penitent　P-89
後悔する [kōkai-suru]　　regret　R-79
後悔する [kōkai-suru]　　repent　R-123
高価な [kōka-na]　　costly　C-415
高価な [kōka-na]　　precious　P-288
高価な [kōka-na]　　dear　D-31
交換 [kōkan]　　exchange　E-192
交換する [kōkan-suru]　　exchange　E-192
交換する [kōkan-suru]　　interchange　I-154
講義 [kōgi]　　lecture　L-59
好奇心の強い [kōkishin-no-tsuyoi]　　curious　C-487, 488, 489
抗議する [kōgi-suru]　　protest　P-382
高貴な [kōki-na]　　noble　N-88
合計 [gōkei]　　sum　S-567
口座 [kōza]　　account　A-42
絞殺する [kōsatsu-suru]　　hang　H-30
鉱山 [kōzan]　　mine　M-165
小牛 [koushi]　　calf　C-9
公衆の [kōshū-no]　　public　P-394
工場 [kōjō]　　factory　F-7
強情な [gōjō-na]　　stubborn　S-528
控除する [kōjo-suru]　　subtract　S-549
行進 [kōshin]　　parade　P-24
行進する [kōshin-suru]　　march　M-54, 55
香水 [kōsui]　　perfume　P-104
洪水 [kōzui]　　flood　F-176
構図する [kōzu-suru]　　compose　C-286
構成する [kōsei-suru]　　constitute　C-342
公正な [kōsei-na]　　righteous　R-198
功績 [kōseki]　　merit　M-127

交接する　[kōsetsu-suru]　　　　　copulate　C-393
光線　[kōsen]　　　　　　　　　　ray　R-32
構造　[kōzō]　　　　　　　　　　frame　F-249
強情な　[gōjō-na]　　　　　　　　obstinate　O-22
強奪する　[gōdatsu-suru]　　　　rob　R-227, 228, 229
紅茶　[kōcha]　　　　　　　　　　tea　T-44, 45
交通　[kōtsū]　　　　　　　　　　traffic　T-252
皇帝　[kōtei]　　　　　　　　　　emperor　E-73
コート　[kōto]　　　　　　　　　coat　C-212
高等学校　[kōtōgakkō]　　　　　　high school　H-109
高等の　[kōtō-no]　　　　　　　　advanced　A-96
口頭の　[kōtō-no]　　　　　　　　oral　O-109
氷　[kōri]　　　　　　　　　　　ice　I-3
合流する　[gōryū-suru]　　　　　merge　M-126
考慮する　[kōryo-suru]　　　　　consider　C-336, 337, 338
氷る　[kōru]　　　　　　　　　　freeze　F-260
口論　[kōron]　　　　　　　　　　quarrel　Q-8
荒廃させる　[kōhaisaseru]　　　　ruin　R-278
コーヒー　[kōhī]　　　　　　　　coffee　C-222
幸福　[kōfuku]　　　　　　　　　happiness　H-33
幸福な　[kōfuku-na]　　　　　　　happy　H-34
公平な　[kōhei-na]　　　　　　　fair　F-17
公平な　[kōhei-na]　　　　　　　just　J-35
候補者　[kōhosha]　　　　　　　　candidate　C-29
高慢な　[kōman-na]　　　　　　　haughty　H-54
高慢な　[kōman-na]　　　　　　　proud　P-384
拷問にかける　[gōmon-ni-kakeru]　torment　T-229
声　[koe]　　　　　　　　　　　voice　V-57
越える　[koeru]　　　　　　　　　exceed　E-187
誤解する　[gokai-suru]　　　　　misunderstand　M-188
コカコーラ　[kokakōra]　　　　　Coca-Cola　C-216
コカコーラ　[kokakōra]　　　　　Coke　C-228
小柄な　[kogara-na]　　　　　　　slight　S-309
ご気げんの悪い　[gokigen-no-warui]　grouchy　G-163
小切手　[kogitte]　　　　　　　　check　C-131
呼吸　[kokyū]　　　　　　　　　　breath　B-230
呼吸　[kokyū]　　　　　　　　　　respiration　R-151
こぐ　[kogu]　　　　　　　　　　row　R-265
黒人　[kokujin]　　　　　　　　　Negro　N-45, 46
ごく小さい　[goku-chiisai]　　　　minute　M-175
ごく小さい　[goku-chiisai]　　　　tiny　T-194, 195
黒板　[kokuban]　　　　　　　　　blackboard　B-165
穀類　[kokurui]　　　　　　　　　grain　G-108
ここ　[koko]　　　　　　　　　　here　H-95
午後　[gogo]　　　　　　　　　　afternoon　A-107
心地よい　[kokochiyoi]　　　　　pleasant　P-208
小言を言う　[kogoto-o-yuu]　　　scold　S-69, 70, 71, 72
ここまで　[kokomade]　　　　　　thus far　T-175
心　[kokoro]　　　　　　　　　　mind　M-159, 160, 163
心からの　[kokorokarano]　　　　cordial　C-398
心の狭い　[kokoro-no-semai]　　　narrow-minded　N-14
心の広い　[kokoro-no-hiroi]　　　broad-minded　B-250
試みる　[kokoromiru]　　　　　　attempt　A-297, 298
試みる　[kokoromiru]　　　　　　try　T-297, 298
こじき　[kojiki]　　　　　　　　beggar　B-96
こじき　[kojiki]　　　　　　　　moocher　M-213
こじき　[kojiki]　　　　　　　　panhandler　P-14
こしょう　[koshō]　　　　　　　pepper　P-93
個人の　[kojin-no]　　　　　　　private　P-332
こじんまりとして居心地のよい
　　[kojinmari-toshite-igokochi-no-yoi]
　　　　　　　　　　　　　　　cozy　C-442
こする　[kosuru]　　　　　　　　rub　R-267

し

しかめっつらをする　[shikamettsura-o-suru]　make a face　M-24
士官　[shikan]　sergeant　S-153
時間　[jikan]　hour　H-170
時間　[jikan]　time　T-186, 187, 188, 189
志願者　[shigansha]　volunteer　V-62
磁器　[jiki]　porcelain　P-249
しきたり　[shikitari]　tradition　T-251
敷地　[shikichi]　site　S-278
司教　[shikyō]　bishop　B-158, 159
司教冠　[shikyō-kan]　mitre　M-189
刺激する　[shigeki-suru]　excite　E-194
試験　[shiken]　examination　E-181
試験　[shiken]　test　T-89
事故　[jiko]　accident　A-33
思考　[shikō]　thought　T-150, 151
地獄　[jigoku]　hell　H-86, 87
自己中心主義　[jikochūshin-shugi]　egotism　E-33, 34, 35
仕事　[shigoto]　job　J-16
仕事　[shigoto]　task　T-33
仕事　[shigoto]　work　W-171
仕事場　[shigotoba]　workshop　W-173
視察する　[shisatsu-suru]　inspect　I-128
支社　[shisha]　affiliate　A-101
磁石　[jishaku]　magnet　M-11
思春期　[shishunki]　adolescence　A-90
辞書　[jisho]　dictionary　D-150, 151
地震　[jishin]　earthquake　E-15
自信のある　[jishin-no-aru]　positive　P-254, 255
静かな　[shizuka-na]　quiet　Q-25, 26
静かな　[shizuka-na]　still　S-487
静かにさせる　[shizukani-saseru]　hush　H-205
静かにして下さい　[shizuka-ni-shite-kudasai]　keep quiet　K-2, 3
静かにしなさい　[shizuka-ni-shinasai]　be quiet　B-122, 123
沈む　[shizumu]　sink　S-270, 271
自制　[jisei]　temperance　T-69
私生活　[shiseikatsu]　privacy　P-330
私生児　[shiseiji]　bastard　B-49
自然な　[shizen-na]　natural　N-17
子孫　[shison]　descendant　D-106
子孫　[shison]　offspring　O-49
自尊心　[jisonshin]　pride　P-315
舌　[shita]　tongue　T-218
時代　[jidai]　age　A-112
下手の　[shitade-no]　underhand　U-18
親しい　[shitashii]　friendly　F-270
親しみやすい　[shitashimiyasui]　amiable　A-161
したたる　[shitataru]　drip　D-311
下に　[shita-ni]　beneath　B-114
下に　[shitani]　below　B-109, 110, 111
下の　[shita-no]　down　D-294
七面鳥　[shichimen-chō]　turkey　T-301, 302
歯痛　[shitsū]　toothache　T-224
しっかりした　[shikkarishita]　solid　S-364
しっかり定着させる　[shikkari-teichaku-saseru]　fasten　F-62
四旬節　[shikkusetsu]　Lent　L-72
実行する　[jikkō-suru]　perform　P-100
実行する　[jikkō-suru]　practice　P-278, 279
実際の　[jissai-no]　actual　A-67
実質的な　[jisshitsuteki-na]　substantial　S-547
しっと深い　[shitto-bukai]　jealous　J-5
指定保留地　[shiteihoryūchi]　reservation　R-139
支店　[shiten]　branch　B-222

しゃれた [shareta]	swell S-635, 636
シャベル [shaberu]	shovel S-226
しゃべる [shaberu]	talk T-22, 23, 24
シャワー [shawā]	shower S-229
自由 [jiyū]	liberty L-89
自由な [jiyū-na]	free F-257, 258
週 [shū]	week W-64, 65
十 [jū]	ten T-75
十億 [jūoku]	billion B-147
収穫 [shūkaku]	harvest H-47, 49
習慣 [shūkan]	custom C-498
習慣 [shūkan]	habit H-1
習慣 [shūkan]	practice P-280
習慣 [shūkan]	rule R-279
習慣ずける [shūkan-zukeru]	accustom A-50
宗教 [shūkyō]	religion R-100
十五分 [jūgofun]	quarter-hour Q-10
終始一貫した [shūshiikkan-shita]	consistent C-340
十字架 [jūjika]	cross C-463
終止する [shūshi-suru]	cease C-86
終止符 [shūshifu]	period P-107
収集する [shūshū-suru]	collect C-233
住所 [jūsho]	address A-76, 77
住所 [jūsho]	domicile D-265
修正する [shūsei-suru]	correct C-409
修正する [shūsei-suru]	modify M-198
重大な [jūdai-na]	grave G-126
集団 [shūdan]	group G-165, 166
集中する [shūchū-suru]	concentrate C-293
姑 [shūtome]	mother-in-law M-231
収入 [shūnyū]	income I-65
重複の [jūfuku-no]	duplicate D-332, 333
充分な [jūbun-na]	adequate A-79
充分な [jūbun-na]	ample A-167
充分な [jūbun-na]	sufficient S-560
十分に [jūbun-ni]	enough E-110
十分の一 [jūbun-no-ichi]	tithe T-200
終油の秘蹟 [shūyu-no-hiseki]	extreme unction E-234
重要な [jūyōna]	important I-39, 40
重要な [jūyōna]	vital V-54, 55
修理 [shūri]	repair R-120
修理する [shūri-suru]	mend M-110
主教区 [shukyōku]	diocese D-171
主権 [shuken]	majesty M-22
祝祭 [shukusai]	feast F-81
熟思する [jukushi-suru]	contemplate C-355
熟した [jukushita]	ripe R-210
淑女 [shukujo]	lady L-6
熟達した [jukutatsu-shita]	adept A-78
祝福 [shukufuku]	benediction B-116, 117
祝福する [shukufuku-suru]	bless B-172, 173
手術 [shujutsu]	operation O-96, 97
種々の [shuju-no]	diverse D-240, 241
主題 [shudai]	subject S-540
主張する [shuchō-suru]	advocate A-99
主張する [shuchō-suru]	maintain M-20
熟考する [jukkō-suru]	ponder P-238
出席する [shusseki-suru]	attend A-299
出頭させる [shutto-saseru]	summon S-573, 574
首都 [shuto]	capital C-42
手りゅう弾 [shuryūdan]	grenade G-153
種類 [shurui]	kind K-16

主婦 [shufu]	housekeeper H-172
種別に分ける [shubetsu-ni-wakeru]	assort A-285
主要な [shuyō-na]	essential E-142
手腕 [shuwan]	skill S-287
瞬間 [shunkan]	moment M-201
殉教者 [junkyōsha]	martyr M-59
純潔 [junketsu]	innocence I-115
巡査 [junsa]	cop C-392
ショー [shō]	show S-228
章 [shō]	chapter C-114
錠 [jō]	lock L-134, 135
譲位 [jōi]	abdicate A-7
上院 [jōin]	senate S-137
上院議員 [jōingiin]	senator S-138
女王 [jōō]	queen Q-11
障害 [shōgai]	obstacle O-21
紹介する [shōkai-suru]	introduce I-183
蒸気 [jōki]	steam S-473
正気でない [shōki-de-nai]	insane I-121
商業 [shōgyō]	trade T-250
象限 [shōgen]	quadrant Q-1
証拠 [shōko]	evidence E-174
証拠 [shōko]	proof P-370
証拠 [shōko]	witness W-157
正午 [shōgo]	noon N-101
正午 [shōgo]	midday M-139
小冊子 [shōsasshi]	booklet B-194
称賛 [shōsan]	praise P-282
正直な [shōjiki-na]	honest H-145
正直に [shōjiki-ni]	frankly F-253
生じる [shōjiru]	happen H-31, 32
生じる [shōjiru]	yield Y-13
少女 [shōjo]	maiden M-14
上昇 [jyōshō]	ascension A-266
招待 [shōtai]	invitation I-194
招待された [shōtai-sareta]	invited I-196
招待する [shōtai-suru]	invite I-195
承諾する [shōdaku-suru]	accept A-32
上達する [jōtatsu-suru]	improve I-50
冗談 [jōdan]	joke J-22
女中 [jochū]	maid M-13
焦点を合わせる [shōten-o-awaseru]	focus F-187
衝突 [shōtotsu]	bump B-269
衝突する [shōtotsu-suru]	collide C-235, 236
商人 [shōnin]	merchant M-123
承認 [shōnin]	admission A-85
承認する [shōnin-suru]	admit A-87
情熱 [jōnetsu]	passion P-45, 46
上品な [jōhin-na]	elegant E-58
上品な [jōhin-na]	gracious G-105
丈夫な [jōbu-na]	stout S-504
譲歩する [jōho-suru]	cede C-87
情報を流す [jōhō-o-nagasu]	tip off T-197
消防士 [shōbōshi]	fireman F-148
証明 [shōmei]	testimony T-93
賞与 [shōyo]	award A-325
勝利 [shōri]	triumph T-285, 286
勝利 [shōri]	victory V-37, 38
省略 [shōryaku]	omission O-66, 67
省略する [shōryaku-suru]	abbreviate A-4, 5
除外する [jogai-suru]	exclude E-197
書簡 [shokan]	epistle E-129

死んだ [shinda] — dead D-25, 26
身体の [shintai-no] — physical P-148
深度 [shindo] — depth D-103
振動 [shindō] — vibration V-33
伸縮性のある [shinshuku-sei-no-aru] — elastic E-46
真に理解する [shin-ni-rikai-suru] — realize R-45
侵入する [shinnyū-suru] — infiltrate I-91
侵入する [shinnyū-suru] — trespass T-274
死ぬべき運命の [shinubeki-unmei-no] — mortal M-225
信念 [shinnen] — belief B-101
信念 [shinnen] — faith F-20
新年 [shinnen] — New Year N-71
心配 [shinpai] — anxiety A-198
心配する [shinpai-suru] — anxious A-200
心配する [shinpai-suru] — concern C-298
心配な [shinpai-na] — anxious A-199
審判 [shinpan] — umpire U-10
神秘 [shinpi] — mystery M-274
新聞 [shinbun] — newspaper N-67
しんぼう [shinbō] — patience P-52, 53
進歩しない [shinposhinai] — not improve N-126
審問 [shinmon] — hearing H-69
新約聖書 [shinyakuseisho] — New Testament N-68, 69, 70
信用できる [shinyōdekiru] — credible C-455
信用するな [shiñyō-suru-na] — don't believe D-273
信頼 [shinrai] — confidence C-312
信頼 [shinrai] — trust T-295
心理学 [shinrigaku] — psychology P-392, 393
診療所 [shinryōjo] — infirmary I-93, 94

す

巣 [su] — nest N-55
酢 [su] — vinegar V-45
水泳者 [suieisha] — swimmer S-641
すいか [suika] — watermelon W-44
水彩 [suisai] — watercolor W-43
水夫 [suifu] — seaman S-103
水平な [suihei-na] — level L-86
水曜日 [suiyōbi] — Wednesday W-63
数 [sū] — number N-132, 133
数学 [sūgaku] — mathematics M-68
枢機卿 [sūkikei] — cardinal C-50
スーツ [sūtsu] — suit S-563
スーツケース [sūtsukēsu] — suitcase S-565
崇拝 [sūhai] — worship W-187
崇拝する [sūhai-suru] — adore A-93
スープ [sūpu] — soup S-379
数秒前 [sūbyō-mae] — few seconds ago F-106
スェーデン人 [suēden-jin] — Swede S-628
スカート [sukāto] — skirt S-292, 293
姿を消す [sugata-o-kesu] — fade away F-10
スカンク [sukanku] — skunk S-294
すき [suki] — plow P-214
救う [sukuu] — save S-45
すぐ隣りの [sugu-tonari-no] — adjacent A-80
すぐに [sugu-ni] — immediately I-217
すぐり [suguri] — currant C-491
すぐれた [sugureta] — superior S-584
スケートする [sukēto-suru] — skate S-281
少し [sukoshi] — little L-122, 123

少し　〔sukoshi〕　　　　　　　　　　　some　S-366
少しの　〔sukoshi-no〕　　　　　　　　　few　F-104
スコットランド人　〔sukottorandojin〕　　Scot　S-76, 77, 78
すず　〔suzu〕　　　　　　　　　　　　　tin　T-193
涼しい　〔suzushii〕　　　　　　　　　　cool　C-390
すっぱい　〔suppai〕　　　　　　　　　　sour　S-380
すっぱい　〔suppai〕　　　　　　　　　　tart　T-32
ステッチ　〔sutecchi〕　　　　　　　　　stitch　S-491
捨てる　〔suteru〕　　　　　　　　　　　abandon　A-2, 3
ストッキング　〔sutokkingu〕　　　　　　stocking　S-492, 493
ストライク　〔sutoraiku〕　　　　　　　　strike　S-518
スパイ　〔supai〕　　　　　　　　　　　　spy　S-433, 434, 435
スパゲティ　〔supagetti〕　　　　　　　　spaghetti　S-387
すばやい　〔subayai〕　　　　　　　　　　quick　Q-23
すばらしい　〔subarashii〕　　　　　　　　great　G-137, 138
すばらしい　〔subarashii〕　　　　　　　　magnificent　M-12
すばらしい　〔subarashii〕　　　　　　　　wonderful　W-165
すばらしい事　〔subarashii-koto〕　　　　marvel　M-60
スプレー　〔supurē〕　　　　　　　　　　spray　S-427
スペイン　〔supein〕　　　　　　　　　　Spain　S-388
スペイン人　〔supeinjin〕　　　　　　　　Spaniard　S-389
スペード　〔supēdo〕　　　　　　　　　　spade　S-386
〜すべきである　〔〜subeki-dearu〕　　　ought to　O-138
全て　〔subete〕　　　　　　　　　　　　altogether　A-150
全ての　〔subete-no〕　　　　　　　　　　entire　E-117
すべる　〔suberu〕　　　　　　　　　　　skid　S-286
すべる　〔suberu〕　　　　　　　　　　　slide　S-307, 308
すぼませる　〔subomaseru〕　　　　　　　deflate　D-68
ズボン　〔zubon〕　　　　　　　　　　　pants　P-15
ズボン　〔zubon〕　　　　　　　　　　　trousers　T-291
スポンヂ　〔suponji〕　　　　　　　　　　sponge　S-424
住む　〔sumu〕　　　　　　　　　　　　　reside　R-144
すり切れた　〔surikireta〕　　　　　　　　worn　W-176, 177
スリッパ　〔surippa〕　　　　　　　　　　slipper　S-312
すりつぶす　〔suri-tsubusu〕　　　　　　　mash　M-64
〜する　〔〜suru〕　　　　　　　　　　　do　D-254
ずるい　〔zurui〕　　　　　　　　　　　　cunning　C-483
ずるい　〔zurui〕　　　　　　　　　　　　sly　S-315, 316, 317
〜するつもりである　〔〜suru-tsumori-de-aru〕　intend　I-148
鋭い　〔surudoi〕　　　　　　　　　　　　sharp　S-178, 179
〜するな　〔〜suruna〕　　　　　　　　　do not　D-269, 270
座って下さい　〔suwattekudasai〕　　　　　be seated　B-66
座る　〔suwaru〕　　　　　　　　　　　　sit　S-275, 276
座る　〔suwaru〕　　　　　　　　　　　　sit down　S-277
寸法を取る　〔sunpō-o-toru〕　　　　　　measure　M-84

せ

セーター　〔sētā〕　　　　　　　　　　　sweater　S-627
セールスマン　〔sērusuman〕　　　　　　　salesman　S-23
生家　〔seika〕　　　　　　　　　　　　　home　H-142
正確な　〔seikaku-na〕　　　　　　　　　　accurate　A-46, 47
正確な　〔seikaku-na〕　　　　　　　　　　exact　E-176, 177
正確な　〔seikaku-na〕　　　　　　　　　　precise　P-289
世紀　〔seiki〕　　　　　　　　　　　　　century　C-96
正義　〔seigi〕　　　　　　　　　　　　　justice　J-38, 39
税金　〔zeikin〕　　　　　　　　　　　　　impost　I-43
税金　〔zeikin〕　　　　　　　　　　　　　tax　T-39, 40
請求する　〔seikyū-suru〕　　　　　　　　charge　C-117
制限する　〔seigen-suru〕　　　　　　　　restrict　R-167
性交　〔seikō〕　　　　　　　　　　　　　sexual intercourse　S-165

性交する〔seikōsuru〕 make love M-29, 30
成功する〔seikō-suru〕 succeed S-551
製材所〔seizaisho〕 sawmill S-51
精査する〔seisa-suru〕 probe P-338, 339
聖ざん〔seizan〕 Eucharist E-150
聖ざん式〔seizanshiki〕 Holy Communion H-137, 138
性質〔seishitsu〕 character C-115, 116
成熟させる〔seijyuku-saseru〕 mature M-70
聖書〔seisho〕 Bible B-135, 136, 137
聖書〔seisho〕 Holy Scriptures H-141
正常〔seijō〕 normal N-103
聖職〔seishoku〕 holy orders H-140
精神〔seishin〕 spirit S-416
聖人〔seijin〕 saint S-15, 16
精神の〔seishin-no〕 mental M-115
精神の弱い〔seishin-no-yowai〕 feebleminded F-87
精神不安定な〔seishinfuantei-na〕 mentally unbalanced M-117, 118, 119, 120, 121
精神病医〔seishinbyōi〕 psychiatrist P-391
精神病になる〔seishinbyō-ni-naru〕 mental breakdown M-116
製図〔seizu〕 model (n) M-196
整然とした〔seizen-to-shita〕 orderly O-122
製造〔seizō〕 manufacture (n) M-49
製造する〔seizō-suru〕 manufacture (v) M-49
聖体〔seitai〕 Communion, Holy C-262, 263
ぜいたくな〔zeitaku-na〕 extravagant E-233
生徒〔seito〕 pupil P-410, 411, 412
聖堂〔seidō〕 temple T-72
青年〔seinen〕 lad L-4
聖灰水曜日〔seihai suiyōbi〕 Ash Wednesday A-269
政府〔seifu〕 government G-99
制服〔seifuku〕 uniform U-30
征服する〔seifuku-suru〕 subdue S-539
征服する〔seifuku-suru〕 conquer C-326
聖別〔seibetsu〕 consecration C-333
正方形の〔seihōkei-no〕 square S-437
聖母マリア〔seibo-maria〕 Mary M-62
聖母マリア〔seibo-maria〕 Virgin Mary V-49
（聖母マリアの）無原罪の御宿り
〔(seibo-maria-no)mugenzai-no-onyadori〕 Immaculate Conception I-25
生命〔seimei〕 life L-98, 99
声明〔seimei〕 statement S-460
生命のない〔seimei-no-nai〕 insensate I-125
誓約〔seiyaku〕 pledge P-211
聖約〔seiyaku〕 Testament T-90, 91, 92
生理になる〔seiri-ni-naru〕 menstruate M-113
聖礼〔seirei〕 sacrament S-5
世界〔sekai〕 globe G-58, 59
世界〔sekai〕 world W-174
世界中〔sekaijū〕 around the world A-253
世界の〔sekai-no〕 international I-167
せがむ〔segamu〕 insist I-127
咳〔seki〕 cough C-417, 418
席〔seki〕 seat S-107
石炭〔sekitan〕 coal C-210
責任〔sekinin〕 obligation O-14
責任〔sekinin〕 responsibility R-155, 156
赤面する〔sekimen-suru〕 blush B-187
世代〔sedai〕 generation G-26
節〔setsu〕 paragraph P-25
説教〔sekkyō〕 sermon S-155
説教する〔sekkyō-suru〕 preach P-285
石けん〔sekken〕 soap S-344, 345, 346, 347

接合する　［setsugō-suru］　　　　　connect　C-323
接種する　［sesshu-suru］　　　　　　inoculate　I-117
接触　［sesshoku］　　　　　　　　　contact　C-351, 352
節制の　［sessei-no］　　　　　　　　temperate　T-70
絶対の　［zettai-no］　　　　　　　　absolute　A-23
設置する　［setchi-suru］　　　　　　install　I-130
絶頂　［zecchō］　　　　　　　　　　peak　P-66
切望　［setsubō］　　　　　　　　　　lust　L-180
切望する　［setsubō-suru］　　　　　crave　C-448
説明する　［setsumei-suru］　　　　　explain　E-220, 221
絶妙な　［zetsumyō-na］　　　　　　　exquisite　E-228
設立する　［setsuritsu-suru］　　　　establish　E-144
設定する　［settei-suru］　　　　　　institute　I-133, 134
せと物　［setomono］　　　　　　　　china　C-152
背中　［senaka］　　　　　　　　　　back　B-4
狭い　［semai］　　　　　　　　　　　narrow　N-13
セミコロン　［semikoron］　　　　　　semicolon　S-134
攻める　［semeru］　　　　　　　　　attack　A-295
ゼロ　［zero］　　　　　　　　　　　zero　Z-4, 5
ゼロックス　［zerokkusu］　　　　　　Xerox　X-1
世話をする　［sewa-o-suru］　　　　　care　C-53, 54
世話をする　［sewa-o-suru］　　　　　mind　M-181
世話をする　［sewa-o-suru］　　　　　take care of　T-15, 16, 17
線　［sen］　　　　　　　　　　　　　line　L-110
千　［sen］　　　　　　　　　　　　　thousand　T-154
船員　［senin］　　　　　　　　　　　sailor　S-13, 14
選挙する　［senkyo-suru］　　　　　　elect　E-49
宣教　［senkyō］　　　　　　　　　　mission　M-183, 184
先月　［sengetsu］　　　　　　　　　　last month　L-22
宣言する　［sengen-suru］　　　　　　declare　D-44
宣言する　［sengen-suru］　　　　　　proclaim　P-345
前後に　［zengoni］　　　　　　　　　back and forth　B-5
せんさく好きな　［sensaku-zukina］　　nosy　N-111, 112, 113
前進する　［zenshin-suru］　　　　　　advance　A-95
前進する　［zenshin-suru］　　　　　　go ahead　G-71
先週　［senshū］　　　　　　　　　　last week　L-24
先生　［sensei］　　　　　　　　　　　teacher　T-47
先祖　［senzo］　　　　　　　　　　　ancestors　A-169, 170
戦争　［sensō］　　　　　　　　　　　war　W-20
選択　［sentaku］　　　　　　　　　　choice　C-157
洗たく機　［sentakuki］　　　　　　　washing machine　W-30
洗たくばさみ　［sentakubasami］　　　clothespin　C-202
船長　［senchō］　　　　　　　　　　captain　C-45
セント　［sento］　　　　　　　　　　cent　C-92
戦闘　［sentō］　　　　　　　　　　　battle　B-56
先導者　［sendosha］　　　　　　　　　leader　L-45
全能の　［zennō-no］　　　　　　　　　almighty　A-138
全般的な　［zenpanteki-na］　　　　　universal　U-37
全部の　［zenbu-no］　　　　　　　　　all　A-127, 128
全部の　［zenbu-no］　　　　　　　　　whole　W-110
前方に　［zenpō-ni］　　　　　　　　　ahead　A-117
前方に　［zenpō-ni］　　　　　　　　　onward　O-87
全滅させる　［zenmetsu-saseru］　　　annihilate　A-180
前夜　［zenya］　　　　　　　　　　　eve　E-157
洗礼　［senrei］　　　　　　　　　　　baptism　B-30
洗礼者　［senrei-sha］　　　　　　　　Baptist　B-31
染料　［senryō］　　　　　　　　　　　dye (color)　D-340

そ

象　［zō］　　　　　　　　　　　　　elephant　E-59
像　［zō］　　　　　　　　　　　　　image　I-19

像　[zō]　statue　S-462
相違　[sōi]　difference　D-156
騒音　[sōon]　din　D-168
騒音　[sōon]　noise　N-92
そうか　[sōka]　that's it　T-103
双眼鏡　[sōgankyō]　binoculars　B-151
増強する　[zōkyōsuru]　reinforce　R-86
総計の　[sōkei-no]　total　T-233
総合大学　[sōgōdaigaku]　university　U-38, 39, 40
相互の　[sōgo-no]　mutual　M-270, 271
葬式　[sōshiki]　funeral　F-293
掃除する　[sōji-suru]　clean　C-186
掃除する　[sōji-suru]　sweep　S-631
操縦士　[sōjūshi]　pilot　P-174
装飾　[sōshoku]　ornament　O-135, 136
装飾する　[sōshoku-suru]　trim　T-279, 280
装飾的な　[sōshokuteki-na]　fancy　F-41
想像　[sōzō]　fiction　F-108
想像　[sōzō]　imagination　I-20
創造者　[sōzō-sha]　creator　C-454
創造する　[sōzō-suru]　create　C-453
想像する　[sōzō-suru]　imagine　I-22
ソーダー　[sōdā]　soda pop　S-354
ソーダ水　[sōdāsui]　soda water　S-355
相談相手　[sōdan-aite]　counselor　C-421
相談する　[sōdan-suru]　confer　C-306
相談する　[sōdan-suru]　consult　C-347
相談する　[sōdan-suru]　counsel　C-420
贈呈する　[zōtei-suru]　present　P-299
騒動　[sōdō]　row　R-266
贈与する　[sōyo-suru]　bestow　B-130
創立する　[sōritsu-suru]　found　F-236
促進する　[sokushin-suru]　promote　P-368
属する　[zoku-suru]　belong　B-106
測定　[sokutei]　gage　G-1
速度　[sokudo]　speed　S-408
束縛する　[sokubaku-suru]　fetter　F-102
側微計　[sokubikei]　micrometer　M-138
測量技師　[sokuryōgishi]　surveyor　S-607
ソケット　[soketto]　socket　S-350
底　[soko]　bottom　B-206
そこから　[sokokara]　thence　T-116
そこで　[sokode]　there　T-119, 120
組織　[soshiki]　system　S-651
阻止する　[soshi-suru]　check　C-129, 130
僧職を授ける　[soshoku-o-sazukeru]　ordain　O-118
注ぐ　[sosogu]　pour　P-269
育てる　[sodateru]　raise　R-21
育てる　[sodateru]　rear　R-51
ソックス　[sokkusu]　sock(s)　S-351, 352
卒業する　[sotsugyō-suru]　graduate　G-106, 107
沿って　[sotte]　along　A-141
ぞっとする　[zotto-suru]　shocked　S-203, 204
ぞっとする　[zotto-suru]　thrill　T-163, 164
外へ　[sotoe]　out　O-141, 142
その　[sono]　its　I-220
その後の　[sonogo-no]　subsequent　S-543
そばに　[sobani]　by　B-286
祖父　[sofu]　grandfather　G-111, 112
祖母　[sobo]　grandmother　G-113, 114
そよ風　[soyokaze]　breeze　B-232
空　[sora]　sky　S-295, 296

そらす [sorasu] deflect D-70
空を飛ぶもの [sora-o-tobumono] flier F-172
そる [soru] shave S-182
それ [sore] it I-214, 215, 216
それ [sore] that T-100, 101, 102
それ以来 [soreirai] ever since E-167
それ以来 [soreirai] thenceforth T-117
それから [sorekara] from then on F-281
それから [sorekara] then T-114, 115
それ自身 [sorejishin] itself I-221
それにもかかわらず [sorenimokakawarazu] nevertheless N-61
それ故に [soreyueni] therefore T-121, 122, 123
それる [soreru] deviate D-135, 136
尊敬する [sonkei-suru] respect R-150
尊敬する [sonkei-suru] revere R-182, 183
存在 [sonzai] presence P-297
存在する [sonzai-suru] exist E-206
存続する [sonzoku-suru] persist P-122, 123
そんな [sonna] such S-555

た

第一の [daiichi-no] first F-149, 150
大英帝国 [daieiteikoku] Great Britain G-139
大学 [daigaku] college C-234
大かっさい [dai-kassai] acclamation A-36
退却 [taikyaku] retreat R-178
大工 [daiku] carpenter C-61
体育館 [taikukan] gym G-183
退屈させる [taikutsu-saseru] bore B-196
退屈な [taikutsu-na] boring B-198
退屈な [taikutsu-na] tedious T-54
対決する [taiketsu-suru] confront C-315
太鼓 [taiko] drum D-318
対抗者 [taikōsha] opponent O-99
滞在 [taizai] stay S-464, 465
第三の [daisan-no] tertiary T-87, 88
大司教 [daishikyō] archbishop A-237
対して [taishite] against A-110
対照 [taishō] contrast C-371
対照させる [taishō-saseru] contrast C-370
退職する [taishoku-suru] resign R-147
代数学 [daisūgaku] algebra A-124
大旋風 [daisenpū] tornado T-230
怠惰 [taida] sloth S-313
怠惰 [taida] laziness L-40
だいだい色 [daidai-iro] orange O-112
怠惰な [taidana] lazy L-42
態度 [taido] attitude A-301
大統領 [daitōryō] president P-303
台所 [daidokoro] kitchen K-24, 25
大破壊 [daihakai] havoc H-59
タイピスト [taipisuto] typist T-317
代表的な [daihyōteki-na] representative R-130
タイプする [taipu-suru] type T-316
大変災の [daihensai-no] catastrophic C-74
逮捕 [taiho] arrest A-258
大砲 [taihō] cannon C-33, 34
題目 [daimoku] theme T-112
題目 [daimoku] title T-201
ダイヤの札 [daiya-no-fuda] diamond D-146

頼む [tanomu]	ask A-271
タバコ [tabako]	cigarette C-172
タバコ [tabako]	tobacco T-206
旅 [tabi]	journey J-25, 26, 27
旅 [tabi]	trip T-282, 283, 284
多分 [tabun]	perhaps P-105
食べ尽くす [tabetsukusu]	consume C-348
食べる [taberu]	eat E-22
玉 [tama]	ball B-17, 18
球 [tama]	orb O-115
球 [tama]	sphere S-413
卵 [tamago]	egg E-32
だまされ安い [damasare-yasui]	gullible G-180
だまされやすい人 [damasare-yasui-hito]	sucker S-556
魂 [tamashii]	soul S-377
だます [damasu]	cheat C-127, 128
だます [damasu]	defraud D-71
だます [damasu]	fool F-197, 198
玉ねぎ [tamanegi]	onion O-80, 81
ためらう [tamerau]	hesitate H-102
保つ [tamotsu]	uphold U-53
便り [tayori]	tidings T-178
頼る [tayoru]	depend D-94, 95, 96
頼る [tayoru]	rely R-102, 103
堕落 [daraku]	degeneration D-72
たる [taru]	barrel B-38
誰 [dare]	who W-108
誰か [dareka]	anyone A-204
誰か [dareka]	someone S-367
誰でも [daredemo]	whoever W-109
誰の [dareno]	whose W-115
たわむれ [tawamure]	fun F-290
嘆願する [tangan-suru]	entreat E-120
短気 [tanki]	ill temper I-17
短気な [tanki-na]	irritable I-205
短期の [tanki-no]	transient T-263
探求 [tankyū]	quest Q-16
単語 [tango]	word W-170
誕生 [tanjō]	birth B-153, 154, 155
誕生日 [tanjō-bi]	birthday B-156
たんす [tansu]	chest C-141
ダンス [dansu]	dance D-8
団体 [dantai]	organization O-124, 125
単調な [tanchō-na]	grind G-160
単調な [tanchō-na]	monotonous M-207, 209
探偵 [tantei]	detective D-123, 124
断念する [dannen-suru]	renounce R-117

ち

地域 [chiiki]	area A-242
小さい [chiisai]	little L-122, 123
小さい [chiisai]	small S-319, 320
チーズ [chīzu]	cheese C-136
誓い [chikai]	oath O-2
誓い [chikai]	vow V-65
誓いを立てる [chikai-o-tateru]	take oath T-18
誓う [chikau]	swear S-621
近く [chikaku]	near N-26, 27
知覚 [chikaku]	sensation S-144
知覚する [chikaku-suru]	perceive P-94, 95
近くに [chikaku-ni]	close (to) C-198

丁度　[chōdo]	just　J-36
丁度今　[chōdo-ima]	just now　J-40, 41
ちううネクタイ　[chō-nekutai]	bow tie　B-212
長老教会員　[chōrōkyōkaiin]	Presbyterian　P-295
直接の　[chyokusetsuno]	immediate　I-26
直立した　[chyokuritsu-shita]	erect　E-137
チョコレート　[chokorēto]	chocolate　C-156
チョッキ　[chokki]	vest　V-31
ちょっと　[chotto]	minute　M-174
ちょっと後で　[chotto-ato-de]	after a while　A-106
ちょっと考えて下さい　[chotto-kangaete-kudasai]	just think of it!　J-42
ちょっと前に　[chotto-mae-ni]	just a moment ago　J-37
地理学　[chirigaku]	geography　G-35
沈黙　[chinmoku]	silence　S-255, 256

つ

追突（する）　[tsuitotsu(suru)]	crash　C-447
費す　[tsuiyasu]	spend　S-412
墜落する　[tsuiraku-suru]	fall　F-27
通知する　[tsūchi-suru]	notify　N-124, 125
通訳する　[tsūyaku-suru]	interpret　I-168
通路　[tsūro]	hall　H-14
使い込み　[tsukaikomi]	embezzlement　E-69
使い尽くされた　[tsukaitsuku-sareta]	exhausted　E-203
使い尽くす　[tsukaitsukusu]	consume　C-349
使い古した　[tsukaifurushita]	worn out　W-178
使う　[tsukau]	use　U-64
仕える　[tsukaeru]	wait on　W-8
捕える　[tsukamaeru]	catch　C-75, 76, 77
つかむ　[tsukamu]	hold　H-129
つかむ　[tsukamu]	seize　S-122
疲れさせる　[tsukare-saseru]	exhaust　E-202
疲れさせる　[tsukare-saseru]	tire　T-198
疲れた　[tsukareta]	weary　W-60
月　[tsuki]	month　M-210
月　[tsuki]	moon　M-214, 215
次の　[tsugi-no]	next　N-73, 74
突く　[tsuku]	pick　P-153, 154
着く　[tsuku]	reach　R-34
継ぐ　[tsugu]	splice　S-421
つぐないの日　[tsugunai-no-hi]	day of atonement　D-21
作る　[tsukuru]	fabricate　F-2
作る　[tsukuru]	make　M-23
作る　[tsukuru]	model (v)　M-196
つけ物　[tsukemono]	pickle　P-156
告げ口する者　[tsugeguchisuru-mono]	telltale　T-67, 68
告げる　[tsugeru]	inform　I-99, 100
頭痛　[zutsū]	headache　H-65
続き　[tsuzuki]	sequel　S-152
続く　[tsuzuku]	last　L-19
続ける　[tsuzukeru]	proceed　P-343
慎しみ深い　[tsutsushimi-bukai]	modest　M-197
つっつく　[tsuttsuku]	prod　P-349
包み　[tsutsumi]	package　P-2
つづる　[tsuzuru]	spell　S-410
常に　[tsuneni]	always　A-151
角　[tsuno]	horns　H-157
翼　[tsubasa]	wings　W-139
つばを吐く　[tsuba-o-haku]	spit　S-417
つぶす　[tsubusu]	squash　S-440

手袋 [tebukuro]	glove(s) G-66
テレビ [terebi]	television T-63
テレビジョン [terebijyon]	TV T-308
手を切る [te-o-kiru]	part from P-36
手をたたく [te-o-tataku]	clap C-179
手をふる [te-o-furu]	wave W-46
手渡す [tewata-su]	surrender S-604, 605
天 [ten]	heaven H-78
点 [ten]	point P-224
電機で殺す [denki-de-korosu]	electrocute E-56
電気の [denki-no]	electric E-51
伝言 [dengon]	message M-129
天使 [tenshi]	angel A-172
天真らんまんな [tenshinranman-na]	naive N-4
伝染性の [densensei-no]	contagious C-353
伝達 [dentatsu]	communication C-261
伝達する [dentatsu-suru]	communicate with C-260
テント [tento]	tent T-82
伝統 [dentō]	heritage H-98
電動機 [dendōki]	electric motor E-53
伝道者 [dendōsha]	preacher P-286
天然痘 [tennentō]	smallpox S-322
天火 [tenpi]	oven O-145
転覆 [tenpuku]	capsize C-44
電報 [denpō]	telegram T-57, 58
デンマーク [denmāku]	Denmark D-89
デンマーク人 [denmāku-jin]	Dane D-9
展覧する [tenran-suru]	display D-220
展覧する [tenran-suru]	exhibit E-204
電話 [denwa]	phone P-140, 141
電話 [denwa]	telephone T-61, 62

と

戸 [to]	door D-284
ドイツの [doitsu-no]	German G-37
ドイツ人 [doitsujin]	German (people) G-37
説いて～させる [toite～saseru]	induce I-86
搭 [tō]	tower T-246
遠い [tōi]	remote R-109
同意 [dōi]	accord A-40
同意語 [dōigo]	synonym S-649
同意する [dōi-suru]	agree A-115
同意する [dōi-suru]	concur C-302
同意する [dōi-suru]	consent C-335
どういたしまして [dōitashimashite]	you're welcome Y-20, 21
同一の [dōitsu-no]	identical I-8
陶器 [tōki]	ceramics C-97
統治者 [tōji-sha]	governor G-100
投資する [tōshi-suru]	invest I-190
同情 [dōjō]	sympathy S-648
同情の厚い [dōjō-no-atsui]	sympathetic S-646
トーストする [tōsuto-suru]	toast T-204
同性愛者 [dōseiaisha]	queer Q-13
同性愛の男 [dōseiai-no-otoko]	fairy F-19
どうぞ [dōzo]	please P-209
到着 [tōchaku]	arrival A-260
ドーナツ [dōnatsu]	doughnut D-293
逃避 [tōhi]	refuge R-77
投票 [tōhyō]	vote V-64
動物 [dōbutsu]	animal A-177, 178

〜と言う名　［〜to-yūna］	named　N-7
土曜日　［doyōbi］	Saturday　S-43
とら　［tora］	tiger　T-181
捕える　［toraeru］	catch　C-75
ドラ・サール教職会　［do-ra-saaru-kyōshyoku-kai］	Christian Brothers　C-164
トランク　［toranku］	trunk　T-294
トランプ　［toranpu］	card　C-49
トランプをする　［toranpu-o-suru］	card playing　C-51
トランプをする　［toranpu-o-suru］	playing cards　P-205
鳥　［tori］	bird　B-152
鶏　［tori］	fowl　F-243
取り合わせた　［toriawaseta］	assorted　A-286
取り替える　［torikaeru］	replace　R-125
取り消しする　［torikeshi-suru］	cancel　C-28
取り消す　［torikesu］	revoke　R-188
取りこわす　［torikowasu］	demolish　D-85
取り付ける　［toritsukeru］	attach　A-294
取り逃がす　［torinigasu］	miss　M-179
取り残された　［torinokosareta］	stranded　S-506
取り除く　［torinozoku］	remove　R-110
努力　［doryoku］	effort　E-29, 30
努力　［doryoku］	endeavor　E-88
取る　［toru］	take　T-9
ドル　［doru］	dollar(s)　D-263, 264
トルコ　［toruko］	Turkey　T-303
奴隷　［dorei］	slave　S-299
ドレスメーカー　［doresumēkā］	dressmaker　D-305
どれだけ　［doredake］	how many?　H-178
どれでも　［doredemo］	any　A-201, 202
泥の多い　［doro-no-ōi］	muddy　M-256
泥棒　［dorobō］	burglar　B-271
泥棒　［dorobō］	robber　R-230
泥棒　［dorobō］	stealer　S-472
泥棒　［dorobō］	thief　T-130, 131
トロンボーン［toronbōn］	trombone　T-289
戸を開いて下さい　［to-o-akete-kudasai］	open the door　O-92
どんぐり　［donguri］	acorn　A-55
どんなに　［donnani］	how　H-174
どんぶり　［donburi］	bowl　B-210
どん欲な　［donyokuna］	avaricious　A-318

な

内観　［naikan］	introspection　I-185
ナイフ　［naifu］	knife　K-27, 28, 29
内部の　［naibu-no］	inside　I-126
尚　［nao］	besides　B-127
尚　［nao］	moreover　M-219
長い　［nagai］	long　L-145
内へ　［nakae］	within　W-155
長くつ下　［nagakutsushita］	hose　H-160, 161
中にはいる　［naka-ni-hairu］	come between　C-249
仲間　［nakama］	circle　C-175
仲間　［nakama］	peer　P-78
仲間同士　［nakamadōshi］	fellowship　F-96
眺める　［nagameru］	view　V-42
泣く　［naku］	weep　W-68, 69
泣く　［naku］	cry　C-479, 480
慰める　［nagusameru］	console　C-341
亡くなった　［nakunatta］	gone　G-82, 83, 84
殴り倒す　［naguri-taosu］	knock down　K-32

嘆き [nageki]	grief	G-155, 156
嘆く [nageku]	mourn	M-244
投げ出す [nagedasu]	throw(n) out	T-170
投げる [nageru]	throw	T-167, 168
投げる [nageru]	pitch	P-185
情け深い [nasakebukai]	benevolent	B-120
なし [nashi]	pear	P-68
成し遂げる [nashitogeru]	accomplish	A-38, 39
成し遂げる [nashitogeru]	achieve	A-52, 53
～なしに [～nashini]	without	W-156
なぜ [naze]	why	W-117
なぜならば [nazenaraba]	because	B-81
ナチ [nachi]	Nazi	N-25
夏 [natsu]	summer	S-572
納得させる [nattoku-saseru]	convince	C-387
なでる [naderu]	stroke	S-521, 522
等々 [nadonado]	et cetera	E-146
七 [nana]	seven	S-160
何 [nani]	what	W-83
何か [nanika]	anything	A-205
何か [nanika]	something	S-368
何も知らない [nani-mo-shiranai]	know nothing	K-38
何もない [nanimonai]	nothing	N-119, 120, 121, 122
ナプキン [napukin]	napkin	N-9
生意気な [namaiki-na]	saucy	S-44
名前 [namae]	name	N-6
鉛 [namari]	lead	L-44
波 [nami]	wave	W-45
涙 [namida]	tear	T-49
滑らかな [namerakana]	smooth	S-330
納屋 [naya]	barn	B-37
悩む [nayamu]	fret	F-267
悩む [nayamu]	worry	W-181, 182, 183
並んで [narande]	side by side	S-243
鳴る [naru]	ring	R-204
馴れた [nareta]	tame	T-28
縄 [nawa]	rope	R-252, 253
汝 [nanji]	thou	T-149
汝の者 [nanji-no-mono]	thine	T-136

に

二 [ni]	two	T-312
臭い [nioi]	scent	S-62
匂いのよい [nioi-no-yoi]	fragrant	F-247
～に遅れる [～ni-okureru]	fall behind	F-29
～に溺れる [～ni-oboreru]	fall for	F-30
苦い [nigai]	bitter	B-162
苦さ [nigasa]	bitterness	B-163
似かよっている [nikayotteiru]	similar	S-261
～に関して [～ni-kanshite]	concerning	C-300
肉 [niku]	flesh	F-171
肉 [niku]	meat	M-85
肉汁 [nikujiru]	gravy	G-128
憎む [nikumu]	hate	H-52, 53
逃げる [nigeru]	escape	E-140
逃げる [nigeru]	flee	F-170
逃げる [nigeru]	run away	R-284
にこにこした [nikoniko-shita]	cheerful	C-135
二・三ヵ月中に [nisankagetsu-naini]	in a few months	I-54
二・三日前 [nisannichi-mae]	few days ago	F-105
二・三日内に [nisannichi-nai-ni]	in a few days	I-53

二・三年内に [nisannen-uchi-ni]	in a few years I-55
西 [nishi]	west W-80
にじみ出させる [nijimidasaseru]	perspire P-129, 130
二週間 [nishūkan]	two weeks T-315
二週間で [nishūkan-de]	in two weeks I-186
〜に属する [〜ni-zoku-suru]	belong to B-107
〜に対して [〜ni-taishite]	versus V-28
日没 [nichibotsu]	sunset S-581
〜に注意する [〜ni-chūi-suru]	give attention (to) G-50
日曜日 [nichiyōbi]	Sunday S-577, 578
〜について [〜ni-tsuite]	about A-14
日光 [nikkō]	sunshine S-582
日本 [nippon]	Japan J-3
日本の（日本人）[nippon-no(nipponjin)]	Japanese J-4
似ている [niteiru]	like L-104
二度 [nido]	twice T-309
二度と〜しない [nidoto〜shinai]	never again N-60
〜になる [〜ninaru]	become B-83
二倍の [nibai-no]	double D-288
〜にはいる [〜ni-hairu]	enter E-113
二番目 [nibanme]	second S-108
鈍い [nibui]	dull (not sharp) D-325
〜に面する [〜ni-men-suru]	face F-4
〜にもかかわらず [〜nimo-kakawarazu]	despite D-118
〜にもかかわらず [〜 nimo-kakawarazu]	in spite of I-129
荷物 [nimotsu]	luggage L-176
ニューイングランド [nyūingurando]	New England N-63
ニューオリンズ [nyūorinzu]	New Orleans N-65
入会させる [nyūkai-saseru]	affiliate A-100
入金する [nyūkin-suru]	deposit D-100, 101
ニュージャージー [nyūjyājī]	New Jersey N-64
入場 [nyūjō]	admission A-84
ニュース [nyūsu]	news N-66
ニューヨーク [nyūyōku]	New York N-72
柔和な [nyūwa-na]	meek M-97
尿 [nyō]	urine U-62
〜によって [〜ni-yotte]	by B-287
〜によって決定する [〜ni-yotte-kettei-suru]	hinge H-116
〜によれば [〜ni-yoreba]	according (to) A-41
庭 [niwa]	garden G-13
庭 [niwa]	yard Y-1, 2
にわ鳥 [niwatori]	chicken C-144
人形 [ningyō]	doll D-261, 262
人間の [ningen-no]	human H-184
人間性 [ningensei]	humanity H-186
認証された [ninshō-sareta]	authentic A-313
人情のある [ninjō-no-aru]	humane H-185

ぬ

縫う [nuu]	sew S-163
盗み [nusumi]	robbery R-233
盗み [nusumi]	theft T-107, 108, 109
盗む [nusumu]	steal S-469, 470, 471

ね

根 [ne]	root R-251
願う [negau]	request R-134, 135
ネクタイ [nekutai]	necktie N-35
ネクタイ [nekutai]	tie T-180

ねこ　[neko]　cat　C-72
ねじ　[neji]　screw　S-91, 92
ねじ回し　[nejimawashi]　screwdriver　S-93
ねじまわし　[nejimawashi]　wrench　W-201
寝過ごす　[nesugosu]　oversleep　O-152
ねずみ　[nezumi]　rat　R-26
値段　[nedan]　cost　C-414
妬んで　[netande]　envious　E-121
熱　[netsu]　fever　F-103
熱　[netsu]　heat　H-76, 77
熱心な　[nesshin-na]　zeal　Z-1
熱心な　[nesshin-na]　eager　E-4
熱中　[netchū]　enthusiasm　E-114
熱烈な　[netsuretsuna]　ardent　A-239
～ねばならない　[～nebanaranai]　must　M-268
眠い　[nemui]　sleepy　S-304
眠っている　[nemutte-iru]　asleep　A-275
眠り　[nemuri]　sleep　S-301
狙い　[nerai]　aim　A-119
狙う　[nerau]　aim　A-119
寝る　[neru]　go to bed　G-96, 97
寝る　[neru]　sleep　S-302
値をつける　[ne-o-tsukeru]　bid　B-140
粘土　[nendo]　clay　C-184
粘板岩　[nenbanseki]　slate　S-298
年齢　[nenrei]　age　A-111

の

～の間　[～no-aida]　between　B-133
～の間に　[～no-aida-ni]　during　D-334
～の後に付いて行く　[～no-atonitsuite-yuku]　follow　F-190
脳　[nō]　brain　B-221
～の上に　[～no-ueni]　above　A-16
～の上に　[～no-ueni]　over　O-146, 147
農場　[nōjō]　farm　F-47, 48, 49
～の後ろに　[～no-ushironi]　behind　B-98
能力　[nōryoku]　ability　A-10
能力　[nōryoku]　capacity　C-41
能力　[nōryoku]　faculty　F-8
能力のある　[nōryoku-no-aru]　capable　C-40
～の階級を下げる　[～no-kaikyū-o-sageru]　demote　D-88
～の価値のある　[～no-kachi-no-aru]　worth　W-191
～の代りに　[～no-kawari-ni]　instead of　I-131, 132
のこぎり　[nokogiri]　saw　S-49, 50
～のごとく　[～no-gotoku]　as　A-264
～の事を言う　[～no-koto-o-iu]　mention　M-122
残り　[nokori]　rest　R-161, 162
残り　[nokori]　remainder　R-105
残りの　[nokori-no]　left　L-62
残る　[nokoru]　remain　R-104
～の下に　[～no-shitani]　under　U-16, 17
～のせいにする　[～no-seini-suru]　attribute　A-307, 308
除く　[nozoku]　eliminate　E-63
覗く　[nozoku]　peep　P-77
覗く　[nozoku]　pry　P-389
～の側に　[～no-sobani]　beside　B-126
望む　[nozomu]　hope　H-153
望む　[nozomu]　want　W-19
～の為に　[～no-tameni]　for　F-204
後に　[nochi-ni]　later　L-29

のどの渇き [nodo-no-kawaki]　thirst　T-142
～の中に [no-nakani]　amid　A-162
～の中に [～no-naka-ni]　in　I-52
～の中に [～no-nakani]　into　I-180
延ばす [nobasu]　defer　D-64
野原 [nohara]　field　F-111, 112
～の分野で [～no-bunya-de]　in the field of　I-176
述べる [noberu]　state　S-459
～の方へ [～no-hōe]　toward　T-242, 243, 244
～の方を好む [～no-hō-o-konomu]　prefer　P-291
昇る [noboru]　ascend　A-265
登る [noboru]　climb　C-192, 194
のぼる [noboru]　rise　R-212, 213, 214
～の前に [～no-maeni]　before　B-92, 93
～のまわり [no-mawari]　around　A-252
のみ [nomi]　chisel　C-155
のみ [nomi]　flea　F-167, 168, 169
飲む [nomu]　drink　D-309, 310
飲む [nomu]　swallow　S-618, 619
～のようだ [～no-yōda]　appear　A-216, 218
～のようだ [～no-yōda]　look　L-150
～のようだ [～no-yōda]　seem　S-121
のり [nori]　glue　G-67
乗る [noru]　ride　R-192
ノルウェー [noruwē]　Norway　N-108
ノルウェー人 [noruwējin]　Norwegian　N-109
のろう [norou]　curse　C-494, 495, 496

は

葉 [ha]　leaf　L-46
歯 [ha]　teeth　T-55
歯 [ha]　tooth　T-223
パーセント [pāsento]　percent　P-96
パーティ [pātī]　party　P-38, 39, 40
ハープ [hāpu]　harp　H-46
はい [hai]　yes　Y-9
肺 [hai]　lungs　L-179
パイ [pai]　pie　P-165, 166
灰色の [haiiro-no]　gray　G-129, 130, 131
肺炎 [haien]　pneumonia　P-220
バイオリン [baiorin]　violin　V-47
バイオリン [baiorin]　fiddle　F-109
背景 [haikei]　background　B-7
廃止する [haishi-suru]　abolish　A-12, 13
歯医者 [haisha]　dentist　D-90
買収する [baishū-suru]　bribe　B-233
売春婦 [baishunfu]　harlot　H-43
売春婦 [baishunfu]　prostitute　P-379
売春婦 [baishunfu]　strumpet　S-527
売春婦 [baishunfu]　whore　W-114
排せつ物 [haisetsubutsu]　feces　F-83
配達する [haitatsu-suru]　deliver　D-82
配当 [haitō]　dividend　D-246
はい登る [hainoboru]　scramble　S-88
パイプ [paipu]　pipe　P-181
配分する [haibun-suru]　apportion　A-228
配分する [haibun-suru]　share　S-177
俳優 [haiyū]　actor　A-65
はえ [hae]　fly　F-185
生える [haeru]　grow　G-167

破壊　[hakai]　　　　　　　　　　　wreck　W-200
破壊する　[hakai-suru]　　　　　　destroy　D-119
ばかな　[bakana]　　　　　　　　　foolish　F-199
馬鹿な　[baka-na]　　　　　　　　daft　D-4
馬鹿な　[baka-na]　　　　　　　　dull (dumb)　D-325
馬鹿な　[baka-na]　　　　　　　　dumb　D-328
馬鹿な　[baka-na]　　　　　　　　silly　S-258
馬鹿な　[baka-na]　　　　　　　　stupid　S-535, 536
馬鹿にする　[baka-ni-suru]　　　　mock　M-195
はがね　[hagane]　　　　　　　　　steel　S-476
墓場　[hakaba]　　　　　　　　　　grave　G-125
ばからしい　[bakarashi-i]　　　　　absurd　A-29
計り　[hakari]　　　　　　　　　　gauge (n)　G-23
はかり　[hakari]　　　　　　　　　scale　S-55, 56
計る　[hakaru]　　　　　　　　　　gauge (v)　G-23
計る　[hakaru]　　　　　　　　　　weigh　W-70, 71
吐き出す　[hakidasu]　　　　　　　expectorate　E-210
吐き気　[hakike]　　　　　　　　　nausea　N-22
吐く　[kaku]　　　　　　　　　　　vomit　V-63
博愛　[hakuai]　　　　　　　　　　charity　C-120
迫害する　[hakugai-suru]　　　　　persecute　P-117
拍手かっさいする　[hakushu-kassai-suru]　applaud　A-221
白状する　[hakujō-suru]　　　　　　confess　C-308
ばく大な　[bakudai-na]　　　　　　enormous　E-109
白鳥　[hakuchō]　　　　　　　　　swan　S-620
爆発する　[bakuhatsu-suru]　　　　explode　E-224
白墨　[hakuboku]　　　　　　　　　chalk　C-104
はげの　[hage-no]　　　　　　　　bald　B-16
箱　[hako]　　　　　　　　　　　　box　B-213
運び去る　[hakobisaru]　　　　　　take away from　T-14
運ぶ　[hakobu]　　　　　　　　　　convey　C-383
はさみ　[hasami]　　　　　　　　　scissors　S-68
はさみ　[hasami]　　　　　　　　　shears　S-184, 185
破産した　[hasanshita]　　　　　　broke　B-253
破産する　[hasan-suru]　　　　　　bankrupt　B-27
橋　[hashi]　　　　　　　　　　　　bridge　B-234, 235
麻疹　[hashika]　　　　　　　　　　measles　M-83
はしご　[hashigo]　　　　　　　　ladder　L-5
恥じて　[hajite]　　　　　　　　　ashamed　A-267
始まる（める）[haji-maru(meru)]　begin　B-97
初めから　[hajimekara]　　　　　　all along　A-130
初めの　[hajime-no]　　　　　　　initial　I-104
始める　[hajimeru]　　　　　　　　initiate　I-105
始める　[hajimeru]　　　　　　　　start　S-455
馬車　[basha]　　　　　　　　　　carriage　C-62
馬車　[basha]　　　　　　　　　　chariot　C-119
場所　[basho]　　　　　　　　　　place　P-188
走る　[hashiru]　　　　　　　　　run　R-281, 282
恥ずかしがりや　[hazukashigariya]　bashful　B-43
恥ずかしさ　[hazukashisa]　　　　shame　S-170
バスケットボール　[basukettobōru]　basketball　B-48
旗　[hata]　　　　　　　　　　　　banner　B-28
旗　[hata]　　　　　　　　　　　　flag　F-157
バター　[batā]　　　　　　　　　　butter　B-280
裸の　[hadaka-no]　　　　　　　　bare　B-34, 35
裸の　[hdaka-no]　　　　　　　　　nude　N-131
裸の　[hadaka-no]　　　　　　　　naked　N-5
肌着　[hadagi]　　　　　　　　　　underwear　U-24
働く　[hataraku]　　　　　　　　　toil　T-210
八　[hachi]　　　　　　　　　　　eight　E-38
蜂　[hachi]　　　　　　　　　　　bee　B-87
八番目の　[hachibanmeno]　　　　eighth　E-39

はつか大根 〔hatsuka-daikon〕	radish R-12
はつかねずみ 〔hatsuka-nezumi〕	mouse M-246, 247
はっきりした 〔hakkiri-shita〕	plain P-191
はっきりしない 〔hakkiri-shinai〕	vague V-6
はっきりしない 〔hakkiri-shinai〕	unclear U-15
罰金 〔bakkin〕	fine F-135
罰金 〔bakkin〕	penalty P-82
発見する 〔hakken-suru〕	discover D-201
発行する 〔hakkō-suru〕	publish P-395, 396
罰する 〔bassuru〕	punish P-407, 408, 409
バッター 〔battā〕	batter B-55
発達 〔hattatsu〕	development D-134
発達 〔hattatsu〕	progress P-359
発達する 〔hattatsu-suru〕	develop D-131, 132
はったり 〔hattari〕	bluff B-185
バット 〔batto〕	bat B-51
発表する 〔happyō-suru〕	announce A-181
発明者 〔hatsumei-sha〕	inventor I-189
発明する 〔hatsumei-suru〕	invent I-187, 188
パテ 〔pate〕	putty P-428
はと 〔hato〕	pigeon P-171
花 〔hana〕	blossom B-180
花 〔hana〕	flower F-180
鼻 〔hana〕	nose N-110
花が咲く 〔hanaga-saku〕	bloom B-179
話 〔hanashi〕	tale T-20
話し手 〔hanashite〕	speaker S-393
離す 〔hanasu〕	disjoin D-214
話す 〔hanasu〕	speak S-392
話す 〔hanasu〕	tell T-64
鼻であしらう 〔hana-de-ashirau〕	snub S-343
バナナ 〔banana〕	banana B-21, 22
離れて 〔hanarete〕	off O-38, 39
花輪 〔hanawa〕	wreath W-199
はにかんだ 〔hanikanda〕	shy S-237
ハヌカ 〔hanuka〕	Chanukah C-112
はねる 〔haneru〕	leap L-51
幅の広い 〔haba-no-hiroi〕	broad B-249
幅の広い 〔haba-no-hiroi〕	wide W-119
歯ブラシ 〔haburashi〕	toothbrush T-225
葉巻 〔hamaki〕	cigar C-170, 171
場面 〔bamen〕	scene S-61
場面 〔bamen〕	stage S-443
早い 〔hayai〕	rapid R-24
速い 〔hayai〕	fast F-60
速い 〔hayai〕	swift S-639
早く 〔hayaku〕	early E-9
払う 〔harau〕	pay P-57, 58, 59
パラシュート 〔parashūto〕	parachute P-22
針 〔hari〕	needle N-40
針金 〔harigane〕	wire W-143, 144
春 〔haru〕	spring S-430
はるかに 〔harukani〕	far F-43
パレード 〔parēdo〕	parade P-23
バレーボール 〔barēbōru〕	volleyball V-60
晴れた 〔hareta〕	fine F-134, 137
ハレルヤ 〔hareruya〕	hallelujah H-15
ハワイ 〔hawai〕	Hawaii H-60
ハワイ人 〔hawai-jin〕	Hawaiian H-61
パン 〔pan〕	bread B-226
番 〔ban〕	turn T-305
繁栄する 〔hanei-suru〕	prosper P-378

ひ

秒 [byō]　second S-110
費用 [hiyō]　expense E-213
病院 [byōin]　hospital H-162, 163
美容院 [biyōin]　beauty parlor B-79
ひょいと飛ぶ [hyoi-to-tobu]　hop H-151, 152
評価する [hyōka-suru]　evaluate E-154, 155
病気 [byōki]　illness I-16
病気 [byōki]　sickness S-240
病気 [byōki]　disease D-206, 207
病気な [byōki-na]　ill I-15
病気の [byōki-no]　sick S-239
評決 [hyōketsu]　verdict V-25
表現 [hyōgen]　expression E-226
表紙 [hyōshi]　cover C-434, 435, 436, 437
美容師 [biyōshi]　hairdresser H-5
表示する [hyōji-suru]　indicate I-74
病人 [byōnin]　patient P-56
費用のかかる [hiyō-no-kakaru]　expensive E-214
開く [hiraku]　open O-88, 89
比率 [hiritsu]　proportion P-376
比率 [hiritsu]　ratio R-30
ひる [hiru]　leech L-60
昼寝 [hirune]　nap N-8
疲労 [hirō]　fatigue F-70
拾い上げる [hiroiageru]　pick up P-159
広げる [hirogeru]　expand E-208
広げる [hirogeru]　spread S-428, 429
広く [hiroku]　widespread W-121
貧乏 [binbō]　poverty P-270, 271
ピンポン [pinpon]　Ping-Pong P-178
ピンポン [pinpon]　table tennis T-4

ふ

フィート [fīto]　foot F-201
不意に発言する [fui-ni-hatsugen-suru]　ejaculate E-44
フィラデルフィア [firaderufia]　Philadelphia P-137
フィンランド [finrando]　Finland F-144
風変りな [fūgawari-na]　eccentric E-23
フォーク [fōku]　fork F-225
フォートコピー [fōtokopī]　photocopy P-142
深い [fukai]　deep D-56
不快な [fukaina]　obnoxious O-17
不確定な [fukakuteina]　uncertain U-13
付加する [fuka-suru]　annex A-179
不可能な [fukanō-na]　impossible I-41, 42
不機嫌な [fukigen-na]　cross C-462
吹き散らす [fukichirasu]　blow away B-183
無器用さ [bukiyō-sa]　clumsiness C-206
無器用な [bukiyō-na]　clumsy C-208
無器用な [bukiyō-na]　green G-150
吹く [fuku]　blow B-181
服 [fuku]　gown G-101
福音 [fukuin]　gospel G-92, 93
複合の [fukugō-no]　multiple M-260
複雑にする [fukuzatsuni-suru]　complicate C-284
不具者 [fugusha]　cripple C-457
複写する [fukusha-suru]　mimeograph M-157
復讐 [fukushū]　revenge R-181
服従 [fukujū]　obedience O-4
複数 [fukusū]　plural P-218

フランスの [furansu-no]	French F-261
振り動かす [furiugokasu]	flirt F-174
振り掛ける [furikakeru]	sprinkle S-432
震える [furueru]	shiver S-201, 202
無礼な [bureina]	impolite I-38
プレスする [puresu-suru]	press P-304
触れる [fureru]	touch T-234
風呂 [furo]	bath B-52
ブローチ [burōchi]	brooch B-254
ブローチ [burōchi]	pin P-176
プロテスタント [purotesutanto]	Protestant P-383
文 [bun]	sentence S-149
分解させる [bunkai-saseru]	dissolve D-230
分割する [bunkatsu-suru]	divide D-244, 245
紛失した [funshitsu-shita]	missing M-181, 182
噴出する [funshutsu-suru]	erupt E-139
文通する [buntsū-suru]	correspond C-410
分配する [bunpai-suru]	distribute D-234, 235
分野 [bunya]	field F-113, 114
分裂 [bunretsu]	fracture F-246
分裂させる [bunretsu-saseru]	disrupt D-227

へ

平穏 [heion]	calm C-16, 17
兵器 [heiki]	arms A-250
平均 [heikin]	average A-319
平均 [heikin]	mean M-80
平行 [heikō]	parallel P-26
兵籍に入れる [heiseki-ni-ireru]	enlist E-108
兵卒 [heisotsu]	private P-333
平和 [heiwa]	peace P-61
ページ [pēji]	page P-4
ベール [bēru]	veil V-20
ペダル [pedaru]	pedal P-72
ベッド [beddo]	bed B-85
別に [betsuni]	apart A-207
ペテン [peten]	deceit D-38
ペニー [penī]	penny P-91
へび [hebi]	snake S-331
ヘブライ語聖書 [heburaigo-seisho]	Hebrew Bible H-81
ヘブル書 [heburu-sho]	Hebrews H-82
部屋 [heya]	room R-248, 249
ヘヤーピン [heyāpin]	hairpin H-6
ヘヤーブラシ [heyāburashi]	hairbrush H-4
減らす [herasu]	reduce R-74
減る [heru]	deplete D-99
ペン [pen]	pen P-79
弁解 [benkai]	excuse E-199
弁解 [benkai]	plea P-206
変化のある [henka-no-aru]	varied V-17
ペンキを塗る [penki-o-nuru]	paint P-6
勉強 [benkyō]	study S-533
ペンキヤ [penki-ya]	painter P-8
弁護士 [bengoshi]	attorney A-302
弁護士 [bengoshi]	lawyer L-39
便所 [benjo]	toilet T-211
ペンチ [penchi]	pliers P-213
ベンチ [benchi]	bench B-112
扁桃腺手術 [hentōsen-shujutsu]	tonsillectomy T-220
変な [hen-na]	odd O-35
変な [hen-na]	weird W-74

ほ

保安官 [hoankan]	sheriff S-190
ぽいと投げる [poi-to-nageru]	toss T-232
棒 [bō]	rod R-241
棒 [bō]	stick S-484
ボーイスカウト [bōisukauto]	Boy Scout B-217
法王 [hōō]	Pope P-246
崩壊 [hōkai]	breakdown B-228
崩壊 [hōkai]	collapse C-231
妨害する [bōgai-suru]	impede I-32
宝冠 [hōkan]	coronet C-406
ほうき [hōki]	broom B-255
放棄する [hōki-suru]	cast off C-70
放棄する [hōki-suru]	discard D-187, 188, 189
放棄する [hōki-suru]	relinquish R-101
方向 [hōkō]	direction D-174, 175
奉公する [hōkō-suru]	serve S-157
帽子 [bōshi]	hat H-51
暴食 [bōshoku]	gluttony G-68
方針 [hōshin]	policy P-233, 234
包帯 [hōtai]	bandage B-23
ボート [bōto]	boat B-190
暴動 [bōdō]	riot R-207
冒涜する [bōtoku-suru]	blaspheme B-168, 169, 170
放任する [hōnin-suru]	let alone L-79
奉納 [hōnō]	oblation O-13
豊富 [hōfu]	abundance A-30
豊富 [hōfu]	plenty P-212
報復する [hōfuku-suru]	retaliate R-170, 171
豊富な [hōfu-na]	abundant A-31
方法 [hōhō]	fashion F-58
方法 [hōhō]	manner M-45, 46
方法 [hōhō]	method M-132
訪問 [hōmon]	visit V-53
抱擁する [hōyō-suru]	embrace E-70
ポーランド [pōrando]	Poland P-229
法律 [hōritsu]	law L-37
法律の [hōritsu-no]	legal L-64
ボーリング [bōringu]	bowl B-211
法令 [hōrei]	decree D-52
法令 [hōrei]	statute S-463
吠える [hoeru]	bark B-36
ほお [hoo]	cheek C-133
捕獲する [hokaku-suru]	capture C-47
他の [hoka-no]	other O-137
牧師 [bokushi]	father F-68
牧師 [bokushi]	minister M-169
牧師 [bokushi]	pastor P-50
牧師 [bokushi]	priest P-316, 317, 318, 319
牧師 [bokushi]	reverend R-184
北西 [hokusei]	northwest N-107
北東 [hokutō]	northeast N-106
ポケット [poketto]	pocket P-221
保険 [hoken]	insurance I-143
保護眼鏡 [hogogankyō]	goggles G-79
保護する [hogo-suru]	protect P-380
星 [hoshi]	star S-454
欲しがる [hoshigaru]	covet C-438, 439
干し草 [hoshigusa]	hay H-62
干し草 [hoshigusa]	mow (n) M-252, 253
欲しくない [hoshikunai]	don't want D-283

干しすもも　[hoshisumomo]　　　　prune　P-388
保証　[hoshō]　　　　　　　　　　guarantee　G-169, 170
細い　[hosoi]　　　　　　　　　　fine　F-136
細い　[hosoi]　　　　　　　　　　thin　T-134, 135
保蔵する　[hozōsuru]　　　　　　preserve　P-302
保存する　[hozon-suru]　　　　　keep　K-1
ボタン　[botan]　　　　　　　　　button (n)　B-283, 284
ボタンを止める　[botan-o-tomeru]　button (v)　B-283, 284
墓地　[bochi]　　　　　　　　　　cemetery　C-91
欲する　[hossuru]　　　　　　　　wish　W-147, 148
ほっそりした　[hossori-shita]　　slender　S-305
ほっそりした　[hossori-shita]　　slim　S-310
没頭させる　[bottō-saseru]　　　engross　E-105
没頭する　[bottō-suru]　　　　　engross　E-104
ホットドック　[hottodoggu]　　　hot dog　H-165
ホテル　[hoteru]　　　　　　　　hotel　H-166
施しをこう　[hodokoshi-o-kou]　ask alms　A-274
ほとんど　[hotondo]　　　　　　almost　A-139
ほとんど　[hotondo]　　　　　　nearly　N-28
骨　[hone]　　　　　　　　　　　bone　B-192
炎　[honoo]　　　　　　　　　　flame　F-158
帆船　[hobune]　　　　　　　　　sailboat　S-11
微笑む　[hohoemu]　　　　　　　smile　S-325
誉める　[homeru]　　　　　　　　commend　C-259
ぼやけた　[boyaketa]　　　　　　blurry　B-186
掘る　[horu]　　　　　　　　　　dig　D-163, 164
彫る　[horu]　　　　　　　　　　engrave　E-103
本　[hon]　　　　　　　　　　　book　B-193
盆　[bon]　　　　　　　　　　　tray　T-271
ポンド　[pondo]　　　　　　　　pound　P-266, 267
本当の　[hontō-no]　　　　　　　genuine　G-34
ポンプ　[ponpu]　　　　　　　　pump　P-400, 401
ぼんやりした　[bonyari-shita]　　absent-minded　A-22

ま

毎週の　[maishū-no]　　　　　　weekly　W-67
毎年の　[maitoshi-no]　　　　　　yearly　Y-4
毎日　[mainichi]　　　　　　　　every day　E-170
毎日の　[mainichi-no]　　　　　　daily　D-5
毎年　[mainen]　　　　　　　　　every year　E-172
マイル　[mairu]　　　　　　　　mile　M-151
前掛　[maekake]　　　　　　　　apron　A-234
前の　[mae-no]　　　　　　　　　front　F-282
前の　[mae-no]　　　　　　　　　previous　P-311
負かす　[makasu]　　　　　　　　defeat　D-59
まがった　[magatta]　　　　　　stooped　S-496
巻き毛　[makige]　　　　　　　　curl　C-490
巻きこむ　[makikomu]　　　　　　involve　I-197
撒き散らす　[makichirasu]　　　scatter　S-60
負けた　[maketa]　　　　　　　　beaten　B-75
負けた　[maketa]　　　　　　　　defeated　D-60
曲げる　[mageru]　　　　　　　　bend　B-113
まことに　[makotoni]　　　　　　verily　V-26
まことに　[makotoni]　　　　　　very　V-30
混ざる　[mazaru]　　　　　　　　mingle　M-167, 168
真面目な　[majimena]　　　　　　earnest　E-11
魔術師　[majyutsushi]　　　　　magician　M-9
増す　[masu]　　　　　　　　　　increase　I-66
増す　[masu]　　　　　　　　　　multiply　M-261
麻酔剤　[masuizai]　　　　　　　narcotic　N-10

マスクメロン [masukumeron]	muskmelon M-267
貧しい [mazushii]	poor P-241, 242, 243
混ぜる [mazeru]	mix M-191
叉 [mata]	also A-143, 144
又 [mata]	too T-222
まだ [mada]	yet Y-11, 12
まだ〜しない [mada〜shinai]	not yet N-128
又は [matawa]	or O-107, 108
町 [machi]	town T-247
間違え [machigae]	mistake M-187
待つ [matsu]	wait W-5
マッチ [macchi]	match M-67
抹消する [masshō-suru]	remove R-112
真直ぐな [massuguna]	straight S-505
〜まで [〜made]	till T-185
〜まで [〜made]	until U-48
窓 [mado]	window W-136
まともな [matomo-na]	decent D-40
窓を開けて下さい [mado-o-akete-kudasai]	open the window O-93
学ぶ [manabu]	learn L-52
間に合わせの [maniawase-no]	makeshift M-35
マニキュア [manikyua]	nail polish N-3
マネージャー [maneijā]	manager M-43
真似する [mane-suru]	mimic M-158
真似る [maneru]	imitate I-23
まばたく [mabataku]	wink W-140
まぶしくする [mabushiku-suru]	dazzle D-22
魔法 [mahō]	magic M-8
まま父 [mamachichi]	stepfather S-481
まま母 [mamahaha]	stepmother S-482
豆 [mame]	bean(s) B-64
豆の支え棒 [mame-no-sasaebō]	beanpole B-65
間もなく [mamonaku]	by and by B-288
守る [mamoru]	defend D-62
守る [mamoru]	guard G-171
眉をひそめる [mayu-o-hisomeru]	frown F-283
迷う [mayou]	stray S-510
真夜中 [mayonaka]	midnight M-141
丸い [marui]	round R-263, 264
丸太 [maruta]	log L-138
稀な [marena]	rare R-25
稀に [mareni]	seldom S-123
回す [mawasu]	direct D-172, 173
満期になる [manki-ni-naru]	expire E-218
満期になる [manki-ni-naru]	due D-324
満足 [manzoku]	satisfaction S-39
満足した [manzoku-shita]	content C-361
真中 [mannaka]	midst M-142

み

見えること [mierukoto]	vision V-51, 52
見降ろす [miorosu]	look down L-154
見返る [mikaeru]	look back L-153
磨く [migaku]	polish P-235
磨く [migaku]	shine S-194
右 [migi]	right R-196
ミサエル [misaeru]	missile M-180
短い [mijikai]	short S-218
水 [mizu]	water W-40, 41
湖 [mizuumi]	lake L-8

水かき [mizukaki] — paddle P-3
未熟な [mijuku-na] — unskilled U-47
水たまり [mizutamari] — pool P-240
見捨てる [misuteru] — forsake F-229, 230, 231
水庖瘡 [mizubōsō] — chickenpox C-145
店 [mise] — shop S-215
店 [mise] — store S-498
未成年者 [miseinensha] — minor (n) M-170
見せびらかす [misebirakasu] — show off S-230, 231
見せる [miseru] — show S-227
見出し [midashi] — caption C-46
道 [michi] — road R-225
道 [michi] — street S-511
道 [michi] — way W-49
満ちた [michita] — full F-288, 289
導く [michibiku] — lead L-43
三つ編 [mitsuami] — braid B-220
見つける [mitsukeru] — detect D-122
見つける [mitsukeru] — find F-131
見積る [mitsumoru] — estimate E-145
認める [mitomeru] — appreciate A-229
認める [mitomeru] — concede C-288
認める [mitomeru] — recognize R-64
緑色の [midori-iro-no] — green G-149
皆 [mina] — everybody E-169
港 [minato] — harbor H-35
南 [minami] — south S-381
南アメリカ [minami-amerika] — South America S-382
醜い [minikui] — homely H-143, 144
醜さ [minikusa] — ugliness U-1, 2, 3
身につけている [minitsuketeiru] — wear W-58, 59
見本 [mihon] — sample S-31
耳 [mimi] — ear E-7
耳の痛み [mimi-no-itami] — earache E-8
耳のきこえない [mimi-no-kikoenai] — deafness D-29
耳の遠い [mimi-no-tooi] — hard-of-hearing H-39
耳をかたむける [mimi-o-katamukeru] — hark H-42
脈博 [myakuhaku] — pulse P-399
明後日 [myōgonichi] — day after tomorrow D-18
未来 [mirai] — future F-299
未来に [mirai-ni] — in the future I-177
魅力的な [miryokuteki-na] — attractive A-306
見る [miru] — look L-149
見る [miru] — see S-116
ミルウォーキー [miruwōkī] — Milwaukee M-156
魅惑する [miwaku-suru] — fascinate F-56, 57
民主主義者 [minshushugisha] — democrat D-84
民族 [minzoku] — people P-92

む

無 [mu] — naught N-18, 19, 20
無意味な事 [muiminakoto] — nonsense N-100
無学の [mugaku-no] — ignorant I-13
昔々 [mukashimukashi] — once upon a time O-71
無関心 [mukanshin] — indifference I-75
むく [muku] — pare P-29
報いる [mukuiru] — render R-114, 115
無限の [mugen-no] — infinite I-92
無効にする [mukō-ni-suru] — annul A-188
向う見ずの [mukōmizu-no] — reckless R-61

むさぼり食う　[musabori-kuu]　devour　D-143
虫　[mushi]　bug　B-265
虫　[mushi]　worm　W-175
無視する　[mushi-suru]　disregard　D-226
無視する　[mushi-suru]　ignore　I-14
むし歯　[mushiba]　cavity　C-85
矛盾する　[mujun-suru]　contradict　C-368
難しい　[muzukashii]　hard　H-36
息子　[musuko]　son　S-370
結び目　[musubime]　knot　K-34
娘　[musume]　daughter　D-16
無責任な　[musekinin-na]　irresponsible　I-203, 204
無駄口をきく　[mudaguchi-o-kiku]　tattle　T-35, 36
無駄な　[mudana]　vain　V-7
無駄にする　[muda-nisuru]　waste　W-34, 35
むち　[muchi]　whip　W-101
無中になる　[muchū-ni-naru]　apply　A-225
胸　[mune]　chest　C-140
謀叛　[muhon]　rebel　R-54
村　[mura]　village　V-43
紫色の　[murasakiirono]　purple　P-418

め

目　[me]　eye　E-236
姪　[mei]　niece　N-82
命じる　[meijiru]　bid　B-139, 141
命じる　[meijiru]　command　C-256
名声　[meisei]　fame　F-36
明白な　[meihaku-na]　apparent　A-214
明白な　[meihaku-na]　clear　C-187
明白な　[meihaku-na]　explicit　E-222, 223
名誉　[meiyo]　honor　H-147, 148
命令する　[meirei-suru]　order　O-119
迷惑させる　[meiwaku-saseru]　bother　B-204, 205
雌牛　[meushi]　cow　C-440
目がね　[megane]　eyeglasses　E-237
目がね　[megane]　glasses　G-56
目がね　[megane]　spectacles　S-399
メキシコ人　[mekishikojin]　Mexican　M-135
メキシコの　[mekishiko-no]　Mexican　M-135
盲の　[mekurano]　blind　B-174
召使い　[meshitsukai]　servant　S-156
雌犬　[mesuinu]　bitch　B-160
メソジスト教徒　[mesojisuto-kyōto]　Methodist　M-133
目立つ　[medatsu]　prominent　P-362, 363, 364
目に見える　[menimieru]　visible　V-50
目の前に　[me-no-maeni]　before　B-91
目まい　[memai]　dizziness　D-252
目まいがする　[memai-ga-suru]　dizzy　D-253
メロディー　[merodī]　melody　M-102
メロン　[meron]　melon　M-103
免許　[menkyo]　license　L-91, 92
免除　[menjo]　absolution　A-25, 26
雌鶏　[mendori]　hen　H-91

も

申し込む　[mōshikomu]　propose　P-377
申し出る　[mōshideru]　offer　O-42, 43

モーター [mōtā] — motor M-241
もう1つの [mōhitotsuno] — another A-191
盲目 [mōmoku] — blindness B-175
木材 [mokuzai] — lumber L-177, 178
黙想する [mokusō-suru] — meditate M-94
目的 [mokuteki] — goal G-72
目的 [mokuteki] — objective O-12
目的 [mokuteki] — purpose P-419, 420, 421
黙認する [mokunin-suru] — acquiesce A-56
木曜日 [mokuyōbi] — Thursday T-173
潜る [moguru] — dive D-238, 239
もしも [moshimo] — if I-12
もたれる [motareru] — recline R-63
持ちこたえる [mochikotaeru] — maintain M-19
持つ [motsu] — have H-55, 56, 57
持って来る [motte-kuru] — bring B-246
もっと [motto] — more M-218
もっと遠い [motto-tōi] — further F-295, 296
もっと遠く [motto-tōku] — farther F-54
最も [mottomo] — most M-227
最も [mottomo] — ultimate U-7
最も遠い [mottomo-tōi] — farthest F-55
最も年上の [mottomo-toshi-ueno] — eldest E-48
最も良い [mottomo-yoi] — best B-128
もっと悪い [motto-warui] — worse W-184, 185, 186
モップ [moppu] — mop M-217
元の [moto-no] — original O-132
戻る [modoru] — return R-180
物 [mono] — thing T-137
物語 [monogatari] — story S-502
物語る [monogataru] — narrate N-11
～もまた～でない [～mo-mata～de-nai] — nor N-102
木綿 [momen] — cotton C-416
桃 [momo] — peach P-63, 64, 65
燃やす [moyasu] — kindle K-17
森 [mori] — woods W-168
モルヒネ [moruhine] — morphine M-224
モルモン教(徒) [morumonkyō-(to)] — Mormon M-221
漏れる [moreru] — leak L-48
門 [mon] — gate G-18
問題 [mondai] — problem P-340, 341, 342
問題外にそれて [mondaigai-ni-sorete] — go off the track G-90

や

やぎ [yagi] — goat G-73
野球 [yakyū] — baseball B-42
野牛 [yagyū] — buffalo B-264
野球帽子 [yakyūbōshi] — cap C-39
約 [yaku] — about A-15
焼く [yaku] — bake B-12
焼く [yaku] — burn B-273
焼く [yaku] — broil B-252
役員会 [yakuinkai] — board B-188
約束 [yakusoku] — promise P-365, 366, 367
役人 [yakunin] — officer O-48
薬品 [yakuhin] — drug D-317
優しい [yasashii] — gentle G-31
優しい [yasashii] — kind K-15
優しい [yasashii] — soft-hearted S-359
野心 [yashin] — ambition A-156

安い [yasui]	cheap C-125, 126
やすり [yasuri]	file F-121
野生の [yasei-no]	wild W-124, 125
やせこけた [yasekoketa]	skinny S-291
やせている [yaseteiru]	lean L-49, 50
やって来る [yatte-kuru]	come on C-250
雇う [yatou]	employ E-77
宿屋 [yadoya]	inn I-114
屋根 [yane]	roof R-247
やぶ [yabu]	bush B-275
野望な [yabō-na]	ambitious A-157, 158
山 [yama]	mountain M-243
止める [yameru]	give up G-52
やり続ける [yaritsuzukeru]	persevere P-120
柔かい [yawarakai]	soft S-358
柔かい [yawarakai]	tender T-78, 79, 80

ゆ

唯一の [yuiitsu-no]	only O-82
唯一の [yuiitsu-no]	sole S-363
憂うつ [yūutsu]	melancholy M-101
誘拐する [yūkai-suru]	abduct A-8
誘かいする [yūkai-suru]	kidnap K-12
勇敢な [yūkan-na]	brave B-223
勇気 [yūki]	courage C-425
勇気づける [yūki-zukeru]	encourage E-83
勇気を失わせる [yūki-o-ushinawaseru]	discourage D-198, 199
夕刻 [yūkoku]	evening E-159
ユーゴスラビア [yūgosurabia]	Yugoslavia Y-27
言うことを聞かない [yūkoto-o-kikanai]	disobey D-217
有罪と判定する [yūzai-to-hantei-suru]	damn D-6
有罪の [yūzai-no]	guilty G-177, 178
優秀な [yūshū-na]	excellent E-188
優勝者 [yūshōsha]	champion C-106
夕食 [yūshoku]	supper S-589
郵送する [yūsō-suru]	mail M-16
郵送する [yūsō-suru]	post P-262
雄大な [yūdai-na]	grand G-109, 110
誘導する [yūdō-suru]	conduct C-304, 305
誘導する [yūdō-suru]	motivate M-236
有能な [yūnō-na]	competent C-275
郵便 [yūbin]	mail M-15
裕福な [yūfuku-na]	rich R-191
雄弁家 [yūbenka]	orator O-114
有名な [yūmei-na]	celebrated C-89
有名な [yūmei-na]	renowned R-118
ユーモア [yūmoa]	humor H-191
幽霊 [yūrei]	ghost G-43
誘惑する [yūwaku-suru]	entice E-116
誘惑する [yūwaku-suru]	tempt T-73
床 [yuka]	floor F-177
雪 [yuki]	snow S-342
輸送 [yusō]	transportation T-265
輸送する [yusō-suru]	transport T-264
ユダヤ教 [yudaya-kyō]	Judaism J-29
ユダヤ教の男の成人式 [yudaya-kyō-no-otoko-no-seijin-shiki]	Bar Mitzvah B-33
ユダヤ教 メーズーザ [yudaya-kyō mēzūzā]	mezuzah M-137
ユダヤ人 [yudayajin]	Jew J-12
ユダヤ人用のパン [yudayajinyō-no-pan]	matzoth M-71

ユダヤ聖書 [yudayaseisho]	Jewish Bible J-14
指 [yubi]	finger F-138
指ぬき [yubinuki]	thimble T-133
指輪 [yubiwa]	ring R-203
弓 [yumi]	bow(s) (of archer) B-208
弓(バイオリンの) [yumi(baiorin-no)]	bow(s) (of violin) B-209
弓形の [yumigata-no]	arch A-236
夢 [yume]	dream D-303
揺りいす [yuriisu]	rocking chair R-238, 239
許す [yurusu]	allow A-134
許す [yurusu]	forgive F-223, 224
許す [yurusu]	pardon P-28
許せない [yurusenai]	unforgivable U-27
緩める [yurumeru]	relax R-97, 98
揺れ [yure]	quake Q-4
揺れる [yureru]	shake S-167
揺れる [yureru]	swing S-642

よ

良い [yoi]	good G-85, 86
用意する [yōi-suru]	get ready G-41
用意する [yōi-suru]	provide P-386, 387
用意する [yōi-suru]	prepare P-292, 293, 294
用意できた [yōidekita]	ready R-40, 41, 42, 43
容易な [yōina]	easy E-20, 21
容易にする [yōi-ni-suru]	facilitate F-6
容器 [yōki]	container C-354
陽気 [yōki]	gaiety G-2, 3
陽気な [yōki-na]	gay G-24
陽気な [yōki-na]	merry M-128
陽気な [yōki-na]	jolly J-23
要求する [yōkyū-suru]	demand D-83
容姿 [yōshi]	figure F-120
幼児 [yōji]	infant I-90
養子(養女)にする [yōshi(yōjo)ni-suru]	adopt A-92
用心 [yōjin]	caution C-83
要点をつかむ [yōten-o-tsukamu]	summarize S-568
洋服ピン [yōfukupin]	pin P-175
洋服ブラシ [yōfukuburashi]	clothesbrush C-201
洋服屋 [yōfukuya]	tailor T-8
予防注射 [yobō-chūsha]	vaccination V-4
羊毛 [yōmō]	wool W-169
要約する [yōyaku-suru]	condense C-303
予期する [yoki-suru]	anticipate A-194
浴室 [yokushitsu]	bathroom B-54
抑制する [yokusei-suru]	control C-374, 375
良くない [yokunai]	no good N-90, 91
欲望 [yokubō]	desire D-114, 115
予言 [yogen]	prophecy P-372
予言する [yogen-suru]	predict P-290
横切って [yokogitte]	across A-59
横切る [yokogiru]	cross C-464, 465
横切る [yokogiru]	intersect I-174
汚す [yogosu]	soil S-361
汚す [yogosu]	stain S-444
横たわる [yokotawaru]	lie L-96
横にそれる [yoko-ni-soreru]	sidetrack S-244
よごれた [yogoreta]	dirty D-177
横笛 [yokobue]	fife F-116
酔った [yotta]	drunk D-319

呼びリン [yobirin]	bell B-103
よびリン [yobirin]	doorbell D-285
呼ぶ [yobu]	call C-12, 13
予報 [yohō]	forecast F-212
予防する [yobō-suru]	prevent P-309
読む [yomu]	read P-36, 37, 38
予約 [yoyaku]	appointment A-227
予約 [yoyaku]	engagement E-98
～より少ない [～yorisukunai]	less L-75
より低い [yori-hikui]	beneath B-115
～よりも [～yorimo]	than T-96
より良い [yoriyoi]	better B-132
より良く [yoriyoku]	better B-132
夜 [yoru]	night N-83
夜遅く [yoruosoku]	late at night L-27
喜ばせる [yorokobaseru]	gratify G-123, 124
喜び [yorokobi]	delight D-80
喜び [yorokobi]	joy J-28
喜ぶ [yorokobu]	rejoice R-90
喜こんで [yorokonde]	willing W-129, 130, 131
宜しい [yoroshii]	all right A-135
宜しい [yoroshii]	O.K. O-57, 58
弱い [yowai]	frail F-248
弱い [yowai]	weak W-53
酔わせる [yowaseru]	intoxicate I-181
弱った [yowatta]	feeble F-86
四十五分 [yonjūgofun]	three-quarters of an hour T-159
四分の一 [yonbun-no-ichi]	quarter Q-9
四分の三 [yonbun-no-san]	three-fourths T-157

ら

ライオン [raion]	lion L-113
来月 [raigetsu]	next month N-77
来週 [raishū]	next week N-78, 79
来年 [rainen]	next year N-80
ライノタイプ [rainotaipu]	Linotype L-112
らい病 [raibyō]	leprosy L-74
ライフル銃 [raifurujū]	rifle R-195
ラクダ [rakuda]	camel C-20
落第する [rakudai-suru]	fail F-13
落第する [rakudai-suru]	flunk F-181
落胆した [rakutan-shita]	dejected D-73
ラケット [raketto]	racket R-9
ラジオ [rajio]	radio R-10, 11
ラテンの [raten-no]	Latin L-31, 32
らば [raba]	mule M-258
ラビ(ユダヤ教の牧師) [rabi(yudayakyō-no-bokushi)]	rabbi R-1, 2

り

利益 [rieki]	benefit B-118
利益 [rieki]	gain G-4, 5
利益 [rieki]	profit P-356
理解する [rikai-suru]	comprehend C-287
理解する [rikai-suru]	understand U-20, 21
陸 [riku]	land L-11
利口な [rikō-na]	bright B-240
利口な [rikō-na]	clever C-188, 189
利己主義な [rikoshugi-na]	selfish S-129, 130, 131

る

れ

ろ

廊下 [rōka]	corridor C-411
労苦 [rōku]	travail T-267
ろうそく [rōsoku]	candle C-30
労働 [rōdō]	labor L-1
労働者 [rōdōsha]	worker W-172
浪費する [rōhi-suru]	squander S-436
ローマ教皇 [rōmakyōkō]	pontiff P-239
ローマ教皇の [rōmakyōkō-no]	papal P-17
ローマ人 [rōmajin]	Roman R-245
ローラースケート [rōrāsukēto]	roller skating R-244
六 [roku]	six S-279
ロケット [roketto]	rocket R-237
ロザリオ [rozario]	rosary R-254, 255
ロシア [roshia]	Russia R-288
ロスアンゼルス [rosuanzerusu]	Los Angeles L-160
魯鈍 [rodon]	moron M-223
ロバ [roba]	donkey D-268
論議 [rongi]	discussion D-205
論議する [rongi-suru]	debate D-34
論証する [ronshō-suru]	demonstrate D-87
論争 [ronsō]	controversy C-376
論争する [ronsō-suru]	dispute D-225
論理学 [ronrigaku]	logic L-139

わ

ワイン [wain]	wine W-137, 138
和解 [wakai]	propitiation P-375
若い [wakai]	young Y-18
わがままな [wagamama-na]	willful W-128
分りました [wakari-mashita]	I see I-208
分りました [wakarimashita]	oh, I see! O-53
分る [wakaru]	aware of A-326
別れる [wakareru]	part P-33, 34
わき水 [wakimizu]	spring S-431
惑星 [wakusei]	planet P-198
分け前 [wakemae]	share S-176
分ける [wakeru]	separate S-150, 151
ワゴン [wagon]	wagon W-4
わし [washi]	eagle E-6
ワシントン [washinton]	Washington W-31, 32
忘れる [wasureru]	forget F-221, 222
話題 [wadai]	topic T-227
私 [watakushi]	I I-1, 2
私 [watakushi]	me M-76
私自身 [watakushi-jishin]	myself M-273
私の [watakushi-no]	my M-272
私のもの [watakushi-no-mono]	mine M-164
私も [watakushi-mo]	me, too M-134
私を見なさい [watakushi-o-minasai]	look at me L-152
罠 [wana]	trap T-266
喚きたてる [wamekitateru]	bawl out B-59
喚く [wameku]	bawl B-57, 58
笑い [warai]	laughter L-35, 36
笑う [warau]	laugh L-33
割合 [wariai]	rate R-28
割る [waru]	crack C-443
悪い [warui]	bad B-9, 10

Portuguese-English Index

adivinhar	guess G-172, 173, 174, 175	
adjacente	adjacent A-80	
admirar	admire A-82, 83	
admissão	admission A-84	
admitir	admit A-87	
adolescencia	adolescence A-90	
adoração	worship W-187	
adorar	adore A-93	
adornar	adorn A-94	
adotar	adopt A-92	
adquirir	acquire A-58	
adversidade	hard times H-41	
advertir	forewarn F-219	
advertir	admonish A-88, 89	
advertir	warn W-23	
advogado	attorney A-302	
advogado	lawyer L-39	
afagar	stroke S-522	
afastar	sidetrack S-244	
afastar	remove R-110, 111, 112	
afligir-se	fret F-267	
afogar-se	drown D-315, 316	
Africa	Africa A-703	
afundar-se	sink S-270, 271	
agarrar	tackle T-6	
agarrar	grab G-102	
agonia	agony A-114	
agora	now N-130	
agora mesmo	just now J-40, 41	
agradar	gratify G-123, 124	
agradável	pleasant P-208	
agrimensor	surveyor S-607	
água	water W-40, 41	
água forte	etch E-147	
água-di-colínia	cologne C-239	
agudo	sharp S-180, 181	
águia	eagle E-6	
agulha	needle N-40	
ái de mim	alas A-123	
ainda	still S-486	
ainda	yet Y-11, 12	
ainda não	not yet N-128	
ainda que	although A-149	
ajoelhar-se	kneel K-26	
ajudar	help H-90	
ajudar	aid A-118	
ajustar	adjust A-81	
alaranjado	orange O-110, 111, 112	
alce americano	moose M-216	
alce	elk E-64	
aldeia	village V-43	
alegre	gay G-24	
alegre	cheerful C-135	
alegre	merry M-128	
alegria	joy J-28	
alegria	gaiety G-2, 3	
aleijado	cripple C-457	
alelúia	hallelujah H-15	
alem disso	besides B-127	
alem (de)	beyond B-134	
alemão	German G-37	
alento	breath B-230	
alerta	wide awake W-120	
alfabeto	alphabet A-142	
alfabeto manual	manual alphabet M-48	
alface	lettuce L-84, 85	
alfaiate	tailor T-8	
alfinete	pin P-175	
álgebra	algebra A-124	
algodão	cotton C-416	
alguem	someone S-367	
alguma vez	ever E-163, 164, 165	
algumas vezes	sometime(s) S-369	
alguns	some S-366	
alicate	pliers P-213	
alimentar	feed F-88, 89	
alimento	food F-195, 196	
alinhar	queue Q-22	
alinhavar	baste B-50	
alistar	enlist E-108	
alívio	relief R-99	
alma	soul S-377	
altar	altar A-145, 146	
alterar	alter A-147	
altercação	quarrel Q-8	
altivo	haughty H-54	
alto	high H-104, 105, 106, 107	
alto	loud L-165	
alto	tall T-25, 26, 27	
alto	top T-226	
altura	height H-84, 85	
aluir	cave in C-84	
aluno	pupil P-410, 411, 412	
amalgamar	merge M-126	
amanhã	tomorrow T-217	
amante	lover L-170	
amante	fond F-193, 194	
amarelo	yellow Y-7	
amargo	bitter B-162	
amável	amiable A-161	
amável	kind K-15	
amável	nice N-81	
ambição	ambition A-156	
ambicioso	ambitious A-157, 158	
ambiente	environment E-122, 123	
ambos	both B-203	
ameixa seca	prune P-388	
amém	amen A-159	
amendoim	peanut P-67	
América	America A-160	
América do Norte	North America N-105	
amigo	friend F-269	
amistoso	friendly F-270	
amoldar	fashion F-58	
amor	love L-169	
amostra	sample S-31	
amplo	ample A-167	
ancinho	rake R-22	

andaime	scaffold S-53	apuntar	put down P-425
andar	story S-503	aqui	here H-95
andar de rastos	scramble S-88	aquiescer	acquiesce A-56
andar furtivamente	sneak S-337	ar	air A-120
anel	ring R-203	arado	plow P-214
anelar	long L-146	aranha	spider S-414
anexar	annex A-179	árbitro	umpire U-10
ângulo	angle A-174	árbitro	referee R-76
animal	animal A-177, 178	arbusto	bush B-275
aniquilar	annihilate A-180	arcebispo	archbishop A-237
anjo	angel A-172	arco	arch A-236
ano	year Y-3	ardente	ardent A-239
ano novo	new year N-71	ardor	zeal Z-1
ansiar	crave C-448	ardósia	slate S-298
ansiedade	anxiety A-198	área	area A-242
antecipar	anticipate A-194	argumentar	argue A-243
anteontem	day before yesterday D-19	árido	arid A-245
		aritmética	arithmetic A-248
antepassados	ancestors A-169, 170	armadilha	trap T-266
anterior	previous P-311	armário	closet C-199
antes	rather R-29	armas	arms A-250
antes	before B-91, 92, 93	armazenar	store S-499, 500
antes de	ahead A-117	aroma	scent S-62
antigo	antique A-196	arquivar	file F-121
anual	annual A-187	arrepender-se	repent R-123
anual	yearly Y-4	arrotar	belch B-100
anular	annul A-188	arroz	rice R-190
anunciar	announce A-181	arruinaco	broke B-253
ao contrário	on the contrary O-84	arruinar	ruin R-278
ao lado de	beside B-126	arrumar	arrange A-255
ao longo de	along A-141	arte	art A-262
ao seu critério	up to you U-59	artista	artist A-263
apagar	erase E-136	árvore	tree T-273
apalpar	feel F-90	asa	wings W-139
apanhar	gather G-19, 20	ascenção	ascension A-266
apanhar	pick up P-159	ascender	ascend A-265
apanhar	catch C-75, 76, 77	ascensor	elevator E-61, 62
aparar	pare P-29	Ásia	Asia A-270
aparatus	apparatus A-213	áspero	rugged R-277
aparecer	appear A-217, 218	aspiração	aim A-119
aparente	apparent A-214	aspirar	aspire A-276
apesar de	in spite of I-129	aspirar a	aim A-119
apesar disso	nevertheless N-61	assar	broil B-252
apetite	appetite A-220	assassínio	murder M-264
apinhado	crowded C-469	assento	seat S-107
aplaudir	applaud A-221	assim	thus T-174
apodrecer	rot R-257	assinalar	point P-224
apoplético	stroke S-521	assinar	subscribe S-541
aposta	wager W-1	assinar	sign S-246
aposta	bet B-131	assistir	attend A-299
apostar	gamble G-10	associação	association A-284
apreciar	appreciate A-229	associar	associate A-282, 283
apreender	arrest A-258, 259	assombrar	astonish A-288
aprender	learn L-52	assoviar	whistle W-105, 106
aprender de memória	memorize M-107, 108	assumir	assume A-287
apresentar	introduce I-183	assunto	subject S-540
apresentar	present P-300	astuto	shrewd S-232
apressar	hustle H-206	astuto	sly S-315, 316, 317
apressar	urge U-60, 61	astuto	cunning C-483
apressar-se	hurry H-199	atacar	attack A-295
aprovação	approbation A-231	ataque cardíaco	heart attack H-73

atar	tie T-179	azedo	sour S-380
até	until U-48	azul	blue B-184
até	up to V-57		
até	till T-185		
até aqui	thus far T-175	**B**	
até aqui	so far S-356		
atender	pay attention to P-60	bacana	swell S-635, 636
atender	give attention to G-50	bafetada	slap S-297
atingir	attain A-296	bagagem	baggage B-11
atirar	throw T-167, 168, 169	bagagem	luggage L-176
atirar com flechas	archery A-238	baixo	low L-171, 172
atitude	attitude A-301	baixo	shallow S-169
ator	actor A-65	baixo	base B-39, 40, 41
atrair	attract A-303	baixo	short S-218, 219
atrás	back B-3	balança	balance B-14, 15
atrás de	behind B-98	balança	scale S-54, 55, 56
atrasado	behind time B-99	balançar(se)	swing S-642
atrasado	tardy T-31	baleia	whale W-82
atrasar-se	fall behind F-29	banana	banana B-21, 22
atraso	delay D-74	banco	bench B-112
atrativo	attractive A-306	bandagem	bandage B-23
atraves de	across A-59	bandeira	banner B-28
atravessar	cross C-464, 465	bandeira	flag F-157
atrevido	saucy S-44	bandeja	tray T-271
atribuir	attribute A-307, 308	bandido	bandit B-25
atriz	actress A-66	banho	bath B-52
atraves de	through T-166	banquete	banquet B-29
atuar	act A-60	bar mitzvah	Bar Mitzvah B-36
audição	hearing H-68	barato	cheap C-125, 126
auditório	audience A-309, 310	barato	inexpensive I-89
aumentar	increase I-66	barba	beard B-70, 71
aumentar	raise R-19	barbante	string S-519
aumento	raise R-19	barbear-se	shave S-182
ausência	absence A-18, 19	barco	boat B-190
ausente	away A-327	barril	barrel B-38
ausente	out O-141, 142, 143	barro	clay C-184
Austrália	Australia A-312	barulho	clutter C-209
autêntico	authentic A-313	basear	base B-39, 40, 41
autêntico	genuine G-34	basebol	baseball B-42
automóvel	automobile A-315	bastante	enough E-110
autoridade	authority A-314	bastardo	bastard B-49
auxiliar	assist A-280	batalha	battle B-56
auxiliar	give assistance G-49	batata	potato P-265
avaliar	evaluate E-154, 155	batatas fritas	French fried potatoes F-262
avançado	advanced A-96	bate	bat B-51
avançar	advance A-95	bater	beat B-72, 73, 74
avaro	avaricious A-318	bater	knock K-31
ave	bird B-152	bater	rap R-23
ave	fowl F-243	bater	pound P-268
avental	apron A-234	batismo	baptism B-30
averia	breakdown B-228	batista	Baptist B-31
aversão	dislike D-215	batom	lipstick L-115
aviador	flier F-172	baú	trunk T-294
aviador	aviator A-320	bebê	baby B-1
avião	airplane A-121, 122	bêbedo	drunk D-319
avião	plane P-195, 196, 197	beber	drink D-309, 310
ávido	greedy G-145, 146, 147	bebida	liquor L-117, 118
ávido	eager E-4	beijo	kiss K-21, 22, 23
avô	grandfather G-111, 112	belo	fine F-134
avó	grandmother G-113, 114	bem	well W-76
azedo	tart T-32	bem de saúde	well W-77

bem-vindo	welcome W-75	brando	soft S-358
benção	benediction B-116, 117	bravo	brave B-223
benefício	benefit B-118, 119	breve	brief B-236, 237
benevolente	benevolent B-120	brilhante	bright B-238, 239, 240, 241
besteira	humbug H-190		
bexiga louca	chickenpox C-145	brilhar	glisten G-57
bezerro	calf C-9	brilhar	shine S-194
bíblia	Bible B-135, 136, 137	brincar	frolic F-279
biblioteca	library L-90	brinco	earring E-12
bicicleta	bicycle B-138	brindar a	toast T-205
bico de ave	beak B-63	brisa	breeze B-232
bilhete	ticket T-176, 177	broche	brooch B-254
bilhetes	bills B-148, 149	brônzeaco	tan T-29
bilião	billion B-147	buraco	hole H-131, 132
binóculo	binoculars B-151	burro	donkey B-268
binóculo de teatro	opera glasses O-94		
biruta	off the beam O-50		
bís	encore E-81		**C**
bisavô	great grandfather G-140		
		cabeça	head H-64
bisavó	great grandmother G-141	cabeleireiro	hairdresser H-5
		cabelo	hair H-3
bisbilhotar	gossip G-94	cabo	point P-226
biscoitinho	cookie C-389	cabo de esquadra	corporal C-407
biscoito duro	cracker C-445, 446	cabra	goat G-73
bispo	bishop B-158, 159	caçar	chase C-121
bizarro	queer Q-12	caçar	hunt H-198
blasfemar	blaspheme B-168, 169, 170	cachimbo	pipe P-181, 182
		cachorro quente	hotdog H-165
bobagem	nonsense N-100	caçoar	kid K-11
boca	mouth M-248	caçoar	tease T-51, 52, 53
bochecha	cheek C-133	cada	each E-1
boda	wedding W-62	cada dia	every day E-170
boiar	float F-175	cada um	each one E-2
bola	ball B-17	cadêia	chain C-100
bola	ball B-18	cadêia	jail J-1
bola ao cesto	basketball B-48	cadeira	chair C-101, 102, 103
bolo	cake C-3, 4, 5	cadeira de balanço	rocking chair R-238, 239
bolo	pool P-240		
bolota	acorn A-55	cadela	bitch B-160
bolso	pocket P-221	café	coffee C-222
bom	good G-85, 86	cair	fall F-27, 28
bomba	pump P-400, 401	caixa	box B-213
bombeiro	fireman F-148	calado	keep quiet K-2, 3
bondoso	soft-hearted S-359	calamitoso	calamitous C-6
boné	cap C-39	calças	pants P-15
boneca	doll D-261, 262	calças	trousers T-291
bonito	pretty P-307	calcular	reckon R-62
bonito	handsome H-28	calcular	estimate E-145
boquiaberto	open-mouthed O-91	calcular	figure F-119
borboleta	bow tie B-212	calcular	calculate C-7
borboleta	butterfly B-281	cálculo	calculus C-8
borda	shore S-217	Califórnia	California C-10
borracha	rubber R-268, 269, 270	calor	heat H-76, 77
bosque	woods W-168	caloteiro	crook C-461
bosque	forest F-216	caluniar	backbite B-6
bossa	bump B-269	calvário	Calvary C-18, 19
botão	button B-283, 284	calvo	bald B-16
box	box B-214	cama	bed B-85
boy scout	Boy Scout B-217	câmara	camera C-21, 22
braço	arm A-249	camaradagem	fellowship F-96
branco	white W-107	cambiar	exchange E-192

chorar	weep W-68, 69	começar	commence C-258
chumbo	lead L-44	começar	begin B-97
chuva	rain R-17	comer	eat E-22
chuveiro	shower S-229	comerciante	merchant M-123
cidadão	citizen C-177	comestiveis	groceries G-161
cidade	city C-178	cómico	comic C-253
cidade	town T-247	como	as A-264
ciência	science S-66, 67	como	how H-174
cigarro	cigarette C-172	como está o senhor?	how are you? H-175
cinco	five F-153	comoda	chest C-141
cinco de nós	five of us F-154	comodo	cozy C-442
cinema	cinema C-173	compaixão	compassion C-269
cinema	movies M-250	compaixão	sympathy S-648
cínico	cynic C-503	companhia	company C-267
cinzelar	chisel C-155	comparar	compare C-268
cinzento	gray G-129, 130, 131, 132	compêndio	textbook T-95
		competente	competent C-275
circulação	traffic T-252	competir	compete C-273, 274
círculo	circle C-174, 175	completar	complete C-282, 283
cirurgia	surgery S-599	complicar	complicate C-284
cirurgião	surgeon S-598	compôr	compose C-286
cisne	swan S-620	comprar	buy B-285
citação	quotation Q-31	comprar	purchase P-413
citar	cite C-176	compreender	include I-63
ciumento	jealous J-5	compreender	comprehend C-287
clandestinamente	underhand U-18	compreender	understand U-20, 21
claro	clear C-187	comprometido	engaged E-96, 97
classe	class C-180	comunicação	communication C-261
cliente	client C-190, 191	comunicação sexual	sexual intercourse S-165
clube	club C-205		
coagir	coerce C-218, 219	comunicar	communicate with C-260
cobiçar	covet C-438, 439		
cobra	snake S-331, 332, 333, 334, 335, 336	comunidade	community C-265, 266
		conceber	conceive C-290, 291, 292
cobra cascavel	rattlesnake R-31		
cobrir	cover C-434, 435, 436, 437	conceder	concede C-288
		conceder	grant G-115, 116
coca	Coca-Cola C-216	conceito	concept C-295, 296
cochichar	whisper W-104	concentrar	concentrate C-293
codorniz	quail Q-2, 3	concertar	fix F-155
coelho	rabbit R-3, 4	concluir	conclude C-301
coincidir	coincide C-225, 226	concordar	concur C-302
coisa	thing T-137	condenar	damn D-6
cola	glue G-67	conduzir	conduct C-304, 305
colapso nervoso	mental breakdown M-116	conexão	connection C-324
		conferência	conference C-307
colar	necklace N-34	conferência	lecture L-59
colarinho	collar C-232	conferir	confer C-306
colêra	anger A-173	conferir	bestow B-130
colete	vest V-31	confessar	confess C-308
colheita	harvest H-47, 48, 49	confiança	confidence C-312
colher	spoon S-425	confiança	trust T-295
colidir	collide C-235, 236	confidencial	private P-332
colina	hill H-110	confirmação	confirmation C-313
colocar	place P-188, 189	confissão	confession C-310
coluna por um	single file S-269	confissão	admission A-84
com	with W-150	conformar-se	comply C-285
com os músculos entorpecidos	muscle-bound M-265	confôrto	comfort C-251
		confrontar	confront C-315
com respeito a	concerning C-300	confundir	confuse C-316
combater	combat C-245	conotar	connote C-325
começar	start S-455	consagração	consecration C-333

consciência	conscience C-328, 329, 330	corda	rope R-252, 253
consciente	aware of A-326	cordão de sapato	shoelaces S-208
conscio	conscious C-331	cordeiro	lamb L-9
consecutivo	consecutive C-334	cordel	twine T-311
conselho	advice A-97	cordial	cordial C-398
consentir	consent C-335	Corea	Korea K-39
consertar	mend M-110, 111	cornos	horns H-157
considerar	consider C-336, 337, 338	coroa de titular	coronet C-406
consignar	consign C-339	coroar	crown C-470, 471, 472
consistente	consistent C-340	corpo	body B-191
consolar	console C-341	corpulento	stout S-504
constante	persevere P-118, 119, 120, 121	corredor	corridor C-411
		corredor	hall H-14
constituir	constitute C-342	correio	mail M-15, 16
constranger	compel C-270, 271	corrente	current C-493
construir	build B-266	correr	run R-281, 282
construir	construct C-344, 345	correto	right R-198
consultar	consult C-347	correto	correct C-408, 409
consumir	consume C-348, 349	corrida	race R-6, 7, 8
conta	account A-42	corrigir	correct C-408, 409
contacto	contact C-351, 352	corrupto	corrupt C-412
contagioso	contagious C-353	cortar	cut-off C-502
contar	count C-422	cortar	cut C-499
contar	tell T-64	corte	court C-427
contar di	tell about T-65	corte	score S-73
contemplar	contemplate C-355	cortejar	court (ing) C-430
contender	contend C-358, 359, 360	cortês	courteous C-428
		cortês	polite P-237
contento	content C-361	cortina	curtain C-497
continuar	continue C-366, 367	coruja	owl O-155
conto	tale T-20	coser	sew S-163
contra	versus V-28	cosméticos	cosmetics C-413
contra	against A-110	costa	coast C-211
contradizer	contradict C-368	costa	seaside S-105
contrastar	contrast C-370, 371	costas	back B-3, 4
contribuir	contribute C-372	costume	custom C-498
contribuir	chip (in) C-154	costume	practice P-278, 279, 280
contrição	contrition C-373		
controlar	control C-374, 375	costureira	dressmaker D-305
controvérsia	controversy C-376	côuve	cabbage C-1
convencer	convince C-387	covarde	coward C-441
conveniente	suitable S-564	covocar	convene C-377
conversa	talk T-22, 23, 24	côxo	lame L-10
conversacão	conversation C-379, 380	cozer no forno	bake B-12
		cozido a ponto	medium M-96
converter	convert C-382	cozinha	kitchen K-24, 25
convicção	conviction C-384, 385, 386	cozinheiro	cook C-388
		cozinheiro-chefe	chef C-137
convidar	invite I-195	crédulo	gullible G-180
convite	invitation I-194	crédulo	sucker S-556
cooperar	cooperate C-391	creme	cream C-452
copiar	copy C-394, 395, 396	crença	belief B-101
copo	glass G-54, 55	crepúscolo	twilight T-310
copular	copulate C-393	crescer	grow G-167
coquetear	flirt F-174	criada	maid M-13
cor	color C-241, 242, 243	criança	child C-147
cor-de-rosa	pink P-179	crianças	children C-148
coração	heart H-71, 72	criar	create C-453
coragem	courage C-425	criar	raise R-20, 21
corda	cord C-397	criar	rear R-51
		crime	crime C-456
		crisma	confirmation C-314

desalojar

desamparar

desaparcer

desaparecer

desaparecer

desaparecido

desapontado

desapontar

desatender

desbotar

descanso

descartar

descendência

descendente

descer

descer

descer

descobrir

descobrir

desconexar

desconfiança

descontente

descortês

descrença

descrever

descuidado

descuidado

desculpar

desculpar-se

desde

desde então

desde então

desde então

desdem

desejar

desejar

desejoso

desempregado

desenhar

desenvolver-se

desequilibrado

desesperar

desfigurar

desfilar

desfile

desgosto

desgostoso

desigual

desinflar

deslizar

deslumbrar

desmaiar

desmaiar

desmoronar-se

desnecessário

desobedecer

evict   E-173

forsake   F-229, 230,
    231

vanish   V-15

disappear   D-180

fade away   F-10

gone   G-82, 83, 84

disappointed   D-182,
    183

disappoint   D-181

disregard   D-226

fade   F-9

rest   R-161, 162

discard   D-187, 188,
    189

offspring   O-49

descendant   D-106

descend   D-104, 105

go down   G-78

get off   G-40

discover   D-201

detect   D-122

disconnect   D-196

distrust   D-236

discontented   D-197

impolite   I-38

disbelief   D-185, 186

describe   D-109, 110,
    111

careless   C-59

heedless   H-83

excuse   E-199

apologize   A-209, 210

since   S-265

thenceforth   T-117

from then on   F-281

ever since   E-167

scorn   S-74, 75

desire   D-114, 115

wish   W-147, 148

anxious   A-199

idle   I-10

draw   D-298

develop   D-131, 132

mentally unbalanced
    M-117, 118, 119, 120,
    121

lose hope   L-162

deface   D-58

parade   P-23, 24

parade   P-23, 24

disgust   D-208

displeased   D-221

unlike   U-44

deflate   D-68

slide   S-307, 308

dazzle   D-22

faint   F-15, 16

pass out   P-47

collapse   C-231

unnecessary   U-45, 46

disobey   D-217

desobediente

desonesto

desordem

despachar

despedir

despedir

despertar

desperto

despesas

desprender

desprezar

desprezo

dessatisfazer

desterrar

destro

destro

destruir

destruir

desviar

desviar-se

deter(-se)

deteriorar

determinar

detestar

detetive

Detroit

Deus

devagar

devaneio

dever

dever

deve

dever

deveras

deveria

devoção

devorar

devoto

dez

dia

diabo

diácono

diamante

diante de

diário

diarréia

dicionário

diferença

diferir

difícil

difícil

diga para mim

dilatar

diligência

diminuto

dinamarquês

dinheiro

diocese

direção

naughty   N-21

dishonest   D-212

disorder   D-218

dispatch   D-219

discharge   D-190, 191

fire   F-147

arouse   A-254

awake   A-323

expense   E-213

detach   D-121

despise   D-116, 117

contempt   C-356, 357

dissatisfaction   D-228

banish   B-26

adept   A-78

clever   C-188, 189

destroy   D-119

perish   P-109, 110

deflect   D-70

deviate   D-135, 136

halt   H-19

deteriorate   D-125

determine   D-127

detest   D-128, 129

detective   D-123, 124

Detroit   D-130

God   G-75

slow   S-314

daydream   D-20

duty   D-337

owe   O-154

must   M-268

obligation   O-14, 15, 16

indeed   I-69

ought to   O-138

devotion   D-142

devour   D-143

devout   D-144

ten   T-75

day   D-17

devil   D-138

deacon   D-23, 24

diamond   D-145, 146,
    147

before   B-91, 92, 93

daily   D-5

diarrhea   D-148

dictionary   D-150, 151

difference   D-156

defer   D-64

difficult   D-159, 160,
    161

hard   H-36, 37

tell me   T-66

expand   E-208

diligence   D-165, 166

minute   M-175

Dane   D-9

money   M-203, 204,
    205

diocese   D-171

direction   D-174, 175

direito — straight S-505
dirigir — direct D-172, 173
disciplinar — discipline D-193, 194, 195
discípulo — disciple D-192
discordar — disagree D-179
discursar — orate O-113
discurso — discourse D-200
discurso — address A-75
discurso — speech S-404, 405
discussão — discussion D-205
discutir — discuss D-203
disparar — shoot S-212, 213
disparo — shot S-221
dispersar — scatter S-60
disposto — willing W-129, 130, 131
disputar — dispute D-225
disputar sôbre ninharias — split hairs S-422
disputar sôbre ninharias — hairsplitting H-9
dissipar — waste W-34, 35
dissolver — dissolve D-230
distância — distance D-231
distração — distraction D-233
distraido — absent-minded A-22
distribuir — distribute D-234, 235
diversão — fun F-290
diverso — diverse D-240, 241
diversos — sundry S-579
divertido — amusing A-168
dívida — obligation O-14, 15, 16
dividendo — dividend D-246
dividir — divide D-244, 245
divino — divine D-247
divorciar — divorce D-249, 250, 251
dizer — say S-52
dizino — tithe T-200
do que — than T-96
dobrar — bend B-113
dobrar — fold F-189
doce — sweet S-632
doces — candy C-31, 32
doença — disease D-206, 207
doente — ill I-15
doente — patient P-56
doente — sick S-239
doer — hurt H-200, 201, 202, 203
dois — two T-312
dois pontos — colon C-240
dólar — dollar D-263, 264
doméstico — servant S-156
domicílio — residence R-145, 146
domicílio — domicile D-265
dominar o marido — henpeck H-93
domingo — Sunday S-577, 578
dona de casa — housekeeper H-172
donzela — maiden M-14
dor — pain P-5

dor — sorrow S-373
dor — ache A-51
dor — grief G-155, 156
dor de cabeça — headache H-65
dor de dentes — toothache T-224
dor de ouvido — earache E-8
dormido — asleep A-275
dormir — sleep S-301, 302
dormir demais — oversleep O-152
dormitar — doze D-295
doughnut — doughnut D-293
doutor — doctor D-255
doutrina — doctrine D-256, 257
doutrinar — indoctrinate I-81
drama — drama D-297
droga — drug D-317
duas vezes — twice T-309
dum lado para outro — back and forth B-5
duplicar — duplicate D-332, 333
duplo — double D-288
durante — during D-334
durante o ano todo — all year (round) A-137
durar — wear W-59
durar — last L-19
duro — hard H-36, 37
duro de ouvido — hard-of-hearing H-39
duvidar — doubt D-289, 290, 291

E

e — and A-171
é (voce) — are A-240, 241
é (ele) — is I-206, 207
ebanista — cabinetmaker C-2
edifício — building B-267
educação — education E-25
educar — educate E-24
efeito — effect E-27, 28
egoísta — selfish S-129, 130, 131
egotismo — egotism E-33, 34, 35
ela — she S-183
ela mesma — herself H-101
elástico — rubber R-268, 269, 270
elástico — elastic E-46
êle — he H-63
êle mesmo — itself I-221
êle mesmo — himself H-112
electrocutar — electrocute E-56
elefante — elephant E-59
elegante — elegant E-58
eleger — elect E-49
êles — they T-126
êles — themselves T-113
elétrico — electric E-51
elevar — elevate E-60
eliminar — eliminate E-63
eliminar — remove R-110, 111, 112
elogiar — commend C-259
em — into I-180

em	in I-52	enterro	funeral F-293
em redor de	around A-252	entrancar	splice S-421
em seguida	immediately I-27	entrar	enter E-113
em vez de	instead of I-131, 132	entre	between B-133
emancipar	emancipate E-65	entrecruzar-se	intersect I-174
embaixo	down D-294	entregar	render R-114, 115
embaraçar	embarrass E-66	entregar	deliver D-82
embriagar	intoxicate I-181	entretanto	meantime M-82
emigrar	migrate M-149	entusiasmo	enthusiasm E-114
emoção	emotion E-71, 72	enviar	send S-139, 140
empedernido	hard-boiled H-38	enxada	hoe H-126
empregar	employ E-77	epíscopal	Episcopal E-127
emprego	job J-16	epístola	epistle E-129
empréstimo	loan L-129, 130	época	epoch E-130
emprestar	lend L-70, 71	época	age A-112
empurrar	push P-423	era uma vez	once upon a time O-73
emudecido	dumfounded D-329, 330	eremita	hermit H-99
		erigir	erect E-137
en volta do mundo	around the world A-253	errado	wrong W-207
		errar o alvo	miss M-179
enamorar-se	fall in love with F-31	erro	mistake M-187
encalhado	stranded S-506	erro	error E-138
encarcerar	imprison I-49	erupçao	erupt E-139
encher	fill F-123	ervilha	peas P-69
encomendar	order O-119	esbanjar	squander S-436
encontrar	run up against R-287	escada	stair(s) S-445, 446
encontrar	meet M-98	escada de mão	ladder L-5
encontrar	encounter E-82	escapar	escape E-140
encontro	meeting M-99, 100	escaparse	slip away S-311
encorajar	encourage E-83	escarnecer	sneer S-338
encurralar	corner C-403	escassez	dearth D-32
endereço	address A-76, 77	escasso	scarce S-58
endossar	indorse I-83, 84, 85	escocês	Scot S-76, 77, 78
enfadonho	tedious T-54	escola	school S-65
ênfase	emphasis E-74	escolha	choice C-157
enfermaria	infirmary I-93, 94	escolher	choose C-160, 161
enfermeira	nurse N-136	esconder(-se)	hide H-103
enforcar	hang H-29	escova de cabelo	hairbrush H-4
enfrentar	face F-4	escova de calçado	shoebrush S-207
enganar	cheat C-127, 128	escova de dentes	toothbrush T-225
enganar	fool F-197, 198	escova de roupa	clothesbrush C-201
enganchar	hitch H-123	escovar	brush B-260, 261, 262, 263
engano	hoax H-125		
engano	deceit D-38	escravo	slave S-299
engasgar-se	choke C-158, 159	escrever	write W-205
engolir	swallow S-618, 619	escrever a máquina	type T-316
engraçadinho	cute C-500, 501	escritório	office O-46
engraçado	funny F-294	escudo	shield S-191, 193
engrinaldar	trim T-279, 280	esculpir	sculpt S-96
enorme	enormous E-109	esculpir	carve C-68
enorme	huge H-183	escultor	sculptor S-97
enquanto(que)	while W-97	escuro	dark D-14
enraivecer	enrage E-111	escutar	listen L-121
enrubescer	flush F-182	esfera	sphere S-413
ensinar	teach T-46	esforçar-se	endeavor E-88
então	then T-114, 115	esforço	effort E-29, 30, 31
entardecer	evening E-159	esfregão de rosto	washcloth W-28
entediar	bore B-196	esfregar	rub R-267
entender mal	misunderstand M-188	esgotado	exhausted E-203
enternecer-se	feel touched F-94	esgotar	exhaust E-202
enterrar	bury B-274	esgotar	deplete D-99

esgrimir	fence F-100	estrago	havoc H-59
esguio	slender S-305	estranho	strange S-507, 508
esmagar	squash S-440	estranho	weird W-74
esmalte de unhas	nail polish N-3	estreito	narrow N-13
espaço	space S-385	estrela	star S-454
espada	sword S-644	estrépito	racket R-9
espantar	scare S-59	estrito	strict S-515, 516
espanto	fright F-272	estudante	student S-531, 532
especial	special S-395	estudo	study S-533
especializar	specialize S-396	estúpido	stupid S-535, 536
específico	specific S-398	estúpido	thick-skulled T-129
espectro	ghost G-43	estúpido	dull D-325
especular	speculate S-400, 401	estúpido	dumb D-328
espelho	mirror M-177	et cétera	et cetera (etc) E-146
espelho	looking glass L-156	eternidade	eternity E-148, 149
esperar	hope H-153	eu compreendo	I see I-208
esperar	wait W-5	eu mesmo	myself M-273
esperar	expect E-209	eu tambem	me too M-134
espesso	thick T-127	evacuar	evacuate E-152
espetáculo	show S-228	evadir (-se)	evade E-153
espião	spy S-433, 434, 435	evangelho	gospel G-92, 93
espiar	pry P-389	evidência	evidence E-174
espinho	thorn T-147	evitar	avoid A-321, 322
espírito	spirit S-416	evitar	shun S-233
espirrar	sneeze S-339	exacto	just J-35, 36
esplêndido	splendid S-418, 419, 420	exagerar	exaggerate E-179, 180
		exame	examination E-181, 182, 183
esplêndido	great G-137, 138		
esponja	sponge S-424	exame	test T-89
espreitar	peek P-73, 74	examinar	examine E-185
esquecer	forget F-221, 222	exato	exact E-176, 177
esquema	scheme S-63	exato	accurate A-46, 47
esquerdo	left L-61	exceder	exceed E-187
esquilo	squirrel S-442	exceder	surpass S-600
esquisito	odd O-35	excelente	excellent E-188
essencial	essential E-142	excêntrico	eccentric E-23
êsses	those T-148	exceto	except E-189
está bem	all right A-135	excitar	excite E-194
esta noite	tonight T-219	excluir	exclude E-197
estabelecer	establish E-144	excremento	feces F-83
estaçao	station S-461	executar	perform P-100, 101
estacionar	park P-30	exemplo	example E-186
estada	stay S-464, 465, 466, 467	exercitar	drill D-308
		exercito	army A-251
estanho	tin T-193	exibição	display D-220
estar	be B-60, 61, 62	exibir	exhibit E-204
estar com sono	sleepy S-304	exigir	demand D-83
estar de acordo	agree A-115	existir	exist E-206
estar de pé	stand S-449, 450, 451	expectorar	expectorate E-210
estar farto de	sick of S-241	expedir	forward F-234
estar sentado	sit S-275, 276	expelir	expel E-211, 212
estátua	statue S-462	expelir	throw out T-170
estatutos	statute S-463	experiência	experience E-215, 216
estender	extend E-229	expirar	expire E-218
êstes	these T-125	explicar	explain E-220, 221
estiagem	drought D-314	explícito	explicit E-222, 223
esticar o pescoço	rubberneck R-271, 272	explodir	explode E-224
estirar-se	stretch S-514	expressão	expression E-226
estrada	road R-225	expulsar	cast out C-71
estragar	mar M-52, 53	extinguir-se	die out D-154
estragar	spoil S-423	extinto	extinct E-231

extravagante	extravagant E-233	felicitar	congratulate C-319, 320
exultação	exultation E-235	feliz	happy H-34
		feliz	glad G-53
	F	fêmea	female F-97
		fenda	crack C-443
fábrica	factory F-7	fénix	phoenix P-139
fabricar	fabricate F-2	feno	hay H-62
fábula	fable F-1	feriado	holiday H-133
faca	knife K-27, 28, 29	férias	vacation V-3
faça o que manda	practice what you preach P-281	ferido	wound W-197
		ferir	injure I-107, 108
fácil	easy E-20, 21	feroz	fierce F-115
facilitar	facilitate F-6	ferrador	blacksmith B-166
faculdade	faculty F-8	ferro	iron I-201
fadiga	fatigue F-70	ferro de passar roupa	flatiron F-162
falar	speak S-392	festa	feast F-81
falar	talk T-22, 23, 24	festa	party P-38, 39
falhar	flunk F-181	fiar	spin S-415
falido	bankrupt B-27	fiar-se	rely R-102, 103
falso	false F-32, 33	ficar	remain R-104
falta	lack L-3	ficar	stay S-464, 465, 466, 467
faltar ao dever	shirk S-199		
fama	fame F-36	ficção	fiction F-108
família	family F-37, 38	fidelidade	fidelity F-110
fanfarronar	bluff B-185	fiel	faithful F-21, 22, 23
fantasia	fancy F-42	fígado	liver L-126
farinha de aveia	oatmeal O-3	figura	figure F-120
farinha	flour F-178, 179	fila	line-up L-111
fascinar	fascinate F-56, 57	filactério	phylacterie P-147
fatia	slice S-306	Filadélfia	Philadelphia P-137
fatigar	tire T-198	filha	daughter D-16
fato completo	suit S-563	filho	son S-370
favoravelmente disposto	sympathetic S-646	filiar	affiliate A-100, 101
		filosofia	philosophy P-138
favorecer	favor F-74	fim	end E-84, 85, 86, 87
favorito	favorite F-75, 76, 77	final	final F-126, 127
faz calor	hot weather H-169	finalmente	eventually E-162
fazenda	farm F-47, 48, 49	finanças	finances F-130
fazer	do D-254	fincado	stuck S-529, 530
fazer	make M-23	Finlândia	Finland F-144
fazer careta	make a face M-24	fino	fine F-136
fazer compras	shop S-214	firme	fast F-61
fazer croché	crochet C-460	física	physics P-150
fazer lembrar	remind R-108	físico	physical P-148
fazer mal	harm H-44, 45	fita	tape T-30
fazer meia	knit K-30	fixar	fasten F-62
fazer ostentação	show off S-230, 231	flôr	flower F-180
fazer saber	let know L-80, 81	florescer	bloom B-179
fazer-se	become B-83	focar	focus F-187
fazer sinal com a mão	wave W-46	fogo	fire F-146
fé	faith F-20	foguete	rocket R-237
febre	fever F-103	foice grande	scythe S-99
fechado a chave	locked L-136	folha	leaf L-46, 47
fechar	shut S-234	folheto	pamphlet P-12
fechar	close C-197	fome	famine F-39
fechar bem	shut up S-235, 236	fonte	fountain F-239
fechar(v)	lock L-134, 135	fonte	spring S-431
feijão	bean B-64	fora	out O-141, 142, 143
feio	homely H-143, 144	força	strength S-512
feito	deed D-55	força	force F-210, 211
feiura	ugliness U-1, 2, 3	força de alma	fortitude F-233

forçado	far-fetched F-46	galo	cock C-217
forma	form F-226	galo	rooster R-250
forma	shape S-174, 175	galocha	overshoes O-151
formoso	beautiful B-77	gancho	hook H-150
fornicar	fornicate F-228	ganhar	gain G-4, 5
forno	oven O-145	ganhar	earn E-10
fortalecer	fortify F-232	ganso	goose G-91
forte	strong S-523, 524	garantia	guarantee G-169, 170
fósforo	match M-67	garção	waiter W-7
fotocópia	photocopy P-142	garfo	fork F-225
fotografar	take a picture T-12	garoto	kid K-10, 11
fotografia	photograph P-143, 144, 145	gás	gas G-15
		gasolina	gas G-16
fraco di espírito	feeble minded F-87	gastar	consume C-348, 349
frágil	frail F-248	gastar	spend S-412
fragrante	fragrant F-247	gato	cat C-72
francamente	frankly F-253	gaveta	drawer D-300
francês	French F-261	gelar	freeze F-260
franco	frank F-251	geleia	jam J-2
frango	chicken C-144	gélido	frozen F-284
fratura	fracture F-246	gelo	ice I-3
fraude	fraud F-254	gênero	kind K-16
fraudulento	fraudulent F-256	generoso	generous G-27, 28
freira	nun N-135	gente	people P-92
frente	front F-282	geografia	geography G-35
frequente	frequent F-264	geometria	geometry G-36
frequentemente	often O-51	geração	generation G-26
fresco	cool C-390	ginasio	gym G-183
frígido	frigid F-274	ginásio	high school H-109
frigir	fry F-287	ginástica	exercise E-200
frio	cold C-229	girafa	giraffe G-45
friorento	chilly C-149	giz	chalk C-104
frisar	curl C-490	globo terrestre	globe G-58, 59
frívolo	frivolous F-275	glória	glory G-64, 65
frívolo	trifling T-277	glorioso	glorious G-63
frustrado	frustrated F-286	golfe	golf G-81
fruta	fruit F-285	golpe	blow B-182
fugir	flee F-170	golpear	hit H-120, 121
fugir	run away R-284	golpear	hit 122
fumar	smoke S-326, 327	golpear	strike S-517
funcionar	function F-291	goma de mascar	gum G-181
fundamento	foundation F-237	gonzo	hinge H-115
fundamento	basis B-45, 46	gordo	fat F-63, 64
fundar	found F-236	gordura	fat F-65
fundo	bottom B-206	gorduroso	fatty F-71
fundo	background B-7	gorjeta	tip T-196
fundos	funds F-292	gostar de	fond F-193, 194
furar	drill D-306, 307	gostar de	like L-103, 105
furar	pierce P-168	gosto	taste T-34
fúria	fury F-298	gotejar	drip D-311
furioso	mad M-4	governar	govern G-98
furtivamente	on the sly O-85	governar	rule R-279, 280
furto	theft T-107, 108, 109	governo	government G-99
futebol	soccer S-349	gozar	enjoy E-106
futebol	football F-202, 203	Grã-Bretanha	Britain B-247
fuzil	gun G-182	Grã-Bretanha	Great Britain G-139
		graça	grace G-103, 104
		gracejo	joke J-22
G		gracioso	gracious G-105
		graduar-se	graduate G-106, 107
		grampo de papel	paper clip P-19
galante	beau B-76	grampo para o cabelo	hairpin H-6
galinha	hen H-91		

granada — grenade G-153
grande — great G-135, 136
grande — big B-142, 143
grande — large L-16
grandioso — grand G-109, 110
grato — grateful G-122
gravar — engrave E-103
gravata — necktie N-35
gravata — tie T-180
grave — weighty W-73
grave — grave G-126
graxa — grease G-133
grego — Grecian G-143
greve — strike S-518
grinalda — wreath W-199
gritar — yell Y-6
gritar — bawl B-57, 58
gritar — cry C-481
gritar — shout S-225
gritar alto — scream S-90
gritar aplausos — cheer C-134
groselha — currant C-491
grosseiro — rough R-259, 260, 261
grotesco — grotesque G-162
grudar — stick S-483
grupo — group G-165, 166
grupo de pessoas — circle C-174, 175
guarda civil — cop G-392
guarda-chuva — umbrella U-9
guardanapo — napkin N-9
guardar — keep K-1
guardar — guard G-171
guerra — war W-20
guiar — guide G-176
guiar — drive D-312
guiar — lead L-43
guitarra — guitar G-179
guinchar — squeal S-441
gula — gluttony G-68

H

ha — ago A-113
ha alguns dias — few days ago F-105
ha alguns segundos — few seconds ago F-106
ha pouco — while ago, a W-98, 99, 100
habilidade — ability A-10
habilidade — skill S-287
hábito — habit H-1
hamburguesa — hamburger H-20, 21
harpa — harp H-46
Hawáii — Hawaii H-60
Hebreu — Hebrew H-80
herança — heritage H-98
heresia — heresy H-96
hesitar — hesitate H-102
hino — hymn H-207, 208
hipócrita — hypocrite H-209, 210
histérico — hysterical H-211
história — history H-118, 119

história — story S-502
hoje — today T-207
Holanda — Holland H-134, 135
holandês — Dutch D-335, 336
homem — man M-40
homosexual — queer Q-13
honorários — fee F-85
honra — honor H-147, 148
honrado — honest H-145
hora — hour H-170
horizonte — horizon H-155
hospital — hospital H-162, 163
hotel — hotel H-166
humanidade — humanity H-186
humano — humane H-185
humano — human H-184
humilde — humble H-187, 188, 189
humorismo — humor H-191
húngaro — Hungarian H-194

I

idade — age A-111
ideia — idea I-7
idêntico — identical I-8
identificar — identify I-9
idiota — moron M-223
ídolo — idol I-11
ignorante — ignorant I-13
igreja — church C-168, 169
igual — equal E-131
ilha — island I-209, 210
ilustrar — illustrate I-18
ima — magnet M-11
imaculada conceição — Immaculate Conception I-25
imaculado — immaculate I-24
imagem — image I-19
imaginação — imagination I-20
imaginar — imagine I-22
imediato — immediate I-26
imenso — immense I-28
imitar — imitate I-23
imitar — mimic M-158
imobilizar — pin P-177
imodesto — immodest I-29
imparcial — impartial I-31
impedir — impede I-32
impedir — prevent P-309
impedir — hinder H-113
impelir — impel I-33, 34
imperador — emperor E-73
imperativo — imperative I-35
imperito — unskilled U-47
impertinente — fresh F-265, 266
implicar — imply I-37
implorar — implore I-36
implorar — beseech B-125
importante — important I-39, 40
impossível — impossible I-41, 42

imposto	duty D-338	inspecionar	inspect I-128
imposto	tax T-39, 40	instalar	install I-130
impostor	impostor I-44	instituir	institute I-133, 134
impregnar	impregnate I-45	instruir	instruct I-136
impressão digital	fingerprint F-140	instrumento	instrument I-139
impressionar	impress I-46	insultar	insult I-140, 141, 142
imprestável	worthless W-192, 193	inteiro	entire E-117
imprimir	print P-326	inteiro	whole W-110, 111
impuro	impure I-51	intelecto	intellect I-144
imundo	filthy F-125	intelectual	intellectual I-145
inanição	starvation S-456	intelectual	highbrow H-108
incapaz	unable U-12	inteligente	bright B-238, 239, 240, 241
incerto	uncertain U-13		
inchar	swell S-637	inteligente	intelligent I-147
incidente	incident I-59	intelligente	smart S-323
inclinação	inclination I-60	intenção	intent I-151
incomodar	trouble T-290	intencional	willful W-128
incomodar	disturb D-237	intensidade	intensity I-149
incomodar	bother B-204, 205	intercambio	interchange I-154
incredulidade	incredulity I-67	interceptar	intercept I-153
indecisão	indecision I-68	interesse	interest I-155, 156, 157, 158, 159
independência	independence I-70		
indicador de lugar	usher U-67	internacional	international I-167
indicar	indicate I-74	interpretar	interpret I-168
indiferença	indifference I-75	interrogação	query Q-14, 15
indignado	indignant I-77	interrogar	interrogate I-169, 170
indio	Indian I-72, 73	interromper	interrupt I-173
indistinto	unclear U-15	intervir	interfere I-164
indistinto	blurry B-186	introspecção	introspection I-185
individuo	individual I-79, 80	inundação	overflow O-150
índole	character C-115, 116	inundação	flood F-176
indolência	sloth S-313	invejoso	envious E-121
indulgência	indulgence I-87	inventar	devise D-140, 141
industrioso	industrious I-88	inventar	invent I-187, 188
induzir	induce I-86	inverno	winter W-141, 142
infante	infant I-90	inverter capital	invest I-190
inferno	hell H-86, 87	investigar	investigate I-191, 192
infiltrar	infiltrate I-91	ir	go G-69, 70
infinito	infinite I-92	ir buscar	fetch F-101
influência	influence I-95, 96, 97, 98	ir devagar	lag L-7
		ira	ire I-198
informar	inform I-99, 100	irado	angry A-175
inglês	Englishman E-102	irascível	hot-headed H-167
inicial	initial I-104	irmã	sister S-272, 273
iniciar	initiate I-105	irmão	brother B-256, 257
inimigo	enemy E-95	irrefletido	thoughtless T-153
inimigo	foe F-188	irresponsável	irresponsible I-203, 204
injeção	injection I-106	irritável	irritable I-205
injeção	shot S-221	isso	that T-100, 101, 102
injustiça	injustice I-110	isto	this T-145
injusto	unjust U-41	italiano	Italian I-217
injusto	unfair U-25, 26		
inocência	innocence I-115		
inocular	inoculate I-117		**J**
inquérito	examination E-181, 182, 183		
		jactar-se	boast B-189
inquieto	anxious A-200	jactar-se	brag B-219
inquieto	restless R-165	janela	window W-136
insensível	insensate I-125	jantar	dine D-169
inseto	insect I-123, 124	jantar	dinner D-170
inseto	bug B-265	Japão	Japan J-3
insistir	insist I-127	japonês	Japanese J-4

jarda

jardim

jaritataca

jato

Jerusalem

jesuita

Jesus

jogar

jogar

jogar cartas

jogo

jogo de bola

jornal

jovem

jovial

judaismo

judeu

jugo

julgar

junta

juntamente

juntar

juntos

juramento

jurar

jurar

justiça

justo

justo

justo

yard   Y-2

garden   G-13

skunk   S-294

jet   J-11

Jerusalem   J-8

Jesuit   J-9

Jesus   J-10

pitch   P-185

play   P-202

card playing   C-51

game   G-11

bowling   B-211

newspaper   N-67

young   Y-18

jolly   J-23

Judaism   J-29

jew   J-12

yoke   Y-14

judge   J-30

board   B-188

altogether   A-150

join   J-17, 18, 19, 20

together   T-209

oath   O-2

swear   S-621

sworn   S-645

justice   J-38, 39

just   J-35, 36

righteous   R-200

fair   F-17

L

lã

lá

labor

laço

lado

lado a lado

ladrão

ladrão

ladrar

lago

lagosta

lágrima

lamacento

lamentar

lamentar-se

lanterna elétrica

lápis

lar

larãnja

largo

largo

lascívia

lata

latim

latrocínio

lavagem

lavar os pratos

wool   W-169

there   T-119, 120

labor   L-1

bow   B-208

side   S-242

side by side   S-243

burglar   B-271

thief   T-130, 131

bark   B-35

lake   L-8

lobster   L-132

tear   T-49

muddy   M-256

rue   R-276

mourn   M-244

flashlight   F-159

pencil   P-85

home   H-142

orange   O-110, 111, 112

broad   B-249

wide   W-119

lust   L-180

can   C-25

Latin   L-31, 32

holdup   H-130

wash   W-25, 26, 27

dish wash (ing)   D-213

lazer

leal

leão

legal

legar

legislatura

lei

leite

lembrar-se de

lenço

lenho

leopardo

lepra

ler

leste

levantar-se

levantar-se

levantar-se

levar

levar

levar a conta di

leve

liberação

liberdade

libertar

libra

lição

licença

ligar

lima

limão

limbo

limite

limusine

limpar

limpar c soalho

limpo

limpo

Lincoln

lingua

lingua

linha

linha

linotipo

líquido

liso

lisonjear

lista

lista longa

livre

livro

lixa

lobo

locação

locomotiva

lógica

logo

loja

loja

longe

longe

leisure   L-66

loyal   L-175

lion   L-113

legal   L-64

bequeath   B-121

legislature   L-65

law   L-37

milk   M-154

remember   R-107

handkerchief   H-25

log   L-138

leopard   L-73

leprosy   L-74

read   R-36, 37, 38

east   E-16

arise   A-246, 247

get up   G-42

rise   R-212, 213, 214

carry   C-64, 65

take away from   T-14

charge   C-117, 118

light   L-101

liberation   L-88

liberty   L-89

deliver   D-81

pound   P-266, 267

lesson   L-77

license   L-91, 92

bind   B-150

file   F-121

lemon   L-67, 68, 69

limbo   L-106

limit   L-107

limousine   L-108

clean   C-185, 186

mop   M-217

neat   N-29

clean   C-185, 186

Lincoln   L-109

language   L-13, 14

tongue   T-218

thread   T-155

line   L-110

Linotype   L-112

liquid   L-116

smooth   S-330

flatter   F-163, 164

list   L-119, 120

long list   L-148

free   F-257, 258

book   B-193

sandpaper   S-34

wolf   W-159

location   L-133

locomotive   L-137

logic   L-139

by and by   B-288

shop   S-215

store   S-498

off   O-38, 39

far   F-43

longo	long L-145
Los Ângeles	Los Angeles L-160
louco	insane I-121
louco	nuts N-138, 139, 140
louco	mad M-5
louco	crazy C-449, 450, 451
louvor	praise P-282
lua	moon M-214, 215
lugar	place P-188, 189
luta	wrestling W-202
lutar	struggle S-526
lutar	fight F-117, 118
Lutero	Luther L-181
luva	glove G-66
luz	light L-100

M

má índole	ill temper I-17
maça	batter B-55
maça	apple A-223
macaco	ape A-208
macaco	monkey M-206
macante	boring B-198
macho	male M-38
madeira	wood W-167
madrasta	stepmother S-482
madrinha	godmother G-77
maduro	ripe R-210
maduro	mature M-70
mãe	mother M-229, 230
mãe	mama M-39
magia	magic M-8
magnánimo	magnanimous M-10
magnífico	magnificent M-12
magoar	hurt H-200, 201, 202, 203
magro	lean L-49, 50
magro	skinny S-291
maior	elder E-47
mais	plus P-219
mais	more M-218
mais longe	farther F-54
mais tarde	later L-28, 29
majestade	majesty M-22
mala	suitcase S-565
maleta	valise V-11
maluco	daft D-4
mancha	stain S-444
mandamentos	commandments C-257
mandar	command C-256
mandar	bid B-139, 141
maneira	manner M-45
manejar	manage M-41
manhã	morning M-222
manhã	forenoon F-214
manso	meek M-97
manso	tame T-28
manteiga	butter B-280
manter	maintain M-19

manual	manual M-47
manufacturar	manufacture M-49
manutenção	maintenance M-21
mão	hand H-23, 24
mapa	map M-51
maquilagem	make-up M-36
máquina	machine M-1
máquina	engine E-99
máquina de cortar grama	lawn mower L-38
máquina de lavar	washing machine W-30
maquinaria	machinery M-3
mar	sea S-100
maravilha	marvel M-60
maravilha	wonder W-162
maravilhoso	wonderful W-165
marcar	mark M-56
marchar	march M-54, 55
marido	husband H-204
marinheiro	seaman S-103
marinheiro	sailor S-13, 14
martelo	hammer H-22
mártir	martyr M-59
mas	but B-279
mascar	chew C-142
mastigar	masticate M-66
matar	kill K-13
matar	slay S-300
matemática	mathematics M-68
matéria	matter M-69
matrimônio	marriage M-57
mau	bad B-9, 10
mau	evil E-175
mau	wicked W-118
me enuoa	make me disgusted M-31
mecánico	mechanic M-86, 87
medalha	medal M-89
média	average A-319
mediano	median M-92
medicamento	medicine M-93
medir	measure M-84
medir	scale S-54, 55, 56
medir	gauge G-23
meditar	meditate M-94
medo	fear F-78, 79
medroso	fearful F-80
meia	sock(s) S-351, 352
meia	stocking S-492, 493
meia hora	half-hour H-13
meia-noite	midnight M-141
meias	hose H-160, 161
meigo	mild M-150
meio	middle M-140
meio	mean M-80
meio	midst M-142
meio	half H-11, 12
meio-dia	midday M-139
meiodia	noon N-101
melaço	molasses M-200
melância	watermelon W-44

melancolia	melancholy M-101	moeda	coin C-223, 224
melão	melon M-103	moeda corrente	currency C-492
melão de cheiro	muskmelon M-267	moer	grind G-159
melhor	best B-128	mofar	mock M-195
melhor	better B-132	molhado	wet W-81
melhorar	improve I-50	molho	gravy G-128
melodia	melody M-102	momento	moment M-201
membro	member M-105, 106	monótono	monotonous M-207, 208, 209
memória	memory M-109		
mencionar	mention M-122	montanha	mountain M-243
mendigar	ask alms A-274	morango	strawberry S-509
mendigar	beg B-94, 95	morar	reside R-144
mendigo	panhandler P-14	morar	dwell D-339
menina	girl G-46	morder	bite B-161
menor	minor M-170	morfina	morphine M-224
menos	minus M-171, 172, 173	moribundo	dying D-341
menos	less L-75, 76	mormão	Mormon M-221
menosprezar	snub S-343	morrer	expire E-219
mensagem	message M-129	morrer	die D-152, 153
menstruação	menstruate M-113	mortal	mortal M-225
mental	mental M-115	mortificação	mortification M-226
mente	mind M-159, 160, 163	morto	dead D-25, 26
mentir	lie L-94, 95	mosca	fly F-185
mentirinha	fib F-107	mostrar	show S-227
mentiroso	liar L-87	motim	riot R-207
merecer	deserve D-113	motivar	motivate M-236
meretriz	harlot H-43	motivo	motive M-238, 239, 240
mergulhar	dive D-238, 239		
mérito	merit M-127	motocicleta	motorcycle M-242
mes	month M-210	motor	motor M-241
mes passado	last month L-22	motor	electric motor E-53
mesa	table T-2, 3	mover(-se)	move M-249
mesclar	mix M-191	movimento	motion M-233
mesquinho	stingy S-488, 489, 490	mudável	changeable C-110
meta	goal G-72	mudo	mute M-269
metal	metal M-130, 131	mudo	speechless S-406
meter-se	meddle M-90, 91	muito	very V-30
metodista	Methodist M-133	muito	much M-255
método	method M-132	muito	lot L-164
metralhadora	machine gun M-2	muito difundido	widespread W-121
mexicano	Mexican M-135	muitos	many M-50
micrómetro	micrometer M-138	mula	mule M-258
mil	thousand T-154	mulher	wife W-123
milagre	miracle M-176	mulher	woman W-160
milha	mile M-151	multa	penalty P-82
milhão	million M-155	multa	fine F-135
milho	corn C-401	multidão	crowd C-468
militar	military M-153	multiplicar	multiply M-261, 262
Milwaukee	Milwaukee M-156	múltiplo	multiple M-260
mim	me M-76	mundo	earth E-13
mina	mine M-165	mundo	world W-174
minuto	minute M-174	muro	wall W-14, 15
misericórdia	mercy M-124, 125	música	music M-266
missão	mission M-183, 184	mutuamente	each other E-3
mistério	mystery M-274	mútuo	mutual M-270, 271
misturar-se	mingle M-167, 168		
mitra	mitre M-189		
mocão	motion M-232	**N**	
moda	stylish S-538		
modelo	model M-196	na moda	fashionable F-59
modesto	modest M-197	nabo	turnip T-306
modificar	modify M-198	nação	nation N-16

nada	naught N-18, 19, 20	New Jersey	New Jersey N-64
nada	nothing N-119, 120, 121, 122	ninho	nest N-55
nadar	swim S-640	no	knot K-34
naif	naive N-4	no meio de	amid A-162
namorada	sweetheart S-633, 634	nobre	noble N-88
não	no N-86	noção	notion N-127
não	not N-114, 115	noite	night N-83
não	no N-87	nome	name N-6
não crer	don't believe D-273	nomear	appoint A-226
não diga	don't tell D-282	nordeste	northeast N-106
não faça	do not D-269, 270	normal	normal N-103
não fazer caso de	ignore I-14	noroeste	northwest N-107
não feito	not done N-117	norte	north N-104
não gostar de	don't care for D-277	Noruega	Norway N-108
não importa	doesn't matter D-258	nos	us U-63
não importa	make no difference M-33	nos	we W-51, 52
		nos mesmos	ourselves O-140
não importar-se	don't care D-274, 275, 276	nosso	our N-139
		notar	note N-118
não judio	Gentile G-29	notícias	tidings T-178
não melhorar	not improve N-126	notificar	notify N-124, 125
não poder	cannot C-35, 36	Nova Inglaterra	New England N-63
não querer	don't want D-283	Nova Iorque	New York N-72
não saber	don't know D-279	Nova Orleans	New Orleans N-65
não saber nada	know nothing K-38	novato	green G-150
não ter gosto para	no taste for N-116	nove	nine N-84
narcótico	narcotic N-10	nove de nós	nine of us N-85
narcótico	dope D-287	novidade	novelty N-129
narigudo	nosy N-111, 112, 113	novo	new N-62
nariz	nose N-110	novo testamento	New Testament N-68, 69, 70
narrar	narrate N-11		
nascer	born B-199, 200, 201	noz	nut N-137
nascer do sol	sunrise S-580	nu	nude N-131
nascido	nee N-36	nu	naked N-5
nascimento	birth B-153, 154, 155	nu	bare B-33, 34
natal	Christmas C-166, 167	número	number N-132, 133
natural	natural N-17	numeroso	numerous N-134
náusea	nausea N-22	nunca	never N-59
navalha de barbear	razor R-33	nunca mais	never again N-60
navio	ship N-197	nuvem	cloud C-204
navio a vapor	steamer S-474		
nazi	Nazi N-25		
necessário	necessary N-30, 31		**O**
necessidade	need N-37, 38, 39		
negação	negation N-41	o	it I-214, 215, 216
negar	deny D-91, 92	o	oh O-52
negativo	negative N-42	o	the T-104
negligente	reckless R-61	o dia todo	all day A-131
negligeuciar	neglect N-44	o Egito	Egypt E-36
negócio	concern C-299	o êle	him H-111
negócios	business B-276	o eu vejo	oh I see O-53
negro	Negro N-45, 46	O.K.	O.K. O-57, 58
nem	neither N-49	o mais velho	eldest E-48
nem	nor N-102	o menos	least L-54
nenhum	none N-96, 97, 98, 99	o mesmo	same S-27, 28, 29
nenhum	no N-86, 87	o meu	mine M-164
nervo	nerve N-51	o meu	my M-272
nervoso	nervous N-52	o senhor	lord L-159
nesse meio tempo	in the meantime I-178	o senhor	you Y-16, 17
neutral	neutral N-58	o seu	your Y-19
neve	snow S-342	o seu	their T-110
		o seu	his H-117

o seu	hers H-100	operar	operate O-95
o seu	her H-94	opinião	opinion O-98
obedecer	mind M-162	oponente	opponent O-99
obediência	obedience O-4	opor-se	oppose O-105
obeso	obese O-6	oportunidade	opportunity O-100, 101, 102, 103, 104
objetar	object O-9, 10		
objetivo	objective O-12	oposto	opposite O-106
objeto	object O-8, 9, 10	oposto	reverse R-185, 186
oblação	oblation O-13	oração	sentence S-149
obrigação	obligation O-14, 15, 16	orador	orator O-114
obrigado	bound B-207	orador	speaker S-393
obrigado	thank you T-99	oral	oral O-109
obscuro	obscure O-18	orbe	orb O-115
observação	remark R-106	órbita	orbit O-116, 117
observar	observe O-19, 20	ordem	order O-119
observar	watch (observe) W-36, 37	ordenado	orderly O-122
		ordenado	salary S-21
obstáculo	obstacle O-21	ordenar	order O-119
obstáculo	block B-176	ordenar	ordain O-118
obstinado	obstinate O-22	ordens sacerdotais	holy orders H-140
obter	obtain O-24	orelha	ear E-7
obter	procure P-348	organização	organization O-124, 125
obter	achieve A-52, 53		
obter	get G-39	orgulho	pride P-315
óbvio	obvious O-25	orgulhoso	proud P-384
ocasião	opportunity O-100, 101, 102, 103, 104	orientacão	orientation O-127
		oriental	Oriental O-126
ocasião	occasion O-26	origem	origin O-128, 129, 130
ocasional	occasional O-27	original	original O-132
oceano	ocean O-31, 32	orina	urine U-62
ocorrer	occur O-30	ornamento	ornament O-135, 136
oculista	oculist O-34	os	them T-111
óculos di proteção	goggles G-79	os Estados Unidos	United States U-35
óculos	glasses G-56	osso	bone B-192
óculos	eyeglasses E-237	ostra	oyster O-157
óculos	spectacles S-399	ou	or O-107, 108
ocupado	busy B-277, 278	ou . . . ou	either E-41, 42, 43
ódio	hate H-52, 53	ouro	gold G-80
odioso	obnoxious O-17	outono	autumn A-316, 317
odor	odor O-36	outono	fall F-25, 26
oeste	west W-80	outra vez	again A-109
ofender	offend O-40	outro	another A-191
oferecer	offer O-42, 43	outro	other O-137
oferecer	extend E-229, 230	outrora	formerly F-227
oferta	bid B-140	ouve	hark H-42
oferta	offering O-45	ouvir	hear H-68
oficial	officer O-48	ovelha	sheep S-186
oficina	workshop W-173	ovo	egg E-32
oh	oh O-52		
oitavo	eighth E-39		
oito	eight E-38		**P**
olear	oil O-54		
óleo	oil O-55	pá	shovel S-226
olhadela	peep P-77	pá	paddle P-3
olhar	look L-149, 150	pá	spade S-386
olhar fixo	gaze G-25	paciência	patience P-52, 53
olho	eye E-236	pacote	package P-2
omissão	omission O-66, 67	padeiro	baker B-13
onda	wave W-46	padrasto	stepfather S-481
onde	where W-91, 92	padrinho	godfather G-76
ontem	yesterday Y-10	pagar	pay P-57, 58, 59
operação	operation O-96, 97	página	page P-4

pai	father F-66, 67, 68	patim de rodas	roller skating R-244
pais	country C-424	patinar	skate S-281
pais	land L-11, 12	patinar	ice-skating I-6
Paises Baixos, os	Netherlands N-56, 57	pátio	yard Y-2
paixão	passion P-45, 46	pato	duck D-323
palavra	speech S-404, 405	pau	stick S-483
palavra	word W-170	paz	peace P-61
palestrar	chat C-124	pé	foot F-200
pálido	pale P-11	peagem	toll T-214
palito	beanpole B-65	peça	play P-203
palmada	smack S-318	peca	room R-248, 249
pancada violenta	swipe S-643	pecado	sin S-264
panqueca	pancake P-13	peculiar	peculiar P-71
pão	bread B-226	pedaço	piece P-167
pão doce	muffin M-257	pedal	pedal P-72
pão-duro	tightwad T-182, 183, 184	pedir	request R-134, 135
		pedir	ask (for) A-271, 272, 273
papa	pope P-246		
papa	dad D-2	pedir un emprego	apply A-224
papai	papa P-16	pedra	stone S-494, 495
papal	papal P-17	pegador de roupa	clothespin C-202
papel	paper P-18	pegar	seize S-122
par	pair P-10	peito	chest C-140
par	peer P-78	peixe	fish F-151, 152
para	for F-204, 205	pelar	peel P-75, 76
para	toward T-242, 243, 244	pele	skin S-289, 290
		película	film F-124
para a direita	right R-198	pena	pen P-79
para sempre	forever F-218	penalidade	penalty P-80, 81, 82
pára-quedas	parachute P-22	pendente	pending P-86
parafuso	screw S-91, 92	pendurar	hang H-29
paragem	stop S-497	pênis	penis P-88
parágrafo	paragraph P-25	penetrar	penetrate P-87
paralelo	parallel P-26	penhor	pledge P-211
parasito	parasite P-27	penitência	penance P-83, 84
parecer	look L-149, 150	penitenciário	penitentiary P-90
parecer	seem S-121	penitente	penitent P-89
parecer	appear A-216	pensamento	thought T-150, 151
parente	kin K-14	pensar	think T-138
parente	relative R-95	pentear	comb C-244
parentesco	relationship R-93, 94	pequeno	tiny T-194, 195
parir	bear B-67, 68	pequeno	little L-122, 123
parreira	grapevine G-119	pequeno	small S-319, 320
parte	part P-32, 33, 34, 35	pequeno	petty P-136
parte	share S-176, 177	pequeno	slight S-309
participar	participate P-37	pequeno almoço	breakfast B-229
partir	depart D-93	pera	pear P-68
pasar ao lado de	pass by P-43	perceber	perceive P-94, 95
páscoa	Easter E-17, 18, 19	percha	perch P-98
pascua hebraica	Passover P-48	perdão	pardon P-28
pasmar	flabbergasted F-156	perder	lose L-161
pasmar	amaze A-154	perder a calma	flip the lid F-173
passado	past P-49	perder o direito a	forfeit F-220
passar	pass P-42	perder-se	stray S-510
passar	go by G-74	perdoar	forgive F-223, 224
passar a ferro	iron I-202	perecer	perish P-109, 110
passar a ferro	press P-304, 305, 306	perfeito	perfect P-99
passeio	walk W-13	pérfido	false-faced F-34
passo	step S-478, 479, 480	perfume	perfume P-104
passo	pace P-1	perfurar	bore B-196, 197
pastor	minister M-169	pergunta	question Q-17
pastor	pastor P-50	perguntar	inquire I-118, 119, 120

pouco	little P-122, 123	procissão	procession P-344
pouco depois	after a while A-106	proclamar	proclaim P-345
poucos	few F-104	procrastinar	procrastinate P-347
poupar	save S-45	procurar	seek S-120
praguejar	curse C-494, 495, 496	procurar	look for L-155
praguejar	swear S-622, 623, 624	procurar	try T-297, 298
prata	silver S-259, 260	produzir	produce P-350, 351, 352, 353
prateleira	shelf S-187		
praticar	practice P-278, 279, 280	proeminente	prominent P-362, 363, 364
prato	plate P-201	profecia	prophecy P-372
prato	dish D-211	profissão	profession P-354, 355
prazo-dado	appointment A-227	profissão	occupation O-29
prazo-dado	engagement E-98	profissão	field F-113, 114
preceito	precept P-287	profundidade	depth D-103
precioso	precious P-288	profundo	deep D-56
preciso	precise P-289	prognosticar	forecast F-212
preço	price P-313, 314	programa	program P-357, 358
preço	charge C-117, 118	progresso	progress P-359
predicar	preach P-285	proibir	prohibit P-361
predizer	predict P-290	proibir	forbid F-206, 207
prefirir	prefer P-291	proibir	ban B-20
prego	nail N-2	projetil	missile M-180
preguiça	laziness L-40	promessa	promise P-365, 366, 367
preguiçoso	lazy L-42		
prêmio	award A-325	promover	promote P-368
prender	arrest A-258, 259	pronto	ready R-40, 41, 42, 43
prender	pin P-177	propiciação	propitiation P-375
prensar	press P-304, 305, 306	próprio	proper P-371
preparar	prepare P-292, 293, 294	propor	propose P-377
		proporção	proportion P-376
preparar-se	get ready G-41	propósito	purpose P-419, 420, 421
presbitério	Presbyterian P-295		
presença	presence P-297	proprio	own O-156
presente	present P-300	propugnar	boost B-195
presente	gift G-44	prosperar	prosper P-378
preservar	preserve P-302	prosseguir	go ahead G-71
presidente	president P-303	prostituta	prostitute P-379
pressa	haste H-50	prostituta	strumpet S-527
pressão	stress S-513	proteger	protect P-380
prestar juramento	take oath T-18	protesta	protest P-382
presunsoso	swell-headed S-638	protestante	Protestant P-383
pretensioso	snob S-341	prova	proof P-370
preto	black B-164	provável	probable P-336
prevaricar	prevaricate P-308	proveito	profit P-356
prevenir alguém	tip off T-197	proveito	benefit B-118, 119
prima	cousin C-432, 433	prover	provide P-386, 387
primário	primary P-320	provisório	makeshift M-35
primavera	spring S-430	próxima semana	next week N-78, 79
primeiro	first F-149, 150	próximo	next N-73, 74, 75, 76
princesa	princess P-322		
principal	principal P-323, 324	próximo ano	next year N-80
principal	main M-17	proximo mes	next month N-77
principal	chief C-146	psicologia	psychology P-392, 393
príncipe	prince P-321	psiquiatra	psychiatrist P-391
princípio	principle P-325	publicar	publish P-395, 396
prisão	prison P-329	público	public P-394
privilégio	privilege P-335	pular	jump J-33, 34
problema	problem P-340, 341, 342	pulga	flea F-167, 168, 169
		pulmões	lungs L-179
proceder	proceed P-343	pulsação	heartbeat H-74, 75

referir	refer R-75	responder	answer A-192, 193
reforçar	reinforce R-86	responsabilidade	responsibility R-155, 156
reformar-se	mend M-110, 111		
refrear	check R-129, 130, 131, 132	resposta	response R-154
		ressusciação	resurrection R-169
refugio	refuge R-77	restante	remainder R-105
regalo	present P-299	restante	left L-62
regozijar	rejoice R-90	resto	rest R-161, 162
regra	rule R-279, 280	restringir	restrict R-167
regressar	return R-180	resumir	summarize S-568
regulação	regulation R-83	retaliar	retaliate R-170, 171
regular	regulate R-82	retardar	retard R-174
regular	regular R-81	retirar	retire R-175, 176, 177
regular	fair F-18	retirar	withdraw W-151, 152, 153, 154
rei	king K-19		
reincidir	relapse R-91	retiro	retreat R-178
reitor	rector R-68	retomar	resume R-168
rejeitar	reject R-88	retraguarda	rear R-50
rejeitar	cast off C-70	retrospecção	retrospection R-179
relação	relation R-92	reunião	meeting M-99, 100
relâmpago	lightning L-102	reunir	collect C-233
relativo	relative R-96	reunir (-se)	assemble A-277
relaxar	relax R-97, 98	reunir-se	gather G-19, 20
religião	religion R-100	revelar	develop D-131, 132
relógio	clock C-196	reverendo	reverend R-184
relógio	watch (timepiece) W-38, 39	reverso	reverse R-185, 186
		revista	magazine M-7
relógio de pulso	wristwatch W-204	reviver	revive R-187
remar	row R-265	revogar	revoke R-188
remir	redeem R-71, 72	revoltante	revolting R-189
remoto	remote R-109	rezar	pray P-283
remover	remove R-110, 111, 112	rico	rich R-191
		ridículo	ridicule R-193
renda	income I-65	rifle	rifle R-195
render-se	yield Y-13	rincão	corner C-402, 403
render-se	surrender S-604, 605	rio	river R-222, 223, 224
		riqueza	wealth W-56
renome	renowned R-118	rir	laugh L-33
renunciar	renounce R-117	rir-se de	make fun of M-26
reparar	repair R-120	riscado	striped S-520
repartir	share S-176, 177	riscar	expunge E-227
repartir	apportion A-228	riso	laughter L-35, 36
repetir	repeat R-121	rival	rival R-211, 212, 213, 214
repreender	bawl out B-59		
repreender	admonish A-88, 89	rivalizar	vie V-39, 40, 41
repreensão	reprimand R-131	rixa	row R-266
representar	represent R-129	robusto	sturdy S-537
representar	act A-60	rocha	rock R-235, 236
representativo	representative R-130	rociar	sprinkle S-432
republicano	republican R-133	roda	wheel W-88
repugnar	loathe L-131	rodear	surround S-606
reserva	reservation R-139	rolar	roll R-242, 243
reservar	reserve R-141, 142, 143	rolha	cork C-399
		romão	Roman R-245
resfriado	cold C-230	romper	break B-227
resistir a	resist R-148	rosário	rosary R-254, 255
resmungar	nag N-1	rotina diária	grind G-160
resolverse	resolve R-149	roubar	rob R-227, 228, 229
respeitar	respect R-150	roubar	steal S-469, 470, 471
respiração	respiration R-151	roubo	robbery R-233
responder	respond R-152	roupa	clothes C-200
responder	reply R-126, 127	roupa de baixo	underwear W-24

rua	street S-511	São José	Saint Joseph S-18
ruborizar-se	blush B-187	sapateiro	shoemaker S-209
rude	rude R-273, 274	sapateiro	cobbler C-214
ruido	noise N-92	sapato	shoe S-205, 206
ruido	din D-168	saraiva	hail H-2
ruim	mean M-78	sarampo	measles M-83
ruina	wreck W-200	sargento	sergeant S-153
		Satanás	Satan S-37
		satélite	satellite S-38
S		satisfação	satisfaction S-39
		saúde	health H-66
sábado	Saturday S-43	se	if I-12
sábado dos hebreus	Sabbath S-2, 3, 4	se	whether W-94
sabão	soap S-344, 345, 346, 347	secção	section S-115
		seco	dry D-322
sabedoria	wisdom W-145	secretário	secretary S-114
saber	know K-35	século	century C-96
sábio	scholar S-64	sede	thirst T-142
saboroso	savory S-48	seduzir	entice E-116
saca-rolhas	corkscrew C-400	segar	mow M-252, 253
sacerdote	father F-68	segredo	secret S-113
sacerdote	priest P-316, 317, 318, 319	seguinte	next N-73, 74, 75, 76
		seguir	follow F-190
sacramento	sacrament S-5	segunda-feira	Monday M-202
sacrifício	sacrifice S-6	segundo	second S-108
sacrílego	sacrilegious S-7	segundo	according to A-41
sacudida	jolt J-24	seguro	insurance I-143
sacudir	shake S-167	seguro	sure S-596
sagrada escritura	Holy Scriptures H-141	seis	six S-279
saia	skirt S-292, 293	selecionar	select S-124, 125, 126
saída	exit E-207	seleto	exquisite E-228
sair clandestinamente	leave clandestinely L-57, 58	selo	stamp S-447, 448
		selo	seal S-101, 102
sair de	leave L-55	selvagem	wild W-124, 125
sal	salt S-24, 25	sem	minus M-171, 172. 173
sala (de visitas)	living room L-128		
salada	salad S-20	semana	week W-64, 65
salão de beleza	beauty parlor B-79	semear	seed S-117, 118, 119
salário	wage(s) W-2	semear	sow S-384
salmo	psalm P-390	semelhante	similar S-261
salsicha	frankfurter F-252	semelhante	like L-104
saltar	hop H-151, 152	semelhante	alike A-125
saltar	leap L-51	seminário	seminary S-135, 136
salvação	salvation S-26	sempre	always A-151
salvar	save S-45	senado	senate S-137
salvar	rescue R-137	senda	path P-51
salve	hello H-88, 89	senda	trail T-255
salvo	safe S-9	senha	check C-131, 132
sancionar	endorse E-90, 91, 92	senhor	lord L-158
sandália	sandals S-33	senhora	madam M-6
sandwiche	sandwich S-35	senhora	lady L-6
sangrar	bleed B-171	sensação	sensation S-144
sanguessuga	leech L-60	sensível	sensitive S-147
santificado	hallowed H-16, 17	senso	sense S-145
santificar	sanctify S-32	sentar-se	sit down S-277
Santa Comunhão	Holy Communion, H-137, 138	sente-se	be seated B-124
		sentir	feel F-90, 91
santo	saint S-15, 16	sentir	regret R-79
santo	holy H-136	separado	apart A-207
são	hale H-10	separar	disjoin D-214
São Francisco	San Francisco S-36	separar	part P-32, 33, 34, 35
São João	Saint John S-17	separar	separate S-150, 151

separar-se	part from P-36	soneca	nap N-8
sepultura	grave G-125	sonho	dream D-303
sequela	sequel S-152	sono	sleep S-301, 302
ser candidato	run for office R-285	sopa	soup S-379
ser reprovado	fail F-11, 12, 13	soprar	blow away B-183
série	series S-154	sorrir	smile S-325
sério	earnest E-11	sortido	assorted A-286
sério	grave G-127	sortir	assort A-285
sermão	sermon S-155	sorvete	ice cream I-4, 5
serra	saw S-49, 50	sou	am A-152, 153
serra de vaivém	jig saw J-15	suave	gentle G-31
serraria	saw mill S-51	subjugar	subdue S-539
serrote	handsaw H-26	submergir	plunge P-217
servir	serve S-157	submeter-se	bow B-209
servir	wait on W-8	subornar	bribe B-233
sete	seven S-160	subsequente	subsequent S-543
seu	its I-220	substancia	substance S-545, 546
sexta-feira	Friday F-268	substancial	substantial S-547
significação	significance S-248, 249	substituir	replace R-125
significar	signify S-251	substituto	substitute S-548
silêncio	silence S-255, 256	subtrair	subtract S-549
silêncio	hush H-205	sueco	Swede S-628
silencioso	quiet Q-25, 26	suéter	sweater S-627
silencioso	noiseless N-93	suficiente	sufficient S-560
sim	yes Y-9	sugerir	suggest S-562
simples	plain P-191, 192	sujar	soil S-360
simples	simple S-262, 263	sujo	nasty N-15
sincero	sincere S-266, 267	sujo	dirty D-177
sino	bell B-103, 104, 105	sujo	foul F-235
sinónimo	synonym S-649	suor	sweat S-684, 685
sistema	system S-651	superar	overcome O-149
sítio	site S-278	superintendente	superintendant S-583
só	lone L-141	superintender	supervise S-587
só	alone A-140	superior	superior S-584
soar	ring R-204	superlativo	superlative S-585
sobre	over O-146, 147	súplica	supplication S-590
sobre	on O-68	súplica	plea P-206
sobre	upon U-56	suplicar	entreat E-120
sobrenatural	supernatural S-586	supor	suppose S-594
sobretudo	overcoat O-148	suportar	endure E-93, 94
sobrinha	niece N-82	suportar	bear B-69
sobrinho	nephew N-50	suposto	so-called S-348
sóbrio	temperate T-70	surdo	deaf D-27, 28
soda	soda pop S-354	surpreender	surprise S-601, 602
sofrer	suffer S-557, 558, 559	suspeita	suspicion S-615
sol	sun S-576	suspeitar	suspect S-608, 609
soldado	soldier S-362	suspender	suspend S-610, 611
soldado raso	private P-333	sustentar	maintain M-20
soletrar	spell S-410	sustentar	sustain S-616
solicitude	concern C-298	sustentar	support S-591, 592, 593
solidão	privacy P-330		
sólido	solid S-364	suster	uphold U-53
solitário	lonely L-142, 143		
solo	soil S-360		
solo	dirt D-176		**T**
solteiro	bachelor B-2		
solto	loose L-157	tabaco	tobacco T-206
som	sound S-388	tábua	lumber L-177, 178
soma	sum S-567	tacanho	tightwad T-182, 183, 184
somar	add A-70, 71, 72, 73		
sombra	shadow S-166	tacanho	narrow-minded N-14
sondar	probe P-338, 339	tagarelar	tattle T-35, 36

tal	such S-555	tesouras de tosquia	shears S-184, 185
talo	stem S-477	tesoureiro	treasurer T-272
também	too T-222	testamento	testament T-90, 91, 92
também	also A-143, 144	testemunha ocular	witness W-157
tambor	drum D-318	testemunho	testimony T-93
tampa	lid L-93	tia	aunt A-311
tapeçaria	upholstery U-54	tigo	thee T-106
tarde	afternoon A-107	tigre	tiger T-181
tardio	late L-26	tijela	bowl B-210
tarefa	task T-33	tímido	bashful B-43
tartaruga	turtle T-307	tímido	timid T-192
tartaruga	tortoise T-231	tímido	shy S-237
tato	touch T-234	tinta	ink I-111, 112
taverna	inn I-114	tintura	dye D-340
táxi	taxi T-43	tio	uncle U-14
teatro	theatre T-105	tipografia	printshop P-328
tecer	weave W-61	tirar	drag D-296
teimoso	stubborn S-528	título	title T-201
telefone	phone P-140, 141	toalette	toilet T-211
telefone	telephone T-61, 62	toalha	towel T-245
telegrãma	telegram T-57, 58	toalha de mesa	tablecloth T-4
televisão	television T-63	todavia	however H-176, 177
telhado	roof R-247	todo	all A-127, 128
tema	theme T-112	todo o mundo	everybody E-169
tema	exercise E-201	todos os	every E-168
temor	dread D-301	todos os anos	every year E-172
temperança	temperance T-69	tolerar	tolerate T-212, 213
temperatura	temperature T-71	tolice	folly F-192
tempestada	storm S-501	tolo	foolish F-199
templo	temple T-72	tolo	silly S-258
tempo	time T-186, 187, 188, 189	tomada	electric outlet E-54
		tomar	take T-9
temporaca	season S-106	tomar emprestado	borrow B-202
tencionar	intend I-148	tomar pílula	take a pill T-13
tenda	tent T-82	tomate	tomato T-215, 216
tender	tend T-76	tópico	topic T-227
tênis	tennis T-81	torcedura	sprain S-426
tênis de mesa	Ping-Pong P-178	tormentar	worry W-181, 182, 183
tenro	tender T-78, 79, 80	tormento	torment T-229
tentar	tempt T-73	torrada	toast T-204
tentar	attempt A-297, 298	torre	tower T-246
teoria	theory T-118	torta	pie P-165, 166
ter	have H-55, 57	tosse	cough C-417, 418
ter	hold H-129	total	total T-233
ter cuidado	be careful B-80	touro	bull B-268
ter de	have to H-58	trabalhar	toil T-210
ter êxito	succeed S-551	trabalhar	run R-283
ter medo	afraid A-102	trabalho	work W-171
ter vergonha	ashamed A-267	tradição	tradition T-251
terca-feira	Tuesday T-300	tragédia	tragedy T-253
terceiro	third T-139, 140, 141	trança	braid B-220
terminar	terminate T-83	tranquilo	calm C-16, 17
termómetro	thermometer T-124	tranquilo	still S-486, 487
terra	earth E-14	transbordar	run over R-286
terra	ground G-164	transferir	transfer T-261, 262
terra	land L-11, 12	transitório	transient T-263
terrível	awful A-328	transportar	transport T-264
terrível	dreadful D-302	transportar	convey C-383
terrível	terrible T-84	transporte	transportation T-265
terror	terror T-85, 86	trasgredir	trespass T-274
teso	rigid R-202	trazer	bring B-246
tesoura	scissors S-68	trem	train T-256

tremer	shiver S-201, 202	vagância	vacancy V-1
tremor	quake Q-4	vagão	wagon W-4
trepar	climb C-192, 193, 194	vagar	roam R-226
tres	three T-156	vagina	vagina V-5
tres semanas	three weeks T-161	vago	vague V-6
tres veces	three times T-160	vagões de comboio	cars C-66
triángulo	triangle T-275	vaguear	wander W-16, 17
triciclo	tricycle T-276	vaidade	vanity V-16
trigonometria	trigonometry T-278	vaidoso	conceited C-289
trilho	track T-249	vale	vale V-9
triáde	trinity T-281	valentão	tough T-238, 239, 240
trinta	thirty T-144	valer	worth W-191
triste	mournful M-245	válido	valid V-10
triste	sad S-8	valioso	valuable V-13
tristeza	gloom G-60	vão	vain V-7
triunfo	triumph T-285, 286	vapor	steam S-473
troca	trade T-250	vara	rod R-241
trombone	trombone T-289	variado	varied V-17
trovão	thunder T-172	variola	smallpox S-322
tu	thou T-149	vários	several S-162
tua	thine T-136	vários	various V-18
tubo	pipe P-181, 182	varrer	sweep S-631
tubo di ajustamento	pipe-fitting P-183	vassoura	broom B-255
tufão	tornado T-230	vazar	leak L-48
tumulto	turmoil T-304	vazio	empty E-79, 80
		vazio	void V-58
		veado	deer D-57
		vela	candle C-30
		vela de navio	sailboat S-11

U

uisque	whiskey W-102, 103	velho	old O-59
ulterior	further F-295, 296	velho testamento	Old Testament O-62,
último	ultimate U-7		63, 64, 65
último	last L-17, 18	velocidade	speed S-408
um	one O-72, 73	vencer	beat B-72, 73, 74
um	a A-1	vencer	conquer C-326
um ao outro	one another O-74	vencer	win W-133, 134
uma vez	once O-69	vencido	due D-324
úmido	moist M-199	vencido	beaten B-75
úmido	damp D-7	venda	sale S-22
unha	fingernail F-139	vender	sell S-132
união	union U-32	vender	vend V-21
união (a)	Union (the) U-33	veneno	poison P-227, 228
único	sole S-363	venerar	revere R-182, 183
único	only 82	ventania	gale G-6
unidade	unity U-36	ventar	blow B-181
uniforme	uniform U-30	vento	wind W-135
unir	attach A-294	ver	see S-116
universal	universal U-37	verão	summer S-572
universidade	university U-38, 39, 40	verbal	verbal V-23, 24
universidade	college C-234	verdadeiro	true T-292
untar	anoint A-189, 190	verdadeiro	actual A-67
urso	bear B-66	verde	green G-149
usado	worn W-176, 177	veredicto	verdict V-25
usar	use U-64	vergonha	shame S-170
uva	grape G-117, 118	verme	worm W-175
		vermelho	red R-69
		verossímil	credible C-455

V

		versos	verse V-27
		verter	pour P-269
vaca	cow G-440	vertiginoso	dizzy D-253
vacilação	waver W-47, 48	véspera	eve E-157
vacinação	vaccination V-4	vestido	dress D-304

vestido	gown G-101	voar	fly F-183, 184
vestido	frock F-276	vocação	vocation V-56
vestir	wear W-58	você mesmo	yourself Y-23
vestuário	garment G-14	volleyball	volleyball V-60
veu	veil V-20	volontário	volunteer V-62
via férrea	track T-248	volta	turn T-305
via férrea	railroad R-14, 15	volume	volume V-61
viado	fairy F-19	vomitar	vomit V-63
viagem	trip T-282, 283, 284	vontade	will W-127
viagem	journey J-25, 26, 27	votar	vote V-64
viajar	travel T-268, 269, 270	voto	vow V-65
viajar pendindo carona	hitchhike H-124	voz	voice V-57
vibração	vibration V-33	vulcão	volcano V-59
vibrar	thrill T-163, 164		
vice-presidente	vice president V-34		
vida	life L-98, 99	**W**	
videira	vine V-44		
vidro	glass G-54	Wáshington	Washington W-31, 32
vigilante	open-eyed O-90		
vinagre	vinegar V-45		
vingar	revenge R-181	**X**	
vinho	wine W-137, 138		
violar	violate V-46	xarope	syrup S-650
violino	violin V-47	xerife	sheriff S-190
vir	come C-246, 247, 248	Xerox	Xerox X-1
virgem	virgin V-48	xícara	cup C-484
Virgem Maria	Mary M-62	xilofone	xylophone X-4
vírgula	comma C-255		
visão	vision V-51, 52		
visita	visit V-53	**Y**	
visível	visible V-50		
vista	view V-42	Yugoslávia	Yugoslavia Y-27
vista	sight S-245		
vital	vital V-54, 55		
vitória	victory V-37, 38	**Z**	
viver	live L-124		
viver em paz	peace of mind P-62	zangado	cross C-463
vivo	alive A-126	zebra	zebra Z-3
vizinhança	vicinity V-36	zero	zero Z-4, 5
vizinho	neighbor N-47		

Russian-English Index

А

а	but B-279
абзац	paragraph P-25
абсолютный	absolute A-23
авария	breakdown B-228
авария	wreck W-200
авматор	aviator A-320
Авраам	Abraham A-17
Австралия	Australia A-312
автомобиль	automobile A-315
авторитет	authority A-314
агония	agony A-114
ад	hell H-86, 87
Адам	Adam A-69
адвокат	lawyer L-39
адрес	address A-76, 77
азбука	alphabet A-142
Азия	Asia A-270
актёр	actor A-65
актриса	actress A-66
алгебра	algebra A-124
аллилуия	hallelujah H-15
алмаз	diamond D-145, 146, 147
алтарь	altar A-145
алфавит	alphabet A-142
амбиция	ambition A156
Америка	America A-160
американский олень	moose M-216
амер. монета в 1 цент	penny P-91
аминь	amen A-159
ангел	angel A-172
англичанин	Englishman E-102
Англия	England E-100
анкета	questionnaire Q-21
антик	antique A-196
античная вещь	antique A-196
апельсин	orange O-110, 111, 112
аплодировать	applaud A-221
аппарат	apparatus A-213
аппетит	appetite A-220
арап	Negro N-45, 46
арахис	peanut P-67
арбуз	watermelon W-44
арестовать	arrest A-259
арифметика	arithmetic A-248
арка	arch A-236
армия	army A-251
арфа	harp H-46
архиепископ	archbishop A-237
ассоциация	association A-284
атаковать	attack A-295
атлас	Satan S-37
Африка	Africa A-103
ах!	O! O-1
ах! я понимаю	Oh, I see O-53

Б

бабочка	butterfly B-281
бабушка	grandmother G-113, 114
багаж	baggage B-11
базис	basis B-45, 46
бакался	groceries G-161
банан	banana B-21, 22
бандаж	bandage B-23
бандит	bandit B-25
банкет	banquet B-29
банкротство	bankruptcy B-27
бант	bow B-208
баня	bath B-52
баптист	Baptist B-31
барабан	drum D-318
бар мицва	bar mitzvah B-36
баскетбол	basketball B-48
басня	fable F-1
башмак	shoe, (-s) S-205, 206
башня	tower T-246
беда	trouble T-290
бедность	poverty P-270, 271
бедный	poor P-241, 242, 243
бедственный	calamitous C-6
бежать	flee F-170
бежать	run R-281, 282
без	minus M-172
безводный	arid A-245
безопасный	safe S-9
безрассудный	reckless R-61
безрассудство	folly F-192
без средств	stranded S-506
безумный	daft D-4
безумный	insane I-121
белка	squirrel S-442
белый	white W-107
бензин	gas G-16

вкус	taste T-34	воскресение	resurrection R-169
drecysq (jxty')	delicious D-78, 79	воскресенье	Sunday S-577, 578
влагалище	vagina V-5	воспаление легких	pneumonia P-220
владеть	possess P-257, 258	воспитание	education E-25
влажный	moist M-199	воспитывать	educate E-24
влияние	influence I-95, 96, 97, 98	воспитывать	rear R-51
влюбляться	fall in love with F-31	воспоминание	memory M-109
вместе	together T-209	восставать	rebel R-54
вместительность	capacity C-41	восток	east E-16
вместо	instead of I-131, 132	восточный	oriental O-126
вмешиваться	meddle M-90, 91	восхищаться	admire A-82, 83
внебрачный ребенок	bastard B-49	восход солнца	sunrise S-580
вне себя	off the beam O-50	восьминог	octopus O-33
вниз	down D-294	восьмной	ahead A-117
внизу	below B-109, 110, 111	впереди	onward O-87
вносить	contribute C-372	вперед	impress I-46
внутреннее		впечатлевать	last year L-25
рассматривание	introspection I-185	в прошлом году	injection I-106
внутри	inside I-126	впрыскивание	enemy E-95
внушать (мысли, мнение)	indoctrinate I-81	враг	run R-283
во время	during D-334	вращаться	pest P-133
вода	water W-40, 41	вредитель	harm H-44, 45
водопроводчик	plumber P-216	вредить	time T-187
военный	military M-153	время	forenoon F-214
вожжи	reins R-87	время до полудня	ever E-163, 164, 165
возбуждать	arouse A-254	всегда	universal U-37
возбуждать	excite E-194	всеобщий	all A-127, 128
возвращать	return R-180	всё	nevertheless N-61
возвышать	elevate E-60	всё-таки	all morning A-132
воздвигать	erect E-137	всё утро	by and by B-288
воздерживаться	abstain A-27	в скором времени	recall R-55, 56
воздержанность	abstinence A-28	вспоминать	explode E-224
воздух	air A-120	вспыхивать	stand S-450, 451
возле	besideB-126	вставать	meeting M-100
возлюбленный, -ая	sweetheart S-633, 634	встреча	meet M-98
возможность	possibility P-259	встречать	all night A-133
возможный	possible P-260	всю ночь	every E-168
вознесение	ascension A-266	всякий	everybody E-169
возобновлять	resume R-168	всякий	while W-97
возраст	age A-111	в то время как	Tuesday T-300
война	war W-20	вторник	second S-108
войско	army A-251	второй	veil V-20
вокзал	station S-461	вуаль	volcano V-59
вокруг	around A-252	вулкан	enter E-113
волейбол	volleyball V-60	входить	yesterday Y-10
волк	wolf W-159	вчера	you Y-16
волна	wave W-45	вы	choose C-160, 161
волонтёр	volunteer V-62	выбирать	pick P-153, 154
волос(ы)	hair H-3	выбирать	choice C-157
воля	will W-127	выбор	sprain S-426
вонючка	skunk S-294	вывихнуть	evacuate E-152
воображать	conceive C-290, 291	выводить	remove R-112
воображать	imagine I-22	выводить	peek P-73, 74, 77
воображение	imagination I-20	выглядывать	reprimand R-131
вообще	altogether A-150	выговор	profit P-356
вор	thief T-131	выгода	promote P-368
воровать	steal S-469, 470, 471	выдвигать	drawer D-300
ворота	gate G-18	выдвижной ящик	advanced A-96
воротник	collar C-232	выдвинутый	manufacture M-49
вопрос	query Q-14, 15	выделывать	challenge C-105
вопрос	question Q-17	вызов	summon S-573, 574
вопросник	questionnaire Q-21, 397	вызывать	win W-133, 134
восемь	eight E-38	выиграть	score S-73
восьмой	eighth E-39	выиграть очко	miscarriage M-178
		выкидыш	

Д

для	for F-204
дно	bottom B-206
до	until U-48
добиваться	aspire A-276
доброволец	volunteer V-62
добро пожаловать!	welcome W-75
добрый	decent D-40
добрый	kind K-15
добывать	procure P-348
доверие	trust T-295
довольно	rather R-29
довольный	content C-361
доверие	confidence C-312
дождь	rain R-17
дозволять	grant G-115
доказательство	proof P-370
доктор	doctor D-255
доктрина	doctrine D-256, 257
дол(ина)	vale V-9
долбить клювом	peck P-70
долг	duty D-337
долженствовать	must M-268
должно	must M-268
должный	due D-324
доллар	dollar(s) D-263, 264
долото	chisel C-155
доля	share S-176
доля	portion P-250
дом	home H-142
дом	house H-171
домашняя туфля	slipper S-312
допрашивать	interrogate I-169, 170
допускать	admit A-87
допускать	tolerate T-212
допущение	admission A-85
дорога	road R-225
дорогой	expensive E-214
досаждать	annoy A-183, 184
до свидания	goodbye G-87, 88
до сих пор	so far S-356
доставать	procure P-348
доставить	deliver D-82
доставлять	provide P-386, 387
достаточный	enough E-110
достигать	attain A-296
достигать	reach R-34
достоинство	worth W-191
достойный веры	credible C-455
досуг	leisure L-66
доход	income I-65
дочь	daughter D-16
драгоценный	precious P-288
дразнить	tease T-51, 52, 53
драма	drama D-297
дремать	doze D-295
дрова	wood W-167
дрожать	quake Q-4
дрожать	shiver S-201, 202
друг	friend F-269
друг друга	each other E-3
другой	other O-137
дуга	arch A-236
думать	think T-138
дурацкий	foolish F-199

дурачить	fool F-197, 198
дурное расположение духа	ill temper I-17
дуть	blow B-181
дух	breath B-230
дух	spirit S-416
духи	perfume P-104
духи	scent S-62
душ	shower S-229
душа	soul S-377
душистый	fragrant F-247
дым	smoke S-327
дыня	melon M-103
дыня	muskmelon M-267
дыра	hole H-131, 132
дыропробивной станок	punch press P-406
дыхание	respiration R-151
дюйм	inch I-57, 58
дядя	uncle U-14

Е

Евангелие	gospel G-92, 93
еврей	Hebrew H-80
еврейская Пасха	Passover P-48
Египет	Egypt E-36
его	him H-111
его	his H-117
его	its I-220
еда	meal M-77
единообразный	uniform U-30
единственный	only O-82, 83
единство	unity U-36
её	her H-94
её	hers H-100
её	its I-220
ежегодный	yearly Y-4
ежедневный	daily D-5
енот	raccoon R-5
епархия	diocese D-171
епископ	bishop B-158, 159
епископский	episcopal E-127
епитимья	penance P-83, 84
ересь	heresy H-96
если	if I-12
если не	unless U-43
естественный	natural N-17
есть	eat E-22
ехать верхом	ride R-192
ещё	yet Y-11, 12
ещё не	not yet N-128
ещё раз	again A-109

Ж

жадный	greedy G-145, 146, 147
жажда	thirst T-142
жаждать	crave C-448
жалованье	salary S-21
жаловать	confer C-306
жаловать	grant G-116
жаловаться	complain C-279, 280

жалость	pity P-187	зависеть	depend D-94, 95, 96
жареный картофель	French fried potatoes F-262	зависеть от	hinge H-116
жарить	fry F-287	завистливый	envious E-121
жарить на рашпере	broil B-252	завлекать	entice E-116
жаркий	hot H-164	завтра	tomorrow T-217
жарко	hot weather H-169	завтрак	breakfast B-229
жать	press P-306	заглавие	title T-201
жать	reap R-47, 48, 49	заглядывать	peek P-73, 74, 77
ждать	wait W-5	заголовок	caption C-46
жевательная резинка	gum G-181	загонять в тупик	corner C-403
жевать	chew C-142	задача	task T-33
желать	wish W-147, 148	задержка	delay D-74
желать (сильно)	covet C-438, 439	задняя сторона	rear R-50
железная дорога	railroad R-14, 15, 16	задыхаться	choke C-158, 159
железо	iron I-201	зажигать	kindle K-17
жена	wife W-123	зажимка	clothespin C-202
женитьба	marriage M-57	заказывать	order O-120
женский	female F-97	заканчивать	complete C-282, 283
женщина	woman W-160	закат	sunset S-581
жертва	sacrifice S-6	заклад	bet B-131
жертвоприношение	oblation O-13	заключать в тюрьму	imprison I-149
жестокий	cruel C-475, 476, 477	закон	law L-37
жестокосердный	hard-boiled H-38	законный	legal L-64
жестняка	can(ning) C-25	законодательная власть	legislature L-65
жёлтый	yellow Y-7	закрывать	close C-197
жёлудь	acorn A-55	закулисный	underhand U-18
жёсткий	rigid R-202	залог	pledge P-211
жёсткий	tough T-238, 239, 240	замазка	putty P-428
живой	alive A-126	замедлять	retard R-174
животное	animal A-177, 178	заменять	substitute S-548
жидкость	liquid L-116	замечание	remark R-106
жизнь	life L-98, 99	замечательный	swell S-635, 636
жил-был	once upon a time O-71	замечать	note N-118
жилет	vest V-31	замещать	substitute S-548
жилище	domicile D-265	замёрзший	frozen F-284
жир	fat F-65	занавес	curtain C-497
жираф	giraffe G-45	заниматься	apply A-225
жирный	fatty F-71	заносить	skid S-286
жительство	residence R-145, 146	занятие	occupation O-29
жить	live L-124	занятой	busy B-277, 278
жить согласно своим		запад	west W-80
взглядам	practice what you preach P-281	западня	trap T-266
		запасать	store S-499, 500
журнал	magazine M-7	запах	odor O-36
		запертый	locked L-136
		запирать	lock L-134, 135
	З	записки	bill(s) B-148, 149
		заповеди	commandments C-257
		заповедь	precept P287
за	at A-292	запоздалый	tardy T-31
за	behind B-98	запрещать	forbid F-206, 207
за	for F-204	запугивать	bluff B-185
забавный	amusing A-168	запускать	neglect N-44
забастовка	strike S-518	запястье	wrist W-203
заблуждение	mistake M-187	запятая	comma C-255
забор	fence F-98, 99	заработная плата	wage(s) W-2
заботиться о ком-либо	take care of T-15, 16, 17	зарабатывать	earn E-10
заботливый	careful C-58	заразный	contagious C-353
забывать	forget F-221, 222	засевать	seed S-118
заведовать	operate O-95	заслуживать	deserve D-113
заведующий	superintendent S-583	заспаться	oversleep O-152
завет	testament T-90	заставлять	impel I-33, 34
завещать	bequeath B-121	застенчивый	bashful B-43
завивать	curl C-490	застенчивый	timid T-192

И

Л

М

мармелад	jam J-2
маршировать	march M-54, 55
масло	butter B-280
масло	oil O-55
мастерская	workshop W-173
мастерство	field F-113, 114
математика	mathematics M-68
материя	matter M-69
матрос	sailor S-13, 14
мать	mother M-229, 230
махать	wave W-46
мачеха	stepmother S-482
машина	machine M-1
машина для стрижки травы	lawn mower L-38
машины	machinery M-3
медаль	medal M-89
медведь	bear B-66
медицинская сестра	nurse N-136
медленный	slow S-314
медлительность	sloth S-313
между	amid A-162
между	between B-133
между тем	in the meantime I-178
мексиканский	Mexican M-135
мел	chalk C-104
меланхолия	melancholy M-101
меласса	molasses M-200
мелкий	fine F-136
мелкий	minute M-175
мелкий	petty P-136
мелкий	shallow S-169
мелодия	melody M-102
мельчайший	minute M-175
менее	less L-75
менструация	menstruate M-113
меньший	least L-54
меньший	less L-75
меня	me M-76
менять	change C-108, 109
менять	exchange E-192
мерить	measure M-84
мести	sweep S-631
местность	site S-278
место	place P-188, 189
место	seat S-107
местоположение	location L-133
месяц	moon M-214, 215
месяц	month M-210
металл	metal M-130, 131
метательное орудие	missile M-180
метла	broom B-255
метод	method M-132
методист	Methodist M-133
механик	mechanic M-86, 87
меч	sword S-644
мечта	daydream D-20
мешать	hinder H-113
мешать	mix M-191
мешкать	fall behind F-29
мёрзнуть	freeze F-260
мёртвый	dead D-25, 26
мигать	wink W-140
микрометр	micrometer M-138

миллион	million M-155
миловидный	cute C-500, 501
милосердие	charity C-120
милосердие	mercy M-124, 125
Милуоки	Milwaukee M-156
милый	nice N-81
миля	mile M-151
минус	minus M-171, 173
минута	minute M-174
мир	peace P-61
мир	world W-174
миссия	mission M-183,184
митра	mitre M-189
младенец	infant I-90
мне	me M-76
мнение	opinion O-98
много	many M-50
много	much M-255
многократный	multiple M-260
многочисленный	numerous N-134
множественный	plural P-218
могила	grave G-125
могущественный	mighty M-148
модель	model M-196
модный	stylish S-538
может быть	perhaps P-105
можно	may M-73, 74
мозг	brain B-221
мой	my M-272
мокрый	wet W-81
молить	beseech B-125
молиться	pray P-283
молния	lightning L-102
молодой	young Y-18
молоко	milk M-154
молокосос	sucker S-556
молоток	hammer H-22
молоть	grind G-159
молчание	silence S-255, 256
молчи	keep quiet K-2, 3
молчи	shut up S-235, 236
мольба	supplication S-590
момент	moment M-201
монахиня	nun N-135
монета	coin(s) C-223, 224
монотонность	grind G-160
монотонный	monotonous M-207, 208, 209
моргать	wink W-140
море	sea S-100
мороженое	ice cream I-4, 5
морфин	morphine M-224
моряк	seaman S-103
москоть	drug D-317
мост	bridge B-234
мотив	motive M-238, 239, 240
мотор	electric motor E-53
мотор	motor M-241
мотоцикл	motorcycle M-242
мотыга	hoe H-126
моцион	exercise E-200
моча	urine U-62
мочь	can C-24
мощь	might M-144

настойчиво продолжать persist P-122
настольный теннис ping-pong P-178
настоящий real R-44
насущный vial V-54, 55
нахальный fresh F-265, 266
нахмуриваться frown F-283
находить find F-131
натуральный natural N-17
натянутый far-fetched F-46
наука science S-66, 67
недавно a while ago W-98, 99, 100
недавний recent R-58
не делайте! don't D-271, 272
неделя week W-64, 65
недоверчивость distrust D-236
недовольный discontented D-197
недовольный displeased D-221
недоимки arrears A-257
недолгий сон nap N-8
не дома out O-143
недонос miscarriage M-178
недопонимать misunderstand M-188
недорогой inexpensive I-89
недоставать lack L-3
недостаток dearth D-32
недостаток deficiency D-65
нежный tender T-78, 79, 80
независимость independence I-70
не за что you're welcome Y-20, 21
не знать don't know D-279
неимение deficiency D-65
нейтральный neutral N-58
неквалифицированный unskilled U-47
некоторые several S-162
некоторые some S-366
некрасивый homely H-143, 144
нелепый absurd A-29
неловкий clumsy C-208
неловкость clumsiness C-206
не любить don't care for D-277
немецкий German G-37
немного погодя after a while A-106
немой mute M-269
не мочь cannot C-35, 36
ненавидеть detest D-128, 129
ненависть hate H-52, 53
не нравиться no taste for N-116
ненужный unnecessary U-45
неопределённый vague V-6
неответственный irresponsible I-203, 204
не понимать misunderstand M-188
не попасть в miss M-179
не поправляться not improve N-126
непорочное зачатие Immaculate Conception I-25
непорочный pure P-414, 415
непослушный naughty N-21
непосредственный immediate I-26
непостоянный changeable C-110
неправильный wrong W-207
неприкреплённый loose L-157
нерасположение dislike D-215
нерв nerve N-51

нервное расстройство mental breakdown M-116
нервный nervous N-52
нерешительность indecision I-68
неровный rough R-259, 260, 261
не сделано not done N-117
не скажите don't tell D-282
несколько several S-162
несколько some S-366
несколько дней тому назад a few days ago F-105
несколько секунд тому назад a few seconds ago F-106
нескромный immodest I-29
несмотря на despite D-118
несовершеннолетний minor M-170
не соглашаться disagree D-179
неспособный unable U-12
несправедливость injustice I-110
несправедливый unfair U-25, 26
не спящий awake A-323
несчастный случай accident A-33
нет no N-86
нет no N-87
не уважать disregard D-226
неуверенный uncertain U-13
неугомонный restless R-165
неудовольствие dissatisfaction D-228
неуклюжесть clumsiness C-206
неуклюжий clumsy C-208
не улучшаться not improve N-126
не хотеть don't want D-283
нечестный corrupt C-412
нечестный dishonest D-212
нечестный человек crook C-461
нечистый impure I-51
нечувствительный insensate I-125
неясный unclear U-15
ни neither N-49
Нидерланды Netherlands N-56, 57
нижнее бельё underwear U-24
низкий low L-171, 172
никогда never N-59
никогда больше never again N-60
никто none N-96, 97, 98, 99
нить thread T-155
ничего doesn't matter D-258
ничего nothing N-119, 120, 121, 122
ничего не знать know nothing K-38
ничего не стоящий worthless W-192, 193
ничего себе fair F-18
ничто nothing N-119, 120, 121, 122
нищий panhandler P-14
но but B-279
Новая Англия New England N-63
новизна novelty N-129
новичок green G-150
новости tidings T-178
новый new N-62
Новый Год New Year N-71
Новый завет New Testament N-68, 69, 70
Новый Орлеан New Orleans N-65

нога	foot F-200
нога	leg L-63
ноги	feet F-95
ноготь	fingernail F-139
нож	knife K-27, 28, 29
ножницы	scissors S-68
ножницы	shears S-184, 185
номер	number N-132, 133
Норвегия	Norway N-108
норд-вест	northwest N-107
норд-ост	northeast N-106
нормальный	normal N-103
нос	nose N-110
носить	carry C-64, 65
носить	wear W-58
носовой платок	handkerchief H-25
носок	sock(s) S-351, 352
ночь	night N-83
нравиться	like L-103, 105
нужда	need N-37, 38, 39
нужный	necessary N-30, 31
нуль	zero Z-4, 5
нынешний	present P-301
нырять	dive D-238, 239
нырять	plunge P-217
Нью-Джерси	New Jersey N-64
Нью-Йорк	New York N-72

О

щ	O! O-1
щ, об	about A-14
оба	both B-203
обвинять	accuse A-48, 49
обдумывать	consider C-336, 337, 338
обед	dinner D-170
обед	meal M-77
обедать	dine D-169
обезображивать	deface D-58
обезьяна	monkey M-206
обескураживать	discourage D-198, 199
обеспечивать	provide P-386, 387
обет	vow V-65
обещать	promise P-365, 366, 367
обжорство	gluttony G-68
обивка	upholstery U-54
обилие	plenty P-212
обитать	dwell D-339
облако	cloudz C-204
облегчать	facilitate F-6
облегчение	relief R-99
облигация	obligation O-16
обман	fraud F-254
обман	hoax H-125
обманный	fraudulent F-256
обмануть	take advantage of T-10, 11
обманщик	impostor I-44
обманывать	cheat C-127, 128
обманывать	kid K-11
обменивать	trade T-250
обменивать(ся)	interchange I-154
обмывать(ся)	wash W-26, 27

обнимать	hug H-182
ободрять	encourage E-83
обожать	worship W-187
обонять	smell S-324
образ	image I-19
образец	sample S-21
обратно	back B-3
обратное	reverse R-185
обращать внимание	give attention (to) G-50
обращать внимание на	pay attention (to) P-60
обращаться	apply A-224
обрезать	snu S-343
обрезать	cut off C-502
обсуждать	discuss D-203
обсуждать прошлое	look back L-153
обсуждение	discussion D-205
общественный	public P-394
община	community C-265, 266
объединённый фонд	pool P-240
объектив	objective O-12
объявлять	announce A-181
объяснять	explain E-220, 221
объяснять	illustrate I-18
обыскивать	search S-104
обычай	custom C-498
обыгрывать	beat B-73
обязанность	obligation O-15
обязанный	bound B-207
обязательство	obligation O-14
овсяная мука	oatmeal O-3
овца	sheep S-186
огонь	fire F-146
огород	garden G-13
ограничивать	restrict R-167
огромный	huge H-183
одежда	garment G-14
одеколон	cologne C-239
один	alone A-140
один	one O-72, 73
одинаково	alike A-125
одинокий	lone L-141, 142, 143
один раз	once O-69
однако	however H-176, 177
однообразная работа	grind G-160
однообразный	uniform U-30
одобрение	approbation A-231
одобрять	commend C-259
одобрять (восклицаниями)	acclaim A-34, 35
одолжать	lend L-70, 71
ожерелье	necklace N-34
оживать, -лять	revive R-187
ожидать	expect E-209
озабоченность	anxiety A-198
озабоченный	anxious A-200
озеро	lake L-8
означать	signify S-251
О. К.	O. K. O-57, 58
оказия	occasion O-26
оказывать внимание на	pay attention (to) P-60
оканчивать	conclude C-301
оканчиваться	expire E-218
океан	ocean O-31, 32
окно	window W-136
око	eye E-236

около	around A-252	особый	specific S-398
окончить учебное заве-		оспа	smallpox S-322
дение, университет	graduate G-106, 107	оставаться	stay S-466, 467
окрестности	vicinity V-36	оставлять	forsake F-229, 230, 231
окружать	surround S-606	оставлять за собой	leave L-56
окружение	environment E-122, 123	остальной	left L-62
олень	deer D-57	останавливать(ся)	stop S-497
оленьи рога	antlers A-197	остаток	rest R-161, 162
олово	tin T-193	осторожный	careful C-58
омар	lobster L-132	остриё	point P-225
он	he H-63	остров	island I-209, 210
она	she S-183	острог	jail J-1
она сама	herself H-101	остроумный	smart S-323
онемевший	speechless S-406	отсрочивать	postpone P-263
они	they T-126	острый	sharp S-178, 179
оно	it I-214, 215, 216	осуждать	find fault F-132, 133
он сам	himself H-112	от	from F-280
опасность	danger D-10, 11	отбирать	select S-124, 125, 126
операция	operation O-96, 97	отбиться	stray S-510
описывать	describe D-109, 110, 111	отбывать	leave L-55
оплакивать	mourn M-244	отвергать	reject R-88
оплодотворить	impregnate I-45	ответ	answer A-192, 193
оппонент	opponent O-99	ответственность	responsibility R-155, 156
определить	appoint A-226	отвечать	answer A-192, 193
определять	define D-66, 67	отвёртка	screwdriver S-93
определять	determine D-127	отвлекать	sidetrack S-244
опрыскивать	spray S-427	отвратительный	revolting R-189
опускать(ся)	sink S-270, 271	отвращение	disgust D-208
опустошать	deplete D-99	отдалённый	remote R-109
опустошение	havoc H-59	отдельно	apart A-207
опухоль	bump B-269	отделять	detach D-121
опыт(ность)	expirience E-215, 216	отделять(ся)	part P-33, 34
опять	again A-109	отдёргивать	withdraw W-152, 154
оранжевый	orange O-112	отдыхать	rest R-159, 160
оратор	orator O-114	отзываться	respond R-152
ораторствовать	orate O-113	отец	father F-66, 67
орбита	orbit O-116, 117	отказывать(ся)	refuse R-78
организация	organization O-124, 125	отказываться	decline D-47
орех	nut N-137	отказываться	renounce R-117
орёл	eagle E-6	отказываться от долж-	
ориентация	orientation O-127	ности	resign R-147
орнамент	ornament O-135, 136	откладывать	postpone P-263
оружие	arms A-250	откладывать (со дня	
осадить	snub S-343	на день)	procrastinate P-347
освещение	light L-100	отклик	response R-154
освобождать	deliver D-81	отклонять	deflect D-70
освобождение	liberation L-88	отклоняться от прямого	
освящать	sanctify S-32	пути	deviate D-135, 136
освящение	benediction B-116, 117	откровенно	frankly F-253
освященный	hallowed H-16, 17	откровенный	frank F-251
осень	autumn A-316, 317	открывать	detect D-122
осёл	donkey D-268	открывать	discover D-201
оскорблять	insult I-140, 141, 142	открывать	open O-88, 89
ослабевать	decline D-45, 46	открывать дверь	open the door O-92
ослеплять	dazzle D-22	открывать окно	open the window O-93
ослушиваться	disobey D-217	отлагать	defer D-64
осматривать	inspect I-128	отличный	swell S-635, 636
осмеивать	ridicule R-193, 194	отложить	put off P-427
основание	basis B-45, 46	отменять	abolish A-12, 13
основной	principal P-324	отменять	annul A-188
основывать	base B-39, 40	отмечать	mark M-56
основывать	establish E-144	отмороженный	frozen F-284
особа	individual I-79, 80	отнимать	take away from T-14
особа	person P-124	относительно	concerning C-300

равнодушие	indifference I-75
равный	equal E-131
равный	peer P-78
рад	glad G-53
радио	radio R-10, 11
радость	delight D-80
радость	joy J-28
радоваться	rejoice R-90
раз	time T-189
разбитый	defeated D-60
разбить	defeat D-59
разбой	robbery R-233
разбойник	bandit B-25
разваливаться	collapse C-231
развалина	ruin R-278
развеять	blow away B-183
развиваться	develop D-131, 132
развлечение	distraction D-233
развлечение	fun F-290
развлечение	recreation R-67
разводить	divorce D-249, 250, 251
развязанный	loose L-157
разговор	conversation C-379, 380
разговор	talk T-23, 24
раздавить	squash S-440
разделять	apportion A-228
раздражительный	irritable I-205
раздуваться	swell S-637
разинув рот от удивления	open-mouthed O-91
раз(лич)ный	sundry S-579
различный	diverse D-240, 241
размышление о прошлом	retrospection R-179
размышлять	consider C-336, 337, 338
разница	difference D-156
разноимённый	unlike U-44
разнообразный	varied V-17
разнообразный	various V-18
разные	varied V-17
разные	various V-18
разорённый	broke B-253
разочарованный	disapointed D-182, 183
разочаровывать	disapoint D-181
разрезать	rip R-208, 209
разум	intellect I-144
разуметь	comprehend C-287
разъединять	disconnect D-196
разъединять	disjoin D-214
разъярять	enrage E-111
ракета	rocket R-237
рама	frame F-249
рана	wound W-197
ранний	early E-9
раньше	before B-91, 92
раскиваться	repent R-123
раскаивающийся	penitent P-89
раскаяние	contrition C-373
размышлять	meditate M-94
распинать (на кресте)	crucify C-474
распределять	distribute D-234, 235
распространять(ся)	spread S-428, 429
распылять	spray S-427
рассеянный	absent-minded A-22
рассказ	story S-502
рассказывать	narrate N-11
расследовать	probe P-338, 339
рассматривать	reckon R-62
рассматривать	contemplate C-355
расстаться	part from P-36
расстраивать	frustrated F-286
расстройство	clutter C-209
рассыпать	scatter S-60
растворять	dissolve D-230
растение	plant P-199
растить	grow G-167
расточать	waste W-34, 35
расточительный	extravagant E-233
растягивать	expand E-208
растянуть	sprain S-426
расходиться	differ D-155
расходы	expense E-213
расширять	expand E-208
расширять	extend E-229
рвать(ся)	tear T-48
рвение	zeal Z-1
рвота	vomit V-63
реабилитация	rehabilitation R-84
реактивный самолёт	jet J-11
реакция	reaction R-35
ребёнок	child C-147
ребёнок	kid K-10
реванш	revenge R-181
ревнивый	jealous J-5
регистрировать (документы)	file F-122
регулировать	regulate R-82
регулярный	regular R-81
редиска	radish R-12
редкий	rare R-25
редко	seldom S-123
резать	cut C-499
резвиться	frolic F-279
резервировать	reserve R-141, 142
резец	chisel C-155
резина	rubber R-268
резинка	rubber R-269
река	river R-222, 223, 224
ректор	rector R-68
религия	religion R-100
ремонтировать	repair R-120
репа	turnip T-306
республиканец	republican R-133
рефери	umpire U-10
рехнувшийся	nuts N-138, 139, 140
рецепт	prescription P-296
рецидив	relapse R-91
речь	discourse D-200
речь	speech S-404, 405
решать	decide D-42
решать(ся)	resolve R-149
решаться на что	make up one's mind M-37
римский	Roman R-245
рис	rice R-190
рисовать	draw D-298
робкий	shy S-237
ровно через месяц	this month T-146
ровный	even E-158

С

сено	hay H-62	скрытно уходить, уезжать	leave clandestinely L-57, 58
сердечный	cordial C-398		
сердечный припадок	heart attack H-73	скудный	scarce S-58
сердитый	angry A-175	скульптор	sculptor S-97
сердить	anger A-173	скунс	skunk S-294
сердце	heart H-71, 72	скупой	stingy S-488, 489, 490
серебро	silver S-259, 260	скучный	boring B-198
середина	midst M-142	слабоумный	feeble-minded F-87
серединный	median M-92	слабоумный	moron M-223
серединный	middle M-140	слабый	weak W-53
сержант	sergeant S-153	слабый (очень)	woefully weak W-158
серия	series S-154	слава	glory G-64, 65
серый	gray G-129, 130, 131, 132	славный	glorious G-63
		сладкий	sweet S-632
серьга	earring E-12	след	track T-249
серьёзность	earnest E-11	следовало (бы)	ought to O-138
серьёзный	grave G-127	следовать	follow F-190
сестра	sister S-272, 273	следующая неделя	next week N-78, 79
сесть	sit down S-277	следующий	next N-73, 74
сечь	whip W-101	слеза	tear T-49
сеять	sow S-384	слезать	get off G-40
сжимать	condense C-303	слепой	blind B-174
сигара	cigar C-170, 171	сливки	cream C-452
сигарета	cigarette C-172	словарь	dictionary D-150, 151
сиделка	nurse N-136	словесный	oral O-109
сиденье	seat S-107	словесный	verbal V-23, 24
сидеть	sit S-275, 276	слово	word W-170
сила	force F-210, 211	сложить	fold F-189
сила	might M-144	слон	elephant E-59
сила	strength S-512	слуга	servant S-156
сила воли	will power W-132	служанка	maid M-13
сила души	fortitude F-233	служить	serve S-157
сильный	strong S-523, 524	случай	chance C-107
сильный ветер	gale G-6	случай	event E-161
синий	blue B-184	случай	occasion O-26
синоним	synonym S-649	случайная встреча	encounter E-82
сироп	syrup S-650	случайность	accident A-33
система	system S-651	случайный	occasional O-27
скажите мне	tell me T-66	случаться	happen H-31, 32
сказать	tell T-64	слушай	hark H-42
скакать	hop H-151, 152	слушание	hearing H-69
скала	rock R-235, 236	слушатели	audience A-309, 310
скамья	bench B-112	слушать	listen L-121
скатерть	tablecloth T-4	слушаться	mind M-162
скверный	nasty N-15	слышать	hear H-68
сквозь	through T-166	смазка	grease G-133
скептик	skeptic S-282, 285	смазывать	oil O-54
скидывать	deduct D-54	смежный	adjacent A-80
складывать	add A-70, 71	смелость	courage C-425
складывать	fold F-189	смертный	mortal M-225
скоблить	scrape S-89	смех	laugh L-33
сковывать	fetter F-102	смешивать	mingle M-167, 168
скользить	slide S-307, 308	смешной	funny F-294
сколько?	how many? H-178	смётывать	baste B-50
сколько денег?	how much money? H-180	смирный	meek M-97
		смородина	currant C-491
сколько лет?	how old? H-181	смотреть	look L-149
сколько это стоит?	what is the price? W-85	смотреть за	mind M-161
скорбный	sorrowful S-374	смотреть за кем-либо	take care of T-15, 16, 17
скорость	speed S-408	смотреть на	look at L-151
скорый	fast F-60	смотреть назад	look back L-153
скрепка	paper clip P-19	смотреть свысока	look down L-154
скрипка	violin V-47	смутный	vague V-6
скромный	modest M-197		

станция   station S-461
стараться   try T-297, 298
старый   old O-59
старший   elder E-47
старший   eldest E-48
статут   statute S-463
статуя   statue S-462
стать в тупике   stuck S-529, 530
ствол   stem S-477
стебель   stem S-477
стежок   stitch S-491
стекло   glass G-54
стелющееся растение   vine V-44
стена   wall W-14, 15
стенной шкаф   closet C-199
стенные часы   clock C-196
с тех пор   since S-265
с тех пор   thenceforth T-117
стиральная машина   washing machine W-30
стирать   wash W-25
стих   verse V-27
стихотворение   poem P-222
сто   hundred H-193
с того времени   thenceforth T-117
стоимость   worth W-191
стойко продолжать   persevere P-120
стол   table T-2
столетие   century C-96
столица   capital C-42
столкнуться   collide C-235, 236
столяр   cabinetmaker C-2
сторона   side S-242
стоять   stand S-449
стоять лицом к лицу   confront C-315
стоять на коленях   kneel K-26
стоящий   worth W-191
страдать   suffer S-557, 559
страна   country C-424
старание   endeavor E-88
страница   page P-4
странный   strange S-507, 508
странствовать   roam R-226
страсть   passion P-46
страх   terror T-85, 86
страхование   insurance I-143
страшный   dreadful D-302
стрельба из лука   archery A-238
стрелять   shoot S-212, 213
стремиться   anxious (to) A-199
строгий   strict S-515, 516
строить   build B-266
строфа   verse V-27
стряпчий   attorney A-302
студент   student S-531
стул   chair C-101, 102, 103
ступень(ка)   step(s) S-479, 480
стучать   knock K-31
стыд   shame S-170
стыдиться   ashamed A-267
стыдливый   bashful B-43
суббота   Saturday S-43
судить   judge J-30
судья   referee R-76
суетность   vanity V-16

суетный   vain V-7
сук   branch B-222
сука   bitch B-160
сумасшедший   crazy C-449, 450, 451
суматоха   turmoil T-304
сумерки   twilight T-310
сумма   sum S-567
суммировать   summarize S-568
сундук   trunk T-294
суп   soup S-379
сутул(оват)ый   stooped S-496
сухой   dry D-322
сушёная слива   prune P-388
существенный   essential E-142
существенный   substantial S-547
существовать   exist E-206
сфера   sphere S-413
схватить   seize S-122
схватывать   grab G-102
схема   scheme S-63
сходиться   convene C-377
сходный   alike A-125
сцена   scene S-61
сцена   stage S-443
счастливый   happy H-34
счёт   account A-42
считать   count C-422
с широко раскрытыми
(от удивления) глазами   open-eyed O-90
съедать   consume C-348
сын   son S-370
сыр   cheese C-136
сырой   damp D-7
сыщик   detective D-123, 124
сюрприз   surprise S-601, 602, 603

Т

табак   tobacco T-206
таинство   sacrament S-5
тайна   secret S-113
тайна   mystery M-274
тайный   underhand U-18
так   thus T-174
также   also A-143, 144
таким образом   thus T-174
так называемый   so-called S-348
такой   such S-555
такси   taxi T-43
тальк   powder P-272, 273
там   there T-119, 120
танцевать   dance D-8
тарелка   plate P-201
таять   melt M-104
твёрдый   hard H-37
твой   thine T-136
творить   make M-23
театр   theatre T-105
тебе   thee T-106
тебя   thee T-106
текущий   current C-493
телевидение   television T-63
телевизор   television T-63

У

убирать	remove R-110, 111	умирающий	dying D-341
уборная	toilet T-211	умножать	multiply M-261, 262
уважать	respect R-150	умный	clever C-188, 189
уважать	revere R-182, 183	умный	strong-minded S-525
уведомлять	inform I-99, 100	умолять	beg B-95
увеличивать	increase I-66	умопомешанный	mentally unbalanced
уверенный	sure S-596		M-117, 118, 119, 120, 121
увещевать	admonish A-89	умственный	mental M-115
увиливать	shirk S-199	универсальный	universal U-37
увольнять	discharge D-190, 191	университет	university U-38, 39, 40
увы	alas A-123	уничтожать	annihilate A-180
угадать	guess G-172, 173, 174, 175	уничтожать	annul A-188
		уносить	remove R-110, 111
уговаривать	coax C-213	унылость	gloom G-60
угол	corner C-402	унылый	dejected D-73
уголь	coal C-210	упаковка	package P-2
удаляться	withdraw W-151, 153	упасть в обморок	faint F-15, 16
удар	blow B-182	упорно добиваться	persevere P-118, 119, 121
удар	stroke S-521	упорный	stubborn S-528
ударить	rap R-23	употреблять	use U-64
удар кулаком	punch P-404, 405	управлять	conduct C-304
ударять	hit H-120, 121, 122	управлять	drive D-312
удваивать	duplicate D-332, 333	управлять	govern G-98
удерживать	check C-129, 130	упражнение	exercise E-201
удивлять	amaze A-154	упражняться	practice P-278, 279
удить рыбу	fish F-152	упрямый	obstinate O-22
удлинять	extend E-229	упускать	fail F-11, 12
удобное время	opportunity O-100, 104	упущение	omission O-66, 67
удобный случай	opportunity O-101, 104	ураган	tornado T-230
удобство	comfort C-251	уродство	ugliness U-1, 2, 3
удовлетворение	satisfaction S-39	урожай	harvest H-47, 48, 49
удовлетворять	gratify G-123, 124	урождённая	nee N-36
уединённый	lonely L-141, 142, 143	урок	lesson L-77
уехать	depart D-93	усердие	zeal Z-1
ужас	terror T-85, 86	усиливать	reinforce R-86
ужасный	terrible T-84	усилие	effort E-29, 30, 31
ужин	dinner D-170	усложнять	complicate C-284
ужин	supper S-589	уста	mouth M-248
узел	knot K-34	уставший от	sick of it S-241
узкий	narrow N-13	усталость	fatigue F-70
узких взглядов	narrow-minded N-14	устный	oral O-109
узнавать	recognize R-64	устный	verbal V-23, 24
уйти не прощаясь	slip away S-311	устраивать	arrange A-255
указывать	indicate I-74	устрица	oyster O-157
указывать на	point P-224	уступать	concede C-288
укладка	package P-2	уступать	yield Y-13
украшать	trim T-279, 280	утешать	console C-341
украшение	ornament O-135, 136	утка	duck D-323
укреплять	fortify F-232	утаивать	embezzle E-68
уксус	vinegar V-45	утомительный	tedious T-54
улица	street S-511	утомлённый	weary W-60
уличное движение	traffic T-252	утомлять(ся)	tire T-198
улучшать	improve I-50	утро	morning M-222
улучшать(ся)	mend M-111	утюг	flatiron F-162
улыбка	smile S-325	ухо	ear E-7
ум	mind M-159, 160, 163	уходить	leave L-55
уменьшать	decrease D-50	уходить в отставку	retire R-177
умеренность	temperance T-69	уход с работы, со службы	quit Q-27
умеренный	mild M-150	участвовать	participate P-37
умеренный	temperate T-70	учащийся	learner L-53
умереть	die D-152, 153	учебник	textbook T-95
умерщвление	mortification M-226	ученик	disciple D-192
умилостивление	propitiation P-375	ученик	pupil P-410, 412
умирать	expire E-219		

часть	part P-32	шеф-повар	chef C-137
часы	watch W-38, 39	шёпот	whisper W-104
чаш(к)а	bowl B-210	шип	thorn T-147
чашка	cup C-484	шипучий напиток	soda pop S-354
чек	check C-131	широкий	wide W-119
человеческий	human H-184	широко распространён-	
человечество	humanity H-186	ный	widespread W-121
человечный	humane H-185	шить	sew S-163
чем	than T-96	школа	school S-65
чемодан	suitcase S-565	шланг	water hose W-43
чемпион	champion C-106	шлёпать	spank S-391
чепуха	humbug H-190	шляпа	hat H-51
червь	worm W-175	шнурки для ботинок	lace L-2
через	across A-59	шоколад	chocolate C-156
через	through T-166	шотландец	Scot S-76, 77, 78
черепаха	tortoise T-231	шпага	sword S-644
чернила	ink I-111, 112	шпаклёвка	putty P-428
чесать	comb C-244	шпилька	hairpin H-6
честный	honest H-145	шпион	spy S-433, 434, 435
честолюбивый	ambitious A-157, 158	штамповочный пресс	punch press P-406
честолюбие	ambition A-156	штаны	pants P-15
честь	honor H-147, 148	штепсельная розетка	electric outlet E-54
четверг	Thursday T-173	штопать	darn D-15
четверть	quarter Q-9	штопор	corkscrew C-400
четверть часа	quarter-hour Q-10	штраф	penalty P-82
четвёртый	fourth F-242	шум	noise N-92
четыре	four F-240	шум	row R-266
чёрный	black B-164	шутка	joke J-22
чётки	rosary R-254, 255	щека	cheek C-133
Чикаго	Chicago C-143	щётка для волос	hairbrush H-4
чинить	mend M-110	щипцы	pliers P-213
чистилище	purgatory P-416		
чистить башмаки	shine shoes S-195		
чистить щёткой	brush B-260, 261, 262, 263	**Э**	
чистый	clean C-185	эгоистичный	selfish S-129, 130, 131
читать	read R-36, 37, 38	эгоизм	egotism E-33, 34, 35
чихать	sneeze S-339	экзамен	examination E-181
член	member M-105, 106	экипаж	carriage C-63
чмокать губами	smack S-318	экономка	housekeeper H-172
чёрт	devil D-138	эксцентричный	eccentric E-23
что?	what W-83	эластичный	elastic E-46
что нового	what's new W-86	элеватор	elevator E-61, 62
чувствительный	sensitive S-147	элегантный	elegant E-58
чувствовать	feel F-91	электрический	electric E-51
чудной	grotesque G-162	эмансипировать	emancipate E-65
чудо	miracle M-176	эмоция	emotion E-71, 72
чулки	hose H-160, 161	эмфаза	emphasis E-74
чулок	stocking(s) S-492, 493	энергичный	strong-minded S-525
чуять	smell S-324	энтузиазм	enthusiasm E-114
		эпоха	epoch E-130
		этаж	story S-503
Ш		эти	these T-125
		это	it I-214, 215, 216
шабаш	sabbath S-2, 3, 4	это(т)	that T-100, 101, 102
шаг	pace P-1	эффект	effect E-27, 28
шайка	gang G-12	эшафот	scaffold S-53
шар	ball B-17, 18		
швед	Swede S-628		
шелуха	peel P-75, 76	**Ю**	
шериф	sheriff S-190		
шероховатый	rugged R-277	юбка	skirt S-292, 293
шерсть	wool W-169	юг	south S-381
шесть	six S-279	Югославия	Yugoslavia Y-27

Spanish-English Index

A

a	at A-292
a	to T-202, 203
a caballo	horseback H-159
a pesar de	despite D-118
a discreción de vd.	up to you U-59
a la derecha	right R-196
a lo largo de	along A-141
a medio asar	medium M-96
a medio camino	midway M-143
a menos que	unless U-43
a pesar de	in spite of I-129
a través de	through I-166
a través de	across A-57
abajo	below B-109, 110, 111
abajo	down D-294
abandonar	abandon A-2, 3
abandonar	relinquish R-101
abatido	dejected D-73
abatido	depressed D-102
abdicar	abdicate A-7
abeja	bee B-87
abogado	attorney A-302
abogado	lawyer L-39
perecer	perish P-109, 110
abolir	abolish A-12, 13
abonarse	subscribe S-542
aborrecer	abhor A-9
aborto	miscarriage M-178
abra la puerta	open the door O-92
abra la ventana	open the window O-93
Abrahán	Abraham A-17
abrazar	embrace E-70
abrazar	hug H-182
abreviar	condense C-303
abreviar	abbreviate A-4, 5
abrigo	cloak C-195
abrigo	shelter S-188
abrir	open O-88, 89
absolución	absolution A-25, 26
absoluto	absolute A-23
absorber	engross E-105
abstenerse	abstain A-27
abstinencia	abstinence A-28
abstraido	absent-minded A-22
absurdo	absurd A-29

abuela	grandmother G-113, 114
abuelo	grandfather G-111, 112
en abundancia	plenty P-212
abundancia	abundance A-30
aburrido	boring B-198
aburrido	tedious T-54
aburrir	bore B-196
abusar de	take-advantage of T-10, 11
acabado	done D-266, 267
acabar	finish F-142, 143
acalambrado	muscle bound M-265
acariciar	petting P-135
acautelar	caution C-83
accidente	accident A-33
acción	deed D-55
aceitar	oil O-54
aceite	oil O-55
aceptar	accept A-32
acerca de	about A-14
acerca de	concerning C-300
acercarse (a)	approach A-230
acero	steel S-476
ácido	acid A-54
aclamar	acclaim A-34, 35
acomodador	usher U-67
acompañar	accompany A-37
acompañar	attach A-294
aconsejar	counsel C-420
acontecer	happen H-31, 32
acontecimiento	event E-161
acordarse de	remember R-107
acorralar	corner C-402, 403
acostarse	go to bed G-96, 97
acostumbrarse	accustom A-50
actitud	attitude A-301
actor	actor A-65
actriz	actress A-66
actuar	act A-60
acuerdo	accord A-40
acumular	accumulate A-43, 44, 45
acusar	accuse A-48, 49
Adán	Adam A-69
adecuado	adequate A-79
adelante	onward O-87
además	moreover M-219

añadir	add A-70, 71, 72, 73	apuntar	put down P-425
anaquel	shelf S-187	apurarse	hustle H-206
anaranjado	orange O-110, 111, 112	aquí	here H-95
ancho	wide W-119	arado	plow P-214
ancho	broad B-249	araña	spider S-414
ancho de un pelo	hair's-breadth H-8	árbitro	umpire U-10
andamio	scaffold S-53	árbitro	referee R-76
andar furtivamente	sneak S-337	árbol	tree T-273
anexar	annex A-179	arbusto	bush B-275
ángel	angel A-172	archivar	file F-122
ángulo	angle A-174	arco	arch A-236
anhelar	long L-146	ardiente	ardent A-239
anillo	ring R-203	ardilla	squirrel S-442
animal	animal A-177, 178	área	area A-242
animar	encourage E-83	arete	earring E-12
aniquilar	annihilate A-180	argumentar	argue A-243
año	year Y-3	árido	arid A-245
año nuevo	new year N-71	aritmética	arithmetic A-248
ansiedad	anxiety A-198	armario	closet C-199
ante	elk E-64	armas	arms A-250
anteayer	day before yesterday D-19	arpa	harp H-46
		arrepentirse	repent R-123
anteojos	glasses G-56	arrestar	arrest A-258, 259
anteojos	spectacles S-399	arriba	up U-52
antepasados	ancestors A-169, 170	arrodillarse	kneel K-26
anterior	previous P-311	arrojar	throw T-167, 168
antes	before B-91, 92, 93	arroz	rice R-190
antes	formerly F-227	arruinado	broke B-253
antes de	ahead A-117	arruinar	ruin R-278
anticipar	anticipate A-194	arte	art A-262
antiguo	antique A-196	artista	artist A-263
Antiguo Testamento	Old Testament O-62, 63, 64, 65	arzobispo	archbishop A-237
		asar	broil B-252
antiparras	goggles G-79	ascender	ascend A-265
anual	annual A-187	ascensión	ascension A-266
anual	yearly Y-4	ascensor	elevator E-61, 62
anular	annul A-188	asco me da	make me disgusted M-31
anunciar	announce A-181		
aparato	apparatus A-213	asentir	acquiesce A-56
aparcar	park P-30	aserradero	saw mill S-51
aparecer	appear A-217, 218	asesinato	murder M-264
aparente	apparent A-214	así	thus T-174
apartar	remove R-110, 111, 112	Asia	Asia A-270
		asiento	seat S-107
apetecer	crave C-448	asistir	attend A-299
apetito	appetite A-220	asistir	assist A-280
aplaudir	applaud A-221	asociación	association A-284
aplaudir	clap C-179	asociar	associate A-282, 283
aplazar	postpone P-263	asombrar	astonish A-288
aplazar	put off P-427	asombrar	amaze A-154
aplicarse	apply (oneself) A-225	asomo	peep P-77
apoplejía	stroke S-521	aspiración	aim A-119
apostar	gamble G-10	aspirar	aim A-119
apreciar	appreciate A-229	aspirar	aspire A-276
appremiar	urge U-60, 61	astas	antlers A-197
aprender	learn L-52	astuto	cunning C-483
aprender de memoria	memorize M-107, 108	astuto	sly S-315, 316, 317
apresurarse	hurry H-199	astuto	shrewd S-232
aprobación	approbation A-231	asumir	assume A-287
aprobar	endorse E-90, 91, 92	asunto	subject S-540
apuesta	bet B-131	ataque cardíaco	heart attack H-73
apuesta	wager W-1	atar	tie T-179

boca   mouth   M-248
bodas   wedding   W-62
bofetada   slap   S-297
bolsillo   pocket   P-221
bomba   pump   P-400, 401
bombero   fireman   F-148
bonito   pretty   P-307
boquiabierto   open-mouthed   O-91
borracho   drunk   D-319
borrar   delete   D-75, 76, 77
borrar   erase   E-136
bosque   forest   F-216
bosque   woods   W-168
botón   button   B-283, 284
boxear   box   B-214
boy scout   Boy Scout   B-217
brazo   arm   A-249
breve   brief   B-236, 237
brillante   bright   B-238, 239, 240, 241
brillar   glisten   G-57
brillar   shine   S-194
brindar a   toast   T-205
brisa   breeze   B-232
broche   brooch   B-254
broma   joke   J-22
bromear   kid   K-11
bronceado   tan   T-29
bueno   fine   F-134
bueno   good   G-85, 86
búho   owl   O-155
buñuelo   doughnut   D-293
buque de vapor   steamer   S-474
burlarse de   make fun of   M-26
burro   donkey   D-268
buscar   look for   L-155
buscar   search   S-104

C

caballero   gentleman   G-32
caballo   horse   H-158
cabello   hair   H-3
cabeza   head   H-64
cabezudo   thick-skulled   T-129
cabo   point   P-226
cabo   corporal   C-407
cabra   goat   G-73
cacahuete   peanut   P-67
cada   each   E-1
cada día   every day   E-170
cada uno   each one   E-2
cadena   chain   C-100
caer   fall   F-27, 28
café   coffee   C-222
caja   box   B-213
cajetilla   package   P-2
cajón   drawer   D-300
calabaza   pumpkin   P-402, 403
calabaza   squash   S-439
calamitoso   calamitous   C-6

calcetín   sock(s)   S-351, 352
calcular   calculate   C-7
calcular   figure   F-119
cálculo   calculus   C-8
caliente   warm   W-21, 22
caliente   hot   H-164
California   California   C-10
calle   road   R-225
calle   street   S-511
cállese   hush   H-205
calor   heat   H-76, 77
calumniar   backbite   B-6
Calvario   Calvary   C-18, 19
calvo   bald   B-16
cama   bed   B-85
cámara fotográfica   camera   C-21, 22
camaradería   fellowship   F-96
cambiar   exchange   E-192
cambiar   change   C-108, 109
camello   camel   C-20
camino   way   W-49
camisa   shirt   S-200
campamento   camp   C-23
campana   bell   B-103, 104, 105
campeón   champion   C-106
campo   country   C-423
campo   field   F-111, 112
Canadá   Canada   C-26
cancelar   cancel   C-28
canción   song   S-371
candidato   candidate   C-29
canoa   canoeing   C-37
cañón   cannon   C-33, 34
cansado   weary   W-60
cantar   sing   S-268
cantar   chant   C-111
cantidad   amount   A-165, 166
cantidad   quantity   Q-6, 7
capacidad   capacity   C-41
capataz   foreman   F-213
capaz   capable   C-40
capilla   chapel   C-113
capital   capital   C-42, 43
capitán   captain   C-45
capítulo   chapter   C-114
capturar   capture   C-47
cara   face   F-3
carácter   character   C-115, 116
caramba   wow   W-198
carbón   coal   C-210
cárcel   jail   J-1
cardenal   cardinal   C-50
caries   caries   C-60
caridad   charity   C-120
carne   flesh   F-171
carne   meat   M-85
carne de vaca   beef   B-88
caro   expensive   E-214
caro   dear   D-30, 31
carpintero   carpenter   C-61
carrera   race   R-6, 7, 8
carro   wagon   W-4

colgar	hang H-29	concluir	conclude C-301
colina	hill H-110	conducir	conduct C-304, 305
collar	necklace N-34	conejo	rabbit R-3, 4
colocar	place P-188, 189	conexión	connection C-324
colocar	arrange A-255	conferencia	conference C-307
colonia	cologne C-239	conferencia	lecture L-59
color	color C-241, 242, 243	conferencia	talk T-22, 23, 24
columpiar	swing S-642	conferir	confer C-306
coma	comma C-255	conferir	bestow B-130
combatir	combat C-245	confesar	confess C-308
combinar	merge M-126	confesión	confession C-310
comenzar	commence C-258	confesión	admission A-84
comenzar	begin B-97	confianza	confidence C-312
comenzar	start S-455	confidencial	private P-332
comer	eat E-22	confinaza	trust T-295
comerciante	merchant M-123	confirmación	confirmation C-313
comestibles	groceries G-161	conformarse	comply C-285
cómico	comic C-253	confort	comfort C-251
comida	meal M-77	confrontar	confront C-315
comida al aire libre	picnic P-161, 162	confundir	confuse C-316
como	how H-174	confundir	stumped S-534
como	as A-264	confusión	clutter C-209
cómo está vd?	how are you? H-175	congratular	congratulate C-319, 320
cómoda	chest C-141		
cómodo	cozy C-442	connotar	connote C-325
compañía	company C-267	consagración	consecration C-333
comparar	compare C-268	consciente	conscious C-331
compasión	compassion C-269	consciente	aware of A-326
compasión	sympathy S-648	consecuente	consistent C-340
compeler	compel C-270, 271	consecutivo	consecutive C-334
competente	competent C-275	consejo	advice A-97
competir	compete C-273, 274	consentir	consent C-335
complacer	gratify G-123, 124	conserva	jam J-2
completar	complete C-282, 283	considerar	consider C-336, 337, 338
complicar	complicate C-284		
componer	compose C-286	consignar	consign C-339
componer	fix F-155	consolar	console C-341
comprar	buy B-285	constituir	constitute C-342
comprar	purchase P-413	construir	construct C-344, 345
comprender	include I-63	construir	build B-266
comprender	comprehend C-287	consultar	consult C-347
comprometido	engaged E-96, 97	consumir	consume C-348, 349
computar	reckon R-62	contacto	contact C-351, 352
comunicación	communication C-261	contagioso	contagious C-353
comunicación sexual	sexual intercourse S-165	contar	count C-422
		contar	tell about T-65
comunicar	communicate C-260	contar con	rely R-102, 103
comunidad	community C-265, 266	contemplar	contemplate C-355
comunión	Communion, Holy C-262, 263	contender	contend C-358, 359, 360
comunión	confirmation C-314	contento	content C-361
con	with W-150	continuar	continue C-366, 367
con retraso	behind time B-99	continuar	persist P-122, 123
concebir	conceive C-290, 291, 292	contra	against A-110
		contra	versus V-28
conceder	concede C-288	contradecir	contradict C-368
conceder	grant G-115, 116	contrastar	contrast C-370, 371
concentrar	concentrate C-293	contribuir	contribute C-372
concepto	concept C-295, 296	contribuir con su cuota	chip (in) C-154
concertar	mend M-110, 111	contrición	contrition C-373
conciencia	conscience C-328, 329, 330	controlar	control C-374, 375
		controversia	controversy C-376

convencer	convince C-387	crédulo	sucker S-556
conveniente	suitable S-564	creencia	belief B-101
convenir	convene C-377	creerse gran cosa	swell-headed S-638
conversación	conversation C-379, 380	creíble	credible C-455
		crepúsculo	twilight T-310
convertir	convert C-382	criada	maid M-13
convicción	conviction C-384, 385, 386	criado	servant S-156
		criar	raise R-20, 21
convidar	invite I-195	crimen	crime C-456
convite	invitation I-194	cristianismo	Christianity C-165
convocar	summon S-573, 574	cristiano	Christian C-163
cooperar	cooperate C-391	Cristo	Christ C-162
copiar	copy C-394, 395, 396	crítica	criticism C-458
copular	copulate C-393	criticar	find fault F-132, 133
coquetear	flirt F-174	crucificar	crucify C-474
coraje	courage C-425	cruel	cruel C-475, 476, 477
corazón	heart H-71, 72	cruz	cross C-462
corbata	necktie N-35	cuadrado	square S-437
corbata	tie T-180	cuadrante	quadrant Q-1
corbatín	bow tie B-212	cuadro	picture P-163, 164
corcho	cork C-399	cual	which W-96
cordero	lamb L-9	cualquier	any A-201, 202
cordial	cordial C-398	cuando	when W-89
cordón de zapato	shoelaces S-208	cuánto dinero	how much money H-180
Corea	Korea K-39		
coronar	crown C-470, 471, 472	cuántos	how many H-178
coronilla	coronet C-406	cuántos años	how old H-181
corpulento	stout S-504	cuaquero	Quaker Q-5
correcto	correct C-408, 409	cuaresma	Lent L-72
correcto	right R-198	cuarto	quarter Q-9
corredor	hall H-14	cuarto	fourth F-242
corredor	corridor C-411	cuarto de baño	bathroom B-54
corregir	correct C-408, 409	cuarto de hora	quarter-hour Q-10
correo	mail M-15, 16	cuatro	four F-240
correoso	tough T-238, 239, 240	cubrir	cover C-434, 435, 436, 437
correr	run R-281, 282		
corriente	current C-493	cuchara	spoon S-425
corrupto	corrupt C-412	cuchichear	whisper W-104
cortadora de césped	lawnmower L-38	cuchillo	knife K-27, 28, 29
cortar	cut-off C-502	cuello	collar C-232
corte	court C-427	cuenco	bowl B-210
cortejar	court(ing) C-430	cuenta	account A-42
cortés	courteous C-428	cuenta abierta	charge C-117, 118
cortés	polite P-237	cuento	tale T-20
cortina	curtain C-497	cuerda	twine T-311
corto	short S-218, 219	cuerda	cord C-397
corto de miras	narrow-minded N-14	cuerda	rope R-252, 253
cosa	thing T-137	cuerdecilla	string S-519
cosecha	harvest H-47, 48, 49	cuernos	horns H-157
coser	sew S-163	cuerpo	body B-191
cosméticos	cosmetics C-413	cuestionario	questionnaire Q-21
costa	cost C-414	cuidadoso	careful C-58
costa	coast C-211	cuidar	mind M-161
costa	seaside S-105	cuidar	tend T-76
costoso	costly C-415	cuidar de	take care of T-15, 16, 17
costumbre	custom C-498		
costumbre	practice P-278, 279, 280	cuidar de	care C-53, 54
		culebra	snake S-331, 332, 333, 334, 335, 336
costurera	dressmaker D-305		
crear	create C-453	culebra de cascabel	rattlesnake R-31
crecer	grow G-167	culpa	fault F-72, 73
crédulo	gullible G-180	culpable	guilty G-177, 178

culpar	blame B-167
cultivar	raise R-20, 21
curiosear	rubberneck R-271, 272
curioso	curious C-487, 489

D

dados	dice D-149
dama	lady L-6
dañar	hurt H-200, 201, 202, 203
dañar	harm H-44, 45
dar	render R-114, 115
dar	extend E-230
dar	give G-47, 48
dar aviso secreto a	tip off T-197
dar patadas	kick K-7
darse cuenta de	realize R-45
de	of O-37
de	from F-280
de aquí para allá	back and forth B-5
de buen corazón	soft-hearted S-259
de cualquier modo	anyhow A-203
de hombros anchos	broad shouldered B-251
de moda	fashionable F-59
de nada	you're welcome Y-20, 21
de ningún valor	no good N-90, 91
de veras	indeed I-69
de vez en cuando	once in a while O-70
de voluntad débil	weak-minded W-54
debajo de	beneath B-114, 115
debate	debate D-34
deber	duty D-337
deber	must M-268
deber	owe O-154
deber	obligation O-14, 15, 16
debiera	ought to O-138
débil	hopelessly weak H-154
débil	feeble F-86
débil	weak W-53
débito	debit D-35
decaer	decay D-37
decente	decent D-40
decepcionado	disappointed D-182, 183
decepcionar	disappoint D-181
decidirse	decide D-42
decidirse	make up one's mind M-37
decir	say S-52
decir	tell T-64
declarar	state S-459
declarar	declare D-44
declinar	decline D-45, 46
decorar	decorate D-48, 49
decrépito	decrepit D-53
decretar	decree D-51, 52
dedal	thimble T-133
dedo	finger F-138

dedo del pie	toe T-208
deducir	deduct D-54
defecar	defecate D-61
defender	defend D-62
deficiencia	deficiency D-65
definir	define D-66, 67
defraudar	defraud D-71
degeneración	degeneration D-72
dejar	quit Q-27
dejar	part from P-36
dejar	leave L-56
dejar caer	drop D-313
dejar de	fail F-11, 12, 13
delantal	apron A-234
delante de	before B-91, 92, 93
deleite	delight D-80
deletrear	spell S-410
delgado	slender S-305
delgado	thin T-134, 135
delicioso	delicious D-78, 79
deme	give me G-51
demócrata	democrat D-84
demoler	demolish D-85
demonio	demon D-86
demostrar	demonstrate D-87
dentista	dentist D-90
dentro	inside I-126
dentro de	within W-155
depender	depend D-94, 95, 96
depositar	deposit D-100, 101
derecho	straight S-505
derramar	spread S-428, 429
derrapar	skid S-286
derretir	melt M-104
derribar	knock down K-32
derrotado	defeated D-60
derrotar	defeat D-59
desafío	challenge C-105
desairar	snub S-343
desalentar	discourage D-198, 199
desalojar	evict E-173
desamparar	forsake F-229, 230, 231
desaparecer	disappear D-180
desaparecido	gone G-82, 83, 84
desarrollarse	develop D-131, 132, 133
desatender	disregard D-226
desatino	folly F-192
desayuno	breakfast B-229
desbordamiento	overflow O-150
desbordar	run over R-286
descanso	rest R-161, 162
descartar	cast off C-70
descartar	discard D-187, 188, 189
descendiente	descendant D-106
descendiente	offspring O-49
desconectar	disconnect D-196
desconfianza	distrust D-236
descontento	discontented D-197
descontento	dissatisfaction D-228

descortés	impolite I-38	destruir	destroy D-119
describir	describe D-109, 110, 111	desunir	disjoin D-214
		desvanecerse	fade away F-10
descubrir	detect D-122	desvanecerse	vanish V-15
descubrir	discover D-201	desviar	sidetrack S-244
descuidado	careless C-59	desviar	deviate D-135, 136
descuidado	heedless H-83	desviar	deflect D-70
descuidar	neglect N-44	detective	detective D-123, 124
desde	since S-265	detener	arrest A-258, 259
desde	thence T-116	detener(se)	halt H-19
desde entonces	thenceforth T-117	deteriorar	deteriorate D-125
desde entonces	from then on F-281	determinar	determine D-127
desde que	ever since E-167	detestar	detest D-128, 129
desdén	scorn S-74, 75	detestar	loathe L-131
desear	desire D-114, 115	detrás de	behind B-98
desear	wish W-147, 148	Detroit	Detroit D-130
desechar	cast out C-71	deuda	obligation O-14, 15, 16
desemejante	unlike U-44	devoción	devotion D-142
deseoso	anxious A-199	devorar	devour D-143
desequilibrado	mentally unbalanced M-117, 118, 119, 120, 121	devoto	devout D-144
		día	day D-17
		día de fiesta	holiday H-133
desesperar	lose hope L-162	diablo	devil D-138
desfalcar	embezzle E-68	diácono	deacon D-23, 24
desfigurar	deface D-58	diamante	diamond D-145, 146, 147
desfile	parade P-23, 24		
desgarrar	rend R-113	diario	daily D-5
deshonesto	dishonest D-212	diarrea	diarrhea D-148
desinflar	deflate D-68	diccionario	dictionary D-150, 151
deslizar	slide S-307, 308	diente	tooth T-223
deslumbrar	dazzle D-22	dientes	teeth T-55
desmaña	clumsiness C-206	diestro	clever C-188, 189
desmañado	clumsy C-208	diestro	adept A-78
desmañado	awkward A-329	diez	ten T-75
desmayarse	faint F-15, 16	diezma	tithe T-200
desmayarse	pass out P-47	diferencia	difference D-156, 158
desnudo	naked N-5	diferir	differ D-155
desnudo	nude N-131	diferir	defer D-64
desnudo	bare B-33, 34	difícil	difficult D-159, 160, 161
desobedecer	disobey D-217		
desocupado	idle I-10	difícil	hard H-36, 37
desorden	disorder D-218	dígame	tell me T-66
despachar	dispatch D-219	dilatar	expand E-208
despachurrar	squash S-440	diligencia	diligence D-165, 166
despacio	slow S-314	Dinamarca	Denmark D-89
desparramar(se)	scatter S-60	dinamarqués	Dane D-9
despedir	discharge D-190, 191	dinero	money M-203, 204, 205
despedir	fire F-147		
despertar	arouse A-254	diócesis	diocese D-171
despertar	wake up W-12	Diós	God G-75
despierto	awake A-323	dirección	address A-76, 77
desplomarse	collapse C-231	dirección	direction D-174, 175
desplome	crash C-447	dirigir	direct D-172, 173
despreciar	despise D-116, 117	disciplinar	discipline D-193, 194, 195
desprecio	contempt C-356, 357		
desprender	detach D-121	discípulo	disciple D-192
después de	after A-104, 105	discurso	discourse D-200
desquitarse	retaliate R-170, 171	discurso	address A-75
destenirse	fade F-9	discurso	speech S-404, 405
desterrar	banish B-26	discusión	discussion D-205
destornillador	screwdriver S-93, 94	discutir	discuss D-203

diseñar   draw   D-298
disentir   disagree   D-179
disgustado   displeased   D-221
disgusto   disgust   D-208
disminuir   decrease   D-50
disolver   dissolve   D-230
disparar   shoot   S-212, 213
disparo   shot   S-221
dispensar   excuse   E-199
dispuesto   willing   W-129, 130, 131
disputar   dispute   D-225
distancia   distance   D-231
distracción   distraction   D-233
distribuir   distribute   D-234, 235
diversión   fun   F-290
diverso   diverse   D-240, 241
diversos   sundry   S-579
divertido   amusing   A-168
divertido   funny   F-294
dividendo   dividend   D-246
dividir   divide   D-244, 245
divino   divine   D-247
divorciar   divorce   D-249, 250, 251

doblar   bend   B-113
doblar   fold   F-189
doble   double   D-288
doctor   doctor   D-255
doctrina   doctrine   D-256, 257
doctrinar   indoctrinate   I-81
dólar   dollar   D-263, 264
doler   hurt   H-200, 201, 202, 203
dolor   pain   P-5
dolor   ache   A-51
dolor   grief   G-155, 156
dolor   sorrow   S-373
dolor de cabeza   headache   H-65
dolor de muelas   toothache   T-224
dolor de oído   earache   E-8
domicilio   domicile   D-265
domicilio   residence   R-145, 146
dominar (marido)   henpeck   H-93
domingo   Sunday   S-577, 578
doncella   maiden   M-14
donde   where   W-91, 92
dormido   asleep   A-275
dormir   sleep   S-301, 302
dormitar   doze   D-295
dos   two   T-312
dos puntos   colon   C-240
dos veces   twice   T-309
drama   drama   D-297
droga   drug   D-317
dudar   doubt   D-289, 290, 291
dulce   sweet   S-632
dulces   candy   C-31, 32
duplicar   duplicate   D-332, 333
durante   during   D-334
durar   wear   W-59

durar   last   L-19
durar   persevere   P-118, 119, 120, 121
duro   hard   H-36, 37

E

ebanista   cabinetmaker   C-2
echar a perder   spoil   S-423
echar al correo   mail   M-15, 16
echar fuera   throw out   T-120
económico   inexpensive   I-89
edad   age   A-111
edificio   building   B-267
educación   education   E-25
educar   educate   E-24
efecto   effect   E-27, 28
Egipto   Egypt   E-36
egoísta   selfish   S-129, 130, 131
egotismo   egotism   E-33, 34, 35
ejecutar   perform   P-100, 101
ejemplo   example   E-186
ejercitar   drill   D-308
ejercito   army   A-251
él   he   H-63
el   the   T-104
el mío   mine   M-164
el mismo   same   S-27, 28, 29
el mismo   himself   H-112
el señor   lord   L-159
el suyo   hers   H-100
el suyo   their   T-110
el uno al otro   each other   E-3
elástico   elastic   E-46
elástico   rubber   R-268, 269, 270
elección   choice   C-157
eléctrico   electric   E-51
electrocutar   electrocute   E-56
elefante   elephant   E-59
elegante   elegant   E-58
elegir   elect   E-49
elevar   elevate   E-60
eliminar   eliminate   E-63
eliminar   remove   R-110, 111, 112
ella   she   S-183
ella misma   herself   H-101
ellos   they   T-126
ellos mismos   themselves   T-113
emancipar   emancipate   E-65
embriagar   intoxicate   I-181
embromar   tease   T-51, 52, 53
embuste   fib   F-107
emigrar   migrate   M-149
emocion   emotion   E-71, 72
emocionar   thrill   T-163, 164
empalmar   splice   S-421
emparedado   sandwich   S-35
empedernido   hard-boiled   H-38
emperador   emperor   E-73

G

garantía	guarantee G-169, 170	grosella	currant C-491
gas	gas G-15	grosero	rough R-259, 260, 261
gasolina	gas G-16	grotesco	grotesque G-162
gastado	worn W-176, 177	grupo	group G-165, 166
gastar	spend S-412	guadaña	scythe S-99
gastar	consume C-348, 349	guadañar	mow M-252, 253
gastos	expense E-213	guante	glove G-66
gatear	scramble S-88	guapo	handsome H-28
gato	cat C-72	guardar	guard G-171
generación	generation G-26	guardar	keep K-1
género	kind K-16	guerra	war W-20
generoso	generous G-27, 28	guiar	lead L-43
gente	people P-92	guiar	guide G-176
geografía	geography G-35	guiar	drive D-312
geometría	geometry G-36	guiñar	wink W-140
gimnasio	gym G-183	guirnaldas	wreath W-199
girar sobre	hinge H-116	guitarra	guitar G-179
globo	globe G-58, 59	gusano	worm W-175
gloria	glory G-64, 65	gustarle a	like L-103, 105
glorioso	glorious G-63	gusto	taste T-34
glotonería	gluttony G-68		
gobernar	govern G-98		
gobierno	government G-99	**H**	
golf	golf G-81		
golocha	overshoes O-151	haber	have H-56
golpe	blow B-182	había una vez	once upon a time O-73
golpear	pound P-266, 267	habilidad	skill S-287
golpear	rap R-23	habilidad	ability A-10
golpear	hit H-120, 121, 122	habitar	dwell D-339
golpear	strike S-517	hábito	habit H-1
gordo	fat F-63, 64	hablar	speak S-392
gorra	cap C-39	hablar	talk T-22, 23, 24
gotear	drip D-311	hace	ago A-113
gotear	leak L-48	hace calor	hot weather H-169
governar	rule R-279, 280	hace poco	while ago, a W-98, 99, 100
gozar	enjoy E-106		
gozne	hinge H-115	hace unos días	few days ago F-105
grabar	engrave E-103	hace unos segundos	few seconds ago F-106
gracia	grace G-103, 104	hacer	do D-254
gracias	thank you T-99	hacer	make M-23
gracioso	gracious G-105	hacer calceta	knit K-30
graduarse	graduate G-106, 107	hacer crochet	crochet C-460
Gran Bretaña	Great Britain G-139	hacer ejercicio	exercise E-200
Gran Bretaña	Britain B-247	hacer muecas	make a face M-24
granada	grenade G-153	hacer saber	let know L-80, 81
grande	great G-135, 136	hacer señas	beckon B-82
grande	big B-142, 143	hacerse	become B-83
grande	large L-16	hacía	toward T-242, 243, 244
grandioso	grand G-109, 110		
granizo	hail H-2	hallar	find F-131
granja	farm F-47, 48, 49	hambre	famine F-39
grasa	fat F-65	hamburguesa	hamburger B-20, 21
grasa	grease G-133	harina	flour F-178, 179
grasiento	fatty F-71	harina de avena	oatmeal O-3
grave	grave G-126	hasta	till T-185
griego	Grecian G-143	hasta	up to U-57
grieta	crack C-443	hasta	until U-48
gris	gray G-129, 130, 131, 132	hasta aquí	thus far T-175
		hasta aquí	so far S-356
gritar	cry C-481	Hawaii	Hawaii H-60
gritar	shout S-225	hebreo	Hebrew H-80
gritar	yell Y-6	helado	frozen F-284

inducir	induce I-86	interrogar	interrogate I-169, 170
inducir	entice E-116	interrogacion	query Q-14, 15
indulgencia	indulgence I-87	interrumpir	interrupt I-173
industrioso	industrious I-88	intervenir	interfere I-164
inexperto	unskilled U-47	introspección	introspection I-185
infante	infant I-90	inundación	flood F-176
infierno	hell H-86, 87	inventar	devise D-140, 141
infiltrar	infiltrate I-91	inventar	invent I-187, 188
infinito	infinite I-92	inverso	reverse R-185, 186
influencia	influence I-95, 96, 97, 98	invertir(fondos)	invest I-190
		investigación	research R-138
informar	inform I-99, 100	investigar	investigate I-191, 192
ingenuo	naive N-4	invierno	winter W-141, 142
Inglaterra	England E-100	inyección	injection I-106
inglés	Englishman E-102	inyección	shot S-221
inicial	initial I-104	ir	go G-69, 70
iniciar	initiate I-105	ir de compras	shop S-214
injusticia	injustice I-110	ir por	fetch F-101
injusto	unfair U-25, 26	ira	ire I-198
injusto	unjust U-41	Irlanda	Ireland I-199
inmaculada concepción	Immaculate Conception I-25	irresponsable	irresponsible I-203, 204
		irritable	irritable I-200
inmaculado	immaculate I-24	isla	island I-209, 210
inmediato	immediate I-26	Italia	Italy I-218, 219
inmenso	immense I-28	italiano	Italian I-217
inmodesto	immodest I-29	izquierda	left L-61
inmovilizar	pin P-177		
innecesario	unnecessary U-45, 46		
inocencia	innocence I-115		**J**
inocular	inoculate I-117		
inquieto	restless R-165	jabón	soap S-344, 345, 346, 347
inquieto	anxious A-200	jactarse	brag B-219
inquietud	concern C-298	jactarse	boast B-189
inquietud	worry W-181, 182, 183	Japón	Japan J-3
insecto	bug B-265	japonés	Japanese J-4
insecto	insect I-123, 124	jardín	garden G-13
insensible	insensate I-125	jefe de cocina	chef C-137
inservible	worthless W-192, 193	Jerusalén	Jerusalem J-8
insistir	insist I-127	jesuíta	Jesuit J-9
insolente	saucy S-44	Jesús	Jesus J-10
inspeccionar	inspect I-128	jirafa	giraffe G-45
inspeccionar	supervise S-587	joven	young Y-18
instalar	install I-130	jovial	jolly J-23
instar	coax C-213	judaísmo	Judaism J-29
instituir	institute I-133, 134	judío	Jew J-12
instruir	instruct I-136	juego	game G-11
instrumento	instrument I-139	jueves	Thursday T-173
insultar	insult I-140, 141, 142	jugar	play P-202
intelecto	intellect I-144	jugar a los bolos	bowl B-211
intelectual	intellectual I-145	jugar al naipe	card playing C-51
inteligente	intelligent I-147	junta	board B-188
inteligente	bright B-238, 239, 240, 241	juntar	join J-17, 18, 19, 20
		juntos	together T-209
intensidad	intensity I-149	juramento	oath O-2
intento	intent I-151	jurar	swear S-621
intercambio	interchange I-154	jurar	sworn S-645
interceptar	intercept I-153	justicia	justice J-38, 39
interés	interest I-155, 156, 157	justo	just J-35, 36
interés	interest I-158, 159	justo	righteous R-200
internacional	international I-167	justo	fair F-17
interpretar	interpret I-168	juzgar	judge J-30

L

la China	China C-151
la mayor parte	most M-227
la vuelta al mundo	around the world A-253
labor	labor L-1
laca de uñas	nail polish N-3
lado	side S-242
lado a lado	side by side S-243
ladrar	bark B-35
ladrón	burglar B-271
ladrón	thief T-130, 131
lago	lake L-8
lágrima	tear T-49
lamentar	mourn M-244
lamentarse	rue R-276
lana	wool W-169
langosta	lobster L-132
lapiz	pencil P-85
lapiz de labios	lipstick L-115
largo	long L-145
lata	can C-24
latido	heartbeat H-74, 75
látigo	whip W-101
latín	Latin L-31, 32
lavado	wash W-25, 26, 27
lavar los platos	dishwashing D-213
lazo	bow B-208
leal	loyal L-175
lección	lesson L-77
leche	milk M-154
lechuga	lettuce L-84, 85
leer	read R-36, 37, 38
leer los labios	read lips R-39
legal	legal L-64
legar	bequeath B-121
legislatura	legislature L-65
lejos	off O-38, 39
lejos	far F-43
lengua	language L-13, 14
lengua	tongue T-218
lenguaje	speech S-404, 405
leño	log L-138
lentes	eyeglasses E-237
león	lion L-113
leopardo	leopard L-73
lepra	leprosy L-74
levantarse	rise R-212, 213, 214
levantarse	get up G-42
levantarse	arise A-246, 247
ley	law L-37
liberación	liberation L-88
libertad	liberty L-89
libertar	deliver D-81
libra	pound P-266, 267
libre	free F-257, 258
libro	book B-193
licencia	license L-91, 92
ligar	bind B-150
ligero	light L-101
ligero	slight S-309

lima	file F-121
limbo	limbo L-106
límite	limit L-107
limón	lemon L-67, 68, 69
limousina	limousine L-108
limpiar	clean C-185, 186
limpiar el suelo	mop M-217
limpio	clean C-185, 186
Lincoln	Lincoln L-109
linea	line L-110
linotipia	Linotype L-112
linterna eléctrica	flashlight F-159
líquido	liquid L-116
liso	smooth S-330
lisonjear	flatter F-163, 164
lista	list L-119, 120
lista larga	long list L-148
listo	ready R-40, 41, 42, 43
listo	smart S-323
lo	it I-214, 215, 216
lo (el)	him H-111
lobo	wolf W-159
loco	crazy C-449, 450, 451
loco	nuts N-138, 139, 140
loco	mad M-5
loco	insane I-121
locomotora	locomotive L-137
lodoso	muddy M-256
lógica	logic L-139
lograr	achieve A-52, 53
los	them T-111
Los Ángeles	Los Angeles L-160
los Estados Unidos	United States U-35
lucha	wrestling W-202
luchar	struggle S-526
luchar	fight F-117, 118
luego	by and by B-288
lugar	place P-188, 189
lujuria	lust L-180
luna	moon M-214, 215
lunes	Monday M-202
lustrar zapatos	shine shoes S-195
Lutero	Luther L-181
luz	light L-100

LL

llama	flame F-158
llamado	recall R-55, 56
llamado	called C-14
llamaco	so-called S-348
llamar	call C-12, 13
llano	even C-158
llanura	plain P-191, 192
llave	key K-6
llave	wrench W-201
llegada	arrival A-260
llegar a	reach R-34
llenar	fill F-123
lleno	full F-288, 289
lleno de gente	crowded C-469

llevar	carry C-64, 65	maravilla	marvel M-60
llevar	wear W-58	maravilla	wonder W-162
llevarse	take away T-14	maravilloso	wonderful W-165
llorar	weep W-68, 69	marbete	check C-132
llorar	cry C-479, 480	marcar	mark M-56
lluvia	rain R-17	marchar	march M-54, 55
		marchar	parade P-23, 24

M

		marco	frame F-249
		marica	fairy F-19
		marido	husband H-204
macho	male M-38	marinero	seaman S-103
madera	lumber L-177, 178	marinero	sailor S-13, 14
madera	wood W-167	mariposa	butterfly B-281
madrastra	stepmother S-482	martes	Tuesday T-300
madre	mother M-229, 230	martillo	hammer H-22
madrina	godmother G-77	mártir	martyr M-59
maduro	mature M-70	más	more M-218
maduro	ripe R-210	más	plus P-219
mágico	magic M-8	más allá de	beyond B-134
magnánimo	magnanimous M-10	más bien	rather R-29
magnífico	magnificent M-12	más lejos	farther F-54
maíz	corn C-401, 405	más tarde	later L-28, 29
majestad	majesty M-22	mascar	chew C-142
mal	evil E-175	masilla	putty P-428
mal humorado	cross C-463	masticar	masticate M-66
maldecir	damn D-6	matar	slay S-300
maleta	suitcase S-565	matar	kill K-13
maleta	valise V-11	matemáticas	mathematics M-68
malgastar	squander S-436	material	matter M-69
malgastón	waste W-34, 35	matrimonio	marriage M-57
malo	wicked W-118	mayor	elder E-47
malo	bad B-9, 10	el mayor	eldest E-48
mamá	mama M-39	mecánico	mechanic M-86, 87
mañana	morning M-222	mecedora	rocking chair R-238, 239
mañana	forenoon F-214		
mañana	tomorrow T-217	medalla	medal M-89
mancha	stain S-444	media	stocking S-492, 493
mandamientos	commandments C-257	media hora	half-hour H-13
mandar	bid B-139, 141	mediano	median M-92
mandar	command C-256	medianoche	midnight M-141
manejar	manage M-41	medias	hose H-160, 161
manejar	run R-283	medicamento	medicine M-93
manera	manner M-45	medio	middle M-140
mano	hand H-23, 24	medio	mean M-80
manso	meek M-97	medio	midst M-142
manso	tame T-28	medio	half H-11, 12
mantel	tablecloth T-4	medio sordo	hard-of-hearing H-39
mantener	maintain M-19	mediodía	midday M-139
mantenimiento	maintenance M-21	mediodía	noon N-101
mantequilla	butter B-280	medir	scale S-54, 55, 56
manual	manual M-47	medir	measure M-84
manufacturar	manufacture M-49	medir	gauge G-23
manzana	apple A-223	meditar	meditate M-94
mapa	map M-51	mejicano	Mexican M-135
mapache	raccoon R-5	mejilla	cheek C-133
mapurite	skunk S-294	mejor	best B-128
maquillaje	make-up M-38	mejor	better B-132
máquina	machine M-1	mejorar	improve I-50
máquina	engine E-99	melancolía	melancholy M-101
máquina de lavar	washing machine W-30	melocotón	peach P-63, 64, 65
maquinaria	machinery M-3	melodía	melody M-102
mar	sea S-100	melón	muskmelon M-267

melón	melon M-103	mojado	wet W-81
memoria	memory M-109	molaza	molasses M-200
mencionar	mention M-122	moler	grind G-159
mendigar	ask alms A-274	molestar	bother B-204, 205
mendigar	beg B-94, 95	molestar	disturb D-237
mendigo	panhandler P-14	molestar	trouble T-290
menor	less L-75	momento	moment M-201
menor de edad	minor M-170	moneda	coin C-223, 224
menos	minus M-171, 172, 173	moneda corriente	currency C-492
menos	less L-76	monja	nun N-135
menos	least L-54	mono	monkey M-206
mensaje	message M-129	mono	cute C-500, 501
menstruación	menstruate M-113	mono	ape A-208
mental	mental M-115	monótono	monotonous M-207, 208, 209
mente	mind M-159, 160, 163		
mentir	lie L-94, 95	montaña	mountain M-243
mentiroso	liar L-87	montar	ride R-192
menudo	minute M-175	morder	bite B-161
merecer	deserve D-113	morfina	morphine M-224
mérito	merit M-127	moribundo	dying D-341
mes	month M-210	morir	die D-152, 153
mes pasado	last month L-22	mormón	Mormon M-221
mesa	table T-2, 3	mortal	mortal M-225
meta	goal G-72	mortificación	mortification M-226
metal	metal M-130, 131	mosca	fly F-185
meterse	meddle M-90, 91	mostrar	show S-227
metodista	Methodist M-133	motivar	motivate M-236
método	method M-132	motivo	motive M-238, 239, 240
mezclar	mix M-191		
mezclar	mingle M-167, 168	motocicleta	motorcycle M-243
mezquino	stingy S-488, 489, 490	motor	motor M-241
mi	my M-272	motor	electric motor E-53
mí	me M-76	mover(se)	move M-249
micrómetro	micrometer M-138	movimiento	motion M-233
miedo	fear F-78, 79	mozo	waiter W-6, 7
miembro	member M-105, 106	muchacha	girl G-46
mientras(que)	while W-97	muchacho	boy B-215, 216
miércoles	Wednesday W-63	muchedumbre	crowd C-468
miércoles de ceniza	Ash Wednesday A-269	mucho	much M-255
mil	thousand T-154	mucho	lot L-164
milagro	miracle M-176	muchos	many M-50
militar	military M-153	mudable	changeable C-110
milla	mile M-151	mudo	mute M-269
millón	million M-155	mudo	speechless S-406
Milwaukee	Milwaukee M-156	mueca	grimace G-158
mina	mine M-164	muerto	dead D-25, 26
minuto	minute M-174	muestra	sample S-31
mirar	look L-149	mujer	wife W-123
mirar fixo	gaze G-25	mujer	woman W-160
misericordia	mercy M-124, 125	mula	mule M-258
misión	mission M-183, 184	multa	penalty P-82
mismo	itself I-221	multa	fine F-135
misterio	mystery M-274	multiple	multiple M-260
mitra	mitre M-189	multiplicar	multiply M-261, 262
mición	motion M-232	mundo	earth E-13
moda	stylish S-538	mundo	world W-174
modelo	model M-196	muñeca	wrist W-203
moderado	mild M-150	muñeca	doll D-262
modesto	modest M-197	muro	wall W-14, 15
modificar	modify M-198	música	music D-266
mofar	mock M-195	mutuo	mutual M-270, 271
mofarse	sneer S-338	muy	very V-30

N

nabo	turnip T-306
nacer	born B-199, 200, 201
nacido	nee N-36
nacimiento	birth B-153, 154, 155
nación	nation N-16
nada	naught N-18, 19, 20
nada	nothing N-119, 120, 121, 122
nadar	swim S-640
naranja	orange N-110, 111, 112
narcótico	narcotics N-10
narcótico	dope D-287
narisón	nosy N-111, 112, 113
nariz	nose N-110
narrar	narrate N-11
nata	cream C-452
natural	natural N-17
náusea	nausea N-22
navaja de afeitar	razor R-33
navidad	Christmas C-166, 167
navío	ship S-197
nazi	Nazi N-25
necesario	necessary N-30, 31
necesidad	need N-37, 38, 39
necio	silly S-258
negación	negation N-41
negar	deny D-91, 92
negarse	decline D-47
negativo	negative N-42
negocio	concern C-299
negocios	business B-276
negro	black B-164
negro	Negro N-45, 46
nervio	nerve N-51
nervioso	nervous N-52
neutral	neutral N-58
New Jersey	New Jersey N-64
ni	neither N-49
ni	nor N-102
nido	nest N-55
nieve	snow S-342
ningún	none N-96, 97, 98, 99
ninguno	no N-86
niño	kid K-10
niño	child C-147
niños	children C-148
no	not N-114, 115
no	no N-87
no creer	don't believe D-273
no diga	don't tell D-282
no gustarle	don't care for D-277
no hacer caso de	ignore I-14
no hecho	not done N-117
no importa	make no difference M-33
no importa	doesn't matter D-258
no importarle	don't care D-274, 275, 276
no judio	Gentile G-29

no lo haga	do not D-269, 270
no mejorar	not improve N-126
no poder	cannot C-35, 36
no querer	don't want D-283
no saber	don't know D-279
no saber nada	know nothing K-38
no ser a su gusto	no taste for N-116
noble	noble N-88
noche	night N-83
noción	notion N-127
nombrado	named N-7
nombrar	appoint A-226
nombre	name N-6
nordeste	northeast N-106
normal	normal N-103
nordeste	northwest N-107
norte	north N-104
Norteamérica	North America N-105
Noruega	Norway N-108
nos	us U-63
nosotros	we W-51, 52
nosotros mismos	ourselves N-140
notar	note N-118
noticias	tidings T-178
notificar	notify N-124, 125
novato	green G-150
novedad	novelty N-129
nube	cloud C-204
nudo	knot K-34
nuestro	our N-139
Nueva Inglaterra	New England N-63
Nueva Orleáns	New Orleans N-65
Nueva York	New York N-72
nueve	nine N-84
nueve de nosotros	nine of us N-85
nuevo	new N-62
Nuevo Testamento	New Testament N-68, 69, 70
nuez	nut N-137
numero	number N-132, 133
numeroso	numerous N-134
nunca	never N-59
nunca jamas	never again N-60

O

o	o O-1
o	or O-107, 108
O. K.	O. K. O-57, 58
o . . . o	either E-41, 42, 43
obedecer	mind M-162
obediencia	obedience O-4
obeso	obese O-6
obispo	bishop B-158, 159
objetar	object O-9, 10
objetivo	objective O-12
objeto	object O-8
oblación	oblation O-13
obligación	obligation O-14, 15, 16
obligado	bound B-207
obscuro	dark D-14

observación	remark R-106	órdenes sagradas	holy orders H-140
observar	observe O-19, 20	oreja	ear E-7
observar	watch (observe) W-36, 37	organización	organization O-124, 125
obstáculo	obstacle O-21	orgullo	pride P-315
obstinado	obstinate O-22	orgulloso	proud P-384
obstinado	strong-minded S-525	orientación	orientation O-127
obtener	obtain O-24	oriental	Oriental O-126
obtener	procure P-348	origen	origin O-128, 129, 130
obtener	get G-39	original	original O-132
obvio	obvious O-25	orilla	shore S-217
ocasión	opportunity O-100, 101, 102, 103, 104	orina	urine U-62
		ornamento	ornament O-135, 136
ocasión	occasion O-26	oro	gold G-80
ocasional	occasional O-27	oscuro	obscure O-18
océano	ocean O-31, 32	oso	bear B-66
ocho	eight E-38	ostra	oyster O-157
ocio	leisure L-66	otoño	autumn A-316, 317
octavo	eighth E-39	otoño	fall F-25, 26
oculista	oculist O-34	otorgar	grant G-115, 116
ocupación	occupation O-29	otra vez	again A-109
ocupado	busy B-277, 278	otro	another A-191
ocurrir	occur O-30	otro	other O-137
odio	hate H-52, 53	oveja	sheep S-186
oeste	west W-80		
ofender	offend O-40		
ofensivo	obnoxious O-17		**P**
oferta	offering O-45		
oferta	bid B-140	paciencia	patience P-52, 53
oficial	officer O-48	padrastro	stepfather S-481
oficina	office O-46	padre	father F-66, 67
ofrecer	offer O-42, 43	padre	father F-68
oh	oh O-52	padrino	godfather G-76
oh ya veo	oh I see O-53	pagar	pay P-57, 58, 59
oiga	hark H-42	página	page P-4
oir	hear H-68	país	land L-11, 12
ojo	eye E-236	país	country C-424
oler	smell S-324	Paises Bajos, los	Netherlands N-56, 57
olla	pot P-264	pala	shovel S-226
olor	odor O-36	pala	paddle P-3
olor	scent S-62	pala	spade S-386
olvidar	forget F-221, 222	palabra	word W-170
omisión	omission O-66, 67	pálido	pale P-11
onda	wave W-46	palillo	stick S-484
operación	operation O-96, 97	palmada	smack S-318
operar	operate O-95	palpar	feel F-91
opinión	opinion O-98	pan	bread B-226
oponente	opponent O-99	pan dulce	muffin M-257
oponer	oppose O-105	panadero	baker B-13
oportunidad	opporunity O-100, 101, 102, 103, 104	pandilla	gang G-12
		paño para lavarse	washcloth W-28
opuesto	opposite O-106	pantalones	trousers T-291
opuesto	reverse R-185, 186	pantalones	pants P-15
oración	sentence S-149	pañuelo	handkerchief H-25
orador	orator O-114	papá	dad D-2
orador	speaker S-393	papa	papa P-16
oral	oral O-109	papa	pope P-246
orbe	orb O-115	papal	papal P-17
órbita	orbit O-116, 117	papel	paper P-18
orden	order O-119	papel de lija	sandpaper S-34
ordenado	orderly O-122	papera	mumps M-263
ordenar	ordain O-118	par	pair P-10

pesado	heavy H-79	poder	may M-72, 73, 74
pesado	weighty W-73	poder	power P-274, 275
pesar	weigh W-70, 71	poderío	might M-144, 146
pesaroso	sorrowful S-374	poderoso	mighty M-148
pescar	fish F-151, 152	podrido	rotten R-258
pesquisa	quest Q-16	poema	poem P-222
peste	pest P-133	policía	police P-231
petirrojo	robin R-234	policía	cop C-392
pez	fish F-151, 152	política	policy P-233, 234
piano	piano P-152	pollo	chicken C-144
picar	pick P-153	Polonia	Poland P-229
picar	peck P-70	polvos	powder P-272, 273
picar	prod P-349	ponderar	ponder P-238
pícaro	naughty N-21	poner	put P-424
pichón	pigeon P-171	ponerse de pie	stand S-449, 450, 451
pico	peak P-66	pontífice	pontiff P-239
pico	beak B-63	por	by B-287
pie	foot F-200	por ciento	percent P-96
piedad	pity P-187	por favor	please P-209
piedra	stone S-494, 495	por lo tanto	hence H-92
piel	skin S-289, 290	por lo tanto	therefore T-121, 122, 123
pierna	leg L-63		
pies	feet F-95	por qué	why W-117
pieza	play P-203	porcelana	china C-152
pieza	room R-244, 245	porcelana	porcelain P-249
pífano	fife F-116	porción	portion P-250
píldora	pill P-173	porque	because B-81
piloto	pilot P-174	portalámparas	socket S-350
pimienta	pepper P-93	porvenir	future F-299
pintar	paint P-6, 7	posada	inn I-114
pinza	clothespin C-202	poseer	possess P-257, 258
pío	pious P-180	posibilidad	possibility P-259
pipa	pipe P-181, 182	posible	possible P-260
piso	story S-503	posición	position P-251, 252, 253
pistola	pistol P-184		
pizarra	slate S-298	positivo	positive P-254, 255
plan	plan P-193, 194	posterior	rear R-50
plancha	flatiron F-162	postizo	fake F-24
planchar	press P-304, 305, 306	practicar	practice P-278, 279, 280
planchar	iron I-202		
planeta	planet P-198	precepto	precept P-287
plano	level L-86	precio	price P-313, 314
plano	flat F-160	precio	charge C-117, 118
planta	plant P-199, 200	precioso	precious P-288
plata	silver S-259, 260	preciso	precise P-289
plátano	banana B-21, 22	predecir	predict P-290
platicar	chat C-124	predicar	preach P-285
plato	dish D-211	predique con el	
plato	plate P-201	ejemplo	practice what you preach P-281
plomero	plumber P-216		
plomo	lead L-44	preferir	prefer P-291
pluma	pen P-79	pregunta	question Q-17
plural	plural P-218	preguntar	inquire I-118, 119, 120
población	population P-247	preguntar	ask A-271, 272, 273
pobre	poor P-241, 242, 243	preguntarse	wonder W-161, 163
pobre de espíritu	feeble-minded F-87	premio	award A-325
pobreza	poverty P-270, 271	prende	pin P-177
poco	little L-122, 123	prensar	press P-304, 305, 306
poco claro	unclear U-15	preparar	prepare P-292, 293, 294
poco después	after a while A-106		
pocos	few F-104	prepararse	get ready G-41
poder	can C-24	presbiterio	Presbyterian P-295

resfriado	cold C-230	romper	break B-227
resistir a	resist R-148	ropa	clothes C-200
resolverse	resolve R-149	ropa interior	underwear W-24
respetar	respect R-150	rosado	pink P-179
respiración	respiration R-151	rosario	rosary R-254, 255
responder	reply R-126, 127	rudo	rude R-273, 274
responder	respond R-152	rueda	wheel W-88
responder	answer A-192, 193	rueda	circle C-174, 175
responsabilidad	responsibility R-155, 156	ruido	noise N-92
		ruidoso	loud L-165
respuesta	response R-154	ruín	mean M-78
restante	left L-62	ruina	havoc H-59
resto	rest R-161, 162	ruina	wreck W-200
resto	remainder R-105	Rusia	Russia R-288
restringir	restrict R-167	rutina diaria	grind G-160
resumir	summarize S-568		
resurrección	resurrection R-169		
retardar	retard R-174		**S**
retirar	retire R-175, 176, 177		
retirar	withdraw W-151, 152, 153, 154	sábado	Saturday S-43
		sábado hebraico	Sabbath S-2, 3, 4
retiro	retreat R-178	saber	know K-35
retozar	frolic F-279	sabiduría	wisdom W-145
retraso	delay D-74	sabio	scholar S-64
retrete	toilet T-211	sabroso	savory S-48
retrospección	retrospection R-179	sacacorchos	corkscrew C-400
reunión	meeting M-99, 100	sacar fotografías	take a picture T-12
reunir	collect C-233	sacerdote	father F-68
reunirse	assemble A-277	sacerdote	priest P-316, 317, 318, 319
reunirse	gather G-19, 20		
revelar	develop D-131, 132	saco	coat C-212
reverencia	bow B-209	sacramento	sacrament S-5
reverendo	reverend R-184	sacrificio	sacrifice S-6
revista	magazine M-7	sacrilegio	sacrilegious S-7
revivir	revive R-187	sacudida	jolt J-24
revocar	revoke R-188	sacudir	shake S-167
rey	king K-19	sagrada escritura	Holy Scriptures H-141
rezagarse	lag L-7	sal	salt S-24, 25
rezar	pray P-283	sala	living room L-128
rico	rich R-191	salario	wage(s) W-2
ridículo	ridicule R-193	salchicha	frankfurter F-252
rifle	rifle R-195	salida	exit E-207
riña	row R-266	salida del sol	sunrise S-580
rincón	corner C-402, 403	salir	leave L-55
río	river R-222, 223, 224	salir clandestinamente	leave clandestinely L-57, 58
riqueza	wealth W-56		
risa	laughter L-35, 36	salmo	psalm P-390
rival	rival R-215, 216, 217, 218	salón de belleza	beauty parlor B-79
		salsa	gravy G-128
rivalizar	vie V-39, 40, 41	saltar	hop H-151, 152
rizar(se)	curl C-490	saltar	leap L-51
robar	steal S-469, 470, 471	saltar	jump J-33, 34
robar	rob R-227, 228, 229	salteamiento	holdup H-130
robo	robbery R-233	salud	health H-66
roca	rock R-235, 236	salvación	salvation S-26
rociar	spray S-427	salvaje	wild W-124, 125
rociar	sprinkle S-432	salvar	save S-45
rodar	roll R-242, 243	salvar	rescue R-137
rodear	surround S-606	salvo	safe S-9
rodrigón	beanpole B-65	San Francisco	San Francisco S-36
rojo	red R-69	sandalia	sandals S-33
romano	Roman R-245	sandía	watermelon W-44

sangrar	bleed B-171	sepultura	grave G-125
sanguijuela	leech L-60	sequía	drought D-314
sano	hale H-10	ser candidato	run for office R-285
santificado	hallowed H-16, 17	ser reprobado	fail F-11, 12, 13
santificar	sanctify S-32	serie	series S-154
santo	saint S-15, 16	serio	earnest E-11
Santo José	Saint Joseph S-18	serio	grave G-127
Santo Juan	Saint John S-17	sermón	sermon S-155
santos	saints S-19	serrucho	handsaw H-26
santo	holy H-136	servilleta	napkin N-9
sarampión	measles M-83	servir	serve S-157
sargento	sergeant S-153	servir	wait on W-6
sastre	tailor T-8	sheriff	sheriff S-190
Satán	Satan S-37	sí	yes Y-9
satélite	satellite S-38	si	whether W-94
satisfacción	satisfaction S-39	si	if I-12
sección	section S-115	siempre	always A-151
seco	dry D-322	siéntese usted	be seated B-124
secretario	secretary S-114	sierra	saw S-49, 50
secreto	secret S-113	sierra de vaivén	jig saw J-15
secreto	privacy P-330	siesta	nap N-8
secuela	sequel S-152	siete	seven S-160
sed	thirst T-142	siglo	century C-96
segar	mow M-252, 253	significado	significance S-248, 249
segar	reap R-47, 48, 49	significar	signify S-251
seguir	follow F-190	siguiente	next N-73, 74, 75, 76
seguir adelante	go ahead G-71	silbar	whistle W-105, 106
según	according to A-41	silencio	silence S-255, 256
segunco	second S-108	silencio	be quiet B-122, 123
segundo	second S-110	silencioso	quiet Q-25, 26
seguro	insurance I-143	silencioso	noiseless N-93
seguro	sure S-596	silla	chair C-101, 102, 103
seis	six S-279	simpático	nice N-81
selecta	select S-124, 125, 126	sin	minus M-171, 172, 173
sello	seal S-101, 102	sin embargo	nevertheless N-61
sello	stamp S-447, 448	sin embargo	however H-176, 177
semana	week W-64, 65	sincero	sincere S-266, 267
sembrar	sow S-384	sinónimo	synonym S-649
sembrar	seed S-117, 118, 119	siquiatra	psychiatrist P-391
semejante	similar S-261	sistema	system S-651
semejante	like L-104	sitio	location L-133
semejante	alike A-125	sitio	site S-278
semilla	seed (n) S-117, 118, 119	sobornar	bribe B-233
		sobre	over O-146, 147
seminario	seminary S-135, 136	sobre	on O-68
seña con la mano	wave W-46	sobre	upon U-56
senado	senate S-137	sobrenatural	supernatural S-586
señalar	point P-224	sobrepasar	surpass S-600
sencillo	plain P-191, 192	sobretodo	overcoat O-148
sencillo	simple S-262, 263	sobrevenir	befall B-90
sendero	path P-51	sobrina	niece N-82
señor	lord L-158	sobrino	nephew N-50
señora	madam M-6	socarrón	underhand U-18
sensación	sensation S-144	soda	soda pop S-354
sensitivo	sensitive S-147	sofocarse	choke C-158, 159
sentarse	sit down S-277	sol	sun S-576
sentido	sense S-145	soldado	soldier S-362
sentir	regret R-79	soldado raso	private P-333
sentir	feel F-91	solicitar	seek S-120
separado	apart A-207	solicitar	apply A-224
separar	part P-32, 33, 34, 35	solido	solid S-365
separar	separate S-150, 151	solitario	lonely L-142, 143

solo   lone   L-141
solo   alone   A-140
sólo   only   O-82
sólo uno   only one   O-83
soltero   bachelor   B-2
sombra   shadow   S-166
sombrero   hat   H-51
soñar   ring   R-204
sondear   probe   P-338, 339
sonido   sound   S-378
sonreir   smile   S-325
sonrojarse   flush   F-182
sonrojarse   blush   B-187
sopa   soup   S-379
soplar   blow away   B-183
soportar   bear   B-69
sordo   deaf   D-27, 28
sorprender   surprise   S-601, 602,
                          603
sospecha   suspicion   S-615
sospechar   suspect   S-608, 609
sostener   sustain   S-616
sostener   support   S-591, 592,
                          593
sostener   uphold   U-53
sostener   maintain   M-20
soy   am   A-152, 153
su   his   H-117
su   her   H-94
su   its   I-220
su   your   Y-19
suave   gentle   G-31
subsiguiente   subsequent   S-543
substancia   substance   S-545, 546
substancial   substantial   S-547
substituir   replace   R-125
subyugar   subdue   S-539
sucio   nasty   N-15
sucio   filthy   F-125
sucio   dirty   D-177
sucio   foul   F-235
sudor   sweat   S-625, 626
sueco   Swede   S-628
suela   dirt   D-176
sueldo   salary   S-21
suelo   soil   S-360
suelo   floor   F-177
suelto   loose   L-157
sueño   sleep   S-301, 302
sueño   dream   D-303
sueter   sweater   S-627
suficiente   sufficient   S-560
sufrir   suffer   S-557, 558, 559
sugerir   suggest   S-562
sujetapapeles   paper clip   P-19
suma   sum   S-567
sumar   add   A-70, 71, 72, 73
superar   overcome   O-149
superintendente   superintendant   S-583
superior   superior   S-584
superlativo   superlative   S-585
súplica   supplication   S-590

súplica   plea   P-206
suplicar   beseech   B-125
suplicar   entreat   E-120
suponer   suppose   S-594
sur   south   S-381
Suramérica   South America   S-382,
                          383
surtido   assorted   A-285, 286
suspender   suspend   S-610, 611
sustituto   substitute   S-548
sustraer   subtract   S-549

T

tabaco   tobacco   T-206
tacaño   tightwad   T-182, 183,
                          184
tacto   touch   T-234
tajar   cut   C-499
tal   such   S-555
taladrar   bore   B-197
taladrar   drill   D-306, 307
taller   workshop   W-173
tallo   stem   S-477
también   too   T-222
también   also   A-143, 144
tambor   drum   D-318
tapa   lid   L-93
tapar la boca   shut up   S-235, 236
tapicería   upholstery   U-54
tarde   late   L-26
tarde   afternoon   A-107
tarea   exercise   E-201
tarea   task   T-33
tarjeta   card   C-49
taxi   taxi   T-43
taza   cup   C-484
té   tea   T-44, 45
te   thee   T-106
teatro   theatre   T-105
tejado   roof   R-247
tejer   weave   W-61
teléfono   telephone   T-61, 62
teléfono   phone   P-140, 141
telegrama   telegram   T-57, 58
televisión   television   T-63
tema   theme   T-112
tema   topic   T-227
temblor   quake   Q-4
temerario   reckless   R-61
temeroso   fearful   F-80
temperatura   temperature   T-71
tempestad   storm   S-501
templado   temperate   T-70
templanza   temperance   T-69
templo   temple   T-72
temporada   season   S-106
temprano   early   E-9
tenedor   fork   F-225
tener   have   H-55, 57
tener   hold   H-129

W

X

Y

Z